*W*HAT THE EXPERTS ARE SAYING . . .
ABOUT NEOCONNED AGAIN

"Deconstructs the war on Iraq as part of the neocon blueprint for consolidating the American Empire."

> —Marjorie Cohn, J.D.
> Professor at Thomas Jefferson School of Law; Executive
> Vice President of the National Lawyers Guild; and U.S.
> representative to the executive committee of the American
> Association of Jurists

"Much more than just a critique of the U.S. invasion and occupation of Iraq, this volume effectively dissects broad aspects of U.S. foreign policy – both of the current Bush Administration and those administrations that preceded it. Contributions by academics and political figures, by former military and other U.S. security personnel and others document the increasingly imperial thrust of U.S. policy and the corrupting influence of that policy from Abu Ghraib in Iraq to the corruption of the media. The overall message of the book, however, goes beyond a concern about U.S. foreign and security policy. It also raises the fundamental question of the possibility of maintaining democratic institutions in the United States itself in the face of the lying, misrepresenting, and fear-mongering that has characterized U.S. policy."

> —Roger E. Kanet, Ph.D.
> Professor of Political Science and Political Developments in
> Central & Eastern Europe, University of Miami

"In the wake of re-election the Bush administration is busy rewriting history to suggest that any problems connected with the Iraq war are unavoidable by-products of U.S. willingness to employ its limited resources in the service of freeing an oppressed people and ridding the world of terrorism. The publication of *Neo-CONNED!* and *Neo-CONNED! Again* is perfectly timed to arrest this attempt to transform moral blindness and strategic incompetence into a fable of excessive self-sacrifice. This remarkable two-volume collection of essays and interviews provides the most comprehensive coverage of the war and its aftermath available anywhere. These books make it abidingly clear that divorcing power from accountability is an invitation to tragedy."

> —George W. Downs, Ph.D.
> Dean of Social Science and Professor of Politics, New York
> University

"*Neo-CONNED! Again* has appeared not a moment too soon. The Bush administration has become ever bolder in its efforts to invent a depraved and hostile world that needs liberation. It succeeds in its deceptions and cover-ups to the American people about the war in Iraq because contrary voices are silent, intimidated, or outshouted. The superb essays in *Neo-CONNED! Again* by a stellar cast of scholars and policy intellectuals can help turn the tide against the Bush administration's crusade to help make the world safe for freedom."

—Lloyd Rudolph, Ph.D.
Professor of Political Science Emeritus, University of Chicago

"*Neo-CONNED! Again* contains many arguments against the war in Iraq, including that it has caused needless suffering and that it has worsened, not reduced, threats to U.S. and international security. Contributors include theologians, reporters, lawyers, military and intelligence personnel, and diplomats. Their aim is to frighten us awake, and they succeed."

—Jessica Stern, Ph.D.
John F. Kennedy School of Government at Harvard University; Lecturer in Public Policy with the Belfer Center for Science and International Affairs; and author of *Terror in the Name of God*

"The contrast between the richness and depth of these discussions and the coverage given to the Iraq war debate in our leading national media is especially striking."

—Hayward R. Alker, Ph.D.
John A. McCone Professor of International Relations, University of Southern California

"*Neo-CONNED! Again* is an important collection of articles converging from all over the political spectrum. Collectively they make a powerful case that neoconservative delusions of world domination are bad for Iraq, bad for Israel, bad for peace and prosperity, bad for our secular ideals and institutions, bad for the basic spiritual principles of love and justice, and therefore bad for America. It is particularly effective in undermining the immoral arguments they and their supporters have made justifying our violent and deadly intrusion into the lives of so many who have never done anything to harm us."

—Gus diZerega, Ph.D.
Visiting Assistant Professor, Department of Government, St. Lawrence University

"Thank goodness somebody has the courage to publish such a collection of intelligent and truly patriotic condemnations of the insanity of the United States' criminal onslaught against Iraq. From the criminality of the onslaught itself, may as many minds as possible be further opened to the wickedness of the global plan behind it: the agents of the Antichrist are instrumentalizing the United States of America!"

—Richard Williamson
Catholic Bishop and Director, Seminario Nuestra Señora, Corredentora, Argentina

"*Neo-CONNED! Again* looks behind the mask of lies and propaganda to reveal to Americans a clearer picture of what has truly gone on in befuddled and invasive Iraqi wars."

—Mgr. Raymond Ruscitto
Catholic Priest, Kingsburg, CA

"These two volumes, this compendium, is of enormous value, indispensable. No Catholic school, college or university library should be without it, nor anyone engaged in teaching the traditional Catholic faith and its doctrines on justice and peace. They bring together sound theology and trustworthy observation of fact from many sources not usually found in Catholic publications, like Naomi Klein, Robert Fisk, Noam Chomsky, and Michael Ratner. When the Catholic Church in the U.S. catches up with the worldwide Church, Light in the Darkness Publications will deserve an important share of the credit."

—Tom Cornell
Editor, *The Catholic Worker*

"An incisive series of critical interventions into the dreadfully misguided conflict in Iraq."

—Simon Critchley, Ph.D.
Professor of Philosophy, Department of the Graduate Faculty,
New School Universiity

"In the two volumes of *Neo-CONNED!*, editors Sharpe and O'Huallachain have pulled off a tour de force: they have brought together a dazzling compilation of essays and essayists in which the whole is actually greater than the sum of the parts. The first volume, *Just War Principles: A Condemnation of War in Iraq*, provides a thoughtful assessment of the U.S. invasion of Iraq by eminent scholars and practitioners of religion, philosophy, and ethics. With authors drawn from all parts of the political map, this volume explores the 'just war' tradition and its interpretation and application in the case of Iraq. The second volume, *Hypocrisy, Lawlessness, and the Rape of Iraq*, looks at the war in Iraq from myriad political viewpoints, including but not limited to the clash between modern international law and outdated policies of empire, the role of economics, the military campaign, the intelligence failures, and the question of how to meet the new danger of terrorism. Combined, the two volumes provide food for the mind, the heart, the soul, and the day-to-day political activity of any responsible citizen. A must-read for just about everyone – educators and academics, journalists and political wonks, and people of faith."

—Randall Caroline Forsberg, Ph.D.
Director, Institute for Defense and Disarmament Studies
(idds.org), specialist on alternative security policies, former
adviser to Presidents Bush (41) and Clinton, and co-founder
of the Nuclear Weapon Freeze Campaign

"This fascinating two-volume work presents a comprehensive, highly informative critique of the background and motivation of the U.S.-sponsored war on Iraq. The coverage is broad, ranging from detailed refutation of the administration's rationale for war, to evaluation of the war from a just war perspective, to reactions from military participants and intelligence specialists, and to an evaluation of the influence of Leo Strauss, *eminence grise* of the neoconservatives. Future historians will frequently consult this important book; thinking Americans should read it now."

—Ambassador Jonathan Dean (ret.)
Former Ambassador heading U.S. Delegation to NATO
Warsaw Pact Negotiations on Mutual and Balanced Force
Reductions; and adviser on International Security Issues,
Union of Concerned Scientists

"The war in Iraq was a very unnecessary war falsely sold to the American people by a small minority called neoconservatives, who really are not conservative at all. This war has led to massive foreign aid, contributed to huge deficit spending, placed almost the entire burden of enforcing UN resolutions on our taxpayers and military, and has greatly expanded federal power. Worst of all, it has caused death or very serious injury to thousands of young Americans. These books hopefully will be read by many thousands and play an important role in helping make sure that our nation is never again so eager to go to war."

—John Duncan
U.S. Congressman (R-Tenn., 2nd district)

"*Neo-CONNED!* and *Neo-CONNED! Again* are two books that are a must read for anyone that wants to gain a deeper understanding of just what this nation is currently faced with under the leadership of the Bush Administration and its bevy of advisors. Light in the Darkness Publications has brought together a diverse group of some of the nation's best and brightest thinkers, representing just about every political and ideological background one can think of. The end results are two of the best books I have seen disseminating how this nation was neoconned into invading and occupying Iraq. It is the diversity of writers, from Republicans on the right, to liberal Democrats on the left that gives *Neo-CONNED!* and *Neo-CONNED! Again* their force and power. Both are essential for any and all who want to gain a better understanding of just what has been done in our names."

—Jack Dalton
Co-editor, *Project for the Old American Century*
(www.oldamericancentury.org)

"Careful study of the essays collected in *Neo-CONNED!* and *Neo-CONNED! Again* will deter the phony use of traditional Catholic Social Teaching to excuse modern warmongering."

—Kathy Kelly
Authoress, producer, and Secretary, *Voices in the Wilderness*

"Why the war on Iraq is wrong and how we got into it is described from many points of reference in this fascinating, readable and useful collection. One group of contributions, 'The Professionals Speak,' should be read by all interested persons, whether for or against the war. The contribution to this segment from Col. W. Patrick Lang, USA (ret.), is mandatory reading for its convincing evidence of impeachable offenses."

—Howard N. Meyer
Civil rights and peace historian, and author of *The World Court in Action*

"As a wife and mother, I was one of only two deputies in the Berlusconi government to vote against the deployment of Italian troops to Iraq. The extensive documentation provided in these two volumes, along with the tremendous misery conferred unjustly upon too many Iraqi, Italian and American families since – especially the women and children – confirms daily my belief that my vote was the correct one. Unjust war *never* leads to freedom and justice, but rather to dead, wounded and orphaned – and huge profits for the weapons industries."

> —Alessandra Mussolini
> Member of the Italian Parliament (1993–2004) from Naples for Alleanza Nazionale; Member of the European Parliament (2004) from Central Italy for Alternativa Sociale; and member of the European Parliament's Freedom and Justice Committee

"Despite having several Jewish contributors, Noam Chomsky, Immanuel Wallerstein, Jeff Steinberg, and others, these two books will no doubt attract the toxic smear of 'anti-Semitism' – a smear which as Pat Buchanan reminds us, as have many others, is designed to nullify public discourse by smearing and intimidating foes and censuring and blacklisting them and any who publish them. For that very reason, Light in the Darkness Publications is to be commended, as are their contributors, for bearing witness to the grave crimes committed in our name. Americans, particularly those who claim to be Catholic or Christian, who truly claim to love their country owe it to themselves and their children to read these books. If they do so with an open mind, they will be disinclined to align their patriotism and religion with the designs of the neocon establishment."

> —Anthony S. Fraser
> Editor, *Apropos*, Scotland

"I am in total agreement with the contents of *Neo-CONNED!* and *Neo-CONNED! Again*. Since 1982 I have been trying to warn people about what goes on behind the scenes in the quest for a New World Order dictatorship. Wherever there is war, the participants are merely pawns acting out their planned part in this programme. I hope and pray that these books will be the instruments, therefore, that will save at least some lives from the slaughter that is coming. At Fatima in 1917, the Mother of God prophesized everything that would happen if people did not turn away from sin – and the countless wars that have taken place since are the result. Let every man and woman who reads these books do whatever is possible so that Good may triumph and Evil be overcome.

> —Deirdre Manifold
> Irish Catholic authoress, lecturer, publisher, and radio personality

"Clarification and de-mystification about Iraq and U.S. foreign policy come together in these two volumes. Whoever reads this collection of papers will get a compelling picture about one of the great tragedies of our time."

> —Hans von Sponeck
> Former UN Humanitarian Coordinator for Iraq

"The United States began by creating a new enemy: Islam. Then, they initiated campaigns against both Arabs and Muslims based on the excuse of 'Islamic terror.' They claimed that Islam was at the root of terrorism. They humiliated millions of men and women using the weapons of propaganda, psychological warfare and manipulation. The primary beneficiary, Israel, applauded all this. In the evolution of its foreign policy – and in spite of the opposition expressed by several governments – the United States has benefited greatly from the complicity of what may be conveniently called 'the international community.' Huge numbers of servile news media have carefully hidden from sight all the lies. Today what makes this illegal war even more appalling is to watch the U.S. shamelessly use for its own ends an election held under duress being presented as a step towards democracy. The only possible response is that numerous voices are raised – like those in these volumes – which denounce the cowardice of those who govern us, protest against these crimes, and break the silence. The time has come for people throughout the world, who overwhelmingly opposed this war, to insist that accounts be settled with these criminals and their allies."

> —Silvia Cattori
> Independent journalist, Switzerland

"American foreign policy is forced to conform to Zionist pressure-group ideology, which dictates to politicians and policymakers to further Israeli imperialism in the Middle East. Nowhere is this more evident than in the current Iraq war and no better illustration of this ideology is presented than the two volumes, *Neo-CONNED!* and *Neo-CONNED! Again.* The Iraq war should be viewed not as a singular event, but as a greater and expansive Israeli-Palestinian crisis. President Bush has the power to end the reign of terror right now if he is willing to break clean from the stranglehold of the Zionist lobby. Politically, it is a hard choice, but ultimately a sensible and realistic one that would bring about true peace and justice in the Middle East."

> —Brig. Gen James J. David, USANG (ret.)
> Georgia Army National Guard and graduate, U.S. Army's
> Command and General Staff College

"Truly a unique contribution in intellectual diversity and critical thinking that gives full meaning to the patriotic tradition. Together the two volumes constitute a direct challenge to the jingoists who seek to monopolize the discourse on violence, in particular war and terrorism. The breadth and depth of the analysis puts its value far beyond the Iraq situation."

> —Beau Grosscup
> Public speaker on terrorism and author,
> *The Newest Explosions in Terrorism*

"These two volumes carry with them both breadth and depth. At the heart of the chapters lies a concern for the justice (or want of it) of wars. I have nowhere come across a finer set of analyses of theories of just war from which scholars and activists might quarry useful material for dealing with war and its old and new weapons in our time. Alongside the central concern there are fine individual studies: Robert Fisk's historical piece on the original putting together of Iraq in the wake of the break-up of the Ottoman Empire offers almost incredible parallels with the present war; Stephen Sniegoski's linking of the neoconservatives, Israel, and 9/11 is carefully chronicled; several chapters take up the issue of Christian Zionism as well as the tensions between conservatives and liberals within the American Catholic Church. Several authors demystify the 'war on terror' construct, and they show that the issue of weapons of mass destruction was dishonestly and carelessly used. Overall, these volumes deal thoroughly with the impact of the neoconservatives on American and global politics but they also provide reflections that transcend those immediate concerns."

—James M. O'Connell, Ph.D.
Professor Emeritus of Peace Studies, University of Bradford, England

"That a Catholic press is publishing this compendium of arguments against the unjust war against Iraq is an indication of the power of the current hegemonic order where too many mainstream presses continue to roll over. With contributions from left and right, religious and secular, military, and civilian, *Neo-CONNED!* and *Neo-CONNED! Again* are more than valuable resources, they are valuable weapons for fighting against the neoconservative drive for empire."

—Jodi Dean, Ph.D.
Associate Professor of Political Science, Hobart-William Smith Colleges, Geneva, N.Y., and author, *Publicity's Secret: How Technoculture Capitalizes on Democracy*

"If you've been looking for intellectual and political support for your worries about American involvement in Iraq and beyond, look no further. In *Neo-CONNED!* and *Neo-CONNED! Again,* you will find two ample volumes of essays that dissect and unmask the underlying neoconservative political and rhetorical machinations behind the War on Iraq. This approach is augmented by a thorough study of Catholic just-war theory, from its earliest roots to the present day. Authors range from big names like Patrick Buchanan and Noam Chomsky to a wide and multi-faceted range of voices from the military, political, and intelligence establishments. Western involvement in Iraq is analyzed from World War I to the present. The vast array of information and perspective would challenge anyone who glibly supports our war efforts as just and noble."

—John Norris, Ph.D.
Assistant Professor of Theology, University of Dallas

"In the face of continuing administration denials of reality and morality, *Neo-CONNED!* and its companion volume *Neo-CONNED! Again* are essential reading on law, just war theory and the catastrophe in Iraq. Current international law on war divides into *jus ad bellum* and *jus in bello* and these books show how virtually every aspect of both sets of laws were and are being violated. More important, the critiques from the perspective of just war theory developed through sixteen centuries of Church teaching illuminate what leaders should have known and considered before entering into this tragically misguided enterprise. As is forcefully argued, the Iraq war is both imprudent and immoral. These books are must reading for anyone teaching or writing about the world we live in and moral choice."

—Michael T. Corgan, Ph.D.
Associate Professor, Director of Undergraduate Studies, Department of International Relations, Boston University

"These two crackling volumes will speak to general readers, students, and academics alike. They provide a source of extraordinary scope on the invasion of Iraq, by writers of varied backgrounds ranging from theologians and political analysts to investigative reporters and military experts. Re-examining the facts surrounding the decision to invade and its aftermath is only part of the coverage, which ranges from the war-makers' neoconservatism and other motivations, to just-war critiques, history, the issues of pre-emptive attacks, and reflections on both Christian Zionism and Muslim fundamentalism."

—Peter Juviler, Ph.D.
Professor Emeritus and Special Lecturer, Barnard College of
Political Science, Columbia University

"These two volumes don't just make a compelling argument against the morality of the U.S.'s war on Iraq, the essays herein make a convincing one. It's too bad that the men and women in power in D.C. and London don't care for moral arguments that come to conclusions other than their own, especially when those arguments (such as those inside these volumes) include facts the rulers prefer to ignore. Any world citizen who has questions about the justice of the Iraq war should read this collection."

—Ron Jacobs
Member, Burlington Anti-war Coalition, University of
Vermont; public speaker, Movement History, Civil Liberties,
U.S. Foreign Policy; and author, *The Way the Wind Blew: A
History of the Weather Underground*

"*Neo-CONNED!* shocks and awes the sentient reader with Volume I's devastating moral and ethical critiques of the current war in Iraq and Volume II's armor-piercing political and ideological analyses. Books not bombs, indeed."

—Wally Goldfrank, Ph.D.
Professor of Sociology, University of California, Santa Cruz

"It's all right here. Future historians, seeking to untangle the spaghetti plate of deceit, machinations, and bungling that led to this needless war, will find their work has already been done. It's all right here."

—Charles Goyett
KXXT talk show host, Phoenix, Arizona

"The two volumes that Light in the Darkness Publications has prepared on the just war and the war in Iraq clearly express that, throughout its long history, the Church has always been aware of the challenge which the world presents. The work of Light in the Darkness Publications is a testimony to this awareness, and it also makes us aware of the necessity to reflect on the reality of world affairs."

—Daniela Parisi
Professor of History of Economic Thought, Faculty of
Economics
Catholic University of the Sacred Heart, Milan, Italy

"For those who believe in the sacredness of the universal human family, in international law, in means being consistent with ends, in justice, and only in just wars, *Neo-CONNED!* and *Neo-CONNED! Again* are must reads. The neocons conned us once. These volumes will help to ensure they don't get away with it a second time."

—Jesse L. Jackson, Jr.
U.S. Congressman (D-Ill., 2nd district)

"Light in the Darkness Publications has assembled the most critical collection of Iraq war commentary to date. Clearly assembled and comprehensive, the volume is a central reading for all those who seek to understand the role played by neoconservatives in rallying the war engines. With hard-hitting contributions from former military officers, scientists, diplomats, journalists, lawyers and other Middle East experts, this book offers something new for all readers. Above all, this provocative collection reminds us of the need to continue to think critically in these deeply troubled times."

        —Julie Mertus, Ph.D.
          Author of *Bait and Switch: Human Rights and U.S. Foreign
          Policy*; and Professor of International Relations and Ethics,
          American University

"The American Congress and people have been 'neoconned' by a group of ideologues who seek to remake the world through the use of force. Though they may masquerade as 'conservatives,' there is nothing conservative about ignoring our Founding Fathers' admonitions against meddling in the affairs of foreign countries and going abroad seeking monsters to slay. This book does a valuable service in reminding American citizens that, if we want to retain our way of life, we must study history and we must repudiate those who seek to destroy our Republic."

        —Ron Paul, M.D.
          U.S. Congressman (R-Tex., 14th district)

"The unfortunate thing about this collection of important essays – other than the fact that they had to be written at all – is that those who need to read them, those who blindly support everything the Bush administration does out of ideological fervor, will not. People, for the most part today, are not interested in any opinion that does not buttress their own. What's done is done, but hopefully the writing contained herein can help discredit the philosophy that has wrought so much death, destruction and shame on this great, once good, nation and rid us of it for the next generation."

        —Andy Prutsok
          Publisher, *Suffolk News-Herald*

"The editors of these two volumes have done a prodigious job in collecting essays from a wide range of highly qualified commentators on American policy in Iraq and the Middle East. The essays take us beyond headlines and sound bites, offering thoughtful, thorough and very readable analyses from a variety of points of view. They should be required reading for all Americans."

        —Tom Morgan, Ph.D.
          Director, Center for the Study of Peace and Justice, College of
          St. Scholastica, Duluth, Minn.

"Though these books take as their target the neocons, these essays raise issues far more important then whether the neocons are right or wrong about Iraq. Anyone who wants to think seriously about the war on Iraq in terms of the ethical challenge presented by that war needs to read these volumes."

        —Stanley Hauerwas, Ph.D.
          Gilbert T. Rowe Professor of Theological Ethics, Duke Divinity
          School, and *TIME Magazine* Theologian of the Year, 2001

"If events since 9/11 could be described as globally paradigmatic, this comprehensive, cutting-edge, twin volume captures the moral essence of these times. Especially, the text does an excellent job articulating the sorely needed alternative perspective of the Bush Doctrine and the Bush Wars. Certainly, both volumes of *Neo-CONNED!* are required reading for the dynamic international relations and comparative politics classroom."

—Rita Kiki Edozie, Ph.D.
Assistant Professor, Comparative Politics and International
Relations, University of Delaware

"The views represented here are the unwanted side of a policy debate that never took place. It is, in effect, a chronicle of things left unsaid. Mainstream media, given its intellectual bias, has proven itself to be the enemy of rational public policy. Attempting to set the record straight, this book demonstrates the need for open discourse, lest our foreign policy be dictated by interests not our own, It is a must read for every honest mind within our policy making ranks."

—Jude P. Dougherty, Ph.D.
Dean of the School of Philosophy, The Catholic University
of America, Washington, DC; Editor, *Review of Metaphysics*;
and Editor, *Studies in Philosophy* and *History of Philosophy*

"Founded on moral principle, steeped in fact, argued with force, this remarkable collection presents a forceful condemnation of U.S. policy in Iraq. Every American ought to read it."

—Joshua Cohen, Ph.D.
Professor of Political Philosophy, Massachusetts Institute of
Technology, and Editor, *Boston Review*

"This lively anthology contains a broad range of criticisms of the Second Gulf War and of the rationales offered by the so-called 'neocon' intellectual movement. These lucid, ideologically diverse, and always passionate essays should provoke fresh thinking in any reader – regardless if a supporter or opponent of the war."

—Cyrus Ernesto Zirakzadeh, Ph.D.
Professor of Comparative Politics and History of Political
Thought, University of Connecticut, and author of *Social
Movements in Politics: A Comparative Study*

"These books are not about anti-Americanism, but about how all true friends of America need to know and disseminate this indictment of a profoundly unjust and mistaken war."

—Anthony Coughlan, Ph.D.
Senior Lecturer Emeritus in Social Policy, Trinity College,
Dublin, Ireland

"This anthology of anti-war materials will quickly become a counterrevolutionary classic. In an age of fifth-rate, pseudo-intellectual resistance literature from self-appointed critics, it is gratifying to see an array of intellectually solid, self-sacrificing idealists set their faces against this rotten System we are all forced to live under. The editors of these volumes deserve the highest intellectual respect and regard for their intuitive good taste. Few who finish these volumes will be able to escape having their political universes reoriented."

—M. Raphael Johnson, Ph.D.
Former lecturer, Political Theory and International Relations, University of Nebraska, Lincoln; former Editor, *The Barnes Review*; and Director of Academics, Government Educational Foundation

"This is an extremely valuable collection of commentaries on the War in Iraq, featuring some of our most astute observers of U.S. foreign policy. I recommend it as a treasure trove of information and ideas."

—Howard Zinn
Historian, playwright, social activist; writer, *The Progressive Magazine*; and one-time political scientist and historian, Boston University, Spelman College

"These volumes serve a number of purposes that serve America's national interests. First, the authors included here are among the best in their fields; their essays provide what should be, for Americans, an unnerving dissection of neoconservatism and the dangers towards which it is leading our country. Second, the essays are excellent correctives to the uneducated, distorted, or simply fabricated definitions of the "principles of American foreign policy" that are offered by the neo-Wilsonian and neoconservative theorists. Third, and most important, the volumes show beyond doubt that a person can question the content and application of contemporary U.S. foreign policy and yet remain a loyal American citizen, faithful to the tenets of the nation's founders, and ready at all times to defend the United States. Well Done."

—Michael Scheuer
Former Chief, Bin Laden Unit, Counterterrorist Center, CIA, and author ("Anonymous") of *Imperial Hubris: Why the West Is Losing the War on Terror* and *Through Our Enemies' Eyes: Osama bin Laden, Radical Islam, and the Future of America*

"Experts already consider President Bush's ill-fated invasion of Iraq as one of history's greatest strategic blunders. In these outstanding collections of essays from Light in the Darkness Publications, authors ranging from professors at U.S. war colleges to theologians to journalists to Middle East experts expose the false claims of neoconservatives, who have deceived Americans and, in a gratuitous act of naked aggression, destroyed the reputation of the United States. Reading these valuable essays is the complete antidote to the propagandistic bombast that flows from the Oval Office."

—Paul Craig Roberts
Former Assistant Secretary to the Treasury in the Reagan administration; syndicated columnist; and former Associate Editor, *Wall Street Journal*

"The U.S. state has a long history of aggressive war, but the neocons add a strain of lunacy missing since Wilson. Congratulations to Light in the Darkness Publications for defending peace at this dangerous time."

—Lew Rockwell
Director, Ludwig von Mises Institute

"This is a very important collection for at least two reasons. First, it shows that there are limits to the propaganda and deception practiced by the Bush administration. You cannot fool all the people all the time. Most of the world was against this war before it started and they are still against it – and this collection tells us why. The second reason that this collection is important is that it helps to distance Christianity from the war crimes of the Bush administration, which pretends that it is fighting a war for God, Truth, and Justice."

—Shadia Drury, Ph.D.
Canada Research Chair in Social Justice, University of
Regina, Saskatchewan, Canada

"These cogent essays constitute a devastating moral, legal, and political case against the war in Iraq – the most catastrophic U.S. foreign policy decision since Vietnam. If I had the power to make members of the Bush administration and of Congress read one thing about this abhorrent war of choice, this would be it."

—Thomas G. Weiss, Ph.D.
Presidential Professor and Director, Ralph Bunche Institute
for International Studies, CUNY Graduate Center

"The invasion of Iraq in 2003, without the backing of the United Nations, was a disaster whose consequences we will all have to live with for decades. I have not yet seen a more comprehensive collection of sophisticated and detailed critical perspectives, encompassing a very wide range of authoritative arguments against the war and aspects of its aftermath."

—Ken Booth, Ph.D.
E.H. Carr Professor and Head of Department of International
Politics, University of Wales, and former Chairman and first
President, British International Studies Association

"Clearly a monumental but also a timely effort, which must needs be presented to America while the iron is still hot, before events overtake these findings and the guilty are permitted to slide into temporary obscurity."

—Col. J. Richard Niemela, USAF (ret.)

"The books are a collection of important articles on the real nature of the Iraq war, from the lies of the Bush administration to the naked violations of international humanitarian law. Highly recommended to every concerned American!"

—John H. Kim
UN NGO Representative, International Fellowship of
Reconciliation

NEOCONNED AGAIN

The public was told that Saddam posed an imminent threat. If that claim was fraudulent, the selling of the war is arguably the worst scandal in American political history.

> —Paul Krugman
> *New York Times*, June 2003

War is a racket. It always has been. It is possibly the oldest, easily the most profitable, surely the most vicious. It is the only one international in scope. It is the only one in which the profits are reckoned in dollars and the losses in lives.

> —Major General Smedly D. Butler, USMC
> *War Is a Racket*, 1935

AD DEUM IUSTITIÆ

*To the thousands of Iraqi dead and wounded,
to their families, and to the entire Nation at the
cradle of civilization – all victims of tragic and
diabolical Anglo-American aggression.*

*To the British and American widows and
orphans whose dear ones have been sacrificed
on the vain altar of cynical statecraft.*

*And to George Bush, Tony Blair, Dick Cheney, Richard
Perle, Donald Rumsfeld, Paul Wolfowitz, and the rest of the
ideologues and hypocrites, both famous and obscure,
who have orchestrated the unjust and unnecesary
war in Iraq. We implore God to have mercy on their
souls for the ocean of innocent blood they have spilled
in pursuit of their ambitions and nightmares.*

*T*O THE READER

The two volumes of *Neo-CONNED!* have one purpose: to bring together the best minds on the Iraq War and everything pertaining to it. We have, in consequence, assembled an eclectic group, spanning the political, religious, and professional spectrum. We submit that the result is a tremendous intellectual and analytical dynamic, hitherto unavailable in the vitally important debate over war and peace.

The appearance of a contributor in either of our two volumes implies *no endorsement* by that contributor of anything beyond the words attributed to him or her; it particularly does not imply endorsement of any other contributor's work, either in these pages or in other fora. Whether the various contributors agree, in whole or part, with any of the pieces contained in this work beyond their own is a matter for each contributor; it should certainly not be assumed. The fact that our authors come from widely divergent philosophical, political, and religious backgrounds ought to make this obvious.

As for our own views, they do not, strictly speaking, appear in this volume. In compiling and editing the *Neo-CONNED!* texts, we have, of course, sought to produce a coherently integrated whole. Nevertheless, our authors speak for *themselves* throughout. While most grateful for their participation, and feeling, of course, a general sympathy for what they have contributed, we do not necessarily subscribe to their each and every view as expressed either in these volumes or in their writings in other places, on other subjects. No doubt the contributors would feel the same about our own view of things.

These works are about *Iraq*, and Iraq alone. We believe that they vindicate the principles of the Catholic just-war tradition, which convict the war in Iraq of manifest injustice. We pray that these volumes serve the cause of Truth, for it is in that spirit that they are presented.

The Editors

neo-CONNED! AGAIN

Hypocrisy, Lawlessness, and the Rape of Iraq

The illegality and the injustice of the second Gulf War

D. L. O'Huallachain & J. Forrest Sharpe • Editors

Light IN THE Darkness PUBLICATIONS
AN IMPRINT OF IHS PRESS

Vienna, Virginia • 2005

ISBN-10: 1-932528-05-9
ISBN-13: 978-1-932528-05-3

Library of Congress Cataloging-in-Publication Data

Neo-conned! again : hypocrisy, lawlessness, and the rape of Iraq : the illegality and
    the injustice of the Second Gulf War / editors, D.L. O'Huallachain and J. Forrest
    Sharpe ; foreword by Joseph Cirincione ; introduction by Scott Ritter.
        p. cm.
    ISBN 1-932528-05-9 (alk. paper)
    1. Iraq War, 2003-   --Causes. 2. Iraq War, 2003-   --Public opinion. 3.
    Public opinion--United States. 4. Illegality--Case studies. 5. Hypocrisy--Political
    aspects--United States--Case studies. 6. United States--Military policy. 7.
    Conservatism--United States. 8. War on Terrorism, 2001-   . I. O'Huallachain,
    D. L. II. Sharpe, J. Forrest.
    DS79.76.N46 2005
    956.7044'31--dc22

                                                                            2005016071

Printed in the United States of America.

Light in the Darkness Publications is an imprint of IHS Press.
IHS Press is the only publisher dedicated exclusively to the
Social Teachings of the Catholic Church. For information on
current or future titles, contact IHS Press at:

        toll-free phone/fax: 877.447.7737 (877-IHS-PRES)
            e-mail: info@ihspress.com
            e-mail: info@lidpubs.com

CONTENTS

THE PROFESSIONALS SPEAK IV:
A SCIENTIST AND A DIPLOMAT

DEFYING WORLD ORDER: REACTIONS
FROM VATICAN AND UN PERSPECTIVES

PROPPING UP A DYING GIANT:
AMERICAN ECONOMIC AND MILITARY SURVIVAL TACTICS

ONE GOOD SCANDAL DESERVES ANOTHER:
THE SNOWBALLING OF AMERICAN LAWLESSNESS

www.albasrah.net

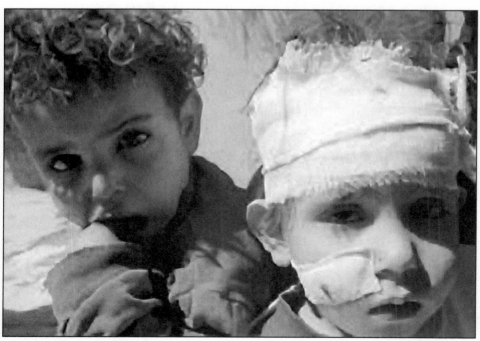

www.informationclearinghouse.info

... the whole world knows by now that Iraq has lost well over a million of its people as a direct result of the sanctions that have been in place for eight years. ... Many critics seem to think the government of Iraq is supposed to stand idle while watching a whole generation of its people melt away like snowflakes. ...

Iraq will never be able to satisfy UNSCOM because it is being asked to prove the negative: that it does not have any more weapons. There is, of course, no way Iraq can prove that it has nothing if it has nothing. How many more Iraqis will have to die because Richard Butler's team has not yet found another document, which cannot be located because there is no such document in the first place? The inspectors are searching for a black cat in a dark room where the cat does not exist.

... many American officials have stated that even if Iraq complies with the Security Council's resolutions, the United States will not approve the lifting of sanctions. The declared goal of Washington is to remove the current government of Iraq. WE WONDER IF THIS GOAL IS IN LINE WITH THE LETTER AND SPIRIT OF INTERNATIONAL LAW AND THE UNITED NATIONS RESOLUTIONS. *Iraq continues to believe that the resolutions are used by the United States as a cover for an illegal political agenda. The allocation of money to the Central Intelligence Agency for subversion in Iraq is just a unit in this series. One might wonder why Iraq should continue being part of this futile and endless game.*

... many high-ranking American officials keep speaking about Iraq as being a threat to American interests and the region. We would like to assure these officials, and through them the American people, that Iraq is eager to live in peace with its neighbors and the world. But Iraq will not submit to intimidation, bullying, and coercion. Peace will come only through dialogue based on mutual respect for the principles of independence, sovereignty, and the observance of international law.

—Nizar Hamdoon, former Iraqi Ambassador
to the UN, "A Black Cat in a Dark Room,"
New York Times, August 20, 1998

The Greatest Con of Our History

· · · · · · · · · ·

Joseph Cirincione

WITH SO MANY scholars presenting so much material in this book, it would perhaps be impossible to agree with everything the authors say. What is important is that they are saying it.

Americans are speaking out against the greatest con in the history of the American presidency. The President, the vice president, and their senior officials willfully and systematically misled the American people and our closest allies on the most crucial question any government faces: Must we go to war?

Not one of the dozens of claims our officials made about Iraq's alleged stockpiles of chemical and biological weapons, missiles, unmanned drones, or most importantly, Iraq's nuclear weapons and ties to al-Qaeda, was true. Yet no one in the administration has been held accountable for the hundreds of false statements or – if they made the statements in good faith – for their faulty judgments and incompetence. Almost all the key officials are still in office for the administration's second term. Several have received awards or promotions.

We now know that during the buildup to the 2003 Iraq War, Saddam Hussein did not have any of these weapons, did not have production programs for manufacturing these weapons, and did not have plans to restart programs for these weapons. The most that Charles Duelfer, head of the Iraq Survey Group, was able to tell Congress in October 2004 was that Saddam might have had the "intention" to restart these programs at some point. The evidence for even this claim is largely circumstantial and inferential.

The administration, having extended the search for these weapons past the November 2004 elections, officially ended it in January 2005. The search found no evidence that the weapons were destroyed shortly before the war or moved to Syria, as some still claim. They never existed. As Duelfer reported, the weapons and facilities had been destroyed by the United Nations inspectors and U.S. bombing strikes in the 1990s, and he found no evidence of "concerted efforts to restart the program."

There is now a coordinated effort underway to reframe the rationale for the Iraq War, to claim that we went to war to promote democracy, or to save the Iraqi people, or, most recently, as part of the struggle to end tyranny. Weapons, we are told, were just one of the reasons. As Senator Carl Levin of Michigan pointed out on the Senate floor on January 25, 2005, in opposition to the confirmation of Condoleeza Rice as secretary of state, this is an attempt to rewrite history.

> The simple fact is that before the war, the administration repeatedly and dramatically made the case for war on the issue of Iraq possessing and continuing to develop weapons of mass destruction, and the likelihood that it would provide those weapons to terrorists like al-Qaeda. For Dr. Rice to suggest that there were many other, equally compelling, reasons to go to war simply does not square with the reality of how the administration persuaded the American people and the Congress of the need for war. Her suggestion is an effort to revise the history of the administration's presentations to the American people.

Indeed, the President's final speech to the American people as the war began was entirely about the urgent need to disarm Saddam. He mentioned human rights and democracy only in passing near the conclusion of his remarks.

The key document in the administration's campaign, the report that convinced many Americans, was the CIA *White Paper on Iraq's Weapons of Mass Destruction Programs*. The White Paper was hurriedly produced and distributed to the public in October 2002 as an unclassified version of the now-infamous National Intelligence Estimate (NIE) that was given to Congress in the same month, just a few days before the vote to authorize the use of force. These two documents convinced the majority of congressional members, experts, and journalists that Saddam had a powerful and growing arsenal.

I have *pored* over these two deeply flawed documents (for the January 2004 Carnegie study, *WMD in Iraq: Evidence and Implications*). There is not one claim in the reports that proved true, except the finding that Saddam was highly unlikely to transfer any weapons to terrorist groups – a finding that the administration ignored and was not included in the public White Paper.

One brief example serves to demonstrate the way the information, faulty to begin with, was shaped to present the worst possible case to the American people. The first paragraph of the White Paper concludes that Iraq "probably will have a nuclear weapon during this decade." This claim was then repeated endlessly to the public with much talk of "mushroom clouds." But the classified NIE only said that Iraq *might* acquire a bomb some time between 2007 and 2009. A danger, but not a threat that required war in March 2003. The estimate itself was wildly wrong (there was no program, there was no bomb), but by dropping the dates, officials who honestly believed the estimate could be right frightened the public into believing Saddam might already have a bomb. The danger was urgent. We had to act. We had no choice but to terminate the UN inspections and invade.

Officials knew or should have known that this was not true at the time. But dissenters to the worst-case scenarios were ignored. Caveats and qualifications were discarded. Only those who supported the policy were allowed into the decision-making circles, or as Patrick Lang reports later in this book, only those "who drank the Kool-Aid" got to sit at the table.

Anger over this unnecessary war, of course, is not confined to the authors of this book. The majority of Americans do not believe the war in Iraq has been worth the heavy cost paid. During the debate on the Rice nomination, many respected senators took to the floor to denounce the administration's deceptions. Senator Mark Dayton of Minnesota said Rice had briefed him at the White House before the vote to authorize the use of force. He said most of what Rice told him was wrong. " I don't like to impugn anyone's integrity," he said, "but I really don't like being lied to, repeatedly, flagrantly, intentionally. It's wrong. It's undemocratic. It's un-American. And it's dangerous." Senator Carl Levin said, "Voting to confirm Dr. Rice as Secretary of State would be a stamp of approval for her participation in the distortions and exaggerations of intelligence that the administration used to initiate the war in Iraq, and the hubris which led to their inexcusable failure to plan and prepare for the aftermath of the overthrow of Saddam Hussein with tragic ongoing consequences."

Rice was confirmed, as the majority of the Senate urged the opposition to "look to the future" and not to "dwell on the past." We ignore the past at our peril, however, for similar methods and warnings are cropping up in the debate over Iran. Those who favor military action are again making the threat appear closer than it is by minimizing the substantial technological and engineering obstacles that Iran must overcome to be able to enrich uranium and manufacture a weapon. Those who favor diplomatic solutions, even our closest allies, are given short shrift. The United States is standing aside from the efforts of the European Union to negotiate an end to Iran's nuclear program and, by this inaction, it will doom the effort. We will undoubtedly hear stories of the brutality of the Iranian regime, coupling the danger of Iran someday getting nuclear weapons with the President's call to end tyranny. There may well be an orchestrated campaign to build support for an attack on Iran that will be as determined as the campaign to build support for the invasion of Iraq.

Those who hope not to repeat the mistakes of the past would do well to read the informed accounts of recent history contained in this valuable volume.

Joseph Cirincione
Director for Non-Proliferation
Carnegie Endowment for International Peace
January 2005

Oil, War, and Things Worth Fighting For
• • • • • • • • •
Scott Ritter

O N THE EVE of America's invasion of Iraq, I watched with great interest the debate between arch-hawk Richard Perle and arch-dove Dennis Kucinich (then a Presidential hopeful) on NBC's *Meet the Press* (February 23, 2003). One exchange in particular caught my attention. Mr. Kucinich, when asked about the fundamental motivation for the Bush administration's push for war with Iraq, said, " . . . the fact is that, since no other case has been made to go to war against Iraq, for this nation to go to war against Iraq, oil represents the strongest incentive." Then Richard Perle retorted: "I find the accusation that this administration has embarked upon this policy for oil to be an outrageous, scurrilous charge for which, when you asked for the evidence, you will note there was none. There was simply the suggestion that, because there is oil in the ground and some administration officials have had connections with the oil industry in the past, therefore, it is the policy of the United States to take control of Iraqi oil. It is a lie, Congressman. It is an out and out lie."

In the past, I used to resist the suggestion that Bush's war with Iraq was about oil. It just didn't seem to make any sense. Oil is about business, and business is about making money. Any oil man worth his salt would know that it makes better business sense to invest $50 billion in Iraqi oilfield refurbishment over five years, raising production rates from the current level of 1.5 million barrels per day to an estimated 7 million, than it would to spend $200 billion – the current low end of the costs of the Iraq war – to invade Iraq, knowing that the end result would likely be the destruction of the Iraqi oil production infrastructure. Yet when I heard Richard Perle making the same argument, I was suddenly suspicious. He is, after all, not just a manipulator of truth, but he is in fact anti-truth – especially when it comes to Iraq. So I decided to re-examine my stance on the war-for-oil thesis, and found that the case for such a link becomes quite clear, once subjected to closer scrutiny.

In 2003, Richard Perle chaired the influential Defense Policy Board (DPB), and used the access to the inner circle of American power that this non-governmental position enjoys to wield considerable influence over senior policy makers both at home and abroad. While this position does have its limits, there is no denying that the former chairman of the DPB serves as the ideological focus for the neoconservatives currently populating the elected and politically-appointed ranks of the Defense Department. As such, Perle was only too aware of the post-war plans for the multi-billion dollar reconstruction bonanza that was to be unleashed once the Pentagon assumed military governorship of occupied – or in Perle-speak, "liberated" – Iraq.

Those lucrative contracts were to be doled out exclusively to U.S. and U.S.-allied companies. Bids were already accepted, on a no-competition basis, *before* the war, from companies such as Halliburton. Among those deals were contracts for oil field refurbishment and operations, which meant that for a period of at least two to five years, Iraq's oil would be – *as it is today* – under the control of American oil companies, operating under the umbrella of a U.S. military government, or a U.S. military-backed government, if one accepts as legitimate the highly questionable elections of January 30, 2005. Given the dearth of national security justifications for the war, how could our war in Iraq be about anything other than oil? The current – and remorselessly rising – $200 billion price tag for war will prove a boon for defense contractors who produce the weapons of war, while the post-war "need" for reconstruction and refurbishment will provide billions of dollars more in government-funded contracts, assuming that the American military can create sufficient "peace" to allow any construction to take place. This orgy of war-related spending and profit-taking translates into a massive economic incentive program for defense- and oil-sector businesses (sectors historically close to the Bush-Cheney White House) while the American taxpayer foots the bill.

There is, in fact, a far more substantial case for linking the Bush war with Iraq to oil than there ever was for linking Saddam Hussein to Bin Laden. The Bush-Harkin, Cheney-Halliburton, Condi Rice-Chevron links are beyond dispute, while Secretary Powell's artfully constructed case regarding Saddam-Bin Laden, built around the conveniently shadowy figure of Abu Musab Zarqawi, collapsed like a house of cards when it became known that Powell misrepresented French-supplied intelligence on the subject. Audio tapes from Osama Bin Laden, encouraging the Muslim world to rise up in support of the Iraqi people, also fingered Saddam Hussein as an apostate, someone worthy of being overthrown. The revelations about the Pentagon's post-war plans regarding U.S. control of Iraqi oil reveals the goals of Team Bush to be little more than crude throwbacks to the economically-motivated imperialism of the nineteenth century.

That these are not mere personal sentiments may be gauged from an article by Ray McGovern, posted at *Truthout.com* on February 14, 2005. Entitled, "We Need The Oil, Right? So What's the Problem?" his piece deals directly with the oil factor from the perspective of someone with decades of service (in the CIA) to the American national interest.

His argument is worth noting in some detail.

> Canadian writer Linda McQuaig, author of *It's the Crude, Dude*, has noted that decades from now it will all seem a no-brainer. Historians will calmly discuss the war in Iraq and identify oil as one of the key factors in the decision to launch it. They will point to growing U.S. dependence on foreign oil, the competition with China, India, and others for a world oil supply with terminal illness, and the fact that (as former Deputy Secretary of Defense Paul Wolfowitz has put it) Iraq "swims on a sea of oil." It will all seem so obvious as to provoke little more than a yawn.
>
> But that will be then. Now is now. How best to explain the abrupt transition from early-nineties prudence to the present day recklessness of this administration? How to fathom the continued cynicism that trades throwaway soldiers for the chimera of controlling Middle East oil
>
> In August 1992, Dick Cheney, who was then the secretary of defense – Dick Cheney under a very different President Bush – was asked to explain why U.S. tanks did not roll into Baghdad and depose Saddam Hussein during the Gulf War. Cheney said: "I don't think you could have done that without significant casualties . . . . And the question in my mind is how many additional casualties is Saddam worth? And the answer is not that damned many . . . . And we're not going to get bogged down in the problems of trying to take over and govern Iraq."
>
> Later, then-CEO Dick Cheney of Halliburton found himself focusing on different priorities. In the fall of 1999 he complained: "Oil companies are expected to keep developing enough oil to offset oil depletion and also to meet new demand . . . . So where is this oil going to come from? Governments and national oil companies are obviously in control of 90 percent of the assets . . . . The Middle East with two-thirds of the world's oil and the lowest cost is still where the prize ultimately lies."

McGovern then gets to the heart of the issue by asking this question: "What had changed in the seven years between Cheney's two statements?" Here's his answer:

- The U.S. kept importing more and more oil to meet its energy needs.
- Energy shortages drove home the need to ensure/increase energy supply.
- Oil specialists concluded that "peak oil" production was but a decade away, while demand would continue to zoom skyward.
- The men now running U.S. policy on the Middle East appealed to President Clinton in January 1998 to overthrow Saddam Hussein or "a significant portion of the world's supply of oil will be put at hazard."

- In October 1998 Congress passed and Clinton signed a bill declaring it the sense of Congress that "it should be the policy of the United States to support efforts to remove the regime headed by Saddam Hussein."

McGovern then concludes this crucial part of his piece: "Shortly after George W. Bush entered the White House in January 2001, Vice President Cheney's energy task force dragged out the maps of Iraq's oil fields."

Another famous weapons inspector evidently had the same thought process. An April 6, 2005, *Associated Press* wire quoted Hans Blix as saying – in reference to the possibility that the invasion of Iraq was motivated by oil – "I did not think so at first." He went on to say, however, that "the U.S. is incredibly dependent on oil," and that perhaps we "wanted to secure oil in case competition on the world market becomes too hard."

We should not, however, trivialize the war with Iraq as being *simply* about oil, since doing so gives the Bush administration a break it doesn't deserve. For above all this is a war of ideology, of a conflict between neoconservative unilateralism and the broader concept of self-determination as espoused by our founding fathers and implied in the Constitution of the United States. Team Bush argues that its policies are designed to defend American democracy, that the Constitution cannot be seen as a suicide pact, a "limiting" feature to be exploited by potential enemies of the state. The argument, however, rings hollow, much like the Vietnam-era argument that "we had to destroy the village in order to save the village."

No, the Bush administration's war is a frontal assault on international law and on the U.S. Constitution, through its illegal war of aggression in Iraq. It should serve as a wake-up call to all Americans, who ought to reflect on the oath of office taken by all those who serve our nation to uphold and defend the Constitution against all enemies – foreign *and* domestic. In a sense, the Constitution is a suicide pact, because without it we are no longer the United States of America, but some empty shadow of a nation that has lost its heart and soul. It is high time that the American people rallied to the defense of what defines them as a nation, with the understanding that the domestic threat to our national existence posed by the wrongheaded policies of the Bush administration far outweighs any possible foreign threat – real or imagined – posed by people like Saddam Hussein and bin Laden.

While a somewhat convincing case can be made for linking the Bush war to oil interests, it should nevertheless be understood that in opposing this war with Iraq we are doing far more than saying "no blood for oil." We are defending the rule of law and the American way of life. And that, in my opinion, *is* a fight worth fighting.

The essays and analysis contained in the volume that follows (and those in its companion and predecessor, *Neo-CONNED!*) are representative of the reality that not everyone in America has abandoned the obligations that patriotic citizens have to our great nation. They are testimony to the fact that many are still willing to stand up and speak out – even during these dark times, when to do so invites ridicule, invective, and worse. All Americans should read both of these books carefully, and reflect upon what they contain. And then they should resolve not to stand idly by, but rush to defend our country and the common good.

Scott Ritter
former Chief Weapons Inspector,
UN Special Commission (UNSCOM)
February 2005

Before I vote for this resolution for war, a war in which thousands, perhaps tens of thousands or hundred of thousands of people may die, I want to make sure that I and this Nation are on God's side.

I want more time. I want more evidence. I want to know that I am right, that our Nation is right, and not just powerful.

—Senator Robert Byrd (D-W.Va.),
October 10, 2002, before the Senate,
prior to the vote on war in Iraq

An Exercise in Critical Thinking: Today's Sharpest Minds Tackle the War and Its Context

THE EDITORS' GLOSS: This chapter (adapted from the authors' book *Imperial Crusades*) argues that the American war against Iraq included a decade of sanctions of questionable legality, and bombing of undoubted illegality – illegal because the "no-fly zones" (NFZs) it purported to enforce were not authorized or created by the UN, as Tariq Aziz pointed out in 1993. What these "NFZs" offered was a pretext for the 2003 war, and even a chance to begin it in 2002. As Robert Dreyfuss reported in *The American Prospect* (December 30, 2002), Point 8 of UN Resolution 1441 – Iraq's "last chance" – forbade Iraq from carrying out "hostile acts directed against . . . any member state taking action to uphold any Council resolution." The U.S. saw this as a reference to the NFZs: if the Iraqis fired on American planes patrolling the NFZs, this point would provide, it was claimed, grounds for war.

The "hot" war of 2003 actually began in 2002 with increased air strikes during "NFZ patrols," with the hope that Saddam would strike back and provoke "retaliation." Michael Smith writes (June 23, 2005, *London Sunday Times*) that a recently released memo has British Defense Secretary, Geoff Hoon, confirm "that 'the U.S. had already begun "spikes of activity" to put pressure on the regime.'" NFZ bombing increased from virtually nothing in March–April 2002 to 54.6 tons in September. This was all part of the "Plan B," developed in the event of a failure of "Plan A," which Smith also detailed: "British officials hoped the [weapons inspections] ultimatum could be framed in words that would be so unacceptable to Hussein that he would reject it outright." Another memo (see *Los Angeles Times*, June 15, 2005) confirmed that the British ambassador, Christopher Meyer, had "told [U.S. Deputy Defense Secretary] Wolfowitz that UN pressure and weapons inspections could be used to trip up Hussein."

The recent revelation (*Washington Post*, August 3, 2005) of a 2002 finding signed by President Bush, creating a CIA-backed paramilitary force of Iraqi exiles ("the Scorpions"), trained at bases in Jordan and sent before the war to "cities such as Baghdad, Fallujah and Qaim to give the impression that a rebellion was underway and to conduct light sabotage," completes a dishonest and despicable picture.

As Michael Smith put it, the real news isn't the famed "Downing Street Memo" but rather "the shady April 2002 deal to go to war, the cynical use of the UN to provide an excuse, and the secret, illegal air war [conducted] without the backing of Congress."

C H A P T E R

1

The Thirteen Years' War
. . . .
Alexander Cockburn and Jeffrey St. Clair

THE "WAR," OFFICIALLY designated by the U.S. government as such and inaugurated with the "decapitation" strike of March 19, 2003, was really only a change of tempo in the overall war on Iraq. It commenced with the sanctions imposed by the UN and by a separate U.S. blockade in August of 1990, stretching through the first "hot" attack of January 16, 1991, on through the next twelve years, 1990–2003: a long war, and a terrible one for the Iraqi people.

ONE

On April 3, 1991, the UN Security Council approved Resolution 687, the so-called mother of all resolutions, setting up the Sanctions Committee, dominated by the United States.

It is vital to understand that the first "hot" Gulf War was waged as much against the people of Iraq as against the Republican Guard. The U.S. and its allies destroyed Iraq's water, sewage and water-purification systems and its electrical grid. Nearly every bridge across the Tigris and Euphrates was demolished. They struck twenty-eight hospitals and destroyed thirty-eight schools. They hit all eight of Iraq's large hydropower dams. They attacked grain storage silos and irrigation systems.

Farmlands near Basra were inundated with saltwater as a result of allied attacks. More than 95 per cent of Iraq's poultry farms were destroyed, as were 3.3 million sheep and more than 2 million cows. The U.S. and its allies bombed textile plants, cement factories and oil refineries, pipelines and storage facilities, all of which contributed to an environmental and economic nightmare that continued nearly unabated over the twelve years.

When confronted by the press with reports of Iraqi women carting home buckets of filthy water from the Tigris river, itself contaminated with raw sewage from the bombed treatment plants, an American general shrugged his shoulders and said: "People say, 'You didn't recognize that the bombing was going to have an effect on water and sewage.' Well, what were we trying to do with sanctions: help out the Iraqi people? What we were doing with the attacks on the infrastructure was to accelerate the effect of the sanctions."

After this first "hot" war in early 1991, with Iraq's civilian and military infrastructure in ruins, the sanctions returned, as an invisible army of what we could call "external occupation," with a vise grip: the intent was to keep Iraq from rebuilding not only its army but the foundations of its economy and society.[1]

Despite the efforts of outfits such as Voices in the Wilderness, embargoes don't draw the same attention as salvoes of cruise missiles or showers of cluster bombs. But they're infinitely more deadly, and the perpetrators and executives deserve to end up on trial as war criminals as richly as any targeting officer in the Pentagon.

By 1998, UN officials working in Baghdad were arguing that the root cause of child mortality and other health problems was no longer simply lack of food and medicine but lack of clean water (freely available in all parts of Iraq prior to the Gulf War) and of electrical power, now running at only 30 per cent of the pre-bombing level, with consequences for hospitals and water-pumping systems that can be all too readily imagined.

Many of the contracts vetoed at the insistence of the U.S. by the Sanctions Committee were integral to the repair of water and sewage systems. By some estimates, the bombings from the Gulf War inflicted nearly $200 billion worth of damage to the civilian infrastructure of Iraq. "Basically, anything with chemicals or even pumps is liable to get thrown out," one UN official revealed.

The sanctions, then, served as a pretext to bring this hidden war home to the Iraqi people, to "soften them up" from the inside, as one Pentagon official put it. The same trend was apparent in the power supply sector, where around 25 per cent of the contracts were vetoed. This meant not only were homes without power, but also hospitals, schools, the infrastructure of everyday life.

But even this doesn't tell the whole story. UN officials referred to the "complementarity issue," meaning that items approved for purchase would

---

1. See the comprehensive discussion of the sanctions applied to Iraq between the wars by Judge Marc Bossuyt and Prof. Joy Gordon on pp. 89–96 and 97–133, respectively, of the companion to the present volume, *Neo-CONNED!*.

be useless without other items that had been vetoed. For example (as *CounterPunch* reported at the time) the Iraqi Ministry of Health ordered $25 million worth of dentist chairs. This order was approved by the Sanctions Committee, except for the compressors, without which the chairs were useless and consequently gathered dust in a Baghdad warehouse.

These vetoes served as a constant harassment, even over petty issues. In February 2000 the U.S. moved to prevent Iraq from importing 15 bulls from France. The excuse was that the animals, ordered with the blessing of the UN's humanitarian office in Baghdad to try to restock the Iraqi beef industry, would require certain vaccines which (who knows?) might be diverted into a program to make biological weapons of mass destruction.

For sheer sadistic bloody-mindedness, however, the interdiction of the bulls pales beside an initiative of the British government, which banned the export of vaccines for tetanus, diphtheria and yellow fever on the grounds that they too might find their way into the hands of Saddam's biological weaponeers. It had been the self-exculpatory mantra of U.S. and British officials that "food and medicine are exempt from sanctions." As the vaccine ban shows, this, like so many other pronouncements on Iraq, turns out to be a lie.

Indeed, the sanctions policy was always marked by acts of captious cruelty. Since 1991, the U.S. and Britain slapped their veto on requests by Iraq for infant food, ping-pong balls, NCR computers for children's hospitals for blood analysis, heaters, insecticide, syringes, bicycles, nail polish and lipstick, tennis balls, children's clothes, pencil sharpeners and school notebooks, cotton balls and swabs, hospital and ambulance radios and pagers, and shroud material.

TWO

But the prolonged onslaught on the Iraqi people by the sanctions did not mean that direct military attack stopped in March of 1991. Indeed, though it received scant attention in the press, Iraq was hit with bombs or missiles an average of every three days since the ceasefire that purportedly signaled the end of the first Gulf War. Its feeble air defense system was shattered and its radars were jammed and bombed; its air force was grounded, the runways of its airports were repeatedly cratered; its navy, primitive to begin with, was destroyed. The nation's northern and southern territories were occupied by hostile forces, armed, funded and overseen by the CIA.

COCKBURN & ST. CLAIR

Every bit of new construction in the country was scrutinized for any possible military function by satellite cameras capable of zooming down to a square meter. Truck and tank convoys were zealously monitored. Troop locations were pinpointed. Bunkers were mapped, the coordinates programmed into the targeting software for bunker-busting bombs.

Iraq after the Gulf War wasn't a rogue state. It was a captive state. This daily military harassment was the normal state of play, but there were also more robust displays of power. In June of 1993, Bill Clinton okayed a cruise missile strike on Baghdad, supposedly in response to an alleged and certainly bungled bid by Iraqi agents to assassinate George Bush the first on his triumphal tour of Kuwait.

Twenty-three cruise missiles were launched at Baghdad from two ships in the Persian Gulf. With deadly imprecision, eight of the missiles hit a residential suburb of Baghdad killing dozens of civilians, including one of Iraq's leading artists, Leila al-Attar.

Then in December of 1998 another raid on Baghdad was launched, this one timed to divert attention from the House of Representatives' vote on the question of Clinton's impeachment. This time more than 100 missiles rained down on Baghdad, Mosul, Tikrit, and Basra, killing hundreds. Clinton's chief pollster, Stan Greenberg, imparted the welcome news that the bombings had caused Clinton's poll numbers to jump by 11 points. When in doubt, bomb Iraq.

The message was not lost on Bush. In late February of 2001, less than a month into office, Bush let fly with two dozen cruise missiles on Baghdad, a strike that Donald Rumsfeld described as an "act of protective retaliation." And alongside these attacks the CIA was busy sponsoring assassination bids and, with sometimes comical inefficiency, trying to mount coups against Saddam Hussein.

After five years of sanctions Iraq was in desperate straits. The hospitals filled with dying children, while medicines necessary to save them were banned by the U.S. officials in New York supervising the operations of the Sanctions Committee. Half a million children had died in the time span. The mortality rates were soaring with terrifying speed. The infant mortality rate had gone from 47 per 1,000 in 1989 to 108 per 1,000 in 1996. For kids under five the increase in the rate was even worse, from 56 per 1,000 in 1989 to 131 per 1,000 in 1996. By 1996 the death count was running at 5,000 children a month, to which Madeleine Albright made the infamous comment, "we think the price is worth it."

THREE

One might think this carefully planned and deadly onslaught on a civilian population, year after year, surely was retribution enough for Saddam's invasion of Kuwait. But what allowed the ultra-hawks in Washington to press for another hot war on Iraq was Saddam's personal survival as Iraqi dictator. Though the aims of the war party were much broader, the brazen survival of Saddam was always the pretext.

On July 8, 1996, the Institute for Advanced Strategic and Political Studies sent a strategy memo to Israel's new Prime Minister, Benjamin Netanyahu. Grandly titled "A Clean Break: A New Strategy for Securing the Realm" (the realm in this instance being Israel), the memorandum had among its sponsors several notorious Washington characters, some of them accused more than once down the years of being agents of influence for Israel, including Richard Perle and Douglas Feith.

Among the recommendations for Netanyahu were these:

> . . . roll-back some of [Israel's] most dangerous threats. This implies a clean break from the slogan "comprehensive peace" to a traditional concept of strategy based on balance of power . . . .
>
> Change the nature of [Israel's] relations with the Palestinians, including upholding the right of hot pursuit for self-defense into all Palestinian areas . . . .
>
> Israel can shape its strategic environment, in cooperation with Turkey and Jordan, by weakening, containing, and even rolling back Syria. This effort can focus on removing Saddam Hussein from power in Iraq – an important Israeli strategic objective in its own right – as a means of foiling Syria's regional ambitions.

Within a few short months this strategy paper for Netanyahu was being recycled through the agency of a Washington bucket shop called the Project for a New American Century, which was convened by William Kristol with infusions of cash from the right-wing Bradley Foundation. The PNAC became a roosting spot for a retinue of DC neocons, headlined by Donald Rumsfeld, Dick Cheney, and Paul Wolfowitz.

On the eve of Clinton's 1998 State of the Union address, Rumsfeld and Wolfowitz sent Clinton a letter on PNAC stationery urging the President to overhaul radically U.S. policy toward Iraq. Instead of the slow squeeze of sanctions, Rumsfeld and Wolfowitz declared that it was time for Saddam to be forcibly evicted and Iraq reconstructed along lines favorable to U.S. and Israeli interests. The UN be damned. "We are writing you because we are convinced that current American policy toward Iraq is not succeeding, and that we may soon face a threat in the Middle East more serious than any we have known since the end of the cold war," the letter blared.

> In your upcoming State of the Union Address, you have an opportunity to chart a clear and determined course for meeting this threat. We urge you to seize that opportunity, and to enunciate a new strategy that would secure the interests of the U.S. and our friends and allies around the world. That strategy should aim above all at the removal of Saddam Hussein's regime from power .... American policy cannot continue to be crippled by a misguided insistence on unanimity in the UN Security Council.

In all likelihood, the strategy outlined in the letter was aimed not at Clinton, the lame duck, but at Gore, who Wolfowitz, Rumsfeld, *et al.* believed might be more receptive to this rhetoric.

They had reason for hope. One of the PNAC's members was James Woolsey, former CIA head and long-time Gore advisor on intelligence and military matters. And it worked. As the campaign season rolled into action Gore began to distance himself from Clinton on Iraq. He embraced the corrupt Ahmad Chalabi and his Iraqi National Congress, indicted the Bush family for being soft on Saddam and called for regime topple.

Had Gore been elected he likely would have stepped up the tempo of military strikes on Iraq within weeks of taking office.

FOUR

After seizing power, the Bush crowd didn't have to wait long to draw Iraqi blood. Less than a month after taking office, cruise missiles pummeled Baghdad, killing dozens of civilians. Then came the attacks of 9/11. Just hours into that day of disaster, Rumsfeld convened a meeting in the war room. He commanded his aides to get "best info fast. Judge whether good enough to hit S.H." – meaning Saddam Hussein – "at same time. Not only U.B.L." – the initials used to identify Osama bin Laden. "Go massive." Notes taken by these aides quote him as saying: "sweep it all up. Things related and not." The notes were uncovered by David Martin of CBS News.

The preparations for overthrowing Saddam began that day, under the pretense that Saddam was somehow connected to bin Laden's Wahhabite kamikazes. Rumsfeld knew then that the connection was illusory, and, despite lots of bluster and digging, it didn't become any more substantial over the next year and a half.

In the months that preceded the second "hot" war, started on March 19, 2003, many a theory was advanced for the prime motive of the war party. Was it the plan of the pro-Israel neocon hawks? Was it all about oil and (a sub-variant) because Saddam was insisting on being paid for his oil in euros? Was it, in the wake of 9/11, a peremptory message about U.S. power (this is the current White House favorite)? Was it essentially a subject change from the domestic economic slump?

The answer is the essentially unconspiratorial one that it was a mix. Bush's initial policy in his first fumbling months in office was far from the chest-pounding stance of implacable American might that it became after 9/11 changed the rule book. 9/11 is what gave the neocons their chance, and allowed them to push forward and eventually trump the instincts of a hefty chunk of the political and corporate elites.

For many in these elites, the survival of Saddam Hussein was a small blip on the radar screen. For a résumé of what preoccupied these elites, here's a useful account from Jeffrey Garen, who was Clinton's first under secretary of commerce for international trade, writing in *Business Week*:

> The biggest issues the administration faced were not military in nature but competition with Japan and Europe, financial crises in Latin America and Asia, negotiations over the North American Trade Agreement, and the establishment of the World Trade Organization and China's entrance into it. In Washington's eyes, the policies of the IMF, the World Bank, and the WTO were bigger issues than the future of NATO. The opening of Japan's markets was more critical than its military posture in Asia. The rating that Standard & Poor's gave to Indonesia was of greater significance than sending our military advisers there. We pushed deregulation and privatization. We mounted massive trade missions to help U.S. companies win big contracts in emerging markets. Strengthening economic globalization became the organizing principle for most of our foreign policy. And American corporations were de facto partners all along the way.

That's a fair account of how the agenda looks, from the imperial battlements. Run the show as best you can, but don't rock the boat more than you have to. Acting too blatantly as prime world gangster, dissing the Security Council, roiling the Arab world, prompting popular upheavals in Turkey, all counted as boat-rocking on a dangerous scale.

By the end of half a year's national debate on the utility of attacking Iraq, business leaders were still chewing their fingernails and trembling at the economic numbers; the *New York Times* was against war and George Jr. had lost the support of his father, who issued a distinct rebuke during a question-and-answer session at Tufts in mid-spring. George Senior's closest associates, James Baker and Brent Scowcroft, similarly expressed disagreement.

But against this opposition, domestic political factors proved paramount and overwhelming. The post-9/11 climate offers the American right its greatest chance since the first days of the Reagan administration, maybe even since the early 1950s, to set in blood and stone its core agenda: untrammeled exercise of power overseas, and at home roll-back of all liberal gains since the start of the New Deal. And not just that, but an opportunity too to make a lasting dent in the purchase on Jewish support and money held since Truman by the Democratic Party.

FIVE

These are the prizes, and so it was never in doubt, since the morning hours of 9/11, that the Bush regime would attack Iraq and *eventually* bring home the head of Saddam. But what the regime needed immediately, and got, was not the head, but the image of the head, wrapped in the U.S. flag. That came with the images of Iraqis – actually a small knot of Chalabi's supporters plus some journalists – cheering U.S. troops in the Baghdad square in front of the Palestine Hotel on April 9 as they hauled down Saddam's statue in one small portion of that square, itself sealed off by three U.S. tanks.[1] As for the looting, it's entirely in character for U.S. planners to have had plans for the "attrition of Iraqi national self-esteem," but also we wouldn't discount local initiative, probably with inside help, in looting the archeological museum and the National Library.

The non-discovery of the weapons of mass destruction was and remains a huge embarrassment for both Bush and Blair. The British *Independent* (April 20, 2003) carried the following huge frontpage banner headlines: "SO WHERE ARE THEY, MR BLAIR? NOT ONE ILLEGAL WARHEAD. NOT ONE DRUM OF CHEMICALS. NOT ONE INCRIMINATING DOCUMENT. NOT ONE SHRED OF EVIDENCE THAT IRAQ HAS WEAPONS OF MASS DESTRUCTION IN MORE THAN A MONTH OF WAR AND OCCUPATION."

CounterPunch tends to agree with the assessment of the Russian commentator "Venik," who remarked when the "hot war" ended that, as in the initial U.S. engagement in Afghanistan, the prime U.S. weapon of mass destruction was the dollar.

---

1. Interested readers can go to http://www.counterpunch.org/statue.html and see for themselves.

We have read many highly detailed accounts of how, in the first week of April, the impending siege of Baghdad turned into a cakewalk, and though we don't believe most of those details, we do agree that there were some big pay-offs and U.S. guarantees of assisted flight. Indeed here at *CounterPunch* we wonder whether some of those billion-dollar stashes found by U.S. troops in Baghdad were not U.S. pay-off money that speeded the departure of the Republican Guard's commanders, duly followed by the defection of the prudent troops.

Iraq's thirteen years' war is not over. That's obvious enough, and we expect many long years of travail and struggle lie ahead for those millions of people in the cradle of civilization. We will report on them to the best of our ability. Readers (and CounterPunchers especially) should not neglect, in pondering those thirteen years, the fact that U.S. officials spent years knowingly making decisions that spelled certain death to hundreds of thousands of the poorest Iraqi civilians, the bulk of them children.

CHAPTER
1
postscript

Some Final Thoughts
• • • • • • • • • •

Alexander Cockburn

FIRST, I THINK the left needs to get a lot more hard-eyed about what the actual function of the UN is.

Nikita Khrushchev wrote in his incomparable memoirs that Soviet admirals, like admirals everywhere, loved battleships, because they could get piped aboard in great style amid the respectful hurrahs of their crews. It's the same with the UN, now more than ever reduced to the servile function of after-sales service provider for the United States, on permanent call as the mop-up brigade. It would be a great step forward if several big Third World nations were soon to quit the United Nations, declaring that it has no political function beyond ratifying the world's present distasteful political arrangements.

The trouble is that national political elites in pretty much every UN-member country – now 191 in all – yearn to live in high style for at least a few years, and in some cases for decades, on the Upper East side of Manhattan and to cut a dash in the General Assembly. They have a deep material stake in continuing membership, even though in the case of small, poor countries the prodigious outlays on a UN delegation could be far better used in some decent domestic application, funding orphanages or local crafts back home.

Barely a day goes by without some Democrat piously demanding "an increased role" for the UN in whatever misadventure for which the U.S. requires political cover. Howard Dean built his candidacy on clarion calls for the UN's supposedly legitimizing assistance in Iraq. Despite the political history of the nineties many leftists still have a tendency to invoke the UN as a countervailing power. When all other argument fails they fall back on the International Criminal Court, an outfit that should by all rights have the same credibility as a beneficial institution as the World Bank or Interpol.

On the issue of the UN, I can boast a record of matchless consistency. As a toddler I tried to bar my father's exit from the nursery of our London flat when he told me he was leaving for several weeks to attend, as diplomatic correspondent of the *Daily Worker*, the founding conference of the UN in San Francisco. Despite my denunciation of all such absence-prompting conferences (and in my infancy there were many), he did go.

He wrote later in his autobiography, *Crossing the Line*, that

> [t]he journey of our special train across the Middle West was at times almost intolerably moving. Our heavily laden special had some sort of notice prominently displayed on its sides indicating it was taking people to the foundation meeting of the United Nations. From towns and lonely villages all across the plains and prairies, people would come out to line the tracks, standing there with the flags still flying at half-mast for Roosevelt on the buildings behind them, and their eyes fixed on this train with extraordinary intensity, as though it were part of the technical apparatus for the performance of a miracle . . . . On several occasions I saw a man or woman solemnly touch the train, the way a person might touch a talisman.

It was understandable that an organization aspiring to represent All Mankind and to espouse Peace should have excited fervent hopes in the wake of a terrible war, but the fix was in from the start, as Peter Gowan reminds us in a spirited essay in *New Left Review* for November/December 2003. The Rooseveltian vision was for an impotent General Assembly with decision-making authority vested in a Security Council without, in Gowan's words, "the slightest claim to rest on any representative principle other than brute force," and of course dominated by the United States and its vassals. FDR did see a cosmopolitan role for the UN; not so Truman and Acheson who followed Nelson Rockefeller's body-blow to the nascent UN when, as assistant secretary of state for Latin American affairs, the latter brokered the Chapultepec Pact in Mexico City in 1945, formalizing U.S. dominance in the region through the soon-to-be familiar regional military-security alliance set up by Dean Acheson in the next period.

These days the UN has the same restraining role on the world's prime imperial power as did the Roman Senate in the fourth century AD, when there were still actual senators spending busy lives bustling from one cocktail party to another, intriguing to have their sons elected quaestor and so forth, deliberating with great self-importance and sending the Emperor pompous resolutions on the burning issues of the day.

For a modern evocation of what those senatorial resolutions must have been like, read the unanimous Security Council resolution on October 15,

2003, hailing the U.S.-created "Governing Council of Iraq," and trolling out UN-speak to the effect that the Security Council *"welcomes* the positive response of the international community to the establishment of the broadly representative council"; *"supports* the Governing Council's efforts to mobilize the people of Iraq"; *"requests* that the United States on behalf of the multinational force report to the Security Council on the efforts and progress of this force." Signed by France, Russia, China, UK, U.S., Germany, Spain, Bulgaria, Chile, Mexico, Guinea, Cameroon, Angola, Pakistan and Syria. As Gowan remarks, this brazen twaddle evokes "the seating of Pol Pot's representatives in the UN for fourteen years after his regime was overthrown by the DRV."

Another way of assaying the UN's role in Iraq is to remember that it made a profit out of its own blockade and the consequent starvation of hundreds of thousands of Iraqi babies in the 1990s. As a fee for its part in administering the "Oil-for-Food" Program, the UN helped itself to two per cent off the top. (On more than one account members of the UN-approved Governing Council, whose most conspicuous emblem was the bank looter Ahmad Chalabi, were demanding a far heftier skim in the present looting of Iraq's national assets.)

Two months before the October 2003 resolution, the U.S.'s chosen instrument for selling the Governing Council, UN Special Envoy Vieira de Mello, was blown up in his office in Baghdad by persons with a realistic assessment of the function of the UN. Please, my friends, no more earnest calls for "a UN role," at least not until the body is radically reconstituted along genuinely democratic lines. As far as Iraq is concerned, all occupying forces should leave, with all contracts concerning Iraq's national assets and resources written across the last nine months repudiated, declared null and void, illegal under international covenant.

And finally, there is the matter of imperial motive. So why did the U.S. want to invade Iraq in 2003 and finish off Saddam? There are as many rationales as there were murderers on Christie's Orient Express. In the end my mind goes back to something my friend the political scientist Doug Lummis wrote from his home in another outpost of the Empire, in Okinawa at the time of the first onslaught on Iraq at the start of the nineties.

Iraq, Lummis wrote, had been in the eighties a model of an oil-producing country thrusting its way out of the Third World, with its oil nationalized, a good health system, and an efficient bureaucracy cowed from corrupt practices by a brutal regime. The fundamental intent of the prime imperial power was to thrust Iraq back, deep and ever deeper into Third-World indigence, and of course to re-appropriate Iraq's oil.

In the fall of 2003 I was in London and for a weekend enjoyed the hospitality of the first-class journalist Richard Gott, also of his wife Vivienne. At one point our conversation turned to this question of motive, and I was interested to hear Gott make the same point as Lummis, only about the attack of 2003. I asked him why he thought this, and Gott recalled a visit he'd made to Baghdad in the very early spring of 2003.

This was a time when the natural and political inclination of most opponents of the impending war was to stress the fearful toll of the sanctions imposed from 1990 onwards. Gott had a rather different observation, in part because of his experience in Latin America. Baghdad, he said, looked a lot more prosperous than Havana. "It was clear today," Gott wrote after his visit, "from the quantity of goods in the shops, and the heavy traffic jams in the urban motorways, that the sanctions menace has been effectively defeated. Iraq is awakening from a long and depressing sleep, and its economy is clearly beginning to function once more. No wonder it is in the firing line."

Eyes other than Gott's no doubt observed the same signs of economic recovery. Iraq was rising from the ashes, and so, it had to be thrust down once more. The only "recovery" permitted would be on Uncle Sam's terms. Or so Uncle Sam, in his arrogance, supposed.

Then, in January 2004, former U.S. Treasury Secretary Paul O'Neill disclosed that George Bush had come into office planning to overthrow Saddam Hussein. MSNBC promptly polled its audience with the question, "Did O'Neill betray Bush?"

Was that really the big question? The White House had a sharper nose for the real meat of Leslie Stahl's *60 Minutes* interview with O'Neill and Ron Suskind, the reporter who based much of his exposé of the Bush White House, *The Price of Loyalty,* on 19,000 government documents O'Neill provided him.

What bothered the White House is one particular National Security Council document shown in the *60 Minutes* interview, clearly drafted in the early weeks of the new administration, which showed plans for the post-invasion dispersal of Iraq's oil assets among the world's great powers, starting with the major oil companies.

For the brief moment it was on the TV screen one could see that this bit of paper, stamped "Secret," was undoubtedly one of the most explosive documents in the history of imperial conspiracy. Here, dead center in the camera's lens, was the refutation of every single rationalization for the attack on Iraq ever offered by George W. Bush and his co-conspirators, including Tony Blair.

That NSC document told *60 Minutes*'s vast audience the attack on Iraq was not about national security in the wake of 9/11. It was not about weapons of mass destruction. It was not about Saddam Hussein's possible ties to Osama bin Laden. It was about stealing Iraq's oil, the same way the British stole it three quarters of a century earlier. The major oil companies drew up the map, handed it to their man George, helped him (through such trustees as James Baker) steal the 2000 election, and then told him to get on with the attack.

O'Neill said that the Treasury Department's lawyers okayed release of the document to him. The White House, which took 78 days to launch an investigation into the outing of Valerie Plame as a CIA officer, clearly regarded the disclosure of what Big Oil wanted as truly reprehensible, as opposed to endangering the life of Ms. Plame.

Forget about O'Neill "betraying" Bush. How about Bush lying to the American people? It's obvious from that document that Bush, on the campaign trail in 2000, was as intent on regime change in Iraq as was Clinton in his second term and as Gore was publicly declaring himself to be.

Here's Bush in debate with Gore October 3, 2000:

> If we don't stop extending our troops all around the world in nation-building missions, then we're going to have a serious problem coming down the road. I'm going to prevent that.

The second quote is from a joint press conference with Tony Blair on January 31, 2003. Bush's reply:

> Actually, prior to September 11, we were discussing smart sanctions. We were trying to fashion a sanctions regime that would make it more likely to be able to contain somebody like Saddam Hussein. After September 11, the doctrine of containment just doesn't hold any water. The strategic vision of our country shifted dramatically because we now recognize that oceans no longer protect us, that we're vulnerable to attack. And the worst form of attack could come from somebody acquiring weapons of mass destruction and using them on the American people. I now realize the stakes. I realize the world has changed. My most important obligation is to protect the American people from further harm, and I will do that.

In his cabinet meetings before 9/11 Bush may, in O'Neill's words, have been like a blind man in a room full of deaf people. But, as O'Neill also says, in those early strategy meetings Bush did say the plan from the start was to attack Iraq, using any pretext. Bush's language about "smart sanctions" from the press conference at the start of last year was as brazen and far more momentous a lie as any of those that earned Bill Clinton the Republicans' impeachment charges.

THE EDITORS' GLOSS: The idea that people are innocent until proven guilty, entitled to equitable treatment at the hands of others or the government, entitled to a reasonably free exercise of rights to expression, religious worship, and the like – these are all elements of whatever is left of the positive image of Britain and the United States in the world today.

Yet history shows that these nations frequently departed from the noblest aspects of their legal and political traditions to pursue what they hypocritically maintained was "a higher good," if not mere "national interest." Robert Fisk's historical sketch of Iraq, published in *The Independent*, June 17, 2004, is one choice example of this attempt to "civilize" at gunpoint, and is chillingly similar to the experiment America is conducting there today. As Maurizio Blondet illustrates in the chapter that follows – and as sketched philosophically by Prof. Claes Ryn later – the willingness of the U.S. to follow, some 80 years later, in Britain's footsteps stems from a tragic commitment to an amorphous and ideological "democracy," at the expense of the principles – such as self-determination and political integrity – that such a democracy is supposed to support and defend. It is a commitment whose *in*sincerity is to be found not in the fine print of much-publicized declarations, but in its brutal application to nations and peoples who would prefer not to embrace such a kind of "democracy."

CHAPTER
2

Iraq, 1917
· · · · · · · · ·
Robert Fisk

ON THE EVE of our "handover" of "full sovereignty" to Iraq, this is a story of tragedy and folly and of dark foreboding. It is about the past-made-present, and our ability to copy blindly and to the very letter the lies and follies of our ancestors. It is about that admonition of antiquity: that if we don't learn from history, we are doomed to repeat it. For Iraq 1917, read Iraq 2003. For Iraq 1920, read Iraq 2004 or 2005.

Yes, we have given "full sovereignty" to Iraq. That's also what the British falsely claimed more than 80 years ago. Come, then, and confront the looking glass of history, and see what America and Britain will do in the next 12 terrible months in Iraq.

Our story begins in March 1917 as 22-year-old Private 11072 Charles Dickens of the Cheshire Regiment peels a poster off a wall in the newly captured city of Baghdad. It is a turning point in his life. He has survived the hopeless Gallipoli campaign, attacking the Ottoman empire only 150 miles from its capital, Constantinople. He has then marched the length of Mesopotamia, fighting the Turks yet again for possession of the ancient caliphate, and enduring the grim battle for Baghdad. The British invasion army of 600,000 soldiers was led by Lieutenant-General Sir Stanley Maude, and the sheet of paper that caught Private Dickens's attention was Maude's official "Proclamation" to the people of Baghdad, printed in English and Arabic.

That same 11" by 18" poster, now framed in black and gold, hangs on the wall a few feet from my desk as I write this story of empire and dark prophecy. Long ago, the paper was stained with damp – "foxed," as booksellers say – which may have been Private Dickens's perspiration in the long hot Iraqi summer of 1917. It has been folded many times; witness, as his daughter Hilda would recall 86 years later, to its presence in his army knapsack over many months.

In a letter to me, she called this "his precious document," and I can see why. It is filled with noble aspirations and presentiments of future tragedy; with the false promises of the world's greatest empire, commitments and good intentions; and with words of honour that were to be repeated in the same city of Baghdad by the next great empire more than two decades after Dickens's death. It reads now like a funeral dirge:

> Proclamation . . . . Our military operations have as their object, the defeat of the enemy and the driving of him from these territories. In order to complete this task I am charged with absolute and supreme control of all regions in which British troops operate; but our armies do not come into your cities and lands as conquerors or enemies, but as liberators . . . . Your citizens have been subject to the tyranny of strangers . . . and your fathers and yourselves have groaned in bondage. Your sons have been carried off to wars not of your seeking, your wealth has been stripped from you by unjust men and squandered in different places. It is the wish not only of my King and his peoples, but it is also the wish of the great Nations with whom he is in alliance, that you should prosper even as in the past when your lands were fertile . . . . But you, people of Baghdad . . . are not to understand that it is the wish of the British Government to impose upon you alien institutions. It is the hope of the British Government that the aspirations of your philosophers and writers shall be realised once again, that the people of Baghdad shall flourish, and shall enjoy their wealth and substance under institutions which are in consonance with their sacred laws and with their racial ideals . . . . It is the hope and desire of the British people . . . that the Arab race may rise once more to greatness and renown amongst the peoples of the Earth . . . . Therefore I am commanded to invite you, through your Nobles and Elders and Representatives, to participate in the management of your civil affairs in collaboration with the Political Representative of Great Britain . . . so that you may unite with your kinsmen in the North, East, South and West, in realising the aspirations of your Race.
>
> (signed) F.S. Maude, Lieutenant-General,
> Commanding the British Forces in Iraq.

Private Dickens spent the First World War fighting Muslims, first the Turks at Suvla Bay at Gallipoli and then the Turkish army – which included Iraqi soldiers – in Mesopotamia. He spoke "often and admirably," his daughter would recall, of one of his commanders, General Sir Charles Munro, who at 55 had fought in the last months of the Gallipoli campaign and then landed at Basra in southern Iraq at the start of the British invasion.

But Munro's leadership did not save Dickens's sister's nephew, Samuel Martin, who was killed by the Turks at Basra. Hilda remembers: "My father told of how, killing a Turk, he thought it was in revenge for the death of his 'nephew.' I don't know if they were in the same battalion, but they were a similar age, 22 years."

In all, Britain lost 40,000 men in the Mesopotamian campaign. The British had been proud of their initial occupation of Basra. More than 80 years later, Shameem Bhatia, a British Muslim whose family came from Pakistan, would send me an amused letter, along with a series of 12 very old postcards, which were printed by *The Times of India* in Bombay on behalf of the Indian YMCA. One of them showed British artillery amid the Basra date palms; another a soldier in a pith helmet, turning towards the camera as his comrades tether horses behind him; others the crew of a British gunboat on the Shatt al-Arab river, and the Turkish-held town of Kurna, one of its buildings shattered by British shellfire, shortly before its surrender. The ruins then looked, of course, identical to the Iraqi ruins of today. There are only so many ways in which a shell can smash through a home.

As long ago as 1914, a senior British official was told by "local [Arab] notables" that "we should be received in Baghdad with the same cordiality [as in southern Iraq] and that the Turkish troops would offer little if any opposition." But the British invasion of Iraq had originally failed. When Major-General Charles Townshend took 13,000 men up the banks of the Tigris towards Baghdad, he was surrounded and defeated by Turkish forces at Kut al-Amara. His surrender was the most comprehensive of military disasters, ending in a death march to Turkey for those British troops who had not been killed in battle.

The graves of 500 of them in the Kut War Cemetery sank into sewage during the period of United Nations sanctions that followed Iraq's 1990 invasion of Kuwait, when spare parts for the pumps needed to keep sewage from the graves were not supplied to Iraq. Visiting the cemetery in 1998, my colleague Patrick Cockburn found "tombstones . . . still just visible above the slimy green water. A broken cement cross sticks out of a reed bed . . . . A quagmire in which thousands of little green frogs swarm like cockroaches as they feed on garbage."

Baghdad looked much the same when Private Dickens arrived in 1917. Less than two years earlier, a visitor had described a city whose streets "gaped emptily. The shops were mostly closed . . . . In the Christian cemetery east of the high road leading to Persia, coffins and half-mouldering skeletons were floating. On account of the Cholera which was ravaging the town [three hundred people were dying of it every day] the Christian dead were now being buried on the new embankment of the high road, so that people walking and riding not only had to pass by but even to make their way among and over the graves . . . . There was no longer any life in the town."

The British occupation was dark with historical precedent. There was, of course, no "cordial" reception of British troops in Baghdad. Indeed, Iraqi troops who had been serving with the Turkish army but who "always entertained friendly ideas towards the English" were jailed – not in Abu Ghraib, but in India – and found that while in prison there they were "insulted and humiliated in every way." These same prisoners wanted to know if the British would hand Iraq over to Sherif Hussein of the Hejaz – to whom the British had made fulsome and ultimately mendacious promises of "independence" for the Arab world if he fought alongside the Allies against the Turks – on the grounds that "some of the Holy Moslem Shrines are located in Mesopotamia."

British officials believed that control of Mesopotamia would safeguard British oil interests in Persia (the initial occupation of Basra was ostensibly designed to do that) and that "clearly it is our right and duty, if we sacrifice so much for the peace of the world, that we should see to it we have compensation, or we may defeat our end" – which was not how Lt-Gen Maude expressed Britain's ambitions in his famous proclamation in 1917.

Earl Asquith was to write in his memoirs that he and Sir Edward Grey, the British foreign secretary, agreed in 1915 that "taking Mesopotamia . . . means spending millions in irrigation and development." Which is precisely what President George Bush was forced to do only months after his illegal invasion in 2003.

Those who want to wallow in even more ghastly historical parallels should turn to the magnificent research of the Iraqi scholar Ghassan Attiyah, whose volume on the British occupation was published in Beirut long before Saddam's regime took over Iraq, at a time when Iraqi as well as British archives of the period were still available. Attiyah's *Iraq, 1902–1921: A Socio-Political Study,* written 30 years before the Anglo-American invasion, should be read by all Western "statesmen" planning to occupy Arab countries.

As Attiyah discovered, the British, once they were installed in Baghdad, decided in the winter of 1917 that Iraq would have to be governed and reconstructed by a "council" formed partly of British advisers "and partly of representative non-official members from among the inhabitants." The copycat 2003 version of this "council" was, of course, the Interim Governing Council, supposedly the brainchild of Maude's American successor, Paul Bremer.

Later, the British thought they would like "a cabinet half of natives and half of British officials, behind which might be an administrative council, or some advisory body consisting entirely of prominent natives." The traveller and scholar Gertrude Bell, who became "oriental secretary" to the British military occupation authority, had no doubts about Iraqi public opinion: "The stronger the hold we are able to keep here the better the inhabitants will be pleased .... They can't conceive an independent Arab government. Nor, I confess, can I. There is no one here who could run it."

Again, this was far from the noble aspirations of Maude's proclamation issued 11 months earlier. Nor would the Iraqis have been surprised had they been told (which, of course, they were not) that Maude strongly opposed the very proclamation that appeared over his name, and which in fact had been written by Sir Mark Sykes – the very same Sykes who had drawn up the secret 1916 agreement with F. Georges-Picot for French and British control over much of the post-war Middle East.

But, by September 1919, even journalists were beginning to grasp that Britain's plans for Iraq were founded upon illusions. "I imagine," the correspondent for *The Times* wrote on 23 September,

> that the view held by many English people about Mesopotamia is that the local inhabitants will welcome us because we have saved them from the Turks, and that the country only needs developing to repay a large expenditure of English lives and English money. Neither of these ideals will bear much examination. ... From the political point of view we are asking the Arab to exchange his pride and independence for a little Western civilisation, the profits of which must be largely absorbed by the expenses of administration.

Within six months, Britain was fighting a military insurrection in Iraq and David Lloyd George, the Prime Minister, was facing calls for a military withdrawal. "Is it not for the benefit of the people of that country that it should be governed so as to enable them to develop this land which has been withered and shrivelled up by oppression? What would happen if we withdrew?" Lloyd George would not abandon Iraq to "anarchy and confusion." By this stage, British officials in Baghdad were blaming the violence on "local political agitation, originated outside Iraq," suggesting that Syria might be involved.

Come again? Could history repeat itself so perfectly? For Lloyd George's "anarchy," read any statement from the American occupation power warning of "civil war" in the event of a Western withdrawal. For Syria – well, read Syria.

A.T. Wilson, the senior British official in Iraq in 1920, took a predictable line. "We cannot maintain our position ... by a policy of conciliation of extremists. Having set our hand to the task of regenerating Mesopotamia, we must be prepared to furnish men and money.... We must be prepared ... to go very slowly with constitutional and democratic institutions."

There was fighting in the Shiite town of Kufa and a British siege of Najaf after a British official was murdered. The British demanded "the unconditional surrender of the murderers and others concerned in the plot," and the leading Shiite divine, Sayed Khadum Yazdi, abstained from supporting the rebellion and shut himself up in his house. Eleven of the insurgents were executed. A local sheikh, Badr al-Rumaydh, became a target. "Badr must be killed or captured, and a relentless pursuit of the man till this object is obtained should be carried out," a British political officer wrote.

The British now realised that they had made one big political mistake. They had alienated a major political group in Iraq – the ex-Turkish Iraqi officials and officers. The ranks of the disaffected swelled. For Kufa 1920, read Kufa 2004. For Najaf 1920, read Najaf 2004. For Yazdi, read Grand Ayatollah Ali al-Sistani. For Badr, read Muqtada al-Sadr.

In 1920, another insurgency broke out in the area of Fallujah, where Sheikh Dhari killed a British officer, Col. Leachman, and cut rail traffic between Fallujah and Baghdad. The British advanced towards Fallujah and inflicted "heavy punishment" on the tribe. For Fallujah, of course, read Fallujah. And the location of the heavy punishment? Today it is known as Khan Dari – and it was the scene of the first killing of a U.S. soldier by a roadside bomb in 2003.

In desperation, the British needed "to complete the façade of the Arab government." And so, with Winston Churchill's enthusiastic support, the British gave the throne of Iraq to the Hashemite King Faisal, the son of Sherif Hussein, a consolation prize for the man the French had just thrown out of Damascus. Paris was having no kings in its own mandated territory of Syria. Henceforth, the British government – deprived of reconstruction funds by an international recession, and confronted by an increasingly unwilling soldiery, which had fought during the 1914–18 war and was waiting for demobilisation – would rely on air power to impose its wishes.

There are no kings to impose on Iraq today (the former Crown Prince Hassan of Jordan pulled his hat out of the ring just before the invasion), so we have installed Iyad Allawi, the former CIA "asset," as Prime Minister in the hope that he can provide the same sovereign wallpaper as Faisal once did. Our soldiers can hide out in the desert, hopefully unattacked, unless they are needed to shore up the tottering power of our present-day "Faisal."

And so we come to the immediate future of Iraq. How are we to "control" Iraq while claiming that we have handed over "full sovereignty"? Again, the archives come to our rescue. The Royal Air Force, again with Churchill's support, bombed rebellious villages and dissident tribesmen in Iraq. Churchill urged the employment of mustard gas, which had been used against Shiite rebels in 1920.

Squadron Leader Arthur Harris, later Marshal of the Royal Air Force and the man who perfected the firestorm destruction of Hamburg, Dresden and other great German cities in the Second World War, was employed to refine the bombing of Iraqi insurgents. The RAF found, he wrote much later, "that by burning down their reed-hutted villages, after we'd warned them to get out, we put them to the maximum amount of inconvenience, without physical hurt [sic], and they soon stopped their raiding and looting . . . . "

This was what, in its emasculation of the English language, the Pentagon would now call "war lite." But the bombing was not as surgical as Harris's official biographer would suggest. In 1924, he had admitted that "they [the Arabs and Kurds] now know what real bombing means, in casualties and damage; they know that within 45 minutes a full-sized village can be practically wiped out and a third of its inhabitants killed or injured."

T. E. Lawrence – Lawrence of Arabia – remarked in a 1920 letter to *The Observer* that "it is odd that we do not use poison gas on these occasions." Air Commodore Lionel Charlton was so appalled at the casualties inflicted on innocent villagers that he resigned his post as Senior Air Staff Officer Iraq because he could no longer "maintain the policy of intimidation by bomb." He had visited an Iraqi hospital to find it full of wounded tribesmen. After the RAF had bombed the Kurdish rebel city of Sulaymaniyah, Charlton "knew the crowded life of these settlements and pictured with horror the arrival of a bomb, without warning, in the midst of a market gathering or in the bazaar quarter. Men, women and children would suffer equally."

Already, we have seen the use of almost indiscriminate air power by the American forces in Iraq: the destruction of homes in "dissident" villages, the bombing of mosques where weapons are allegedly concealed, the slaughter-by-air-strike of "terrorists" near the Syrian border, who turned out to be a wedding party. Much the same policy has been adopted in the already abandoned "democracy" of Afghanistan.

As for the soldiers, we couldn't ship our corpses home in the heat of the Middle East 80 years ago, so we buried them in the great North Wall Cemetery in Baghdad, where they lie to this day, most of them in their late teens and twenties. We didn't hide their coffins. Their last resting place is still there for all to see today, opposite the ruins of the suicide-bombed Turkish embassy.

As for the gravestone of Samuel Martin, it stood for years in the British war cemetery in Basra with the following inscription: "In Memory of Private Samuel Martin 24384, 8th Bn, Cheshire Regiment who died on Sunday 9 April 1916. Private Martin, son of George and Sarah Martin, of the Beech Tree Inn, Barnton, Northwich, Cheshire."

In the gales of shellfire that swept Basra during the 1980–88 war with Iran, the cemetery was destroyed and looted and many gravestones shattered beyond repair. When I visited the cemetery in the chaotic months after the Anglo-American invasion of 2003, I found wild dogs roaming between the broken headstones. Even the brass fittings of the central memorial had been stolen. *Sic transit gloria.*

www.einswine.com

THE EDITORS' GLOSS: The "West" has given much of immense value to the world. Traditions of achievement in law, government, science, the arts, craftsmanship and religion are just a few examples. Yet that very history acts as a severe temptation to pride and self-satisfaction for modern politicians, like George Bush and Tony Blair, who see themselves as heirs to those traditions, although grasping nothing of their spirit. Such traditions provide them with the opportunity to pose as the defenders of "civilization" from "its enemies" – those who "hate freedom" – even while employing methods of war and "diplomacy" that contradict everything those traditions stand for. When the "West" that Bush and Blair claim to represent betrays its own origins, when it replaces loyalty to religious and moral ideals with a fanatical attachment to an ideology of "freedom" and obsession with the external machinery of plutocratic "democracy," it appears rightly to many people – not merely Muslims – as the "Great Satan."

The shift in the orientation of the "West" has its roots in a number of different but converging forces, all of which are evident in the contemporary treatment of Iraq. This is what makes the case of Iraq so tragically interesting and illustrative, and Blondet's piece so compelling.

Blondet quotes the neoconservative Edward Luttwak, who pushed for war with Iraq in 1990 and was quite candid about why. He was no less honest in 2003, even admitting that the focus on al-Qaeda and WMD stemmed not from the facts themselves, but from the fact that the Bush administration could not admit openly that its real desire was to dispose of Saddam Hussein. "Cheney was forced into this fake posture of worrying about weapons of mass destruction," Luttwak told *Mother Jones* reporters Vest and Dreyfuss. "The ties to Al Qaeda? That's complete nonsense."

Given the change in American foreign policy evident in the post-9/11 era, we thought that readers would appreciate a postscript excerpt from Blondet's book, *Who Really Governs America?*, dealing with Dr. Luttwak's best-selling *Coup d'État*. In view of the widespread suspicion that the Bush administration, or parts of it, has "hijacked" the Pentagon and much of the American political structure, the excerpt will provide food for thought for those who want to think for themselves in these dangerously unstable times.

CHAPTER
3

Global Democracy . . .
Through Superior Firepower
• • • • • • • • • •
Maurizio Blondet

I T WAS 1991. President George H. W. Bush had opened a war of words with President Saddam Hussein of Iraq, a war that was becoming more likely by the hour to become a war of death and destruction. The situation throughout the world was tense, with television stations, newspapers and magazines presenting the arguments of pundits, analysts and "experts" of every conceivable kind around the clock. The sun never set on the propaganda barrage that sought to convince world public opinion that an international coalition was necessary to evict the Iraqi Armed Forces from the tiny Gulf State of Kuwait.

At the same time there was a steady buildup of American and "coalition" troops in the Gulf, accompanied by colossal volumes of arms and ammunition. Within a few months, nearly half a million men stood poised to confront Iraq.

Yet, strange as it may seem in retrospect, there were people in Europe who were not wholly convinced that Bush was serious about launching a war in an area of the world that is volatile, one might even say predisposed towards instability because of historical, political and economic circumstances. Was this another, though much more elaborate, case of saber-rattling designed to get Saddam to back down, leave Kuwait with his tail between his legs, and bring crushing humiliation upon him in the eyes of the Arab world? Who could I ask for an informed view on this question?

I put through a call to Dr. Edward Luttwak, the internationally renowned author, lecturer, historian, military strategist and Pentagon consultant. Well-known in political circles in Italy, he had studied the military power of the Roman Empire here and was thus well able to express himself in Italian. I asked him whether the White House really was prepared to invade Iraq with all its attendant risks? "We are very serious," he answered. He continued: "We are going to bomb Iraq back into the Stone Age!" But why is this necessary, I answered, finding Luttwak's bluntness somewhat at variance with his reputation for subtle thinking and expression. Almost warming to the subject, he continued:

> Saddam is not like the Saudi Princes who spend the bulk of their lives outside of their country, and who fritter away the Kingdom's oil profits on prostitutes and bottles of champagne in Paris. No, Saddam is building railways! Creating electrical networks! Highways and other important elements of a serious State infrastructure! After eight years of war against the Iranian regime of Khomeini, he desperately needs to demobilize his Republican Guard, which incorporates so many of his technical elite, in order to rebuild the war-devastated country. These people are his technicians, his engineers. If they are put to work in the way Saddam wishes, they will rapidly make Iraq the most advanced power in the region, and we cannot allow this to happen.

It was an incredible statement, a statement of pure power politics, and for the first time in my life I came up against the notion that the United States was not what it proclaimed itself to be. It had always told the world that it saw itself as on a mission to combat poverty and illiteracy, injustice and tyranny; and now here was a high-ranking American official stating as bluntly as language allowed him that America not only did not want to see Iraq develop, but that it actually sought to undo what development it had already achieved. For many in Latin America, none of this would be real news given the turbulent and violent intervention – largely covert – of the United States in the countries of this continent, which Washington power-brokers like to consider as their "backyard." But for many in Europe it was a blinding revelation, an angel of light suddenly being transformed into something demonic!

Yet some time spent in historical reflection brought to the foreground the fact that the United States had *always* shown its hostility to the develop- ment of modern and efficient states and societies in the Middle East – with one exception, of course, Israel. In the fifties, many dictators and strong- men – mainly drawn from the Arab and Muslim armed forces of the region – came to power, men who were not of an Islamic fundamentalist disposition, but were rather men who sought to open up their societies to the benefits of modern technology and organization. They were men who believed in great national development, and who were, for the most part, also pro-American. Gamal Abdul Nasser in Egypt, a figure of huge importance in Arab his- tory, intended to transform Egypt and thereafter the Arab world, and at the beginning he sought to involve the Americans in this process. The Shah of Iran, too, was a modernizer and was staunchly pro-American. Even Col. Muammar Qathafi of Libya was originally open to the West. These men and their visions were distinct and often contradictory, but they shared certain common features. They sought to use modern means to transform the lives of their respective peoples; they sought to bring this change about in conjunction with the Western powers, especially America; and they had little or no time for Islamic fundamentalism as distinct from Islam as a system of religious beliefs. Thus, for example, Qathafi insisted that young girls be sent to school – a very un-Islamist idea.

But one by one they fell foul of the United States, with the Americans overthrowing some of these regimes, and pushing the rest into the arms of the Soviet Union. The result was that Arabs like Nasser and Qathafi became characterized as "Commies" by a hostile Western media. Furthermore it was the United States which did everything to bring Ayatollah Khomeini to power in Iran; and which preferred the crude Pakistani-instructed "Koranic students" of the Taliban to take control of Afghanistan, rather than Ahmad Shah Masood who was a potential unifier and modernizer of the country. First he opposed the Soviets, then he opposed the Taliban, and in the process became something of a popular myth. He was a bold man with a good sense of strategy whose popularity went beyond the ethnic groups of the country, even extending to the majority Pashtuns. Needless to say this forward-looking man was assassinated probably on the orders of our old CIA-created friend, Osama bin Laden. And who has been the prop and master of the tyrannical, oppressive and corrupt Wahhabite monarchy in Saudi Arabia? The Americans.

As I reflected on this history – which is crystal clear and yet largely unknown it seems – down the years since, I happened upon a recent statement made by Anupama Rao Singh, who was UNICEF's representative in Iraq, made to the journalist, John Pilger, in an interview. He said: "In 1989, the literacy rate in Iraq was 95%; and 93% of the population had free access to modern health facilities. Iraq had reached a stage where the basic indicators we use to measure the overall well-being of human beings, including children, were some of the best in the world. Now it is among the bottom 20%. In 10 years, child mortality has gone from one of the lowest in the world, to the highest." In other words, Iraq was on its way to joining the First World, on its way to becoming a beacon and model for the rest of the Middle East – a *source of endless problems* for those determined to ensure that corruption, oppression and dependency remained the dominant atmosphere in the region through the careful maintenance and manipulation of so-called "pro-Western governments."

But why should the powers-that-be have such a policy towards the Arabs? One possible, and very obvious, answer is oil. The oil cartels have a preference in dealing with ignorant clerics and corrupt hypocrites because neither the one nor the other has any conception, any vision, of dragging their societies and their peoples out of the mire of backwardness. Faced by intelligent Arab leaders, such oil men have to go nose to nose with those who understand the strategic and commercial importance of oil within the framework of the global economy, and thus have to pay up more in prices per barrel and in royalties. Since "money makes the world go around" for the oil barons, it is far better and *cheaper* to deal with those who lack knowledge, or with those whose peccadilloes really don't cost very much.

Another possible, if less obvious to the man-in the-street, answer is Israel and its "need" for security. If Saddam's regime had been left untouched, and if the President had continued the plans for development that he had implemented in the Seventies and early Eighties, it is pretty plain that within a decade or two he would have been in a position to confront Israel on militarily credible terms. This is not speculation on my part, but something that was declared quite candidly by a transitional member of Dubya's first term team, Philip Zelikow. A former Chairman of the President's Foreign Intelligence Advisory Board before being nominated to the Commission of Inquiry for the September 11 attack, he told a panel of foreign policy experts at the University of Virginia on September 19, 2002, that an attack against Iraq was imminent – note the date and note, too, that it shows that no matter what Saddam and his government did things would not change! – and that it was therefore imperative that the world be persuaded that Saddam possessed an arsenal of weapons of mass destruction ready to be used against America. To this select group, he declared truthfully: "Why would Iraq attack America or use nuclear weapons against us? I'll tell you what I think the real threat is, and actually has been since 1990 – it is the threat to Israel. And this is the threat that dare not speak its name, because the Europeans do not care deeply about that threat, I tell you frankly. And the American government does not want to lean too hard on it rhetorically, because it is not a popular sell."

It is almost certainly the case that the Europeans do not care very much about the threat to Israel, but is it because we are "anti-Semites"? No, it is probably because we are well informed of the fact that Israel has built a nuclear arsenal of several hundred weapons capable of being delivered across a wide area of the Mediterranean Sea and the Middle East. In simple terms, we Europeans are in the frontline of the Israeli threat to *our* civilization whatever the hype involved in "our shared values and history." And is it not peculiar that the only state in the entire region which does possess weapons of mass destruction, and which is public knowledge, receives no criticism of any sort however mild? Israel is a racist, fundamentalist state at war in practical terms with all its neighbors – be it hot or cold war, or even commercial and psychological war – it is armed to the teeth in a way that wholly overshadows all of its neighbors *put together*, and *still* it does not feel secure enough. Be it remembered that it was Israel which began this terrible regional arms race, and now it is having to come to terms with its created nightmare – the possibility of neighboring states seeking parity. Thus we have a potent, well-armed neighbor in Israel; and is it any real surprise that countries like France and Italy have little "sympathy" for Israel's security when they could so easily be affected by radioactive fall-out should Israel ever strike out against its nightmares? Zelikow is right: Israel is not "a popular sell" in Europe. Obstinately, we Europeans happen to believe that Israel would feel far safer in every sense if it were to try and come to terms with her Arab neighbors on the basis of justice and honesty, beginning with a just peace for the scandalously treated and abandoned Palestinian people.

We see, then, that the unilateral war of aggression launched by America against a sovereign state is due to the converging interests of the Israeli and Oil Lobbies. To these two must be added the American military-industrial complex for whom *all* war is good business in terms of sales, profits and publicity. Of course it does not follow that the interests of these Americans necessarily coincide with the interests of the American people. "Homeland" is a very nebulous idea to corporate dealers who see the goal of life as being determined by money. And it is precisely because they are so fixated on the biblical "root of all evil" that many Europeans have grave doubts about the sincerity of American businessmen-turned-statesmen, who proclaim that their intention is to bring "stability and democracy to Iraq." It is no secret that the Bush administrations have been choc-a-bloc with "former" businessmen, and that these men have profited immensely from the Iraq war; and no doubt they intend to do so in the other wars that are bound to come their way as the neoconservatives live out their folly at the expense of the rest of the world. As long as Israel feels "secure" – at least for the moment – and as long as companies like Halliburton continue to rake in monstrous profits, what difference does it make to the businessmen-statesmen that Iraq is plunging into what could be a semi-permanent chaos, and the sons and daughters of working class Americans will continue to come home in body bags?

The fact remains, of course, that the Americans were out to get Saddam come what may; and they wanted him out of the way for many reasons, but perhaps one of them has not been as clearly articulated as it should have been. In the autumn of 2000, Saddam Hussein took an action that can only be viewed as a declaration of war on American mega-business when he announced that he would be pricing Iraqi oil in euros not dollars. To an outsider it would have seemed a decision of little consequence, but to a serious player it had tremendous implications. On November 6, 2000, Radio Free Europe – the CIA funded operation – giggled that Saddam's move would result in bad business for Saddam given the then weakness of the euro. Yet Saddam was to wipe the grin of their faces as the euro gained strength and rose some 35% in valuation against the dollar. Needless to say, other oil-producing countries began to show an interest. Mr. Javad Yariani, Chairman of the Department of Market Analysis for OPEC said in August 2002, whilst visiting Spain, that "Since the Nineties, more than 80% of the monetary exchanges, and half of global exports, has been denominated in dollars, and the American currency makes up about 60% of all currency reserves. This forces all countries to keep large amounts of dollars in their reserves, amounts which are disproportionate in comparison with the "weight" of the United States in the global economy." He went on: "The commercial links between OPEC countries and Europe are stronger than those between the USA and OPEC. Almost 45% of our imports come from Europe, and OPEC is the primary exporter of oil to the European Union. In future, it could well become possible to price oil in euros . . . and this could attract bigger and much-needed investment into the Middle East . . . . Perhaps time is on our [EU and OPEC] side." One has only to consider this for a moment to realize why Bush kept repeating that "time is running out," and although Saddam has been removed from the scene the threat to the dollar has not. In late October 2004, Vladimir Putin, wondering out loud no doubt, suggested to the EU that if other things could be arranged between Russia and the EU to their mutual benefit, it might indeed be a very positive thing to price oil in euros. If that idea ever begins to take shape, perhaps we will live to see the day that the countries of Europe, including Russia, will be designated " rogue states" and become a candidate to be bombed back to the Stone Age.

This essay began with a shocking quotation from Dr. Edward Luttwak. It might be objected, of course, that in the Second Gulf War he took a position "against" the Bush Jr. administration, and thus, in a sense, his comments in 1991 are rather out of date or irrelevant today. That would be true *if* Luttwak were *against* the war, but a study of his comments does not bear this out. What he says is that he doubts that this is the *right way* of achieving the declared aims of the American government. He worries about the effect of unilateral action on allies, on friends, on international relations. But this is not the same thing as worrying about the end. It is not that he opposed the attack on Iraq because it is illegal and unjust, but because the methods used may be waking up vast numbers of people to the threat that the United States poses to the rest of the world. *It is an argument about means not end; it is an argument about style not substance.*

Other people in the American establishment have been playing the same tune, both on television and in the *op-ed* columns of influential dailies. We might mention Henry Kissinger, James Schlesinger, Brent Scowcroft, Zbigniew Brzezinski and R. James Woolsey in this connection. The media present their musings as "opposition" to Bush Jr., but it is nothing of the sort. It is all a question of approach. Nor should we be surprised that this crowd are mouthing the same things, for they are all part and parcel of the little-publicized, not-for-profit Centre for Strategic and International Studies (CSIS) based in Washington and set up in the 1960s. It is made up of "luminaries" from the Republican and Democratic Parties (including one Senator John Kerry!), ex-government officials, ex-CIA directors, military men, and high-level bureaucrats, and is funded according to the CSIS by corporations and foundations to the tune of $25 million! Thus, while Luttwak is presenting his highly nuanced view of the Iraq war, we find his fellow CSIS adviser, Arnaud de Borchgrave, editing the fervently pro-war *Washington Times*, a journal owned by the CIA-funded and created by Moonies whose connections with dirty money and Israel are long and deep. Nor is this a simple coincidence, for Luttwak sits alongside Michael "creative destruction" Ledeen on Dr. Joseph Churba's International Security Council which is stacked with neoconservative warmongers. At the end of the day every conceivable view – other than the resolutely anti-Iraq war view – is catered for in the American media, from the manic, blood-lust ravings of a Ledeen through to the "thoughtful" – "this is a hard case, to be sure" – dribblings of a Luttwak, and which combine to give the impression that Rambo and Mother Teresa have teamed up to "get Saddam and the other bad guys." Believe it if you will. Believe it if you can.

CHAPTER
3
postscript

On Luttwak's *Coup d'État: A Practical Handbook*
· · · · · · · · · ·
Maurizio Blondet

I T IS NOT a recent book. Published by Harvard University Press in 1968, it is entitled *Coup d'État: A Practical Handbook*. Its author is Edward Luttwak, the well-known military expert who was an adviser on National Security to Ronald Reagan. He is Jewish, an ultra-conservative, and a militarist with known links to the CIA, to friends in the Pentagon, to the military-industrial complex, and, naturally, to JINSA.

We will seek to present crucial passages from this old book, limiting ourselves to italicizing and commenting upon the ideas which could have been in the minds of those – if our hypothesis is correct – who orchestrated the tragedy of September 11.

Chapter 1: What is a Coup d'État?

A coup d'état is not necessarily assisted by either the intervention of the masses, or, to any significant degree, by military-type force. The assistance of these forms of direct force would no doubt make it easier to seize power, but it would be unrealistic to think that they would be available to the organizers of a coup.

If a coup does not make use of the masses, or of warfare, what instrument of power will enable it to seize control of the State? The short answer is that the power will come from the State itself.

A coup consists of the infiltration of a small but critical segment of the State apparatus, which is then used to displace the government from its control of the remainder [JINSA infiltrated the Pentagon in precisely this manner].

Chapter 2: When is a Coup d'État Possible?

First of all, Luttwak lists the necessary "preconditions":

1. The social and economic conditions of the target country must be such as to confine political participation to a small fraction of the population [this is the case in America where non-voters are the majority].

2. The target State must be substantially independent and the influence of foreign powers in its internal political life must be relatively limited [the United States is the only State remaining that enjoys these conditions].

3. The target State must have a political centre. If there are several centres these must be identifiable and they must be politically, rather than ethnically, structured. If the State is controlled by a non-politically organized unit [like the CFR, the representative of business] the coup can only be carried out with its consent or neutrality.

Already in the Preface, Luttwak underlined as essential the fact that the perpetrators of a coup must be able to count upon "the absence of a politicised community," upon the apathy of the public. "The dialogue between the rulers and the ruled [upon which democratic legitimacy is founded] can only take place if there is a large enough section of society which is sufficiently literate, well fed and secure to 'talk back.'" But "without a politicised population, the State is nothing other than a machine. Then the coup d'état becomes feasible because, like every machine, one can take control of everything by grasping the essential levers." Now Luttwak identifies this "machine" in the Bureaucracy.

The growth of modern bureaucracy has two implications which are crucial to the feasibility of the coup: the development of a clear distinction between the permanent machinery of State and the political leadership [which changes], and the fact is, like most large organizations, the bureaucracy has a structured hierarchy with definite chains of command . . . .

The importance of this development lies in the fact that if the bureaucrats are linked to the political leadership, an illegal seizure of power must take the form of a "Palace Revolution," *and it essentially concerns the manipulation of the person of the ruler. He can be forced to accept policies or advisers, he can be killed or held captive,* but whatever happens the Palace Revolution can only be conducted from the "inside" and by "insiders" [in these pages, we have seen nothing but the work of insiders surrounding a weak President].

The State bureaucracy has to divide its work into clear-cut areas of competence, which are assigned to different departments. Within each department there must be an accepted chain of command, and standard procedures have to be followed. Thus a given piece of information, or a given order, is followed up in a stereotyped manner, and if the order comes from the appropriate source, at the appropriate level, it is carried out . . . . The apparatus of the State is therefore to some extent a "machine" which will normally behave in a fairly predictable and automatic manner.

A coup operates by taking advantage of this machine-like behaviour; during the coup, because it uses parts of the State apparatus to seize the controlling levers; afterwards because the value of the "levers" depends on the fact that the State is a machine.

Who are the best conspirators? Here is how Luttwak describes them:

All power, all participation, is in the hands of the small educated elite, and therefore radically different from the vast majority of their countrymen, practically a race apart. The masses recognize this and they also accept the elite's monopoly on power, unless some unbearable exaction leads to desperate revolt . . . . Equally, they will accept a change in government, whether legal or otherwise. After all, it is merely another lot of "them" taking over [this is precisely the case of American society: a great mass of badly educated people, remains passive because of need, accepts the new capitalist flexibility so as to hold on to or find work].

Thus, after a coup . . . the majority of the people will neither believe nor disbelieve . . . . This lack of reaction is all the coup needs on the part of the people to stay in power.

The lower levels of the bureaucracy will react – or rather fail to react – in a similar manner and for similar reasons: the "bosses" give the orders, can promote or demote and, above all, are the source of that power and prestige . . . . After the coup, the man who sits at district headquarters will still be obeyed – whether he is the man who was there before or not – so long as he can pay the salaries . . . .

For the senior bureaucrats, army and police officers, the coup will be a mixture of dangers and opportunities. For the greater number of those who are not too deeply committed, the coup will offer opportunities rather than dangers. They can accept the coup and, being collectively indispensable, can negotiate for even better salaries and positions.

As the coup will not usually represent a threat to most of the elite, the choice is between the great dangers of opposition and the safety of inaction. All that is required in order to support the coup is, simply, to do nothing – and that is what will usually be done.

Thus, at all levels, the most likely course of action following a coup is acceptance . . . . This lack of reaction is the key to the victory of the coup.

Chapter 3: The Strategy of a Coup d'État

If we were revolutionaries, wanting to destroy the power of some of the political forces, the long and often bloody process of revolutionary attrition can achieve this. Our purpose is, however, quite different: *we want to seize power within the present system*, and we shall only stay in power if we embody some new status quo supported by those very forces which a revolution may seek to destroy . . . . This is perhaps a more efficient method, and certainly a less painful one, than that of a classic revolution [this is a perfection description of the neoconservative coup d'état].

Though we will try to avoid all conflict with the "political" forces, some of them will almost certainly oppose a coup. But this opposition will largely subside when we have substituted our new status quo for the old one, and can enforce it by our control of the State bureaucracy and security forces. We shall then be carrying out the dual task of imposing our control on the machinery of State while at the same time *using it to impose our control on the country at large.*

As long as the execution of the coup is rapid, *and we are cloaked in anonymity,* no particular political faction will have either a motive, or opportunity, to oppose us.

Chapter 4: The Planning of the Coup d'État

Whether it is a two party system, as in much of the Anglo-Saxon world, where parties are in effect coalitions of pressure groups, or whether they are the class or religion-based parties of much of continental Europe, *the major political parties in developed and democratic countries will not present a direct threat to the coup.* Though such parties have mass support at election time, neither they nor their followers are versed in the techniques of mass agitation. The comparative stability of political life has deprived them of the experience required to employ direct methods, and the whole climate of their operation revolves around the concept of periodic elections.

Though some form of confrontation may be inevitable, it is essential to avoid bloodshed, because this may well have crucial negative repercussions amongst the personnel of the armed forces and the police.

Chapter 5: The Execution of the Coup d'État

With detailed planning, there will be no need for any sort of headquarters structure in the active stage of the coup: for if there is no scope for decision-making there is no need for decision-makers and their apparatus. *In fact, having a headquarters would be a serious disadvantage: it would constitute a concrete target for the opposition and one which would be both vulnerable and easily identified. . . .* We should avoid taking any action that will clarify the nature of the threat and thus reduce the confusion that is left in the defensive apparatus of the regime . . . . The leaders of the coup will be scattered among the various teams. [As we can see Luttwak is theoretically discussing an invisible coup d'état: the infiltrated coup participants speak with the voice of the legitimate government, of that which they have seized. On September 11, let's remember, the immediate entourage of President Bush were not thinking of an Arab attack, but of a military coup d'état. It is for this reason that the President was taken to a secure location for 10 hours].

In the period immediately after the coup, they [the high level Civil Servants and Military Commanders] will probably see themselves as isolated individuals whose careers, and even lives, could be in danger. This feeling of insecurity may precipitate two alternative reactions, both extreme: they will either step forward to assert their loyalty to the leaders of the coup or else they will try to foment or join in the opposition against us. Both reactions are undesirable from our point of view. Assertions of loyalty will usually be worthless since they are made by men who have just abandoned their previous, and possibly more legitimate, masters. Opposition will always be dangerous and sometimes disastrous. Our policy towards the military and bureaucratic cadres will be to reduce this sense of insecurity. *We should establish direct communications with as many of the more senior officers and officials as possible to convey one principal idea in a forceful and convincing manner: that the coup will not threaten their positions in the hierarchy and the aims of the coup do not include a reshaping of the existing military or administrative structures* [this appears to be exactly the task of JINSA].

The masses have neither the weapons of the military nor the administrative facilities of the bureaucracy, but their attitude to the new government established after the coup will ultimately be decisive. Our immediate aim will be to enforce public order, but our long-term objective is to gain the acceptance of the masses so that physical coercion will not longer be needed . . . . *Our far more flexible instrument will be our control over the means of mass communication . . . . In broadcasting over the radio and television services our purpose is not to provide information about the situation, but rather to affect its development by exploiting our monopoly of these media.* [This is exactly what the American mass media has done since September 11.]

[The action of the media] will be achieved by conveying the reality and strength of the coup instead of trying to justify it [the emotional blow of the collapse of the World Trade Centre was presented with plenty of "reality" and "force" by CNN]. We will have fragmented the opposition so that each individual opponent would have to operate in isolation. In these circumstances, the news of any further resistance against us would act as a powerful stimulant to further resistance by breaking down this feeling of isolation. *We must, therefore, make every effort to withhold such news. If there is in fact some resistance . . . we should strongly emphasize that it is isolated, the product of the obstinacy of a few misguided or dishonest individuals who are not affiliated to any party or group of significant membership.* The constant working of the motif of isolation, and the emphasis on the fact that law and order have been reestablished, should have the effect of making resistance appear as dangerous and useless.

There will arise, Luttwak says, *"the inevitable suspicions that the coup is a product of the machinations of the Company* [American slang for the CIA]. *This can only be dispelled by making violent attacks on it . . . and the attacks should be all the more violent if these suspicions are in fact justified . . . . We shall make use of a suitable selection of unlovely phrases* [for example, anti-Americanism? Anti-Semitism?]. Even if their meanings have been totally obscured by constant and deliberate misuse, *they will be useful indicators of our impeccable nationalism."*

It seems to this author that these paragraphs describe, with shocking precision, all that has taken place in America since September 11.

THE EDITORS' GLOSS: We were told recently by a "conservative" colleague that he "wouldn't cross the street to read anything that Noam Chomsky writes." But then this is, sadly, what passes for political discussion these days. "I don't listen to *him*," the saying goes. But never mind that: what about what he *says*?

This is the approach we believe readers, whether fans or critics of Prof. Chomsky's work, should take to what follows. Happily, his essay, adapted from a talk given to the Royal Institute of Philosophy in London on May 19, 2004, aims at some lowest-common-denominator principles that even our "I-wouldn't-cross-the-street" colleague should be able to appreciate. Chomsky's target is the hypocrisy of the "West," the "West" being that Anglo-American democracy machine which draws its life-blood not from Chaucer, Cervantes, Chopin, and Christ, but from corporations, banks, and armies.

Heaven knows Chomsky has plenty of material to work with, but he doesn't ask for too much in making his point. Only that the "West" hold itself to standards to which it expects others to adhere. Study after study reveals that this is seen as a reasonable request – both within the "West" and without – and one which we must take to heart if we really wish to avoid further provoking those who have had enough of our double-standards. Speaking at the Baker Institute for Public Policy at Rice University, pollster John Zogby said recently that many Arabs continue to "love Americans, but hate American policy." It's what we do and not who we are or what we believe that makes the difference.

CHAPTER
4

Simple Truths, Hard Problems:
Some Thoughts on Terror, Justice, and Self-Defense
• • • • • • • • •
Prof. Noam Chomsky, Ph.D.

TO DISPEL ANY false expectations, I really am going to keep to very simple truths, so much so that I toyed with suggesting the title "In Praise of Platitudes," with an advance apology for the elementary character of what follows. The only justification for proceeding along this course is that the truisms are widely rejected, in some crucial cases almost universally so. And the human consequences are serious, in particular, with regard to the hard problems I have in mind. One reason why they are hard is that moral truisms are so commonly disdained by those with sufficient power to do so with impunity, because they set the rules.

The guiding principle is elementary. Norms are established by the powerful, in their own interests, and with the acclaim of responsible intellectuals. These may be close to historical universals. I have been looking for exceptions for many years. There are a few, but not many.

Sometimes the principle is explicitly recognized. The norm for post-World War II international justice was established at Nuremberg. To bring the Nazi criminals to justice, it was necessary to devise definitions of "war crime" and "crime against humanity." Telford Taylor, chief counsel for the prosecution and a distinguished international lawyer and historian, has explained candidly how this was done:

> Since both sides in World War II had played the terrible game of urban destruction – the Allies far more successfully – there was no basis for criminal charges against Germans or Japanese, and in fact no such charges were brought . . . . Aerial bombardment had been used so extensively and ruthlessly on the Allied side as well as the Axis side that neither at Nuremberg nor Tokyo was the issue made a part of the trials.[1]

---

1. Telford Taylor, *Nuremberg and Vietnam: an American Tragedy* (Chicago: Quadrangle

The operative definition of "crime" is: "Crime that you carried out but we did not." To underscore the fact, Nazi war criminals were absolved if the defense could show that their U.S. counterparts carried out the same crimes.

The Nuremberg Tribunal is commonly described by distinguished figures in the field of international law and justice as "the birth of universal jurisdiction."[1] That is correct only if we understand "universality" in accord with the practice of the enlightened states, which defines "universal" as "applicable to others only," particularly enemies.

The proper conclusion at Nuremberg and since would have been to punish the victors as well as the vanquished foe. Neither at the postwar trials nor subsequently have the powerful been subjected to the rules, not because they have not carried out crimes – of course they have – but because they are immune under prevailing standards of morality. The victims appear to understand well enough. Wire services report from Iraq that "If Iraqis ever see Saddam Hussein in the dock, they want his former American allies shackled beside him."[2] That inconceivable event would be a radical revision of the fundamental principle of international justice: tribunals must be restricted to the crimes of others.

There is a marginal exception, which in fact underscores the force of the rule. Punishment is permissible when it is a mere tap on the wrist, evading the real crimes, or when blame can be restricted to minor figures, particularly when they are *not like us*. It was, for example, considered proper to punish the soldiers who carried out the My Lai massacre, half-educated, half-crazed GI's in the field, not knowing who was going to shoot at them next. But it was inconceivable that punishment could reach as far as those who planned and implemented Operation Wheeler Wallawa, a mass murder operation to which My Lai was a very minor footnote.[3] The gentlemen in the air-conditioned offices are like us, therefore immune by definition. We are witnessing similar examples right now in Iraq.

One moral truism that should be uncontroversial is the principle of universality: we should apply to ourselves the same standards we apply

Books, 1970).

1. Justice Richard Goldstone, "Kosovo: An Assessment in the Context of International Law," Nineteenth Morgenthau Memorial Lecture, Carnegie Council on Ethics and International Affairs, 2000.

2. Michael Georgy, "Iraqis want Saddam's old U.S. friends on trial," *Reuters*, January 20, 2004.

3. On this and other such operations, based in part on unpublished investigations of *Newsweek* Saigon bureau chief Kevin Buckley, see Chomsky and Edward Herman, *The Political Economy of Human Rights* (Boston: South End Press, 1979), Vol. I.

to others – in fact, more stringent ones. This should be uncontroversial for everyone, but particularly so for the world's most important citizens, the leaders of the enlightened states, who declare themselves to be devout Christians, devoted to the Gospels, hence surely familiar with their famous condemnation of the Hypocrite. Their devotion to the commandments of the Lord is not in question. George Bush reportedly proclaims that "God told me to strike at al-Qaeda and I struck them, and then He instructed me to strike at Saddam, which I did," and "now I am determined to solve the problem of the Middle East,"[1] also at the command of the Lord of Hosts, the War God, whom we are instructed by the Holy Book to worship above all other gods. And as I mentioned, the elite press dutifully refers to his "messianic mission" to solve the problem of the Middle East – in fact the world – following our "responsibility to history to rid the world of evil," in the President's words, the core principle of the "vision" that Bush shares with Osama bin Laden.

This common response of the intellectual culture, some memorable exceptions aside, is entirely natural if we abandon the most elementary of moral truisms, and declare ourselves to be uniquely exempt from the principle of universality. And so we do, constantly. Every day brings new illustrations. The U.S. Senate lent its consent to the appointment of John Negroponte as Ambassador to Iraq, heading the world's largest diplomatic mission, which had the task of handing over "sovereignty" to Iraqis to fulfill Bush's "messianic vision" to bring democracy to the Middle East and the world, so we are solemnly informed. The appointment bears directly on the principle of universality, but before turning to that, we might raise some questions about other truisms, regarding evidence and conclusions.

That the goal of the Iraq invasion is to fulfill the President's messianic vision is simply presupposed in news reporting and commentary, even among critics, who warn that the "noble" and "generous" vision may be beyond our reach. As the London *Economist* posed the problem, "America's mission" of turning Iraq into "an inspiring example [of democracy] to its

---

1. Arnon Regular, *Haaretz*, May 24, 2003, based on minutes of a meeting between Bush and his hand-picked Palestinian Prime Minister, Mahmoud Abbas, provided by Abbas. See also *Newsweek*, "Bush and God," March 10, 2003, with a cover story on the beliefs and direct line to God of the man with his finger on the button; "The Jesus Factor," PBS *Frontline* documentary, on the "religious ideals" that Bush has brought to the White House, "relevant to the Bush messianic mission to graft democracy onto the rest of the world"; Sam Allis, "A Timely Look at How Faith Informs Bush Presidency," *Boston Globe*, February 29, 2004; and White House aides report concern over Bush's "increasingly erratic behavior" as he "declares his decisions to be 'God's will'" (Doug Thompson, publisher, *Capitol Hill Blue*, June 4, 2004).

neighbours" is facing obstacles.[1] With a considerable search, I have not been able to find exceptions in the U.S. media, and with much less search, elsewhere, apart from the usual margins.

One might inquire into the basis for the apparently near universal acceptance of this doctrine in Western intellectual commentary. Examination will quickly reveal that it is based on two principles. First, our leaders have proclaimed it, so it must be true, a principle familiar in North Korea and other stellar models. Second, we must suppress the fact that by proclaiming the doctrine after other pretexts have collapsed, our leaders are also declaring that they are among the most accomplished liars in history, since in leading their countries to war they proclaimed with comparable passion that the "sole question" is whether Saddam had disarmed. But now we must believe them. Also obligatory is the dispatch deep into the memory hole of the ample record of professed noble efforts to bring democracy, justice, and freedom to the benighted.

It is, again, the merest truism that pronouncements of virtuous intent by leaders carry no information, even in the technical sense: they are completely predictable, including the worst monsters. But this truism also fades when it confronts the overriding need to reject the principle of universality.

The doctrine presupposed by Western commentary is accepted by some Iraqis too: one percent agreed that the goal of the invasion is to bring democracy to Iraq according to U.S.-run polls in Baghdad in October 2003 – long before the atrocities in April and the revelations of torture. Another five percent felt that the goal is to help Iraqis. Most of the rest took for granted that the goal is to gain control of Iraq's resources and use Iraq as a base for reorganizing the Middle East in U.S. interests[2] – a thought virtually inexpressible in enlightened Western commentary, or dismissed with horror as "anti-Americanism," "conspiracy theory," "radical and extremist," or some other intellectual equivalent of four-letter words among the vulgar. In brief, Iraqis appear to take for granted that what is unfolding is a scenario familiar from the days of Britain's creation of modern Iraq, accompanied by the predictable and therefore uninformative professions of virtuous intent, but also by secret internal documents in which Lord Curzon and the Foreign Office developed the plans to establish an "Arab

1. "Another Intifada in the Making" and "Bloodier and Sadder," *Economist*, April 17, 2004.

2. Walter Pincus, "Skepticism About U.S. Deep, Iraq Poll Shows, Motive for Invasion Is Focus of Doubts," *Washington Post*, November 12, 2003, and Richard Burkholder, "Gallup Poll of Baghdad: Gauging U.S. Intent," *Government & Public Affairs*, October 28, 2003.

facade" that Britain would rule behind various "constitutional fictions." The contemporary version is provided by a senior British official quoted in the *Daily Telegraph*: "The Iraqi government will be fully sovereign, but in practice it will not exercise all its sovereign functions."[1]

Let us return to Negroponte and the principle of universality. As his appointment as Ambassador[2] reached Congress, the *Wall Street Journal* praised him as a "Modern Proconsul," who learned his trade in Honduras in the 1980s, during the Reaganite phase of the current incumbents in Washington. The veteran *Journal* correspondent Carla Anne Robbins reminds us that in Honduras he was known as "the proconsul," as he presided over the second largest embassy in Latin America, with the largest CIA station in the world – perhaps to transfer full sovereignty to this centerpiece of world power.[3]

Robbins observes that Negroponte has been criticized by human rights activists for "covering up abuses by the Honduran military" – a euphemism for large-scale state terror – "to ensure the flow of U.S. aid" to this vital country, which was "the base for Washington's covert war against Nicaragua." The main task of proconsul Negroponte was to supervise the bases in which the terrorist mercenary army was armed, trained, and sent to do its work, including its mission of attacking undefended civilian targets, so the U.S. military command informed Congress. The policy of attacking such "soft targets" while avoiding the Nicaraguan army was confirmed by the State Department and defended by leading American liberal intellectuals, notably *New Republic* editor Michael Kinsley, who was the designated spokesman for the left in television commentary. He chastised Human Rights Watch for its sentimentality in condemning U.S. international terrorism and failing to understand that it must be evaluated by "pragmatic criteria." A "sensible policy," he urged, should "meet the test of cost-benefit analysis," an analysis of "the amount of blood and misery that will be poured in, and the likelihood that democracy will emerge at the other end" – "democracy" as U.S. elites determine, their unquestionable right. Of course, the principle of universality does not apply: others are not authorized to carry out large-scale international terrorist operations if their goals are likely to be achieved.

---

1. Anton La Guardia, Diplomatic Editor, "Handover Still on Course As UN Waits for New Leader to Emerge," *Daily Telegraph*, May 18, 2004.

2. I.e., before he was nominated and confirmed as director of national intelligence.—Ed.

3. Robbins, "Negroponte Has Tricky Mission: Modern Proconsul," *Wall Street Journal*, April 27, 2004.

On the wall of my office at MIT, I have a painting given to me by a Jesuit priest, depicting the Angel of Death standing over the figure of Salvadoran Archbishop Romero, whose assassination in 1980 opened that grim decade of international state terrorist atrocities, and right before him the six leading Latin American intellectuals, Jesuit priests, whose brains were blown out in 1989, bringing the decade to an end. The Jesuit intellectuals, along with their housekeeper and her daughter, were murdered by an elite battalion armed and trained by the current incumbents in Washington and their mentors. It had already compiled a bloody record of massacres in the U.S.-run international terrorist campaign that Romero's successor described as a "war of extermination and genocide against a defenseless civilian population." Romero had been killed by much the same hands, a few days after he pleaded with President Carter not to provide the junta with military aid, which "will surely increase injustice here and sharpen the repression that has been unleashed against the people's organizations fighting to defend their most fundamental human rights." The repression continued with U.S. aid after his assassination, and the current incumbents carried it forward to a "war of extermination and genocide."

I keep the painting there to remind myself daily of the real world, but it has turned out to serve another instructive purpose. Many visitors pass through the office. Those from Latin America almost unfailingly recognize it. Those from north of the Rio Grande virtually never do. From Europe, recognition is perhaps 10 percent. We may consider another useful thought experiment. Suppose that in Czechoslovakia in the 1980s, security forces armed and trained by the Kremlin had assassinated an Archbishop who was known as "the voice of the voiceless," then proceeded to massacre tens of thousands of people, consummating the decade with the brutal murder of Vaclav Havel and half a dozen other leading Czech intellectuals. Would we know about it? Perhaps not, because the Western reaction might have gone as far as nuclear war, so there would be no one left to know. The distinguishing criterion is, once again, crystal clear. The crimes of enemies take place; our own do not, by virtue of our exemption from the most elementary of moral truisms.

Let us move on to some hard problems. Terrorism poses a number of them. First and foremost, of course, the phenomenon itself, which really is threatening, even keeping to the subpart that passes through the doctrinal filters: *their* terrorism against *us*. It is only a matter of time before terror and WMD are united, perhaps with horrendous consequences, as has been discussed in the specialist literature long before the September 11 atrocities. But apart from the phenomenon, there is the problem of a definition of "terror." That too is taken to be a hard problem, the subject of scholarly literature and international conferences. At first glance, it might seem odd that it is regarded as a hard problem. There are what seem to be satisfactory definitions – not perfect, but at least as good as others regarded as unproblematic: for example, the official definitions in the U.S. Code and Army Manuals in the early 1980s when the "war on terror" was launched, or the quite similar official formulation of the British government, which defines "terrorism" as "the use, or threat, of action which is violent, damaging or disrupting, and is intended to influence the government or intimidate the public and is for the purpose of advancing a political, religious, or ideological cause." These are the definitions that I have been using in writing about terrorism for the past twenty years, ever since the Reagan administration declared that the war on terror would be a prime focus of its foreign policy, replacing human rights, the proclaimed "soul of our foreign policy" before.[1]

On closer look, however, the problem becomes clear, and it is indeed hard. The official definitions are unusable, because of their immediate consequences. One difficulty is that the definition of terrorism is virtually the same as the definition of the official policy of the U.S., and other states, called "counter-terrorism" or "low-intensity warfare" or some other euphemism. That again is close to a historical universal, to my knowledge. Japanese imperialists in Manchuria and North China, for example, were not aggressors or terrorists, but were protecting the population and the legitimate governments from the terrorism of "Chinese bandits." To undertake this noble task, they were compelled, reluctantly, to resort to "counter-terror," with the goal of establishing an "earthly paradise" in which the people of Asia could live in peace and harmony under the enlightened guidance of Japan. The same is true of just about every other case I have investigated. But now we do face a hard problem: it will not do to say that the enlightened states are officially committed to terrorism. And it takes little effort to demonstrate that the U.S. engages in large-scale international terrorism according to its own definition of the term, quite uncontroversially in a number of crucial cases.

There is, then, a hard problem of defining "terrorism," rather like the problem of defining "war crime." How can we define it in such a way as

---

1. See, *inter alia*, my *Pirates and Emperors* (1996; updated edition, Cambridge, Mass.: South End-Pluto, 2002). For a review of the first phase of the "war on terror," see Alexander George, ed., *Western State Terrorism* (New York: Routledge, 1991).

to violate the principle of universality, exempting ourselves but applying it to selected enemies? And these have to be selected with some precision. The U.S. has had an official list of states sponsoring terrorism ever since the Reagan years. In all these years, only one state has been removed from the list: Iraq, in order to permit the U.S. to join the U.K. and others in providing badly needed aid for Saddam Hussein, continuing without concern after he carried out his most horrifying crimes.[1] There has also been one near-example. Clinton offered to remove Syria from the list if it agreed to peace terms offered by the U.S. and Israel. When Syria insisted on recovering the territory that Israel conquered in 1967, it remained on the list of states sponsoring terrorism, and continues to be on the list despite the acknowledgment by Washington that Syria has not been implicated in sponsoring terror for many years and has been highly cooperative in providing important intelligence to the U.S. on al-Qaeda and other radical Islamist groups. As a reward for Syria's cooperation in the "war on terror," last December Congress passed legislation calling for even stricter sanctions against Syria, near unanimously (the Syria Accountability Act). The legislation was recently implemented by the President, thus depriving the U.S. of a major source of information about radical Islamist terrorism in order to achieve the higher goal of establishing in Syria a regime that will accept U.S.-Israeli demands – not an unusual pattern, though commentators continually find it surprising no matter how strong the evidence and regular the pattern, and no matter how rational the choices in terms of clear and understandable planning priorities.

The Syria Accountability Act offers another striking illustration of the rejection of the principle of universality. Its core demand refers to UN Security Council Resolution 520, calling for respect for the sovereignty and territorial integrity of Lebanon, violated by Syria because it still retains in Lebanon forces that were welcomed there by the U.S. and Israel in 1976 when their task was to carry out massacres of Palestinians. The congressional legislation, and news reporting and commentary, overlook the fact that Resolution 520, passed in 1982, was explicitly directed against Israel, not Syria, and also the fact that while Israel violated this and other Security Council resolutions regarding Lebanon for 22 years, there was no call for any sanctions against Israel, or even any call for reduction in the huge unconditional military and economic aid to Israel. The silence for 22

1. Cf. the interview with Jude Wanniski for a slightly differing perspective on the actions Dr. Chomsky is most likely referring to, on pp. 3–79 of the companion to the present volume, *Neo-CONNED!*—Ed.

years includes many of those who now signed the Act condemning Syria for its violation of the Security Council resolution ordering Israel to leave Lebanon. The principle is accurately formulated by a rare scholarly commentator, Steven Zunes: it is that "Lebanese sovereignty must be defended only if the occupying army is from a country the United States opposes, but is dispensable if the country is a U.S. ally."[1] The principle, and the news reporting and commentary on all of these events, again make good sense, given the overriding need to reject elementary moral truisms, a fundamental doctrine of the intellectual and moral culture.

Returning to Iraq, when Saddam was removed from the list of states supporting terrorism, Cuba was added to replace it, perhaps in recognition of the sharp escalation in international terrorist attacks against Cuba in the late 1970s, including the bombing of a Cubana airliner killing 73 people and many other atrocities. These were mostly planned and implemented in the U.S., though by that time Washington had moved away from its former policy of direct action in bringing "the terrors of the earth" to Cuba – the goal of the Kennedy administration, reported by historian and Kennedy adviser Arthur Schlesinger in his biography of Robert Kennedy, who was assigned responsibility for the terror campaign and regarded it as a top priority. By the late 1970s Washington was officially condemning the terrorist acts while harboring and protecting the terrorist cells on U.S. soil in violation of U.S. law. The leading terrorist, Orlando Bosch, regarded as the author of the Cubana airline bombing and dozens of other terrorist acts according to the FBI, was given a presidential pardon by George Bush number one, over the strong objections of the Justice Department. Others like him continue to operate with impunity on U.S. soil, including terrorists responsible for major crimes elsewhere as well for whom the U.S. refuses requests for extradition (from Haiti, for example).

We may recall one of the leading components of the "Bush doctrine" – now Bush 2: "Those who harbor terrorists are as guilty as the terrorists themselves," and must be treated accordingly; the President's words when announcing the bombing of Afghanistan because of its refusal to turn over suspected terrorists to the U.S., without evidence, or even credible pretext as later quietly conceded. Harvard international-relations specialist Graham Allison describes this as the most important component of the Bush Doctrine. It "unilaterally revoked the sovereignty of states that provide sanctuary to terrorists," he wrote approvingly in *Foreign Affairs*, adding that

---

1. Zunes, "U.S. Policy Towards Syria and the Triumph of Neoconservatism," *Middle East Policy*, Spring, 2004.

the doctrine has "already become a de facto rule of international relations." That is correct, in the technical sense of "rule of international relations."

Unreconstructed literalists might conclude that Bush and Allison are calling for the bombing of the United States, but that is because they do not comprehend that the most elementary moral truisms must be forcefully rejected: there is a crucial exemption to the principle of universality, so deeply entrenched in the reigning intellectual culture that it is not even perceived, hence not mentioned.

Again, we find illustrations daily. The Negroponte appointment is one example. To take another, a few weeks ago the Palestinian leader Abu Abbas died in a U.S. prison in Iraq. His capture was one of the most heralded achievements of the invasion. A few years earlier he had been living in Gaza, participating in the Oslo "peace process" with U.S.-Israeli approval, but after the second Intifida began, he fled to Baghdad, where he was arrested by the U.S. army and imprisoned because of his role in the hijacking of the cruise ship Achille Lauro in 1985. The year 1985 is regarded by scholarship as the peak year of terrorism in the 1980s; Mideast terrorism was the top story of the year, in a poll of editors. Scholarship identifies two major crimes in that year: the hijacking of the Achille Lauro, in which one person, a crippled American, was brutally murdered; and an airplane hijacking with one death, also an American. There were, to be sure, some other terrorist crimes in the region in 1985, but they do not pass through the filters. One was a car-bombing outside a mosque in Beirut that killed 80 people and wounded 250 others, timed to explode as people were leaving, killing mostly women and girls; but this is excluded from the record because it was traced back to the CIA and British intelligence. Another was the action that led to the Achille Lauro hijacking in retaliation, a week later: Shimon Peres's bombing of Tunis with no credible pretext, killing 75 people, Palestinians and Tunisians, expedited by the U.S. and praised by Secretary of State Shultz, then unanimously condemned by the UN Security Council as an "act of armed aggression" (US abstaining). But that too does not enter the annals of terrorism (or perhaps the more severe crime of "armed aggression"), again because of agency. Peres and Shultz do not die in prison, but receive Nobel prizes, huge taxpayer gifts for reconstruction of what they helped destroy in occupied Iraq, and other honors. Again, it all makes sense once we comprehend that elementary moral truisms must be sent to the flames.

Sometimes denial of moral truisms is explicit. A case in point is the reaction to the second major component of the "Bush Doctrine," formally enunciated in the National Security Strategy of September 2002, which was at once described in the main establishment journal *Foreign Affairs* as a "new imperial grand strategy" declaring Washington's right to resort to force to eliminate any potential challenge to its global dominance. The NSS was widely criticized among the foreign policy elite, including the article just cited, but on narrow grounds: not that it was wrong, or even new, but that the style and implementation were so extreme that they posed threats to U.S. interests. Henry Kissinger described "The new approach [as] revolutionary," pointing out that it undermines the 17th century Westphalian system of international order, and of course the UN Charter and international law. He approved of the doctrine but with reservations about style and tactics, and with a crucial qualification: it cannot be "a universal principle available to every nation." Rather, the right of aggression must be reserved to the U.S., perhaps delegated to chosen clients. We must forcefully reject the most elementary of moral truisms: the principle of universality. Kissinger is to be praised for his honesty in forthrightly articulating prevailing doctrine, usually concealed in professions of virtuous intent and tortured legalisms.

To add just one last example that is very timely and significant, consider "just-war theory," now undergoing a vigorous revival in the context of the "normative revolution" proclaimed in the 1990s. There has been debate about whether the invasion of Iraq satisfies the conditions for just war, but virtually none about the bombing of Serbia in 1999 or the invasion of Afghanistan, taken to be such clear cases that discussion is superfluous. Let us take a quick look at these, not asking whether the attacks were right or wrong, but considering the nature of the arguments.

The harshest criticism of the Serbia bombing anywhere near the mainstream is that it was "illegal but legitimate," the conclusion of the International Independent Commission of Inquiry headed by Justice Richard Goldstone. "It was illegal because it did not receive approval from the UN Security Council," the Commission determined, "but it was legitimate because all diplomatic avenues had been exhausted and there was no other way to stop the killings and atrocities in Kosovo."[1] Justice Goldstone observed that the Charter may need revision in the light of the report and the judgments on which it is based. The NATO intervention, he explains, "is too important a precedent" for it to be regarded "an aberration." Rather,

---

1. The Independent International Commission on Kosovo, "The Kosovo Report," October 23, 2000 (Oxford: Oxford University Press, 2000), at http://www.palmecenter.se/print _uk.asp?Article_Id=873.

"state sovereignty is being redefined in the face of globalization and the resolve by the majority of the peoples of the world that human rights have become the business of the international community." He also stressed the need for "objective analysis of human rights abuses."[1]

The last comment is good advice. One question that an objective analysis might address is whether the majority of the peoples of the world accept the judgment of the enlightened states. In the case of the bombing of Serbia, review of the world press and official statements reveals little support for that conclusion, to put it rather mildly. In fact, the bombing was bitterly condemned outside the NATO countries, facts consistently ignored.[2] Furthermore, it is hardly likely that the principled self-exemption of the enlightened states from the "universalization" that traces back to Nuremberg would gain the approval of much of the world's population. The new norm, it appears, fits the standard pattern.

Another question that objective analysis might address is whether indeed "all diplomatic options had been exhausted." That conclusion is not easy to maintain in the light of the fact that there were two options on the table when NATO decided to bomb – a NATO proposal and a Serbian proposal – and that after 78 days of bombing, a compromise was reached between them.[3]

A third question is whether it is true that "there was no other way to stop the killings and atrocities in Kosovo," clearly a crucial matter. In this case, objective analysis happens to be unusually easy. There is vast documentation available from impeccable Western sources: several compilations of the State Department released in justification of the war, detailed records of the OSCE, NATO, the UN, a British Parliamentary Inquiry, and other similar sources.

There are several remarkable features of the unusually rich documentation. One is that the record is almost entirely ignored in the vast literature on the Kosovo war, including the scholarly literature.[4] The second is that

1. Goldstone, *loc. cit.*

2. For a review see my *New Military Humanism* (Monroe, Maine: Common Courage Press, 1999).

3. For details, see my *A New Generation Draws the Line* (New York: Verso, 2000), which also reviews how NATO instantly overturned the Security Council resolution it had initiated. Goldstone, *loc. cit.*, recognizes that the resolution was a compromise, but does not go into the matter, which aroused no interest in the West.

4. The only detailed reviews I know of are in my books cited in the two preceding notes, with some additions from the later British parliamentary inquiry in *Hegemony or Survival*.

the substantive contents of the documentation are not only ignored, but consistently denied. I have reviewed the record elsewhere, and will not do so here, but what we discover, characteristically, is that the clear and explicit chronology is reversed. The Serbian atrocities are portrayed as the cause of the bombing, whereas it is uncontroversial that they followed it, virtually without exception, and were furthermore its anticipated consequence, as is also well documented from the highest NATO sources.

The British government, the most hawkish element of the alliance, estimated that most of the atrocities were attributable not to the Serbian security forces, but to the KLA guerrillas attacking Serbia from Albania – with the intent, as they frankly explained, to elicit a disproportionate Serbian response that could be used to mobilize Western support for the bombing. The British government assessment was as of mid-January, but the documentary record indicates no substantial change until late March, when the bombing was announced and initiated. The Milosevic indictment, based on U.S. and U.K. intelligence, reveals the same pattern of events.

The U.S. and UK, and commentators generally, cite the Racak massacre in mid-January as the decisive turning point, but that plainly cannot be taken seriously. First, even assuming the most extreme condemnations of the Racak massacre to be accurate, it scarcely changed the balance of atrocities. Second, much worse massacres were taking place at the same time elsewhere but aroused no concern, though some of the worst could have easily been terminated merely by withdrawing support. One notable case in early 1999 is East Timor, under Indonesian military occupation. The U.S. and U.K. continued to provide their military and diplomatic support for the occupiers, who had already slaughtered perhaps one-fourth of the population with unremitting and decisive U.S.-UK support, which continued until well after the Indonesian army virtually destroyed the country in a final paroxysm of violence in August-September 1999. That is only one of many such cases, but it alone more than suffices to dismiss the professions of horror about Racak.

In Kosovo, Western estimates are that about 2000 were killed in the year prior to the invasion. If the British and other assessments are accurate, most of these were killed by the KLA guerrillas. One of the very few serious scholarly studies even to consider the matter estimates that 500 of the 2000 were killed by the Serbs. This is the careful and judicious study by Nicholas Wheeler, who supports the NATO bombing on the grounds that there would have been worse atrocities had NATO not bombed.[1] The argu-

---

1. Nicholas Wheeler, *Saving Strangers: Humanitarian Intervention and International Society* (Oxford 2000).

ment is that by bombing with the anticipation that it would lead to atrocities, NATO was preventing atrocities, maybe even a second Auschwitz,
many claim. That such arguments are taken seriously, as they are, gives
no slight insight into Western intellectual culture, particularly when we
recall that there were diplomatic options and that the agreement reached
after the bombing was a compromise between them (formally at least).

Justice Goldstone appears to have reservations on this matter as well. He
recognizes – as few do – that the NATO bombing was not undertaken to
protect the Albanian population of Kosovo, and that its "direct result" was
a "tremendous catastrophe" for the Kosovars – as was anticipated by the
NATO command and the State Department, followed by another catastrophe particularly for Serbs and Roma under NATO-UN occupation. NATO
commentators and supporters, Justice Goldstone continues, "have had to
console themselves with the belief that 'Operation Horseshoe,' the Serb
plan of ethnic cleansing directed against the Albanians in Kosovo, had
been set in motion before the bombing began, and not in consequence of
the bombing." The word "belief" is appropriate: there is no evidence in the
voluminous Western record of anything having been set in motion before
the international monitors were withdrawn in preparation for the bombing,
and very little in the few days before the bombing began; and "Operation
Horseshoe" has since been exposed as an apparent intelligence fabrication,
though it can hardly be in doubt that Serbia had contingency plans, at
present unknown, for such actions in response to a NATO attack.

It is difficult, then, to see how we can accept the conclusions of the
International Commission, a serious and measured effort to deal with the
issues, on the legitimacy of the bombing.

The facts are not really controversial, as anyone interested can determine. I suppose that is why the voluminous Western documentary record
is so scrupulously ignored. Whatever one's judgment about the bombing,
not at issue here, the standard conclusion that it was an uncontroversial
example of just war and the decisive demonstration of the "normative revolution" led by the "enlightened states" is, to say the least, rather startling
– unless, of course, we return to the same principle: moral truisms must be
cast to the flames, when applied to us.

Let us turn to the second case, the war in Afghanistan, considered such
a paradigm example of just war that there is scarcely even any discussion
about it. The respected moral-political philosopher Jean Bethke Elshtain
summarizes received opinion fairly accurately when she writes approvingly that only absolute pacifists and outright lunatics doubt that this was

uncontroversially a just war. Here, once again, factual questions arise. First, recall the war aims: to punish Afghans until the Taliban agree to hand over Osama bin Laden without evidence. Contrary to much subsequent commentary, overthrowing the Taliban regime was an afterthought, added after several weeks of bombing. Second, there is quite good evidence bearing on the belief that only lunatics or absolute pacifists did not join the chorus of approval. An international Gallup poll after the bombing was announced (but before it actually began) found very limited support for it, almost none if civilians were targeted, as they were from the first moment. And even that tepid support was based on the presupposition that the targets were known to have been responsible for the September 11 attacks. They were not. Eight months later, the head of the FBI testified to the Senate that after the most intensive international intelligence inquiry in history, the most that could be said was that the plot was "believed" to have been hatched in Afghanistan, while the attacks were planned and financed elsewhere. It follows that there was no detectable popular support for the bombing, contrary to confident standard claims, apart from a very few countries; and of course Western elites. Afghan opinion is harder to estimate, but we do know that after several weeks of bombing, leading anti-Taliban figures, including some of those most respected by the U.S. and President Karzai, were denouncing the bombing, calling for it to end, and charging the U.S. with bombing just to "show off its muscle" while undermining their efforts to overthrow the Taliban from within.

If we also adopt the truism that facts matter, some problems arise; but there is little fear of that.

Next come the questions of just war. At once, the issue of universality arises. If the U.S. is unquestionably authorized to bomb another country to compel its leaders to turn over someone it suspects of involvement in a terrorist act, then, *a fortiori*, Cuba, Nicaragua, and a host of others are entitled to bomb the U.S. because there is no doubt of its involvement in very serious terrorist attacks against them: in the case of Cuba going back 45 years, extensively documented in impeccable sources, and not questioned; in the case of Nicaragua, even condemned by the World Court and the Security Council (in vetoed resolutions), after which the U.S. escalated the attack. This conclusion surely follows if we accept the principle of universality. The conclusion, of course, is utterly outrageous, and advocated by no one. We therefore conclude, once again, that the principle of universality has a crucial exception, and that rejection of elementary moral truisms is so deeply entrenched that even raising the question is considered an unspeakable abomination. That is yet another instructive comment on the reigning intellectual and moral culture, with its principled rejection of unacceptable platitudes.

The Iraq war has been considered more controversial, so there is an extensive professional literature debating whether it satisfies international law and just-war criteria. One distinguished scholar, Michael Glennon of the Fletcher School of Law and Diplomacy, argues forthrightly that international law is simply "hot air" and should be abandoned, because state practice does not conform to it: meaning, the U.S. and its allies ignore it. A further defect of international law and the UN Charter, he argues, is that they limit the capacity of the U.S. to resort to force, and such resort is right and good because the U.S. leads the "enlightened states" (his phrase), apparently by definition: no evidence or argument is adduced, or considered necessary. Another respected scholar argues that the U.S. and U.K. were in fact acting in accord with the UN Charter, under a "communitarian interpretation" of its provisions: they were carrying out the will of the international community, in a mission implicitly delegated to them because they alone had the power to carry it out.[1] It is apparently irrelevant that the international community vociferously objected, at an unprecedented level – quite evidently, if people are included within the international community, but even among elites.

Others observe that law is a living instrument, its meaning determined by practice, and practice demonstrates that new norms have been established permitting "anticipatory self-defense," another euphemism for aggression at will. The tacit assumption is that norms are established by the powerful, and that they alone have the right of anticipatory self-defense. No one, for example, would argue that Japan exercised this right when it bombed military bases in the U.S. colonies of Hawaii and the Philippines, even though the Japanese knew very well that B-17 Flying Fortresses were coming off the Boeing production lines, and were surely familiar with the very public discussions in the U.S. explaining how they could be used to incinerate Japan's wooden cities in a war of extermination, flying from Hawaiian and Philippine bases.[2] Nor would anyone accord that right to any state today,

1. Carston Stahn, "Enforcement of the Collective Will after Iraq," *American Journal of International Law*, Symposium, "Future Implications of the Iraq Conflict," Vol. 97, January, 2003, pp. 804–23. For more on these matters, including Glennon's influential ideas and his rejection of other moral truisms, see my article and several others in *Review of International Studies* Vol. 29, No. 4, October, 2003, and my *Hegemony or Survival* (New York: Henry Holt, 2004).

2. See Bruce Franklin, *War Stars* (New York: Oxford University Press, 1988).

apart from the self-declared enlightened states, which have the power to determine norms and to apply them selectively at will, basking in praise for their nobility, generosity, and messianic visions of righteousness.

There is nothing particularly novel about any of this, apart from one aspect. The means of destruction that have been developed are by now so awesome, and the risks of deploying and using them so enormous, that a rational Martian observer would not rank the prospects for survival of this curious species very high, as long as contempt for elementary moral truisms remains so deeply entrenched among educated elites.

I'm pleased to be here at the American Enterprise Institute. I have some long-time friends here, as you know if you've studied the published wiring diagrams that purport to illuminate the anatomy of the neocon cabal.

> —Douglas Feith, May 4, 2004, addressing the American Enterprise Institute at "Winning Iraq: A Briefing on the Anniversary of the End of Major Combat Operations"

The storm of enthusiasm in "old Europe" is muted.

> —Heidemarie Wieczorek-Zeul, German development minister, March 17, 2005, on the nomination of Paul Wolfowitz, former U.S. deputy defense secretary and chief architect of the Iraq war, as head of the World Bank

Driving the Runaway Train: Neocons, 9/11, and the Pretexts for War

THE EDITORS' GLOSS: In this compelling piece, adapted from *America the Virtuous* as it appeared in the Summer 2003 *Orbis*, Prof. Ryn gets to the heart of the obsession that America has developed with freedom and democracy over the years, under the influence of predominantly neoconservative "thinkers." Not that these ideas or realities are not good things, if correctly understood. Indeed, freedom to fulfill essential duties and pursue one's true end is an absolute good, while the idea of democracy, taken to mean the legitimate participation of citizens in a nation's political life, is extremely laudable.

Yet this "freedom and democracy" vision should emphatically not embrace what *National Review*'s Jonah Goldberg, for instance, sees as the defining note of the current American presidency. "In a literal sense," he noted, "revolutionaries and radicals tend [to] call for the violent overthrow of the government . . . . that is precisely what lies at the core of Bush's revolutionary foreign policy. Bush has already violently overthrown two governments – Iraq and Afghanistan – and he's made it clear that he wouldn't cry in his non-alcoholic beer if a few more regimes went the way of the dodo, with our help." How many soldiers and sailors who sign up to *support and defend the Constitution*, we wonder, want to get into the business of violently overthrowing foreign governments? How many should, whether they want to or not? Should we as a nation be doing so as a matter of national policy?

A tyrant might say "yes," insofar as his goal might be to remake the world according to his own image. But it's a little hard to take when the professed exemplar of "democracy" isn't at all concerned about what the rest of the world's citizens might prefer as forms of government or styles of life in their own backyards.

5

The Ideology of American Empire
• • • • • • • • • •
Prof. Claes G. Ryn, Ph.D.

T
HE PRESIDENT OF the United States has committed his country to goals that will require world hegemony, not to say supremacy. In numerous speeches and statements since September 2001,
President Bush has vowed to wage an exhaustive, final war on terror and
to advance the cause of a better world. "Our responsibility to history is
clear: to answer these attacks and rid the world of evil."[1] In the President's
opinion, the United States represents universal principles. He summarizes
them in the word "freedom." As mankind's beacon of political right, the
United States must, he believes, remove obstacles to freedom around the
world. Accomplishing this task is associated in the President's mind with
using American military might. In June 2002, he informed the Congress
that the "Department of Defense has become the most powerful force for
freedom the world has ever seen."[2] Since 9/11, the U.S. government has
relentlessly mobilized and deployed that force far and wide, with effects
that remain to be seen.

What had happened? In his 2000 presidential campaign, President
Bush had repeatedly called for a more "humble" U.S. foreign policy and
expressed strong reservations about America's undertaking nation building and following a generally interventionist foreign policy. A cynic might
suggest that, having won the presidency partly by appealing to Americans'
weariness of international over-extension, President Bush had now seized
an opportunity to extend his power greatly. A less cynical observer would
note that the 9/11 attacks outraged the President. They aroused nationalis-

---

1. Remarks, National Cathedral, September 14, 2002 (http://www.whitehouse.gov/news/
releases/2001/09).

2. Statement to the U.S. Congress, June 18, 2002 (http://www.whitehouse/gov/news/
releases/2002/06).

tic feelings in him and shifted his focus to world affairs. Since then he has also gained a new sense of the military and other power at his command.

Yet it is not likely that George W. Bush would have changed his stated approach to foreign policy so drastically had he not been affected by a way of thinking about America's role in the world that has acquired strong influence in recent decades, not least in the American foreign policy establishment inside and outside of government. A large number of American political intellectuals, including many writers on American foreign policy, have been promoting what may be called an ideology of empire. Many of them are in universities; some are leading media commentators. Today some of the most articulate and strong-willed have the President's ear.

When the 9/11 terrorists struck, the time had long been ripe for systematically implementing an ideology of empire, but in his election campaign George W. Bush had seemed an obstacle to such a course. He advocated a more restrictive use of American power. If he had done so out of genuine conviction, 9/11 brought a profound change of heart. The already available ideology of empire helped remove any inhibitions the President might have had about an activist foreign policy and helped shape his reaction to the attack. It can be debated to what extent his advisors and speechwriters, who were to varying degrees attracted to the ideology, along with numerous media commentators of the same orientation, were able to channel the President's anger. In any case, President Bush moved to embrace the idea of armed world hegemony. The attack on America could have elicited a much different reaction, such as a surgical and limited response; it became instead the occasion and justification for something grandiose.

In spite of its great influence, the ideology of empire is unfamiliar to most Americans, except in segments that appear disparate but are in fact closely connected. Drawing these connections is essential to assessing the import and ramifications of the evolving Bush Doctrine.

Though heavily slanted in the direction of international affairs, the ideology of American empire constitutes an entire world view. It includes perspectives on human nature, society, and politics, and it sets forth distinctive conceptions of its central ideas, notably what it calls "democracy," "freedom," "equality," and "capitalism." It regards America as founded on universal principles and assigns to the United States the role of supervising the remaking of the world. Its adherents have the intense dogmatic commitment of true believers and are highly prone to moralistic rhetoric. They demand, among other things, "moral clarity" in dealing with regimes that stand in the way of America's universal purpose. They see themselves as champions of "virtue." In some form, this ideology has been present for a long time.

There are similarities between the advocates of the ideology of American empire and the ideologues who inspired and led the French Revolution of 1789. The Jacobins, too, claimed to represent universal principles, which they summed up in the slogan *"liberté, égalité, et fraternité."* The dominant Jacobins also wanted greater economic freedom. They thought of themselves as fighting on the side of good against evil and called themselves "the virtuous." They wanted a world much different from the one they had inherited. The result was protracted war and turbulence in Europe and elsewhere. Those who embody the Jacobin spirit today in America have explicitly global ambitions. It is crucial to understand what they believe, for potentially they have the military might of the United States at their complete disposal.

The philosopher who most influenced the old Jacobins was Jean-Jacques Rousseau (1712–78), who asserted in *The Social Contract* (1762) that "man was born free, but he is everywhere in chains."[1] The Jacobins set out to liberate man. The notion that America's military might is the greatest force for freedom in human history recalls Rousseau's famous statement that those who are not on the side of political right may have to be "forced to be free."

The new Jacobins have taken full advantage of the nation's outrage over 9/11 to advance their already fully formed drive for empire. They have helped rekindle America's long-standing propensity for global involvement. Knowingly or unknowingly, President Bush has become the new Jacobins' leading spokesman, and he is receiving their very strong support. Reflexes developed by American politicians and commentators during the cold war have boosted the imperialistic impulse. Many cold warriors, now lacking the old enemy of communism, see in the goal of a better world for mankind another justification for continued extensive use of American power. President Bush's moralistic interventionism gains additional support and credibility from a number of antecedents in modern American politics. Woodrow Wilson comes immediately to mind. But the current ideology of empire goes well beyond an earlier, more tentative and hesitant pursuit of world hegemony, and it has acquired great power at a new, formative juncture in history.

The most conspicuous and salient feature of the neo-Jacobin approach to international affairs is its universalistic and monopolistic claims. The

---

1. Jean-Jacques Rousseau, *The Basic Political Writings* (Indianapolis: Hackett, 1987), *Social Contract*, Bk. I, Ch. I, p. 141.

University of Chicago's Allan Bloom (1930–92) argued in his best-selling *The Closing of the American Mind* that what he called "the American project" was not just for Americans. "When we Americans speak seriously about politics, we mean that our principles of freedom and equality and the rights based on them are rational and everywhere applicable." World War II was for Bloom not simply a struggle to defeat a dangerous enemy. It was "really an educational project undertaken to force those who did not accept these principles to do so."[1] If America is the instrument of universal right, the cause of all humanity, it is only proper that it should be diligent and insistent in imposing its will.

The new Jacobins typically use "democracy" as an umbrella term for the kind of political regime that they would like to see installed all over the world. In their view, only democracy, as they define it, answers to a universal moral imperative and is legitimate. Bringing democracy to countries that do not yet have it ought to be the defining purpose of U.S. foreign policy. One may call this part of neo-Jacobin ideology "democratism." It has been espoused by many academics, Duke University political scientist James David Barber prominent among them. "The United States should stand up and lead the world democracy movement," he wrote in 1990. "We have made democracy work here; now we ought to make it work everywhere we can, with whatever tough and expensive action that takes."[2]

Numerous American intellectual activists, journalists, and columnists, many of them taught by professors like Bloom and Barber, sound the same theme. It has become so common in the major media, newspapers, and intellectual magazines and has been so often echoed by politicians that, to some, it seems to express a self-evident truth.

Not all who speak about an American global mission to spread democracy are neo-Jacobins in the strict sense of the term. Some use neo-Jacobin rhetoric not out of ideological conviction, but because such language is in the air and appears somehow expected, or because war is thought to require it. Many combine Jacobin ideas with other elements of thought and imagination: rarely, if ever, is an individual all of a piece. Contradictory ideas often compete within one and the same person. The purpose here is not to classify particular persons but to elucidate an ideological pattern, showing how certain ideas form a coherent, if ethically and philosophically questionable, ideology.

---

1. Allan Bloom, *The Closing of the American Mind* (New York: Simon and Schuster, 1987), p. 153.

2. James David Barber, " . . . And Democracy Needs Help," *Washington Post*, January 25, 1990.

New Nationalism

Two writers with considerable media visibility, William Kristol and David Brooks, who label themselves conservatives, have led complaints that the long-standing prejudice among American conservatives against a larger federal government is paranoid and foolish. Big government is needed, Kristol and Brooks contend, because the United States is based on "universal principles." Its special moral status gives it a great mission in the world. In order to pursue its global task, the American government must be muscular and "energetic," especially with regard to military power. Kristol and Brooks call for a "national-greatness conservatism," which would include "a neo-Reaganite foreign policy of national strength and moral assertiveness abroad."[1]

Similarly, foreign policy expert Robert Kagan writes of his fellow Americans: "As good children of the Enlightenment, Americans believe in human perfectibility. But Americans . . . also believe . . . that global security and a liberal order depend on the United States – that 'indispensable nation' – wielding its power."[2]

International adventurism has often served to distract nations from pressing domestic difficulties, but in America today, expansionism is often fueled also by intense moral-ideological passion. Since the principles for which America stands are portrayed as ultimately supranational (for Bloom they are actually opposed to traditional national identity), "nationalism" may not be quite the right term for this new missionary zeal. The new Jacobins believe that as America spearheads the cause of universal principles, it should progressively shed its own historical distinctiveness except insofar as that distinctiveness is directly related to those principles. Though countries confronted by this power are likely to see it as little more than a manifestation of nationalistic ambition and arrogance, it is nationalistic only in a special sense. Like revolutionary France, neo-Jacobin America casts itself as a savior nation. Ideological and national zeal become indistinguishable. "Our nationalism," write Kristol and Brooks about America's world mission, "is that of an exceptional nation founded on a universal principle, on what Lincoln called 'an abstract truth, applicable to all men and all times.'"[3]

---

1. William Kristol and David Brooks, "What Ails Conservatism," *Wall Street Journal*, September 15, 1997.

2. Robert Kagan, "The U.S.-Europe Divide," *Washington Post*, May 26, 2002.

3. Kristol and Brooks, "What Ails," *loc. cit.*

This view of America's role can hardly be called patriotic in the old sense of that word. Neo-Jacobinism is not characterized by devotion to America's concrete historical identity with its origins in Greek, Roman, Christian, European, and English civilization. Neo-Jacobins are attached in the end to ahistorical, supranational principles that they believe should supplant the traditions of particular societies. The new Jacobins see themselves as on the side of right and fighting evil and are not prone to respecting or looking for common ground with countries that do not share their democratic preferences.

Traditionally, the patriot's pride of country has been understood to encompass moral self-restraint and a sense of his own country's flaws. By contrast, neo-Jacobinism is perhaps best described as a kind of ideological nationalism. Its proponents are not precisely uncritical of today's American democracy; Bloom complained that American democracy was too relativistic and insufficiently faithful to the principles of its own founding. But it should be noted that he regarded those principles as "rational and everywhere applicable" and thus as monopolistic. Greater dedication to "American principles" would by definition increase, not reduce, the wish to dictate terms to others.

New Universalism

Having been nurtured for many years in pockets of the academy, American neo-Jacobinism started to acquire journalistic and political critical mass in the 1980s. It was well-represented in the national security and foreign policy councils of the Reagan and Bush Sr. administrations. As Soviet communism was crumbling, it seemed to people of this orientation increasingly realistic to expect an era in which the United States would be able to dominate the world on behalf of universal principles. Missionary zeal and the desire to use American power began to flood the media, the government, and the public policy debate. Columnist and TV commentator Ben Wattenberg offered a particularly good example of this frame of mind when he wrote in 1988 that the prospects for exporting American values were highly propitious. "Never has the culture of one nation been so far-flung and potent." Wattenberg pointed out that "there is, at last, a global language, American."[1]

---

1. Ben Wattenberg, "Chance to Champion Freedom," *Washington Times*, December 1, 1988.

After the cold war, American culture could only spread, he continued, with global sales of American TV shows, movies, and music. "Important newsstands around the world now sell three American daily newspapers. There is now a near-global television news station: Cable News Network." Not mentioned by Wattenberg was that the content being transmitted to the world might be of dubious value and a poor reflection on America and democracy. What intrigued him was the potential to expand American influence by exporting America's culture.

Behind the argument that the United States and its values are models for all peoples lurked the will to power, which was sometimes barely able to keep up ideological appearances. Again by way of example, Wattenberg desired nothing less than world dominance: "It's pretty clear what the global community needs: probably a top cop, but surely a powerful global organizer. Somebody's got to do it. We're the only ones who can." He called "visionary" the idea of "spreading democratic and American values around the world." As if not to appear immodest, he wrote: "Our goal in the global game is not to *conquer* the world, only to *influence* it so that it is hospitable to our values" (emphasis added).[1] Later he urged, "Remember this about American Purpose: a unipolar world is fine, if America is the uni."[2]

In the major media, one of the early and most persistent advocates of an assertive American foreign policy was the columnist and TV commentator Charles Krauthammer. In 1991, for example, he urged "a robust interventionism." "We are living in a unipolar world," he wrote. "We Americans should like it – and exploit it." "Where our cause is just and interests are threatened, we should act – even if . . . we must act unilaterally."[3] This point of view would eventually become a commonplace.

The idea of spreading democracy sometimes took on a religious ardor. In a Christmas column published in 1988, Michael Novak said about the Judeo-Christian tradition that it "instructs the human race to make constant progress . . . . It insists that societies must continually be reshaped, until each meets the measure the Creator has in mind for a just, truthful, free, and creative civilization." All over the world people were "crying out against abuses of their God-given rights to self-determination." The spread of democracy was for Novak a great religious development that he

1. *Ibid.*; "Showdown Time . . . Wake-up Slap," August 8, 1990; and "To Sow Seeds of Freedom," August 1, 1990.
2. Ben Wattenberg, "Peddling 'Son of Manifest Destiny,'" *Washington Times*, March 21, 1990.
3. Charles Krauthammer, "Bless Our Pax Americana," *Washington Post*, March 22, 1991.

compared to God's Incarnation. The "citizens of the world . . . demand the birth of democracy in history, in physical institutions: as physical as the birth at Bethlehem."[1] The enthusiasm of the Christmas season may have inclined Novak to overstatement, but he was clearly eager to have his readers associate democracy with divine intent.

This mode of thinking is in marked contrast to the old Christian tradition. Christianity has always stressed the imperfect, sinful nature of man and warned against placing too much faith in manmade political institutions and measures. St. Augustine (354–430) is only one of the earliest and least sanguine of many Christian thinkers over the centuries who would have rejected out of hand the idea that mankind is destined for great progress and political perfection, to say nothing about the possibility of salvation through politics. Although Christianity has stressed that rulers must serve the common good and behave in a humane manner, it has been reluctant to endorse any particular form of government as suited to all peoples and all historical circumstances. Here Christianity agreed with the Aristotelian view.

The New Democratism

Democratism has long had more than a foothold in American government. A look back in modern history is appropriate. President Woodrow Wilson, with his belief in America's special role and his missionary zeal, gave it a strong push. Harvard professor Irving Babbitt (1865–1933), perhaps America's most incisive and prescient student of modern Western and American culture, commented in the early years of the twentieth century on the imperialistic trend in U.S. foreign policy. Babbitt, the founder of what has been called the New Humanism or American Humanism, was formally a professor of French and comparative literature, but he was also a highly perceptive as well as prophetic observer of social and political developments. He noted that the United States was setting itself up as the great guardian and beneficiary of mankind. "We are rapidly becoming a nation of humanitarian crusaders," Babbitt wrote in 1924. Leaders like Wilson viewed America as abjuring selfish motives and as being, therefore, above all other nations. Babbitt commented:

> We are willing to admit that all other nations are self-seeking, but as for ourselves, we hold that we act only on the most disinterested motives. We have

---

1. Michael Novak, "Human Rights at Christmas," *Washington Times*, December 23, 1988.

not as yet set up, like revolutionary France, as the Christ of Nations, but during the late war we liked to look on ourselves as at least the Sir Galahad of Nations. If the American thus regards himself as an idealist at the same time that the foreigner looks on him as a dollar-chaser, the explanation may be due partly to the fact that the American judges himself by the way he feels, whereas the foreigner judges him by what he does.[1]

By the time of President Wilson the idea had long been common in America that in old Europe conceited and callous elites oppressed the common man. There and elsewhere things needed to be set right. Thomas Jefferson had been a pioneer for this outlook. But from the time of George Washington's warning of the danger of entangling alliances, a desire for heavy American involvement abroad had for the most part been held in check. By the time of Theodore Roosevelt's presidency, it was clear that the wish for American prominence and activism in international affairs had thrown off earlier restraints. Woodrow Wilson reinforced the interventionist impulse, not, of course, to advance selfish American national motives but, as he said, to "serve mankind." Because America has a special moral status, Wilson proclaimed, it is called to do good in the world. In 1914, even before the outbreak of the European war, Wilson stated in a Fourth of July address that America's role was to serve "the rights of humanity." The flag of the United States, he declared, is "the flag, not only of America, but of humanity."[2]

Babbitt pointed out that those who would not go along with Wilson's "humanitarian crusading" were warned that they would "break the heart of the world." Babbitt retorted: "If the tough old world had ever had a heart in the Wilsonian sense, it would have been broken long ago." He added that Wilson's rhetoric, which was at the same time abstract and sentimental, revealed "a temper at the opposite pole from that of the genuine statesman." Wilson's humanitarian idealism made him "inflexible and uncompromising."[3]

---

1. Irving Babbitt, *Democracy and Leadership* (Indianapolis: Liberty Fund, 1979, originally published, 1924), pp. 337, 295. It is a national misfortune that Americans have paid less attention to one of their truly great thinkers than to a number of lesser European lights who impress by their denser, more technical, less essayistic philosophical style.

2. Woodrow Wilson, Thanksgiving Proclamation, Nov. 7, 1917, *The Papers of Woodrow Wilson*, Arthur S. Link *et al.* (Princeton, N.J.: Princeton University Press, 1966–93), pp. 44, 525; and Address at Independence Hall, Philadelphia, *Papers*, pp. 30, 254. For an in-depth study of Woodrow Wilson and his notion of America as servant of mankind, see Richard M. Gamble, "Savior Nation: Woodrow Wilson and the Gospel of Service," *Humanitas*, Vol. XIV, No. 1, 2001.

3. Babbitt, *Democracy*, p. 314.

The Post-Cold War Imperative

The notion that America had a mandate to help rid the world, not least Europe, of the bad old ways of traditional societies with their undemocratic political arrangements has remained a strong influence on American foreign policy. In World War II, FDR's sense of American mission may have been as strong as Wilson's.

For a long time during the cold war, most policy makers and commentators saw that war as a defensive struggle to protect freedom or liberty against totalitarian tyranny. But some of the most dedicated cold warriors were also democratists. They had a vision for remaking the world that differed in substance from that of the Soviet Union and other communist regimes but that was equally universalistic. With the disintegration and collapse of the Soviet Union, these cold warriors did not argue for substantially reducing the American military or the United States' involvement in international affairs. On the contrary, they believed that America should continue to play a large and, in some respects, expanded role in the world; that, as the only remaining superpower, America had a historic opportunity to advance the cause of democracy and human rights. This language had long been gaining currency in the centers of public debate and political power, and soon government officials and politicians in both of the major parties spoke routinely of the need to promote democracy. Many did so in just the manner here associated with neo-Jacobinism. It seemed to them that the American ideology had not only survived the challenge from the other universalist ideology, but had prevailed in a contest that validated the American ideal as applicable in all societies.

The first President Bush thought of himself as a competent pragmatist, but, as is often the case with persons who lack philosophically grounded convictions of their own, he was susceptible to adopting the language and ideas of intellectually more focused and ideological individuals. The rhetoric in his administration about a New World Order often had a distinctly democratist ring, in considerable part probably because of the ideological leanings of speechwriters. In 1991 James Baker, President Bush's secretary of state, echoed a neo-Jacobin refrain when he declared that U.S. foreign policy should serve not specifically American interests but "enlightenment ideals of universal applicability." Whether such formulations originated with Mr. Baker or his speechwriters, the Secretary clearly liked the sound of them. He advocated a "Euro-Atlantic community that extends east from Vancouver to Vladivostok." This "community," he said, "can only be achieved on a democratic basis." The enormous size and political and cultural diversity of the region he described did not give him pause or make him question the United States' willingness or ability to take charge of such a daunting cause. No, the United States should promote "common . . . universal values" in those parts of the world, he said, and "indeed, elsewhere on the globe."[1] American power was there to be used. It seemed appropriate in cases such as these to talk of virtually unlimited political ambition.

The surge of globalist political-ideological aspirations was even more blatantly and pointedly expressed by the Bush Sr. administration in a draft Pentagon planning document that was leaked to the *New York Times*. It had been produced under the supervision of then-Under Secretary of Defense Paul Wolfowitz. The draft plan dealt with the United States' military needs in the post–cold war era, setting forth the goal of a world in which the United States would be the sole and uncontested superpower. The draft plan assigned to the United States "the pre-eminent responsibility" for dealing with "those wrongs which threaten not only our interests, but those of our allies or friends, or which could seriously unsettle international relations." The goal of American world dominance was presented as serving the spread of democracy and open economic systems. American military power was to be so overwhelming that it would not even occur to the United States' competitors to challenge its will.[2] This vision of the future might have seemed the expression of an inordinate, open-ended desire for power and control, uninhibited by the fact that the world is, after all, rather large. But significantly, many commentators considered the vision entirely plausible. The *Wall Street Journal* praised the draft plan in a lead editorial favoring *"Pax Americana."*[3]

Bill Clinton made clear in his 1992 presidential campaign that he would pursue a foreign policy similar to, if not more expansive than, the Bush administration's. In 1993 his Secretary of State-designate, Warren Christopher, addressed a group of neoconservative Democrats, including Penn Kemble, Joshua Muravchik, Peter Rosenblatt, Albert Shanker, and Max Kampelman, to assure them that he would fully back the President's commitments to making promotion of democracy a central tenet of U.S. foreign policy.[4] Christopher's successor, Madeleine Albright, was even

---

1. Secretary of State James A. Baker, speech to the Aspen Institute in Berlin, Germany, June 18, 1991.

2. Patrick E. Tyler, "U.S. Strategy Plan Calls for Insuring No Rivals Develop," *New York Times*, March 8, 1992.

3. *Wall Street Journal*, lead editorial, March 16, 1992.

4. *Washington Post*, January 9, 1993. The designation "neoconservative" for the mentioned individuals is taken from this article.

more comfortable with this stance. Democratist ideology was by now clearly dominant in top policy-making circles in Washington and elsewhere. It both generated and sanctioned an assertive, expansive use of American power.

When running for President, George W. Bush appeared to have substantial qualms about this broad use of American might. He questioned the desire to impose solutions to problems in all regional and local trouble spots around the world, seeming to recognize that such efforts betrayed arrogance and an undue will to power that other countries might resent. His adoption of a wholly different, far more assertive tone after the 9/11 attacks was surely induced in large part by war-like conditions. Although the change was probably motivated more by pragmatic than by ideological considerations, President Bush's rhetoric began to take on a neo-Jacobin coloring, as when he spoke of the "axis of evil," a phrase coined by neoconservative speechwriter David Frum.

In subsequent speeches, the President has often come to resemble Woodrow Wilson in assigning to the United States, the exceptional country, an exceptional mission in the world. He has asserted that an attack upon the United States was an attack upon freedom: "A lot of young people say, well, why America? Why would anybody want to come after us? Why would anybody want to fight a war with this nation? And the answer is because we love freedom. That's why. And they hate freedom."[1] Identifying America with the universal cause of freedom, Bush has even adopted Wilsonian imagery. Echoing Wilson in 1917, he said that the American flag stands "not only for our power, but for freedom."[2] Although the President used the term "freedom" rather than "democracy," which is the one favored by the new Jacobins, he seemed to agree with the notion that any enemy or critic of the United States is an opponent of universal principle. "They have attacked America," he said three days after 9/11, "because we are freedom's home and defender."[3]

---

1. Remarks of President to United Brotherhood of Carpenters and Joiners of America 2002 Legislative Conference, June 19, 2002 (http://www.whitehouse.gov/news/releases/2002/06); Peter Slevin, "The Word at the White House: Bush Formulates His Brand of Foreign Policy," *Washington Post*, June 23, 2002.

2. Remarks of President to West Point Commencement, June 1, 2002 (http://www.whitehouse.gov/ news/releases/2002/06). The same kind of imagery had been used by General George C. Marshall at the Commencement exercises in 1942, and the President began his speech by quoting Marshall, who had expressed the hope that "our flag will be recognized throughout the world as a symbol of freedom on the one hand, and of overwhelming power on the other."

3. Remarks, National Cathedral, September 14, 2001 (http://www.whitehouse.gov/news/

Proponents of American empire had moved with great speed to head off any reluctance on the part of a devastated and disoriented American public to deal quickly and comprehensively with terrorism around the globe. Already on the morning after the attacks, when it was still not clear who was responsible, the *Washington Post* carried an article by Robert Kagan calling for sweeping countermeasures. The U.S. Congress should, Kagan insisted, declare war immediately on the terrorists and any nation that might have assisted them. The situation required that America act with "moral clarity and courage as our grandfathers did [responding to the attack on Pearl Harbor]. Not by asking what we have done to bring on the wrath of inhuman murderers. Not by figuring out ways to reason with, or try to appease those who have spilled our blood."[1] On the same day William Bennett, Jack Kemp and Jeane Kirkpatrick issued a statement calling for war against the "entire" Islamic terrorist network.[2]

If the President thought that American actions might have contributed to the hostility to the United States in the world, he did not, and in the circumstances perhaps could not, say so publicly. What he did say and has said repeatedly is that the United States must be diligent, active, and forceful – preemptive even – in dealing with present or potential threats of terrorism. Paradoxically, given his earlier calls for American humility, he has presided over a massive push for greater American involvement in the world and for a vastly more intrusive role for government in the daily lives of U.S. citizens. In fairness to a politician who is not also an intellectual and a historian, war has its own logic, and it may be premature to draw definitive conclusions about the President's statements and actions in the wake of 9/11, which was an act of war. But the fact is that President Bush's assertive approach and universalistic rhetoric has been seized on by American democratists who have been preparing the ground for a war and for a wider pursuit of empire. Charles Krauthammer praised the President for applying "the fundamental principle of American foreign policy – the promotion of democracy."[3] Political activist and writer Midge Decter pointed out that after 9/11 America could do something to clean up the world. She urged her countrymen "to hang onto what is most important to remember: that our country, the strongest on earth, has been pressed by

releases/2001/09/20010914-2.html).

1. Robert Kagan, "We Must Fight this War," *Washington Post*, September 12, 2001.
2. Statement of three of the co-directors of Empower America, September 12, 2001.
3. Charles Krauthammer, "Peace Through Democracy," *Washington Post*, June 28, 2002.

circumstance – I would say, has been granted the opportunity – to rid the world of some goodly measure of its cruelty and pestilence."[1]

In mid-September 2002, President Bush sent to the U.S. Congress the President's annual statement on strategy, the *National Security Strategy*, which gave clear evidence that he was abandoning his earlier calls for a more "humble" U.S. foreign policy. Though the report was framed as a strategy for combating terrorism, the stated objectives supererogated any need to respond to acute external or internal threats. The report defined what amounted to a new and highly ambitious role for America in the world. Released the day after the President asked the Congress to authorize the use of preemptive military force against Iraq, it provided justifications for American intervention against potential security threats, while also formulating a new and much broader international agenda. The report in effect set forth a doctrine of American armed hegemony. The President justified this ascendancy as serving both America's security needs and its efforts to promote freedom, democracy, and free trade. The *Washington Post* said that the *Strategy* gave the United States "a nearly messianic role." It meant not only acceptance but also extension of the old Wolfowitz draft plan. Indeed, Wolfowitz later became deputy secretary of defense and remained a highly vocal and assertive proponent of American activism around the world. According to the report, America's strength and influence in the world is "unprecedented" and "unequaled." The United States, "sustained by faith in the principles of liberty and the value of a free society," also has "unparalleled responsibilities, obligations, and opportunities" beyond its borders. The report calls for possessing such overwhelming military power as to discourage any other power from challenging American hegemony or developing weapons of mass destruction. It overturns the old doctrines of deterrence and containment. Committing the United States to a much expanded understanding of security, it argues that the United States must reserve the right to act preemptively and unilaterally against potentially threatening states or organizations. But the President approved an even wider goal. The *Strategy* commits the United States to making the world "not just safer but better." In explaining the report, a senior administration official said that besides leading the world in the war against terrorists and "aggressive regimes seeking weapons of mass destruction," the United States should preserve the peace, "extend the benefits of liberty and prosperity through the spread of American values," and promote "good governance." In familiar-sounding words, the report describes America's

---

1. Midge Decter, "Unnecessary Wars," *Imprimis*, September 2002, p. 5.

strategy as a "distinctly American internationalism that reflects the union of our values and our national interests."[1]

A New Kind of War

The foreign policy of George W. Bush's immediate two predecessors, Bush Sr. and Bill Clinton, had a strong Wilsonian tilt. But neither President followed any sustained, consistent strategy. By contrast, the Bush Doctrine as set forth in the *National Security Strategy* and other places commits the United States to a bold, comprehensive, and elaborate foreign policy. The publicly and formally stated U.S. goal, in sum, is to establish global supremacy. The United States would set itself up as the arbiter of good and evil in the world and, if necessary, enforce its judgments unilaterally.

Reservations expressed in Europe and elsewhere about American unilateralism and global aspirations have been scorned and dismissed by proponents of empire as a failure to recognize the need to combat evil in the world. Kenneth Adelman, a former deputy ambassador to the UN and a highly placed advisor on defense to the U.S. government, couched his advocacy of imperial designs in terms of fighting terrorism. "I don't think Europeans should cooperate with the United States as a favor to the United States. They should be very grateful to the United States and cooperate because we have a common enemy – terrorism. In my mind, it's a decisive moment in the conflict between civilization and barbarism."[2]

Since America is at war it is, in a way, not surprising that some of its leaders should be portraying America as being on the side of good and those not eager to follow America's lead as aiding and abetting evil. Stark rhetoric has been used before to get Americans to support or sustain war, but the war aims spoken of today are derived from a consciously universalistic and imperialistic ideology. Therein lies an important difference, and a great danger.

The belief in American moral superiority knows no party lines. In an article critical of the George W. Bush administration's way of preparing for war against Iraq, Richard C. Holbrooke, ambassador to the UN under President Clinton, expressed a view ubiquitous in the American foreign policy establishment: "Over the past 60 years, the United States has consistently combined its military superiority with moral and political lead-

---

1. *National Security Strategy of the United States of America*, September 17, 2002 (http://www.whitehouse.gov/nsc/nss.html) and Karen DeYoung and Mike Allen, "Bush Shifts Strategy From Deterrence to Dominance," *Washington Post*, September 21, 2002.
2. "Six Degrees of Preemption," *Washington Post*, Outlook section, September 29, 2002.

ership."[1] The word "consistently" is telling. The notion that, unlike other nations, America is above moral suspicion, provides the best possible justification for the desire to exercise American power.

It seems to the proponents of the ideology of American empire that, surely, America the virtuous is entitled to dominate the world. Some of them have worked long and hard to make this point of view dominant in American foreign policy. President Bush was merely echoing what others had been saying when he stated: "There is a value system that cannot be compromised, and that is [sic] the values we praise. And if the values are good enough for our people, they ought to be good enough for others."[2]

Many members of the so-called Christian right share the view that America has a special mission, but give this notion a triumphalist religious cast beyond the moralism typical of neo-Jacobin ideology. They believe that the United States, as led by a man of God, has a virtually messianic role to play, especially in the Middle East, where God's chosen people, Israel, must be supported by the United States against their enemies. Breaking sharply with the mainstream of traditional Christianity, which has made a distinction between the things of God and the things of Caesar, this form of religion identifies a particular political power, America, with God's will. George W. Bush's rhetoric has sometimes suggested that he is drawn to such thinking. "Evangelical" Christianity of this kind may rest on rather simplistic theological, biblical, and historical assumptions and arguably have virtually no influence over America's dominant national culture, but it provides considerable political support for neo-Jacobinism, which does have such influence. In its practical effects on United States foreign policy, this religious triumphalism puts a religious gloss on neo-Jacobinism. It does not Christianize U.S. foreign policy, but makes it less humble and more belligerent.

Both in domestic and international affairs the new Jacobins are strongly prejudiced against the traditions of old, historically evolved nations and groups. These only retard the emergence of a new order based on what they consider universal principles. In their view, the distinctive traits of different societies and cultures should yield to the homogeneity of virtuous democracy. The new Jacobins are trying to clear away obstacles to the triumph of their ideology and of their own will to power. They exhibit a revolution-

1. Richard C. Hoolbrooke, "It Did Not Have to Be This Way," *Washington Post*, February 23, 2003.

2. Remarks by President George W. Bush, in taped interview with Bob Woodward, *Washington Post*, Nov. 19, 2002; excerpted from Woodward, *Bush at War* (New York: Simon and Schuster, 2002).

ary mindset that will inexorably lead to disaster. Alongside what President Bush called "history's unmarked graves of discarded lies"[1] lie the graves of the self-righteous, the people whose moralism concealed, even from themselves, their importunate will to power. As Ronald Reagan preached, the idealistic utopians and the well meaning are responsible for some of the world's worst evils. Self-righteousness blinds one to one's own sins.

Even if the opinions examined in this article are assessed in the most generous and charitable spirit, their element of political-ideological imperialism is hard to miss. A philosophically and historically inclined observer is reminded of the terrible and large-scale suffering that has been inflicted on mankind by power-seeking sanctioned or inspired by one or another kind of Jacobin moral and intellectual conceit. Communism, one of the most radical and pernicious manifestations of the Jacobin spirit, has disintegrated, at least as a major political force. But another panacea for the world is taking its place. The neo-Jacobin vision for how to redeem humanity may be less obviously utopian than that of communism. It may strike some as admirably idealistic, as did communism. But the spirit of the two movements is similar, and utopian thinking is utopian thinking, fairly innocuous perhaps if restricted to isolated dreamers and theoreticians but dangerous to the extent that it inspires action in the real world. The concern voiced here is that neo-Jacobinism has come to permeate American public debate and is finally within reach of controlling the military might of the United States.

Prudence, realism, compromise, and self-restraint are indispensable qualities in politics. They have been reflected in traditional American institutions, in great decisions made by American statesmen, and sometimes in American public opinion. They have constituted the first line of defense against all manner of foreign and domestic threats, including surges of passion and eruptions of extremism. Given the atrocities of 9/11 and the need for a firm American response, the prominence of crusaders in the Bush administration is perhaps not surprising. But it is also a sign that needed old American virtues are weakening or disappearing. The continued ascendancy of neo-Jacobinism would have disastrous consequences. By acting under its influence America's leaders may be setting in motion fateful developments that they and their successors will not be able to control.

---

1. Address to Congress, September 20, 2001.

THE EDITORS' GLOSS: There is one fact about the rhetoric that comes from the American political establishment that confirms the truth of Dr. Sniegoski's essay beyond anything we could possibly add. This is the constant, frankly tedious reference to 9/11 in conjunction with the Iraq war. Ideologically and rhetorically, Sniegoski suggests, the neoconservatives, Israel-firsters, and Israeli politicians have sought to portray "regime change" in Iraq as a legitimate response to 9/11, in order to carry it out for various reasons of their own. Anyone inclined to balk at this notion as somehow "anti-Semitic" would do well to read Michael Meacher's article for the British *Guardian* of September 6, 2003, subtitled "The 9/11 attacks gave the U.S. an ideal pretext to use force to secure its global domination," which offers substantial confirmation of Sniegoski's thesis.

Now 9/11 is being offered as the reason why it's essential to "stay the course" in Iraq. As the President told the American Legislative Exchange Council (August 3, 2005), "We're at war with an enemy that attacked us on September 11, 2001 . . . . We're at war against an enemy that, since that day, has continued to kill."

Never mind that the argument from the pro-war crowd *before* the war was that Saddam the secular Ba'athist was a sponsor of "international terrorism," and if not a financier of al-Qaeda at least a moral supporter of the attacks on 9/11. *Now* they maintain that Iraq is the "central front" in the war on terror because it is *not* a clash so much with secular, pro-Saddam Ba'athists as with Islamic fanatics who have allegedly taken the opportunity to strike back at the Great Satan.

The problem for the administration message, however, is that the facts get in the way – notwithstanding "spin" – for those willing to look at them. The "Iraq-equals-war-on-terror" line doesn't hold up now, as Col. de Grand Pré explains later, nor did it do so before the war, as Dr. Sniegoski indicates in what follows. What it *did* do for those who were making the claim, though, is the other – and perhaps more interesting – side of the story.

C H A P T E R
6

Neoconservatives, Israel, and 9/11: The Origins of the U.S. War on Iraq
• • • • • • • • • •
Stephen J. Sniegoski, Ph.D.

T HE NEOCONSERVATIVES WERE the driving force for the war on Iraq. Their leading role has been noted by numerous observers[1] even though noting that role has been condemned as "anti-Semitic,"[2] and thus is considered taboo in certain mainstream circles. The public record clearly reveals that the neocons had a Middle East war agenda that long pre-dated the September 11, 2001, terrorism. Their position also dove-tailed with the goals of the Israeli Right (the Likudniks), which sought to weaken and fragment Israel's Arab and Islamic neighbors so as to enhance Israel's power and security. But it was only the traumatic effects of the 9/11 terrorism that enabled the agenda of the neocons to become the pol-

---

1. Joseph Wilson, *The Politics of Truth: Inside the Lies that Led to War and Betrayed My Wife's CIA Identity* (New York: Carroll & Graf Publishers, 2004), p. 425; Craig R. Eisendrath and Melvin A. Goodman, *Bush League Diplomacy: How the Neoconservatives Are Putting the World at Risk* (Amherst, NY: Prometheus Books, 2004); Stefan Halper and Jonathan Clarke, *America Alone: The Neoconservatives and the Global Order* (Cambridge, U.K.: Cambridge University Press, 2004); Joshua Micah Marshall, "Bomb Saddam?: How the Obsession of a Few Neocon Hawks Became the Central Goal of U.S. Foreign Policy," *Washington Monthly*, June, 2002, online; Michael Lind, "How Neoconservatives Conquered Washington – and Launched a War," *Antiwar.com*, April 10, 2003; Elizabeth Drew, "The Neoocons in Power," *New York Review of Books*, Vol. 50, No. 10, June 12, 2003, online; Michael Hirsh, "The Mideast: Neocons on the Line," *Newsweek*, June 23, 2003, online; Robert Kuttner, "Neocons Have Hijacked U.S. Foreign Policy," *Boston Globe*, September 10, 2003, online; Patrick J. Buchanan, "Whose War?" *The American Conservative*, March 24, 2003, online [see pp. 135–147 of the companion to the present volume, *Neo-CONNED!*—Ed.]; Justin Raimondo, "The Neocons' War," *Antiwar.com*, June 2, 2004; Sam Francis, "An Anti-War Column: Bush Likudniks Seek to Start 'World War IV,'" *Vdare.com*, March 20, 2003; Paul Craig Roberts, "Neo-Jacobins Push for World War IV," *LewRockwell.com*, September 20, 2003; Scott McConnell, "The Struggle Over War Aims: Bush Versus the Neo-Cons," *Antiwar.com*, September 25, 2002.

2. Stephen J. Sniegoski, "The Neoconservative Smoke Screen," April 4, 2003, *The Last Ditch* (http://www.thornwalker.com/ditch/snieg_smoke.htm).

icy of the United States of America. The following essay will detail this development.[1]

Although the term neoconservative is in common usage, a brief description of the group might be helpful. Many of the first generation neoconservatives were originally liberal Democrats, and even Marxists and Trotskyites. They drifted to the right in the 1960s and 1970s as the Democratic Party moved to the anti-war McGovernite left. Concern for Jews and Israel loomed large in their change. They adopted a pronounced anti-Soviet policy as the Soviet Union aided Israel's enemies in the Middle East and prohibited Soviet Jews from emigrating. As political scientist Benjamin Ginsburg puts it:

> One major factor that drew them inexorably to the right was their attachment to Israel and their growing frustration during the 1960s with a Democratic party that was becoming increasingly opposed to American military preparedness and increasingly enamored of Third World causes (e.g., Palestinian rights). In the Reaganite right's hard-line anti-communism, commitment to American military strength, and willingness to intervene politically and militarily in the affairs of other nations to promote democratic values (and American interests), neocons found a political movement that would guarantee Israel's security.[2]

Over the years, due to their media power and support from, or control of, numerous well-funded think tanks, such as – to name a few – the American Enterprise Institute (AEI), the Jewish Institute for National Security Affairs (JINSA), the Hudson Institute, and the Center for Security Policy (CSP), the neocons have taken the dominate position in American conservatism. As historian Paul Gottfried writes regarding neocon power today: "At this point they control almost all Beltway 'conservative' think tanks, the 'conservative' TV channel, the *Wall Street Journal*, the *New York*

---

1. This author produced an earlier piece on the origins of the war on Iraq entitled, "The War on Iraq: Conceived in Israel," *The Last Ditch*, February 10, 2003 (http://www.thornwalker.com/ditch/conc_toc.htm).

2. Benjamin Ginsberg, *The Fatal Embrace: Jews and the State* (Chicago: University of Chicago Press, 1993), p. 231; On the connection between Jews, Zionism, and neoconservativism, see Paul Gottfried, *The Conservative Movement* (New York: Twayne Publishers, 1993); J. J. Goldberg, *Jewish Power: Inside the Jewish Establishment* (Reading, Massachusetts: Addison Wesley Publishing Company, Inc., 1996), pp. 159–162; Peter Steinfels, *The Neoconservatives: The Men Who Are Changing America's Politics* (New York: Simon and Schuster, 1979); Gary Dorrien, *The Neoconservative Mind: Politics, Culture, and the War of Ideology* (Philadelphia: Temple University, 1993); James Neuchterlein, "This Time: Neoconservatism Redux," *First Things*, Vol. 66, October, 1996, pp. 7–8.

Post, and several major presses, together with just about every magazine that claims to be conservative."[1]

In moving over to the right, the neoconservatives have not adopted traditional American conservatism but have changed it to fit their own beliefs and interests. Looking back, Irving Kristol, the "godfather of neoconservatism," maintains that

> the historical task and political purpose of neoconservatism would seem to be this: to convert the Republican party, and American conservatism in general, against their respective wills, into a new kind of conservative politics suitable to governing a modern democracy.[2]

In his 1996 book, *The Essential Neoconservative Reader*, editor Mark Gerson jubilantly observes:

> The neoconservatives have so changed conservatism that what we now identify as conservatism is largely what was once neoconservatism. And in so doing, they have defined the way that vast numbers of Americans view their economy, their polity, and their society.[3]

A more negative evaluation of the neoconservative domination of American conservatism has been made by the evolutionary biologist Kevin MacDonald, who writes that the

> intellectual and cumulative effect of neoconservatism and its current hegemony over the conservative political movement in the United States (achieved partly by its large influence on the media and among foundations) has been to shift the conservative movement toward the center and, in effect, to define the limits of conservative legitimacy. Clearly, these limits of conservative legitimacy are defined by whether they conflict with specifically Jewish group interests . . . . The ethnic agenda of neoconservatism can also be seen in their promotion of the idea that the United States should pursue a highly interventionist foreign policy aimed at global democracy and the interests of Israel rather than aimed at the specific national interests of the United States.[4]

In justifying American support for Israel, Irving Kristol, explicitly eschewed national interest on the grounds that

---

1. Paul Gottfried, "Goldberg Is Not the Worst," *LewRockwell.com*, March 20, 2003.

2. Irving Kristol, "The Neoconservative Persuasion," *The Weekly Standard*, August 25, 2003, online.

3. Mark Gerson, "Introduction," in Gerson, ed., *The Essential Neoconservative Reader* (Reading, Mass.: Addison-Wesley Publishing Company, Inc., 1996), p. xvi.

4. Kevin MacDonald, *The Culture of Critique: An Evolutionary Analysis of Jewish Involvement in Twentieth-Century Intellectual and Political Movements* (Westport, Conn.: Praeger, 1998), pp. 312–313.

large nations, whose identity is ideological, like the Soviet Union of yesteryear and the United States of today, inevitably have ideological interests in addition to more material concerns . . . . That is why we feel it necessary to defend Israel today, when its survival is threatened. No complicated geopolitical calculations of national interest are necessary.[1]

The Middle East position of the neoconservatives has paralleled that of the Israeli right, the Likudniks, which has been that weakening and destabilizing Israel's Arab enemies would, by cutting off external support, ultimately facilitate a solution to the Palestinian demographic problem, which threatens the very *raison d'être* of Israel as an exclusivist Jewish state. An extensive, early articulation of this policy was an article by Oded Yinon, entitled, "A Strategy for Israel in the 1980s," which appeared in the World Zionist Organization's periodical *Kivunim* (Directions) in February 1982. Oded Yinon had been attached to the Foreign Ministry and his article undoubtedly reflected high-level thinking in the Israeli military and intelligence establishment. The article called for Israel to bring about the dissolution of all of the Arab states and their fragmentation into a mosaic of ethnic and sectarian groupings. Yinon believed that this would not be a difficult undertaking because nearly all the Arab states were afflicted with internal religious dissent. In essence, the end result would be a Middle East of powerless mini-states that could in no way confront Israeli power. Lebanon, then facing divisive chaos, was Yinon's model for the entire Middle East. Yinon wrote:

> Lebanon's total dissolution into five provinces serves as a precedent for the entire Arab world including Egypt, Syria, Iraq and the Arabian peninsula and is already following that track. The dissolution of Syria and Iraq later on into ethnically or religiously unique areas such as in Lebanon, is Israel's primary target on the Eastern front in the long run, while the dissolution of the military power of those states serves as the primary short term target.[2]

Note that Yinon sought the dissolution of countries – Egypt and Saudi Arabia – that were allied to the United States.

Yinon looked upon Iraq as a major target for dissolution, and he believed that the then ongoing Iran-Iraq war would promote its break-up. It should be pointed out that Yinon's vision for Iraq seems uncannily like what has actually taken place since the U.S. invasion in 2003. He wrote:

1. Kristol, *loc. cit.*
2. Israel Shahak, trans. & ed., *The Zionist Plan For the Middle East* (Belmont, Mass.: A.A.U.G., 1982), a translation of Oded Yinon, *A Strategy for Israel in the Nineteen Eighties* (http://www.geocities.com/alabasters_archive/zionist_plan.html).

Iraq, rich in oil on the one hand and internally torn on the other, is guaranteed as a candidate for Israel's targets. Its dissolution is even more important for us than that of Syria. Iraq is stronger than Syria. In the short run it is Iraqi power which constitutes the greatest threat to Israel. An Iraqi-Iranian war will tear Iraq apart and cause its downfall at home even before it is able to organize a struggle on a wide front against us. Every kind of inter-Arab confrontation will assist us in the short run and will shorten the way to the more important aim of breaking up Iraq into denominations as in Syria and in Lebanon. In Iraq, a division into provinces along ethnic/religious lines as in Syria during Ottoman times is possible. So, three (or more) states will exist around the three major cities: Basra, Baghdad and Mosul, and Shiite areas in the south will separate from the Sunni and Kurdish north. It is possible that the present Iranian-Iraqi confrontation will deepen this polarization.[1]

The goal of Israeli hegemony was inextricably tied to the expulsion of the Palestinians. According to Yinon, the policy of Israel must be "to bring about the dissolution of Jordan; the termination of the problem of the [occupied] territories densely populated with Arabs west of the [river] Jordan; and emigration from the territories, and economic-demographic freeze in them." He added, "We have to be active in order to encourage this change speedily, in the nearest time." Like many Israeli advocates of transfer, Yinon believed that

Israel has made a strategic mistake in not taking measures [of mass expulsion] towards the Arab population in the new territories during and shortly after the [1967] war .... Such a line would have saved us the bitter and dangerous conflict ever since which we could have already then terminated by giving Jordan to the Palestinians.[2]

In a foreword to his own translation of Yinon's piece, Israel Shahak made the interesting comparison between the neoconservative position and actual Likudnik goals.

The strong connection with neoconservative thought in the USA is very prominent, especially in the author's notes. But, while lip service is paid to the idea of the 'defense of the West' from Soviet power, the real aim of the author, and of the present Israeli establishment is clear: to make an Imperial Israel into a world power. In other words, the aim of Sharon is to deceive the Americans after he has deceived all the rest.[3]

Israeli foreign policy expert Yehoshafat Harkabi critiqued the war/expulsion scenario – "Israeli intentions to impose a *Pax Israelica* on the Middle

---

1. *Ibid.*
2. *Ibid.*
3. *Ibid.*

East, to dominate the Arab countries and treat them harshly" – in his very significant work, *Israel's Fateful Hour,* published in 1988. Writing from a "realist" perspective, Harkabi believed that Israel did not have the power to achieve the goal of *Pax Israelica,* given the strength of the Arab states, the large Palestinian population involved, and the vehement opposition of world opinion. Harkabi hoped that "the failed Israeli attempt to impose a new order in the weakest Arab state – Lebanon – will disabuse people of similar ambitions in other territories."[1] Left unconsidered by Harkabi was the possibility that the United States would act as Israel's proxy to achieve this goal.

The chance to use America as Israel's proxy came with Iraq's occupation of Kuwait in 1990. Iraq had been supported and armed by the United States during its war with Iran during the 1980s and continued to receive such support in the war's aftermath. With Iraq's invasion of Kuwait in August 1990, American policy would swiftly change. President George H. W. Bush denounced Saddam's move and the United States quickly made preparations to send troops to Saudi Arabia to protect the kingdom from an attack that was alleged to be imminent. Israel was ecstatic and called for strong American measures, with President Chaim Herzog even calling upon the United States to use nuclear weapons. But Israel did not fully trust that the United States would carry out a military attack. On December 4, 1990, Israeli Foreign Minister David Levy reportedly threatened the United States ambassador, David Brown, that if the United States failed to attack Iraq, Israel would do so itself.[2]

Neoconservatives took a leading role in promoting a U.S. war against Iraq, setting up the Committee for Peace and Security in the Gulf, co-chaired by Richard Perle along with former New York Democratic Congressman Stephen Solarz, which focused on mobilizing popular and congressional support for a war. Neoconservative war hawks such as Frank Gaffney, Jr., Richard Perle, A. M. Rosenthal, William Safire, and *The Wall Street Journal* emphasized in the media that America's war objective should not be simply to drive Iraq out of Kuwait but also to destroy Iraq's military potential, especially its capacity to develop nuclear weapons, which was Israel's fundamental objective.[3] Patrick J. Buchanan pointed out the link between

---

1. Yehoshafat Harkabi, *Israel's Fateful Hour* (New York: Harper & Row, 1988), pp. 57–58.

2. Andrew and Leslie Cockburn, *Dangerous Liaison: The Inside Story of the U.S.-Israeli Covert Relationship* (New York: Harper Perennial, 1991), pp. 353, 356.

3. Christopher Layne, "Why the Gulf War was Not in the National Interest," *The Atlantic,* July 1991, pp. 55–81.

the neocons advocacy of war and the interests of Israel when he made the controversial remark that "There are only two groups that are beating the drums for war in the Middle East – the Israeli Defense Ministry and its amen corner in the United States."[1]

The Bush administration accepted the arguments that Iraq should not only be forced to leave Kuwait but should also be disarmed of its major weapons, addressing the Israeli goal of maintaining a monopoly of military power in the Middle East. The neocons, however, wanted more: the removal of Saddam Hussein and the American occupation of Iraq. However, despite the urging of then-Defense Secretary Dick Cheney and then-Under Secretary of Defense Paul Wolfowitz to adopt a military plan to invade the heartland of Iraq, this was never done, in part because of the opposition from General Colin Powell, chairman of the Joint Chiefs of Staff, and General Norman Schwarzkopf, the field commander.[2] Moreover, the U.S. had a UN mandate to liberate Kuwait, not to remove Saddam. To attempt the latter would have caused the warring coalition to fall apart. America's coalition partners in the region, especially Turkey and Saudi Arabia, feared that the elimination of Saddam's government would cause Iraq to fragment into warring ethnic and religious groups. This could have involved a Kurdish rebellion in Iraq spreading to Turkey's own restive Kurdish population, while the Iraqi Shiites, falling under the influence of Iran, would increase the threat of Islamic radicalism in the region. In 1998, the first President Bush would explain his reason for not invading Iraq to remove Saddam thus: "We would have been forced to occupy Baghdad and, in effect, rule Iraq. The coalition would instantly have collapsed, the Arabs deserting it in anger . . . . Had we gone the invasion route, the United States could conceivably still be an occupying power in a bitterly hostile land."[3]

Neocons remained dissatisfied with the outcome in Iraq and throughout the 1990s they pushed for the elimination of Saddam Hussein as, apparently, a first step in the destabilization of Israel's enemies throughout the region. A clear illustration of the neoconservative thinking on this subject is a 1996 paper developed by Richard Perle, Douglas Feith, David Wurmser, and others, entitled "A Clean Break: A New Strategy for Securing the

1. American Defamation League, *Anger on the Right: Pat Buchanan's Venomous Crusade*, 1991 (http://www.adl.org/special_reports/pb_archive/pb_1991rpt.pdf).

2. Arnold Beichman, "How the Divide Over Iraq Strategies Began," *Washington Times*, November 27, 2002, p. A18.

3. George Bush and Brent Scowcroft, *A World Transformed* (New York: Alfred A. Knopf, 1998), p. 489.

Realm," and published by an Israeli think tank, the Institute for Advanced Strategic and Political Studies. It was intended as a political blueprint for the incoming government of Benjamin Netanyahu. The paper stated that Netanyahu should "make a clean break" with the Oslo peace process and reassert Israel's claim to the West Bank and Gaza. It presented a plan by which Israel would "shape its strategic environment," beginning with the removal of Saddam Hussein and the installation of a Hashemite monarchy in Baghdad, which would serve as a first step towards eliminating the anti-Israeli governments of Syria, Lebanon, Saudi Arabia, and Iran.[1] It is to be noted that these Americans – Perle, Feith, and Wurmser – were advising a foreign government and that they joined the George W. Bush adminis-tration: Perle was head, and now a member, of the Defense Policy Board; Feith is (outgoing) under secretary of defense for policy; and Wurmser worked first under Feith and then in the State Department, and is now in the Office of the Vice President. It is noteworthy that while in 1996 Israel was to "shape its strategic environment" by removing its enemies, the same individuals have now proposed that the United States alter the Middle East environment by removing Israel's enemies. It would seem that the United States is to serve as Israel's proxy to advance Israeli interests. As newspaper columnist and former senior editor of *Newsweek* and president of United Press International, Arnaud de Borchgrave, maintained: "The 1996 docu-ment provided the strategic underpinnings for Operation Iraqi Freedom seven years later."[2]

A key neoconservative umbrella group that would be in the forefront of urging war on Iraq was the Project for a New American Century (PNAC), which was founded in 1997 to promote a strategy for American military dominance of the globe. The PNAC was initiated by the New Citizenship Project (NCP), which was an affiliate of the Project for the Republican Future, a conservative Republican think tank founded by Bill Kristol. Kristol was the chairman of the PNAC, and Robert Kagan, one of Kristol's close associates as a contributing editor of *The Weekly Standard*, was one of the directors. The NCP and the PNAC were headquartered at 1150 17th St., NW, Washington, D.C., which was also the headquarters of the AEI.[3] Many figures who would become prominent war hawks in the cur-

---

1. The Study Group on a New Israeli Strategy Toward 2000 of the Institute for Advanced `Strategic and Political Studies, "A Clean Break: A New Strategy for Securing the Realm," (http://www.israeleconomy.org/strat1.htm).

2. Arnaud de Borchgrave, "All in the Family," *Washington Times*, September 13, 2004, online.

3. "New Citizen's Project," Disinfopedia (http://www.disinfopedia.org/wiki.phtml?title=New_Citizenship_Project).

rent Bush administration were associated with the PNAC: Dick Cheney, Donald Rumsfeld, I. Lewis Libby, Paul Wolfowitz, Richard Perle, Douglas Feith, Elliot Abrams, John Bolton, Zalmay Khalilzad.[1]

On January 26, 1998, the PNAC sent a letter to President Clinton urging him to take unilateral military action against Iraq and offering a plan to achieve that objective. It especially called on the President not to go through the UN Security Council. "American policy cannot continue to be crippled by a misguided insistence on unanimity in the UN Security Council," the letter said. Among the letter's eighteen signatories were Donald Rumsfeld, Paul Wolfowitz, Zalmay Khalilzad, Elliott Abrams, Richard Armitage, Robert Kagan, Bill Kristol, R. James Woolsey, and Richard Perle.[2]

After the Clinton administration failed to take action on the suggestions, a second open letter to President Clinton dated February 19, 1998, was made public. It included an expanded list of forty names; among those signers added were John Bolton, Douglas Feith, Michael Ledeen, and David Wurmser. It was sent under the banner of the resurrected Committee for Peace and Security in the Gulf, which had played a major role in promoting the 1991 Gulf War. The letter was more detailed than the one of January 26, proposing "a comprehensive political and military strategy for bringing down Saddam and his regime."[3] It continued: "It will not be easy – and the course of action we favor is not without its problems and perils. But we believe the vital national interests of our country require the United States to [adopt such a strategy]."[4]

Unsatisfied with Clinton's response, the Project for the New American Century wrote another letter on May 29, 1998, to former House Speaker Newt Gingrich and Senate Republican Majority Leader Trent Lott, with almost the same signatories as the January PNAC letter to President Clinton, saying that

> U.S. policy should have as its explicit goal removing Saddam Hussein's regime
> from power and establishing a peaceful and democratic Iraq in its place. We

1. PNAC describes itself as follows: "Established in the spring of 1997, the Project for the New American Century is a non-profit, educational organization whose goal is to promote American global leadership. The Project is an initiative of the New Citizenship Project (501c3); the New Citizenship Project's chairman is William Kristol and its president is Gary Schmitt" (http://www.newamericancentury.org/aboutpnac.htm).

2. PNAC Letter to President William J. Clinton, January 26, 1998 (http://www.newamericancentury.org/iraqclintonletter.htm).

3. Publications of the Center for Security Policy No. 98-D 33 (http://www.security-policy.org/papers/1998/98-D33at.html).

4. "Open Letter to the President," February 19, 1998 (http://www.iraqwatch.org/perspectives/rumsfeld-openletter.htm); Frank Gaffney, "End Saddam's Reign of Terror: Better Late Than Never," *National Review Online* (www.nationalreview.com), February 21, 2002.

recognize that this goal will not be achieved easily. But the alternative is to leave the initiative to Saddam, who will continue to strengthen his position at home and in the region. Only the U.S. can lead the way in demonstrating that his rule is not legitimate and that time is not on the side of his regime.[1]

Numerous bills were put forward in Congress to provide aid to the Iraqi opposition to Saddam's regime. Ultimately, President Clinton would only go so far as to support and, in September 1998, sign the Iraq Liberation Act, which allocated $97 million for training and military equipment for the Iraqi opposition. Neoconservatives saw that as insufficient. As Richard Perle wrote, " . . . the administration refused to commit itself unequivocally to a new strategy, raising questions as to whether any meaningful shift had occurred in U.S. policy." The Iraq Liberation Act, nonetheless, was sometimes cited as a legal justification for the American war on Iraq in 2003.[2]

In September 2000, the Project for the New American Century issued a report, "Rebuilding America's Defenses: Strategy, Forces and Resources for a New Century," which envisioned an expanded global posture for the United States. In regard to the Middle East, the report called for an increased American military presence in the Gulf, whether Saddam was in power or not, maintaining that

the United States has for decades sought to play a more permanent role in Gulf regional security. While the unresolved conflict with Iraq provides the immediate justification, the need for a substantial American force presence in the Gulf transcends the issue of the regime of Saddam Hussein."[3]

The report struck a prescient note when it observed that "the process of transformation is likely to be a long one, absent some catastrophic and catalyzing event – like a new Pearl Harbor."[4]

The neoconservative war vision far transcended Iraq, and was openly directed to all the Middle Eastern enemies of Israel, and assumed a common identity with Israel. As David Wurmser wrote in an article that came out in January 2001, just prior to the start of the Bush administration:

1. PNAC Letter to Gingrich and Lott, May 29, 1998 (http://www.newamericancentury.org/iraqletter1998.htm).

2. Seymour Hersh, "The Iraq Hawks," *New Yorker*, December 20, 2001, online; Richard Perle, "Foreword," David Wurmser, *Tyranny's Ally* (Washington, D.C.: AEI Press, 1999), p. xii.

3. Neil Mackay, "Bush Planned Iraq 'Regime Change' Before Becoming President," *Scottish Sunday Herald*, September 15, 2002, online.

4. PNAC, *Rebuilding America's Defenses: Strategy, Forces and Resources for a New Century*, A Report of The Project for the New American Century September 2000, p. 51.

Israel and the United States should adopt a coordinated strategy to regain the initiative and reverse their region-wide strategic retreat. They should broaden the conflict to strike fatally, not merely disarm, the centers of radicalism in the region – the regimes of Damascus, Baghdad, Tripoli, Tehran, and Gaza. That would reestablish the recognition that fighting with either the United States or Israel is suicidal. Many in the Middle East will then understand the merits of being an American ally and of making peace with Israel.[1]

Neoconservatives would come to power with the advent of the George W. Bush presidency. Ironically, the first President Bush was not seen as a friend of Israel and had rejected neoconservative demands that the United States remove Saddam Hussein in the first Gulf War in 1991. The elder Bush and his advisers were seen to be close to oil interests which sought stability in the region in contrast to war. Furthermore, his close confidante and National Security Advisor, Brent Scowcroft, would become a major opponent of the move toward war on Iraq in 2002 and 2003.[2]

While it was assumed that the elder Bush's advisors would control the foreign policy of the younger George Bush, this proved not to be the case. And neoconservatives began to exert their influence in Bush circles early in the campaign. Paul Wolfowitz and Richard Perle managed to obtain leading roles in the Bush foreign policy and national security advisory team for the 2000 campaign. Headed by Soviet specialist Condoleeza Rice, the team was referred to as the "Vulcans" – named after the Roman god Vulcan whose statue graced Rice's hometown of Birmingham, Alabama. The name conveyed the image of toughness and power, as intended.[3]

Bush admitted that he had little knowledge of foreign policy. Nor was it apparent that he had the interest or ability to learn. Journalist Christopher Hitchens would describe Bush in 2000 as "unusually incurious, abnormally unintelligent, amazingly inarticulate, fantastically uncultured, extraordinarily uneducated, and apparently quite proud of all these things."[4] Given his ignorance in foreign policy, it was apparent that George W. Bush would

1. David Wurmser, "Middle East 'War': How Did It Come to This?" *AEI Online*, January 1, 2001.

2. "GOP Backing Out of Iraq Offensive?" *FOX News*, August 16, 2002, online; Todd S. Purdum and Patrick E. Tyler, "Top Republicans Break With Bush on Iraq Strategy," *New York Times*, August 16, 2002, online; Jim Lobe, "Washington Goes to War Over War," *Asia Times*, August 21, 2002, online; Brent Scowcroft, "Don't Attack Iraq," *Wall Street Journal*, August 15, 2002 (online at http://www.ffip.com/opeds081502.htm).

3. James Mann, *Rise of the Vulcans: The History of Bush's War Cabinet* (New York: Viking, 2004), p. x.

4. "Home Stretch Madness," November 4, 2000, quoted at "How Slatesters Voted," *Slate*, November 7, 2000 (http://slate.msn.com/id/93134/).

need to rely heavily on his advisers. "His foreign policy team," neoconservative Robert Kagan observed during the campaign, "will be critically important to determining what his policies are." As columnist Robert Novak noted, "Since Rice lacks a clear track record on Middle East matters, Wolfowitz and Perle will probably weigh in most on Middle East policy."[1]

But neoconservatives had to battle others for access with Bush and do not seem to have won him over to their positions *during* the campaign. Significantly, Bush did not reveal a distinctively neoconservative foreign policy during the 2000 campaign. In fact, he did just the opposite, explicitly eschewing an interventionist foreign policy aimed at changing regimes and societies. Bush frequently criticized the Clinton administration for "nation-building" – an activity dear to the hearts of neoconservatives. Nation building was not the proper role of the military, Bush told a crowd on November 7, 2000, one day before the election. "I'm worried about an opponent who uses nation building and the military in the same sentence. See, our view of the military is for our military to be properly prepared to fight and win war and, therefore, prevent war from happening in the first place."[2] The speech was an explicit criticism of the Clinton administration for allegedly stretching the military too thin with peacekeeping missions in Haiti, Somalia and the Balkans. Moreover, Bush argued, it was just improper for the United States to dominate other countries. As Bush stated in his second presidential debate with Al Gore: "I just don't think it's the role of the United States to walk into a country [and] say, 'We do it this way; so should you.'"[3] Any attempt to dictate to other countries, Bush maintained, would be counterproductive. "If we're an arrogant nation, they'll resent us. If we're a humble nation but strong, they'll welcome us."[4]

Furthermore, during the campaign Bush never suggested that terrorism was a major problem or claimed that Clinton had been lax on this issue. And Bush never placed any emphasis on the danger of Iraq. No mention was made of Saddam's allegedly brutal treatment of his people. Like Al Gore and the Clinton administration, Bush simply said that the United States should continue to contain Iraq through sanctions. In short, Bush's foreign policy views differed fundamentally from those of the neoconser-

1. Ian Urbina, "Rogues' Gallery, Who Advises Bush and Gore on the Middle East?" *Middle East Report* 216, Fall, 2000, online.

2. Terry M. Neal, "Bush Backs Into Nation Building," *Washington Post*, February 26, 2003, online.

3. Quoted in Mann, *Rise of the Vulcans* p. 257.

4. Quoted *ibid.*

vatives. Stefan Halper and Jonathan Clarke in *America Alone: The Neo-Conservatives and the Global Order* observe that "when Bush turned to the neoconservatives after 9/11, he came as a convert, based on intuition and personality rather than deep convictions."[1]

Condoleeza Rice, who headed Bush's foreign policy team, also expressed views that ran quite contrary to the neocon interventionist position on Iraq. In an article in the January-February 2000 issue of *Foreign Affairs*, Rice wrote that "rogue nations" such as Iraq and North Korea "are living on borrowed time, so there need be no sense of panic about them. Rather, the first line of defense should be a clear and classical statement of deterrence – if they do acquire weapons of mass destruction, [they] will be unusable because any attempt to use them will bring national obliteration."[2]

While some neoconservatives served as Bush's foreign policy advisers, the actual favorite candidate for a number of leading neoconservatives during the 2000 campaign was Senator John McCain, Bush's Republican rival in the primaries, who did express openly neoconservative positions.[3] As Franklin Foer, editor of the liberal *New Republic* put it:

> Jewish neoconservatives have fallen hard for John McCain. It's not just unabashed swooner William Kristol, editor of *The Weekly Standard*. McCain has also won over such leading neocon lights as David Brooks, the entire Podhoretz family, *The Wall Street Journal*'s Dorothy Rabinowitz, and columnist Charles Krauthammer, who declared, in a most un-Semitic flourish, "He suffered for our sins."[4]

Most important for the neoconservatives was McCain's advocacy of a policy of "rogue state rollback" that pointed to the enemies of Israel. McCain had been a member of the neoconservative Committee for the Liberation of Iraq and was a leading senatorial sponsor of the Iraq Liberation Act of 1998, which called upon the United States government to press for Saddam's elimination.[5] Antiwar commentator Justin Raimondo sized up the fundamental reason for the neoconservative *The Weekly Standard's*

1. Halper and Clarke, *op. cit.*, p. 135.
2. Quoted in Mann, *Rise of the Vulcans*, p. 259.
3. *Ibid.*
4. Francis Foer, "The Neocons Wake Up: Arguing the GOP," *New Republic*, March 20, 2000, p. 13. See also Charles Krauthammer, "A Winner? Yes," *Washington Post*, February 11, 2000, online.
5. "Committee for the Liberation of Iraq," Nationmaster (http://www.nationmaster.com/encyclopedia/Committee-for-the-Liberation-of-Iraq); Laurie Mylorie, "'Iraq Liberation Act' introduced into Congress," *Federation of American Scientists*, Iraq News, September 29, 1998 (http://www.fas.org/news/iraq/1998/09/980929-in2.htm).

political infatuation with McCain: "Never mind all this doubletalk about 'sacrificing for a cause bigger than yourself' – what the authors of this piece really mean to say is that this is a candidate who will not hesitate to lead his country into war."[1]

Although Bush might not have been the neocons favorite candidate, upon his taking office, neoconservatives would manage to fill key positions in his administration in crucial areas involving defense and foreign policy. On Donald Rumsfeld's staff were Deputy Defense Secretary Paul Wolfowitz and Under Secretary for Policy Douglas Feith. On Cheney's staff, the principal neoconservatives included I. Lewis "Scooter" Libby, Eric Edelman, and John Hannah. (David Wurmser would come aboard, replacing Edelman, in 2003). Vice President Dick Cheney, who had long-time neoconservative connections, played a significant role in shaping administration foreign policy, in part by bringing in neoconservative staff.

Cheney had a key role in the Bush campaign and his selection as Vice-President was, as James Mann points out in his *Rise of the Vulcans*, "of surpassing importance for the future direction of foreign policy. It went further than any other single decision Bush made toward determining the nature and the policies of the administration he would head."[2]

Although never identified as a neoconservative, Cheney was closely connected to the neoconservative elite. Prior to becoming vice president, Cheney had been a member of the board of advisors of the Jewish Institute for National Security Affairs (JINSA) and was a founding member of the neoconservative Project for a New American Century (PNAC). Cheney's wife, Lynne, was a prestigious member of the neoconservative American Enterprise Institute.

Cheney was in charge of the transition team between the election in November 2000 and Bush's inauguration in January 2001, and used that position to staff national security positions with his neoconservative associates. Columnist Jim Lobe writes:

> It was Cheney's choices that prevailed in the appointment of both cabinet and sub-cabinet national-security officials, beginning with that of Donald Rumsfeld as Defense Secretary. Not only did Cheney personally intervene to ensure that Powell's best friend, Richard Armitage, was denied the deputy defense secretary position, but he also secured the post for his own protégé, Paul Wolfowitz. Moreover, it was Cheney who insisted that the ultra-

1. Justin Raimondo, "John McCain and the War Party," *Antiwar.com*, February 14, 2000.
2. Mann, *Rise of the Vulcans*, pp. 252–53.

unilateralist John Bolton be placed in a top State Department arms job – a position from which Bolton has consistently pursued policies that run counter to [Secretary of State] Powell's own views.[1]

Significantly, Cheney created a large national-security staff in his office, constituting a virtual National Security Council in miniature, which has had a major effect in shaping American national policy. Glenn Kessler and Peter Slevin, writing in the *Washington Post*, likened Cheney's office to "an agile cruiser, able to maneuver around the lumbering aircraft carriers of the Departments of State and Defense to make its mark."[2]

Inside the Bush administration the neoconservatives would work to push the United States in the direction of making war on the Middle East enemies of Israel. As national-security analysts Kathleen and Bill Christison put it:

> The issue we are dealing with in the Bush administration is dual loyalties – the double allegiance of those myriad officials at high and middle levels who cannot distinguish U.S. interests from Israeli interests, who baldly promote the supposed identity of interests between the United States and Israel, who spent their early careers giving policy advice to right-wing Israeli governments and now give the identical advice to a right-wing U.S. government, and who, one suspects, are so wrapped up in their concern for the fate of Israel that they honestly do not know whether their own passion about advancing the U.S. *imperium* is motivated primarily by America-first patriotism or is governed first and foremost by a desire to secure Israel's safety and predominance in the Middle East through the advancement of the U.S. *imperium*.[3]

The neoconservatives tried to make an attack on Iraq a key issue in the Bush administration from the very beginning. An influential figure was Paul Wolfowitz, the deputy secretary of defense, who was described by *TIME Magazine* as the "godfather of the Iraq war"[4] and designated "Man of the Year" by the *Jerusalem Post*.[5] Similarly, Bob Woodward writes in his

---

1. Jim Lobe, "Dick Cheney, Commander-in-Chief," *AlterNet.org*, October 27, 2003.

2. Glenn Kessler and Peter Slevin, "Cheney Is Fulcrum of Foreign Policy: In Interagency Fights, His Views Often Prevail," *Washington Post*, October 13, 2002, p. A1; Lind, *loc. cit.*

3. Kathleen and Bill Christison, "Dual Loyalties: The Bush Neocons and Israel," *Colorado Campaign for Middle East Peace*, September 6, 2004 (http://www.ccmep.org/2004_articles/palestine/090604_dual_loyalties.htm).

4. Mark Thompson, "The Godfather of the Iraq War," *Time*, (posted) December 21, 2003, online.

5. Bret Stephens, "Man of the Year," *Jerusalem Post*, October 2, 2003, online. The designation applied to the Jewish year 5763 and to A.D.2002–03.

The Plan of Attack, "The intellectual godfather and fiercest advocate for toppling Saddam was Paul Wolfowitz."[1]

According to Richard Clarke, former terrorism advisor in the Bush administration, Wolfowitz and other neoconservatives in the administration were fixated on Iraq rather than on the far more dangerous terrorist threat coming from al-Qaeda. When, in April 2001, the White House convened a top-level meeting to discuss terrorism, Wolfowitz considered Saddam to be a much more important subject than al-Qaeda, which had been Clarke's focus. According to Clarke, Wolfowitz said he couldn't "understand why we are beginning by talking about this one man bin Laden."[2] The real threat, Wolfowitz insisted, was state-sponsored terrorism orchestrated by Saddam.[3]

In the early period of the Bush administration, Wolfowitz and his neoconservative confreres were spinning plans for an American attack on Iraq. Wolfowitz maintained that the United States military could easily invade southern Iraq and seize the oil fields. This was styled as the "enclave strategy," under which the American foothold in the south would supposedly provide support to the anti-Saddam resistance in the rest of the country to overthrow the dictator. As described by Bob Woodward, Secretary of State Powell rejected Wolfowitz's proposal as "one of most absurd, strategically unsound proposals he had ever heard." Powell's opposition, however, did not stop Wolfowitz and the neoconservatives from continuing to plan an American attack on Iraq. Woodward writes that "Wolfowitz was like a drum that would not stop. He and his group of neoconservatives were rubbing their hands over ideas which were being presented as 'draft plans.'"[4]

Secretary of State Powell's resistance to the neoconservative war agenda underscores the fact, however, that prior to the September 11, 2001, terror events the neoconservatives, though influential, did not control American foreign policy. While Wolfowitz and the neocons were pushing for war against the allegedly dangerous Iraq, both Powell and National Security Advisor Condoleeza Rice were saying that Saddam was no threat to anyone. At a news conference in Cairo, Egypt, on February 24, 2001, Powell said: "He (Saddam Hussein) has not developed any significant capability with respect to weapons of mass destruction. He is unable to project conventional power against his neighbors." On May 15, 2001, in testimony before

---

1. Bob Woodward, *Plan of Attack* (New York: Simon & Schuster, 2004), p. 21.

2. Richard A. Clarke, *Against All Enemies: Inside America's War on Terror* (New York: Free Press, 2004), p. 231.

3. *Ibid.*

4. Woodward, *Plan of Attack*, pp. 21–22.

a subcommittee of the Senate Appropriations Committee, Powell stated that Saddam Hussein had not been able to "build his military back up or to develop weapons of mass destruction" for "the last 10 years." America, he said, had been successful in keeping him "in a box." On July 29, 2001, Rice replied to CNN White House correspondent John King: "But in terms of Saddam Hussein being there, let's remember that his country is divided, in effect. He does not control the northern part of his country. We are able to keep arms from him. His military forces have not been rebuilt."[1] It was only the terror events of September 11 that would give the neocons the opportunity to implement their war agenda.

As the Bush administration came into office in January 2001, press reports in Israel quoted Israeli government officials and politicians speaking openly of mass expulsion of the Palestinians. The new Prime Minister, Ariel Sharon (elected in February 2001), had said in the past that Jordan should become the Palestinian state where Palestinians removed from Israeli territory would be relocated.[2] There was increased public concern about demographic changes that threatened the Jewish nature of the Israeli state. Haifa University professor Arnon Sofer released a study, "Demography of Eretz Israel," which predicted that by 2020 non-Jews would be a majority of 58 percent in Israel and the occupied territories.[3] Moreover, it was recognized that the overall increase in population was going beyond that which the land, with its limited supply of water, could maintain.[4]

It appeared to some that Sharon intended to achieve expulsion through militant means. As one left-wing analyst put it at the time: "One big war with transfer at its end – this is the plan of the hawks who indeed almost

1. Colin L. Powell, "Press Remarks with Foreign Minister of Egypt Amre Moussa," Cairo, Egypt, (Ittihadiya Palace), February 24, 2001 (http://www.state.gov/secretary/rm/2001/933.htm); John Pilger, "Colin Powell Said Iraq Was no Threat," *Daily Mirror*, September 22, 2003 (online at http://www.coldtype.net/Assets/Pilger/JP.26.% 20Sept%2022.pdf); James Ridgeway "Tripping Down Memory Lane," *Village Voice*, October 15–23, 2001, online.

2. Ronald Bleier, "Sharon Routs Bush: Palestinians Now Vulnerable to Expulsion," Demographic, Environmental, and Security Issues Project, Institute for Global Communications, August 2001 (http://desip.igc.org/SharonRoutsBush.html); Bleier, "The Next Expulsion of the Palestinians," Demographic, Environmental, and Security Issues Project, Institute for Global Communications, January 2001 (http://desip.igc.org/TheNextExpulsion.html).

3. Tikva Honig-Parnass, "Israel's Recent Conviction: Apartheid in Palestine Can Only Be Preserved Through Force," *Between the Lines*, September, 2001 (http://www.betweenlines.org/archives/2001/sep/Tikva_Honig-Parnass.htm).

4. Ronald Bleier, "Sharon Gears Up for Expulsion," January 2002 (http://desip.igc.org/SharonGearsUp.html).

reached the moment of its implementation."[1] In the summer of 2001, the authoritative Jane's Information Group reported that Israel had completed planning for a massive and bloody invasion of the Occupied Territories, involving "air strikes by F-15 and F-16 fighter bombers, a heavy artillery bombardment, and then an attack by a combined force of 30,000 men . . . tank brigades and infantry." It would seem that such bold strikes aimed at far more than simply removing Arafat and the PLO leadership. But the U.S. opposed the plan and Europe made equally plain its opposition to Sharon's strategy.[2] As one close observer of the Israeli-Palestinian scene presciently noted in August 2001,

> [I]t is only in the current political climate that such expulsion plans cannot be put into operation. As hot as the political climate is at the moment, clearly the time is not yet ripe for drastic action. However, if the temperature were raised even higher, actions inconceivable at present might be possible.[3]

The September 11 atrocities created the white-hot climate in which Israel could undertake radical measures unacceptable under normal conditions. When asked what the attack would do for U.S.-Israeli relations, former Prime Minister Benjamin Netanyahu blurted out: "It's very good." Then he edited himself: "Well, not very good, but it will generate immediate sympathy." Netanyahu correctly predicted that the attack would "strengthen the bond between our two peoples, because we've experienced terror over so many decades, but the United States has now experienced a massive hemorrhaging of terror." Prime Minister Ariel Sharon depicted Israel as being in the same situation as the United States, referring to the attack as an assault on "our common values" and declaring, "I believe together we can defeat these forces of evil."[4]

In the eyes of Israel's leaders, the September 11 attack had joined the United States and Israel together against a common enemy. That enemy was not in far off Afghanistan, but was geographically close to Israel. Israel's

---

1. Tikvah Honig-Parnass, "Louder Voices of War: Manufacturing Consent at its Peak," *Between the Lines*, Vol. 1, No. 8, July, 2001, quoted in Ronald Bleier, "Sharon Routs Bush," *loc. cit.*

2. *Associated Press*, "Israeli War Plan Revealed," July 12, 2001 (http://www.globalexchange.org/countries/palestine/news2001/ap071201.html); "Israelis Generals' Plan to 'Smash' Palestinians," *Mid-East Realities*, July 12, 2001, online (http://www.middleeast.org/premium/read.cgi?category=Magazine&standalone=&num=278&month=7&year=2001&function=text); Tanya Reinhart, "The Second Half of 1948," *Mid-East Realities*, June 20, 2001 (http://www.middleeast.org/premium/read.cgi?category=Magazine&num=251&month=6&year=2001&function=text).

3. Bleier, "Sharon Routes Bush," *loc. cit.*

4. James Bennet, "Spilled Blood Is Seen As Bond That Draws 2 Nations Closer," *New York Times*, September 12, 2001, p. A22; "Horrific Tragedy, the Media, Palestinian Reaction," Jerusalem Media & Communication Centre (http://www.jmcc.org/new/01/Sep/us.htm).

traditional enemies would now become America's as well. Israel would have a free-hand to deal harshly with the Palestinians under the cover of a "war on terrorism." Palestinian resistance to Israeli occupation could simply be portrayed as "terrorism." Conversely, America would clearly become the enemy of those who previously had focused on Israel.

It is important to recall that in the period before September 11, Israel had been widely criticized in the U.S. and in the Western world for its brutal suppression of the Palestinians. Israeli soldiers, tanks and helicopter gunships were regularly shown on the television battling with Palestinian youths armed with nothing more than sticks and stones. Israeli tanks bulldozed Palestinian farms and homes. Humanitarian groups complained that captured Palestinians were being tortured and abused in Israeli prison cells. The events of September 11 completely transformed this entire picture. In December 2001, the Christian Zionist *Israel Report* summarized the effect of the September 11 terrorist attack:

> Today, Israel has the opportunity to wage total war against its terrorist enemies, with the American government sitting on the sidelines and the American people cheering from the bleachers. What has granted us this opportunity is not simply the horrific tragedy that occurred on September 11, but also the strategic doctrine that has been established in its wake. American-Israeli relations have undergone a sea change over the past three months. The bond of common values is now buttressed by shared experience, transforming our American friends into sympathetic brothers.[1]

For the neocons the horrific tragedy of 9/11 offered the extremely convenient pretext to implement their war agenda for the United States. Immediately after the 9/11 attacks, the neoconservatives began to push publicly for a wider war on terrorism that would immediately deal with Israel's enemies, beginning with Iraq. As neoconservative Kenneth Adelman put it, "At the beginning of the administration people were talking about Iraq but it wasn't doable. There was no heft. That changed with September 11 because then people were willing to confront the reality of an international terrorist network, and terrorist states such as Iraq."[2]

In the immediate aftermath of 9/11, there was internal debate within the administration regarding the scope of the "war on terrorism." According to Bob Woodward's *Bush at War*, as early as the day after the attacks, Secretary of Defense Donald Rumsfeld

---

1. Ron Dermer, "A Strategic Opportunity," *The Israel Report*, December 6, 2001 (http://www.cdn-friends-icej.ca/isreport/dec01/opportunity.html).
2. Quoted in Drew, *loc. cit.*

raised the question of attacking Iraq. Why shouldn't we go against Iraq, not just al-Qaeda? he asked. Rumsfeld was speaking not only for himself when he raised the question. His deputy, Paul D. Wolfowitz was committed to a policy that would make Iraq a principal target of the first round in the war on terrorism.[1]

Woodward continues: "The terrorist attacks of September 11 gave the U.S. a new window to go after Hussein." On September 15, Wolfowitz put forth military arguments to justify a U.S. attack on Iraq rather than Afghanistan. Wolfowitz expressed the view that "Attacking Afghanistan would be uncertain." He voiced the fear that American troops would be "bogged down in mountain fighting . . . . In contrast, Iraq, was a brittle, oppressive regime that might break easily. It was doable."[2] In fact, Wolfowitz immediately envisioned a wider war that would strike a number of countries alleged to support "terrorism."

> [O]ne has to say it's not just simply a matter of capturing people and holding them accountable, but removing the sanctuaries, removing the support systems, ending states who sponsor terrorism. And that's why it has to be a broad and sustained campaign. It's not going to stop if a few criminals are taken care of.[3]

Though left unnamed, it would appear that a large percentage of the terrorist states Wolfowitz sought to "end" were Israel's Middle East enemies.

However, the neoconservatives were not able to achieve their goal of a wider war at the outset. Secretary of State Colin Powell was most adamantly opposed to attacking Iraq, holding that the war should focus on the actual perpetrators of September 11. (It might be added that this was how most Americans actually viewed the war.) Perhaps Powell's most telling argument was his allegation that an American attack on Iraq would lack international support. He held that a U.S. victory in Afghanistan would enhance America's ability to deal militarily with Iraq at a later time, "if we can prove that Iraq had a role" in September 11.[4] Powell hardly hid his contempt for Wolfowitz's call for "ending states" with the retort that "We're after ending terrorism. And if there are states and regimes, nations, that support terrorism, we hope to persuade them that it is in their interest to stop doing that. But I think 'ending terrorism' is where I would leave it and let Mr. Wolfowitz speak for himself."[5]

1. Bob Woodward, *Bush at War*, p. 49.

2. *Ibid.*, p. 83; Ron Suskind, *The Price of Loyalty: George W. Bush, the White House, and the Education of Paul O'Neil* (New York: Simon and Schuster, 2004), p.188.

3. DoD News Briefing – Deputy Secretary Wolfowitz, September 13, 2001 (http://www.defenselink.mil/news/Sep2001/t09132001_t0913dsd.html).

4. Woodward, *Bush at War*, p. 84.

5. Patrick E. Tyler and Elaine Sciolino, "Bush's Advisers Split on Scope Of Retaliation,"

The Bush administration would thus initially target Osama bin Laden in Afghanistan. That did not mean, however, that Iraq would not be a future target. On September 16, 2001, when asked about Iraq on NBC's *Meet the Press*, Vice-President Dick Cheney simply replied that Osama bin Laden was the target "at the moment . . . at this stage."[1] Very significantly, however, while the "war on terrorism" would not begin with an attack on Iraq, military plans were being made for just such an endeavor. A TOP SECRET document outlining the war plan for Afghanistan, which President Bush signed on September 17, 2001, included, as a minor point, instructions to the Pentagon to make plans for an attack on Iraq also, although that attack was not yet a priority.[2]

In short, although the 9/11 atrocities psychologically prepared the American people for the war on Iraq, those horrific events were not sufficient by themselves to thrust America immediately into an attack on Iraq. To bring about the attack on Iraq it was necessary for the neoconservatives to push a lengthy propaganda offensive, which finally would revolve around the alleged weapons of mass destruction (WMD) that threatened the United States. The fact that the neoconservatives were inside the Bush administration, and were in positions to manipulate and even fabricate the intelligence assessments regarding the alleged dire danger of Iraqi WMD, ultimately made the bulk of the American people, Congress, and even a rather ignorant President Bush amenable to the launching of an American attack.[3] The WMD propaganda lies were definitely essential for the launching of war on Iraq, but it was definitely the 9/11 attacks that made the American people susceptible to the massive fear and hysteria over WMD that war propaganda whipped up.

Neoconservatives outside the administration beat the war drums for an attack on Iraq immediately after the 9/11 attacks. On September 20, 2001,

---

New York Times, September 20, 2002, online; Julian Borger, "Washington's Hawk Trains Sights on Iraq," October 15, 2001, online.

1. "Vice-President Appears on *Meet the Press* with Tim Russert," White House, September 16, 2001 (http://www.whitehouse.gov/vicepresident/news-speeches/speeches/vp20010916.html).

2. Glenn Kessler, "U.S. Decision on Iraq Has Puzzling Past," *Washington Post*, January 12, 2002, p. A1; Bob Woodward, *Plan of Attack*, p. 26.

3. James Bamford, *A Pretext for War: 9/11, Iraq, and the Abuse of America's Intelligence Agencies* (New York: Doubleday, 2004), pp. 263–331; Robert Dreyfuss and Jason Vest, "The Lie Factory," *Mother Jones*, January/February 2004, online; Seymour M. Hersh, "Selective Intelligence," *New Yorker*, May 6, 2003, online; Richard Cummings, "War, Lies, and WMDs," *LewRockwell.com*, May 22, 2003; Robert Dreyfuss, "More Missing Intelligence," *The Nation*, July 7, 2003 (posted June 19, 2003), online; Jason Leopold, "Wolfowitz Committee Told White House to Hype Dubious Uranium Claims," *Antiwar.com*, July 17, 2003.

the Project for the New American Century sent a letter to President Bush endorsing the war on terrorism and stressing that the removal of Saddam Hussein was an essential part of that war. They maintained that

> even if evidence does not link Iraq directly to the attack, any strategy aiming at the eradication of terrorism and its sponsors must include a determined effort to remove Saddam Hussein from power in Iraq. Failure to undertake such an effort will constitute an early and perhaps decisive surrender in the war on international terrorism.

Furthermore, the letter opined that if Syria and Iran failed to stop all support for Hezbollah, the United States should also "consider appropriate measures against these known sponsors of terrorism." Also emanating from the letter was the view that Israel was America's crucial ally in the war on terrorism and that therefore its actions should not be criticized. "Israel has been and remains America's staunchest ally against international terrorism, especially in the Middle East. The United States should fully support its fellow democracy in its fight against terrorism. We should insist that the Palestinian Authority put a stop to terrorism emanating from territories under its control and imprison those planning terrorist attacks against Israel." Among the letter's signatories were such neoconservative stalwarts as Bill Kristol, Midge Dector, Eliot Cohen, Frank Gaffney, Robert Kagan, Jeane Kirkpatrick, Charles Krauthammer, Richard Perle, and Norman Podhoretz.[1]

With the Bush administration opting to target Afghanistan first, neoconservatives presented it as simply a first step in a broader Middle Eastern war. In the October 29, 2001, issue of *The Weekly Standard*, Robert Kagan and William Kristol predicted a much wider war on terrorism.

> When all is said and done, the conflict in Afghanistan will be to the war on terrorism what the North Africa campaign was to World War II: an essential beginning on the path to victory. But compared with what looms over the horizon – a wide-ranging war in locales from Central Asia to the Middle East and, unfortunately, back again to the United States – Afghanistan will prove but an opening battle . . . . But this war will not end in Afghanistan. It is going to spread and engulf a number of countries in conflicts of varying intensity. It could well require the use of American military power in multiple places simultaneously. It is going to resemble the clash of civilizations that everyone has hoped to avoid.[2]

Despite their reference to the desire to avoid such a civilizational clash, it seems that Kagan and Kristol looked forward to that gigantic conflagration.

---

1. William Kristol *et al.*, letter to the President, September 20, 2001 (online at PNAC, http://www.newamericancentury.org/Bushletter.htm).

2. Robert Kagan and William Kristol, "The Gathering Storm," *The Weekly Standard*, October 29, 2001, online.

In a November 20, 2001, article in *The Wall Street Journal*, Eliot A. Cohen would dub the conflict "World War IV," a term picked up by other neoconservatives and their critics. ("World War III" had been applied to the cold war.) Cohen proclaimed that "The enemy in this war is not 'terrorism' . . . but militant Islam . . . . Afghanistan constitutes just one front in World War IV, and the battles there just one campaign."[1]

Critics of a wider war in the Middle East were quick to notice the neoconservative war propaganda effort. In analyzing the situation in late September 2001, Scott McConnell wrote:

> For the neoconservatives, however, bin Laden is but a sideshow . . . . They hope to use September 11 as pretext for opening a wider war in the Middle East. Their prime, but not only, target is Saddam Hussein's Iraq, even if Iraq [had] nothing to do with the World Trade Center assault.[2]

However, McConnell mistakenly considered the neocon position to be a minority one within the Bush administration.

> The neocon wish list is a recipe for igniting a huge conflagration between the United States and countries throughout the Arab world, with consequences no one could reasonably pretend to calculate. Support for such a war – which could turn quite easily into a global war – is a minority position within the Bush administration (Assistant Secretary of State [sic] Paul Wolfowitz is its main advocate) and the country. But it presently dominates the main organs of conservative journalistic opinion, the *Wall Street Journal, National Review*, the *Weekly Standard*, and the *Washington Times*, as well as Marty Peretz's neoliberal *New Republic*. In a volatile situation, such organs of opinion could matter.[3]

Expressing a similar view, veteran columnist Georgie Anne Geyer observed:

> The "Get Iraq" campaign . . . started within days of the September bombings . . . . It emerged first and particularly from pro-Israeli hard-liners in the Pentagon such as Deputy Defense Secretary Paul Wolfowitz and adviser Richard Perle, but also from hard-line neoconservatives, and some journalists and congressmen.
>
> Soon it became clear that many, although not all, were in the group that is commonly called in diplomatic and political circles the "Israel-firsters," meaning that they would always put Israeli policy, or even their perception of it, above anything else."

---

1. Eliot A. Cohen, "World War IV," *Wall Street Journal*, November 20, 2001, online.

2. Scott McConnell, "The Struggle Over War Aims: Bush Versus the Neo-Cons," *Antiwar. com*, September 25, 2002.

3. *Ibid.* [N.B.: Wolfowitz was sworn in as Deputy Secretary of Defense over six months before McConnell's piece was written.—Ed.]

Within the Bush administration, Geyer believed that this line of think-ing was "being contained by cool heads in the administration, but that could change at any time."[1]

Although the neoconservatives could not completely get their entire war against the Middle East enemies of Israel begun right away, the events of 9/11 were critical in leading the United States to adopt significant por-tions of their already-existing Middle East war program. This entailed a melding of American and Israeli policy.

And it was not just that the United States would be moving to com-bat Israel's enemies but that it would adopt the same militant, absolutist approach of the Israeli right. Naomi Klein, writing in *The Guardian,* aptly refers to it as "Likudisation of the world." She writes:

> What I mean is that on September 11, George W. Bush went looking for a political philosophy to guide him in his new role as "War President," a job for which he was uniquely unqualified. He found that philosophy in the Likud Doctrine, conveniently handed to him ready-made by the ardent Likudniks already ensconced in the White House. No thinking required . . . . It's not sim-ply that Bush sees America's role as protecting Israel from a hostile Arab world. It's that he has cast the United States in the very same role in which Israel casts itself, facing the very same threat. In this narrative, the U.S. is fighting a never ending battle for its very survival against utterly irrational forces that seek nothing less than its total extermination.[2]

The events of 9/11 had a profound impact on President Bush's psyche, causing him to adopt the neocons pre-packaged simple solution of a war of good versus evil. The idea of a war of good versus evil was undoubtedly in line with Bush's Christian evangelical beliefs. Bush's adoption of the neo-con war agenda provided him with a purpose in life, which he identified as the will of God. As *Washington Post* columnist Dana Milbank writes:

> Bush has come to view his leadership of post 9/11 America as a matter of fate, or of God's will . . . . With that assumption, it is almost impossible to imagine Bush confining the war on terrorism to al-Qaeda. Instead, he quickly embraced the most sweeping foreign policy proposal his most hawkish advis-ers had developed – a vision of American supremacy and preemption of emerg-ing threats – and that policy leads inexorably to Iraq, and beyond.[3]

This neocons' war agenda fitted in not only with Bush's born-again Evangelical Christianity, with its millenarian aspects, but it also meshed

1. Georgie Anne Geyer, "Pro-Israeli, Anti-Arab Campaigns Could Isolate America," *Universal Press Syndicate* (uexpress.com), October 25, 2001.
2. Naomi Klein, "The Likud Doctrine," *The Guardian*, September 10, 2004, online.
3. Dana Milbank, "For Bush, War Defines Presidency," *Washington Post*, March 9, 2003, p. A1.

with the vaunted American frontier values of toughness and simplicity, which Bush consciously tries to emulate. Historian Douglas Brinkley, director of the Eisenhower Center at the University of New Orleans, calls Bush a "rough and ready" President in the mold of Jackson, Polk and Truman.

"He's absorbed those traditions, this very tough-line attitude," Brinkley said. "It's a way for him to get intellectual certainty without getting involved in deeper questions. He can cling tenaciously to a belief. When there's a crisis, he resorts to a tough rhetorical line or threat."[1]

Neoconservatives presented the September 11 atrocities as a lightning bolt to make President Bush aware of his destiny to destroy the evil of world terrorism. In the religious (ironically Christian) terminology of Norman Podhoretz,

> [A] transformed – or, more precisely, a transfigured – George W. Bush appeared before us. In an earlier article in these pages, I suggested, perhaps presumptuously, that out of the blackness of smoke and fiery death let loose by September 11, a kind of revelation, blazing with a very different fire of its own, lit up the recesses of Bush's mind and heart and soul. Which is to say that, having previously been unsure as to why he should have been chosen to become President of the United States, George W. Bush now knew that the God to whom, as a born-again Christian, he had earlier committed himself had put him in the Oval Office for a purpose. He had put him there to lead a war against the evil of terrorism.[2]

In essence, the events of September 11 had transformed George Bush in the way he would look at the world. Stefan Halper and Jonathan Clarke write in *America Alone*:

> The duty-bound, born-again, can-do Texan morphed into a man who drew on those qualities and intensity of those early days to focus a searing rage. He was determined to rally the nation and the civilized world to crush al-Qaeda and the diabolical future it represented. The dynamic forged by the moment distilled the many shades of gray reflecting relations among nations into a black and white Manichean "either you are with us or against us" position. To say that American national security priorities were transformed is an understatement. His declaration of the "war on terror" redefined the strategic landscape. Most significant in terms of the shift was the transition from a "humble" candidate Bush to a President whose administration policy was based on unilateral preemption and millenarian nation building.[3]

Moreover, the neocons in the post 9/11 period were feeding Bush with bogus intelligence. In short, the weight of information provided to Bush

1. *Ibid.*

2. Norman Podhoretz, "In Praise of the Bush Doctrine," *Commentary*, September, 2002 (online at http://www.ourjerusalem.com/opinion/story/opinion20020904a.html).

3. Halper and Clarke, *op. cit.*, pp. 137–38.

naturally moved him in the pro-war direction. It was understandable that a man who knew nothing else would adopt the neocon line that was being handed him, although a curious individual might grasp the neocons' biases. Added to this was the fact that the pro-war policy seemed to have political support and Bush could bask in the praise of his supporters for his firm "leadership." Such positive feedback naturally would tend to convince Bush of the rightness of his pro-war viewpoint.

The Bush administration's post-911 militant, unilateralist position is quite different from what had been the American foreign policy position of the United States in the past. It differs from liberal internationalism in its rejection of international cooperation and international law. A few days after the United States attack on Iraq in March 2003, Richard Perle gleefully celebrated the destruction of internationalism wrought by the American preemptive attack.

> Saddam Hussein's reign of terror is about to end. He will go quickly, but not alone: in a parting irony, he will take the UN down with him. Well, not the whole UN. The "good work" part will survive, the low-risk peacekeeping bureaucracies will remain, the chatterbox on the Hudson will continue to bleat. What will die is the fantasy of the UN as the foundation of a new world order. As we sift the debris, it will be important to preserve, the better to understand, the intellectual wreckage of the liberal conceit of safety through international law administered by international institutions.[1]

The neocon agenda adopted by the Bush administration differs dramatically from the traditional conservative foreign policy position stance in its rejection of maintaining global stability. Stefan Halper and Jonathan Clarke maintain that

> the neoconservatives have taken American international relations on an unfortunate detour, veering away from the balanced, consensus-building, and resource-husbanding approach that has characterized traditional Republican internationalism – exemplified today by Secretary of State Colin Powell – and acted more as a special interest focused on its particular agenda.[2]

By adopting the neocon position of dramatically altering the Middle East status quo, the Bush administration stood in stark contrast to the traditional American position of promoting stability in the area in order to facilitate the flow of oil to the West – though forceful change, of course, meshed perfectly with the long-established Israeli goal of destabilizing its enemies. According

---

1. Richard Perle, "Thank God for the Death of the UN," *The Guardian*, March 21, 2003, online.
2. Halper and Clarke, *op. cit.*, p. 9.

to Kenneth Adelman, "The starting point is that conservatives now are for radical change and the progressives – the establishment foreign policy makers – are for the status quo." Adelman emphasized that "Conservatives believe that the status quo in the Middle East is pretty bad, and the old conservative belief that stability is good doesn't apply to the Middle East. The status quo in the Middle East has been breeding terrorists."[1] In the words of Michael Ledeen: "Creative destruction is our middle name. We do it automatically . . . . It is time once again to export the democratic revolution."[2]

The foreign policy shift by the neocons was not supported by members of the foreign policy elite. Significantly, those cool to the preemptive strike on Iraq included luminaries of the Republican foreign policy establishment such as Brent Scowcroft, who served as national security advisor under Presidents Ford and George H. W. Bush; Lawrence Eagleburger, who served as deputy secretary of state and secretary of state under the first Bush; and James Baker, who served as secretary of state in that administration.[3]

In an op-ed piece in the August 15, 2002, issue of Wall Street Journal, entitled, "Don't Attack Iraq," Scowcroft contended that Saddam was not connected with terrorists and that his weapons posed no threat to the United States. Scowcroft acknowledged that "Given Saddam's aggressive regional ambitions, as well as his ruthlessness and unpredictability, it may at some point be wise to remove him from power." However: "An attack on Iraq at this time would seriously jeopardize, if not destroy, the global counterterrorist campaign we have undertaken."[4]

Also expressing strong opposition to the war on Iraq was Zbigniew Brzezinski, the national security advisor in the Carter administration, who is often wrongly identified by hardline war critics as the central figure in the war cabal.[5] To be sure, Brzezinski explicitly advocated American global dominance in his 1997 work, The Grand Chessboard: American Primacy and its Geostrategic Imperatives.[6] However, during the build up for war,

---

1. Quoted in Drew, loc. cit.

2. Michael Ledeen, "Creative Destruction," National Review Online (www.nationalreview.com), September 20, 2001.

3. "GOP Backing Out of Iraq Offensive?" loc. cit.; Purdum and Tyler, loc. cit.; Jim Lobe, "Washington Goes to War," loc. cit.

4. Scowcroft, loc. cit.

5. Michele Steinberg, "Can the Brzezinski-Wolfowitz Cabal's War Game Be Stopped?" Executive Intelligence Review, December 7, 2001, online.

6. Zbigniew Brzezinski, The Grand Chessboard: American Primacy and its Geostrategic Imperatives (New York: Basic Books, 1997). A similar argument that the control of vital resources is the key to global power and global warfare is presented by Michael T. Klare, Resource Wars: The New Landscape of Global Conflict (New York: Henry Holt, 2001).

he expressed the concern that a unilateral attack on Iraq would serve to undermine America's global interests. What especially troubled him was the havoc America's unilateral march to war was wreaking on America's alliance with Western Europe, which he considered the central element of American global policy, terming it the "anchor point of America's engagement in the world." Brzezinski feared that the "cross-Atlantic vitriol" over America's plan to attack Iraq despite European opposition had left "NATO's unity in real jeopardy." Moreover, the Bush administration's fixation on Iraq interfered with America's ability to engage in other global hotspots, with Brzezinski observing that "there is justifiable concern that the preoccupation with Iraq – which does not pose an imminent threat to global security – obscures the need to deal with the more serious and genuinely imminent threat posed by North Korea." Brzezinski granted that "force may have to be used to enforce the goal of disarmament. But how and when that force is applied should be part of a larger strategy, sensitive to the risk that the termination of Saddam Hussein's regime may be purchased at too high a cost to America's global leadership."[1]

In fact, the entire foreign policy establishment tended to be cool to the war policy, as shown by opposition from within the elite Council on Foreign Relations. As columnist Robert Kuttner wrote in September 2003, " . . . it's still a well-kept secret that the vast foreign policy mainstream – Republican and Democratic ex-public officials, former ambassadors, military and intelligence people, academic experts – consider Bush's whole approach a disaster."[2]

While the neoconservatives never succeeded in winning over the foreign policy elite to their Middle East war agenda, the September 11, 2001, terror events, however, enabled the neoconservatives to gain support from a majority of the American people for their Middle East war agenda. Most importantly, neoconservative policies have received particular support from Americans of a more conservative, patriotic bent.

The 9/11 attacks made the American people angry and fearful. Ordinary Americans wanted to strike back at the terrorist enemy, even though they weren't exactly sure who that enemy was. Many could not distinguish between Saddam and Osama bin Laden. Moreover, they were fearful of more attacks and were susceptible to the administration's propaganda

1. Zbigniew Brzezinski, "Why Unity is Essential," *Washington Post*, February 19, 2003, online.

2. Robert Kuttner, "Neocons Have Hijacked U.S. Foreign Policy," *Boston Globe*, September 10, 2003, online.

that the United States had to strike Iraq before Iraq somehow struck the United States. In other words, the neocons' propaganda found fertile soil in America, though it got virtually nowhere in the rest of the world.

It wasn't that difficult to channel American fear and anger into war against Iraq. Polls and much anecdotal evidence showed a majority of the American people in favor of the war. The support was strongest among the white American working and lower middle class. Blacks opposed the war but not by a substantial margin. Since the September 11 terrorism the popular heroes have been average Americans – policemen, firemen, soldiers. Their perceived heroism had the effect of boosting the self-esteem of average, ordinary white people.[1] The least educated tended to be the most angry and fearful and gave the greatest support to the war.[2]

To conclude, the American war on Iraq and the overall effort calling for regime change in the Middle East reflects a partial adoption of the neoconservative agenda for the area. The war did not reflect any existing agenda of the oil lobby, American militarists, or the Bush family. Although the neoconservatives were influential in political circles, it was only the environment created by the September 11, 2001, terrorist events that enabled the neoconservatives to have the American government adopt, though not yet *totally* adopt, their Middle East war agenda – a war agenda that advances the interests of Israel and has been sought by the Israeli government. The neocons achieved their goal not by winning the support of the American foreign policy elite by virtue of their reasoned arguments, but by providing an agenda that fitted in with the psychological trauma caused by the 9/11 terrorism, and thus captivating President Bush and a significant percentage of the American people.

---

1. Norman Mailer, "We Went to War Just to Boost the White Male Ego," April 29, 2003 (http://www.veteransforpeace.org/We_went_to_war_042903.htm); Mailer, "The White Man Unburdened," *The New York Review of Books*, July 17, 2003, online.

2. Steve Sailer, "Analysis: Which American Groups Back War?" *UPI*, March 20, 2003, online.

THE EDITORS' GLOSS: At the end of the following essay, Justin Raimondo raises a crucial and sensitive issue for those who have opposed the Iraq war and its neoconservative architects. This is the question of the "Jewish" identity of neoconservatism. In the grand scheme of things, the *religious* persuasion of neoconservatives shouldn't matter – and for most of their reasonable critics, it doesn't. Yet the issue continues to arise, and – perhaps revealingly – it is raised most frequently not by critics of the neocons but by the neocons themselves.

A July 2005 article by leading neocon, Michael Ledeen, bemoaned the existence in Britain of "so many complaints that 'Zionists,' 'Likudniks,' 'Jewish hawks,' and – the single epithet that sums up all of the above – 'neocons' had manipulated America and its poodle Blair into the ghastly blunder of Iraq. The BBC has devoted hours of radio and television to slanderous misrepresentations of places like the American Enterprise Institute, where I sit, and of such Jewish luminaries as Richard Perle, Douglas Feith, William Kristol, and Paul Wolfowitz." Senator John Kyl (R-Ariz.) vented a similar lamentation at the CSIS in May 2004. The "conspiracy theory" surrounding the neoconservatives, he said, "has its bigoted overtones: many of the neoconservatives are Jews; they are accused of having favored elimination of Saddam Hussein's regime because of the Iraqi threat to Israel rather than the threat to the United States; therefore, according to these theories, a way had to be found to get George W. Bush to do Israel's bidding."

Where does all this whining leave the *facts*? Religious questions aside, there is still the political reality: American support for Israel has costs. Some people think the costs worthwhile, others think not. That Israel is a self-proclaimed "Jewish state" means that Jewishness will be pivotal whenever reasonable people discuss political support for Israel. It is not surprising that many supporters of Israel are Jewish and feel an obligation to support Israel on a religious and political basis. This is a normal fact of life, where religious, political, social and all kinds of other influences combine to lead people in one direction or another. At any rate, none of this should make "off-limits" the discussion of what motivated the war in Iraq and whether those motivations were right or wrong. To say that discussion of Israel and foreign policy equates to *hatred* of people for their race or religion is silliness at best, *intentionally slanderous* at worst. It's evidently quite good PR, though.

C H A P T E R
7

A Real Hijacking: The Neoconservative Fifth Column and the War in Iraq

• • • • • • • • •

Justin Raimondo

ANY WERE BAFFLED by the Bush administration's fixation on Iraq as the next target in our perpetual "war on terrorism." After all, there was no proven link between Saddam and 9/11 or Iraq and the anthrax scare, no weapons of mass destruction (as we discovered to our chagrin) – so why did the President of the United States go off on such a pronounced tangent, beating the war drums for Gulf War II? Chris Matthews, the columnist who throws a fast *Hardball* on NBC, knew before the shooting ever started and wasn't shy about saying what was behind Dubya's diversion:

> Like Bob Hope and Bing Crosby, a pair of rightist factions in the Bush administration are hoping to take the United States on the road to Baghdad. Unlike the beloved Hope-Crosby "road" pictures, however, the adventure in Iraq is not going to be funny.[1]

Yes, but some were definitely all smiles, among them what Matthews calls the "neoconservative faction" of the administration: namely, Bill Kristol of the *Weekly Standard*, who, with his sometime co-author Robert Kagan, proclaimed in a famous article that the goal of American foreign policy must be "benevolent world hegemony."[2] Matthews dolefully noted that the two of them "write a regular column for the *Washington Post* pushing war with Iraq," as the rest of the neocon chorus dutifully shouted "Amen!" including Frank Gaffney, William Safire, and a host of Washington political operatives deeply embedded in the Bush administra-

---

1. Chris Matthews, "The Road to Baghdad," *San Francisco Chronicle*, March 24, 2002, online.

2. William Kristol and Robert Kagan, "Toward a Neo-Reaganite Foreign Policy," *Foreign Affairs*, July/August, 1996.

tion. One widely-noted example of neocon dominance: as neocon presidential speechwriter David Frum, author of the "axis of evil" phraseology, exited the White House, neocon Joseph Shattan took his place.

Dana Milbank pointed out in the *Washington Post* that a cadre of young neocons dominates the Bush White House corps of speechwriters: Shattan once worked for Kristol, when the latter was shilling for Dan Quayle, a job history young Shattan shares with Bush speechwriter Matthew Scully and Cheney scribe John McConnell.[1] Other Kristolian alumni: Peter Wehner, another Bush speechwriter, and National Security Council wordsmith Matthew Rees. What was odd about Shattan's ascension, however, is that he had just gotten through savaging the Bushies in *National Review* for not being sufficiently pro-Israel. By endorsing a Palestinian state, Bush was exhibiting "America's cowardice and corruption," averred the future White House speechwriter:

"Thanks entirely to the President and his team . . . the campaign to defeat the Islamist challenge has gotten off to a singularly inauspicious start."[2]

After that, naturally, Shattan was vetoed for a job in the administration as a speechwriter for the Energy Department by the munchkins in the Office of Presidential Personnel – and, not so naturally, invited to work at the White House.

Oh, but there's no such thing as a "neocon agenda," *National Review* rushed to reassure us: this is an invention of "the Left." *NR* writer Neil Seeman, a policy analyst at the Canadian Fraser Institute, complained: "After 9/11, terms like 'neoconservative agenda' and 'neoconservative' have acquired a new frisson in the anti-war lexicon."[3]

Seeman goes on to attack none other than Pat Buchanan for firing "the first fusillade." Some "leftist"!

Indeed, the first and loudest complaints against the neocons and their agenda came not from the left but from their critics on the right, not only Pat Buchanan but Tom Fleming of the Rockford Institute and conservative scholar Paul Gottfried: the latter's book, *The Conservative Movement*, chronicles what Gottfried regards as the degeneration of authentic conservatism since the neocons gained the upper hand over traditionalists

---

1. Dana Milbank, "'Bush's Blunder' May Be Kristol's Inside Influence," *Washington Post*, March 19, 2002, online.

2. Joseph Shattan, "Bush's Blunder," *National Review Online* (www.nationalreview.com), October 15, 2002.

3. Neil Seeman, "What 'Neoconservative Agenda?'" *National Review Online* (www.nationalreview.com), March 6, 2002.

and libertarians.[1] My own book, *Reclaiming the American Right: The Lost Legacy of the Conservative Movement* also tells the story of how the limited government and pro-peace conservatism of Senator Robert A. Taft was subverted by a coterie of ex-Stalinists and ex-Trotskyists and made consonant with a right-wing form of social democracy.[2]

This is old news: the neocon-"paleocon" debate has been playing out in the pages of conservative journals for a decade. But Seeman was blissfully oblivious to all this, or pretended to be, and blithely derided the very idea of a neocon agenda as "one of those gems you might find littered in fascinating periodicals with names like the *Journal of Canadian Studies*."[3] Well, uh, not exactly: try *Chronicles* magazine, or *The American Conservative*, which are to *National Review* what real gold is to fool's gold, if you want the real dirt on the neocons.[4]

A major target of the paleocon critique has been the globalist outlook of the neocon faction, whose foreign policy views can be summed up by simply inverting the title of Pat Buchanan's best-selling anti-interventionist tome, *A Republic, Not an Empire*. The paleocons, for their part, abhor war, albeit not on pacifist but on decentralist and libertarian grounds. Kristol and his fellow neo-imperialists have never seen a war they didn't support, even going so far as threatening to abandon the Republicans, during the Clinton era, if they didn't get squarely behind Clinton's rape of Serbia. Kristol called for "cracking Serb skulls" long before Clinton decided to drop bombs on Belgrade.

Kristol and his followers almost did walk out of the GOP to support warhawk John McCain, who, from Day One of the Kosovo war, called for putting in American ground troops, and whose blustering bullying style perfectly embodies the neocon foreign policy. For years, Kristol and his gang has been clamoring for war not only with Iraq, but with the entire Arab Middle East. In the wake of 9/11, they seized their chance, and took the offensive: the smoke had yet to clear from the site of the devastated World Trade Center when Kristol and a coterie of his fellow neocons signed an

---

1. Paul Gottfried, *The Conservative Movement: Social Movements Past and Present* (Detroit MI: Twayne Publishers), December 1, 1992.

2. Justin Raimondo, *Reclaiming the American Right: The Lost Legacy of the Conservative Movement* (Burlingame, Calif.: Center for Libertarian Studies, 1993).

3. Neil Seeman, "What 'Neoconservative Agenda?,'" *National Review Online* (www.nationalreview.com), March 6, 2002.

4. Samuel Francis, "The Real Cabal," *Chronicles*, September, 2003, p. 33.

open letter to the President calling for the military occupation of not only Iraq, but also Syria, Iran, and much of the rest of the Middle East.[1]

Oh, but not to worry, averred Seeman, it wasn't just the neocons because, you see, there was this poll of "opinion leaders," and it showed that the idea of expanding the war to Iraq would be *real* popular if that country could be shown to "support terrorism." (A big "if," but never mind . . . .) So, you see, practically everybody – or, at least, anybody who's anybody – had forgotten all about Osama-bin-What's-his-name, and was at that point just as determined to see U.S. troops take Baghdad – no matter how many killed and wounded – as, say, Charles Krauthammer. "Sorry folks," said Seeman,

> there's no vast right-wing conspiracy here. Curiously, though, the anti-war, anti-neocon cant continues. Neocons are "Washington's War Party"; the neo-cons are implacable and blood thirsty; and so on and so forth. Not so long ago, neoconservatives were a few estranged liberals, mugged by reality. Now they're everywhere, mugging America's entire political agenda? I don't think so.

Who, *us*? Seeman's indignant denial may seem disingenuous to intellectual historians of the Right, who have traced the neoconservatives' promiscuous odyssey from schismatic Trotskyism to the far-right wing of Social Democracy and then into the arms of the conservative establishment. Yet it is perfectly in synch with the conceit that their predecessors on the right – the traditionalists and the libertarians – hardly mattered. In celebrating the complete takeover of conservative institutions by "a few estranged liberals mugged by reality," *Weekly Standard* writer David Brooks once triumphantly declared "We're all neoconservatives now!"[2] So, it seems, they are everywhere, mugging America's entire political agenda – and the number one item on their agenda is war.

Joe Sobran once described the neocons as essentially "pragmatists" who are, at best, "muddled centrists" with "conservative leanings," and as basically lacking any coherent ideology beyond support for the New Deal's stratification of American capitalism and a general feeling that they'd "had enough of liberalism."[3] Sobran is right about their statist inclinations, but wrong on the essential point. The neocons may be all over the map on

---

1. William Kristol *et al.*, "Toward a Comprehensive Strategy: A Letter to the President," September 20, 2001 (online at Project for the New American Century, http://www.newamericancentury.org/Bushletter.htm).

2. Sam Tanenhaus, "When Left Turns Right, It Leaves The Middle Muddled," *New York Times*, September 16, 2000, p. 7.

3. Joseph Sobran, "Staying in the Muddle," *Sobran's Real News of the Month*, September 19, 2000.

domestic policy, exhibiting none of the gut-level distrust of government power that defines the traditional American Right, but on the vital question of foreign policy they have been the most consistently belligerent faction in American politics.

Indeed, warmongering is the very essence of neoconservatism. The first neocons were James Burnham and Max Shachtman, two dissident Trotskyists who turned right starting in 1940, splitting with the left over the question of World War II: Burnham went on to set the tone at *National Review*, and Shachtman had an enormous influence on the slower-moving ex-leftists who became Reaganites in the 1970s and 80s. During the Vietnam era, the leading lights of the neocon movement left the Democratic party when the antiwar McGovernites took over. During the cold war, the neocons were the most militant faction, and they came into policy positions during the Reagan administration, burrowing their way into the National Endowment for Democracy, and, under the aegis of such ex-Democrats as Jeanne Kirkpatrick, into the national security bureaucracy. This marriage of right and ex-left was consummated, symbolically, when President Ronald Reagan awarded the Medal of Freedom to Sidney Hook, a lifelong socialist and fervent anti-Communist.

To such forerunners of neoconservatism as Professor Hook, the heroes of the Old Right – Senator Robert A. Taft, Joe McCarthy, and even Barry Goldwater – were disreputable (to liberals, that is) and therefore beyond the pale. They didn't want to dismantle the Welfare-Warfare State that had grown up in the wake of the New Deal: indeed, they didn't care much about domestic policy, as most of the neocons' attention was directed abroad, at the battlefields of the cold war in Europe and Asia. With the end of the cold war, however, the neocons were temporarily in a funk. What to do?

After all, their primary ideological focus had suddenly, without warning, dissolved before their very eyes, like a mirage in the desert. And what could take the place of the Kremlin in the pantheon of evil? In the neocons' never-ending war-game, a militant Good always requires an even more militant Evil. But no one was quite up to snuff: Slobodan Milosevic was supposed to be "another Hitler," but instead turned out to be a smalltime hoodlum. Saddam Hussein was only a threat to Israel and Kuwait, in spite of the propaganda campaign that tried to paint his regime as the second coming of the Third Reich. Besides, in a post-cold war world that looked forward to a "peace dividend" – remember *that*? – their desperate search for a suitable enemy was more than a little unseemly: it occurred to many, on the right as well as the left, that the neocons were just trying to make trouble (trouble which, in their case, always means war).

9/11 breathed new life into the neocons, and animated them as never before. They immediately sprang into action, taking full advantage of the war hysteria to broaden the scope of the public's anger toward all things Arab. From the beginning, they looked beyond Afghanistan and took a position that was, as they say, more royalist than the King. As the President and his Secretary of State looked to build a broad anti-terrorist coalition, including key Arab countries, the neocons accused him of selling out Israel. And here we come to yet another key element of the neocon agenda, and that is *unconditional* support for Israeli aggression and expansionism. As far as they are concerned, any talk of compromise or conciliation in the Middle East is "appeasement." When Ariel Sharon compared George W. Bush to Neville Chamberlain, and his own nation to poor little Czechoslovakia, neocon Bill Bennett sided with Sharon.[1] Never mind coalition-building: the neocons want nothing less than all-out war between America and the Islamic world, and don't mind at all if Israel is the prime beneficiary.

Chris Matthews was right that the Bush administration is led by a bunch of "oil patch veterans" who have a "sense of entitlement" to the oil reserves of the Persian Gulf. He was also wise to the fact that a war on Iraq could only benefit Israel, and that the neocons were and are more than ready to sell American interests down the river if that is what Israel requires. It scared him that a cabal of ideologues who revel in the idea of waging what they call "World War IV" had worked their way into the White House, and was being given the run of the place. And he was also spot on in his analysis of the mechanics of the neocons' pact with Big Oil. This working alliance is a revamped version of the same right-wing Popular Front that took over the conservative movement in the late 1980s, the union of big business and neoconservative intellectuals that blossomed into lushly funded think tanks, magazines, and front organizations that proliferated like worms after a rain. The neocons crawled up through the ranks during the Reagan era, and began to assert their dominance aggressively on the Right. Having purged most of the libertarians and anyone else in the least bit original or interesting for any number of heresies, the right was short of intellectuals and was more than glad to welcome new recruits with open arms – especially those whose acceptability as former liberals

---

1. Patrick J. Buchanan, "Bush-Bashing by Bill Bennett," *WorldNetDaily.com*, March 22, 2002.

made the *New York Times* and the *Washington Post* begin to take conservatives seriously.

The conservatives of, say, 1952, would find the triumphalist rot trumpeted by our bellicose neocons nothing short of crazy. Invade and conquer the Middle East? I can hear old Bob Taft, who opposed NATO, questioned the Korean War, and – like virtually all conservatives of the day – derided the Marshall Plan as "globaloney," rolling over in his grave. The conservative writer Garet Garrett warned, in 1952, that "we have crossed the boundary that lies between Republic and Empire."[1] But to today's "conservatives" of the neo variety, that's a *good* thing.

In detailing "the conservative crack-up" over the Iraq war, E. J. Dionne writes:

> The isolationist conservatives around Pat Buchanan cannot understand why we went to war in the first place – and they opposed it from the beginning. These conservatives speak explicitly about the "costs of empire," much as the left does. They argue that globalism is really "globaloney" and that being an empire is incompatible with being a republic.[2]

Actually, that's not true. We "isolationists" – conservatives and libertarians alike – understand all too well why we went to war. As Pat Buchanan put it in the run-up to the invasion:

> We charge that a cabal of polemicists and public officials seek to ensnare our country in a series of wars that are not in America's interests. We charge them with colluding with Israel to ignite those wars and destroy the Oslo Accords. We charge them with deliberately damaging U.S. relations with every state in the Arab world that defies Israel or supports the Palestinian people's right to a homeland of their own. We charge that they have alienated friends and allies all over the Islamic and Western world through their arrogance, hubris, and bellicosity . . . .
>
> They charge us with anti-Semitism – i.e., a hatred of Jews for their faith, heritage, or ancestry. False. The truth is, those hurling these charges harbor a "passionate attachment" to a nation not our own that causes them to subordinate the interests of their own country and to act on an assumption that, somehow, what's good for Israel is good for America.

Buchanan named names, tracing the development of the "what's good for Israel is good for America" doctrine to the influential sect known as neoconservatives: ex-leftists who defected from the Democratic party in

1. Garet Garrett, *The People's Pottage* (Boston: Western Islands, 1965), p. 93.
2. E. J. Dionne, Jr., "Iraq and the Conservative Crackup," *Washington Post*, June 1, 2004, p. A23.

the 1960s and 1970s over the Vietnam War, and wormed their way into top GOP policymaking circles, eventually winding up in charge of George W. Bush's foreign policy.[1]

This theme – that an Israeli-centric foreign policy is the real reason for this war – was not looked on with favor when the shooting began. But a year later, by a simple process of elimination, it is the only rational explanation left standing.

They said it was "weapons of mass destruction" in Saddam's possession, and, when those failed to turn up, they fell back on Iraq's alleged responsibility for the 9/11 terrorist attacks. When that canard was debunked, however, the War Party was reduced to claiming that Saddam's tyranny alone was sufficient as a *casus belli*, and that their real goal – their primary goal – is to spread Democracy, Goodness, and Light throughout a region still mired in the Dark Ages. The lengthy foot-dragging before "elections" were called, however, along with Abu Ghraib and Paul Bremer's propensity for acting like a dictator, soon disabused all but the most gullible of such highfalutin' notions.

That left only the truth, and it is this: Israel is the chief beneficiary of this war, with bin Laden coming in a close second. We have opened up an Eastern front on Tel Aviv's behalf, not only eliminating a secular Arab opponent of Israel, but also pressing the Syrians to kowtow to a nuclear-armed Israel, sending tremors through the rest of the Arab world. No sooner had we taken Baghdad, than Israeli Prime Minister Ariel Sharon made his move, ingesting whole hunks of the West Bank under the guise of a "withdrawal," and blithely ignoring muted criticism by the U.S. State Department as his government subsidized yet more "settlements" on Palestinian land. A "Wall of Separation" was built – with U.S. taxpayers' money – to underscore the Likudniks' contempt for world public opinion, and especially American public opinion.

Looked at in purely geopolitical terms, the war in Iraq is diverting the energy, resources, and focused hatred of the Arab "street" away from the Israelis and toward America. In undertaking what promises to be a project of many years, the U.S. invasion has shifted the balance of power – already weighted in Israel's favor, thanks to massive American military aid – decisively and perhaps permanently in favor of the Israelis. Bristling with weaponry, including nuclear arms, and not shy about mobilizing its

---

1. Pat Buchanan, "Whose War?" *The American Conservative*, March 24, 2003, online. [See pp. 135–147 of the companion to the present volume, *Neo-CONNED!.*—Ed.]

international amen corner to defend its interests aggressively, Israel is fast achieving the status of regional hegemon.

Israel seems to be the one exception to the new U.S. theory of global preeminence – what might be called the Wolfowitz Doctrine, since he was one of the first to put it in writing – that no power should rival U.S. hegemony in any region of the world.[1]

Now, it is fair to ask: why *is* that? But not everyone thinks it's fair, or even decent, to ask any such thing.

When General Anthony Zinni, former commander of all U.S. forces in the Middle East, went on national television and told the truth about the key role played by the neocons in dragging us into this unwinnable and increasingly ugly war, the voices of political correctness were raised to a pitch of shrillness not heard since the early 1990s.[2] Back then it was Buchanan – always ahead of his time – who first identified "Israel's amen corner" as the sparkplug and chief inspiration of the War Party, just as the first Gulf War broke out.[3] Now, in the disastrous wake of the Second Gulf War, the rest of the country seems to be catching up with him.

Zinni, a registered Republican who voted for Bush in 2000, reflected the views of a broad swath of the thinking public when he told *60 Minutes*:

> I think it's the worst kept secret in Washington. That everybody – everybody I talk to in Washington has known and fully knows what their agenda was and what they were trying to do.
>
> And one article, because I mentioned the neoconservatives who describe themselves as neoconservatives, I was called anti-Semitic. I mean, you know, unbelievable that that's the kind of personal attacks that are run when you criticize a strategy and those who propose it. I certainly didn't criticize who they were. I certainly don't know what their ethnic religious backgrounds are. And I'm not interested.
>
> I know what strategy they promoted. And openly. And for a number of years. And what they have convinced the President and the secretary to do. And I don't believe there is any serious political leader, military leader, diplomat in Washington that doesn't know where it came from.[4]

Zinni was mercilessly smeared by all the usual suspects, but the mud didn't stick. Instead, it boomeranged, and, instead of isolating him, sud-

1. "Excerpts From Pentagon's Plan: 'Prevent the Re-Emergence of a New Rival,'" *New York Times*, Mar 8, 1992, p. 1.

2. Thomas E. Ricks, "For Vietnam Vet Anthony Zinni, Another War on Shaky Territory," *Washington Post*, December 23, 2003, p. C01.

3. *The McLaughlin Report*, August 26, 1990.

4. "Gen. Zinni: 'They've Screwed Up,'" *60 Minutes*, May 21, 2004, online.

denly everyone was citing him, and defending him, including author Tom Clancy, who has co-written with Zinni a new book that promises to let the cat out of the bag as far as the origins of this war are concerned.[1] While neocon sock-puppets on the order of Jonah Goldberg flailed angrily about, retailing the obligatory innuendoes, *The Forward*, the oldest Jewish newspaper in America, intervened to recognize the new reality, and "The Ground Shifts" was the very apt title of their editorial on the subject:

> As recently as a week ago, reasonable people still could dismiss as anti-Semitic conspiracy mongering the claim that Israel's security was the real motive behind the invasion of Iraq. No longer. The allegation has now moved from the fringes into the mainstream. Its advocates can no longer simply be shushed or dismissed as bigots. Those who disagree must now argue the case on the merits.[2]

Arguing for or against anything strictly on the merits is going to be a whole new experience for the neocons. Smearing their enemies and lying is, for them, a matter of course – it isn't just a matter of tactics, it's part of who and what they are.[3]

As Israeli "settlers" push out the Palestinians under the protection of U.S.-made helicopter gunships and tanks, American soldiers are taking heavy casualties on the Eastern front – and the U.S. homeland gets ready for a "summer of terror." How can anyone make a rational argument that this is in America's national self-interest? It isn't possible, and so the neo-cons have no arguments: only a barrage of lies and smears. Argue their case strictly "on the merits"? It can't be done, unless they want to argue openly that America's interests must be subordinated to Israel's. Strip away the ideological pretenses, the sexed-up "intelligence," and the "patriotic" window-dressing, and what you see is the naked reality of Israel's fifth column in America.

In identifying who dragged us into this war, and why, General Zinni "changed the terms of the debate," says *The Forward*, and "he is not one to be waved off." Not that they agree, exactly. They blame the President, "unilateralism," and the "ideological predilections" of this administration, although they admit that

---

1. Tom Clancy, Tony Zinni, Tony Koltz, *Battle Ready* (London: Grosset & Dunlap, 2004).

2. "The Ground Shifts," *The Forward*, May 28, 2004, online.

3. John G. Mason, "Leo Strauss and the Noble Lie: The Neo-Cons at War," *Logos*, Vol. 3, No. 2, Spring, 2004 (http://www.logosjournal.com/mason.htm).

[t]he truth is, of course, that Zinni is partly right – but only partly. Securing Israel was one of the war hawks' motives, but not the only one, probably not even the main one.[1]

But what were these "ideological predilections" that the Bushies brought with them to the table if not the neoconservative ideology embraced by his top foreign policy advisors and officials – an ideology that, aside from championing a foreign policy aiming at "benevolent global hegemony,"[2] elevates Israel to a special status among America's allies, and advocates unconditional support for the actions of its ultra-rightist government?

Rep. Nita Lowey (D-N.Y.) has made the trenchant point that Bush's policies have made Israel, and Jews worldwide, less safe,[3] but the mantle of victimhood is not so easily surrendered by the radical Zionist faction: this is "blaming the victim," says the Likudnik chorus, a stance that neatly sidesteps the issue of whether or not anyone, Jew or Gentile, feels the least bit safer these days.

According to Jonah Goldberg, the term "neoconservative" – up until now a recognized term in the American political lexicon, meaning "a liberal who's been mugged," a Scoop Jackson Democrat turned Reagan Republican – is just a "code word" for "Jew."[4] But it's too late for special pleading and the usual victimological histrionics just won't do, as Rich Lowry, Goldberg's boss over at *National Review*, makes clear in an interview with columnist Bill Steigerwald in the *Pittsburgh Tribune-Review*:

> With the war on terror, you saw neoconservatives emerging as a distinct tendency within conservatism, mostly on foreign policy; its hallmarks being extreme interventionism, extremely idealistic foreign policy, and emphasis on democracy building and spreading human rights and freedom and an overestimation, in my view, of how easy it is to spread democracy and liberty to spots in the world where it doesn't exist currently.[5]

It seems the neocons aren't creatures of pure myth, the unicorns of the American political bestiary, but living breathing individuals, and, what's more, they're a movement separate and distinct from ordinary unprefixed

---

1. "The Ground Shifts," *loc. cit.*

2. Kristol and Kagan, *loc cit.*

3. "The Ground Shifts," *loc. cit.*

4. Jonah Goldberg, "State of Confusion," *National Review Online* (www.nationalreview.com), May 16, 2003.

5. Bill Steigerwald, "So, What Is a 'Neocon'?" *Pittsburgh Tribune-Review*, May 29, 2004, online.

run-of-the-mill conservatives, with their own doctrines and organizations. So, is it "anti-Semitic" to separate them out from the rest of the Republican Right, and name them "as being the planners and instigators of the war in Iraq?" asks Steigerwald. Lowry's reply is more than a little equivocal:

> No. No. It would be false. It wouldn't necessarily be anti-Semitic. It would be accurate to say that some of the most articulate and powerful expressions of the case for war have come from people who are neoconservatives. So that's not anti-Semitic. But if you take a couple of steps beyond that, you begin to get into territory that is a little shady, I would think.[1]

So Jonah is wrong, at least according to his boss, that merely employing the term "neocon" is the equivalent of shouting *"Sieg Heil!"* at the top of one's lungs. It's amazing to see how far the boundaries of neoconservative political correctness are being stretched, these days, but then Lowry – perhaps remembering how much his magazine depends on the largesse of big neoconservative foundations – snaps back and comes out with this murky business of taking "a couple of steps beyond that." What "steps" is he talking about?

One need only step up to a computer terminal, and read Seymour Hersh's detailed sketch of the "Office of Special Plans,"[2] or perhaps Julian Borger's (in the *Guardian*),[3] and Jim Lobe's piece on *Antiwar.com*,[4] to go beyond merely naming the neocons as the chief culprits in this dirty business of invading and occupying a nation that had never posed a real threat to us. What occurred in the run-up to war was not merely an intellectual debate, as Lowry genteelly pretends, but a battle between two organized factions, one of which had seized the reins of power in Washington, according to Bob Woodward, who writes in *Plan of Attack* that Cheney and the neocons had, in effect, set up "a separate government."[5]

In examining this highly organized effort, and in effect writing the history of what amounted to a coup d'état,[6] a number of reporters, including on-the-scene observers such as Lt. Col. Karen Kwiatkowski, point to an Israeli component as a key element in the intelligence apparatus that

1. *Ibid.*

2. Seymour Hersh, "The Stovepipe," *The New Yorker*, October 27, 2003, online.

3. Julian Borger, "The Spies Who Pushed for War," *The Guardian*, July 17, 2003, online.

4. Jim Lobe, "Pentagon Office Home to Neo-Con Network," *Antiwar.com*, August 7, 2003.

5. Bob Woodward, *Plan of Attack*, (New York: Simon & Schuster, 2004), p. 292.

6. See the interesting discussion by Maurizio Blondet of the idea of coup d'état on pp. 36–41 of the present volume.—Ed.

pushed us into war.[1] Robert Dreyfuss, writing in *The Nation*, cites a former U.S. ambassador with strong ties to the CIA:

> According to the former official, also feeding information to the Office of Special Plans was a secret, rump unit established last year in the office of Prime Minister Ariel Sharon of Israel. This unit, which paralleled [Abram N.] Shulsky's – and which has not previously been reported – prepared intelligence reports on Iraq in English (not Hebrew) and forwarded them to the Office of Special Plans. It was created in Sharon's office, not inside Israel's Mossad intelligence service, because the Mossad – which prides itself on extreme professionalism – had views closer to the CIA's, not the Pentagon's, on Iraq. This secretive unit, and not the Mossad, may well have been the source of the forged documents purporting to show that Iraq tried to purchase yellowcake uranium for weapons from Niger in West Africa, according to the former official.[2]

A Jewish conspiracy? No. An Israeli covert action? Perhaps.

Anti-Semites may see no difference, but, then again, *neither do the neocons*. To them, an attack on the Wolfowitz-Feith-Shulsky Axis of Deception is an attack on "the Jews." But this terminological confusion, as Michael Lind trenchantly pointed out in an excellent essay in *The Nation*, is rooted in journalistic sloppiness and the error of conflating ethnicity and ideology:

> It is true, and unfortunate, that some journalists tend to use "neoconservative" to refer only to Jewish neoconservatives, a practice that forces them to invent categories like "nationalist conservative" or "Western conservative" for Rumsfeld and Cheney. But neoconservatism is an ideology, like paleoconservatism and libertarianism, and Rumsfeld and Dick and Lynne Cheney are full-fledged neocons, as distinct from paleocons or libertarians, even though they are not Jewish and were never liberals or leftists. What is more, Jewish neocons do not speak for the majority of American Jews. According to the 2003 Annual Survey of American Jewish Opinion by the American Jewish Committee, 54 percent of American Jews surveyed disapproved of the war on Iraq, compared with only 43 percent who approved, and American Jews disapproved of the way Bush is handling the campaign against terrorism by a margin of 54-41.[3]

The idea that naming names – identifying specific government officials as tireless advocates of war with Iraq – is the equivalent of painting a swastika on a synagogue door is, as longtime conservative activist Paul Weyrich put it to Steigerwald, "really outrageous." Weyrich's answer to the "anti-

---

1. Karen Kwiatkowski, "Open Door Policy," *The American Conservative*, January 19, 2004, online. [Also see her essay in the present volume, pp. 199–207.—Ed.]

2. Robert Dreyfuss, "More Missing Intelligence," *The Nation*, June 19, 2003, online.

3. Michael Lind, "A Tragedy of Errors" *The Nation*, February 23, 2004, online.

Semite" smear needs to be read and absorbed by all thinking conservatives, especially those who supported the war:

> I really resent the idea that if you question who it is that planned the war – just because you ask questions about them – it is automatically anti-Semitic. It is not. It is legitimate to ask these questions. It is legitimate to have a debate about the legitimacy and effect of this war. If that means questioning some of the people who are involved in it, so be it. The President is a very committed Christian. Should we say that, "Well, we can't question anything that Bush does, because if we did it would be anti-Christian"? That's silly.[1]

Silly – in a sinister kind of way. Political correctness is not entirely a phenomenon of the left, as Rush Limbaugh and his fellow neoconized "conservatives" would have you believe: the right has its own version, which is, in many ways, even more rigid than any campus "speech code." But the failure of the neocons' war is introducing a note of glasnost into the conservative camp, as E. J. Dionne and others are beginning to notice.

As this war pierces the very heart of the nation like a poisoned arrow, the day of the neocons may be over. But I wouldn't count on it. They are nothing if not resilient, and determined. Certainly they are well-funded. But of one thing we can be sure: the tide of opposition to this war – and the policy of imperialism – on moral as well as consequentialist grounds, is rising on the right as well as the left.

1. Steigerwald, *loc. cit.*

THE EDITORS' GLOSS: Illustrating our earlier point – that in a discussion of support for war in Iraq, the ethnicity or religion of those involved in the discussion is secondary at best, if relevant at all – is the fact that there are so many self-professed Christians who frame their perspective on questions of foreign policy around what is or is not good for Israel. One may be permitted to wonder if it's "anti-Semitic" or "anti-Christian" to oppose Christian Zionism?

One thing is certain, as Dr. Lutz makes clear in his article: without support for the Iraq war among Christians, it could not have happened. Israel has the support of those Christians who embrace an "apocalyptic" vision of events in the Middle East, imagining that whatever furthers modern-day Israel's political or foreign-policy agenda is somehow sanctioned by the Almighty. Pat Robertson illustrated this approach nicely when he said, "I see the rise of Islam to destroy Israel and take the land from the Jews and give East Jerusalem to Yasser Arafat. I see that as Satan's plan to prevent the return of Jesus Christ the Lord." (How can mere "men" – or even Satan – prevent the return of God Himself, Pat?)

The refreshing aspect of Lutz's piece is that he demonstrates, conclusively and even authoritatively, that most Christians do not support the line taken by men like Robertson. In fact, the old and venerable Christian tradition directly opposes the Robertson "Christian Zionist" cant and states that the claims of justice apply to Palestinians and Arabs no less than anyone else. It argues, too, that such considerations of justice stem from an essentially Christian view of the world, whose substance is sadly missing in Robertson's "Christianity." That this tradition has much in common with the common sense found *outside* the Christian communion is no coincidence.

8

*Un*just-War Theory:
Christian Zionism and the Road to Jerusalem

Prof. David W. Lutz, Ph.D.

T HE CHRISTIAN TRADITION includes a highly refined theory of just war, by means of which we can judge whether a particular war is moral or immoral. Just-war theory has roots in pre-Christian Greek and Roman philosophers, primarily the Stoics and Cicero, and was developed more fully by Christian scholars such as St. Augustine, St. Thomas Aquinas, Francisco de Vitoria, Francisco Suárez and Hugo Grotius. St. Thomas identified three criteria of just war:

> First, the authority of the sovereign by whose command the war is to be waged. For it is not the business of a private individual to declare war . . . .

> Second, a just cause is required, namely that those who are attacked, should be attacked because they deserve it on account of some fault . . . .

> Third, it is necessary that the belligerents should have a rightful intention, so that they intend the advancement of good, or the avoidance of evil . . . .[1]

Subsequent thinkers have developed additional criteria. Although there is disagreement regarding the number of just-war criteria, seven clearly belong to the tradition:

1. Legitimate Authority: The war must be declared by a legitimate authority, responsible for the common good, not a private citizen.

---

1. St. Thomas Aquinas, *Summa Theologica* (henceforth *ST*), Fathers of the English Dominican Province, trans., II, ii, Q. 40, A. 1.

2. Just Cause: The purpose of the war must be to defend one's country or an ally against aggression. Recently, some just-war theorists have added humanitarian intervention, the defense of innocent persons within another country, as a just cause.

3. Right Intention: The intention must be the restoration of peace, not domination, wealth or revenge.

4. Last Resort: All peaceful means of avoiding the conflict must first be exhausted.

5. Reasonable Hope of Success: It is wrong to bring about death and destruction, and to ask soldiers to sacrifice their lives, in a futile war.

6. Proportionality: The military action must not produce more evil than the good to be achieved; one must avoid using force in excess of that necessary to achieve the objective of the war.

7. Discrimination: Noncombatants may not be directly targeted and care must be taken to minimize killing them indirectly.

The first five are classified as criteria of *jus ad bellum* (the justice of going to war) and the last two as criteria of *jus in bello* (the justice of conducting war), though some writers count proportionality as a *jus ad bellum* criterion. A particular war must satisfy *all* of these criteria in order to be just.

Just War and the War in Iraq

When the invasion of Iraq is evaluated in terms of these criteria, it fails the test. This war was not declared by a legitimate authority, because it was not declared at all.[1] Iraq posed no threat to the United States, nor to

---

1. According to the U.S. Constitution, "the President shall be Commander-in-Chief of the Army and Navy of the United States," but "the Congress shall have Power to declare War." This is one of the "checks and balances" between the three branches of government. But the last time the U.S. Congress declared war against another country was immediately after Pearl Harbor, sixty-four years ago. The precedent of going to war without declaring war was established by President Truman in 1950. General MacArthur commented: "I could not help being amazed at the manner in which this great decision was being made. With no submission to Congress, whose duty it is to declare war, and without even consulting the field commander involved, the members of the executive branch of the government agreed to enter the Korean War" (Douglas MacArthur, *Reminiscences* (New York: McGraw-Hill, 1964)).

any of our allies – unless one regards Israel, which has been caught several times in the act of spying against us, as an ally. We did not exhaust all peaceful alternatives before deciding to go to war. There was a reasonable hope of success, only if success was understood to mean merely removing a tyrant from power, not subsequently restoring the peace. The magnitude of the death and destruction is disproportionate to whatever good may be achieved.

Disintegration of Just-War Reasoning

There is disagreement among Catholics who have attempted to assess the ethical status of our invasion of Iraq in terms of the just-war criteria. Among those who have found it to be just is Robert Royal, of the Faith and Reason Institute. In order to make his case, however, he must argue that just-war theory as we know it is inadequate for the present situation:

> In my view, current weapons technologies, which will inevitably find their way into the hands of some nasty characters around the world, make it inevitable that the world community will have to take strong action to preserve peace and international order. We cannot shirk this responsibility by mechanically invoking traditional categories of last resort and demanding proof of an immediate threat. Our situation is new, and our moral response to it must be as well, not only for Iraq but for the whole post-cold war world.[1]

At all points in history, not just the present, the traditional categories of just-war theory should be invoked prudentially, not mechanically. Furthermore, the just-war tradition is in need of continual development.[2] There is a profound difference, however, between developing a tradition and abandoning it. To say that all nations, not just the United States and her allies, are free to go to war without first exhausting peaceful alternatives and obtaining evidence of an immediate threat would give a green light to far more wars than are permitted by the traditional just-war criteria.

Another innovation of some Catholic just-war theorists is the addition of "comparative justice" to the criteria of *jus ad bellum*. The U.S. Catholic Bishops tell us in "The Challenge of Peace":

> The category of comparative justice is destined to emphasize the presumption against war which stands at the beginning of just-war teaching. In a world of sovereign states recognizing neither a common moral authority nor a cen-

---

1. Robert Royal, "Just War and Iraq," United States Institute of Peace, Special Report 98 (http://www.usip.org/pubs/specialreports/sr98.html).

2. See the article on the development of the Church's teaching on war by Romano Amerio on pp. 427–436 of the companion to the present volume, *Neo-CONNED!*—Ed.

tral political authority, comparative justice stresses that no state should act on the basis that it has "absolute justice" on its side. Every party to a conflict should acknowledge the limits of its "just cause" and the consequent require- ment to use only limited means in pursuit of its objectives. Far from legitimiz- ing a crusade mentality, comparative justice is designed to relativize absolute claims and to restrain the use of force even in a "justified" conflict.[1]

This is an unnecessary innovation and an unfortunate choice of termi- nology. We live at a time when many Christians believe that ethics is rela- tive. According to ethical relativism, ethical truth differs from one person or group of persons to another. The alternative is ethical absolutism, which claims that ethical truth is the same for all of us. Much confusion results from the fact that "absolutism" is sometimes also used to mean that all ethical principles are applicable under all circumstances, and "relativism" to mean that whether we should follow certain ethical principles depends upon the situation. Although Joseph Fletcher's theory of "situation eth- ics" is erroneous, St. Thomas tells us that "human actions are good or evil according to circumstances."[2] Killing another person is wrong under most circumstances, but not in situations such as self-defense and just war. Sexual intercourse between two persons may be either moral or immoral, depending upon how they are related to one another.

In the sense that the ethical status of an action is related to the circum- stances under which it is performed, ethics is indeed "relative." A common error is to start from the fact that there are exceptions to rules such as "Do not kill," and then to conclude that ethics is relative. This is a mistake, because it is true for everyone, without exception, that it is unethical to kill another person, except under certain exceptional circumstances. (Some writers attempt to reduce confusion by making a distinction between "absolutism" and "universalism," though there is no universal agreement about the proper use of these two terms.)

What, then, do the Bishops mean by "absolute" and "relative" when they write that "comparative justice is designed to relativize absolute claims"? Although it is far from clear, they seem to mean that all causes for war are less than totally ("absolutely") just, and that the use of force should be proportionate to the degree of justice of the cause. Thus, if a cause for war is two-thirds just, then the use of force should be limited ("relativized") by one-third. If this interpretation is correct, one of the many problems is

1. U.S. Catholic Bishops, "The Challenge of Peace: God's Promise and Our Response," 1983, p. 93.
2. *ST*, II, i, Q. 18, A 3.

determining how the criterion of comparative justice stands in relation to that of just cause. A cause for war is either just or unjust. If it is merely partially just, then it is not a just cause. The standard is a high one, intended to limit the resort to warfare as a means of solving problems. But it appears that the criterion of "comparative justice" can be satisfied as long as one's cause for war is more just (i.e. less unjust) than that of one's enemy.

All justice is "comparative." Justice is "a habit whereby a man renders to each one his due by a constant and perpetual will."[1] Determining what is due each person requires comparison. Determining whether a cause for war is just or unjust requires comparing the actions of different persons. But it is unclear how the traditional criterion of just cause and the new criterion of "comparative justice" can be reconciled with one another.

In the primary senses of "ethical absolutism" and "ethical relativism," Catholic moral doctrine, including just-war theory, is absolute. Despite the fact that sovereign states recognize neither a common moral authority nor a central political authority, the criteria that determine whether a war is just or unjust are the same for all states. We do not need a new criterion to relativize the absolute character of the traditional criteria, because they already address the presumption against war, the limitation of means in pursuit of objectives, and restraint of the use of force. Nor do we need additional confusion about ethical relativism and ethical absolutism.

Subversion of Just-War Thinking

In addition to writers who are altering the just-war tradition from within, there are others who, from within other moral traditions, maintain the language of "just war." Michael Walzer's *Just and Unjust Wars* is widely regarded as the most important recent treatise on just war. This book, however, is not written within the one moral tradition within which just-war theory was developed and is coherent – that of natural law and moral virtues – but is instead based on the dichotomy between rights and utility, which is what normative ethics is left with following the rejection of the Catholic moral tradition: "The morality I shall expound is in its philosophical form a doctrine of human rights, though I shall say nothing here of the ideas of personality, action, and intention that this doctrine probably presupposes. Considerations of utility play into the structure at many points, but they cannot account for it as a whole."[2]

---

1. *ST*, II, ii, Q. 58, A 1.
2. Michael Walzer, *Just and Unjust Wars: A Moral Argument with Historical Illustrations*

Walzer attempts to write about "just and unjust wars" with what MacIntyre has described as "the fragments of a conceptual scheme."[1] According to Walzer, "Justice and prudence stand in an uneasy relation to one another."[2] This statement confirms that he stands outside the moral tradition within which just-war theory was developed. Within the tradition of natural law and human virtues, as St. Thomas explains, there is no conflict or tension, only harmony and collaboration, between prudence, an intellectual and moral virtue, and the moral virtues themselves, including justice.[3] Walzer, a modern liberal, understands prudence, not as a virtue, but as a principle or motive of action that can conflict with morality.

Walzer also writes about "moral law," but not within the tradition of natural law. For him, "the moral law" is "those general principles that we commonly acknowledge, even when we can't or won't live up to them."[4] As Walzer defines "the moral law," no such thing exists, because, following the rejection by most of us of the Catholic moral tradition, there are no general principles that we commonly acknowledge.[5]

When Walzer applies his incoherent interpretation of just-war theory to the world in which we live, the Middle East in particular, the result is that unjust actions are justified. His bias is readily apparent: "Contemporary terrorist campaigns are most often focused on people whose national existence has been radically devalued: the Protestants of Northern Ireland, the

---

(New York: Basic Books, 1977), p. xvi.

1. Alasdair MacIntyre, *After Virtue: A Study in Moral Theory*, 2nd ed. (Notre Dame, Ind.: University of Notre Dame Press, 1984), p. 2.

2. Walzer, *op. cit.*, p. 67.

3. *ST*, II, i, Q. 58, A.4: "Moral virtue cannot be without prudence, because it is a habit of choosing, i.e., making us choose well. Now in order that a choice be good, two things are required. First, that the intention be directed to a due end; and this is done by moral virtue, which inclines the appetitive faculty to the good that is in accord with reason, which is a due end. Secondly, that man take rightly those things which have reference to the end: and this he cannot do unless his reason counsel, judge and command aright, which is the function of prudence and the virtues annexed to it." *ST*, II, i, Q. 65, A. 1: "One cannot have prudence unless one has the moral virtues: since prudence is *right reason about things to be done*, and the starting-point of reason is the end of the thing to be done, to which end man is rightly disposed by moral virtue."

4. Walzer, *op. cit.*, p. xiii.

5. MacIntyre, *op. cit.*, p. 6: "The most striking feature of contemporary moral utterance is that so much of it is used to express disagreements; and the most striking feature of the debates in which these disagreements are expressed is their interminable character. I do not mean by this just that such debates go on and on and on – although they do – but also that they apparently can find no terminus. There seems to be no rational way of securing moral agreement in our culture." And, one might add, not even an irrational way.

Jews of Israel, and so on."[1] Discussing the history and morality of Catholic-Protestant relations in Ireland and Britain would exceed the scope of this essay. More relevant to the present argument are the simple facts that more Palestinians have been killed by Israeli terrorism than Israelis by Palestinian terrorism, and that the national existence of the Arabs of Palestine has been far more radically devalued than that of the Jews of Israel.

Walzer regards Israel's 1967 Six-Day War as a just war, on the grounds that Egypt was the aggressor:

> Often enough, despite the cunning agents, the theory [of aggression] is readily applied. It is worth setting down some of the cases about which we have, I think, no doubts: the German attack on Belgium in 1914, the Italian conquest of Ethiopia, the Japanese attack on China, the German and Italian interventions in Spain, the Russian invasion of Finland, the Nazi conquests of Czechoslovakia, Poland, Denmark, Belgium, and Holland, the Russian invasions of Hungary and Czechoslovakia, the Egyptian challenge to Israel in 1967, and so on – the twentieth century makes for easy listing.[2]

Although he does not deny that Israel attacked first, Walzer insists that Egypt was the party guilty of aggression:

> The Israeli first strike is, I think, a clear case of legitimate anticipation. To say that, however, is to suggest a major revision of the legalist paradigm. For it means that aggression can be made out not only in the absence of a military attack or invasion but in the (probable) absence of any immediate intention to launch such an attack or invasion.[3]

Noam Chomsky – like Walzer, a Jew; unlike Walzer, a non-Zionist[4] – demonstrates the falsity of the claim that Israel started the war in 1967 in response to aggression:

---

1. Walzer, *op cit.*, p. 203.

2. *Ibid.*, p. 292.

3. *Ibid.*, p. 84.

4. Chomsky believes that Jews and Palestinians should be treated as equals. In response to an interviewer's question in April 2004 – "As a Jew who has also lived on a kibbutz in Palestine, have your views changed at all over the years regarding the Israeli-Palestinian issue?" – he replied: "My views have not changed. The only thing that has changed is that my views back in the 1940s were labeled Zionist, and today they are labeled anti-Zionist. Although my views back then did not represent the majority of Zionist Jews, the idea of forming a democratic state for both Jews and Arabs in Palestine was still considered within the mainstream of debate. Now, any talk of a democratic secular state is considered anti-Zionist" (Ahmed Nassef, "Hug a Jew: Hug Noam Chomsky," *MuslimWakeUp. com*, April 29, 2004).

Walzer offers no argument or evidence to show that the "Egyptian challenge" to Israel stands on a par with the "clear cases" of aggression cited. He simply states that Israel had a "just fear" of destruction – which, even if true, would hardly substantiate his claim. Israeli generals take a rather different view. The former Commander of the Air Force, General Ezer Weizmann, regarded as a hawk, stated that there was "no threat of destruction" but that the attack on Egypt, Jordan and Syria was nevertheless justified so that Israel could "exist according to the scale, spirit and quality she now embodies." Citing corroboratory statements by Chief of Staff Chaim Bar-Lev and General Mattityahu Peled, Amnon Kapeliouk wrote that "no serious argument has been advanced to refute the thesis of the three generals." . . . Furthermore, the interactions leading up to the war included provocative and destructive Israeli actions and threats, which Walzer ignores, alongside of Egyptian and other Arab actions such as the closing of the Straits of Tiran, which Egypt claimed to be an internal waterway.

Among others who, unlike Walzer, have doubts about the Egyptian "challenge" as a "clear case" of aggression is Menachem Begin, who had the following remarks to make: "In June 1967, we again had a choice. The Egyptian Army concentrations in the Sinai approaches do not prove that Nasser was really about to attack us. We must be honest with ourselves. We decided to attack him." Begin of course regards the Israeli attack as justified, "This was a war of self-defense in the noblest sense of the term." But then, it may be recalled that the term "self-defense" has acquired a technical sense in modern political discourse, referring to any military action carried out by a state that one directs, serves or "supports." What is, perhaps, of some interest is that an American democratic socialist dove goes well beyond Menachem Begin in portraying Israel's actions as defense against aggression. However one evaluates these complex circumstances, it is plainly impossible to regard the "Egyptian challenge" as a "clear case" of aggression, on a par with the Nazi conquests, etc. Rather, this is a "clear case" of the style of apologetics adopted by many supporters of Israel.[1]

Disregard of Just-War Thinking

The Joint Service Conference on Professional Ethics (JSCOPE) is an annual, academic conference on the ethics of the profession of arms. Although it is open to everyone and has no official relationship with the Department of Defense, many of the papers presented are by military officers and by those – both military and civilian – who teach military ethics to present and future officers. Consequently, the papers (which may be found at the U.S. Air Force Academy's website) provide a fairly accu-

1. Noam Chomsky, *Fateful Triangle: The United States, Israel, and the Palestinians*, updated ed. (Cambridge, Mass: South End Press, 1999), pp. 100–1.

rate picture of the kind of military ethics that is taught to and believed by American military officers.

Although JSCOPE papers are written within a variety of ethical traditions – Kantian, consequentialist, etc. – most are more or less closely related to the just-war tradition. To take one example, Major Richard C. Anderson of the U.S. Military Academy presented a paper in January 2003 shortly before the invasion of Iraq, entitled "Redefining Just War Criteria in the Post-9/11 World and the Moral Consequences of Preemptive Strikes." He relies primarily on Walzer's rendition of just-war theory (JWT), while observing that it "is unique, in that it gives no mention to the traditional JWT criteria of just cause, proper authority, right intention, reasonable chance of success, proportionality of ends, and last resort."

Major Anderson provides an excerpt from President Bush's 2002 West Point graduation address: "Homeland defense and missile defense are part of stronger security, and they're essential priorities for America. Yet the war on terror will not be won on the defensive. We must take the battle to the enemy, disrupt his plans, and confront the worst threats *before they emerge*" (Anderson's emphasis). He then observes: "President Bush's remarks that day were more than just encouraging words to the newest batch of U.S. Army junior leaders. The remarks signaled a dynamic change in our nation's traditional stance regarding preemption and the justified use of force." Anderson's conclusion is that we should not redefine the criteria of just war:

> In order to maintain the moral justification for our response to the 9/11 attacks, and the threats of the post-9/11 world, we must remain committed to our pre-9/11 understanding of JWT. Although we should certainly reevaluate our security posture, and our political and economic relationships with certain countries, we should not change our moral perspectives regarding the difference between just and unjust wars. If we maintain that human rights and dignity are universally inalienable, then we cannot violate the rights of some in order to secure the rights of others; nor can we violate the rights of nations *before* they actually threaten us. Therefore, our JWT is in need of re-affirmation and clarification, not redefinition.[1]

If decisions about whether to go to war were made by soldiers, rather than by politicians, America would fight fewer unjust wars. But we believe in the constitutional principle of "civilian control of the military" (which,

1. Richard C. Anderson, "Redefining Just War Criteria in the Post 9/11 World and the Moral Consequences of Preemptive Strikes," Joint Services Conference on Professional Ethics, January 24, 2003 (http://www.usafa.af.mil/jscope/JSCOPE03/Anderson03.html).

like the constitutional principle of "separation of church and state," cannot be found in the Constitution). Although they may question the words of their Commanders-in-Chief during academic conferences, American officers obey their commands to go to war. And if our recent Commanders-in-Chief have made any attempt to rely on just-war theory to decide when and when not to start wars, they have succeeded in keeping it secret.

The explanation of the U.S. Government's many decisions to involve us in unjust wars is not that just-war theory has been distorted, but that it has been disregarded. In May 1999 during NATO's U.S.-led aerial war of aggression against Yugoslavia, President Clinton wrote an opinion piece for *The New York Times* entitled "A Just and Necessary War." Despite the title, the text of the article has almost nothing whatsoever to do with just-war theory.[1] I am not aware of any attempt by an official of the U.S. Government to justify the invasion of Iraq to the American people in terms of the criteria of just war. The available evidence leads to the conclusion that most officials of the U.S. Government either do not know or do not care that just-war theory exists.

In fact, President Bush and the U.S. Government decided to launch the unjust war against Iraq for a variety of converging reasons that had little to do with just-war criteria. There was no evidence that, even if Saddam Hussein did possess weapons of mass destruction, he was capable of employing them against the United States, or that he contributed to the attacks of September 11, 2001. Perhaps President Bush wished to finish the job that his father had left uncompleted.[2] He may really believe that

1. William Jefferson Clinton, "A Just and Necessary War," *The New York Times*, May 23, 1999. Clinton comes closest to the criteria of just war when he writes, "When the violence in Kosovo began in early 1998, we exhausted every diplomatic avenue for a settlement." But the criterion of last resort was certainly not satisfied. As Richard Becker points out: "The Rambouillet accord, the U.S./NATO 'peace plan' for Kosovo, was presented to Yugoslavia as an ultimatum. It was a 'take it or leave it' proposition, as Albright often emphasized back in February [1999]. There were, in fact, no negotiations at all, and no sovereign, independent state could have signed the Rambouillet agreement" ("The Rambouillet Accord: A Declaration of War Disguised as a Peace Agreement," (http://www.iacenter.org/rambou.htm)). And George Kenney reports: "An unimpeachable press source who regularly travels with Secretary of State Madeleine Albright told this reviewer that, swearing reporters to deep-background confidentiality at the Rambouillet talks, a senior State Department official had bragged that the United States 'deliberately set the bar higher than the Serbs could accept.' The Serbs needed, according to the official, a little bombing to see reason" ("Rolling Thunder: The Rerun," *The Nation*, June 14, 1999, online).

2. The second Iraq war was a continuation of the first, because there was no peace for Iraq during the interim. In a 1996 television interview, a journalist asked Madeleine Albright, then U.S. Ambassador to the UN, concerning the U.S. sanctions against Iraq: "We have heard that a half million children have died. I mean, that's more children than

it is appropriate to invade and occupy a non-democratic country in order to transform it into a democracy. William Engdahl has documented the role of oil in most of the wars fought by Britain and the United States during the twentieth century,[1] and oil certainly played some role in this first Anglo-American war of the twenty-first century.

The reaction of the average American to the war also had little to do with the traditional just-war doctrine. The evidence even suggests that most American Christians are ignorant of just-war theory. It belongs to a larger moral tradition, that of natural law and human virtues, which has been discarded by most Protestants, as well as by those Catholics who are striving to transform the American Catholic Church into the nation's largest Protestant denomination. Thus a complete explanation of the overwhelming support for the war by American citizens, and American Christians in particular (as well as a complete explanation of the decision to go to war itself), must acknowledge the leading role of a quite different "war theory," which was used to justify support for the present Iraq war. This theory is Zionism, including its "Christian" variant.

What is Zionism?

> "The end of the road is coming eventually in Iraq, and once we reach it we will immediately have to take out another road map, this one showing the way to peace between Israel and the Palestinians. The road to Jerusalem runs through Baghdad."
>
> —Michael D. Evans[2]

"Zionism" is defined by the Israeli Ministry of Foreign Affairs as "the national movement espousing repatriation of Jews to their homeland – the Land of Israel – and the resumption of sovereign Jewish life there."[3] The problem, of course, is that other people had been living in this "homeland"

---

died in Hiroshima. And, you know, is the price worth it?" Albright replied: "I think this is a very hard choice, but the price, we think the price is worth it" ("60 Minutes," May 12, 1996).

1. F. William Engdahl, *A Century of War: Anglo-American Oil Politics and the New World Order* (Wiesbaden: Böttiger Verlag, 1993).

2. "For a 'Christian Road Map,'" *The Israel Report*, April, 2003 (http://christianactionforisrael.org/isreport/apr03/isrep03apr.html). Evans is founder of the Jerusalem Prayer Team and the Evangelical Israel Broadcasting Network. See also Robert Kuttner, "Neocons Have Hijacked U.S. Foreign Policy," *Boston Globe*, September 10, 2003, online.

3. Israeli Ministry of Foreign Affairs, "1997 – The 'Year of Zionism'" (http://www.mfa.gov.il/mfa/history/modern%20history/centenary%20of%20Zionism).

for centuries. Establishing the Jewish state involved killing thousands of Palestinians and driving hundreds of thousands from their ancestral homes. Since then, Zionism has sought to expand and secure the borders of Israel. Wars are fought against neighboring countries – in the past with American weapons and money, at present by American soldiers. Arabs are treated as inferior persons – or as less than persons. Homes are razed, families are deported, children are killed, and when Palestinians retaliate, the media portray Israel as the innocent victim of unprovoked hatred. Although atrocities have been committed by both sides, it is not irrelevant to consider which side set the cycle of violence in motion.

The UN General Assembly adopted a resolution declaring Zionism to be racist in 1975, but repealed it in 1991. The standard response to the charge that Zionism is racist is to change the subject: "A world that closed its doors to Jews who sought escape from Hitler's ovens lacks the moral standing to complain about Israel's giving preference to Jews."[1] Chomsky, however, acknowledges the truth:

> The notorious UN Resolution identifying Zionism as a form of racism can properly be condemned for profound hypocrisy, given the nature of the states that backed it (including the Arab states), and (arguably) for referring to Zionism as such rather than the policies of the State of Israel, but restricted to these policies, the resolution cannot be criticized as inaccurate.[2]

It is important for American Christians who believe they have much in common with Israeli Jews to understand that contemporary Jewish Zionism is primarily a secular ideology, the secularization of Jewish messianism. Moses Hess[3] (1812–1875), an important contributor to the early development of both Marxism and Zionism, was a secular Jew, as were such important Zionist writers and leaders as Leo Pinsker (1821–1891), Theodor Herzl (1860–1904), Chaim Weizmann (1874–1952), Vladimir Jabotinsky (1880–1940) and David Ben-Gurion (1886–1973). When leading Christian fundamentalist, Ralph Reed, writes, "Unique among all nations in history, with the exception of Israel, America was settled by persons of faith,"[4] he makes a remarkable claim. In addition to being false on other counts,

---

1. Alan M. Dershowitz, *Chutzpah* (Boston: Little, Brown, & Co., 1991), p. 241.

2. Chomsky, *op. cit.*, p. 158.

3. Hess's crucial work on the subject, first published in German in 1862, is *Rome and Jerusalem: A Study in Jewish Nationalism*, tr. from the German, with introduction and notes, by Meyer Waxman (New York: Bloch Publishing Company, 1918).—Ed.

4. Ralph Reed, *Politically Incorrect: The Emerging Faith Factor in American Politics* (Dallas: Word Publishing, 1994), p. 63.

this statement is inaccurate regarding Israel. A majority of the Jews who settled Israel and a majority of the Jews living in Israel today were and are secular Jews. Martin Buber (1878–1965), a Jewish philosopher-theologian and Zionist, wrote to Mahatma Gandhi in 1939, "I must tell you that you are mistaken when you assume that in general the Jews of today believe in God and derive from their faith guidance for their conduct."[1] Most Jewish Zionists do not and cannot claim that the Jews have a right to the Promised Land, since that would require belief in a Promisor.[2] Among the sites considered for the Jewish national home before the First World War were Argentina and British East Africa. The subsequent decision to establish the homeland in Palestine was not based primarily upon considerations of Jewish theology. Many religious Jews are non-Zionists or anti-Zionists, on the grounds that the Jewish state should be brought about by divine intervention, not the efforts of secular Jews.[3]

Zionism is promoted in the United States by the powerful pro-Israel lobby, which includes the American Israel Public Affairs Committee, the Zionist Organization of America, the American Jewish Committee, the Simon Wiesenthal Center, the Anti-Defamation League of B'nai B'rith, Americans for a Safe Israel, and the Jewish Institute for National Security Affairs. It is also promoted by the so-called "neoconservatives" – Paul Wolfowitz, Douglas Feith, Richard Perle, *et al.* – who played leading roles in bringing about the invasion of Iraq.

In May 2004, Senator Ernest "Fritz" Hollings of South Carolina wrote for the *Charleston Post and Courier*:

> With 760 dead in Iraq and over 3,000 maimed for life, home folks continue to argue why we are in Iraq – and how to get out. Now everyone knows what was not the cause. Even President Bush acknowledges that Saddam Hussein had nothing to do with 9/11 . . . . Of course there were no weapons of mass

---

1. Martin Buber, "The Land and Its Possessors," in Buber, *Israel and the World: Essays in a Time of Crisis*, 2nd ed. (New York: Schocken Books, 1963), p. 230.

2. Even the Zionism of a religious Jew such as Buber is not based upon the promise of the land, but on the need for Jews to live together: "What is decisive for us is not the promise of the Land, but the demand, whose fulfilment is bound up with the land, with the existence of a free Jewish community in this country. For the Bible tells us, and our inmost knowledge testifies to it, that once more than three thousand years ago our entry into this land took place with the consciousness of a mission from above to set up a just way of life through the generations of our people, a way of life that cannot be realized by individuals in the sphere of their private existence, but only by a nation in the establishment of its society" (Buber, *ibid.*, p. 229).

3. Three organizations of non-Zionist Jews are Jews Not Zionists (http://www.jewsnotZionists.org), Jews Against Zionism (http://www.jewsagainstZionism.com), and Neturei-Karta (http://www.nkusa.org).

destruction. Israel's intelligence, Mossad, knows what's going on in Iraq. They are the best. They have to know. Israel's survival depends on knowing. Israel long since would have taken us to the weapons of mass destruction if there were any or if they had been removed. With Iraq no threat, why invade a sovereign country? The answer: President Bush's policy to secure Israel. Led by [Paul] Wolfowitz, Richard Perle and Charles Krauthammer, for years there has been a domino school of thought that the way to guarantee Israel's security is to spread democracy in the area.[1]

Although it is doubtful that the neoconservatives desire a democratic Iraq, it is true that the purpose of the war was to promote Israel's security. Our Department of "Defense" has become an instrument of Israeli foreign policy, employed to further the aims of Zionism. It may seem remarkable that a member of the U.S. Government would speak so straightforwardly about Israel. But Hollings, who has represented his state in the Senate since 1966, decided to retire from the Senate and spoke candidly during what was his final term.

The standard response to anyone who tells the truth about the pro-Israel lobby, Israel, and Zionism is to accuse him of "anti-Semitism." As retired CIA officer Bill Christison puts it, "Supporters of Bush have launched a two-pronged counterattack, arguing first that the influence of the neocons over U.S. foreign policy is a myth and, second, that if you are dumb enough to believe the myth, it is almost a sure thing that you are also an anti-Semite."[2] Chomsky comments:

> It might be noted that the resort to charges of "anti-Semitism" (or in the case of Jews, "Jewish self-hatred") to silence critics of Israel has been quite a general and often effective device. Even Abba Eban, the highly-regarded Israeli diplomat of the Labor Party (considered a leading dove), is capable of writing that "One of the chief tasks of any dialogue with the Gentile world is to prove that the distinction between anti-Semitism and anti-Zionism [generally understood as criticism of the policies of the Israeli state] is not a distinction at all."[3]

Much progress is being made in accomplishing this task. The "Joint Declaration of the 18th International Catholic-Jewish Liaison Committee

---

1. Ernest F. Hollings, "Bush's Failed Mideast Policy is Creating More Terrorism," *Charleston Post and Courier*, May 6, 2004 (online at http://www.aljazeerah.info/Opinion%20editorials/2004%20opinions/May/8o/Bush's%20failed%20Mideast%20policy%20is%20creating%20more%20terrorism%20By%20Senator%20Ernest%20F%20Hollings.htm).

2. Bill Christison, "Faltering Neo-Cons Still Dangerous: How They Might Influence the Election," *CounterPunch.org*, March 5, 2004.

3. Chomsky, *op. cit.*, p. 15. The parenthetical remark "generally understood as criticism of policies of the Israeli state" is Chomsky's.

Meeting" of July 2004 states: "We draw encouragement from the fruits of our collective strivings which include the recognition of the unique and unbroken covenantal relationship between God and the Jewish People and the total rejection of anti-Semitism in all its forms, including anti-Zionism as a more recent manifestation of anti-Semitism."[1] Anti-Semitism, if understood as hatred of Jews, is a sin, inconsistent with the virtue of charity, without which no one can be saved. But opposing an unethical ideology does not require hating anyone; it may in fact be an act of charity toward its victims. One can be an anti-Zionist without being an anti-Semite, just as one can be a Jew without being a Zionist:

> Jews believe that Adam was created in G-d's image and that he is the common ancestor of all mankind. At this stage in human history, there is no room for privileged people who can do with others as they please. Human life is sacred and human rights are not to be denied by those who would subvert them for "national security" or for any other reason. No one knows this better than the Jews, who have been second-class citizens so often and for so long. Some Zionists, however, may differ. This is understandable because Judaism and Zionism are by no means the same. Indeed they are incompatible and irreconcilable: if one is a good Jew, one cannot be a Zionist; if one is a Zionist, one cannot be a good Jew.[2]

Not surprisingly, Hollings was accused of anti-Semitism. With the courage of a politician freed from the fear that the pro-Israel lobby would destroy a future re-election campaign, he responded on the floor of the Senate:

> I have, this afternoon, the opportunity to respond to being charged as anti-Semitic when I proclaimed the policy of President Bush in the Mideast as not for Iraq or really for democracy.... I can tell you no President takes office – I don't care whether it is a Republican or a Democrat – that all of a sudden AIPAC [the American Israel Public Affairs Committee] will tell him exactly what the policy is.... Yes, I supported the President on this Iraq resolution, but I was misled. There weren't any weapons, or any terrorism, or al-Qaeda. This is the reason we went to war. He had one thought in mind, and that was re-election.[3]

---

1. The 18th International Catholic-Jewish Liaison Committee Meeting, "Joint Declaration," Buenos Aires, July 5–8, 2004.

2. G. Neuburger, "The Difference between Judaism and Zionism" (http://www.jews-notZionists.org/differencejudzion.html).

3. Ernest F. Hollings, "Senator Hollings Floor Statement Setting the Record Straight on his Mideast Newspaper Column," May 20, 2004 (http://hollings.senate.gov/~hollings/statements/2004521A35.html).

Christian Zionism

The Jewish Zionists who succeeded in persuading America to fight a war for the security of Israel owe much of their success to the support of Christian Zionists.[1] Tens of millions of American Christians, most of whom are opponents of secular Jews on issues such as abortion and "homosexual marriage," allied themselves with Jewish Zionists in supporting their country's unjust war of aggression against Iraq. Christian Zionist spokesmen, such as television show host and former presidential candidate Pat Robertson, use the Bible to defend political stances alongside those of secular-Jewish Zionists:

> Israel is the spiritual capitol [sic] of the world. This is what God calls the navel of the earth in the Old Testament. Why are all of the nations so concerned about Israel? I will tell you why. Because it is God's outpost, and it would be, in a sense, a black eye against Him if His plans were frustrated by human beings. And He will not let people frustrate His plan.
> ... There is no such thing as a Palestine state, nor has there ever been. Now we're going to make something that never happened before in contravention to Scripture. God may love George Bush. God may love America. God may love us all, but if we stand in the way of prophecy and try to frustrate what God said in His immutable word, then we're in for a heap of trouble. And I think this is a warning we should all take.
> This road map, as it is set up now, with the United Nations, with the European Union, and with the Russians coming together in the so-called Quartet, these are all enemies of Israel. If we ally ourselves with the enemies of Israel, we will be standing against God Almighty. And that's a place I don't want us to be.[2]

This writer was raised as an evangelical Protestant and Christian Zionist. My childhood memories include the joy with which news of Israel's victory in the Six-Day War was received in my thoroughly Protestant hometown (as well as jokes, such as the one about Egyptian tanks having five speeds, one forward and four reverse). We were witnessing the fulfillment of biblical prophecy. I converted after being introduced to the Catholic intellectual tradition and coming to the realization that Protestantism is fundamentally irrational – a fact that some Protestants acknowledge and regard as a virtue. Many Protestants, not only Lutherans, reject Church Tradition and believe the Bible only. This is irrational, because the doc-

1. Among the more prominent Christian Zionists are Jerry Falwell, Pat Robertson, Gary Bauer, James Dobson, Tim and Beverly LaHaye, Ralph Reed, Franklin Graham, Kay Arthur, and D. James Kennedy.
2. Pat Robertson, "On Israel and the Road Map to Peace," *Christian Broadcasting Network*, 2004 (http://www.patrobertson.com/Teaching/TeachingonRoadMap.asp).

trine of *sola Scriptura* cannot be found in Scripture, only in Protestant tradition. Among the other irrational beliefs of many American fundamentalist and evangelical Protestants – not unrelated to *sola Scriptura* – is Christian Zionism.

A concise statement of the central beliefs of Christian Zionism is provided by Joseph Farah of *WorldNetDaily.com*. He asks – "Why do American Christians support Israel so loyally and enthusiastically?" – and then replies:

> 1. The strong evangelical church in America can read the Bible and see that the Jews' only historic home is in Israel.
> 2. Most Christians understand that Jesus was a Jew who lived in a Jewish state, albeit one under the colonial rule of the Roman Empire.
> 3. They understand that God chose to reveal Himself to the Jewish people and the nation of Israel.
> 4. They don't see a nation of Palestine mentioned in the Old Testament or New – with good reason: it never existed before or since, except in the imaginations of people like Yasser Arafat.
> 5. They believe God made certain promises to the nation of Israel and that today's Jewish state is a manifestation of those promises.
> 6. They understand that their Holy Scriptures indicate God will bless those who bless Israel and curse those who curse it. They don't want to be on the wrong side of that spiritual equation.
> 7. They understand their own salvation, in the person of Jesus, chose to come through the House of David and minister principally to the Jews.
> 8. They grasp that the Jews alone – with the help of God, of course – have made the deserts bloom in that Holy land, just as the prophets predicted.
> 9. They comprehend that the Jews alone formed a free society in the Middle East.
> 10. They can see that Israel has been an ally to the United States and a friend to the free world throughout its 50-year history of rebirth.[1]

The Intertwined Histories of Jewish and Christian Zionism

Although I have distinguished Jewish and Christian Zionism, their respective histories are so intertwined that they should be regarded as a common history. Zionism is a single genus with a variety of species, some religious and some secular, some Jewish and some non-Jewish. The historical roots of Zionism as a political movement are found primarily in the history of Protestantism, only secondarily in Jewish traditions:

> From the days of the Reformation to the ascent of Napoleon III in France and the digging of the Suez Canal, there were no Jewish leaders in the Zionism

---

1. Joseph Farah, "The Jewish Lobby?" *WorldNetDaily.com*, January 27, 2003.

movement, despite repeated British and French attempts to recruit them. The non-Jewish origin of Zionism is further illustrated by the simple fact that the ideas of Restoration developed first in England (with no Jewish population) instead of Germany, Poland, or Russia (where the bulk of European Jewry lived).[1]

A complete account of the origin and development of Zionism would have to include discussion of many factors: geopolitical, commercial, military, etc. In order to understand the kind of Christian Zionism that motivated so many Americans to support the invasion of Iraq, however, it is necessary to focus on theological factors. Christian Zionism can be best understood as the *reductio ad absurdum* of *sola Scriptura*.

Donald Wagner identifies several British, Protestant "proto-Christian Zionists":

> One of the early expressions of fascination with the idea of Israel was the monograph *Apocalypsis Apocalypseos*, written by Anglican clergyman Thomas Brightman in 1585. Brightman urged the British people to support the return of the Jews to Palestine in order to hasten a series of prophetic events that would culminate in the return of Jesus. In 1621, a prominent member of the British Parliament, attorney Henry Finch, advanced a similar perspective when he wrote: "The (Jews) shall repair to their own country, shall inherit all of the land as before, shall live in safety, and shall continue in it forever." Finch argued that based on his interpretation of Genesis 12:3, God would bless those nations that supported the Jews' return.[2]

Among the most important figures in the history of Zionism is John Nelson Darby (1800–82), who left the Anglican priesthood to join the Plymouth Brethren. This "non-denominational" denomination "taught the priesthood of all believers, therefore had no pastor, but depended upon the Holy Spirit for their leadership."[3] It also stood squarely in the tradition of *sola Scriptura*: "In no uncertain terms the Brethren proclaimed the Scriptures to be absolutely inspired by God and the sole authority for faith and practice."[4]

---

1. Mohameden Ould-Mey, "The Non-Jewish Origin of Zionism," *The Arab World Geographer*, Vol. 5, No. 1 (2002), pp. 34–52. Ould-Mey goes on to document the fact that there were indeed some Jews in England during the seventeenth and eighteenth centuries, though extremely few.

2. Donald E. Wagner, "The History of Christian Zionism," *The Daily Star* (Beirut), October 7, 2003, online.

3. Miles J. Stanford, "The Plymouth Brethren – A Brief History" (http://withchrist.org/MJS/pbs.htm).

4. Stanford, *loc. cit.*

Darby contributed to the development of a theological system known as "premillennial dispensationalism" (or "dispensational premillennialism"). It is "dispensational" because Scripture and history are compartmentalized into different dispensations of grace, and "premillennial" because it teaches that the Second Advent of Christ will take place before the millennium. The scriptural authority for compartmentalizing Scripture in this manner is 2 Tim. II:15: "Do your best to present yourself to God as one approved, a workman who has no need to be ashamed, rightly handling [King James Version: 'dividing'] the word of truth." Divorced from Tradition, Scripture can say anything anyone wants it to say.

Although there exists some disagreement among dispensationalists regarding the number of dispensations, the most common listing includes seven:

1. The Age of Innocence (Creation to the Fall).

2. The Age of Conscience (Fall to Noah).

3. The Age of Human Government (Noah to Abraham).

4. The Age of Promise (Abraham to Moses).

5. The Age of Law (Moses to the Crucifixion).

6. The Age of Grace (Crucifixion to the Second Advent).

7. The Age of Christ's Millennial Kingdom.

Among Darby's theological innovations is the "rapture" (popularized today by Tim LaHaye and Jerry Jenkins's series of novels about those "left behind"). At some moment in time, according to this doctrine, all Christian believers will suddenly be removed from the earth. This rapture of the church will be followed by seven years of tribulation, the Battle of Armageddon, the Second Advent of Christ and Christ's thousand-year reign on earth, centered in Jerusalem. Darby's scriptural basis for the doctrine of the rapture is 1 Thess. iv:16–17: "For the Lord himself will descend from heaven with a cry of command, with the archangel's call, and with the sound of the trumpet of God. And the dead in Christ will rise first; then we who are alive, who are left, shall be caught up together with them in the clouds to meet the Lord in the air; and so we shall always be with the Lord." Deriving the rapture from these verses obviously requires extraordinary skill in "reading between the lines."

Darby's theology was criticized by a number of his contemporaries. In an attempt to reconcile it with the Bible, Darby made a distinction between

Scripture intended for Jews and Scripture intended for Christians: "The doctrine of the separation of Israel and the Church, the foundation of dispensationalism, was born out of Darby's attempt to justify his newly fabricated rapture theory with the Bible."[1]

Dispensationalism is opposed to Protestant traditions of "supersessionism" or "replacement theology," according to which the New Covenant has superseded or replaced the Old. For dispensationalists, the Jews continue along a track of prophecy parallel to that of Christians. Darby "placed a restored Israel at the center of his theology, claiming that an actual Jewish state called Israel would become the central instrument for God to fulfill His plans during the last days of history."[2]

Dispensationalists understand that their system conflicts with Catholic theology and with "supersessionism" generally:

> 1 Corinthians 10:32 plainly states that there are three categories of men in the world today: "Give none offense, neither to the Jews, nor to the Gentiles, nor to the Church of God." Obviously, then, Israel is not the same as the church. This is a very, very important matter for the Bible student to understand. Some of the most common errors in theology have come about through confusing the church with Israel.
>
> This is one of the errors of Roman Catholicism. Rome claims to be the new Israel and has adopted many things from the Old Testament dispensation, such as priests, temples, candles, incense, sprinkling of water, and many other things. This is one reason why Rome attempted to take over the Holy Land during the crusades of the Middle Ages. It is also why Rome has opposed Israel's desire to control Jerusalem.[3]

In 1909, Cyrus I. Scofield (1843–1921) published an edition of the King James Bible with premillennial dispensationalist notations. (Scofield read some of Darby's writings while doing time for forgery.) The *Scofield Reference Bible* has been extremely popular among American fundamentalist Protestants ever since and is still available today from Oxford University Press. It contributed to an increase in the interpretation of current events as fulfillment of biblical prophecy and signs of the imminent end of the present dispensation. Among the leading contemporary centers of premillennial dispensationalism are the Moody Bible Institute in Chicago and Dallas Theological Seminary.

---

1. Jack Van Deventer, "Eschaton: The Dispensational Origins of Modern Premillennialism," *Credenda/Agenda*, Vol. 7, No. 3, online.

2. Wagner, *loc. cit.*

3. David Cloud, "Study the Bible Dispensationally," Fundamental Baptist Information Service, October 4, 2004 (http://www.wayoflife.org/fbns/studybible-dispensation.html).

Another chapter in the intertwining of the histories of Protestant and Jewish Zionism is the relationship between Scofield and Samuel Untermeyer (1858–1940), a wealthy New York lawyer and Jewish Zionist. In addition to being Chairman of the American Jewish Committee and President of the American League of Jewish Patriots, Untermeyer also played a leading role in the campaign to involve the U.S. in the First World War against Germany. (The unjust terms of the Treaty of Versailles at the end of that war led to the conditions that prepared the way for Hitler to come to power.) Untermeyer used Scofield, a Kansas City lawyer with no formal training in theology, to inject Zionist ideas into American Protestantism. Untermeyer and other wealthy and influential Zionists whom he introduced to Scofield promoted and funded the latter's career, including travel in Europe. The notations in the *Scofield Reference Bible* are in fact a mix of premillenial dispensationalist and Jewish Zionist (including Kabbalistic) ideas. And, according to a recent book by Michael Collins Piper, some have charged that "Schofield's dispensationalism was actively promoted and funded by the Rothschild family of Europe, for the very purpose of advancing the Zionist cause and for fostering a push for an imperial global order quite similar indeed to the policies being pursued by the "neoconservative" elements in the Bush administration in alliance with the Christian right."[1]

Although theological considerations were not central to the decision by Jewish Zionists to establish their national home in Palestine, since most of them were not theists, the contributions of many British and other Christians to that decision were, in fact, based upon theological beliefs. Arthur Balfour, "the strongest and most influential advocate of Zionism which that movement had,"[2] was a Christian Zionist, raised in a dispensationalist church. His 1917 "Balfour Declaration" calls itself a "declaration of sympathy with Jewish Zionist aspirations" and states that "His Majesty's Government view with favor the establishment in Palestine of a national home for the Jewish people."

The Fuse of Armageddon

In 1970, premillennial dispensationalist Hal Lindsey of Dallas Theological Seminary published a little book entitled *The Late Great Planet Earth*. It has sold more than twenty-five million copies and has contributed significantly to the popularity of Zionism among Christians,

---

1. *The High Priests of War* (Washington, D.C.: American Free Press, 2004), pp 79–80.
2. "Obituary: Balfour a Leader for Half a Century," *New York Times*, March 20, 1930.

including many belonging to Protestant traditions other than premillennial dispensationalism. According to Lindsey, 1948 marked the beginning of the end of the world as we know it:

> Some time in the future there will be a seven-year period climaxed by the visible return of Jesus Christ. Most prophecies which have not yet been fulfilled concern events which will develop shortly before the beginning of and during this seven-year countdown. The general time of this seven-year period couldn't begin until the Jewish people reestablished their nation in their ancient homeland of Palestine.[1]

Israel is, for Lindsey, the "fuse of Armageddon," because three events must take place there before that battle: the restoration of Israel as a nation in Palestine, the repossession of ancient Jerusalem and the sacred sites, and the rebuilding of the temple upon its historic site. Lindsey cites Christ's words in Matthew 24 as his primary scriptural basis for regarding present events in the Middle East as the fulfillment of biblical prophecy: "When Jesus looks into the future and describes the conditions which would prevail at His coming, He puts the Jews back in the land as a nation."[2] Lindsey finds "an extremely important time clue" in Matt. 24, 32–33: "From the fig tree learn its lesson: as soon as its branch becomes tender and puts forth its leaves, you know that summer is near. So also, when you see all these things, you know that He is near, at the very gates." A straightforward reading of these two sentences would seem to be that the meaning of the first is explained by the second. Lindsey, however, provides the following gloss:

> When the signs just given begin to multiply and increase in scope it's similar to the certainty of leaves coming on the fig tree. But the most important sign in Matthew has to be the restoration of the Jews to the land in the rebirth of Israel. Even the figure of speech "fig tree" has been a historic symbol of national Israel. When the Jewish people, after nearly 2,000 years of exile, under relentless persecution, became a nation again on 14 May 1948 the "fig tree" put forth its first leaves. Jesus said that this would indicate that He was "at the door," ready to return. Then He said, "Truly I say to you, *this generation* will not pass away until all these things take place" (Matthew 24:34 NASB). What generation? Obviously, in context, the generation that would see the signs – chief among them the rebirth of Israel. A generation in the Bible is something like forty years. If this is a correct deduction, then within forty years or so of 1948, all these things could take place.[3]

1. Hal Lindsey with C. C. Carlson, *The Late Great Planet Earth* (Grand Rapids, Mich: Zondervan Publishing House, 1970), p. 42.
2. *Ibid.*, p. 53.
3. *Ibid.*, pp. 53–54.

The second event in Lindsey's fuse of Armageddon occurred nineteen years later:

> In March and April of 1967 . . . I said that if this was the time that I thought it was, then somehow the Jews were going to have to repossess old Jerusalem. Many chuckled about that statement. Then came the war of June 1967 – the phenomenal Israeli six-day blitz. I was personally puzzled as to the significance of it all until the third day of fighting when Moshe Dayan, the ingenious Israeli general, marched to the Wailing Wall, the last remnant of the Old Temple, and said, "We have returned to our holiest of holy places, never to leave her again."[1]

Since two of the three events that will precede Armageddon have now taken place, the fuse is short – though apparently not as short as Lindsey expected.

One problem for Christian Zionists who believe that the land that was recently called "Palestine" and is now called "Israel and the Occupied Territories" belongs to the Jews, not the Palestinians, is determining who is a Jew. Lindsey assumes that contemporary Jews are descendants of the Hebrew patriarchs: "We see the Jews as a miracle of history. Even the casual observer is amazed how the descendants of Abraham, Isaac, and Jacob have survived as a distinct race in spite of the most formidable odds. What other people can trace their continuous unity back nearly 4,000 years?"[2] According to Jews, however, one can become a Jew in either of two ways: by being born to a Jewish mother or by converting to Judaism. The matrilineal descendants of converts to the Jewish religion are Jews, even if they do not believe in the Jewish religion. Many Israeli Jews, especially those who immigrated from Russia and other Eastern European countries, are not descendants of Abraham, Isaac, and Jacob, but of converts to Judaism. If Jews have a right to the land of Israel because the Bible says so, does that include descendants of converts to the Jewish religion? What about descendants of "converts" from Christianity to Judaism? Do such Jews have a right to dispossess Palestinian Christians of their land?

Christian Zionist Interpretations of the Iraq War

Although most Christian Zionists supported the invasion of Iraq, there is disagreement among them concerning how exactly it fits into biblical prophecy. The website of Paw Creek Ministries in Charlotte, North

---

1. *Ibid.*, p. 55.
2. *Ibid.*, p. 45.

Carolina tells us that we are conquering and eliminating the enemies of Israel in Iraq:

> Presently, we are eliminating Israel's enemies in Iraq. This is important because Iraq will be the center of the New World Order and Israel will make a treaty with the false messiah. That seven-year treaty will be broken in the middle of the seven years. Jesus said it like this, "When ye therefore shall see the abomination of desolation, spoken of by Daniel the prophet, stand in the holy place, (whoso readeth, let him understand) . . . . For then shall be great tribulation, such as was not since the beginning of the world to this time, no, nor ever shall be" (Matthew 24:15,21). There has to be a truce between the government of Israel and the government of Iraq for this treaty to be enacted and then broken.
>
> Who is the President best fitted to defend Israel, to conquer the enemies in Iraq and to set the stage for prophecy? President George W. Bush is the only man . . . .
>
> Bible Prophecy is unalterable truth set in the halls of heaven. It cannot vary. Israel is going to be safe until the middle of this Great Tribulation but will survive the relentless attack of the Antichrist. Iraq must be in place to become the center of the Antichrist Kingdom. Israel will have America as her defender even when the Antichrist seeks to eliminate every Jew from the face of the earth. The terrorists that claim Allah as their god will help lead this campaign of Jewish eradication, but they will fail.
>
> . . . A Biblical prophecy almost totally unknown by Bible teachers is that the Antichrist will be an Assyrian and that an Assyrian nation will develop at the end of God's judgment. This nation will be one of the three major nations in the Middle East during the millennial reign. The movements in Iraq have already caused the ancient Assyrians that number in the thousands and spread over many nations to start yearning for their own independent self-government and homeland. There has been no self-governed nation of Assyria for over two thousand years, yet the Creator Jehovah has preserved this ancient culture for His End Time plan.
>
> . . . It's exciting to have spiritual eyes capable of watching prophecy being fulfilled.[1]

Exciting indeed! But how can one be confident that one's spiritual vision is clear, when others with spiritual eyes see the situation differently? According to LaHaye, the war is not about conquering and eliminating enemies, but about liberating people who will become neither friend nor foe:

> Dr. Tim LaHaye, co-author of the popular *Left Behind* series of Christian novels, says world events are pointing to the Middle East in general and Israel

---

1. "George W. Bush and Bible Prophecy," April 2004 (http://www.pawcreek.org/articles/pna/GeorgeWBushAndBibleProphecy.htm). The author does not reveal the identity of the "Biblical prophecy almost totally unknown by Bible teachers."

in particular as the center for prophesied future world events. And he says Iraq will play a prominent role in upcoming events leading to Christ's return . . . .

The author and theologian says the war to liberate Iraq will pave the way for that nation eventually to emerge as a world power. As the region comes into its own, he says the people of Iraq will want to develop a distinct identity and in the last days old Babylon will become a sort of "Switzerland" for the world, a neutral country.

According to LaHaye, in chapters 38 and 39 in the book of Ezekiel, the one Arab nation not mentioned among those that come against Jerusalem when God destroys Russia and the Arab world, is Iraq. He says scripture suggests that Iraq is going to rise to prominence, but "won't be involved in that awful destruction that will solve the Arab problem temporarily."

LaHaye feels now is an exciting time to be a Christian because the Rapture is imminent.[1]

It is good to know how LaHaye feels. But it would be better if the rational part of the soul were involved in relating Scripture to the world in which we live.

R. A. Coombes, of *The Alpha-Omega Report,* has a different interpretation of the passage in Ezekiel and believes that America, not Iraq, is old Babylon:

America's invasion of Iraq created American control over the ancient site of Babylon and the old nation of Babylonia. America, in effect, has become "Babylon." This is a fact that has been ignored by most American Bible Prophecy commentators. Today, America controls Babylon as a conquering nation. From a prophetic perspective, America IS Babylon . . . .

It should be obvious to Bible Prophecy commentators that Iraq is not to be the fulfillment of Mystery Babylon prophecies if indeed we are approaching the "Last Days." To that end, some other nation must be Mystery Babylon because Gulf War 2 ruined any possible chance that Iraq might be miraculously transformed into a World Super-Power leader and thus be Mystery Babylon . . . .

The Second Gulf War has not adversely affected the prophecies regarding Israel's Messianic Kingdom boundaries. While contamination by depleted uranium is a current problem, it will be no problem for direct, Divine clean-up work by the Creator-god Himself. In fact, the prophecies indicate probably far greater contamination from the Gog-Magog war than what has taken place so far in Iraq. That will not be a problem for Israel then and the Iraqi "depleted uranium" issue will likely be less of a problem for Israel (See Ezekiel 38–39) . . . .

Gulf War 2 may well have taken western Iraq out of the equation for massive destruction of the Arab alliance of nations led by Iran against Israel. Eastern

---

1. Allie Martin, "'Left Behind' Author Says Iraq Will Be Prominent in End-Times Events," *AgapePress.org*, November 19, 2003.

portions of Iraq – closely aligned now with Iran – may suffer the same results as Iran and other Islamic confederated nations that war against Israel and the Lord. Thus, Gulf War 2 may have played a part in minimizing damage in order that it will be readily absorbed by Israel's Messianic Kingdom.

All told, we can see these elements as important consequences of Gulf War 2 upon Biblical Prophecy . . . . If we stumble across more revelations of this nature, we will bring it to your attention.[1]

It is unsurprising that Christian Zionists disagree with one another in interpreting biblical prophecy, since Protestants disagree with one another regarding every other point of theology. Griffith Thomas commented on the splintering of Darby's Plymouth Brethren into opposing factions, "The Brethren are remarkable people for rightly dividing the Word of Truth and wrongly dividing themselves!"[2] If these mutually-inconsistent interpretations of scriptural prophecy were not relevant to decisions about people's lives, they could be dismissed as nonsense or read for entertainment. But tens of thousands of soldiers and civilians have died as a consequence of our invasion of Iraq.[3] Since this was an unjust war of aggression, those who are responsible for it – with a government of, by, and for the people, not a small number – have innocent blood on their hands. This is no laughing matter.

Christian Zionists and National Policy

To point out that Christian Zionists supported the invasion of Iraq in large numbers is not to subscribe to any "conspiracy theory," according to which all of them did so as part of an orchestrated campaign. There are hundreds of Christian Zionist organizations in the United States.[4] A single

---

1. R. A. Coombes, "Prophetic Implications of Gulf War 2 upon Bible Prophecy," *The Alpha-Omega Report*, December 19, 2004, online.

2. Stanford, *loc. cit.*

3. One team of researchers concluded in October 2004 that "the death toll associated with the invasion and occupation of Iraq is probably about 100,000 people, and may be much higher" (Les Roberts *et al.*, "Mortality Before and After the 2003 Invasion of Iraq: Cluster Sample Survey," *The Lancet*, Vol. 364, 2004, pp. 1857–64, published online October 29, 2004 at http://image.thelancet.com/ extras/04art10342web.pdf). This includes only civilian deaths, not the thousands of Iraqi soldiers who died in defense of their country.

4. The National Unity Coalition for Israel claims to include more than two hundred Jewish and Christian organizations. Among the more important Christian Zionist organizations are the International Christian Embassy Jerusalem, the National Christian Leadership Conference for Israel, Christians for Israel, Christian Friends of Israel, Christian Friends of Israeli Communities, Christians United for Israel, Christian Action for Israel, Stand for Israel, Bridges for Peace, Chosen People Ministries, and the International Christian Zionist Center.

Protestant denomination claims by itself to represent 3.5 million Israel-loving Americans.[1] Tens of millions of American Christians, belonging to a wide variety of religious organizations and theological traditions, supported the war and were influenced in doing so by their theological beliefs.

Opinion polls by various organizations show that the invasion of Iraq was supported by Protestants more than by Catholics, and by evangelical Protestants more than by mainline Protestants: "A nationwide survey March 13–16 [2003] by the Pew Research Center and the Pew Forum on Religion and Public Life showed that 62 percent of Catholics and the same percentage of mainline Protestants support the war . . . . The Pew sample showed 77 percent of evangelical Christians supporting the war."[2]

Estimates of the number of evangelical or "born-again" Protestants in the United States vary widely, with most falling somewhere between 40 and 80 million. Making a precise estimate is complicated by disagreement about what qualifies one for membership in these categories. Whatever the exact count, their numbers are so large that no presidential candidate can avoid taking their views seriously: "U.S. evangelicals, many of whom proudly refer to themselves as Christian Zionists, are clearly on the upswing. According to the Pew Research Center, evangelical Protestants accounted for 23 percent of the entire American electorate, or nearly one out of every four voters, in the recent [2004] election."[3] The percentages of affirmative responses to the Gallup Poll question "Would you describe yourself as a 'born-again' or evangelical Christian?" were 44% in 2001, 46% in 2002, and 42% in 2003.[4]

It may seem surprising that so many "conservative" Protestants are Christian Zionists, when premillennial dispensationalism is only one of a multitude of Protestant traditions. Part of the explanation is that there has evolved a generic evangelicalism of Protestants who find more in com-

---

1. See Ken Silverstein and Michael Scherer, "Born-Again Zionists," *Mother Jones*, September/October 2002, online. The authors quote Thomas Lindberg, pastor of the Memphis First Assembly of God Church, who, reflecting upon a tour he led to Israel, said, " . . . let me say today that we — and when I say 'we,' I represent the Assemblies of God here in America, three and a half million of us, 42 million Assemblies of God people around the globe — we love Israel."

2. Mark O'Keefe, "Church Leaders' Anti-War Message Fails in the Pews," *Newhouse News Service*, April 9, 2003, online.

3. Michael Freund, "Onward Christian Voters," *Jerusalem Post*, November 16, 2004, online.

4. Frank Newport, "A Look at Americans and Religion Today," Gallup Poll, March 23, 2004.

mon with evangelicals of other Protestant traditions than with "liberals" in their own. For example, I was raised within the evangelical wing of the Wesleyan, Methodist tradition, which regards the majority of United Methodists as apostates. But the books I was encouraged to read included more from outside than within the tradition of John Wesley. "Brand loyalty" is small and diminishing among evangelicals. Many search for pastors, churches, books, magazines, radio and television programs that seem to be biblical and meet their needs, with little concern for distinctions among the many subdivisions of Protestant theology. This has enabled Christian Zionist ideas to spread to tens of millions of evangelicals who are not premillennial dispensationalists.

Even in the absence of direct influence on the U.S. Government, Christian Zionists exert influence by their voting power. Their numbers are large and they overwhelmingly support Israel in its relations with its neighbors. According to *The Washington Post*, "In an online survey of U.S. evangelicals after [the March 2004] attack on Sheik Ahmed Yassin, 89 percent of the 1,630 respondents supported the killing of the Hamas leader – compared with the 61 percent of Israelis who supported the attack in a survey by the newspaper *Maariv*."[1] But there is also evidence of more direct influence.

On September 20, 2001, nine days after the al-Qaeda attacks, neoconservative William Kristol of the Project for the New American Century sent a letter to President Bush, calling for the inclusion of Iraq in the war against terrorism: "It may be that the Iraqi government provided assistance in some form to the recent attack on the United States. But even if evidence does not link Iraq directly to the attack, any strategy aiming at the eradication of terrorism and its sponsors must include a determined effort to remove Saddam Hussein from power in Iraq." The letter is signed by several dozen neoconservatives, but also by Christian Zionist Gary Bauer. The inclusion of a leader of several evangelical organizations appears to have been a signal that more than his one vote was behind a policy of military action against Iraq.

Christian Zionist organizations also conduct letter-writing campaigns to communicate their views to our Government: "When Israel invaded the West Bank in April 2002 following the Passover bombings, President Bush urged Ariel Sharon to withdraw from Jenin. Christian Zionists mobilized an email campaign that produced 100,000 letters for Washington. And

---

1. Bill Broadway, "The Evangelical-Israeli Connection," *Washington Post*, March 27, 2004, online.

it worked. Bush never said another word."[1] Other grassroots-level activities by Christian Zionists on behalf of Israel include "spending millions on everything from armored school buses for Israeli children to halogen lights for the army's emergency-rescue service. There are email chains, prayer ministries and grassroots efforts to get the word out that the U.S. must stand united with its ally in the war on terror."[2]

According to *The Washington Post*, "The White House held a private briefing for 141 evangelical Christian leaders March 27 [2003] to discuss the Iraq war and other subjects."[3] President Bush himself is, of course, an evangelical Protestant. His stances on issues such as embryonic stem-cell research and "homosexual marriage" suggest that he is serious about acting in a manner consistent with his theological beliefs. Unfortunately, he has chosen a theological tradition that values Christian Zionist thinking more than just-war theory.

Perhaps the most outspoken evangelical Christian Zionist in our government is House Majority Leader DeLay, who calls himself "an Israeli at heart."[4] In July 2003 he told an audience in Jerusalem: "Brothers and sisters of Israel, be not afraid. The American people stand with you, and so does our President." Aryeh Eldad, a member of the National Union Party, said afterwards, "Until I heard him speak, I thought I was farthest to the right in the Knesset."[5] DeLay strongly supported the invasion of Iraq, and it is reasonable to assume that he used his position to influence other congressmen to do so as well.

In April 2003 DeLay delivered the keynote address at a Stand for Israel rally:

> Something extraordinary is happening on the other side of the world. Hundreds of thousands of trained and dedicated volunteers, an army of virtue, are liberating a nation. Mile by mile, a blood-thirsty dictator's grip on a noble people slips. Town by town, Iraqi families realize what the smiling men in camouflage uniforms have won for them. And day by day, children awaken, for the first morning of their lives, to G-d's freedom. This is the meaning of

---

1. Gary M. Burge, "Christian Zionism, Evangelicals and Israel," The Holy Land Christian Ecumenical Foundation (http://www.hcef.org/hcef/index.cfm/ID/159).

2. Nancy Gibbs, "Is It Good for the Jews?" *TIME Magazine*, July 1, 2002, online.

3. Dana Milbank, "An Answer? Out of the Question," *Washington Post*, April 22, 2003, online.

4. James Bennet, "Palestinians Must Bear Burden of Peace, DeLay Tells Israelis," *New York Times*, July 30, 2003, online.

5. Megan K. Stack, "House's DeLay Bonds with Israeli Hawks," *Los Angeles Times*, July 31, 2003.

Operation IRAQI FREEDOM. *Greater love hath no man than this: that he lay down his life for his friends . . . .*

Americans have defended our freedom for more than 200 years. Israelis have done the same for more than 50. We are opposed by many of the same enemies, who use many of the same tactics. Israel's fight is our fight: against terror, and for humanity . . . .

The United States is the world's defender of freedom, and Israel is one of our greatest allies. We won't allow anyone to reward terrorists and terrorist acts; least of all nations and organizations who appeased Saddam Hussein and who continue to appease Yasser Arafat. This struggle is one of good versus evil; nations and organizations who fail to distinguish between the two disqualify themselves from input on this matter.[1]

Another factor in evangelical influence on our government is the Council for National Policy, which was founded by Christian Zionist Tim LaHaye in 1981, with the assistance of several wealthy individuals. It was intended to be a counterweight to the secular Council on Foreign Relations and to plan the strategy of the "Religious Right." Although some of its several hundred members are Catholics, most are evangelical Protestants. Its thrice-yearly meetings are closed to all but a few non-members. Its stance on many issues is consistent with Catholic doctrine. It is harshly criticized by Americans United for Separation of Church and State, which is an indication that it is doing good work. But, because most of its members are evangelicals, it advocates Christian Zionism.

The Council for National Policy not only plans strategies for shaping policy, but also has contributed tens of millions of dollars to members of Congress. Many of its members hold high positions. Other persons in positions of influence are invited to speak to its members. Texas Governor Bush addressed the Council in 1999 to solicit support for his presidential election campaign. Vice President Cheney and Defense Secretary Rumsfeld attended a meeting of the Council shortly after the invasion of Iraq. Several Bush administration and campaign officials attended a meeting in New York in August 2004, shortly before the Republican Party convention, at which Senate Majority Leader Frist received the Council's Thomas Jefferson award. According to *The New York Times*, former Under Secretary of State Bolton, a leading neoconservative, spoke about plans for Iran at that meeting.[2] Because of the Council for National Policy's some-

---

1. Tom DeLay, Keynote Speech, Stand For Israel Rally, April 2, 2003 (online at http://www.internationalwallofprayer.org/A-173-Tom-DeLays-Speech-Stand-For-Israel-Rally-April-2003.html).

2. David D. Kirkpatrick, "Club of the Most Powerful Gathers in Strictest Privacy," *New York Times*, August 28, 2004, online.

what stealthy manner of conducting business, it is difficult to document the magnitude of its influence on the decision to attack Iraq. But it is certain that it has influence on the Republican Party and that its membership includes leading Christian Zionists.

All in all, Christian Zionists have an aggressive view of their ability (or at least potential) to influence affairs in Washington. As detailed by a substantial piece on Christian Zionism in *Mother Jones*:

> Richard Hellman, a former GOP Senate staffer and born-again Pentecostal, hopes to organize at least 7 million followers as members of his lobbying group, Christians' Israel Public Action Campaign. "Someone once referred to us as AIPAC's little echo," Hellman says with a laugh. "Maybe we'll turn out to be the echo that roared."[1]

Christian Zionists and Israeli Strategy

American Christian Zionists not only influence the U.S. government, but also have close relationships with the Israeli government and Likud party. When the Carter administration pursued a Middle East policy that was less unfavorable to the Palestinians than Likud wished, the Likud party made a strategic shift away from the Democratic Party and toward "conservative" Protestants. (Around the same time, some of the leading American neoconservatives switched their allegiance from the Democratic to the Republican Party.) Yona Malachy's *American Fundamentalism and Israel: The Relation of Fundamentalist Churches to Zionism and the State of Israel,* published by the Institute of Contemporary Jewry at the Hebrew University of Jerusalem in 1978, discussed how Israel could make strategic use of American fundamentalist and evangelical Christians. Likud began developing relationships with selected American Christian Zionist leaders. Menachem Begin's government gave Jerry Falwell a Lear jet for use in his work on Israel's behalf in 1979, and honored him with its Jabotinsky Award for Zionist excellence in 1981.[2] In return, Christian Zionist organizations have donated tens of millions of dollars to promote immigration of Jews to Israel and expansion of Jewish settlements.[3]

---

1. Silverstein and Scherer, *loc. cit.*

2. Michael R. Welton, "Unholy Alliance: Christian Zionists and the Israeli/Palestinian Conflict," *Canadian Dimension*, March/April, 2003, online.

3. See Jonathan Krashinsky, "Zionist Christians Make Solidarity Visit," *Jerusalem Post*, December 7, 2000; Jason Keyser, "Jews, Christians in Uneasy Alliance over Israel," *Associated Press*, March 7, 2002, online; Danielle Haas, "U.S. Christians Find Cause to Aid Israel: Evangelicals Financing Immigrants, Settlements," *San Francisco Chronicle*, July 10, 2002, online; William A. Cook," Ministers of War: Criminals of the Cloth," *CounterPunch.org*,

LUTZ

When Israel bombed Iraq's nuclear reactor in 1981, Begin called Falwell first, then President Reagan. According to the *Executive Intelligence Review*:

> In September 1982, when then-Israeli Defense Minister Ariel Sharon sent tanks into Lebanon and orchestrated the massacres at the Sabra and Shatila Palestinian refugee camps, Begin arranged for Falwell to lead a delegation of American Christian evangelicals to the front line. [Harry Zvi] Hurwitz, Begin's liaison to the Christian Zionists, defended the decision as necessary to offset the "bad propaganda" that the massacres had generated in the United States and Europe.[1]

Falwell promised an American Jewish audience in 1985 that he would "mobilize 70 million conservative Christians for Israel and against anti-Semitism." And Ralph Reed reports meeting with Likud Prime Minister Shamir, while he was director of the Christian Coalition:

> Evangelicals remain some of the strongest supporters of Israel. I saw this first-hand during a trip to the Holy Land in early 1993 as the Israeli government and the PLO completed negotiations on a peace treaty. I met with former Prime Minister Yitzak Shamir and expressed my concerns about the peace process and the need to protect Israeli citizens from terrorist attacks. "You are not the problem," replied Shamir. "You are among our strongest supporters. Whatever problems we have now are caused by Israelis, not Americans."[2]

The close relationships between American evangelical Protestants and Likud continued during the government of Prime Minister Netanyahu:

> Since then all subsequent Likud Prime Ministers have carefully strengthened ties to American evangelicals. In 1996, Benjamin Netanyahu created the Israel Christian Advocacy Council and flew 17 Christian leaders to Israel, where they signed a pledge that "America never, never desert Israel." And in December 2000, Deputy Defense Secretary Paul Wolfowitz, a leading hawk in the Bush administration, spoke to thousands of supporters of Israel at an April rally.[3]

Additionally, as reported by the *Christian Century*:

> When Israeli Prime Minister Benjamin Netanyahu visited Washington [in January 1998], his initial meeting was not with President Clinton but with Jerry Falwell and more than 1,000 fundamentalist Christians. The crowd saluted

---

October 27, 2003; Josef Federman, "Rabbis Express Unprecedented Criticism of American Evangelical Support for Israel," *Associated Press*, May 10, 2004, online.

1. Scott Thompson and Jeffrey Steinberg, "25-Year 'Shotgun Marriage' of Israel's Likud and U.S. Fundamentalists Exposed," *Executive Intelligence Review*, November 29, 2002.

2. Reed, *op. cit.*, p. 21.

3. Silverstein and Scherer, *loc. cit.*

[158]

the Prime Minister as "the Ronald Reagan of Israel," and Falwell pledged to contact more than 200,000 evangelical pastors, asking them to "tell President Clinton to refrain from putting pressure on Israel" to comply with the Oslo accords.[1]

More recently, Prime Minister Sharon "addressed a group of 1,500 Christian Zionists who had traveled to Jerusalem, saying, 'We regard you to be one of our best friends in the world.'"[2]

Given the influence of conservative Christians, it is no surprise that the Israeli Embassy has an "Office of Interreligious Affairs" that hosts monthly briefings for evangelicals, welcomes church bus tours, and organizes breakfasts.

American Jewish groups, no less than the Israeli government, "have increasingly accepted Christian support." In May 2002 the Anti-Defamation League "ran an advertisement in major newspapers that reprinted an article written by Ralph Reed, former head of the Christian Coalition, that was titled 'We People of Faith Stand Firmly With Israel.'" And in July of the same year, the Zionist Organization of America honored Pat Robertson for his work on behalf of Israel.[3]

As surprising as it may be to find Israeli and American Jews accepting fervent support from Bible-believing Christians, where the state of Israel is concerned they show a remarkable broad-mindedness and pragmatism. "Evangelicals have a unique role to play with this administration and in the Republican Party that Jews can't," said Rabbi Yechiel Eckstein, who runs an interfaith alliance. "Jews today see Israel's survival at stake, so they are more willing to put aside domestic concerns."[4] This mentality was confirmed by none other than Abe Foxman, the arch-defender of Jews from Christian (or any other) anti-Semitism. As *TIME Magazine* reported it,

[W]hen a people feels isolated and under attack, it will take all the friends it can get, retorts Abraham Foxman, national director of the Anti-Defamation League. "I don't think it's our business to get at the heart and soul and metaphysics of people as to why they come to support Israel. Some do it for a national-interest point of view, some because of moral issues, some because of theological issues. We don't set standards or conditions for support."[5]

---

1. Donald E. Wagner, "Evangelicals and Israel: Theological Roots of a Political Alliance," *Christian Century*, November 4, 1998, p. 1020.
2. Silverstein and Scherer, *loc. cit.*
3. *Ibid.*
4. Quoted in Nancy Gibbs, "Is It Good for the Jews?" *TIME Magazine*, July 1, 2002, online.
5. *Ibid.*

Echoing these sentiments, Zionist Organization of America president, Morton Klein, maintains that theological differences are small details to overlook in exchange for fervent support for Israel from Christians. "I am willing to make this deal: if they continue to support Israel's prosperity, security, and survival, then if Jesus comes back in the future I will join their parade," Klein says. "Hey, if I was wrong, no problem."[1] What's more, the Jewish concern that Christianity is somehow anti-Semitic, or that Christians harbor veiled (or otherwise) anti-Semitic sentiments, is "mostly a thing of the past" where Christian support for Israel is concerned. "You find hints of anti-Semitism among many non-Jewish groups, and a few evangelicals may have anti-Jewish feelings," Klein reported.

> But I have spoken to dozens of Christian Zionist groups and I have never encountered any anti-Semitism, and I'm a child of Holocaust survivors. Instead, I have found a great love of the Jewish people. I'm thrilled they are helping Israel and I think they are doing a great job. They are more pro-Israel and pro-Zionist than most Jews.[2]

Identifying *specific* connections between American Christian Zionists' support of the invasion of Iraq and their relationships with Israel's government and Likud party is complicated by the fact that, according to the official party line, Israel had nothing to do with this war.[3] The truth is, however, that this war was part of Likud strategy to strengthen Israel's security. The grand strategy of Israeli Zionists includes both the expulsion of Palestinians and the destabilization and fragmentation of neighboring countries. The application of this strategy to Iraq is explained in a 1982 policy paper, "A Strategy for Israel in the Nineteen Eighties," by Oded Yinon, who was attached to Israel's Ministry of Foreign Affairs:

> Iraq, rich in oil on the one hand and internally torn on the other, *is guaranteed as a candidate for Israel's targets*. Its dissolution is even more important for us than that of Syria. Iraq is stronger than Syria. In the short run it is Iraqi power which constitutes the greatest threat to Israel. An Iraqi-Iranian war will tear Iraq apart and cause its downfall at home even before it is able to organize a struggle on a wide front against us. *Every kind of inter-Arab confrontation will assist us in the short run and will shorten the way to the more important aim of breaking up Iraq into denominations as in Syria and in Lebanon.* In Iraq, a division into provinces along ethnic/religious lines as in Syria during

---

1. Silverstein and Scherer, *loc. cit.*

2. *Ibid.*

3. On the falsity of the official party line, see Stephen J. Sniegoski, "The War on Iraq: Conceived in Israel" (http://www.thornwalker.com:16080/ditch/conc_toc.htm), and (http://www.currentconcerns.ch/archive/20030102.php).

Ottoman times is possible. So, three (or more) states will exist around the three major cities: Basra, Baghdad and Mosul, and Shiite areas in the south will separate from the Sunni and Kurdish north.[1]

An updated call for the destabilization of Israel's enemies, "A Clean Break: Strategy for Securing the Realm," was written for Netanyahu by (American) neoconservatives Richard Perle, David Wurmser and Douglas Feith (currently the outgoing under secretary of defense for policy) in 1996. According to this document, the safety of Israel required removing Saddam Hussein from power.

There exists no simple "conspiracy." But there does exist a complex web of interrelationships between Israeli Zionists, American neoconservatives (most of whom are ethnically Jewish), and American Christian Zionists, all of whom collaborated in bringing about the 2003 invasion of Iraq. The strategy, of which the war is a part, was conceived by Israeli Zionists. The key persons in the Bush administration who planned the war were neo-conservatives. But neither of these groups could have achieved its objectives without support from tens of millions of Christian Zionist voters.

Christian Zionism and Catholic Tradition

Although it may be possible to define "Christian Zionism" in such a way that it is consistent with the Catholic Tradition, the Christian Zionism that is so popular among American Protestants is inconsistent with it. According to Sacred Tradition, which cannot contradict Sacred Scripture, the Church is the new Israel, the new people of God. Catholics find the fulfillment of God's Old Testament promises in Christ. The Old Covenant has never been revoked or abrogated, nor has it been superseded or replaced: the New Covenant is the *fulfillment* of the Old Covenant.[2] The Old and

---

1. Oded Yinon, "A Strategy for Israel in the Nineteen Eighties," trans. Israel Shahak; originally published in Hebrew in *Kivunim: A Journal for Judaism and Zionism*, No. 14, February 1982.

2. Although the Old Covenant has never been revoked, abrogated, superseded, or replaced, the ceremonial and judicial precepts of the Old Law have been annulled by the fulfillment of the reality they signified, while the moral precepts of that Law bind forever. Various passages from St. Thomas make this clear: "The mystery of the redemption of the human race was fulfilled in Christ's Passion: hence Our Lord said then: 'It is consummated' (St. Jn. xix:30). Consequently the prescriptions of the Law must have ceased then altogether through their reality being fulfilled. As a sign of this, we read that at the Passion of Christ 'the veil of the temple was rent' (Mt. 27:51)" (*ST*, II, i, Q. 103, A. 3, *ad* 3). And elsewhere, "The judicial precepts did not bind for ever, but were annulled by the coming of Christ" (II, i, Q. 104, A. 3). Additionally, "The Old Law is said to be *for ever* simply and absolutely, as regards its moral precepts; but as regards the ceremonial precepts it lasts for ever in

New Covenants are properly understood, not as divided, but as a unity.[1] As St. Thomas tells us, "Whatsoever is set down in the New Testament explicitly and openly as a point of faith, is contained in the Old Testament as a matter of belief, but implicitly, under a figure."[2] And in both Testaments there is one and the same Faith: "Our faith in Christ is the same as that of the fathers of old."[3] The new Catechism of the Catholic Church adds:

> The Church, as early as apostolic times, and then constantly in her Tradition, has illuminated the unity of the divine plan in the two Testaments through *typology*, which discerns in God's works of the Old Covenant prefigurations of what He accomplished in the fullness of time in the person of His incarnate Son.
>
> Christians therefore read the Old Testament in the light of Christ crucified and risen. Such typological reading discloses the inexhaustible content of the Old Testament; but it must not make us forget that the Old Testament retains its own intrinsic value as Revelation reaffirmed by Our Lord Himself. Besides, the New Testament has to be read in the light of the Old. Early Christian catechesis made constant use of the Old Testament. As an old saying put it, the New Testament lies hidden in the Old and the Old Testament is unveiled in the New.[4]

Consequently, and in sharp contradistinction to dispensational theology:

> Our aim should be to show the unity of biblical revelation (O.T. and N.T.) and of the divine plan, before speaking of each historical event, so as to stress that particular events have meaning when seen in history as a whole – from creation to fulfillment. This history concerns the whole human race and espe-

---

respect of the reality which those ceremonies foreshadowed" (II, i, Q. 103, A. 3). Just as the New Covenant is the fulfillment of the Old Covenant, the New Law is the fulfillment of the Old Law (St. Matt. v:17: "Think not that I have come to abolish the law and the prophets; I have come not to abolish them but to fulfil them"). There is *no* possibility of the Old Law or the Old Covenant continuing to exist today as something distinct from the New, for which reason St. Thomas remarks: "[because] the Old Law betokened Christ as having yet to be born and to suffer, whereas our sacraments signify Him as already born and having suffered . . . [,] It would be a mortal sin now to observe those ceremonies which the fathers of old fulfilled with devotion and fidelity" (II, i, Q. 103, A. 4).

1. The tendency of many Protestant traditions to divorce the Old and New Covenants from one another is related to the other two *"sola's"* of the Protestant Reformation: *sola fide* and *sola gratia*. When the New Covenant is understood to be about faith and grace only, and not also about the fulfillment of the moral precepts of the Law, it becomes more difficult to understand the two Covenants as forming a unity. Thus, the temptation of supersessionism and replacement theology.

2. *ST*, II, i, Q. 107, A. 3.

3. *ST*, II, i, Q. 103, A. 4.

4. *The Catechism of the Catholic Church*, 128–129.

cially believers. Thus, the definitive meaning of the election of Israel does not become clear except in the light of the complete fulfillment (Rom. ix–xi) and election in Jesus Christ is still better understood with reference to the announcement and the promise (cf. Heb. iv:1–11).[1]

Since the Old Covenant has never been revoked, abrogated, superseded or replaced, if the Old and New Covenants were separate, and the Old had not been fulfilled by the New, there would now be two alternative paths to salvation: one for Jews and one for Christians. Some Catholics believe that, after Auschwitz or after *Nostra Aetate,* this is now the case. But the truth remains that, although God has not rejected the Jews, there is only one path to salvation:

> It was in the awareness of the one universal gift of salvation offered by the Father through Jesus Christ in the Spirit (cf. Eph 1:3–14), that the first Christians encountered the Jewish people, showing them the fulfillment of salvation that went beyond the Law . . . .
>
> It must therefore be *firmly believed* as a truth of Catholic faith that the universal salvific will of the One and Triune God is offered and accomplished once for all in the mystery of the incarnation, death, and resurrection of the Son of God.[2]

"Anti-Zionism" and "Anti-Semitism"

According to Shmuel (Samuel) Golding, of the Jerusalem Institute of Biblical Polemics, the very idea that Christians should invite Jews to enter the Church is "anti-Semitic": "[Christian] fundamentalists are hindering and harming the progress that has been made in Christian-Jewish relationships. By their desire to convert the Jew, they prove themselves to be the most anti-Semitic of all Christian groups, for the whole idea of conversion is anti-Semitic." Christians are commanded to "make disciples of all nations, baptizing them in the name of the Father and of the Son and of the Holy Spirit" (St. Matt. xxviii:19). It turns out, however, that the New Testament itself is the source of anti-Semitism: "The roots of Christian anti-Semitism lie within the New Testament . . . . As long as the New Testament continues in print (at least in its present form) the Jew will be

---

1. Commission for Religious Relations with the Jews, "Notes on the Correct Way to Present the Jews and Judaism in Preaching and Catechesis of the Roman Catholic Church," June 24, 1985.

2. Congregation for the Doctrine of the Faith, Declaration *Dominus Iesus* on the Unicity and Salvific Universality of Jesus Christ and the Church, August 6, 2000, §§13–14 (http://www.vatican.va/roman_curia/congregations/cfaith/documents/rc_con_cfaith_doc_20000806_dominus-iesus_en.html).

hated."[1] One item of evidence of New Testament anti-Semitism cited by Golding is St. Mark xvi:16: "He who believes and is baptized will be saved; but he who does not believe will be condemned." Given this definition of "anti-Semitism," Christians can avoid being anti-Semites only by ceasing to be Christians.

The term "anti-Semitic," like its cousins "fascist" and "homophobic," is characterized more by the way it can be used than by its meaning. It has become a weapon to silence defenders of the Christian faith, as well as anyone else within its range. Hatred of Jews, just as hatred of any other person or group of persons, is a grave sin. To oppose attempts by certain Jews – whether secular or religious – to subvert the faith and morals of Christians, however, is not wrong (though it may be done in a manner that is wrong). Nevertheless, anyone who points out the incompatibility of Christianity and Judaism, or of Catholic moral teaching and the moral beliefs of many secular Jews, is tarred as "anti-Semitic." We need to eliminate hatred of persons who disagree with us. At the same time, we are in need of clarity in understanding the points of disagreement.

Although "anti-Zionist" does not have the firepower of "anti-Semitic," it can also be defined and used in various ways. I have stated my profound disagreement with those Catholics who believe that anti-Zionism is a manifestation of anti-Semitism. In doing so, I do not deny that it is possible to define the two terms in such a way that the former is indeed a manifestation of the latter. If one were to define an "anti-Zionist" as one who believes that Israeli Jews should be deported to Europe or pushed into the Mediterranean, then it would be appropriate to regard anti-Zionism as a manifestation of anti-Semitism. But extremely few critics or opponents of Zionism believe that. I do not.

For European Zionists to dispossess Palestinians of their land was an act of colossal injustice. Nevertheless, some might argue, most of the Jews living in Israel today were born there. If we were to say that all Israeli Jews with ancestors who misappropriated land must return to the countries where those ancestors were born, we would also have to say that most Americans must return to Europe, millions of Britons must return to Germany or France, etc. In fact, if we were to look back in time as far as the earliest human conquests, most members of the human race would have to leave the lands of their birth. To call upon them to do so would be silly, as well as unjust. Nevertheless, it is appropriate to ask whether, for

1. Shmuel Golding, "Antisemitism in the New Testament," Jerusalem Institute of Biblical Polemics (http://www.messianic-racism.mcmail.com/ca/antisem/g2.htm).

example, present relations between Americans of European ancestry and the descendants of Native Americans whose land was taken from them are just. Furthermore, determining what justice requires today depends to some degree upon how far back in history the conquest took place, an extremely relevant consideration, in fact, when one compares the rights of long-established European or other countries to their terrories, versus the right of an Israel (or another nation with similar history) to hold land which it seized a mere 50 years ago. Additionally, the fact that it is impossible – or even inappropriate – to "right" all of the wrongs of history does not justify the new wrongs of the present.

Buber wrote to Gandhi in 1939 regarding the latter's "axiomatic statement that a land belongs to its population": "In an epoch when nations are migrating, you would first support the right of ownership of the nation that is threatened with dispossession or extermination; but were this once achieved, you would be compelled, not at once, but after a suitable number of generations had elapsed, to admit that the land 'belongs' to the usurper."[1] But, surely, the position Buber attributes to Gandhi is correct, or at least much closer to being correct than Buber's position that European Jews had a right to a share of the land belonging to Palestinians. It would be unjust today to require descendants of Jews who migrated from Europe sixty-five years ago to return to Europe (though justice does require acknowledging and respecting the rights of the descendants of Arabs whose land was dispossessed sixty-five years ago). But it was unjust sixty-five years ago to claim that Zionists had a right to dispossess Palestinians of their land. And it is unjust today to claim that Zionists have a right to dispossess Palestinians of additional land, to expand the borders of Israel, to treat Arabs as inferior to Jews, to make Israel's borders more secure by means of unjustified military actions, and to ignore the legitimate claims of Palestinians to justice in redressing the injustices of the past century.

To be an anti-Zionist today is not to claim that the Jews must leave the Middle East or that the state of Israel has no right to exist. We may disagree with President Truman's decision to recognize the state of Israel in 1948 (as did many Americans at the time), but we cannot change the fact that it has been recognized by much of the world for more than half-a-century. To be an anti-Zionist today is to believe that our present and future actions regarding relations between Jews and Arabs must be just, and that we must seek appropriate restitution – an act of commutative

---

1. Buber, *op. cit.*, pp. 232–3.

justice – for the unjust actions of the past. Understood in this sense, anti-Zionism is not a manifestation of anti-Semitism. For the International Catholic-Jewish Liaison Committee to say that it is, without explaining that it is using the terms in a manner contrary to their plain meaning, is irresponsible. It implies that Catholics should not be opposed to Zionism. *And to fail to oppose Zionism today is to fail to oppose some profound injustices, including the unjust war of aggression against Iraq.*

Given the history of relations between Catholics and Jews, it is appropriate to seek improvement. Injustices have been committed by both sides. But it is inappropriate to let Jews dictate to Catholics the terms of the improvement, especially when doing so would mean subverting the Catholic tradition. Some Catholics have accepted the position of Golding that it is inappropriate for Christians to invite Jews to convert to Christianity. A 2002 document, which is unofficial but nevertheless represents the views of at least a few of the American Catholic Bishops, contains the following paragraphs:

> While the Catholic Church regards the saving act of Christ as central to the process of human salvation for all, it also acknowledges that Jews already dwell in a saving covenant with God. The Catholic Church must always evangelize and will always witness to its faith in the presence of God's kingdom in Jesus Christ to Jews and to all other people. In so doing, the Catholic Church respects fully the principles of religious freedom and freedom of conscience, so that sincere individual converts from any tradition or people, including the Jewish people, will be welcomed and accepted.
>
> However, it now recognizes that Jews are also called by God to prepare the world for God's kingdom. Their witness to the kingdom, which did not originate with the Church's experience of Christ crucified and raised, must not be curtailed by seeking the conversion of the Jewish people to Christianity. The distinctive Jewish witness must be sustained if Catholics and Jews are truly to be, as Pope John Paul II has envisioned, "a blessing to one another" [John Paul II, "Address on the Fiftieth Anniversary of the Warsaw Ghetto Uprising," April 6, 1993]. This is in accord with the divine promise expressed in the New Testament that Jews are called to "serve God without fear, in holiness and righteousness before God all [their] days" (Luke 1:74–75).[1]

The writers of this document have clearly protected themselves against accusations of "anti-Semitism," but they have done so at the cost of stepping outside the Catholic Tradition. One potential error of Catholics who

---

1. "Reflections on Covenant and Mission: Consultation of The National Council of Synagogues and The Bishops Committee for Ecumenical and Interreligious Affairs, USCCB," August 12, 2002 (online at http://www.gccuic-umc.org/web/webpdf/covenantreflections.pdf).

dialogue with persons of other faiths or no faith is defending the Faith in a manner inconsistent with the virtue of charity. Another potential error is failing to defend the Faith in a manner consistent with the virtue of fortitude and the requirements of Truth. If the objective of the dialogue is conformity with the beliefs of the opponents of Catholicism, it isn't much of a dialogue. To misrepresent one's own position is to disrespect the other party.

Concluding Reflections

In response to Farah's ten points:

1. Christians in America and elsewhere can read the Bible and see that the historic home of Egyptians is Egypt. Most of them understand that this does not give Egyptians living elsewhere a right to steal land belonging to non-Egyptians in Egypt.

2. Of course, Jesus was a Jew. The question of what kind of state He lived in has little relevance to the question of justice in the Middle East today.

3. Christians understand not only that God chose to reveal Himself to the Jewish people, but also that: "There is neither Jew nor Greek, there is neither slave nor free, there is neither male nor female; for you are all one in Christ Jesus. And if you are Christ's then you are Abraham's offspring, heirs according to promise" (Gal. iii:28–29).

4. Christians don't see a nation of USA mentioned in the Old Testament or New. Most also understand that not much follows from this. The name "Palestine" (derived from "Philistine," which *is* mentioned in the Old Testament) has been used as the name of a province of various empires, from the Roman to the Ottoman. The British Mandate of 1923–48 was named "Palestine-Eretz Israel." Justice requires helping the Palestinian people to establish a sovereign state of their own, whatever they decide to call it.

5. Most Christians believe that God made certain promises to the Israelites, and that Jesus Christ is the fulfillment of those promises.

6. Most Christians understand that when God said he would bless those who bless Israel and curse those who curse Israel, He wasn't talking about the secular Jewish state that was established by Zionists in 1948. Christians can read the words of St. John the Baptist: "Bear fruit that befits repentance, and do not presume to say to yourselves, 'We have Abraham as our father'; for I tell you, God is able from these stones to raise up children to Abraham. Even now the axe is laid to the root of the trees; every tree therefore that does not bear good fruit is cut down and thrown into the fire" (St. Matt. iii:8–10; St. Luke iii:8–9). They don't want to place themselves on the wrong side of this "spiritual equation" by supporting the sinful policies of the secular state of Israel and citing Sacred Scripture to justify doing so.

7. Christians also understand, "To the Gentiles also God has granted repentance unto life" (Acts xi:18).

8. Many Christians grasp that it isn't true that the Jewish Zionists took possession of a barren desert. Much of the land that they appropriated had been cultivated by Palestinians for centuries.

9. Most Christians comprehend that "the only democracy in the Middle East" is far from free. There is severe discrimination against Arabs by Jews, and against Sephardic (Iberian), Mizrahi (North African and Middle Eastern), and Ethiopian Jews by Ashkenazi (Germanic and Eastern European) Jews.

10. Many Christians are able to see that American support of Israeli terrorism against Arabs is the root provocation of the recent series of terrorist attacks against the United States. They see no reason to doubt that Osama bin Laden means what he says: "Our terrorism against the United States is blessed, aimed at repelling the oppressor so that America stops its support for Israel."[1]

The road to Jerusalem does not run through Baghdad – if that is understood to mean that removing Saddam Hussein from power and forcing

---

1. Osama bin Laden, transcript of videotaped comments as broadcast by *Aljazeera*, *Reuters News Service*, December 26, 2001, online.

Iraqis to hold elections will improve relations between Israeli Jews and Palestinian Arabs. The road to peace in the Middle East runs through justice, both justice for the Palestinian people whose human rights have been violated and justice in the use of military force by all parties with an interest in the region.

Although Christian Zionism was not the most central issue in the process of my conversion from evangelical Protestantism to Catholicism, it did fit into a larger picture of rejecting irrational beliefs. My beliefs about Israelis and Palestinians began to change ten years ago, five years before I finally converted. I presented a paper at an academic conference in Jerusalem (on "Ethics in the Public Service") and also spent a few days on a whirlwind sight-seeing tour of Israel. The greatest impression of my only visit to the Holy Land was that most of the Jews I met there did not believe in God and hated Palestinians. I began to wonder why I was such a strong supporter of such people.

I skipped one day of the conference in order to visit the Old City. As I was walking back to the hotel on an East Jerusalem side street, I met a Palestinian man. As we approached one another, he stopped, spat on the pavement, and then walked past me. I said nothing, but regretted later that I had not told him I didn't hate him. Then I realized that – as an American citizen, former U.S. Army officer, and evangelical Protestant – I would have been hard-pressed to provide him any evidence that I did not.

Although that trip to Israel did not lead immediately to my conversion, it did spur me to question another piece of the puzzle of my Protestant beliefs. I invite Protestants who are inclined towards Zionist political theology to ask themselves whether it or just-war theory is more consistent with living a Christian life. And I challenge American Catholics – a majority of whom supported our war of aggression against Iraq – to ask themselves whether they have been influenced by Protestant or Jewish thinking (or both) to adopt a position inconsistent with their own Tradition.

THE EDITORS' GLOSS: Dr. Jones's position is a challenging and provocative one, and certainly not one to be rashly dismissed. The essence of his argument is that what masquerades as "conservatism" is not "conservative" at all in any authentic sense. On the contrary, it's a very useful tool in the hands of our political masters.

Undoubtedly, there is room for disagreement with this thesis, but what it highlights is a larger truth that we believe irrefutable. That truth declares that the two mainstream camps – Democrats or Republicans, left or right, liberal or conservative – are essentially the two broken pieces of a dysfunctional political system, both tools of the ruling class. This is the thesis that Gore Vidal gets in so much trouble for, though no one ever proves him wrong.

The list of grievances one might have against one or other camp is indeed long. As far as the war in Iraq is concerned there's plenty of blame to go around. The opposition of the "left" to the war reminds one of the old saying, "with friends like these, who needs enemies?" Excluding the few honest "radicals," the Democrats were worse than useless, John Kerry's inability to articulate a convincing anti-war position – or any position, for that matter – being the perfect example of this. The "conservatives," on the other hand, who are supposed to represent "liberty" and "freedom" against the bureaucratic paternalism and coddling of the liberal welfare state, dutifully lined up to support overthrowing a legal government and waging war to change a society wholesale. The Iraqis who were broadly happy with the way things were evidently didn't qualify for consideration among those to whom Rebublican bombs and bullets bring such "liberty" and "freedom."

All of which is to say that thinking Americans – particularly those that identify with either of the "mainstream" parties – would do well to take a long, hard, objective look at where their loyalties lie, and why. As Dr. Jones says, it's quite possible things are not what they seem. And if they aren't, odds are they're much worse.

Manipulating Catholic Support for the War:
The Black Operation Known as "Conservatism"
• • • • • • • • •

E. Michael Jones, Ph.D.

I N MARCH 2003, with American troops massing on the border with Iraq, Rod Dreher, a Catholic columnist for *National Review*, wrote an article in the *Wall Street Journal* saying that Catholics didn't have to listen to the Pope – who was opposed to the war in Iraq – because of the truly scandalous pedophile issue that has been rocking the Church.

In his article, "Finally, a Rapid Response: Why didn't sex-abuse scandals stir Vatican action the way war has?" *WSJ* online, March 7, 2003, Mr. Dreher opined that "Catholics are not obliged to agree with the Pope on this issue. The rightness or wrongness of this or any particular war is a matter of opinion . . . . The 50% of America's Catholics who stand by their President, and not their Pope, in this matter do not thereby diminish their standing as Catholics." He went on to say that it was "appalling to watch President Bush, who has responsibility for safeguarding 280 million of us from terrorist and terror states being lectured . . . by a Church that would not even protect children from its own rogue priests and the bishops who enabled them."

David Frum of *National Review* went so far as to attack paleoconservatives as traitors in that journal's effort to get Catholics to support the war and disregard what the Pope had said to the contrary. More on Frum later.

All of this was part of a propaganda barrage launched by *neocon*servatives to silence domestic critics of George W. Bush's war on Iraq. A barrage that was aimed at gaining Catholic support for the war by undermining the influence and authority of the Church which stood overwhelmingly in opposition to it. A barrage that had its roots in the editorial offices of some of the country's leading opinion journals, and even in the shadowy depths of the CIA.

Christopher Manion (son of Clarence Manion, former dean of the Notre Dame Law School, a founding father of the post-WW II conservative movement, and one of the original conservative radio broadcasters) was outraged by Dreher's column. "Mr. Dreher's syllogism," Manion wrote, in a piece which appeared on *lewrockwell.com*, "requires that the Pope be a perfect administrator, able to prune away all evil from his bishops and priests before he is qualified to teach anyone – let alone our fine President! – about morality." But what Manion considered the most curious part of Dreher's *Wall Street Journal* article was the by-line that stated: "Mr. Dreher, a Catholic, is a senior writer for *National Review.*"

Why, Manion wondered, was Dreher identified as *a Catholic*? "When I wrote for *National Review* and the *Wall Street Journal*," he said, "I was never identified as 'a Catholic' (although I am), even though I often wrote about issues of ethics, religion and politics. I have never seen other writers there identified by their religious affiliations. Strange."

Strange, indeed. Manion added that his "curiosity is compounded because Mr. Dreher appears to identify himself as a Catholic in order to garner additional authority to condemn the Church as an institution with no moral authority."

Did Dreher do this because he is a bad person? I leave that question, as Mrs. Winterbourne did in *Daisy Miller*, to the metaphysicians. One explanation is that he did it because he was an employee of *National Review*; and the "conservative" network was pulling out all the stops in support of the neocon war in Iraq. That required, to use Chris Manion's phrase, "sliming the Pope."

Now why would someone who identifies himself as a Catholic want to do something like that? The more we probed for answers, the more questions we came up with. So let's start at the beginning: who is Rod Dreher?

Rod Dreher is a relatively new star in the firmament of conservative journalism. He was born in 1976 and grew up in Starhill, Louisiana, near Baton Rouge. He was raised in a nominally Methodist family and attended Louisiana State University, where he got a degree in journalism. While in college he had a religious awakening which led him to become first an Episcopalian, then a Catholic, and then a serious conservative Catholic, as evidenced by the autobiographical articles he wrote for *Touchstone*, which began to appear in June of 2000. In his piece, "Right-wing in New York," in the September 2000 issue, Dreher announced that he had arrived in the Big Apple in 1998 to become a columnist for the *New York Post*. He informed us that – as an indication of his "Catholicity," one supposes – he and his wife Julie "practice Natural Family Planning out of obedience to the Church."

One year later, Dreher was still listed in his *Touchstone* by-lines as a columnist for the *New York Post*. He was also going through some kind of crisis, which he described for *Touchstone* readers in an October 2001 article entitled "Holding my Own in New York." The crisis had to do with 1). his father and 2). whether Dreher should raise his son, Matthew, in a pure but 'culturally backward' place like Louisiana where his career would not thrive, or in New York City, where his career was just beginning to take off. "I'm doing well in my vocation, and have even begun to appear on national TV every couple of weeks. For me, it's onward and upward." But in New York he was apparently subjected to some temptation that he couldn't quite bring himself to articulate beyond his worry that "Matthew will never look up to me in quite the same way as I did to my father."

Why was that? "Because the tasks I and urban dads like me are required to perform aren't as physically arduous" as catfish grabbing and other exploits that Dreher described in his article. But, we wondered, wouldn't little Matthew be proud when his dad "appear[s] on national TV every couple of weeks"? Evidently not. Dreher kept trying to convince himself that it was morally licit to live in New York City, "even though I won't have the opportunity to be a hero to my son in the same way my dad was to me." Well, it may very well be that Dreher wouldn't be a hero to his son, but it's difficult to see why this was a question of geography. Heroism is bound up with morals not geography.

So what was Dreher's reason for remaining in New York City when his child's moral development was apparently at stake? "We live in New York City because we love it, and that's where my job is. In my field, at my level, there is little work for me down South." (Dreher's most recent career move, paradoxically, took him to Dallas, Texas.)

By what means, then, did he resolve the issue? Did he pray to the Holy Ghost for guidance? Did he make a Novena? No, he talked to "a wise old Jewish friend, a life-long veteran of the media biz," who told him that "the impact of any book you write, and of any printed work you do, is enormously magnified by a New York by-line." Moreover, the wise Jew warned him ominously, "once you leave, you're probably not going to be able to come back." So, as a result of this public soul-searching, Dreher came to the conclusion that: "Maybe I have to be unfaithful to my father to be faithful to my Father."

So for Dreher to have a career in journalism, at least journalism in New York, apparently meant that he had to be unfaithful to his father, a man

Dreher admired. One might conclude that journalism as Dreher practices it must involve something less than admirable, a betrayal of what his father believed in, a betrayal of something Dreher believes in as well. Dreher was probably not planning to write piece after piece about his father *per se*, but within a matter of months he wrote a number of articles on the Pope – otherwise known to us as the Holy Father – pieces which were critical of the Pope's opposition to the war in Iraq. Perhaps what Dreher was really telling us was that in order to be the kind of journalist he intends to be, he had to be as unfaithful to the Holy Father as he was to his biological father. Otherwise he, too, may end up back in Louisiana "grabbing catfish."

Two months after this series of articles, Rod Dreher was working for *National Review* (*NR*), where it seems that one of his main editorial duties was, to quote Chris Manion again, "sliming the Pope" as a part of the neo-con propaganda barrage leading up to the invasion of Iraq. It was from this editorial platform that Dreher launched what some characterize as a meteoric rise into the stratosphere of "conservative" punditry.

But before we describe Dreher's journalistic rocket ride, we need to devote a few words to the vehicle. Just what is *National Review*? The answer to that raises a related question: what, in the early days of *National Review*, was "conservatism"? The answer is simple: conservatism (neoconservatism, actually) was a black – as in "covert" – operation. That contention comes from Murray Rothbard, whose arguments can be reviewed online in their entirety under "Neoconservatism: A CIA Front?" at *lewrockwell. com.* Rothbard, who grew up among the Messianic Jewish sects of New York City, and knew them intimately, felt that *National Review* was a CIA front operation and marshals his arguments in the same article.

As he and others have made clear, the CIA was, from its inception, in the business of media manipulation. "Not long after the Central Intelligence Agency was founded in 1947," Rothbard writes, "the American public and the world were subjected to an unprecedented level of propaganda in the service of U.S. foreign policy objectives in the cold war . . . . At its peak the CIA allocated 29 percent of its budget to 'media and propaganda.'" Because of the intensity of the internecine hatred which Communism created, one of the main groups willing, if not positively eager, to grasp the levers of the anti-Stalinist propaganda machine were the Trotskyites.

According to Rothbard, the neoconservatives "moved from cafeteria Trotskyites to apologists for the U.S. warfare state without missing a beat." The CIA established the Congress for Cultural Freedom (CCF) as its premiere anti-Stalinist organization, but that organization's credibility was destroyed when it became known that it was a CIA front. James Burnham, one of the co-founders of *National Review*, worked for the CCF. He was also a former Trotskyite and a CIA agent. Also associated with the CCF was the father of neoconservatism, Irving Kristol. After World War II, Kristol was editor of *Commentary*, the American Jewish Committee's magazine. Then in 1953 he became editor of *Encounter*, which Peter Coleman exposed as a CIA front operation in his largely sympathetic book, *The Liberal Conspiracy*. Kristol at first denied knowing that *Encounter* was a CIA front operation. Later, in his autobiography, he admitted knowing that the CIA was involved but tried to play down the scale of his participation. But Kristol was being disingenuous. As Rothbard points out, Tom Braden, then head of the CIA's International Organizations Division, "wrote in a *Saturday Evening Post* article, a CIA agent always served as editor of *Encounter*."

Now if *National Review*, like *Encounter*, was a CIA front, what purpose did it serve? The answer is simple. *National Review* existed to destroy competing conservatisms. It used conservatism as a way of mobilizing certain groups – as in ethnic groups – such as Catholics, for example, behind government policies. It existed to colonize these groups, to divide and conquer, and, ultimately, to get them to act against their own ethnic interests.

More specifically, *National Review* was created to destroy isolationist conservatism. People who criticized America's march to empire from the conservative point of view were to be demonized and decertified. *NR* has shown undeviating consistency in this regard, the most recent example being David Frum's diatribe against the paleoconservatives, "Unpatriotic Conservatives," in the March 19, 2003, issue. The paleocons, according to Frum "have made common cause with the left-wing and Islamist anti-war movements in this country and in Europe. They deny and excuse terror. They espouse a potentially self-fulfilling defeatism. They publicize wild conspiracy theories. And some of them explicitly yearn for the victory of their nation's enemies."

All of this, according to Frum, flies in the face of the "50-year-old conservative commitment to defend American interests throughout the world, which inspired the founding" of *National Review*.

Murray Rothbard has a slightly different take on the founding of this magazine that became the editorial home of David Frum and Rod Dreher. According to Rothbard, "the idea for *National Review* originated with Willi Schlamm, a hard-line interventionist and feature editor with the Old Right *Freeman*," who was at odds with the isolationism of the right. Revilo Oliver, a friend of the Buckley family, said pretty much the same thing in his autobiography. *National Review,* according to Oliver, "was conceived as a way to put the isolationist *Freeman* out of business. A surreptitious deal was cut with one of the *Freeman* editors (presumably Schlamm) to turn the magazine over to Buckley."

By 1955, the year *National Review* was launched, Buckley had been a CIA agent for some time. One biography of Buckley claims that he served under E. Howard Hunt in Mexico City in 1951. Rothbard says that Buckley was directed to the CIA by Yale Professor Wilmoore Kendall, who introduced him to James Burnham, a consultant to the Office of Policy Coordination, the CIA's covert-action wing. While at Yale, Buckley served as an on-campus informant for the FBI, "feeding," in Rothbard's words, "God only knows what to Hoover's political police."

Virtually everyone associated with the founding of *National Review* was either a former CIA agent or someone in the pay of the CIA. In addition to Buckley, Kendall, and Burnham, that included William Casey, who would go on to become head of the CIA. Casey drew up the legal documents for the new magazine. Of the $500,000 needed to launch the publication, $100,000 came from Buckley's father. The source of the rest of the funding is unaccounted for. It was this and other evidence that led Frank Meyer (see *Culture Wars,* reviews June 2003) to confide privately to Rothbard that he believed that *National Review* was a CIA front.

Another purpose of *National Review* was to purge "bad" conservatives. First, the isolationists and anyone with residual sympathies for the pre-World War II America First movement, including the followers of Father Coughlin, were purged. Then the John Birch Society was purged. Then the Ayn Rand cult was purged. Then Joe Sobran and Pat Buchanan were purged after Buckley denounced them personally as 'anti-Semites.'

A further objective of *National Review* is to run the "conservative black-list." We know this because, as in the case of David Frum's previously mentioned article, the list gets published periodically. I was not included in the Frum attack on the paleoconservatives, probably because I am perceived primarily as a Catholic, not as a paleo; but it became clear to me long ago that I was on their list of "bad" conservatives.

An example of this can be found in Michael Potemra's review of my book, *Monsters from the Id,* in the May 22, 2000, issue of *NR.* In the same issue, a book by Thomas Hibbs is reviewed as being "correct in excoriating *The Exorcist* for its view of the Enlightenment," whereas I am ridiculed for saying essentially the same thing. Potemra goes out of his way to praise my publisher, Spence Publishing, as the up and coming conservative publishing house, but then, as if to help ensure they don't publish me again, he goes equally out of his way to criticize *Monsters* for "the sheer outlandishness of its thesis."

So what's the problem here? The "conservatives" at the *Washington Times* liked *Monsters* and understood its essentially conservative message. Then why was it denounced as "outlandish" in a magazine that calls itself "conservative"? The answer is simple. I have been blacklisted by a movement that does not want to see me offer a competing brand of "conservatism." The point, then, is not what you say, but how you are perceived and by whom. Thus *National Review's* job is to keep certain groups on the "conservative" reservation; and to "excommunicate" anyone who might lead them off that reservation.

One of the main groups to be kept on the reservation is America's Catholics. Kevin Philips articulated his strategy for bringing Catholic ethnics into the Republican Party in his 1969 book *The Emerging Republican Majority*. *National Review* was at work on this project long before Philips wrote his book. If William F. Buckley is famous for a phrase, it is certainly "Mater, Si; Magistra, no," his response to papal encyclicals in general, when they deviated from the "conservative" party line. What the phrase means is that being a "conservative" is supposed to trump anything a Pope says when it comes to determining the views of American Catholics.

The device that was historically used to keep the Catholics in line was anti-Communism, and though Buckley discredited staunch anti-Communists Pat Buchanan and Joe Sobran in the early '90s, the dawn of the 21st century posed a new threat in the person of the Pope. John Paul II was, in no uncertain terms, against the war in Iraq. That meant that Bill Buckley, if he wanted to continue to earn his keep, would somehow have to discredit him too. But how do you discredit the Pope? Events conspired to create what appeared to be a simple, and certainly convenient, answer. You do it by linking him to the homosexual and/or pedophilic priest crisis.

Among the first articles Rod Dreher wrote after arriving at *NR* was a review of Michael Rose's study of American seminaries, *Good-bye, Good Men*. Rose had written a book that accepted, almost uncritically, the testimony of virtually everyone who was ever expelled from a Catholic seminary as evidence of a homosexual conspiracy running the Church.

In spite of *NR's* usual negative position on conspiracy theories, those that coincide with the party line are okay. In his review of Rose's book ("Andrew Sullivan's Gay Problem," *NR Online*, March 13, 2002), Dreher had no problem claiming that a "'lavender Mafia' [was] running much of the institutional church" in America. Once Dreher had written his review, the "conservative" network picked up the drumbeat. Linda Chavez wrote a review for the *Jewish World Review* that was little more than a recap of Dreher's piece. "The Vatican," Chavez concluded darkly, and without a shred of evidence offered in support, "has chosen to ignore this [gay sub-culture] aspect of the scandal."

Dreher's work was then cited by William Buckley himself. But more importantly, as a result of the review, Regnery volunteered to become publisher of what, up until the time of Dreher's piece, was Rose's *self-published* book. Regnery is as venerable a name in American conservatism as *National Review*. Henry Regnery, the firm's now deceased founder, published Buckley's first book, *God and Man at Yale,* as well as Russell Kirk's *The Conservative Mind.*

A recent article in the *New York Press* indicated that Regnery is now an integral part of the allegedly burgeoning conservative publishing network. "Regnery's recent success," the article claimed, "is thanks in part to the market-driven rise of *FOX News.*" Regnery "sell[s] books through *National Review's* website or they try to get the author on to Sean Hannity's afternoon radio show. They can send a direct mail letter to NewsMax subscribers or bring it to Rush's attention. If Rush likes it, he'll tell his 20 million listeners about it." In other words, the conservative network can *create* a phenomenon like *Good-Bye, Good Men* if it suits their purposes.

What are those purposes? In the opinion of Chris Manion,

> Mr. Dreher and his ideological cohorts have been called into battle to discredit all the countries, institutions, leaders, powers, and dominions that dare to question this war, while chasing after renowned moral authorities like Angola and Cameroon with billions in promised bribes, more popularly known as foreign aid and trade concessions.

(The reference to Angola and Cameroon is a reminder of the U.S. attempt to buy off these countries and their crucial votes on the UN Security Council at a time when the Anglo-American aggressors were seeking a fig-leaf of legitimacy for the attack in the form of a second resolution.)

As has been made clear, the editorial policy at *NR*, especially during the period immediately preceding the war in Iraq, was to colonize Catholics by discrediting their leaders; and for Catholics of lower rank who refused to go along with this stunt, other punishments were planned. "If they don't buy that [weapons of mass destruction]," Manion continues, "we'll threaten to brand them with dark and subterranean and totally unprovable anti-Semitism."

Six days after Dreher "slimed" the Pope in the *Wall Street Journal,* David Frum launched his now infamous attack on the paleoconservatives in *National Review.* Both pieces were part of the same neoconservative propaganda barrage in support of the initially successful, but ultimately ill-fated Iraqi war. Why this apparent sense of urgency? Because too many people in general, and too many Catholics in particular, were leaving the conservative reservation.

But the story doesn't stop here. Rod Dreher's writing appeared in *Touchstone* again in March 2003 with this warning: "If 2002 was a bad year for the Catholic Church, just wait for 2003." Was he playing the prophet here, or just telling us about his plans? It seems clear that what Dreher and *National Review* intended to do was employ a divide and conquer strategy among a group that might be termed religious-right, social issues conservatives by heavily promoting books like *Good-Bye, Good Men.* Using this technique against such magazines as *New Oxford Review, Touchstone,* and *Culture Wars,* the neocon smart operatives hoped to open up internal friction among the people who support these publications.

It's time to pull the plug on this brand of "conservatism," whose purpose was and is the conversion of Catholic ethnics, isolationists, and white Southerners into supporters of the warfare state. Those who don't go along will be blacklisted by *National Review*; or will be recruited by divide and conquer tactics.

As the frenzied activity at *National Review* and some other like-minded journals indicates, neoconservatism is fast becoming one more god that failed, just as its mirror image, Communism, failed. It has been a "black operation" from its inception. It's time to pull back the curtain and take a look at this "Wizard of Oz" for what it really is.

THE EDITORS' GLOSS: Many on the "left" who are rightly upset by the support that generic "Christians" gave to the war in Iraq make the mistake – perhaps to some degree understandably – of failing to distinguish between different kinds of Christians, for such differences do exist. They would do well to read Dr. Lutz's piece as a primer on the subject. They would do even better to notice the care with which Kirkpatrick Sale handles the idea of who is a Christian and what Christianity really means.

In the run-up to last year's presidential election, too many folks bought into the metro versus retro "divide," the red-blue battle, and other such thought-killing paradigms. This framework simply precluded serious independent thought. Perhaps it was (and continues to be) fostered by Republicans and Democrats because both have far too big a stake in lucrative, hum-drum politics to let word get out that people don't have to be one or the other. An objection to this pigeon-holing of ideologies was raised in a small North Carolina paper, *The Charlotte Observer*, by journalist Mary Curtis on January 12, 2005. She asked: "Are you a 'Passion of the Christ' person or a 'Fahrenheit 9/11' person? Do you love Mel Gibson and hate Michael Moore, or the other way around?" Her answer contained all the wisdom anyone would need to find his or her way out of today's polarized political mess.

"Silly me," she wrote, "I was not aware that I had to choose."

Neither were we. Believe it or not, there are many "conservative" Christians out there who don't believe in unjust wars, exaggerated CEO salaries, "we're-always-right" foreign policy, or Lt. Gen William Boykin's notion that Bush is "in the White House because God put him there" to lead the "army of God" against "a guy named Satan." (God help us.) Equally, there are those on the "left," religious or not, who are all for social compassion but don't believe in the welfare state or the dissolution of the family. This is the world that transcends the artificial left-right divide and considers, in broader terms, what's right and wrong. This is the world that must be consolidated, strengthened, and united if the peoples of the world are ever going to get something approximating real peace and prosperity.

CHAPTER
10

What the War Is All About
. . . .
Kirkpatrick Sale

WHAT'S IMPORTANT TO know about this war in Iraq is that it is not about oil, or about weapons of mass destruction, or al-Qaeda, or Saddam Hussein – this war is about American global hegemony.

You see, Bush has a dream – or, rather, Cheney, Rumsfeld, Wolfowitz, and that crowd has sold Bush a dream: it is the creation of a world in which all states will be what we call *capitalistic* (though not allowed ever to be as rich as the U.S.) and what we call *democratic* (though the power elite doesn't have to change as long as it allows elections from time to time), and will participate in a global economy on our terms. This is what William Kristol and Robert Kagan, in a 1996 *Foreign Affairs* article, called America's "benevolent global hegemony" – and you know who is defining "benevolent."

This has been the goal of the neoconservative right wing ever since the downfall of the Soviet Union in 1989, and when they came to power with George the First they tried to push it as hard as they could, going so far as to make a war against Iraq for invading a country they told him he could invade; but they never got George to go the whole way. He was for a "new world order," all right, but he didn't think his coalition wanted America to take over Iraq like some colonial power, and he saw no reason to fight a messy war in the streets of Baghdad that might or might not topple Saddam Hussein.

Then comes George the Second, who early on in office was essentially an isolationist – he was opposed to troops in Kosovo, he was against "nation-building," he knew practically nothing of the world beyond the Dallas Cowboys, and he had no notion of an American role in it. But he put into power the old crowd from the days of George the First and made it even more prominent. They started work on him right from the start, but he was a slow learner and nothing much stuck – he didn't even want to have anything to do with the so-called peace process in Israel, nor did he care much about recovering our spy plane when it was forced to land in China.

Then came 9/11, and suddenly everything changed.

Bush could see it all *now*. It wasn't just that there was a terrorist group based in Afghanistan that had brought the war to us. It wasn't just that the U. S. was hated by a whole bunch of Arabs. This was, as he said, "the presence of evil" – sheer "evil," because it was attacking the United States, which was "good." That struck a chord that his Manichean-Christian, born-again mind could understand, which saw things in terms of whether others were "for us" or "against us," and so he declared a war against "evil" – a war not against the terrorists who destroyed two ugly skyscrapers in New York, but against terrorism itself, everywhere in the world, and for all time.

That was all the opening that the global hegemony people needed, and they were right there telling Bush that the war against evil also had to be fought against the "evil" regimes – Iraq, say, and Iran too; and throw in North Korea since one non-Muslim state was needed: a trio that he famously called "the axis of evil." And that was no off-handed phrase – it came from the bottom of his inflamed fundamentalist, American-"Christian" heart, that seeks to rid the world not so much of anti-Christianity but of anti-Americanism; to rid the world of those who, in his words, hate us because "we love freedom . . . and they hate freedom." And as he said at another time, his task was to answer the attacks of 9/11, "and rid the world of evil."

Ridding the world of evil is, of course, a long-standing ideal for Christians, both the intelligent, honest, and reflective ones, and the us-against-them American Manicheans. The former think that the elimination of evil is to be done by teaching the Word of the Prince of Peace, that the seed of righteousness is sown in peace, and that if war is ever to be part of the equation it must meet narrow, rigid, in-practice-almost-impossible-to-meet criteria that ultimately boil down to permitting self defense in specific circumstances. There are some who think that war is itself an evil and the taking of lives is wrong, as God was trying to tell us in the Sixth Commandment. And there are others who think that a "just war" is a convenient cloak for launching a crusade against whoever the "evildoers" *du jour* happen to be, like, for instance, those who "hate freedom," even if that's just a convenient way of saying they criticize America or don't accept its role as dominator of the globe.

In fact it just so happens that George Bush, when he was governor of Texas, would go to a church in Dallas run by a minister who had founded a movement called the Promise Keepers, a fundamentalist sect that pushed a doctrine it called "dominionism." Dominionism held that it was the duty of the forces of Good, guided in their mission knowing God was on their side, to rescue the world from evil and establish the Kingdom of God everywhere, "to restore the earth," as they put it, "to God's control." Bush clearly resonated with that idea; never mind that he had no clear sense – in fact you might say he had an "anti-sense" – of to what degree, in a "God-controlled" world, the United States would be obligated to comply with the requirements of justice, charity, peace, brotherhood, and all those other decent, commonsense things that more reasonable people find articulated in the Bible.

And now here he was, actually able to put that dominionism into practice, with the largest and most powerful military in the world, and no one to prevent or challenge him. It was, as Bob Woodward reported in his book about the war planning,[1] a chance to cast "his mission and that of the country in the grand vision of God's Master Plan." But more: he could do it not just in the name of God but in the name of America, because America was good, and believed in freedom, and was rich and successful, and it would be *its* dominion that would be established in the world: a benevolent . . . "Christian" . . . American . . . global . . . hegemony.

Then Wolfowitz whispered "Iraq" to Rumsfeld, who whispered it to Cheney, who whispered it to Bush, and it was suddenly so obvious. Let us begin the campaign to make the world safe for goodness with a war against that convenient little mustachioed Arab Hitler.

Besides, a war against the Taliban, say, or al-Qaedaistas in Pakistani caves, does nothing to promote the interests of Israel; but the destruction of Iraq would be just the ticket. It is obvious that this was an important secondary motive for the Jewish neocons around Bush, who could put up with his "Christian" rhetoric and pious fundamentalism as long as he invoked the same wrathful God. But it was also something that people like Bush and Cheney could roll with, because the support of Israel is a basic tenet of "Christian" fundamentalism, based on the somewhat wacky idea that there is a God-given obligation to restore the lands of Israel and defeat the enemies of Zion, so that the Second Coming of Christ can occur.[2] So an attack on Saddam would be just the thing, taking out the most aggressive and militarily powerful of Israel's neighbors and providing bases, both

---

1. *Plan of Attack* (New York: Simon & Schuster, 2004).

2. See the lengthy piece on Christian Zionism by Dr. David Lutz on pp. 127–169 of the present volume.—Ed.

military and propagandistic, to spread American influence in the rest of the Middle East on Israel's behalf.

So there we have it. That is why the whole thing has seemed so irrational, because it doesn't have anything to do with rational, real-political calculations. And it doesn't need "weapons of mass destruction," since they were only an excuse for the public and politicians. They had nothing to do with the *real* reason for the war.

Bush doesn't care that there have been at least 175 wars since world War II, at the cost of perhaps 12 million lives, that have brought more misery than stability; or that the greatest user of weapons of mass destruction in history has been the United States; or that at least 10 other nations than Iraq actually *have* nuclear weapons. He doesn't care that he lost the popular election the first time around by half-a-million votes; or that the Joint Chiefs actually opposed the war at first; or that 70 percent of Americans oppose a war with significant casualties; or that the only other world superpower – popular opinion – is totally against him. Why should that distract him? He is on a holy, American mission. Against evil.

And it won't stop with Iraq, as long as Bush is in power. You are forewarned.

THE EDITORS' GLOSS: Naomi Klein's article, adapted from a piece that appeared in *The Nation*, and the postscript by Prof. O'Rourke, which originally appeared in the *Chicago Sun-Times*, demonstrate the fallacy of the "at least Iraq's better off than it was" defense of the war. If their testimony is to be believed – and reports that have been released since indicate that they should be – corruption and graft are, indeed, far worse than they were. One report is "U.S. Mismanagement of Iraqi Funds," prepared by the minority staff of the U.S. House Committee on Government Reform. It is a damning indication of how we approached just one aspect of the Iraqi commercial and financial situation. A *New York Times* report of June 25, 2005, noted an "office originally set up by the U.S. occupation to investigate corruption in Iraq" has, since July 2004, "looked into more than 814 cases of potential wrongdoing, producing 399 investigations that were still open at the end of May." The cases are not even confined to "the Iraqi executive branch, but also sprawl across provincial and city governments." One official said, according to the report, "that corruption had reached 'disastrous proportions' since 2003 and that some countries had been unwilling to send financial aid as a result."

Potentially shady dealings at the macro level are no less disturbing. Laith Kubba, a spokesman for the new Iraqi "Prime Minister," indicated (*Los Angeles Times*, June 6, 2005) that "post-war" Iraq is obliged to reduce public spending under a debt-reduction scheme sponsored by the IMF. Those "in the know" will understand what this means: IMF schemes are often coupled with internal "structural adjustments" and new loans (read debts) that benefit those already atop the international economic pyramid, translating into political and financial oppression of the regular Iraqis by "international" institutions.

More sobering still is a recent statement from John Perkins, author of *Confessions of an Economic Hit Man*, who has detailed the inner workings of debt-reduction and structural-adjustment schemes that the U.S. has sponsored for the last quarter century, the most famous being the deal struck with Saudi Arabia to dollarize oil sales in exchange for guaranteed military, infrastructural, and technological benefits. Perkins told Amy Goodman that "in Iraq we tried to implement the same policy that was so successful in Saudi Arabia, but Saddam Hussein didn't buy." The rest, sadly, is history: " . . . the third line of defense, if the economic hit men and the [CIA] jackals fail . . . is our young men and women, who are sent in to die and kill, which is what we've obviously done in Iraq." As if any of this contributes to "Iraq's being better off than it was."

Risky Business:
The Perils of Profitmongering in Iraq

· · · · · · · · ·

Naomi Klein

I
T WAS 8:40 a.m. on December 3, 2003, and the Sheraton Hotel ballroom thundered with the sound of plastic explosives pounding against metal. No, this was not the Sheraton in Baghdad, it was the one in Arlington, Virginia. And it was not a real terrorist attack, it was a hypothetical one. The screen at the front of the room was playing an advertisement for "bomb resistant waste receptacles": this trash can is so strong, we were told, it can contain a C4 blast. And its manufacturer was convinced that given half a chance, these babies would sell like hotcakes in Baghdad – at bus stations, Army barracks and, yes, upscale hotels. Available in Hunter Green, Fortuneberry Purple, and Windswept Copper.

This was ReBuilding Iraq 2, a two-day gathering of 400 business people itching to get a piece of the Iraqi reconstruction action. They were there to meet the people doling out the cash, in particular the $18.6 billion worth of reconstruction aid approved in November 2003 (as part of an $87 billion Iraq appropriation) to be dispensed in the form of contracts to companies from "coalition partner" countries. The people to meet were from the Coalition Provisional Authority (CPA), its Program Management Office, the Army Corps of Engineers, the U.S. Agency for International Development, Halliburton, Bechtel, and members of Iraq's interim Governing Council. All these players were on the conference program, and delegates had been promised that they would get a chance to corner them at regularly scheduled "networking breaks."

There have been dozens of similar trade shows on the business opportunities created by Iraq's decimation, held in hotel ballrooms from London to Amman. Though the early conferences (by all accounts) throbbed with the sort of cash-drunk euphoria not seen since the heady days before the dotcoms crashed, by the time of ReBuilding Iraq 2 it was apparent that something was not right. Sure, the conference's organizers did the requisite gushing about how "non-military rebuilding costs could be near $500 billion" and that this was "the largest government reconstruction effort since Americans helped to rebuild Germany and Japan after the Second World War."

But for the under-caffeinated crowd staring uneasily at exploding garbage cans, the mood was less gold rush than grim determination. Giddy talk of "greenfield" market opportunities had been supplanted by sober discussion of sudden-death insurance; excitement about easy government money had given way to controversy about foreign firms being shut out of the bidding process; exuberance about CPA chief Paul Bremer's ultra-liberal investment laws had been tempered by fears that those laws could be overturned by a directly elected Iraqi government.

At ReBuilding Iraq 2 it seemed finally to have dawned on the investment community that Iraq was not only an "exciting emerging market"; it was also a country on the verge of civil war. As Iraqis protested layoffs at state agencies and made increasingly vocal demands for general elections, it was becoming clear that the White House's pre-war conviction that Iraqis would welcome the transformation of their country into a free-market dream state may have been just as off-target as its prediction that U.S. soldiers would be greeted with flowers and candy.[1]

I mentioned to one delegate that fear seemed to be dampening the capitalist spirit. "The best time to invest is when there is still blood on the ground," he assured me. "Will you be going to Iraq?" I asked. "Me? No, I couldn't do that to my family."

He was still shaken, it seemed, by the afternoon's performance by ex-CIAer John MacGaffin, who had harangued the crowd like a Hollywood drill sergeant. "Soft targets are us!" he had bellowed. "We are right in the bull's-eye . . . . You must put security at the center of your operation!" Lucky for us, MacGaffin's own company, AKE Group, offered complete counterterrorism solutions, from body armor to emergency evacuations.

Youssef Sleiman, managing director of Iraq initiatives for the Harris Corporation, had a similarly entrepreneurial angle on the violence. Yes,

1. The fact that according to a *BBCNews* report of April 4, 2005, only 20% of the $18.6 billion earmarked for reconstruction had been spent, with half of that going for security, would seem to confirm the point. And *Chicago Tribune* correspondent, Cam Simpson, reporting from Amman, Jordan, at the Rebuild Iraq 2005 conference (held 4–7 April, 2005), noted in her article ("Graft, Fear Bind Iraqis Trying to Do Business," April 10, 2005, online) that many entrepreneurs still fear to cross the border into Iraq "because of continuing violence." Though the nation remains in "dire need of foreign investment," she pointed out, it "still can't offer legitimate letters of credit to foreign business people. Banking is a mess, telecommunications and electricity remain unreliable, and there are still few rules governing commerce."—Ed.

helicopters were falling, but "for every helicopter that falls there is going to be replenishment."

I began to notice that many of the delegates at ReBuilding Iraq 2 were sporting a similar look: Army-issue brush cuts paired with dark business suits. The guru of this gang was retired Maj. Gen. Robert Dees, at that point freshly hired out of the military to head Microsoft's "defense strategies" division. Dees told the crowd that rebuilding Iraq had special meaning for him because, well, he was one of the people who broke it. "My heart and soul is in this because I was one of the primary planners of the invasion," he said with pride. Microsoft was helping develop "e-government" in Iraq, which Dees admitted was a little ahead of the curve, since there was no g-government in Iraq – not to mention functioning phones lines.

No matter. Microsoft was determined to get in on the ground floor. In fact, the company was so tight with Iraq's Governing Council that one of its executives, Haythum Auda, served as the official translator for the council's Minister of Labor and Social Affairs, Sami Azara al-Ma'jun, during the conference. "There is no hatred against the coalition forces at all," al-Ma'jun said, via Auda. "The destructive forces are very minor and these will end shortly . . . . Feel confident in rebuilding Iraq!"

The speakers on a panel about "Managing Risks" had a different message: feel afraid about rebuilding Iraq, very afraid. Unlike previous presenters, their concern was not the obvious physical risks, but the potential economic ones. These were the insurance brokers, the grim reapers of Iraq's gold rush.

It turned out that there was a rather significant hitch in Paul Bremer's bold plan to auction off Iraq while it was still under occupation: the insurance companies weren't going for it. Until that point, the question of who would insure multinationals in Iraq had not been pressing. The major reconstruction contractors like Bechtel were covered by USAID for "unusually hazardous risks" encountered in the field. And Halliburton's pipeline work was covered under a law passed by Bush on May 22, 2003, that indemnified the entire oil industry from "any attachment, judgment, decree, lien, execution, garnishment, or other judicial process."

But with bidding having started on Iraq's state-owned firms, and foreign banks ready to open branches in Baghdad, the insurance issue was suddenly urgent. Many of the speakers admitted that the economic risks of going into Iraq without coverage were huge: privatized firms could be renationalized, foreign ownership rules could be reinstated and contracts signed with the CPA could be torn up.

Normally, multinationals protect themselves against this sort of thing by purchasing "political risk" insurance. Before he got the top job in Iraq

[189]

this was Bremer's business – selling political risk, expropriation, and terrorism insurance at Marsh & McLennan Companies, the largest insurance brokerage firm in the world. Yet in Iraq, Bremer oversaw the creation of a business climate so volatile that private insurers – including his old colleagues at Marsh & McLennan – were simply unwilling to take the risk. Bremer's Iraq was, by all accounts, uninsurable.

"The insurance industry has never been up against this kind of exposure before," R. Taylor Hoskins, vice president of Rutherford International insurance company, told the delegates apologetically. Steven Sadler, Managing Director and Chairman at Marsh Industry Practices, a division of Bremer's old firm, was even more downbeat. "Don't look to Iraq to find an insurance solution. Interest is very, very, very limited. There is very limited capacity and interest in the region."

It was clear that Bremer knew Iraq wasn't ready to be insured: when he signed Order 39, opening up much of Iraq's economy to 100 percent foreign ownership, the insurance industry was specifically excluded. I asked Sadler, a Bremer clone with slicked-back hair and bright red tie, whether he thought it strange that a former Marsh & McLennan executive could have so overlooked the need for investors to have insurance before they enter a war zone. "Well," he said, "he's got a lot on his plate." Or maybe he just had better information.

Just when the mood at ReBuilding Iraq 2 couldn't sink any lower, up to the podium strode Michael Lempres, vice president of insurance at the Overseas Private Investment Corporation (OPIC). With a cool confidence absent from the shell-shocked proceedings so far, he announced that investors could relax: Uncle Sam would protect them.

A U.S. government agency established in 1971, OPIC provides loans and insurance to U.S. companies investing abroad. And while Lempres agreed with earlier speakers that the risks in Iraq were "extraordinary and unusual," he also said that "OPIC is different. We do not exist primarily to generate profit." Instead, OPIC exists to "support U.S. foreign policy." And since turning Iraq into a free-trade zone was a top Bush policy goal, OPIC would be there to help out. Earlier that same day, President Bush had signed legislation providing "the agency with enhancements to its political risk insurance program," according to an OPIC press release.

Armed with this clear political mandate, Lempres announced that the agency was now "open for business" in Iraq, and was offering financing and insurance – including the riskiest insurance of all: political risk. "This is a priority for us," Lempres said. "We want to do everything we can to encourage U.S. investment in Iraq."

The news, at the time unreported, appeared to take even the high-est-level delegates by complete surprise. After his presentation, Lempres was approached by Julie Martin, a political risk specialist at Marsh & McLennan.

"Is it true?" she demanded.

Lempres nodded. "Our lawyers are ready."

"I'm stunned," Martin said. "You're ready? No matter who the govern-ment is?"

"We're ready," Lempres replied. "If there's an expro[priation] on January 3, we're ready . . . . I don't know what we're going to do if someone sinks a billion dollars into a pipeline and there's an expro."

Lempres didn't seem too concerned about those possible "expros," but it was a serious question. According to its official mandate, OPIC func-tioned "on a self-sustaining basis at no net cost to taxpayers." But Lempres admitted that the political risks in Iraq were "extraordinary." If a new Iraqi government were to expropriate and re-regulate across the board, OPIC could be forced to compensate dozens of U.S. firms for billions of dollars in lost investments and revenues, possibly tens of billions. What would happen then?

At the Microsoft-sponsored cocktail reception in the Galaxy Ballroom that evening, Robert Dees urged us "to network on behalf of the people of Iraq." I followed orders and asked Lempres what would happen if "the people of Iraq" decided to seize back their economy from the U.S. firms he had so generously insured. Who would bail out OPIC? "In theory," he said, "the U.S. Treasury stands behind us." That meant the U.S. taxpayer. Yes, them again: the same people who had already paid Halliburton, Bechtel et al, to make a killing on Iraq's reconstruction would have to pay these companies *again*, this time in compensation for their losses. While the enormous profits being made in Iraq were strictly private, it turned out that the entire risk was being shouldered by the public.

For the non-U.S. firms in the room, OPIC's announcement was any-thing but reassuring: since only U.S. companies were eligible for its insur-ance, and the private insurers were sitting it out, how could they compete? The answer was that they likely could not. Some countries might decide to match OPIC's Iraq program. But in the short term, not only had the U.S. government barred companies from non-"coalition partners" from com-peting for contracts against U.S. firms, it had made sure that the foreign firms that were allowed to compete would do so at a serious disadvantage.

The reconstruction of Iraq has emerged as a vast protectionist racket, a neocon New Deal that transfers limitless public funds – in contracts, loans, and insurance – to private firms, and even gets rid of the foreign competition to boot, under the guise of "national security." Ironically, those firms were initially handed this corporate welfare so they could take full advantage of CPA-imposed laws that stripped Iraqi industry of all *its* protections, from import tariffs to limits on foreign ownership. As Michael Fleisher, onetime head of private-sector development for the CPA, said to a group of Iraqi business people (explaining why these protections had to be removed), "Protected businesses never, never become competitive," he said. Somebody should have told that to OPIC and Paul Wolfowitz.[1]

The issue of U.S. double standards came up again at the conference when a CPA representative took the podium. A legal adviser to Bremer, Carole Basri had a simple message: reconstruction was being sabotaged by Iraqi corruption. "My fear is that corruption will be the downfall," she said ominously, blaming the problem on "a thirty-five-year gap in knowledge" in Iraq that had made Iraqis "not aware of current accounting standards and ideas on anti-corruption." Foreign investors, she said, must engage in "education – bring people up to world-class standards."

It is hard to imagine what world-class standards she was referring to, or who, exactly, was supposed to be doing this educating. Halliburton, with its accounting scandals and its outrageous over-billing for gasoline in Iraq? The CPA, whose inspector general generated a report in mid-2004 that triggered 27 criminal cases, and which was reported in early 2005 as having failed to account properly for some $9 billion?[2] On the final day of ReBuilding Iraq 2, the cover headline in our complimentary copies of the *Financial Times* (a conference sponsor) was "Boeing linked to Perle invest-

1. It is worth remembering that the Pentagon, via a December 5, 2003, directive issued by Deputy Secretary of Defense Paul Wolfowitz, barred French, German, and Russian companies from competing for contracts to be awarded as part of the $18.6 billion reconstruction aid package (Douglas Jehl, "A Region Inflamed: The Reconstruction; Pentagon Bars Three Nations From Iraq Bids," *New York Times*, December 10, 2003, p. 1).—Ed.

2. Since the U.S.-led "transformation" of the Iraqi economy, the bad news has only increased. An Iraqi office established originally by the U.S. occupation authority has looked into 814 cases of potential corruption relating to reconstruction funds paid to Iraqi agencies and officials by the U.S., producing 399 investigations (as of May 2005) and 44 arrest warrants for Iraqi government employees. The problems identified include "sweetheart deals on leases, exorbitant contracts for things like garbage hauling, and payments for construction that was never done." The author of a recent report puts questions raised by the investigation's findings in rather understated terms, saying that the information will "fuel the most pessimistic concerns over where the money has gone." See James Glanz, "Iraq Officials Detail Extensive Corruption," *International Herald Tribune*, June 25, 2005, online. [Interested readers should also see the report by the minority staff of the House Committee on Government Reform on the cash delivered to Iraq, and then lost track of: "Rebuilding Iraq: U.S. Mismanagement of Funds," June, 2005 (http://www.democrats.reform.house.gov/Documents/20050621114229-22109.pdf).—Ed.]

ment fund." Perhaps Richard Perle – who had supported Boeing's $18 billion refueling-tanker deal and extracted $20 million from Boeing for his investment fund – was the one to teach Iraq's politicians to stop soliciting "commissions" in exchange for contracts.

For the Iraqi expats in the audience, Basri's was a tough lecture to sit through. "To be honest," said Ed Kubba, a consultant and board member of the American Iraqi Chamber of Commerce, "I don't know where the line is between business and corruption." He pointed to U.S. companies subcontracting huge taxpayer-funded reconstruction jobs for a fraction of what they were getting paid, then pocketing the difference. "If you take $10 million from the U.S. government and sub the job out to Iraqi businesses for a quarter-million, is that business, or is that corruption?"

These were the sorts of uncomfortable questions faced by George Sigalos, director of government relations for Halliburton KBR. In the hierarchy of Iraqi reconstruction, Halliburton is king, and Sigalos sat onstage, heavy with jeweled ring and gold cufflinks, playing the part. But the serfs were getting restless, and the room quickly turned into a support group for jilted would-be subcontractors.

"Mr. Sigalos, what are we going to have to do to get some subcontracts?"

"Mr. Sigalos, when are you going to hire some Iraqis in management and leadership?"

"I have a question for Mr. Sigalos. I would like to ask what you would suggest when the Army says, 'Go to Halliburton,' and there's no response from Halliburton?"

Sigalos patiently instructed them all to register their companies on Halliburton's website. When the questioners responded that they had already done so and still hadn't heard back, Sigalos invited them to "approach me afterward."

The scene afterward was part celebrity autograph session, part riot. Sigalos was swarmed by at least fifty men, who elbowed each other out of the way to shower the Halliburton VP with CD-ROMs, business plans and resumes. When Sigalos spotted a badge from Volvo, he looked relieved. "Volvo! I know Volvo. Send me something about what you can achieve in the region." But the small, no-name players who had paid their $985 entrance fees, there to hawk portable generators and electrical control paneling, were once again told to "register with our procurement office."

There were and are fortunes being made in Iraq, but it seems – as illustrated not least by my experience at the Arlington Sheraton – they are out of reach to all but the chosen few.

CHAPTER
11
postscript

The More Things Change . . .
• • • • • • • • • •
Prof. William O'Rourke

GIVEN THE REALITIES of the war in Iraq – shock and awe, death and destruction, a continuing guerrilla insurgency – it is easy to overlook what in Hollywood is called "the back story," what our government also brought to Iraq when it invaded: we're not just bringing "democracy" to Iraq, we are bringing, without objection, unchecked free-market ideology.

When Paul Bremer, fresh from Kissinger Associates, first arrived in Iraq, the Coalition Provisional Authority made a lot of changes other than just disbanding what was left of the Iraqi army. He annulled all of Saddam Hussein's rules and regulations overseeing the Iraq economy, except one: he kept Saddam's laws banning labor unions.

Tariffs protecting Iraqi industries were cut to a minimum. Foreign ownership of land and most businesses was allowed. Iraq had had a largely self-sustaining economy, but when Bremer's reforms were enacted, all that changed.

Iraq's cement industry found itself being undersold by Jordanian firms after the tariffs were cut, and when cement plants shut down – similar to the permanent death steel mills suffer when closed – they turn into concrete. Iraq is now a cement importer – not a sign of economic efficiency. As one military observer put it, the State Department sent in young economists – many in their first job out of graduate school – to create the free-market economy Bremer and the White House wanted.

When Bremer left in June 2004 he didn't leave behind a new economy, just a destroyed one.

The free-market economy experiment has made Iraq a nation of importers and high unemployment – nearly 50 percent – and the U.S. underwrites endless unemployment insurance. Much of business is still conducted in a cash-and-carry manner. Hundred-dollar bills have been a symbol of the

Iraq war since its very beginning, when caches of them were found squirreled away in various locations. The American military pays compensation in cash for whatever human collateral damage occurs, if relatives of the damage complain.

The new Iraqi government in formation is having trouble deciding how to divide the spoils of the war, though, at this point, the spoils are largely spoiled. Counter to all claims to the contrary, the one industry that remains as it was before the war – in fact, has even improved – is the oil industry, and, although Bremer wanted it privatized, oil was exempted temporarily, though it remains under the protection and control of the U.S. military. In any case, outside investors aren't too eager to risk their capital and employees in such an unsafe environment. Iraq's National Assembly halted its work in March 2005 when it couldn't decide who would be named oil minister.

What the Bush administration is doing domestically – trying to privatize Social Security, continuing tax favors for corporations, changing bankruptcy laws to favor business over individuals, applying free-market ideology wherever possible – has been done with impunity in Iraq.

Wars might be hell, but they have their up side for business. Bechtel and Halliburton might be impeded in the way they do business here in the States, but in Iraq, anything goes. One of the first edicts Bremer signed gave immunity from Iraqi laws to U.S. contractors and other Western firms doing business in Iraq.

Americans are concerned with the suffering of their soldier children, dead and injured and in peril. It is hard to get exercised over spending tax money for other purposes, beyond that of the tardily produced body and Hummer armor – all the equipment and infrastructure large armies require. The last thing on most minds is the fact that the Bush administration has attempted, however ineptly, to remake Iraq in its chosen image: a triumphal business-friendly, free-market paradise, a future Banana Republic, where those in-the-know profit and those on the ground try to figure out what happened to their lives.

It kills me when I hear of the continuing casualties and the sacrifice that's being made. It also kills me when I hear someone say that, well, each one of those is a personal tragedy, but in the overall scheme of things, they're insignificant statistically. Never should we let any political leaders utter those words. This is the greatest treasure the United States has, our enlisted men and women. And when we put them into harm's way, it had better count for something. It can't be because some policy wonk back here has a brain fart of an idea of a strategy that isn't thought out.

They should never be put on a battlefield without a strategic plan, not only for the fighting – our generals will take care of that – but for the aftermath and winning that war. Where are we, the American people, if we accept this, if we accept this level of sacrifice without that level of planning? Almost everyone in this room, of my contemporaries – our feelings and our sensitivities were forged on the battlefields of Vietnam; where we heard the garbage and the lies, and we saw the sacrifice. We swore never again would we do that. WE SWORE NEVER AGAIN WOULD WE ALLOW IT TO HAPPEN. *And I ask you, is it happening again?*

> —Gen. Anthony Zinni, USMC (ret.),
> September 4, 2003, at the Marine Corps
> Association and U.S. Naval Institute Forum

THE PROFESSIONALS SPEAK:
MILITARY REACTIONS TO
OPERATION IRAQI FREEDOM

THE EDITORS' GLOSS: Lt. Col. Kwiatkowski has received flack for her candid reporting about what the Pentagon policy shop she worked in looked like as war with Iraq approached. That she was attacked principally by a civilian ideologue who had a minor role to play in preparing for war from his Pentagon office (where he was on loan from, not surprisingly, the American Enterprise Institute) means that her accounts struck a raw nerve. That the attack comes via *National Review Online* in a May 2004 article full of ad hominem attacks coupled with sanctimonious protests is yet further evidence that she's onto something.

Her article is an intriguing read in its own right. Let us simply point out that she makes a subtle observation towards the end that we think needs emphasizing. "The military brass," she writes, could "have prevented this invasion." As Dr. Lutz observes in a footnote, "civilian control of the military" is something of a loose term. No doubt what it means, and what it is understood to mean, for normal people is that the American people should, through their elected representatives, control the nation's armed forces and establish when and where they will be used. What it tends to become in practice is the subservience of career military professionals to politically appointed hacks who tow a party line and expect their "subordinates" to do the same. This is the picture painted by Kwiatkowski in her description of the workings of the Office of the Secretary of Defense. It is this culture and practice that the military brass should have stood up to, especially in light of its drift towards an illegal war, sold to the American people based upon a pack of lies. But "following orders" is evidently an acceptable answer in this case. After all, they're not the Germans.

An Inside Look at Pentagon Policy-Making in the Run-Up to Gulf War II
• • • • • • • • •

Lt. Col. Karen Kwiatkowski, USAF (ret.)

AT THE PENTAGON these days, often on Friday afternoons, award ceremonies are held for soldiers injured in the Iraq occupation. They limp, hobble and roll, or are pushed up to the front to accept their award and the quiet applause of the Pentagon brass and other staff. These soldiers are mostly in their late teens or early twenties. They have little education, few marketable skills, no financial resources, and appalling and debilitating injuries. Most are on their way to being discharged from the Army or Marines. The overwhelming majority will never again be employed by any agency of the United States government, or by Halliburton or Bechtel for that matter.

But these thousands of injured servicemen and women may be better off than the roughly eighteen-hundred Americans who have been killed in Iraq so far. We are engaged in a preemptive war of occupation, a fourth generation war launched in March 2003 under cover of the dissembling actions of an American President who never understood war, a vice president who might have but had "other priorities," a crew of very focused neoconservative ideologues, and a confused, muddling, and irresponsible Congress.

When Army Captain Russell Burgos returned from the occupation of Iraq, he observed to the *Washington Post* that, "The 'peace' has been bloodier than the war." He compares America in Iraq to Israel's 18-year occupation of Lebanon. He notes, "Some of us were using the Lebanon analogy even before we invaded."[1]

One wonders if the "some of us" thinking of Israel's 18 years in Lebanon included the architects of the preemptive invasion of Iraq. Did Richard

---

1. Thomas Ricks, "U.S. Troops Death Rates Rising in Iraq" *Washington Post*, September 9, 2004, p. A1.

Perle, Paul Wolfowitz, Donald Rumsfeld, Dick Cheney, Douglas Feith, and the united pseudo-intellectual column at the Project for a New American Century, the American Enterprise Institute, and the Washington Institute for Near East Affairs consider the Lebanon occupation before promoting their war?

As Pat Buchanan has so eloquently pointed out, Iraq is indeed "their" war. And for all its costs and blatant immorality, it was a valuable war for neoconservative ideologues, for reasons never shared with the American public. Retired Lieutenant General Jay Garner has said we will occupy Iraq for at least the next 20 or 30 years, in part because we need a powerful military presence in the Middle East. Americans might compare the "liberation" of Iraq to the case in the Philippines almost a century ago. There, too, was a preemptive war based on false stories manipulated by Washington-based warmongers, categorized as liberation, and resulting in a bloody and hated American occupation that lasted well over 30 years. Even General Garner used the Philippine case to explain Iraq "positively" to *Government Executive* magazine in February 2004.[1]

I worked in the Under Secretariat for Defense Policy, the Near East and South Asia (NESA) desk under the International Security Affairs Directorate, from May 2002 to February 2003, during the most heated part of the political preparation and justification for war. Our director was Bill Luti, a retired Navy Captain, armed with a Ph.D. from the Fletcher School and the sponsorship of Dick Cheney. He nominally supervised Abram Shulsky, who served as director of the NESA sister, Office of Special Plans (OSP), a group of 20 or so mostly political appointees convened in the summer of 2003. OSP was apparently chartered to ensure proper development and promulgation of talking points explaining to the unwashed how the upcoming invasion of Iraq was liberation for humanity and democracy, and not a territorial and economic expansion of American – and by extension, Israeli – influence in the region. Shulsky's real "boss," however, appeared to be less the apparatchik Luti and more accurately Paul Wolfowitz, then our deputy secretary of defense; his boss Donald Rumsfeld; and the under secretary for policy, the notoriously pro-Likud and former legal consultant for Turkey and Israel, Douglas Feith. It was a happy family – for those related to the neoconservatives. Every military and civilian professional with actual current cultural and military knowledge of the Middle East was excluded from that inner decision-making circle. And, as in all good

---

1. Amy Svitak Klampe, "Former Iraq Administrator Sees Decades Long U.S. Military Presence in Iraq," *Government Executive*, February 6, 2004.

tragedies, the seeds of pending disaster were sown early, and they were readily apparent to those watching the show.

I and my co-workers – Army and Air Force colonels, Navy captains, senior civilians in Policy and Intelligence, and even the administrative professionals – observed in a kind of paralyzed numbness the march to preemptive war to topple Saddam Hussein, to found a friendly regime in Baghdad (at the time in the person of the clearly anointed Ahmad Chalabi of the Iraqi National Congress), and to establish military bases in the heart of the Middle East in order to better threaten Iran and Syria, and to allow us to vacate Saudi Arabia militarily.

In retrospect, it is amazing to realize that the toppling of Saddam Hussein, threats to the Shiite government in Iran and the secular one in Syria, and the removal of American troops from Saudi Arabian territory are the same goals as those oft-stated by the Wahhabist Sunni radical, Osama bin Laden. But we didn't think in those terms then. Most of us mid-level officers and civilians simply watched in wide-eyed amazement as policy organs in the Pentagon, and in parts of the Departments of State and Energy, were hijacked by neoconservatives: political activists just as committed, organized, and disciplined as those who hijacked four jetliners on September 11.

The Office of Special Plans apparently planned very little for the actual occupation of Iraq. In fact, the office was disbanded a year later, a few months after President Bush declared "Mission Accomplished" in May 2004. To this day, the OSP, and leading neoconservatives have had nothing to offer in terms of occupation guidance, beyond "kill the insurgents." Of course, none of them would actually be doing that dirty work. For them the mission had been accomplished, in the re-creation of a Philippine experience, a Lebanon experience, or the creation of a new West Bank for the United States. The false patriotism and misplaced anger they manipulated in order to justify the invasion of Iraq would, they hoped, translate into a stubborn reluctance among the American people to ever retreat, admit a mistake, or recognize a lie. It was a good gamble for these Machiavellians, among at least 30% of the population.

During the run-up to war, Abe Shulsky was the "approving" official for the talking points that all desk officers (including myself) were mandated to include in their written work. Copy and paste, we were told, no edits or deletes. These talking points on Iraq, WMD, and terrorism were carefully crafted to integrate bits of "intelligence" with lots of wishful thinking on the part of the neoconservatives. Not just for internal use, many of the same "talking points" were publicly repeated by key neoconservative organs in the media, such as the *National Review* and the *Washington Times*, and by pundits like Charles Krauthammer, William Safire, and Bill Kristol. Uncritical editors at the *New York Times* and *Washington Post* filled their news and editorial pages with the government-issued false flags. The President and vice president made numerous speeches in the summer and fall of 2002, lapping from the same dish of tasty fabrications: Saddam worked with al-Qaeda; Iraq assisted in the attacks on the Twin Towers and Pentagon; Iraq recently sought, and even has, deliverable nuclear and active biological capability; and though Iraq had been bombed and sanctioned for over 12 years by the greatest military on earth, was intensively monitored by the global community, and was without an air force or navy, President Bush and his national security advisor, Condoleeza Rice, blithely proclaimed that the threat of Saddam Hussein could be ignored only at the risk of a mushroom cloud rising over rubble in the heartland. Not since the fables collected by Jacob and Wilhelm Grimm have such stories captured the fearful imagination of whole nations.

But these modern Bush-Cheney fantasies lasted less than a year. By summer 2003, the Congress and the American people were shown both evidence and commentary that began to reveal the level of deception disseminated by their own government, from key congressmen, to the President, vice president, and the secretary of defense. By late spring 2004 major newspapers around the country were already publishing *mea culpas* for their vacuous consumption of government lies regarding the reasons for the invasion and occupation of Iraq. Meanwhile, we stay in Iraq, we kill in Iraq, we die in Iraq; we help sow the seeds of future generations of committed anti-Americanism and hatred of Western politics. Iraqi patriots, like those who wrested our own independence from Great Britain centuries ago, will utilize techniques that some call terrorism, but military strategists from Sun Tzu to William Lind understand to be simply the weapons of fourth generation warfare, the methods of combat by the stateless hopefuls against the hopeless state.

Over two years ago, America conducted what is now commonly understood to be an illegal invasion of a sovereign state. The invasion was supported by the majority in a democracy whose post-9/11 fear and anger were callously and calculatedly transferred to another secret enemy – not an enemy of that majority, but an enemy of the frenetic neoconservatives in Washington. It was an evidently undemanding bait and switch operation conducted on a national scale in a country purported to have an educated populace and an independent media.

Today, the political challenge for Washington, especially neoconservative and establishmentarian Washington, is to justify the occupation: one more costly, more deadly, and more resented than even neoconservatives familiar with Israel's costly, deadly, and resented 18-year Lebanon occupation had expected. Today, as Secretary of Defense Rumsfeld shatters the readiness of the National Guard and Reserve, and destroys morale in the standing Army, the neoconservatives and occupation supporters must find new stories to tell as Americans begin to wake up to the reality of Iraq, the wrongness of the occupation, the falseness of the rationale, and the real possibility of a re-institution of the draft.

When I worked in the Pentagon, my military co-workers and I attempted privately to understand the real reasons for the invasion of Iraq, and why it was needed in 2002 or 2003, a time when Saddam Hussein had never been more contained and constrained politically, economically, and militarily. We realized that the "intelligence" being touted in 2002 didn't match what we knew and had known for years about Saddam Hussein's capabilities and intentions. So why invade? Why topple this dictator? And why now? Saddam Hussein was a former ally; the United States purchased 80% of the oil he sold under sanctions, even while bombing his military positions. He was certainly no worse to his people than many current dictators we confer and trade with, and even defend. In fact, Saddam tolerated more religious freedom and education of women than both Pakistan and Saudi Arabia. There were "reasons," however. To sustain the occupation these reasons must be put forward by Bush; and military occupation must be accepted by the United States population as the only option.

Military basing shifts in the Middle East were a key driver for the occupation, and for the awarding of contracts to the Halliburton subsidiary, Kellogg, Brown and Root, and to Bechtel. These are our lead base builders. Base building is the most profitable of the work they have been doing in Iraq, with numerous bases constructed or upgraded to support United States military operations. That we may "safely" leave Saudi Arabia, and "safely" threaten Iran and Syria on behalf of Israeli interests or our own, is a great strategic benefit. But that benefit will be greater still when the ring of American bases, top of the line in some cases, from Bosnia to Kosovo, to Uzbekistan, to Afghanistan, to Iraq is completed. We will then militarily encircle an oil and gas geography that is coveted by many but effectively challengeable by none. In terms of cold war realist theory, if no state can challenge us, and expand to where we are, we are secure. The conceptual flaw on the part of neoconservatives, otherwise intelligent and well-educated people, is their Neanderthal-like perspective that states are the ultimate conception of organization, and that all fights use the same weapons. Just as their intellectual predecessors faded and left only traces of their one-time ascendance, so will go the neoconservatives – but not just yet.

But the war is about more than bases. Saddam Hussein in 2003 was ready to re-enter the community of nations, and all evidence to that effect was well known to the rest of the world. Even the UN inspection regime was satisfied that the level of access and cooperation they had received was satisfactory, and that the sanctions were costing far more in human terms than ever intended or justified. The major nations of the world were preparing to lift sanctions, to trade with Iraq, and to invest in Iraq and take advantage of economic opportunities there – once the most industrially productive of the Arab countries. Plus it was a secular nation where women freely worked outside the home and could supervise men in the workplace, as education, skills and productivity might demand. It was believed by most of the world that sanctions on Iraq should be lifted, and the UN – even the Security Council itself – is only as strong as a shared faith in its mandates. Had the sanctions been lifted either in part or in full with Saddam Hussein in power, only three countries would have been unable to participate in the harvest: the United States and the United Kingdom, who had been busily bombing Iraq for well over a decade, and the tiny but economically strained Israel, a nation Saddam Hussein had clearly deemed an enemy, and against which he supported the Palestinian cause. The sanctions were in fact already collapsing, with many countries, including European Security Council members, actively seeking business arrangements with Iraq. A post-sanction Iraq with Saddam Hussein in charge would not only be costly to the United States, Great Britain, and Israel; it would be unacceptable to American neoconservatives. Regime change was necessary: not for the common Iraqi "suffering" under Saddam Hussein's rule, but for American, British, and Israeli corporations sure to be left out otherwise. A key success for the neoconservative approach in Iraq is that United States, British, and Israeli investment is first, and then contracts with other firms are granted only as the spoils of war, not on productive merit or free competition in the global marketplace.

A final reason, again merging the interests of the United States and Israel – and to a lesser extent the U.K. – has to do with the financial dilemma of George W. Bush's America. Unlike a generation or two ago, even in the big spending years of Nixon, LBJ, and Ronald Reagan, the United States today is a debtor nation which since November 2002 has been running significant monthly current account deficits – at times as much as some $60 billion. Unlike what has happened in the past to countries like Mexico or Argentina, no one on the planet can mandate that the United States implement the "Washington consensus," a ten-step financial repair and dietary program of reduced spending, increased taxes and tax collection, deregulation of industries, and privatization of federal and state assets. The American solution is to print and sell more Treasury bills, hoping against hope that future generations will be able to make good on the promises of today's aging but politically empowered baby boom generation. Treasury bills are purchased by foreign governments, particularly Asian and European, and their central banks. Dollars are thus a large part (but not all) of their investment portfolios. The rise of the Euro was viewed with some trepidation a decade ago, but its managerial overhead and floundering as a favored currency was a calming influence in Washington. But as the debt-laden American economy has slowed in growth and shifted in terms of real exports and real productivity (from a technology and a demographic perspective), the popularity of the dollar as the bank reserve currency of choice has diminished. But there were no worries as long as it was clear that most oil would be traded on the dollar.

Unfortunately for Saddam Hussein, he formally changed the currency Iraq would use for oil exports in November 2000 (almost a year before 9/11). In a post-sanctions oil production environment, this shift in currency was terrifying to those who rely politically on continued monthly purchases of America's debt. Naturally, the first executive order signed by President Bush regarding Iraq in May 2003 changed the oil-trading currency back into dollars, and effectively transferred the oil into American control.

Indeed there were many reasons to invade and occupy Iraq and select a friendly puppet government. But none would have gotten Americans excited; because most Americans believe in free trade and peace, and are not interested in sending their sons and daughters to faraway places to fight a war that really interests only pro-Israel ideologues, banks, and the big corporations. Americans may have a certain fondness for Israel, banks, and corporations, but there were other ways of achieving the salient goals of each of these entities. But the peaceful, trade-oriented ways of accessing Iraqi oil, helping develop the Iraqi economy, making the dollar more attractive, and even negotiating military bases in foreign countries, were not controllable by a small group of neoconservatives. The outcomes could not be guaranteed. So the neocons chose to send us to war instead. Their salient goals, it seems, were all achieved, and are locked up tight. The only uncertainties are which of our sons and daughters gets to die today, and which ones will come home maimed today, as we weather an occupation that is opposed by almost all Iraqis. These uncertainties are not born by neoconservative ideologues. As has been often noted, the ideologues, including Bush and Cheney, have no personal experience with combat, and none of their children serves in uniform.

Could the immoral and illegal invasion of Iraq have been prevented? Of course. Imagine Bill Clinton in a post-Monica Lewinsky environment launching a preemptive war of occupation, with boots on the ground. He barely got his "humanitarian" war in Kosovo, and the whole Washington establishment wanted that one. He dropped a few missiles into Afghanistan, and the chattering classes consumed themselves with "wag the dog" theories of his real motivation. Simple partisan politics between the Congress and the President would have prevented such an invasion.

Could the media have prevented the Iraqi invasion and occupation? Of course. They could have asked the right questions, the hard questions, and challenged the transparently illogical storyline from the White House and the Pentagon. They might have publicly queried our supercilious secretary of defense with real questions of strategy and motivation instead of offering only tentative fawning adoration. The so-called independent American media might have put aside its fear of exclusion, and of being verbally attacked by government talking heads, and found the fortitude to discover and report the truth.

Could the military brass have prevented this invasion? Yes, by insisting privately and stating publicly what the real reasons were for this war and why it was seen as a strategic necessity. Those reasons included the cost and operational constraints of enforcing sanctions on Iraq with air strikes from bases in Kuwait, Turkey, and the 5th Fleet that were draining the readiness of the Air Force and Navy, while the Army was perceived as growing fat and lazy. A discussion of both the real military problem in the Middle East and American strategic goals would have opened the door to real solutions. And none of the best solutions would have included the neoconservative choice of invasion, occupation, and a puppet government.

Could the American people have prevented this invasion? By themselves – without the support of the Congress, the media, and the military leadership – they could not. That, in fact, exemplifies the situation we have observed in the last several years. American democracy, like most others, is vulnerable to the vagaries and incompetence of those who control the mainstream media and to Congressional representatives more concerned with their own political positions than serving the interests of their constituents. Moreover the American people are always vulnerable to a White House willing to use its credibility and bully pulpit to appeal to emotions over logic, to offer colorful fireworks instead of a shed full of split wood to a people in fear of a cold winter.

Our Iraq occupation will end when the American people themselves react to a corporate Washington political establishment by refusing to listen to the marionette media; when we reject the pleas of the President for more time, more money, more lives, and more understanding. It will end when we send a message of disgust to Congress for their utter lack of statesmanship and respect for the Constitution. It will end as returning servicemen and women tell the truth to anyone willing to listen. And it will end when we step up to living as a compassionate people and accept our responsibility to care for the returning soldiers – the physically and mentally disabled ones – who paid too high a price for this narrow, un-American, and immoral agenda.

In ending the occupation of Iraq, and the military and financial manipulation of many lesser countries in the Middle East, we would also fight (and possibly end) terrorism against American interests and friends. In making a moral and a traditionally American choice about how to behave in the world, and without spending a penny or sacrificing one more life, we would be acting as true patriots. Thomas Jefferson and the rest of the Founders would certainly have advised us in this direction.

THE EDITORS' GLOSS: Where Karen Kwiatkowski provides a snap-shot from the battlefield of career military officers serving their civilian, political-appointee masters, Dr. Hickson fills in the historical, cultural, and philosophical background. His sweeping essay drives at – among other things – the issue that we have raised in a number of places: the need for an effective military culture to act as a restraint against those who have effectively hijacked the Defense Department as an instrument not in the service of the national interest, but of a dangerously radical agenda aiming to transform the world by force of arms.

"The common good of the United States would be greatly furthered if there were even just one 'ferociously honest' man within the U.S. mili-tary," Dr. Hickson writes. This is indeed a tall order, but as unlikely as it is, it is even more desperately needed today. When the few men who talked sense – even timidly – to the defense secretary prior to the war can be summarily dismissed for not "playing ball," there is clearly a need for a more deeply honest man who will not just curse the tacti-cal losses but expose the flaws of the whole system. When 20-year-old Navy petty officers are sacrificing their careers and personal comfort in order to avoid participation in a clearly unjust war to uphold the rule of law and moral values, while the four-stars charged with the leader-ship of the entire military establishment have not the courage to "speak truth to power," as the saying goes, something is gravely wrong.

Dr. Hickson's observations contribute to the beginnings of an under-standing of just what that is, and they illustrate how "root and branch" the reformation of the military will have to be.

13

The Moral Responsibility of the U. S. Military Officer in the Context of the Larger War We Are In

• • • • • • • • •

Robert Hickson, USA (ret.), Ph.D.

T HIS ESSAY PROPOSES to consider the long-range effects of a gradually implemented educational reform within the American military culture – a form of re-education that was slowly introduced by the psychological and social scientists after World War II. In a more mitigated form than the German military's *Umerziehung* (i.e., re-education) after World War II, the American military culture seems to have undergone its own transformation and "instrumentalization" in order to become a more useful, non-authoritarian professional cadre in the service of a modern, often messianic, and increasingly imperial democracy.

It would seem that the traditional, more or less Christian, American military culture had to be re-paganized and neo-Machiavellianized and made more philo-Judaic – or at least less patently (or latently) "anti-Semitic."

The Freudian-Marxist "Frankfurt School" doctrines could further build upon the educational reforms which had already been implemented by John Dewey's own theories of pragmatism and instrumentalism. These combined innovations in military, as well as civilian, education would seem to have weakened the intellectual and moral character of the American military officer, and concurrently inclined him to become more technocratic as well as more passive and neutral as an instrument in the service of his civilian masters in a "modern democracy" or a new "messianic *imperium*" with a "globalist, neo-liberal ideology." Indeed, some of these innovations were introduced when I was first being formed as a future military officer.

It was in the autumn of 1960, after Plebe Summer and the test of "Beast Barracks," that I first heard about the revisions that the West Point academic curriculum had recently undergone, and which would be experimentally applied to our incoming class of some eight hundred men. Col. Lincoln's Social Science Department, as it was presented to us, was to be much more influential and more deeply formative than before upon the education of officers. There were to be several more classes now in military psychology, sociology, and leadership, and fewer in strategic military history and concrete military biography. The long-standing and ongoing process of replacing the Humanities with the academic and applied social sciences would, we were told, continue and increase.

At the time – especially at 17 years of age – I had little idea of the implications of these curricular revisions, nor of their underlying soft "logic of scientific discovery," much less an awareness of the growing "soft tyranny" of the Social Sciences and their subtly relativizing "sociology of knowledge" (as in the work of German sociologist, Karl Mannheim). But I do remember reading two mandatory books: Samuel Huntington's *The Soldier and the State* and Morris Janowitz's *The Professional Soldier.* Both of these books, we were told, were to help form the proper kind of officer that was needed in "modern democratic society."

Janowitz had an intellectual background rooted in neo-Marxist "critical theory" as it was first propagated by Max Horkheimer and Theodor Adorno at the Institute for Social Research of the University of Frankfurt in Germany. (This school of thought became more commonly known as "the Frankfurt School.") This internationally networked school of Marxist-Freudian thought – indeed a well-armed ideology – was likewise active in conducting various "studies in prejudice" and quite intensely concerned about the dangers of the "authoritarian personality," especially because this character type supposedly tended to "fascism" and "anti-Semitism." The Frankfurt School "critical theory" claimed to detect and to unmask "anti-democratic tendencies," perhaps most notably in traditional military institutions and their more autocratic cultures – especially because of the recent history of Germany – but also in traditional, well-rooted, religious institutions of the West, i.e., Christian institutions in general and the culture of the Catholic Church most specifically.

The Frankfurt School theorists and activists claimed to want to produce the "democratic personality" – although they had originally (and more revealingly) called it the "revolutionary personality." This purportedly "democratic personality" was to be a fitting replacement for the inordinately prejudiced and latently dangerous "authoritarian personality," which allegedly conduced to the disorder and illness of "anti-Semitism."

The combination of Karl Marx's earlier writings and critical theories and Sigmund Freud's psychiatric theories would be a special mark of this "neo-Marxist critical theory," not only in the writings of Wilhelm Reich and Herbert Marcuse, but also in the "anti-authoritarian" psychology of Erich Fromm.

Morris Janowitz was at the time (1960) a sociologist at the University of Chicago, and he seemed to want to form a "new kind of military professionalism" and a new kind of military officer. That is to say, a military officer who would be a "suitable" instrument to serve those who are truly "governing a modern democracy."

These last few words in quotation marks were taken from a recent essay by the candid Irving Kristol (the neoconservative patriarch and *patronus* and former Trotskyite) who has for some years been writing about, and promoting, "the emerging American *imperium*," first in the *Wall Street Journal* in the mid-1990s.

In the August 25, 2003, issue of the *Weekly Standard*, Kristol wrote a forthright article entitled, "The Neoconservative Persuasion." In this essay he uses words that could also be retroactively applied to the larger, long-range re-education and cultural project of the Frankfurt School, of Morris Janowitz, and of his kind of "neo-military sociologist." Kristol speaks in somewhat elevated but bluntly candid language as follows:

> The *historical* task and political *purpose* of *neoconservatism* [and also of the "new" military sociology and psychology?] would seem to be this: *to convert* the Republican party, and American conservatism [and also the American military culture?] in general, *against their respective wills*, into *a new kind* of conservative politics [and hence a neo-imperial American military and its Global Expeditionary Force?] *suitable to governing a modern democracy*.[1]

In the article Kristol further argues that, "like the Soviet Union of yesteryear," the "United States of today" has "an identity that is ideological" (though he does not specify the content of this purported ideological identity). Therefore, in addition to "more material concerns" and "complicated geopolitical calculations of national interest," the United States, says Kristol, "inevitably" has "ideological interests" and "that is why we [sic] feel it necessary to defend Israel today, when its survival [sic] is threatened." (Israel Shamir, for slightly different reasons, also thinks that Israel is now threatened, at least as a "Jewish supremacist state" or as an "exclusionary, apartheid state.")

---

1. My emphasis added, along with my suggestive insertions in brackets.

[211]

However, is it conceivable that after our anti-authoritarian re-education in America's purportedly tolerant, new "democratic military culture," any active-duty military officers would now be permitted – much less long tolerated – to make any critique or have any moral reservation about this pre-eminent "ideological mission" for America, either for the protection of Israel or for the further expansion of, in Kristol's own words, "the emerging American *imperium*"? It would seem not. The culture of tolerance would seem to be a fiction, especially when truth is taboo. Furthermore, a sign of real power is who effectively controls (or is intimidating about) what is permitted to be discussed and critiqued in open public discourse, and what must not be spoken.

Indeed, to what extent could any general officer or flag officer today even make a strategic argument – much less a principled, moral argument – that such "ideological interests" and permanent missions for America actually undermine true U.S. national interests and the common good? If any younger military officers were openly, or even privately, to make such critical arguments, or were known even to have such principled views, would they not likely be "weeded out" before they could even become general or flag officers? Nonetheless, the American military officer, in his Commissioning Oath, still accepts a high moral obligation when he solemnly swears to defend the (clear and plain, i.e. un-"deconstructed") Constitution of the United States "against all enemies, foreign and domestic."

Therefore, from the vantage point of "the emerging American *imperium*" in 2005, and in light of our seemingly intimidated military culture, one may now better consider the strategic, longer-range cultural project of "anti-authoritarian re-education," which was gradually implemented by way of a reformed "military sociology and psychology." This cultural project was, in fact, slowly implemented, even back in 1960 during the so-called "cold war," and was intended, it would seem, to be part of the quiet and unobtrusive "re-education" (*Umerziehung*) of the "updated" and "progressive" military officer, so as to make him more "suitable" and docile for helping his civilian superiors in governing a modern democracy – which is also now seen to be an emerging American *imperium* more and more "governed" by inaccessible and seemingly intractable oligarchies or new elites. In Antonio Gramsci's terms, a new "cultural hegemony" has been attained, replacing an older, traditional military and political culture with a new ethos and orientation. While the United States was fighting the "cold war" against the more conspicuous revolutionary socialism of the Soviet Union and Red China, the culture was being quietly, indirectly, and "dialectically" captured! After seeing these fruits from the vantage point of 2005, we may soberly ask: to what extent were we cadets being prepared, even back in 1960, to be compliant officers in a "modern imperial democracy," or even a new kind of Praetorian Guard for our new elites and their Proconsuls?

Indeed, it was Samuel Huntington's *The Soldier and the State* which was the second mandatory book for us to read as cadets in 1960 as part of our new curriculum, in addition to the writings of Morris Janowitz. Huntington's book also promoted the ethos of an unquestioningly obedient, properly subordinated, and docile military officer as a compliant instrument in the service of a modern State and "democratic society." Huntington's concept of "civil-military relations" clearly implied that there was not to be a keen intellectual or strategic culture in the U.S. military, and certainly nothing resembling the German General Staff concept of well-educated, strategic-minded, far-sighted, and thinking officers who were to be not only indispensable senior staff officers but also field commanders with high qualities of moral and intellectual leadership. (Even the post-World War II German military culture was permitted to retain the German General Staff concept in its educational system for future officers, but the American military culture was, ironically, not permitted to imitate – or even to know much about – this brilliant achievement. I never learned about it during my studies at West Point except when I was abroad among the German military as an exchange-cadet in the summer of 1962.)

Two other men made indispensable contributions to my deeper understanding of strategic psychological warfare and modern cultural warfare, as well as the historical instances of *Kulturkampf* and the re-education of an enemy: Col. (later Lt. Gen.) Sam V. Wilson and Theodore Ropp.

During the early 1970s, when I studied military history under the Austrian-American professor Theodore Ropp at Duke University, I realized that this great teacher, scholar, and author of *War in the Modern World,* understood not only "battlefield" military history but also the relation of war and society and the subtle influence of war upon larger civilizations and cultures. And he understood these matters in a very profound way. Professor Ropp, who taught many West Point officers in graduate school, cultivated and disciplined the eager minds of his students to take the longer view of various profoundly differentiated military cultures. He especially illuminated these different traditions by way of counter-pointed contrasts and a finely nuanced comparative cultural history of long-standing military institutions, to include their specific martial effects upon civilization as a whole.

[213]

Under the instruction of Professor Ropp, I realized for the first time that something serious, important, and substantial was missing from my formative military education at West Point. Although I had been on the exchange trip with the German military and their cadets, I was then still too young and callow to have a deeper appreciation of the formation of the new German military culture after World War II, in contrast to its earlier history – and not just its Prussian military history. But Professor Ropp helped me and so many other students to understand and savor these deeper matters, for which I am so grateful.

Another important influence in my deeper education was Col. Sam V. Wilson, who in 1969 and 1970 was my mentor. He was also during that time (and during the Vietnam War years in general) the director of studies at the John F. Kennedy Special Warfare Center at Fort Bragg, North Carolina. Sam Wilson was a deep-thinking military officer, especially in the field of irregular warfare and strategic special operations. He, too, made me realize, though in an incipient way, the deeper strategic, moral, and cultural factors in the waging of modern war. West Point, I then realized, had prepared us very little to take this longer, truly strategic, view of military culture, history, and war, even though the Academy had been in fact founded to form and cultivate the discerning mind and moral character of a future *strategos* (the Greek for "general officer"), like the historian Thucydides.

Irving Kristol and Professor Sidney Hook were both involved in "the cultural cold war" as part of the CIA-supported Congress for Cultural Freedom, in which they tried to influence and capture the culture of the so-called "non-Communist left," and to increase its active resistance to the increasingly "anti-Semitic" Stalinist form of Soviet Communism. In like manner, there seems also to have been a quieter "cultural project," by way of the social sciences, to "update" and "transform" the traditionally authoritarian and rigid American military culture into a more "dynamic" and more "democratic form of society." For, as the argument went, a more authoritarian and explicitly Christian military culture also had the danger of being at least latently "anti-Semitic."

Professor Joseph Bendersky's recent book supports this suggestion and intuition. Published in 2000, his book – which contains ironic or sarcastic quotation marks even in his title – is called: *The "Jewish Threat": Anti-Semitic Politics in the U.S. Army.*[1]

---

1. New York: Basic Books, 2000.

Bendersky shows how the "Officers' Worldview, 1900–1939," as well as their dangerously "elitist" views, had to be corrected and transformed, especially in light of "Officers and the Holocaust, 1940–1945" and in light of the "Birth of Israel, 1945–1949" (the quoted periods being also the titles of three of his chapters).

When one finishes reading Bendersky's lengthy and learned (but not entirely intelligent) ideological book, one realizes that a very intelligent psycho-cultural project had been designed and conducted, especially after World War II, to remove and to chasten the "dangerous" propensities of the "elitist" American military culture – especially its sometimes "racist" (and "eugenicist") and un-democratic propensities toward "anti-Semitism." (Bendersky never sharply defines, though, what he means by anti-Semitism, although he implies that it constitutes a kind of *summum malum* – i.e., the greatest of evils.)

In the context of strategic, cultural warfare, Antonio Gramsci, along with Géorg Lukacs, Walter Benjamin, Ernst Bloch, and the whole Frankfurt School apparatus, understood the "cultural channels" of religious and strategic subversion, especially of traditional Western civilization and its once deeply rooted Christian religious culture. In like manner, there seems to have been some well-prepared "cultural warfare" within the United States subtly conducted against the post-World War II military culture and its Christian moral traditions (which included formation in the life of the four cardinal virtues, as distinct from the dialectic of mere "values" and its mostly emotive and subjective "critical thinking.")

Moreover, I am led to make these observations merely as a "fruit inspector." For I have seen the fruits of these cultural and curricular revisions, and I have also seen what was once present and is no longer. I also see the extent to which the truth is taboo concerning these matters. Like other matters of historical inquiry, the matter of the transformation of the American military culture also seems to be "off limits." Investigators are not welcome.

Nonetheless, I have observed the fruits and shall continue to examine the cumulative combination of the deeper causes and agents of this transformation of our military education and culture into something which is more vulnerable to manipulation; and whose moral and intellectual resistance to injustice and other disorders is increasingly "dimmed down."

I have also witnessed – by personal, direct involvement – how little intellectual and moral resistance there now is *within* the military, against our creeping and technocratic neo-Praetorianism in support of our regional military Proconsuls and their civilian masters (both inside and outside of the government). Our military culture is altogether inattentive to an arguably unconstitutional abuse of power; and also to our myopically "un-strategic" and thoroughly irrational involvement in unjust aggressive wars (like Iraq), while we are concurrently and centrifugally over-extended elsewhere throughout the world, and "strutting to our confusion."

The common good of the United States would be greatly furthered, I believe, if there were even just one "ferociously honest" man like Israel Shamir within the U.S. military. This former Israeli commando and immigrant from the former Soviet Union gives many unflinching "reports from reality," which are not easily found in other sources. The reader of this essay will certainly know what I mean if he will only read Shamir's recently published collection of essays entitled *Flowers of Galilee*.[1]

In his candid book, Israel Shamir gives more and deeper cultural and strategic intelligence about Israel than one will find in all of CIA's unclassified translations, available from its gifted, but sometimes overly selective (or self-censoring), Foreign Broadcast Information Service (FBIS). Like the now-deceased Israeli writer and "secular humanist" Israel Shahak – but, I think, even more profoundly so – Israel Shamir is truthful and candid in his manifold analyses and presentation of hard facts, many of which are essentially unknown in the West unless one reads Hebrew.

What Israel Shamir writes gives not only much "ground truth" about Israel and its strategic operations and deceptions, but also larger reports about the "political action of Jewish forces" in the wider world, and keenly vivid "cautionary tales" plus even deeper "parables" – all of which will aid our indispensable knowledge of reality and give good grounds for the United States' strategic "course-correction" in the Middle East and at home.

Israel Shamir's work would be a great example to our own military and intelligence officers. For it has been my constant experience over the years – even as a professor at military colleges and academies, strategic institutes, and universities – that our military and intelligence officers are not formed to grasp, nor even to desire, a deeper cultural and strategic intelligence about foreign countries. That kind of intelligence (hence understanding) is too often depreciated and considered as "soft intelligence" rather than "hard" or "quantifiable" intelligence. As a result, and as we become increasingly secularized as a nation, we cannot easily take the measure of foreign

---

1. Tempe, Ariz.: Dandelion Books, 2004.

THE MORAL RESPONSIBILITY OF THE U.S. MILITARY OFFICER

religious cultures or gauge the importance of religious world-views such as Zionism and Islam.

Furthermore, because much of cultural-strategic intelligence can be reliably derived from unclassified open sources or OSINT (Open Source Intelligence), it is often thought to be too vague and untrustworthy compared to, say, MASINT (Measurement and Signatures Intelligence) or SIGINT (Signals Intelligence) or covert-clandestine HUMINT (Human Intelligence).

Properly conceived and patiently conducted "cultural and strategic intelligence" would, however, illuminate the moral, religious, and deep-cultural factors of foreign strategy and grand strategy. It further reveals another country's own strategic culture (as well as its political culture). For example, in the case of mainland China, one is thereby made more sensitive to Chinese perceptions of its own vulnerable geography and its important "strategic thresholds," and, therefore, its own historical reluctance to have a large blue-water navy.

Moreover, because the U.S. State Department has never, as an institution, had any larger "regional strategies" or "regional orientations" of its foreign policy – as distinct from its focus on policies and strategies designed for individual countries, and to be conducted by our individual resident Embassies (or "country teams") – the U.S. military is placed in an awkward situation, which may even involve it in Constitutional difficulties and illegalities. The senior military officers of major regional combatant commands – such as Central Command (CENTCOM) or Pacific Command (PACOM) – must now act as if by default as Regional Proconsuls, as was the case in imperial Rome, thereby producing many moral difficulties for our purportedly democratic military culture, and its proper subordination to civilian leadership in foreign policy. These senior officers, in their effective role as Proconsuls, appear to be forming, as well as implementing, foreign policy – not an easy mission for a traditional military officer in our culture.

For example, let us consider the case of Dennis Blair. Just before Admiral Blair retired from active duty as Commander-in-Chief of the U.S. Pacific Command (a position now known simply as Commander, U.S. Pacific Command, or CDRUSPACOM), I asked him a question after his strategic luncheon talk at Fort Lesley McNair in Washington D.C., at our National Defense University (NDU). In its essence, my question went something like this:

> To what extent, Admiral Blair, must you effectively act as a Regional Proconsul in the Pacific because our State Department has no coordinated policy and

strategy for the region as a whole? And to what extent are your larger political and grand-strategic missions compromising your role as a military officer under the requirements of our Constitution, and in light of our traditional civil-military relations and customs of proper subordination?

In response to this question, the audience, as well as the gracious Admiral, gasped. The audience then nervously laughed aloud (especially one of Admiral Blair's own classmates from the U.S. Naval Academy – an energetic Marine Major General who was also sitting in the audience)! Admiral Blair then took a deep breath and said: "How can I give you a good answer to your serious question – a truthful answer that you deserve – without getting myself into trouble?" (His initial response and candor with me produced even more pervasive laughter in the room!)

What is important in this context, however, is that our Regional Combatant Commanders (former "CINCs" and now simply "Commanders") and our larger global Functional Unified Commanders (such as our U.S. Special Operations Command – USSOCOM) actually have not just military-strategic but higher grand-strategic missions.

But my deeper argument is that our gradated military educational system – from our formation as cadets up to our higher education at the National Defense University – does not prepare officers for such long-range and culturally sensitive missions, much less clarify the deeper legal and political and Constitutional issues. These issues are illustrated by the case of the recently established "homeland command" (formally known as U.S. Northern Command, or USNORTHCOM) with its domestic as well as Canadian missions, *and* an altogether ambiguous area of responsibility *within* the U.S. – and consequent, but very sensitive, intelligence requirements!

If our military education and deeper-rooted military culture properly prepared our officers to think in these larger, grand-strategic terms, they would now also be much more acutely sensitive to, and discerning of, the moral factors of modern war (and "terrorism"), including the cultural and religious factors of strategy, which are always involved when we are intimately working with other (and often quite alien) civilizations.

In this context we should be reminded of the far-sightedness of Lieutenant General Sam V. Wilson. In 1969 and '70, when he was still a colonel and a formative leader as well, he saw (and said) what was needed in the strategic and cultural formation of U.S. military officers. He was, however (I regret to say), insufficiently appreciated or understood at the time.

Having had many diverse experiences abroad, Col. Wilson long ago realized that the U.S. military needed a cadre of officers who could take the larger (and nuanced) measure of *foreign military cultures* as well as the strategic factors and cultural events of moment in the world. He wanted U.S. military officers to be able to understand foreign strategic and military cultures on their own terms and in the longer light of their own histories and geographies. He knew, as in the case of Turkey and the Turkish General Staff, that some foreign militaries had their own uniquely differentiated and distributed roles within their own societies, and which were in sharp contrast to the roles of a military officer within our own society and traditions. He knew that – *for the common good of the United States* – we needed to understand these often radically different and even incommensurable military traditions.

He also saw that we needed officers who were truly competent in strategic foreign languages (e.g., Chinese, Russian, Japanese, Arabic, Hebrew, Spanish, etc.) and who were desirous and capable of savoring foreign cultures and their histories as a whole – and not just their military institutions and their conduct in war: that is to say, to understand their literature and philosophy and world-view, and their resonant cultural symbols and aspirations. Yet Col. Wilson realized that such officers should also be more than well-educated and deep-thinking "foreign area officers," which were then being formed in our Foreign Area Special Training (FAST) Program. He foresaw that we also needed officers who could intelligently connect different regions of the world and take a longer view of the whole – to understand, for example, "Soviet revolutionary warfare" as a form of "total war," whereby even peace was strategically considered and employed as "an instrument of revolution" (as Major General J.F.C. Fuller also very well understood), and to understand the long-range strategic and religious operations of historic and modern Islamic civilization, in contrast to the strategic cultures of Great Britain, China, and Israel, and their uniquely long-range aspirations.

Col. Wilson's personally designed and implemented strategic-cultural program was called the Military Assistance Overseas Program (MAOP). The initial formation of officers in this program was a six-month course for colonels and lieutenant colonels – and their Navy equivalents – at the Special Warfare Center. (Col. Wilson had assigned me to be an instructor in this new program, and head of the East-Asian Seminar. He also permitted me, because of my experience with several foreign militaries, to attend the course and receive the diploma by way of special exception, because I was then only a captain in our Army Special Forces.)

Originally, Col. Wilson wanted to have the whole program, with its strategic courses, in Washington, D.C., and to be part of the National

Interdepartmental Seminar for long-range strategic and cultural education, which then included the State Department and the Intelligence Community. However, in 1969 – during the Vietnam War – Sam Wilson's important ideas were suspect and frowned upon. They were, indeed, too politically sensitive, even before the development of "the emerging American *imperium."*

Despite support from thoughtful political leaders, Col. Wilson's plan to have the school in Washington was finally rejected because too many people saw that he was – or could easily be perceived to be – forming "men on white horseback," i.e., ambitious military officers who would potentially encroach upon, if not actually *usurp,* the super-ordinate role of their "civilian political masters."

Had Sam V. Wilson been more influential, we would not now, as a nation, have such a passive and unthinking military, or such an invertebrate military culture, or such a shortsighted strategic culture. And our military would be much more intelligently resistant to our neoconservative and pro-imperial civilian masters.

By way of contrast, the American military culture was to be, I regret to say, much more formatively influenced by John Dewey's "pragmatic education," in combination with the Frankfurt School's "critical theory" and subtle anti-authoritarian "re-education." Our traditional military culture was to be more and more uprooted and cut off from its Christian roots, and thereby more and more secularized, re-paganized, and neo-Machiavellianized. This gradually transformed military culture is now conspicuously acquiescent to its neo-Machiavellian, civilian masters and mentors (like Michael Ledeen), in unthinking support of the growing American *imperium* and of the grand-strategy of the "greater Israel" (*Eretz Israel*) not only in the Middle East but throughout the world. Our military officers, in my experience, no longer know, nor reflect upon, nor respectfully consider the criteria and standards of just war, as revealed in the long, articulate tradition of Western Christian civilization. It is now their usual orientation and preference to think and speak in terms of a vague and unspecified "preventive war" or a war of "anticipatory self-defense," both of which concepts are, too often, Orwellian "Newspeak" for the reality of *a war of aggression* – the only specific offense for which the German officers were brought to trial at Nuremberg in 1945.

THE EDITORS' GLOSS: Sometimes when the "usual suspects" protest a war or all wars their demeanor leaves something to be desired. But there's something eminently persuasive about former, or serving, military members doing so – men and women ostensibly willing to give their lives in support and defense of the Constitution. So when they raise concerns about war, their objections should be considered all the more carefully, given that mere "pacifism" is not a likely motive.

It is a shame and an injustice that these service personnel are sometimes dubbed "unpatriotic." Absent clear, treasonable intent, it's not credible to assert that someone who tries to keep his country from waging an unjust or disastrous war is unpatriotic. The contrary makes more sense. Many, too, are suspicious of soldiers' and sailors' judgments about war, on the assumption that joining the service equates to an oath of absolute obedience. The fact is, service men and women remain citizens at all times with a stake in their country's ultimate direction and health, and, even while serving, their obligation to law and morality (which trumps orders that conflict with them) is non-negotiable.

In addition to the four veterans we spoke with, there can be added the voices of a thousand some veterans from all eras who have signed on to a "Veterans Call to Conscience" declaration (www.calltoconscience. net). It reads: "When, in an unjust war, an errant bomb dropped kills a mother and her child it is not 'collateral damage,' it is murder. When, in an unjust war, a child dies of dysentery because a bomb damaged a sewage treatment plant, it is not 'destroying enemy infrastructure,' it is murder. When, in an unjust war, a father dies of a heart attack because a bomb disrupted the phone lines so he could not call an ambulance, it is not 'neutralizing command and control facilities,' it is murder. When, in an unjust war, a thousand poor farmer conscripts die in a trench defending a town they have lived in their whole lives, it is not victory, it is murder." Those who question the premise of the veterans' position should read our companion volume, *Neo-CONNED!*, where the injustice of the Iraq war is argued persuasively and, it seems to us, irrefutably.

C H A P T E R
14
i n t r o d u c t i o n

To War or Not to War, That Is the Question
· · · · · · · · ·
Jack Dalton

I F THERE IS one thing I understand it is simply this: people who once "see" war up close and personal, and look into the abyss, that "Heart of Darkness" of war, they are forever changed – period. Some become very self-defensive and become strong supporters of war. What else can they do? If they do not support war, then they would be compelled to revisit war and come to terms with it. That in itself shakes the very foundations of people's beliefs, and is something a lot of them just do not want, or are unwilling to do; it hurts like hell!

Then there are those like Jim Massey, Mike Hoffman, Kevin Benderman, Dave Bischel, Tim Goodrich, Camilo Mejia, just to name a very few, who have confronted the issue of war's immorality and inhumanity from the perspective of those who have participated in war; and through participation have found war sorely lacking; and due to that have come out in opposition to that participation; and in opposition to war in general as a methodology of solving our problems.

These men are not alone in their outspoken opposition to war, or in their refusals to be further participants in the destruction of their fellow human beings. They are just a few in the growing numbers of people in uniform who are currently taking the very same position.

In fact, over the past year there have been upwards of 300 individuals who have written me saying they will do whatever they have to not to go back to Iraq. And I'm just one person; so how many others have been sent similar letters is anyone's guess, but I would venture to say the numbers are rather large. We know over 5,500 military people have left the country to avoid participation in the war in Iraq. How many more are there we have not heard about? No war escapes this. There were 25,000 that had split by the time Vietnam was over, a few thousand of them declared deserters. Even WWII had 22,000 tried and convicted of desertion. It's just that now, with Iraq, this kind of thing is taking place a lot sooner than with previous wars. And not all of them are going to Canada.

One very important thing we must keep in the forefront of our minds is that these people, the men and women that are starting to refuse deployment or re-deployment to Iraq, are not "nut jobs." Far from it! Not only are they sane, but they have the absolute moral right to choose what they will or will not participate in when their lives are being put on the line and in jeopardy.

In fact, Monica Benderman, Sgt. Kevin Benderman's wife, puts it much better than I in the questions she has posited:

> What is wrong with a country when a man can walk into a military recruiting office, sign on the dotted line, and find himself in a war zone two months later? No one questions his sanity then.
>
> What is wrong with the direction of the world when a man and his wife receive phone calls and emails from all over their country asking them to explain themselves, calling them cowards, wondering if they have ever read the Bible or studied the Scripture, all because that man has chosen to speak out against war and violence, and his wife has chosen to stand with him?
>
> Have we gone so far away from truth that people actually believe war and killing is right, and that a man must be crazy to want to walk away?"

These are powerful words and questions, which have not only got to be pondered, but answered. As a disabled Vietnam veteran (I served from August 1965 to May 1967) and someone who has been an anti-war activist ever since coming back "home" – a term I use loosely – not only do I agree with the anti-war movement within the ranks, I fully support it; and I support those who take this stand.

The men and women in today's military are doing now what it took those who were sent to Vietnam over four years to start doing: opposing war and starting to refuse to participate. Sooner rather than later is a good thing.

As a war veteran, as an American citizen, and as a writer, I fully support those who publicly denounce and refuse to participate in the senselessness of this "legal murder." For, to a large degree, that is what this war is – though it's "legal" only in the minds of those who propel the rest of us into their wars of "choice."

We at the Project for the Old American Century (as opposed to the wing-nuts at the Project for a New American Century), where I am co-editor, have come out strongly against the war and will fully support any and all of the men and women in uniform who, as a matter of conviction, maintain their moral right to stand against it, and who refuse deployment to Iraq or anywhere else the Bush cabal may choose to start another war.

C H A P T E R
14

Hindsight is 20-20:
Iraq and "War on Terror" Veterans on Gulf War II
. . . .

A Roundtable with Chris Harrison, former Army 1ˢᵗ Lt.; Jimmy Massey, former Marine Corps Staff Sgt.; Tim Goodrich, former Air Force Sgt.; and Dave Bischel, former Air Force Sgt.

W**HAT DO YOU** *think of Operation "IRAQI FREEDOM" (OIF)? Do you think it is essentially and morally "wrong"? Ill-advised and imprudent? Neither? Both?*

HARRISON: It was an aggressive action conducted against a country that posed no threat to the U.S. nor to its immediate neighbors, conducted in full violation of international law. It fits the definition of "aggressive war" that was a result of the Nuremberg trials. Furthermore, the occupation has been in violation of international law because it has attempted to transform and privatize the economy of Iraq.

MASSEY: I agree – definitely both. I think that if we continue on the path that we are on now, it's going to continue to be on a downward spiral.

GOODRICH: Though I was fully supportive of Operation ENDURING FREEDOM (OEF), as a typical 21-year old in the military, I began thinking and talking about the coming war in Iraq around October of 2002. That was during my last deployment. I thought to myself that if I was going to have to fight in Iraq, I ought to know about the war. The only tool I had for research was the Internet, but that was enough. I concluded rather quickly that going to war with Iraq would be wrong. I didn't think Iraq was an imminent threat; I didn't think there was a terrorist connection; and frankly I didn't believe the administration's arguments. After 12 years worth of sanctions, it seemed obvious to me that we really had them boxed in.

MASSEY: Right. By the beginning of the war, the Iraqi military had almost completely fallen apart, and the country had become impoverished. Of course the lack of medicine coming into the country – ones to cure even simple diseases – didn't help either. With the country being suppressed by the sanctions, the Iraqi people had no will or means to fight.

GOODRICH: Anyway, in January of this year, I had an opportunity to visit Baghdad with Global Exchange. Seeing everything that I did while I was there certainly confirmed me in my point of view. The condition of the country – no medical supplies, no reconstruction (at least none that I could see in Baghdad), simply talking to people on the street. Though I didn't expect to see as much reconstruction as the administration claims on TV, I at least expected to see something. I was shocked to see nothing. It was obvious that my earlier feeling about the real reasons for the war was correct.

And even as early as January of this year the Iraqi people that I spoke to were against the American occupation. Surprisingly, a small majority supported us coming in initially, I'd say maybe 60%. But after months of nothing happening, they saw what our true intentions were and public opinion turned against us.

BISCHEL: Let me put things into a little broader perspective, guys. We live in Orwellian times, and that is why we let a President, who I think was never even elected in 2000, get our country involved in the Iraqi quagmire. Our two party system is 100% under the control of our country's wealthiest 1%, and therein lies the problem. Our current administration can and will do as it pleases because they think themselves untouchables and above the law. As for the war? Let me be frank – the storyline that drove us into it is total garbage, and in all honesty Bush should be brought up on charges of war crimes, but, of course, it will never happen. As Voltaire once said, "Those that can make you believe absurdities can make you commit atrocities."

LID: *Chris, how did your opinion about the war develop: over time, during service in Iraq, or were you convinced it was wrong from the get-go?*

HARRISON: I imagined the war to be wrong from the beginning. I had already begun to question the true purpose and use of the U.S. military long before this, and it only crystallized my beliefs.

LID: *What about you two, Jimmy and Dave?*

MASSEY: Prior to going to war, I had read every classified and unclassified document that I could find about Iraq. I felt that in order to participate in conquering the country, I had to understand how the American hand has played an important part in the building of Iraq. I knew that the American government has had an impact on the Iraqi people from the very beginning, through covert CIA operations and supplying weapons and tanks for the war against Iran. So, I knew that the war was wrong from the beginning, but over time my experiences in Iraq confirmed my feeling. When I started witnessing first hand the lack of humanitarian support provided and the killing of innocent civilians, I knew for sure that what we were doing there was wrong.

BISCHEL: Well, I used to think the GOP had two individuals of integrity left in it: John McCain and Colin Powell. I found myself wanting to believe the Powell presentation before the United Nations, even though I was still filled with doubt. Time (not the magazine) has proven Powell's presentation to have been nothing more than the same crap handed down to the masses from the beginning. As for McCain, his soul has been bought and paid for by the party. My 11 months in Iraq has reinforced my belief that the war is 100% based on lies. I owe it to fallen Iraqis, Americans, and anybody else caught in the crossfire, to speak out against the war!

LID: Why does no one else share your point of view, if it's as obvious as you suggest?

GOODRICH: Most people believe what's in the headlines and don't reflect on them at all; I don't know a whole lot of people who are willing to research the claims that the newspapers make. For instance, out of 300 in my deployed unit, only three of us discussed it amongst ourselves and tried to get others to think about it. But eventually our superiors told us to be quiet.

At any rate, the way the whole military is, reflection and a "questioning attitude" is something that isn't much used in the military. As you might suspect, obedience is the main virtue that is stressed.

MASSEY: I think you have to understand that the American people are not seeing the facts or the truth about what is going on in Iraq, because the media is very limited in their coverage. Most Americans are too worried about paying for healthcare and prescription drugs and trying to save their job from going overseas. If you're worried about how you are going to put food on the table, you don't have time to care about what is going on in Iraq. The ones who do know – the big corporations and the government – are making a huge profit off the war, and of course they don't want to stop making money.

LID: Were you able to leave the military easily after deciding that the war was wrong? Or did your opinion on the war cause you any hardship in terms of your service in the military? Were you in the position of having to fight while thinking that the war was wrong, and if so, how did you manage to deal with it?

GOODRICH: I spoke out a bit, but was quickly told to keep quiet. I only had six months, so I thought I'd tough it out. While in Saudi I went to a chaplain to ask about what a conscientious objector was, to find out if that was something I needed to do, and he pretty much turned me away, saying, "You're going to get out anyway; why not just hang in there, since the war won't start before you leave."

HARRISON: I filed for classification as a 1-0 conscientious objector prior to the invasion. Surprisingly, this did not lead to any sort of retribution from my commanders or fellow soldiers. My opinion, however, was a minority one and not one that I voiced very loudly while in uniform. I was almost faced with the proposition of deployment to Iraq when my battalion was given a mobilization alert, but in the end they only took four detachments from our battalion.

BISCHEL: It was easy to leave the military after this experience. Frankly, I felt exploited. When I got back to the States, I said on TV that if they try to send me back I'd rather go to prison than fight a war based on lies. I later found out – happily – that I had already completed my Individual Ready Reserve time and I couldn't be called back. How I dealt with being in Iraq was through speaking out while I was there, and through further spiritual development such as prayer, meditation, and looking into philosophies such as Buddhism.

MASSEY: Remembering when I took the oath of enlistment and clearly remembering what we learned in boot camp on the Geneva Conventions, those two things made my decision to leave the Marines very clear. I am not a mercenary. Mercenaries get paid to do operations that are beyond the scope of the Geneva Conventions, such as killing women and children, and bombing civilian areas. When I witnessed those sorts of thing in Iraq, it was very easy to see that the U.S. government was committing war crimes. At that point I knew that I not only had every right to come forward and bring these war crimes to light, but also to leave the Corps.

It wasn't easy, though, to leave the Marines. I felt betrayed. It was kind of like being married for 12 years and waking up on your anniversary and your spouse says to you "I never loved you, I never wanted to be with you and by the way . . . those kids down the hall . . . they aren't even yours." I am happy to say that I never had any physical harm done to me because of my decision, though I was called a coward and a traitor and things like that.

LID: Well, it would seem that it takes an awful lot of courage to make decisions based upon your conscience and your sense of right and wrong in the face of the kinds of peer-pressure that you guys faced. "Coward" isn't exactly the word we'd pick to describe your stance. Anyway, as you all know, the U.S. government does not recognize a "selective" right of conscientious objection. In other words, someone who claims conscientious objection has to believe that all war is wrong, and not just this or that particular war. Do you think the law should be changed to allow a soldier/sailor/airman/marine to object to a war that is obviously unjust – and not participate in it?

HARRISON: Absolutely. As a former CO applicant, I am very familiar with the regulations. The regulations actually have not been changed since the days of the draft, and are meant to apply primarily to people claiming CO to avoid being drafted. The problem with the regulations is that the only war which is really relevant at the time of application is the one that is going on or imminent – everything else is an exercise in hypotheticals. Of course, the military tries to lead you down this slippery slope by asking questions like, "What would you have done about Hitler?" and "What would you have done about the genocide in Rwanda?" Since the current situation is the only one that is relevant, that is the only one that should be dealt with at the time of application. Furthermore, the threshold is an impossibly high one, and a person can be disqualified for simply answering that they would defend themselves if directly attacked.

GOODRICH: But you know, if the law were changed to allow selective CO status, *no one* would have been around to fight this war, because I think that very few people believed in it. Remember that old saying, "what if they had a war and no one came?" That's what this would have been like if the law allowed it.

As an example of what I mean, I've been distributing our Iraq Veterans Against the War pamphlet around Camp Pendleton, a Marine Corps base in California near me. The pamphlet has our mission statement, a list of resources like the GI rights hotline, etc. Of all the Marines that I've distributed the pamphlet to, 95% of them have kept it and seemed interested. Normally I would expect these young enlisted guys, ranking from about private to sergeant, to be very "gung ho" and pro-war. But these pamphlets are kept and read by almost everyone I give them to; they don't throw them away or mock me as a coward or whatever. Which means that many if not most people are open to questioning the war.

MASSEY: I think so too. Though it seems idealistic, in my mind military personnel should be allowed to object to a war that is obviously unjust, and then they should be able to participate in another war that isn't. There are some wars that are driven by greed and money, and but then again there have been some wars that have not been driven by those things. Each war is different. And I think that there should be a panel of civilian taxpaying American citizens who decide whether an individual in the military should be allowed to receive true conscientious objector status. Military personnel exclusively shouldn't be allowed to make that decision any longer.

BISCHEL: As you point out, conscientious objection is believing all war is wrong, and I don't feel that way.

LID: For those of you who did not have to go through a period of opposing the war while in the military, if today you found yourself still on active duty, and commanded to participate in a war you believed to be unjust, what would you do? Would it be different than how you approached the current war in Iraq?

MASSEY: If I were on active duty right now, I would have no choice but to go to Iraq. There are laws that have been placed so that unless you file for CO status, you *have* to go where the military sends you. So, I would play by the rules, and if, when I got over there, I saw with my own two eyes what I saw before, I would do the exact same thing that I did – leave the Marines. I wouldn't change anything that I did this time around.

GOODRICH: I'm not sure what I would have done if I had to stay in for another number of months or years after the war started, because meanwhile I've almost turned into a pacifist. It would be a hard decision, because it wouldn't have been as convenient for me, being that I was able to get out just as the war was starting.

HARRISON: I would definitely refuse and take the court-martial. This is no different than how I approached the war on Iraq, outside of the fact that it took me a long time to sort things out in my mind when I was confronted with all the possibilities.

BISCHEL: Right! Speak out, go to prison if you have to. Whatever it takes.

LID: What would you say to your brothers and sisters who are still on active duty, and who may not have the clear idea that the war is wrong, or who may think it's wrong but not have the courage to do anything about it?

MASSEY: I would tell them to keep a journal of everything that happens while they are in Iraq. From day one in boot camp, we are taught that regardless of rank, if you are a private or you are a general, you can call a cease fire at anytime and anywhere, even on the battlefield. We were also taught that killing innocent civilians is wrong. Sometimes you have to go back to the basics to find your answers. They have the right to refuse to do these things, and they can be protected from the military while doing them.

HARRISON: I'd say that the most important thing in their life that the troops can do is to follow their consciences. Most people who joined the military did so because they believed in the ideals of their country and they saw military service as a way to spread those ideals. The current campaign has nothing to do with spreading those ideals – in fact, it could be argued that it is inhibiting them. Despite what they may think, they have a *huge* support network out there of people that would overwhelmingly help them in any way possible. And when all is said and done, this is not a choice that anyone else can make for them – but they should approach it from the perspective not of worrying about what others may think of them, but what they think each time they look themselves in the mirror – are they confident that they are standing up for what they believe and standing true to their principles?

BISCHEL: To those who can still think for themselves I would say that *dissent is patriotic.* Our numbers – I mean, we free thinkers – are growing and I believe that we already outnumber the brainwashed. We need to lead by able example, speak out against the war no matter what the circumstances. I was ostracized for being an outspoken liberal while in Iraq, and it didn't stop me. Stand your ground my brothers and sisters, for you are absolutely, morally right in taking a stand against the invasion of Iraq.

GOODRICH: You know, people say we're not supporting the troops by calling for them to come home and by calling for them to no longer be used to fight this war, but I beg to differ. The essence of support for the troops is demanding that they come home to be with their families. Those people with the yellow ribbons – how many of them have really done anything to support the troops? How many of them care enough to speak out against an illegal war?

THE EDITORS' GLOSS: Pablo Paredes is an example of what we meant in pointing out that a soldier or a sailor does not turn off his conscience when joining the service. "Now, as far as being a robot . . . 'do as I say and don't question it' and things like that, I think that is a very dangerous situation for a human being, and I don't think you stop being a human being because you become a Navy sailor or an Army soldier," he told one interviewer in December 2004. "Even within the rules that are afforded to us," he went on to say, "we are told if at any time you find an order to be unlawful you have not only a right but a duty not to follow it. And I feel that way about any order that has to do with this war." Perhaps there'd be a much larger number of both Iraqis and American military alive today if just a few thousand had had the courage and vision of Pablo Paredes.

His understanding of principle isn't particularly controversial. "We support the political will," outgoing Joint Chiefs of Staff Chairman Gen. Richard Myers said to an interviewer in May 2005, "and unless it's illegal, immoral, or unethical, we do what we're told to do" (*Los Angeles Times*, May 9, 2005). The question is, what exactly would constitute an illegal, immoral, or unethical war, in Dick Myers's mind, if not this one?

Paredes was court-martialed on May 11, 2005, for missing his ship's movement. Interestingly, the presiding judge at his court-martial seemed to think that there was at least a reasonable case to be made for the illegality of the Iraq war (not to mention others). Marjorie Cohn, a lawyer called for Paredes during the trial, explained: " . . . the military prosecutor was trying to undermine my testimony about the legality of the Iraq war, and he had looked at some of the articles I had written . . . about the illegality of the war in Afghanistan and the war in Yugoslavia, as well. And so he asked me questions like: 'Well, you would also say then that the war in Afghanistan was illegal, right?' He expected me just to have a 'yes' answer, and I think he expected that that would be such a ridiculous response that it would speak for itself." As it turned out, Prof. Cohn made such a case, responding to the government prosecutor's questions, that when the defense asked the judge if the court had any further questions for the witness, the judge replied: "I believe the government has successfully demonstrated a reasonable belief for every service member to decide that the wars in Yugoslavia, Afghanistan, and Iraq were illegal to fight." There can be little wonder why that comment wasn't extensively publicized.

CHAPTER

15

Just Following Orders: One Sailor and His Vision of the Higher Law
• • • • • • • • • •
An Interview with Petty Officer Third Class Pablo Paredes, USN

> "To those who say I should be 'serving my country,'
> I say that what I am doing *is* a vital service to my country."

PABLO, YOU MADE *headlines last December by refusing to get underway with your ship, the USS BONHOMME RICHARD, when it was headed from San Diego to Iraq. That was a bold move on your part, and presumably not one you would have made without having serious thoughts on the war. Can you share some of those?*

PP: Frankly, the military invasion and occupation of Iraq was and is both legally and morally without justification, and should not be tolerated. Unfortunately there are ways of controlling the masses, of fabricating justification, and, as Noam Chomsky puts it, "manufacturing consent."

The Pope condemned the war, while George W. Bush has said that God is on his side. Presented in this manner, most Christians should probably favor the opinion of the person who, by the nature of Christian beliefs, is not only someone closer to God but who in fact is someone understood to be infallible in issues of faith and morality. However, the corporate-controlled media, which bombards the average citizen or Christian so heavily, has found it in its own interest to market Mr. Bush's actions as being in keeping with Christian traditions. Mr. Bush makes headlines daily, and wastes no opportunity to toot the "man of God" horn. The Pope, in comparison, was marginalized, at least in terms of media coverage. I, for one, was quite ignorant of the Pope's public statements on the war in Iraq until after I made my decision. I was informed of them by a very devout Catholic. In this example, the crime, the fabrication of justification, the manufacturing of consent comes by way of omission. No journalist covering any press conference or presidential address or speech, after reporting on the President's claim that God is on his side, has ever reported the Pope's position. This is one example of how the masses have been controlled.

The ongoing war in Iraq is, as I see it, frankly a crime against humanity. Reflecting on the December 2004 earthquake in the Pacific, it is hard not to compare its effects – the greatest of which was the terrible tsunami – and the war. And that's when it hits you. There was nothing we could do to prevent the thousands and thousands of deaths that this tsunami claimed, but in Iraq our leaders have actually chosen the needless, tragic body count that continues to increase. Millions of people across Asia – and worldwide – are asking themselves, "Why did this have to happen?" and, "How can we prevent more deaths of innocent people?" In the case of the Tsunami victims, these questions have no answers. However, in Iraq, the answer to the first question continues to change. And the second has a definite and plausible response that our leaders fail to acknowledge.

LID: In your interview with Amy Goodman shortly after your ship set sail without you, you made a specific reference to the fact that you consider any orders received that have to do with this war to be unlawful. That seems to be the logical conclusion of what you've said above. True?

PP: Every understanding I have of our constitution has led me to believe that the right to declare war is furnished only to our Congress, and not to our President. I also understand that to engage in war, and not just to deploy military forces for a purpose much less grave than war, there must be a specific declaration of war. I have researched these beliefs and found them to be accurate. Therefore, according to the document that governs this great country, this war is, in fact, illegal.

Now within our country, if the three branches of government that act as checks and balances to each other find no illegitimacy in the war in Iraq, then it is conceivable to say that our laws have been compromised by our government for reasons that it found to be worthwhile. Now while I disagree – and so do millions – this government is, I suppose, at liberty to govern and interpret laws within its borders.

International law, however, is in no way subject to being compromised unilaterally. The UN Charter contains strict guidelines as to the circumstances under which war is legal. The United States signed the UN charter, and the Senate ratified it. A number of the articles in the charter dictate that if and when a nation is to deploy armed forces, regardless of the purpose, the UN Security Council must vote its consent. The UN Security Council did not approve the U.S.-lead war in Iraq. By acting against the laws that govern the international theatre, we not only broke a tradition of over five decades in which only when an international consensus of the necessity of war was reached did a nation declare war, but we also set a most dangerous precedent: defying the laws that govern our planet whenever a nation strong enough to do so feels it is necessary.

This war by domestic and international standards is without question illegal. Therefore any order that is complicit in carrying out the execution of this war is irrefutably illegal. The same government that, at Nuremburg, prosecuted individuals for carrying out unlawful orders in an illegal war[1] should not only tolerate but in fact expect and demand that its military personnel object to and defy illegal orders. My actions of December 6, 2004, were not only the actions of a human being endowed with a conscience, but in fact were my duty as a member of the United States Navy.

LID: That's all very clear to you, but a shocking number of your fellow Servicemen and women don't see it that way. Has your insight into these things always been so clear and decisive? If not, what brought you to this clarity of vision in this case?

PP: My thoughts on our country's involvement in foreign relations weren't always as clear as I feel they are now. Until age 18, I was the typical American kid. I could name every player in the National Basketball Association; I could easily identify every hip-hop artist; I spent a considerable amount of my life playing video games; but I couldn't for the life of me tell you anything about the situation in the Middle East or even the history of my own Latin America. None of these things made me odd among my peers. In fact, to some extent my interest in my own culture and heritage made me a little more aware than the average American teenager. Then at 18 I decided college was for the wealthy and my options were limited to the workforce and the military. I saw the military as a bridge to an education.

My first two years in the military did not serve to change my perspective much at all. However, at the two-year mark, I received orders to Yokosuka, Japan. Thus began a new education for me. I found myself often surrounded by foreigners who were very interested in the perspective of an American sailor. I found myself being asked to take part in countless discussions, the subjects of which I was quite ignorant. The shame of this ignorance led me to devour every piece of literature I could find on subjects ranging from U.S. foreign policy to Latin American history to politi-

---

1. See the interesting references to Nuremberg's condemnation of wars of aggression – or "crimes against the peace" – by Prof. Chomsky, Dr. Hickson, and Dr. Doebbler on pp. 43–59, 209–220, and 797–817, respectively, of the present volume.

cal science. This sudden urge led to an enormous increase in awareness on my part of the numerous aspects of the current political landscape. From this point of view I can't really see an alternative to concluding that this war is immoral, illegal, and a crime against humanity.

Realizing that it took me a considerable amount of time in a foreign country in order to develop my own understanding of politics and history, I then began to wonder, what was it about the U.S. of A. that kept me from developing this kind of awareness before. Figuring this out became my new drive. One thing I slowly became aware of was what corporate power is, and how it can affect a society. A corporation has a duty only to its shareholders to produce and to generate profit. In practice corporations put obedience to this duty even ahead of their obligation to obey the law.

Once I came to realize that these are the very specific aims of a corporation, and that every means of readily available, mass-media information in this country is essentially dependent upon a corporation for its existence, it becomes crystal clear that the information the average American absorbs is that which corresponds, ultimately, to the economic needs of the corporate entity by which that information is produced and disseminated. Taking all of this into account, along with the sheer size of the military-industrial complex, I arrived at the conclusion that it is nearly impossible for the mainstream media to objectively report on a range of issues, including the war in Iraq. This was my conclusion in searching for an understanding of why my perspective as an American was initially so limited.

So, in answer to your question, I had the opportunity – rare for an American – to consume alternative, non-privatized forms of information and news while I was overseas. I think that this is what gave me the ability today to see this war as so clearly, clearly illegal.

LID: Why do you think others haven't followed your course of action? Lack of courage?

PP: Well, to believe that a lack of courage is at the root of people's willingness to participate in the war assumes that they thoroughly understand the geo-political climate and the underlying economic influences that drive it. I would venture to say that as these truths become clear to the American public, the dissent will multiply.

In the military, there is a significant amount of closet dissent. Rather than judge those who, for whatever reason, cannot publicly denounce the war, I call on those who dissent and who do not feel hampered to be a voice for themselves and those who cannot speak out.

LID: As you are aware, the U.S. Government does not recognize a "selective" right of Conscientious Objection. In other words, someone who claims conscientious objection has to believe that all war is wrong, and not just this or that particular war. Do you think the law should be changed to allow a soldier/sailor/airman/marine to object to and not participate in a war that is obviously unjust?

PP: "Obviously" unjust would still, ultimately, be a matter of opinion. In one man's opinion every war is obviously unjust; in someone else's opinion all but one war may have been unjust in the past; in still another's opinion, all wars have been just except for the one in Iraq. The point is that, practically speaking, I don't think the military can afford to allow a service member to choose, based on his opinion, which war to participate in. As for "official" conscientious objection, the way CO guidelines are currently formulated, they apply to only a very select number of people; there are many that it should not and does not include. But in theory, regardless of how "practically" difficult it is, it would seem reasonable and necessary to make an allowance for anyone who has a grave conflict of conscience – one that he cannot ignore – to request such status and to have the right to make his case.

Don't forget, though, that beyond conscientious objection there are other military provisions that are applicable to this kind of situation, at least in theory (if not in practice). I mean the duty of a service member to disobey unlawful orders. The fundamental problem is, of course, proving an order is unlawful, as apposed to simply saying that a service member *felt* the order was unlawful. No doubt the military would rarely *feel* an order to be unlawful; so what it or a service member *feels* should probably be irrelevant. What should matter is whether the service member had sufficient reason to believe it was unlawful. In this way a service member aware of the Geneva Conventions could protest an Abu-Ghraib type order without worry. And a service member aware of the UN charter, as well as basic notions of international law, could protest any order linked to the current war in Iraq without fear of being convicted of disobeying an order that in the military's opinion is lawful.

LID: Notwithstanding your own clear views on the subject, you have been called a deserter and a disgrace. But it's hard for us to not have respect for someone like yourself who risks everything to follow his conscience. Do you think that you are doing anything that you should be punished for, or do you think rather that the law should support what you are doing?

PP: Sadly, it is our commander in chief who is doing something *he* should be punished for. Our government has *deserted* democracy and the rule of law. The massacre of however many thousands of people in Iraq is the *disgrace*. These are all crimes worthy of prosecution. I have chosen to refuse to participate in them. I don't see any reason for punishing anyone who acts on his conscience, especially when that conscience is backed up by law and fact.

Besides, the law does support what I am doing. It says that no country can make preemptive war without the backing of the UN Security Council. Military law says no service member should obey an unlawful order. The implementation and interpretation of law may work against me, and I may be labeled things like "deserter" and "felon," but history will speak differently of actions like Camilo Mejia's[1] and mine.

I know that calling a spade a spade is unpopular, and it can have serious repercussions in today's society. But it is the only way I can live with myself. It is the only way I can one day face my children and grandchildren and dare to tell them about right and wrong and to teach them how a man should lead his life. Beyond my personally vested interest, it is necessary for those in positions like mine to take advantage of them in a united assault on the institutions and accepted ideologies that have created this war on Iraq, as well as the aggression played out against Afghanistan and the countless attacks that might follow suit. If rank and file individuals won't sacrifice a little for the end of oppression by military means, then that end will never come. The exiles and political prisoners of the Vietnam resistance era are tribute to this theory.

LID: People have said that it's "disloyal" of you to leave your fellow Sailors and Soldiers behind to get shot at while you sit out the war. That you take yourself out of harm's way only to leave your comrades in it. What do you say to that?

PP: There is no man or woman doing my job in today's Navy who will be shot at or bombed. My trade was one of the safest jobs I have ever had. My co-workers will be working on electronics, without me, in an air conditioned space, far from the acts of war that go on in Iraq. They will not hold M-16's or dig trenches or throw grenades. I think this is very important. The easiest way to discredit my protest is to say that I was afraid for

---

1. See the short letter of former Army Staff Sgt. Camilo Mejia in the companion to the present volume, *Neo-CONNED!*, on pp. 375–377, detailing generally his reasons for attempting to become a recognized conscientious objector in response to the war in Iraq.

my own safety, that I am a coward, or that I abandoned my fellows on the battlefield. This plays on the misconception that many people have that all branches and jobs within the military are some kind of infantry. The fact is, infantry is one of many jobs, and the Navy doesn't have an infantry. The marines and the army conduct ground warfare, while the Navy sails ships and provides naval support, whether it be transport or radar detection or a platform from which to send aircraft, etc. I worked on a missile system which was created to defend my ship in case of an air strike, whether incoming aircraft or missiles. This system has been in our Navy over 30 years and has yet to be used in any way other than in practice. Not to mention that the Iraqi insurgents are hardly an aerial threat. This further illustrates how safe my job was.

One thing that is not common knowledge is that there are incredible benefits to being on a ship deployed to the gulf for six months. The lowest ranking sailor can take home around ten thousand dollars, thanks to special pay and the absence of taxes on pay in a war zone. I think it is important for people to know this, so that they are aware that my decision is one that not only cannot be attributed to cowardice, but in fact takes a willingness to sacrifice major benefits, and a preparedness to face possible courts-martial, conviction, and confinement.

There are also infantrymen who feel that this war is unjust and who do not want to loose their souls doing something they know to be criminal. To say that if these men decide to follow their conscience, they are "disloyal," is nothing but propaganda.

LID: Anything that you'd like to add? Anything you want to say that we didn't cover?

Before there were political parties, and a left and right side of the political spectrum, there was humanity. After this trend in history, which has led to so much violence, I hope there will still be a human race left. I hope that we as members of the human race can realize that life is more important than anything that party politics can offer. Ultimately, Life should be the most important issue in all of our hearts. Whether it belong to "Our Troops," Iraqi civilians, Iraqi resistance forces, Palestinians. South East Asians, Africans, Central American, Cuban, or any of the oppressed whom I have not studied enough to be aware of, must always be the most valuable and protected possession of humanity.

THE EDITORS' GLOSS: Al Lorentz may be just a "simple soldier," but he is a perceptive one. He accurately pins the ultimate blame for the Iraq fiasco on the Bush administration which is, as he says, "more concerned with its image than it is with reality." Would to God that all our so-called military "scholars" were as perceptive.

Andrew Bacevich, a Boston University professor and West Point graduate, is the author of a critique entitled *The New American Militarism*. Word is his book is a fair one, but if the logic it contains is anything like that in his recent column (*Washington Post*, June 28, 2005), it leaves much to be desired. In his piece he lambastes Lt. Gen. Sanchez, former ground commander in Iraq, for having left the "insurgency" stronger than it was before he took command. Sanchez used the wrong tactics, he says. We are not Sanchez apologists, especially since he bears much of the responsibility for Abu Ghraib, but it's hard to find fault with his approach to Iraq. He vowed in December 2003, as Bacevich notes, to use "whatever combat power is necessary to win." Being a combat officer trained in armor, one would expect him to take that approach. *Sanchez is not a diplomat*, nor does his job description, as commander of the Army's V Corps, demand that he be one. Bacevich complains, though, that, "rather than winning Iraqi hearts and minds, [Sanchez] alienated them." Bacevich then *claims* to take the non-politically correct hard line of firm military accountability: Sanchez should retire in disgrace; he didn't "accomplish the mission."

You'd think the "scholar" Bacevich would know better. But this is *safe* politically "incorrect" territory. It pretends to talk tough *while swallowing the insane Bush-administration Iraq project*. If Bacevich really wanted to talk tough, he should have skewered Sanchez – or Dick Myers and Tommy Franks, more appropriately – for accepting a mission that was inappropriate for "combat power." Soldiers, as members of the Defense Department, are trained to fight and, ideally, win; but *they win wars, not hearts and minds*. If Bush was looking to contract an outfit to persuade Iraqis that they should "gladly" support the overthrow of their recognized government through foreign invasion, and turn their country over to Shiite terrorists and Kurdish separatists, he should have hired the spin doctors at the Rendon Group (see Chapter 34), not the U.S. Army. It's a scandal that our young men and women were put in this situation, and that their senior leaders were complicit in putting them there. It's no less of one when our long-gray-line of "professional" military thinkers push this nonsense and let the culprit politicians off the hook.

CHAPTER 16

The Case of Staff Sgt. Al Lorentz

• • • • • • • • •

Lt. Col. Karen Kwiatkowski, USAF (ret.)

A L LORENTZ IS a non-commissioned officer in the Army Reserves, who in September 2004 was serving in Iraq. At that time he decided that somebody ought to say something about what was really happening there. And so he wrote a crystal-clear, succinct article on Iraq that was published on *LewRockwell.com*. Within days it had traveled across America and around the world. And back.

In the eyes of the Pentagon and the White House, writing that article was his first mistake. Entitling it "Why We Cannot Win" was his second.

Al's article was simply his factual, personal assessment of what was – and as of this writing still is – happening in Iraq. He revealed no classified information. Far more detail on tactical and strategic challenges had already been provided by retired military officers like Marine Gen. Tony Zinni and Army Gen. Eric Shinseki, and former director of the NSA, William Odom. Al certainly wrote nothing more damning than what was previously released and published in part by the CIA as well as the U.S. House and Senate regarding conditions and future possibilities in Iraq.

For writing this article, Lorentz was isolated, reprimanded, and threatened by the chain of command with jail time for violation of U.S. Code, Title 18, §2388 – "willfully causing or attempting to cause insubordination, disloyalty, mutiny, or refusal of duty, in the military forces of the U.S."; and for violation of Article 134 of the Uniform Code of Military Justice – "making a statement with the intent to promote disloyalty or disaffection toward the U.S. by any member of the Armed forces."

He became the target of a Department of Defense-wide smear campaign that I heard about via emails from active duty soldiers and officers from Iraq to Alabama. They had "heard things" about Al – nasty things – that they just "thought I should know." And the Pentagon also threatened to charge Al with conducting partisan political activity, as if standing up against bad judgment, creative mendacity, and sheer idiocy in foreign policy is "partisan."

But while Al was being punished directly by the military and indirectly through the orchestrated military public affairs smear campaign, something happened. Retired generals of the likes of Joseph Hoar and Brent Scowcroft; commentators from the left, right and center; and even members of the hand picked Iraqi governing council in Baghdad, all began to voice much the same kinds of concerns that Al had raised.

And six months after Al's article, even many of the neoconservatives who had dreamed up the deceits and deceptions for the Iraq war, and who, with George W. Bush's help, turned it into a real live disaster, began criticizing the administration on these same counts.

The Iraq invasion and occupation has been a nuclear-strength credibility buster for George W. Bush, his neoconservative advisors, and the Pentagon brass that went along with them in hopes of advancing their careers. On the other hand, as a long-serving soldier in the field in Iraq, "Big Al," as he is known affectionately, has credibility to spare: he is truthful, he puts his country first, and he honors the Constitution. Batting zero in all three of these categories, it is no wonder that Bush, his war advisors, and the Pentagon brass became more than a little agitated over Al's article.

In that article that follows Al lists five why we cannot win in Iraq. And as a senior military officer I maintain that he is absolutely, if tragically, correct. Sun Tzu and Clausewitz alike would recognize his perceptiveness and appreciate his strategic understanding. Meanwhile, thousands die or are maimed, and billions of our hard-earned tax dollars are wasted.

Victory in Iraq – if such is ever claimed by Washington – won't be "winning" as defined by Webster, or anyone else. The permanent military bases and American corporate advantage in some future Iraq may provide this administration its Pyrrhic victory. But no one will call it winning.

The non-commissioned officer has always been the backbone of the American military. This has never been more true than today, when so many commissioned officers in key positions are more politicized and less courageous than ever before. But Al is still, as of this writing, under overt and veiled threat to stay quiet. He has paid, and continues to pay, a great price for telling the truth.

Read his article. Then read it again. You'll see why I see Big Al as one of those people – they are few and far between, today – who sacrifice their personal peace, prosperity, and security so that others might have a better peace, a greater security, and a more authentic prosperity. We call them heroes.

C H A P T E R
16

Why We Cannot Win
. . . .
Staff Sgt. Al Lorentz, USAR

BEFORE I BEGIN, let me state that I am a soldier currently deployed in Iraq, I am not an armchair quarterback. Nor am I some politically idealistic and naïve young soldier, I am an old and seasoned non-commissioned officer with nearly 20 years under my belt. Additionally, I am not just a soldier with a muds-eye view of the war, I am in Civil Affairs and as such, it is my job to be aware of all the events occurring in this country and specifically in my region.

I have come to the conclusion that we cannot win here for a number of reasons. Ideology and idealism will never trump history and reality.

When we were preparing to deploy, I told my young soldiers to beware of the "political solution." Just when you think you have the situation on the ground in hand, someone will come along with a political directive that throws you off the tracks.

I believe that we could have won this un-Constitutional invasion of Iraq and possibly pulled off the even more un-Constitutional occupation and subjugation of this sovereign nation. It might have even been possible to foist democracy on these people who seem to have no desire, understanding or respect for such an institution. True the possibility of pulling all this off was a long shot and would have required several hundred billion dollars and even more casualties than we've seen to date but again it would have been possible, not realistic or necessary, but possible.

Here are the specific reasons why we cannot win in Iraq.

First, we refuse to deal in reality. We are in a guerrilla war, but because of politics, we are not allowed to declare it a guerrilla war and must label the increasingly effective guerrilla forces arrayed against us as "terrorists, criminals and dead-enders."

This implies that there is a zero sum game at work, i.e. we can simply kill X number of the enemy and then the fight is over, mission accomplished, everybody wins. Unfortunately, this is not the case. We have few tools at our disposal and those are proving to be wholly ineffective at fighting the guerrillas.

The idea behind fighting a guerrilla army is not to destroy its every man (an impossibility since he hides himself by day amongst the populace). Rather the idea in guerrilla warfare is to erode or destroy his base of support.

So long as there is support for the guerrilla, for every one you kill two more rise up to take his place. More importantly, when your tools for killing him are precision guided munitions, raids and other acts that create casualties among the innocent populace, you raise the support for the guerrillas and undermine the support for yourself. (A 500-pound precision bomb has a casualty-producing radius of 400 meters minimum; do the math.)

Second, our assessment of what motivates the average Iraqi was skewed, again by politically motivated "experts." We came here with some fantasy idea that the natives were all ignorant, mud-hut dwelling camel riders who would line the streets and pelt us with rose petals, lay palm fronds in the street and be eternally grateful. While at one time there may have actually been support and respect from the locals, months of occupation by our regular military forces have turned the formerly friendly into the recently hostile.

Attempts to correct the thinking in this regard are in vain; it is not politically correct to point out the fact that the locals are not only disliking us more and more, they are growing increasingly upset and often overtly hostile. Instead of addressing the reasons why the locals are becoming angry and discontented, we allow politicians in Washington, D.C. to give us pat and convenient reasons that are devoid of any semblance of reality.

We are told that the locals are not upset because we have a hostile, aggressive, and angry Army occupying their nation. We are told that they are not upset at the police state we have created, or at the manner of picking their representatives for them. Rather, we are told they are upset because a handful of terrorists, criminals, and dead enders in their midst have made them upset, that and of course the ever convenient straw man of "left-wing media bias."

Third, the guerrillas are filling their losses faster than we can create them. This is almost always the case in guerrilla warfare, especially when your tactics for battling the guerrillas are aimed at killing guerrillas instead of eroding their support. For every guerrilla we kill with a "smart bomb" we kill many more innocent civilians and create rage and anger in the Iraqi community. This rage and anger translates into more recruits for the guerrillas and less support for us.

We have fallen victim to the body count mentality all over again. We have shown a willingness to inflict civilian casualties as a necessity of war without realizing that these same casualties create waves of hatred against us. These angry Iraqi citizens translate not only into more recruits for the guerrilla army but also into more support of the guerrilla army.

Fourth, their lines of supply and communication are much shorter than ours and much less vulnerable. We must import everything we need into this place; this costs money and is dangerous. Whether we fly the supplies in or bring them by truck, they are vulnerable to attack, most especially those brought by truck. This not only increases the likelihood of the supplies being interrupted. Every bean, every bullet and every bandage becomes infinitely more expensive.

Conversely, the guerrillas live on top of their supplies and are showing every indication of developing a very sophisticated network for obtaining them. Further, they have the advantage of the close support of family and friends and traditional religious networks.

Fifth, we consistently underestimate the enemy and his capabilities. Many military commanders have prepared to fight exactly the wrong war here.

Our tactics have not adjusted to the battlefield and we are falling behind.

Meanwhile the enemy updates his tactics and has shown a remarkable resiliency and adaptability.

Because the current administration is more concerned with its image than it is with reality, it prefers symbolism to substance: soldiers are dying here and being maimed and crippled for life. It is tragic, indeed criminal that our elected public servants would so willingly sacrifice our nation's prestige and honor as well as the blood and treasure to pursue an agenda that is ahistorical and unconstitutional.

On the brink of war, and in front of the whole world, the United States government asserted that Saddam Hussein had reconstituted his nuclear weapons program, had biological weapons and mobile biological weapon production facilities, and had stockpiled and was producing chemical weapons. All of this was based on the assessments of the U.S. Intelligence Community. And not one bit of it could be confirmed when the war was over.

—Commission on the Intelligence Capabilities of the United States Regarding Weapons of Mass Destruction, March 31, 2005

THE PROFESSIONALS SPEAK II:
THE INTELLIGENCE COMMUNITY AND
THE INTELLIGENCE DEBACLE

THE EDITORS' GLOSS: This piece, originally published in the Summer 2004 *Middle East Policy Journal*, along with its companion in this section by Ray McGovern, pretty much says it all. We were sold a bill of goods, and none of it was a product of "intelligence failure." The failure was one of integrity, honesty, and basic respect for the good of the nation, the reputation of the American people, and the lives and limbs of the members of their armed forces.

As Dr. Sniegoski demonstrated, there was a political push for war that had little to do with the professional demands of statecraft. That political push translated into pressure, of various shades, on America's intelligence apparatus to come up with the "right answer." A classic, tragic, life-and-death case of "when I want your opinion I'll give it to you." What a shame; a scandal; and *an outrage*.

Looking back over the past decade, Dave Lindorff wrote for *Counterpunch*: "Everyone agreed that it was not the sex. It was the lying, right?" Obviously, he was referring to our recently impeached President. "The audacious bending of the meaning of the word 'is' and the word 'sex.' Right?" Well how about the meanings of the words "we *know* Saddam has WMD"; the meaning of words "imminent threat"; the meaning of "reveal the identity of Valerie Plame"; the meaning of "no one authorized torture"? The list seems endless. "Has lying ever been practiced so blatantly," Lindorff continues, "as it is being practiced today in the White House? . . . Where is the public outcry demanding that [Bush] be called to account for his shameless and bloody deception of the American public and the Congress?" Where indeed.

God bless Congresswoman Barbara Lee (D-Calif.) for at least asking the question. She's got a Resolution of Inquiry in the works, "requesting the President and directing the Secretary of State to transmit to the House of Representatives not later than 14 days after the date of the adoption of this resolution all information in the possession of the President and the Secretary of State relating to communication with officials of the United Kingdom between January 1, 2002, and October 16, 2002, relating to the policy of the United States with respect to Iraq."

What's the betting that obfuscation and still more lies will be the order of the day?

C H A P T E R
17

Drinking the Kool-Aid: Making the Case for War with Compromised Integrity and Intelligence

• • • • • • • • •

Col. W. Patrick Lang, USA (ret.)

T HROUGHOUT MY LONG service life in the Department of Defense, first as an army officer and then as a member of the Defense Intelligence Senior Executive Service, there was a phrase in common usage: "I will fall on my sword over that." It meant that the speaker had reached a point of internal commitment with regard to something that his superiors wanted him to do and that he intended to refuse even though this would be career suicide. The speaker preferred career death to the loss of personal honor.

This phrase is no longer widely in use. What has taken its place is far more sinister in its meaning and implications. "I drank the Kool-Aid" is what is now said. Those old enough to remember the Jonestown tragedy know this phrase all too well. Jim Jones, a self-styled "messiah" from the United States, lured hundreds of innocent and believing followers to Guyana, where he built a village, isolated from the world, in which his Utopian view of the universe would be played out. He controlled all news, regulated all discourse and expression of opinion, and shaped behavior to his taste. After a time, his paranoia grew unmanageable and he "foresaw" that "evil" forces were coming to threaten his "paradise." He decided that these forces were unstoppable and that death would be preferable to living under their control. He called together his followers in the town square and explained the situation to them. There were a few survivors, who all said afterward that within the context of the "group-think" prevailing in the village, it sounded quite reasonable. Jim Jones then invited all present to drink from vats of Kool-Aid containing lethal doses of poison. Nearly all did so, without physical coercion. Parents gave their children the poison and then drank it themselves. Finally Jones drank. Many hundreds died with him.

What does drinking the Kool-Aid mean today? It signifies that the person in question has given up personal integrity and has succumbed to the prevailing group-think that typifies policymaking today. This person has become "part of the problem, not part of the solution."

What was the "problem"? The sincerely held beliefs of a small group of people who think they are the "bearers" of a uniquely correct view of the world, sought to dominate the foreign policy of the United States in the Bush 43 administration, and succeeded in doing so through a practice of excluding all who disagreed with them. Those they could not drive from government they bullied and undermined until they, too, had drunk from the vat.

What was the result? The war in Iraq. It is not anything like over yet, and the body count is still mounting. As of August 2005, there were 1847 American soldiers dead, thousands wounded, and tens (if not a hundred) of thousands Iraqis dead, though the Pentagon is not publicizing the number. A PBS special on *Frontline* concerning Iraq mentioned that senior military officers had said of General Franks, "He had drunk the Kool-Aid." Many intelligence officers have told the author that they too drank the Kool-Aid and as a result consider themselves to be among the "walking dead," waiting only for retirement and praying for an early release that will allow them to go away and try to forget their dishonor and the damage they have done to the intelligence services and therefore to the republic.

What we have now is a highly corrupted system of intelligence and policymaking, one twisted to serve specific group goals, ends and beliefs held to the point of religious faith. Is this different from the situation in previous administrations? Yes. The intelligence community (the information collection and analysis functions, not "James Bond" covert action, which should properly be in other parts of the government) is assigned the task of describing reality. The policy staffs and politicals in the government have the task of creating a new reality, more to their taste. Nevertheless, it is "understood" by the government professionals, as opposed to the zealots, that a certain restraint must be observed by the policy crowd in dealing with the intelligence people. Without objective facts, decisions are based on subjective drivel. Wars result from such drivel. We are in the midst of one at present.

The signs of impending disaster were clear from the beginning of this administration. Insiders knew it all along. Statements made by the Bush administration often seem to convey the message that Iraq only became a focus of attention after the terrorist attacks on 9/11. The evidence points in another direction.

Sometime in the spring of 2000, Stephen Hadley, formerly deputy to Condoleeza Rice at the National Security Council (NSC), briefed a group of prominent Republican party policymakers on the national-security and foreign-policy agenda of a future George W. Bush administration. Hadley was one of a group of senior campaign policy advisers to then-Texas Governor Bush known collectively as "the Vulcans." The group, in addition to Hadley, included Rice, Paul Wolfowitz, and Richard Perle and had been assembled by George Shultz and Dick Cheney beginning in late 1998, when Bush first launched his presidential bid.

Hadley's briefing shocked a number of the participants, according to Clifford Kiracofe, a professor at the Virginia Military Institute, who spoke to several of them shortly after the meeting. Hadley announced that the "number-one foreign-policy agenda" of a Bush administration would be Iraq and the unfinished business of removing Saddam Hussein from power. Hadley also made it clear that the Israel-Palestine conflict, which had dominated the Middle East agenda of the Clinton administration, would be placed in the deep freeze.

Dr. Kiracofe's account of the pre-election obsession of the Vulcans with the ouster of Saddam Hussein is corroborated by former U.S. Treasury Secretary Paul O'Neill's memory of the first meetings of the Bush National Security Council, which he attended in late January and early February of 2001. Ron Suskind's book, *The Price of Loyalty*, based on O'Neill's memory and notes, tells us of an NSC meeting, ten days into the Bush administration, at which both the Israel-Palestine and Iraq situations were discussed.

Referring to President Clinton's efforts to reach a comprehensive peace between the Israelis and the Palestinians, President Bush declared, "Clinton overreached, and it all fell apart. That's why we're in trouble. If the two sides don't want peace, there's no way we can force them. I don't see much we can do over there at this point. I think it's time to pull out of the situation."

Next, Condoleeza Rice raised the issue of Iraq and the danger posed by Saddam's arsenal of weapons of mass destruction. A good deal of the hour-long meeting was taken up with a briefing by CIA Director George Tenet on a series of aerial photographs of sites inside Iraq that "might" be producing WMD. Tenet admitted that there was no firm intelligence on what was going on inside those sites, but at the close of the meeting, President Bush tasked Secretary of Defense Donald Rumsfeld and Joint Chiefs of Staff Chairman Hugh Shelton to begin preparing options for the use of U.S. ground forces in the northern and southern no-fly zones in Iraq to support an insurgency to bring down the Saddam regime. As author Ron Suskind summed it up: "Meeting adjourned. Ten days in, and it was about Iraq. Rumsfeld had said little, Cheney nothing at all, though both men clearly had long entertained the idea of overthrowing Saddam." If this was a decision meeting, it was strange. It ended in a presidential order to prepare contingency plans for war in Iraq.

Surely, this was not the first time these people had considered this problem. One interesting thing about those at the meeting is that no one present or in the background had any substantive knowledge of the Middle East. It is one thing to have traveled to the area as a senior government official. It is another to have lived there and worked with the people of the region for long periods of time. People with that kind of experience in the Muslim world are strangely absent from Team Bush. In the game plan for the Arab and Islamic world, most of the government's veteran Middle East experts were largely shut out. The Pentagon civilian bureaucracy of the Bush administration, dominated by an inner circle of think-tankers, lawyers and former Senate staffers, virtually hung out a sign, "Arabic Speakers Need Not Apply." They effectively purged the process of Americans who might have inadvertently developed sympathies for the people of the region.

Instead of including such veterans in the planning process, the Bush team opted for amateurs brought in from outside the Executive Branch who tended to share the views of many of President Bush's earliest foreign-policy advisors and mentors. Because of this hiring bias, the American people got a Middle East planning process dominated by "insider" discourse among longtime colleagues and old friends who ate, drank, talked, worked and planned only with each other. Most of these people already shared attitudes and concepts of how the Middle East should be handled. Their continued association only reinforced their common beliefs. This created an environment in which any shared belief could become sacrosanct and unchallengeable. A situation like this is, in essence, a war waiting for an excuse to happen. If there is no "imminent threat," one can be invented, not as a matter of deliberate deception, but rather as an artifact of group self-delusion. In normal circumstances, there is a flow of new talent into the government that melds with the old timers in a process both dynamic and creative. This does not seem to have happened in the Bush 43 administration. Instead, the newcomers behaved as though they had seized control of the government in a silent coup. They tended to behave in such a way that civil servants were made to feel that somehow they were the real enemy, barely tolerated and under suspicion. There seemed to be a general feeling among the newcomers that professional intelligence people somehow just did not "get it." To add to the discomfort, the new Bush team began to do some odd things.

Information Collection

Early in the Bush 43 administration, actions began that clearly reflected a predisposition to place regime change in Iraq at the top of the foreign-policy agenda. Sometime in January 2001, the Iraqi National Congress (INC), the opposition group headed by Ahmad Chalabi, began receiving U.S. State Department funds for an effort called the "Information-Collection Program." Under the Clinton administration, some money had been given to Iraqi exiles for what might be called agit-prop activities against Saddam's government, but the INC (Chalabi) had not been taken very seriously. They had a bad reputation for spending money freely with very little to show for it. The CIA had concluded that Chalabi and his INC colleagues were not to be trusted with taxpayers' money. Nevertheless, Chalabi had longstanding ties to a group of well-established anti-Saddam American activists who were installed by the Bush administration as leading figures of the politically appointed civilian bureaucracy in the Pentagon and in the Office of the Vice President.

Those ties paid off. The Information-Collection Program, launched in the early months of the Bush administration, was aimed at providing funds to the INC for recruiting defectors from Saddam's military and secret police, and making them available to American intelligence. But what the program really did was to provide a steady stream of raw information useful in challenging the collective wisdom of the intelligence community where the "War with Iraq" enthusiasts disagreed with the intelligence agencies. If the President and Congress were to be sold the need for war, information had to be available with which to argue against what was seen as the lack of imagination and timidity of regular intelligence analysts. To facilitate the flow of such "information" to the President, a dedicated apparatus centered in the Office of the Vice President created its own intelligence office, buried in the recesses of the Pentagon, to "stovepipe" raw data to the White House, to make the case for war on the basis of the testimony of self-interested émigrés and exiles.

At the time of the first Gulf War in 1991, I was the defense intelligence officer for the Middle East in the Defense Intelligence Agency. This meant that I was in charge of all DIA substantive business for the region. In discussions at the time of the victorious end of that campaign and the subsequent Shiite and Kurdish revolts in Iraq, it became abundantly clear that the same people who later made up the war party in the Bush 43 administration were not completely reconciled to the failure of U.S. forces to overthrow the Saddam regime. In spite of the lack of UN sanction for such an operation and the probable long-term costs of the inevitable American occupation of Iraq, the group later known as the neocons seemed deeply embittered by the lack of decisive action to remove the Iraqi dictator. Soon after the dust settled on Operation Desert Storm, the first Bush administration helped launch the Iraqi National Congress (INC). The INC was initially an umbrella of anti-Saddam groups largely composed of Kurdish and Shiite organizations. In the beginning, the CIA provided seed money as a result of presidential direction, and a private consulting firm, the Rendon Group, provided the initial public-relations support. To this day, one of the Rendon advisors to the INC, Francis Brooke, serves as the INC's chief Washington lobbyist.

Chalabi's American connections played a dominant role in the INC's evolution over the next dozen years. At the University of Chicago, Chalabi had been a student of Albert Wohlstetter, a hard-line Utopian nuclear-war planner who had been the dissertation adviser to another University of Chicago Ph.D., Paul Wolfowitz. Wohlstetter had also been a mentor to Richard Perle. In the summer of 1969, Wohlstetter arranged for both Wolfowitz and Perle to work for the short-lived Committee to Maintain a Prudent Defense Policy, a Washington-based group co-founded by two icons of American cold war policy, Dean Acheson and Paul Nitze. Wolfowitz and Perle remained close collaborators from that time forward.

Chalabi, an Iraqi Shiite Arab, had fled Iraq in 1958, just after the overthrow of the royal Hashemite government. His father and grandfather had held cabinet posts in the British-installed Hashemite regime. Before coming to the United States to obtain a doctorate, Chalabi lived in Jordan, Lebanon and Britain. He returned to Beirut after obtaining his doctorate, but in 1977, he moved to Jordan and established a new company, the Petra Bank, which grew into the second largest commercial bank in the country. Twelve years later, the Jordanian government took over the bank and charged Chalabi, who fled the country, with embezzling $70 million. In 1992, Chalabi was tried and convicted in absentia and sentenced to 22 years at hard labor. One of the persistent stories concerning this scandal is that Chalabi's Petra Bank was involved in arms sales to Iran during the Iran-Iraq War, and that Saddam Hussein discovered this and pressured King Hussein of Jordan to crack down on Chalabi.

Shortly after his hasty departure from Jordan, Chalabi, with the backing of his neocon allies in Washington, most notably, Paul Wolfowitz, Richard Perle and Professor Bernard Lewis of Princeton, helped launch the INC. Chalabi had first been introduced to Perle and Wolfowitz in 1985 by their mutual mentor, Albert Wohlstetter. Bernard Lewis met Chalabi in 1990 and soon thereafter asked his own allies inside the Bush 41 administration, including Wolfowitz's Pentagon aide Zalmay Khalilzad, to help boost the Iraqi exile. Another future Bush 43 Iraq War player also met Chalabi about that time. General Wayne Downing was first introduced to Chalabi in 1991, when Downing commanded the Joint Special Operations Command (JSOC) at Fort Bragg, North Carolina.

In November 1993, Chalabi presented the newly inaugurated Clinton administration with a scheme for the overthrow of the Saddam Hussein regime. Dubbed "End Game," the plan envisioned a limited revolt by an insurgent force of INC-led Kurds and Shiites in the oil regions around Basra in the south and Mosul and Kirkuk in the north. The "End Game" scenario: at the first sign of revolt against Saddam, there would be a full-scale insurrection by military commanders, who would overthrow the Saddam clique and install a Washington- and Tel Aviv-friendly, INC-dominated regime in Baghdad. The plan was based on a belief that Iraq was ripe for revolt and that there were no units in the armed forces that would fight to preserve Saddam's government. Since the same units had fought to keep Saddam in power during the Kurdish and Shiite revolts of a few years before, it is difficult to see why the sponsors of End Game would have thought that. A limited effort to implement End Game ended in disaster in 1995, when the Iraqis did fight to defeat the rebels and the Iraqi Army killed over 100 INC combatants. From that point on, both the CIA and DIA considered Chalabi "persona non grata." The CIA also dropped all financial backing for Chalabi, as the INC, once an umbrella group of various opposition forces, degenerated into little more than a cult of personality, gathered together in London, where Chalabi and his small group of remaining INC loyalists retreated.

In spite of this, neoconservatives inside the United States, largely in exile during the Clinton administration, succeeded in influencing the Congress enough to obtain passage of the "Iraq Liberation Act of 1998," largely to revive Chalabi's End Game scheme. Now retired, Gen. Downing, along with retired CIA officer Duane "Dewey" Clarridge of Iran-contra fame, became military "consultants" to Chalabi's INC and then drafted their own updated version of the Chalabi plan, now dubbed "the Downing

Plan." It was different in name only. The Downing-Clarridge plan insisted that a "crack force" of no more than 5,000 INC troops, backed by a group of former U.S. Army Special Forces soldiers (Green Berets), could bring down the Iraq Army. "The idea from the beginning was to encourage defections of Iraqi units," Clarridge insisted to *The Washington Post.* "You need to create a nucleus, something for people to defect to. If they could take Basra, it would be all over." It is difficult to understand how a retired four-star army general could believe this to be true.

In subsequent congressional testimony, then-Central Command head General Anthony Zinni (USMC) denounced the Downing scheme in no uncertain terms, warning that it would lead to a "Bay of Goats," adding that, by his most recent counts, there were 91 Iraqi opposition groups. None of them had "the viability to overthrow Saddam." Elsewhere he mocked Chalabi and the INC as "some silk-suited, Rolex-wearing guys in London." Despite CIA and uniformed military repudiation of End Game, the Downing Plan and other variations on the same theme, the neoconservative group continued to crank out advocacy for Chalabi's proposed revolution.

On February 19, 1998, a group of neocons calling themselves the Committee for Peace and Security in the Gulf issued an "Open Letter to the President" (this was before the passage of the Iraq Liberation Act) calling for the implementation of yet another revised plan for the overthrow of Saddam. The letter was remarkable in that it adopted some of the very formulations that would later be used by Vice President Cheney and other current administration officials to justify the preventive war in Iraq that commenced on March 20, 2003. The letter stated:

> Despite his defeat in the Gulf War, continuing sanctions, and the determined effort of UN inspectors to root out and destroy his weapons of mass destruction, Saddam Hussein has been able to develop biological and chemical munitions . . . . This poses a danger to our friends, our allies, and to our nation.

Equally striking were the recommendations in the letter. Chapter and verse, the document called for the implementation of the Downing Plan with a few added wrinkles. After demanding that the Clinton administration recognize a "provisional government of Iraq based on the principles and leaders of the Iraqi National Congress (INC)," the letter called for the creation of INC-controlled "liberated zones" in the north and south of the country; the lifting of sanctions in those areas and the release of billions of dollars of frozen Iraqi government funds to the INC; the launching of a "systematic air campaign" against the Republican Guard divisions and the military-industrial infrastructure of Iraq; and the prepositioning of U.S.

ground-force equipment "so that, as a last resort, we have the capacity to protect and assist the anti-Saddam forces in the northern and southern parts of Iraq."

The letter was co-authored by former Congressman Stephen Solarz (D-N.Y.) and Richard Perle. The signers included some people merely sympathetic to the cause of Iraqi freedom and a pantheon of Beltway neocons, many of whom would form the core of the Bush administration's national security apparatus: Elliot Abrams, Richard Armitage, John Bolton, Stephen Bryen, Douglas Feith, Frank Gaffney, Fred Ikle, Robert Kagan, Zalmay Khalilzad, William Kristol, Michael Ledeen, Bernard Lewis, Peter Rodman, Donald Rumsfeld, Gary Schmitt, Max Singer, Casper Weinberger, Paul Wolfowitz, David Wurmser, and Dov Zakheim. Some of these gentlemen may have had cause to reconsider their generosity in signing this document. This was in February 1998. A month after the release of the letter, Paul Wolfowitz and Gen. Wayne Downing briefed a group of U.S. senators on the INC war scheme. The senators at the meeting may also have cause to regret their subsequent sponsorship of the Iraq Liberation Act. This law clearly set the stage for renewed fighting in the Middle East in 2003.

The Bush-Cheney "Clean Break"

A core group of neoconservatives, including Vulcans Paul Wolfowitz and Richard Perle, came into the Bush administration fully committed to the overthrow of the Saddam Hussein regime in Baghdad as the number-one foreign-policy priority for the United States, but they found it necessary to spend much of the first nine months in bureaucratic combat with the State Department, the Joint Chiefs of Staff and the CIA, all of whom remained unconvinced that Saddam posed any serious threat to American strategic interests. At the first NSC meeting of the new administration, Colin Powell argued that the existing sanctions regime against Iraq was ineffective, and he promoted the idea of a change to "smart sanctions." These would zero in on vital military technologies that might enable Saddam to rebuild his military machine, which had been devastated by Desert Storm, a decade of sanctions, no-fly-zone bombing sorties, six years of UN inspections, and the 1998 Operation Desert Fox 70-hour bombing campaign.

Arguments like this were hard to deal with for those completely convinced of the necessity of a new government in Baghdad. But Colin Powell cast a mighty shadow on the American political scene, and his military credentials were formidable. If there had not been a cataclysmic event that tipped the balance, it is possible that the war party would never have won the struggle to have their point of view accepted as policy. It was the attacks on New York and Washington on September 11, 2001, that provided the neocons with the opportunity to turn dreams into reality. In a war-cabinet meeting at the presidential retreat at Camp David four days after the 9/11 attacks, Deputy Defense Secretary Paul Wolfowitz made an appeal for an immediate American military invasion of Iraq in retaliation for the terrorist attacks. Wolfowitz argued that attacking Afghanistan would be uncertain. He worried about 100,000 American troops getting bogged down in mountain fighting in Afghanistan indefinitely. In contrast, he said, Iraq was a brittle, oppressive regime that might break easily. He said that Iraq was "doable." He estimated that there was a 10–50 percent chance Saddam was involved in the September 11 terrorist attacks (this, of course, is a judgment that he was not involved). The United States "would have to go after Saddam at some time if the war on terrorism was to be taken seriously." Wolfowitz's pitch for war against Iraq, rather than against the Afghan strongholds of Osama bin Laden's al-Qaeda, was rejected at the Camp David session, and two days later, on September 17, President Bush signed a two-and-a-half page directive marked "TOP SECRET," which spelled out the plan to go to war against Afghanistan. The document also ordered the Pentagon to begin preparing military options for an invasion of Iraq.

Instantly, the neocon apparatus inside the Pentagon and in the office of Vice President Dick Cheney seized upon the opportunity represented by the authorization. On September 19, 2001, the Defense Policy Board (DPB) convened a closed-door meeting to discuss Iraq. Vulcan Richard Perle chaired the DPB. In the past, the board had been recruited from defense experts from both parties and with a broad range of views. In contrast, Perle's DPB had become a neocon sanctuary, including such leading advocates of war on Saddam as former Speaker of the House Newt Gingrich (R-Ga.), former CIA Director James R. Woolsey (a Democrat, but nevertheless a longstanding member of the neocon group), former arms control adviser Ken Adelman, former Under Secretary of Defense Fred C. Ikle, and former Vice President Dan Quayle. Wolfowitz and Defense Secretary Donald Rumsfeld attended the September 19 session. The speakers at the event, who aggressively advocated U.S. military action to overthrow Saddam Hussein, were Ahmad Chalabi and Princeton professor Bernard Lewis.

One consequence of the DPB meeting was that former CIA Director Woolsey was secretly dispatched by Wolfowitz to London to seek out evidence that Saddam Hussein was behind the 9/11 attacks and the earlier 1993 attack on the World Trade Center. Part of Woolsey's mission involved making contact with INC officials to get their help in further substantiating the link between hijacker Mohammed Atta and Iraqi intelligence. This theory was the brainchild of Laurie Mylroie, a scholar completely "in tune" with neocon thinking. According to news accounts at the time, Woolsey's actions drew the attention of police officials in Wales, who contacted the U.S. embassy to confirm that Woolsey was on "official U.S. government business," as he claimed. It was only then that Secretary of State Colin Powell and CIA Director Tenet found out about Woolsey's mission.

By October 2001, Under Secretary of Defense for Policy Douglas Feith had established a two-man intelligence cell inside his office with the job of combing the intelligence community's classified files to establish a pattern of evidence linking Saddam Hussein to al-Qaeda and the 9/11 attacks. The permanent, statutory agencies of the national intelligence community could not support such beliefs on the basis of what they saw in their own files. Therefore, some other means was sought to obtain the conclusion that the Iraqi government had been involved in 9/11. The team's mission was to cull the massive holdings of the intelligence database and to uncover intelligence reports accumulated on the subject of Iraq-al-Qaeda links. The issue of whether or not the intelligence agencies considered these reports to be true was thought immaterial. Not surprisingly, some of the sweetest cherries picked in the data searches came from informants provided by the INC's "Information Collection Program." The team in Feith's office was later more formally constituted as the "Policy Counterterrorism Evaluation Group."

This kind of single-minded intensity in pursuing his goals was nothing new for Feith. In July 1996, he had been a principal author of a study prepared for Israeli Prime Minister Benjamin Netanyahu. This paper advocated abrogation of the Oslo accords and the launch of a new regional balance-of-power scheme based on American-Israeli military dominance with a subsidiary military role for Turkey and Jordan. The study was produced by the "Institute for Advanced Strategic and Political Studies" (IASPS), a Jerusalem-based Likud-party-linked think tank, and was called "A Clean Break: A New Strategy for Securing the Realm." In it, Feith and company wrote, "Israel can shape its strategic environment, in cooperation with Turkey and Jordan, by weakening, containing and even rolling back Syria. This effort can focus on removing Saddam Hussein from power in Iraq – an important Israeli strategic objective in its own right – as a means of foiling Syria's regional ambitions." The study-group leader was Richard Perle. Other members of the team included Charles Fairbanks Jr., a longtime friend of Paul Wolfowitz since their student days together at the University of Chicago; and David Wurmser, an American Enterprise Institute Middle East fellow, and his wife, Meyrav Wurmser, who headed the Washington, D.C., office of the Middle East Media Research Institute (MEMRI). Her boss in that group was a retired Israeli intelligence officer, Yigal Carmon. On July 8, 1996, Richard Perle presented the "Clean Break" document to Netanyahu, who was visiting Washington. Two days later, the Israeli Prime Minister unveiled the document as his own regional foreign-policy design in a speech before a joint session of the U.S. Congress.

The initial team selected by Feith to conduct the cherry picking data search in the Pentagon consisted of "Clean Break" co-author David Wurmser and Michael Maloof. Maloof was a career Pentagon bureaucrat who had joined forces with Perle during the Reagan years, when Perle was a Pentagon official. At that time Maloof was a deputy to Stephen Bryen. The existence of the Wurmser-Maloof unit was kept a secret within the Pentagon for more than a year. Only on October 24, 2002, did Defense Secretary Rumsfeld formally announce that he had commissioned what *The Washington Post* called "a small team of defense officials outside regular intelligence channels to focus on unearthing details about Iraqi ties with al-Qaeda and other terrorist networks." The unveiling of the "Policy Counterterrorism Evaluations Group," as Pentagon officials dubbed it, coincided with a move by Rumsfeld to take over directly the financing and management of the INC's "Information Collection Project" from the State Department, which had developed serious reservations about maintaining an "off the reservation" intelligence operation.

Rumsfeld defensively told the Pentagon press corps on October 24, 2002, "Any suggestion that it's an intelligence-gathering activity or an intelligence unit of some sort, I think would be a misunderstanding of it." But former CIA case officer and AEI fellow Reuel Marc Gerecht, a relatively late recruit to the neocon cause, could barely conceal his enthusiasm in discussing the group: "The Pentagon is setting up the capability to assess information on Iraq in areas that in the past might have been the realm of the agency (CIA). They don't think the product they receive from the agency is always what it should be." Gerecht was then consulting with the Policy Counterterrorism Evaluation Group. In September 2001, the State Department inspector general issued a scathing audit of the INC, charging that the group had failed to account for how it was spending its U.S. government cash. "The Information Collection Project" was singled out as one of the particular problem cases. According to the audit, there was no accounting for how informants were paid or what benefit had been derived from their work. As a result of the audit, the State Department placed severe restrictions on the INC, suspended some payouts, and insisted that an outside auditor co-sign for all funds drawn by the group.

It was not until June 2002 that the State Department loosened the restrictions on the INC's cash flows. By then, the drive for a war against Iraq was in high gear inside the Pentagon civilian bureaucracy, and Feith and company (as opposed to the State Department) sought direct control over the INC, particularly the informant program.

No Saddam-al-Qaeda Ties

The overwhelming view within the professional U.S. intelligence community was (and is) that there was no Saddam Hussein link to the 9/11 terrorists. Admiral Bob Inman, who served in both Democratic and Republican administrations as head of the Office of Naval Intelligence, Director of the National Security Agency and Deputy Director of the CIA, bluntly stated,

> There was no tie between Iraq and 9/11, even though some people tried to postulate one . . . . Iraq did support terror in Israel, but I know of no instance in which Iraq funded direct, deliberate terrorist attacks on the United States.

Vincent Cannistraro, who headed the CIA's counterterrorism office before his retirement in 1990, maintains close ties to the intelligence community to this day. He debunks the Saddam-9/11 claims:

> The policymakers already had conceits they had adopted without reference to current intelligence estimates. And those conceits were: Saddam was evil, a bad man, he had evil intentions, and they were greatly influenced by neoconservative beliefs that Saddam had been involved with the sponsorship of terrorism in the United States since as early as 1993, with the first World Trade Center bombing . . . . None of this is true, of course, but these were their conceits, and they continue in large measure to be the conceits of a lot of people like Jim Woolsey.

This, he added, is not the view of the intelligence community:

> No, no, no. The FBI did a pretty thorough investigation of the first World Trade Center bombing, and while it's true that their policy was to treat terrorism as a law-enforcement problem, nevertheless, they understood how the first World Trade Center bombing was supported . . . and had linkages back to Osama bin Laden. He was of course, not indicted . . . because the FBI until recently believed that you prosecuted perpetrators, not the sponsors. In any event they knew there was no Saddam linkage. Laurie Mylroie promoted a lot of this, and people who came in [to the Bush administration], particularly in the Defense Department – Wolfowitz and Feith – were acolytes, promoting

her book, *The Study of Revenge*, particularly in the Office of Special Plans, and the Secretary's Policy Office. In any event, they already had their preconceived notions .... So the intelligence, and I can speak directly to the CIA part of it, the intelligence community's assessments were never considered adequate.

The Office of Special Plans

Some time before the 9/11 attacks, Vice President Cheney dispatched one of his Middle East aides, William Luti, over to the Pentagon as deputy under secretary of defense for Near East and South Asian affairs (NESA). Luti, a retired Navy captain, is a member of the neocon group recruited by Albert Wohlstetter. They had met in the early 1990s, when Luti was part of an executive panel of advisers to the chief of naval operations.

Parenthetically, I received what seems to have been an exploratory recruiting visit from Dr. Wohlstetter and his wife, Roberta. In 1992, the Wohlstetters unexpectedly arrived at my doorstep at the Pentagon with the news that a mutual friend, now a senior personage in the Pentagon, had told them to visit me. There followed an hour and a half of conversation involving European and world history, philosophy and a discussion of the various illustrious people who were friends and associates of the Wohlstetters. Roberta Wohlstetter went so far as to show me various books that they and their friends had written. An unspoken question seemed to hang in the air. After a while they became impatient with my responses and left, never to return. Clearly, I had failed the test. At the time, I only vaguely knew who these people were and did not really care, but since they have become so important to this story, I have inquired of various people who might have received similar visits and found that this was not uncommon. An old academic colleague of Wohlstetter has also told me that the couple had done similar things in the university setting.

In any case, Luti landed a job as a military aide to Speaker of the House Gingrich from 1996 to 1997. There, he worked with Air Force Col. William Bruner, another active-duty military officer on loan to the speaker. Still on active duty when the Bush 43 administration came into office, Luti worked in the vice president's office as part of a shadow National Security Council staff, under the direction of Cheney's chief of staff and chief policy aide, I. Lewis "Scooter" Libby.

Libby was a Yale Law School protégé of Paul Wolfowitz. Beginning in the 1980s, Libby followed Wolfowitz into the Reagan and Bush 41 administrations. When he was not working for Uncle Sam or Wolfowitz, Libby was the law partner/protégé of Richard Nixon's personal attorney, Leonard

Garment. Under his direction, for a period of 16 years, on and off, Libby was the attorney for fugitive swindler and Israeli Mossad agent, Marc Rich. In the first Bush administration, Libby served with Wolfowitz in the policy office of then-Defense Secretary Cheney, where he gained some notoriety as one of the principal authors, along with Wolfowitz and Zalmay Khalilzad, of the draft 1992 "Defense Planning Guidance" that advocated preventive war and the development of a new arsenal of mini-nuclear weapons, to be used against Third World targets thought to be developing WMD arsenals.

Midway through 2001, Luti retired from the Navy and took a civilian Pentagon post as head of NESA. Under normal circumstances, NESA is a Pentagon backwater, responsible primarily for arranging bilateral meetings with military counterparts from a region stretching "from Bangladesh to Marakesh." Before the war, the NESA staff worked daily with the defense intelligence officer for the Near East, South Asia and Counterterrorism. This was the most senior officer in DIA for that region and the person responsible for seeing that NESA was well provided with intelligence information. During the early Luti period at NESA, the DIO was Bruce Hardcastle. There were DIOs for each of the major regions of the world; Hardcastle happened to be the man for the Middle East. I knew Hardcastle and respected his work. He had been a middle-level analyst in DIA when I held the job of DIO for the Middle East.

Abruptly last year, the Defense Department dismantled the entire DIO system. It now seems likely that frictions that developed between Luti and Hardcastle were a significant factor in this destruction of a very worthwhile intelligence-analytic system. Historically, the DIO oversaw all of the regional analysts and assets of DIA, but reported directly to the director of the DIA, avoiding bureaucratic and managerial duties while retaining responsibility for all analysis within his or her geographical domain. The roots of the friction between Hardcastle and Luti were straightforward: Hardcastle brought with him the combined wisdom of the professional military intelligence community. The community had serious doubts about the lethality of the threat from Saddam Hussein, the terrorism links and the status of the Iraqi WMD programs. Luti could not accept this. He knew what he wanted: to bring down Saddam Hussein. Hardcastle could not accept the very idea of allowing a desired outcome to shape the results of analysis.

Even before the Iraq desk at NESA was expanded into the "Office of Special Plans" in August 2002, Luti had transformed NESA into a de facto arm of the vice president's office. While the normal chain of command for NESA ran through Under Secretary for Policy Feith and up to Deputy

Secretary Wolfowitz and Secretary Rumsfeld, Luti made it clear that his chain of command principally ran directly up to Scooter Libby, Cheney's chief of staff. We are lucky enough to have a description of this relationship from a participant in the business of the office itself.

Lt. Col. (ret.) Karen Kwiatkowski (USAF), who served at NESA from June 2002 to March 2003, provides an interesting perspective. She says she was "shocked to learn that Luti was effectively working for Libby . . . . In one of the first staff meetings that I attended there," she recalled, "Bill Luti said, 'Well, did you get that thing over to Scooter? Scooter wants this, and somebody's got to get it over to him, and get that up to him right away.' After the meeting, I asked one of my co-workers, who'd been there longer, 'Who is this Scooter?' I was told, 'That's Scooter Libby over at the OVP (Office of the Vice President). He's the Vice President's chief of staff.' Later I came to understand that Cheney had put Luti there."

Kwiatkowski learned that OSP personnel were participating, along with officials from the DIA and CIA, in the debriefings of Chalabi-delivered informants. John Trigilio, a DIA officer assigned to NESA, confirmed it to her in a heated discussion.

> I argued with him [Trigilio] after the President's Cincinnati speech (in October 2002). I told him that the President had made a number of statements that were just not supported by the intelligence. He said that the President's statements are supported by intelligence, and he would finally say, "We have sources that you don't have." I took it to mean the sources that Chalabi was bringing in for debriefing . . . . Trigilio told me he participated in a number of debriefs, conducted in hotels downtown, or wherever, of people that Chalabi brought in. These debriefs had Trigilio from OSP, but also CIA and DIA participated . . . . If it (the information) sounded good, it would go straight to the OVP or elsewhere. I don't put it out of possibility that the information would go straight to the media because of the (media's) close relationship with some of the neoconservatives. So this information would make it straight out into the knowledge base without waiting for intelligence (analysts) to come by with their qualifications and reservations.

NESA/OSP apparently carried the cherry-picking methods of the smaller Policy Counterterrorism Evaluation Group to a new level of effectiveness, according to Lt. Col. Kwiatkowski.

> At the OSP, what they were doing was looking at all the intelligence they could find on WMD. That was the focal point, picking bits and pieces that were the most inflammatory, removing any context that might have been provided in the original intelligence report, that would have caused you to have some pause in believing it or reflected doubts that the intelligence community had, so if the intelligence community had doubts, those would be left out . . . . They would

take items that had occurred many years ago, and put them in the present tense, make it seem like they occurred not many years ago . . . . But they would not talk about the dates; they would say things like, "He has continued since that time" and "He could do it tomorrow," which of course, wasn't true . . . . The other thing they would do would be to take unrelated events that were reported in totally unrelated ways and make connections that the intelligence community had not made. This was primarily in discussing Iraq's activities and how they might be related to al-Qaeda or other terrorist groups that might be against us, or against Israel . . . . These kinds of links would be made. They would be made casually, and they would be made in a calculated way to form an image that is definitely not the image that anyone reading the original reports would have. The summaries that we would see from Intelligence did not match the kinds of things that OSP was putting out. So that is what I call propaganda development. It goes beyond the manipulation of intelligence to propaganda development.

A number of people have made the observation that Lt. Col. Kwiatkowski did not have sufficient access to have seen what was going on with intelligence materials. The previous paragraphs would seem to disprove that idea.

Kwiatkowski also knows a lot about Luti's efforts to exclude DIO Bruce Hardcastle from the briefings to foreign military officials. Luti ordered that Hardcastle was not to be included in briefings on Iraq, its WMD, and its links to terrorism. Instead, the Iraq desk of NESA, and later the Office of Special Plans, would produce "talking points" which, Luti insisted, were to be the only briefings provided on Iraq. Kwiatkowski says,

With the talking points, many of the propagandistic bullets that were given to use in papers for our superiors to inform them – internal propaganda – many of those same phrases and assumptions and tones, I saw in Vice President Cheney's speeches and the President's speeches. So I got the impression that those talking points were not just for us, but were the core of an overall agenda for a disciplined product, beyond the Pentagon. Over at the vice President's office and the *Weekly Standard*, the media, and the neoconservative talking heads and that kind of thing – all on the same sheet of music.

Lt. Col. Kwiatkowski identified Abram Shulsky as the principal author of the NESA/OSP talking points on Iraq. Shulsky was one of the Pentagon's "defense intellectuals" who had been involved on the periphery of intelligence work since the late 1970s, when he first came to Washington as an aide to Senator Daniel Patrick Moynihan (D-N.Y.). He also worked for Senator Henry "Scoop" Jackson (D-Wash.). Shulsky shared a common background with Paul Wolfowitz. Both men had graduated from the University of Chicago and had studied under Leo Strauss. In 1999, Shulsky, along with his fellow Chicago alumnus and Strauss protégé Gary Schmitt, founder of the "Project for the New American Century" (PNAC), wrote an essay entitled, "Leo Strauss and the World of Intelligence," which attacked American intelligence-community icon Sherman Kent for failing to understand that all intelligence work ultimately comes down to deception and counterdeception. For Shulsky (as expressed in his article), the goal of intelligence is to serve the needs of policymakers in making possible the attainment of policy goals. Intelligence, he wrote, "was the art of deception." Shulsky seems to have set out to use the OSP as the means for providing the Bush administration policymakers all the ammunition they needed to get their desired results. Interestingly, neither Shulsky nor the great majority of the people employed at one time or another by all these ad hoc intelligence groups were people with any previous experience of intelligence work. They were former congressional staffers, scholars and activists of one kind or another. They were people embarked on a great adventure in pursuit of a goal, not craftsmen devoted to their art.

Subverting and Subduing the Professionals

Supporting the statements of Kwiatkowski and others about the pipeline of unevaluated information that flowed straight into the hands of Vice President Cheney and other key policymakers, there is extant a June 2002 letter from the INC's Washington office addressed to the Senate Appropriations Committee that argues for the transfer of the "Information Collection Program" from the State Department to the Defense Intelligence Agency's Defense HUMINT Service (a service I was instrumental in founding). In a clumsy act of indiscretion, the letter's author explained that there was already a direct flow of information from the INC into the hands of Bill Luti and John Hannah, the latter being Scooter Libby's deputy in Cheney's office.

Armed with the INC product, Vice President Cheney made a series of visits to the CIA headquarters at Langley to question agency analysts who were producing assessments that did not match the material that had been funneled to him through Luti and Hannah. The vice president also made personal visits to many members of Congress, to persuade them, in the autumn of 2002, to grant the President the authority to go to war with Iraq. One leading Democratic senator says that Cheney sat in his office and made what now appear to be greatly exaggerated claims about Saddam's nuclear weapons program. The fear of Saddam's possessing a nuclear bomb compelled the senator to vote in favor of granting the war powers.

Part of the "Saddam bomb plot" tale came from Khadir Hamza, an Iraqi nuclear scientist who defected in 1994 and settled in the United States through the assistance of the INC. Hamza initially went to work for the Institute for Science and International Security, a think tank headed by former UN weapons inspector David Albright. According to a May 12, 2003, *New Yorker* interview with Albright by Seymour Hersh, Hamza and his boss drafted a 1998 proposal for a book that would have exposed how Saddam's quest for a nuclear bomb had "fizzled." There were no takers. But two years later, Hamza co-authored a very different book, with Jeff Stein, vastly exaggerating Saddam's nuclear weapons program. This, despite the fact that, in 1995, Saddam Hussein's son-in-law, General Hussein Kamel, who was the head of Iraq's weapons agency, escaped to Jordan with a large collection of Iraqi government documents showing how little was left of Iraqi WMD programs. Kamel was interviewed by a team of UN weapons inspectors headed by Rolf Ekeus, chairman of the UN teams, and he confirmed that the inspections had, in effect, uprooted most of what was left of the Iraqi WMD program after the 1991 Gulf War.

It is telling that, in the more than two-year run-up to the March 2003 invasion of Iraq, nobody in the Bush administration sought to commission a National Intelligence Estimate (NIE) on Saddam Hussein's WMD programs. Perhaps it is unsurprising that they did not want such an estimate. An estimate, if conducted over a period of months, would undoubtedly have revealed deep skepticism about the threat posed by Saddam's weapons program. It would have exposed major gaps in the intelligence picture, particularly since the pullout of UN weapons inspectors from Iraq at the end of 1998, and it would have likely undercut the rush to war. It was only as a result of intense pressure from Senator Bob Graham (D-Fla.), chairman of the Senate Select Committee on Intelligence, that the intelligence community was finally tasked, in September 2002, to produce an NIE on Saddam's WMD programs. The report was to be rushed to completion in three weeks, so it could reach the desks of the relevant congressional committee members before a vote on war-powers authorization scheduled for early October, on the eve of the mid-term elections. As the NIE went forward for approval, everyone knew that there were major problems with it.

The issue of the Niger yellowcake uranium precursor had been a point of controversy since late 2001, when the Italian secret service, SISMI, reported to their American, British and Israeli counterparts that they had obtained documents on Niger government letterhead indicating that Iraq had attempted to purchase 500 tons of yellowcake. The yellowcake lead had been reported to the vice president by his CIA daily-briefing officer, and Cheney had tasked the CIA to dig deeper. Obviously, if the case could be made that

Saddam was aggressively seeking nuclear material, no one in Congress could justifiably oppose war. The story proved to be a hoax. In February 2002, the CIA dispatched former Ambassador Joseph Wilson to Niger to look into the report. Wilson had served in several African countries, including Niger, and had also been the U.S. chargé d'affaires in Baghdad, at the time of the Iraqi invasion of Kuwait. He knew all the players. After several days of meetings in Niger, he returned to Washington and was debriefed by the CIA. The yellowcake story simply did not check out. Case closed.

Contrary to Wilson's expectations, variations on the matter continued to creep into policy speeches by top administration officials. Although CIA Director Tenet personally intervened to remove references to the discredited African uranium story from President Bush's early October 2002 speech in Cincinnati, Ohio, promoting the overthrow of Saddam Hussein, bogus yellowcake information appeared in a December 19, 2002, State Department "fact sheet" on Saddam's failure to disclose his secret WMD programs. As we all know, President Bush's January 2003 State of the Union speech contained the now infamous 16 words citing British intelligence claims about Saddam's seeking uranium in Africa.

For Greg Thielmann, who retired in September 2002 from his post as director of the Strategic, Proliferation and Military Affairs Office at the State Department's Intelligence Bureau, the issue of the aluminum tubes was an even more egregious case of policymakers' contamination of the intelligence process than the Wilson yellowcake affair. His position is:

> What was done with the aluminum tubes was far worse than what was done with the uranium from Africa. Because the intelligence community had debated over a period of months, and involved key scientists and engineers in the National Laboratories – and foreigners as well – in a long and detailed discussion. The way I would have characterized it, if you had asked me in July 2002, when I turned over the leadership of my office, there was a growing consensus in the intelligence community that this kind of aluminum was not suitable for the nuclear weapons program. So I was really quite shocked to see – I was just retired – the National Intelligence Estimate say that the majority of agencies came to the opposite interpretation, that it was going into the nuclear weapons program.

Even with this "majority" view, Thielmann points out that anyone at the White House or the National Security Council who was genuinely seeking the truth would have seen through the subterfuge and drawn the proper conclusion:

> If they had read the NIE in October, it is transparent that there were different views in the intelligence community. They could have read, for example,

that the Department of Energy and the State Department INR believed that the aluminum tubes were not going into the nuclear weapons program and instead were going into conventional artillery rockets. And, if one assumes a modicum of intelligence understanding at the NSC, they should know that the agency that is most able to judge on this would be the Department of Energy. They control all the laboratories that actually over the years have enriched uranium and built centrifuges.

Thielmann also had an important observation about the Office of Special Plans and the other intelligence boutiques that Cheney and Rumsfeld and Wolfowitz had established inside the Pentagon's policy shop:

> It was a stealth organization. They didn't play in the intelligence community proceedings that our office participated in. When the intelligence community met as a community, there was no OSP represented in these sessions. Because, if they had done that, they would have had to subject their views to peer review. Why do that when you can send stuff right in to the vice president?

The NIE Contamination

Two other major INC-foisted fabrications made their way into the NIE and from there into policy speeches by top Bush administration officials, including the President, the vice president, and the secretaries of Defense and State. The first involved claims that Iraq had mobile biological-weapons labs that could produce deadly agents. The declassified version of the October 2002 NIE stated, "Baghdad has mobile facilities for producing bacterial and toxin BW agents; these facilities can evade detection and are highly survivable. Within three to six months, these units probably could produce an amount of agent equal to the total that Iraq produced in the years prior to the Gulf war." The same claim was a dramatic highlight of Colin Powell's February 5, 2003, presentation before the Security Council.

But, a subsequent review of the intelligence files – long after the NIE had been produced – revealed that the sole source for the mobile-lab story was an Iraqi military defector, a major, who had been produced by the INC via the "Information Collection Program." The CIA and DIA had both given warnings about the defector, after concluding that he was a fabricator. But, as CIA Director Tenet would later admit in a February 2004 speech at Georgetown University, those warnings fell on deaf ears. The fabrication judgment was shown to be correct after the U.S. invasion, when two of the mobile labs were captured. They were, as other Iraqi sources had claimed, mobile facilities for producing hydrogen for weather balloons.

A somewhat different fiasco occurred on the issue of the equally inflammatory claim that Iraq had unmanned airborne vehicles (UAVs), outfitted to deliver biological and chemical weapons. Allegations about the UAVs surfaced in early September 2002, prompting both CIA Director Tenet and Vice President Cheney to visit House and Senate leaders on the day Congress reconvened after the Labor Day recess to present their new "smoking gun" argument for war. The UAV story appeared in President Bush's October 7, 2002, speech in Cincinnati. It was also featured in Colin Powell's Security Council presentation four months later. Powell warned the Council then that "Iraq could use these small UAVs, which have a wingspan of only a few meters, to deliver biological agents to its neighbors or, if transported, to other countries, including the United States."

Yet the declassified version of the October 2002 NIE, while reporting that "Baghdad's UAVs could threaten Iraq's neighbors, U.S. forces in the Persian Gulf and, if brought close to or into the United States, the U.S. homeland," also noted that "the Director, Intelligence, Surveillance and Reconnaissance, U.S. Air Force, does not agree that Iraq is developing UAVs primarily intended to be delivery platforms for chemical and biological warfare (CBW) agents. The small size of Iraq's new UAV strongly suggests a primary role of reconnaissance, although CBW delivery is an inherent capability." Indeed, the specifications of the Iraqi UAVs, known to U.S. Air Force Intelligence, proved that they were ill-suited for CBW dissemination. According to several news accounts, even the formulation that "CBW delivery is an inherent capability" was foisted upon the Air Force during the negotiating sessions over the final wording of the NIE.

The subversion of the intelligence process was death by a thousand cuts, a cumulative process of badgering in which the pipeline of disinformation from the INC, through OSP, to the desk of the vice president played a decisive role.

Vincent Cannistraro puts it this way:

> Over a long period of time, there was a subtle process of pressure and intimidation until people started giving them what was wanted . . . . When the Senate Intelligence Committee interviewed, under oath, over 100 analysts, not one of them said, "I changed my assessment because of pressure" . . . . The environment was conditioned in such a way that the analyst subtly leaned toward the conceits of the policymakers . . . . The intelligence community was vulnerable to the aggressiveness of neoconservative policymakers, particularly at the Pentagon and at the VP's office. As one analyst said to me, "You can't fight something with nothing, and those people had something. Whether it was right or wrong, fraudulent or specious, it almost didn't make any difference, because the policymakers believed it already, and if you didn't have hard countervailing evidence to persuade them, then you were at a loss."

Lt. Col. Dale Davis (USMC, ret.) concurs that the intelligence process was badly subverted by a "political operation." Davis, through March 2004, headed International Programs at the Virginia Military Institute. A fluent Arabic speaker, he has served throughout the Arab world. Davis initially said that he did not think that the intelligence analysts were pressured, "per se":

> They created an organization that would give them the answers they wanted. Or at least piece together a very compelling case by rummaging through all the various intelligence reports and picking out the best, the most juicy, but quite often the most flimsy pieces of information . . . . By creating the OSP, Cheney was able to say, "Hey, look at what we're getting out of OSP. How come you guys aren't doing as well? What is your response to what this alternative analysis that we're receiving from the Pentagon says?" That's how you do it. You pressure people indirectly.

The Countdown

> "Why on earth didn't [Saddam] let the inspectors in and avoid the war?"
> —Senator Pat Roberts[1]

Senator Pat Roberts of Kansas is the Republican chairman of the Senate Select Committee on Intelligence, which was charged with investigating the misuse of intelligence prior to the Iraq war, the failures of intelligence, the Iraqi National Congress, and the Office of Special Plans.[2] The answer

---

1. Quoted by Paul Krugman in a *New York Times* column, February 6, 2004.

2. As of July 2005 "phase II" of the Roberts-led investigation – the phase that was supposed to look not at the alleged "failures" of the intelligence community but at the political use made by the administration of the intelligence that they claim to have had in persuading the American public to support going to war in Iraq – has still not occurred, in spite of repeated promises from the committee chairmen to conduct it. Democrats are now taking the lead – though one wonders if it's too little, too late, or whether the administration will respond one way or the other – in pushing the "use of intelligence" part of the investigation forward. The congressional Democrats' efforts include (1) a June 22, 2005, letter from Senator John Kerry (D-Mass.) and nine of his colleagues to the chairmen of the Senate Select Committee on Intelligence requesting the second phase of the investigation, promised in February 2004, that was to look into "the use of intelligence by policy makers, the comparison of pre-war assessments and post-war findings, the activities of the Policy Counterterrorism Evaluation Group (PCTEG) and the Office of Special Plans in the Office (OSP) of the Under Secretary of Defense for Policy, and the use of information provided by the Iraqi National Congress"; (2) the holding up of the nomination of a replacement for Defense Under Secretary for Policy Douglas Feith by Senator Carl Levin (D-Mich.) in order to coerce the Bush administration into turning over documents Levin has requested relating to his own investigation into the OSP; (3) the investigation (and resultant report, *vide infra*, p. 285, note 1) by Levin's staff into the use that OSP made of intelligence regarding alleged ties between Iraq and al-Qaeda; (4) the construction of a comprehensive database of misleading Bush-administration statements regarding Iraq during the run-up to the war by the minority office of the House Committee on Government Reform, and as directed by the

to his question is simple: Saddam did let the inspectors in, at a level of cooperation that was unprecedented. The question that Senator Roberts should really be asking is, "Why didn't it matter?"

It should have been a dire warning to the U.S. Congress when the man who had been convicted of lying to Congress during the Iran-contra affair – Elliot Abrams – was put in charge of the Middle East section of the NSC staff. One underestimated talent of the neocon group in the run-up to this war was its ability to manipulate Congress. They were masters of the game, having made the team in Washington in the 1970s on the staffs of two of the most powerful senators in recent decades, New York's Patrick Moynihan and Washington's Henry "Scoop" Jackson. The old boy's club – Abe Shulsky at OSP, Deputy Secretary of Defense Paul Wolfowitz, Under Secretary of Defense for Policy Douglas Feith, Middle East Desk Officer at the NSC Elliot Abrams, Defense Policy Board Chairman Richard Perle – had not only worked together in their early government years in these two Senate offices, but they had stayed together as a network through the ensuing decades, floating around a small number of businesses and think tanks, including the American Enterprise Institute and the openly neo-imperialist Project for a New American Century. The neocons were openly contemptuous of Congress, as they were of the UN Security Council. And a number of tricks and manipulations of the congressional process have now been exposed. But was the trickery planned? Was it a well-orchestrated obfuscation, an accident or coincidence? What is the evidence?

First, there was the consistent refusal to provide witnesses and information to the U.S. Senate, especially regarding the projected costs of the war and the lack of opportunities to question key players such as General Jay Garner, who was appointed by the Defense Department to be the first head of the U.S. provisional authority in Iraq. There was also the subtle hiding of the objections of the Department of Energy and the State Department's Bureau of Intelligence and Research (INR) in the NIE of October 2002. One congressional source explained that the classified NIE was made available in its entirety to only a select few members of Congress. There were verbal

---

ranking member of the Committee, Congressman Henry Waxman (D-Calif.); (5) the informal hearing held by several House Democrats on allegations arising from the "Downing Street Memo" (DSM) (see Ray McGovern's essay following the present one, pp. 277–305); (6) a Resolution of Inquiry introduced by Congresswoman Barbara Lee (D-Calif.) and co-sponsored by 39 House Democrats, requesting DSM-related information from the executive branch, and (7) Congressman Conyers's letter, signed by over 120 House Democrats and several hundred thousand individuals, requesting that President Bush provide information on what he knew, when he knew it, as it relates to the infamous memo.—Ed.

briefings and an elaborate process to access the document in a secure location. But it was never clear that the 27-page unclassified version that was available to every office was missing any crucial information.

There were also false statements to Congress about providing the UN inspectors all the intelligence that might have helped them locate the Iraqi WMD and programs. Senator Carl Levin of Michigan has accused the administration, and especially CIA Director Tenet, of withholding information because "the truth" – that the United States had withheld the locations of 21 high- and middle-priority sites – might have slowed down the drive for war. The truth might have convinced Congress to take action to delay military action until the inspections were completed.

The March 7, 2003, appearance by the chairmen of UNMOVIC (Hans Blix) and the IAEA (Mohamed ElBaradei) before the UN Security Council was a disaster for the neoconservatives. The Iraqis and Saddam Hussein had "accelerated" cooperation with the United Nations, said Dr. Blix. Blix told the Council that Iraq had made a major concession: they had agreed to allow the destruction of the Al-Samoud ballistic missiles. "We are not watching the breaking of toothpicks," Blix said. "Lethal weapons are being destroyed . . . . The destruction undertaken constitutes a substantial measure of disarmament – indeed, the first since the middle of the 1990s."

The Al Samoud, a massive missile seven meters long weighing two tons with its warhead, was being destroyed, without the slightest obstruction or even complaint from the Iraqis. Major Corrine Heraud, a French woman who served as the chief weapons inspector for UNMOVIC in this operation and who had also served from 1996 with UNSCOM, says that the level of cooperation from the Iraqis was unprecedented, something that she never would have expected and did not encounter during the 1996–98 inspections. Each missile cost more than $1 million, estimates Maj. Heraud, who also cautions that this would be equivalent to a much higher amount in Western dollars, considering the difficulty that Iraq encountered in buying materials and parts, due to the UN sanctions. Yet, to President Bush, the destruction of the Al Samoud, a missile often mistaken in photographs for the better-known SCUD missile, was meaningless. The missile destruction, said Bush, was a "campaign of deception." For the UN inspectors, Bush's words were a shock. "We didn't know what to make of this," an UNMOVIC official said.

"Blix came down hard on the Iraqis, and we actually were in the process of destroying all these Al Samoud missiles," says Greg Thielmann, the former head of the WMD section of INR. "As soon as the Iraqis agreed to do that, I sighed a big sigh of relief. I thought, the UN inspectors are working;

we've stared Saddam down; we've forced him to do what he desperately didn't want to do, in that area of activity that was of most concern to us." Thielmann believes that the Al Samoud incident shows that the administration was so intent on war that this compliance with the inspections "made no difference."

But it was after the next presentation, by IAEA chairman Mohammed ElBaradei, that "all hell broke loose" in Washington. ElBaradei, in his statement, sank the U.S. intelligence community's prestigious NIE, President Bush's State of the Union address, and Colin Powell's February 5 address to the UN Security Council with one blow. ElBaradei was calm in what he had to say: "Based on thorough analysis, the IAEA has concluded, with the concurrence of outside experts, that these documents, which form the basis for reports of recent uranium transactions between Iraq and Niger are, in fact, not authentic." The Niger yellowcake documents were forgeries. Then, ElBaradei told the press that an IAEA staff member had, in fact, used the common search engine Google to determine, within hours, that the Niger documents, which had been passed on to the U.S. embassy in Rome through an anonymous source, were fakes! Members of Congress then began to grumble. In light of the contradictions, a bill was introduced demanding that the administration disclose the intelligence reports that were the basis for the statements made by Bush, Cheney, Rumsfeld and Powell about the Iraqi WMD threat. It was still locked in committee when the war began.

The destruction of the Al Samoud missiles continued. It was not only missiles, reports UNMOVIC chief weapons inspector Corrine Heroud, it was engines, launchers, training missiles and missiles still in production that were destroyed. Heroud, called "the terminator" in her native France for her expertise in destroying missiles, described the delicate process of disarming the missiles, then crushing them over and over till they "were a pancake" that was then encased in concrete and buried.

How did the White House respond to these instances of effective work by the United Nations in Iraq? In the final weeks of the countdown to war, the administration's actions resembled nothing so much as some of the madder scenes from Alice in Wonderland. The fact that the documents the administration had used to "prove" that Iraq was working on nuclear weapons were forged only led to greater insistence that Iraq was a danger. The absence of discovery of WMD by the UN inspectors was only further evidence that the Iraqis were the greatest deceivers in history and that they had succeeded in concealing their location. The destruction of the Al Samoud missiles was just more evidence of a "grand deception."

George Tenet has now told us, on February 5, 2004, exactly one year after he and Colin Powell drank the Kool-Aid at the UN Security Council, that there was no imminent danger. The administration spin-doctors immediately responded to this statement by saying that nobody from the administration ever claimed there was an "imminent danger."

On March 7, 2003, Mohammed ElBaradei spoke to the UN Security Council in an open session watched by tens of millions of Americans and countless congressional and government offices. He said:

> In conclusion, I am able to report today that, in the area of nuclear weapons – the most lethal weapons of mass destruction – inspections in Iraq are moving forward. One, there is no indication of resumed nuclear activities in those buildings that were identified through the use of satellite imagery as being reconstructed or newly erected since 1998, nor any indication of nuclear-related activities at any inspected sites. Second, there is no indication that Iraq has attempted to import uranium since 1990. Third, there is no indication that Iraq has attempted to import aluminum tubes for use in centrifuge enrichment. Moreover, even had Iraq pursued such a plan, it would have encountered practical difficulties in manufacturing centrifuges out of the aluminum tubes in question. Fourth, . . . there is no indication to date that Iraq imported magnets for use in a centrifuge enrichment programme.
>
> After three months of intrusive inspections, we have to date found no evidence or plausible indication of the revival of a nuclear weapons programme in Iraq . . . . I should note that, in the past three weeks, possibly as a result of ever-increasing pressure by the international community, Iraq has been forthcoming in its cooperation, particularly with regard to the conduct of private interviews and in making available evidence that contributes to the resolution of matters of IAEA concern.

On March 16, 2003, the neocons struck back with the heavy artillery. Vice President Dick Cheney appeared on *Meet the Press*. When pressured by Tim Russert about Iraq's nuclear danger, Cheney retorted:

> We know he has been absolutely devoted to trying to acquire nuclear weapons. And we believe he has, in fact, reconstituted nuclear weapons (emphasis mine). I think Mr. ElBaradei frankly is wrong. And I think if you look at the track record of the International Atomic Energy Agency on this kind of issue, especially where Iraq's concerned, they have consistently underestimated or missed what it was Saddam Hussein was doing. I don't have any reason to believe they're any more valid this time than they've been in the past.

On March 17, 2003, President George W. Bush went on national television to tell Saddam and his sons, "They have 48 hours to get out of town." No new evidence or reason was given. It was the ultimate imperial moment.

On March 19, 2003, the bombs began to fall.

THE EDITORS' GLOSS: Following the completion of the Presidential Commission's March 31, 2005, report on WMD intelligence, Senator Pat Roberts (R-Ks.) of the intelligence committee said, " . . . we have now heard it all regarding prewar intelligence . . . . it would be a monumental waste of time to re-plow this ground any further." Promises were made on Capitol Hill that there would be a second phase of inquiry by the Senate to determine how "faulty" (read misrepresented) intelligence was used by the Bush administration to mislead the American public. Now we are told there's no reason to "re-plow" this ground. But the dirt continues to come out, indicating that re-plowing is precisely what's needed.

First there's the recent report that, in 2001, intelligence was provided by a credible source to a 20-year-plus veteran CIA agent indicating that Baghdad dropped segments of its nuclear program in the mid-90s, but the agency refused to share that information with senior policymakers or other agencies. Then there's a comment that Roberts made on *Meet the Press*, April 10, 2005, that a statement he received indicated that "some of the activities [in the Office of Special Plans] may have been illegal [and that] everybody down there got a lawyer." Finally there's the denial (the hard-nosed might call it a "lie") of Secretary Rumsfeld, on *Face the Nation*, March 14, 2004, before Bob Schieffer and Thomas Friedman, that he said Iraq was an "immediate threat":

SCHIEFFER: If they did not have these weapons of mass destruction . . . why then did they pose an immediate threat to us, to this country?

RUMSFELD: Well, you're the—you and a few other critics are the only people I've heard use the phrase "immediate threat." I DIDN'T. The President didn't. And it's become kind of folklore that that's what's happened . . . .

SCHIEFFER: You're saying that nobody in the administration said that.

RUMSFELD: I—I can't speak for nobody—everybody in the administration and say nobody said that.

SCHIEFFER: Vice president didn't say that? The . . .

RUMSFELD: Not—if—if you have any citations, I'd like to see 'em . . . .

FRIEDMAN: [quoting a Rumsfeld statement] "No terrorist state poses a greater or more immediate threat to the security of our people and the stability of the world and the regime of Saddam Hussein in Iraq."

Telling the story of how credible this bloody farce has been from the start is Rumsfeld's "persuasive" reply to Schieffer and Friedman: "Mm-hmm. It—my view of—of the situation was that he—he had—we—we believe, the best intelligence that we had and other countries had and that—that we believed and we still do not know—we will know." Right.

CHAPTER
18

Sham Dunk:
Cooking Intelligence for the President
• • • • • • • • •

Ray McGovern

LET'S REVIEW. It was bad intelligence that forced an unwitting President to invade Iraq, right? The sad fact that so many Americans believe this myth is eloquent testimony to the effectiveness of the White House spin machine. The intelligence was indeed bad – shaped that way by an administration determined to find a pretext to effect "regime change" in Iraq. Senior administration officials – first and foremost Vice President Dick Cheney – played a strong role in ensuring that the intelligence analysis was corrupt enough to justify," *ex post facto*, the decision to make war on Iraq. It is not altogether clear how witting President George W. Bush was of all this, but there is strong evidence that he knew chapter and verse. Had he been mouse trapped into this "preemptive" war, one would expect some heads to roll. None have. And where is it, after all, that the buck is supposed to stop?

The intelligence-made-me-do-it myth has helped the Bush administration attenuate the acute embarrassment it experienced early last year when the *casus belli* became a *casus* belly laugh. When U.S. inspector David Kay, after a painstaking search to which almost a billion dollars – and many lives – were given, reported that there had been no "weapons of mass destruction" (WMD) in Iraq since 1991, someone had to take the fall. Elected was CIA director George Tenet, the backslapping fellow from Queens – always eager to do whatever might be necessary to play with the bigger kids. For those of you just in from Mars, the grave danger posed by Iraqi "weapons of mass destruction" was what President Bush cited as the *casus belli* for invading Iraq. It was only after Kay had the courage to tell the truth publicly that Bush fell back on the default rationale for the war – the need to export democracy, about which we are hearing so much lately.

Not surprisingly, the usual suspects in the mainstream media that played cheerleader for the war are now helping the President (and the media) escape blame. "Flawed intelligence that led the United States to invade Iraq was the fault of the U.S. intelligence community," explained the *Washington Times* last July 10, after regime loyalist Senator Pat Roberts (R-Kan.), chairman of the *Senate Select Committee on Intelligence*, released his committee's findings.[1] Nine months later, after publication of similar findings[2] by a commission handpicked by the President, the *Washington Post's* lead headline was "Data on Iraqi Arms Flawed, Panel Says." The date was, appropriately, April Fools Day, 2005. In a word, they are playing us for fools. The remarkable thing is that most folks don't seem able, or willing, to recognize that – or even to mind.

On May 1, 2005, a highly sensitive document published by *The Sunday Times* of London provided the smoking gun showing that President Bush had decided to make war on Iraq long before the National Intelligence Estimate was produced to conjure up "weapons of mass destruction" there and mislead Congress into granting authorization for war. The British document is classified "SECRET AND STRICTLY PERSONAL – U.K. EYES ONLY." And small wonder. It contains an official account of Prime Minister Tony Blair's meeting with top advisers on July 23, 2002, at which Sir Richard Dearlove, head of MI6 (the U.K. equivalent to the CIA) – simply "C" in the written document – reported on talks he had just held in Washington with top U.S. officials. (Blair has now acknowledged the authenticity of the document.)

As related in the document, Dearlove told Blair and the others that President Bush wanted to remove Saddam Hussein through military action, that this "was seen as inevitable," and that the attack would be "justified by the conjunction of terrorism and WMD." He continued: *". . . but the intelligence and facts were being fixed around the policy"* (emphasis added), and tacked on yet another telling comment: "There was little discussion in Washington of the aftermath after military action." British Foreign Secretary Jack Straw concurred that Bush had made up his mind to take military action, but noted that finding justification would be challenging, for "the case was thin." Straw pointed out that Saddam was not threatening his neighbors, and his WMD capability was less than that of Libya, North Korea, or Iran.

---

1. *Report on the U.S. Intelligence Community's Prewar Intelligence Assessments on Iraq,* July 7, 2004.

2. *Report of The Commission on the Intelligence Capabilities of the United States Regarding Weapons of Mass Destruction,* March 31, 2005.

As head of MI6, Dearlove was CIA Director George Tenet's British counterpart. We Veteran Intelligence Professionals for Sanity (VIPS) have been saying since January 2003 that the two intelligence chiefs' marching orders were to "fix" the intelligence "around the policy." It was a no-brainer. Seldom, however, does one acquire documentary evidence that this – the unforgivable sin in intelligence analysis – was used by the most senior government leaders as a way to "justify" a prior decision for war. There is no word to describe our reaction to the fact that the two intelligence chiefs quietly acquiesced in the corruption of our profession on a matter of such consequence. "Outrage" doesn't even come close.

Denial: Not an Option

What has become painfully clear since the trauma of 9/11 is that most of our fellow citizens have felt an overriding need to believe that administration leaders are telling them the truth and to ignore all evidence to the contrary. Many Americans seem impervious to data showing that it was the administration that misled the country into this unprovoked war and that the "intelligence" was conjured up well after the White House decided to effect "regime change" in Iraq (or introduce democracy, if you favor the default rationale) by force of arms.

I have been asking myself why Americans find it so painful to delve deeper and let their judgment be influenced by the abundance of evidence showing this to be the case. Perhaps it is because most of us know that responsible citizenship means asking what might seem to be "impertinent" questions, ferreting out plausible answers, and then – if necessary – rectifying the situation and ensuring it does not happen again. Resistance, however, is strong. At work – in all of us to some degree – is the same convenient denial mechanism that immobilized so many otherwise conscientious German citizens during the 1930s, enabling Germany to launch its own unprovoked wars and curtail civil liberties at home. Taking action, or just finding one's voice, entails risk; denial is the more instinctive, easier course.

So, fair warning. If you prefer denial, you may wish to page directly to the next chapter. No hard feelings.

Iraq: Prime Target from the Start

Was the intelligence bad? It was worse than bad; it was corrupt. But what most Americans do not realize is that the intelligence adduced had nothing to do with President Bush's decision to make war on Iraq.

On January 30, 2001, just ten days after his inauguration, when George W. Bush presided over the first meeting of his National Security Council (NSC), he made it clear that toppling Saddam Hussein sat atop his to-do list, according to then Secretary of the Treasury Paul O'Neil sworn in earlier that day. (The Treasury Secretary is by statute a full member of the NSC.) O'Neil was thoroughly confused: why Saddam, why now, and why was this central to U.S. interests, he asked himself. The NSC discussion did not address these questions. Rather, at the invitation of then-National Security Advisor Condoleezza Rice, George Tenet showed a grainy overhead photo of a factory in Iraq that he said might produce either chemical or biological material for weapons. Might. There was nothing – in the photo, or in other intelligence sources – to support that conjecture, but it was just what Doctor Rice ordered. The discussion then turned from unconfirmed intelligence, to which targets might be best to begin bombing in Iraq. Tenet had shown his mettle. The group was off and running; the planning began in earnest. And not only for war. O'Neil says that two days later the NSC reconvened to discuss Iraq, and that the deliberations included not only planning for war, but also for how and with whom to divide up Iraq's oil wealth.

Saddam and al-Qaeda

Seven months later, the terrorist attacks of 9/11 raised the question of possible Iraqi complicity, and on 9/12 White House terrorism adviser Richard Clarke experienced rather crass pressure directly from the President to implicate Saddam Hussein. To his credit, Clarke resisted. This did not prevent the White House from playing on the trauma suffered by the American people and falsely associating Saddam Hussein with it. Following Clarke's example, CIA analysts also held their ground for many months, insisting that there was no good evidence of such an association. Lt. Gen. Brent Scowcroft, national security advisor to the first President Bush and chairman of the President's Foreign Intelligence Advisory Board until just a few months ago, supported them by stating publicly that evidence of any such connection was "scant," while Defense Secretary Donald Rumsfeld was saying it was "bulletproof." And President Bush said flat out a year after 9/11, "You cannot distinguish between al-Qaeda and Saddam when you talk about the war on terror." The 9/11 Commission has now put the lie to those claims, but the PR campaign has been enduringly effective. According to a recent poll, most Americans have not been able to shake off the notion, so artfully fostered by the administration and the compliant media, that Saddam Hussein played some role in the events of 9/11. (This, even though the President himself, in a little noticed remark on September 17, 2003, admitted for the first and only time that there was "no evidence Hussein was involved" in the 9/11 attacks.)

Weapons of Mass Destruction

Unable to get enough intelligence analysts to go along with the carefully nurtured "noble lie" that Iraq played a role in 9/11, or even that operational ties existed between Iraq and al-Qaeda, the administration ordered up a separate genre of *faux* intelligence – this time it was "weapons of mass destruction." This was something of a challenge, for in the months before 9/11, Condoleezza Rice and then-Secretary of State Colin Powell had said publicly that Saddam Hussein posed no security threat. On February 24, 2001, for example, Powell said, "Saddam Hussein has not developed any significant capability with respect to weapons of mass destruction. He is unable to project conventional power against his neighbors." And just six weeks before 9/11, Condoleezza Rice told *CNN:* " . . . let's remember that his [Saddam's] country is divided, in effect. He does not control the northern part of his country. We are able to keep his arms from him. His military forces have not been rebuilt." Conveniently, the U.S. media pressed the delete button on these statements.

And, as is well known, after 9/11 "everything changed" – including apparently Saddam's inventory of "weapons of mass destruction." We were asked almost immediately to believe that WMD wafted down like manna from the heavens for a soft landing on the sands of Iraq. Just days after 9/11, Defense Secretary Rumsfeld began promoting the notion that Iraq might have weapons of mass destruction and that "within a week, or a month, Saddam could give his WMD to al-Qaeda." (This is an early articulation of the bogus "conjunction of terrorism and WMD," now immortalized in the minutes recording Richard Dearlove's report to Tony Blair ten months later, as the way the attack on Iraq would be "justified.") And it was not long before the agile Rice did a demi-pirouette of 180 degrees, saying, "Saddam was a danger in the region where the 9/11 threat emerged." By the summer of 2002, the basic decision for war having long since been taken, something persuasive had to be conjured up to get Congress to authorize it. Weapons of mass *deception,* as one wag called them, were what the doctor ordered. The malleable Tenet followed orders to package them into a National Intelligence Estimate, which Colin Powell has admitted was prepared specifically for Congress.

What about the CIA? Sadly, well before the war, truth took a back seat to a felt need on the part of then-CIA Director George Tenet to snuggle up to power – to stay in good standing with a President, vice president, and secretary of defense, all of whom dwarfed Tenet in pedigree, insider experience, and power; and all hell-bent and determined to implement "regime change" in Iraq.

So What Really Happened?

In our various oral and written presentations on Iraq, Veteran Intelligence Professionals for Sanity (VIPS) colleagues and I took no delight in exposing what we saw as the corruption of intelligence analysis at CIA. Nothing would have pleased us more than to have been proven wrong. As it turned out, we did not know the half of it. Last year's Senate Intelligence Committee report on prewar intelligence assessments on Iraq showed that the corruption went far deeper than we had thought. Both Senator Pat Roberts and the latest presidential panel have insisted, disingenuously, that no intelligence analysts complained about attempts to politicize their conclusions. What outsiders do not realize is that each of those analysts was accompanied by a "minder" from Tenet's office, minders reminiscent of the ubiquitous Iraqi intelligence officials that Saddam Hussein insisted be present when scientists of his regime were interviewed by UN inspectors. The hapless Democrats on Roberts's committee chose to acquiesce in his claim that political pressure played no role – this despite the colorful testimony by the CIA's ombudsman that never in his 32-year career with the agency had he encountered such "hammering" on CIA analysts to reconsider their judgments on operational ties between Iraq and al-Qaeda. It is no surprise that the President's own commission parroted the Roberts's committee's see-no-evil findings regarding politicization, even though the commission's report is itself replete with examples of intelligence analysts feeling the political heat.

Last July, George Tenet resigned for family reasons the day before the Senate committee issued its scathing report. He left behind an agency on life support – an institution staffed by careerist managers and thoroughly demoralized analysts embarrassed at their own naiveté in having believed that the unvarnished truth was what they were expected to serve up to their masters in the agency and the White House.

The Senate report and now the presidential commission's findings have performed masterfully in letting the White House off the hook. With copious instances of unconscionable intelligence missteps to draw from, it was, so to speak, a slam dunk – hardly a challenge to pin all the blame on intelligence. George had supplied the petard on which they hoisted him – and the intelligence community. The demonstrated malfeasance and misfeasance are a sharp blow to those of us who took pride in working in an agency where our mandate – and our orders – were to speak truth to power; an agency in which we enjoyed career protection from retribution from powerful policymakers who wished to play fast and loose with intelligence; an agency whose leaders in those days usually had the independence, integrity, and courage to face down those who would have us sell out in order to "justify" policies long since set in train.

Off-Line "Intelligence": The Pentagon's Office of Special Plans

The various committees and commissions assessing intelligence performance on Iraq avoided investigating the Pentagon's Office of Special Plans (OSP), whose de facto chain of command, from division chief to commander-in-chief, was a neocon dream come true: from Abram Shulsky to William Luti to Douglas Feith to Paul Wolfowitz to Donald Rumsfeld to Dick Cheney and George W. Bush. Journalist Seymour Hersh rightly calls this a stovepipe. It is also a self-licking ice cream cone. The lower end of this chain paid for and then stitched together bogus "intelligence" from the now thoroughly discredited Ahmad Chalabi and his Pentagon-financed Iraqi National Congress. Then Shulsky, Luti, and Feith cherry-picked "confirmation" from unevaluated reports on Iraq from other agencies, and served up neatly packaged, alarming sound-bites to "Scooter" Libby, Cheney's chief of staff. Whereupon Libby would scoot them right in to Cheney for him to use with the President, the Congress, and the media. But what about the CIA and the rest of our $40 billion intelligence establishment? Tenet and his crew were seen as far too timid, not "forward leaning" enough. The attitude in the world of the OSP was a mixture of chutzpah and naiveté: after our cakewalk into Baghdad, let the intelligence analysts eat cake.

Since this was all done off-line, and not, strictly speaking, as part of the activities of the "intelligence community," it could conveniently be ignored in the various inquiries into intelligence performance on Iraq[1] – effectively

---

1. The Senate Intelligence Committee's investigation into the Iraq intelligence debacle was supposed to look into the use/misuse of intelligence by administration officials in their public statements. Senator Roberts was successful in postponing that part of the inquiry until after the November 2004 election, in return for a promise to pursue it as "phase II" of the committee's investigation. In March 2005 Roberts dismissed the need for "phase II," but when Democrats on the committee objected to his reneging, he expressed

letting the Defense Department off the hook, while putting the spotlight on CIA and other intelligence professionals. Also ignored was the OSP-like operation[1] of Israeli Prime Minister Ariel Sharon's office and its role in providing "intelligence," possibly including the famous forgeries – in which neocon operative Michael Ledeen reportedly played a key role – regarding Iraq's alleged attempts to acquire "yellowcake" uranium.

Even though quintessential Republican loyalist Pat Roberts character-ized the activities of the Office of Special Plans as possibly "illegal," official responses to queries about the rogue OSP have ducked the issue. Some, like Senator John Kyl[2] and Paul Wolfowitz, the former deputy secretary of defense, maintain that the OSP provided a valuable service by exercising initiative and challenging the assumptions of the intelligence community. Cherry-picking intelligence, according to them, is simply taking a hard look at the intelligence community's analysis and "going against the grain" in an effort to think creatively and critically about conclusions made by analysts. The problem is that the OSP was pushing the same *wrong* conclu-sion vis-à-vis the danger posed by Iraq that those most politicized within the intelligence community were pushing. The OSP – like Tenet and Co. – ignored the analysts' conclusions in favor of feeding the administration what it wanted to hear. Call it "thinking outside the box" if you like; it was also acting out of bounds.

The other response from the Pentagon is equally disingenuous. Rumsfeld, Wolfowitz, and Feith have argued that OSP activity was merely an effort by two individuals to assist the Department of Defense in reviewing intel-ligence on Iraq in order to "assist [Feith] in developing policy recommen-dations." There is, of course, a multi-billion dollar Defense Intelligence Agency with the charter to do just that, but, to their credit, DIA analysts could not always be counted on to cook the intelligence to the Rumsfeld/ Wolfowitz/Feith recipe. And, while Rumsfeld keeps repeating that the OSP assisted Feith in "developing policy recommendations," it is no secret that the policy – "regime change" by force in Iraq – came well before the "intel-ligence." The OSP simply worked hard to provide the nation's leadership with "evidence" that such a policy should be pursued. Seymour Hersh and

---

reluctant willingness to go forward. "Phase 2" was also supposed to look into the role of the Office of Special Plans. Time will tell. [Also *vide supra*, p. 271, note 2.—Ed.]

1. Reported on by Robert Dreyfuss in the July 7, 2003, issue of *The Nation* and a July 17, 2003, piece in *The Guardian* by Julian Borger.

2. "DoD's Role in Pre-War Iraq Intelligence: Setting the Record Straight," remarks for the Center for Strategic and International Studies, May 3, 2004.

others[1] have reported credibly on this effort by the OSP to discredit the analysis of the intelligence community and to push its own, much more sinister picture of Iraq's capabilities and intentions.

Having to contend with Feith-based "intelligence" from the OSP and its powerful patrons greatly increased political pressure on intelligence analysts throughout the community to come up with conclusions that would "justify" policy decisions. Worst of all, George Tenet lacked the courage to stand up to Feith, Wolfowitz, and Rumsfeld. Neither would Porter Goss, Tenet's successor, have the backbone to go to the mat with Rumsfeld (or his own patron, Dick Cheney) on the role of the OSP, as was made clear when this whole question arose during Goss's nomination hearings. It was clear, for that matter, that Goss would not go to the mat over anything else either.

The Cancer of Careerism

Within the intelligence community, the ethos in which fearless intelligence analysis prospered began to evaporate big-time in 1981, when CIA Director William Casey and his protégé Robert Gates in effect institutionalized the politicization of intelligence analysis. Casey saw a Russian under every rock and behind every "terrorist," and summarily dismissed the idea that the Soviet Union could ever change. Gates, a former analyst of Soviet affairs, knew better, but he quickly learned that parroting Casey's nonsense was a super-quick way to climb the career ladder. Sadly, many joined the climbers, but not all. Later, as CIA director, Gates adhered closely to the example of his avuncular patron Casey. In an unguarded moment on March 15, 1995, Gates admitted to *Washington Post* reporter Walter Pincus that he had watched Casey on "issue after issue sit in meetings and present intelligence framed in terms of the policy he wanted pursued."

In the early eighties, after Casey became director, many bright analysts quit rather than take part in cooking intelligence-to-go. In contrast, those inspired by Gates's example followed suit and saw their careers prosper. By the mid-nineties senior and mid-level CIA managers had learned well how to play the career-enhancing political game. So it came as no surprise that director John Deutch (1995–96) encountered little opposition

---

1. See Seymour Hersh, "Selective Intelligence," *The New Yorker*, May 12, 2003, online; Julian Borger, "The Spies Who Pushed for War," *The Guardian*, July 17, 2003, online; Robert Dreyfuss and Jason Vest, "The Lie Factory," *Mother Jones*, January/February, 2004, online; *Report on the U.S. Intelligence Community's Prewar Intelligence Assessments on Iraq*, July 7, 2004, pp. 361–636; and Senator Carl Levin, *Report of an Inquiry into the Alternative Analysis of the Issue of an Iraq-al-Qaeda Relationship*, October 21, 2004, *passim*.

when he decided to cede the agency's world-class imagery analysis capability – lock, stock, and barrel – to the Department of Defense. True, all of Deutch's line deputies sent him a memo whimpering their chagrin over his giving away this essential tool of intelligence analysis. Only his statutory Deputy Director of Central Intelligence, George Tenet, thought it a great idea. (Tenet set the tone even in those days, by repeatedly referring to his boss – often in his presence – as "the great John Deutch.")

Deutch went ahead and gave imagery analysis away, apparently out of a desire to ingratiate himself with senior Pentagon officials. (No other explanation makes sense. He had made no secret of his ambition to succeed his good friend and former colleague William Perry as soon as the latter stepped down as secretary of defense.) But still more shameless was Deutch's order to agency subordinates to help the Pentagon cover up exposures to chemicals that accounted, at least in part, for the illnesses of tens of thousands of Gulf-War veterans. Sadly, with over a decade's worth of the go-along-to-get-along ethos having set in among CIA managers, Deutch could blithely disregard the whimpers, calculating (correctly) that the whimperers would quietly acquiesce.

Corruption is contagious and has a way of perpetuating itself. What we are seeing today is largely the result of senior management's penchant for identifying and promoting compliant careerists. Deutch did not stay long enough to push this trend much farther; he did not have to. By then functionaries like John McLaughlin, who was Tenet's deputy director, and whose meteoric rise began with Gates, had reached very senior positions. In September 2002, when Tenet and McLaughlin were asked to cook to Cheney's recipe a National Intelligence Estimate on Iraq's putative "weapons of mass destructive," they were able to tap a number of willing senior co-conspirators, and what emerged was by far the worst NIE ever produced by the U.S. intelligence community. Several of the key managers of that estimate were originally handpicked by Gates for managerial positions. These include not only McLaughlin but also National Intelligence Officer Larry Gershwin, who gave a pass to the infamous "Curveball" – the main source of the "intelligence" on Iraq's biological weapons program – and Alan Foley who led those who mishandled analysis of the celebrated (but non-nuclear-related) aluminum tubes headed for Iraq and the forged documents about Iraqi efforts to acquire uranium from Niger. More recently, a rising star who grew up in this ambience explained to me, "We were not politicized; we were just leaning forward, given White House concern over Iraq." Far from being apologetic, he actually seemed to have persuaded himself that "leaning forward" is not politicization!

Leaning Forward . . . or Backward

Since then McLaughlin and Tenet have been accused by senior CIA officers of the operations directorate of suppressing critical information that threw strong doubt on the reliability of Curveball and his "biological weapons trailers." That highly dubious information was peddled by then-Secretary of State Colin Powell – with artists' renderings on the big screen, no less – at the UN on February 5, 2003.

If the accusers are telling the truth, what could McLaughlin and Tenet have been thinking in failing to warn Powell? Clearly, someone should ask them – under oath. Perhaps it was what intelligence officers call "plausible denial," one of the tricks of the trade to protect senior officials like Powell. (He could not be accused of lying about what he didn't know.) But could CIA's top two officials have thought the truth would not eventually get out? It seems likely that their thinking went something like this: when Saddam falls and the Iraqis greet our invading forces with open arms and cut flowers, who at that victorious point will be so picayune as to pick on the intelligence community for inaccuracies like the absence of the "biological weapons trailers?" I don't know where they got the part about the open arms and cut flowers – perhaps it came from the Office of Special Plans.

What Casey Begat

Casey begat Gates. And Gates begat not only John McLaughlin but also many others now at senior levels of the agency – notably the malleable John Helgerson, CIA's inspector general. No one who worked with these three functionaries for very long was surprised when Helgerson acquiesced last summer in the suppression of his congressionally mandated report on intelligence and 9/11. In December 2002 Helgerson was directed by Congress to determine "whether and to what extent personnel at all levels should be held accountable" for mistakes that contributed to the failure to prevent the attacks on 9/11. After 18 months, his report was finally ready in the spring of 2004, and it identified individual officers by name. But many of those officers had records of the umpteen warnings they had provided the White House before 9/11, not to mention painful memories of the frustration they felt when they and Richard Clarke were ignored. It would have been far too dangerous to risk letting that dirty linen hang out on the line with the approach of the November election.

To his credit, knowing the report was ready, House Intelligence Committee Chairman Peter Hoekstra (R-Mich.) asked Helgerson to release it to the committee. In an August 31, 2004, letter, Helgerson told Hoekstra that then-Acting Director John McLaughlin had broken with usual practice and told him not to distribute his report. The tenacious chairman of the Senate Intelligence Committee, Pat Roberts, called the postponement "uncommon but not abnormal." His meaning is clearer than it might seem. Indeed, it is not abnormal. The whole episode was just further confirmation that Roberts takes his orders from the White House, that checks and balances are out the window, and that people like Helgerson can still be counted upon to play along to get along. Helgerson's report has still not been released. And it may be some time before it is, for the CIA Inspector General's job jar is full to overflowing. Managing inquiries into alleged CIA involvement in torture and "extraordinary renderings," and now into *L' Affaire* Curveball as well, Helgerson is a busy man. But don't hold your breath; these things take time.

Defining Politicization

An unusually illustrative first-hand example of politicization of intelligence became available in relation to the recent nomination of former Under Secretary of State John Bolton to be U.S. ambassador to the UN, with the declassification and release to the Senate Foreign Relations Committee of email exchanges involving his office. In one of those emails, obtained in April by *The New York Times*, Frederick Fleitz, then principal aide to Bolton, proudly told his boss that he had instructed State Department intelligence analyst Christian Westermann on whose prerogative it properly is to interpret intelligence. Said Fleitz (who we now know was a CIA analyst on loan to Bolton), "I explained to Christian that it was a *political judgment as to how to interpret* this data [on Cuba's biological warfare capability], and the intelligence community should do as we asked" (emphasis mine).

Were it not for the numbing experience of the past four years, we intelligence professionals, practicing and retired, would be astonished at the claim that how to interpret intelligence data is a political judgment. But this is also the era of the Rumsfeld maxim: "Absence of evidence is not evidence of absence," and the Cheney corollary: "If you build it, they will come" – meaning that intelligence analysts will come around to any case that top administration officials may build. All it takes is a few personal visits to CIA headquarters and a little arm-twisting, and the analysts will be happy to conjure up whatever "evidence" may be needed to support Cheneyesque warnings that "they" – the Iraqis, the Iranians, it doesn't matter – have "reconstituted" their nuclear weapons development program.

George Tenet, however docile, could not have managed the cave-in on Iraq all by himself. Sadly, he found willing collaborators in the generation of CIA managers who bubbled to the top under Casey and Gates. In other words, Tenet was the "beneficiary" of a generation of malleable managers who prospered under CIA's promotion policies starting in the early eighties.

Why dwell on Gates? Because, a careerist in both senses of the word, he bears the lion's share of responsibility for institutionalizing the corruption of intelligence analysis. It began big-time when he was chief of the analysis directorate under Casey. Since this was well known in intelligence circles in late 1991 when President George H. W. Bush nominated Gates to be CIA director, all hell broke loose among the rank and file. Former Soviet division chief Mel Goodman had the courage to step forward to give the Senate Intelligence Committee chapter and verse on how Gates had shaped intelligence analysis to suit his masters and his career. What followed was an even more intense controversy than that precipitated in April by the equally courageous Carl Ford, former director of intelligence at the State Department, who spoke out strongly and knowledgeably against John Bolton's attempts to skew intelligence to his own purposes.

At the hearings on Gates, Goodman was joined at once by a long line of colleague analysts who felt strongly enough about their chosen profession to put their own careers at risk by testifying against Gates's nomination. They were so many and so persuasive that, for a time, it appeared they had won the day. But the fix was in. With a powerful assist from George Tenet, then staff director of the Senate Intelligence Committee, members approved the nomination. Even so, 31 senators found the evidence against Gates so persuasive that, in an unprecedented move, they voted against him when the nomination came to the floor.

"Centrifuge/Subterfuge Joe"

A corrupted organization also breeds people like "centrifuge/subterfuge Joe." Although it was clear to us even before we created VIPS in January 2003 that the intelligence on Iraq was being cooked to the recipe of policy, not until the Senate report of July 2004 did we learn that the recipe included outright lies. We had heard of "Joe," the nuclear weapons analyst in CIA's Center for Weapons Intelligence and Arms Control, and had learned that his agenda was to "prove" that the infamous aluminum tubes sought by Iraq were to be used for developing nuclear weapons. We did not know that he and his CIA associates deliberately cooked the data – including that from rotor testing ironically called "spin tests."

"Who could have believed that about our intelligence community, that the system could be so dishonest," wondered the normally soft-spoken David Albright, a widely respected authority on Iraq's moribund nuclear program. We in VIPS share his wonderment. I am appalled – and angry. You give 27 years of your professional life to an institution whose main mission – to get at the truth – you are convinced is essential for orderly policy making, and then you find it has been corrupted. You realize that your former colleagues lacked the moral courage to rebuff efforts to enlist them as accomplices in gross deception – deception that involved hoodwinking our elected representatives in Congress into giving their blessing to an unnecessary war. Even Republican stalwart Senator Pat Roberts has said that, had Congress known before the vote for war what his committee has since discovered, "I doubt if the votes would have been there."

Catering to "The Powers That Be"

It turns out that only one U.S. analyst had met with the Iraqi defector appropriately codenamed "Curveball" – the sole source of the scary fairy tale about alleged mobile biological weapons factories. This analyst, in an email to the deputy director of CIA's Task Force on Weapons of Mass Destruction, raised strong doubts regarding Curveball's reliability before Colin Powell highlighted his claims at the United Nations on Feb. 5, 2003.

I became almost physically ill reading the cynical response from the deputy director of the Task Force: "As I said last night, let's keep in mind the fact that this war's going to happen regardless of what Curveball said or didn't say, and the powers that be probably aren't terribly interested in whether Curveball knows what he's talking about."

This brought to consciousness a painful flashback to early August 1964. My colleague analysts working on Vietnam knew that reports of a second attack on U.S. destroyers in the Tonkin Gulf were spurious, but were prevented from reporting that in the next morning's publication. The director of current intelligence "explained" that President Johnson had decided to use the non-incident as a pretext to escalate the war in Vietnam and added, "We do not want to wear out our welcome at the White House." So this kind of politicization is not without precedent – and not without similarly woeful consequences. Still, in those days it was the exception, rather than the rule.

George Tenet's rhetoric about "truth" and "honesty" in his valedictory last July 2004 has a distinctly Orwellian ring. Worse still, apparently "Centrifuge/Subterfuge Joe," the above-mentioned deputy director, and their co-conspirators get off scot-free. Senator Roberts has stressed, "It is very important that we quit looking in the rearview mirror and affixing blame and, you know, pointing fingers." And, besides, they were only doing what they knew Roberts's patrons in the White House wanted. And, if they were cashiered, would they sing? John McLaughlin, who became acting director when Tenet left, willingly played his part. He told the press that he saw no need to dismiss anyone as a result of what he said were honest, limited mistakes. But what about the dishonest ones? It is enough to make one wonder what it would take to get fired. Tell the truth?

Forecast: Mushroom Cloudy

As we have seen, the standard line on why things went so wrong is that administration officials were taken in by intelligence on Iraq that turned out to be wrong. Senator Roberts put it concisely when he spoke with reporters in March: "If you ask any member of the administration, 'why did you make that declarative statement?' . . . basically, the bottom line is they believed the intelligence and the intelligence was wrong."

Again, you would not know it from our domesticated mainstream press, but this does not stand up to close scrutiny. Take the ubiquitous mushroom clouds that, we were warned, could come to us as the "first evidence" that Iraq had a nuclear weapon. On October 7, 2002, the President pulled out all stops in a major speech in Cincinnati. Associating Saddam Hussein with 9/11 and claiming that he would be "eager" to use a nuclear weapon against us, Bush warned, "Facing clear evidence of peril, we cannot wait for the final proof – the smoking gun – that could come in the form of a mushroom cloud." Condoleezza Rice parroted that line the next day, and the Pentagon spokeswoman did likewise on October 9. It was no coincidence that Congress voted on October 10 and 11 to authorize war.

Those of us who worked with former CIA deputy director John McLaughlin know that he is an amateur magician. In the fall of 2002 he had a chance to learn from a real pro. For it was Vice President Dick Cheney who conjured up the mushroom clouds. Indeed, it was Cheney, not Saddam Hussein, who "reconstituted" Iraq's nuclear weapons development; and he did it out of thin air.

There was nothing but forgery, fallacy, and fairy tales to support key assertions in Cheney's speech of August 26, 2002. The most successful midwife of fairy tales, Ahmad Chalabi, later bragged about facilitating the spurious claims of WMD in Iraq. He said, "Saddam is gone . . . . What was said before is not important . . . . We are heroes in error."

Cheney and the Son-in-Law

Cheney's August 26 address provided the recipe for how the intelligence was to be cooked in September. The speech, in effect, provided the terms of reference and conclusions for a National Intelligence Estimate (NIE) commissioned at the behest of Congress a few weeks later and completed on October 1, 2002. That NIE, nick-named "The Whore of Babylon," has been (aptly) criticized as one of the worst ever prepared by U.S. intelligence. But it did the job for which it was produced; i.e., to deceive Congress out of its constitutional prerogative to declare or otherwise authorize war. During September 2002, the intelligence community dutifully conjured up evidence to support Cheney's alarmist stance. The vice president claimed:

> . . . We now know that Saddam has resumed his efforts to acquire nuclear weapons. Among other sources, we've gotten this from the firsthand testimony of defectors – including Saddam's own son-in-law, who was subsequently murdered at Saddam's direction. Many of us are convinced that Saddam will acquire nuclear weapons fairly soon.

That statement was highly misleading. Saddam's son-in-law, Hussein Kamel, had been in charge of Iraq's nuclear, chemical, biological, and missile programs before he defected in 1995. But what Kamel told us then was that *all that weaponry had been destroyed* at his command in the summer of 1991. And everything *else* he told us checked out, including particularly valuable information on Iraq's earlier biological weapons programs. Now we know he was telling us the truth on the 1991 destruction of weapons, as well.

Many in the intelligence community knew of Cheney's playing fast and loose with the evidence and the administration's campaign to deceive Congress. Most just held their noses; sadly, no one spoke out.

Cheney's misleading reference to Kamel calls to mind the unbridled chutzpah in vogue during the march to war. This was no innocent mistake. Even if the vice president's staff had neglected to show him the debriefing report on Kamel, the full story became public well before the invasion of Iraq. A veteran reporter for *Newsweek* obtained the transcript of the debriefing in which Kamel said bluntly, "All weapons – biological, chemical, missile, nuclear – were destroyed." *Newsweek* broke the story on February 24, 2003, more than three weeks before the war began. But this news struck a discordant note amid the cheerleading for war, and the mainstream media suppressed it. Even now that Kamel's assertion has been proven correct, the press has not corrected the record.

The NIE: First None; Then Cooked

That there was no National Intelligence Estimate on Iraq's "weapons of mass destruction" before Cheney's preemptive speech of August 26, 2002, speaks volumes. The last thing wanted by the policymakers running the show from the Pentagon and the Office of the Vice President was an intelligence estimate that might complicate their plans for "regime change" in Iraq. Since it was abundantly clear that no estimate was wanted, none was scheduled. This was clearly the course George Tenet preferred, and his lieutenants were happy to acquiesce. It got them all off the horns of a distasteful dilemma – namely, having to choose between commissioning an honest estimate that would inevitably call into serious question the White House/Pentagon ostensible rationale for war on Iraq, or ensuring that an estimate was cooked to the recipe of policy – that is, massaged to justify an earlier decision for war.

As noted above, forcing "regime change" in Iraq – intelligence or no, legal or no – was a top priority from day one of the George W. Bush administration. The attacks of 9/11 were a fillip to military planning to invade Iraq after the brief sideshow in Afghanistan. On August 29, 2002, after three months of war exercises conducted by the Pentagon, President Bush approved "Iraq goals, objectives and strategy," and the juggernaut started rolling in earnest. We know this from a Pentagon document titled "Operation IRAQI FREEDOM Strategic Lessons Learned," a report prepared in August 2003 for the Joint Chiefs of Staff and stamped SECRET. The report was obtained by the *Washington Times* in late summer 2003, and Rowan Scarborough – no liberal he – wrote the story. Remarkably, it got virtually no play in other media.

Until September 2002, George Tenet was able to keep his head way down, in the process abnegating his responsibility as principal intelligence adviser to the President. Tenet probably calculated (by all indications correctly) that the President would be just as pleased not to have complications introduced after he had already decided for war and set military deployments in motion. And so the director of central intelligence, precisely at a time when he should have been leaning hard on intelligence analysts throughout the community to prepare an objective estimate, danced away from doing one until it was forced on him. He then made sure that the estimate's findings were the kind that would be welcome in the White House and Pentagon.

In mid-September 2002, as senior officials began making their case for war, it occurred to them that they needed to do what George H. W. Bush did before the first Gulf War; i.e., seek the endorsement of Congress. Senator Richard Durbin (D-Ill.) alerted Senator Bob Graham (D-Fla.), then-chairman of the Senate Select Committee on Intelligence, to the fact that no National Intelligence Estimate had been written. Awakened from his sleep, watchdog Graham wrote to Tenet requesting an NIE. Tenet asked the White House, and got the go-ahead – on one condition: that the estimate's judgments had to parallel those in Cheney's August speech. To his discredit, Tenet saluted and immediately chose a trusted aide, Robert Walpole, to chair the estimate and do the necessary. Walpole had just the pedigree. In 1998 he had won Donald Rumsfeld's favor by revising an earlier estimate to exaggerate the strategic threat from countries such as North Korea. The key conclusions (since proven far too alarmist) of that National Intelligence Estimate met Rumsfeld's immediate needs quite nicely, greasing the skids for early deployment of a multi-billion-dollar, unproven antiballistic missile system.

Aiming to Please

Walpole came through again in September 2002 – this time on Iraq, and in barely three weeks (such estimates normally take several months). An honest National Intelligence Estimate on "Iraq's Continuing Programs for Weapons of Mass Destruction" would not have borne that title, but rather would have concluded that there was no persuasive evidence of "continuing programs." But that, of course, was not the answer desired by those who had already decided on war. Thus, a much more ominous prospect was portrayed, including the "high-confidence" (but erroneous) judgments that Iraq had chemical and biological weapons and was reconstituting its program to develop nuclear weapons.

Although those widely publicized judgments differed sharply with the statements of senior intelligence and policy officials the year before (a highly curious fact that U.S. media ignored), they dovetailed nicely with Cheney's claims. In an apologia released a year later by the Central Intelligence Agency, Stuart Cohen, another Gates protégé and Walpole's immediate boss as acting head of the National Intelligence Council, contended that the writers were "on solid ground" in how they reached their judgments; and, defying credulity, some of those involved still make that argument.

Without Fear or Favor ... or with Lots of Both?

Sorry to say, CIA analysis can no longer be assumed to be honest – to be aimed at getting as close to the truth as one can humanly get. Now, I can sense some of you readers smirking. I can only tell you – believe it or not – that truth *was* the currency of analysis in the CIA in which I was proud to serve. But that was B.C. (before Casey).

Aberrations like the Tonkin Gulf cave-in notwithstanding, the analysis directorate before Casey was widely known as a place in Washington where one could normally go and expect a straight answer unencumbered by any political agenda. And we were hard into some very controversial – often critical – national security issues. It boggles my mind how any President, and particularly one whose father headed the CIA, could expect to be able to make informed judgments on national-security and foreign-policy issues without the ability to get candid, straightforward intelligence analysis.

In 2004, the vice president insisted on having "some additional, considerable period of time to look [for weapons of mass destruction] in all the cubbyholes and ammo dumps . . . where you'd expect to find something like that." ("Cubbyholes?" The vice president's very vocabulary betrays a *tabula rasa* on military matters.) Speaking at Georgetown University in 2004, George Tenet put it this way: "Why haven't we found the weapons? I have told you the search must continue and it will be difficult." Difficult indeed. But now, the expensive, prolonged search has found nothing. Mistake or willful deception, the jig is up. Tenet, mercifully, has gone away – at least until he starts pushing his book. (No wish to steal his thunder, but a good source tells me Tenet's book says, "Condi made me do it.")

The alarming thing is that Cheney is now looking in the cubbyholes of Iran.

Blaming (and "Fixing") the Intelligence Community

The current administration approach is, as we've seen, to place all blame on the intelligence community – and then to insist upon bureaucratic "reform." But the problem is not organizational diagrams; it is lack of integrity and professionalism. Lt. Gen. William Odom, one of the country's most highly respected and senior intelligence officers, now retired, put a useful perspective on last summer's politically driven rush into wholesale intelligence reform. In a *Washington Post* op-ed on August 1, 2004, he was typically direct in saying, "No organizational design will compensate for incompetent incumbents." I believe he would be the first to agree that the adjectives "careerist and sycophantic" should be added to "incompetent," for incompetence often is simply the handmaiden of those noxious traits.

For the surest way to produce incompetent incumbents is by promoting folks more interested in career advancement than in performing professionally and speaking truth to power. And a major part of the problem is the failure of the 9/11 Commission and Congress to hold accountable those whose misfeasance or malfeasance led to the disasters of 9/11 and Iraq.

Now, more than two years and tens of thousands of lives after the invasion of Iraq, I marvel at the ease with which the White House has succeeded in getting Congress to scapegoat the intelligence community. All it takes is "a few good men" – like Senate Intelligence Committee Chairman (and former Marine) Pat Roberts, living out the Marine Corps motto, *Semper Fi* – always faithful.

But faithful to what? Faithful, first and foremost, to the party, in what – let us be frank – has become to all intents and purposes a one-party state. That pejorative label, you may recall, is what we used to pin on the dictatorship in the U.S.S.R., where there were no meaningful checks and balances. There has been a dangerous slide in that direction in the U.S.

What is required is character and integrity, not a re-jiggered organizational chart. Those who sit atop the intelligence community need to have the courage to tell it like it is – even if that means telling the President his so-called "neoconservative" tailors have sold him the kind of suit that makes him a naked mockery (wardrobe by the imaginative designer, Ahmad Chalabi).

Enter John Negroponte

A major step in intelligence "reform" came on February 17, 2005, with the President's announcement that he had selected John Negroponte for the newly created post of director of national intelligence and his subsequent confirmation in the post by the Senate on April 21.

Is Negroponte up to being a fearless director of national intelligence? Will he be able to overcome decades of being a super-loyal "team player," implementing whatever policies the White House thrust upon him? Is there a chance he will summon the independence to speak to the President without fear or favor – the way we were able to do in the sixties and seventies?

It is, of course, too early to tell. Suffice it to say at this point that there is little in his recent government service to suggest he will buck his superiors, even when he knows they are wrong – or even when he is aware that the course they have set skirts the constitutional prerogatives of the elected representatives of the American people in Congress. Will he tell the President the truth, even when the truth makes it clear that administration policy is failing – as in Iraq? We shall have to wait and see.

The supreme irony is that President Bush seems blissfully unaware that the corruption that Vice President Dick Cheney, Defense Secretary Donald Rumsfeld, and he have fostered in the intelligence community – politicization that seems certain to continue, intelligence community reform or no – has frittered away an indispensable resource for the orderly making of foreign policy. Institutional politicization at the CIA is now virtually complete. It pains me to see how many senior careerists at CIA and elsewhere have made a career (literally) of telling senior officials in the White House and elsewhere what they think the White House wants to hear.

If that is the template John Negroponte chooses, and if he contents himself with redrawing organizational diagrams, the security of our country is in even greater danger. If, on the other hand, Negroponte intends to ensure that he and his troops speak truth to power – despite the inevitable pressure on them to trim their analytical sails to existing policy – he has his work cut out for him. At CIA, at least, he will have to cashier many careerists at upper management levels and find folks with integrity and courage to move into senior positions. And he will have to prove to them that he is serious. The institutionalization of politicization over the last two dozen years has so traumatized the troops that the burden of proof will lie with Negroponte.

His prior career and lack of experience in managing a large organization offer slim hope that he is up to that task. Let us remember, though, that even at the bottom of Pandora's box lies hope. Negroponte is likely to be faced immediately with strong challenges. From what can be discerned of Bush's intentions vis-à-vis Iran, for example, it appears altogether likely that the challenge of speaking truth on this issue will be Negroponte's first acid test. Let us hope that a combination of integrity and self-interest will win the day. Awareness of what happened to the hapless George Tenet may give Negroponte pause before saluting smartly and marching off in his footsteps. One can only hope that Negroponte will forget that Tenet earned a Medal of Freedom for his servility.

Show Me Your Company . . .

Negroponte is best known to most of us as the ambassador to Honduras with the uncanny ability to ignore human rights abuses so as not to endanger congressional support for the attempt to overthrow the duly elected government of Nicaragua in the mid-1980s. His job was to hold up the Central-American end of the Reagan administration's support for the Contra counterrevolutionaries, keeping Congress in the dark when that was deemed necessary.

Stateside, Negroponte's opposite number was Elliot Abrams, then assistant secretary of state for inter-American affairs, whose influence has recently grown by leaps and bounds in the George W. Bush administration. Convicted in October 1991 for lying to Congress about illegal support for the Contras, Abrams was pardoned, along with former Defense Secretary Casper Weinberger (also charged with lying to Congress), former National Security Advisor Robert McFarlane, and three CIA operatives. Indeed, their pardons came cum laude, with President George H. W. Bush stressing that "the common denominator of their motivation . . . was patriotism." Such "patriotism" has reached a new pinnacle in his son's administration, as a supine Congress no longer seems to care very much about being misled.

The younger President Bush completed Elliot Abrams's rehabilitation in December 2002 by bringing him back to be his senior adviser for the Middle East, a position for which the self-described neoconservative would not have to seek congressional confirmation. Immediately, his influence with the President was strongly felt in the shaping and implementation of policy in the Middle East, especially on the Israel-Palestine issue and Iraq. In January of this year, the President made him his deputy assistant for national security affairs and deputy national security advisor for global democracy strategy, where he can be counted on to overshadow – and outmaneuver – his boss, the more mild-mannered Stephen Hadley.

It is a safe bet Abrams had a hand in recruiting his erstwhile partner-in-crime, so to speak, for director of national intelligence. There is little doubt, in my opinion, that he passed Negroponte's name around among neoconservative colleagues to secure their approval. On the day Negroponte was nominated, FOX News Channel commentator Charles Krauthammer granted him a dubious distinction. Krauthammer noted that Negroponte "was ambassador to Honduras during the Contra War . . . and he didn't end up in jail, which is a pretty good attribute for him. A lot of others practically did."

Organizational "Reform" Won't Cut It

No amount of reform, however – not even the promotion of pedigreed loyalists from the Reagan era – can remedy what is essentially the root of the problem. Over and over again we hear the plaintive plea for better information sharing among the various intelligence agencies – and for a single individual, now Negroponte, to make it happen. We keep hearing this plea because it furthers the notion that the poor intelligence on Iraq was essentially an "accident," that it was a function of bad intelligence work, and is to be remedied by intelligence reform. The truth is that the main problem was *corrupted* intelligence work, caused not by a broken system but by men and women with broken character, most of whom knew exactly what they were doing.

The NIE on Iraq, for instance, was out-and-out dishonest. It provided the cover story for a war launched for a twin purpose: (1) to gain an enduring strategic foothold in the oil-rich Middle East, and (2) to eliminate any possible threat to Israeli dominance of the region. While these aims are generally consistent with longstanding American policy objectives, no previous U.S. administration thought it acceptable to use war to achieve them.

And, on Occasion, Candor Slips Through

These, of course, were not the reasons given to justify placing U.S. troops in harm's way, but even the most circumspect senior officials have had unguarded moments of candor. For example, when asked in May 2003 why North Korea was being treated differently from Iraq, then-Deputy Defense Secretary Paul Wolfowitz responded, "Let's look at it simply . . . . [Iraq] swims on a sea of oil." Basking in the glory of "Mission Accomplished" shortly after Baghdad had been taken, he also admitted that the Bush administration had focused on weapons of mass destruction to justify war on Iraq "for bureaucratic reasons." It was, he added, "the one reason everyone could agree on" – meaning, of course, the one that could successfully sell the war to Congress and the American people. And in another moment of unusual candor – this one before the war – Philip Zelikow, a member of the President's Foreign Intelligence Advisory Board from 2001 to 2003, more recently executive director of the 9/11 Commission, and now a senior State Department official, discounted any threat from Iraq to the U.S. Instead, Zelikow pointed to the danger that Iraq posed to Israel as "the unstated threat – a threat that dare not speak its name . . . because it is not a popular sell." In this connection, General Brent Scowcroft recently noted that the President has in fact been "mesmerized" by Israeli Prime Minister Ariel Sharon, and that Sharon has Bush "wound around his little finger."

The (real) twin purpose for the war leaps out of neoconservative literature and was widely understood from Canada to Europe to Australia. Australian intelligence, for example, boldly told the government in Canberra that the focus on weapons of mass destruction was a red herring to divert attention from the "more important reasons" behind the neoconservatives' determination to launch this war of choice. It strains credulity to suppose that what was clear in Canberra could have escaped the attention of senior intelligence officials in America. They knew it all too well. And, sadly, they proved all too eager to serve up to their masters what was clearly wanted – an ostensible *casus belli:* "weapons of mass destruction" in Iraq. Sycophancy has no place in intelligence work, and certainly not in matters of war and peace.

It bears repeating that the unforgivable sin in intelligence analysis is telling the policymaker what he/she wants to hear – justifying with cooked "intelligence" what they have already decided to do. And that, in a nutshell, is what happened on Iraq. CIA credibility has taken a major hit, and it is far from certain that the agency can recover. It used to be that, in such circumstances, one would look to Congress to conduct an investigation. But the highly partisan intelligence committees of Congress have given new meaning to the word "oversight."

Character Counts

It is important to understand, as we follow the continuing "reform" process, that the real culprit is a failure of leadership in both the executive branch and Congress, not a structural fault.

I served under nine CIA directors, four of them at close remove. And I watched the system *work* more often than malfunction. Under their second hat as Director of Central Intelligence (DCI), those directors *already had the necessary statutory authority* to coordinate effectively the various intelligence agencies and ensure that they did not hoard information. All that was needed were: (1) a strong leader with integrity, courage, a willingness to knock noses out of joint when this was unavoidable, and no felt need to be a member of the "President's team"; and (2) a President who would back him up when necessary. Sadly, it has been over 24 years since the intelligence community has had a director – and a President – fitting that bill.

When President-elect Jimmy Carter asked Adm. Stansfield Turner, then-commander of the Sixth Fleet, to be director of central intelligence, Turner shared his concern at assuming responsibility for the entire intelligence community absent unambiguous authority to discharge those responsibilities. An executive order signed by Carter delineating and strengthening the authorities implicit in the National Security Act of 1947 was all Turner needed. And on those few occasions when that did not suffice (let's say the FBI was caught hoarding intelligence information useful to CIA analysts), Turner would not hesitate to go directly to the President for his help in rectifying the situation. And the problem would be fixed.

No shrinking violet, Admiral Turner was not overly concerned about putting noses out of joint; he didn't need the job. Unlike his more timid successors, he would have been a match for Defense Secretary Rumsfeld, the consummate insider. If Turner were to learn that the Pentagon – or the vice president's growing empire, for that matter – had set up small "intelligence" offices of their own – like the Office of Special Plans, there would have been hell to pay. Turner would have asked Carter to put a quick end to it. It is no secret that both George Tenet and Porter Goss have been obsequious toward Rumsfeld, and Negroponte's comments at his nomination hearings strongly suggest that he will follow suit. A friend who knows Rumsfeld, Goss, and Negroponte well has quipped, "Goss will lead Negroponte down the garden path, and Rumsfeld will eat Negroponte's lunch."

The analysts in the trenches will still be there, of course, and some will keep trying to tell it like it is – whatever the hierarchy above them might look like at any given time. In the before-Casey days, at least, we had career protection for doing so. And so we did. Anything short of that would have brought the equivalent of professional censure and ostracism by our own colleagues. And if, for example, a senior policymaker were to ask a briefer if there were good evidence of weapons of mass destruction in Iraq, and we knew that serious analysts we trusted thought not, we would simply say, "No."

Danger to Civil Liberties Grows

One important reality that gets lost in all the hand wringing about problems in sharing intelligence among agencies is the fact that the CIA and the FBI are separate and distinct entities for very good reason – first and foremost, to avoid infringement on the civil liberties of American citizens. So a red flag should go up when, under the intelligence reform legislation, the director of national intelligence will have under his aegis not only the entire CIA but also a major part of the FBI. Under existing law, the CIA has no police powers and its operatives are generally enjoined against collecting intelligence information on American citizens. Since citizens' constitutional protections do not sit atop the list of CIA priorities and its focus is abroad, it pays those protections little heed. In contrast, FBI personnel, for judicial and other reasons, are trained to observe those protections scrupulously and to avoid going beyond what the law permits. That accounts, in part, for why FBI agents at the Guantánamo detention facility judged it necessary to report the abuses they witnessed. Would they have acted so responsibly had they been part of a wider, more disparate environment in which the strict guidelines reflecting the FBI's ethos were not universally observed?

It is an important question. In my view, the need to protect the civil liberties of American citizens must trump other exigencies when rights embedded in the Constitution are at risk. The reorganization dictated by the latest reform legislation cannot be permitted to blur or erode constitutional protections. That would be too high a price to pay for hoped-for efficiencies of integration and scale. Rather, there is a continuing need for checks and balances and – especially in law enforcement – clear lines of demarcation *within* the executive branch as well as outside it. Unfortunately, the structure and functions of the oversight board created by the most recent intelligence legislation make a mockery of the 9/11 Commission's insistence that an *independent* body be established to prevent infringement on civil liberties. Sadly, the Privacy and Civil Liberties Oversight Board created by the new law has been gutted to such a degree that it has become little more than a powerless creature of the President.

The concern over endangering civil liberties is fact-based. In discussing it we are not in the subjunctive mood. No one seemed to notice, but on June 16, 2004, when CIA director Porter Goss was chairman of the House Intelligence Committee, he actually introduced legislation that would have given the President new authority to direct the CIA to conduct law-enforcement operations *inside* the United States – including arresting American citizens. This legislation would have reversed the strict prohibition in the National Security Act of 1947 against such CIA activities in the U.S. Goss's initiative got swamped by other legislation in the wake of the 9/11 Commission report. More recently, Goss's answers to Senators' questions regarding CIA interrogation techniques and the use of torture have been disingenuous and, at times, transparently evasive. For the most part, Senators and Representatives have allowed themselves to be diddled by such evasive testimony. And with the U.S. media thoroughly domesticated, there is essentially no one to hold the administration accountable. The White House, the congressional intelligence committees, and the media simply tell us that we should await the results of another ongoing investigation on torture, this one led by CIA Inspector General John Helgerson!

Second Wind for COINTELPRO?

Some of us are old enough to remember operation COINTELPRO, in which the FBI, CIA, Army Intelligence, and other agencies cooperated closely in provocative and often unlawful actions targeting civil rights leaders like Dr. Martin Luther King, Jr., protesters against the Vietnam War, and a wide range of left- and right-wing groups. We thus have a real-life reminder of what can happen when lines of jurisdiction are blurred and super-patriots are given carte blanche to pursue U.S. citizens in time of war. History can repeat itself.

A year and a half ago, FBI guidance to local police anticipating peace marches in Washington, D.C., and protest demonstrations in Miami blurred the line between legitimate protesters and "terrorists." Local authorities and police were advised, for example, to watch for telltale behavior like raising money via the Internet, or going limp upon arrest. Such behavior, they were told, were signs that they might be dealing with "terrorists."

Let's be clear. There is in this country an already discernible trend toward the establishment of a national security state of the kind I closely observed during my career as an analyst of Soviet affairs. Our intelligence and security establishment has come to resemble more and more what the Russians called their all-powerful "organs of public safety," which were – pure and simple – tools of the ruling party. If this trend continues here, it is entirely conceivable that civil liberties may come to be regarded as an artifact of the past. Attorney General Alberto Gonzales may even feel free to characterize laws protecting them as "obsolete" or "quaint" – adjectives he applied to provisions of the Geneva Conventions. Gonzales, you may recall, was the chief White House counsel who advised President Bush that he could disregard with impunity the Geneva Conventions' prohibitions, and also have a "reasonable" chance of avoiding subsequent prosecution under U.S. law, specifically the War Crimes Act (18 U.S.C. §2441) of 1996.

The January 25, 2002, torture-is-not-only-okay-but-necessary memorandum from Gonzales to President Bush is just one of several signs that the President has been advised by his lawyers that – to put it simply – he is above the law. He has acted on that advice and there is plenty of disquieting evidence that he intends to continue doing so. If you have read down this far, you probably are among those who have succeeded in overcoming the common resistance to admitting that to yourself.

And yet we keep hearing the glib denial, "It could not happen here." Please tell your friends it has already begun to happen here. Tell them it is time for all of us to wake up and do something about it.

In Sum

Intelligence reform in a highly charged political atmosphere – laced with a pinch of hysteria – gathers a momentum of its own. The reform bill Congress passed late last year creates more problems than it solves, largely because the changes do not get to the heart of the main problem. Again, what is lacking is not a streamlined organizational chart, but integrity. Character counts.

My own recommendations – for any who might be interested – include some simple organizational changes, but have mostly to do with integrity.[1] The leadership sets the tone, and one very important lesson leaping out of the performance of intelligence on Iraq is that greater care needs to be exercised in selecting intelligence community leaders. Next, the process of creating relevant, timely, apolitical National Intelligence Estimates needs to be improved and inoculated against politicization, with managers held accountable for their performance.

Organizational changes. Imagery analysis should be returned, agenda-free, to the CIA, after languishing in the Department of Defense for the past nine years, so that chicken coops can once again be distinguished from missile storage facilities, and imagery can again act as a check on information peddled by dubious émigré sources. Had professional imagery analysts been able to report their findings without fear of their ultimate master, Defense Secretary Rumsfeld, the tenuousness of the evidence on weapons of mass destruction in Iraq could have been injected into the debate. (Remember? Rumsfeld said he knew where they were!)

In addition, CIA must rebuild its independent media analysis capability. The Analysis Group of the agency's Foreign Broadcast Information Service (FBIS) filled that role after Pearl Harbor for more than 50 years, and enjoyed wide respect in government and academe, before shortsighted senior CIA

---

1. See "A Compromised Central Intelligence Agency: What Can Be Done" in *Patriotism, Democracy and Common Sense: Restoring America's Promise At Home and Abroad* (Rowman & Littlefield, New York, 2004).

managers disbanded it a decade ago. Both the 9/11 Commission and the more recent presidential commission led by Judge Lawrence Silberman and former Senator Chuck Robb recommended new emphasis on media analysis, and the Silberman-Robb panel even proposed creating a separate "directorate" for that purpose. That is hardly necessary. All that is needed is (1) to acknowledge that it was a huge mistake to abolish FBIS's Analysis Group, and (2) to reconstitute it, staffing it with supervisors who are familiar with the tools of the exacting but fruitful discipline of media analysis. Such expertise could, for example, give the President and his advisers a better understanding of terrorism and what breeds it (beyond the "they hate our democracy" mantra).

"You Will Know the Truth ... "

Chiseled into the marble wall at the entrance to CIA Headquarters is: "You will know the truth, and the truth will set you free." This was the ethos of the intelligence analysis directorate during most of the 27 years I spent there.

The experience of the past four years suggests a visit might be in order to ensure that the inscription has not been sandblasted away. Many of us alumni are astonished that, of the hundreds of analysts who knew in 2002 and 2003 that Iraq posed no threat to the U.S., not one had the courage to blow the whistle and warn about what was about to happen. And even Paul O'Neil and Richard Clarke, who are to be commended for eventually speaking out, waited until it was too late to stop the administration from launching an unprovoked war.

This is by no means a water-over-the-dam issue. If plans go forward for an attack on Iran, it may become necessary for those intelligence professionals with the requisite courage to mount their own preemptive strike against the kind of corrupted intelligence that greased the skids for war on Iraq. That this would mean going to the press, preferably with documentation, is a sad commentary. But no alternatives with any promise are available. The normal channel for such redress, the inspector generals of the various agencies, is a sad joke. And the prospect for any appeal to the intelligence lapdog/watchdog intelligence committees of Congress is equally sad – and even more feckless.

The only defensible war is a war of defense.

—G. K. Chesterton, *Autobiography*, 1937

THE PROFESSIONALS SPEAK III: WAR COLLEGE PROFESSORS APPLY THEIR EXPERTISE

THE EDITORS' GLOSS: For a coherent, comprehensive, and persuasive dissection of the strategic viability of the "war on terror," one need look no further than Dr. Record's incisive comments in the following interview. Were Dr. Record a French liberal, his perspective could easily be dismissed by ad hominem arguments accusing him of a deep-seated anti-Americanism, carefully sidestepping the fact that the substance of what he says would still be unimpeachable. The fact is, however, that Dr. Record is a respected professional in the U.S. military academic community, a professor at the Department of Strategy and International Security at the U.S. Air Force's Air War College in Montgomery, Ala., and a recipient of a doctorate from the Johns Hopkins School of Advanced International Studies. In other words, he's neither a lightweight nor a blowhard.

His analysis of the mistake of mixing Iraq up with the Bush administration's "war on terror" cuts to the heart of the problem that Iraq poses for the U.S. at this very moment. As people increasingly discover that by removing Saddam – who is now starting to look like a master statesman in his governorship of a terribly divided and difficult country in the light of the evident incompetence of both Washington and its puppet regime in Baghdad – we have unleashed a whole slew of far more challenging and dangerous problems, the administration has to resort to ever more bloated rhetoric defending what is going on in Iraq in terms of 9/11. For a root analysis of what a disaster this was and remains, Dr. Record's analysis is unparalleled.

CHAPTER
19

The "War on Terror": Ingenious or Incoherent?
• • • • • • • • • •
An Interview with Prof. Jeffrey Record, Ph.D.

PROFESSOR, ON MAY 1, *2003, President Bush announced, perhaps prematurely, the end to "major combat operations" from aboard the USS ABRAHAM LINCOLN. He also said that "the battle of Iraq is one victory in a war on terror that began on September the 11, 2001, and still goes on." This statement is surprising, because many people – ourselves included – imagined Iraq to be something separate from the government's declared "war on terror."*

JR: Strategically, Operation IRAQI FREEDOM was not part of the Global War on Terrorism, or "GWOT"; rather, it was a war-of-choice distraction from the war of necessity against al-Qaeda. Indeed, it will be much more than a distraction if the United States fails to establish order and competent governance in post-Saddam Iraq. Terrorism expert Jessica Stern, in August 2003, warned that the bombing of the UN headquarters in Baghdad was "the latest evidence that America has taken a country that was not a terrorist threat and turned it into one." How ironic it would be that a war initiated in the name of the GWOT ended up creating "precisely the situation the administration has described as a breeding ground for terrorists: a state unable to control its borders or provide for its citizens' rudimentary needs."[1] Former CIA Director of Counterterrorism Operations and Analysis Vincent Cannistraro agrees: "There was no substantive intelligence information linking Saddam to international terrorism before the war. Now we've created the conditions that have made Iraq the place to come to attack Americans."[2]

---

1. Jessica Stern, "How America Created a Terrorist Haven," *New York Times*, August 20, 2003, online.
2. Quoted in John Walcott, "Some in Administration Uneasy Over Bush Speech," *Philadelphia Inquirer*, September 19, 2003, online.

Iraq and the "War on Terror"

LID: So if there was initially no connection between terrorism and Iraq, then it wasn't necessarily a good idea to treat Iraq as if it were part of the GWOT – especially if we've now made it one by invading the country.

JR: The conflation of al-Qaeda and Saddam Hussein's Iraq as a single, undifferentiated terrorist threat was a strategic error of the first order because it ignored critical differences between the two in character, threat level, and susceptibility to U.S. deterrence and military action. The result has been an unnecessary preventive war of choice against a deterred Iraq that has created a new front in the Middle East for Islamic terrorism and diverted attention and resources away from securing the American homeland against further assault by an undeterrable al-Qaeda. The war against Iraq was not integral to the GWOT, but rather a detour from it. Moreover, Operation IRAQI FREEDOM saddled the U.S. armed forces, especially the U.S. Army, with costly and open-ended imperial policing and nation-building responsibilities outside the professional military's traditional mission portfolio. The major combat operational phase of the war against Iraq unexpectedly and seamlessly morphed into an ongoing insurgent phase for which most U.S. ground combat forces are not properly trained.

LID: So you really think that the war in Iraq was an unnecessary *expanding of the GWOT?*

JR: Yes. In conflating Saddam Hussein's Iraq and Osama bin Laden's al-Qaeda, the administration unnecessarily expanded the GWOT by launching a preventive war against a state that was not at war with the United States and that posed no direct or imminent threat to the United States, at the expense of continued attention and effort to protect the United States from a terrorist organization with which the United States *was* at war.

LID: You say "preventive" war: what do you mean by that, exactly?

JR: According to the Defense Department's official definition of the term, Operation IRAQI FREEDOM was a preventive war, *which traditionally has been indistinguishable from aggression,* not a preemptive attack, which in contrast to preventive war has international legal sanction under strict conditions. Preemption is "an attack initiated on the basis of incontrovertible evidence that an enemy attack is imminent." Preventive war is "a war initiated in the belief that military conflict, while not imminent, is inevitable, and that to delay would involve greater risk."[1]

---

1. See Joint Publication 1-02, *DoD Dictionary of Military and Associated Terms*

LID: Now if the war in Iraq was really unnecessary, how is it that it became part of the administration's approach to dealing with terrorism?

JR: Frankly, the goals of the GWOT also encompass regime change, forcible if necessary, in rogue states, and in the case of at least Iraq, the transformation of that country into a prosperous democracy as a precursor to the political transformation of the Middle East.

LID: Forcible regime change? That seems a little disturbing, given not only George Washington's parting recommendation to the nascent America that she avoid "entangling alliances," but also the sense most Americans have that we approach other nations in an equitable, "live and let live" kind of fashion.

JR: Threatening or using force to topple foreign regimes is nothing new for the United States. During the 20th century, the United States promoted the overthrow of numerous regimes in Central America and the Caribbean, and occasionally in the Eastern Hemisphere (e.g., in Iran in 1953, South Vietnam in 1963, the Philippines in 1986).

LID: Incredible. At any rate the GWOT is about a lot more than just dealing one-on-one with bin Laden?

JR: Absolutely. Let me summarize it for you this way: the GWOT ledger of goals – war aims – thus far includes:

(1) destroy the perpetrators of 9/11 – i.e., al-Qaeda;

(2) destroy or defeat other terrorist organizations of global reach, including the nexus of their regional and national analogs;

(3) delegitimize and ultimately eradicate the phenomenon of terrorism;

(4) transform Iraq into a prosperous, stable democracy; and,

(5) transform the Middle East into a region of participatory self-government and economic opportunity.

Vague and Overly Broad Strategy

LID: How likely is it that we'll be able to achieve this list of goals, which, as it stands, seems pretty sweeping?

JR: My sense is that most of the GWOT's declared objectives are unrealistic and condemn the United States to a hopeless quest for absolute secu-

(Washington, D.C.: Department of Defense), April 12, 2002, pp. 333, 336.

rity. As such, the GWOT's goals are also politically, fiscally, and militarily unsustainable.

LID: Can you elaborate on what you mean by a "hopeless quest" for absolute security? Evidently you think that winning the kind of war we've set ourselves up for is beyond the realm of possibility.

JR: Sound strategy mandates threat discrimination and reasonable harmonization of ends and means. The GWOT falls short on both counts. Indeed, it may be misleading to cast the GWOT as a war; the military's role in the GWOT is still a work in progress, and the military's "comfort level" with it is in any event problematic. Moreover, to the extent that the GWOT is directed at the phenomenon of terrorism, as opposed to flesh-and-blood terrorist organizations, it sets itself up for strategic failure. Terrorism is a recourse of the politically desperate and militarily helpless, and, as such, it is hardly going to disappear. The challenge of grasping the nature and parameters of the GWOT is certainly not eased by the absence of a commonly accepted definition of terrorism or by the depiction of the GWOT as a Manichaean struggle between good and evil, "us" versus "them."

Additionally, the nature and parameters of the GWOT remain frustratingly unclear. The administration has postulated a multiplicity of enemies, including rogue states, weapons of mass destruction (WMD) proliferators, terrorist organizations, and terrorism itself. It has also, at least for the purposes of mobilizing and sustaining domestic political support for the war on Iraq and other potential preventive military actions, conflated them as a general, undifferentiated threat. In so doing, the administration has arguably subordinated strategic clarity to the moral clarity it seeks in foreign policy, and may have set us on a path of open-ended and unnecessary conflict with states and non-state entities that pose no direct or imminent threat to the United States.

LID: Indeed. You've raised a number of interesting points here, and maybe we can discuss them separately in some detail. Your last point is rather shocking in its breadth.

JR: Yes, threat conflation makes the GWOT a war on an "enemy" of staggering multiplicity: in terms of numbers of entities (dozens of terrorist organizations and terrorist states); types (non-state entities, states, and failed states); and geographic loci (al-Qaeda alone is believed to have cells in 60 countries). The global war on terrorism is moreover not only a war against practitioners of terrorism but also against the phenomenon of terrorism itself. The goal is the elimination of both terrorists and the method of violence they employ. *National Strategy for Combating Terrorism* speaks of the imperative "to eradicate terrorism" and states that "Defeating terrorism is our nation's primary and immediate priority. It is 'our calling,' as President Bush has said."[1] Indeed.

> We must use the full influence of the United States to delegitimize terrorism and make clear that all acts of terrorism will be viewed in the same light as slavery, piracy, or genocide: behavior that no responsible government can condone or support and all must oppose. In short, with our friends and allies, we aim to establish a new international norm regarding terrorism requiring non-support, non-tolerance, and active opposition to all terrorists.[2]

This objective essentially places the United States at war with all terrorist organizations, including those that have no beef with the United States. As such, this objective is both unattainable and strategically unwise. It is unattainable because of the sheer number and variety of terrorist organizations. It is strategically unwise because it creates unnecessary enemies at a time when the United States has more than enough to go around. As strategist Stephen Van Evera observes of the administration's response to the 9/11 attacks:

> Defining it as a broad war on terrorism was a tremendous mistake. It should have been a war on al-Qaeda. Don't take your eye off the ball. Subordinate every other policy to it, including the policies toward Russia, the Arab-Israeli conflict, and Iraq. Instead, the administration defined it as a broad war on terror, including groups that have never taken a swing at the United States and never will. It leads to a loss of focus . . . . And you make enemies of the people you need against al-Qaeda.[3]

The GWOT Isn't a "War" in the Traditional Sense

LID: You mentioned also that the military's role in the GWOT is a "work in progress." With such a state of flux, does it even make sense for the GWOT to be a "war" on terror? Is it proper to speak of it in this way, if even the military is not sure yet of what its role is?

JR: By traditional standards of what constitutes a war, the GWOT, like the drug war, insofar as it encompasses the military's participation, qualifies as a "military operation other than war," or MOOTW (to employ an

---

1. *National Strategy for Combating Terrorism* (Washington, D.C.: The White House), February 2003, p. 15.

2. *Ibid.*, pp. 23–24.

3. Nicholas Lemann, "The War on What?" *The New Yorker*, September 16, 2002, p. 41.

officially discarded but very useful term.) To be sure, the GWOT has so far encompassed two major military campaigns, in Afghanistan and Iraq, but those campaigns were part of a much broader grand strategy and struggle that has mobilized all elements of national power as well as the services of many other countries. The proper analogy here may be the cold war, a much larger and longer contest than the occasional hot wars – e.g., the Korean and Vietnam conflicts – that were waged on its behalf.

LID: But rather than refer to the military's participation in the response to terrorism as a military operation other than war, we seem committed in fact to making it into one.

JR: American political discourse over the past several decades has embraced "war" as a metaphor for dealing with all kinds of "enemies," domestic and foreign. One cannot, it seems, be serious about dealing with this or that problem short of making "war" on it. Political administrations accordingly have declared "war" on poverty, illiteracy, crime, drugs – and now terrorism. Even political campaign headquarters have "war rooms," and "war" is a term used increasingly to describe bitter partisan disputes on Capitol Hill. "War" is perhaps the most over-used metaphor in America.

LID: And making the response to terror into a "war" is to succumb, at least to some extent, to this tendency towards hyperbole?

JR: Well, traditionally war has involved military operations between states or between a state and an insurgent enemy for ultimate control of that state. In both cases the primary medium for war has been combat between fielded military forces, be they regular (state) or irregular (non-state) forces. Yet terrorist organizations do not field military forces as such and, in the case of al-Qaeda and its associated partners, are trans-state organizations that are pursuing non-territorial ends. As such, and given their secretive, cellular, dispersed, and decentralized "order of battle," they are not subject to conventional military destruction. Indeed, the key to their defeat lies in the realms of intelligence and police work, with military forces playing an important but nonetheless supporting role.

LID: So thinking about a "war" on terrorism in the traditional way makes about as much sense as imaging a "war" on obesity to be a war in the traditional sense, as one commentator, Elizabeth Wilmshurst of the U.K., pointed out.

JR: These "wars" on terrorism and drugs are not really wars as most Americans, including the professional military, have come to understand the meaning of the term since the United States became a world power.

LID: Essentially because terrorism is a method of warfare, and not a nation or group of people that we can declare war on, right?

JR: Yes, the chief problem with any attempt to eradicate the phenomenon of terrorism is that terrorism is not a proper noun. Like guerrilla warfare, it is a *method* of violence, a *way* of waging war. How do you defeat a technique, as opposed to a flesh-and-blood enemy? You can kill terrorists, infiltrate their organizations, shut down their sources of cash, wipe out their training bases, and attack their state sponsors, but how do you attack a method? A generic war on terrorism "fails to make the distinction between the differing objectives of those who practice terrorism and the context surrounding its use," observes Robert Worley. "Failing to make the necessary distinctions invites a single, homogenous policy and strategy."[1] Again, one is reminded of the lack of threat discrimination that prompted U.S. intervention in the Vietnam War.

LID: Not to mention that there's no real measure of success in the GWOT.

JR: Right. The ultimate measure of success will be diminished incidence and scope of terrorist attacks – i.e., non-occurring events. From an analytical standpoint this is an unsatisfactory measure of success. As in the case of gauging the success of deterrence, which also rests on non-events, there is no way to prove a cause and effect relationship. Moreover, even manifestly disruptive counterterrorist operations can have self-defeating unintended consequences.

"Terrorism" Is Substantially Undefined

LID: Another problem is the lack of a clear definition of "terrorism," is it not?

JR: Sound strategy requires, of course, a clear definition of the enemy. The GWOT, however, is a war on something whose definition is mired in a semantic swamp. Even inside the U.S. Government, different departments and agencies use different definitions reflecting different professional perspectives on the subject.[2] A 1988 study counted 109 definitions of terror-

1. D. Robert Worley, *Waging Ancient War: Limits on Preemptive Force* (Carlisle Barracks, PA: Strategic Studies Institute, U.S. Army War College), February 2003, p. 8.
2. Bruce Hoffman, "Defining Terrorism," in Russell D. Howard and Reid L. Sawyer, eds., *Terrorism and Counterterrorism: Understanding the New Security Environment* (Guilford, Conn.: McGraw-Hill/Dushkin, 2003), pp. 19–20.

ism that covered a total of 22 different definitional elements.[1] Terrorism expert Walter Laqueur also has counted over 100 definitions and concludes that the "only general characteristic generally agreed upon is that terrorism involves violence and the threat of violence."[2] Yet terrorism is hardly the only enterprise involving violence and the threat of violence. So does war, coercive diplomacy, and barroom brawls. At any rate, the current U.S. national security strategy defines terrorism as simply "premeditated, politically motivated violence against innocents."[3]

LID: Which begs the question of who is "innocent" and by what standards innocence is determined, and by whom.

JR: Yes. For instance, the U.S. firebombing of Japanese cities in 1945 certainly terrified their inhabitants, many of whom were women and children who had nothing to do with Japan's war effort.

LID: And which also raises the question about whether, according to the popularly accepted notion of "terrorism," a state can ever be guilty of a terrorist act, or if it's always – by definition – the "disenfranchised" individuals who are the terrorists.

JR: The Defense Department officially defines terrorism as the "calculated use of unlawful violence to inculcate fear; intended to coerce or intimidate governments or societies in pursuit of goals that are generally political, religious, or ideological."[4] The U.S. *National Strategy for Combating Terrorism* places similar emphasis on terrorism as a non-state phenomenon directed against the state and society; terrorism is "premeditated, politically motivated violence perpetrated against non-combatant targets by sub-national groups or clandestine agents."[5] The problem with both these definitions is that they exclude state terrorism, which since the French Revolution has claimed far more victims – in the tens of millions – than terrorism perpetrated by non-state actors. The lethality of the likes of al-Qaeda, the Tamil Tigers, and Sendero Luminoso pales before the gov-

---

1. Alex P. Schmid, Albert J. Jongman, *et al.*, *Political Terrorism: A New Guide to Actors, Authors, Concepts, Data Bases, Theories, and Literature* (New Brunswick, N.J.: Transaction Books), 1988, pp. 5–6.

2. Walter Laqueur, *The New Terrorism: Fanaticism and the Arms of Mass Destruction* (New York: Oxford University Press, 1999), p. 6.

3. George W. Bush, *The National Security Strategy of the United States of America* (Washington, D.C.: The White House), September 2002, p. 5.

4. *Department of Defense Dictionary of Military and Associated Terms* (Washington, D.C.: Department of Defense), April 2001, p. 428.

5. *National Strategy for Combating Terrorism, op. cit.*, p. 1.

ernmental terrorism of Stalinist Russia, Mao's China, Pol Pot's Cambodia, etc. Moreover, by excluding state terrorism, these definitions give states facing violent internal challenges – even challenges based on legitimate grievances – the benefit of the moral doubt, and in so doing invite such states to label their internal challenges "terrorism" and to employ whatever means they deem necessary, including the terrorism of counterterrorist operations of the kind practiced by the French in Algeria and the Russians in Chechnya.

LID: All of which means that, more or less, whoever is in the definitional "driver's seat" makes sure, in deciding who is and who isn't a terrorist, that terrorism is defined in a way that makes the terrorists somebody other than "us."

JR: I'd certainly say that the contemporary language on terrorism, perhaps inadvertently, has become, as Conor Gearty puts it, "the rhetorical servant of the established order, whatever and however heinous its own activities are." Because the administration has cast terrorism and terrorists as always the evilest of evils, what the terrorist does

> is always wrong [and] what the counter-terrorist has to do to defeat them is therefore invariably, necessarily right. The nature of the [established] regime, the kind of action that is possible against it, the moral situation in which violence occurs – none of these complicating elements matters a jot against the contemporary power of the terrorist label.[1]

Thus Palestinian terrorism is condemned, while Ariel Sharon is hailed as a man of peace. Richard Falk observes that:

> "Terrorism" as a word and concept became associated in U.S. and Israeli discourse with anti-state forms of violence that were so criminal that any method of enforcement and retaliation was viewed as acceptable, and not subject to criticism. By so appropriating the meaning of this inflammatory term in such a self-serving manner, terrorism became detached from its primary historical association dating back to the French Revolution. In that formative setting, the state's own political violence against its citizens, violence calculated to induce widespread fear and achieve political goals, was labeled as terrorism.[2]

One Man's Terrorist Is Another Man's Freedom Fighter

LID: That's very insightful. Why do you think there's this "definitional mire" that surrounds the notion of "terrorism"?

---

1. Conor Gearty, "Terrorism and Morality," *RUSI Journal*, October, 2002, pp. 36–37.
2. Richard Falk, *The Great Terror War* (New York: Olive Branch Press, 2003), pp. xiii–xiv.

JR: It stems in large measure from differing perspectives on the moral relationship between objectives sought and means employed. It is easy for the politically satisfied and militarily powerful to pronounce all terrorism evil regardless of circumstance, but, like it or not, those at the other end of the spectrum are bound to see things differently. Condemning all terrorism as unconditionally evil strips it of political context and ignores its inherent attraction to the militarily helpless. This is not to condone terrorism; it is simply to recognize that it can reflect rational policy choice.

LID: This is reminiscent of the recent report from the Defense Science Board's Task Force on Strategic Communications, which criticized the communications strategy that we employ in support of the GWOT. They said that Muslims don't "hate our freedom," but rather they "hate our policies." Which would seem to us to imply, as a conclusion, that even those who employ terrorism aren't freedom-hating lunatics but rather desperate political militants who are acting – if with regrettable methods – towards rational ends.

JR: Look, terrorism – like guerrilla warfare – is a form of irregular warfare,[1] or "small war" so defined by C. E. Callwell in his classic 1896 work, *Small Wars, Their Principles and Practice*, as "all campaigns other than those where both sides consist of regular troops."[2] As such, terrorism, like guerrilla warfare, is a weapon of the weak against a "regular" (i.e., conventional) enemy that cannot be defeated on his own terms or quickly. Absent any prospect of a political solution, what options other than irregular warfare, including terrorism (often a companion of guerrilla warfare), are available to the politically desperate and militarily helpless?

LID: Not many. Are you suggesting that terrorism might even be justified under certain circumstances?

JR: Let me answer your question with a question. Was Jewish terrorism against British rule in Palestine, such as the 1946 Irgun bombing attack (led by future Nobel Peace Prize Winner Menachem Begin) on the King David Hotel in Jerusalem (killing 93, including 17 Jews),[3] justified as a means of securing an independent Jewish state? Laqueur responds to the question in these terms: "Terrorism may be the only feasible means of

---

1. See James D. Kiras, "Terrorism and Irregular Warfare," in James Baylis, James Wirtz, Eliot Cohen, and Colin S. Gray, *Strategy in the Contemporary World, An Introduction to Strategic Studies* (New York: Oxford University Press, 2002), pp. 208–232.

2. C. E. Callwell, *Small Wars, Their Principles and Practice*, 3rd ed. (Lincoln, NE: University of Nebraska Press), 1996, p. 21.

3. Martin Gilbert, *Israel, A History* (New York: William Morrow, 1998), pp. 135–146.

overthrowing a cruel dictatorship, the last resort of free men and women facing intolerable persecution."[1]

LID: Then terrorism isn't "wrong" in all cases?

JR: I'm not saying that. As you know, most governments in the world today regard terrorism as illegitimate. But what I am saying is that morally black and white choices are scarce in a gray world. One man's terrorist can in fact be another's patriot. "Is an armed Kurd a freedom fighter in Iraq but a terrorist in Turkey?" asks Tony Judt. "Were al-Qaeda volunteers terrorists when they joined the U.S.-financed war [against the Soviets] in Afghanistan?"[2]

The Unvarnished Truth of the Administration's Approach

LID: Let's get back to Iraq for a moment. Aside from the numerous problems with the GWOT itself, as you've indicated, there is still the question of how the war in Iraq ended up being a part of it, when you've indicated that it wasn't a necessary war but rather one of choice, and a distraction at that. You said that "regime change" is one of the tools in the GWOT "tool kit." What's the thinking behind this?

JR: The administration believes that a politically transformed Iraq and Middle East is a GWOT imperative because it believes that the fundamental source of Islamist terrorism, including that of 9/11, is the persistence in the region of politically repressive regimes incapable of delivering economic modernity. For the administration, the political status quo in the Middle East is no longer acceptable because it produced the Islamist extremism that produced 9/11. This is why Deputy Secretary of Defense Paul Wolfowitz declared in late July 2003 that "the battle to win the peace in Iraq now is the central battle in the war against terrorism,"[3] and why National Security Advisor Condoleezza Rice argues that "a transformed Iraq can become a key element in a very different Middle East in which the ideologies of hate will not flourish."[4] The President himself endorsed this objective before the war, in his February 26, 2003, speech before the neoconservative American Enterprise Institute. "A liberated Iraq can show

---

1. Laqueur, *op. cit.*, p. 8.

2. Tony Judt, "America and the War," in Robert B. Silvers and Barbara Epstein, eds., *Striking Terror, America's New War* (New York: New York Review of Books, 2002), p. 21.

3. Quoted in Walter Pincus, "Wolfowitz: Iraq Key to War on Terrorism," *Washington Post*, July 28, 2003, online.

4. Condoleezza Rice, "Transforming the Middle East," *Washington Post*, August 7, 2003, online.

the power of freedom to transform that vital region by bringing hope and progress to the lives of millions .... A new [democratic] regime in Iraq could serve as a dramatic example of freedom for other nations in the region." The President went on to cite the success of the United States in transforming defeated postwar Germany and Japan into democratic states, noting that, at the time, "many said that the cultures of Japan and Germany were incapable of sustaining democratic values."[1] For the administration, the connection between tyranny and terrorism, and between "freedom" and the absence of terrorism, is clear. In his September 7, 2003, televised address to the nation, the President stated:

> In Iraq, we are helping ... to build a decent and democratic society at the center of the Middle East .... The Middle East will become a place of progress and peace or it will be an exporter of violence and terror that takes more lives in America and in other free nations. The triumph of democracy and tolerance in Iraq, in Afghanistan and beyond would be a grave setback for international terrorism. The terrorists thrive on the support of tyrants and the resentments of oppressed peoples. When tyrants fall, and resentment gives way to hope, men and women in every culture reject the ideologies of terror and turn to the pursuits of peace. Everywhere that freedom takes hold, terror will retreat.[2]

LID: And what chance of success, in your view, does this crusade to re-shape the Middle East really have?

JR: Leaving aside the inherent perils of making analogies between the hypothetical future experience of Iraq and the Middle East and the past experience of Germany and Europe, the assumption seems to be that democracy is so catching that the establishment of just one big one in the Middle East will trigger a rush to emulate it. The basis on which this democratic domino theory rests has never been explicated, however. Is it hope? Neoconservative ideological conviction? How would democracy spread to the rest of the region?

LID: Good question. Is the thinking behind the answer credible?

JR: The problem with this new domino theory is the same as the problem with the old one: it assumes that states and societies are essentially

---

1. "In the President's Words: 'Free People Will Keep the Peace of the World.'" Transcript of President Bush's speech to the American Enterprise Institute (AEI, Washington, D.C.), February 26, 2002; *New York Times*, February 27, 2002, online. Also see Philip H. Gordon, "Bush's Middle East Vision," *Survival*, Spring 2003, pp. 131–153; and George Packer, "Dreaming of Democracy," *New York Times Magazine*, March 2, 2003, pp. 44–49, 60, 90, 104.

2. Excerpted from the text of President Bush's September 7, 2003, speech, reprinted in "Bush: 'We Will Do What Is Necessary,'" *Washington Post*, September 8, 2003, online.

equal in vulnerability to the "threat" (i.e., democracy in the Middle East today, Communism in Southeast Asia in the 1960s). It ignores local circumstance, societal differences, separate national histories, and cultural asymmetries.

LID: Besides, is America really serious when it talks about wanting a spread of democracy?

JR: The rhetoric certainly ignores the prospect of those opposed to democracy using the democratic process to seize power, as did Hitler in Germany in 1933. "One man, one vote, one time." It was this very threat of Islamists using democracy to win power that provoked the suppression of budding democratic institutions in Algeria in the early 1990s. Indeed, fear of an Islamist electorate accounts in no small measure for the persistence of autocracy in Algeria, Egypt, Pakistan, and Saudi Arabia. Are U.S. strategic interests in the Muslim world really better served by hostile democracies than by friendly autocracies?

Non-proliferation: Cooperative or Coercive

LID: So in the midst of all this vague and frankly incoherent rhetoric surrounding the GWOT and the Iraq war, what are we really trying to accomplish?

JR: The conflation of rogue states, terrorism, and WMD, coupled with the administration's preventive war against Saddam Hussein's Iraq for the purpose of disarming that country, make the GWOT as much a war on nuclear proliferators – at least ones the United States does not like –as it is a war against terrorism itself. Because the administration sees a nexus between terrorism and WMD, the GWOT is a global counter-proliferation war, an aggressive supplement to, perhaps even a substitute for, the arms control regime established by the nuclear Non-Proliferation Treaty (NPT) of 1968.

LID: What was that regime all about?

JR: The NPT regime is essentially a bargain between nuclear "haves" and "have-nots." In exchange for foreswearing development of nuclear weapons, the have-nots obligate the haves to provide the knowledge and assistance to develop nuclear energy for non-military purposes, and in turn the have-nots agree to have their programs inspected by the International Atomic Energy Agency. Inspections are, however, conducted only at sites declared by the host state, thus permitting a determined violator to launch a nuclear weapons program at a secret site.

LID: Has this approach worked?

JR: The NPT regime and its associated efforts have been remarkably successful in retarding nuclear weapons proliferation. Since 1968, only five states have acquired nuclear weapons. Of the five, three (Israel, India, and Pakistan) were not signatories to the NPT, and one (South Africa) relinquished its weapons and joined the NPT. The fifth (North Korea) has been twice caught cheating and has now entered negotiations. Additionally, the United States has successfully encouraged several states (Argentina, Brazil, South Korea, and Taiwan) to cease work on suspected nuclear weapons programs and other states (Belarus, Kazakhstan, and Ukraine) to give up nuclear weapons they inherited from the Soviet Union. The United States has also extended nuclear deterrence to such key allies as Germany and Japan that might otherwise have felt compelled to develop their own arsenals.

LID: So why did we depart from this successful approach?

JR: Well, one can speculate that the 9/11 attacks, which admittedly raised the specter of nuclear-armed terrorism, afforded an *already predisposed* administration the political opportunity to shift to a new counter-proliferation policy based on threatened and actual preventive military action. "We will not permit the world's most dangerous regimes and terrorists to threaten us with the world's most destructive weapons," declares *National Strategy to Combat Weapons of Mass Destruction.*[1] That document also states: "Effective interdiction is a critical part of the U.S. strategy to combat [proliferation of] WMD and their delivery means. We must enhance [U.S.] capabilities . . . to prevent the movement of WMD materials, technology, and expertise to hostile states and terrorist organizations."[2] The administration is even promoting development of a new generation of small, "bunkerbusting" nuclear weapons designed to threaten or destroy rogue state underground nuclear facilities.

LID: How successful do you think this new aggressive, military approach to non-proliferation is going to be?

JR: It seems to me that the value of threatened or actual preventive military action may be limited to target states, like Iraq, that are incapable of either offering effective military resistance or placing at risk assets highly valued by the United States and its allies.

---

1. *National Strategy to Combat Weapons of Mass Destruction* (Washington, D.C.: The White House), December 2002, p. 1.

2. *Ibid.*, p. 2.

LID: So what will be the result in the case of the others – i.e., the states that do have the ability, as you say, to "offer effective military resistance or place at risk assets highly valued by the United States and its allies"?

JR: Those states may instead be *deterring the United States* rather than being deterred. "What North Korea shows is that deterrence is working," observed Joseph S. Nye, Jr., in January 2003. "The only problem is that we are the ones being deterred."[1] Iraq, though dwarfed by North Korea as a proliferator and by Iran as a sponsor of terrorism, was selected because it was a military pushover. According to Robin Cook, the former British Foreign Minister who resigned over the decision to go to war with Iraq, "The truth is that the U.S. chose to attack Iraq not because it posed a threat but because the U.S. knew Iraq was weak and expected its military to collapse."[2]

LID: So the message that our potential enemies take away from this is that they may as well have weapons of mass destruction, since we ignore those who have them and attack those that don't.

JR: Well, bear in mind that rogue states want WMD – especially the nuclear variety – for a variety of reasons, not the least of which is self-protection against enemies also armed or seeking to arm themselves with nuclear weapons. The United States is the greatest of those enemies. It is therefore not unreasonable to assume that rogue states view acquisition of nuclear weapons as a deterrent to U.S. military attack on them or at a very minimum as a means of raising the price of an American attack. Take Iran for an example. Iranian interest in nuclear weapons began under the Shah and was stimulated by having a hostile nuclear superpower (the Soviet Union) to the north, an aspiring hostile nuclear power (Iraq) to the west, and yet another nuclear aspirant (Pakistan) to the east. Throw in a nuclear-armed Israel and a history of violence, instability, and war in the region, and later, a U.S. declaration of Iran as "evil," and you get a perfectly understandable explanation for Iran's nuclear ambitions.

LID: Understandable indeed. And it would seem that one of the distinctions that our policy fails to deal with is the difference between having WMD and using them.

---

1. Quoted in Michael Dobbs, "N. Korea Tests Bush's Policy of Preemption," *Washington Post*, January 6, 2003, online. It is not clear that small and vulnerable nuclear arsenals deter superpower military action. See Lyle J. Goldstein, "Do Nascent WMD Arsenals Deter? The Sino-Soviet Crisis of 1969," *Political Science Quarterly*, Number 1, 2003, pp. 59–79.

2. Robin Cook, "Iraq's Phantom Weapons and Iran," *New Perspectives Quarterly*, Summer 2003, p. 29.

JR: Right. The main issue is whether the United States can, via threatened preventive military action, deter rogue states from *pursuing the acquisition* of nuclear weapons and – failing that – whether it can militarily deprive such states of the means of doing so. There is no evidence that successful deterrence of the *use* of nuclear weapons in wartime can be extended to their *acquisition* in peacetime. On the contrary, threatened preventive war may actually *encourage* proliferation. Moreover, considerable disagreement surrounds the potential effectiveness of proposed new nuclear weapons designed to destroy subterranean nuclear weapons facilities. In any event, the development and certainly the use of such weapons could in the long run prove catastrophically counterproductive to the goal of halting proliferation by undermining or demolishing the NPT regime and the now universally respected moratorium on nuclear weapons testing.

The Sane Approach to Iraq – Deterrence and Non-proliferation Agreements

LID: So what's the "sane" answer to dealing with regimes that are, in general, hostile to our interests and that might want to obtain mass-casualty-producing weapons?

JR: Unlike terrorist organizations, rogue states, notwithstanding administration declamations to the contrary, *are subject to effective deterrence and therefore do not warrant status as potential objects of preventive war and its associated costs and risks.* One does not doubt for a moment that al-Qaeda, had it possessed a deliverable nuclear weapon, would have used it on 9/11. But the record for rogue states is clear: none has ever used WMD against an adversary capable of inflicting unacceptable retaliatory damage.

Saddam Hussein did use chemical weapons in the 1980s against Iranian infantry; however, he refrained from employing such weapons against either U.S. forces or Israel during the Gulf War in 1991, and he apparently abandoned even possession of such weapons sometime later in the decade.[1] For its part, North Korea, far better armed with WMD than

1. See Rolf Ekeus, "Iraq's Real Weapons Threat," *Washington Post*, June 29, 2003, online; Bob Drogin, "The Vanishing," *New Republic*, July 21, 2003, online; John Barry and Michael Isikoff, "Saddam's Secrets," *Newsweek*, June 30, 2003, online; Walter Pincus and Kevin Sullivan, "Scientists Still Deny Iraqi Arms Programs," *Washington Post*, July 31, 2003, online; Michael R. Gordon, "Weapons of Mass Confusion," *New York Times*, August 1, 2003, online; David Kelly, "Regime's Priority Was Blueprints, Not Arsenal, Defector Told," *Los Angeles Times*, April 26, 2003. online; and Joseph Curl, "Bush Believes Saddam Destroyed Arms," *Washington Times*, April 26, 2003, online.

Saddam Hussein's Iraq, has for decades repeatedly threatened war against South Korea and the United States but has yet to initiate one.

LID: So you're saying that these two regimes didn't act because they were being successfully deterred?

JR: Again, I'll respond with a question. How is their inaction to be explained *other* than by successful deterrence? There is no way of proving this, of course, but there is no evidence that Saddam Hussein ever intended to initiate hostilities with the United States once he acquired a nuclear weapon; if anything, rogue state regimes see in such weapons a means of deterring *American* military action against *themselves*.

LID: It seems like common sense, but is this just your opinion or do others whose opinions don't seem to run counter to "prevailing wisdom" share this perspective?

JR: Example: Condolezza Rice, just a year before she became national security advisor, voiced confidence in deterrence as the best means of dealing with Saddam. In January of 2000 she published an article in *Foreign Affairs* in which she declared, with respect to Iraq, that "the first line of defense should be a clear and classical statement of deterrence – if they do acquire WMD, their weapons will be unusable because any attempt to use them will bring national obliteration." She added that rogue states "were living on borrowed time" and that "there should be no sense of panic about them."[1] My gloss on this would be to ask: if statelessness is a terrorist enemy's "most potent protection," then is not "stateness" a rogue state's most potent strategic liability?

LID: It would seem to be. Speaking of our "terrorist enemies," is there a way to approach them with realism and sanity, much the way you've outlined the approach that could have been taken towards Iraq?

JR: Sure. We should not allow an insistence on moral clarity to trump strategic discrimination. Even if all terrorism is evil, most terrorist organizations do not threaten the United States. Many pursue local agendas that have little or no bearing on U.S. interests. Should the United States, in addition to fighting al-Qaeda, gratuitously pick fights with the Basque Euzkadi Ta Askatasuna (E.T.A. [Fatherland and Liberty]), the Sri Lankan Tamil Tigers, the Provisional Wing of the Irish Republican Army, the Islamic

---

1. Condoleezza Rice, "Promoting the National Interest," *Foreign Affairs*, January/ February, 2000, p. 61.

Movement of Uzbekistan, Sendero Luminoso, Hamas, and Hezbollah? Do we want to provoke national- and regional-level terrorist organizations that have stayed out of America's way into targeting U.S. interests and even the American homeland?

LID: Of course not. But the problem in fact lies in the nature of the organizations you just listed, doesn't it? Those groups don't believe in "terror" in the abstract, nor in wreaking havoc and striking fear in the hearts of innocent people for no reason. We've touched on that earlier. In most cases they have a specific, local, and – from their point of view – legitimate grievance, right?

JR: As I said, most governments in the world today already regard terrorism as illegitimate. The problem is that there are countless millions of people around the world who are, or believe they are, oppressed, and have no other recourse than irregular warfare – including terrorism – to oppose oppression. They do not regard terrorism as illegitimate. Indeed, they do not regard what they are doing as terrorism. "The difference between the revolutionary and the terrorist," Palestine Liberation Organization Chairman Yasser Arafat declared before the UN General Assembly in 1974, "lies in the reason for which he fights. For whoever stands by a just cause and fights for the freedom and liberation of his land from the invaders, the settlers and colonialists, cannot possibly be called a terrorist."[1] (Similarly, the recently executed anti-abortion terrorist Paul Hill denied that killing an abortionist was even an act of violence, much less terrorism. "I was totally justified in shooting the abortionist, because he was actually the one perpetrating the violence," he told Jessica Stern. "I would not characterize force being used to defend the unborn as violence."[2])

LID: But you've quoted a couple of extremists here. Is there really a coherent logic behind your understanding?

JR: Bruce Hoffman, the world-class terrorism scholar and RAND Corporation vice president, who holds a doctorate in International Relations from Oxford, observes that "terrorists perceive themselves as reluctant warriors, driven by desperation – and lacking any viable alternative – to violence against a repressive state, a predatory rival ethnic or nationalist group, or an unresponsive international order."[3] Point being, for the

1. Quoted in Hoffman, *op. cit.*, pp. 11–12.
2. Jessica Stern, *Terror in the Name of God, Why Religious Militants Kill* (New York: HarperCollins, 2003), p. 169.
3. *Ibid.*, p. 14.

Hamas suicide bomber, no Israeli is innocent; all Israelis are enemies, and to blow them up in buses and discos is an heroic act of war against a hated oppressor. As long as irregular warfare, including terrorism, remains the only avenue of action open to the politically despondent and the militarily impotent, it will continue to be practiced regardless of how many governments view it as illegitimate. Terrorism can be a logical strategic choice for those who have no attractive alternatives.[1] It is well and good to counsel those with grievances to seek political solutions, but this is hardly useful advice if there is no political process available for doing so.

Parting Thoughts

LID: So what does the future hold, in your view?

JR: If the U.S. insists on continuing to view its effort in Iraq as a component in the GWOT (President Bush, in his September 7, 2003, address to the nation called Iraq "the central front" of the GWOT[2]), then it is certainly the largest component in terms of monetary cost, military manpower committed, and strategic risk. The sustainability of the GWOT therefore hinges very significantly on the sustainability of present U.S. policy in Iraq. The question then, is the following: will the American people and their elected representatives go the distance in Iraq?

LID: That indeed is the question. Before we let you go, Professor, give us, in summary, your parting thought on the strategic viability of the "war on terror."

JR: Certainly. The global war on terrorism as presently defined and conducted is strategically unfocused, promises much more than it can deliver, and threatens to dissipate U.S. military and other resources in an endless and hopeless search for absolute security. The United States may be able to defeat, even destroy, al-Qaeda, but it cannot rid the world of terrorism, much less evil.

---

1. See Martha Crenshaw, "The Logic of Terrorism: Terrorist Behavior as the Product of Strategic Choice," in Howard and Sawyer, *op. cit.*, pp. 55–67.
2. "Bush: 'We Will Do What Is Necessary,'" *loc. cit.*

THE EDITORS' GLOSS: All that really needs to be said by way of introduction to Dr. Pelletière's contribution is that its credibility cannot be impugned. The piece first appeared in the *New York Times* on January 31, 2003 – by no means an indication that it's the truth, the whole truth, and nothing but the truth (witness Judith Miller's stellar "reporting"). But it is something of an event when the largely pro-war paper finds an opposing argument significant enough to print on its op-ed page. Pelletière was the CIA's senior political analyst on Iraq during the Iran-Iraq war, and was a professor at the Army War College from 1988 to 2000. During the same period he served as the Middle East expert at the War College's Strategic Studies Institute. A solid argument can easily be made that not too many in this country are more familiar with the circumstances surrounding the Iran-Iraq war and developments immediately thereafter. The Halabja gassing thus occurs right in the heart of Dr. Pelletière's academic and professional career.

All this isn't a guarantee of anything, of course, but it has, we believe, massive weight in a debate that has for too long been characterized by superficiality and subterfuge. Those who are interested in finding out more should consult the lengthy interview with Jude Wanniski called "The (Bogus) Case Against Saddam" which leads off our companion volume, *Neo-CONNED!*. It is largely composed of other sources beyond Wanniski's opinion that confirm Pelletière's perspective. The bottom line is that the "gassing" charges that have re-surfaced since Saddam was deposed, after the al-Qaeda and WMD myths were debunked, are themselves at the very least *questionable*. Should some 2,000 Americans and untold Iraqis have died for that?

A War Crime or an Act of War?

• • • • • • • • • •

Stephen C. Pelletière, Ph.D.

I T WAS NO surprise that President Bush, lacking smoking-gun evidence of Iraq's weapons programs, used his 2003 State of the Union address to re-emphasize the moral case for an invasion: "The dictator who is assembling the world's most dangerous weapons has already used them on whole villages, leaving thousands of his own citizens dead, blind or disfigured."

The accusation that Iraq has used chemical weapons against its citizens is a familiar part of the debate. The piece of hard evidence most frequently brought up concerns the gassing of Iraqi Kurds at the town of Halabja in March 1988, near the end of the eight-year Iran-Iraq war. President Bush himself has cited Iraq's "gassing its own people," specifically at Halabja, as a reason to topple Saddam Hussein.

But the truth is, all we know for certain is that Kurds were bombarded with poison gas that day at Halabja. We cannot say with any certainty that Iraqi chemical weapons killed the Kurds. This is not the only distortion in the Halabja story.

I am in a position to know because, as the Central Intelligence Agency's senior political analyst on Iraq during the Iran-Iraq war, and as a professor at the Army War College from 1988 to 2000, I was privy to much of the classified material that flowed through Washington having to do with the Persian Gulf. In addition, I headed a 1991 Army investigation into how the Iraqis would fight a war against the United States; the classified version of the report went into great detail on the Halabja affair.

This much about the gassing at Halabja we undoubtedly know: it came about in the course of a battle between Iraqis and Iranians. Iraq used chemical weapons to try to kill Iranians who had seized the town, which is in northern Iraq not far from the Iranian border. The Kurdish civilians who died had the misfortune to be caught up in that exchange. But they were not Iraq's main target.

And the story gets murkier: immediately after the battle the United States Defense Intelligence Agency investigated and produced a classified report, which it circulated within the intelligence community on a need-to-know basis. That study asserted that it was Iranian gas that killed the Kurds, not Iraqi gas.

The agency did find that each side used gas against the other in the battle around Halabja. The condition of the dead Kurds' bodies, however, indicated they had been killed with a blood agent – that is, a cyanide-based gas – which Iran was known to use. The Iraqis, who are thought to have used mustard gas in the battle, are not known to have possessed blood agents at the time.

These facts have long been in the public domain but, extraordinarily, as often as the Halabja affair is cited, they are rarely mentioned. A much-discussed article in *The New Yorker* last March[1] did not make reference to the Defense Intelligence Agency report or consider that Iranian gas might have killed the Kurds. On the rare occasions the report is brought up, there is usually speculation, with no proof, that it was skewed out of American political favoritism toward Iraq in its war against Iran.

I am not trying to rehabilitate the character of Saddam Hussein. He has much to answer for in the area of human rights abuses. But accusing him of gassing his own people at Halabja as an act of genocide is not correct, because as far as the information we have goes, all of the cases where gas was used involved battles. These were tragedies of war. There may be justifications for invading Iraq, but Halabja is not one of them.

In fact, those who really feel that the disaster at Halabja has bearing on today might want to consider a different question: why was Iran so keen on taking the town? A closer look may shed light on America's impetus to invade Iraq.

We are constantly reminded that Iraq has perhaps the world's largest reserves of oil. But in a regional and perhaps even geopolitical sense, it may be more important that Iraq has the most extensive river system in the Middle East. In addition to the Tigris and Euphrates, there are the Greater Zab and Lesser Zab rivers in the north of the country. Iraq was covered with irrigation works by the sixth century A.D., and was a granary for the region.

---

1. Jeffrey Goldberg, "The Great Terror," *The New Yorker*, March 25, 2002, online.

Before the Persian Gulf war, Iraq had built an impressive system of dams and river control projects, the largest being the Darbandikhan dam in the Kurdish area. And it was this dam the Iranians were aiming to take control of when they seized Halabja. In the 1990s there was much discussion over the construction of a so-called Peace Pipeline that would bring the waters of the Tigris and Euphrates south to the parched Gulf states and, by extension, Israel. No progress has been made on this, largely because of Iraqi intransigence. With Iraq in American hands, of course, all that could change.

Thus America could alter the destiny of the Middle East in a way that probably could not be challenged for decades – not solely by controlling Iraq's oil, but by controlling its water. Even if America didn't occupy the country, once Mr. Hussein's Ba'ath Party is driven from power, many lucrative opportunities would open up for American companies.

All that is needed to get us into war is one clear reason for acting, one that would be generally persuasive. But efforts to link the Iraqis directly to Osama bin Laden have proved inconclusive. Assertions that Iraq threatens its neighbors have also failed to create much resolve; in its present debilitated condition – thanks to United Nations sanctions – Iraq's conventional forces threaten no one.

Perhaps the strongest argument left for taking us to war quickly is that Saddam Hussein has committed human rights atrocities against his people. And the most dramatic case is the accusations about Halabja.

Before we go to war over Halabja, the administration owes the American people the full facts. And if it has other examples of Saddam Hussein gassing Kurds, it must show that they were not pro-Iranian Kurdish guerrillas who died fighting alongside Iranian Revolutionary Guards. Until Washington gives us proof of Saddam Hussein's supposed atrocities, why are we picking on Iraq on human rights grounds, particularly when there are so many other repressive regimes Washington supports?

We are working these days on very, very serious issues of war and peace, life or death. We are not working on potatoes.

> —Nathalie Loiseau, French embassy spokeswoman, March 2003, on the substitution of "freedom fries" for "French fries" on all House of Representatives menus at U.S. congressional cafeterias

I wish it had never happened.

> —Congressman Walter B. Jones (R-N.C.), in retrospect, May 2005, on the "freedom fries" initiative, which he sponsored

THE PROFESSIONALS SPEAK IV:
A SCIENTIST AND A DIPLOMAT

THE EDITORS' GLOSS: Several unique points are raised by Dr. Prather that aren't routinely considered in the debate surrounding the war in Iraq. Much is made – and we'd be the last to deny this – of the neoconservative push for war with Saddam that seems to have come to fruition under Bush 43. But Prather offers a healthy reminder, adding some detail to the picture painted by Cockburn and St. Clair in Chapter 1 (and by Dr. Joy Gordon in *Neo-CONNED!*), that the U.S. position throughout the Clinton administration tended towards "regime change" in Iraq, and was no less a violation of the UN Charter and principles of equity and justice then than it was and is under the current regime.

Then there's Congress. Congress too is guilty of capitulation in the face of Bush-administration machinations. It had a chance to pull the plug on the march to war against Iraq, because its resolution authorizing the President to use force in Iraq was contingent upon him notifying them that further diplomatic action wasn't an option. He did so, but, Prather argues, they should have known better. Sadly the whole exchange of documents between the White House and Congress seems like a dramatic paper trail covering a fait accompli.

The end result of this fiasco – from Prather's perspective – is a world that is less safe than it was when the International Atomic Energy Agency had access to Iraq and its nuclear-program-related materials under effective surveillance. A tribute to Bush's "triumph" is the October 1, 2004, report from the IAEA indicating that it "continues to be concerned about the widespread and apparently systematic dismantlement that has taken place at sites previously relevant to Iraq's nuclear program." In other words, materials that were accounted for by the IAEA in Iraq now are not accounted for. "The disappearance of such equipment and materials may be of proliferation significance," the report said. Call it yet another Iraq war "success" story.

CHAPTER
21

Neocons & Loose Nukes
• • • • • • • • •
Gordon Prather, Ph.D.

IT WAS JOHN Kerry's best shot, but evidently most Americans – especially those living safely in the heartland – did *not* want a President whose Number One Priority is keeping nukes out of the hands of terrorists.

Keeping nukes out of the hands of terrorists certainly hasn't been President Bush's Number One Priority. On the contrary, Bush's application of the Bush Doctrine of preemptive strikes has actually increased – substantially – the chances that a few hundred thousand Americans will be nuked by terrorists.

In particular, when Bush II became President, North Korea was a signatory to the Nuclear Non-Proliferation Treaty (NPT), and *all* its nuclear facilities and nuclear materials were "frozen" under the terms of a bilateral U.S.-Democratic People's Republic of Korea agreement and subject to continuous monitoring by the International Atomic Energy Agency.

When Bush II became President, Iraq was an NPT signatory, and *all* its nuclear facilities and nuclear materials had been destroyed, removed from Iraq, or rendered harmless by the IAEA under the terms of UN ceasefire-implementing resolutions.

Hence, when Bush II became President, if there were any countries in the world that could be certified to be nuke-free, North Korea and Iraq headed the list.

Furthermore, both wanted desperately – and "desperately" is not too strong a term – to have their diplomatic and trade relations with the United States "normalized." You see, officially, a state of war still exists between North Korea and us after more than 50 years; one existed with Iraq for more than twelve. And a state of something close to war has existed with Iran for more than twenty.

Isn't that ridiculous? Or is it tragic?

As Kerry suggested, voters should have looked at the mess Bush II had got us in to by sand-bagging the IAEA – alleging that the Iraqi and North Korean governments were producing nukes even though subject to the IAEA Safeguards regime – and by accusing the Iraqi and North Korean regimes of being so evil as to give those alleged nukes to terrorists willingly.

When confronted with those allegations, guiltless – so far as the IAEA could determine – but *defiant* North Korea decided that it was better to have nukes than not to have them. So North Korea threw the IAEA inspectors out and began recovering the weapons-grade plutonium that had been under IAEA padlock and seal.

Guiltless – so far as the IAEA could determine – but *defenseless* Iraq reacted by throwing itself on the mercy of the international court of world opinion and of the UN Security Council. A lot of good it did them.

Establishing American Hegemony

Bush II had brought with him to power the folks who call themselves "neoconservatives." Also known as neocons, they are more appropriately called neocrazies.

Denied a military "victory" in the cold war by the collapse of the Warsaw Pact and the Soviet Union, the neocons were, nevertheless, determined to establish an American hegemony. In particular, the existing governments in Iraq, Iran, North Korea, and elsewhere were to be removed – by force, if necessary – and replaced by American puppet regimes.

But how to get the support of the American people for the removal – by force, if necessary – of all those regimes? Convince them that Iraq, Iran, North Korea, and other anti-American regimes had – or would soon have – nukes and that these evil regimes would give those nukes to terrorists who would, in turn, use them against them?

Okay, but how to convince the American people that those regimes were evil? And how to convince them that the IAEA – whose inspectors were monitoring these nations' peaceful nuclear programs to ensure they were not converted into nuke programs – is incompetent?

Well, fortunately for the neocons, there had been for many years well-organized and well-funded organizations like Greenpeace and Human Rights Watch.

"Human-rights" organizations – and their media sycophants – would be used by the neocons to demonize the existing governments in Iraq, Iran, and North Korea.

"Anti-nuclear power" organizations – and their media sycophants – would be used by the neocons to challenge the credibility and authority of the IAEA Safeguards regime, and, thereby, challenge the "peacefulness" of IAEA Safeguarded programs.

Loose Nukes

So, scroll back in time to the disintegration of the Warsaw Pact in 1989.

Hallelujah! Dancing in the streets! The prospect of Armageddon in central Europe was no more.

Hence, both the Soviet Union and the United States began to withdraw from service the tens of thousands of nukes that had been specifically developed and deployed to fight that battle.

Two years later, with the Soviet Union on the verge of economic collapse, Russian officials came to "lobby" the U.S. Congress. By then, the vast majority of Soviet nukes had been returned to Russia. Those that had not – the "strategic" nukes that were deployed atop ballistic missiles in Ukraine and Kazakhstan – were already slated to be "eliminated" under the Lisbon Protocol negotiated by Secretary of State James Baker.

The Russian delegation told Senator Sam Nunn *et al.* that they wanted to dismantle the tens of thousands of Soviet nukes excess to Russian needs, recover the fissile material (essentially pure U-235 uranium and Pu-239 plutonium) from those dismantled nukes, and then store it until they could eventually dispose of it as reactor fuel.

The problem was, the Russians didn't have the money to do all of that. Would Congress help?

Rarely has Congress responded so quickly to any request. The "Nunn-Lugar" Soviet Nuclear Threat Reduction Act was attached to the Conventional Forces in Europe Treaty Implementation Act of 1991, which just happened to be pending before the Senate.

Nunn-Lugar began by noting "that Soviet President Gorbachev has requested Western help in dismantling nuclear weapons and President Bush has proposed United States cooperation on the storage, transportation, dismantling, and destruction of Soviet nuclear weapons."

Nunn-Lugar then declared "that it is in the national security interest of the United States to facilitate on a priority basis the transportation, storage, safeguarding, and destruction of nuclear and other weapons in the Soviet Union, its republics, and any successor entities, and to assist in the prevention of weapons proliferation."

Bush Senior was immediately authorized to "reprogram" up to $400 million from funds already appropriated for that fiscal year to the Department of Defense (DoD) to implement Nunn-Lugar.

Planning for American Hegemony

Now, in 1992, Dick Cheney was secretary of defense and Paul Wolfowitz was under secretary for policy.

Periodically, the under secretary develops for the secretary a top-secret document entitled Defense Planning Guidance. The document is supposed to be "threat driven." Once developed and approved, the secretary issues it to the military Departments and to the Joint Chiefs of Staff. It tells them what their "force structure" needs to be as well as the manpower, weapons, equipment, and logistical support that will be required to meet the "threat."

So when the *New York Times* revealed in 1992 some contents of Wolfowitz's Defense Planning Guidance – which "envisioned a future in which the United States could, and should, prevent any other nation or alliance from becoming a great power" – there was understandably quite a flap, here and abroad, in and out of government.

Those kinds of statements belong – if anywhere – in National Security Strategy documents, developed by the National Security Council staff under the direction of the President's national security advisor. National Security Strategy documents are supposed to inform Defense Planning Guidance, not the other way around.

But surely Cheney and the neocons shared the Bush-Baker and Nunn-Lugar view that nukes getting into the hands of terrorists was the Number One threat to our national security, right? They were anxious to implement Nunn-Lugar as soon as possible, weren't they?

Apparently not. Then or now.

In fact, Cheney and Wolfowitz may have decided to implement Nunn-Lugar maliciously.

You see, the U.S. and Russian division of responsibilities for nukes and nuclear energy were similar. The Soviet Ministry of Defense was the customer for Soviet nukes and the Ministry of Atomic Energy – MinAtom – was the supplier. MinAtom was also the entity that provided fuel for nuclear power reactors. Similarly, DoD is the customer for U.S. nukes and the Department of Energy (DoE) is the supplier. Until recently, DoE was the U.S. entity that provided fuel for nuclear power reactors.

When a U.S. nuke is determined by DoD to be obsolete or excess to requirements, it is returned to the supplier, DoE, for disposal. Similarly, the Soviet nukes determined to be in excess of the Russian Defense Ministry's needs had been returned to Russia's MinAtom for disposal.

Hence, the optimum way to have provided Nunn-Lugar assistance to Russia would have been for DoE – not DoD – to have been our Nunn-Lugar agent. Unfortunately, it was several years before Congress got around to authorizing DoE's entities to deal directly with their MinAtom counterparts.

Enter Clinton

But then, just as the Nunn-Lugar funds began to flow, the Bush-Quayle administration was turned out of office. So now, with Clinton in power and the neocons gone from the Pentagon, we could proceed to apply correctly and expeditiously the Nunn-Lugar solution to "loose nukes"; still widely acknowledged to be the Number One Threat to our national security – right?

Wrong!

For one thing, the neocons weren't all gone from the Pentagon. Richard Perle – a neo-crazy if ever there was one – had been a member of the influential Defense Policy Board all during the Bush-Quayle administration and remained there through both Clinton-Gore administrations. He was soon joined by Wolfowitz and various other card-carrying neocons.

For another, the Republicans soon took control of both Senate and House and many Republicans were not happy with the prospect of helping the only other nuke superpower optimize – and perhaps modernize – its nuke arsenal.

As a result, of the billions of "Nunn-Lugar" dollars that have been appropriated over the years, the vast majority of it was spent by DoD – most of that going to DoD contractors – with only a small fraction ever being spent in Russia by MinAtom.

The Nuke Disarmament Activists

In any event, for the anti-nuclear entourage that Clinton brought to power, *our* national security was not as important as world peace. For Greenpeace, the thousands of nukes – yea, even the hundreds of nuclear power plants – in our hands were more of a threat to world peace than a few "loose" nukes in the hands of terrorists.

So, Clinton made it quite clear that he intended to pursue "a treaty on general and complete disarmament under strict and effective international control" as required by Article VI of the NPT.

Whereas Cheney's neocons had essentially declined to implement Nunn-Lugar as intended, Clinton's Greenpeace entourage actually hijacked Nunn-

Lugar, transforming it from a nuke proliferation prevention program into a nuke *disarmament* program.

Although not required to do so, Clinton unilaterally subjected our "excess" cold-war nuke materials and nuke facilities to the full NPT-IAEA Safeguards regime.

Clinton expected all other nations having nukes to follow our example.

Russia did – somewhat reluctantly – once Clinton and the Republican Congress made it clear that the promised Nunn-Lugar assistance was contingent upon it.

At the 40th IAEA General Conference in 1997, Director General Hans Blix announced the U.S.-IAEA-Russia Trilateral Agreement. We and the Russians each committed to dispose of 34 tons of weapons-grade plutonium, "transparently" and permanently, under the watchful eyes of the IAEA.

But, the Russians intended to make mixed-oxide (MOX) reactor fuel out of their excess weapons-grade plutonium. Once that was gone, they intended to continue making MOX from plutonium recovered from the "spent-fuel" of ordinary nuclear power reactors.

Hence, the Trilateral Agreement essentially committed us to fund the "recycling" of spent fuel. Greenpeace had long argued that the plutonium recovered from power plant spent-fuel could be used to make nukes. That's scientific nonsense, of course, but their argument had been translated into law by President Jimmy Carter.

The "no-recycling" activists so objected to the Trilateral Agreement that Clinton never asked Congress for the funds needed to implement it.

As if that weren't enough, taking a page from the neocon's 1992 grand strategy, Clinton had begun pushing the boundaries of NATO eastward, toward the walls of the Kremlin.

Also, at the urging of human-rights activists and the neocons, Clinton bashed the Russians for their efforts to suppress Islamic terrorist activities in Chechnya.

Clinton further angered the Russians by attempting to achieve regime change in Kosovo-Bosnia from 20,000 feet, imperiling Russia's Slavic brethren, the Serbs, on the ground.

As a result, when Clinton and his human rights entourage and his anti-nuclear entourage left office, the Russian loose nuke threat was at least as bad as when he entered.

Return of the Neocons

Worse, on Clinton's "watch," there had been added the Pakistani "loose" nuke threat. Pakistan had surprised everyone in 1998 by testing a half-dozen or so fairly sophisticated nukes just days after India – defying Clinton – had tested several of their own.

The prospect that the next India-Pakistani conflict would involve nukes was bad enough, but Bush II inherited a far worse problem. Nuke-armed Pakistan openly supported the ruling Taliban in neighboring Afghanistan, and the Taliban openly provided refuge to Osama bin Laden and al-Qaeda.

Moreover, Bush II inherited in Iraq a Gulf War mess made far worse by Clinton, the human rights activists, and the neocons.

In 1991, in the aftermath of the Gulf War, the IAEA had discovered the remains of a well-funded – but nevertheless unsuccessful – Iraqi program to enrich uranium to be used to produce nukes.

Iraq had agreed, as a condition of the Gulf War ceasefire, to accept UN Security Council sanctions and to allow the IAEA to preside over the complete destruction of *all* Iraqi nuclear programs, peaceful or otherwise. Furthermore, the IAEA was to continue monitoring Iraq in perpetuity to ensure that Iraq made no attempt to resurrect those programs.

But, in 1998, at the urging of the neocons, Clinton sand-bagged the IAEA – which had certified Iraq to be nuke free – by bombing Saddam's palaces in and around Baghdad. The neocons claimed they had "intelligence" that Saddam was conducting a nuke development program beneath his palaces – the only places the IAEA had not requested to look at.

So, Bush II inherited a situation in Iraq wherein the IAEA continued to verify Iraq's compliance with its IAEA Safeguards agreement, but where Clinton and the anti-nuclear activists had badly undercut the value of an IAEA "seal of approval."

Finally, Bush II inherited Clinton's Agreed Framework, wherein North Korea – which had already produced enough weapons-grade plutonium to make a half-dozen nukes, but had not yet chemically recovered it – had agreed to "freeze" all its nuclear programs, subject to IAEA locks, seals, and continuous environmental monitoring.

Enter the Axis of Evil

It soon became apparent – at least to Iraq, Iran, and North Korea – that Bush II intended to impose "regime change" on them, and that the rationale would be that each "evil" regime had an illicit nuke development program that the IAEA had been unable – and never would be able – to uncover.

The neocons had begun making these charges about Iraq, Iran, and North Korea during the Clinton-Gore administrations.

In particular, they had been charging that the conventional nuclear power reactor the Russians were building at Bushehr in Iran could easily be operated – even though subject to IAEA Safeguards – so as to produce weapons-grade plutonium for use in a nuke.

In order to make these ridiculous charges stick, the competence of the IAEA had to be attacked, and the authority of the IAEA itself destroyed.

That authority suffered a severe blow when Clinton totally ignored the IAEA report made weeks earlier, on October 7, 1998, to the UN Security Council that:

> The verification activities have revealed no indications that Iraq had achieved its programme objective of producing nuclear weapons or that Iraq had produced more than a few grams of weapon-usable nuclear material or had clandestinely acquired such material.
>
> Furthermore, there are no indications that there remains in Iraq any physical capability for the production of weapon-usable nuclear material of any practical significance.

The value of an IAEA "clean bill of health" took another severe blow in March 2003 when Bush II launched his preemptive invasion against Iraq.

Only days before the Bush invasion, IAEA Director General ElBaradei had reported to the UN Security Council that he had "to date found no evidence or plausible indication of the revival of a nuclear weapons programme in Iraq."

ElBaradei went on to refute the three specific charges that Bush and other high administration officials had made. To wit:

> There is no indication of resumed nuclear activities in those buildings that were identified through the use of satellite imagery as being reconstructed or newly erected since 1998, nor any indication of nuclear-related prohibited activities at any inspected sites.
>
> There is no indication that Iraq has attempted to import uranium since 1990.
>
> There is no indication that Iraq has attempted to import aluminum tubes for use in centrifuge enrichment. Moreover, even had Iraq pursued such a plan, it would have encountered practical difficulties in manufacturing centrifuges out of the aluminum tubes in question.

The Clinton preemptive attack on Baghdad was seven years ago and the Bush preemptive invasion of Iraq over two years ago. Result? The IAEA has been totally vindicated.

But now ElBaradei and the IAEA are under fire again by the neocons over Iran. Not content to accuse the IAEA of incompetence, they had accused ElBaradei of being in cahoots with Saddam Hussein. They are now accusing ElBaradei of being in cahoots with the Iranian mullahs.

The neocons are claiming – as they have claimed for the last decade – that Iran has a secret nuke development program that the IAEA hasn't found and is *incapable* of finding. And now, in keeping with the attempt to discredit the IAEA, it has come to light (as reported in the December 13, 2004, issue of the *Washington Post*) that the U.S. has been tapping ElBaradei's phone in hopes of finding reason – like not dealing effectively with the Iranians – to block his third term at the IAEA's helm. The irony of it all is – as Ray McGovern has pointed out in a March 2005 column (based on a *Washington Post* report by Dafna Linzer) – that, "in 1976 – with Gerald Ford President, Dick Cheney his chief of staff, Donald Rumsfeld secretary of defense, Paul Wolfowitz responsible for non-proliferation at the Arms Control and Disarmament Agency, and Henry Kissinger national security advisor," the Ford administration *agreed* to let Iran pursue a nuclear energy program to meet its future energy needs.

Meanwhile, the Iranians have taken the route chosen by the Iraqis two years ago and have thrown themselves on the mercy of the court of world opinion. That might work for Iran. The British were on Bush's side in Iraq. They're on Iran's side this time.

The Iranians opened up completely to the IAEA. ElBaradei has recently reported to the IAEA Board of Governors that as a result of a two-year-long exhaustive and intrusive inspection he has found *no indication* that the Iranians have or ever had a nuke program.

Enter Congress

Just as it isn't fair to blame Bush II for everything the neocons have done – especially during the Clinton-Gore administrations – it isn't fair to let Congress off the hook, either. Neither Bush II nor Clinton would ever have been able to change – or even threaten to change – the governments of Iraq, North Korea, and Iran if they had not been aided and abetted by Congress.

And Congress would never have aided and abetted the neocons if they had not been influenced by the "human rights" activists, the "anti-nuclear" activists, and the disarmament crowd.

In passing the Iran and Libya Sanctions Act of 1996 for Clinton – which was renewed in 2001 for Bush II – Congress found (among other things) that:

> The efforts of the Government of Iran to acquire weapons of mass destruction and the means to deliver them and its support of acts of international terrorism endanger the national security and foreign policy interests of the

United States and those countries with which the United States shares common strategic and foreign policy objectives.

In signing the Iraq Liberation Act of 1998 President Clinton said:

> This Act makes clear that it is the sense of the Congress that the United States should support those elements of the Iraqi opposition that advocate a very different future for Iraq than the bitter reality of internal repression and external aggression that the current regime in Baghdad now offers.

In passing the Resolution Authorizing the Use of U.S. Armed Forces Against Iraq of 2002, Congress found (among other things) that:

> Iraq persists in violating resolutions of the United Nations Security Council by continuing to engage in brutal repression of its civilian population thereby threatening international peace and security in the region, by refusing to release, repatriate, or account for non-Iraqi citizens wrongfully detained by Iraq, including an American serviceman, and by failing to return property wrongfully seized by Iraq from Kuwait;

and that

> . . . members of al-Qaeda, an organization bearing responsibility for attacks on the United States, its citizens, and interests, including the attacks that occurred on September 11, 2001, are known to be in Iraq.

Then, of course, there is the International Religious Freedom Act of 1998 which cited Iran, Iraq, and North Korea as "countries of particular concern" for whom the President may invoke all sorts of economic sanctions.

There is also the North Korea Human Rights Act of 2004, which, among other things, established within the U.S. Department of Homeland Security the "Weapons of Mass Destruction Informant Center" to ensure that foreigners who have information on weapons of mass destruction receive the proper visas and provide information to the appropriate agencies of the U.S. government.

North Korea has repeatedly, and recently formally, accused the United States of using "human rights" as a pretext to try to destroy its political system, and said that it has therefore been forced to increase its "self-defensive deterrent force."

But, it is important to note that – the influence of the human-rights activists on Congress notwithstanding – all the public opinion polls showed that Americans would not support an invasion and occupation of Iraq or Iran or North Korea just because of "human rights" abuses.

Hence, the Resolution Authorizing the Use of U.S. Armed Forces Against Iraq of 2002 required the President to make available to Congress his "determination" that reliance by the United States "on further diplomatic or other peaceful means alone will not adequately protect the national security of the United States against the continuing threat posed by Iraq."

There can be no doubt that the congressional leadership – at a minimum – knew perfectly well that Bush II had *not* met the requirements set out in their resolution. They knew that the "determination" he sent them was based upon "intelligence" long since thoroughly discredited by the UN inspectors on the ground in Iraq.

Furthermore, they knew from the testimony before the UN Security Council in the days, weeks, and months before Bush II made his "determination" that Iraq was *in substantial compliance* with all Security Council disarmament resolutions, and was, hence, not a threat to anyone, especially the United States.

All our congressional representatives knew Bush II had launched a war of aggression, not sanctioned either by the UN Security Council or by the Congress.

But, Bush II got away with it.

Hence, Bush II has successfully challenged the authority and seriously damaged the effectiveness of the International Atomic Energy Agency and the UN Security Council, and made congressmen – including John Kerry – look like fools.

If ever terrorists somehow get their hands on a North Korean nuke and use it against us, there will be no question as to who is principally to blame for that. Bush II!

He is the President who unilaterally abrogated Clinton's Agreed Framework. He is the President who is responsible for North Korea withdrawing from the NPT. He is the President who went ahead and invaded Iraq knowing that North Korea had restarted its weapons-grade plutonium producing reactor. He is the President who made invading Iraq his Number One Priority, even before he became President. He is the President who *didn't* make keeping nukes out of hands of terrorists his Number One Priority.

Well, it's been thirteen years since the Russian delegation first came to us for help in keeping nukes from getting loose. Because of the billions of "Nunn-Lugar" dollars spent on programs that had nothing to do with nukes – to say nothing of the hundreds of billions spent invading Iraq to keep Saddam from giving his non-existent nukes to terrorists – by all accounts the loose nuke threat is greater now than it has ever been.

THE EDITORS' GLOSS: This open letter by Roger Morris originally appeared on May 20, 2004, in *Salon.com*. It does not mince words regarding what he sees as the disastrous consequences for America of the Bush administration's approach to foreign affairs. More important than that, though, is the concern Morris evidently has for both integrity and professionalism. It is this, more than any perspective on what "the Republicans are up to" or how "the Democrats are simply playing partisan politics," that makes Morris's stark words both inspiring and tragic.

His letter speaks of *responsibility*. As we have noted elsewhere regarding the role of the professional military and those in the intelligence community, Morris reminds those in the foreign-service branch of the government's employ that "just doing their job" cannot, ultimately, be a legitimate answer to the crisis facing the "new" American approach to foreign affairs. How could it be so? If men and women witness in private, in whatever form, the kind of scandals that only occasionally make the news – think Gitmo, Abu Ghraib, etc. – and remain silent for fear of the powers-that-be, of what use to America is the kind of service we are getting from them? If there is no core of integrity, of honor, of humility, of Christian values at work in such an important field of the nation's life, then what we have is a putrid body politic masquerading as government, with salaries acting as a kind of Ten Commandments. "Every cable you write to or from the field," he says, "every letter you compose for Congress or the public, every memo you draft or clear, every budget you number, every meeting you attend, every testimony you give extends your share of the common disaster." Never were truer words said, for the buck stops with everyone in a position of proportionate influence when the question is one of life and death.

As Morris notes: it is well past time for professionals in government service to consider their duty to the reigning administration in light of their higher duty to the common good of the nation. Let us all, collectively, wherever we are and whatever we do, figure out how to mend the political mess we're in, and restore a culture of honor and responsibility in government life that is immune – as much as possible – from the attempts of any merely partisan, elected official to tamper with it.

A Call to Conscience
. . . .
Roger Morris

DEAR TRUSTEES,

I am respectfully addressing you by your proper if little-used title. The women and men of our diplomatic corps and intelligence community are genuine trustees. With intellect and sensibility, character and courage, you represent America to the world. Equally important, you show the world to America. You hold in trust our role and reputation among nations, and ultimately our fate. Yours is the gravest, noblest responsibility. Never has the conscience you personify been more important.

A friend asked Secretary of State Dean Acheson how he felt when, as a young official in the Treasury Department in the 1930s, he resigned rather than continue to work for a controversial fiscal policy he thought disastrous – an act that seemed at the time to end the public service he cherished. "Oh, I had no choice," he answered. "It was a matter of national interest as well as personal honor. I might have gotten away with shirking one, but never both." As the tragedy of American foreign policy unfolded so graphically over the past months, I thought often of Acheson's words and of your challenge as public servants. No generation of foreign affairs professionals, including my own in the torment of the Vietnam War, has faced such anguishing realities or such a momentous choice.

I need not dwell on the obvious about foreign policy under President Bush – and on what you on the inside, whatever your politics, know to be even worse than imagined by outsiders. The senior among you have seen the disgrace firsthand. In the corridor murmur by which a bureaucracy tells its secrets to itself, all of you have heard the stories.

You know how recklessly a cabal of political appointees and ideological zealots, led by the exceptionally powerful and furtively doctrinaire Vice President Cheney, corrupted intelligence and usurped policy on Iraq and other issues. You know the bitter departmental disputes in which a deeply politicized, parochial Pentagon overpowered or simply ignored any opposition in the State Department or the CIA, rushing us to unilateral aggressive war in Iraq and chaotic, fateful occupations in both Iraq and Afghanistan.

You know well what a willfully uninformed and heedless President you serve in Bush, how chilling are the tales of his ignorance and sectarian fervor, lethal opposites of the erudition and open-mindedness you embody in the arts of diplomacy and intelligence. Some of you know how woefully his national security advisor fails her vital duty to manage some order among Washington's thrashing interests, and so to protect her President, and the country, from calamity. You know specifics. Many of you are aware, for instance, that the torture at Abu Ghraib was an issue up and down not only the Pentagon but also State, the CIA and the National Security Council staff for nearly a year before the scandalous photos finally leaked.

As you have seen in years of service, every presidency has its arrogance, infighting and blunders in foreign relations. As most of you recognize, too, the Bush administration is like no other. You serve the worst foreign policy regime by far in the history of the republic. The havoc you feel inside government has inflicted unprecedented damage on national interests and security. As never before since the United States stepped onto the world stage, we have flouted treaties and alliances, alienated friends, multiplied enemies, lost respect and credibility on every continent. You see this every day. And again, whatever your politics, those of you who have served other Presidents know this is an unparalleled bipartisan disaster. In its militant hubris and folly, the Bush administration has undone the statesmanship of every government before it, and broken faith with every presidency, Democratic and Republican (even that of Bush I), over the past half century.

In Afghanistan, where we once held the promise of a new ideal, we have resumed our old alliance with warlords and drug dealers, waging punitive expeditions and propping up puppets in yet another seamy chapter of the "Great Game," presuming to conquer the unconquerable. In Iraq – as every cable surely screams at you – we are living a foreign policy nightmare, locked in a cycle of violence and seething, spreading hatred continued at incalculable cost, escaped only with hazardous humiliation abroad and bitter divisions at home. Debacle is complete.

Beyond your discreetly predigested press summaries at the office, words once unthinkable in describing your domain, words once applied only to the most alien and deplored phenomena, have become routine, not just at the radical fringe but across the spectrum of public dialogue: "American empire," "American gulag." What must you think? Having read so many of your cables and memoranda as a foreign service officer and then on the NSC staff, and so many more later as a historian, I cannot help wondering how you would be reporting on Washington now if you were posted in the U.S. capital as a diplomat or intelligence agent for another nation. What would the many astute observers and analysts among you say of the Bush regime, of its toll or of the courage and independence of the career official-dom that does its bidding?

"Let me begin by stating the obvious," Senator Jack Reed (D-R.I.) said at the Abu Ghraib hearing the other day. "For the next 50 years in the Islamic world and many other parts of the world, the image of the United States will be that of an American dragging a prostrate naked Iraqi across the floor on a leash." The senator was talking about you and your future. Amid the Bush wreckage worldwide, much of the ruin is deeply yours.

It is your dedicated work that has been violated – the flouted treaties you devotedly drew up and negotiated, the estranged allies you patiently cultivated, the now-thronging enemies you worked so hard to win over. You know what will happen. Sooner or later, the neoconservative cabal will go back to its incestuous think tanks and sinecures, the vice president to his lavish Halliburton retirement, Bush to his Crawford, Texas, ranch – and you will be left in the contemptuous chancelleries and back alleys, the stiflingly guarded compounds and fear-clammy, pulse-racing convoys, to clean up the mess for generations to come.

You know that showcase resignations at the top – Defense Secretary Donald Rumsfeld or flag officers fingered for Abu Ghraib – change nothing, are only part of the charade. It is the same with Secretary of State Colin Powell, who may have been your lone relative champion in this perverse company, but who remains the political general he always was, never honoring your loss by giving up his office when he might have stemmed the descent.

No, it is you whose voices are so important now. You alone stand above ambition and partisanship. This administration no longer deserves your allegiance or participation. America deserves the leadership and example, the decisive revelation, of your resignations.

Your resignations alone would speak to America the truth that beyond any politics, this Bush regime is intolerable – and to an increasingly cynical world the truth that there are still Americans who uphold with their lives and honor the highest principles of our foreign policy.

Thirty-four years ago this spring, I faced your choice in resigning from the National Security Council over the invasion of Cambodia. I had been involved in fruitful secret talks between Henry Kissinger and the North Vietnamese in 1969–1970, and knew at least something of how much the invasion would shatter the chance for peace and prolong the war – though I could never have guessed that thousands of American names would be added to that long black wall in Washington or that holocaust would follow in Cambodia. Leaving was an agony. I was only beginning a career dreamed of since boyhood. But I have never regretted my decision. Nor do I think it any distinction. My friends and I used to remark that the Nixon administration was so unprincipled it took nothing special to resign. It is a mark of the current tragedy that by comparison with the Bush regime, Nixon and Kissinger seem to many model statesmen.

As you consider your choice now, beware the old rationalizations for staying – the arguments for preserving influence or that your resignation will not matter. Your effectiveness will be no more, your subservience no less, under the iron grip of the cabal, especially as the policy disaster and public siege mount. And your act now, no matter your ranks or numbers, will embolden others, hearten those who remain and proclaim your truths to the country and world.

I know from my own experience, of course, that I am not asking all of you to hurl your dissent from the safe seats of pensioners. I know well this is one of the most personal of sacrifices, for you and your families. You are not alone. Three ranking Foreign Service officers – Mary Wright, John Brady Kiesling and John Brown – resigned in protest of the Iraq war last spring. Like them, you should join the great debate that America must now have.

Unless and until you do, however, please be under no illusion: every cable you write to or from the field, every letter you compose for Congress or the public, every memo you draft or clear, every budget you number, every meeting you attend, every testimony you give extends your share of the common disaster.

The America that you sought to represent in choosing your career, the America that once led the community of nations not by brazen power but by the strength of its universal principles, has never needed you more. Those of us who know you best, who have shared your work and world, know you will not let us down. You are, after all, the trustees.

Respectfully,
Roger Morris

When will this President's most theologically articulate supporters admit that the absence of weapons of mass destruction and the absence of compelling evidence of a link with al-Qaeda mean there was no just cause for this war, and that the incompetence and duplicity of the current administration mean that there was no competent authority for this war? If, alternatively, the war's agile Catholic defenders think getting rid of Saddam counts as a just cause, they have some serious rewriting of the tradition to do. Most of all, as George Weigel reminds us, they must explain their moral muteness in a time of war.

—Peter Dula, "The War in Iraq: How Catholic Conservatives Got it Wrong," *Commonweal*, December 3, 2004

DEFYING WORLD ORDER: REACTIONS FROM VATICAN AND UN PERSPECTIVES

THE EDITORS' GLOSS: Neoconservative Catholics generally reacted with disgust at the efforts – ineffective though they were – of the Catholic hierarchy in the U.S. and around the world to stave off the Iraq war. Appeals to the UN were hateful both to them and (in what is as remarkable a case of "strange bedfellows" as will be found) to some "ultra-conservative" Catholics clustered around bizarre outfits such as Tradition in Action and Tradition, Family, Property. Like it or not, the calls coming from Catholic prelates for working on the U.S.-U.K.-Iraq problem through the medium of the UN were *not inconsistent* with what the Catholic tradition says about the need for nations to conduct foreign affairs with regard not only to the national interest but also to international law as well. The next chapter should make clear just how consistent the UN Charter is with the just-war tradition. Furthermore, whatever is valuable in current international law can be traced back to the sterling work done by Spanish Jesuits and other Catholic thinkers over the last several hundred years, so much so that a rejection of their work is a rejection of them, and potentially of the Catholic faith as well.

Another reaction to the anti-war efforts of Catholics on the part of their "conservative" co-religionists were accusations of "pacifism" and a willingness to "appease" a "tyrant" simply in order to "save lives." The conservative Charley Reese put these assertions to rest with his characteristic frankness: "Let me spell it out for the mentally impaired: people are anti-war because they do not wish to see anyone die – our soldiers, their soldiers, our civilians, or their civilians. Anti-war is pro-life."

The problem, of course, is that so many – and neoconservatives, Catholic or otherwise, are some of the worst offenders in this regard – find it impossible to examine an issue with openness and objectivity rather than with mindless partisan loyalty. A political system and climate that enabled Catholics and others of good will and common sense to approach issues without pigeon-holing their perspectives into pre-approved positions would go a long way towards restoring some sanity to Anglo-American political life. Phil Berryman, writing in the Philadelphia Catholic Peace Fellowship newsletter, was driving at just this when he wrote (speaking of the "red-blue," left-right divide) that "the 'red' worldview that divides the world into 'enemies' and 'friends' and elevates the United States to a privileged position above the other 95% of humanity is profoundly un-Catholic . . . . [But] I am not saying that Catholicism is simply equated with a 'blue' worldview. We are poorly served by a political process that simplifies complex issues into overall ideological packages."

23

The Iraq War and the Vatican

• • • • • • • • •

Mark and Louise Zwick

THE MOST CONSISTENT and frequent promoter of peace in our time was Pope John Paul II. Specifically, from Iraq War I to Iraq War II, he has echoed the voice of Paul VI crying out before the United Nations in 1965: War No More, War Never Again!

John Paul II stated before the 2003 invasion of Iraq by the United States that this war would be a defeat for humanity which could not be morally or legally justified.

In the weeks and months before the war began not only the Holy Father, but also one Cardinal and Archbishop after another at the Vatican, spoke out against a "preemptive" or "preventive" strike, declaring that the just-war theory could not justify such a war. Archbishop Jean-Louis Tauran said that such a "war of aggression" is a crime against peace. Cardinal Renato Martino, who used the same words in calling the possible military intervention a "crime against peace that cries out for vengeance before God," also criticized the pressure that the most powerful nations exerted on the less powerful ones in the UN Security Council to support the war. The Pope spoke out almost every day against war and in support of diplomatic efforts for peace. Cardinal J. Francis Stafford, at the time President of the Pontifical Council for the Laity and the highest ranking U. S. prelate in Rome, sharply criticized the U.S. government's push for military strikes on Iraq, saying the war would be morally unjustified and a further alarming example of increased global use of violent force. Vatican officials suggested that such a war would be illegal. John Paul II sent his personal representative, Cardinal Pio Laghi, a friend of the Bush family, to remonstrate with the U.S. President before the war began. Pio Laghi said publicly at that time that such a war would be illegal and unjust. The message: God is not on your side if you invade Iraq.

After the United States began its attacks against Iraq, on one of the few occasions in which the U. S. secular media picked up the comments from

Rome, *FOX News* reported the immediate comments of the Holy Father made in an address at the Vatican to members of an Italian religious television channel, Telespace: "When war, as in these days in Iraq, threatens the fate of humanity, it is ever more urgent to proclaim, with a strong and decisive voice, that only peace is the road to follow to construct a more just and united society," John Paul said. "Violence and arms can never resolve the problems of man."

As talk escalated about a U. S. attack on Iraq, Cardinal Joseph Ratzinger, the Prefect of the Vatican Congregation for the Doctrine of the Faith, began stating unequivocally that "the concept of a 'preventive war' does not appear in the *Catechism of the Catholic Church.*" His comments had been published as early as September 2002 and were repeated several times as war seemed imminent.

Cardinal Ratzinger recommended that the three religions who share a heritage from Abraham return to the Ten Commandments to counteract the violence of terrorism and war: "The Decalogue is not the private property of Christians or Jews. It is a lofty expression of moral reason that, as such, is also found in the wisdom of other cultures. To refer again to the Decalogue might be essential precisely to restore reason."

Cardinal Ratzinger noted that the preparation of a new shorter, simpler version of the *Catechism of the Catholic Church* would probably include revisions to clarify the section on just war, as the official version had done against capital punishment in a civilized society. Ratzinger heads up the Commission to write the new catechism. In an interview with *Zenit* on May 2, 2003, the Cardinal restated the position of the Holy Father on the Iraq war (II) and on the question of the possibility of a just war in today's world:

> There were not sufficient reasons to unleash a war against Iraq. To say nothing of the fact that, given the new weapons that make possible destructions that go beyond the combatant groups, today we should be asking ourselves if it is still licit to admit the very existence of a "just war."

Americans were largely unaware of the depth and importance of the opposition of Church leaders to an attack on Iraq, since for the most part the mainstream media did not carry the stories. In the same way, many Americans were unaware that Pope John Paul II spoke against the first Gulf War 56 times, since media in the United States omitted this from the coverage on the war.

In the past few years, Catholic neoconservatives have been attempting to develop a new philosophy of just war which would include what they called "preventive war." George Weigel has published major articles defending this position since 1995. *First Things* magazine published his articles and editorially agreed with this point of view. The George W. Bush administration used these writings to defend the strike against Iraq.

Shortly before the war began, through the U.S. Ambassador to the Vatican, President Bush sent Michael Novak to Rome to try to justify the war to the Pope and Vatican officials. Since with one voice Rome had already publicly rejected the argument for a preventive war, Novak took the approach that a war on Iraq would not be a preventive war, but a continuation of a "just war," which was Iraqi War I, and actually a moral obligation. He argued that it was also a matter of self-defense, that Saddam Hussein had weapons of mass destruction, was an unscrupulous character, and therefore it was only a matter of time before he took up with al-Qaeda and gave them such weapons.

Novak did not succeed in convincing Church leaders – in fact, some commentators reflected that his efforts might have had the opposite effect. Novak's credibility in this argument was perhaps undermined by his employment at the American Enterprise Institute, heavily funded by oil companies, some of whom began advertising in the *Houston Chronicle* for employees to work in Iraq even before the war began. Administration officials denied for months that the goal of the war on Iraq was related to oil. On June 4, 2003, however, *The Guardian* reported the words of the U.S. deputy defense secretary, Paul Wolfowitz (one of the major architects of the war). Wolfowitz had earlier commented that the urgent reason given for the war, weapons of mass destruction, was only a "bureaucratic excuse" for war. At an Asian security summit in Singapore he this time declared openly that the real reason for the war was oil. Asked why a nuclear power such as North Korea was being treated differently from Iraq, where weapons of mass destruction had not been found, the deputy defense minister said: "Let's look at it simply. The most important difference between North Korea and Iraq is that economically, we just had no choice in Iraq. The country swims on a sea of oil."

One eloquent, perceptive commentator described the neoconservatives' new just-war theory as corruption, rather than development, of dogma, noting that there was some considerable irony in the Pope's biographer and trusted confidant, George Weigel, arguing against the Pope that a war on Iraq would be just according to new "developed and extended" just-war principles, while the "rebellious," ultraconservative Society of St. Pius X, using old, undeveloped and unextended just-war principles, argued that a war against Iraq would not be just. Those who had carefully read Weigel's papal biography, however, would not have been surprised at his opposition to John Paul II's unflagging efforts toward the avoidance of a war that would cause so much suffering to the Iraqi people and the deaths of many American soldiers, as well as further inflame mistrust and hatred of the "Christian" West. In what was in many ways a glowing biography, Weigel delivered a devastating attack on the Pope for his diplomatic failure to join forces with the first President George Bush and the United Nations in conducting the Gulf War. In his book Weigel declared that both the Holy Father and the Vatican had lacked the "rigorous empirical analysis" to present and apply the just-war theory to that particular war, and dismissed the repeated appeals for peace immediately before and during the war as "not meeting the high standards set in the previous twelve years of the pontificate."

Violations of just-war principles in the attack on Iraq abounded. Bombing included such targets as an open market and a hotel where the world's journalists were staying. While most television and newspaper reports in the United States minimized coverage of deaths and injuries to the Iraqi people, reports of many civilian casualties did come out. CBS news reported on April 7 stories of civilians pouring into hospitals in Baghdad, threatening to overwhelm medical staff, and the damage inflicted by bombs which targeted homes: "The old, the young, men and women alike, no one has been spared. One hospital reported receiving 175 wounded by midday. A crater is all that remains of four families and their homes – obliterated by a massive bomb that dropped from the sky without warning in the middle afternoon." The Canadian press carried a Red Cross report of "incredible" levels of civilian casualties from Nasiriyah, of a truckload of dismembered women and children arriving at the hospital in Hilla from that village, their deaths the result of "bombs, projectiles." Only much later would the scandal of the abuse of prisoners of war by U. S. soldiers be made public. Reportedly, many of those prisoners had simply been swept up off the streets of Iraq, another example of the suffering of innocent bystanders during the war.

John Paul II sought to distance the Catholic Church from George W. Bush's idea of the manifest Christian destiny of the United States, and especially to avoid the appearance of a clash of Christian civilization against Islam. *Zenit* reported that in his Easter Sunday message of 2003 John Paul II "implored for the world's deliverance from the peril of the tragic clash between cultures and religions." The Pope also sent his message to terrorists: "Let there be an end to the chain of hatred and terrorism which threatens the orderly development of the human family."

At the Ash Wednesday Mass in 2003 John Paul II referred to the root causes of war and terrorism, emphasizing the theme that peace comes with justice, as he had so often pointed out before: "There will be no peace on earth while the oppression of peoples, injustices and economic imbalances, which still exist, endure." He insisted that changes in structures, economic and otherwise, must come from conversion of hearts: "For the desired structural changes to take place, external initiatives and interventions are not enough; what is needed above all is a joint conversion of hearts to love." On several occasions the Holy Father mentioned that in order to address the scourge of terrorism world-wide, there must be progress in peace in the Middle East between Israel and Palestinians.

Catholic World News quoted the Latin-rite Bishop of Baghdad, Bishop Jean-Benjamin Sleimaan, as saying in the Italian daily *La Repubblica* that the Pope's high-profile opposition to a war on Iraq has helped to avoid a sort of Manichaeism that would set up an opposition between the West and the East, in which Christianity is linked to the West and Islam to the East.

The success of John Paul II's efforts to distance the Catholic Church from any "crusade" against Islam or clash of civilizations was apparent in al-Sadr's request that the Vatican mediate talks with the United States in the August 2004 standoff between U. S. forces, together with those of the provisional government the U. S. had set up in Iraq, and Shiite Iraqi cleric Muqtada al-Sadr's militia at the holy shrine in the city of Najaf. The United States government apparently rejected this idea, continuing to present al-Sadr as a radical who was unreasonable, refusing to recognize that there might be any validity to his opposition movement which rejected a government which was not democratically elected and inadequately represented the Iraqi people. As it turned out the revered Grand Ayatollah Ali al-Sistani was apparently able to solve the crisis.

In his 2004 World Day of Peace message the Pope called for a reform of the United Nations to strengthen it in order to avoid war. That message expressed the heart of his philosophical and theological perspective on war and peace: "The end never justifies the means." Even the traditional just-war theory had been construed and misrepresented by many governments to justify wars over the centuries. The "end" in so many cases has been power, domination, and increased wealth, achieved through the means of violence.

The Vatican has made very clear its tremendous commitment to peace and its sound rejection of the idea of expanding the just-war theory. The statements of the Holy Father against war especially give Catholic Workers much encouragement in their pursuit of the means of nonviolence. The Holy Father falls into the tradition of Dorothy Day, and one can only imagine her joy.

THE EDITORS' GLOSS: On September 12, 2002, President Bush asked the UN General Assembly, in reference to Iraq: "Are Security Council resolutions to be honored and enforced, or cast aside without consequence? . . . We want the resolutions of the world's most important multilateral body to be enforced." A year and a half later, when it was more than clear that the WMD and al-Qaeda charges were essentially devoid of substance, neoconservatives like George Weigel scrambled to piece together a persuasive justification for the war in Iraq. On April 21, 2004, he asked himself this hypothetical question: " . . . if you knew then what you know now, would you have made the same call?" His answer:

> We know some things now that we also knew then. We know Saddam Hussein was in material breach of the "final" UN warning, Resolution 1441; his formal response to 1441 was a lie. We know he had the scientists, the laboratories, and the other necessary infrastructure for producing weapons of mass destruction [WMD]. We know he was seeking long-range ballistic missiles (again in defiance of the UN) to deliver biological, chemical, and perhaps nuclear weapons.

This obsession with UN requirements is hypocritical at best, given the willingness of both Bush administration officials and its supporters (like Weigel) to ignore the more binding statues of the UN: that is to say, its founding Charter. References to resolution after resolution (not to mention the oil-for-food "scandal" which sent neocons into orbit because Saddam and others allegedly had the temerity to ignore the requirements of a UN-managed program) ring a little hollow when regime-change advocates ignore the Charter's Article 2, which reads: "All Members shall refrain in their international relations from the threat or use of force against the territorial integrity or political independence of any state." As international law scholars Nicole Deller and John Burroughs make perfectly clear (in this expanded and updated iteration of an article originally appearing in the Winter 2003 *Human Rights*), it is the Charter that governs relations between nations that have signed and ratified it, and the force of any Security Council resolution must always be understood in light of the document of positive international law that gives those resolutions whatever force they possess.

So how credible is it for Bush and Co. to run roughshod over the UN Charter and then maintain that their regime-change operation was based upon their unilateral enforcement of UN decrees? "Hypocrisy" is not even the half of it.

24

The United Nations Charter and the Invasion of Iraq

• • • • • • • • • •

John Burroughs, J.D., Ph.D., and Nicole Deller, J.D.

THE UNITED STATES' formal claim that the invasion of Iraq complied with international law relied on United Nations Security Council resolutions. In a March 20, 2003, letter to the United Nations, U.S. Ambassador John Negroponte asserted that coalition forces had commenced military operations in order to secure Iraq's compliance with disarmament obligations laid down by the Security Council in a series of resolutions beginning with resolution 687 of April 3, 1991, and culminating in resolution 1441 of November 8, 2002.[1] The underlying, substantive rationale for the war was the emphatic U.S. articulation of a novel doctrine of self-defense articulating a right to take preemptive military action against threats arising from possession or development of nuclear, biological, or chemical weapons coupled with links to terrorism, "even if uncertainty remains as to the time and place of the enemy's attack."[2]

Taken on their own terms, both U.S. rationales have been fatally undermined by the post-invasion failure to discover significant programs to develop nuclear, biological, and chemical weapons and missiles, stocks of chemical and biological weapons or materials, or Ba'athist regime links to global terrorism.[3] The collapse of the factual underpinnings for the rationales should not obscure an essential, larger point: the doctrine of

1. Letter dated March 20, 2003, from the Permanent Representative of the United States of America to the United Nations addressed to the President of the Security Council, S/2003/351.

2. George W. Bush, *The National Security Strategy of the United States of America* (Washington, D.C.: The White House), September 2002, p. 15.

3. See Barton Gellman, "Iraq's Arsenal Was Only on Paper: Since Gulf War, Nonconventional Weapons Never Got Past the Planning Stage," *Washington Post*, January 7, 2004, online.

preemptive war, and the related assertion of a right to enforce Security Council resolutions on disarmament, are contrary to international legal constraints on use of force, traditionally known as *jus ad bellum*, and now embodied in the United Nations Charter.

The UN Charter is a treaty of the United States, and as such forms part of the "supreme law of the land" under the U.S. Constitution.[1] The Charter is the highest treaty in the world, superseding states' conflicting obligations under any other international agreement.[2] Adopted in the wake of World War II and proclaiming the determination "to save succeeding generations from the scourge of war," the Charter established a prohibition on the use of force to resolve disputes among states. Article 2(4) bans the threat or use of force (1) against the territorial integrity of a state, (2) against the political independence of a state, and (3) in any other manner inconsistent with the purposes of the United Nations. The Charter contains two exceptions to the prohibition, authorizing the Security Council to use force on behalf of the United Nations to maintain peace and security, and recognizing the right of self-defense against an armed attack. These are the only bases for legitimate use of force generally accepted in present-day international law.

Self-Defense Under the UN Charter

We turn first to the underlying rationale for the invasion of Iraq, self-defense. Article 51 of the UN Charter provides in part: "Nothing in the present Charter shall impair the inherent right of individual or collective self-defense if an armed attack occurs against a member of the United Nations, until the Security Council has taken measures necessary to maintain international peace and security." The use of "inherent" acknowledges that the Charter does not create a right to self-defense; rather, the right preexists the Charter and is fundamental to the system of states. But the Charter also strictly limits self-defense, in that the triggering condition for its exercise is the occurrence of an armed attack.

This limitation prompted an ongoing debate whether the right to use force in anticipation of an attack, which existed prior to the Charter, remains in effect. Some scholars believe Article 51 should be read literally

---

1. U.S. Constitution, Article VI, Clause 2. Regarding the role of the UN Charter and international law and treaty regimes generally in U.S. law and foreign policy, see Nicole Deller, Arjun Makhijani, and John Burroughs, eds., *Rule of Power or Rule of Law? An Assessment of U.S. Policies and Actions Regarding Security-Related Treaties* (New York: Apex Press, 2003) pp. 1–18.

2. UN Charter, Art. 103.

and therefore the right of anticipatory self-defense has been terminated. Others believe that the reference to "inherent right" expresses an intent not to limit the right of self-defense under customary international law.[1] States generally have been reluctant to acknowledge a right of anticipatory self-defense under the Charter, preferring if necessary to interpret "armed attack" broadly to include actions incident to launching an attack.[2]

The right to anticipatory self-defense under customary law has never been unlimited. One generally recognized formulation dating from the mid-nineteenth century is that set forth by Daniel Webster, that the necessity for action must be "instant, overwhelming, and leaving no choice of means, and no moment for deliberation."[3] Since then, and especially since World War II, capabilities to launch devastating attacks with little advance warning have improved dramatically. Nonetheless, scholars have continued to affirm Webster's restraints on legitimate self-defense, recognizing their value in inhibiting resort to war. A recent edition of a leading treatise states that self-defense may justify use of force under the following conditions: an attack is immediately threatened; there is an urgent necessity for defensive action; there is no practicable alternative, particularly when another state or authority that legally could stop or prevent the infringement does not or cannot do so; and the use of force is limited to what is needed to prevent the infringement.[4]

Assuming its continued relevance, application of the doctrine of anticipatory self-defense in the months preceding the invasion of Iraq should have been straightforward. The United States accused Iraq of retaining stocks of chemical and biological weapons and materials and of reconstituting the chemical, biological, and nuclear weapons and missile programs that were terminated or at least severely disrupted by the post-Gulf War inspections. However, no definitive evidence was presented to establish Iraq's possession of such weapons or missiles, or their current use to threaten the United States or other states. In his February 15, 2003, briefing of the Security Council, Secretary of State Colin Powell focused

---

1. A standard definition of customary international law is that it consists of universally binding rules based on general and consistent practices of states followed out of a sense of legal obligation.

2. See Christine Gray, *International Law and the Use of Force* (Oxford, New York: Oxford University Press, 2000), pp. 111–115.

3. Letter from Daniel Webster, U.S. Secretary of State, to British Lord Ashburton, August 6, 1842, regarding the 1837 *Caroline* affair.

4. *Oppenheim's International Law*, Robert Jennings and Sir Arthur Watts, eds., 9th ed. (Harlow, Essex: Longmans Group U.K., Ltd., 1992), p. 412.

on alleged program activities, and the "evidence" he presented seemed thin at the time, a perception borne out by its later discrediting. The UN Monitoring, Verification and Inspection Commission (UNMOVIC) made it very clear that only *uncertainty* existed as to such matters as whether Iraq had fully destroyed stocks of chemical and biological weapons and materials.[1] Given UNMOVIC's stance, especially in view of the fact that states were requested to provide relevant information to UNMOVIC, any plea that U.S. and other intelligence agencies reasonably believed Iraq retained such weapons is unpersuasive. In any event their possession, taken alone, would not suffice to demonstrate a threat of imminent attack. Similarly, the International Atomic Energy Agency (IAEA) publicly and emphatically confirmed what was common knowledge among specialists, namely that the Iraqi nuclear weapons program had been successfully dismantled under IAEA monitoring in the early 1990s.[2]

Seen from a larger perspective, the months of ongoing, public deliberations on Iraq strongly suggested that there was no immediate threat; only part of that time was required for the build-up of U.S. military forces. Further, absent an imminent attack, nonviolent options such as negotiation and verification of claimed compliance with disarmament and nonproliferation norms should be pursued in all cases of suspected acquisition of banned weapons. This follows from the doctrine of anticipatory self-defense, which in Webster's formulation allows force only if there is "no choice of means," and, more broadly, from the UN Charter, which requires the peaceful resolution of disputes when possible. Finally, since the 1990 Iraqi invasion of Kuwait, the Security Council had asserted its authority with respect to Iraq, most centrally by imposing disarmament obligations. Under Article 51, once "the Security Council has taken measures necessary to maintain international peace and security" the right of self-defense is terminated.

In short, it was manifest prior to the invasion of Iraq that conditions, even liberally interpreted, for exercise of any right to anticipatory self-defense were far from being met. The history with respect to Iraq should strengthen resistance to the general U.S. doctrine claiming the right to act militarily against states based on potential threats arising from states' possession or development of non-conventional weapons together with links to terrorism. Although the doctrine has been in gestation for over a decade,

1. See Hans Blix, *Disarming Iraq* (New York: Pantheon Books, 2004), pp. 177–178 and *passim*.
2. *Ibid.*

it was given great impetus by the September 11 terrorist attacks. This is true even though expanding the scope of self-defense was not necessary to legitimize the military operations undertaken in Afghanistan in response to the attacks; these are generally acknowledged to fall under the existing right of self-defense. The Bush administration, however, contends that September 11 demonstrates that threats facing the United States, especially from non-conventional weapons, have reached a magnitude that demands a far-reaching revision of *jus ad bellum*.[1]

The articulation of what amounts to a doctrine of preventive war has met with a great deal of resistance. A rule permitting a military response to an uncertain threat absent immediate danger or exhaustion of peaceful alternatives is a standard ripe for abuse that would destabilize the UN Charter system of restraints on use of force that protects all states. Preventive war undertaken unilaterally by states also appears contrary to international law predating the Charter. The International Military Tribunal sitting at Nuremberg rejected defendants' arguments that Germany was entitled to attack Norway to forestall an Allied invasion, finding that no such invasion was imminent.[2] Defenders of the new doctrine point to the 1981 Israeli air strike against the Osirak nuclear reactor in Iraq as an example of a beneficial preventive military action. In terms of the legality of the action, the Security Council condemned the strike as a violation of the UN Charter and of the "norms of international conduct."[3] From a practical standpoint, whether the strike aided in protecting Israel against an Iraqi nuclear weapons capability remains in dispute; it may have strengthened Iraqi resolve to pursue a concealed program. Whatever the assessment of the balance of factors affecting medium-term Israeli security, it is also true that one case does not justify a rule; the consequences for long-term regional and global security must be weighed in considering general application of a doctrine of preventive war.[4]

---

1. For an examination of possible techniques to effect such revision, see Michael Byers, "Preemptive Self-defense: Hegemony, Equality, and Strategies of Legal Change," *The Journal of Political Philosophy*, Harlow, Essex Vol. 11, No. 2, 2002, pp. 171–190. For a critique of the U.S. doctrine arguing that the answer to the potential spread of nuclear weapons is not preventive war but rather global abolition of nuclear arsenals, see Peter Weiss and John Burroughs, "Weapons of Mass Destruction and Human Rights," *Disarmament Forum* No. 3, 2004, pp. 26–28.

2. *United States v. Goering*, 6 Federal Rules of Decision (1946), pp. 100–101.

3. Resolution 487, June 19, 1981.

4. See Thomas Graham, Jr., "Is International Law Relevant to Arms Control? National Self-Defense, International Law, and Weapons of Mass Destruction," *Chicago Journal of International Law*, Vol. 4, No. 1, Spring, 2003, pp. 11–12.

Security Council Authorization of Force

The only generally recognized legitimate use of force other than self-defense is that directed or authorized by the Security Council to restore or maintain international peace and security. Chapter VII of the UN Charter establishes that force may be used for this purpose when the Security Council has determined the existence of a threat to peace, a breach of peace, or an act of aggression, and efforts to address the matter using measures short of force have failed or would be futile. In the post-cold war era, Security Council resolutions regarding Somalia, Haiti, Rwanda, the Darfur region of Sudan, and other states have established that "international peace and security" encompasses situations of humanitarian emergency or massive human rights violations which may be largely internal to a state but nonetheless are deemed to have adverse consequences for regional or global security. The Charter originally envisaged that states would make their troops and facilities available for Security Council use pursuant to Article 43, essentially creating a standing force, but that arrangement never materialized. Instead, the Security Council delegates its authority to willing states on an ad hoc basis.

A central issue is whether a state or group of states may legally conduct military operations not expressly authorized by the Security Council. The issue was highlighted sharply by the 1999 U.S./NATO bombing of Yugoslavia and is at the forefront of the debate over the invasion of Iraq. In the Yugoslavia case, the United States argued, albeit not very strongly, that the use of force was implied by resolutions condemning Yugoslavia's conduct in Kosovo. Given that Russia and/or China was likely to veto an explicit authorization of use of force, this argument carries little weight. Despite the lack of Security Council authorization, the action received considerable international support as a humanitarian intervention, evidenced in part by the 12–3 vote in the Security Council against a resolution condemning the bombing then under way.

Indeed, some generally contend that non-Security Council authorized military action to prevent genocide, crimes against humanity, and other gross human rights violations is lawful under human rights clauses of the UN Charter, the Genocide Convention, and other international law. One influential report, *The Responsibility to Protect*, has called intervention for human protection purposes "an emerging norm" growing out of international law and state practice.[1] The report holds that Security Council

---

1. International Commission on Intervention and State Sovereignty, *The Responsibility*

authorization for interventions must be sought, but if the Council fails to act in response to threats of genocide, ethnic cleansing, and comparable large-scale human rights abuses, other entities may legitimately authorize intervention, including the UN General Assembly and regional organizations. This view has been strengthened by widespread criticism of the abject failure of the Security Council and major states to respond effectively to ethnically-motivated killings on a vast scale in Rwanda and Bosnia. Many states, especially those in the developing world that fear major power interference in their affairs, oppose arguments tending to legitimize intervention. It is fair to say, though, that should the Security Council continue to prove unable to act to prevent massive atrocities, pressure will build for recognition of the lawfulness of humanitarian intervention by regional organizations and coalitions of states.

In the case of Iraq, humanitarian intervention was not a principal rationale for the invasion. While in the past the Ba'athist regime at a minimum had committed serious violations of human rights and humanitarian law,[1] there was no contention that large-scale atrocities were presently occurring or impending. The question posed, rather, is whether there was *implied* Security Council authorization for military action to compel Iraqi compliance with disarmament obligations. Shortly before the war was launched, together with Britain the United States sought a Security Council resolution that would have declared that Iraq had missed its "final opportunity" to comply with disarmament requirements laid down by the Security Council in resolution 1441. Given that resolution 1441 recalled that the Council had "repeatedly warned Iraq that it will face serious consequences as a result of its continued violations," a resolution making that declaration would have been widely understood to authorize military action. But

---

to Protect (2001).

1. See, e.g., Amnesty International, "Iraq: 'Disappearances': Unresolved cases since the early 1980s," October 1997; Amnesty International, "The Middle East: Fear, flight, and forcible exile," September 1997; United Nations Development Fund for Women, "Iraq: Gender Profile," (examining both pre- and post-war situations, collecting sources, online at www.womenwarpeace.org/iraq/iraq.htm). Human Rights Watch's contention, contested by some [see the interview with Jude Wanniski on pp. 3–79 of the companion to the present volume, *Neo-CONNED!*—Ed.], is that the violations of human rights and humanitarian law were so massive and deliberate as to amount to crimes against humanity and, in relation to the Kurds, genocide. See *Justice for Iraq: A Human Rights Watch Policy Paper*, December 2002; Human Rights Watch/Middle East, *Iraq's Crime of Genocide: The Anfal Campaign Against the Kurds* (New Haven: Yale University Press, 1995); Human Rights Watch/Middle East, *Endless Torment: the 1991 Uprising in Iraq and its Aftermath* (New York: Human Rights Watch, 1992). Humanitarian law is the set of rules imposing limits on the conduct of warfare and occupation. Most centrally, it prohibits attacks against civilians and attacks which indiscriminately harm civilians.

despite determined lobbying, the United States and Britain were unable to muster the required majority of nine members of the 15-member Council. Further, one of the five permanent members, France, signaled that it was prepared to veto the proposed resolution.

Consequently, the United States and Britain had to fall back on the argument that military action was authorized by resolution 1441 and prior resolutions, if *in their view* Iraq failed to fulfill disarmament requirements. That indeed had been the U.S. position all along. The Bush administration contended that because resolution 1441 "decides that Iraq has been and remains in material breach of all relevant resolutions," the United States already had the authority to use force to ensure compliance with the new inspection regime should the Security Council choose not to use force. The logic behind the assertion was that (1) the Security Council previously authorized force in response to Iraq's invasion of Kuwait; (2) authorization was suspended only pursuant to a cease-fire codified by Resolution 687; (3) Iraq is in breach of the cease-fire terms; and (4) the authorization therefore remains in effect.

This argument, together with the underlying rationale of the need for a preemptive strike against a gathering threat, received support from some international lawyers, especially in the United States.[1] But the vast majority of international lawyers, certainly outside the United States, were far from persuaded, with good reason, as explained below.[2] The prevailing rejection of U.S. arguments is well illustrated by the extraordinary readiness of UN Secretary-General Kofi Annan to continue to publicly state that the war was "not in conformity with the UN Charter" and, when pressed, was "illegal."[3]

---

1. E.g., John Yoo, "International Law and the War in Iraq," *American Journal of International Law*, Vol. 97, No. 3, July, 2003, pp. 563–576; Ruth Wedgwood, "The Fall of Saddam Hussein: Security Council Mandates and Preemptive Self-Defense," *ibid.*, pp. 576–585. See also the article by the State Department legal adviser, William H. Taft IV, and Todd Buchwald, Assistant Legal Adviser for Political-Military Affairs, State Department, "Preemption, Iraq, and International Law," *ibid.*, pp. 557–563.

2. Statements of international lawyers opposing the impending war as illegal include "International Appeal by Lawyers and Jurists Against the 'Preventive' Use of Force," February 15, 2003, coordinated by the International Association of Lawyers Against Nuclear Arms (www.lcnp.org/global/LawyersandJuristsAppeal.htm) and a January 15, 2003, open letter to the Security Council by the International Commission of International Law Jurists (online at www.eurolegal.org/useur/bbiraqwar.htm). See also C.G. Weeramantry, *Armageddon or Brave New World? Reflections on the Hostilities in Iraq* (Colombo, Sri Lanka: Weeramantry International Centre for Peace Education and Research, 2003). Weeramantry is a former vice president of the International Court of Justice.

3. Patrick E. Tyler, "UN Chief Ignites Firestorm By Calling Iraq War 'Illegal,'" *New York Times*, September 17, 2004, online.

At the most basic level, it is for the Security Council, not individual states, to decide whether and how to enforce its resolutions.[1] Presumably the United States would not accept that other members of the Council could decide, over U.S. objections, to take military action to compel compliance with Council resolutions. Resolution 1441 refers to "serious consequences" of Iraqi non-compliance, but also provides that the Council "upon receipt of a report" of Iraqi non-compliance will convene "to consider the situation." While the United States purported to make such a report in Powell's presentation, none was received from UNMOVIC or the IAEA, and as noted above, the Council publicly and unambiguously declined to approve the U.S./British proposed resolution that would have been understood to authorize force. Further, when resolution 1441 was adopted, Russia, France, China, Mexico, Ireland, Colombia and other states noted that it provided for no "automaticity" or "hidden triggers" regarding use of force without further Council authorization. Finally, the last paragraph of the resolution stated that the Council "[d]ecides to remain seized of the matter."

The U.S. and British invocation of prior resolutions is also unavailing. Resolution 687 required that Iraq end its long-range missile and its chemical, biological, and nuclear weapons programs and account for having done so, but the Security Council reserved for itself the power to make determinations regarding enforcement of the cease-fire terms. Paragraph 34 of the resolution states that the Council "[d]ecides to remain seized of the matter and to take such further steps as may be required for the implementation of the present resolution and to secure peace and security in the area." Since then, although the Security Council repeatedly has found Iraq to be in a state of non-compliance, it has not clearly and specifically authorized the use of force to achieve compliance. When the Security Council has authorized force in other situations, it has employed language universally understood to authorize force, *e.g.*, "all necessary means." This applied to use of force in Korea in 1950; ejection of Iraq from Kuwait in 1990; and in Somalia, Haiti, Rwanda, and Bosnia in the 1990s. Further, the Security Council has expressly authorized force only in response to actual invasion, large-scale violence, or humanitarian emergency, not to potential threats of the kind the United States claimed were posed by Iraq. The U.S. claim

---

1. See Blix, *op. cit.*, p. 268. Head of UNSCOM prior to the war and an international lawyer, Blix writes: "There is something strange about the argument that the authority of the Security Council could be upheld by a minority of states in the Council ignoring the views of the majority. Can the will of the world be enforced by an action (in this case preemptive) by one or a few states, even when this action runs counter to the expressed will of the world?"

that material breach by Iraq provides a basis for termination of the cease-fire ignores the fact that the Gulf War was an action authorized by the Security Council, not a state-versus-state conflict. Accordingly, only the Security Council could determine whether to end the cease-fire. As Jules Lobel and Michael Ratner wrote in a seminal and prescient 1999 article, for the Security Council to maintain international peace and security credibly, it must "retain strict control over the initiation, duration and objectives of the use of force."[1]

Claims of implied authorization of force should be examined critically in light of the fundamental principles of the UN Charter.[2] The Charter gives priority to the peaceful settlement of disputes and the non-use of force. The Article 2(4) prohibition on the threat or use of force has been described by the International Court of Justice as a peremptory norm of international law from which states cannot derogate.[3] Strained interpretations of Security Council resolutions, especially when opposed, as in the case of Iraq, by a majority of other Council members, cannot overcome those fundamental principles. Rather, given the values embedded in the Charter, the burden is on those who claim use of force has been authorized.[4] The United States failed to meet that burden.

Conclusion

The question naturally arises, what difference does it make that international lawyers, or even the UN secretary-general, declare the illegality of an action by the world's most powerful state? One answer is that by undermining the legitimacy of the U.S. occupation, it may influence political developments in Iraq and the region. But it is also the case that there are no readily identifiable consequences, legal or other, for the states and their leaders responsible for launching the invasion. In this respect, the main aspiration is to affect future decisions about use of force.

---

1. Jules Lobel and Michael Ratner, "Bypassing the Security Council: Ambiguous Authorizations to Use Force, Cease-Fires and the Iraqi Inspection Regime," *American Journal of International Law*, Vol. 93, No. 1, January, 1999, p. 125.

2. *Ibid*, p. 128 and *passim*; Peter Weiss, "Presentation on the Illegality of the War," World Tribunal on Iraq, New York session, May 8, 2004 (www.worldtribunal-nyc.org/Document/index.htm).

3. *Nicaragua v. United States*, 1986 ICJ 14, ¶190.

4. Rabinder Singh, QC, Alison Macdonald, Matrix Chambers, London, "Legality of Use of Force Against Iraq: Opinion," September 10, 2002, p. 31 (online at www.lcnp.org/global/IraqOpinion10.9.02.pdf).

It is certainly true that weakness of enforcement with respect to issues of war and peace is endemic to the current international order. Most importantly, the body charged with the responsibility to govern use of force, the Security Council, remains subject to the veto power of the United States and other permanent members, and those states or their allies have often been principal actors in uses of force. The International Court of Justice is a suitable venue for redress against transgressing states only to the extent that involved states have accepted or would accept its jurisdiction. The United States withdrew from its jurisdiction in the wake of the 1980s case brought by Nicaragua challenging U.S. support for Nicaraguan counterrevolutionary forces. The International Criminal Court will not have jurisdiction over individuals accused of the crime of aggression unless and until agreement is reached on definition of the crime and the treaty creating the court is amended, a process that will take at least a decade and probably longer. Moreover, the United States refuses to join the treaty, limiting, though not excluding, circumstances under which the court can have jurisdiction over U.S. nationals.

Because international ability and will to respond to violations after they have occurred remain limited, it is crucial there be in-depth deliberation on the compatibility of future uses of force with international law prior to their initiation, within governments, in the United Nations, and in the public sphere. Concerning the United States in particular, it is imperative to build respect for international law within U.S. political culture, so that compliance with basic international obligations and constructive participation in international institutions can be effectively promoted by U.S. civil society as well as in international forums. Among other things, respect for international law requires rejection of two premises of the invasion of Iraq: that the United States has the right to engage in preventive war against states asserted to pose potential threats; and that the United States may enforce Security Council resolutions absent express authorization by the Council.

THE EDITORS' GLOSS: Article I.8 of the Constitution gives Congress the power to "constitute Tribunals inferior to the Supreme Court ... define and punish ... Offenses against the Law of Nations ... and make Rules concerning Captures on Land and Water." But on November 13, 2001, President Bush issued a "Military Order" granting *himself* the power to detain and try by "military commission" – for "violations of the laws of war and other applicable laws" – anyone *he determines* is or was in al-Qaeda, "engaged in, aided or abetted, or conspired to commit, [undefined] acts of international terrorism," or "knowingly harbored one or more" individuals in these categories. As the Order was developed, the usual suspects (David Addington, vice president's counsel; John Yoo, Justice Department lawyer; Timothy Flanigan, former deputy White House counsel) overruled military, State, and Justice Department experts – who wanted criminal or courts-martial proceedings for 9/11 and "war on terror" (GWOT) suspects – because GWOT intelligence might be hard to get if defense lawyers and due-process got in the way ("After Terror, a Secret Rewriting of Military Law," *New York Times*, October 24, 2004).

The legality of so removing individuals from the criminal or military justice system was challenged by attorneys on behalf of Salim Hamdan. D. C. District Court Judge James Robertson stopped the commissions in November 2004 (see pp. 480-2). The government appealed and pressed ahead, an insider blaming Cheney for its intransigence (*New York Times*, March 27, 2005: "Cheney is still driving a lot of this"). Meanwhile, some of the commission's defense lawyers and even military *prosecutors* complained of its "marginal" cases and "half-assed effort" (*AFP*, August 1, 2005). But on July 15 – in spite of 17 "friend of the court" briefs on Hamdan's side from retired JAGs, generals, and admirals; a Constitutional historian at the Library of Congress; and numerous international-, national-security-, and military-law academics and lawyers – the government won a reversal from a D. C. Appeals Court three-judge panel; it argued that the "Geneva Convention cannot be judicially enforced."

One of the three judges met the President for an interview the day before, and on July 20 he was nominated to the Supreme Court. It might be coincidental that John Roberts was tapped for the Court five days after he joined the decision that the President's "construction and application of treaty provisions is entitled to great weight." Alternatively, Bruce Shapiro, writing in *The Nation* (July 20, 2005), suggests that Roberts's interview with the President was his oral exam, and the *Hamdan* decision was the "essay question." Evidently he passed.

25

Legal Nonsense: The War on Terror and its Grave Implications for National and International Law
· · · · · · · · · ·
An Interview with Prof. Francis Boyle, J.D., Ph.D.

I N YOUR RECENT *interview with Bill O'Reilly, he said that we had the right to roll into Afghanistan essentially (and simply) because bin Laden is a bad guy, and the Afghans were not cooperating. Do you see our refusal to make a traditional declaration of war against Afghanistan as a matter of convenience? Does it get us off the hook, morally and legally, from having to obey the normal rules of how wars are conducted and declared between one state and another?*

FB: I think they had already planned to go to war against Afghanistan beforehand, and it is abundantly clear from the so-called offer made by President Bush to the Afghan government that it was not really made in good faith. They were looking for a pretext, they got it, and they went to war.

LID: Do you think they would have been caught off guard if Afghanistan had given way on all their demands?

FB: It was reported on *CounterPunch.org* that they did, in fact, offer to turn over bin Laden, but this offer was never followed up. It is clear that bin Laden was a pretext, and 9/11 was a pretext. They needed a pretext to go to war against Afghanistan and Iraq, and they created the conditions to make it possible. It also seems to me that they knew the 9/11 attacks were going to happen, but that's another story.

LID: Indeed. There's a lot about the mainstream story of 9/11 that doesn't make sense, but that is, as you say, another story. What struck us, as all this unfolded, was how non-traditional our approach to the whole thing was. They could have made an argument to make a real declaration of war against Afghanistan, but it seems to us that this approach was intentionally avoided.

FB: I think Bush did seek a declaration along the lines of what Roosevelt got from Congress on December 8, 1941. The reason he sought it was that it would have made him a constitutional dictator. Fortunately, Congress did not give Bush a formal declaration of war, but he did try. Had he gotten one all the provisions of the U.S. Code would have applied, which give the President sweeping powers during a state of declared war.

LID: So you say "fortunately" because of the powers of the U.S. Code that would have been granted to the President?

FB: The book *Presidential Power* by Arthur Miller explains how, with a formal declaration of war by Congress, as happened in December 1941 and also in WWI, the President essentially becomes a constitutional dictator. He can pretty much do what he wants.

LID: That's interesting. Although there are negative ramifications for how the prisoners are treated in an undeclared war, it sounds like one of the "benefits" has been that at least we avoided having a dictatorship on our hands in America – or at least more of one than we currently suffer.

FB: It could have been a lot worse. Senator Byrd pointed out that the authorization that the President did get was not a formal declaration of war, but rather a limited authorization and subject to all the requirements of the War Powers resolution. He was not given a blank check.

LID: Do you know how well he did in meeting any of those requirements?

FB: Ha! That's a good one. The problem is that the President does not care. He believes clearly that he is above the Constitution of the United States. He has made it clear that he is not limited by anyone. But the fact remains that it is up to Congress to enforce its own war powers. The Constitution, Article I, Section 8, gives the power to Congress to go to war, not to the President. It is up to Congress to enforce this in the first instance, and ultimately for the American people to enforce this in default by Congress. This is why I started my campaign for impeachment. I called Ramsey Clark to discuss starting an impeachment campaign against the President over the war in Afghanistan. He felt that the public support was not there at that time, because the President had been very successful in brainwashing the American people into supporting what he was doing. But, in August 2002 Cheney began making his speeches against Iraq and the situation and atmosphere began to change. It appeared to be the same scenario they had pursued in Gulf War I under Bush Senior.

LID: In following your impeachment efforts, we saw that you are waiting on an equivalent to Congressman Henry B. Gonzalez (D-Tex.), who – I think many Americans don't know this – worked with you to attempt an impeachment of Bush 41 over the first Gulf War.

FB: We are pressuring Congress. We need one member of Congress to propose a bill. Congressman Conyers did have a discussion on March 13, 2003, with 40 or 50 of his top advisors. He called Ramsey and me, inviting us to state the case for putting in immediate bills of impeachment against Bush, Cheney, Rumsfeld, and Ashcroft to try to head off the war. We did the best we could. The merits were debated quite extensively. The people there did not really disagree with us on the merits of impeachment but rather on the political practicality. John Podesta was there on behalf of the Democratic National Committee arguing that proposing a bill of impeachment might hurt the Democratic candidate in 2004. That is where we stand now. I think that advice was wrong. But I did not argue the point. I just argued the constitutional merits of impeachment. No one really disagreed with that. They were merely concerned with how it would play out in the November 2004 elections. Of course the Democrats were clobbered, but Ramsey and I agreed before the election to push forward, and that is what we are doing.

LID: Do you have any hopefuls in terms of the Congressional sponsorship that you need?

FB: Any one of them could do it. It's up to the people to pressure their representatives to put one in. But with the offensive, the destruction, and the killing in Fallujah – this is a crime against humanity. We have already lost some 1800 military people thanks to Bush, Cheney, Rumsfeld, and others. It seems to me that we owe it to those fallen troops to file bills of impeachment, and to make it clear that we are going to try to hold these war criminals to account not only for the dead U.S. soldiers, but also for the more than 100,000 dead Iraqis. If we do not act, this war is going to get well and truly out of control. General Shinseki publicly testified that we need several hundred thousand troops to occupy Iraq. He has been proven right. The troops there are sitting ducks, and what we need to do is get our troops out of harms way.

LID: On another subject – but speaking of resisting war criminals and their crimes – we understand that you were able to act as counsel for 28-year-old former Staff Sgt. Camilo Mejia, who was sentenced on May 21, 2004, to one year in prison for refusing to return to fight in Iraq.

FB: That's right. He was the first resister. He saw everything, and was even asked to participate in the torture being conducted. He came back home on leave and after much soul-searching realized he could not continue in good conscience to participate in an illegal war. He filed for conscientious objector status as a result. He was court marshaled for desertion! Though he was the first to do so, he is unlikely to be the last. The Pentagon decided to make an example of him, to make a point to the rest of the troops who are beginning to get very restless. He is, of course, a hero, the first Amnesty-International-declared prisoner of conscience in America linked to this war.

LID: A couple of thoughts on the legal background. We came across a comment made by Dr. Elizabeth Wilmshurst in England, who as you know resigned her post as deputy legal adviser to the Foreign & Commonwealth Office in the U.K. over the illegality of the Iraq war. She said, "lawyers hate the phrase 'war on terror.'" Do you share that sentiment?

FB: If you see my book, Destroying World Order, there is a whole chapter entitled "Preserving the Rule of Law in the War on International Terrorism." It is mere propaganda, a slogan that the Bush people have come up with to justify aggression, their own terrorism, war crimes, and torture elsewhere round the world. There is no generally accepted definition of terrorism. In practical terms, anyone who opposes what the U.S. does becomes "a terrorist." The USSR did much the same thing after they invaded Afghanistan. Powerful governments as a rule call their opponents "terrorist," thereby seeking some kind of "moral high ground."

LID: For the Soviets, Osama bin Laden would have been a "terrorist extraordinaire" when he was involved in resisting their efforts to take over Afghanistan. But now the shoe is on the other foot.

FB: Let's be clear about all this. Bin Laden is our guy. The Carter administration, as well as the Reagan people, worked hand-in-glove with bin Laden and the CIA. That's where he and al-Qaeda came from! As long as he was fighting the Soviet Union, he was "a freedom fighter," part of the Mujahideen. But once these Islamic warriors turned against the U.S. and its view of the world – assuming that they ever believed it – they became "terrorists" overnight. These terms are devoid of any substance. They are designed, quite simply, to squash dissent. We used to throw around the term "Communist" a lot in the old days, even when the accused were very far from being such. It was a convenient way of ridding oneself of problems through the use of the smear technique.

LID: You mentioned that one of the real problems making this war on terror so vague, so sweeping and so meaningless – to the point of allowing it to encompass just about anything the Bushites want it to – is that all the normal protections afforded to people on the opposite side of an armed force can be twisted, manipulated, or just dispensed with.

FB: It's dehumanizing to Arabs, Blacks, Muslims, Asians, Coloreds. We cannot forget the racist element of the war here, very much like Vietnam. In Vietnam, we had to dehumanize them in order to kill them – so we called them "gooks." Now instead of looking at these people as human beings, with grievances and a cause that they have not made known to our people but might like to, we call them "terrorists." We dehumanize them in order to make it easier for the American people to do terrible things to them that we otherwise would not be doing in all likelihood. I doubt seriously that we would be treating white Christians or white Jews this way. These terrorists, as we call them, are throwaway people.

LID: Of course in Serbia and Kosovo, it was the other way around. It was white Christians who were being attacked in another illegal and unjust war for their alleged crimes against Muslims, never mind that the faction that we supported were real terrorists, i.e., the KLA. In that light it simply seems like the terrorists are always whomever we've chosen to oppose in whatever the conflict de jour is. Now speaking of Kosovo – just to digress for a second – our sense is that the legal background for the assault on Serbia was just as specious as that used in the war against Iraq.

FB: I agree with you. In fact, in that same book mentioned above there is a chapter on humanitarian intervention in which I also condemn the arguments used to justify the Serbia intervention.

LID: Now there may have been some argument that the Serbia bombing was a "humanitarian effort" to protect Muslims and Kosovars, though we would agree with you that it was an entirely bogus pretext. But that shows, doesn't it, that we will pick up whatever flag is useful – "humanitarian aid," "WMDs," "terrorism" – to accomplish our other aims?

FB: All of these wars, Afghanistan and Iraq – and our less well-known military interventions elsewhere of late – have one thing in common: oil and natural gas. That is what all this "imperial hubris" is about. We are running out of these things, things so vital to our economy. The Pentagon knows it, and so they are scrambling to get whatever oil and natural gas they can find – whether it's in Central Asia, Afghanistan, Iraq, Columbia, Jibouti, or the Suez Canal. They are now planning military intervention on the west coast of Africa because oil and gas have been found there. If you look at all they are doing – not what they are saying, but what they are doing – they are deploying forces all over the world where there is oil and gas to be had. There is no deployment, however urgent the situation, where there is no oil and gas.

LID: Let's give some thought, if we may, to the Guantánamo detainees. One thing that has struck us as problematic – and it goes all the way back to 9/11 – is that, in the context of the "war on terror," Uncle Sam is making an informal declaration of war against irregular forces all over the globe. Anyone with a gun who does not sympathize with the American way of life, or the politics of the government, is automatically deemed "an enemy." Correct us if we are wrong, but under the normal process of declaring war, the opposing sides' troops are recognized as lawful combatants who are guaranteed certain rights. Here, where we are picking a fight with all the irregular forces of the world, they are immediately deprived of their rights – or so it seems to us. It appears that much of the Geneva Conventions have been set aside and that POW rights have effectively been ignored and nullified. If this is so, it seems to be the height of hypocrisy.

FB: It is most definitely the case. What that is going to do is react to the disadvantage of our own men and women in the armed forces, because what we have done is to send a message that we don't care about the Geneva Convention – and that can only expose our armed forces to grave harm and danger. Battle is bad enough, but if they get wounded or captured the only protection our people have is the Geneva Convention. If we are now saying we just don't care about any of this in Afghanistan, Iraq, Gitmo, then there is no kind of protection for our armed forces. Even Secretary of State Powell pointed this out in a memo to Bush. I regret to say you will likely see outright savagery being inflicted on our armed forces – and certainly to the extent that we are inflicting it on our opponents. The U.S. Marine filmed shooting dead a wounded resistance fighter in a mosque in Fallujah has set a dangerous precedent. It says, in effect, that if you are an Iraqi fighting the occupation and you are caught, you are likely to get your head blown off. What hope, then, is there for wounded or captured American troops in Iraqi hands?

LID: A lot of media coverage has been given to the tribunals in Gitmo, variously termed "Combatant Status Review Tribunals" and "Administrative Review Boards" – not to mention the infamous military commissions established under the President's Military Order of November 13, 2001. The heated discussion is all about whether or not these tribunals are sufficient to provide for the rights of the detainees. Our sense is that they don't come close, because of clear obligations on the part of those doing the detaining (i.e., us) to provide for a Geneva Article 5 tribunal, which passes a judgment on whether people should be held as POWs or not – and until those tribunals are conducted, the detainees are supposed to be presumed to be POWs and afforded POW rights. Something our government has conspicuously not done.

FB: These kangaroo courts – I'm talking "military commissions" now – were opposed by the professional military lawyers in the Judge Advocate General's (JAG) office at the Pentagon. They were opposed by the professional international lawyers in the State Department. The only lawyers who supported these kangaroo courts were right wing, war-mongering lawyers that inhabited the office of White House counsel Alberto Gonzales – now attorney general – and John Ashcroft at the Department of "Injustice." That is to say, none of the professionals who know anything at all about human rights or the laws of war. As I said, even the professional military lawyers were against these courts. As you know, in late November 2004 the federal district judge in Washington, D.C., struck the whole thing down, though in July 2005 it was rehabilitated by an appeals court for the D.C. circuit in a frankly ridiculous decision. Though in the district case – *Hamdan v. Rumsfeld* – the judge applies the law as it should have been applied in the first place.[1]

LID: What are the details of these recent decisions?

FB: The first decision simply struck down the kangaroo court procedure down at Gitmo. That decision was then overturned on the basis that the Geneva Conventions are not "self-executing," though honestly, what good

---

1. See the discussion of military commissions and related tribunals in chapter 29 and its postscripts, on pp. 443–489 of the present volume.—Ed.

is a right if it cannot be protected in the courts? When the Department of Justice first made the appeal, they were probably hopeful that they'd get it to the Supreme Court, which the Bushites control; now it looks like that might happen, as the attorneys for Hamdan have themselves appealed. Do remember, by the way, that it was the five Republican justices that gave the presidency to Bush Jr. in 2000 to begin with, and started this whole problem. After that happened the Democrats were derelict in their duty by not putting in Bills of Impeachment against those five Supreme Court Justices. They rolled over and played dead, just as Gore and Kerry have done. What good are they?

LID: On a side (but related) note, one of the pretexts we have heard that was supposed to have justified our aggression in Afghanistan is the phrase, "Afghanistan is a failed state." It appears everywhere in the political literature on the subject and it seems to say that, as a consequence, the norms of international law between one sovereign State and another simply don't apply. Would you say that is gibberish?

FB: Yes, it means nothing. It's just a category, a description, pulled out of thin air and developed.

LID: The Afghans don't see things the way we do, so they can be dismissed as a nonentity, right?

FB: Yes. In fact we were actually negotiating with the Taliban government in Afghanistan during the Clinton administration about the construction of a huge oil pipeline through their territory, and it appears that Clinton was about to establish diplomatic relations with them.

LID: So, Afghanistan being a "failed state" did not impede that process!

FB: Not at all. All we cared about was getting into that Central Asian oil field and raking in big money.

LID: On the legal question of one sovereign state versus another, many commentators and public figures – Robin Cook, Kofi Annan, Elizabeth Wilmshurst, and yourself to name but a few – have come out in black and white saying the aggression against Iraq was illegal. This is also the opinion of some hundreds of international lawyers around the globe that have made statements on various occasions.[1] Even Richard Perle conceded that international law would have "gotten in the way" of the Iraq invasion, had it been

1. *Vide supra*, p. 368, note 2.—Ed.

obeyed. What this means, at least from our point of view, is that we deposed by force of arms a legitimate government, recognized as such throughout the world, and that consequently the government that was in place is still the legitimate government at least de jure if not de facto. Do you agree?

FB: Yes. Under the laws of war as codified in U.S. Army Field Manual 2710, we did indeed depose the legitimate government of Iraq. The U.S. and Britain are – still – what is known as the "belligerent occupants" of Iraq. The so-called Allawi government was nothing more than a puppet government. But the laws of war do not prohibit us from establishing a puppet government if that is what we want as occupiers. Again, under the above law, we are responsible for the behavior of that puppet government. We have displaced the legitimate government of Iraq and have imposed a puppet government – twice. What happens now depends on if and when the belligerent occupation by the U.S. and U.K. ends, and if the Iraqi people themselves have an opportunity to reestablish their own government. It's important to keep this in mind, despite all the talk about the transfer of sovereignty, democracy, and elections. That's all nonsense. The sovereignty resides in the hands of the Iraqi people. They never lost it in the first place. It was never ours to transfer. A belligerent occupant does not obtain sovereignty. Sovereignty remains with people and with the state that is occupied. We never had anything to transfer to Allawi. He remained at all times the puppet head of a puppet government. The January 2005 elections did nothing but establish another puppet government, no matter who did or did not participate, and in what numbers.

LID: And any so-called trial of former members of the legitimate government conducted under the auspices of this puppet government – particularly if the occupying forces are still there – is very problematic as well.

FB: They are simply more kangaroo court proceedings. Clearly there are procedures. Saddam is a prisoner of war. Prisoners of war under the Third Geneva Convention can be tried for the commission of war crimes, but they are subject to all the protections of the third Geneva Convention. In this situation Saddam would be entitled to a trial in the form of a court-martial under the Uniform Code of Military Justice. Clearly he will not get that. He will get a kangaroo summary procedure and then they will take him out and kill him. Several of the so-called Iraqi human rights people involved in setting up these kangaroo courts have already said as much. Saddam will not get a fair trial. Of that there can be very little doubt.

LID: Are there any other important points of which we should be aware?

FB: Before the start of the war against Iraq, President Putin of Russia and Walter Cronkite both publicly stated that if Bush went to war against Iraq, he could set off a third world war – and that is the situation we find ourselves in now. This is an extremely volatile area of the world. Two-thirds of the world's energy resources are there – the very thing that we are going after. That that is what we are doing is very clear to Russia, Europe, China, India, Pakistan. It's very clear we are going all out for the oil and the gas in order to control the future of the world's economy. The longer we, the American people, let this go on, the more we risk a wider regional war that could easily degenerate into a world war.

LID: Rumsfeld's favorite words for the Iraqi resistance is "extremist," "terrorist," etc. We assume there is no question that the Iraqis who are defending themselves from occupation have every legitimate right to do so, regardless of what outside influence there may or may not be in Iraq?

FB: This is clearly an illegal and criminal war being waged by Bush Jr. and Tony Blair. So, of course, the Iraqi people have a right to resist an illegal, criminal war under international law. That's the danger in all of this. Hitler got away with marching into Austria and Czechoslovakia, but then he went into Poland and that led to the start of WWII. Here we have Bush who has waged two wars now, in Afghanistan and Iraq. He is now threatening Syria, Iran, and North Korea. We have a very similar situation here. Either the current situation is brought under control, or they launch one more aggressive war. That could start a chain reaction leading to a regional war – and perhaps to another world war.

LID: Let's hope we can reverse the tide before that happens.

FB: I think we have to, and that is why Ramsey and I are pressing ahead with impeachment. Remember, and this is very important, Nixon won a landslide victory against McGovern in 1972. Massachusetts was against him, but the rest of the country supported him. Yet he and Agnew were out of office less than two years later. So, that is the scenario that I think we must pursue with respect to Messrs. Bush and Cheney.

www.einswine.com

www.informationclearinghouse.info

The [next] priority for change – the first element of a new politics for the United States – is in our policy toward the world. Too much and for too long, we have acted as if our great military might and wealth could bring about an American solution to every world problem.

—Robert F. Kennedy, U.S. Attorney General
and presidential candidate, 1968

PROPPING UP A DYING GIANT: AMERICAN ECONOMIC AND MILITARY SURVIVAL TACTICS

THE EDITORS' GLOSS: It is a frightening thought for many Americans. The idea that someday the United States won't be the "biggest," the "best," the most powerful, the leader of a more-or-less global *Pax Americana*. But it is probably historically inevitable. Greece, Rome, Spain, Britain – all examples of great powers that have come and gone.

The funny thing is – and a paradox for "worried" imperial Americans – England, Spain, Italy, and Greece are still fantastic places to visit and, in many respects, wonderful places to live. The pizza, the art, and the wine in Italy are not less appreciable because Italy is not managing the foreign affairs of all Europe. The cultural traditions of law and civilization refined by the British Empire are not of less value because the "empire" has been reduced to modest proportions. The works of Sophocles, Aeschylus, Homer, Plato, and Aristotle still represent some of the greatest intellectual achievements of all time, notwithstanding Athens's modern confinement to a small island. The cathedrals, the hills, and the Rioja of Spain are no less delightful as a result of the independence of South America. Many of these cultural treasures pertain, though, to a side of life that many – certainly not all – Americans fail, in many ways, to appreciate. They have little to do with speed, size, power. They have a lot, however, to do with what makes life worth living.

The point is, being a humble country – a proud but cooperative member of the family of nations – is not such a bad thing. Some would say it's a natural thing. Some would also say it's where the U.S. is headed, willing or no. A balanced perspective would urge us towards willingness, knowing that the life of a nation doesn't end with the eclipse of empire. The unbalanced one, which currently guides our "ship of state" – as Wallerstein puts it – is less resigned to facts and more convinced that "imperial America" is the only America possible and desirable. This view threatens everyone, but above all Americans. Prof. Wallerstein's perspective on this problem follows, in what first appeared as the introductory chapter to his book *Alternatives*.

C H A P T E R
26

In Her Death Throes:
The Neoconservative Attempt to Arrest
the Decline of American Hegemony
• • • • • • • • •
Prof. Immanuel Wallerstein, Ph.D.

THE GREATEST THREAT to the United States today – its liberty, its security, its prosperity, its future – is the United States. For at least thirty years, the United States had already been wandering uncertainly and hesitatingly down a slippery incline, when George W. Bush decided to rush full speed ahead. As a result, the U.S. is in immediate danger of falling badly, perhaps fracturing itself. After the dramatic and terrible September 11 attack on the United States, Bush listened to his covey of hawks, and declared a "war on terrorism" – one in which he told the whole world that it was either "with us or against us" and one, he said, that the United States would "surely win." This bravura was the public face of just about the worst strategy the U.S. government could have adopted, not only weakening the United States and the world considerably in the subsequent years but also strengthening all those forces it was ostensibly designed to destroy.

How did the United States come to place itself in such a disastrous position? It was surely not inevitable. The hawks around George W. Bush were determined to transform the world, and they have, but not at all in the way they hoped. The basic premise of the Bush hawks was that the U.S. had been in a slow decline for at least thirty years – which is true. In their analysis, however, this decline was the result of a weak and faulty policy of successive Presidents, therefore reversible. All the U.S. needed to do, they argued, was to flex seriously its considerable military muscle, abandon all pretense of multilateral consultation with hesitant and weak allies, and proceed to intimidate both dubious friends and hostile enemies alike, and the U.S. would be in the world driver's seat again. This, however, was not at all true.

The U.S. decline is structural, the result of the predictable loss of the enormous economic edge the United States temporarily had after 1945 vis-à-vis everyone, including all the other so-called industrialized countries. In a capitalist system, such an edge – especially the outsized advantage the U.S. had in the 1950s and 1960s – is impossible to maintain, since others can and will copy the technology and organization that make it momentarily possible. This is exactly what happened. By circa-1970, Western Europe and Japan had brought their economic structures to the point where they were more or less competitive with the U.S. structures – in their home markets, in the home market of the United States, and in the markets of the rest of the world. The decline from the giddy but passing economic dominance and therefore hegemony in the world-system that the U.S. experienced is something one lives with, adjusts to, and makes the best of. The decline of an erstwhile hegemonic power is really less about its own decline than about the rise of the others. Thus its decline is initially only relative (it commands an ever-smaller proportion of world value produced and capital accumulated). And the decline can be slow. But it is not something that can be reversed in any fundamental way. Once the hegemonic peak has been reached and then passed, it cannot be regained. Trying to restore the glorious past only hastens the pace of the decline.

The hawks do not see it that way. They have the vision of an imperial America always on top, always impregnable, virtually by moral right. They believe that supremacy in the economic and political arenas can be imposed and reimposed *manu militari*. The position of the hawks has been so egregiously arrogant that they could not get their way for a long time. Quite the contrary. Instead, in the thirty years after 1970, from Nixon to Carter to Reagan to Clinton, the U.S. government did its best to deal with an increasingly difficult situation with the strategy that I call "soft multilateralism."

The primary object of this strategy was to slow down as much as possible the process of decline of U.S. primacy in the world that had resulted from the loss of the once-unquestioned supremacy of the United States in industrial production. The three main pillars of this Nixon-to-Clinton strategy were (1) *partnership*: the attempt to keep our allies from striking off on independent political (and military) paths by emphasizing past politico-moral debts and continuing common enemies, and offering them a right of prior consultation on new initiatives in their role as "partners"; (2) *nuclear oligopoly*: maintenance of the status quo in the list of nuclear powers by persuading and/or intimidating middle powers (especially Third

World countries) to avoid pursuing any and all roads to nuclear proliferation; and (3) *globalization:* the reorganization of world economic macrostructures by persuading and pressuring countries of the South – the peripheral zones located primarily in Asia, Africa and Latin America – to renounce protectionist, developmentalist policies in favor of opening their economic frontiers, especially their financial borders. I call these policies *soft* multilateralism because the U.S. was always ready to go unilateral if it thought it had to. It simply did not say so out loud, in the hope that going it alone would not be necessary. The United States counted on its ability to "lead"- that is, to persuade others to endorse the decisions that the U.S. favored and which best served U.S. interests.

What one can say about this Nixon-to-Clinton strategy, pursued over thirty years, is that it was partially successful, in that the decline of the U.S. was indeed slowed down, but of course never reversed. The neocons, however, saw the glass as half-empty rather than half-full. They therefore proposed to improve the score in the pursuit of the same three objectives by using a new, tougher line. For a long time, their views were considered adventurous and outside the mainstream. And they were very frustrated, even with the Reagan administration. The attack of September 11, however, gave them at last the excuse they needed to implement their program, which had been advertised in advance in the 2000 report issued by the Project for a New American Century. Indeed, they had promoted an invasion of Iraq unceasingly since 1997. After 9/11, they went into high gear and the regime in power was ready to move forward. When, eighteen months later, U.S. troops entered Baghdad, they celebrated wildly. Now, they thought, all good things would follow. This program, imposed on the U.S. Congress and public in general through deception, manipulation, and demagoguery, has in fact been disastrous – above all, for the United States, which is far weaker today on the world scene than it was before September 11.

The hawks expected that the war in Iraq would be easily consummated. It has proved to be slow and draining, a continuing bleeding of lives and money with no immediate prospect of closure. The hawks expected that the traditional U.S. allies would respond to the display of military strength and determination by abandoning their hesitant steps toward political independence. Today, instead, the Paris-Berlin-Moscow axis, only a remote possibility in 2000, has become a continually developing reality with which Washington must deal. For the first time in history, Canada was not willing to participate in a war fought by its two closest allies, the United States and Great Britain. Today, the U.S.'s once-firm allies in East

Asia – Japan and South Korea – dragged their feet about sending troops to Iraq to help out the U.S. because public opinion at home was so hostile to the idea, and both countries insisted that the troops they did send would not be engaged in combat operations. The hawks expected that, once Iraq had been divested of weapons of mass destruction, others like Iran and North Korea would abandon their pretensions to nuclear weaponry. But the U.S. found no weapons of mass destruction in Iraq, and both North Korea and Iran have clearly speeded up rather than slowed down their programs of obtaining a nuclear arsenal, even as they make not too meaningful gestures about inspections. And the U.S. finds that it can't really do very much about it.

The true lesson of the invasion of Iraq concerns the *limitations* of the huge military power of the United States. Of course, today, the U.S. is far ahead of any other country – and, certainly, of a weak country like Iraq – in military strength. Of course, the U.S. is able to win battlefield operations. And, up to a point, it can deal with the threat of covert operations by non-state hostile groups, although this requires constant expensive vigilance and an appreciation that the ability to prevent such attacks will always be less than perfect. Some of them will succeed.

But in the end one has to be able to control the situation politically. War, as Clausewitz reminded us, is only the continuation of politics by other means. It is not a substitute for politics. Military prowess is hollow without political strength. And politically, the United States is weaker, not stronger, as a result of the Iraq war. Let us analyze this zone by zone.

Let us start with Europe. Ever since 1945, the alliance with Europe, Western Europe, was supposed to be the Rock of Gibraltar on which U.S. foreign policy was based. Europe, it was said, shared U.S. values. The dominant groups in the United States were all of European extraction. The cultural ties were deep. And of course, there were all kinds of institutional ties – military (NATO), economic (first the Marshall Plan, later OECD), political (G-7, the Trilateral Commission). If there were quarrels from time to time (particularly with France), these were in the end minor. When the chips were down, Western Europe and the U.S. were believed by both to be on the same side – as the joint bearers of the Judeo-Christian legacy, as the heirs of Greece and Rome, as the Free World versus the Communist world, as the North versus the South. All this was in fact largely true.

Relations now, however, have become quite frayed. No doubt, lip service is still being paid to the alliance, but the seeds of distrust are deep. The neocons basically scorn contemporary Europe, and have spread their views to a much larger U.S. public. They see Europeans as too pacifist (even cow-ardly), too addicted to the welfare state, too ready to appease the Muslim world, too "old-fashioned" (recall Rumsfeld's famous characterization of those less enthusiastic toward the U.S.'s Iraq policies as the "old Europe"). That many American people have felt this way about Europe is nothing new. What is new is that the view became official policy.

What this public proclamation of disdain did was trigger a European response that will not be easy to overcome. Many journalists speak in a facile manner about rampant "anti-Americanism" in Europe, especially in France. This is a gross exaggeration and, in many respects, actually less true of France than of other parts of Europe. But to frame the discussion in this way is to miss the cultural reality. Until 1945, Europe was in cultural terms the parent, or at least the elder sibling, of the United States, and this was the view not only of Europeans but of Americans themselves. Europeans tended to think of Americans as cultural adolescents, rebellious but naive. The Second World War changed all that. The United States emerged as the world's hegemonic power, the economic powerhouse, the political protec-tor of Western Europe against the Soviet Union, and in cultural terms the new center of Western, indeed of world, culture.

In the thirty or so years of American hegemony after 1945, the United States learned to hone its cultural rough edges; it tried to cease being Graham Greene's "ugly American." And Europeans learned to accept, even admire, the United States – for its technology, to be sure, but even for its political philosophy. Still, even among the most pro-American of Europeans, the switch in relative cultural status rankled. As European economic self-con-fidence rose again, and as Europe began to construct itself politically, there commenced a strong drive to reassert an autonomous, powerful cultural presence in the world that would be distinctively European. Thanks to Bush, this drive, so natural and so evident, has now come to be defined as one that should and will distinguish itself very clearly from the United States – culturally, and therefore politically as well as economically. Europe and the United States are now going their separate ways. They are not enemies, but the days of automatic alliance – at any level – are forever over.

The story of Russia is different. The collapse of the Soviet Union, though considered a positive thing by many, perhaps even most, Russian citizens, represented nonetheless a striking downgrading of Russian power in the world-system. This was most particularly evident in the military arena. As a consequence, Russia not only had to restructure itself internally, with all the difficulties that entailed, but also had to reposition itself on the world scene. The 1990s, the Yeltsin decade, is not one on which Russians look back with enthusiasm. During this period, Russia suffered a lowering of its standard of living, severe internal polarization, the financial crisis of 1997, the crumbling of its military strength and morale, and internal threats to the unity of the residual Russian Federation (most notably the continuing war in Chechnya).

When Putin came to power in 2000, his program was clearly the restoration not only of internal order and economic growth within Russia but of Russian power in the world-system. The question was how to do it, and in particular what diplomatic stance to take. Putin obviously did not want to recreate a cold war antagonism toward the United States. He flew to Crawford, Texas, to make a deal with George W. Bush. What he wanted most of all was to be accepted by the U.S. once again as a major player on the world scene. But behind all the flowery language, equality on the world scene was the one thing Bush was not ready to concede to Russia. So Putin began to play the field, seeking better relations in all directions – Western Europe (particularly Germany), China, India. And of course, he wished to reassert a central role for Russia in the Middle East, a continuing priority of Russian foreign policy since at least the eighteenth century.

The Iraq war was a decisive moment, crystallizing the results of three years of tentative outreach. For what Bush did, in effect, was to tell Russia that the U.S. did not consider it a major player even in the Middle East (and therefore, implicitly, not anywhere). Indeed, the United States used the occasion of the Iraq war to create and/or deepen the U.S.'s ties with countries formerly part of the Soviet Union – Central Asian countries in particular, but also Georgia and Azerbaijan. Far from reaffirming Russia's role, the U.S. was in fact working further to diminish it. France and Germany on the other hand reached out to Russia – as a permanent member of the Security Council, but also, no doubt, as a counterweight to the pro-American tendencies of the east-central European countries.

What had always been a theoretical possibility – a Paris-Berlin-Moscow axis – was stimulated into existence by the unilateralist pretensions of the Bush regime. The difficult initial building-blocks of this alliance were put into place by George W. Bush. The rest of the construction will be done by the three countries. As with all such structures, once consolidated, it will be hard to tear down. The world has passed from a theoretical possibility to a practical process.

As for the Muslim world, it has been a problem for the United States for all of the last half-century. This is the case for two reasons: the active and ever-greater commitment of the United States to Israel – not merely to its right to exist but to its ongoing policies vis-à-vis the Palestinians and the Arab world in general; and the continuing active intervention of the United States in the region because of the importance of its oil deposits. Bush did not create these tensions. What he has done is worse. He has undone the basic mechanism by which the U.S. government and most regimes in the region had hitherto managed to keep the tensions under some control. This mechanism was U.S. collusion in the deliberate ambiguity of the governments of the region in their public stance vis-à-vis the United States. In practice, they did most of what the United States wanted them to do (including at the military level) while frequently employing a quite different public rhetoric and, most important, allowing the multiple movements hostile to the United States (now grouped under the loose label of "terrorist" movements) to continue to work and even flourish within their borders.

The game of ambiguity was a constantly dangerous one for the regimes, as Anwar Sadat learned to his peril. The governments had to be very careful not to tilt too far in one direction or the other. But on the whole it was a possible game to play, and it satisfied the needs of the United States. Two regimes in particular were crucial in this regard: Saudi Arabia and Pakistan. It is therefore no accident that Osama bin Laden made it clear that the actions of his group, and most notably the September 11 attack, had as its primary objective the bringing down of these two regimes. What he hoped would happen, and it obviously did, was that the United States would react by insisting that these regimes end their ambiguity in the light of 9/11. It called upon them to throw themselves publicly and fully into the "war against terrorism." The U.S. largely succeeded with Pakistan, but thus far only partially with Saudi Arabia. The problem is that, once the veil of ambiguity is torn asunder, it cannot be easily restored. We shall see if the two regimes can survive. Any replacement regimes will be far less friendly to the United States.

At the same time, the hawks in Israel have taken advantage of the unprecedented level of support they have gotten from the Bush regime to destroy the Palestinian Authority, which had also been playing the same game of ambiguity. The Oslo accords may never have achieved their objective of an agreed-upon two-state outcome, but the real point here is that the world cannot go back to anything like the Oslo accords. It has been said for the last thirty years that only the United States could mediate the Israeli-Palestinian dispute. It seems to me that what Bush has done is to achieve the exact opposite. The United States is now totally compromised, and if there is ever to be a political resolution of the dispute, which seems increasingly unlikely, it will come about only if the United States is *not* involved in the process.

Latin America has been considered by the United States to be the latter's backyard, its private hunting-ground and zone of prime influence. The Monroe Doctrine dates, after all, from 1823. The Latin American revolutionary wave of the 1960s, which challenged U.S. dominance, was brought in check by the mid-1970s. As of 2000, the U.S. government could feel relatively relaxed about the political evolution of the continent. The governments were in civilian hands, the economic frontiers were largely open, and, except for Cuba, no government was hostile.

By 2004, the tone of the continent had radically changed. There are two reasons for this. On the one hand, the Bush regime overplayed the U.S. hand by deciding to push full steam ahead with the proposed Free Trade Area of the Americas (FTAA) at the very moment that Latin American governments found themselves in great economic difficulties as a result of the 2000 – 2003 recession. In particular, there was the spectacular crash of Argentina, the poster-child of the International Monetary Fund (IMF) of the 1990s. This crash affected not merely the working classes but the middle classes as well, who massively lost their savings and saw their standard of living collapse. The net outcome of three years of changing governments, popular insurrections, and general turmoil was a populist government that openly thumbed its nose at the IMF and has gotten away with it, to the great applause of the Argentinian people.

There have been parallel leftward thrusts elsewhere in Latin America with varying degrees of strength. In Brazil, economically the most important country, the Partido dos Trabalhadores (Workers Party), under Lula, won the elections. And while Brazil is not (yet) thumbing its nose at the IMF (to the dismay of many of Brazil's intellectuals), it is leading the struggle against the FTAA and acquiring support in this action from governments across the continent that had been expected to react more conservatively. Indeed, Brazil's brilliant diplomatic effort is moving Latin America toward a collective autonomy it has never known before.

If this has been possible, and this is the second reason for the change in atmosphere, it is because the United States has been so overwhelmed with its concentration on and difficulties in Iraq and the Middle East in general that it has been unable to expend the effort it traditionally did to hold Latin American resistance in check. This not only accounts for its surprisingly vacillating policy in Venezuela but also explains why it could not persuade either Mexico or Chile, among the Latin American governments most friendly toward the U.S., to support it in its quest for a Security Council resolution on Iraq in February 2003.

Are there not any bright spots? The Bush regime thinks it can point to three: east-central Europe, India, and Israel. In general, the countries of east-central Europe have had deeply pro-American policies ever since the collapse of the Soviet Union. The United States represented for them protection against the possible resuscitation of both Communism and Russia as an imperialist state as well as the nirvana of consumer wealth. They were not at all attuned to the West European need to separate themselves culturally and politically from the United States. Quite the contrary. Such sentiments of course predate George W. Bush and, indeed, had already begun to wane in the last years of Clinton. What Bush has done is to seize the opportunity of the so-called war on terrorism to pursue an active campaign of establishing military bases and other forms of active political cooperation in this region as well as in former Soviet republics in Central Asia and the Caucasus.

So, as the West European and the Russian reaction to these American intrusions takes concrete form, it is forcing choices on the east-central European countries that they would happily avoid. The situation is similar to the United States' forcing the end of ambiguity in the Muslim world. It amounts to a lose-lose option for the countries involved. And in the long run, Western Europe and Russia have more leverage than the United States, since the U.S. cannot supply the kind of economic assistance demanded by the populations of these countries. Nor is the U.S. ready to treat east-central Europe to the same relaxed visa arrangements it offers Western Europe, which is bitter news for these governments. Therefore, even in what seems to be the sunny climes of east-central Europe and Central Asia, the United States has set itself up for a fall that, when it occurs, will smash the possibility of the slow development of relations on which previous U.S. regimes had built their hopes and strategies.

India is a similar case in point. The basis of an improved relationship between India and the United States has been India's hope and expectation, first, that the U.S. would reverse its historic tilt toward Pakistan and, second, that the U.S. would give India a sizable slice of the technological pie because of the latter's vast supply of skilled personnel in the most profitable sectors of the world-economy. But, as in east-central Europe and Central Asia, the United States, by implicitly over-promising, has set itself up for a fall. For India is, in the medium run, a competitor in informatics and pharmaceutics and not an ally. And the U.S. cannot afford to loosen its ties with Pakistan. Quite the contrary. Its headache is that Pakistan might decide to loosen its ties with the United States. In any case, India is now responding to Brazilian seduction to create a Third World economic alliance.

As for Israel, the Bush administration has tied itself so closely to the fate of the Sharon/Likud regime that it risks going under when the regime does. And this is just a matter of time. The U.S. has shed the last vestige of any pretense toward being the neutral mediator. It will thereby find itself squeezed out of the equation.

There remains one last zone, East Asia – in many respects the most crucial for the future of the United States. And here, too, the Bush regime has shown itself to be most imprudent, although perhaps a bit more wary and cautious than in other regions. China is holding a very strong hand. It is a powerhouse of industrial growth. It is steadily gaining military strength. And it is conducting a foreign policy designed to create strong ties in East and Southeast Asia. Given the Bush economic policy at home, which has led to a massive and ever-growing deficit and imbalance of trade, the United States finds itself more dependent on China than the other way around. It needs continued Chinese purchase of U.S. Treasury bonds. And while there are good reasons for China to do this in its own interests, the policy is one that has negative implications for China and, in any case, is not the only possible one. So the U.S. finds itself unable to take a tough line with China on anything really important. Meanwhile, Japan is making an economic comeback. And the two Koreas are moving very slowly, but somewhat ineluctably, toward closer ties, perhaps even reunification.

Ten years from now it will be clear that what Bush has hastened is the creation of an East Asian zone of entente and, therefore, a powerful limit to U.S. power and authority in this region of the world. It is not that East Asia will necessarily be hostile to the United States. Rather, Bush has ensured that the future geo-political and geo-economic alliance of East Asia and the United States, faced with a resurgent Europe (which includes Russia), will be arranged more on East Asian terms than on U.S. terms.

As the United States loses manufacturing and white-collar jobs (especially in information technology and even biotechnology) to East Asia and Europe, it will seek to hold on to its one remaining strength, which is in the financial arena. And here the dollar is crucial. The dollar has gone up and down vis-à-vis other strong currencies for the last fifty years, but this has been largely the United States' doing. The strength of the dollar has always been a function not of its exchange rate but of the fact that it has been the only reserve currency in the world since 1945. And the reason for this has been not U.S. economic strength but U.S. political strength. Governments and capitalists across the world have felt safest holding dollars. And they have been correct in making this judgment until now.

The crazy economic policies of the Bush regime are bringing this political strength to an end. Given the incredible deficits that the Bush regime has been accumulating (and they are threatening to go much higher), governments and capitalists are no longer certain that the safe place to hold their money is in dollars. And of course, objectively, they are wise not to be certain. It is a matter of political and economic judgment and psychological comfort. This process is one that suddenly tilts and, once tilted, will not right itself. We can expect that this tilt will occur within the next few years. It is hard to see how it can be stopped now. After that, there will be no safe currency, with all the implications this has for economic chaos. But geopolitically, this circumstance will remove the last, surest lever with which the United States has been able to put pressure on other countries.

None of the foregoing was, as I have said, inevitable. The trends were always there, but they were unfolding slowly. What might have taken thirty years to come to pass, Bush has ensured will occur in five or ten. And instead of the soft landing that might have been possible, the United States is in for a very hard landing. The question now is not how this situation can be reversed – it no longer can – but what would be an intelligent way to handle the very rough waters through which the ship of state is passing.

THE EDITORS' GLOSS: William Engdahl's thesis is a controversial one, but it is no less feasible for being so. One suspects that it would prove impossible to ascribe to the dollar-euro conflict alone the ultimate cause of the invasion of Iraq. Indeed, much of what else is contained in this book would contradict that exclusive interpretation. But human actions are rarely the product of single motives; more often than not they stem from numerous factors. As for the Iraq war, Engdahl's point is that currency may certainly have been one of them. We spoke to Prof. William Anderson of Frostburg State University's College of Business about Engdahl's position. He had the same impression. "To surmise that it was the dollar issue that drove the invasion is tough to prove. One can talk about motives, but who knows what the real reasons were." Nevertheless, he also said that "I do agree with the overall contention of the author. I had heard the dollar theory from someone whom I respect, so I was not surprised by what I read."

Some of those we know who make their living studying financial markets and money politics second Engdahl's view. One is Brad King, president of King Money Management, Inc., who had this to say: "F. William Engdahl thinks out of the box. More often than not, anything obvious is obviously wrong if it comes from the political-money axis of Washington-New York. He claims the Iraq war is much more about whether or not oil – the life blood of modern civilization – will be sold in dollars or euros. Since the Federal Reserve was founded in 1913, the dollar has lost 95% of its purchasing power, but now it is in danger of a final meltdown, resulting in sharply higher interest rates, and a skyrocketing cost of living. Enron, Worldcom, and Arthur Andersen are only the tips of the debt-bergs and cooked books. Mr. Engdahl shares the good company of Warren Buffett who also thinks we should thoughtfully prepare for a major currency devaluation of the almighty United States dollar. Like the 1970s, the price of oil and gold is rapidly rising again, and, like the 1970s, there is war on the same Middle East stage set, with the same bad actors."

Meanwhile Bill Murphy of the Gold Anti-Trust Action Committee notes in general that "America has become a nation of double-speak." He explained to us that "the elitists in New York and Washington preach one thing to the world and the American public, and do another to satisfy their own hidden agendas. The surreptitious rigging of the gold price over the last decade to the detriment of the poor in sub-Saharan Africa is one example. As are the real reasons for the invasion of Iraq, so well articulated in this piece."

A New "American Century"?
Iraq and the Hidden Euro-Dollar Wars

• • • • • • • • •

F. William Engdahl

S OME TWO YEARS following the fall of Saddam Hussein's regime in Iraq, it is clear to most in the world that Washington did not risk such a war in order to deal with any threat from weapons of mass destruction, nor was Iraq a base for the Osama bin Laden's al-Qaeda organization. That left the very real question: why would the United States risk so much in terms of its international relations and its role as a defender of democracy and freedom to wage the brutal Iraq war?

One very crucial reason for the U.S. action has been virtually ignored in public discussion: namely, the strategic importance of the dollar to Washington's global role, to its very ability to finance future wars. Specifically, the role of the U.S. dollar as the world's primary reserve currency for world trade and financial transactions is the crucial issue at stake.

Despite the apparent swift U.S. military success in Iraq, the U.S. dollar has yet to benefit as a safe haven currency, two years after the fall of Baghdad. This was an unexpected development, as many currency traders had expected the dollar to strengthen on the news of a U.S. win. Capital continues to flow out of the dollar, largely into the euro. Many are beginning to ask whether the objective situation of the U.S. economy is far worse than the stock market would suggest. The future of the dollar is far from a minor issue of interest only to banks or currency traders. It stands at the heart of *Pax Americana,* or as it is called, the "American Century," the system of arrangements on which America's role in the world rests.

Yet, even as the dollar continues steadily dropping against the euro, Washington appears to be deliberately worsening the dollar's fall by its calculated public comments. What is taking place is a power game of the highest geopolitical significance, the most fateful perhaps since the emergence of the United States in 1945 as the world's leading economic power.

The coalition of interests which converged on war against Iraq as a strategic necessity for the United States included not only the vocal and highly visible neoconservative hawks around Defense Secretary Rumsfeld and his deputy, Paul Wolfowitz. It also included powerful interests on whose global role American economic influence depends – such as the influential energy sector around Halliburton, ExxonMobil, ChevronTexaco, and other giant multinationals. It also included the huge American defense industry interests around Boeing, Lockheed-Martin, Raytheon, Northrup Grumman, and others. The issue for these giant defense and energy conglomerates is not simply a few fat contracts from the Pentagon to rebuild Iraqi oil facilities and line the pockets of Dick Cheney or others. It is a game for the very continuance of American power in the coming decades of the new century. That is not to say that profits are not made in the process, but those are purely by-products of the global strategic issue.

In this power game, least understood is the role of preserving the dollar as the world reserve currency as a major driving factor contributing to Washington's power calculus over Iraq in the past months. American domination in the world ultimately rests on two pillars – its overwhelming military superiority, especially on the seas; and its control of world economic flows, through the role of the dollar as the world's reserve currency. More and more it is clear that the Iraq war was more about preserving the second pillar – the dollar role – than the first, the military. In the dollar role, oil is a strategic factor.

"American Century": The Three Phases

If we look back over the period since the end of World War II, we can identify several distinct phases of evolution of the American role in the world. The first phase, which began in the immediate post-war period (1945–1948) and the onset of the cold war, could be called the Bretton Woods Gold Exchange system.

Under the Bretton Woods system, in the immediate aftermath of the war, the order was relatively tranquil. The United States had emerged from the war clearly as the sole superpower, with a strong industrial base and the largest gold reserves of any nation. The initial task was to rebuild Western Europe and to create an Atlantic alliance against the Soviet Union. The role of the dollar was directly tied to that of gold. So long as America

enjoyed the largest gold reserves, and the U.S. economy was the most productive and efficient producer, the entire Bretton Woods currency structure, from French Franc to British Pound Sterling and German Mark, was
stable. Dollar credits were extended, along with Marshall Plan assistance
and credits, to finance the rebuilding of war-torn Europe. American companies, among them oil multinationals, gained nicely from dominating the
trade at the onset of the 1950s. Washington even encouraged creation of
the Treaty of Rome in 1958 in order to boost European economic stability,
and create larger U.S. export markets in the bargain. For the most part,
this initial phase of what *TIME Magazine* publisher Henry Luce called the
"American Century," in terms of economic gains, was relatively "benign"
for both the U.S. and Europe. The United States still had the economic
flexibility to move.

This was the era of American liberal foreign policy. The United States
was the hegemonic power in the Western community of nations. As it
commanded overwhelming gold and economic resources, compared with
Western Europe or Japan and South Korea, the United States could well
afford to be open in its trade relations to European and Japanese exports.
The trade-off was European and Japanese support for the role of the United
Sates during the cold war. American leadership was based during the 1950s
and early 1960s less on direct coercion and more on arriving at consensus,
whether in GATT trade rounds or on other issues. Organizations of elites,
such as the Bilderberg meetings, were organized to share the evolving consensus between Europe and the United States.

This first, more benign phase of the "American Century" came to an
end by the early 1970s.

The Bretton Woods Gold Exchange began to break down as Europe got
on its feet economically and began to become a strong exporter in the mid-
1960s. The growing economic strength of Western Europe coincided with
soaring U.S. public deficits, as Johnson escalated the tragic war in Vietnam.
All during the 1960s, France's de Gaulle began to take its dollar export earn-
ings and demand gold from the U.S. Federal Reserve, legal under Bretton
Woods at that time. By November 1967 the drain of gold from U.S. and
Bank of England vaults had become critical. The weak link in the Bretton
Woods Gold Exchange arrangement was Britain, the "sick man of Europe."
The link broke when Sterling was devalued in 1967. That merely accelerated
the pressure on the U.S. dollar, as French and other central banks increased
their call for U.S. gold in exchange for their dollar reserves. They calculated
that with the soaring deficits from the war in Vietnam, it was only a matter

of months before the United States itself would be forced to devalue against gold, so better to get their gold out at a high price.

By May 1971 the drain of U.S. Federal Reserve gold had become alarming, and even the Bank of England joined the French in demanding U.S. gold for their dollars. That was the point where, rather than risk a collapse of the gold reserves of the United States, the Nixon administration opted to abandon gold entirely, going to a system of floating currencies in August 1971. The break with gold opened the door to an entirely new phase of the "American Century." In this new phase, control over monetary policy was, in effect, privatized, with large international banks such as Citibank, Chase Manhattan, or Barclays assuming the role that central banks had had in the gold system, but entirely without gold. "Market forces" now could determine the dollar. And they did so with a vengeance.

The free floating of the dollar, combined with the 400% rise in OPEC oil prices in 1973 after the Yom Kippur War, created the basis for a second phase of the "American Century," the petro-dollar phase.

Recycling Petro-dollars

In the mid-1970s, the "American Century" system of global economic dominance underwent a dramatic change. An Anglo-American oil shock suddenly created enormous demand for the floating dollar. Oil importing countries from Germany to Argentina to Japan were all faced with *how* to export in dollars to pay their expensive new oil import bills. OPEC oil countries were flooded with new oil dollars. A major share of these oil dollars came to London and New York banks, where a new process was instituted. Henry Kissinger termed it "recycling petro-dollars." The recycling strategy was discussed already in May 1971 at the Bilderberg meeting in Saltsjoebaden, Sweden. It was presented by American members of Bilderberg, as detailed in the book *Mit der Ölwaffe zur Weltmacht*.[1]

OPEC suddenly was choking on dollars it could not use. U.S. and U.K. banks took the OPEC dollars and re-lent them as petro-dollar bonds or loans to countries of the third world desperate to borrow dollars to finance oil imports. The buildup of these petro-dollar debts by the late 1970s laid the basis for the third world debt crisis of the 1980s. Hundreds of billions

---

1. Wiesbaden: Edition Steinherz, 2002. The English translation of the book is available in a new edition: *A Century of War: Anglo-American Oil Politics and the New World Order* (London: Pluto Press, Ltd., 2004). Chapters 9 and 10 detail the creation and impact of the petro-dollar recycling scheme and the secret 1973 Saltsjoebaden meeting of the Bilderberg group in preparing the oil shock.

of dollars were recycled between OPEC, the London and New York banks, and back to third world borrowing countries.

By August 1982 the chain finally broke and Mexico announced it would likely default on repaying petro-dollar loans. The third world debt crisis began when Paul Volcker and the U.S. Federal Reserve had unilaterally hiked U.S. interest rates in late 1979 to try to save the failing dollar. After three years of record high U.S. interest rates, the dollar was "saved," but the entire developing sector was choking economically under usurious U.S. interest rates on their petro-dollar loans. To enforce debt repayment to the London and New York banks, the banks brought in the IMF to act as the "debt policeman." Public spending for health, education, and welfare was slashed on IMF orders to ensure the banks got timely debt service on their petro-dollars.

The petro-dollar hegemony phase was an attempt by the United States establishment to slow down its geopolitical decline as the hegemonic center of the post-war system. The IMF "Washington Consensus" was developed to enforce draconian debt collection on third world countries, force them to repay dollar debts, prevent the economic independence of the nations of the south, and keep the U.S. banks and the dollar afloat. The Trilateral Commission was created by David Rockefeller and others in 1973 in order to take account of the emergence of Japan as an industrial giant, and to try to bring Japan into the system. Japan, as a major industrial nation, was a major importer of oil. Japanese trade surpluses from export of cars and other goods were used to buy oil in dollars. The remaining surplus was invested in U.S. Treasury bonds, to earn interest. The G-7 was founded to keep Japan and Western Europe inside the U.S. dollar system. From time to time into the 1980s, various voices in Japan would call for three currencies – dollar, German mark, and yen – to share the world reserve role. It never happened. The dollar remained dominant.

From a narrow standpoint, the petro-dollar phase of hegemony seemed to work. Underneath, it was based on an ever-worsening decline in living standards across the world, as IMF policies destroyed national economic growth and broke open markets for globalizing multinationals seeking cheap production outsourcing in the 1980s and especially into the 1990s.

Yet, even in the petro-dollar phase, American foreign economic policy and military policy were dominated by the voices of traditional liberal consensus. American power depended on negotiating periodic new arrangements in trade or other issues with its allies in Europe, Japan, and East Asia.

[403]

A Petro-euro Rival?

The end of the cold war and the emergence of a new "single Europe" and the European Monetary Union in the early 1990s began to present an entirely new challenge to the "American Century." It took some years, more than a decade after the 1991 Gulf War, for this new challenge to emerge full-blown. The present Iraq war is only intelligible as a major battle in the new, third phase of securing American dominance. This phase has already been called "democratic imperialism," a favorite term of Max Boot and other neoconservatives. As Iraq events suggest, it is not likely to be very democratic, but it is definitely likely to be imperialist.

Unlike the earlier periods after 1945, in the new era U.S. freedom to grant concessions to other members of the G-7 is gone. Now raw power is the only vehicle to maintain American long-term dominance. The best expression of this argument comes from the neoconservative hawks around Paul Wolfowitz, Richard Perle, William Kristol, and others.

The point to stress, however, is that the neoconservatives enjoy such influence since September 11 because a majority in the U.S. power establishment finds their views useful to advance a new aggressive U.S. role in the world.

Rather than work out areas of agreement with European partners, Washington increasingly sees euro-land as the major strategic threat to American hegemony, especially the "old Europe" of Germany and France. Just as Britain in decline after 1870 resorted to increasingly desperate imperial wars in South Africa and elsewhere, so the United States is using its military might to try to advance what it can no longer achieve by economic means. Here the dollar is its Achilles heel.

With the creation of the euro over the past five years, an entirely new element has been added to the global system, one which defines what we can call a third phase of the "American Century." This phase, in which the latest Iraq war plays a major role, threatens to bring a new malignant or imperial phase to replace the earlier phases of American hegemony. The neoconservatives are open about their imperial agenda, while more traditional U.S. policy voices try to deny it. The economic reality faced by the dollar at the start of the new century defines this new phase in an ominous way.

There is a qualitative difference emerging between the two initial phases of the "American Century" – those of 1945–1973 and 1973–1999 – and the new phase of continued domination in the wake of the September 11 attacks and the Iraq war. Post-1945 American power before now, was predominately that of a hegemon. While a hegemon is the dominant power in an unequal distribution of power, its power is not generated by coercion alone, but also by consent among its allied powers. This is because the hegemon is compelled to perform certain services to the allies such as military security or regulating world markets for the benefit of the larger group, itself included. An imperial power has neither obligations to allies nor the freedom to meet them; it has only the raw dictates of how to hold on to its declining power – what some call "imperial overstretch." This is the world which neoconservative hawks around Rumsfeld and Cheney are suggesting America has to dominate with a policy of preemptive war.

A hidden war between the dollar and the new euro currency for global hegemony is at the heart of this new phase.

To understand the importance of this unspoken battle for currency hegemony, we first must understand that since the emergence of the United States as the dominant global superpower after 1945, U.S. hegemony has rested on two un-challengeable pillars. First, the overwhelming U.S. military superiority over all other rivals. The United States today spends on defense more than three times the total of all the members of the European Union, some $396 billion versus $118 billion in 2002, and more than the next 15 largest nations combined. Washington plans an added $2.1 trillion on defense over the next several years. No nation or group of nations can come close in defense spending. China is at least 30 years away from becoming a serious military threat. No one is serious about taking on U.S. military might.

The second pillar of American dominance in the world is the dominant role of the U.S. dollar as reserve currency. Until the advent of the euro in late 1999, there was no potential challenge to this dollar hegemony in world trade. The petro-dollar has been at the heart of dollar hegemony since the 1970s. Dollar hegemony is strategic to the future of American global pre-dominance, in many respects as important, if not more so, as overwhelming military power.

Dollar Fiat Money

The crucial shift took place when Nixon took the dollar off a fixed gold reserve to float against other currencies. This removed the restraints on printing new dollars. The limit was only how many dollars the rest of the world would take. By firm agreement with Saudi Arabia, as the largest OPEC oil producer (the "swing producer"), Washington guaranteed that the world's largest commodity, oil, essential for every nation's economy, the basis of all transport and much of the industrial economy, could only be purchased in world markets in dollars. The deal had been fixed in June 1974 by Secretary of State Henry Kissinger, establishing the U.S.-Saudi Arabian Joint Commission on Economic Cooperation. The U.S. Treasury and the New York Federal Reserve would "allow" the Saudi central bank, SAMA, to buy U.S. Treasury bonds with Saudi petro-dollars. In 1975 OPEC officially agreed to sell its oil only for dollars. A secret U.S. military agreement to arm Saudi Arabia was the *quid pro quo*.[1]

Until October 2000, no OPEC country dared violate the dollar price rule. So long as the dollar was the strongest currency, there was as well little reason to do so. But October was when French and other euro-land members finally convinced Saddam Hussein to defy the United States by demanding, for Iraq's "Oil-for-Food" oil, not dollars, "the enemy currency" as Iraq named it, but euros. On October 31, 2000, the UN Security Council Committee on relations between Iraq and Kuwait, which was charged with monitoring the "Oil-for-Food" Program, approved the request from Iraq earlier that month to denominate its oil sales in euros, beginning on November 6, 2000.[2] The euros would be deposited in a special UN account of the leading French bank, BNP Paribas. The U.S. government's Radio Liberty ran a short wire on the news, and the story quickly faded.[3]

This little-noted Iraqi move to defy the dollar in favor of the euro was, in itself, insignificant. Yet if it were to spread, especially at a point when the dollar was already weakening, it could create a panic sell-off of dollars by foreign central banks and OPEC oil producers. In the months before the latest Iraq war, hints in this direction were heard from Russia, Iran, Indonesia, and even Venezuela. An Iranian OPEC official, Javad Yarjani, delivered a detailed analysis of how OPEC at some future point might sell its oil to the E.U. for

---

1. An interesting narrative – though it is just one perspective – of how this U.S.-Saudi cooperation was brought about can be found on pp. 81–96 of John Perkins's book, *Confessions of an Economic Hit Man* (San Francisco: Berrett-Koehler Publishers, Inc., 2004).—Ed.

2. Letter dated March 26, 2001, from the Chairman of the Security Council Committee established by resolution 661 (1990) concerning the situation between Iraq and Kuwait, Security Council document S/2001/321, and Charles Recknagel, "Iraq: Baghdad Moves to Euro," *Radio Free Europe/Radio Liberty*, November 1, 2000, online.

3. The wire was picked up for about 48 hours by CNN and other media and promptly vanished from the headlines. Since William Clark's article, "The Real But Unspoken Reasons for the Upcoming Iraq War" appeared on the Internet on February 2, 2003, a lively online discussion of the oil-euro factor has taken place, but outside occasional references in the London *Guardian*, little in the mainstream media has been said of this strategic-background factor in the Washington decision to move against Iraq.

euros, not dollars. He spoke in April 2002 in Oviedo, Spain at the invitation of the E.U. All indications are that the Iraq war was seized on as the easiest way to deliver a deadly preemptive warning to OPEC and others not to flirt with abandoning the petro-dollar system in favor of one based on the euro.

Informed banking circles in the City of London and elsewhere in Europe privately confirm the significance of the Iraqi move from the petro-dollar to the petro-euro. "The Iraq move was a declaration of war against the dollar," one senior London banker told me recently. "As soon as it was clear that Britain and the U.S. had taken Iraq, a great sigh of relief was heard in London City banks. They said privately, 'now we don't have to worry about that damn euro threat.'"

Why would something so small be such a strategic threat to London and New York, or to the United States, that an American President would apparently risk fifty years of global alliance relations, and more, to make a military attack whose justification could not even be proved to the world?

The answer is the unique role of the petro-dollar in underpinning American economic hegemony.

How does it work? So long as almost 70% of world trade is done in dollars, the dollar is the currency which central banks accumulate as reserves. But central banks, whether in China or Japan or Brazil or Russia, do not simply stack dollars in their vaults. Currencies have one advantage over gold. A central bank can use it to buy the state bonds of the issuer, the United States. Most countries around the world are forced to control trade deficits or face currency collapse. Not the United States. This is because of the dollar's reserve currency role, and the underpinning of that reserve role is the petro-dollar. Every nation needs to get dollars to import oil, some more than others. This means their trade targets dollar countries, above all the U.S.

Because oil is an essential commodity for every nation, the petro-dollar system demands the build-up of huge trade surpluses in order to accumulate dollar surpluses. This is the case for every country but one – the United States, which controls the dollar and prints it at will or fiat. Because today the majority of all international trade is done in dollars, countries must go abroad to get the means of payment they cannot themselves issue. The entire global trade structure today works around this dynamic, from Russia to China, from Brazil to South Korea and Japan. Everyone aims to maximize dollar surpluses from their export trade.

To keep this process going, the United States has agreed to be "importer of last resort," because its entire monetary hegemony depends on this dollar recycling.

The central banks of Japan, China, South Korea, Russia, and the rest all buy U.S. Treasury securities with their dollars. This in turn allows the United States to have a stable dollar, far lower interest rates, and run a well over $500 billion annual balance-of-payments (or current account) deficit with the rest of the world.[1] The Federal Reserve controls the dollar printing presses, and the world needs its dollars. It is as simple as that.

The U.S. Foreign-Debt Threat

But, perhaps it's not so simple. It is a highly unstable system, as U.S. trade deficits and net debt or liabilities to foreign accounts are now well over 22% of GDP as of 2000, and climbing rapidly. The net foreign indebtedness of the United States – public as well as private – is beginning to explode ominously. In the past three years since the U.S. stock collapse and the re-emergence of budget deficits in Washington, the net debt position, according to a recent study by the Pestel Institute in Hanover, has almost doubled. In 1999, the peak of the dot.com bubble fury, U.S. net debt to foreigners was some $1.4 trillion. By the end of this year, it will exceed an estimated $3.7 trillion![2] Before 1989, the United States had been a net creditor, gaining more from its foreign investments than it paid to them in interest on Treasury bonds or other U.S. assets. Since the end of the cold war, the United States has become a net foreign debtor nation to the tune of $3.7 trillion! This is not what Hilmar Kopper would call "peanuts."

It does not require much foresight to see the strategic threat of these deficits to the role of the United States. With an annual current account (mainly trade) deficit of $500 or $600 billion, some 5% of GDP, the United States must import or attract at least $1.4 billion[3] every day to avoid a dollar collapse and keep its interest rates low enough to support the debt-burdened corporate economy. That net debt is getting worse at a dramatic pace. Were France, Germany, Russia, and a number of OPEC oil countries now to shift even a small portion of their dollar reserves into euros to buy

---

1. The preliminary figure for the current account deficit for the year 2004, as reported by the Bureau of Economic Analysis, was $665.9 billion. Some suggest that the most recent figures, based upon the first part of 2005, indicate an annual rate of current account deficit of up to 7% of GDP, or about $700 billion.—Ed.

2. As of December, 2004, the *total debt* of the U.S. (personal, business, and government – local, state, and federal) was over 400% of GDP! The external portion of that debt as a percentage of GDP was up to 24% as of the end of 2003 – somewhere around $3 trillion – and is projected to be 64% by 2014.—Ed.

3. This figure of the *daily* capital inflow requirement over the last several years has been reported variously as anywhere between $1.2 and 5 billion.—Ed.

bonds from Germany, France, or the like, the United States would face a strategic crisis beyond any other of the post-war period. It would seem reasonable and accurate to conclude that one of the most hidden strategic reasons for the decision to go for "regime change" in Iraq was to preempt this financial and economic threat to the dollar and to the United States. It is as simple and as cold as that. The future of America's sole superpower status depended on preempting the threat emerging from Eurasia and euro-land especially. Iraq was and is a chess piece in a far larger strategic game, one for the highest stakes.

The Euro Threatens American Hegemony

When the euro was launched at the end of the last decade, leading E.U. government figures, bankers from Deutsche Bank's Norbert Walter, and French President, Jacques Chirac, went to major holders of dollar reserves – China, Japan, Russia – and tried to convince them to shift out of dollars and into euros, at least a part of their reserves. However, that proposed move clashed with the need to devalue the too-high euro so that German exports could stabilize euro-land growth. The euro therefore fell until 2002.

With the debacle of the bursting U.S. dot.com bubble, the Enron and World.com finance scandals, and the recession in the U.S., the dollar began to lose its attraction for foreign investors. The euro gained steadily until the end of 2002. Then, as France and Germany prepared their secret diplomatic strategy in the UN Security Council to block war, rumors surfaced that the central banks of Russia and China had quietly begun to dump dollars and buy euros. The result was a dollar free-fall on the eve of war. The stage was set should Washington lose the Iraq war, or should it turn into a long, bloody debacle.

But Washington, leading New York banks, and the higher echelons of the U.S. establishment clearly knew what was at stake. Iraq was not about ordinary chemical or even nuclear weapons of mass destruction. The "weapon of mass destruction" was the threat that others would follow Iraq and shift to euros out of dollars, creating a mass destruction of the United States' hegemonic economic role in the world. As one economist termed it, an end to the dollar reserve role would be a "catastrophe" for the United States. Interest rates of the Federal Reserve would have to be pushed higher than in 1979 when Paul Volcker raised rates above 17% to try to stop the collapse of the dollar then. Few realize that the 1979 dollar crisis was also a direct result of moves by Germany and France under Schmidt and Giscard to defend Europe, along with the selling of U.S. Treasury bonds by Saudi Arabia and others to protest Carter administration policy. It is also worth recalling that after the Volcker dollar rescue, the Reagan administration, backed by many of today's neoconservative hawks, began huge U.S. military defense spending in order to challenge the Soviet Union.

Eurasia Versus the Anglo-American Island Power

This fight over petro-dollars and petro-euros, which started in Iraq, is by no means over, despite the apparent victory there of the United States. The euro was created by French geopolitical strategists to establish a multi-polar world after the collapse of the Soviet Union. The aim was to balance the overwhelming dominance of the U.S. in world affairs. Significantly, French strategists rely on a British geopolitical strategist, namely, Sir Halford J. Mackinder,[1] to develop their rival power alternative to the U.S.

---

1. Halford John (later Sir Halford) Mackinder (1861–1947) was the most prominent British academic geographer of his time. He joined the London School of Economics upon its foundation in 1895, directed the School from 1903 to 1908, and served there variously as reader and professor through 1925. In 1886 he was admitted to the Royal Geographical Society (RGS). He also held posts at Oxford University and the University of London. He was principal of the University Extension College of Christ Church College (of Oxford University) in Reading; his work there was instrumental in the later founding of the University of Reading. He was active in British politics and was a Member of Parliament from 1910 to 1922 for Camlachie, Glasgow. Francis P. Sempa, in his biographical sketch of Mackinder, reports that "[n]o one understood better the important relationship between geography and world history than the great British geographer, Halford John Mackinder." His important works, besides his 1904 paper, all deal with his constant theme, connecting geography with the study of history and geopolitics in order to demonstrate the strategic importance of geography. They include "The Scope and Methods of Geography," presented to the RGS on January 31, 1887 (*Proceedings of the R. G. S.*, Vol. 9, 1887, pp. 141–60, reprinted London: Royal Geographical Society, 1951), *Britain and the British Seas* (New York: D. Appleton & Co., 1902), *Democratic Ideals and Reality: A Study in the Politics of Reconstruction* (first published, London, Constable and Co. Ltd., 1919). The last significant statement of his views is "The Round World and the Winning of the Peace," *Foreign Affairs*, July, 1943. He was awarded the Charles P. Daley Medal by the American Geographical Society at the American Embassy in London on March 31, 1944. On the occasion Ambassador John Winant remarked that Mackinder was the first scholar who fully enlisted geography as an aid to statecraft and strategy. In 1945 he was awarded the Patron's Medal by the RGS; the Society's president noted that "[a]s a political geographer his reputation is . . . worldwide." Mackinder's work has been referenced by individuals such as career "geopoliticians" Zbigniew Brzezinski and Henry Kissinger, strategic historians Paul Kennedy and Colin Gray, and others, including Eugene Rostow, Robert Nisbet, and former U.S. State Department geographer George J. Demko. Sempa concludes his biographical essay of Mackinder by saying that "[m]ore than fifty years [after his death,] statesmen and strategists still operate in Mackinder's world."—Ed.

In February of 2003, a French intelligence-connected newsletter, *Intelligence Online*, published a piece called, "The Strategy Behind the Paris-Berlin-Moscow Tie." Referring to the UN Security Council bloc of France-Germany-Russia which tried to prevent the U.S.-British war in Iraq, the Paris report notes the recent efforts of European and other powers to create a counter-power to that of the United States. Referring to the new ties of France with Germany and more recently with Putin, they note:

> [A] new logic and even dynamic seems to have emerged. An alliance between Paris, Moscow and Berlin, running from the Atlantic to Asia, could foreshadow a limit to U.S. power. For the first time since the beginning of the 20th century, the notion of a world heartland – the nightmare of British strategists – has crept back into international relations.[1]

Mackinder, the father of British geopolitics, wrote in his remarkable paper, "The Geographical Pivot of History," written for the Royal Geographical Society and delivered thereto on January 25, 1904, that the only possible threat to the naval supremacy of Britain would be the control of the Eurasian heartland, from Normandy, France, to Vladivostok, Russia, by a single power or united bloc. British diplomacy until 1914 was based on preventing any such Eurasian threat. At that time the threat was the expansion policy of the German Kaiser eastwards with the Baghdad Railway and the buildup of the German Navy under Tirpitz. World War I was the result. Referring to the ongoing efforts of the British and later the Americans to prevent a Eurasian combination as rival, the Paris intelligence report stressed:

> That strategic approach [i.e., to create Eurasian heartland unity] lies at the origin of all clashes between Continental powers and maritime powers [U.K., U.S. and Japan] .... It is Washington's supremacy over the seas that, even now, dictates London's unshakeable support for the U.S. and the alliance between Tony Blair and Bush.

Another well-connected French journal, ReseauVoltaire.net, wrote on the eve of the Iraq war that the dollar was "the Achilles heel of the USA."[2] An understatement, to put it mildly.

---

1. "The Strategy Behind the Paris-Berlin-Moscow Tie," *Intelligence Online*, No.447, February 20, 2003. *Intelligence Online* Editor, Guillaume Dasquie, is a French specialist on strategic intelligence and has worked for French intelligence services on the bin Laden case and other investigations. His reference to French Eurasian geopolitics clearly reflects high-level French thinking.

2. *Reseau voltaire.net*, "Suprematie du dollar: Le Talon d'Achille des USA," appeared April 4, 2003. It provides a French analysis of the vulnerability of the dollar system on the eve of Iraq war.

Iraq Was Planned Long Before

This threat of a euro policy emerging among France, Iraq, and other countries led some leading circles in the U.S. policy establishment to begin thinking of preempting threats to the petro-dollar system well before Bush was even President. While Perle, Wolfowitz, and other key neoconservatives played a leading role in developing a strategy to preserve the faltering system, a new consensus was also being shaped around major figures of the traditional cold war establishment, such as Rumsfeld and Cheney.

In September 2000, during the first Bush presidential campaign, a small Washington think-tank – the Project for a New American Century – released a major policy study: "Rebuilding America's Defenses: Strategies, Forces, and Resources for a New Century." The report is useful to better understand present administration policy in many areas. On Iraq it states:

> The United States has sought for decades to play a more permanent role in Gulf regional security. While the unresolved conflict with Iraq provides the immediate justification, the need for a substantial American force presence in the Gulf transcends the issue of the regime of Saddam Hussein.

This PNAC paper is the essential basis for the September 2002 "National Security Strategy of the United States of America." The PNAC's paper supports a

> blueprint for maintaining global U.S. pre-eminence, precluding the rise of a great power rival, and shaping the international security order in line with American principles and interests. The American Grand Strategy must be pursued as far into the future as possible.

Further, the U.S. must, "discourage advanced industrial nations from challenging our leadership or even aspiring to a larger regional or global role."

The PNAC membership in 2000 reads like a roster of the Bush administration today. It included Cheney and his wife Lynne Cheney; neoconservative Cheney aide Lewis Libby; Donald Rumsfeld; and Rumsfeld's former deputy, Paul Wolfowitz. It also included NSC Middle East head, Elliott Abrams; John Bolton of the State Department;[1] Richard Perle; and William Kristol. Former Lockheed-Martin vice president, Bruce Jackson, and ex-CIA head James Woolsey were also on board, along with Norman Podhoretz, another founding neocon. Woolsey and Podhoretz speak openly of being currently involved in "World War IV."

1. Currently nominated U.S. ambassador to the United Nations.—Ed.

It is becoming increasingly clear to many that the war in Iraq is about preserving a bankrupt "American-Century" model of global dominance. It is also clear that Iraq is not the end. What is not yet clear and must be openly debated around the world is how to replace the failed petro-dollar order with a just, new system for global economic prosperity and security.

U.S. "Dollarizes" Post-war Iraq

With no fanfare and little media attention, shortly after the fall of Baghdad Washington moved to reestablish the dollar as the currency of Iraq and to take full control over the Iraqi economy. France and other European members of the UN feebly tried to keep a UN weapons inspection program in place to allow the UN to continue supervision of the "Oil-for-Food" Program. The Pentagon and the U.S. State Department rode roughshod over the UN and brought the dollar back as currency in post-war Iraq. Indeed, Washington flew planeloads of dollars into the country to pay Iraqi civil servants, just to be certain the dollar reigned supreme in the new Iraq.

The brief struggle between "old Europe" and the U.S.-U.K. coalition was covered in a *Newsweek* story carried only on the Internet, detailing the American desire to do away with "Oil-for-Food" and its related bureaucratic requirement coupling the disarmament of Iraq to euro-denominated oil sales. The stakes on both sides were amply explained, as were the "cover stories" for the opposing positions.

> Nobody in an official capacity on either side of the Atlantic wants to say . . . in so many words [that "it's the dollar vs. the euro"]. We say that the war isn't over, that it's our job – and only our job – to continue the search for weapons of mass destruction and to bring stability to Iraq with an interim government. The Europeans and the United Nations insist that they should resume the task of searching for WMDs. Until that issue is settled, they say, international sanctions can't formally end. (France is only proposing to "suspend" them.)
>
> In fact, the dispute isn't about WMDs at all. It's about something else entirely: who gets to sell – and buy – Iraqi oil, and what form of currency will be used to denominate the value of the sales. That decision, in turn, will help decide who controls Iraq, which, in turn, will represent yet another skirmish in a growing global economic conflict. We want a secular, American-influenced pan-ethnic entity of some kind to control the massive oil fields (Iraq's vast but only real source of wealth). We want that entity to be permitted to sell the oil to whomever it wants, denominated in dollars. We want those revenues – which would quickly mount into the billions – to be funneled into the rebuilding of the country, essentially (at least initially) by American companies. Somewhere along the line, British, Australian and perhaps even Polish companies would

get cut in (Poland provided troops). President Bush doesn't dare sell the war as a job generator, but it may, in fact, produce more than a few.

The Europeans and the United Nations want the inspections regime to resume because as long as it is in place, the UN "Oil-for-Food" Program remains in effect. Not only does France benefit directly – its banks hold the deposits and its companies have been involved in the oil sales – the entire EU does as well, if for no other reason than many of the recent sales were counted not in dollars but in euros. The United Nations benefits because it has collected more than a billion dollars in fees for administering the program. As long as the 1990 sanctions remain in effect, Iraq can't "legally" sell its oil on the world market. At least, to this point, tankers won't load it without UN permission, because they can't get insurance for doing so.

Sometime in the next few weeks, push will come to shove. There are storage tanks full of Iraqi crude waiting in Turkish ports . . . . Meanwhile, if the rest of the world tries to block any and all Iraq oil sales, it's possible that American companies will find a way to become the customer of first and last resort.

And we'll pay in dollars.[1]

On May 22, 2003, push came to shove, and the UN passed Resolution 1483, on Washington's demand, creating a U.S.-British administered "Development Fund for Iraq." In practical terms, that resolution quietly ended the "Oil-for-Food" Program and reverted Iraqi oil sales from euros back to dollars.[2] The following month, the *Financial Times* reported that Iraq was "back into the international oil market for the first time since the war," moving to sell 10 million barrels of oil to the highest bidder, and "switch[ing] the transaction back to dollars – the international currency of oil sales."

As noted earlier, one prominent City of London banker this author spoke with at that time related, off-the-record, that City bankers were confident that the threat to the dollar as currency for world oil trade was over, now that Iraqi oil would again sell for dollars, and that Washington had demonstrated with its military "shock and awe" what might happen to other oil-rich regimes considering bolting from the dollar. Yet, two years later, the issue remains far from settled.

Iraq Was Not the End

The central banks of China and Japan, the second and third largest importers of oil after the United States, also hold the world's largest

1. "In Round 2, It's the Dollar vs. Euro," *Newsweek* "web exclusive," posted at *www.msnbc.com*, April 23, 2003.

2. The extremely limited media coverage of the shift back to dollar-denominated oil sales included an article in the *Financial Times* by Carol Hoyos and Kevin Morrison, "Iraq Returns to International Oil Market," June 5, 2003, online, and the *Newsweek* "web exclusive."

reserves of dollars. China holds more than $540 billion in dollars, mostly in the form of U.S. Treasury bonds and notes, to earn interest. Japan holds even more. Officially, as of the end of 2004, both central banks held a combined $1.3 trillion in U.S. dollars. The Central Bank of Russia, largely owing to its significant export of oil and gas amid rising prices, held some $121 billion in dollar reserves at the end of 2004. Each of those central banks openly warned Washington to stop talking down the dollar, and each central bank, in the last weeks of 2004, suggested that a decision to shift out of dollar reserves into a greater share of euros was being considered.

On December 6, 2004, the Bank for International Settlements of Basle, Switzerland, a central bank umbrella organization, reported what it termed a "subtle but noticeable shift" reducing their dollar deposits in favor of euros. "Since the third quarter of 2001," the BIS report stated, "oil revenue seems to have been channeled increasingly into euro and other currency deposits."[1] In an article published the same day, the *Financial Times* reported that "[m]embers of the Organisation of Petroleum Exporting Countries have cut the proportion of deposits held in dollars from 75 per cent in the third quarter of 2001 to 61.5 per cent." The piece went on to explain that

Middle Eastern central banks have reportedly switched reserves from dollars to euros and sterling to avoid incurring losses as the dollar has fallen and prepare for a shift away from pricing oil exports in dollars alone.[2]

Private Middle East investors are believed to be worried about the prospect of U.S.-held assets being frozen as part of the war on terror, leading to accelerated dollar-selling after the re-election of President George W. Bush.

The BIS data, in the organisation's quarterly review, state that OPEC countries' stock of dollar-denominated deposits has fallen by 4 per cent in cash terms since 2002 in spite of OPEC revenues' surging to record levels this year.[3]

1. *NewsMax Wires*, December 7, 2004.

2. Jim Turk, writing at *GoldMoney.com* on February 18, 2004, noted that "it seems clear that OPEC and the other oil exporters are already pricing crude oil in terms of euros, at least tacitly." His comment is based upon a detailed review of a Department of Commerce report entitled "U.S. International Trade in Goods and Services." Turk notes that, according to that date, "the price of crude oil in terms of euros is essentially unchanged throughout [the] 3-year period [2001–2003]." His analysis says, "As the dollar has fallen, the dollar price of crude oil has risen. But the euro price of crude oil remains essentially unchanged throughout this 3-year period. It does not seem logical that this result is pure coincidence. It is more likely the result of purposeful design, namely, that OPEC is mindful of the dollar's decline and increases the dollar price of its crude oil by an amount that offsets the loss in purchasing power OPEC's members would otherwise incur. In short, OPEC is protecting its purchasing power as the dollar declines." Hence his conclusion that "OPEC and the other oil exporters are already pricing crude oil in terms of euros."—Ed.

3. Steve Johnson, and Javier Blas, "OPEC Sharply Reduces Dollar Exposure," *The*

A senior banker at BNP Paribas bank, interestingly the same bank which had held the custody account in euros for Iraq under the "Oil-for-Food" Program, also told the *Financial Times*, "After the re-election of George Bush, the Middle East started to sell dollars like crazy due to the fears of assets being frozen."

Yet the selling of dollar assets *alone* is not a mortal threat to dollar hegemony. What is such a threat, however, is the potential loss of the role of the dollar as the sole currency for world oil trade, as Washington fully realizes.

It is instructive to review the world map in terms of Washington's statements as to its wishes for possible "regime change." Venezuela, which had repeatedly supported the shift of OPEC oil trade to euros, has been named by a number of hawks close to the Bush administration as a priority. Sudan has been as well, and there China has built a major oil pipeline to secure urgently needed oil imports.[1] The intense involvement of Washington in the outcome of the Ukraine Presidential elections in November 2004 and the re-run in December reportedly had much to do with the central role of Ukraine as a transit point for Russian oil and gas, and Eurasian political domination by Washington.[2]

Even more ominously, Iran quietly began accepting euros for its oil exports to the E.U. in the spring of 2003,[3] and has publicly discussed the creation of an oil-trading market for OPEC and the Middle East, which "could threaten the supremacy of London's International Petroleum Exchange,"[4] and which would most likely be denominated in euros.[5] It is common knowledge at this point that the country remains high on the regime-change hit list of the Pentagon and White House.

When U.S. civilian administrator Paul Bremer III left Iraq in July 2004, as head of the U.S.-created Coalition Provisional Authority, he handed

Financial Times, December 6, 2004, online.

1. Gordon Prather, "Decision 2004: Iran or Sudan?" *Antiwar.com*, July 31, 2004.

2. F. William Engdahl, "Washington's interest in Ukraine: Democracy or Energy Geopolitics?" Centre for Research on Globalisation (*www.globalresearch.ca*), December, 20 2004 (http://www.globalresearch.ca/articles/ENG412A.html).

3. C. Shivkumar, "Iran offers oil to Asian union on easier terms," *The Hindu Business Line*, June 16, 2003, online.

4. Terry Macalister, "Iran Takes on West's Control of Oil Trading," *The Guardian*, June 16, 2004, online. Macalister further reports that London's IPE was "bought in 2001 by a consortium that includes BP, Goldman Sachs, and Morgan Stanley."

5. William Clark, "The Real Reasons Why Iran is the Next Target: The Emerging Euro-Denominated International Oil Marker," Centre for Research on Globalisation (*www.globalresearch.ca*), October 27, 2004.

nominal control of Iraq to an interim Iraqi caretaker regime under former CIA asset Iyad Allawi.

Before leaving, Bremer, on orders from Washington, signed into force some 100 new laws. The purpose was to ensure that any future Iraqi regime remain faithful to U.S. economic wishes, and that Washington would control every aspect of Iraqi national sovereignty. The laws, known as the 100 Orders, dramatically reorganized Iraq's economy on American-mandated "free-market" lines. They ordered the privatization of some 200 state companies, and allowed 100% foreign ownership of Iraqi businesses, coupled with the unrestricted ability to withdraw profits, tax-free, from Iraq.

No future Iraqi government, however elected, can undo the U.S. laws. To ensure so, Bremer named U.S.-chosen administrators to oversee every State Ministry for a period of 5 years. Little wonder that some Iraqis were skeptical about the outcome of the "elections."

Now, as Iraq continues in more-or-less a state of internal chaos, and the American "regime-change" hit list is being refined (and potentially acted upon), it is more important than ever to rethink the entire post-war monetary order anew. The present French-German-Russian alliance, to create a counterweight to the United States, requires not merely a French-led version of the petro-dollar system, i.e., some petro-euro system that continues the bankrupt "American Century" with only a French accent and euros replacing dollars. That would only continue to destroy living standards across the world, adding to both human waste and soaring unemployment in industrial as well as developing nations. We must entirely rethink what began briefly with some economists during the 1998 Asian crisis. We must develop the basis of a new monetary system, one which *supports* human development and does not destroy it.

I don't care about international law. I don't want to hear the words "international law" again. We are not concerned with international law.

—Unidentified military president of a
Combatant Status Review Tribunal,
Guantánamo Bay, Cuba, as revealed by
transcripts in April 2005

The President is not a tribunal.

—Judge James Robertson, U.S. District Court
for Washington, D.C., November 8, 2004,
on the insufficiency of the President's
determination as to the status of detainee
Salim Ahmed Hamdan in light of the
requirement of Geneva Convention III,
Article 5

We are aware that this decision does not make it easier to deal with the reality. This is the fate of democracy, as not all means are acceptable to it, and not all methods employed by its enemies are open to it. Sometimes, a democracy must fight with one hand tied behind its back. Nonetheless, it has the upper hand. Preserving the rule of law and recognition of individual liberties constitute an important component of its understanding of security. At the end of the day, they strengthen its spirit and strength and allow it to overcome its difficulties.

—Aharon Barak, president, Supreme Court
of Israel, on the court's decision in *Pub.
Comm. Against Torture in Isr. v. Gov't of
Israel* (53(4) P.D. 817, 845), holding that the
violent interrogation of a suspected terrorist
is not lawful even if thought necessary to
save human lives

One Good Scandal Deserves Another: The Snowballing of American Lawlessness

THE EDITORS' GLOSS: When the President's military commissions were developed, Patrick Philbin, a deputy in the DoJ Legal Counsel's office, sent a memo to Alberto Gonzalez saying that the 9/11 attacks were "plainly sufficient" to invoke the laws of war. The opinion created the "war on terror" (GWOT), illustrating, in the President's words, "new thinking in the law of war." So the GWOT rolls on; "...extremists...are being hunted down on every continent by an unprecedented global coalition," Secretary Rumsfeld reminds us (*Financial Times*, August 1, 2005). Yet these "extremists" are frequently mere *suspects*; applying the laws of war to one-on-one pursuits of alleged criminals has made the CIA and U.S. special forces judge, jury, and executioner, "licensed" to conduct doubtful drone strikes in Yemen (November 2002), Pakistan (May 2005), and elsewhere, or pluck people from around the globe and send them to Gitmo where the Geneva Conventions (GC) are said not to apply.

Dr. Rona (who speaks for himself, not for his former (the ICRC) or current (Human Rights First) employer) addresses the error of approaching the GWOT as an "armed conflict," and the bluster of its defenders who lament preoccupation "with whether we are treating captured cut-throats nicely enough" (Thomas Sowell, June 8, 2005). Never mind "nicely": what about the law? Readers should consult Rona's footnotes; they are gems refuting current "thinking." One cites Jean Pictet, the *authoritative* GC commentator, refuting the notion that so-called "terrorists" aren't covered by them: "Every person in enemy hands must have some status under international law . . . . There is no intermediate status; nobody in enemy hands can be outside the law."

The most important of Rona's points is that "'war on terror' is a rhetorical device having no legal significance." What matters are facts on the ground. Elizabeth Wilmshurst, an ex-British Foreign Office deputy legal adviser, made the same point; so did a U.S. judge speaking to "shoe-bomber" Richard Reid: "You are not an enemy combatant, you are a terrorist. You are not a soldier in any army . . . . " The Spanish attorney general got it right, too: "The fight against terrorism is not to be seen as a war, because the terrorists aren't combatants, they're delinquents and criminals and the fight needs to be fought with legal proceedings and procedures."

John Ashcroft warned that America's enemies were diverting attention from the "military offensive abroad" to the "legal defensive at home." Abu Ghraib and other scandals point to the exact contrary: attention to the law at home, and abroad, seems to be *exactly* what's required.

The Law of Armed Conflict and the "War on Terror"

· · · · · · · · · ·

Gabor Rona, J.D., Ll.M.

T HE TITLE OF a panel I recently participated in at the American Enterprise Institute – "Developing a Legal Framework to Combat Terrorism" – assumes the need for a new legal framework to fill a large void in order to combat terrorism successfully. While there will always be room for tinkering around the margins of any legal framework, the implication that a new one needs to be developed specifically to combat terrorism is doubtful. At the very least, we should be skeptical of the view that the existing complementary frameworks of criminal law, human rights law, the web of multilateral and bilateral arrangements for interstate cooperation in police work and judicial assistance, and the law of armed conflict fail to provide tools necessary to combat terrorism.

Critics of the status quo seem to have honed in on the law of armed conflict – historically referred to as the laws of war or *jus in bello*, and now known as international humanitarian law, or IHL[1] – as the weak link in this chain. In reality, for many of the same reasons that truth is said to be the first casualty in war, IHL is increasingly misapplied, misinterpreted, misunderstood, and maligned. Let me offer a view on what IHL actually does and does not cover, what it permits and prohibits. In so doing I will hope to lay a foundation for understanding why that body of law is worthy

---

1. International Committee of the Red Cross, "International Humanitarian Law" (http://www.icrc.org/Web/Eng/siteeng0.nsf/htmlall/section_ihl_in_brief), defining "international humanitarian law" as "a set of rules which seek, for humanitarian reasons, to limit the effects of armed conflict. It protects persons who are not or are no longer participating in the hostilities and restricts the means and methods of warfare." Its central purpose is to limit and prevent human suffering in times of armed conflict. The rules are to be observed not only by governments and their armed forces, but also by armed opposition groups and any other parties to a conflict. The four Geneva Conventions of 1949 and their two Additional Protocols of 1977 are the principal instruments of IHL.

of our respect, why it should not be invoked where it does not apply, and why it must be obeyed when properly invoked.

I. The Existence and Fields of Application of IHL: International and Non-international Armed Conflict

The world is a complicated place, made no less so by law and lawyers. The collected wisdom of my professional ancestors has, over the course of human history, described (rather than invented) a number of constructs by which we govern our affairs: criminal and civil law, domestic and international law, laws of war and laws applicable in peace, etc. These constructs are not alternatives to be chosen at will, like the dishes in alternative columns of a Chinese restaurant menu. Their existence and applicability is not subject to, nor should their utility be made subject to, the shifting concepts of momentary taste or convenience.

It is unfortunate that I need to defend the very existence of IHL, but there are those who have recently questioned whether such a thing exists. Let me put that question to rest quickly and firmly. International humanitarian law, the law of armed conflict, the *jus in bello,* dates back to the time man first decided against a scorched earth policy or fighting to the death. More recently, it has been codified into international treaties, the most prominent of which are the Geneva Conventions (GCs). It has also been incorporated into domestic laws that, for example, criminalize the prohibitions contained in the GCs – thus we have war crimes under national law.[1] It is also reflected in the universally acknowledged body of customary law – that which binds states even in the absence of international or domestic codification, and which has been described as what states do out of a sense of legal obligation.[2]

To distinguish between the realms to which IHL does and does not belong is to distinguish between war and peace or, to be more precise, between the existence and absence of armed conflict. What do we mean by "armed conflict"? The term (the legal term for war) is not directly defined in the GCs (the internationally agreed-upon rules of warfare), but it is generally understood to involve the use of force between two or more states (international armed conflict), or a certain threshold of violence between a state and armed groups, or between armed groups within a state (non-international armed conflict).

---

1. See, for example, United States War Crimes Act of 1996, 18 U.S.C §2441 (2000).

2. Jack L. Goldsmith and Eric A. Posner, "A Theory of Customary International Law," *University of Chicago Law Review,* Vol. 66, 1999, pp. 1113, 1116–17.

IHL covers these two types of armed conflict, international and non-international. The first, involving the use of armed force between states,[1] is relatively easy to discern, since the frequency, duration, and degree of violence are not relevant. The second type, non-international or internal armed conflict, involves rebels fighting against a state or against other rebels within a state, or such conflict spilling over borders into other states.[2] By contrast with international armed conflict, questions of means and methods, frequency, duration, and degrees of violence are critical to determining the existence of internal armed conflict.[3] In the internal context, these threshold issues *are the only means of distinguishing peacetime* (which might include crime, riots, and sporadic acts of violence that may or may not be organized to varying degrees) *from war.*[4] Identification of parties – a given in international armed conflict – is also an essential, though sometimes elusive, requisite of internal armed conflict.[5]

II. Application of the Laws of War Is Restricted to War

IHL, like criminal and human rights law, reflects a compromise, balancing the interests of state security against the interests of humanity and individual liberty. In wartime, the interests of state security can more precisely be defined as those dictated by military necessity. On the one hand, in order to prevent unnecessary suffering, belligerents are bound to observe rules that regulate the conduct of hostilities and the treatment of persons in the power of the enemy. On the other hand, IHL elevates the essence of war – targeting certain people and objects – into a limited right, but only for persons designated as "privileged combatants," such as soldiers in an army, and only against legitimate military objectives, including

1. Common Art. (CA) 2 of Geneva Convention (GC) I for the Amelioration of the Condition of the Wounded and Sick in Armed Forces in the Field (1949), 6 U.S.T. §3114 (1956); GC II for the Amelioration of the Condition of the Wounded, Sick, and Shipwrecked Members of Armed Forces at Sea (1949), 6 U.S.T. §3217 (1956); GC III relative to the Treatment of Prisoners of War (1949), 6 U.S.T. §3316 (1956); and GC IV relative to the Protection of Civilian Persons in Time of War (1949), 6 U.S.T. §3516 (1956). See also Protocol Additional (AP) I to the GCs of 12 August 1949, and relating to the Protection of Victims of International Armed Conflicts, 16 I.L.M. §1391 (1977).

2. Lindsay Moir, *The Law of Internal Armed Conflict* (Cambridge: Cambridge University Press, 2002), pp. 33–34. See also CA 3 of GC I; GC II; GC III; GC IV; and AP II, relating to the Protection of Victims of Non-International Armed Conflicts, Art. 1, 16 I.L.M. §1442 (1977).

3. Moir, *op. cit.*, pp. 34–42.

4. AP II, Art. 1.

5. Moir, *op. cit.*, pp. 36–38.

persons, be they soldiers or civilians, who take an active part in hostilities. (Those who take part in hostilities without such a privilege are criminals subject to prosecution and punishment; they do not, however, thereby forfeit whatever rights they may enjoy under humanitarian, human rights, or criminal law.) IHL also permits internment without trial of POWs – soldiers who fight for the enemy – and of civilians who take part in hostilities or who pose a serious security risk even without taking part in hostilities.[1]

In peacetime, the balance between interests of state security and humanity is, thankfully, struck at a different point than in wartime. For this reason, it is important that the law of armed conflict be restricted in application to armed conflict, since in peacetime, domestic and international criminal and human rights law prohibits and punishes extra-judicial killing, and generally requires that detained persons be entitled to contest their detention in a meaningful fashion involving due process of law.

In other words, where the *lex specialis* of IHL is active – in war – the exceptional prerogatives of the law of armed conflict override some of the protections provided by other legal regimes, such as criminal law and human rights law.[2] These exceptional legal prerogatives, such as targeting and detention without trial, must remain just that – exceptional.

What is the exception? War.

When actions such as terrorism and counterterrorism occur beyond the scope of war, the alleged actors – such as terrorists – may not be subjected to lethal force and detention, except under circumstances and subject to conditions permitted by domestic and international criminal and human rights law. Fiddling with the boundaries or, more accurately, with the overlap between IHL and other legal regimes – in order to extend the right provided by IHL to target or detain without trial a "terrorist" or other person who is not acting in the context of an armed conflict – can have profound, long-term, and decidedly "un-humanitarian" consequences on the delicate balance between state and personal security, human rights, and civil liberties.[3]

---

1. GC IV, Arts. 42, 43.

2. See, for example, Universal Declaration of Human Rights (UDHR), Arts, 3, 9–11; General Assembly Resolution No. 217A (III), UN Doc A/810, pp. 136–37 (1948); International Covenant on Civil and Political Rights (ICCPR) (1966), Arts. 6, 9, 14, 6 I.L.M. §§368, 370–73 (1967); American Convention on Human Rights (ACHR) (1969), Arts. 4, 7, 8; 1144 UN Treaty Ser. 123, 145–46, 147–48 (1979).

3. Carsten Stahn, "International Law at a Crossroads? The Impact of September 11," *Heidelberg Journal of International Law*, Vol. 62, 2002, p. 195, citing W. J. Fenrick, "Should the Laws of War Apply to Terrorists?" *American Society of International Law Proceedings*, Vol. 79, 1985, p. 112: "[T]here are times and places when it is appropriate to apply other regimes such as the criminal law of a State at peace . . . . Premature applica-

III. What the Critics Are Asking For

Some critics of IHL and of the International Committee of the Red Cross (ICRC) claim that the traditional IHL structure of international and non-international armed conflict must now give way to recognition of a new type of war, in which transnational armed groups attack civilians in an effort to undermine state structures.[1] These critics contend that the right to target persons and to detain them without trial – the hallmarks of the traditional law of armed conflict – must now be made applicable to this new type of conflict, since traditional peacetime tools of criminal law and interstate police and judicial cooperation are not up to the task.[2]

The official U.S. view is that an international armed conflict is in fact under way, spanning the globe and pitting certain countries against terrorists.[3] This conflict will end once "terrorism" or "the terrorists" are defeated. In the meantime, the laws of armed conflict prevail over the entire planet – meaning the application of IHL concepts of "targeting" and detention without the usual restraint of judicial intervention. In this world, instead of merely arresting a suspected terrorist on the street and charging him with a crime, the U.S., if it considered him an "enemy combatant," would be within its rights to shoot and/or detain him without trial.

IV. The Answer

The phrase "war on terror" is a rhetorical device having no legal significance. There is no more logic to automatic application of the laws of armed conflict (and the privileges it bestows upon belligerents) to the "war on terror" than there is to a "war on drugs," a "war on poverty," or a "war

---

tion of the laws of war may result in a net increase in human suffering, because the laws of war permit violence prohibited by domestic criminal law."

1. See, for example, James R. Schlesinger *et al.*, *Final Report of the Independent Panel to Review DoD Detention Operations*, pp. 86–87, 92 (2004).

2. *Ibid.*, pp. 27–31.

3. On the other hand, President Bush and others speaking on behalf of the U.S. administration have clearly suggested that some aspects of the "war on terror" will not involve armed conflict, permitting us to conclude that in their view those aspects, at least, will not be covered by IHL. On September 20, 2001, President Bush said in an Address to a Joint Session of Congress and the American People, "The war will be fought not just by soldiers, but by police and intelligence forces, as well as in financial institutions" (http://www.whitehouse.gov/news/releases/2001/09/20010920–8.html). National Security Advisor Condoleezza Rice stated on a *FOX News* broadcast on November 10, 2002: "We're in a new kind of war, and we've made it very clear that this new kind of war will be fought on different battlefields" (http://www.foxnews.com/story/0,2933,69783,00.html).

on cancer." "Terror" or "terrorism" cannot be a party to an armed conflict. This is why despite a publicized "'war' on drugs" the law provides for suspected drug dealers to be arrested and put on trial, rather than summarily executed or detained without charge.

Blanket criticism of the law of armed conflict for its failure to cover all terrorism is akin to assailing the specialized law of corporations for its failure to address all business disputes. Furthermore, it is a stretch to suggest that recognition of America's right to defend itself against the perpetrators of the September 11 attacks amounts to acceptance of a "war paradigm" for everyone and everything considered "terrorist." Simply put, suspected terrorists captured in connection with that which is truly armed conflict may certainly be detained under IHL, and are therefore entitled to the rights that IHL provides such detainees. Terrorist suspects detained beyond the bounds or armed conflict are covered by other applicable laws, such as domestic and international criminal and human rights laws.

Though U.S. officials and other analysts have asserted that the so-called "Global War on Terror" (GWOT) is an international armed conflict, in many cases the GWOT does not measure up to criteria which determine when armed conflict exists: it is not a conflict between states, the territorial boundaries of the conflict are undefined; the beginnings are amorphous and the end indefinable; and, most importantly, the non-state parties are unspecified and unidentifiable entities that are not entitled to belligerent status. Indeed, war does not exist merely by virtue of being declared. It exists, and the laws of war apply, when facts on the ground establish the existence of armed conflict, regardless of any declaration or lack thereof.[1]

The U.S. and allied military interventions in Afghanistan and Iraq are, for example, wars to which the international law of international armed conflict applies. And the conflicts in Colombia, Congo, and Sri Lanka are, or were, wars to which the international law of non-international armed conflict applies. While these true armed conflicts and the so-called GWOT may or may not overlap, the law of armed conflict can only be applied to that which is truly armed conflict. That which is not remains governed by domestic and international criminal and human rights laws.

There is a good reason for this division of legal labor: the law of armed conflict affords rights and imposes responsibilities on warring parties that are legally exceptional. It is therefore essential that the criteria for

---

1. See Gabor Rona, "Interesting Times for International Humanitarian Law: Challenges from the 'War on Terror,'" *Fletcher Forum of World Affairs*, Summer/Fall, 2003, pp. 55–74.

determining the existence of armed conflict be accurately and rigorously applied. An examination of those criteria insofar as the GWOT is concerned, and from the standpoint of a non-international armed conflict, which takes account of non-state armed groups operating against a state, will demonstrate just how much of it actually falls outside of the boundaries of recognized armed conflict, notwithstanding claims by the U.S. to enjoy belligerent privileges afforded by IHL.

1. Identification of parties

The essential humanitarian function of IHL is carried out through the parties to the conflict. They have rights and responsibilities. There can be no IHL conflict without identifiable parties.

"Terror" or "terrorism" cannot be a party to the conflict. As a result, a war on terror cannot be an IHL event. It has been suggested that wars against proper nouns (e.g., Germany and Japan) have advantages over those against common nouns (e.g., crime, poverty, terrorism), since proper nouns can surrender and promise not to do it again. IHL is not concerned with the entitlement to engage in hostilities or the promise not to do so again (the "*jus ad bellum*"). Rather, it concerns the conduct of hostilities and the treatment of persons in the power of the enemy (the "*jus in bello*"). But there is still a strong connection to IHL in this observation. There can be no assessment of rights and responsibilities under IHL in a war without identifiable parties. The concept of a "party" suggests a minimum level of organization required to enable the entity to carry out the obligations of law.[1]

A terrorist group can conceivably be a party to an armed conflict and a subject of IHL, but the lack of commonly accepted definitions is a hurdle. What exactly is terrorism? What is a terrorist act? Does terrorism include state actors? How is terrorism distinguished from mere criminality? How has the international community's reaction to terrorism differed from its treatment of mere criminality; from its traditional treatment of international and non-international armed conflict?

There are numerous conventions and other authorities that treat these questions, but none, as of yet, provides a comprehensive definition of "terrorism" or "terrorist acts."[2] Negotiations on a Comprehensive Convention

---

1. Gerald I. A. D. Draper, "The Geneva Conventions of 1949," *Rec de Cours*, Vol. 114, 1965, p. 90.

2. I acknowledge, but exclude as unhelpful, the definition of terrorism found in the 1937 Convention for the Prevention and Punishment of Terrorism: " . . . criminal acts

on International Terrorism[1] are proceeding, but with considerable difficulty, in no small part due to an inability to reach agreement on the definition of terrorism. Terrorism is not a legal notion.[2] This very fact indicates the difficulty, if not impossibility, of determining how terrorism and responses to it may be identified historically or defined within a legal regime. For example, when the United States in 1998 was still engaged in the negotiations to establish a permanent International Criminal Court in Rome, it took a position against inclusion of terrorism in the court's statute on the grounds that a definition was not achievable. Without international consensus on these questions, how can one determine, for purposes of assigning legal consequences, who are the parties to the GWOT and which branch, if either, of IHL should apply?[3]

We are all now familiar with the refrain that one man's terrorist is another man's freedom fighter. The need for criteria to distinguish terrorists from freedom fighters is more than academic. It may be critical to the determination of whether IHL can apply, and if so, whether it is the rules of international armed conflict or those of non-international armed conflict that will govern. The reason is simply that hostilities directed against a government and undertaken by a belligerent group seeking self-determination may qualify as an international armed conflict under Additional Protocol (AP) I to the GCs, while the same conduct of a group with different aims will not.[4]

This does not, of course, mean that IHL cannot apply to the conduct of persons responsible for the September 11 attacks.[5] On the other hand, the

---

directed against a State or intended to create a state of terror in the minds of particular persons, or a group of persons or the general public." A comprehensive list of treaties on terrorism can be found at http://untreaty.un.org/English/Terrorism.asp).

1. UNGA Res. 51/210, 17 December 1996. See *Measures to Eliminate International Terrorism*, Report of the Working Group, A/C.6/56/L.9, October 29, 2001.

2. Hans-Peter Gasser, "Acts of Terror, 'Terrorism,' and International Humanitarian Law," *International Review of the Red Cross*, Vol. 84, September, 2002, pp. 553–554: "It is much more a combination of policy goals, propaganda, and violent acts – an amalgam of measures to achieve an objective."

3. Chibli Mallat, "September 11 and the Middle East: Footnote or Watershed in World History?" *Crimes of War Project*, September 2002 (http://www.crimesofwar.org/sept-mag/sept-home.html): "The problem is that terrorism as a concept remains so ill-defined that the idea of attacking it systematically transforms the use of violence – in international and domestic law the prerogative of States – into an open-ended project of endless war. And that, surely, is inconceivable, unless the American government now means to prosecute a series of wars to end all violence in the world."

4. AP I, Art. 1(4).

5. Stahn, *op. cit.*, pp. 192–194.

attacks do not, per force, amount to armed conflict which would trigger the application of IHL. In addition to other criteria mentioned below, the non-state participants must qualify as belligerents or insurgents – a status of doubtful applicability to a group not associated with any specific territory.[1] One commentator has suggested that armed attacks by al-Qaeda, which is neither a state, nation, belligerent, nor insurgent group (as those terms are understood in international law), can trigger a right of selective and proportionate self-defense under the UN Charter against those directly involved in such armed attacks. However, neither these attacks nor the use of military force by a state against such attackers can create a state *of war under international law.*[2] Another commentator has asked: "Should the events of September 11 be considered an 'act of war'? It depends on whether a government was involved."[3]

2. Identification of territory

The rules applicable to non-international armed conflict – historically thought of as involving rebels within a state against the state or against other rebels – are found in Common Article 3 (CA 3) to the GCs and in AP II to the GCs; the scope of application of these rules is also found in CA 3 and in Article 1 of AP II.

While CA 3 does not require territorial control by the non-state party in the case of a non-international armed conflict, the conflict must still occur "in the territory" of a High Contracting Party to the GCs. Some analysts construe this requirement to mean that the conflict must be limited to the

---

1. *Ibid.*, p. 189. See also M. Cherif Bassiouni, "Legal Control of International Terrorism: A Policy-Oriented Assessment," *Harvard International Law Journal*, Vol. 43, 2002, p. 83.

2. Jordan J. Paust, "There is No Need to Revise the Laws of War in Light of September 11," American Society of International Law Task Force on Terrorism, November, 2002), citing *Pan American Airways, Inc. v. Aetna Casualty & Surety Co.*, 505 F2d 989, 1013–1015 (2d Cir 1974): "The United States could not have been at war with the Popular Front for the Liberation of Palestine [PFLP], which had engaged in terrorist acts as a nonstate, nonbelligerent, noninsurgent actor." Cf., however, Yoram Dinstein, "IHL on the Conflict in Afghanistan," American Society of International Law Proceedings, Vol. 96, 2002, p.: " . . . a terrorist attack from the outside constitutes an 'armed attack' under Art. 51 of the (UN) Charter."

3. Eyal Benvenisti, "Terrorism and the Laws of War: September 11 and its Aftermath," *Crimes of War Project*, September 21, 2001 (http://crimesofwar.org/expert/attack-apv. html). See also *The Prosecutor v. Dusko Tadic*, Decision on the defence motion for interlocutory appeal on jurisdiction, IT-94–1-AR72; and Dinstein, *op. cit.*, p. 24, citing *Nicaragua v. United States*, 1986 ICJ 14, and the General Assembly's Consensus Definition of Aggression, General Assembly Resolution 3314 (XXIX), Art. 3(g) (1974).

territory of a signatory to the GCs, a so-called High Contracting Party.[1] For this element alone, terrorist attacks on civilian targets in New York may suffice, but retaliation against alleged terrorists in Yemen, for example (i.e., the targeted killing in November 2002 by a CIA-launched, unmanned drone missile), may not.[2] This is *not* because Yemen is not a party to the GCs. It is. Rather, *it is because CA 3 is of questionable application to an isolated, targeted killing of persons outside of U.S. territory.*

3. Relationship of events to an identified conflict

The strike in Yemen on November 4, 2002, highlights another element. "Acts of war" is an understandable, perhaps inevitable, description of the September 11 attacks. However, this rhetorical reaction does not answer the question of whether or not those attacks and the response to them are part of an armed conflict, i.e., that they have a sufficient nexus to an armed conflict. For example, there should be no doubt that the military confrontation in Afghanistan following the September 11 attacks was (and perhaps remains) an armed conflict. And a case can be made that the September 11 attacks are a part thereof. But it does not necessarily follow that the targeted killing of terrorist suspects by U.S. authorities in Yemen a year after the September 11 attacks falls within that conflict and, therefore, is an event to which IHL applies.

4. Identification of beginning and end of armed conflict

According to the jurisprudence of the International Criminal Tribunals for the former Yugoslavia[3] and Rwanda,[4] as well as under the definitions of the permanent International Criminal Court,[5] hostile acts must be "protracted" in order for the situation to qualify as an "armed conflict." In fact, the Yugoslavia Tribunal has specifically stated that the reason for this

---

1. Moir, *op. cit.*, p. 31.

2. For analysis of the legal consequences of the killings in Yemen, see Anthony Dworkin, "The Yemen Strike: The War on Terrorism Goes Global," *Crimes of War Project*, November 14, 2002 (http://crimesofwar.org/onnews/news-yemen.html).

3. *The Prosecutor v. Dusko Tadic*, para. 70, p. 37 (1995).

4. *The Prosecutor v. Jean Paul Akayesu*, ICTR-96–4-T, para. 619 (1998).

5. The Rome Statute of the International Criminal Court (ICC), UN Doc. A/CONF.183/9 dated 17 July 1998, 37 I.L.M. §999–1019 (1998), Art. 8.2(f), contains this requirement, which may be seen as an expression of the drafter's belief that "protracted" is a defining element of non-international armed conflict, or merely that ICC jurisdiction is triggered only in case a non-international armed conflict is protracted.

requirement is to exclude the application of IHL to acts of terrorism.[1] On the other hand, the Inter-American Commission on Human Rights says that intense violence of brief duration will suffice.[2] Likewise, it remains to be seen whether the mere gravity of damage resulting from the September 11 attacks will, in retrospect, become a "decisive point of reference for the shift from the mechanisms of criminal justice to the instruments of the use of force."[3]

Whether or not the conflict needs be protracted, and whether or not intensity can take the place of duration, the beginning and end must be identifiable to know when IHL is triggered, and when it ceases to apply.

V. GWOT Cannot Be Across-the-Board "Armed Conflict"

The most important and most commonly forgotten element is that application of CA 3, like all other aspects of IHL, *depends on the existence of a particular quality of hostilities* that amount to armed conflict. And yet, nowhere in the GCs or APs is the term "armed conflict" defined. Where the question arises – "Is there a state of international armed conflict (i.e., between or among states)?" – the analysis is relatively easy. The answer is "yes" whenever there is "[a]ny difference arising between two States and leading to the intervention of armed forces."[4]

The determination of non-international armed conflict, however, is more complex. One can start with the disqualifying criteria of AP II, Article 1.2 (internal disturbances and tensions such as riots, etc.),[5] but they are hardly precise. One can proceed to the inclusive criteria of the ICRC Commentary, but there is no consensus on their legal authority. The ICRC Commentary also appears to presume that the non-state party to the conflict is acting within a determinate territory in revolt against, and attempt-

---

1. *The Prosecutor v. Zejnil Delalic* (Celebici Camp case), Judgment, IT-96–21, para. 184, (1998).

2. See, *Abella Case*, Inter-American Commission on Human Rights, Report No. 55/97, Case No. 11.137, November 18, 1997, paras. 155–156.

3. Stahn, *op. cit.*, p. 188.

4. See Jean S. Pictet, *Commentary: First Geneva Convention for the Amelioration of the Condition of the Wounded and Sick in Armed Forces in the Field* (Geneva: ICRC, 1952), p. 32. The "difference arising between two States" language suggests the requirement of a *casus belli*. This interpretation is not universally shared.

5. AP II, Part I (Scope of this Protocol), Art. 1 (Material field of application), para. 2: "This Protocol shall not apply to situations of internal disturbances and tensions, such as riots, isolated and sporadic acts of violence and other acts of a similar nature, as not being armed conflicts."

ing to displace, its own government. Must military means be used? Can the line between military and non-military means be neatly drawn? This potential criterion is related to the question of intensity, which has been suggested as an alternative to the requirement that the conflict be "protracted." Traditionally, acts of international terrorism were not viewed as crossing the threshold of intensity required to trigger application of the laws of armed conflict.[1] Some authority to the contrary is suggested by historical precedents involving the use of military force against extraterritorial non-state actors as indicative of "war." But these examples *still fail to make the case* that use of such force necessarily triggers the law of armed conflict.[2]

VI. Having Their Cake and Eating It Too

The GCs stipulate that if you are detained by an enemy state at war with your state, then you will fall into one of two categories: POW or civilian internee.[3] Pursuant to the belief that detainees in the "war on terror" should not be entitled to any legal protections that the law of armed conflict might provide them, a new, third status – one that essentially places detainees outside the framework of IHL – has been proposed. The designation of such persons as "enemy combatants" is used to displace both POW and civilian-internee status. At the same time, individual protections under criminal and human rights law are denied on the basis that those laws do not apply in armed conflict.[4] Thus, detainees are rendered into the infamous "legal black hole."

---

1. Stahn, *op. cit.*, p. 192, citing Elizabeth Chadwick, *Self-Determination, Terrorism and the International Humanitarian Law of Armed Conflict* (Boston: M. Nijhoff, 1996), p. 128, and noting the United Kingdom's denial of existence of armed conflict in Northern Ireland. In fact, the UK's ratification of AP I was accompanied by a statement that the term "armed conflict" is distinguishable from the commission of ordinary crimes including acts of terrorism whether concerted or in isolation.

2. See, Robert Goldman, "Terrorism and the Laws of War: September 11 and its Aftermath," *Crimes of War Project*, September 21, 2001 (http://crimesofwar.org/expert/attack-apv.html), noting the 1805 U.S. military action in Tripoli against the Barbary Pirates and that of 1916 in Mexico against Pancho Villa and his band.

3. Jean S. Pictet, *Commentary: Fourth Geneva Convention relative to the Protection of Civilian Persons in Time of War* (Geneva: ICRC, 1958), p. 51: "Every person in enemy hands must have some status under international law: he is either a prisoner of war and, as such, covered by the Third Convention, a civilian covered by the Fourth Convention, or again, a member of the medical personnel of the armed forces who is covered by the First Convention. *There is no* intermediate status; nobody in enemy hands can be outside the law" (emphasis in original).

4. Schlesinger, *op. cit.*, pp. 81–82.

It is, of course, absolutely correct that persons who are not members of armed forces or assimilated militias, and whose hostile acts violate the most fundamental principle of IHL – namely, that civilians may not be attacked – are not entitled to be designated POWs, a status reserved for lawful combatants.[1] In that event, they default into the legal status of persons covered by the Fourth Geneva Convention.[2] As such, and unlike lawful combatants, they can be prosecuted for the mere fact of having taken part in hostilities.[3] Like lawful combatants, they can also be prosecuted for war crimes, such as the targeting of civilians.[4]

But the U.S. administration claims the privileges conferred by invoking IHL, while refusing to accept its commensurate burdens. Most exemplary in this regard are instances of targeting carried out by the U.S. military or paramilitary forces, and the status of detainees in U.S. military custody.

Targeting beyond the bounds of armed conflict

Since an international armed conflict under IHL must be between two or more states, the better terminology for those aspects of the so-called GWOT that do amount to armed conflict and that cross state boundaries, but that do not implicate two or more governments as parties to the conflict, would be "transnational" or "interstate."[5] The decision of the United States to refer to the GWOT as an international armed conflict is neither insignificant nor innocent. The U.S. view, if accepted as a statement of law, would serve as a global waiver of domestic and international criminal and human rights laws that regulate, if not prohibit, killing. Turning the whole world into a rhetorical battlefield cannot legally justify, though it may in practice set the stage for, a claimed license to kill people or detain them without recourse to judicial review anytime, anywhere. This is a privilege that, in reality, exists under limited conditions and may only be exercised by lawful combatants and parties to armed conflict.

---

1. GC III, Art. 4. Thus, and despite repeated assertions to the contrary made by some commentators, the ICRC has never claimed that Guantánamo detainees are axiomatically entitled to POW status.

2. Pictet, *Commentary: Fourth Geneva Convention*, p. 51.

3. See AP I, Art. 43 (granting a lawful combatant's privilege and, by necessary implication, excluding civilians from this privilege).

4. GC I, Arts. 49–50; GC II, Arts. 50–51; GC III, Arts. 129–130; GC IV, Arts. 146–147.

5. The exception to the "between States" requirement for international armed conflict is armed conflicts "in which peoples are fighting against colonial domination and alien occupation and against racist regimes in the exercise of their right to self-determination . . . " These are deemed international armed conflict by AP I, Art. 1.4.

In war, soldiers may be targeted whenever doing so creates a military advantage – in other words, almost always. Civilians, on the other hand, may not be targeted unless they are taking an active part in hostilities.[1] Since terrorists are likely to be civilians, they can benefit from the fact that it is unlawful to target them whenever they are not actively engaged in hostile behavior. The attack by a missile reportedly launched from a CIA-operated drone on an SUV containing al-Qaeda suspects in Yemen highlighted the debate on this point. It was argued that the civilian legal framework of arrest, criminal charges, and trials is simply "impractical" in dealing with terrorist groups of global organization and reach.[2]

But where does that argument lead? It leads to O'Hare International Airport in Chicago, where U.S. citizen Jose Padilla was arrested and ultimately designated an enemy combatant, now having been held essentially incommunicado, in indefinite detention without trial or even without charge, for three years in a military brig.[3] And it leads not only to such detentions, but also to the potential for targeted killings, either in the deserts of Yemen or the streets of Chicago. When asked whether, consistent with the laws of war, terrorist suspects could be targeted, the U.S. Department of Defense deputy general counsel for international affairs, Charles Allen, said they could.[4] This is true with two critical caveats: one, only if it is truly in the context of armed conflict, and two, only if the suspects are actively engaged in hostilities. I understand that this second caveat frustratingly permits terrorists to play a kind of "peek-a-boo" game with the authorities, but I also believe that limiting the circumstances in which targeted killing is lawful, even in war, is a valid tradeoff when the alternative is a permanent, global free-fire zone against an amorphous enemy.

The targeted killing of suspected terrorists in Yemen is a case in point. The killings are of dubious legality under IHL for several reasons. First, unless the event is part of an armed conflict, IHL does not apply, and its

---

1. AP I, Art. 51, paras. 2–3.

2. "CIA Drones' Attack on Car in Yemen Was Justified," *Dallas Morning News*, November 13, 2002, p. 16A.

3. Gina Holland, "Supreme Court to Rule on Terrorism Case Involving U.S.-born 'Dirty Bomb' Suspect," *Associated Press*, February 20, 2004.

4. Charles Allen made it clear that the U.S. military saw the same rules governing the global war with al-Qaeda as traditional, "battlefield" wars: "When we have a lawful military target that the commander determines needs to be taken out, there is by no means a requirement under the law of armed conflict that we must send a warning to these people, and say, 'You may surrender rather than be targeted.'" Anthony Dworkin, "Law and the Campaign Against Terrorism: The View from the Pentagon," December 16, 2002 (http://www.crimesofwar.org/onnews/news-pentagon.html).

provisions recognizing a privilege to target may not be invoked. The event must then be analyzed under other applicable legal regimes.[1] Second, even if IHL applies, the legality of the attack is questionable because the targets were not directly participating in hostilities at the time they were killed,[2] and because the attackers' right to engage in combat is doubtful.[3]

Extra-judicial detention in a legal "black hole"

The GCs are constructed so as to provide for no gaps in its coverage of enemy soldiers and civilians. The notion that someone who fails to qualify for POW status is therefore beyond the coverage of the GCs is incorrect. An enemy national is either a POW covered by the Third Geneva Convention, or a civilian covered by the Fourth.[4]

In the recent war in Afghanistan – clearly an international armed conflict to which GC III Relative to the Treatment of Prisoners of War applies – the United States took the position that no detainees are entitled to prisoner of war (POW) status.[5] This is despite the plain language of GC III, Article 4.1, which states that POWs are members of the armed forces of a party to the conflict who have fallen into the power of the enemy. The United States has asserted that even the Taliban are not entitled to POW status since they failed to have a fixed, distinctive sign (uniforms) and did not conduct their operations in accordance with the laws and customs of war. These disqualifying factors are part of GC III, Article 4.2, which applies to militias and volunteer corps and not to regular members of the armed forces, who are covered by Article 4.1.

---

1. Sweden's Foreign Minister, Anna Lindh, used the term "summary execution" and further stated: "Even terrorists must be treated according to international law. Otherwise, any country can start executing those whom they consider terrorists." Quoted in Walter Pincus, "Missile Strike Carried Out With Yemeni Cooperation; Official Says Operation Authorized Under Bush Finding," *Washington Times*, November 6, 2002, p. A10.

2. See, AP I, Art. 51.3. The U.S. position on this point is difficult to discern. The Yemen attack notwithstanding, the U.S. State Department remains critical of Israeli targeted killings of Palestinian militants. See Press Briefing by State Department Spokesman Richard Boucher, November 5, 2002.

3. The criteria of GC III, Art. 4, that the United States invokes to deny POW status to detainees it deems "unlawful combatants" would also appear to apply to the CIA. The CIA is not part of the armed forces of the United States. Only members of the armed forces of a party to the conflict (other than medical personnel and chaplains) are combatants, entitled to participate directly in hostilities. AP I, Art. 43.2.

4. Pictet, *Commentary: Fourth Geneva Convention, loc. cit.*

5. This view is probably correct as to al-Qaeda members detained in relation to the Afghan conflict. It is certainly correct as to others detained outside the context of armed conflict.

Even if these disqualifying criteria are relevant to regular members of armed forces, as some analysts suggest, their application is subject to two more provisions: GC III, Article 5, which calls for the convening of a "competent tribunal" to determine POW status in case of doubt, and the even more specific language of U.S. Army regulations calling for "competent tribunal" determinations upon request of the detainee.[1] Both of these authorities can only be construed to require individualized determinations. (Several writers have accused the ICRC of claiming that all detainees are entitled to POW status;[2] actually, all the ICRC has ever claimed is that detainees are entitled by the Conventions to an individualized determination of status in the event of doubt.[3]) Because the U.S. administration has chosen not to make public any specific allegations, I do not pretend to know what it knows about the Taliban's alleged failure to conduct their operations in accordance with the laws and customs of war. It is obvious, however, that if the mere commission of war crimes by one or more members of armed forces can disqualify them all from entitlement to POW status, then there would never be a POW. Such an interpretation cannot stand, since it would defeat the very purposes for which the status of POW exists in IHL.

Having denied its Guantánamo detainees POW status under GC III, the United States also rejects application of GC IV for the protection of civilians, thus leaving them in a legal vacuum. This issue is clouded in emotional rhetoric that has far overshadowed the facts. The right of all persons to recognition before the law is a fundamental, non-derogable human right.[4] Consistent with that right, the ICRC Commentary takes the position that all armed conflict detainees are "protected persons" either under GC III or GC IV.[5]

The idea of granting "protected person" status to "terrorists" is apparently unacceptable to the U.S. administration. But first, not all detainees are terrorists. Those who are mere members of the enemy armed forces

---

1. Section 1–6(b) Army Regulation 190–8, "Enemy Prisoners of War, Retained Personnel, Civilian Internees and Other Detainees, Headquarters Departments of the Army, the Navy, the Air Force, and the Marine Corps" (Washington, D.C., October 1, 1997).

2. See, for example, Schlesinger, *op. cit.*, pp. 86–87.

3. "International Humanitarian Law and Terrorism: Questions and Answers," ICRC press release, May 5, 2001 (http://www.icrc.org/Web/Eng/siteengO.nsf/ iwpList74/ OF32B7E3BB38DD26C1256E8A0055F83E).

4. ICCPR, Arts. 4.2 and 16.

5. Pictet, *Commentary: IV Geneva Convention*, p. 51. Note, however, that nationals of the detaining authority and of neutral and co-belligerent states are not "protected persons." See GC IV, Art. 4. Nevertheless, even they must have some legal status. See ICCPR, *ibid.*

– the Taliban – are presumptively entitled to POW treatment "until such time as their status has been determined by a competent tribunal."[1] Second, others are civilians who may or may not have committed criminal (e.g., terrorist) acts. To recognize their entitlement to "protected person" status under GC IV in no way prohibits their interrogation and detention for the duration of the conflict, so long as they remain a security risk.[2] Nor does it prohibit their prosecution and imprisonment beyond the temporal bounds of the conflict, if convicted of a crime.[3] They may even be subject to execution.[4] However, while they may be killed in battle, detained without trial for the duration of the armed conflict, or tried and sentenced for any "terrorist" acts, they may not be held outside of any legal framework.

On the other hand, the U.S. avails itself of the right in armed conflict to detain individuals without recourse to lawyers in ways that constitute a fundamental misapplication of that right. For example, there are two categories of detainees in Guantánamo for whom long-term detention without any judicial or administrative review is not permitted by international law. First are those lawfully captured in the post-September 11 international armed conflict in Afghanistan, which ended with the installation of the Karzai government in June 2002. To the extent that hostilities continue, they amount either to an internal armed conflict or to something less than armed conflict altogether. Either way, these detainees are entitled to an individualized procedure to challenge the basis of their detention. It is ironic that the U.S. correctly claims a right under the laws of war to detain certain people for the duration of an armed conflict, but then shirks its obligation under the very same laws to provide them with a hearing.

Second are those, taken prisoner in far-flung places such as Zambia, who are suspected of terrorist criminal activity beyond any connection with armed conflict, and are "rendered" into U.S. custody without legal process. To subject them to the rules of detention in war contradicts both the letter and spirit of international law. People who commit hostile acts against U.S. interests may be criminals, but are not necessarily enemy combatants. Those who commit hostile acts in the context of armed conflict may be enemy combatants, but are not necessarily criminals. Only those who commit hostile acts in the context of armed conflict but are not regular soldiers, or "privileged" combatants, can properly be considered

---

1. GC III, Art. 5.
2. GC IV, Arts. 42, 78.
3. GC IV, Arts. 64–68.
4. GC IV, Art. 68.

"unlawful" or "unprivileged" combatants. While they may be prosecuted for unlawful acts of belligerence, such people, despite U.S. assertions to the contrary, may not be denied protections of the law of armed conflict and other applicable laws.

The U.S. is, furthermore, proceeding with plans to subject prisoners to military commission trials, citing the GC provision that prisoners of war be tried by military courts. How can it do so while maintaining that no detainees are entitled to POW status? That aside, the U.S. risks throwing into the military-trial pot people whose alleged crimes have no connection with armed conflict, as understood in IHL. Such people can and should face trial, but not by military courts.

Interrogation

It has been argued that granting POW status would impede effective interrogation because POWs are not obliged to provide more than the most basic identifying information.

This position is incorrect for two reasons. First, it misconstrues the distinction between POWs and civilian internees, implying that the essential point is the varying kinds of techniques that may be employed in interrogation. On the contrary, the essential difference between the two is that, since the law of armed conflict allows the taking of life, regular soldiers and assimilated militia are exempt in wartime from the operation of otherwise applicable criminal laws that prohibit and punish killings, so long as the victim is a legitimate military objective. Civilians, on the other hand, possess no such right and continue to be subject to criminal laws for their hostile acts in wartime, as in peacetime. This is an essential complement to the most fundamental principle of the law of armed conflict, the principle of distinction, which provides that only military objectives may be targeted and that the civilian population may not be targeted.[1] To protect civilians who take no part in hostilities from becoming targets, it is essential that civilians who do unlawfully take part thus lose their immunity from targeting and are liable to criminal punishment. While both soldiers and civil-

---

1. Hans-Peter Gasser, "International Humanitarian Law," in Hans Haug, ed, *Humanity for All: The International Red Cross and Red Crescent Movement* (Bern: Paul Haupt Publishers, 1993), p. 504: "Parties to a conflict shall at all times distinguish between the civilian population and combatants in order to spare the civilian population and property. Neither the civilian population nor civilian persons shall be the object of attack. Attack shall be directed solely against military objectives." See also Jean S. Pictet, *The Principles of International Humanitarian Law* (Geneva: ICRC, 1967), pp. 27–34, discussing the fundamental principles of IHL.

ians may be tried and punished for war crimes, soldiers entitled to POW status are otherwise deprived of their liberty not for reasons of culpability, but merely to prevent their return to battle.[1] Both, however, are equally protected from torture and cruel, inhuman, and degrading treatment by the GCs;[2] by the customary laws of war applicable to both international and internal armed conflict;[3] and by international human rights law.[4]

There is a second reason why it is, in my view, incorrect to suggest that the GCs need to be reworked or ignored on the ground that they prohibit "serious" interrogation. This argument confuses what interrogators are allowed to ask, and how they are allowed to ask it, with what detainees are required to provide. In fact, there are no limits to what an interrogator may ask or what a detainee may volunteer, whether he or she is a POW or civilian. There are, however, limits on how information may be obtained.[5] The assertion that granting POW status would tie the hands of the investigator is merely a discreet way of suggesting that civilians may lawfully be subjected to interrogation techniques not available against POWs. This is false; non-POWs may not lawfully be subjected to interrogation techniques that may not be used against POWs.[6] To assert the contrary is to embark down a slippery slope that could lead to abuses.

Further considerations

Some have asserted that al-Qaeda and Taliban fighters are ineligible for the protections of the GCs because they do not, themselves, obey the rules.[7] Leaving aside the question of whether they do or don't, although it is absolutely clear that targeting civilians who take no part in hostilities is

1. See, Gasser, *ibid.*, p. 524: "Being a prisoner of war is in no way a form of punishment."

2. CA 3 of GC I; GC II; GC III; GC IV. See also GC I, Arts. 12, 50; GC II, Arts. 12, 51; GC III, Arts. 13, 14, 17, 52, 130; GC IV, Arts. 27, 32, 147.

3. Military and Paramilitary Activities (*Nicaragua v. United States*), 1986 ICJ 113–14, ¶218 (June 27, 1986). See also *Prosecutor v. Auto Furundzija*, 38 I.L.M. §317, ¶¶153–57 (ICTY 1998). The International Criminal Tribunal for the Former Yugoslavia also considered the prohibition of torture as belonging to *jus cogens*.

4. ICCPR, Art. 5; Convention Against Torture and Other Cruel, Inhuman or Degrading Treatment or Punishment, Arts. 2, 4, 23 I.L.M. §§1027, 1028 (1984).

5. See, ICRC, "ICRC Reactions to the Schlesinger Panel Report," August 9, 2004 (http://www.icrc.org/Web/Eng/siteengO.nsf/html/64MHS7).

6. See, GC IV, Art. 27, AP I, Art. 75 and CA 3. See also "Request by the Center for Constitutional Rights and the International Human Rights Law Group for Precautionary Measures under Art. 25 of the Commission's Regulations on Behalf of Unnamed Persons Detained and Interrogated by the United States Government," filed with the Inter-American Commission on Human Rights, February 13, 2003.

7. Schlesinger, *op. cit.*, p. 82.

a war crime, it is well settled that the obligations imposed by the GCs are not subject to reciprocity, so long as both parties to the conflict are also parties to the Conventions.[1] It is true that expectations of reciprocal treatment for my soldiers detained by my enemy create a strong incentive for me to obey the rules. But the purposes of International Humanitarian Law are just that, humanitarian. In contract law, if I fail to deliver the widgets, you are excused from paying for them. But in war, my failure to obey the law does not, and cannot, provide you with license to do likewise. Were it otherwise, the rules would likely never be obeyed. Besides, the argument that adherence to rules that terrorists ignore somehow puts them at an unfair advantage is questionable. We have graphically seen what little is gained and how much is lost by sidestepping legal constraints.

Furthermore, the idea that a "just war" confers upon its prosecutors more rights than a "war of aggression" is untenable for the very simple reason that wars generally do not feature self-confessed aggressors. Even if the "good" and "evil" are easily distinguishable, there is no justification for application of a lesser standard of protection to members of the "evil" group, who are not, or are no longer, taking part in hostilities. The absurdity of the proposition that the army, citizens, and members of the aggressor group – or the group that is said by its enemy to be "clearly" in the wrong in the case of armed conflict – should rightfully be subject to cruelties that it may not impose upon its enemy underscores why the *jus ad bellum* is distinct from, rather than consanguineous to, the *jus in bello*. The very essence of *jus ad bellum* is the distinction between just and unjust cause – between entitlement and prohibition to wage war. *Jus in bello,* on the other hand, rightfully recognizes no such distinction. While one party may be a sinner and the other a saint under *jus ad bellum,* the *jus in bello* must and does bind the aggressor and the aggressed equally.[2]

---

1. CA 1 of GC I; GC II; GC III; GC IV: "The High Contracting Parties undertake to respect and to ensure respect for the present Convention in all circumstances."

2. See, Dino Kritsiosis, "On the *Jus ad Bellum* and *Jus in Bello* of Operation ENDURING FREEDOM," American Society of International Law Proceedings, Vol. 96, 2002, p. 35, referring to the distinct spheres, histories, methodological traditions, stages of development, and circumstances of application of these two legal regimes: "As represented in the UN Charter, the laws of the *jus ad bellum* proceed from the general prohibition of the threat or use of force by member States of the United Nations 'in their international relations' (Art. 2(4))," while the *jus in bello* of the (GCs and APs) applies to such use of force. Thus, the Preamble to AP I declares that "the provisions of the Geneva Conventions and of this protocol must be fully applied in all circumstances to all persons who are protected by those instruments, without any adverse distinction based on the nature or origin of the armed conflict or on the causes espoused by or attributed to the Parties to the conflict."

VII. Conclusion

Critics of IHL and of humanitarian organizations like the ICRC have perhaps succeeded in one respect by sowing seeds of doubts about the continued relevance of the Geneva Conventions. But it now seems that *because* the Conventions are all too relevant, because, for example, their application triggers criminal responsibility for grave breaches, i.e., war crimes, their application is being denied.[1] It is on this level that the debate must be joined.

At stake are not merely the rights of persons in any single nation's custody and that nation's reputation for fair dealing. What of the ability and credibility of great powers to exert moral authority on others? What of the practices, and excuses put forth by, violators of the law around the globe? Why shouldn't any accused before the Yugoslavia or other tribunals now claim exemption from the limits imposed by international law, including the GCs? How does one now respond to the accusation that a double standard is no standard at all?

These are the questions that must be addressed before we rush to the conclusion that there is a need to develop a new legal framework to combat terrorism, or that the present framework is inadequate and so may be ignored. The proper frameworks already exist. One of them is the law of armed conflict, or IHL, and it will do the job it was designed to do, namely to strike a proper balance between the interests of state security and individual liberty, but only if we resist applying it where it does not belong and properly apply it where it does belong.

Where terrorism and the battle against it amount to armed conflict, the law of armed conflict must be applied. But when aspects of the "war on terror" do not fit within the definition of armed conflict, it is in everyone's interest that domestic and international law is respected. Furthermore, the inapplicability of humanitarian law to those aspects of the so-called GWOT that do not meet criteria for classification as armed conflict should be viewed as a benefit rather than an obstacle or as a collision between conflicting legal regimes. Ultimately, it would weaken both liberty and security to expand the right to kill people and detain them without trial to situations beyond those envisaged by the law of armed conflict. These distinctions are not mere legal nuances. People's lives and the integrity of the rule of law hang in the balance.

---

1. See, for example, Memorandum from John Yoo, Deputy Assistant Attorney General and Robert J. Delahunty, Special Counsel, United States Department of Justice, to William J. Haynes II, General Counsel, Department of Defense, January 9, 2002.

THE EDITORS' GLOSS: Pentagon spokesman Larry DiRita recently bragged of the DoD having detained and interrogated 70,000 people as part of the "war on terror." He didn't mention how those detainees were treated, or how their detentions were viewed in light of the law. President Bush's perspective is typically unpersuasive: "the only thing I know for certain is that these are bad people." An English saint and lawyer once commented on the same charge: "there's no law against that!" This is Joseph Margulies's perspective, too.

U.S. detention policy and practice remain abominable. One example is Murat Kurnaz, a German national seized in Pakistan in 2001, and assessed "a member of al Qaeda and an enemy combatant" by a military panel (*Washington Post*, March 27, 2005). The now-declassified evidence for his detention (originally "too sensitive to release to the public") indicates that "U.S. military intelligence and German law enforcement . . . concluded there was no information that linked Kurnaz to al-Qaeda, any other terrorist organization, or terrorist activities." D.C. District Court Judge Joyce Hens-Green said it was "one of the most troubling military abuses of due process" among Gitmo cases she has reviewed. The detention was based on a single document that, she said, "fails to provide significant details to support its conclusory allegations, does not reveal the sources for its information, and is contradicted by other evidence in the record."

Another example is Maher Arar, a Canadian seized by the U.S. at JFK airport NYC while in transit to Damascus. He was sent to Syria and detained for 10 months. The government is seeking dismissal of his lawsuit against it because it would "force the government to reveal classified information" (*AP*, August 11, 2005). It further argued that "foreign citizens who change planes at airports in the United States can legally be seized, detained without charge, deprived of access to a lawyer or the courts, and even denied basic necessities like food" (*New York Times*, August 10, 2005). No wonder even "conservative" lawyers are lining up for Gitmo detainee cases from the Center for Constitutional Rights (CCR). "The most satisfying part of my life [recently]," says Tina Foster, who connects lawyers and detainees for the CCR, "is hearing from super-right-wing Republican lawyers who want to find a client to represent."

When Margulies's piece was first published (*Virginia Quarterly Review*, Fall 2004), there were 600 detainees at Gitmo; today there are about 520. Two of his clients – Shafiq Rasul (of *Rasul v. Bush* fame) and Asif Iqbal – were released during the litigation it describes.

29

A Prison Beyond the Law
· · · · · · · · ·

Joseph Margulies, Esq.

NOT LONG AFTER September 11, 2001, the administration began to develop plans for a prison at the Guantánamo Bay Naval Station, in Cuba. Though modeled physically on maximum-security prisons in the United States, this facility – with a maximum capacity of 1100 inmates – would not hold convicted criminals. In fact, most of the inmates at this prison would never be charged with a crime, let alone convicted. The prison would house the people seized in ostensible connection with the war on terrorism, most of whom would never be brought before a tribunal of any kind, and would never be given an opportunity to secure their release by establishing their innocence. Designated "enemy combatants" by the President, they would be held without legal process, consigned to live out their days in isolation until the administration saw fit to release them.

This was the prison my colleagues and I challenged in *Rasul v. Bush*. On behalf of four prisoners – two from Britain and two from Australia – lawyers with the Center for Constitutional Rights and I filed an application in federal court seeking a writ of habeas corpus. Habeas acts as a check on Executive detention by forcing the sovereign to justify a prisoner's detention in open court. Sometimes called the Great Writ, habeas has been part of our law for more than 200 years and is one of the only protections of individual liberty enshrined in the Constitution (as opposed to the protections subsequently added in the Bill of Rights). Consistent with this historic purpose, we argued that the United States had to establish the lawfulness of our clients' detention by a fair process.

No small amount of confusion has attended the litigation in *Rasul*, and it is perhaps important to note what is not at stake. We did not argue – and have never argued – that the administration could not detain people seized in connection with the war on terrorism. We argued only that they could not detain them without some process to determine whether the detention was lawful. Nor did we argue that this process must include all the trappings of a federal criminal trial. We sought only a lawful and fair process that comported with the core understanding of habeas: notice and an opportunity to be heard before an impartial court that made timely decisions based on fixed and transparent standards. Finally, we did not ask that our clients be brought to the federal courthouse while this process unfolded. Instead, we asked that the federal court provide us access to our clients at Guantánamo, so they could be heard through us.

The litigation in *Rasul* has generated a host of intriguing issues, any one of which is worth considerable attention. There is, for example, the matter of the prisoners themselves. So far, the United States has success-fully kept most of the Guantánamo inmates in the dark about the litiga-tion. The argument in favor of complete secrecy runs something like this: the Administration believes that September 11 represents a failure of the intelligence community. While we may never know whether, with bet-ter intelligence, the United States could have prevented the attacks that morning, the administration believes that better intelligence is essential to preventing more attacks in the future. Since we lack reliable informants on the ground, we must get this intelligence by any means available to us, including interrogations of the people seized during the war.

According to the administration, effective interrogations require that the prisoner be separated from all outside influence. Terrorists, they argue, have been trained to resist the conventional blandishments to cooperate, and will withhold all useful information so long as they believe help is on the way. A successful interrogation, therefore, requires that prisoners become convinced that their welfare depends entirely on their interroga-tors. The only link to the outside world is the contact permitted by the cap-tors. No family member, no member of the press, and certainly no attorney, can visit with the inmates, who under all circumstances must not learn of any litigation filed on their behalf, for fear that the knowledge will fortify them in what the administration takes to be their unbending determina-tion to resist interrogation. To implement this vision, the administration needed a place where it could conduct interrogations free from any inter-ference by the outside world – and in particular, by a court and its dreaded accoutrement: lawyers.

The upshot of this logic is that, so far as I am aware, *Rasul* is the only case in United States history in which litigants have been deliberately kept unaware that their fate is being decided by the United States Supreme Court.[1]

---

1. I am frequently asked how we could represent clients who have been held incom-

Ironically, the problem with this argument is that it proves too much and too little. It proves too little because it assumes the critical fact in contention – viz., that the person being interrogated belongs in prison. The argument assumes that – operating in an unconventional conflict, where forces are not arrayed in traditional battlefields, where the enemy may be indistinguishable in appearance from any disengaged civilian, where the United States claims it may find its foe anywhere in the world, and where (by hypothesis) the military suffers from a lack of reliable intelligence on the ground – the administration has made the right decision to detain this person in the first place. In reflecting on the relative value of this assumption, we are well to recall the military's own estimate that perhaps 80% of the people imprisoned during the insurgency in Iraq are innocent.[1] And in Iraq, all the inmates were seized in a single country during a relatively brief period. The prison at Guantánamo, by contrast, houses inmates seized from across the globe, over a period of years.[2]

In any case, armed with this questionable assumption, the military takes the prisoner's refusal to disclose intelligence information as evidence

---

municado. Federal law allows a petitioner to seek habeas relief through a "next friend." The next friend, who is usually a relative or other person with a close relationship to the inmate, can maintain an action when the inmate is incompetent or unable to act on his own behalf. In our case, the detainees obviously could not file the litigation themselves, nor could they seek counsel. They were, however, occasionally allowed to write censored letters to their families, which were delivered by the International Red Cross. When the families heard from their loved ones, they contacted lawyers overseas, who eventually got in touch with us. By this device, though I have represented my clients since February 2002, I have never met them.

1. See, e.g., Jess Bravin, "The Fight For Iraq: Army Report Omitted Prison Details," *Wall Street Journal*, June 4, 2004, p. A6. The *Journal* quotes a report prepared by Lt. Col. Robert Chamberlain, intelligence chief for the Army's Joint Readiness Training Center, who found that prisons in Iraq were severely overcrowded, but that approximately 80% of the prisoners were innocent. According to Col. Chamberlain, "It's like the Roach Motel, 'they can check in but they never check out!'" Col. Chamberlain's assessment was omitted from the portion of the report originally made public by the Department of Defense. See also Maj. Gen. Antonio M. Taguba (Coalition Forces Land Component Command), Article 15–6 Investigation of the 800 Military Police Brigade, March 9, 2004 (http://news.findlaw.com/hdocs/docs/iraq/tagubarpt.html).

2. The domestic experience after September 11 should likewise give us pause. In June 2003 the Inspector General of the Justice Department issued a report on the post-September 11 detentions of foreign nationals in this country. Between September 11 and August 2002, the administration detained 738 foreign nationals in connection with ongoing investigations into the terrorist attacks. None of these people were charged with an offense related to September 11, and the overwhelming majority were cleared of any connection to terrorism. U.S Department of Justice, Office of the Inspector General, *The September 11 Detainees: A Review of the Treatment of Aliens Held On Immigration Charges In Connection with the Investigation of the September 11 Attacks*, April, 2003) (released June 2, 2003); see also David Cole, *Enemy Aliens* (New York: New Press, 2003).

of his rigorous and disciplined training, and not as evidence that he has no information to disclose. The only solution, therefore, is to conduct both more and better interrogations. In that respect, the reasoning is reminiscent of the logic pressed to support the Japanese internments during World War II: the fact that there had been no fifth column activity or acts of sabotage prior to the internments merely confirmed that such activity had been planned for a later date. In all events, the supporters of internment never took the absence of any untoward activity as evidence that they were mistaken about the risk in the first place.[1]

Yet the administration's argument also proves too much. Even if we assume the various premises are correct – that the military has seized the right person, and that extended isolation and complete dependence is the sine qua non of a successful interrogation – the government's argument posits an interrogation that never ends, since the moment the interrogation ends, so does the justification for the strict isolation. For many of the Guantánamo prisoners, the isolation has now gone on for over two years, with no apparent end in sight. Perhaps as importantly, the argument stakes its claim on the singular importance of intelligence gathering. If that is indeed the test, then conditions which increase the likelihood of what the administration defines as a "successful" interrogation will be viewed sympathetically, while conditions that diminish the likelihood will be viewed with skepticism. This argument, however, leads seamlessly – albeit not inevitably – to the sickening abuses recently uncovered at Abu Ghraib and other military facilities.

A few examples may bring this problem into sharper focus. In the first Gulf War, military lawyers were present at every detention center. These attorneys were carefully trained in the laws governing the proper treatment of detainees, and were allowed to monitor any interrogation from behind a one-way mirror. They were also authorized to intervene if any interrogation crossed the line. By design, however, their monitoring was surreptitious, and neither the interrogator nor the detainee knew whether any particular session would be monitored. In the present conflict, however, the administration has curtailed this practice, apparently because it believed lawyers might interfere with aggressive interrogations.[2]

---

1. See, e.g., *Final Report, Japanese Evacuation From The West Coast* (1942), p. 34: "The very fact that no sabotage has taken place to date is a disturbing and confirming indication that such action will be taken." The report was prepared by Lt. Gen. J. L. DeWitt, the military official in charge of the relocations.

2. See Report of the Association of the Bar of the City of New York, *Human Rights Standards Applicable To The United States' Interrogation of Detainees*, June 4, 2004,

But even while the administration removed JAG lawyers, whose presence acted as a potential brake on overzealous interrogators, it endorsed an extremely controversial approach to interrogations at Guantánamo. In September 2002 when the administration had grown impatient with the lack of intelligence coming from Guantánamo, it authorized interrogators to become more aggressive. According to press accounts, at least one prisoner was held under water until he believed he would drown. And in March 2003 a team of administration lawyers concluded the President could authorize the military to torture detainees with impunity, and that the domestic and international laws prohibiting torture were subject to a type of crude cost-benefit analysis, and could be discarded if it was discovered they interfered with what the administration believed was an effective interrogation technique.[1]

Another issue worth further exploration is the unprecedented nature of the detentions. Again, so far as I am aware, the detentions at Guantánamo mark the first time in United States history that the military has relied on a systematic program of indefinite detention without legal process. Defenders of the current detentions point out that the United States has detained people in every prior conflict, and that is of course correct; during the Second World War, the U.S. military detained over four hundred thousand German and Italian prisoners in the United States. But these prisoners enjoyed the protections of an extant legal system – the 1929 Geneva Conventions – which the United States observed to the letter.[2] As importantly, and unlike the present conflict, the nature of the hostilities during the Second World War substantially minimized the risk that the military would capture an innocent civilian. The military could fairly assume, in other words, that the soldier across the field in the slate gray uniform was in fact a member of a belligerent force who could be lawfully held for the duration of the conflict, without the need for further

---

p. 12, n. 22: "[S]enior JAG officers [report] that the prior practice of having JAG officers monitor interrogations in the field for compliance with law and regulations had been curtailed at the direction of senior officials."

1. Neil Lewis and Eric Schmitt, "Lawyers Decided Bans on Torture Didn't Bind Bush," *New York Times*, June 8, 2004, p. A1; James Risen, David Johnston, and Neil A. Lewis, "The Struggle For Iraq: Detainees; Harsh CIA Methods Cited In Top Qaeda Interrogations," *New York Times*, May 13, 2004, online; Tim Golden and Don Van Natta, Jr., "U.S. Said to Overstate Value of Guantánamo Detainees," *New York Times*, June 21, 2004, p. A1; *New York Times*, A Guide To The Memos On Torture (available at www.nytimes.com/ref/international/24MEMO-GUIDE.html as of June 2005).

2. See Arnold Krammer, *Nazi Prisoners of War in America* (New York: Stein & Day, 1979).

process. But administration officials acknowledge that no such confidence surrounds the present conflict.[1]

Defenders of Guantánamo also maintain that wartime detentions are inherently indefinite, if only because one can never predict when a particular conflict will end. This too is undeniably true, but in prior conflicts, the event which marked the end of a particular campaign could be readily ascertained, which made it a relatively simple matter to recognize when a wartime restriction crossed the line from reasonable to abusive. Furthermore, since a nation's defeat marked the end of its ability to maintain an army, it also became reasonably clear when the military should repatriate prisoners. But the war on terrorism pits us against an ideology. How do we know when we have vanquished an idea? What marks the moment when armies doing battle with deeply held convictions may finally set down their arms, secure in the knowledge that the conflict has run its course? I venture the end of such a conflict will not be marked by an armistice signed on the deck of the Missouri. But if this reality makes it difficult to know when the conflict is over, and if it means, as the administration has suggested, that the measure of this conflict will be in decades, and not years, doesn't it also make it more important that people who have been seized by mistake be provided some means by which they may establish their innocence and secure their release?[2]

---

1. See Golden and Van Natta, *loc. cit.*: a former Secretary of the Army was told "by a senior military official at the base that only a third to a half of the detainees appeared to be of some value . . . ." Other programs of wartime imprisonment are likewise distinguishable from the imprisonments at Guantánamo. During the Civil War, for instance, Lincoln unilaterally suspended the writ of habeas corpus and the Union Army seized and detained thousands of citizens without process. See, e.g., Mark Neely, *The Fate of Liberty: Abraham Lincoln and Civil Liberties* (Oxford: Oxford University Press, 1991); William Rehnquist, *All The Laws But One: Civil Liberties in Wartime* (New York: Vintage 1998). Scholars continue to debate whether Lincoln's actions were lawful, but setting the constitutional issues to one side for the moment, it remains the case that most of these prisoners were detained for relatively short periods and released. In addition, the prisoners were not held incommunicado; they were allowed to interact both with other prisoners, and with their families. And finally, Congress substantially circumscribed the effect of Lincoln's suspension with the Habeas Corpus Act of 1863, which prevented indefinite detentions without legal process. *Ex Parte Milligan*, 4 Wall. 2, 132–33 (1866) (Taney, C.J., concurring); Rehnquist, *op. cit.*,pp. 129–131; Neely, *op. cit.*, pp. 202–3. Even the discredited Japanese internments offer no precedent for the Guantánamo detentions; on the same day the Supreme Court approved the detentions, they also held that detainees who could establish their loyalty were entitled to their release. *Korematsu v. United States*, 323 U.S. 214 (1944); *Ex Parte Endo*, 323 U.S. 283 (1944).

2. The Secretary of the Army recently suggested the war on terrorism "is a little bit like having cancer. You may get it in remission, but it's never going to go away in our lifetime" ("Army Chief Likens Terror Threat To Cancer," *Associated Press*, June 15, 2004, online).

There is also the nagging suspicion that much of our current musings about Guantánamo amount to little more than the first draft of history – that despite recent disclosures, almost everything worth knowing about the detentions will not be known for many years. At least, that seems to be one of the important lessons of recent scholarship. We learned only in 1983, when Peter Irons published *Justice At War*, that many of the justifications given by the military for the Japanese internments had in fact been untrue. His important work led ultimately to the judicial decisions vacating the convictions of Fred Korematsu and Gordon Hirabayashi.[1] Likewise, when the military first began transporting prisoners to Guantánamo, Vice President Cheney described them as "the worst of a very bad lot," a characterization echoed by others in the administration. Yet as of this writing, over one hundred have been released, none has been tried, and in recent published reports, senior administration officials have admitted that the administration greatly overstated the intelligence value of the Guantánamo detainees. Privately, administration officials acknowledge that a substantial number of the prisoners are likely innocent, an acknowledgment they have made publicly about the prisoners in Iraq. I suspect we will one day know considerably more about the detentions at Guantánamo than we do today.[2]

Finally, there is the opportunity for engaging speculation – but little more than speculation at this early stage – about whether, in the sober light of day, the architects of the post-9/11 detentions will come to regret their role. This is obviously related to the preceding question, since regret may accompany full disclosure. In any case, there is ample precedent for such ex post contrition, the most prominent example of which emerges from the debacle of the Japanese internments. Within weeks of Pearl Harbor,

---

1. Peter Irons, *Justice At War* (Oxford: Oxford University Press, 1983). For the court decisions, see *Korematsu v. United States*, 584 F. Supp. 1406 (N.D. Cal. 1984) (vacating conviction); *Hirabayashi v. United States*, 828 F.2d 591 (9 Cir. 1987) (vacating conviction for violating curfew); *Hirabayashi v. United States*, 627 F. Supp. 1445 (W.D. Wash. 1986) (vacating conviction for violating exclusion order). More recently, Jane and Harry Scheiber have performed much the same service with their painstaking and eminently readable account of martial law in Hawaii during the Second World War – a five-year period of unprecedented restriction on the civil liberties of citizens and foreign nationals alike, restrictions that the military insisted to the end were critical to our success in the Pacific. Harry N. Scheiber and Jane L. Scheiber, "Bayonets in Paradise: A Half-Century Retrospect on Martial Law in Hawaii, 1941–1946," *University of Hawaii Law Review*, Vol. 19, No. 1, Fall, 1997.

2. The cover sheet of one recently leaked memorandum, which argued that President Bush was not bound by the legal prohibitions on torture, indicated the document was to remain classified for ten years. See also Golden and Van Natta, *loc. cit.*

the Republican Attorney General of California became an enthusiastic and vocal supporter of internment. In January 1942, he warned ominously that the large number of Japanese Americans living on the West Coast "may be the Achilles Heel of the entire civilian defense effort. Unless something is done it may bring about a repetition of Pearl Harbor."[1]

Days later, the Attorney General was among the first to suggest the argument mentioned above – that the very absence of sabotage by Japanese Americans proved that sabotage was imminent: "It seems to me that it is quite significant that in this great state of ours we have had no fifth column activities and no sabotage reported. It looks very much to me as though it is a studied effort not to have any until the zero hour arrives."[2] Over the next several months, he proposed a veritable laundry list of anti-Japanese clichés to support internment. It was only many years later that Earl Warren, whose eventual tenure as Chief Justice became synonymous with an activist, liberal Supreme Court, would admit his error.

"I have since deeply regretted the removal order and my own testimony advocating it," Warren wrote in his memoirs. "It was wrong to react so impulsively without positive evidence of disloyalty, even though we felt we had a good motive in the security of our state. It demonstrates the cruelty of war when fear, get-tough military psychology, propaganda, and racial antagonism combine with one's responsibility for public security to produce such acts."[3] In an interview shortly before his death, Warren was moved to tears as he recalled the faces of the children separated from their parents during the relocations.[4] For now, one can only wonder whether the leading actors in today's tragedy, some of whom presumably look with disgust on the pictures of tortured and humiliated detainees, will likewise come to regret their role in creating the prison at Guantánamo Bay.

All of these are important topics, and I hope one day to have the opportunity to give them the careful attention they deserve. But as pressing as these questions may be, I would suggest they are merely the consequences

---

1. Jacobus TenBroek, Edward N. Barnhart, Floyd W. Matson, *Japanese American Evacuation and Resettlement: Prejudice, War and the Constitution* (Berkeley, University of California Press, 1958), p. 83 (quoting *Monterey Press Herald*, January 30, 1942). For a discussion of the same quote, see G. Edward White, *Earl Warren: A Public Life* (New York: Oxord University Press, 1982), p. 69 (quoting *Associated Press* news release, January 30, 1942).

2. TenBroek *et al.*, *op. cit.*, p. 84 (quoting Hearings, 77 Congress, 2nd sess., House Select Committee Investigating National Defense Migration (Washington: G.P.O., 1942)).

3. Earl Warren, *The Memoirs of Earl Warren* (New York: Doubleday 1977), p. 149.

4. White, *op. cit.*, p. 77.

of an earlier decision. The more important task, and my interest in this essay, is to consider causes rather than effects, and to reflect on the determination by the United States to create a prison beyond the law.

Ruminations on the Fear of Flying

Let me introduce the topic this way: flying can be extremely dangerous. During certain maneuvers, pilots may become so disoriented that they cannot trust their senses. Every instinct in their body will tell them that their life depends on taking a certain action. But tragically, their instincts during these periods cannot be trusted, and what they believe to be the only safe option may be precisely what kills them. By some estimates, this phenomenon, called spatial disorientation or SD, accounts for ten percent of all general aviation accidents, and ninety percent of the accidents attributable to SD are fatal. It is the most likely explanation for the crash that killed John F. Kennedy, Jr. In these moments, pilots must learn to disregard their instincts and to trust their instruments instead.[1]

As I reflect on the tension between civil liberty and national security, and on the particular example of this tension in the present conflict, I have found spatial disorientation a useful metaphor. It suggests the essence of the hysteria that periodically grips the nation, without casting it in pejoratives. As Chief Justice Warren's experience demonstrates, it is the sad fact that honorable, well-intended public servants, who in normal circumstances are steadfast in their commitment to the Constitution and the rule of law, nonetheless find themselves capable of simply reprehensible conduct during times of crisis.

---

1. Spatial disorientation (SD) is a well-recognized phenomenon. Among others, the United States Air Force Research Lab maintains an elaborate website dedicated to providing information about SD. See http://www.spatiald.wpafb.af.mil/index.aspx. Michael Baker, technical editor of *Flying Safety*, authored a useful primer available at this site which dispels certain common myths about SD: "Contrary to some popularly held notions, it isn't just the operator of high-performance aircraft, or the inexperienced flier, who is susceptible to the deadly effects of SD. SD is a phenomenon that transcends aircraft flight characteristics (high-performance or not), experience levels, affiliation (military or civil aviation), and aircraft type (large or small aircraft, fixed- or rotary-wing) . . . . In one of the most common – and dangerous – varieties of SD, the pilot doesn't know that he doesn't know which way is up. It is said there are two types of pilots: those who have experienced SD and those who don't know they've experienced SD." Michael Baker, "A Primer on Spatial Disorientation" (http://www.spatiald.wpafb.af.mil/There_Was.aspx?NID=1). The National Traffic Safety Board concluded the "probable cause" of Kennedy's fatal accident was "[t]he pilot's failure to maintain control of the airplane during a descent over water at night, which was a result of spatial disorientation" (http://www.ntsb.gov/pressrel/2000/000706.htm).

Every significant military conflict has had its singular example: during the Civil War, Lincoln suspended the writ of habeas corpus nationwide and resorted to military trials for civilians. During the First World War, thousands of people were tried, convicted, and sentenced to lengthy terms of imprisonment for the crime of speaking against the war, even when their supposedly seditious remarks had no remote capacity to affect the war effort. After the war, the Palmer Raids became synonymous with government hysteria. The Japanese internments represent one of the darkest chapters in our nation's history. The excesses of McCarthyism are still fresh, and the abuses uncovered by the Church Committee are a matter of recent history. A number of scholars have elaborated on this phenomenon, and the ground is by now well traveled.[1] On these occasions, otherwise thoughtful officials lost their moral compass, and held to their misguided judgments to the bitter end.

In the calm light of day, we look back at these periods with a deep and abiding regret, and berate ourselves in public displays of contrition. In the main, however, I believe we do a disservice when we cast these episodes in moralistic terms, as though the actors, faced with a clear choice between good and evil, calmly chose the latter. With notable exceptions, I no more believe this captures reality than the suggestion that a pilot who suffers from spatial disorientation chooses to crash. Political actors trapped in a tightening spiral of wartime hysteria simply cannot trust their instincts. They make their choices not because they fail to appreciate what they are doing, but because they believe they are doing precisely what must be done to preserve the nation. And typically they cling to their choices with a con-

---

1. As with all things Lincoln, a number of scholars have pondered the lawfulness of his various wartime actions. See, e.g., Rehnquist, *op. cit.*; Daniel Farber, *Lincoln's Constitution* (Chicago: University of Chicago Press, 2003); J. G. Randall, *Constitutional Problems Under Lincoln*, rev. ed. (Urbana: University of Illinois, 1951, originally published 1926). For a discussion of the Espionage and Sedition Act prosecutions during and immediately after World War I, see Zachariah Chafee, *Free Speech in the United States* (Clark, N. J.: Lawbook Exchange 2001, originally published Cambridge: Harvard University Press, 1941). A good primer on the Palmer Raids and the hysteria of the Red Scare can be found in Robert K. Murray, *Red Scare: A Study in National Hysteria: 1919–1920* (Minneapolis: University of Minnesota Press, 1955). The literature on the Japanese internments is simply voluminous. Some of the most important work is TenBroek *et al.*, *op. cit.*; Irons, *op. cit.*; Eugene Rostow, "The Japanese American Cases – A Disaster," *Yale Law Journal*, Vol. 54, 1945, p. 489. The literature on McCarthy and the House Un-American Activities Committee (HUAC) is similarly rich, but one author that discusses them in the context of the present conflict is David Cole (*op. cit.*). For a chilling account of four decades of domestic surveillance, see *Final Report of the Select Committee to Study Governmental Operations with Respect to Intelligence Activities*, S. Rep. No. 94–755, 94 Congress, 2nd Session (1976) (the "Church Committee").

fidence that may be mistaken as arrogance – even when they are terribly mistaken.

But the fact that actors may not have made a moral choice does not mean that circumstances present no moral obligations. Every pilot owes an obligation to himself and his passengers to be familiar with the phenomenon of spatial disorientation, and must learn to recognize the conditions most apt to produce it. And he must agree to abide by certain rules, including the obligation to maintain his instruments in good working order, and to trust them throughout his flight, even when his senses tell him to do otherwise. In short, while the pilot who misapprehends reality may be relieved of his moral obligation to make rational choices, he can certainly be faulted if he deliberately fails to prepare for the day when his judgment may become impaired. And we would be deeply dismayed if a pilot were to disable his instruments precisely when he is most likely to become disoriented. In short, and if I may be allowed to mix my metaphors, we do not blame Ulysses for his madness at the Sirens' call, but we would certainly have taken a dim view of his actions had he not ordered his men to tie him to the mast.

The Creation of a Prison Beyond the Law

With this metaphor in mind, consider the administration's rather unusual specifications: on the one hand, they believed they needed a secure facility where prisoners could be held in isolation from any outside influence, perhaps for decades to come. On the other hand, the inmates had to be readily accessible to the intelligence officials involved in the global campaign against al-Qaeda, which could at various times include the FBI, the CIA, the National Security Agency, and military intelligence. Ideally, the prison would not be in one of the fifty states, since doing so would place it within the potential supervision of a federal court. At the same time, however, it would be best if the prison were not within any foreign country, so the administration could plausibly argue that events at the prison did not fall within the jurisdiction of any foreign or international court. Isolated, but accessible; controlled by the United States, but beyond the reach of her courts; part of the United States, but not in the United States.

In the days after September 11, administration attorneys set to work devising a legal response to these unusual demands. In a remarkable development, we learned of their handiwork when two memos were leaked to the press and disclosed to the public. The first memo, written by Deputy

Assistant Attorney Generals Patrick Philbin and John Yoo, and dated December 28, 2001, addressed "whether a federal district court would properly have jurisdiction to entertain a petition for a writ of habeas corpus filed on behalf of an alien detained at the U.S. naval base at Guantánamo Bay, Cuba." The second memo, written by Yoo and Special Counsel Robert Delahunty and dated two weeks after the first, discussed whether prisoners captured in connection with the war in Afghanistan were protected by the laws of armed conflict, including the Geneva Convention.[1]

Taken together, these memos set out a veritable blueprint for the creation of a prison beyond the law. Both of them deserve careful scrutiny, as do the several memos that followed in their wake; for our purposes, however, the jurisdiction memo is the most important.[2] As an initial matter, it is apparent from the jurisdiction memo that the 'preferred' result – that is, the outcome viewed as most desirable by the administration – was a conclusion that the detainees were beyond the jurisdiction of a federal court. Indeed, the memo explicitly cautions that a contrary result could "interfere with . . . the system that has been developed" by the administration by allowing a federal court to review, among other things, "whether and what international law norms may or may not apply to the conduct of the war in Afghanistan." In other words, from the earliest days of the war on terror, the administration wanted to place these prisoners, and the lawfulness of Executive conduct, beyond the reach of a civil court.

To reach the desired result, Yoo and Philbin relied almost entirely on *Johnson v. Eisentrager*, a case involving German soldiers captured in China during the closing weeks of World War II. Their analysis of the decision, however, is dangerously simplistic. After Germany surrendered but while Japan fought on, the United States captured 27 Germans in China and charged them with assisting the Japanese army, in violation of the laws of war. At trial, the prisoners were represented by counsel and had the right to discover and introduce evidence, to call and confront witnesses, and to make opening and closing statements. After a trial that lasted months, six of the prisoners were acquitted and released, while 21 were sentenced to prison. Later they sought habeas relief in Washington, claiming their

---

1. Yoo and Delahunty are no longer with the administration; Yoo has returned to his position on the faculty of Berkeley Law School and Delahunty has joined the faculty of the University of St. Thomas Law School, in St. Paul, Minnesota. As of this writing, Philbin remains with the Department of Justice.

2. As we now know, these memos were the intellectual foundation for several subsequent memos that purported, among other things, to release the President and officers acting at his direction from domestic and international prohibitions against the use of torture.

trial had been unlawful. In Johnson, the Supreme Court disagreed, holding their trial had been fair, and that they had no right to habeas.

At first blush, it is hard to see how Johnson could help the administration, since the prisoners at Guantánamo, unlike the prisoners in Johnson, have been detained for more than two years with no process. It is one thing to hold that war criminals tried, convicted, and sentenced by a lawful commission, who had a full and fair opportunity to demonstrate their innocence and secure their release, could not seek further review in a civilian court. It is quite another to extend that holding to people who have never been charged.

But Yoo and Philbin relied on other language in Johnson to support their conclusion. In its opinion, the Supreme Court described post-war China (where the crime and trial took place) as an area subject to martial law; it described Germany (where the prisoners were eventually incarcerated) as enemy occupied territory. Collectively, the Court variously described the two areas as outside our "territorial jurisdiction," or beyond our "sovereignty." Without elaborating on which of these appellations was controlling, the Court suggested that the circumstances in Johnson placed the prisoners beyond the jurisdiction of a federal court.

Seizing on some of this language, Yoo and Philbin point to our lease with Cuba for the base at Guantánamo. Under the lease, the United States has "complete jurisdiction and control" over Guantánamo, but Cuba retains "ultimate sovereignty." These terms are not defined. Still, Yoo and Philbin rely on this language to argue that Guantánamo is no different than post-war Germany and China, since all could be described as beyond our "sovereignty." Neither the history nor the present reality of Guantánamo Bay is relevant to this argument, nor is the undeniable difference between Guantánamo and an active theater of military operations: under the lease, Cuba retains some undefined and indiscernible quantum of "sovereignty" over the base, and that – at least for Philbin and Yoo – was conclusive. It is worth examining this contention in more detail.

In 1901, after the Spanish-American War, the United States occupied Cuba. We offered to end the occupation, but only if Cuba included in its constitution a number of clauses drafted by the United States.[1] Known

---

1. Leland H. Jenks, *Our Cuban Colony* (New York: Vanguard Press, 1928), pp. 77–79. The President signed the Platt Amendment March 2, 1901, and it was presented to the Cuban Government the following day: "Their relations to the United States had been settled forever. They had only to vote the articles into their constitution. Until they did so, Cuba was clearly to be regarded as unpacified. The American Army of occupation would remain. The Cubans were entirely free to agree or disagree. They were entirely

as the Platt Amendment, these provisions forced Cuba to agree "that the United States may exercise the right to intervene" in Cuba and her affairs, and that Cuba would "embody the foregoing provisions in a permanent treaty with the United States." Cuba reluctantly added the provisions, verbatim, as an appendix to her constitution June 12, 1901.[1]

One provision of the Platt Amendment (and therefore of the Cuban constitution) required that Cuba "sell or lease to the United States the lands necessary for coaling or naval stations." Two years later, in 1903, Cuba leased Guantánamo Bay to the United States. The lease included the curious provisions identified by Professors Yoo and Philbin: the United States would exercise "complete jurisdiction and control," while Cuba retained "ultimate sovereignty."[2] The lease is indefinite, and cannot be terminated without the consent of the United States, which has repeatedly declared its intention to remain as long as it sees fit. Guantánamo is apparently the only United States military base in the world where the United States exercises complete and exclusive jurisdiction and control in perpetuity.

In light of this history, it is not surprising that the United States has long considered Guantánamo "practically . . . a part of the government of the United States." Solicitor General Olson, who represented the United States before the Supreme Court in *Rasul*, once described the base as part of our "territorial jurisdiction" and "under exclusive United States jurisdiction."[3] The Executive determines who may enter and leave the base, and enjoys the power under the lease "to acquire . . . any land or other property therein by purchase or by exercise of eminent domain." The United States is required under the lease to maintain "permanent fences" around the perimeter of the base. Inside these fence, however, the base enjoys all the trappings of a small American city; it is larger than Manhattan and more than half the size of the District of Columbia.

Congress has often extended federal statutes to Guantánamo and federal courts routinely take jurisdiction over disputes that arise from the base.[4] United States law governs the conduct of all who are present on

---

free to secure such independence as was possible under the Platt Amendment or to continue under the military administration. After several vain attempts to find a more palatable alternative, they added the provisions, word for word, as an 'appendix' to their constitution, June 12, 1901" (*ibid.*, pp. 77–78.)

1. *Ibid.*, pp. 80–82.

2. Agreement for the Lease to the United States of Lands in Cuba for Coaling and Naval Stations, February 23, 1903, Art. III, T.S. No. 418 (Agreement).

3. First quote see 25 Op. Att'y Gen. 157 (1904); Olson quote see 6 Op. O.L.C. 236, 242 (1982) (opinion of Asst. Attorney General Olson).

4. See, e.g., *Kirchdorfer, Inc. v. United States*, 6 F.3d 1573, 1583 (Fed. Cir. 1993) (find-

the base, and violations of criminal statutes are prosecuted in the government's name.[1] Equally important, Cuba's laws are wholly ineffectual in Guantánamo. The Castro government has long characterized the United States presence as illegal and refuses to cash the annual rent payment of $4,085 the United States has tendered pursuant to the lease.[2] "Ultimate sovereignty," however, apparently does not imply any actual authority, as the United States has ignored Cuba's complaints.

In sum, the arguments advanced by Yoo and Philbin reduce to the claim that the unexplained use of the term "ultimate sovereignty" in the lease with Cuba means that Guantánamo – despite all appearances to the contrary – is in fact no different than enemy occupied territory or an area subject to martial law. During the litigation in *Rasul*, this argument came to be known as "the Guantánamo fiction."

If the jurisdiction memo placed the prisoners beyond the protection of the federal courts, it was the Geneva Convention memo that literally placed them beyond the law. In this memo, Yoo and Delahunty constructed an elaborate argument that the prisoners at Guantánamo were not entitled to the protections of either the Geneva Convention, or customary international law. [Customary international law refers to those principles that have achieved such universal acceptance among the nations of the world – like the prohibition on torture – as to have the force of law.] Yet at the same time, Yoo and Delahunty concluded that while the prisoners did not enjoy any protections under the laws of war, they could be subjected to its disabilities, including both punishment as war criminals and indefinite detention. Yoo and Delahunty acknowledged that this result could seem "counter-intuitive," but defended it as "a product of the President's Commander-in-Chief and Chief Executive powers to prosecute the war effectively."

A comprehensive critique of the Geneva Convention memo is beyond the scope of this essay. But it is also unnecessary for our purposes, since certain deficiencies are apparent. First, the memo suffers from an obvious logical lacuna. Yoo and Delahunty argue that prisoners at Guantánamo have no rights because Taliban and al-Qaeda fighters, for a variety of rea-

---

ing violation of Takings Clause by Navy at Guantánamo); *Burtt v. Schick*, 23 M.J. 140 (U.S.C.M.A. 1986) (granting writ of habeas corpus and holding that impending court-martial proceeding on Guantánamo would constitute double jeopardy, in violation of 10 U.S.C. § 844(a)).

1. See, e.g., *United States v. Lee*, 906 F. 2d 117 (4 Cir. 1990).

2. *Bird v. United States*, 923 F. Supp. 338, 341 n.6 (D. Conn. 1996); Anita Snow, "Cuba Attacks Guantánamo Use for Prisoners," *Washington Post*, December 27, 2003, p. 14.

sons, do not enjoy the protections of either the Geneva Convention or cus-tomary international law. But this argument collapses if the prisoners are not associated with these groups. In other words, the argument suffers from the same myopia that clouds the administration's entire approach to the Guantánamo detentions – viz., it assumes the military has seized the right people.

The Geneva Convention explicitly accounts for the possibility that the military may capture a person whose status is not immediately clear, and who may in fact be innocent. In that event, the Convention requires that "any doubt" regarding the person's status must be resolved by a "competent tribu-nal," and that all detainees enjoy POW status until such a tribunal determines otherwise. Furthermore, and perhaps more importantly, the United States military has adopted a comprehensive set of regulations that implement this requirement. These regulations trace their origin to the Vietnam War, the first major conflict when the military regularly captured people whose status under the Convention was in doubt. Rather than allow innocent detainees to languish in custody, the military created "Article 5" tribunals to resolve all doubtful cases. At these tribunals, detainees enjoyed the "fundamental rights considered to be essential to a fair hearing," including the right to notice and an opportunity to be heard through counsel. Today, these regula-tions are binding on all branches of the Armed Forces, and Article 5 hear-ings have become a settled part of military practice; if an Article 5 tribunal determines the detainee is innocent, he must be immediately released.[1] In their memo, Yoo and Delahunty did not discuss this portion of the Geneva Convention, nor did they mention the relevant military regulations.

Second, and far more ominously, the Geneva Convention memo seri-ously misperceives the nature of the Commander-in-Chief power. Yoo and Delahunty advance the notion of an imperial presidency to its absolute limit. They suggest not only that the Commander-in-Chief has uncon-strained power over the detainees, but that any attempt by Congress to rein in this power would likely be unconstitutional. If this is correct, then the courts as well must bow to Executive power in this arena.

---

1. The relevant provision of the Convention can be found at Geneva Convention III, Art. 5, 6 U.S.T. §3324, 75 U.N.T.S. §142; the military regulation is codified at *Enemy Prisoners of War, Detained Personnel, Civilian Internees, and Other Detainees*, U.S. Army Regulation 190–8 (applicable to the Departments of the Army, Navy, the Air Force, and the Marines Corps), October 1, 1997. For a discussion of the history and current use of these provisions, see Frederic L. Borch, *Judge Advocates in Combat* (Washington, D.C.: U.S. Army Center of Military History, 2001); Howard S. Levie, *Prisoners of War* (Newport, R.I.: Naval War College Press, 1978).

If such an argument were accepted, it would reverse a line of decisions that date from virtually the dawn of the Republic. It was 1804 when the Supreme Court first struck down unilateral Executive action taken by the President in his capacity as Commander-in-Chief. Since that time, the law has developed with unmistakable clarity: "What are the allowable limits of military discretion, and whether or not they have been overstepped in a particular case, are judicial questions." Or, as Chief Justice Stone put it somewhat more recently, executive branch action is not "proof of its own necessity." The notion that the President, simply by assuming the mantle of Commander-in-Chief, may disregard Congress, the federal courts, and the binding obligations of international treaties is simply breathtaking.[1]

* * * * *

It is important to understand the combined effect of these memos. The Geneva Convention memo removed the detainees from the protections of the laws of war. But the jurisdictional memo ensured that no other legal regime could be put in its place. The detainees would not enjoy the benefit of an extant legal system specifically designed to protect people seized during armed conflict, but nor would they be able to secure the benefit of whatever protections might derive from a federal court. *Et voilà* – a prison beyond the law.

In the years to come, much will be written about these memos, and the others that followed in their wake. There is, for instance, an undeniable Alice In Wonderland quality to some of the reasoning: in the first memo, Yoo and Philbin argued that Guantánamo was beyond the jurisdiction of a United States court because it is outside our sovereignty. Yet in a later memo, administration lawyers argued that because Guantánamo is within the United States, Executive officials are not constrained by federal laws against torture, since they operate only in a foreign country. Reasoning like this is apparently the price of a dance with the devil.

And what do we distill from the fact that the memos themselves are so simplistic? If nothing else, it is unfortunate the administration had to rely on such ill-considered recommendations. We can only wonder whether a more thoughtful treatment of the issues – one that paid greater heed to the lessons of prior wartime excesses, for instance – would have led to a different result. Still, in keeping with the view expressed earlier, we should probably not be overly critical of the authors; it must be allowed that they were

---

1. First quote: *Sterling v. Constantin*, 287 U.S. 378, 401 (1932); second quote: *Duncan v. Kahanamoku*, 327 U.S. 304, 336 (1946) (Stone, C. J., concurring).

working under the same pressure that bedeviled so many before them. In that light, their work illustrates yet again "how war can upset a first-class thinker."[1]

But there is a more fundamental objection to these memos. In the middle of a conflict – precisely when history cautions us that we are least apt to be thinking clearly – the administration set about disabling the very instruments that mark our commitment to the rule of law: that the military must always be subject to civilian rule; that the proper limits of military discretion are ultimately, and always, judicial questions; that armed conflict – and particularly the treatment of prisoners – is not a descent into lawless anarchy, but is governed by carefully negotiated and reciprocal obligations; and that restraints on individual liberty must be subject to review by some impartial tribunal. Now was no time for flying blind.

Rasul v. Bush: The Supreme Court Weighs In

Every year, the Supreme Court agrees to review only a tiny fraction of the cases clamoring for its attention. For that reason, some lawyers believe, not without reason, that the most important document in a case is the one that petitions the Court to accept review, called the Petition for Writ of Certiorari. The Petition in *Rasul* went through perhaps a dozen drafts, and in the final product, we tried to capture not simply the legal reasons for review, but the moral consequences if the Court remained silent. In other words, we tried to convey what it would mean to the prisoners if the Court allowed the administration to create and maintain a prison beyond judicial scrutiny.

Certainly it would mean that prisoners could be tortured with impunity. But I was writing before the disclosures about Abu Ghraib, and we had no evidence that the prisoners at Guantánamo had been mistreated in the same manner. It would also mean that scores of innocent people could be left to languish. But this was before we learned that other military facilities were filled beyond capacity with innocent people. And because we had not been given access to our clients, we knew only what we could piece together from the fragmented accounts of families and friends, most of whom did not know how or why their relatives had been arrested.

---

1. Chafee, *op. cit.*, p. 108, note 3 (referring to contemporary attempts to defend the now-discredited Supreme Court decision in *Abrams v. United States*, 250 U.S. 616 (1919)). And of course, it is worth recalling that, at least with respect to the jurisdictional argument, the view of Guantánamo expressed by Yoo and Philbin had prevailed in the lower courts.

But in the end, I realized my greatest concern was that the administration would simply forget about them, "in the vain hope the world will as well."[1] The administration may have expected the country would eventually turn its attention elsewhere. In time, the prisoners would settle into the mind-numbing routine that characterizes prison life across the country. Nameless and faceless, lost to a world that would gradually grow indifferent, they would be left to "drift through life rather than live, the prey of aimless days and sterile memories."[2]

On November 10, 2003, the Supreme Court agreed to review the case. Later in the term, the Court also agreed to review cases involving the detention of two U.S. citizens, Jose Padilla and Yasser Hamdi. Padilla had been seized at O'Hare Airport in Chicago; Hamdi was allegedly seized in Afghanistan. Both were imprisoned at a brig in Charleston, South Carolina. Like the prisoners at Guantánamo, the President had dubbed them "enemy combatants" and, by nothing more than his ipse dixit, claimed they could be held without charges or access to counsel, and without allowing them an opportunity to be heard by a impartial tribunal, for as long as he saw fit. Formally, the three cases – *Rasul*, *Padilla*, and *Hamdi* – asked whether, and to what extent, the judiciary could police the bounds of the Commander-in-Chief power to detain people seized in apparent connection with the war on terrorism. But on the level of more immediate concern to the prisoners, they would determine whether the administration could detain people beyond the law.[3]

On the next-to-last day of the Term, the Court issued its decisions in all three cases. The holdings can only be described as a stinging rebuke to the administration. Eight members of the Court rejected the administration's position in *Hamdi*. Writing for a plurality of four, Justice O'Connor tersely reminded the administration that "[a] state of war is not a blank check for the President." The Commander-in-Chief power, she noted, is not a

---

1. *Rasul v. Bush*, No. 03–334, Petition for Writ of Certiorari, p. 13.

2. Albert Camus, *The Plague* (New York: Modern Library, 1948), p. 66

3. There were important differences between the cases. Relying on *Johnson v. Eisentrager*, the administration in *Rasul* claimed the prisoners were entirely beyond the jurisdiction of the federal courts. In *Padilla* and *Hamdi*, the administration agreed the federal courts had jurisdiction over the cases, but argued that the administration's explanation of why the two were being held – offered in the form of hearsay affidavits from an official with the Department of Defense – proved conclusively that the detentions were lawful. The prisoners could not contest the allegations made in these affidavits, and the court had to accept them as true. Jennifer Martinez, one of Padilla's lawyers, discusses his case in "Jose Padilla and the War on Rights," *Virginia Quarterly Review*, Volume 80, Number 4, Fall, 2004, online.

license to "turn our system of checks and balances on its head." In the words of Justice Souter, the President seems to have forgotten that he "is not Commander-in-Chief of the country, only of the military."

And the most passionate rebuke to the administration's position in *Hamdi* may have come from its most conservative member. Joined by Justice Stevens, Justice Scalia reminded the administration that democracy dies behind closed doors: "If civil rights are to be curtailed during wartime, it must be done openly and democratically, as the Constitution requires, rather than by silent erosion." To prosecute his habeas action, Hamdi must be given prompt notice of the allegations against him, and an opportunity to be heard. And if the administration cannot prove its claims, Yasser Hamdi must be released.

The administration fared no better in *Rasul*, where the Court held, by a 6–3 margin, that our clients could invoke the protection of the federal courts to determine whether their detention was lawful. The Court quickly dispatched the "Guantánamo fiction" that had prevailed in the lower courts, concluding the federal court in the District of Columbia had jurisdiction, notwithstanding the fact that Cuba retained "ultimate sovereignty" over Guantánamo Bay. For more than two years, we had argued the courts should look to the reality of events at Guantánamo, rather than some mythical notion of Cuban sovereignty. The Supreme Court agreed. "What matters," Justice Kennedy explained, "is the unchallenged and indefinite control that the United States has long exercised over Guantánamo Bay. From a practical perspective, the indefinite lease of Guantánamo Bay has produced a place that belongs to the United States." At the same time, the Court also rejected the outrageous suggestion that the President, in his capacity as Commander-in-Chief, could detain foreign nationals at Guantánamo indefinitely, "without access to counsel and without being charged with any wrongdoing." Lest anyone misunderstand, the Court made plain that such detention was "unquestionably" illegal.[1]

Students and scholars will study these decisions for years to come. Within months, a trickle of law review articles will begin to appear; in time, the trickle will likely increase to a flood. These articles will parse the decisions with meticulous care, debating every aspect of the various decisions – whether they vindicate the rule of law or dangerously limit the President's war power; what they resolve, what they leave for another

---

1. In a 5–4 decision, the Court in *Padilla* held that the case should have been filed in South Carolina instead of New York. But the decision in *Hamdi* leaves no doubt that Padilla will be entitled to relief once he files in the proper venue.

day; whether they were litigated well or poorly. I suppose I will join in this debate. For now, however, I would close this essay with the penultimate sentence of the majority opinion in *Rasul*:

> What is presently at stake is only whether the federal courts have jurisdiction to determine the legality of the Executive's potentially indefinite detention of individuals who claim to be wholly innocent of wrongdoing.

As the Court well knew when it "answer[ed] this question in the affirmative," much more was at stake in this case. By its decision, the Court reaffirmed – for all time, one fervently hopes – that at least so long as we would call ourselves a democracy, we can never tolerate a prison beyond the law.

THE EDITORS' GLOSS: Joseph Margulies was kind enough to pen the following few words of introduction to the excerpt we've included from Amnesty International's report on Guantánamo Bay.

The following summary of recent developments in the Guantánamo litigation accurately summarizes the state of play since the Supreme Court decision in *Rasul*. As I write, we are heading toward a second round of appellate litigation in the D.C. Circuit, and may be back in the Supreme Court before long. Over 500 prisoners continue to languish at the base – nearly the same number as before *Rasul* – and thousands more at similar prisons around the world. Unfortunately, AI's thoughtful and trenchant critique was overshadowed by the controversy that erupted from their description of Guantánamo as a "gulag." While I disagree with that characterization, and would not have described the base in that way, the tyranny of labels should not distract us from a serious discussion of this matter. The staff at AI, along with other talented researchers at organizations such as Human Rights First, have written excellent accounts of virtually every aspect of the Bush administration's failed detention policy, and it would be a terrible shame if we dismiss their reports simply because we take issue with some of their language.

More importantly, the lesson seems at last to be getting through. Thomas Friedman recently called for President Bush to shut Guantánamo down (*New York Times,* May 27, 2005). Senator Biden (D-Del.) echoed the call days later ("Biden Urges U.S. to Take Steps to Close Prison at Guantánamo," *Associated Press,* June 6, 2005). Two days after that, former President Carter made the same plea ("Carter: Close down Guantánamo," *Associated Press,* June 7, 2005) The next day, President Bush acknowledged that his administration was "exploring all alternatives" to the base ("U.S. Wants Gitmo Prisoners Held at Home," *Associated Press,* June 9, 2005).

We shall see. Events may yet confirm the judgment of Dr. King, who reminded us that "the arc of the moral universe is long, but it bends towards justice." Meanwhile, my own take – essentially as I presented it to the Senate Judiciary Committee – on the Combatant Status Review Tribunal, created in response to *Rasul*, follows the AI selection.

Joseph Margulies
Chicago, Illinois
June 9, 2005

29

Seeking to Render *Rasul* Meaningless

. . . .

Amnesty International

I N THE SPACE of two weeks in January 2005, two diametrically opposed responses to the same question of law were handed down by judges on the same federal court in Washington, D.C. The first displayed a troubling degree of deference to attempts by the executive branch to ignore its human rights obligations, while the second showed a welcome respect for human rights. The U.S. administration supports the former ruling and rejects the latter. It should change direction.

Responses to Habeas Corpus Petitions

Each of the two judges in question – Judge Richard Leon and Judge Joyce Hens Green of the District Court for the District of Columbia – was faced with petitions from detainees labeled as "enemy combatants" and held in indefinite executive detention in Guantánamo. The petitions were asking the judges to issue writs of habeas corpus so that the detainees could challenge the lawfulness of their detention, a basic protection under international law against arbitrary arrest, torture and "disappearance," also explicitly provided in the U.S. Constitution (Article 1, Section 9).[1] The petitions had been filed following the U.S. Supreme Court's decision of 28 June 2004, *Rasul v. Bush*, which held that the federal courts "have jurisdiction to consider challenges to the legality of the detentions of foreign nationals captured abroad in connection with hostilities and incarcerated at Guantánamo Bay."[2] The decision was widely welcomed as a first step to restoring the rule of law to Guantánamo,[3] but the U.S. administration has

---

1. Also widely considered to be provided elsewhere within the Constitution, for instance in the requirement of "due process of law" in the Fifth and Fourteenth Amendments.

2. *Rasul v. Bush*, 000 U.S. 03–334 (2004).

3. For example, at a press conference in Geneva on December 10, 2004, the UN High

sought to drain it of real meaning, and to keep any review of the detentions as narrow and as far from a judicial process as possible.

In a press release issued immediately after the *Rasul* ruling, the U.S. Justice Department interpreted it as holding that "individuals detained by the United States as enemy combatants have certain procedural rights to contest their detention."[1] The Department's use of the word "procedural," rather than "substantive," is telling. It would later argue in the D.C. District Court that the Guantánamo detainees had no grounds under constitutional, federal or international law on which to challenge the lawfulness of their detention. In other words, according to the administration's Kafkaesque vision for Guantánamo, the *Rasul* ruling should be interpreted as mandating no more than a purely procedural right – the detainees could file habeas corpus petitions, but only in order to have them necessarily dismissed. Any further action would be an "unprecedented judicial intervention into the conduct of war operations, based on the extraordinary, and unfounded, proposition that aliens captured outside this country's borders and detained outside the territorial sovereignty of the United States can claim rights under the U.S. Constitution."[2] This was the same position the administration had adopted before the *Rasul* ruling.

The administration has done nothing to facilitate the Guantánamo detainees' access to legal counsel so that they can file petitions to challenge the lawfulness of their detention. Moreover, in the cases where individuals do have lawyers for their habeas corpus appeals, there is concern that the authorities have tried to undermine the relationships between detainees and their counsel. In addition, it would appear that the detaining authorities have offered little or no practical advice to the detainees about how they might go about seeking a lawyer.

Ten days after the *Rasul* ruling, the Department of Defense announced the formation of the Combatant Status Review Tribunal (CSRT) to "serve as a forum for detainees to contest their status as enemy combatants."[3]

Commissioner for Human Rights expressed relief at the Supreme Court's decision, noting that the U.S. courts had historically played a leadership role in the protection of civil liberties. The UN Working Group on Arbitrary Detention also welcomed the ruling. UN Doc. E/CN.4/2005/6, December 1, 2004, para. 64.

1. Statement of Mark Corallo, Director of Public Affairs, regarding the enemy combatant cases. Department of Justice news release, June 28, 2004.

2. *Hicks v. Bush*. Response to petitions for writ of habeas corpus and motion to dismiss or for judgment as a matter of law and memorandum in support. In the U.S. District Court for the District of Columbia, October 4, 2004.

3. Combatant Status Review Tribunal order issued. U.S. Department of Defense News Release, July 7, 2004.

The Pentagon asserted that the CSRT's procedures were intended to "reflect the guidance the Supreme Court provided" in *Rasul v. Bush* coupled with another ruling issued on the same day, *Hamdi v. Rumsfeld*.[1] The latter decision concerned Yaser Esam Hamdi, a U.S. citizen captured in the armed conflict in Afghanistan and held without charge or trial as an "enemy combatant" on the U.S. mainland. The plurality in the split *Hamdi* decision said that "due process demands that a citizen held in the United States as an enemy combatant be given a meaningful opportunity to contest the factual basis for that detention before a neutral decisionmaker." The *Hamdi* plurality held that "the threats to military operations posed by a basic system of independent review are not so weighty as to trump a citizen's core rights to challenge meaningfully the government's case and to be heard by an impartial adjudicator."

With this reference to "military operations" in mind, it should be stressed that the CSRT was not devised to conduct battlefield determinations of the status of detainees. It was devised more than two years *after* detentions began, for use thousands of miles away from the point of capture, regardless of whether that capture occurred on the battlefield of an international conflict long since over or *on the street of a city in a country not at war in the first place.*

Meanwhile, in Afghanistan, where some detainees have been in U.S. custody for more than a year, not even the CSRT process is being applied. Once detainees in the custody of the U.S. Department of Defense in Afghanistan are designated as an "enemy combatant," they have an initial review of that status by a commander or designee within 90 days of being taken into custody. After that, "the detaining combatant commander, on an annual basis, is required to reassess the status of each detainee. Detainees assessed to be enemy combatants under this process remain under DoD control until they no longer present a threat."[2]

The administration's penchant for secrecy and disregard for the fundamental rights of detainees is further displayed in the rules for the

---

1. *Hamdi v. Rumsfeld*, 03–6696, decided June 28, 2004. The Pentagon said: "The Supreme Court held that the federal courts have jurisdiction to hear challenges to the legality of the detention of enemy combatants held at Guantánamo Bay. In a separate decision – involving an American citizen held in the United States (i.e. *Hamdi*) – the Court also held that due process would be satisfied by notice and an opportunity to be heard, and indicated that such process could properly be provided in the context of a hearing before a tribunal of military officers." Department of Defense, Combatant Status Review Tribunals.

2. USA's Periodic Report to the UN Committee against Torture, May 6, 2005 (http://www.state.gov/g/drl/rls/45738.htm), Annex 1.

Combatant Status Review Tribunal. The detainees had no access to legal counsel (only to a "personal representative" – a military officer) or to classified evidence to assist them in the CSRT process, yet the burden was on the detainee to disprove his "enemy combatant" status:

> Following the hearing of testimony and the review of documents and other evidence, the Tribunal shall determine in closed session by majority vote whether the detainee is properly detained as an enemy combatant. Preponderance of the evidence shall be the standard used in reaching this determination, but there shall be a rebuttable presumption in favor of the government's evidence.[1]

The CSRT – a panel of three "neutral" military officers – was "free to consider any information it deems relevant and helpful," including "hearsay evidence, taking into account the reliability of such evidence in the circumstances." Evidence extracted under torture or other coercion was not excluded. As the principal deputy associate attorney general of the U.S. Justice Department argued to Judge Richard Leon:

> If in fact information came to the CSRT's attention that was obtained through a non-traditional means, even torture by a foreign power, I don't think that there is anything in the due process clause [of the U.S. Constitution], even assuming they were citizens, that would prevent the CSRT from crediting that information for purposes of sustaining the enemy combatant class[ification].[2]

The July 7, 2004, order establishing the CSRT was intended "solely to improve management within the Department of Defense concerning its detention of enemy combatants at Guantánamo Bay Naval Base, Cuba, and is not intended to, and does not, create any right or benefit, substantive or procedural, enforceable at law, in equity, or otherwise by any party against the United States . . . ."[3] Guantánamo began receiving "war on terror" detainees following legal advice from the Justice Department that "a district court cannot properly entertain an application for a writ of habeas corpus by an enemy alien detained at Guantánamo Bay Naval Base, Cuba."[4]

1. Memorandum for the Secretary of the Navy. Subject: Order establishing Combatant Status Review Tribunal. Signed by Paul Wolfowitz, Deputy Secretary of Defense, July 7, 2004.

2. *Benchellali et al v. Bush et al.* Transcript of motion hearing before the Honorable Richard J. Leon, U.S. District Judge, in the U.S. District Court for the District of Columbia, December 2, 2004.

3. Memorandum for the Secretary of the Navy. Subject: Order establishing Combatant Status Review Tribunal. Signed by Paul Wolfowitz, Deputy Secretary of Defense, July 7, 2004.

4. Re: Possible habeas jurisdiction over aliens held in Guantánamo Bay, Cuba.

The *Rasul* ruling showed otherwise, but the administration has refused to admit that this legal advice, like the legal advice on torture contained in other previously secret administration memorandums, disregarded international law and fundamental human rights standards. The CSRT process is an improvised, minimalist response to the U.S. Supreme Court's rulings designed to keep the lawfulness of the detentions away from judicial or other external scrutiny for as long as possible.

The CSRT Order added that nothing contained in it should be construed to "limit, impair, or otherwise affect" the President's Commander-in-Chief powers. This has been reflected in the subsequent statistics. On 29 March 2005, the authorities announced that they had completed all the CSRTs for the current detainees in Department of Defense custody in Guantánamo.

- Of the 558 CSRT decisions finalized by March 29, 2005, all but 38 (93 percent) affirmed that the detainee was indeed an "enemy combatant" as broadly defined by the Order.

- Amnesty International's review of 60 cases filed in the D.C. District Court by April 2005 reveals that most were decided inside a single day, and that in all 58 cases which gave the voting details, the CSRT panel was unanimous in finding the detainee to be an "enemy combatant." These 58 cases were all finalized in late 2004.

- Eighty-four percent of the cases (32 out of 38) where the detainee was found *not* to be an "enemy combatant" were decided later than February 1, 2005, *after* Judge Joyce Hens Green ruled that the CSRT process was inadequate and unconstitutional, but *before* the appeal against her decision was heard. In its April 27, 2005, brief appealing to the U.S. Court of Appeals for the District of Columbia Circuit to overturn Judge Green's ruling, the government emphasized these 38 cases as a sign of a constitutionally fair system. The brief did not point out – or explain whether it was pure coincidence – that all but six of them had been decided after Judge Green's finding that the CSRT process was unlawful.[1]

Memorandum for William J. Haynes, II, General Counsel, Department of Defense, from John C. Yoo, Deputy Assistant Attorney General, U.S. Department of Justice, December 28, 2001. Although the memorandum concluded that no federal court could "properly entertain" a habeas corpus petition from a Guantánamo detainee, it warned that there was some possibility that a court could do so.

1. *Al Odah et al. v. USA et al.* Opening brief for the United States *et al.* In the United States Court of Appeals for the District of Columbia Circuit, April 27, 2005, p. 51. The USA also noted these 38 cases in its Second Periodic Report to the UN Committee against Torture.

• This sudden and marked increase in findings that a detainee was no longer an "enemy combatant" also coincided with a period during which the Pentagon was said to be looking to reduce the number of detainees held at the base in the wake of the administration's losses in the courts, including by "outsourcing" detentions to other countries.

Creating procedures that bypass international norms and avoiding judicial scrutiny for its actions should be unacceptable to any government which believes that fundamental human-rights principles are non-negotiable, as the U.S. claims to. As Judge Green said in her recent ruling on the Guantánamo detainees:

> Of course, it would be far easier for the government to prosecute the war on terrorism if it could imprison all suspected "enemy combatants" at Guantánamo Bay without having to acknowledge and respect any constitutional rights of detainees. That, however, is not the relevant legal test.... Although this nation unquestionably must take strong action under the leadership of the Commander-in-Chief to protect itself against enormous and unprecedented threats, that necessity cannot negate the existence of the most basic fundamental rights for which the people of this country have fought and died for well over two hundred years.

For consistency's sake, it had been agreed to have a single judge, Judge Joyce Hens Green, a senior judge appointed to the court in 1979, resolve issues common to the Guantánamo cases.[1] Thus, when the government filed its motion to dismiss the petitions for a writ of habeas corpus, the motion being common to all the cases, other judges on the court transferred this issue to Judge Green. However, Judge Richard Leon declined to participate in this arrangement. He subsequently became the first judge to issue a ruling interpreting the *Rasul* decision.[2] He sided with the government and dismissed the petitions.

On January 19, 2005, just over three years after the Guantánamo detentions began, Judge Leon in essence determined that whereas under the Supreme Court ruling Guantánamo detainees have the right to *petition* federal courts for a habeas corpus writ, they nevertheless do not have the right to *obtain* such writs. He ruled that there was "no viable legal theory"

1. United States District Court for the District of Columbia, Resolution of the Executive Session, September 15, 2004.

2. *Khalid v. Bush*, Memorandum opinion, U.S. District Court for the District of Columbia, January 19, 2005 (http://www.dcd.uscourts.gov/opinions/2005/Leon/2004-CV-1142~7:40:40~3–2-2005-a.pdf).

by which he could issue writs of habeas corpus to foreign detainees held without charge or trial in the naval base. In Judge Leon, appointed to the court by President George W. Bush in 2002, the administration found an ally for its position that *the "war on terror" is a global armed conflict* and that under the President's Commander-in-Chief powers, individuals broadly defined as "enemy combatants" could be picked up by the U.S. anywhere in the world and be subjected to executive detention for the duration of the "war." He agreed with the government that the detainees have no rights under constitutional law to challenge the lawfulness of their detention because they are non-resident foreign nationals captured abroad and held in a naval base whose "ultimate sovereignty" was Cuba's.[1] Similarly, he concluded that they had no rights under federal or international law. He seemed satisfied to give the government the benefit of the doubt on the question of torture and ill-treatment, despite the mounting evidence of such abuses by U.S. forces in the "war on terror."[2]

A Judge with Security Credentials
Takes a More Critical View

Judge Joyce Hens Green, who stressed that she had served as the chief judge of the United States Foreign Intelligence Surveillance Court, "the focus of which involves national security and international terrorism," cast an apparently far more critical eye over the situation.[3] Her decision,

---

1. The USA occupies the Guantánamo base under a 1903 lease, in which "the United States recognizes the continuance of the ultimate sovereignty of the Republic of Cuba over the [leased areas]," while the "Republic of Cuba consents that during the period of occupation by the United States . . . the United States shall exercise complete jurisdiction and control over and within said areas." In 1934, the two parties entered into a treaty whereby, absent their agreement to amend or repeal the lease, it would remain in effect as long as the USA "shall not abandon the . . . naval station of Guantánamo."

2. USA: Guantánamo: Trusting the Executive, Prolonging the Injustice, AI Index: AMR 51/030/2005, January 26, 2005 (http://web.amnesty.org/library/Index/ENGAMR 510302005). [See also the comprehensive piece on the torture and abuses at Abu Ghraib and elsewhere by Col. Dan Smith on pp. 509–552 of the present volume.—Ed.]

3. The Foreign Intelligence Surveillance Court was created under the Foreign Intelligence Surveillance Act (FISA) of 1978. It used to have seven judges on it, but the USA PATRIOT Act of 2001 amended FISA to increase the number to 11. Among the current 11 are Judges Coleen Kollar-Kotelly and James Robertson of the D.C. District Court. The former ruled against the Guantánamo detainees on the question of jurisdiction which was subsequently reversed by the U.S. Supreme Court in *Rasul v. Bush* on June 28, 2004. She noted at the time that her opinion "should not be read as stating that these aliens do not have some form of rights under international law." The ruling of Judge Robertson in November 2004 led to suspension of trials by military commission (see p. 477ff).

handed down on 31 January 2005, offered the detainees and their families hope that justice will yet be done and their legal limbo ended.[1]

Judge Green noted that the Guantánamo detainees seeking habeas corpus relief included men taken into custody as far away from Afghanistan as Gambia, Zambia, Bosnia and Thailand. She wrote that "although many of these individuals may never have been close to an actual battlefield and may never have raised conventional arms against the United States or its allies, the military nonetheless has deemed them detainable as 'enemy combatants.'" She noted that the government had chosen to submit to the court as factual support for the detentions only CSRT records, despite claiming that the detainees' cases had been subjected to unspecified "multiple levels" of administrative review. The "nature and thoroughness" of these alleged multiple levels of review, she said, must be called into "serious question."[2] CSRT proceedings had only commenced from late July 2004, at which point most of the detainees had already been held for more than two years.[3]

Unlike Judge Leon, Judge Green rejected the government's argument that the detainees have no substantive rights, concluding that they must have more than just the procedural right "to file papers in the Clerk's Office." She rejected the government's notion – which lay behind its choice of Guantánamo as a location for "war on terror" detentions – that because Cuba retains "ultimate sovereignty" over Guantánamo, U.S. Supreme Court precedent meant that the detainees have no rights under the U.S. Constitution. On this point, she noted the irony that, while the Cuban government had claimed that the U.S. was violating the human rights of the Guantánamo detainees and had demanded their humane treatment, the U.S. government "does not appear to have conceded the Cuban government's sovereignty over these matters." The executive will only point to Cuba's "sovereignty" over the base when it suits the U.S. agenda.

---

1. In re Guantánamo detainee cases, Memorandum Opinion Declining in Part and Granting in Part Respondents' Motion to Dismiss or Grant for Judgment as a Matter of Law in the U.S. District Court for the District of Columbia, January 31, 2005 (http://www.dcd.uscourts.gov/opinions/2005/Green/2002-CV-299~8:57:59~3-2-2005-a.pdf).

2. Despite the administration's claims about "multiple levels of review," it appears that numerous individuals have been detained in Guantánamo on flawed intelligence, their release only coming after many months if not years of detention. Some detainees, for example Salim Ahmed Hamdan (see below), were reportedly "sold" to the USA by individuals in Afghanistan and Pakistan – the CIA was reportedly offering U.S.$5,000 for al-Qaeda suspects.

3. The final CSRT hearing was held on January 22, 2005.

In the *Rasul* ruling, the Supreme Court majority had said in a footnote:

> Petitioners' allegations – that, although they have engaged neither in combat nor in acts of terrorism against the United States, they have been held in Executive detention for more than two years in territory subject to the long-term, exclusive jurisdiction and control of the United States, without access to counsel and without being charged with any wrongdoing – *unquestionably describe custody in violation of the Constitution or laws or treaties of the United States* (emphasis added).

The government argued to Judge Leon that "it is not for us to speculate . . . on the basis of mood music from the [*Rasul*] opinion."[1] In his subsequent ruling dismissing the Guantánamo detainees' petitions, Judge Leon characterized the reliance of the petitioners on the footnote as "misplaced and unpersuasive."

Judge Green, however, adopted a different stance, writing that "it is difficult to imagine that the Justices would have remarked that the petitions 'unquestionably describe custody in violation of the Constitution or laws or treaties of the United States' unless they considered the petitioners to be within a territory in which constitutional rights are guaranteed." Thus, Judge Green ruled, "it is clear that Guantánamo Bay must be considered the equivalent of a U.S. territory in which fundamental constitutional rights apply." Specifically, she held that the detainees had the Fifth Amendment right not to be deprived of liberty without due process of law.

Judge Green said that a relevant factor in the Guantánamo cases is the potential length of the incarcerations. She noted that the administration was asserting the right to hold "enemy combatants" until the "war on terror" is over or the executive determines that the individual no longer poses a threat to national security. She noted that the government had been unable to inform her of how long it believed the "war on terror" might last, or even how it will determine when it has ended. She continued:

> At a minimum, the government has conceded that the war could last several generations, thereby making it possible, if not likely, that "enemy combatants" will be subject to terms of life imprisonment at Guantánamo Bay. Short of the death penalty, life imprisonment is the ultimate deprivation of liberty, and the uncertainty of whether the war on terror – and thus the period of incarceration – will last a lifetime may be even worse than if the detainees had been tried, convicted, and definitively sentenced to a fixed term.

---

1. *Benchellali et al v. Bush et al.* Transcript of motion hearing before the Honorable Richard J. Leon, U.S. District Judge, in the U.S. District Court for the District of Columbia, December 2, 2004.

At the end of his Combatant Status Review Tribunal on 1 September 2004, Yemeni national Fahmi Abdullah Ahmed said:

> Just know that I have been here for three years and have [not] been in touch with my family. I don't think this is just and it's not right for the American legal system to not allow people to talk to their families. It is a very small right that is allowed to all detainees around the world.[1]

The tribunal president responded that "we are here today to determine your enemy combatant status, and that alone is what we focus our attention on today." On that same day, the panel of three military officers unanimously decided that Fahmi Abdullah Ahmed was an "enemy combatant," as has been done in 519 other cases. He remains held without charge or trial or access to his relatives.[2]

The Administration's Response

The conflict between Judge Green's and Judge Leon's interpretations of the detainee's post-*Rasul* rights will have to be resolved in a higher court, either the U.S. Court of Appeals for the District of Columbia Circuit, or possibly in the U.S. Supreme Court. At the end of April 2005, the administration filed its opening brief in the Court of Appeals arguing that Judge Green's opinion should be overturned. Its arguments show an administration in an unapologetic mood, in continuing pursuit of unfettered executive authority under the President's war powers as Commander-in-Chief, and disregarding international law and standards. Among its arguments are that:

(1) The due process clause of the U.S. Constitution's Fifth Amendment "is inapplicable to aliens captured abroad and held at Guantánamo Bay, Cuba." This, the government argues, repeating its pre-*Rasul* position, is because the "United States is not sovereign over Guantánamo Bay" and U.S. Supreme Court precedent makes it clear that the applicability of the Fifth Amendment to aliens "turns on whether the United States is sovereign, not

---

1. *Ahmed et al. v. Bush et al.* CSRT unclassified factual returns. In the U.S. District Court for the District of Columbia.

2. Principle 19 of the UN Body of Principles for the Protection of All Persons under Any Form of Detention or Imprisonment states: "A detained or imprisoned person shall have the right to be visited by and to correspond with, in particular, members of his family and shall be given adequate opportunity to communicate with the outside world, subject to reasonable conditions and restrictions as specified by law or lawful regulations." Rule 37 of the UN Standard Minimum Rules for the Treatment of Prisoners states: "Prisoners shall be allowed under necessary supervision to communicate with their family and reputable friends at regular intervals, both by correspondence and by receiving visits."

whether it merely exercises control, over the territory at issue." Moreover, "to construe a single, oblique footnote as implicitly overruling decades of settled precedent would be utterly implausible . . . ." In addition,

> [I]f the courts were to second-guess an Executive Branch determination regarding who is sovereign over a particular foreign territory, they would not only undermine the President's lead role in foreign policy, but also compromise the very capacity of the President to speak for the Nation with one voice in dealing with other governments.

(2) Even if the Fifth Amendment did apply to foreign nationals held at Guantánamo, the CSRT procedures would exceed whatever due process requirements there were. The CSRT process, the administration argues, "manifestly satisfies the requirements of due process (if any) in the unique context of ongoing armed hostilities." Moreover, the CSRT procedures criticized by Judge Green "are not constitutionally problematic." The need for deference to the executive on the question of withholding classified information and legal counsel from the detainees is "greatly magnified here, where the issue is not the administration of domestic prisons, but the Executive Branch carrying out incidents of its war-making function."

(3) The definition of "enemy combatant" is not overbroad, as Judge Green found. According to the administration, "although there may be difficult calls at the margin, that has been true in every war, and . . . the determination of who are enemy combatants is a quintessentially military judgment entrusted primarily to the Executive Branch." The executive, the executive argues, "has a unique institutional capacity to determine enemy combatant status and a unique constitutional authority to prosecute armed conflict abroad and to protect the Nation from further terrorist attacks. By contrast, the judiciary lacks the institutional competence, experience, or accountability to make such military judgments at the core of the war-making powers. These concerns are especially pronounced given the unconventional nature of the current war and enemy . . . ."

(4) On the question of the Geneva Conventions, Judge Green "should have deferred to the view of the Executive as to whether the treaty was intended to grant those captured during an armed conflict judicially enforceable rights." Judge Green's contention that the Taliban detainees should have been presumed to have prisoner of war status is "inconsistent with the deference owed to the President as Commander-in-Chief."[1]

---

1. *Al Odah et al. v. USA et al.* Opening brief for the United States *et al.* In the United States Court of Appeals for the District of Columbia Circuit, April 27, 2005 (internal quotation marks omitted).

Thus, at every step, the executive continues to place obstacles in the way of the detainees having their cases subjected to judicial scrutiny. It continues to appeal every decision that goes against it. By continuing its bid for unfettered executive power, rather than heed the ever-mounting criticism, it is inflicting further damage on the rule of law, human rights principles, and the international reputation of the U.S. Meanwhile, the detainees are kept in a legal black hole created by the U.S. administration. Forced to share in this limbo, their families are subjected to what may amount to cruel, inhuman, or degrading treatment.[1] *The situation remains a human rights scandal.*

The Administrative Review Board

For any detainee affirmed as an "enemy combatant" by the Combatant Status Review Tribunal – except those pending trial by military commission – it will be up to another purely administrative process to review each case once a year to determine if the detainee should be released, transferred to the custody of another country, or continue to be detained. The Administrative Review Board (ARB) process will consist of

> an administrative proceeding for consideration of all relevant and reasonably available information to determine whether the enemy combatant represents a continuing threat to the U.S. or its allies in the ongoing armed conflict against al-Qaeda and its affiliates and supporters (e.g., Taliban), and whether there are other factors that could form the basis for continued detention (e.g., the enemy combatant's intelligence value and any law-enforcement interest in the detainee).[2]

As with the CSRT, the detainee will have no access to legal counsel or to secret evidence, and there is no rule excluding evidence extracted under

---

1. Amnesty International has spoken to many relatives of Guantánamo detainees who themselves are in deep distress from the lack of transparency and information about their loved ones and their inability to visit them. In other contexts, the suffering of the relatives of the "disappeared" has been found by the UN Human Rights Committee to amount to torture or cruel, inhuman, or degrading treatment. Similar cruelty is inflicted upon the relatives of people held in indefinite virtual incommunicado detention without charge or trial. See *Maria del Carmen Almeida de Quinteros, on behalf of her daughter, Elena Quinteros Almeida, and on her own behalf v. Uruguay*, Communication No. 107/1981 (September 17, 1981), UN GAOR Supp. No. 40 (A/38/40) p. 216 (1983), para. 14. Regional human rights courts reached similar conclusions, see for instance Velasquez Rodriguez Case, Compensatory Damages (Art. 63(1) American Convention on Human Rights), Judgment of July 21, 1989 Inter-Am.Ct.H.R. (Ser. C) No. 7 (1990), para. 51; *Kurt v. Turkey*, Case No. 15/1997/799/1002 Judgment of 25 May 1998, paras. 133–4.

2. Implementation of administrative review procedures for enemy combatants detained at U.S. Naval Base Guantánamo Bay, Cuba. Department of Defense, September 14, 2004.

torture or other coercion. In the case of the CSRT, the decision is made by the panel of three military officers; for the ARB, the panel makes a recommendation to the Designated Civilian Official (DCO) overseeing the process, who takes the final decision.

In addition to labeling Guantánamo detainees as broadly-defined "enemy combatants" in a broadly-defined global "war" the end of which it can neither predict nor define, the U.S. administration has repeatedly labeled the detainees as "killers" and "terrorists," in violation of the presumption of innocence. This label has been pinned to all detainees, including those subsequently released without any evidence made available that they had committed any wrongdoing. At the same time, the administration states that the reason that a detainee may find himself in Guantánamo Bay is not necessarily because he is guilty of any offense, but because he might commit an offense in the future or might have knowledge of or association with such unlawful activities.[1]

Military Commissions

Military commissions, meanwhile, established under the Military Order on the Detention, Treatment, and Trial of Certain Non-Citizens in the War Against Terrorism signed by President Bush on 13 November 2001, provide for the prosecution of "enemy combatants who violate the laws of war." The administration sees the military commissions as "entirely creatures of the President's authority as Commander-in-Chief . . . and are part and parcel of the conduct of a military campaign."[2] In essence, the proposed military commissions are a case of the law being made and administered by the executive.

In the context of the "war on terror," the U.S. administration defines both the enemy and the war very broadly. In its *Hamdi* decision of June 28, 2004, the U.S. Supreme Court noted that "the government has never provided any court with the full criteria that it uses in classifying individuals as ['enemy combatants']." The administration subsequently wrote the CSRT Order of July 7, 2004, which states that

---

1. For example, at a military commission pre-trial hearing for Salim Ahmed Hamdan in Guantánamo Bay on August 24, 2004, the military prosecutor asked a military commission panel member, "Do you understand that just because someone was transported to Guantánamo does not mean that they are guilty of an offense?"

2. Potential legal constraints applicable to interrogations of persons captured by U.S. Armed Forces in Afghanistan. Memorandum for William J. Haynes, II, General Counsel, Department of Defense, from Jay S. Bybee, Assistant Attorney General, U.S. Department of Justice, February 26, 2002.

the term "enemy combatant" shall mean an individual who was part of or supporting Taliban or al-Qaeda forces or partners. This includes any person who has committed a belligerent act or has directly supported hostilities in aid of enemy armed forces.

In her January 2005 ruling, Judge Joyce Hens Green concluded that this overbroad definition of "enemy combatant," with its use of the word "includes," showed that the government considers that it can subject to indefinite executive detention even individuals who had never committed a belligerent act or who never directly supported hostilities against the U.S. or its allies. This, she gleaned from the government, could include "a little old lady in Switzerland" whose charitable donation to an orphanage in Afghanistan ends up supporting al-Qaeda.[1]

As already noted, the UN Independent Expert on the Protection of Human Rights and Fundamental Freedoms while Countering Terrorism wrote in his recent report that: "However States conceive of the struggle against terrorism, it is both legally and conceptually important that acts of terrorism not be invariably conflated with acts of war."[2] Yet the Pentagon's instructions for the military commissions extend the concept of armed conflict to include "a single hostile act or attempted act," or conspiracy to carry out such acts, a definition so broad that it could encompass many acts that would normally fall under the jurisdiction of the ordinary criminal justice system. The instructions specifically state:

This element does not require a declaration of war, ongoing mutual hostilities, or confrontation involving a regular national armed force. A single hostile act or attempted act may provide sufficient basis so long as its magnitude or severity rises to the level of an "armed attack" or an "act of war," or the num-

---

1. During a hearing in her court on December 1, 2004, Judge Green had asked the government a series of hypothetical questions to ascertain how broadly it interpreted its detention powers. The government responded that it could subject to indefinite executive detention: "'A little old lady in Switzerland who writes checks to what she thinks is a charity that helps orphans in Afghanistan, but [what] really is a front to finance al-Qaeda activities'; a person who teaches English to the son of an al-Qaeda member; and a journalist who knows the location of Osama bin Laden, but refuses to disclose it to protect her source." In front of Judge Leon, the Principal Deputy Associate Attorney General suggested that in the example of the Swiss woman, he had been misquoted and that what he had said was that "in the fog that is often the case in these situations that it would be up to the military applying its process and in going through its classification function to determine who to believe. If in fact this woman, there was some reason to believe this woman did know she was financing a terrorist operation, that would certainly merit a detention both theoretically and practically." The government's position would still be that she could be held indefinitely without charge or trial or judicial review of the merits of her case.

2. UN Doc. E/CN.4/2005/103, February 7, 2005, para. 17.

ber, power, stated intent, or organization of the force with which the actor is associated is such that the act or attempted act is tantamount to an attack by an armed force. Similarly, conduct undertaken or organized with knowledge or intent that it initiate or contribute to such hostile act or hostilities would satisfy the requirement.[1]

Despite these broad definitions, by March 2005, only four people had been charged under the Military Order. This small number could be for any of several reasons – a dearth of evidence against the detainees even given the fact that the military commission rules allow a conviction on lesser standards of evidence than pertain in the ordinary courts; a preference on the part of the U.S. administration for detention without trial; or official sensitivity in the face of the widespread international criticism about the military commission process, even from close allies.

Military commission proceedings against two U.K. nationals were suspended following the widespread public concern in the U.K. that followed their naming under the Military Order in July 2003.[2] From facing the possibility of being charged with war crimes and tried by military commission with the power to sentence them to death, the two detainees in question, Feroz Abbasi and Moazzam Begg, were transferred to the U.K. in January 2005 and released. Their cases further illustrate how the U.S. has detained people, indefinitely and in cruel conditions, against whom whatever evidence it has is considered by other governments to be inadequate, unreliable, or inadmissible even for a simple felony, let alone war crimes. It also suggests a political as well as an additionally arbitrary aspect to the detention – namely that any detainee's treatment depends upon the response and influence of his home government.

As well as the four detainees already charged, another nine detainees have been determined by President Bush to be subject to the Military Order, but had not been charged as of early April 2005.[3] One of these nine

---

1. Department of Defense. Military commission instruction no.2: Crimes and elements for trials by military commission. Section 5(c).

2. According to the Pentagon, President Bush decided on July 18, 2003, "to discuss and review potential options for the disposition of British detainee cases and not to commence any military commission proceedings against British nationals pending the outcome of those meetings [with the U.K. authorities]." DoD statement on British detainee meetings, Department of Defense news release, July 23, 2003.

3. Presidential military order applied to nine more combatants. Department of Defense news release, July 7, 2004. [Navy Lt. Cmdr. Charles Swift confirmed AI's report of the status of those charged under the military commission in his June 15, 2005, testimony before the Senate Judiciary Committee. "It has been nearly four years since the horrific attacks of September 11, 2001. Not a single person has been prosecuted in the Military Commission. Only four people have been charged. Of those four, none can be said to be

detainees has been transferred to his country of nationality and released.[1] His identity, or the identity of the other eight and whether they are held in Guantánamo, remain unknown. Another reason why the administration may be delaying charging them or any others is because it is waiting for resolution of the litigation over the legality of these commissions in the U.S. federal courts. In November 2004, the post-*Rasul* petition for a writ of *habeas corpus* filed with District of Columbia District Judge James Robertson on behalf of Salim Ahmed Hamdan, challenging the lawfulness of the U.S. administration's plans to try this Yemeni detainee, led to the suspension of the military commissions.

Judge Robertson reasoned that Salim Ahmed Hamdan, captured during the international armed conflict in Afghanistan, should have been presumed to be a prisoner of war until a "competent tribunal" determined otherwise, as required under Article 5 of the Third Geneva Convention. The judge pointed out that as a presumed prisoner of war, Hamdan could not be tried by a military commission; under Article 102 of the Third Geneva Convention "a prisoner of war can be validly sentenced only if the sentence has been pronounced by the same courts according to the same procedure as in the case of members of the armed forces of the Detaining Power." U.S. forces would normally be tried by court-martial under the Uniform Code of Military Justice (UCMJ). "The Military Commission is not such a court," stressed Judge Robertson; "Its procedures are not such procedures."

Judge Robertson ruled that, even if a "competent tribunal" determined that Salim Ahmed Hamdan was not a prisoner of war, he could not be tried by military commission because their rules were unlawful. Specifically, the treatment of classified or otherwise "protected" information did not meet the necessary standards. Judge Robertson pointed out that, in front of a military commission,

> The accused himself may be excluded from proceedings ... and evidence may be adduced that he will never see (because his lawyer will be forbidden to disclose it to him). Thus, for example, testimony may be received from a confidential informant, and Hamdan will not be permitted to hear the testimony, see the witness's face, or learn his name. If the government has information developed by interrogation of witnesses in Afghanistan or elsewhere, it can offer such evidence in transcript form, or even as summaries of transcripts. The [commission authorities] may receive it in evidence if it meets the "reasonably probative" standard but forbid it to be shown to Hamdan.

a high-ranking member of al Qaeda or anything close to it." See http://judiciary.senate.gov/testimony.cfm?id=1542&wit_id=4361.—Ed.]

1. USA's Second Periodic Report to the UN Committee against Torture.

Judge Robertson pointed out that "such a dramatic deviation" from the U.S. constitutional right to a fair trial "could not be countenanced in any American court," and added that the right to trial "in one's presence" is "established as a matter of international humanitarian and human rights law."[1] However, he said that he needed to look no further than to the fact that, at least in this critical respect, the rules for the military commissions were contrary to, or inconsistent with, the requirements for U.S. courts-martial which allow the defendant to be present in all proceedings except during the panel's deliberation and vote.

Judge Robertson emphasized that this issue was far from hypothetical, pointing out that Salim Ahmed Hamdan had already been excluded from parts of the commission panel selection process and that the government

1. Including under Art. 14 of the International Covenant on Civil and Political Rights (ICCPR) and Art. 75 of Protocol Additional I to the Geneva Conventions. The latter has long been considered by the USA to reflect customary international law, but the current administration, as part of its pursuit of unfettered executive power and disregard for international law, has refused to accept the applicability of this norm. The Pentagon's Working Group Report on Detainee Interrogations in the Global War on Terrorism: Assessment of Legal, Historical, Policy, and Operational Considerations, April 4, 2003 (http://www.defenselink.mil/news/Jun2004/d20040622doc8.pdf), states that among the international instruments not binding on the USA is Art. 75 of the First Additional Protocol to the Geneva Conventions, overturning the USA's long-held recognition of the "fundamental guarantees" of Art. 75 as reflecting customary international law. (Cf. remarks by M. Matheson, U.S. State Department deputy legal adviser, in "The Sixth Annual American Red Cross-Washington College of Law Conference on International Humanitarian Law: A Workshop on Customary International Law and the 1977 Protocols Additional to the 1949 Geneva Conventions," *American University Journal of International Law & Policy*, Vol. 2, 1987, pp. 415, 425–426, cited in Theodor Meron, *Human Rights and Humanitarian Norms as Customary Law* (New York: Clarendon Press, 1989), p. 65. The deputy legal adviser stated that "the United States will consider itself legally bound by the rules contained in Protocol I only to the extent that they reflect customary international law, either now or as it may develop in the future" (*ibid.*, p. 420). Similarly, the U.S. Army's Judge Advocate General's School has indicated that Art. 45 of Protocol I is consistent with customary international law. Judge Advocate General's School, U.S. Army, *Operational Law Handbook*, JA 422, p. 18–2 (1997) (stating that "the U.S. views [Art. 45] as customary international law"). Five years later, a revised version of this manual (Judge Advocate General's School, U.S. Army, *Operational Law Handbook*, ch. 2 (2002)) stated that the U.S. viewed Art. 45 as "customary international law or acceptable practice though not legally binding," but no evidence was cited or exists demonstrating that the customary rule of international law codified in Art. 45 has been abrogated.) Art. 75 prohibits, inter alia, physical and mental torture, outrages upon personal dignity, in particular humiliating and degrading treatment, as well as trial by any tribunal other than "an impartial and regularly constituted court respecting the generally recognized principles of regular judicial procedure." While not expressly referring to the right to appeal to a higher tribunal, it states that "no provision of this Article may be construed as limiting or infringing any other more favorable provision granting greater protection, under any applicable rules of international law." Consistent with the Human Rights Committee's General Comment 31, then, this would include the provisions of the ICCPR, which does include such right to appeal.

had already indicated that he would be excluded from two days of his trial during which the prosecution would present evidence against him.

Judge Robertson abstained on the question of whether such a trial would violate common Article 3 of the Geneva Conventions, which prohibits trials by any tribunal other than "a regularly constituted court affording all the judicial guarantees which are recognized as indispensable by civilized peoples." However, as Judge Robertson noted elsewhere in his opinion, the International Court of Justice has said that the protections of Common Article 3 "constitute a minimum yardstick" reflecting "elementary considerations of humanity."

An Illusion of Lawful Process
• • • • • • • • •
Joseph Margulies, Esq.

M Y COMMENTS IN what follows are directed at the unlawful nature of the Combatant Status Review Tribunals, or CSRTs, held in Guantánamo. They take *Rasul* as the starting place, and consider some of the problems that have arisen since the case was decided by the Supreme Court roughly one year ago. *Rasul* reaffirmed a simple, but indispensable principle of constitutional democracy: there is no prison beyond the law. After *Rasul*, prisoners seized in ostensible connection with the war on terror cannot be held in a legal black hole, subject to whatever conditions the military may devise for so long as the President sees fit, with no opportunity to demonstrate their innocence and secure their release. Instead, federal courts have the authority and responsibility to determine for themselves the lawfulness of a prisoner's continued incarceration.

But the promise of *Rasul* remains unfulfilled. Within days of the decision, the military announced the creation of the Combatant Status Review Tribunals. The CSRTs create nothing more than the illusion of a lawful process. As I said in my argument to Judge Joyce Hens Green in the federal district court in December 2004, the CSRT mocks this nation's commitment to due process, and it is past time for this mockery to end.

I will address three aspects of the CSRTs: the failure to provide an adequate process; the willingness to rely on evidence secured by torture; and the superficial similarity to so-called Article 5 hearings.

The CSRT Is the Perfect Storm of Procedural Inadequacy

Drawing from a universe of potential procedures, the military has adopted the worst features available to it, and combined them in a grotesque parody of due process.

First, the CSRT applies an overly expansive definition of "enemy combatant," one that sweeps within its reach wholly innocent or inadvertent conduct. In the Supreme Court in this case, the government defined "enemy combatant" as a person who "is part of or supporting forces hostile to the United States and engaged in an armed conflict against the United States."[1] But in the CSRT, the military unilaterally took it upon itself to change this definition from the conjunctive to the disjunctive, and now an "enemy combatant" is anyone who is part of or supporting forces or who engaged in armed conflict. Moreover, that "support" may be entirely accidental or unintentional, as for instance, contributing to a charity without realizing its connection to the Taliban.[2] No amount of due process can rescue a system that simply asks the wrong question.

Second, using this expansive definition, the CSRT presumes the accuracy of the military intelligence it receives, placing the burden on the prisoner to disprove his status.[3]

Third, though the prisoner has the burden, the tribunal relies on secret evidence withheld from him.[4]

Fourth, this evidence may have been secured by torture or other forms of coercive interrogation. I discuss this particular problem in more detail below.

Fifth, the prisoner – a foreign national who has been held for months or years virtually incommunicado – must confront and overcome this secret evidence without the benefit of counsel.[5]

And finally, the CSRT routinely denies the prisoner the opportunity to uncover and present evidence that would prevent a miscarriage of justice. In the same way, the CSRT consistently refuses to inquire into the reliability or provenance of the evidence offered by the military.[6]

The result is simply this: the CSRT asks the wrong question, and then applies a wholly deficient process to produce consistently unfair and arbitrary results.

* * * *

1. Brief for the Respondents, *Rasul et al. v. Bush et al.*, 124 S.Ct. 2686 (2004), pp. 5–6.

2. *In re Guantánamo Detainee Cases*, 355 F.Supp.2d, pp. 482, 475 (D.D.C. 2005).

3. *Implementation of Combatant Status Review Tribunal Procedures for Enemy Combatants Detained at Guantánamo Bay Naval Base, Cuba*, July 29, 2004, §§(g)(11)–(12) (http://www.defenselink.mil/news/Jul2004/d20040730comb.pdf).

4. *In re Guantánamo Detainee Cases*, 355 F.Supp.2d, pp. 468–472.

5. *Ibid.*, p. 468.

6. *Ibid.*, p. 473.

In its court papers, the government makes much of the fact that, viewed in isolation, each procedural piece of the CSRT has been applied in other hearings. It is worth examining that contention in more detail.

Certainly it is true, for instance, that some proceedings do not provide for the assistance of counsel. But not where the government also places the burden on the prisoner to disprove secret evidence, or where an adverse determination may lead to permanent loss of liberty.

Likewise it is true that some proceedings rely, although very rarely, on secret information withheld from the claimant. But not where the prisoner has the burden of disproving the very evidence he cannot see, must do it without the assistance of counsel, and where his failure may lead to his permanent incarceration. And even in the examples relied on by the government, the entire body of evidence was at least reviewed by an Article III court. Here it is not.

Certainly there are cases where the government places some restrictions on the right to prepare and present evidence. But not where the government may rely on evidence secured by torture, then prevent any impartial inquiry into the reliability of this evidence.

There are cases where the issue was decided by a 3-member panel, whether military or otherwise. But not where superiors have explicitly and repeatedly prejudged the issue, and the burden is on the prisoner to rebut that prejudgment.

In sum, let me be as blunt as I can. I am aware of no case, and the government has cited to none, where a potentially permanent loss of liberty is made to depend on a process so devoid of procedural fairness, a process so apt to produce an unjust or arbitrary result. Whether viewed in isolation or in their entirety, the procedures used by the CSRT are a mockery of our commitment to due process.

For the First Time in U.S. History, the Government Is Allowed to Imprison People Based on Evidence Secured by Torture

Each of the various pieces of the CSRT puzzle could be the subject of considerable testimony. Let me focus on one: the CSRT relies on evidence that may have been secured by torture or other forms of coercive interrogations, with no inquiry into its reliability.

The record in these cases indicates the "evidence" against most prisoners consists largely of their uncorroborated statements to interrogators, or the uncorroborated statements of other prisoners. Yet we know several things that should give us pause: we know the government uses interrogation techniques beyond that authorized by the Geneva Conventions;[1] we know the government has repeatedly revised and expanded the permissible interrogation techniques allowed at Guantánamo;[2] we know *from the government* that a number of prisoners have been abused in various ways;[3] and we know that a substantial number of prisoners allege they have been tortured and mistreated, at Guantánamo and elsewhere.[4]

Despite this, the CSRT makes no provision to exclude this evidence – or even to inquire into its reliability – nor does the government suggest otherwise.

Let me discuss one case in particular. I represent Mr. Mamdouh Habib. Mr. Habib was seized in Pakistan and rendered to Egypt, where he was held for 6 months. The U.S. government, through the Department of State, has long decried use of torture by Egyptian authorities. While he was in Egypt, Mr. Habib was subjected to diabolical tortures that have now been described in a number of public documents, including the decision by Judge Green.[5]

Yet the CSRT, based entirely on his uncorroborated statements, found him to be an "enemy combatant." Mr. Habib told the CSRT that his statements had been secured by torture, and the CSRT took his allegations seriously enough that it directed the government to investigate, but that investigation is not part of the CSRT, which merely presumed the accuracy of the military's evidence, as it must do under the rules.[6]

I met repeatedly with Mr. Habib, and we intended to press his allegations very vigorously. Five days after the allegations about his rendition and mis-

---

1. See, e.g., *Final Report of the Independent Panel to Review DOD Detention Operations* ("The Schlesinger Report"), August, 2004.

2. See, e.g., Appendix A of the testimony presented by the author before the Senate Judiciary Committee, "Chronology of United States Policy on Torture and Interrogations," June 15, 2005 (http://judiciary.senate.gov/), along with the article by Col. Dan Smith on pp. 509–552 of the present volume.—Ed.

3. See, e.g., Appendix B of the author's testimony, *ibid.*, "Summary of United States Government Documents Evidencing Detainee Torture and Abuse."

4. See, e.g., Amnesty International USA, *Guantánamo and Beyond: The Continuing Pursuit of Unchecked Executive Power*, AI Index No. AMR 51/063/2005, May 13, 2005, online [*vide infra*, p. 698, note 1, for URL—Ed.] ; Physicians for Human Rights, *Break Them Down: Systematic Use of Psychological Torture by U.S. Forces*, 2005 (http://www.phrusa.org/research/torture/pdf/psych_torture.pdf).

5. *In re Guantánamo Detainee Cases*, 355 F.Supp.2d, p. 473.

6. *Ibid.*

treatment came to light, however, the Department of Defense announced that Mr. Habib would be released, and he is now back in Australia with his family.

Mr. Habib's case is not unusual.

Prisoners who have been released report that the Bosnian-Algerians were repeatedly tortured at Guantánamo, and at least one of the Algerians, Mr. Ait Idir, told the CSRT he had been beaten by the guards at the base. The CSRT conducted no inquiry.[1]

Mr. al-Rawi and Mr. El-Banna, seized in Africa, allege they were beaten for weeks at a time in US custody.[2] Mr. Martin Mubanga alleges he was tortured.[3] The CSRT made no inquiry into these allegations.

The CSRT regarding Faruq Ali Ahmed relied on testimony from a detainee who, according to personal representative "has lied about other detainees to receive preferable treatment and to cause them problems while in custody." Yet the CSRT undertakes no inquiry at all. It merely presumes the testimony of the other prisoner to be true.[4]

In the CSRT regarding Mr. Al-Kandari, the legal advisor to the CSRT, says "the evidence considered persuasive by the Tribunal is made up almost entirely of hearsay evidence recorded by unidentified individuals with no first-hand knowledge of the events they describe."[5]

Any process that allows evidence that may have been secured by torture or abuse to go unexamined, and uses that evidence to support a man's imprisonment, has no place in American law.

The Superficial Similarity to an Article 5 Hearing Does Not Rescue the CSRT

Finally, let me address the superficial similarity between the CSRT and so-called Article 5 hearings.

---

1. See Mustafa Ait Idir, Unclassified Summary of the Basis for Tribunal Decision, *Boumediene et al. v. Bush et al.*, Civil Action No. 04-cv-1166 (D.D.C.) (RJL).

2. See Bisher al-Rawi, Classified Summary of Basis for Tribunal Decision, Unclassified Summary of Basis for Tribunal Decision, *El-Banna et al. v. Bush et al.*, Civil Action No. 04-cv-1144 (D.D.C.) (RR).

3. See Martin Mubanga, Unclassified Summary of Basis for Tribunal Decision, *ibid.*

4. See Faruq Ali Ahmed, Unclassified Summary of Basis for Tribunal Decision, *Abdah et al. v. Bush et al.*, Civil Action No. 04-cv-1254 (D.D.C.) (HHK).

5. See al-Kandari, Unclassified Summary of Basis for Tribunal Decision, *Al-Odah et al. v. United States of America et al.*, Civil Action No. 02-cv-0828 (D.D.C.) (CKK).

As a number of courts have now recognized, the CSRT and Article 5 hearings serve radically different purposes, and operate under entirely different circumstances.[1] The Article 5 hearing takes place in the field, immediately after capture, and is designed to make a swift, "rough-and-ready" determination of the prisoner's legal status so that he may be treated appropriately:

> If he is determined to be a prisoner of war, he is given POW status and treated in accordance with the Geneva Conventions;
>
> If there is reason to believe he has committed a war crime, he is turned over for military prosecution;
>
> If there is reason to believe he violated civilian law, he is turned over to civilian authorities for domestic prosecution;
>
> And if he is innocent, he is returned to the place of capture and released.

In other words, an adverse determination at an Article 5 hearing *leads either to detention under the Geneva Conventions, or to the additional process* appropriate to the prisoner's legal status. This additional process helps insure against an unjust result. Because the Article 5 hearing is undertaken quickly, in the field, and followed by appropriate legal process, it may be summary in form.

By contrast, the CSRT is undertaken months or years after arrest or capture, thousands of miles from the battlefield, after scores of interrogations. Furthermore, an adverse determination in a CSRT is not followed by additional legal process; the prisoner will have no further opportunity to demonstrate his innocence. Yet this determination can lead to a permanent loss of liberty under uniquely severe conditions. Just as the Article 5 hearing may be summary because it is followed by additional process that guards against arbitrary outcomes, the CSRT must be robust because it is followed by what may be life imprisonment under singularly onerous conditions.

Yet despite the differences between the CSRT and an Article 5 hearing – differences that call for *more* procedural protections in the CSRTs, there are in fact fewer in the CSRT than in an Article 5 hearing:

In a CSRT, the burden is on the prisoner to disprove his status. In an Article 5, by contrast, the prisoner is presumed to be a POW.

---

1. See, e.g., *Hamdan v. Rumsfeld*, 344 F.Supp.2d, p. 152 (D.D.C. 2004).

In a CSRT, the entire senior military and civilian chain of command has repeatedly prejudged the result, and declared the prisoners to be "enemy combatants." Indeed, they have been described as "the worst of the worst," and "trained killers." In an Article 5 hearing, by contrast, the prisoner begins the hearing as a POW protected by the Geneva Conventions. In every other adjudicative context, due process calls for a hearing followed by an announcement of the result; here, senior officials announced the result, then assigned junior officers to hold the hearing.

I, and the other lawyers involved in these cases, welcome the recent inquiry by the Senate Judiciary Committee. We hope by the Committee's guidance and oversight we are able to fulfill the promise of *Rasul*, and demonstrate once again that we are a nation of laws, and not of men.

THE EDITORS' GLOSS: Jeff Steinberg's article stands on its own merits as a credible sketch of what the "Niger uranium-Joe Wilson-Valerie Plame-Karl Rove-White House" affair is all about. Let us, therefore, offer a word as to why we've included a postscript by Jacob Weisberg on what some might consider a tangential issue: how reporters Judith Miller of the *New York Times* and Matthew Cooper of *TIME* fared in the investigation into the Plame identity leak.

Few besides Weisberg and a number of perceptive bloggers saw the real problems with the arguments that were made in defense of Judith Miller's alleged stand on the sanctity of reporter-source confidentiality, in which she refused to cooperate with the pertinent grand jury investigation. Much of the mainstream "liberal" press, which subserviently went along with war at the outset and only begrudgingly admitted, after the fact, a lack of discrimination in separating fact from fiction, held up Miller as an icon of principle, single-handedly defending the First Amendment from those out to destroy it. Never mind that she was one of the biggest supporters of war and was largely responsible for popularizing some of the most outrageous lies in the pre-war period. Perhaps the timidly anti-war mainstream media saw her defense as a way to absolve themselves of their own sins on the war, speciously arguing that she – like them – was just reporting what she was told by "confidential" and anonymous "sources." Ignored by the mainstream media was the fact that her silence was a practical defense of a White House operation designed to punish Joe Wilson and deter future critics from coming forward. This presumably explains why the "conservative" press and "right-wing" pundits (e.g., William Safire) were so ready to jump on the "canonize Judith Miller" bandwagon, despite her liberal – though rabidly pro-war – credentials.

At any rate, the idea that the "principle" of "journalistic confidentiality" is an absolute, non-negotiable good, which trumps considerations of law, justice, and morality, is patently outrageous. The idea is so ridiculous, in fact, that one might have just cause to be suspicious of those who defend it. It's almost as if this absurd idea, and the debate that's surrounded it, is yet another creation of the spin machine, designed to achieve other less obvious ends. It has happened before.

CHAPTER
30

Far, Far Worse Than Watergate:
The "Outing" of Valerie Plame
• • • • • • • • •

Jeffrey Steinberg

WATERGATE HAD ITS "Deep Throat," that Nixon-era information source that helped bring down a presidency. In the Valerie Plame case, the revelation by columnist Robert Novak that she was a covert CIA agent was supposedly based on leaked information from "senior White House officials." But, as of this writing, they, unlike Deep Throat, remain unnamed.

Over the course of the past decade, Americans have been shocked by a number of spy scandals, involving fairly senior officers of the armed forces, the Central Intelligence Agency and the Federal Bureau of Investigations. The two most egregious cases involved CIA agent Aldrich Ames and FBI counterintelligence officer Robert Hanssen. Both men are serving life sentences for betraying their country's secrets and undercover agents to the Soviet Union and the post-USSR Russian Federation.

The Ames and Hanssen cases sparked a national debate: what drives such men and women to commit acts of treason – especially acts which include betraying the identities of American intelligence agents and assets who are almost certain to face sudden death if captured? There is no easy or pat answer to the question. How, then, is one to judge the Valerie Plame case? Former Nixon White House Counsel John Dean, now a respected Republican lawyer and judicial analyst, has described the leaking of Ms. Plame's identity as an undercover CIA officer by "senior White House officials" as a crime "worse than Watergate."

There is no doubt he is right. Indeed, he may prove to be a master of understatement. From July 14, 2003, the day Valerie Plame's name and her CIA status first appeared in a nationally syndicated column by Robert Novak, I have been doggedly pursuing the story. I have interviewed dozens of sources of varying degrees of knowledge about the case,[1] compared notes with many other investigators and interested parties, and followed all of the twists and turns of the Bush administration's damage control efforts. Valerie Plame's husband, former Ambassador Joseph Wilson, a central player in the entire affair, has, in the intervening months, written an autobiography, with much detail about the background to the leak. In 2004, during an appearance at the Miller Center for Public Policy at the University of Virginia, Wilson presented a detailed timeline of the events; and the Senate Select Committee on Intelligence produced a lengthy report on the intelligence "failures" leading up to the Iraq invasion of March 2003, containing a detailed timeline, culled from documents and witnesses, that sheds further light on the story.

As I write this analysis, the grand jury is literally "still out" on a case that, in many respects, is of more grave consequence than the Ames and Hanssen cases. For here we are dealing with still-serving members of the executive branch of the U.S. federal government – indeed employees in the Office of the President of the United States. These are individuals with the highest levels of security clearance, who, it appears, betrayed a secret intelligence officer's identity out of political revenge. As a result, a senior career officer, with two decades of expertise hunting down weapons of mass destruction, has been taken out of action. Her many contacts, built up over years of dangerous overseas work as a "non-official cover" officer, have all been jeopardized by the leak. And the cover of a longstanding CIA proprietary company, at the heart of the U.S. government's efforts to track WMD, has been blown. One of my intelligence sources indicated that the CIA is conducting a damage assessment of the Plame leak, and that there are suspicions that overseas assets of the front company where she worked as a "non-official cover" officer, were arrested and, in at least one case, probably tried and executed.

In short, the Valerie Plame case is a story of national betrayal, petty vengeance by senior government officials, and a diminishing of America's capabilities to detect dangerous weapons of mass destruction. The case

---

1. Individuals I've interviewed include several high-ranking current members of the U.S. intelligence community, a number of former senior U.S. intelligence officials, four retired U.S. military intelligence officers, a former Israeli intelligence officer, and a wide array of journalists who specialize in national security affairs. A colleague of mine also interviewed four members of the Defense Policy Board and several former U.S. Ambassadors to Middle Eastern and African countries.

suggests a degree of cynicism and political manipulation by senior government officials on a scale perhaps never before seen in the history of our proud nation.

Saddam's "Bomb"

While Afghanistan was the first target, war planning for an Iraq action was authorized by the Bush administration within days of 9/11. Although skepticism ran deep within the ranks of professional military commanders, intelligence officers, and diplomats about Saddam's ties to the 9/11 attacks and the need or justification for regime change in Baghdad, the neoconservatives who dominate the Pentagon civilian bureaucracy and the "shadow national security council" housed in the office of Vice President Dick Cheney were not about to miss the opportunity of a lifetime to implement their longstanding fantasies to redraw the map of the Middle East, starting in Baghdad.

Two issues stood out as the basis for justifying a U.S. military invasion to overthrow Saddam Hussein. First it was argued, on the flimsiest of "proof," that Saddam Hussein had been the secret architect of the al-Qaeda attacks on September 11. Second, that Saddam Hussein had been secretly amassing an arsenal of weapons of mass destruction, for use against Israel, against Iraq's Arab and Muslim neighbors, and against Iraq's own people. While the U.S. intelligence community overwhelmingly rejected any Saddam links to al-Qaeda and 9/11, there were deep divisions over just how far along Saddam had got in his pursuit of WMD, following the 1998 departure of UN weapons inspectors, who had virtually rid Iraq of WMD during their seven years of on-the-ground inspections.

According to the Senate Select Committee on Intelligence in October 2001, U.S. intelligence officials began receiving reports that Iraq had been secretly seeking to purchase large amounts of yellowcake, a precursor to enriched uranium, from the African state of Niger. Initial reports had been provided to U.S., British, and other intelligence services by the Italian military intelligence agency, SISMI, which, according to Vincent Cannistraro, was itself fed the documents by a questionable source. When word of the purported Iraq-Niger yellowcake transactions reached the office of Vice President Dick Cheney, he tasked his CIA briefing officer to pursue the lead further. For Cheney, the architect of the Bush administration's war drive against Baghdad, any evidence of Saddam advancing his efforts to acquire a nuclear bomb was worth its weight in gold.

In February 2002, the CIA responded by dispatching Joseph Wilson to Niger to pursue the story. (A trip, by the way, for which Wilson was not paid a salary, debunking the suggestion from some quarters that this had been some kind of choice assignment due to his wife's influence.) Wilson was the perfect choice for the mission. He had been a career foreign service officer in Africa for years. He had served in Niger, and had developed close working ties to some of the people who would have necessarily been involved in any secret yellowcake sales, had any taken place. Furthermore, as the number two diplomat at the U.S. embassy in Baghdad in 1991, he had been the last American official to meet face-to-face with Saddam Hussein, just weeks before the January 1991 invasion. And he had been given one of the highest diplomatic medals from President George H.W. Bush for his service in Iraq. If anyone could dig out the truth about the Niger-Iraq allegations, it was Joe Wilson.

Following an exhaustive briefing from CIA and State Department officers, Wilson arrived in Niger in February 2002. He conferred with the U.S. ambassador in Niger, Barbara Owens-Kirkpatrick, who voiced her skepticism about the purported yellowcake transaction. He also spoke with former top Niger military officials, and all of the largely French-administered safeguards, aimed at keeping tight controls on the entire yellowcake production. His conclusion: the Niger-Iraq yellowcake transaction was, in all likelihood, not true.

Unbeknownst to Wilson, now retired Marine General Carlton Fulford, Jr., then deputy commander of the U.S. European Command (EUCOM), also paid a visit to Niger in February. But his mission, undertaken in response to an invitation from the ambassador's office in Niger, was to relay to the Nigerian President, Mamadou Tandja, Washington's concern that al-Qaeda – not Saddam Hussein – was seeking yellowcake. The general recounted that neither the Pentagon nor the many intelligence agencies he was in constant contact with ever raised the prospect of Saddam seeking uranium from an African country. "If there was a question [of Iraqi procurements from Africa]," Fulford said, "I would have been made aware of it." He wasn't. And the U.S. Ambassador to Niger also filed her own report to the State Department, which reached identical conclusions.

Upon his return to Washington, Wilson was debriefed by the CIA. To this day, he is convinced, according to his public remarks at a University of Virginia forum attended by this author, that the results of his mission were reported directly back either to Vice President Dick Cheney or to his chief of staff and chief national security aide, I. Lewis "Scooter" Libby. Wilson cannot say for certain whether the vice president's office received a written report from CIA, or whether the report-back took the form of a verbal briefing by the CIA's briefing officer, assigned to Cheney. In an interview later that year conducted with Josh Marshall of the *Talking Points Memo* blog (www.talkingpointsmemo.com), Wilson said he was sure that Cheney would not have known that it was he, Wilson, who was the original fact-finder. But in the same interview Wilson made it clear that because the vice president was the one who had asked for the report, it would have come back to him in some fashion or other. Wilson has absolutely no doubt that, by March 2002, Vice President Dick Cheney was personally aware that the Niger-Iraq story was, in all likelihood, a hoax.

The Run-Up To War

During the summer of 2002, the Bush administration put the Iraq war plan on the front burner. Yet there was significant resistance to a U.S. military invasion to oust Saddam Hussein. On August 15, Gen. Brent Scowcroft, the alter ego of former President George H.W. Bush, and the chairman of G. W. Bush's President's Foreign Intelligence Advisory Board (PFIAB), penned an op-ed, warning that an invasion of Iraq would be unjustified, and would constitute a major disruption of the War on Terror. Former Bush Sr. Secretary of State, James Baker III, penned a similar piece on August 26.

In response, Vice President Cheney personally launched a counter-offensive in late August. Speaking at the annual convention of the Veterans of Foreign Wars (VFW) in Nashville, Tennessee, Cheney asserted, " . . . we now know that Saddam has resumed his efforts to acquire nuclear weapons." Throughout the autumn of 2002, other senior Bush administration officials picked up the Cheney line that Saddam had to be stopped before his quest for weapons of mass destruction resulted in a nuclear mushroom cloud.

Cheney may have ignored Wilson's findings, but the CIA did not. When President Bush scheduled a speech in Cincinnati, Ohio, for October 7, 2002, and intended to reference Saddam's alleged attempt to acquire "500 metric tons of uranium oxide from . . . Africa," Director of Central Intelligence George Tenet challenged its accuracy, and the statement was removed from the speech.

Despite the serious CIA and DIA reservations about the Niger yellowcake allegations, neoconservative hardliners in the Bush administra-

STEINBERG

tion continued to press their "Big Lie" campaign. In December 2002, the U.S. State Department issued a fact sheet in response to Iraq's 20,000-page submission to the United Nations Security Council on the status of its WMD programs. The State Department document critiqued the fact that Iraq's "Declaration [to the UN] ignore[d] efforts to procure uranium from Niger," and the fact sheet further asked, "Why is the Iraqi regime hiding their uranium procurement?" Perhaps not surprisingly, it has since come to light – via a State Department Inspector General chronology provided to the House Committee on Government Reform – that John Bolton, former under secretary of state for arms control and international security, tasked the Bureau of Non-proliferation, a subordinate office to his own, with preparing the document, *in spite of the fact that State denied his participation* in a letter to Congressman Henry A. Waxman on September 25, 2003.

The proverbial crap hit the fan in late January 2003, when President Bush, in his State of the Union address, cited British intelligence sources to assert that Iraq was attempting to obtain uranium from Africa to build a bomb. Dr. Robert Joseph, a Richard Perle neocon protégé on the National Security Council staff, had pressed the CIA's Weapons Inspection, Non-proliferation and Arms Control Center (WINPAC) for acceptable wording to promote the widely discredited notion that Saddam was well advanced in his quest to obtain a nuclear bomb. The result was the infamous "16 words": "The British government has learned that Saddam Hussein recently sought significant quantities of uranium from Africa."

Joe Wilson heard President Bush's State of the Union address and was, according to his own book-length account, stunned that the President was still promoting the African yellowcake allegations nearly a year after Wilson's mission to Niger. Wilson knew that at least three other African states were capable of producing yellowcake uranium precursor, and therefore concluded that Bush was not necessarily referring to the Niger allegations. But to be on the safe side, he made a series of discreet inquiries to former State Department colleagues and people at the CIA who had sent him to Africa. Thanks to the controversy sparked by President Bush's State of the Union speech, the CIA, which had all along been skeptical of the Iraq-Niger yellowcake story, now, belatedly set out to trace the origins of the tale.

As it turned out, someone at the Niger embassy in Rome had passed documents to the Italian security service, SISMI allegedly detailing Iraqi efforts to procure the large quantity of yellowcake uranium precursor covertly. SISMI had then informed the U.S., British, and other intelligence services about the contents of the documents.

Now, in early 2003, the CIA first obtained copies of the documents, and, eventually, the originals. Parenthetically, the Italian magazine *Panorama*, owned by Italian Prime Minister Silvio Berlusconi, had obtained copies of the documents and shared them with the U.S. embassy in Rome. Upon closer inspection, the *Panorama* reporter and her editor decided *not* to publish a story, due to their own skepticism about the documents' authenticity.

Shortly after obtaining the original documents, the CIA made them available to the International Atomic Energy Agency (IAEA), the United Nations agency leading the on-the-ground search for Iraq's nuclear weapons program. On March 7, 2003, even as the Bush administration was putting the final forces in place for the invasion of Iraq, IAEA head Dr. Mohamed ElBaradei delivered devastating public testimony in front of the United Nations Security Council, in effect pronouncing Iraq free of any nuclear weapons program, secret or otherwise. Dr. ElBaradei also announced that a brief analysis of the Niger documents revealed that they were shoddy forgeries: "The IAEA has concluded," he said, "with the concurrence of outside experts, that these documents . . . are not in fact authentic."

At this point, Wilson took his first public step. In an interview with CNN, 24 hours after Dr. ElBaradei's UN testimony, he made a veiled reference to his own Niger mission. He suggested that if the Bush-Cheney White House did a review of their own files, they would find that they already had evidence discrediting the Niger yellowcake tale.

Within days of Wilson's CNN appearance, a well-placed source reported, a meeting took place in the office of Vice President Dick Cheney to assess the Wilson allegations and map out a counter-attack. A "get Joe Wilson" team was activated to profile the former diplomat – and his family. That March 2003 meeting (occurring on the 8th or 9th) unleashed the chain of events that now is the subject of a Federal grand jury probe, headed by Special Counsel Patrick Fitzgerald.

As of this writing (in July 2005), Fitzgerald has, for more than 18 months, been investigating whether senior Bush officials knowingly leaked the name of covert CIA operative Valerie Plame. The seeming lack of progress may be due in part to the fact that Fitzgerald, in addition to being special counsel, retains his job as U.S. attorney for the northern district of Illinois. It is a position that, according to John Dean, former White House general counsel in the Nixon administration, who has been following the

Plame leak, "is typically a very demanding full-time job." Moreover, Dean points out that federal regulations state that a special counsel "shall be selected from outside the United States Government," a restriction that would clearly preclude the selection of an active U.S. attorney, who ultimately reports to the attorney general. "Those Justice Department regulations had a purpose," Dean put it, "and it was to avoid conflicts of interest and divided loyalties. Now, we are stuck with both."

The top Democrat on the Senate Intelligence Committee, Jay Rockefeller IV (D-W. Va.), tried to get the FBI to conduct an investigation of the Niger uranium document forgery itself. On March 14, 2003, he wrote to the director of the FBI with the hope that such an investigation would help "allay any concerns" as to who was involved in preparing the forged documents. He expressed particular concern over "the possibility that the fabrication of these documents may be part of a larger deception campaign aimed at manipulating public opinion and foreign policy regarding Iraq." Rockefeller's Republican counterpart, Pat Roberts of Kansas, did not sign the letter, indicating to the press through a spokeswoman that while the Senate Intelligence Committee would look into the forgery, it would be "inappropriate for the FBI to investigate at this point." The committee did eventually look at the Niger uranium issue in conjunction with the larger WMD intelligence investigation ordered on July 7, 2004. The report resulting from that investigation even included "additional views" of Senators Roberts, Orrin Hatch (R-Utah), and Christopher Bond (R-Mo.) on Joe Wilson's role in the discussion of the Niger uranium documents, in which they complained of his "media blitz" and the many statements he made that, they alleged, "had no basis in fact." Their "additional" findings were far from uncontested, though. Joe Wilson replied to some of them in a letter published at *Salon.com* (among other places) on July 16, 2004, in which he strongly refuted the assertions they made.

Two days after Rockefeller's letter to the FBI, Cheney asserted, in an interview on *Meet the Press*, that ElBaradei was frankly "wrong." He also attacked the IAEA's record on Iraq. In what was later explained away as a slip of the tongue, Cheney openly charged that Saddam Hussein had "reconstituted nuclear weapons." He also assured the American people that U.S. soldiers would be greeted by the Iraqi people as liberators, and that the regular Iraqi army and even portions of the Republican Guard would simply "step aside."

Then on July 6, 2003, Joe Wilson penned an op-ed in the *New York Times,* in which he recounted his Niger mission and criticized the Bush administration for rushing to war on the basis of shoddy information. The op-ed was a shot heard round the world. Wilson appeared on scores of TV shows and gave many more radio and print interviews. His decision to surface publicly with his criticism of the Bush administration's "Big Lie" campaign to justify the Iraq invasion was the catalyst for a much larger dissent, further fueled by the intensification of the insurgency against the American occupation of Iraq.

Eight days after the Wilson *New York Times* op-ed appeared – and three days after George Tenet admitted that the 16 words "did not rise to the level of certainty which should be required for presidential speeches" – *Chicago Sun-Times* syndicated columnist Robert Novak penned a story, "outing" Ambassador Wilson's wife, Valerie Plame, as a CIA officer, citing two unnamed "senior White House sources." Under a 1980s law, the Intelligence Identities Protection Act of 1982 (50 U.S.C. §421 *et seq.*), it is a felony crime for any government official to reveal publicly the identity of an undercover U.S. intelligence officer, punishable by a maximum jail sentence of 10 years and a substantial fine.

From the moment the Novak column appeared, it has been in the power of President George W. Bush to get to the bottom of the sordid affair. He not only chose *not* to find out the identities of the leakers and banish them from his administration, he also cavalierly told reporters he did not expect to be *able* to identify the sources of the leak.

Perhaps no single event since the arrest of Jonathan Pollard for indulging in "friendly" espionage for Israel so angered the professional intelligence community. According to several current and former CIA officers I interviewed, CIA Director George Tenet was warned that, if he did not pressure the Justice Department to open a full investigation into the Plame leak, the Bush administration would be hit with a string of highly damaging leaks about White House interference in the intelligence process. The Justice Department, then under the direction of John Ashcroft, stalled on even opening an investigation for months. But still more months passed, however, before the Attorney General recused himself and allowed a special counsel to be appointed by the Deputy Attorney General, Robert Comey. As an aside, it's interesting to note that on June 3, 2004, a White House spokesman confirmed that President Bush consulted with a non-government attorney, who the President indicated he would retain, should it be necessary to do so, for advice in the Plame case. A lawyer that John Dean spoke to suggested that this move almost certainly indicates the President has some knowledge of the issue. "It would *not* seem that the President needs to consult personal counsel, thereby preserving the attorney-client privilege, if he has no knowledge about the leak," the lawyer told Dean.

Personally, I have no doubt that the Valerie Plame leak was an act of political treachery hatched in the office of Vice President Dick Cheney – with his tacit or explicit authorization. I have no doubt that "senior officials" in Dick Cheney's office, including Lewis Libby, John Hannah, and David Wurmser, know precisely what was done. There is good reason to believe that several members of the Defense Policy Board, formerly chaired by Richard Perle, also have intimate knowledge of the sequence of events leading to the publication of the Novak story.

A colleague and I contacted Perle, James Woolsey, Kenneth Adelman, and Helmut Sonnenfeldt to determine whether any of them had participated in discussions about Joe Wilson and Valerie Plame prior to the Novak article. Sonnenfeldt told my colleague that, to his knowledge, no such discussion had taken place at a formal session of the Defense Policy Board, but he could not say, for certain, that no such discussion had occurred among board members. Woolsey responded to email queries by denying that the board had even met during the summer of 2003; however, the query concerned meetings that would have taken place between March and June of 2003. When he was asked to respond about meetings prior to July, he refused to comment.

As of June 2005, Special Counsel Patrick Fitzgerald had reportedly completed much of the substantive investigative work. Over the course of his investigation, I am told, Patrick Fitzgerald assembled a clear picture of the crime, including the pivotal role of senior officials in the office of Vice President Dick Cheney. In the course of Fitzgerald's investigation, two journalists – Judith Miller of the *New York Times* and Matthew Cooper of *TIME Magazine* – were subpoenaed to appear before the grand jury. They refused to testify on grounds that the First Amendment to the U.S. Constitution shielded them from having to talk about their confidential sources; Chief Judge Thomas F. Hogan, of the U.S. District Court for the District of Columbia, didn't buy that, and decided in October 2004 to hold them in contempt. He did let them stay out of jail while an appeals process worked itself out, but, as Hogan said in the courtroom at the end of June 2005 – quoting Lewis Carroll's Walrus from the sequel to *Alice in Wonderland* – "The time has come." The Supreme Court refused, on June 27, 2005, to hear the journalists' appeal, following a rejection of their First Amendment argument by a three-judge panel from the D.C. Appellate Court in February, and the April rejection of their request for a full-court re-hearing. *TIME* turned over Cooper's notes with the hope that jail time for him would be avoided, but Judith Miller and Co. decided to play "hard-ball" with the court. She was sent to jail on July 6, 2005, for contempt, and could remain there through October, when the term of the grand jury in the case expires. What at first glance seems most peculiar about the report-ers' relationship to the case is their willingness to take the fall to protect Bush-administration sources. (As we note below, however, it is not, per-haps, as strange as it first seems.) While they and other watchdog groups have turned this into another journalists'-rights case, the facts would seem to point in the other direction. As Fitzgerald himself told Judge Hogan in the courtroom, "This case is not about a whistleblower . . . . [It's] about a potential retaliation *against* a whistleblower." Even Eric Burns of *FOX News* (of all places) said on FOX's *Studio B* on June 30, 2005, that he didn't understand why the two journalists were willing to take such heat, "hiding behind a principle," just to keep the potential commission of a crime confi-dential, and to help cover up the alleged "dirty politics" of the Bush admin-istration. "Why would we assume that the right of a journalist to protect sources is in all cases a more positive good," he asked (as paraphrased by a blogger at *newshounds.us*), than "[t]he right of people to know if politics is being played at a dirty level?"[1]

Given how long it continues to take Fitzgerald to produce indictments that are assuredly forthcoming, much speculation has appeared in the media claiming that there may in fact be no crime involved in the leaking of Valerie Plame's identity. Law experts and senior intelligence commu-nity officials have assured me that this is hogwash. The appointment of Fitzgerald as an independent counsel would never have happened, I have been told, were there any doubt that a serious crime had been committed. The question facing the prosecutor is not whether a crime was committed. The question is: can he produce witnesses who will testify about the crime, beyond the details provided by Cooper's notebook? And if not, will he take on the vice president of the United States on the basis of a circumstantial case and a pattern of forensic evidence alone? Time will tell.

What Cooper's notebook did lead to so far is a flurry of discussion surrounding the role of Karl Rove, who, we now know for sure, spoke to Cooper about Plame, though he claims not to have mentioned her name and therefore not to have "revealed" her identity. The evidence that has recently surfaced also appears to confirm that Vice Presidential Chief of

---

1. See the postscript to the present chapter for more on this issue.—Ed.

Staff I. Lewis Libby was an additional source of the leak to Novak, besides whatever Rove may have provided. Both men were part of a White House "plumbers unit" called the White House Iraq Group, which was formed by Presidential Chief of Staff Andrew Card in August 2002, expressly to lead the propaganda offensive to win support for the invasion of Iraq and the overthrow of Saddam Hussein's government.[1]

Existence of the WHIG was not lost on Independent Counsel Patrick Fitzgerald. In one of the first subpoenas he issued, in January 2004, he demanded the records of the WHIG, during the period of the Wilson op-ed and the outing of his wife. Fitzgerald also demanded telephone records from the White House and from the President's jet, Air Force One, during a Presidential visit to Africa. During that flight, Secretary of State Colin Powell, who was accompanying the President, received a copy of a June 10, 2003, State Department memo on the "Niger yellowcake" affair, which identified "Valerie Wilson" as a CIA officer involved in work on weapons of mass destruction. The memo was delivered to Secretary Powell in the immediate aftermath of the Joe Wilson op-ed in the *New York Times*. Prosecutor Fitzgerald, according to news accounts, believed that the memo may have been circulated to White House staff traveling with the President and Secretary Powell, and this may have been how the information got into the hands of Rove.

Adding to the significance of the June 10th memo is the fact that the paragraph containing Valerie Wilson's name was clearly market "secret," denoting that at least some of the paragraph's contents were classified, and that none of it could be revealed to anyone but those possessing both a valid clearance and a need to know. This classification should have been a clear indication to White House officials, prior to the Novak leak, that Valerie Plame Wilson was an undercover CIA officer whose cover was classified. In retrospect it presumably implicates them in a clear violation of the 1982 intelligence identities act.

The importance of the WHIG's emergence at the center of the Fitzgerald investigation cannot be underestimated. Judith Miller was one of the chief assets of the WHIG in the media. The WHIG was launched following the publication of the August 2002 op-eds by Brent Scowcroft and James Baker opposing any invasion of Iraq. It met weekly in the White House Situation Room to map out the war-propaganda campaign, and Miller was one of the journalists most frequently used to get out administration-cooked scare stories about Saddam Hussein's alleged quest for nuclear weapons. The idea of the Saddam nuclear bomb threat was the most compelling accusa-

---

1. See Col. Gardiner's piece (p. 638) on the WHIG's place in the war's PR network.—Ed.

tion that Cheney and others used to arm-twist members of Congress into voting to grant President Bush war powers in October 2002. It is likely that Miller's refusal to testify – and her current jail time – have more to do with her "special relationship" to the WHIG than to the Plame leak per se, given that she never published an article about Plame.

Another recent twist in the saga is the growing evidence that John Bolton, currently the Bush recess apointee as UN Ambassador and the former State Department chief arms control negotiator, may also have had a role in the Plame leak. Bolton's chief of staff, Fred Fleitz, a CIA officer on loan to the State Department from the Agency, may have known Valerie Plame's identity, according to several sources, and passed it along to Lewis Libby via John Bolton.

So far, however, much of this is speculation and behind-the-scenes deduction. John Dean wrote on October 3, 2003, at *Salon.com* that he strongly encourages Joe Wilson and Valerie Plame to file a civil lawsuit, perhaps against Karl Rove, to force evidence to the surface. Dean points out that, in the wake of the Watergate break-in of 1972, Democratic National Committee Chairman Larry O'Brien filed a civil suit against the Committee to Reelect the President, the organization directly implicated in the Watergate break-in. Dean – at the White House at the time – says that the civil suit caused more anxiety among the Nixon inner circle than any probes underway at the Justice Department. Perhaps the current President and vice president can also count on their political-appointee Justice Department officials to run interference. But a civil suit, with discovery, might pry open doors that would otherwise be shut.

Meanwhile, Ambassador Wilson's take on the "outing" of his wife is that it was a warning – a "shot across the bow" – aimed at intelligence analysts and professionals who might have contemplated speaking candidly about pressure they felt to shape their conclusions according to preconceived administration positions on Iraq's WMD. As he pointed out to Josh Marshall in his September 16, 2003, interview, Congress was at the time encouraging anyone who felt pressured to speak up. Wilson feels the move against his wife was a message: "Should you decide to come forward, you too could be looking at this." In fact he had respected journalists tell him that the White House was trying to get them off of the trail of how the infamous "16 words" got into the State of the Union address, and onto how the CIA position of his wife made his own testimony on the Niger yellowcake issue somehow suspect. He remembers one comment specifically: "White House sources insist the real story here is not the 16 words, it's Wilson and his wife." This, plus the fact that – according to *Newsweek* for October 13, 2003 – Chris Matthews of MSNBC called Wilson and told him, "I just got off the phone with Karl Rove, who said your wife was fair game," would seem to support Wilson's interpretation of events.

Some people are convinced that the government prosecutors already know the names, whether they be Rove, Libby, or others, of the "senior White House officials" involved. "But surely they know already," opined columnist William Raspberry in an article in the May 9, 2005, *Washington Post*. "Novak isn't talking about it, but it's inconceivable to me that they haven't talked to him and learned who tipped him; otherwise he'd be the one on the hot seat." Raspberry's commonsense position has become more and more accepted, as recent discussions in the media have tended to circle around the obvious disparity between the prosecutorial attention that Cooper and Miller have gotten and the relative inattention to Novak. Some have speculated that perhaps Novak has been left alone because of the relationship between the source of his information and those running the investigation. Still others, on the other hand, like Novak's "conservative" friends, have called for him to explain what's kept him out of trouble; columnist William Safire demanded, for instance, that Novak write a column "explaining how his two sources . . . managed to get the prosecutor off his back." Novak said at the time, in reply, that he'd "write a column when the case is closed" and "tell everything I know." But many have speculated that his public outburst on CNN's *Inside Politics* on August 4, 2005 – where host Ed Henry later admitted that he "had told [Novak] in advance that we were going to ask him about the CIA leak case" – is proof positive that the pressure on Novak continues to mount, and perhaps he's not enjoying it.

Whether Raspberry is right or whether, like Deep Throat, the identity of the actual leakers will remain unknown for decades (if not forever) – media speculation and our own investigation and deduction notwithstanding – this great blemish on the American body politic will not go away. No doubt it will haunt those who carried out this act of political vindictiveness – presumably team Bush, including Libby, Rove, and maybe Cheney and others – for years to come. One way or another, whether in a formal court of law, in an impeachment trial before the U.S. Senate, or through the tribunal of public opinion, the true authors and instigators of the Plame leak must be found and, for their high crimes and misdemeanors, brought to justice.

CHAPTER
30
postscript

The Anonymity Trap
• • • • • • • • •
Jacob Weisberg

I T'S BEEN OPEN season on Norm Pearlstine since the Time, Inc., editor-in-chief decided to turn over Matthew Cooper's notes to Special Prosecutor Patrick Fitzgerald. In the *New York Times*, Frank Rich accused Pearlstine of elevating corporate interests over press freedom. *Times* media columnist David Carr went on to chide him for transforming *TIME* "into a lifestyle bible that often leaves the more ambitious stories to others." The *New York Observer* contributed a savage précis of Pearlstine's entire career.

This attack speaks more to journalistic groupthink than to any real moral or legal reasoning. Pearlstine hasn't argued his case beyond the quotes he has supplied in a couple of interviews, but he's clearly struggled with the issue more deeply than *New York Times* publisher Arthur Sulzberger Jr., whose decision on the other side evinces no difficulty and no doubt. Can the nation's leading newspaper really find it an easy call to defy the nation's high court when faced with a ruling it doesn't like? Is corporate disobedience – which would have been a new one on Thoreau and King – really a principle the *Times* wants to establish?

Pearlstine's conclusion that having traveled every legal avenue on behalf of its view of the First Amendment, a publication should obey the law seems persuasive to me. Indeed, this was the *Times'* own position in the landmark Pentagon Papers case, in which the paper clearly would have complied with the Supreme Court's ruling and withheld publication had it lost – even though a far more fundamental right was at issue than today.

But Pearlstine's thoughtful and courageous rejection of the view of the journalistic establishment of which he is (or was) a pillar doesn't go far enough. There's a strong argument that journalists at *TIME* and elsewhere should not just cough up the names of the Valerie Plame leakers in court, but share them with their own readers as well.

Journalists make a fetish of anonymous sources. They do so for reasons ethical, psychological, and anthropological, including genuine principle, the lure of heroism, and – especially in Washington – a culture of status based on access to inside information.

But let's ignore the ulterior motives and focus on the principle Judith Miller has so forcefully asserted by going to prison. To Miller and the *Times*, confidentiality is the trump value of journalism, one that outweighs all other considerations, including obedience to the law, the public interest, and perhaps even loyalty to country.

This is indeed a strong principle, but it is a misguided one. In the Mafia, keeping confidences is the supreme value. In journalism, the highest value is the discovery and publication of the truth. When this paramount value comes into conflict with others – such as following the law, keeping your word, and so on – hard choices have to be made.

Thoughtful journalists sometimes do choose the value of revealing truth over the value of confidentiality. One example: testifying to the Iran-contra committee in 1987, Oliver North defended lying to Congress by citing what he claimed were congressional leaks of classified information. As an illustration, North cited details about the capture of the PLO terrorists who had hijacked the Achille Lauro in 1985. Jonathan Alter pointed out in *Newsweek* that North himself had leaked the details of that military operation to a *Newsweek* reporter. Alter's argument for outing North was that reporters who knew North was the leaker shouldn't be party to his deception.

There are other examples of journalists unilaterally declaring a source's promised anonymity inoperative. In his book Uncovering Clinton, Michael Isikoff put Linda Tripp's off-the-record dealings with him on the record. His argument was that Tripp's grand jury testimony about their conversations had subsequently become public, so it would be ridiculous to continue to suppress his version. Bob Woodward was always planning to name Deep Throat after he died. His argument was the interest of history. In 1988, Milton Coleman of the *Washington Post* revealed that Jesse Jackson had used the terms "hymie" and "hymietown" in a private conversation with him. His argument was that prejudice on the part of a presidential candidate was too important to keep secret. In various instances, publications have fingered campaign operatives attempting to leak negative stories about opposing candidates, on the theory that the fact of the dishing was dishier than the dirt being dished.

The argument for reporters outing the Plame leakers combines elements of several of these examples, and is slightly different from any of them. Talking to a source "on background" cannot be an offer of blanket immunity in all circumstances. If someone goes off the record to offer a journalist a bribe, or threaten violence, the importance of what the source has told a reporter may simply supersede the promise to keep mum. To take an extreme example, any reporter of integrity would reveal off-the-record information about an upcoming terrorist attack or serious crime. In the Plame case, the crime under investigation consists in speaking to reporters. No plausible shield law would, or should, protect a reporter in this situation, because there's no way for a prosecutor to develop a case against a perpetrator without evidence from the recipients of the leak. The *New York Times* might argue that the law against leaking undercover CIA agents' names should be repealed. But the paper can't coherently argue that the law should be enforced and that its own reporter should prevent its enforcement.

The argument against ever outing sources is instrumental. Insiders won't leak to the press if they can't rely on a reporter's pledge of confidentiality, the argument goes, and so the public's interest in discovering wrongdoing ultimately won't be served. This is mostly humbug. As most modern presidents have discovered, leakers are a hardy breed. They act from various motives, of which unalloyed public-spiritedness is probably the rarest. Outing the Plame leakers wouldn't undermine the use of confidential sources. It would merely put leakers on notice that their right to lie and manipulate the press is not absolute and not sacred.

THE EDITORS' GLOSS: The U.S. approach to the "war on terror"(GWOT) and its "detainees" has tarnished and undermined its conduct in Iraq too. Driven by media and Bush-administration rhetoric, which insists that Iraq is part of the GWOT and those fighting U.S. occupation are "terrorists," we have lost all sense of what the law of armed conflict is about. Importing interrogation techniques from Gitmo and Afghanistan, where by our own admission they are permitted because the Geneva Conventions (GC) don't (sic) apply there, to Iraq, where they do, constitutes a crime against the law of war. Our detention of family members of insurgents to compel their surrender (documented by Col. Herrington, December 2003, and the Army Lessons Learned Center, May 2004; soldiers even left a note in one case (*Washington Post*, July 28, 2003): "If you want your family released, turn yourself in") is both a clear violation of GC Art. 34 ("The taking of hostages is prohibited") and further fruit of the "GCs-don't-apply" mentality.

The "torturegate" mendacity appears pervasive. Lt. Gen. Sanchez said before a Senate Committee (May 19, 2004) he "never approved" fear-inducement as an interrogation technique, but his own September 14, 2003, memo approves item "E": "significantly increasing fear level in a detainee." At the same hearing, Maj. Gen. Miller denied discussing his visit to Iraq with DoD intelligence officials ("I had no direct discussions with Secretary Cambone or General Boykin") but said to lawyers in August 2004 (*Chicago Tribune*, July 15, 2005) that he "out-briefed" Cambone "following [his] return in the fall." Perhaps the reality is becoming clear to these men. As Air Force deputy JAG, Maj. Gen. Jack Rives, wrote in an explosive memo discussing acceptable interrogation methods, the "more extreme interrogation techniques . . . amount to violations of domestic criminal law" (*New York Times*, July 28, 2005). This is consistent with his service counterparts' advice, and some in the FBI (*Newsweek*, August 8, 2005). Liz Holtzman, NYC lawyer and ex-Congresswoman, says that "everyone up the chain of command, including the President, could be liable under the [1996] War Crimes Act for ordering or engaging in murder, torture, or the inhuman treatment of prisoners in Iraq."

As Col. Smith notes, when "investigations" *confirm* activities that are "degrading and abusive," but *don't* violate "U.S. law or policy," those *who drafted the policy* should be in the dock, not just those who acted on it. If the law is ever enforced, John Yoo's cavalier dismissal of the issue based on Bush's re-election – "the debate is over" – could prove presumptuous.

C H A P T E R
31

A Torture(d) Web
· · · · · · · · ·
Col. Dan Smith, USA (ret.)

> "What we know is only the tip of an iceberg."
> —Prof. Theo van Boven,
> former UN Special Rapporteur on Torture

THE STATEMENTS IN Army Regulation 190-8 and international law are unambiguous: "The inhumane treatment of enemy prisoners-of-war, civilian internees, [and] retained personnel is prohibited and is not justified by the stress of combat or deep provocation."

The counterclaim is that these rules were crafted in another age, for another reality, for another enemy – that on September 11, 2001, the enemy, and the world, changed forever.

The shame of Guantánamo Bay (GTMO), Afghanistan, and Abu Ghraib goes well beyond those who have been or will be criminally charged or otherwise disciplined, and beyond the U.S. armed forces. Shortly after September 11, officials at the very highest levels of the U.S. government – including those entrusted with enforcing the law – actively searched for ways to circumvent customary and codified prohibitions against maltreatment and torture of individuals captured or otherwise detained during armed hostilities.

Though the effort had been ongoing for some time, its extent became clear only in June 2004. Attorney General John Ashcroft, appearing before the Senate Judiciary Committee on June 8, flatly refused to provide a copy of two memoranda originated by his department's Office of Legal Counsel dealing with protections accorded various classes of detainees under the Geneva Conventions (GC) of 1949. Partisan maneuvering in the Senate to obtain or block access to 23 related documents so supercharged the issue that the White House judged the controversy would not abate as long as it continued to withhold documents. News media calculated the White

House alone released a two-inch thick stack of papers, with other documents coming from the Justice Department (DoJ) and the Pentagon.

Among the latter was a meticulous Defense Department (DoD) memo parsing the language of the GC, the Convention Against Torture, the Constitution, U.S. Army publications on interrogation techniques, and U.S. law. The memo, prepared by DoD civilians, so dismayed senior uniformed lawyers that, two weeks after the memo was completed, a number of them sought the assistance of the New York branch of the American Bar Association to stop what was manifestly an ill-conceived effort to circumvent the 1949 GC, which had eliminated technicalities in earlier international law that could be used to deny detainees status as "protected persons" as provided for in the 1949 revisions.[1]

The Legal Evidence

By the time the torrent abated, twelve letters and memoranda plus one report were on the Internet. Six of these originated in DoJ, one was a letter signed by President Bush, and six – including an 85-page report – originated in the Pentagon. There was also a one-page press briefing paper listing allowed interrogation techniques for GTMO detainees. These documents revealed none of the reported ambivalence of the highest ranking military lawyers about the new rules promulgated by the Pentagon pertaining to permitted and prohibited methods of interrogating detainees, whether prisoners of war or members of that new category declared by President Bush – "unlawful combatants."[2]

---

1. Scott Horton, currently chairman of the Committee on International Law of the New York branch of the American Bar Association, confirmed to the author in a September 15, 2004, conversation that he met personally with the Service Judge Advocates General (JAGs) who went to see him in May of 2003. At the time he chaired the Association's Human Rights Committee.

2. Among the papers released were only three of the 23 requested by Senators, and none dealt with techniques used by the Central Intelligence Agency (CIA), which is conducting its own internal investigation. The documents made public at that time are:
- a January 22, 2002, memo from Department of Justice (DoJ) Assistant Attorney General Jay Bybee to White House Counsel Alberto Gonzales and Department of Defense (DoD) General Counsel William Haynes. The memo held that Afghanistan was a "failed state" and that this gave the President grounds to "suspend" U.S. obligations to Afghanistan under international treaties – including the GC;
- a February 1, 2002, letter from Attorney General John Ashcroft to President Bush outlining two options justifying the position that the GC did not apply to either Taliban or al-Qaeda fighters in U.S. custody. One option was deemed to offer more conclusive "protection" against interventions by U.S. courts;
- a February 7, 2002, DoJ memo (Bybee) to White House Counsel Gonzales stating that the President could issue a "determination" that captured Taliban were not entitled to

Since 1949, the U.S. has fought major wars in Korea, Vietnam, and the Gulf and captured or otherwise interned or detained thousands of individuals. While the chronology of memos and reports presents what was happening, it does not go to the deeper – the *moral* – question of why. It is as if the effort to subvert the GC and other international prohibitions against torture "started without starting."

Whereas most Americans will evaluate a moral choice in terms of what will produce the greatest good or minimize evil, these memos reveal a conscious effort to dissect or "deconstruct" the meaning of rules designed to ensure respect for fundamental human dignity – with the sole aim of undercutting the legal restraints which safeguard moral conduct in war.[1] One well-known example of deconstruction is President Clinton's

prisoner-of-war status;
- a February 7, 2002, memo from the President in which he claims the right to withhold Geneva Convention guarantees from captured Afghan fighters but decides not to apply his decision "at this time";
- a February 26, 2002, DoJ memo (Bybee) to DoD (Haynes) concerning applicability of constitutional protections in a court of law to prisoners' statements made during interrogation;
- an August 1, 2002, DoJ memo (Bybee) to White House Counsel Gonzales advising that interrogation methods employed against al-Qaeda captives would not contravene the Convention against Torture and were not subject to the jurisdiction of the International Criminal Court;
- an August 1, 2002, DoJ memo (Bybee) to White House Counsel Gonzales asserting that under certain conditions, torture of suspected terrorists could be "legally defended." (When these documents were made public on June 22, 2004, the Department of Justice disavowed this memo);
- a December 2, 2002, DoD memo (Haynes), approved by Secretary of Defense (SECDEF) Donald Rumsfeld, specifying interrogation methods that could be employed against detainees at Guantánamo Bay;
- a January 15, 2003, DoD memo (Rumsfeld) to the Commander, U.S. Southern Command, rescinding the December 2, 2002 memo's standing approval to employ some interrogation methods at Guantánamo, but permitting special requests to use more coercive techniques for specific prisoners if the request is meticulously justified;
- a January 15, 2003, DoD memo (Rumsfeld) to General Counsel Haynes directing him to assemble a working group to review all policies relating to interrogations;
- a January 17, 2003, DoD memo (Haynes) to the USAF General Counsel appointing her as chairwoman of the working group requested by Rumsfeld;
- an April 4, 2003, DoD report by the working group, including recommendations on what methods to allow;
- an April 16, 2003, DoD memo (Rumsfeld) to Commander, U.S. Southern Command reaffirming interrogation methods approved for routine use at Guantánamo and methods whose use required his specific assent;
- an undated one-page list of interrogation techniques approved and employed at Guantánamo provided to media on June 22, 2004.
All of these documents can be accessed online at http://www.washingtonpost.com/wp-dyn/articles/A62516-2004Jun22.html.

1. In oversimplified terms, "deconstruction" is the process of textual analysis to uncover all possible meanings by re-arranging relationships (e.g., relative importance) among

response to a question in his grand jury deposition about his relationship with Monica Lewinsky: "It depends on what the meaning of the word 'is' is. If 'is' means 'is and never has been' that's one thing – if it means 'there is none,' that was a completely true statement." Imagine the difference for arms control negotiations – or the evaluation rejecting Saddam Hussein's December 2002 denial that he had unconventional weapons that led to war – if policy makers had to differentiate between "is and never has been" and "there is none."

The thrust of the discussions was to develop an argument that torture is really not torture unless the "right" (really the wrong) circumstances exist. Thus, the memos assert, if physical pain is not "severe" or is a mere by-product of efforts to elicit information from a detainee, then there is no question of whether the acts constitute torture. One Justice Department memorandum implies that there is a threshold of pain that must be crossed for torture to exist, pain "equivalent in intensity to the pain accompanying serious physical injury, such as organ failure, impairment of bodily function, or even death." Similarly, psychological assaults that do not result in "significant" long-term damage (which could not be known until the "long-term" is reached), or which do not "penetrate to the core of an individual's ability to perceive the world around him" or "substantially [interfere] with his cognitive abilities, or fundamentally alter his personality," are *not* torture.[1]

These opinions, together with the claim that the President in his role as commander-in-chief is not bound by either U.S. or international rules prohibiting torture, run directly counter to what the Army teaches its interrogators, counter to what U.S. practice has been for more than three decades, and counter to what the nations of the world, including the United States, have agreed in the GC. If the United States claims exemption or immunity for "national security," what is to prevent other commanders-in-chief from doing the same? To what higher standard will the President appeal to prevent the torture of captured U.S. service members in future wars?

---

structural elements, and then non-judgmentally, and non-hierarchically, highlighting the differences. (Wags assert that the process theoretically produces unlimited variations and outcomes leading to an infinity of meanings – which is to say the result is meaningless.)

1. Elsewhere, the Justice Department memo is inherently contradictory. On one hand, it contends that an act taken out of the context in which it occurs would be "difficult" to brand as torture. Yet it lists objectively (without context) seven techniques that the courts have ruled to be torture regardless of context.

Attorney General Ashcroft, appearing before the Senate Judiciary Committee on June 8, 2004, stated that President Bush had never issued orders that "would require or direct" violations of the GC against torture. But the very fact that key government officials even considered the possibility of ignoring the Conventions, let alone developed and circulated "rationales" to circumvent the rules, reinforces the world's perception that the U.S. will ignore "civilized" norms whenever it chooses – thereby making it as morally bereft as its enemies.

The Military Lawyers Speak

Though the documents that were eventually released in June 2004 did not include any indication that the concerns of the military lawyers and other top military brass were considered, the JAGs did eventually have their "day in court." Though the nomination and subsequent confirmation of White House Counsel Alberto Gonzales as new attorney general following John Ashcroft's resignation confirmed that clear lines between allowed and prohibited acts would be no more forthcoming in the second George W. Bush administration than in the first, the hearings for Gonzales's confirmation at least provided an opportunity for the concerns of some recently retired senior military leaders, some senior JAGs, to be heard. Gonzales's nomination was publicly opposed in a January 4, 2005, press gathering by 12 retired generals and admirals who, in stark terms, decried his role in the torture policy formulation.[1] These included three retired four-stars: a former chairman of the Joint Chiefs of Staff, a former commander of U.S. Central Command (CENTCOM), a former chief of staff of the Air Force; and several senior retired military lawyers: two former Navy judge advocates general, a former Navy inspector general, a former Marine Corps senior legal advisor, and a former chief judge of the Army Court of Criminal Appeals. The group's spokesman, former CENTCOM commander and retired Marine Corps Gen. Joseph Hoar, expressed "deep concern" about the nomination as it was still unclear what role Gonzales actually had in determining the policy on torture. The former Army appeals court judge, retired Brig. Gen. James Cullen, was more direct: "I think he's had such an appalling departure from good judgment."

---

1. Independently but also on January 4, 2005, more than 225 religious leaders voiced "grave concern" about Bush's choice, insisting that the nominee "denounce the use of torture under any circumstances."

In their open letter to the Senate Judiciary Committee for Gonzales's
January 6, 2005, confirmation hearing, the officers pointed out that he
"played a significant role in shaping U.S. detention and interrogation operations in Afghanistan, Iraq, GTMO, and elsewhere. Today," they continued,

> it is clear that these operations have fostered greater animosity toward the
> United States, undermined our intelligence gathering efforts, and added to
> the risks facing our troops serving around the world. Before Mr. Gonzales
> assumes the position of Attorney General, it is critical to understand whether
> he intends to adhere to the positions he adopted as White House Counsel, or
> chart a revised course more consistent with fulfilling our nation's complex
> security interests, and maintaining a military that operates within the rule
> of law.

Of particular concern to the admirals and generals was the fact that

> . . . Mr. Gonzales wrote to the President on January 25, 2002, advising him
> that the GC did not apply to the conflict then underway in Afghanistan. More
> broadly, he wrote that the "war on terrorism" presents a "new paradigm [that]
> renders obsolete Geneva's" protections.

Even more disturbing, they noted, was that

> the White House decision to depart from the GC in Afghanistan went hand in
> hand with the decision to relax the definition of torture and to alter interroga-
> tion doctrine accordingly. Mr. Gonzales's January 2002 memo itself warned
> that the decision not to apply Geneva Convention standards "could undermine
> U.S. military culture which emphasizes maintaining the highest standards of
> conduct in combat, and could introduce an element of uncertainty in the sta-
> tus of adversaries." Yet Mr. Gonzales then made that very recommendation
> with reference to Afghanistan, a policy later extended piece by piece to Iraq.

Finally, they took strong issue with "[a] series of memos that were prepared at [Gonzales's] direction in 2002 recommend[ing] official authorization of harsh interrogation methods, including water-boarding, feigned
suffocation, and sleep deprivation . . . . these memos," they continued,

> ignored established U.S. military policy, including doctrine prohibiting
> "threats, insults, or exposure to inhumane treatment as a means of or aid to
> interrogation." Indeed, the August 1, 2002, Justice Department memo analyz-
> ing the law on interrogation references health care administration law more
> than five times, but never once cites the U.S. Army Field Manual on inter-
> rogation. The Army Field Manual was the product of decades of experience
> – experience that had shown, among other things, that such interrogation
> methods produce unreliable results and often impede further intelligence col-
> lection. Discounting the Manual's wisdom on this central point shows a dis-

turbing disregard for the decades of hard-won knowledge of the professional American military.

Abu Ghraib: Unweaving the Web

There is a sad and ironic note struck in the officers' January 2005 letter when they point out that Gonzales himself admitted that refusing to grant Geneva Convention protection could "introduce an element of uncertainty in the status of adversaries." The fruits of this uncertainty are well known, as these officers pointed out:

> Sadly, the uncertainty Mr. Gonzales warned about came to fruition. As James R. Schlesinger's panel reviewing Defense Department detention operations concluded earlier this year, these changes in doctrine have led to uncertainty and confusion in the field, contributing to the abuses of detainees at Abu Ghraib and elsewhere . . . .

The fruits of this uncertainty include the at least 58 individuals who were implicated in the Abu Ghraib horror, either as direct participants, as knowing about but failing to report the abuses, or otherwise bearing "responsibility" without "culpability" for the 66 incidents substantiated by the August 24, 2004, "Final Report of the Independent Panel to Review DoD Detention Operations" (the Schlesinger panel). Of these, eight occur at Guantánamo, three in Afghanistan, and 55 at Abu Ghraib. They also include the cases beyond those indicated in the premature "final report." An Army report, dated August 23, 2004, and released on August 25, the day after the Schlesinger panel's report was released, documented 44 cases at Abu Ghraib. Then, in December 2004, a leaked memo dated June 25, 2004, from Vice Admiral Lowell Jacoby, head of the Defense Intelligence Agency to Stephen Cambone, under secretary of defense for intelligence, implicated Navy special operations personnel (of Task Force 62-6) in the physical abuse of prisoners as well as in threatening DIA civilians if they told anyone of abuses seen at Abu Ghraib.

Additional reports, and information that continues to come out in the press, indicate still more "fruits" of "uncertainty in the status of adversaries." The so-called Church report, more exactly a "review of DoD detention operations and detainee interrogation techniques," released on March 10, 2005, examined 71 confirmed criminal cases of abuse in Afghanistan, Iraq, and GTMO, and noted, as of September 30, 2004, another 130 open cases with investigations ongoing. Press reports have revealed that FBI agents visiting Abu Ghraib witnessed and reported abuses that took place in the last three months of 2003, and that the CIA directed its agents to stay away from interrogations conducted by the military in which "harsh techniques" were used. On August 30, 2004, it was reported that Lt. Gen Ricardo S. Sanchez, Commander, Combined and Joint Task Force 7 (CJTF-7), sent a secret cable to his superior at U.S. Central Command outlining aggressive interrogation techniques that he then intended to authorize. Sanchez's September 14, 2003, memo – the text of which was obtained via an American Civil Liberties Union (ACLU) Freedom of Information Act (FOIA) request[1] – confirms his order to use dogs, stress positions, and disorientation. Further documents obtained via FOIA request also revealed FBI agents complaining of tactics such as the shackling of detainees to the floor for more than 24 hours at a time, without food and water; draping a detainee in an Israeli flag; and the use of growling dogs. On October 27, 2004, Amnesty International (AI) released a report which cited a late 2004 memo from the JTF-170 (Guantánamo) commander requesting approval to use interrogation techniques such as

> stress positions, isolation, sensory deprivation, hooding, 20-hour interrogations, stripping, forced grooming, use of dogs to inspire fear, exposure to cold water or weather, death threats and use of wet towel and dripping water to induce the misperception of suffocation.[2]

On March 21, 2005, Senator Carl Levin (D-Mich.) released a memo, contained in the material provided via the December 2004 ACLU FOIA request, that was originally released in a version redacted by DoJ according to its own and DoD's guidance. Of note in the newly available, un-redacted memo was an assessment by an FBI agent that intelligence resulting from interrogations was "suspect at best," and a note of the fact that Justice Department officials were so bothered by issues surrounding interroga-

---

1. This FOIA request resulted in the delivery of 1200 pages of documents, including, according to the *Independent*, reporting on April 3, 2005, "reports of brutal beatings and sworn statements that soldiers were told to 'beat the f*** out of' prisoners.'" ACLU's FOIA lawsuit was joined by Physicians for Human Rights, Veterans for Common Sense, Veterans for Peace, and the Center for Constitutional Rights. The ACLU and other advocacy groups have obtained over 30,000 pages of documents concerning abuses through a Freedom of Information Act lawsuit, online at www.aclu.org/torturefoia. An update on the status of the lawsuit from the Center for Constitutional Rights noted, in late January 2005, that thousands more pages were to be expected in the following months.

2. AI, *Human Dignity Denied: Torture and Accountability in the "War On Terror,"* AI Index No. AMR 51/145/2004, October 27, 2004, p. 172. The requested techniques were largely approved (with several of those noted reserved for specific, case-by-case approval) by the DoD memo of December 2, 2002 (*vide supra*, p. 510, note 2). It is worth pointing out that the Haynes memo said that "all Category III techniques [i.e., those that were reserved for case-by-case approval] may be legally available."

tion methods that they went to DoD Counsel William J. Haynes II with their concerns in an attempt to dissuade DoD from the practices to which they objected. In a meeting that FBI officials had with Maj. Gen. Geoffrey D. Miller, commander of Joint Task Force Guantánamo from September 2002 to March 2004, and another Army general, in an effort to resolve those concerns, both sides agreed that the FBI had its rules, and DoD had marching orders from Secretary Rumsfeld. The generals felt "they had a job to do," the memo reported.

Meanwhile, still more reports reveal continued "fruits of uncertainty" as to the status of detainees. Officials have indicated – as of March 2005 – that at least 108 people have died in U.S. custody in Iraq and Afghanistan, and 26 of those are confirmed or suspected criminal homicides. Other reports document the "rendition" by the CIA of possibly 150 people from the U.S. to countries strongly suspected of using torture as an interrogation tool.

More Than Just Numbers

The statistics themselves are notable, but they fail to convey the truly human tragedy that the torture and abuse scandal represents, regardless of *who* is accountable or *how* it happened. Reports that have come out, such as those by Maj. Gen. Antonio Taguba, dated June 8, 2004, have detailed the use of techniques such as:

> ... breaking chemical lights and pouring the phosphoric liquid on detainees; pouring cold water on naked detainees; beating detainees with a broom handle and a chair; threatening male detainees with rape; allowing a military police guard to stitch the wound of a detainee who was injured after being slammed against the wall in his cell; sodomizing a detainee with a chemical light and perhaps a broom stick, and using military working dogs to frighten and intimidate detainees with threats of attack, and in one instance actually biting a detainee.

Since then, other press accounts have detailed incidents such as the death of Manadel al-Jamadi, who was captured by Navy SEALs during a joint CIA-special operations mission in November 2003. He was found dead, suspended by his wrists, handcuffed behind his back – a position known as "Palestinian hanging," according to investigative files from the Army and the CIA's Office of Inspector General. An Army guard was quoted in these reports as having told investigators that blood gushed from al-Jamadi's mouth "as if a faucet had been turned on" when he was lowered to the ground. Jerry Hodge, the military pathologist who autopsied al-Jamadi last year, told the CIA's Inspector General's office – again according to the same report – that "the position that al-Jamadi was placed [in] for interrogation together with the hood (covering his head) was 'part and parcel' of the homicide." Hodge found broken ribs and bruised lungs consistent with "slow, deliberate application of force," such as someone kneeling on his chest or holding him down with the soles or heels of their boots. (The Navy SEAL charged in the case with assault, dereliction of duty, conduct unbecoming an officer, and making false statements, Lt. Andrew K. Ledford, was acquitted of wrongdoing on May 27, 2005.)

Still other disturbing reports detail the beating of GTMO detainee, Mustafa Ait Idir, who was left with scars and partial facial paralysis, according to a lawsuit filed on April 13, 2005. Other reports from GTMO include descriptions of detainees who were struck with chairs, sexually assaulted, and forced to eat meals out of a toilet. Reports coming out of Afghanistan are no better. A recent series by *New York Times* reporter Tim Golden – based upon a nearly 2,000-page file recording a criminal investigation into the brutal deaths of two detainees, Messrs. Habibullah and Dilawar, at the Bagram Collection Point, and which led to 7 Army criminal charges – notes sworn statements attesting to a female interrogator stepping on the neck of a prostrate detainee and kicking another in the genitals;

> . . . a shackled prisoner being forced to roll back and forth on the floor of a cell, kissing the boots of his two interrogators as he went . . . . [and] another prisoner . . . made to pick plastic bottle caps out of a drum mixed with excrement and water as part of a strategy to soften him up for questioning.[1]

The Army coroner who conducted the autopsy in the case of one of the Bagram deaths offered a sobering assessment: "I've seen similar injuries in an individual run over by a bus."[2]

Robert Fisk, the veteran Middle East reporter, recently provided just a sketch of what he has heard from numerous interviews:

> A vast quantity of evidence has now been built up on the system which the Americans have created for mistreating and torturing prisoners. I have interviewed a Palestinian who gave me compelling evidence of anal rape with wooden poles at Bagram – by Americans, not by Afghans.
> Many of the stories now coming out of Guantánamo – the sexual humiliation of Muslim prisoners, their shackling to seats in which they defecate and

---

1. Tim Golden, "In U.S. Report, Brutal Details of 2 Afghan Inmates' Deaths," *New York Times*, May 20, 2005, online. Golden points out what he calls a "final horrific detail" of Dilawar's death: "Most of the interrogators had believed Mr. Dilawar was an innocent man who simply drove his taxi past the American base at the wrong time."
2. *Ibid.*

urinate, the use of pornography to make Muslim prisoners feel impure, the female interrogators who wear little clothing (or, in one case, pretended to smear menstrual blood on a prisoner's face) – are increasingly proved true. Iraqis whom I have questioned at great length over many hours, speak with candor of terrifying beatings from military and civilian interrogators, not just in Abu Ghraib but in U.S. bases elsewhere in Iraq.

At the American camp outside Fallujah, prisoners are beaten with full plastic water bottles which break, cutting the skin. At Abu Ghraib, prison dogs have been used to frighten and to bite prisoners.[1]

The CIA has had its fair share of bad press, as well. Most notorious is the Salt Pit case, in which Afghan guards paid by and under the supervision of CIA were ordered by a new agent to strip an uncooperative detainee, chain him to the floor and leave him overnight without blankets; they then dragged him naked over the floor before putting him in his cell. By the morning he was frozen. He was buried in an unmarked, unacknowledged cemetery used by Afghan forces. Other reports, notably a February 14, 2005, piece by Jane Mayer for the *New Yorker*, have detailed the transfer of some 150 people suspected of terrorism to the custody of foreign governments known to use torture in interrogations, and the existence of CIA prisons being operated in Thailand, Qatar, and Afghanistan.[2] Others document insistence by CIA agents that prisoners in Iraq be "kept off the books" and out of reach of Red Cross inspectors, becoming so-called "ghost detainees."

Putting all this together, with a detailed chronology, are several good websites and a new book, *The Torture Papers* (Cambridge: Cambridge University, 2005). The book's "minutely detailed chronological narrative ... which has appeared piecemeal in other publications, possesses," according to a February 8, 2005, *New York Times* review of it, "an awful and powerful cumulative weight."

Accountability

In an effort to get to the bottom of the scandal, the government has spent a significant amount of time and effort. The Pentagon calculated that there had been, as of early December 2004, 18 congressional hearings and more than 39 congressional staff briefings on the abuse scandal. The

1. "America's Shame, Two Years on from 'Mission Accomplished,'" *The Independent*, May 9, 2005, online.

2. Another noteworthy report regards a Swedish parliamentary investigation into the clandestine transport of two Egyptian terrorist from Sweden to Egypt by the CIA. See Craig Whitlock, "New Swedish Documents Illuminate CIA Action," *Washington Post*, May 21, 2005 online.

SMITH

above-mentioned Schlesinger report itself cited nine major reports that formed the basis of its review of DoD detention operations, including the well-known Miller and Taguba reports. Five others, including the Church report and a three-star investigation appointed on February 28, 2005, to look into GTMO abuse complaints lodged by the FBI, have since been completed. Still ongoing are various DoJ and Army Criminal Investigation Command investigations, and the CIA inspector general is also reportedly investigating about a half-dozen cases of suspected abuse.

The completed investigations cite leadership failures – inadequate oversight and unclear guidance from senior officers – as factors contributing to a morally permissive attitude within detention facilities. Clearly, commanders are directly responsible for what is done and what is not done within their command. Here a basic rule, practiced by every successful leader, comes into play: what the boss emphasizes sets the tone, especially in a hierarchical organization like the military.

Failings of leadership turn on the practical and pragmatic, not the ethical, which comes under tremendous pressure in war. Combat places great psychological stress on troops at the same time that actions normally forbidden – killing – are sanctioned by the state in its defense. The pressures to succumb to "operational necessity" at the expense of individual ethics can be daunting, and success in resisting these pressures may turn on a combination of a solid ethical foundation reinforced by the unambiguous commitment of leaders and commanders at all levels to – and their emphasis upon – high moral standards. Considering this latter element, constraints against mistreating detainees that should have been in play were missing because of unclear policies, exceptions to and expansion of permitted "techniques," and the migration of these techniques from one venue (GTMO) to another (Abu Ghraib).

For this reason did the Schlesinger report note that "military and civilian leaders at the Department of Defense share . . . responsibility" for command failures. It cites an "unclear chain of command" established by CJTF-7; "poor leadership and lack of supervision"; and a failure of Sanchez and his deputy, Maj. Gen. Walter Wojdakowski, "to ensure proper staff oversight." (The Fay-Jones report also said that Sanchez "failed to ensure proper staff oversight.") The Schlesinger document also mildly admonishes those in the Pentagon – the chairman of the Joint Chiefs of Staff, his Joint Staff, and the Office of the Secretary of Defense – for failing to anticipate what could (and did) happen after Saddam's fall, and for being unprepared to respond rapidly to changed circumstances on the ground. The most that the March 2005 Church report ultimately was willing to say – *at least the part released publicly* – was that there were "missed opportunities" for things to be done differently.

. . . Or Lack Thereof

Notwithstanding the money and man-hours spent trying to get to the bottom of the abuses, none of these investigations seriously looked *upward* into the civilian Pentagon and White House circles. While the Schlesinger report did possess the broad charter to review detention operations on a DoD-wide basis, it confined its findings largely to platitudes about leaders sharing a "burden of responsibility." The other reports have, in general, characterized the behavior of those responsible for the cases of torture and detainee abuse as the actions of a few "bad apples." Part of this characterization may stem from the focus of most investigations on one aspect of what John Dean has called "Torturegate," to the exclusion of the broader picture. The Taguba report looked at Military Police operations; the Fay-Jones report looked at Military Intelligence (MI) operations; the Church report considered only interrogation operations and omitted a review of senior official accountability; and the April 1, 2005, Schmidt-Furlow report on the FBI allegations confined itself to evaluating whether certain activities were approved by Army or secretary of defense policy, *admittedly* begging the question as to the "legal validity" of the policy itself. During the March 10, 2005, press briefing in which the Church report was rolled out, Vice Adm. Church was asked whether those responsible for failures and what he called "missed opportunities" would be held accountable. In a statement that seems scandalous for a senior and highly decorated officer, Church remarked, "I don't think you can hold anybody accountable for a situation that maybe if you had done something different, maybe something would have occurred differently."

No wonder, then, that this report was widely called a whitewash. Even the Republican chairman of the Senate Armed Services Committee, Senator John Warner (R-Va.), said, when the report was released, that "there has not been finality as to the assessment of accountability."[1] Senator Carl Levin (D-Mich.) also expressed dismay over what he considered to be the incompleteness of the Church report.

> There's been no assessment of accountability of any senior officials, either within or outside of the Department of Defense . . . . I can only conclude that

1. Frank Davies, "Report on Prisoner Abuse Raises Questions of Accounrability," *Knight Ridder*, March 10, 2005, online.

the Defense Department is not able to assess accountability at senior levels, *particularly when investigators are in the chain of command of the officials whose politics and actions they are investigating* [emphasis mine].[1]

A *Washington Post* editorial dated March 13, 2005 – aptly entitled "More Excuses" – made similar observations: " . . . no genuinely independent investigator has been empowered to connect these decisions and events and conclude where accountability truly should lie." The same piece noted the refusal of Senator Pat Roberts (R-Kan.), Chairman of the Intelligence Committee, to investigate credible reports of "torture, abuse, and homicide by the CIA in a clandestine network of overseas prisons, a scandal for which there has been no public accounting, much less accountability." Roberts has since shown no sign of having changed his mind; in response to a renewed call for investigation into behavior of CIA and other interrogators by Senator Rockefeller (D-W. Va.), also of the Intelligence Committee, Roberts simply stated: "I am fast losing patience with what appears to me to be almost a pathological obsession with calling into question the brave men and women on the front lines of the war on terror."

Roberts's position notwithstanding, calls for accountability have been forthcoming since the abuse scandal broke, and no doubt will continue to be. Almost a year ago, the American Bar Association (ABA), at the annual meeting of its House of Delegates on August 9, 2004, called for the creation of an "independent, bipartisan commission with subpoena power to prepare a full account of detention and interrogation practices carried out by the United States [and] to make public findings."[2] An even more significant call came on August 4, 2004, the day before the ABA's annual meeting began. It was directed to the White House by a group of lawyers, law professors, and public-interest and human-rights groups – including representatives from the Alliance for Justice, Human Rights Watch, Human Rights First, Physicians for Human Rights, and the American Civil Liberties Union – in the form of a memorandum signed by, among others, 12 former judges, eight American Bar Association presidents, six former Congressmen, former law school deans, former state and national attorneys general, numerous senior law professors, and others.

The signatories indicate, in their memo, that "the administration's memoranda, dated January 9, 2002, January 25, 2002, August 1, 2002, and April 4, 2003, ignore and misinterpret the U.S. Constitution and laws, interna-

---

1. *Ibid.*

2. American Bar Association, *Report to the House of Delegates,* August 9, 2004.

tional treaties and rules of international law." Further serious charges are enumerated in the memo as follows:

> ... the most senior lawyers in the Department of Justice, the White House, the Department of Defense, and the vice president's office have sought to justify actions that violate the most basic rights of all human beings . . . .
>
> These memoranda and others like them seek to circumvent long established and universally acknowledged principles of law and common decency. The memoranda approve practices that the United States itself condemns in its annual Human Rights Report. No matter how the memoranda seek to redefine it, torture remains torture.
>
> ... The unprecedented and under-analyzed claim that the Executive Branch is a law unto itself is incompatible with the rule of law and the principle that no one is above the law.
>
> The lawyers who prepared and approved these memoranda have failed to meet their professional obligations . . . . the lawyer has a . . . duty, as an officer of the court and as a citizen, to uphold the law.
>
> Enforcement of all of our laws depends on lawyers telling clients not only what they can do but also what they can not do. This duty binds all lawyers and especially lawyers in government service. Their ultimate client is not the President or the Central Intelligence Agency, or any other department of government but the American people. When representing all Americans, government lawyers must adhere to the Constitution and the rule of law.

The demand for a serious investigation and a real assessment of accountability concludes the memorandum. "We therefore," the signatories wrote,

> ... [c]all for an appropriate inquiry into how and why such memoranda were prepared and by whom they were approved, and whether there is any connection between the memoranda and the shameful abuses that have been exposed and are being investigated at Abu Ghraib prison in Baghdad and at other military prisons.

An even more formal call for an investigation into senior-level accountability has more recently come from a group of exasperated Democratic members of Congress – 51 of them, in fact, led by John Conyers, Jr. (D-Mich.), ranking member of the House Judiciary Committee. In a letter to Attorney General Alberto Gonzalez dated May 12, 2005, the members call for a special counsel to get to answer, once and for all, whether

> high-ranking officials within the Bush administration violated the War Crimes Act, 18 U.S.C. §2441, or the Anti-Torture Act, 18 U.S.C. §234, by allowing the use of torture techniques banned by domestic and international law at recognized and secret detention sites in Iraq, Afghanistan Guantánamo Bay and elsewhere.[1]

---

1. See the text of the letter at the website for the Democratic Members of the House

Their motive for requesting such a move by Gonzales is not surprising. "One year and 10 investigations after we first learned about the atrocities committed at Abu Ghraib," they point out, "there has yet to be a comprehensive, neutral and objective investigation with prosecutorial authority of who is ultimately responsible for the abuses there and elsewhere." Though it was not widely reported, they had already asked once, on May 20, 2004, for a special counsel to be appointed, though they received no reply from then-Attorney General Ashcroft. "The need for a special counsel is more important than ever," they write,

> as the administration and military have repeatedly exonerated high-ranking officials, or declined to even investigate their actions, even as other official investigations linked the policy decisions by these officials to the crimes that occurred at Abu Ghraib. The administration's haphazard and disjointed approach to these investigations appears to have insulated those in command and prevented a full account of the actions and abuses from being determined.

A second reason for appointment of a special counsel is to avoid a situation where the administration is expected to investigate itself, as others have pointed out. "A special counsel is necessary," they indicate,

> not only because high-ranking administration officials, including Cabinet members, are implicated, but also because you personally, and the Department of Justice generally, may have participated in this conspiracy to violate the War Crimes Act.

They further point out how previous inquiries

> were not empowered to impose punishments on those it found culpable, and . . . were not empowered to examine the role of high-ranking officials, including members of the administration, in the perpetuation of these abuses."

The only adequate approach, they emphasize, is an independent and properly empowered investigation:

> While Lynndie England and other low-ranking officers have pleaded guilty, those who ordered and authorized their actions appear to have been protected by the military and this administration. Because so many high level officials, including you, have been implicated in these events, the only way to ensure impartiality is through the appointment of a Special Counsel. Indeed, our nation's integrity is at stake.

Committee on the Judiciary (http://www.house.gov/judiciary_democrats/letters/agspecialcounseltortureltr51205.pdf).

Meanwhile, in the absence of higher-level and more independent investigations, addressing the issue of senior-leader accountability has been left to "amateur" and "watchdog" investigators, who, through their own examination of documents, events, and interrelationships have come up with a different picture from that portrayed by the official inquiries. AI's report of May 2005, *Guantánamo and Beyond,* provides a sadly accurate account of abuses based upon firsthand testimony from Combatant Status Review Tribunal transcripts, FBI memos, and U.K. investigations, one of which confirms outright the use of hooding, sleep and food deprivation, and stress positions in Iraq through May of 2004.[1] Tim Golden's recent piece on the Bagram detainee deaths paints a disturbing picture of what went on routinely at the former air base, notwithstanding the incredible remark of then-Lt. Gen. Daniel McNeill (now a four-star), the U.S. commander in Afghanistan at the time, that he had "no indication" that abuse by soldiers contributed to the deaths, and that interrogation methods were "in accordance with . . . generally accepted . . . interrogation techniques."[2] The *Torture Papers,* furthermore, is said by the above-noted *Times* review to "blow to pieces" the argument that the abuses at Abu Ghraib and elsewhere are the failings of a bunch of bad apples and not a reflection of a larger problem. "In fact," the reviewer writes,

> the book provides a damning paper trail that reveals, in uninflected bureaucratic prose, the roots that those terrible [Abu Ghraib] images had in decisions made at the highest levels of the Bush administration – decisions that started the torture snowball rolling down the slippery slope of precedent by asserting that the United States need not abide by the GC in its war on terror.[3]

It is interesting to note the review's later summary of just what kind of accountability has been demanded of the senior leadership in the Bush administration by their commander-in-chief. "What happened to higher-up architects and consultants on administration policy?" the reviewer asks.

> Mr. Rumsfeld . . . twice offered to resign over the Abu Ghraib scandal and was twice turned down by President Bush. Mr. Bybee, who defined torture as pain equivalent to "organ failure," was nominated by Mr. Bush to the Ninth Circuit

---

1. U.K. Intelligence and Security Committee, *The Handling of Detainees by U.K. Intelligence Personnel in Afghanistan, Guantánamo Bay, and Iraq,* March 2005, para. 47, quoted by AI, *Guantánamo and Beyond: The Continuing Pursuit of Unchecked Executive Power,* AI Index No. AMR 51/063/2005, May 13, 2005, p. 90 [*vide infra,* p. 698, note 1, for URL—Ed.].

2. Golden, *loc. cit.,* and Tim Golden, "Army Faltered in Investigating Detainee Abuse," *New York Times,* May 22, 2005, online.

3. Michiko Kakutani, "Following a Paper Trail to the Roots of Torture," *New York Times,* February 8, 2005.

Court of Appeals and took his seat there in 2003. Michael Chertoff, who in his capacity as head of the Justice Department's criminal division advised the CIA on the legality of coercive interrogation methods, was selected by President Bush to be the new secretary of homeland security. William J. Haynes II, the Department of Defense's chief legal officer, who helped oversee Pentagon studies on the interrogation of detainees, was twice nominated by President Bush to the Fourth Circuit Court of Appeals. And Mr. Gonzales, who used the words "obsolete" and "quaint" in reference to the GC, was confirmed . . . as attorney general, the nation's top legal post.

As for the general officers recently exonerated by the Army inspector-general report, Lt. Gen. Sanchez remains head of the Army's V Corps, though Rumsfeld has equivocated as to what the future looks like for him.[1] Maj. Gen. Walter Wojdakowski, former CJTF-7 Deputy Commander under Sanchez, is now acting Deputy Commanding General, U.S. Army Europe (a spot normally reserved for three-star officers), and Maj. Gen. Barbara Fast, former chief intelligence officer (C2) for CJTF-7, is Commanding General and Commandant of the Army Intelligence Center. Maj. Gen. Geoffrey Miller, former commander of both the Guantánamo Bay and Abu Ghraib facilities, is now Assistant Chief of Staff of the Army for Installation Management. Though the generals investigating the FBI allegations recommended that Miller be admonished for failing to supervise the interrogation of one "high-value" detainee, Gen. Bantz J. Craddock, commander of U.S. Southern Command, questioned the report's conclusion and refused to discipline Miller.

Karpinski and a "Few Rotten Apples"?

The only general officer to be punished thus far in conjunction with the abuse at Abu Ghraib is Janis Karpinski, formerly a brigadier general and now an Army colonel. The results of the investigation by Lt. Gen. Stanley E. Green, the Army Inspector General (IG), recommending her punishment were released by anonymous Army spokesmen late on a Friday – April 22, 2005. The IG report, "designed to be the Army's *final word* on the responsibility of senior leadership in relation to the abuses" (emphasis mine),[2] exonerated the other general officers higher up the chain – Wojdakowski, Fast – along with

---

1. " . . . everyone does not go on to another post," he said; " . . . [I]t gets tight at the top. And he is clearly a person in an important position at the present time; has been in the past, and he's a person who would be considered in the future." See Defense Department Briefing with Secretary of Defense and Gen. Richard Myers, Chairman of the Joint Chiefs of Staff, April 26, 2005 (http://www.defenselink.mil/transcripts/2005/tr20050426-secdef2601.html).

2. Josh White, "Top Army Officers Are Cleared in Abuse Cases," *Washington Post*, April 23, 2005, p. A1.

Col. Mark Warren, the CJTF-7 Staff Judge Advocate, calling "unsubstantiated" the suggestion that they failed to prevent or stop abuses. Interestingly, the findings of the Green investigation exactly reflect the prediction made to investigative journalist Seymour Hersh, over a year ago, regarding the probable results of earlier investigations. Scott Horton, an international law and human rights expert, and a New York City Bar Association official who has interacted with numerous military and legal professionals as the detainee abuse story has developed, told Hersh, "Rumsfeld has completely rigged the investigations. My friends say we should expect something akin to the [earlier] Army IG report – 'just a few rotten apples.'"[1]

Not surprisingly, the April 2005 announcement prompted yet another plea for an investigation capable of looking up as well as down the chain of command. In a press release from the American Civil Liberties Union, Executive Director Anthony D. Romero commented:

> These findings only show that the President must appoint a special counsel – who is not beholden by rank or party and who is able to look up the military chain of command .... The Army has released thousands of pages of internal documents – after months of stonewalling – that clearly show that the command breakdown that led to these abuses was more than the work of one scapegoated officer.[2]

To his credit, Senator Warner also issued a statement, pointing out how it is "absolutely essential to determine what went wrong, up and down the chain of command, both civilian and military."[3]

It was widely reported in the media that, as a result of Green's investigation, Karpinski was "recommended for punishment for the failures that led to abuses at the Abu Ghraib prison"[4] and that she was in fact demoted to colonel – approved by President Bush on May 5, 2005 – "in the abuse of detainees at Abu Ghraib prison."[5] In spite of the exoneration of her seniors, many have considered her punishment as at least a step towards holding someone accountable for the abuses that occurred. The strange fact is, however, that though Karpinski's performance of duty was found to

1. Seymour Hersh, *Chain of Command: The Road From 9/11 to Abu Ghraib* (New York: HarperCollins, 2004), p. 70.

2. American Civil Liberties Union, "ACLU Denounces Internal Army Review of Abuses," April 23, 2005 (http://www.aclu.org/SafeandFree/SafeandFree.cfm?ID=18098&c=206).

3. White, *loc. cit.*

4. *Ibid.*; see also Reuters, "U.S. Officer Blames Superior over Abu Ghraib Abuse," *San Diego Union-Tribune*, May 12, 2005, online.

5. Dave Moniz, "Gen. Karpinski Demoted in Prison Scandal," *USA Today*, May 5, 2005, online.

be "lacking," the statement released by the Army on May 5 indicated that "the investigation determined that *no action or lack of action on her part contributed specifically to the abuse of detainees at Abu Ghraib*"(emphasis mine).[1] She was reprimanded instead for an as yet unexplained "dereliction of duty," and – believe it or not – for shoplifting.

Josh White noted in his *Washington Post* report that it seems "Pentagon officials are trying to have it both ways." They want credit for taking the Abu Ghraib scandal seriously, without conceding that a general officer who was removed from the day-to-day running of the prison could be held truly accountable for what went on in the prison. Such a concession might implicate those well above Karpinski. Her lawyer, Neal A. Puckett, agreed: "I think they're trying to have it both ways. They are severing the chain of command right at her eyeball level, and not letting it go higher."[2]

Aside from Karpinski, several other officers either have been or will be reprimanded. According to the Army:

> . . . 27 officers, including Karpinski, received punishments ranging from court-martial to letter of reprimand.
> The officers include one colonel, four lieutenant colonels, three majors, 10 captains and six lieutenants.[3]

In addition, several lower-ranking enlisted have or will receive punishments, ranging so far from 10 years of confinement to forfeiture of a half-month's pay. These punishments, along with Karpinski's demotion and the high-profile trials of individuals such as Jeremy Sivits, Charles Graner, Ivan Frederick, Javal Davis, Megan Ambuhl, Lynndie England, and Sabrina Harman, are signals to many of the Army's willingness to hold individuals accountable. A *Christian Science Monitor* article from early June 2005 reports some 370 U.S. government investigations into abuses resulting in roughly 130 punishments of varying severity.[4] The narrow focus of these numerous criminal and disciplinary proceedings, however, begs the question of what official policy was when these so-called "few rotten apples" committed various forms of abuse. In the case of Col. Thomas Pappas, the former commander of the 205th Military Intelligence Brigade who was fined, reprimanded, and relieved of command for dereliction of duty, his punishment was the specific result of just "two instances relating to interrogation

---

1. *Ibid.*

2. White, *loc. cit.*

3. Moniz, *loc. cit.*

4. Peter Grier, "The Image War Over U.S. Detainees," *Christian Science Monitor*, June 6, 2005, online.

operations at Abu Ghraib, Iraq, in late 2003 and early 2004."[1] In spite of the political usefulness of his punishment, it would be a stretch to suggest that it represents a real acceptance of accountability by senior government officials. If anything, the facts would bear a contrary interpretation. It – along with Karpinski's demotion and the other soap-opera-like trials of the junior enlisted (a May 10, 2005, *New York Times* piece said appropriately that England's trial was "a spectacle worthy of *As the World Turns*") – seems more like a convenient distraction. Regardless of who did what – indeed all of these individuals may in fact be guilty of specific violations – hammering a few dozen folks for a few dozen specific actions seems to miss the point.

The frustration many no doubt feel in watching the abuse scandals unfold – along with the candidly flawed approach to investigating them – was well captured by a *New York Times* editorial that appeared a month after the exoneration of Karpinski's colleagues:

> The administration has provided nothing remotely like a full and honest accounting of the extent of the abuses at American prison camps in Iraq, Afghanistan, and Guantánamo Bay, Cuba. It has withheld internal reports and stonewalled external inquiries, while clinging to the fiction that the abuse was confined to isolated acts, like the sadistic behavior of one night crew in one cellblock at Abu Ghraib. The administration has prevented any serious investigation of policy makers at the White House, the Justice Department, and the Pentagon by orchestrating official probes so that none could come even close to the central question of how the prison policies were formulated and how they led to the abuses.[2]

Probable Cause

The impetus behind calls for a significant and serious investigation into the responsibility of the highest authorities for Abu Ghraib and similar misconduct is not in any way nullified by any of the judicial or non-judicial punishment that has been or will be meted out. There is plenty of evidence that the abuses that took place at Abu Ghraib during the latter part of 2003 were indeed the result of a specific policy, if not concrete direction, from individuals at the top of the chain of command. Regardless of whether a few "bad apples" went overboard, the question that remains, and that is perhaps most of interest to average people, is whether the self-professed "good apples" might have been out of bounds as well. And no trial that is obsessed with just "two specific instances" and one individual at a time is going to determine that.

---

1. Lisa Burgess, "Colonel in Charge of Interrogators Is Punished in Abu Ghraib Scandal," *Stars and Stripes*, May 12, 2005, online.
2. "Patterns of Abuse," *New York Times*, May 23, 2005, online.

Numerous facts, reports, and statements from individuals close to the Abu Ghraib events point to the involvement of senior officials in decisions that indirectly or even directly contributed to abuse. Notwithstanding the memos produced by DoJ and DoD, which in and of themselves are incriminating, there are a number of compelling reasons why the "few bad apple" line is not persuasive, and why senior individuals should be investigated with the power and independence to do so fully.

The "bad apple" line – firstly – doesn't make a lot of sense. Karpinski related a number of reasons why during the course of her very credible and persuasive interview with *The Signal,* which she gave on July 4, 2004.[1] The military police (MPs) in her command were thoroughly trained at their mobilization stations on GC requirements as part of their pre-deployment training. They also trained occasionally throughout the year – training which included sessions by included Karpinski's brigade and battalion JAG officers. Interestingly, Karpinski relates that her MPs frequently questioned her JAGs "[b]ecause their prisoners [were] asking questions. *And the reasons they were asking questions was because every prisoner was provided with a copy of the Geneva-Hague conventions in their language"* (emphasis mine).[2] Copies of GC requirements were posted on the wall of the cellblocks in each one of the compounds, and even on the concertina wire, she noted. Lack of familiarity with their requirements hardly seems feasible.

The dates of the pictures of abuse didn't make sense to her either. Assuming the photos that were made public were taken in October 2003, the MPs guarding the wings where the abuse took place *would have been there only three weeks,* as they were newly assigned to Abu Ghraib at that point.

> "[They] served successfully in another location for about eight months," Karpinski said, and "moved to Abu Ghraib . . . but that would mean that in three weeks, [they] get their feet on the ground, go to work, and decide that they could do these things and get away with it because they felt so comfortable with their surroundings? I don't believe it."[3]

Their assignment to the cellblocks where the abuse took place – 1A and 1B – was odd as well, she said. Normally individuals would be allocated by squad according to the judgment of the first sergeant, who would know the strength of the different squads. In the case of 1A and 1B, "That didn't happen . . . . it was two from the first squad, three from the second squad." This suggests that the individuals were "hand picked" for interrogation support,

---

1. Janis Karpinski, Interview with Leon Worden, *The Signal,* July 4, 2004, online.
2. *Ibid.*
3. *Ibid.*

as outlined by Maj. Gen. Geoffrey Miller during his visit to the prison from August 31 to September 9, 2003. Karpinski says convincingly:

> ... I know, sincerely, I know in my heart, that these MPs were instructed to do what they did, what has been widely published in photograph form. And they believed that the orders that they were being given, were being given by people authorized to give them those orders.

Critics of Karpinski's point of view suggest the MP's "should have known better," no matter if they were ordered to do what they did or not (implicitly acknowledging that they probably *were* ordered to do something they shouldn't have).[1] But, as an interesting *Washington Monthly* article on Abu Ghraib noted in November of 2004, how likely is that any of the junior enlisted personnel – or even the junior officers – would have felt comfortable questioning orders, especially given that "the memoranda from the White House [had] stamped the interrogation tactics with the imprimatur of legality"?[2]

> It may be unrealistic to expect that a junior enlisted soldier such as England, or even her immediate supervisor, Staff Sgt. Ivan Frederick, would have the knowledge or the temerity to contradict [orders to interrogate prisoners coercively] when they were given. The effect of the Bush administration's exhaustively creative research into breaking the rules was virtually to ensure that every player in this tragedy went along and followed orders.[3]

As noted earlier, the investigations into the treatment of detainees take as a given the legality of this Bush-administration position. The most recent report (Schmidt-Furlow), dealing with the FBI allegations of abuse at GTMO, exonerated most of the individuals investigated on the grounds that their acts were not "in violation of Army Field Manual 34-52 and DoD guidance."[4] But interrogations conducted *within the parameters* of that guidance in fact resulted in a "high-value" detainee being subjected to

> 160 days of segregation from other detainees, 48 of 54 consecutive days of 18- to 20-hour interrogations, and the creative application of authorized interrogation techniques [such as r]equiring the subject ... to be led around by a leash tied to his chains, placing a thong on his head, wearing a bra, insulting

---

1. Mary Hall, a former military judge, was quoted in a *Christian Science Monitor* piece to the effect that the Abu Ghraib courts-martial "are a blunt reminder to even the newest private that they have a duty to just say 'no'" (Faye Bowers, "Abu Ghraib's Message for the Rank and File," May 6, 2005, online). Which raises the question: should have said "no" *to what?*

2. Phillip Carter, "The Road to Abu Ghraib," *Washington Monthly*, November, 2004, online.

3. *Ibid.*

4. Lt. Gen. Randall Schmidt and Brig. Gen. John Furlow, *Final Report, Investigation into FBI Allegations of Detainee Abuse at Guantánamo Bay, Cuba, Detention Facility*, April 1, 2005, p. 1.

his mother and sister [they were called "whores"], being forced to stand naked in front of a female interrogator for five minutes, and using strip searches as an interrogation technique . . . .[1]

Although the Schmidt-Furlow investigation concluded that the "cumulative effect" of these actions constituted "degrading and abusive treatment," it also said that they "did not rise to the level of prohibited inhumane treatment," and that "every technique employed . . . was legally permissible." Gen. Schimdt followed this up by asserting, at the July 13, 2005, Senate Armed Services Committee hearing convened to hear testimony on his report, that "no torture occurred."[2] But if the law itself was the enabler in this case for technically "legal" treatment which Schmidt and Furlow – somewhat contradictorily – said Gen. Miller should have "limited," the responsibility rests clearly with those who promulgated the law, and not with those who followed it. As Senator Levin put it during the hearing, "It is clear from the report that detainee mistreatment was not simply the product of a few rogue military police in a night shift."[3] That's also the perspective of one of the soldiers accused of the prisoner abuse detailed by Tim Golden for the *New York Times*: "I just don't understand how, if we were given the training to do this, you can say that we were wrong and should have known better."[4]

Aside from the commonsense objections to the "bad apple" approach, there is also a plethora of eyewitness and second-hand reported testimony about the involvement of very high authorities within DoD. This is not to say that senior generals committed acts of abuse. But they may quite credibly have ordered or at least consciously created the conditions for it. (The point was hinted at with some wit by Senator John McCain (R-Ariz.) when, during an April 28, 2005, Congressional hearing on defense intelligence, he raised a question about the Army's plan to release a revised interrogations manual barring techniques employed in Abu Ghraib and elsewhere. McCain didn't see how the Army and DoD could acknowledge, implicitly, that doctrine and leadership played a role in the prison abuses – by revising the manual and specifically addressing the Abu Ghraib techniques – while at the same time refusing to admit any failing on the part those at the top of the chain of command. As the senator put it to Under Secretary Cambone during the hearing: "So we didn't do anything wrong,

1. *Ibid.*, p. 20.

2. Associated Press, "Investigators Recommended Disciplining Gitmo Commander," *CNN International*, July 13, 2005, online.

3. *Ibid.*

4. Tim Golden, "Abuse Cases Open Command Issues at Army Prison," *New York Times*, August 8, 2005, online; see also Golden, "In U.S. Report," *loc. cit.*

but we won't do it again."[1] McCain's skepticism is probably warranted: the approval authority for the new Army manual, thanks to her position as head of the Army Intelligence Center in Arizona, is Barbara Fast, who "played an extensive role in developing policies and practices for the interrogation center at Abu Ghraib."[2])

As noted above, Maj. Gen. Miller and another general officer told an FBI agent plainly that they got their marching orders from Rumsfeld. Importing interrogation techniques to Abu Ghraib, in order to improve intelligence collection, lay behind Miller's personal visit to the prison. (GTMO interrogations reportedly employed methods unrestricted by GC protections, under the assumption that detainees there were not entitled to GC prisoner of war status.) "Rumsfeld pointed out [in a summer, 2003, intelligence briefing][3] that Gitmo was producing good intel," a *Newsweek* report stated.

> So he directed Steve Cambone, his under secretary for intelligence, to send Gitmo commandant Miller to Iraq to improve what they were doing out there. Cambone in turn dispatched his deputy, Lt. Gen. William (Jerry) Boykin – later to gain notoriety for his harsh comments about Islam – down to Gitmo to talk with Miller and organize the trip.[4]

This is confirmed by a *Washington Post* report indicating that the trip was authorized by "a memo signed on Aug. 18, 2003, [by] the Pentagon's Joint Staff, acting on a request from Defense Secretary Donald H. Rumsfeld and his top intelligence aide, Stephen A. Cambone."[5] It was also recently confirmed by Maj. Daivd Dienna, testifying at an Article 32 hearing for soldiers accused of prisoner abuse in Iraq. "We understood that [Miller] was sent over by the secretary of defense," he said, and that training teams were sent to Abu Ghraib "to take these interrogation techniques, other techniques they were using in Guantánamo and try to incorporate them in Iraq."[6] Scott Horton, in expert testimony submitted to a German court in Karlsruhe on January 31, 2005, for a lawsuit against senior U.S. officials

1. Bowers, *loc. cit.*

2. Eric Schmitt, "In New Manual, Army Limits Tactics in Interrogation," *New York Times*, April 28, 2005, online.

3. Scott Horton, report to the German Federal Prosecutor, January 28, 2005, online (*vide infra*, note 48).

4. John Barry, Michael Hirsh, and Michael Isikoff, "The Roots of Torture," *Newsweek*, May 24, 2004, online.

5. Jeffrey R. Smith, "Memo Gave Intelligence Bigger Role," *Washington Post*, May 21, 2004, p. A17.

6. Andrea F. Siegel, "Prison in Iraq Imported Interrogation Methods, Former Warden Testifies," *Newsday.com*, July 28, 2005.

filed by the Center for Constitutional Rights (CCR) in New York, confirms the visit and its origin as well. "[T]his simple fact," he writes, "well known to many senior officers involved in the process, is consciously suppressed in all official reports issued by DoD."[1] Drawing out the consequences of the meeting with Rumsfeld and Miller's assignment, Horton continues:

> ... the decision to introduce the Guantánamo techniques (or "Gitmoize") – consciously crafted in evasion of the requirements of the GC – and to introduce them to Iraq, where the Conventions clearly applied, rested on the express and unlawful order of Rumsfeld.[2]

Karpinski attests to Miller's visit as well. "Gen. Miller was one of several visitors that we got that came for a review of our operations," she said.

> But ... Gen. Miller came to visit the military intelligence officer of the headquarters; that was Brig. Gen. [Barbara] Fast. And he was there to help them enhance and improve their interrogation operations. The reason we were included at any point in his visit was because he wanted to visit several of my prison facilities ....
> [D]uring the in-brief, he made reference several times to his plans to "Gitmoize" the interrogation operations. And he was the commander down at Guantánamo Bay; he was extremely successful, apparently, in getting actionable intelligence from the interrogations that were being conducted there. And he was going to use that template of operations in Iraq.[3]

Interestingly, DoD's own Schlesinger report records that during his visit to Iraq, Miller brought with him the interrogation guidance approved for GTMO (the April 16, 2003, memo from the secretary of defense), and noted specifically that it applied to "unlawful combatants" and not to Iraq, where GC protections were recognized by the U.S. The report further notes, however, that Sanchez's September 14, 2003, memorandum authorized interrogation techniques even beyond those authorized for GTMO.[4] Perhaps this subtle willingness to approach the interrogation of combatants in Iraq the way that interrogation of GTMO "unlawful combatants" was conducted is exactly the kind of "uncertainty" as to "adversary status" that Gonzalez referred to in the memo cited in January 2005 by the military JAGs. First hand testimony suggests that this uncertainty existed among the rank and file, and contributed to its share of abuse.[5] Detainees in Afghanistan were

---

1. Horton, *loc. cit.*
2. *Ibid.*
3. Karpinski, *loc. cit.*
4. Schlesinger, *op. cit.*, p. 9.
5. See the comment made by an Army Staff Sgt. in response to a reprimand he received in

also treated "exceptionally" based on the belief that GC protections didn't apply there, according to recent reports.[1] Most troubling is the fact that this uncertainty as to detainees "status" should never in the first place have been construed by the U.S. as authorizing an exemption, in the case of so-called "enemy combatants," from the duty of interrogators and military police to refrain from subjecting detainees to torture or to cruel, degrading, or inhumane treatment. As a recent *Boston Globe* editorial puts it, "international and U.S. anti-torture laws allow no such exemptions."[2]

Beyond Miller, Karpinski implicated "Gen. Fast, Gen. Sanchez, [and Stephen A.] Cambone, [under secretary of defense for intelligence]. I don't know if it stops at Cambone, but I believe that he was orchestrating it, he was directing," she said to *The Signal*.[3]

Seymour Hersh is no less explicit in his reporting for the *New Yorker*:

> The roots of the Abu Ghraib prison scandal lie . . . in a decision, approved last year by Secretary of Defense Donald Rumsfeld, to expand a highly secret operation, which had been focused on the hunt for al-Qaeda, to the interrogation of prisoners in Iraq.[4]

Later in the same article, he writes of his own sources – claimed to be reliable, experienced, and informed – who indicate that even the White House was aware of the plan to have Miller "Gitmoize" the Abu Ghraib intelligence operation.

> . . . a Pentagon consultant . . . spread the blame. "The White House subcontracted this to the Pentagon, and the Pentagon subcontracted it to Cambone," he said. "This is Cambone's deal, but Rumsfeld and Myers approved the program." When it came to the interrogation operation at Abu Ghraib, he said, Rumsfeld left the details to Cambone.[5]

November 2003 for failing to properly supervise soldiers conducting detainee operations: "Comments made by senior leaders regarding detainees, such as 'They are not [POWs]. They are terrorists and will be treated as such . . . ' have caused a great deal of confusion as to the status of the detainees" (quoted by AI, *Guantánamo and Beyond, op. cit.*, p. 29).

1. Golden, "In U.S. Report," *loc. cit.*, explains how, "with President Bush's final determination in February 2002 that the Conventions did not apply to the conflict with al-Qaeda and that Taliban fighters would not be accorded the rights of prisoners of war, the interrogators believed they 'could deviate slightly from the rules,'" according to a Utah Army reservist, Sgt. James A. Leahy. "There was the Geneva Conventions for enemy prisoners of war, but nothing for terrorists," Leahy told Army investigators. Golden notes also that senior intelligence officers said that detainees "were to be considered terrorists until proved otherwise."

2. "The Torture Line," *Boston Globe*, May 21, 2005, online. [See also the clear discussion of this point by Gabor Rona in the article on pp. 421–441 of the present volume.—Ed.]

3. Karpinski, *loc. cit.*

4. Seymour Hersh, "The Grey Zone," *The New Yorker*, May 24, 2004, online.

5. *Ibid.*

In his book, *Chain of Command,* Hersh also confirms the involvement of Lt. Gen. Boykin. "After the scandal became public," he writes, "I was repeatedly told that Boykin had been involved, on behalf of Cambone, in the policies that led to the abuse at Abu Ghraib."[1]

Hersh additionally notes the testimony of a source who maintained that the "sexual humiliation and the posed photographs" may have initially been intended – and for a "serious" purpose.

> It was thought that some prisoners would do anything – including spying on their associates – to avoid dissemination of the shameful photos to family and friends. The government consultant [source] said, "I was told that the purpose of the photographs was to create an army of informants, people you could insert back in the population." The idea was that they would be motivated by fear of exposure, and gather information about pending insurgency action . . . .[2]

Other details include the fact – noted in a Center for Public Integrity report – that Lt. Col. Steven Jordan, head of the Joint Interrogation and Detention Center where intelligence operations were consolidated in September 2003, "told investigators that the interrogation center had been put together at the direction of the White House";[3] and the fact that Charles Graner, during the sentencing phase of his January 2005 court-martial, persuasively (though unconvincingly) argued that senior intelligence officers ordered detainees to be roughed up so they would be easier to interrogate.[4]

A Special Access Program?

As if it weren't enough that there is first hand testimony and credible reporting as to the complicity of high authorities in decisions that set the stage for what transpired at Abu Ghraib, there's more. Seymour Hersh has detailed the possible export to Iraq of an alleged program with very tightly controlled and compartmented security – a "special-access program" or SAP, into which individuals from the nation's special operations and intelligence communities would be "read" in order to participate in the timely interrogation of, or strike missions against, "high value" targets in the "global war on terror." These missions, Hersh notes, could take place anywhere in the world with only Rumsfeld's permission, based upon prior

1. Hersh, *Chain of Command,* p. 52.

2. Hersh, "The Grey Zone," *loc. cit.*

3. Alexander Cohen, "The Abu Ghraib Supplementary Documents," Center for Public Integrity Special Report, October 8, 2004 (http://www.publicintegrity.org/report.aspx?aid=396&sid=100).

4. "Graner Gets Ten Years," *CBS News/Associated Press,* January 15, 2005, online.

agreement between the various agencies – NSA, CIA, DoD, etc. – and using
CIA interrogation sites around the world, along with commandos from the
nation's special operations forces. The intelligence-gathering ability of this
program was highly regarded within the Pentagon, according to Hersh's
sources. "The intelligence would be relayed to the SAP command center in
the Pentagon in real time," he wrote, "and sifted for those pieces of information critical to the 'white,' or overt, world."[1]

When Rumsfeld became exasperated with the lack of intelligence desired
for combating the insurgency in Iraq, Hersh's intelligence source notes,

> [he] and Cambone . . . expanded the scope of the sap, bringing its unconven-
> tional methods to Abu Ghraib. The commandos were to operate in Iraq as they
> had in Afghanistan. The male prisoners could be treated roughly, and exposed
> to sexual humiliation."[2]

Soon after, "[Gen.] Miller was 'read in' – that is, briefed – on the special-
access operation," Hersh's source claims, and military intelligence personnel were incorporated after after that.

> Cambone then made [a] crucial decision . . . : not only would he bring the sap's
> rules into the prisons; he would bring some of the Army military-intelligence
> officers working inside the Iraqi prisons under the sap's auspices. "So here are
> fundamentally good soldiers – military-intelligence guys – being told that no
> rules apply," the former official, who has extensive knowledge of the special-
> access programs, added. "And, as far as they're concerned, *this is a covert opera-
> tion, and it's to be kept within Defense Department channels*" (emphasis mine).[3]

Hersh maintains that the SAP's existence was in fact confirmed to him by
a ranking member of Congress, after his May 2004 *New Yorker* article on the
subject was published.[4] That said, it is perhaps impossible – at least for anyone without blanket access to high-level government officials and highly classified records – to confirm the veracity of the suggestion that Abu Ghraib is
really the fallout from a covert program, called (among other things) "Copper
Green," which according to Hersh's sources, "encouraged physical coercion
and sexual humiliation of Iraqi prisoners in an effort to generate more intelligence about the growing insurgency in Iraq."[5] Nevertheless, two aspects of
the story make it seem at least credible. The first is the number of facts that
fit this picture, though taken by themselves they might seem unrelated. The

1. Hersh, "The Grey Zone," *loc. cit.*
2. *Ibid.*
3. *Ibid.*
4. Hersh, *Chain of Command*, p. 47.
5. Hersh, "The Grey Zone," *loc. cit.*

second is the degree to which the reviews and criminal proceedings that have thus far dealt with the Abu Ghraib abuses scrupulously (perhaps consciously?) avoid a serious investigation into whether or not the program that Hersh has portrayed actually exists. The completed and ongoing investigations could not be better tailored to protect the existence of the program.

Karpinski's testimony is one part of the set of facts that fit the larger picture of a SAP for aggressive interrogations. She believes that the pictures "were staged and set up to be used to show to a detainee as they were getting ready to undergo interrogation." It might be a way to get information "more quickly and more efficiently from a new detainee," if he were threatened with images projected on a screen or printed "in living color" of what happened to his friends – and what might happen to him.[1]

An additional argument in favor of the SAP's existence emerges from a comparison of those in Iraq who would likely have been "read in" to the program, against those who have in fact been implicated (even if exonerated thus far) in contributing to the abuses that occurred. Many of the same individuals are found in both groups.

The event that set things in motion – Lt. Gen. Boykin's trip to GTMO – was known not only to the traveler but also to Rumsfeld, Cambone, and Miller. Karpinski's testimony indicates that once Miller arrived in Iraq from GTMO, he worked directly with the commander – Sanchez – and Sanchez's intelligence chief, Barbara Fast. Karpsinski further indicated that Miller planned to adopt Abu Ghraib for his intelligence gathering operation, telling her, "Ric Sanchez said I could have whatever facility I wanted, and I want Abu Ghraib, and we're going to train the MPs to work with the interrogators."[2]

The interrogators he refers to were those he brought with him from GTMO. A *New York Times* report confirmed, that "[a]ccording to a military officer on the Miller delegation to Iraq, interrogation teams from Guantánamo took part in interrogations at Abu Ghraib . . . . "[3] Karpinski again says the same thing:

> Gen. Miller . . . talked about his interrogators, the ones that he was going to send up from Guantánamo Bay and the ones that he brought with him, that they knew what the rules were, and that they would share them with the interrogation team.[4]

---

1. Karpinski, *loc. cit.*

2. *Ibid.*

3. Douglas Jehl and Andrea Elliott, "Cuba Base Sent Its Interrogators to Iraqi Prison," *The New York Times*, May 29, 2004, online.

4. Karpinski, *loc. cit.*

Karpinski wasn't the only one given to understand that Miller intended his interrogators to train the MI personnel and the MPs. Pappas, then head of the 205th MI Brigade, told her that was his understanding as well, according to her *Signal* interview: "We're supposed to have these interrogators that he's sending up from Guantánamo Bay, and they're going to give some kind of training to my interrogators and to your MPs."[1] By mid or late September, she remembered, the maximum-security cells where the abuse would occur – in cellblocks 1A and 1B – were being run by MI, and Pappas, who worked directly for Fast, the intelligence chief, was living at the prison. It thus came as no surprise to her when Sanchez, the CJTF-7 commander, issued an order (on November 19, 2003) making Pappas the commander of the prison, even though it was staffed by MPs who worked for her, because by that time the MI personnel had been running the interrogations in the high-security areas for two months.[2] What is apparent is a gradual move by MI, following Miller's visit from GTMO, to take over operations at Abu Ghraib.

Karpinski remembers specifically a conversation she had with Pappas following the promulgation of the order placing him in charge of the prison. "[Fast] wanted Abu Ghraib" Pappas told her, "and she wanted the interrogation operation run a certain way, and this was her solution."[3] A later conversation she had with Fast elicited a similar remark, illustrating Fast's central position in intelligence decisions there: " . . . we're going to run interrogations the way we want them run."

Part of running interrogations according to MI desires was selecting a few MPs to learn whatever techniques were necessary to support the new interrogation methods. It was up to Miller's imported "interrogation teams and the interrogators to tell the MPs what they needed them to do,"[4] Karpinski said. Miller specifically told her, in fact, as far as she remembers, "[W]e're going to select the MPs who can do this, and they're going to work specifically with the interrogation team." Her suspicion was that those implicated in the abuse scandal were, in fact, "six or seven individuals who may have been specifically selected. *Because they were likely to participate . . .* " (emphasis mine).[5]

1. *Ibid.*

2. A *New York Times* report, "Afghan Policies on Questioning Prisoners Taken to Iraq," by Douglas Jehl and Eric Schmitt, dated May 21, 2004, available online, confirmed that "Colonel Pappas . . . moved his headquarters to Abu Ghraib in September and was the top Army officer at the prison."

3. Karpinski, *loc. cit.*

4. *Ibid.*

5. *Ibid.*

Two other individuals who have been the subject of scrutiny worked directly for Fast, the intelligence chief in Iraq. One was Lt. Col. Steven Jordan, head of the Joint Intelligence and Debriefing Center (JIDC) at Abu Ghraib, where many interrogations were conducted by MI personnel. He "[told] investigators that he acted in a liaison role and ultimately reported to Major General Barbara Fast, the head of intelligence operations at Coalition headquarters."[1] The second was Col. Stephen Boltz, the second-ranking MI officer in Iraq, just under Fast. His guidance regarding interrogations was reflected in an email from a MI captain:

> The gloves are coming off gentlemen regarding these detainees, Col Boltz has made it clear that we want these individuals broken. Casualties are mounting and we need to start gathering info to help protect our fellow soldiers from any further attacks.[2]

Still others, according to a *Baltimore Sun* report from 2004, claimed to work directly and exclusively for Fast:

> Some of the intelligence officers and civilian contractors at the prison said they were on special assignments for Fast or worked directly for her. "They would play the 'General Fast card,' saying they only reported to her," said a military intelligence soldier who served at Abu Ghraib.[3]

Finally – among those potentially "read in" to a SAP – there is the question of other units that likely would have been part of the alleged program and that have recently been implicated in assisting with the "migration" of interrogation techniques from elsewhere into Iraq. The JDIC, under Lt. Col. Jordan, was stood up by (once again) Barbara Fast – then a one-star – in September 2003. Some of the personnel assigned to support intelligence operations there were part of the 519th MI battalion, which had run interrogations in Afghanistan in late 2002.[4] In Afghanistan they copied interrogation rules "almost verbatim" from the July 15, 2003, "Battlefield Interrogation Team and Facility Policy" of Joint Task Force 121, a secretive Special Operations

1. Cohen, *loc. cit.*

2. Mark Danner, *Torture and Truth; America, Abu Ghraib and the War on Terrorism* (New York: The New York Review of Books, 2004), p. 33, quoted by Human Rights Watch, *Getting Away with Torture?*, April 2005, online.

3. Tom Bowman, "General Faces Abu Ghraib Scrutiny," *Baltimore Sun*, July 15, 2004, online.

4. Douglas Jehl and Eric Schmitt, "Afghan Policies on Questioning Prisoners," *loc. cit.*; see also the report by Lt. Gen. Anthony R. Jones and Maj. Gen. George R. Fay, *Investigation of Intelligence Activities at Abu Ghraib*, August 23, 2004, p. 21. Tim Golden also confirms the role of the operations officer leading interrogations at Bagram in Afghanistan, Army Capt. Carolyn A. Wood, in exporting techniques from there to Abu Ghraib, where she was sent in July 2003 after serving at Bagram for a year. See Golden, "In U.S. Report," *loc. cit.*

Forces/CIA mission seeking former government members in Iraq.[1] It would be reasonable to assume that JTF-121 was cut in on any special interrogation program, given the sensitiveness and importance of its mission. Support for such a supposition is found also in Hersh's book, where he says – without naming the task force – that, according to his intelligence source, "the SAP was involved in a few assignments in Iraq . . . ," where "CIA and other American special forces operatives secretly teamed up to hunt for Saddam Hussein and – without success – for Iraqi weapons of mass destruction."[2]

The Schlesinger report also detailed the adoption by the 519th MI battalion of a February 2003 document, "Special Operation Forces Standard Operating Procedures," prepared in response to a data call from the Pentagon for an interrogations procedures working group report. The officer in charge of the company in Iraq from the 519th "prepared draft interrogation guidelines that were a near copy of the Standard Operating Procedure created by SOF."[3] Again, it is reasonable to speculate that the SOF procedures may have benefited from guidelines that existed within the confines of the alleged special access program.

The Fay report highlights a similar process. When, in September 2003, CJTF-7 requested that the judge advocate from the 205th MI brigade, commanded by Pappas, produce a set of interrogation rules, the draft submitted was based upon the April 16, 2003, secretary of defense interrogation memo (originally drafted specifically for GTMO interrogations) that Miller brought with him when he visited Abu Ghraib. This draft reply was then sent to the 519th MI battalion for coordination, and the 519th added "the use of dogs, stress positions, sleep management, sensory deprivation, and yelling, loud music and light control" from its own 2003 interrogations memo.[4]

Other snippets of fact fit the picture of a special access program that included Abu Ghraib interrogations. An *NBC News* report of May 20, 2004, alleged the existence in Iraq of the Battlefield Interrogation Facility (BIF) – maintained by Army Delta Force personnel at Baghdad airport – where "the normal rules of interrogation don't apply."[5] Of note is the claim of "top U.S. military and intelligence sources" that Rumsfeld,

1. Douglas Jehl and Eric Schmitt, "Army's Report Faults General in Prison Abuse," *New York Times,* August 27, 2004, online.

2. Hersh, *Chain of Command,* p. 56.

3. Independent Panel to Review DoD Detention Operations, *Final Report,* August, 2004, p. 9.

4. Jones and Fay, *op. cit.,* p. 25.

5. Campbell Brown, "New Front in Iraq Detainee Abuse Scandal?" *NBC News,* May 20, 2004, online (http://www.msnbc.msn.com/id/5024068).

through other top Pentagon officials, directed the U.S. head of intelligence in Iraq, Gen. Barbara Fast, and others to bring some of the methods used at the BIF to prisons like Abu Ghraib, in hopes of getting better intelligence from Iraqi detainees.[1]

As head of the JIDC, Lt. Col. Jordan promulgated a policy allowing the CIA to conduct interrogations without the presence of Army personnel.[2] A former Navy SEAL, Dan Cerrillo, testifying at the court-martial trial of Navy Lt. Andrew Ledford – the SEAL accused in conjunction with the death of al-Jamadi – said that he beat another prisoner because he believed he was being directed to do so by CIA personnel.[3] Seymour Hersh's *New Yorker* piece also documents the presence of "[h]ard-core special operatives, some of them with aliases, [who] were working in the prison." Though

> [t]he military police assigned to guard the prisoners wore uniforms ... many others – military intelligence officers, contract interpreters, CIA officers, and the men from the special-access program – wore civilian clothes.[4]

This is consistent with the testimony of Karpinski, who recalls escorting a general officer to an interrogation facility and chatting there with some individuals in civilian clothes. "Are you local?" she remembers asking one.

> Because he looked like he was Kuwaiti. I said, "Are you an interpreter?" He said, "No, I'm an interrogator." And I said, "Oh, are you from here?" And he said, "No, actually, I'm from Israel." And I was kind of shocked. And I think I laughed. And I said, "No, really?" And he said, "No, really, I am."[5]

Other reports raise similar concerns. A January 13, 2005, wire report indicated that the White House *admitted* to having "urged Congress to drop a legislative proposal that would have curbed the ability of U.S. intelligence to use extreme interrogation tactics."[6] Furthermore, a 13-page confidential report was submitted by retired Col. Stuart A. Herrington to general officers in Iraq as early as December 2003, saying "that members of an elite military and CIA task force were abusing detainees."[7] One may

---

1. *Ibid.*

2. Jones and Fay, *op. cit.*, p. 44.

3. Seth Hettena, "CIA Official and Ex-SEAL Give Differing Accounts of Prisoner Abuse at Court-Martial," *San Diego Union-Tribune*, May 24, 2005, online.

4. Hersh, "The Gray Zone," *loc. cit.*

5. Karpinski, *loc. cit.*

6. *Reuters*, January 13, 2005, online.

7. *Criminal Complaint Against the United States Secretary of Defense Donald Rumsfeld et al.*, update, Center for Constitutional Rights, January 27, 2005. See Josh White, "U.S. Generals in Iraq Were Told of Abuse Early, Inquiry Finds," *Washington Post*, December 1, 2004, p. A1.

be forgiven for wondering how much more evidence there is, conforming to the pattern of an extremely secret interrogation program responsible for the Abu Ghraib mess, that still hasn't been released.

Damage Control

Whether a SAP covering the Abu Ghraib interrogations existed or not, the efforts that the U.S. government seems to have gone to in order to keep the damning details about the policy and practicalities of interrogation in Iraq out of the public eye is extraordinary. The Horton testimony is particularly revealing in this regard. His impression is that

> the highest profile cases in which the severest sanctions are sought consistently involve those soldiers who through neglect or oversight permitted photographic evidence of the crimes at Abu Ghraib to become public knowledge. Several soldiers I interviewed told me that they had a clear understanding from this process, that it wasn't the abuse of prisoners which was being punished . . . .[1]

Furthermore, Horton claims to have been informed by senior officers that high-ranking individuals were protected from significant investigation due to their knowledge of Rumsfeld's connection with the scandal. The names of those shielded, according to Horton, are those who would have also had certain knowledge of the operation of any special access program, if one existed.

> [C]ertain senior figures whose conduct in this affair bears close scrutiny were explicitly "protected" or "shielded" by withholding information from investigators or by providing security classifications which made such investigation impossible. The individuals "shielded," I was informed, included MG Geoffrey Miller, MG Barbara Fast, COL Marc Warren, COL Steven Boltz, LTG Sanchez and LTG William ("Jerry") Boykin. In each case, the fact that these individuals possessed information on Rumsfeld's involvement was essential to the decision to "shield" them.[2]

Horton reported as well that criminal proceedings reflect a similar desire to shield senior officials. The Ft. Hood prosecutions, he says, "are further marked by a conscious obstruction of efforts by the defense to prove that they were acting in reliance upon orders up the chain of command." Col. James L. Pohl, the presiding judge, declined all requests that certain senior officers be immunized so as to compel their testimony.[3] This fact is born out by a comment that Charles Graner's defense lawyer, Guy Womack, made

---

1. Horton, *loc. cit.*
2. *Ibid.*
3. *Ibid.*

indicating that he was hampered from trying to prove that Graner had been ordered by intelligence agents to do what he did in order to make the prisoners easier to interrogate. As he told *CBS News,* "None of those superiors came into court, none were questioned, and we were precluded from even bringing them into court because they invoked their right to remain silent."[1] Horton also notes his belief that Senator Warner was threatened with political retaliation by leading Republicans "if he carried through with his plan to conduct real hearings." When Horton proposed witnesses to be interviewed by SASC staff, he was told, he says, "that Senator Warner has assured Rumsfeld that the Committee will conduct no independent investigation of these matters."[2]

Karpinski relates stories that are similarly disturbing. When the International Committee of the Red Cross (ICRC) visited Abu Ghraib, she wasn't involved in dealing with the report of their findings until the eleventh hour. The "usual suspects" dealt with the ICRC findings: " . . . it was already reviewed by the military intelligence people and Col. (Marc) Warren, the CJTF-7 staff judge advocate, before they even presented it to me." The only reason she was asked to bottom-line the report, she says, was to help CJTF-7 avoid scrutiny for having transferred command of the prison to military intelligence personnel.[3]

Finally, there is the disturbing story of Sgt. Frank Ford, a counterintelligence agent in the California National Guard's 223rd Military Intelligence (M.I.) Battalion who was stationed in Samarra, Iraq. On June 15, 2003, he told his commanding officer that he had witnessed five incidents of torture and abuse of Iraqi detainees at his base, and requested a formal investigation. Thirty-six hours later Ford was ordered to submit to a psychiatric evaluation, diagnosed with combat stress, and evacuated outside the country. The evaluation at first diagnosed him as "completely normal," and a non-commissioned officer witness claims that Ford's company commander "became enraged when he read the initial medical report finding nothing wrong with Ford and intimidated the psychiatrist into changing it." Reportedly the psychiatrist was told "that it was a 'C.I. [counterintelligence] or M.I. matter' and . . . that she had to change her report and get Ford out of Iraq."[4]

Hersh's sources maintain that the "damage control" surrounding the alleged special access program is unsurprising. "If General Miller had

1. *CBS News/Associated Press, loc. cit.*

2. Horton, *loc. cit.*

3. Karpinski, *loc. cit.*; see Douglas Jehl and Neil A. Lewis, "U.S. Disputed Protected Status of Iraq Inmates," *New York Times*, May 23, 2004, online.

4. David DeBatto, "Whitewashing Torture?" *Salon.com*, December 8, 2004.

been summoned by Congress to testify" (as he was), his intelligence source pointed out,

> he, like Rumsfeld and Cambone, would not have been able to mention the special-access program. "If you give away the fact that a special-access program exists," the former intelligence official told me, "you blow the whole quick-reaction program."[1]

The problem is that the program got out of control at Abu Ghraib; "[t]he photos," one of Hersh's sources commented, "turned out to be the result of the program run amok."[2] Something clearly needed to be done, for complete silence was just not an option, regardless of the desire to preserve the alleged program and insulate senior officials. The focus on a half dozen junior enlisted folks, along with a few officers – to the exclusion of the real leadership – seems consistent with the Pentagon's possible desire to salvage the aggressive interrogation program. Indeed, Karpinski has said, even since her demotion, that she's "not convinced" that abuse has necessarily ceased. It's possible, she told ABC's *Nightline* on May 12, 2004, "Maybe people who are orchestrating have [simply] gotten smarter and have gotten better."[3] Indeed, Hersh's sources would agree with any suggestion that the crackdown on wayward enlisted reservists is simply grist for the public mill. "Rumsfeld's explanation to the White House," one of Hersh's sources related, was that "'We've got a glitch in the program. We'll prosecute it.' *The cover story was that some kids got out of control*" (emphasis mine).[4]

The Burden of Accountability

Given the repeated calls from congressional and other professional sphere for a serious look into the actual level of responsibility for the torture and abuse scandals, special access program notwithstanding, one might wonder why – in the *Post's* words – "no genuinely independent investigator has been empowered" to connect the dots and hold high level officials accountable. Indeed all the action at this point has focused on low-level operators and a rather "dispensable" woman Army reservist.

Perhaps what is discouraging the executive branch from launching a truly independent and empowered investigation – especially if its complic-

---

1. Hersh, "The Gray Zone," *loc. cit.*

2. *Ibid.*

3. United Press International, "Abu Ghraib General Says She's 'Scapegoat,'" *Washington Times*, May 13, 2005, online.

4. Hersh, "The Gray Zone," *loc. cit.*

ity in the scandal is as significant as reporters like Hersh make it out to be – is the thought of the price that senior officials stand to pay should a full review of their accountability ever be conducted. In this light it is perhaps unsurprising that Secretary Rumsfeld dismissed the call for a special counsel to investigate the abuses and their context independently; "to go back into all of the things that's [sic] already been reviewed by everybody else doesn't make sense," he said, reinforcing the point by reminding viewers of a Sunday talk show that the GTMO detainees are "bad people."[1] One cannot help thinking, in fact, that the Army IG's exoneration of Sanchez (along with Craddock's defense of Miller) is just another useful impediment to any eventual reckoning. To be sure, if Sanchez's September 2003 memo authorizing dogs and high fear inducement aren't enough to land him in the dock, the DoD and DoJ memos wouldn't seem to be either.

While cries of "war crimes" are too easily dismissed as the ravings of the leftist, lunatic, anti-Bush fringe, many serious and thoughtful professionals have admitted that the memos noted above provide damning evidence of a complicity to commit torture or abuses or in some fashion to break the law. John Dean called the Bybee memo "'smoking-gun' level evidence of a war crime."[2] The House Judiciary Committee Democrats say, in their May 12, 2005, letter to Attorney General Gonzalez, "it is clear that a *prima facie* violation of federal criminal law exists," and that "high-ranking administration officials, including the Defense Secretary, as well as high-ranking military officials . . . are potentially subject to criminal prosecution . . . . " Liz Holtzman, a former New York comptroller and Congresswoman who was on the House Judiciary Committee when letters of impeachment were drafted for President Nixon, thinks that if any senior government officials "directed or authorized murder, torture or inhuman treatment of prisoners or, possibly, if they permitted such conduct to continue after they knew about it," they could be held accountable for war crimes. Additionally, following two days of hearings at the London School of Economics in November 2003, a panel of eight international law professors decided there was "sufficient evidence" for the International Criminal Court prosecutor to investigate senior U.K. officials for crimes against humanity committed in Iraq.

---

1. Rumsfeld's comments were made on NBC's *Meet the Press* and *FOX News Sunday*, respectively, on June 26, 2005, and quoted in an *Associated Press* wire syndicated in *USA Today* the same day (available online).

2. See also the testimony of Rear Adm. John Hutson, former Navy Judge Advocate General, included as a postscript to the present chapter.—Ed.

As stated earlier, on November 30, 2004, the Center for Constitutional Rights (CCR) in New York filed a complaint with the Federal Prosecutor's Office in Karlsruhe, Germany, under the doctrine of "universal jurisdiction," whereby suspected war criminals may be prosecuted irrespective of where they are located.[1] The action was joined by the *Fédération Internationale des Droits de l'Homme* (comprising 116 human rights organizations in almost 100 countries), Lawyers Against the War, and the International Legal Resources Center. The German prosecutor at first refused to take the case because he believed that the United States would investigate the matter itself; this would make the "universal jurisdiction" argument unnecessary. In response to this refusal, the CCR filed an appeal on January 31, 2005, and included with it the expert testimony of Scott Horton. His testimony concluded:

> I have formed the opinion that no such criminal investigation or prosecution would occur in the near future in the United States for the reason that the criminal investigative and prosecutorial functions are currently controlled by individuals who are involved in the conspiracy to commit war crimes.

Though the German court replied negatively to the appeal on February 10, 2005, Horton's opinion in this matter is still worth considering.[2] It — along with his comments on other aspects of the Abu Ghraib scandal — is not to be scoffed at; his credentials are impressive.[3] Michael Ratner, director of the CCR, explained the basis for Horton's finding, which is worth reading in its entirety.[4]

---

1. According to a Center for Constitutional Rights report, officials named in the complaint include Defense Secretary Donald Rumsfeld, Attorney General and former White House Counsel Alberto Gonzales, former CIA Director George Tenet, Under Secretary of Defense Stephen Cambone, Major General Geoffrey Miller, and Lieutenant General Ricardo Sanchez.

2. Some have opined that the German court quickly decided the January 31, 2005, appeal due to the planned attendance of Defense Secretary Rumsfeld at the Munich Conference on Security Policy, February 11–13, 2005. The fact that the filing comprised hundreds of pages of material makes it unlikely that it was reviewed with adequate thoroughness. See the report on the German court's decision from the CCR, "Center for Constitutional Rights Blasts Ruling of German Prosecutor Refusing to Hear War Crimes Case Against Rumsfeld," February 10, 2005 (http://www.ccr-ny.org/v2/reports/report.asp?ObjID=b2SxCfTLl0&Content=518).

3. From the, January 28, 2005, report by Horton filed with the German Federal Prosecutor: "I am an attorney at law admitted to practice in the courts of the State of New York since 1982, and an adjunct professor of law at Columbia University in the City of New York, where I lecture in international law and international humanitarian law, and currently conduct the seminar on the treatment of detainees under international humanitarian law. I also chair the Committee on International Law of the Association of the Bar of the City of New York and have previously chaired two other committees. I am a former officer and current director of the International Law Association."

4. See http://www.ccr-ny.org/v2/legal/september_11/docs/ScottHortonGermany013105.pdf.

First, Horton pointed out that the Department of Defense was under the control of defendant Secretary of Defense Rumsfeld who therefore had "effective immunity." Second, he found that the criminal investigations pursuant to army regulations look only down the chain of command and not up, and thus eliminate any "meaningful inquiry into the criminal misconduct of the defendants." Third, he found that the criminal investigations were influenced from above with the "intention of producing a 'whitewash' exculpating those up the chain of command." Fourth, he found that the responsibility of the legislative branch to investigate had been abdicated, since Senator John Warner, chairman of the Senate Armed Services Committee, "was threatened [by other Republicans] with sharp political retaliation if he carried through on his plans to conduct real hearings." Fifth, he found that the Attorney General controls war crimes prosecutions under the U.S. War Crimes Act and that since former Attorney General Ashcroft was "complicit in a scheme for the commission of war crimes" he had not undertaken a criminal investigation. Alberto Gonzales, the current Attorney General, Horton said, was the "principal author of a scheme to undertake war crimes" and was motivated in writing his January 25, 2002, memo by a fear of prosecution for war crimes, which he sought to evade in that memo.[1]

Ratner is optimistic that eventually the right people will be held accountable for their actions, even if that accountability is not generated through more of the administration-directed investigations and reports. "Although we have not yet been able to hold high-level officials accountable, it will happen," he says. "It may not happen this year or even next year, but eventually . . . justice will be done."[2] The fact noted the January 27, 2005, update his office filed with the German court four days later – that over 11,000 letters of support for the lawsuit have been sent to the court – may be one reason he is optimistic.

Efforts by others are moving ahead as well. Also on November 30, 2004, Gail Davidson, co-chairwoman of Lawyers Against the War, brought seven Canadian criminal code charges in the Vancouver Provincial Court against President Bush while he was visiting Canada. There she presented evidence to support her contention that Bush should be held criminally responsible for counseling, aiding, and abetting torture at the Abu Ghraib prison and at GTMO.

On March 1, 2005, the American Civil Liberties Union and Human Rights First, a New York-based group, filed a 77-page civil suit against

---

1. Michael Ratner, "From Magna Carta to Abu Ghraib: Detention, Summary Trial, Disappearances and Torture in America," the Clara Boudin Lecture at the City College of New York, spring 2005 (http://www.ccr-ny.org/v2/reports/report.asp?ObjID=FCYIOrS07g&Content=543).
2. *Ibid.*

Rumsfeld on behalf of eight military detainees in Iraq and Afghanistan. The plaintiffs allege that Rumsfeld "formulated, approved, directed, or ratified the torture or other cruel, inhuman or degrading treatment . . . as part of a policy, pattern, or practice." The *Georgia Straight* of Vancouver, Canada, reported on April 7, 2005, that "a great deal of work went into preparing this case. Lawyers worked with human-rights and humanitarian organizations in Iraq and Afghanistan to identify people who had been mistreated in U.S. detention centers." The clients were then interviewed extensively.

Hina Shamsi, a New York lawyer with Human Rights First, commented to the *Straight* that "although there [have] been other lawsuits filed on behalf of detainees for abuse suffered in U.S. detention facilities, none of those have focused on the policy-making role of a top U.S. official." She also noted the role of the suit in putting the pieces of the whole picture together in a way that official investigations have not. "What we have done here is connect the dots. We connect the creation of interrogation policies and the beginning of abuse in Afghanistan with the migration of those policies to Iraq."

Most remarkable are the individuals who have joined this lawsuit as pro-bono co-counsels: Rear Adm. John D. Hutson, USN, (ret.), former judge advocate general of the Navy;[1] Brig. Gen. James Cullen, USA (ret.); former chief judge of the U.S. Army Court of Criminal Appeals; Bill Lann Lee, chairman of the Human Rights Practice Group at Lieff, Cabraser, Heimann & Bernstein, LLP; and former assistant attorney general for civil rights at the Department of Justice. With former senior military lawyers taking on high-profile lawsuits against a sitting secretary of defense, the ramifications of the Abu Ghraib and related torture and abuse scandals cannot be underestimated.

Guantánamo Bay: Still Cutting Corners

What many thought at the time would be the last chapter in this saga unfolded at GTMO where "unlawful combatants" are kept. In June 2004, post-September 11 barriers to due process were struck down by the Supreme Court when it ruled that the detainees had a right to petition federal courts for a habeas corpus hearing.[2]

---

1. Rear Adm. Hutson's detailed analysis of several of the administration's notorious torture and GC memos follows Col. Smith's piece as a postscript.—Ed.

2. See the essay by Joesph Margulies, Esq., on the legal effort to obtain due-process rights for the Guantánamo Bay detainees on pp. 443–463 of the present volume.—Ed.

Reaction in the Pentagon's top civilian echelons suggests they had not anticipated the Court's ruling. In an apparent effort to blunt the fairness of any habeas corpus proceeding which, on a level playing field, might lead to the release of the detained petitioner, then-Deputy Defense Secretary Paul Wolfowitz signed a new directive creating "Combatant Status Review Tribunals" to evaluate whether a detainee's categorization as an "enemy combatant" was still valid.

On the surface, this might seem to be a step forward in restoring the basic rights of the detainees. But in contradiction to U.S. legal tradition enshrined in the Constitution and international norms set forth in the GC, the Wolfowitz directive specifies that the tribunal will approach each review with a "rebuttable presumption" favoring the government's assertion and its evidence that the detainee is an enemy combatant. That is, the presumption in each review is "guilty until proven innocent," which places the burden on the detainee to disprove the government's "evidence" – in a process where "normal" legal supports (e.g., a qualified attorney) are denied. By the end of March 2005, of more the 558 detainees whose cases were "reviewed," all but 38 were deemed by the tribunals to pose a continuing threat to the U.S.

Past and Future: From Afghanistan to Abu Ghraib and Back Again

In a recent post at *Tomdispatch.com*, media commentator and watchdog Tom Engelhardt persuasively chronicled the way in which coverage of the prison abuse scandals has mirrored the government's investigations into them: both continue to follow the "bad apple" approach, insisting that abuses do not reflect a policy of intentional, aggressive, frankly tortuous interrogations, but simply the misdeeds of a few rogue interrogators. Engelhardt's point is an interesting one: by reporting only on government-sponsored reviews, most journalists have no choice but to follow this "'bad apple' school of journalism," which is based largely on "various military or official investigations of what the military, intelligence agencies, and the Bush administration have done."

His suggestion for getting past this approach is to look to where unpalatable truth is often likely to be found. Doing so reveals a rather disturbing pattern of increasing numbers of detentions and interrogations in Afghanistan, from where the "aggressive" methods of interrogation are believed to have migrated to Iraq, through the facility at GTMO. "Problems are indeed continuing," Engelhardt writes, "in a form that simply cannot be read about in the mainstream media in this country." He cites reports, such as one by Emily Bazelon from the March/April 2005 issue of *Mother Jones*, that suggest a disturbing, continuing pattern.

> Hundreds of prisoners have come forward, often reluctantly, offering accounts of harsh interrogation techniques including sexual brutality, beatings, and other methods designed to humiliate and inflict physical pain. At least eight detainees are known to have died in U.S. custody in Afghanistan, and in at least two cases military officials ruled that the deaths were homicides. Many of the incidents were known to U.S. officials long before the Abu Ghraib scandal erupted; yet instead of disciplining those involved, the Pentagon transferred key personnel from Afghanistan to the Iraqi prison.
>
> . . . Even now, with the attention of the media and Congress focused on Abu Ghraib and Guantánamo, the problems in Afghanistan seem to be continuing . . . . The Afghan commission and Human Rights Watch, as well as a smaller group, the Washington, D.C.-based Crimes of War Project, have also gathered evidence on detainee abuse at American "forward operating bases" near Kandahar, Gardez, Khost, Orgun, Ghazni, and Jalalabad. Investigators estimate that in each of these places, between 5 and 20 prisoners are held at a time, compared to as many as 200 at Bagram.

Another report Engelhardt cites is one by Adrian Levy and Cathy Scott-Clark for the British *Guardian*. "They do what any good reporter should do," he says. "They attempt to put together the pieces of the jigsaw puzzle, take in the overall picture, and then draw the necessary conclusions." The conclusions are not encouraging:

> Prisoner transports crisscross the country between a proliferating network of detention facilities. In addition to the camps in Gardez, there are thought to be U.S. holding facilities in the cities of Khost, Asadabad and Jalalabad, as well as an official U.S. detention center in Kandahar, where the tough regime has been nicknamed "Camp Slappy" by former prisoners. There are 20 more facilities in outlying U.S. compounds and fire bases that complement a major "collection center" at Bagram air force base . . . . More than 1,500 prisoners from Afghanistan and many other countries are thought to be held in such jails, although no one knows for sure because the U.S. military declines to comment.[1]

Their conclusion is speculation, but it may accurately reflect a future as disturbing as the recent past.

> What has been glimpsed in Afghanistan is a radical plan to replace Guantánamo Bay. When that detention center was set up in January 2002, it was . . . beyond the

---

1. "One Huge U.S. Jail," *The Guardian*, March 19, 2005, online.

reach of the U.S. Constitution and even the GC. That all changed in July 2004. The U.S. Supreme Court ruled that the federal court in Washington had jurisdiction to hear a case that would decide if the Cuban detentions were in violation of the U.S. Constitution, its laws or treaties . . . . Guantánamo was [soon] bogged down in domestic lawsuits. It had lost its practicality. So a global prison network built up over the previous three years, beyond the reach of American and European judicial process, immediately began to pick up the slack. The process became explicit . . . when the Pentagon announced that half of the 540 or so inmates at Guantánamo are to be transferred to prisons in Afghanistan and Saudi Arabia.

Conclusion

At both Guantánamo and Abu Ghraib, the ethical question is really the old one of whether the ends justify the means – in this case, whether, with only limited time to gain information that would save the lives of comrades in the field or to prevent "another September 11," inhumane treatment during interrogation is justified. Although it does not say so, the Schlesinger panel suggests that in this scenario, treatment that does not cause permanent harm – inflicting pain to "teach a lesson" or when it becomes clear that information will not be divulged – is permitted under a "minimum harm rule" as suggested in the exchanges between the White House, Justice, and the Pentagon.

Such ambiguity begs the question of how and where to draw the line for "minimum" or "allowable" harm beyond which interrogation will not proceed. The psychologies of power, friendship, nationality, and hatred, all of which come into play in interrogations, can best be constrained by clear lines between allowed and prohibited actions. The drawing of those lines should not be left to any single country or be attempted during hostilities when passions can warp judgment. Yet the Schlesinger report implies that this is the prerogative of the U.S. as it admonishes the ICRC to update its thinking to face "new realities."

The President has repeatedly told the public that, after September 11, 2001, the U.S. confronted a new reality. But there is an even newer reality that the nation faces as a result of the Iraq war and the "post-war" insurgency: the fact that war can bring out the very worst as well as the best. What is most distressing are the growing numbers of U.S. military personnel standing trial not for abuse but for murder.

All of which points to the observation of the great Roman philosopher-general-emperor, Marcus Aurelius, as the solely acceptable rule of conduct: "If it is not right do not do it; if it is not true do not say it."

CHAPTER
31
postscript

A Voice in the Wilderness for the Rule of Law
• • • • • • • • • •
Rear Adm. John Hutson, USN (ret.), J.D.

ON JANUARY 6, 2005, I testified before the United States Senate Committee on the Judiciary at the hearing for confirmation of Alberto Gonzales as Attorney General of the United States. Having dedicated most of my professional life to military service, it was not an insignificant event for me to testify in opposition to the confirmation of an administration nominee for high office. I did not do it lightly, because involved in the confirmation of the Bush administration's nominee for Attorney General are issues about which I feel very strongly.

In a very real way, this nomination presaged the next four years for this country because more than any other discipline, it is the Rule of Law that directs our future. The Attorney General of the United States should be the chief enforcer of that Rule of Law. My opposition to his nomination focused primarily on Judge Gonzales's January 25, 2002, memorandum, with a subject line which read, "DECISION RE APPLICATION OF THE GENEVA CONVENTION ON PRISONERS OF WAR TO THE CONFLICT WITH AL QAEDA AND THE TALIBAN."

One of the few things Judge Gonzales got right in this infamous memo is his statement that "[t]he Attorney General is charged by statute with interpreting the law for the Executive Branch. This interpretive authority extends to both domestic and international law." Given the analysis that follows in that same memo, the fact that he has now been confirmed in that very position should be of great concern to us all. Perhaps more than any other cabinet officer, the Attorney General has cherished public responsibilities to the people, distinct from the role of legal or political advisor to any particular President.

In this memo, Judge Gonzales states that

> this new paradigm [the war against terrorism] renders obsolete Geneva's strict limitation on questioning of enemy prisoners and renders quaint some of its

provisions requiring that captured enemy be afforded such things as commissary privileges, scrip . . . , athletic uniforms, and scientific instruments.

He further urges the President to disregard it because he argues that adherence would restrict the war effort and potentially create criminal liability for war crimes.

In addition, other legal analyses were drafted by administration officials which Judge Gonzales did not repudiate – at least not on the record – until his testimony on January 6, 2005. These memoranda defined torture very narrowly, the defenses to torture broadly, and gave the President carte blanche in prosecuting the war on terror.

I believe Judge Gonzales's January 25 memorandum was narrow minded, shallow and overly legalistic in its analysis, shortsighted in its implications, and altogether ill advised. Candidly, it was too clever by half, and frankly, just plain wrong. Wrong legally, morally, practically, and diplomatically. Moreover and importantly, it and the other memoranda it drew from and formed the basis for – the Bybee memorandum (January 22, 2002, from Assistant Attorney General Jay Bybee), the Yoo memorandum (August 1, 2002, from Deputy Assistant Attorney General John Yoo), and the legal analysis from the DoD Working Group (April 4, 2003) – when taken together, "set the conditions" for the horrific events that followed. They took the United States from the role we have held for generations on the world stage as the avatar for the Rule of Law and proponent of human rights to being just another nation trying to evade our legal obligations. I believe they place our troops and our citizens in even greater harm's way by lowering the bar on acceptable conduct and fueling bitterness and resentment that encourages recruits to the enemy's cause. They weaken our coalition and remove long held limitations on the most destructive of all human endeavors – warfare.

The January 2002 memo from Judge Gonzales concludes that the Geneva Convention Relative to the Protection of Prisoners of War (GPW) does not apply to the conflict in Afghanistan against the Taliban and their partners, al-Qaeda, but in this it is also incorrect. Afghanistan is a party to the Convention. The United States fought the Taliban as the de facto government of Afghanistan, in control of 90% of the country, and its armed forces as the "regular armed forces" of a party to the Convention. Those facts entitled Taliban and al-Qaeda combatants from Afghanistan to a determination on a case-by-case basis of their status as prisoners of war. Moreover, any detainee not entitled to POW status is nevertheless entitled to basic humanitarian protections guaranteed by the Geneva Conventions and customary international law. This is the position taken by the State Department, but rejected by Judge Gonzales.

Judge Gonzales began his rationale for this erroneous position by stating that the "war against terror is a new kind of war." That may be. But the war in Afghanistan was not new in any fundamental way. The Geneva Conventions could be applied to that war without any great difficulty, just as we applied them in Iraq and every war we have fought since World War II. They are all new kinds of wars at the time you fight them, with new enemies, new weapon systems, and new tactics and strategies.

The Conventions are designed to apply in all armed conflict and the immediate aftermath of armed conflict. They are designed to apply to combatants – persons taking direct part in hostilities and regular members of the armed forces. There simply is no case for concluding that the Geneva Conventions were obsolete regarding the war in Afghanistan. They formed the proper applicable law and concluding they did not was simply incorrect.

Although it may still be in our self-interest, it is difficult to apply the Geneva Conventions to a terrorist when he is not taking part in an armed conflict because the Conventions were not intended to apply to those settings. Criminal law is designed to apply to violent, unlawful acts outside the situation of intense inter-group armed hostilities, i.e. war. Fundamentally, Judge Gonzales's problems with the Geneva Conventions stem from his attempt to *apply the wrong law to the problem of terrorism.*

As he should have anticipated, but apparently didn't, his error was compounded as the war on terror expanded to Iraq and included American citizens as enemy combatants. Once he reduced his legal analysis to simply that the Geneva Conventions don't apply to terrorists without explaining what law, if any, does apply, he created a downward spiral of unruliness from which we have not yet pulled out.

His memo is slightly over three pages long. Almost one full page is devoted to listing and rationalizing his two reasons for concluding that the Conventions do not apply:

- preserving flexibility, and
- "substantially reduce[ing] the threat of domestic criminal prosecution under the War Crimes Act (18 U.S.C. §2441)."

Then on less than one half page, 21 lines, Judge Gonzales listed seven reasons why the Conventions should apply. These are:

- since 1949 the United States has never denied their applicability
- unless they apply, U.S. could not invoke the GPW if enemy forces threatened or in fact mistreated our forces
- if they don't apply, the War Crimes Act could not be used against the enemy
- turning away from the Conventions would invoke "widespread condemnation among our allies and in some domestic quarters"
- doing so would also encourage other countries to look for technical "loopholes" in future conflicts
- other countries would be less inclined to turn over terrorists or provide legal assistance to us if we deny applicability of the Conventions;

And finally (notable for its understatement):

- "A determination that GPW does not apply to al-Qaeda and the Taliban could undermine U.S. military culture which emphasizes maintaining the highest standards of conduct in combat, and could introduce an element of uncertainty in the status of adversaries."

The paragraph of the memo which discusses the interplay between Section 2441 of the War Crimes Act and the Geneva Conventions is particularly striking. To his credit, Judge Gonzalez was remarkably frank and candid. Without apparent embarrassment, he asserted as one of the chief reasons to not invoke the Conventions the argument that such action "reduces the threat of domestic criminal prosecution under the War Crimes Act (18 U.S.C. §2441)." He essentially opined that the Conventions create problems because "grave breaches" of the Conventions would constitute war crimes under the domestic legislation that, unlike the Conventions themselves, is enforceable in U.S. courts. He said, " . . . it would be difficult to predict with confidence what action might be deemed to constitute violations of the relevant provisions of the GPW." He referenced as examples of this problem the difficulty he saw in defining such phrases from the Conventions as "outrages upon personal dignity" and "inhuman treatment." Later in that paragraph he offered, " . . . it is difficult to predict the needs and circumstances that could arise in the course of the war on terrorism."

His meaning is clear. We don't want to make ourselves liable under the War Crimes Act via "grave breaches" of the Geneva Conventions because we can't predict whether we may need to engage in what may be defined as outrages on personal dignity and inhuman treatment during the war on terror. This is a stunning observation. It certainly undermines good order and discipline within the military. More importantly, if we can't define those terms, how can we expect the enemy to do so? How can we ever demand that they not engage in such conduct having now said the prohibitions are incapable of definition?

A careful, honest reading reveals that the legal analysis of the January 2002 memo is very result-oriented. It appears to start with the conclusion that we don't want the Geneva Conventions to apply in the present situation, and then it reverse engineers the analysis to reach that conclusion. That approach may be appropriate for a criminal defense counsel who starts with the proposition that the client is not guilty and figures out how to best present that case, but it is not the kind of legal thoughtfulness one would expect from the legal counsel to the commander-in-chief.

It is also shortsighted, and very oriented to the immediate situation. It considers only the events at that moment in time and space. It fails to adequately consider the practical implications of characterizing the relevant provisions of the Geneva Conventions as "obsolete" and "quaint." Once those words were written down they rang a bell that cannot be un-rung. If the Geneva Conventions were obsolete and quaint in 2002, they are obsolete and quaint for all time. Those two words will come back to haunt us forever, or until the Conventions are "modernized." The problem is that it's a bit like going to war with the Army you have, not the Army you would like to have. These are the rules that we went to war with. We must make them work. We must live, or die, with them.

The Bush administration should officially and unequivocally repudiate Judge Gonzales's erroneous position on the applicability of the Geneva Conventions. It is not the case that the Conventions are obsolete in regulating armed conflict. Perhaps they can be improved and updated to deal with the new face of asymmetrical warfare, and the administration should work for that; but in the meantime they are the binding law and they serve us well. If new international law is needed for the struggle against terrorism, then that law should be developed, too, but do not throw out the Geneva Conventions because Judge Gonzalez's poor legal analysis couldn't make them fit.

The United States has supported the Geneva Conventions and urged other nations to do so for over half a century. Now, suddenly, they are characterized by the President's counsel as quaint and obsolete. He argues they may impede our freedom to commit what might otherwise be violations of our own War

Crimes Act; we don't want this outdated international law to inhibit our ability to outrage human dignity and engage in inhuman treatment.

In physics the law of entropy holds that through time any system will degrade to disorder and ultimately to chaos unless there is an outside force that ensures order in the system. That applies equally to the solar system, the community of nations, and to the United States. The outside force ensuring world order is the regime of international treaties, obligations and customary international law. Without adherence to these, we will surely devolve to disorder through time.

This is particularly true in wartime. War is simply the state of the ultimate, but hopefully temporary, disorder. Its only value is to provide the time and space necessary for real solutions to take place – diplomatic, economic, political, and social. War is not a solution in itself and cannot be used to justify national misbehavior or loss of national integrity.

In disagreements or arguments between individuals, it is important that they not act in a manner that so poisons their relationship that it cannot recover. The same is true with nations. It is easy to act with integrity in peacetime when things are going smoothly. *The true test of national integrity is in wartime.* We must wage war in such a way that we are able ultimately to resume peace.

The Geneva Conventions envision an end to the hostilities and to the destruction of war. They envision a return to peace. They provide a framework for the conduct of the war that will enable the peace to be sustained and flourish. We must not be deterred just because our enemy in a war on terror doesn't comply with the Conventions. Our unilateral compliance will aid in the peace process. Moreover, it should have been understood that violation of the Conventions, or ignoring them, *doesn't help bring an end to the war.* To the contrary, as we have seen, this only adds ferocity to the fighting and lengthens the war by hardening the resolve of the enemy. Our flagrant disregard for the Conventions only serves as a recruiting poster for this enemy and for our enemies for generations to come.

To do otherwise than comply with the Geneva Conventions under all circumstances risks waging such an unlimited war that we are no longer perceived to be a nation that values the Rule of Law or supports human rights. Other nations learn from our actions more than our words. If we move away from the Geneva Conventions and toward unlimited warfare, our own troops are imperiled in this war and future wars by our enemies who will follow suit.

If the United States complies with the rules of conduct as laid out by the Geneva Conventions, we can endeavor to force others, including our enemies, to comply as well. The converse is also true. If we fail to live up to the aspirations of the Geneva Conventions, we will have served as the wrong kind of role model. We will have stepped down from the pulpit from which we can preach adherence to the Rule of Law in war.

In the wake of World War II, the U.S. leadership advocated the adoption and reaffirmation of the Conventions because they served the ultimate interest of the United States. Eisenhower, Truman, Marshall, Senator Vinson and others envisioned another step in the historical journey toward the quintessential oxymoron, civilized warfare. They supported the warfighting concepts contained in the Geneva Conventions because those rules would protect U.S. troops in the field. *Their concern was to safeguard our troops from mistreatment by the enemy,* not to protect the enemy from mistreatment by U.S. forces. Judge Gonzales's memorandum completely eviscerated the original vision of the Geneva Conventions.

Where GPW talks about scrip, athletic uniforms, commissaries and the like, American proponents were thinking of *the treatment we could demand for U.S. prisoners of war,* not how we should avoid providing those amenities to enemy prisoners we held. Far from being quaint, these stand as bulwarks protecting U.S. troops who are captured.

Our disregard for the Conventions will likely deter potential future allies from joining us. If we comply with the Geneva Conventions only when it's convenient, who will fight alongside us? The answer is only other nations that also don't want to be hamstrung by so-called quaint and obsolete rules. We will become an outlaw nation that wages unlimited warfare, and only like-minded renegade nations will fight with us.

Since World War II, and looking into the foreseeable future, United States armed forces are more forward-deployed both in terms of numbers of deployments and numbers of troops than all other nations combined. What this means in practical terms is that adherence to the Geneva Conventions is more important to us than to any other nation. We should be the nation demanding adherence under any and all circumstances because we will benefit the most.

Judge Gonzales also bears responsibility, along with others, for the memoranda that were written to inform those in government and the military about the definitions of torture, defenses, and authority of the President acting as Commander-in-Chief. The Bybee and Yoo memoranda are chilling. They read as though they were written in another country, one that does not honor the Rule of Law or advocate on behalf of human rights. They contained an air of desperation: this is the worst war ever and justifies almost anything in order to win. The concept is that as long as you are a smart enough lawyer, you can find an argument to justify anything. Torture is limited to "inflict(ing) pain that is difficult to endure . . . equivalent in intensity to the pain accompanying serious physical injury, such as organ failure, impairment of bodily functions, or even death" (Bybee Memo).

Even if you surpass that lofty standard, your defenses include "necessity" and "self-defense" (meaning defense of the nation, not personal self-defense). Basically, anything that inhibits the President's discretion is unconstitutional and anything that carries it out is permitted.

No mention is made of U.S. military regulations. All services have their own regulations relating to these issues. The U.S. Army Field Manual 34-52 is representative. It states:

> U.S. policy expressly prohibits acts of violence or intimidation, including physical or mental torture, threats, insults, or exposure to inhumane treatment as a means of or aid to interrogation. Such illegal acts are not authorized and will not be condoned by the U.S. Army. Acts in violation of these prohibitions are criminal acts punishable under the U.C.M.J. If there is doubt as to the legality of a proposed form of interrogation not specifically authorized in this manual, the advice of the command judge advocate should be sought before using the method in question.

Although Judge Gonzales would surely consider it quaint and obsolete, this is long-standing U.S. military doctrine.

Significantly, these opinions and legal arguments weren't written in some law review article or in an op-ed piece to stimulate national debate. They were written to inform the President as Commander-in-Chief. Unfortunately, we saw the result of that kind of situational, shortsighted legal analysis.

This advice given to the President by Judge Gonzales was not offered with an eye to protecting American troops, as it may seem to be upon a superficial consideration. In both the short term and the long term, this advice doesn't protect our armed forces; it imperils them. It enables them to engage in the sort of reprehensible conduct we have seen, and it will enable our enemy to also engage in such conduct with impunity.

There are two great spines that run down the back of military discipline. They are accountability and the chain of command. These profound concepts are separate, but related. The concept of accountability means that you may delegate authority, but you can never delegate responsibility. Responsibility always remains with the person in charge.

The chain of command enables the military to operate effectively and efficiently. For good or evil, what starts at the top drops like a rock down the chain of command. Soldiers, sailors, Marines, and airmen execute the orders of those at the top of the chain and adopt their attitude. Consequently, *those at the top have a legal and moral responsibility to protect their subordinates.* We don't want the subordinates to feel compelled to second guess the legality, morality, or wisdom of what is decided above them in the chain of command.

If the message that is transmitted is that the Geneva Conventions don't apply to the war on terror, then that is the message that will be executed. The law and over 200 years of U.S. military tradition say *that those at the top are responsible for the consequences.* Law isn't practiced in a vacuum. It's practiced in real life. This isn't just a quaint academic exercise. It affects human beings and the world order.

The United States is now without a peer competitor. This places an awesome responsibility on us because there is no nation or coalition of nations that can forestall our national will. By in large, we can do what we want in the world if we rely solely on military might. Therefore, it is incumbent upon us to also rely on our integrity as a nation in making decisions about the role we will play. It doesn't make us small or weak to voluntarily inhibit our free will; indeed, it is an indication of great strength and discipline.

The war on terror may be crucial to our survival. But we will survive, and there will be other wars to fight in the future just as there have always been in the past. We cannot lose our soul in this fight. If we do, even if we win the military battles, the victories will by Pyrrhic, and we will have lost the war.

The question before the Court and you, Gentlemen of the jury, is not of small or private concern. It is not the cause of one poor printer, nor of New York alone, which you are now trying. No! . . . It is the best cause. It is the cause of liberty. And I make no doubt but your upright conduct this day will not only entitle you to the love and esteem of your fellow citizens, but every man who prefers freedom to a life of slavery will bless and honor you as men who have baffled the attempt of tyranny, and by an impartial and uncorrupt verdict have laid a noble foundation for securing to ourselves, our posterity, and our neighbors, that to which nature and the laws of our country have given us a right: to liberty of both exposing and opposing arbitrary power (in these parts of the world at least) BY SPEAKING AND WRITING TRUTH.

> —Andew Hamilton, attorney, August 4, 1735, arguing on behalf of his client, John Peter Zenger, accused of publishing "seditious libels" in his *New York Weekly Journal*, though it was not denied by the court or the prosecution that what he printed was true

So Much for the Fourth Estate: Our Imperial Press

THE EDITORS' GLOSS: Tom Engelhardt, who runs the perceptive and insightful *Tomdispatch.com*, points to a fundamental issue that societies like ours – where "the people" allegedly call the shots on matters of national interest – face when going to war. What side is the press on? Ours is almost exclusively on the side of putting facts and legitimate debate well below "rallying around the President in time of war." This may not be a unique event in the history of nations. Nevertheless, one wonders how well this approach serves the truth, the people, or the real good of the nation. It is especially ironic in view of the self-aggrandizing claims of our "fearless" press corps to be the "watchdog" of society, the domestic frontline protecting freedom from the encroachment of tyranny, and the singular honest broker holding the powerful to account.

As it turns out, the press has throughout the entire Iraq war debacle accepted the Bush-administration line that war was the necessary and right course for America. Sometimes a nation's leaders can be wrong, and if there's any value in having a free press, one would think it would be in exploring all the facts and perspectives surrounding a case such as Iraq, where the potential error of the nation's leaders can be costly and deadly. Yet the facts suggest that the press in large measure cooperated more than willingly with a blatant propaganda campaign waged by the White House to encourage people to support what would have been unthinkable had all the facts been discussed publicly. It has also adopted the deceitful rhetoric of the basic Bush-administration position: *we* and our handful of puppets are "Americans and Iraqis," while *they* are "terrorists." But can our journalists really be that credulous and, frankly, that incompetent? This insanity is what Tom Engelhardt explores, and he does so persuasively.

CHAPTER
32

Chronicles of Abdication:
Press Coverage of the War in Iraq
• • • • • • • •
Tom Engelhardt

EVERY NOW AND then, an article catches my eye that seems to sum up the worst of Washington-based access journalism ("just the spin, ma'am") in our imperial press. On Friday, the morning of the second presidential debate, just such a piece, "Pentagon Sets Steps to Retake Iraq Rebel Sites," made it onto the front-page of my hometown newspaper and I thought it might be worth taking a little time to consider it.

1. Yellow Journalism: "Anonymous" Lives and Thrives in Washington

Written by two veteran *New York Times* correspondents, Thom Shanker and Eric Schmitt, it began, "Pentagon planners and military commanders have identified 20 to 30 towns and cities in Iraq that must be brought under control before nationwide elections can be held in January, and have devised detailed ways of deciding which ones should be early priorities, according to senior administration and military officials."

There, right in paragraph one, were those unnamed "senior administration and military officials" who so populate our elite press that they sometimes present crowd-control problems. These are the people our most prestigious newspapers just love to trust and who, anonymous as they are, make reading those papers a ridiculous act of faith for the rest of us. At a time when Senator Kerry had accused the Bush administration of not having a "plan" for Iraq, other than "more of the same," here was a piece that claimed exactly the opposite. Such a plan, the "U.S. National Strategy for Supporting Iraq," was detailed; it had been written over the summer and represented a "six-pronged strategy"; it embodied a "new" approach for the U.S. in Iraq "approved at the highest levels of the Bush administration" – and the confirmation of the truth and accuracy of all this was that lovely little kicker at the end of a sentence: "officials said." According to Schmitt and Shanker, "the officials" (born, I assume, to Mr. and Mrs. Official) called the plan "a comprehensive guideline to their actions in the next few months."

A "comprehensive guideline" – and this only got you through paragraph two of a front-page column of print and two more columns on page 12 (the catch-all page which held the rest of the Iraq news that day); 30 paragraphs, 1,593 words on the "plan," including convenient-for-the-administration "news" that "President Bush has been briefed on it, administration officials said." (This, by the way, on the same day that the *Times* allowed former Coalition Provisional Authority head L. Paul Bremer to write "What I Really Said About Iraq," an op-ed in which he ate crow for his embarrassing comments that week at an insurance convention in West Virginia. These had confirmed Democratic criticisms that from second one the Bush administration had not put enough troops on the ground. Bremer was, he told *Times* readers, putting his remarks "in the correct context." What he actually did, while re-pledging his fealty to George Bush and his "vision" for Iraq, was to re-edit subtly those "remarks," as Joshua Marshall pointed out at his *Talkingpointsmemo.com* website. What, according to the *Washington Post*, Bremer had originally said was: "The single most important change – the one thing that would have improved the situation [in Iraq] – would have been having more troops in Iraq at the beginning *and throughout*." In the *Times* op-ed, he reworded that critique thusly: "I believe it would have been helpful to have had more troops *early on* to stop the looting that did so much damage to Iraq's already decrepit infrastructure." But I digress.)

A reading of the Shanker and Schmitt piece does not reveal whether either journalist actually laid eyes on the plan they were describing; certainly, as their sources described it to them, it sounded like a remarkably empty, even laughable, set of "classified directives" to make the front-page. For instance, there is this choice passage: "For each of the cities identified as guerrilla strongholds or vulnerable to falling into insurgent hands, a set of measurements was created to track whether the rebels' grip was being loosened by initiatives of the new Iraqi government, using such criteria as the numbers of Iraqi security personnel on patrol, voter registration, economic development and health care."

It's a passage that does at least contain eerie echoes of the Vietnam War. Then, our military "measured" everything from dead bodies to "enemy base areas neutralized" and toted it all up in either the Hamlet Evaluation System (after which hamlets in South Vietnam were rated A – "A super hamlet. Just about everything going right in both security and development" – to E – "Definitely under VC control. Local [government] officials and our advisers don't enter except on military operation"), or in the many indices of the Measurement of Progress system. All of this was then quantified in elaborate "attrition" charts and diagrams with multi-colored bar graphs illustrating various "trends" in death and destruction and used to give visiting politicians or the folks back in Washington a little more fantasy news on the "progress" being made in the war.

As in Vietnam, this sort of thing in Iraq is sure to prove laughable on the ground because the territories being "measured" are largely beyond the reach of American intelligence or governmental control. Such "measurements," if ever actually carried out, will likely prove to be desperately surreal affairs, except back home where they may, as in the *New York Times*, have their uses.

Similarly, consider the six "prongs" of the new strategy (on which the President has been briefed), as related by various "officials." These turn out to be such brain-dazzling "basic priorities" as: "to neutralize insurgents, ensure legitimate elections, create jobs and provide essential services, establish foundations for a strong economy, develop good governance and the rule of law and increase international support for the effort." Homer Simpson, were he a *Times* reader, would surely have said, "Doh!"

Or here's another gem of supposed front-page-worthy wisdom from the "plan," as "summarized" by "one senior administration official": "Use the economic tools and the governance tools to separate out hard-core insurgents you have to deal with by force from those people who are shooting at us because somebody's paying them $100 a week." Now, it's true that military people in Iraq officially lump together terrorist groups with the home-grown and increasingly substantial Iraqi resistance and call them all "anti-Iraqi forces" (the troops we are training are, of course, the "Iraqi forces"). But if our military or civilian leaders really believe that all they have to do is use those "governance" and "economic tools" to separate the "hard-core" from unemployed Iraqis being paid to kill, then our whole counterinsurgency effort is already brain-dead and it's not just our President and a few neocons who are living in a world of fantasy spin. The other, more logical conclusion might be that this dazzling document, worth a front-page scoop and tons of *Times* granted anonymity, is in fact largely a propaganda document rather than a planning one. If the speakers – you can't quite give them the dignity or integrity of calling them leakers – had real confidence in the plan, wouldn't they have wanted their real names associated with it?

Almost the only substantive information in the piece comes not in quotes from squadrons of unnamed officials, but in the form of periodic caveats from Schmitt and Shanker, two old pros, about the unplanned and completely disastrous situation in Iraq. ("As American military deaths have increased in Iraq and commanders struggle to combat a tenacious insurgency . . . .")

On close inspection, the plan, news of which was evidently offered exclusively to the *New York Times*, proves to be a strange mix of fantasy and emptiness, at least as reported in the imperial paper of choice. But there's no question that getting it onto the front page of the *Times* with the media equivalent of immunity was a modest coup for the Bush administration. First of all, the front page of the *Times* ratified that there is such a "plan" at a moment when the administration had been embarrassed by Iraq's devolution into reconstruction-less chaos and the loss of significant portions of the country to the insurgents. Under the circumstances, this was a small domestic triumph of planning.

Then, there was the hint in the piece that the administration was also putting in place a withdrawal strategy, another kind of (fantasy?) "plan." After the January 2005 election in Iraq, American forces were to be downsized a brigade at a time "if the security situation improves and Iraqi forces show they can maintain order" – a theme Donald Rumsfeld picked up on a weekend visit to a Marine base in Iraq. ("The United States may be able to reduce its troop levels in Iraq after the January elections if security improves and Iraqi government forces continue to expand and improve, Defense Secretary Donald H. Rumsfeld said Sunday.")

Then there was the generally administration-friendly language of the piece in which one of those "senior administration officials" could be quoted without comment as saying, "We're doing kinetic strikes in Fallujah." Kinetic strikes? Is that what our daily bombing of Fallujah is? Or how about this sentence: "While the broad themes are not new, senior officials now make no secret that those missions have not been carried out successfully during the first year following the end of major combat operations." Major combat operations? That has an oddly familiar ring to it – not surprisingly, since it was the President's much-quoted phrase in his now infamous *Top Gun* landing and speech on the *USS Abraham Lincoln*. But can we any longer believe that the year after the taking of Baghdad saw no "major combat operations"?

Of course, this is not in the normal sense reporting, or rather it's run-of-the-mill access reportage from our imperial capital. "Pentagon Sets Steps to Retake Iraq Rebel Sites" is essentially a stalking horse for the Bush administration, but to grasp fully what this means it's necessary to leave the ostensible news in the piece and turn to the far more interesting subject of the piece's sourcing. Sixteen hundred words and only one person – Lt. Gen. Wallace C. Gregson, the Marine commander in the Middle East – is quoted by name. ("We can start demonstrating that the course that Prime Minister Allawi's government is on, is the one that will bring peace, stability and prosperity to Iraq.") Poor sucker, he obviously didn't know how this game was meant to be played, and so he alone might someday find himself accountable for what he's quoted as saying.

Last February, perhaps feeling the sting of criticism for its pre-war coverage of the Bush administration and weapons of mass destruction in Iraq, the *Times* expanded its previous sourcing rules in an official document entitled, "Confidential News Sources." Essentially, that document instituted a more elaborate version of policies already in use, calling among other things for more extensive descriptive labels for anonymous sources ("The word 'official' is overused, and cries out for greater specificity.") and more fulsome descriptions of how and why the paper offered its grant of anonymity.

The document began:

> The use of unidentified sources is reserved for situations in which the newspaper could not otherwise print information it considers reliable and newsworthy. When we use such sources, we accept an obligation not only to convince a reader of their reliability but also to convey what we can learn of their motivation – as much as we can supply to let a reader know whether the sources have a clear point of view on the issue under discussion .... Exceptions will occur in the reporting of highly sensitive stories, when it is we who have sought out a source who may face legal jeopardy or loss of livelihood for speaking with us. Similarly they will occur in approaches to authoritative officials in government who, as a matter of policy, do not speak for attribution. On those occasions, we may use an offer of anonymity as a wedge to make telephone contact, get an interview or learn a fact.

It also contained the following line, which the Shanker and Schmitt piece would seem to contravene: "We do not grant anonymity to people who use it as cover for a personal or partisan attack." But perhaps using a new "plan" to gain partisan advantage in an election campaign doesn't come under the category of "partisan attack," even when the journalists themselves acknowledge this to be the case in their piece. For paragraphs five and six of the article do offer a description of how the piece came about, indicating for one thing that the *Times* approached the administration, asking for an answer to the question, "Is there a plan for Iraq?" Shanker and Schmitt added the following on the people granted anonymity and on their motivations:

> The three military officers who discussed the plan have seen the briefing charts for the new strategy, and the three civilian officials who discussed it were involved in deliberations that resulted in the strategy. The civilians, in particular, agreed to discuss the newest thinking in part to rebut criticism from the campaign of Senator John Kerry that the administration has no plan for Iraq.

In this light, then, let's take a look at the sourcing of this piece of hot "news." Here are the various anonymous-sourcing descriptive words and phrases used in the piece (with multiple uses in parentheses):

> *Senior administration and military officials; senior officials; the officials (2); these officials; military officials; administration officials (2); senior administration, Pentagon, and military officials; the three military officers who discussed the plan; the three civilian officials who discussed it; the civilians; one [or a] senior administration official (4); one American official; one Pentagon official; American diplomats and commanders in Iraq; Defense Department and other administration officials; commanders; American commanders; Lt General Wallace C. Gregson.*

In other words, 77 words in a 1,600-word piece (not even counting words that naturally go with such sourcing descriptions as "says" or "said") were devoted to 17 different formulations of anonymity. Even with wings, a Daedalus facing the *Times* on Friday morning would never have made his way out of this verbal labyrinth. Not only is there no way for a non-insider to tell much about the three senior military officers and the three senior civilian officials who seem to have been the main sources for the paper, but, as the piece goes on, it becomes almost impossible to tell whether "one American official" or "Defense Department and other administration officials" are these six people or other sources entirely.

For knowledgeable Washington media or political insiders, perhaps it's not terribly difficult to sort out more or less who was speaking to Shanker and Schmitt. The question is: why is it important that the rest of us not know? What made this piece worthy of such a blanket grant of anonymity, except the fact that "Important Administration Figures" were willing to speak on conditions of anonymity about a subject they were eager to put before the public? Under these circumstances, what anonymous sourcing offers is largely a kind of deniability. The "sources" will remain unaccountable for policy statements and policy that may soon enough prove foolish or failed. We're clearly not talking of the leaking of secrets here, but of the leaking of advantageous publicity material.

This is, of course, an every day way of life in the world of the Washington media. My own feeling is that anonymity should generally be confined to protecting the physical or economic well-being of someone, usually a subordinate and/or a whistleblower, who might otherwise suffer from publicly saying something of significance to the rest of us. Hardly the situation of a group of high government and military officials trying to spin the public via a major newspaper. If you read the *Times*, the *Washington Post* or another major paper (the *Wall Street Journal* largely excepted) and want to check out the anonymity game, just pick up your morning rag and start counting. The practice is startlingly widespread, once you start to look for it, and was roundly attacked in the pages of the *New York Times* last June by the paper's own Public Editor or ombudsman, Daniel Okrent. In "An Electrician From the Ukrainian Town of Lutsk," he called for turning "the use of unidentified sources into an exceptional event."

Jack Shafer of the on-line magazine *Slate* wrote a sharp follow-up column on the subject of anonymity ("Journalists have become so comfortable with anonymous sourcing that they're often the first ones to propose it"), suggesting that Washington's reporters felt comfortable as "kept men and women." On the off-chance that this wasn't true, he extended the following offer: "If you cover a federal department or agency and want to drop a dime on your manipulative handlers, send me email at pressbox@hotmail.com. Name your anonymous briefer and point me to a press account of the briefing, and I'll do the rest." Two weeks later, Okrent issued a challenge of his own to the five largest papers and the *Associated Press* to "jointly agree not to cover group briefings conducted by government officials and other political figures who refuse to allow their names to be used." And then life went on.

The Shanker and Schmitt piece was certainly typical of a modern form of yellow journalism, a good example of the sort of front-page "access" articles you're likely to find any week at any of our major papers. Space on the front-page of the *New York Times* is, after all, a valuable commodity. As we saw before the invasion of Iraq, it's been particularly valuable for the

Bush administration, since the *Times* is considered a not-so-friendly outlet – and, as a consequence, confirmation of anything on its front page can be useful indeed.

Undoubtedly, a stew of factors helps explain the appearance of pieces like this. The urge of reporters to make the front-page with a scoop is powerful and easily played upon by administration officials who can, of course, hand the same "story" off to, say, reporters from the *Washington Post*, if conditions aren't met. These are, in other words, bargaining situations and our imperial press, paper by paper, is seldom likely to be in the driver's seat as long as its directors set such an overwhelming value on anything high officials might be willing to say, no matter under what anonymous designations. That much of this is likely to fall into the category of lie and spin can hardly be news to journalists. But it's a way of life. In this context, what the grant of anonymity represents, if you think about it for a moment, is a kind of institutional kow-tow before the power of the imperial presidency.

Under these circumstances, that the *Times* approached the administration and not vice-versa on the question of a "plan" for Iraq hardly matters. Imagine, for a minute, a tourist approaching a three-card monte game on the streets of New York and suggesting to the con man running it that perhaps they should all play cards. After all, if you can spot your mark coming, all the better that he approaches you.

This would obviously have been a very different story if it had said, for instance, that Paul Wolfowitz and/or Condoleezza Rice and/or Donald Rumsfeld and/or Joint Chiefs head Gen. Richard Myers and/or any of their underlings had by name made such statements. Without the grant of anonymity, the statements in this piece would, ironically enough, have looked far more like what they are: spin, lies, and fantasy.

What does anonymity actually do, other than counter-intuitively establish the authority of sources who would have far less authority in their own skins? Through anonymity of this sort, what the press protects is not its sources, but its deals. For all of us locked out – and we *are* locked out of our own newspapers – there's no way of knowing what those deals were. But behind an article like this are house rules (and we're talking White House here), whether explicit or implicit.

For administration figures, this is an all-gain, no-pain situation. For reporters, it gets them on the front page and in line for the next set of "stories," some of which might even be real. It keeps them in the game. Shanker and Schmitt are old pros. They normally do good, solid work. But they, like the rest of the press, live in the imperial capital of our planet. They play by the rules because their newspaper plays by (and dictates) those rules. And the rules driving them are not only cowardly but set up to drive them into the arms of any administration.

What the Shanker and Schmitt piece about the Pentagon's "plan" did was to put this bit of Bush-spin into circulation for the administration in the election season. As it turned out, it wasn't a major matter. It didn't play a part in the second presidential debate. It just proved a small, passing part of the administration's scene-setting for its version of a presidential campaign. At this moment, with so many angry bureaucrats, officials, and military officers in Washington and parts of the CIA – to take but one example – at war with the administration, Washington is a sieve with a tidal basin of information leaking out of every hole. Given that this is a wounded administration, its story right now is but one – still powerful – competing version of the news in our press.

But the Shanker and Schmitt piece should remind us, whether for the second Bush administration or any other administration, that the way of life that made much of pre-war mainstream journalism a stalking horse for the administration's mad policies and outlandish interpretations of reality is still alive and kicking. The rules of the house and the way of doing business are deeply embedded in the journalistic way of life. The allure of the imperial presidency is still powerful. Official lies, official spin, and anonymous officials are the entwined axis of evil of imperial journalism.

2. Which War Is This Anyway?

"Every country and every people has a stake in the . . . resistance, for the freedom fighters . . . are defending principles of independence that form the basis of global security and stability."

"The war . . . was in itself criminal, a criminal adventure. This crime cost the lives of about a million [people], a war of destruction was waged against an entire people . . . . This is what lies on us as a terrible sin, a terrible reproach. We must cleanse ourselves of this shame that lies on our leadership."[1]

Freedom Fighters and Rebels

Consider this as a description:

The "rebels" or "freedom fighters" are part of a nationwide "resistance movement." While many of them are local, even tribal, and fight simply

---

1. For the source of each of these quotes, see the end of this chapter.—Ed.

because they are outraged by the occupation of their country, hundreds of others among the "resistance fighters" – young Arabs – are arriving from as far away as "Lebanon, Syria, Egypt and Jordan," not to speak of Saudi Arabia and Algeria, to engage in jihad, ready as one of them puts it, to stay in the war "until I am martyred." Fighting for their "Islamic ideals," "they are inspired by a sense of moral outrage and a religious devotion heightened by frequent accounts of divine miracles in the war." They slip across the country's borders to fight the "invader" and the "puppet government" its officials have set up in the capital in their "own image." The invader's sway, however, "extends little beyond the major cities, and even there the . . . freedom fighters often hold sway by night and sometimes even by day."

Sympathetic as they may be, the rebels are badly overwhelmed by the firepower of the occupying superpower and are especially at risk in their daring raids because the enemy is "able to operate with virtual impunity in the air." The superpower's soldiers are sent out from their bases and the capital to "make sweeps, but chiefly to search and destroy, not to clear and hold." Its soldiers, known for their massive human rights abuses and the cruelty of their atrocities, have in some cases been reported to press "on the throats of prisoners to force them to open their mouths while the guards urinate into them, [as well as] setting police dogs on detainees, raping women in front of family members and other vile acts."

On their part, the "guerrillas," armed largely with Russian and Chinese rifles and rocket propelled grenade launchers, have responded with the warfare of the weak. They have formed car-bombing squads and use a variety of cleverly constructed wheelbarrow, bicycle, suitcase, and roadside bombs as well as suicide operations performed by volunteers chosen from among the foreign jihadists. They engage in assassinations of, for example, university intellectuals and other sabotage activities in the capital and elsewhere aimed at killing the occupying troops and their sympathizers. They behead hostages to instill fear in the other side. Funding for the resistance comes, in part, from supporters in sympathetic Islamic countries, including Saudi Arabia. However, "if the Mujahideen are ever to realize their goal of forcing [the occupiers] out, they will need more than better arms and training, more than their common faith. They will need to develop a genuinely unified resistance . . . . Above all, the analysts say, they will need to make the war . . . even costlier and more difficult for the [occupiers] than it is now."

It's easy enough to identify this composite description, right? Our war in Iraq, as portrayed perhaps in the Arab press and on Arab websites. Well, as it happens, *actually not*. All of the above (with the exception of the material on bombs, which comes from Steve Cull's book *Ghost Wars*, and on the beheading of hostages, which comes from an Amnesty International report) is from either the statements of American officials or coverage in either the *Washington Post* or the *New York Times* of the Afghan anti-Soviet jihad of the 1980s, fostered, armed, and funded to the tune of billions of dollars by the Central Intelligence Agency with the help of the Saudi and Pakistani intelligence services.

Well, then try this one:

Thousands of troops of the occupying power make a second, carefully planned "brutal advance" into a large city to root out Islamic "rebels." The first attack on the city failed, though it all but destroyed neighborhoods in a "ferocious bombardment." The soldiers advance behind "relentless air and artillery strikes." This second attempt to take the city, the capital of a "rebellious province," defended by a determined "rebel force" of perhaps 500–3,000, succeeds, though the fighting never quite ends. The result? A "razed" city, "where virtually every building has been bombed, burned, shelled beyond recognition or simply obliterated by war"; a place where occupying "soldiers fire at anything that moves" and their checkpoints are surrounded by "endless ruins of former homes and gutted, upended automobiles." The city has been reduced to "rubble" and, for the survivors, "rebel" fighters and civilians alike, it and surrounding areas are now a "killing field." The city lacks electricity, water, or much in the way of food, and yet the rebels hold out in its ruins, and though amusements are few, "on one occasion, a . . . singer came and gave an impromptu guitar concert of patriotic and folk tunes [for them]."

In the carnage involved in the taking of the city, the resistance showed great fortitude. "'See you in paradise,' [one] volunteer said. 'God is great.'" Hair-raising news reports from the occupied city and from refugee camps describe the "traumatized" and maimed. ("Here in the remains of Hospital Number Nine – [the city's] only hospital with electricity – she sees a ceaseless stream of mangled bodies, victims of gunfire and shellings"); press reports also acknowledge the distance between official promises of reconstruction and life in the gutted but still resistant city, suggesting "the contrast between the symbolic peace and security declared by [occupation] officials and the city's mine-ridden, bullet-flying reality." Headlines don't hesitate to highlight claims made by those who fled and survived – "Refugees Describe Atrocities by Occupation Troops" – and reports bluntly use the label given the acts of the occupiers by human rights organizations

– "war crimes." Such organizations are quoted to devastating effect on the subject. The rebels may be called "bandits" by the occupiers, but it's clear in news reports that they are the ones to be admired.

No question of the sources here at least. Obviously the above is a composite account of the American assault on Fallujah taken from Arab press reports or sympathetic Arab websites. As it happens, if you believed that, you'd be zero for two. In fact, all of the above is taken from contemporary press accounts of the Russian assault on Grozny, the capital of Chechnya, in January 2000 in the *Washington Post*, the *New York Times*, or the *Boston Globe*.

How to Tell a Terrorist

I put together these descriptions from American reports on the Afghan anti-Soviet jihad of the 1980s, written in the midst of the cold war, and on the second battle for Grozny ten years after the cold war ended, because both seemed to have certain eerie similarities to events in Iraq today, though obviously neither presents an exact analogy to our Iraqi war. Both earlier moments of reportage do, however, highlight certain limitations in our press coverage of the war in Iraq.

After all, in the case of Afghanistan in the 1980s, there was also a fractured and fractious rebellion against an invading imperial superpower intent on controlling the country and setting up its own regime in the capital. The anti-Soviet rebellion was (like the present one in Iraq) conducted in part by Islamic rebels, many of whom were extremist Sunni jihadists (and some of whose names, from Osama bin Laden to Gulbuddin Hekmatyar, remain significant today). The Afghan guerrilla war was backed by that other superpower, the United States, for a decade through its spy agency, the CIA, which promoted methods that, in the Iraq context, would be called "terrorism."

In the case of the Russian assault on Grozny, the capital of the breakaway region of Chechnya, you also have an imperial power, if no longer exactly a superpower, intent on wresting a city – and a "safe haven" – from a fractious, largely Islamist insurgency and ready to make an example of a major city to do so. The Russian rubblizing of Grozny may have been more extreme than the American destruction of Fallujah (or so it seems), but the events remain comparable. In the case of Grozny, the American government did not actively back the rebels as they had in Afghanistan; but the Bush Sr. administration, made up of former cold warriors who had imbibed the idea of "rolling back" the Soviet Union in their younger years, was certainly sympathetic to the rebels.

What, then, are some of the key differences I noticed in reading through examples of this reportage and comparing it to the products of our present embedded state? Let me list four differences – and suggest a question that might be in the back of your mind while considering them: to what degree are American reporters as a group destined to follow, with only modest variation, the paths opened for them by our government's positions on its wars of choice?

1. *Language*: Those in rebellion in Iraq today are, according to our military, "anti-Iraqi forces" (a phrase that, in quotes, often makes it into news pieces and is just about never commented upon by reporters); others over the months, most of them also first issuing from the mouths of U.S. officials, have been "dead-enders," "bitter enders," "Ba'athist remnants," "terrorists" (especially with forces or acts associated in any way with Abu Musab al-Zarqawi), rarely "guerrillas," and most regularly (and neutrally), "insurgents" who are fighting in an "insurgency."

The Afghans in the 1980s, on the other hand, were almost invariably in "rebellion" and so "rebels" as headlines at the time made clear – Leslie Gelb, "Officials Say U.S. Plans to Double Supply of Arms to Afghan Rebels," the *New York Times*. They were part of a "resistance movement" and as their representatives could write op-eds for our papers, the *Washington Post*, for instance, had no hesitation either about headlining Matthew D. Erulkar's op-ed of January 13, 1987, "Why America Should Recognize the Afghan Resistance," or identifying its author as working "for the Afghan resistance."

But the phrase "Afghan resistance" or "the resistance" was no less likely to appear in news pieces, as in an October 22, 1983, report by *Post* reporter William Branigin, "Feuding Guerrilla Groups Rely on Uneasy Pakistan." Nor, as in James Rupert's "Dreams of Martyrdom Draw Islamic Arabs to Join Afghan Rebels" (*Washington Post*, July 21, 1986), was there any problem calling an Islamic "fundamentalist party" that was part of the "Afghan Jihad" a "resistance party." President Ronald Reagan at the time regularly referred to fundamentalist Afghans and their Arab supporters as "freedom fighters" (while the CIA, through the ISI, the Pakistani intelligence service, shuttled vast sums of money and stores of weaponry to the most extreme of the Afghan jihadists parties). "Freedom fighter" was commonly used in the press, sometimes interchangeably with "the Afghan resistance" – as in a March 12, 1981, piece by *Post* columnist Joseph Kraft, "The Afghan

Chaos" ("Six different organizations claiming to represent Afghan free-dom fighters . . . . ").

As for the Chechens in Grozny in 2000, they were normally referred to in U.S. news accounts as "rebels": "separatist rebels," "rebel ambushes," "a rebel counterattack," and so on. ("Rebel," as anyone knows who remembers American rock 'n' roll or movies of the 1950s and 60s, is a positive term in our lexicon.) Official Russian terms for the Chechen rebels, who were fighting grimly like any group of outgunned urban guerrillas in a man-ner similar to the Sunni guerrillas in Iraq today – "bandits" or "armed criminals in camouflage and masks" – were quoted, but then (as "anti-Iraqi forces" and other Bush administration terms are not) put in context or contrasted with Chechen versions of reality.

In a typical piece from CNN, you could find the following quote: "'The [Russians] aren't killing any bandits,' one refugee said after reach-ing Ingushetia. 'They're killing old men, women and children. And they keep on bombing – day and night.'" In a Daniel Williams piece in the *Washington Post*, the Russian government's announcements about the fighting in Grozny have become a "daily chant," a phrase that certainly suggests how the reporter feels about their accuracy.

Here's a quote from a discussion in a *Washington Post* editorial of an Associated Press photograph of the destruction in Grozny. The photograph was described elsewhere as "a pastel from hell" and was evidently of a sort we've seen far too little of in our press from either Fallujah or the Old City of Najaf:

"Russian leaders announced with pride Sunday that their armed forces had captured Grozny, the capital of Chechnya, five months into their war to subdue that rebellious province. Reports from the battle zone suggested that the Russians had not so much liberated the city as destroyed it . . . . Grozny resembles nothing so much as Stalingrad, reduced to rubble by Hitler's troops before the Red Army inflicted a key defeat that Russian schoolchildren still celebrate . . . . All in all, this is not likely to be a victory that Russian schoolchildren will celebrate generations hence."

Similar writing certainly isn't likely to be found on American editorial pages today when it comes to the "razing" of Fallujah, nor are those strong adjectives like "brutal," once wielded in the Grozny accounts, much to be found at present.

2. *Testimony*: Perhaps the most striking difference between news stories about the Afghan revolt, the destruction of Grozny, and the destruction of Fallujah may be that in the cases of the first two, American reporters

were willing, even eager, to seek out refugee accounts, even if the refugees were supporters of the rebels or rebels themselves. Such testimony
was, for instance, regularly offered as evidence of what was happening in
Grozny and more generally in Chechnya (even when the accounts couldn't
necessarily be individually confirmed). So the *Post's* Daniel Williams, for
instance, in "Brutal Retreat From Grozny Led to a Killing Field" (February
12, 2000) begins by following Heda Yusupova, mother of two "and a cook
for a group of Chechen rebels" as she flees the city. ("[She] froze in her
tracks when she heard the first land mine explode. It was night, and she
and a long file of rebels were making a dangerous retreat from Grozny,
the Chechen capital, during the final hours of a brutal Russian advance.
Another explosion. Her children, ages 9 and 10, screamed . . . . ") It's a piece
that certainly puts the Russian assault on Grozny in a striking perspective.
And in this it's typical of the accounts I've read.

Post reporter Sharon LaFraniere, for example, wrote a piece on June 29,
2000, bluntly entitled, "Chechen Refugees Describe Atrocities by Russian
Troops" in which she reported on "atrocities" in what the Russians labeled
a "pro-bandit village." ("'I have never imagined such tortures, such cruelty,' [the villager] said, sitting at a small table in the dim room that has
housed her family here for nearly three years. 'There were a lot of men who
were left only half alive.'") And when Russian operations against individual
Chechens were described, it was possible to see them through Chechen
eyes: "Three times last month, Algayeva said, Russian soldiers broke in,
threatening to shoot the school's guard. They smashed doors, locks and
desks. The last time, May 20, they took sugar, plates and a brass bell that
was rung at school ceremonies."

As in a February 29, 2000, *Boston Globe* piece, "Chechen Horror," it was
also possible for newspapers to discuss editorially both "the suffering of
the Chechens" and the way "the United States and the rest of the international community can no longer ignore their humanitarian obligation to
alleviate – and end – [that suffering]."

The equivalent pieces for Iraq are largely missing though every now and
then – as with an Edward Wong piece in the *New York Times* on life in resistant Sadr City, Baghdad's huge Shiite slum – there have been exceptions.
Given the dangers Western reporters face in Iraq and the constricting system of "embedding" that generally prevails, when you read of Americans
breaking into Iraqi homes, you're ordinarily going to see the event from
the point of view of the troops (or at least in their company). Iraqi refugees
– upwards of 250,000 of whom may have been driven from Fallujah alone

– have not been much valued in our press for their testimony. There is a deep irony in this, since the Bush administration launched its war, citing mainly exile – that is, refugee – testimony.

We know, of course, that it's difficult for American reporters to go in search of such testimony in Iraq, but not impossible. For instance, Dahr Jamail, a determined freelance journalist whose work can be found on-line at ZNET, the *New Standard,* or his own blog, recently managed to interview refugees from Fallujah and their testimony sounds remarkably like the Grozny testimony from major American newspapers in 2000: "The American warplanes came continuously through the night and bombed everywhere in Fallujah! It did not stop even for a moment! If the American forces did not find a target to bomb, they used sound bombs just to terrorize the people and children. The city stayed in fear; I cannot give a picture of how panicked everyone was.")

For the "suffering of the Iraqis," you need to turn to the periodic "testimony" of Iraqi bloggers like the pseudonymous Riverbend of Baghdad Burning or perhaps Aljazeera. The suffering we actually hear most about in our press is, as Naomi Klein indicated in a powerful piece, American suffering, in part because it's the American troops with whom our reporters are embedded, with whom they bond, and fighters on battlefields anywhere almost invariably find themselves in grim and suffering circumstances. In this context, there has been some striking reporting – as in the Fallujah pieces from Tom Lasseter, one of Knight Ridder's superb journalists, embedded with a company of soldiers in Fallujah. But we're still talking about American suffering, or Iraqi suffering within that context.

3. *Human-rights evidence*: The reports from Grozny in particular (see above) often make extensive use of the investigations of human rights groups of various sorts (including Russian ones) and reporters then were willing to put the acts of the Russians in Grozny (as in Afghanistan) in the context of "war crimes," as indeed they were. In Iraq, on the other hand, while pieces about human rights reports about our occupation can sometimes be found deep in our papers, the evidence supplied by human rights groups is seldom deployed by American reporters as an evidentiary part of war pieces.

4. *"Terrorism"*: Finally, though many more points could be made, it's interesting to see how, in different reporting contexts and different moments, the term "terrorism" is or is not brought to bear. In Grozny, for instance, the "rebels" used "radio-controlled land mines" and assassinated Chechens who worked for the Russians (just as Iraqi insurgents and

terrorists explode roadside IEDs and assassinate those who work for the Americans) and yet the Chechens remained (until recent times) "rebels."

On this topic, though, Afghanistan is of special interest. There, as Steve Coll tells us in his riveting book *Ghost Wars*[1] (pp. 128–135), the CIA organized terror on a major scale in conjunction with the Pakistani ISI which trained "freedom fighters" in how to mount car-bomb and even camel-bomb attacks on Soviet officers and soldiers in Russian-occupied cities (techniques personally "endorsed," according to Coll, by CIA Director William Casey). The CIA also supplied the Afghan rebels with long-range sniper rifles (meant for assassinations) and delayed-timing devices for plastic explosives. "The rebels fashioned booby-trapped bombs from gooey black contact explosives, supplied to Pakistani intelligence by the CIA, that could be molded into ordinary shapes or poured into innocent utensils." Kabul cinemas and cultural shows were bombed and suicide operations mounted using Arab jihadis. "Many tons of C4 plastic explosives for sabotage operations" were shipped in and the CIA took to supplying so-called "dual-use" weapons systems that could be used against military targets "but also in terror attacks and assassinations." Much of this was known, at least to some degree, at the time (and some reported in press accounts), and yet the Afghans remained "freedom fighters" and a resistance movement, even after the Afghan jihad began to slip across the other Pakistani border into Indian Kashmir.

So It Goes

What changed? What made these people, according to our press, "terrorists." The answer is, of course, that we became their prime enemy and target. Coll offers this comment (p. 145): "Ten years later the vast training infrastructure that [the Pakistani ISI] built with the enormous budgets endorsed by NSDD-166 [the official American plan for the Afghan jihad] – the specialized camps, the sabotage training manuals, the electronic bomb detonators, and so on – would be referred to routinely in America as 'terrorist infrastructure.' At the time of its construction, however, it served a jihadist army that operated openly on the battlefield, attempted to seize and hold territory, and exercised sovereignty over civilian populations" – in Soviet Afghanistan, that is.

Similarly, former Prime Minister Iyad Allawi, one of our men of the moment in Baghdad, was not so long ago a CIA-directed "terrorist," as the

---

1. New York: Penguin Press, 2004.

New York Times reported on its front page (to no effect whatsoever). In the early 1990s, the exile organization Allawi ran, the Iraq National Accord, evidently planted car bombs and explosive devices for the CIA in the Iraqi capital (including in a movie theater) in an attempt to destabilize Saddam Hussein's regime.

In the Afghan anti-Soviet war, the CIA looked favorably indeed upon the recruitment of thousands of Arab jihadists and eagerly supported a particularly unsavory and murderous Afghan extremist warlord, Gulbuddin Hekmatyar, who refused at the time to travel to Washington and shake the hand of our "infidel" President, Ronald Reagan – and who today fights American troops in untamed Afghanistan. Though, as it turned out, the "freedom fighters" fell on each other's throats even as Kabul was being taken, and then, within years, some of them turned on their former American patrons with murderous intent. No figure tells the story better, I think, than this one: "In 1971 there had been only nine hundred madrassas [Islamic schools] in all of Pakistan. By the summer of 1988 there were about 8,000 official religious schools and an estimated 25,000 unregistered ones, many of them clustered along the Pakistan-Afghanistan frontier and funded by wealthy patrons from Saudi Arabia and other Gulf states." As the novelist Kurt Vonnegut might say, so it goes.

The Russians in Afghanistan and Chechnya were indeed brutes and committed war crimes of almost every imaginable sort. The language of the American press, watching the invading army of a former superpower turn the capital city of a small border state into utter rubble, was appropriate indeed, given what was going on. In both Afghanistan and in Iraq, on the other hand, where the American government was actively involved, reporters generally – and yes, there are always exceptions – have followed the government's lead with the terminology – "freedom fighter" versus "terrorist" – falling into place as befit the moment, even though many of the acts being described remained the same.

The press is always seen as a weapon of war by officials, and it is so seen by the Pentagon and the Bush administration today. Reporters and editors obviously feel that, and the pressures that flow from it in all sorts of complex ways. Whether consciously or not, it's striking how such perceptions shade and limit even individual stories, alter small language choices, and the nature of what passes for evidence. In the context of Iraq, the testimony of refugees may not be much valued in the American press, for instance, but the testimony of generals is. And so, to give a simple example, when Bradley Graham of the *Washington Post* reports on a "surge of detainees" from recent U.S. operations in Fallujah and elsewhere that is "putting stress" on U.S. prisons in Iraq and "providing the biggest test yet of new facilities and procedures adopted in the wake of the Abu Ghraib prison scandal this past spring," who does he quote on the subject – don't worry, we can handle it, all is going well – but Major General Geoffrey Miller, the former commandant of Guantánamo (of all places) and the man who reputedly brought "Guantánamo methods" to Abu Ghraib before the torture and abuse scandal broke. None of this is even mentioned, of course; nor, unlike in the stories from Grozny, do we hear from any of those detainees who might have recently passed through Abu Ghraib and had the enviable chance to see movies there or use its library. ("For the most cooperative prisoners, there are movies and a library.")

Read Graham's report for yourself. If you believe it, I have a bridge in Brooklyn I'd like to sell you. Try then to imagine a similar piece, written without question or quibble, about the Russian equivalents of General Miller in either Afghanistan or Chechnya. So it goes.

[NOTE: The sources for quotes used throughout this piece are:

Two leading quotes: Ronald Reagan, Proclamation 4908 – Afghanistan Day, March 10, 1982; and "father" of the Russian H-bomb and human rights activist Andrei Sakharov, addressing the Soviet Congress of People's Deputies as Soviet Troops withdrew from Afghanistan, quoted in Coll, *Ghost Wars*, p. 177.

Composite Afghan paragraphs: James Rupert, "Dreams of Martyrdom Draw Islamic Arabs to Join Afghan Rebels," *Washington Post*, July 21, 1986; Ronald Reagan, "Statement on the Situation in Afghanistan," December 27, 1981, *Public Papers of the Presidents of the United States* (Washington: Federal Register Division, National Archives and Records Service, General Services Administration); Leslie Gelb, "Officials Say U.S. Plans to Double Supply of Arms to Afghan Rebels," *New York Times*, November 28, 1984; Joseph Kraft, "The Afghan Chaos," *Washington Post*, March 12, 1981; Orrin G. Hatch, "Don't Forget the Afghans," *New York Times*, November 22, 1985; Steve Coll, *Ghost Wars*; Amnesty International, "Afghanistan: Making Human Rights the Agenda," November, 2001; William Branigin, "Feuding Guerrilla Groups Rely on Uneasy Pakistan," *Washington Post*, October 22, 1983.

Composite Grozny paragraphs: Daniel Williams, "Brutal Retreat From Grozny Led to a Killing Field," the *Washington Post*, February 12, 2000; Michael Wines, "In the Remains of Grozny, the Remains of Living," *New York Times*, December 4, 2001; Sharon LaFraniere, "Despite Russian Assurance of Safety, Chechen Capital Lives Under Siege," *Washington Post*, June 25, 2001; LaFraniere, "Chechen Refugees Describe Atrocities by Russian Troops," *Washington Post*, June 29, 2001; "Chechen Horror," *Boston Globe*, February 29, 2000.]

THE EDITORS' GLOSS: This enlightening contribution from two thoughtful scholars at the Center for Media and Democracy might come as a shock to those who are fortunate enough not to have to watch much television. This chapter, adapted from their book, *Weapons of Mass Deception*, is a stark look at the ditto-head, "no-spin" culture of neocon broadcasting, along with some interesting research and a few telling statistics, the most important of which might well be this from the Gulf War I era: "The more TV people watched, the less they knew . . . . Despite months of coverage, most people do not know basic facts about the political situation in the Middle East, or about the recent history of U.S. policy towards Iraq." The study quoted also revealed "a strong correlation between knowledge and opposition to the war. The more people know, in other words, the less likely they were to support the war policy."

On February 17, 2003, the British *Guardian* ran a revealing piece about print coverage in the English-speaking world outside the U.S. Its secondary headline said it all: "Rupert Murdoch argued strongly for a war with Iraq in an interview this week. Which might explain why his 175 editors around the world are backing it too." What the *Guardian* and Stauber and Rampton pieces highlight is a problem that has long been lamented by media "watchdogs" but ignored by the general public. People think they're getting "news" offered by independent, "fiercely objective" reporters. What they actually get is spin and, worse, a wholesale endorsement of the government's position, rather than a candid look at the pros and cons of government policies.

There is a bright spot, though. The *Guardian* piece reported that in at least one of Murdoch's papers – the relatively tiny Papua New Guinea *Courier Mail* – a voice of some sanity was heard as America and Britain marched to war in February 2003. "The UN inspectors have so far not found any weapons of mass destruction in Iraq. How can a civilised country attack another country without any proof of misconduct?" What a breath of fresh air!

Unfortunately it was just a letter to the editor.

33

Weapons of Mass Deception: The Air War
• • • • • • • • • •

John Stauber and Sheldon Rampton

THE NEWS MEDIA offer two basic services to people who are trying to understand the world: information gathering and information filtering. For people who are trying to *change* the world, the media provide a third essential service: publicity. These days, the service of information gathering has been supplanted to a significant degree by the Internet, where it is now possible to access information and opinions instantly about a wide range of topics from a virtually infinite choice of sources. The task of *filtering* all that information, however, has become more important than ever. The broadcast media claim that they deserve the attention of their audiences because their information is produced by professional journalists with expertise and ethical standards that enable them to separate the wheat from the chaff.

In reality, each media outlet filters the news according to a set of priorities and biases that are often not disclosed to its audience. The FOX News Network, for example, pretends to offer "fair and balanced" reporting in which "we report, you decide." To see what this means in practice, read the following excerpt from a "fair and balanced" interview conducted by Bill O'Reilly, who calls his program, *The O'Reilly Factor,* a "no spin zone." On February 24, 2003, O'Reilly interviewed Jeremy Glick, whose father was one of the people killed on September 11.[1] Unlike O'Reilly, Glick opposed the war in Iraq and had joined with thousands of other Americans in signing a public declaration to that effect. For space reasons, we have edited the exchange, but this excerpt will give you the flavor:

> O'REILLY: You are mouthing a far left position that is a marginal position in this society, which you're entitled to.

---

1. The Jeremy Glick who appeared on *The O'Reilly Factor* is the son of Barry Glick, a 51-year-old worker at Port Authority. He is not related to Jeremy Glick, the 31-year-old passenger of Flight 93 who is believed to have fought the hijackers and prevented them from crashing the plane into its intended target.

GLICK: It's marginal – *right*.

O'REILLY: You're entitled to it, all right, but you're – you see, even – I'm sure your beliefs are sincere, but what upsets me is I don't think your father would be approving of this.

GLICK: Well, actually, my father thought that Bush's presidency was illegitimate.

O'REILLY: Maybe he did, but . . .

GLICK: I also didn't think that Bush . . .

O'REILLY (cuts him off): . . . I don't think he'd be equating this country as a terrorist nation as you are.

GLICK: Well, I wasn't saying that it was necessarily like that.

O'REILLY: Yes, you are . . . . All right. I don't want to . . .

GLICK: Maybe . . .

O'REILLY (cuts him off again): I don't want to debate world politics with you.

GLICK: Well, why not? This is about world politics.

O'REILLY: Because, number one, I don't really care what you think . . . .

GLICK: But you do care because you . . .

O'REILLY (cuts him off again): No, no. Look . . .

GLICK: The reason why you care is because you evoke 9/11 . . .

O'REILLY (cuts him off again): Here's why I care.

GLICK: . . . to rationalize . . .

O'REILLY (interrupts again): Here's why I care . . .

GLICK: Let me finish. You evoke 9/11 to rationalize everything from domestic plunder to imperialistic aggression worldwide . . . .

O'REILLY: You keep your mouth shut when you sit here exploiting those people . . . . You have a warped view of this world and a warped view of this country.

GLICK: Well, explain that. Let me give you an example of a parallel –

O'REILLY (cuts him off again): No, I'm not going to debate this with you, all right.

GLICK: Well, let me give you an example of parallel experience. On September 14 –

O'REILLY: No, no. Here's – here's the . . .

GLICK: On September 14 –

O'Reilly cuts him off several more times; whatever happened on September 14, Glick never gets the chance to say.

O'REILLY: Man, I hope your mom isn't watching this.

GLICK: Well, I hope she is.

O'REILLY: I hope your mother is not watching this because you – that's it. I'm not going to say anymore.

GLICK: OK.

O'REILLY: In respect for your father . . .

GLICK: On September 14, do you want to know what I'm doing?

O'REILLY: Shut up! Shut up!

GLICK: Oh, please don't tell me to shut up.

O'REILLY: As respect – as respect – in respect for your father, who was a Port Authority worker, a fine American, who got killed unnecessarily by barbarians . . .

GLICK: By radical extremists who were trained by this government . . .

O'REILLY: Out of respect for him . . .

GLICK: . . . not the people of America.

O'REILLY: . . . I'm not going to . . .

GLICK: . . . The people of the ruling class, the small minority.

O'REILLY (to his producer): Cut his mike. I'm not going to dress you down anymore, out of respect for your father. We will be back in a moment with more of THE FACTOR.[1]

Reasoned debates between people with opposing views can provide a useful way of clarifying and understanding the issues that separate them, but viewers who watched *The O'Reilly Factor* came away with no better understanding of the respective worldviews of Glick and O'Reilly than they had before watching the show. As O'Reilly stated, he doesn't really *care* what Glick thinks, and he assumes that his viewers don't care either. Why have him as a guest at all, then? Because what the program is really offering is not discussion but *entertainment* – the voyeuristic, sadistic thrill of watching someone get beat up, just like a bullfight or World Wrestling Smackdown. O'Reilly's viewers understand this point implicitly. On the day of the broadcast, *FreeRepublic.com,* a conservative web site, received postings from O'Reilly fans who gloated over the exchange with comments including the following:

"O'Reilly wanted to kick that little punk's ass!"

"I was waiting for Bill to punch him out. What a piece of crap Glick is."

"It was very entertaining."

"Bill should have $itch-slapped that punk-@ss fool."

"His family will never know how lucky they are that it was O'Reilly only telling him to shut up. Had it been me or my husband, I think America would have been witness to a murder on-air and few juries would have convicted us!"[2]

Of the 219 comments posted to this discussion thread (not counting comments that were deleted because the moderator considered them excessive), 31 advocated subjecting Glick to some form of actual physi-

---

1. *The O'Reilly Factor,* February 4, 2003, Transcript #020404cb.256, available on the LEXIS-NEXIS news database. Also see http://www.thismodernworld.com/weblog/mtarchives/week_2003_02_02.html.

2. See http://www.freerepublic.com/focus/news/836052/posts.

cal violence or humiliation. For O'Reilly and his fans, television is a form of combat – specifically, the "air war." This fact is implicit in O'Reilly's description of his program as "no-spin zone" – a deliberate reference to the "no-fly zones" that U.S. jets imposed over Iraqi airspace. As O'Reilly himself has said, a "no-fly zone" and a "no-spin zone" are "the same thing. Violate the rules, get shot down."[1]

The Patriotism Police

Bill O'Reilly's fan club at FreeRepublic.com represents the "ground war" that accompanies his air war against "liberal media bias." The ground war – grassroots organizing and pressure – is directed by well-funded organizations such as the Media Research Center (MRC), a conservative "media watchdog." MRC has an annual budget of $7.8 million – roughly ten times the budget of Fairness and Accuracy in Reporting (FAIR), the most prominent media watchdog on the left.[2] MRC sends out daily email alerts to its list of more than 11,000 followers, detailing the alleged thought crimes of media figures such as Dan Rather and Peter Jennings, encouraging the followers to rain complaints onto networks that fail to toe the correct line on Iraq and other issues. In the wake of 9/11, this lobbying took on new intensity. The *New York Times* reported in September 2001 that TV networks were "increasingly coming under criticism from conservatives who say they exhibit a lack of patriotism or are overly negative toward the government." As MSNBC president Erik Sorenson told the *Times*, "Any misstep and you can get into trouble with these guys and have the Patriotism Police hunt you down."[3]

Other attacks on the press have come directly from the Bush administration. After television personality Bill Maher made remarks following 9/11 that were perceived as critical of past U.S. bombing campaigns, White House Press Secretary Ari Fleischer told journalists that Americans "need to watch what they say, what they do. This is not a time for remarks like this; there never is."[4] In response to complaints about restrictions on

---

1. Bill O'Reilly, "Using Quasi-Prostitutes to Sell Sneakers," *FOX News*, February 25, 2003, online.

2. Media Research Center, IRS Form 990, 2001 (http://documents.guidestar.org/2001/541/429/2001–541429009–1–9.pdf); Fairness and Accuracy in Reporting, IRS Form 990 for fiscal year ending June 30, 2002 (http://documents.guidestar.org/2002/133/392/2002-133392362-1-9.pdf).

3. Jim Rutenberg and Bill Carter, "Network Coverage a Target of Fire from Conservatives," *New York Times*, November 7, 200, online.

4. Press briefing by Ari Fleischer (transcript), White House Office of the Press Secretary, September 26, 2001 (http://www.whitehouse.gov/news/releases/2001/09/20010926–5.html).

civil liberties, Attorney General John Ashcroft testified before Congress, characterizing "our critics" as "those who scare peace-loving people with phantoms of lost liberty; my message is this: your tactics only aid terrorists – for they erode our national unity and diminish our resolve. They give ammunition to America's enemies, and pause to America's friends. They encourage people of good will to remain silent in the face of evil."[1]

Dennis Pluchinsky, a senior intelligence analyst with the U.S. State Department, went further still in his critique of the media. "I accuse the media in the United States of treason," he stated in an opinion article in the *Washington Post* that suggested giving the media "an Osama bin Laden award" and advised, "The President and Congress should pass laws temporarily restricting the media from publishing any security information that can be used by our enemies."[2]

FOX Network owner Rupert Murdoch has brilliantly exploited the current political environment, in which even extreme nationalistic rhetoric is accepted and popular, while liberals and critics of the White House are pressured to walk softly and carry no stick at all. In addition to FOX, Murdoch owns a worldwide network of 140 sensationalist tabloid newspapers – 40 million papers a week, dominating the newspaper markets in Britain, Australia and New Zealand – all of which adopted editorial positions in support of war with Iraq.[3] In the United States, his *New York Post* called France and Germany an "axis of weasel" for refusing to support Bush's war plans and published a full-page cover doctored photo with the heads of weasels superimposed over the faces of French and German ministers at the United Nations.[4] In France, his paper distributed a story calling French President Jacques Chirac a "worm," illustrated by a large graphic of a worm with Chirac's head.[5]

This sort of imagery has historical precedents. Author Sam Keen, who examined the iconography of war in his 1986 book, *Faces of the Enemy*, notes that during wartime, countries frequently produce cartoons, posters

1. Testimony of Attorney General John Ashcroft, Senate Committee on the Judiciary, December 6, 2001 (http://www.justice.gov/ag/speeches/2001/1206transcriptsenate judiciarycommittee.htm).

2. "They Heard It All Here, And That's the Trouble," *Washington Post*, June 16, 2002 (online at http://foi.missouri.edu/terrorismfoi/theyhearditall.html).

3. Roy Greenslade, "Their Master's Voice," *Guardian*, February 17, 2003, online.

4. "The New York Post Captures the Mood of the Extreme Right," *Global Beat*, Center for War, Peace and the News Media, New York University, February 17–24, 2003 (http://www.nyu.edu/globalbeat/index021703.html).

5. Ciar Byrne, "Sun's French Stunt Called 'Disgusting,'" *The Guardian*, February 21, 2003, online.

and other art that attempts to dehumanize their enemies by "exaggerating each feature until man is metamorphosized into beast, vermin, insect . . . . When your icon of the enemy is complete you will be able to kill without guilt, slaughter without shame."[1] The use of this extreme imagery against erstwhile allies simply for refusing to endorse the U.S. war push represented, in symbolic terms, the Murdoch media's interpretation of the Bush doctrine that "if you are not with us, you are with the terrorists."

At MSNBC, meanwhile, a six-month experiment to develop a liberal program featuring Phil Donahue ended just before the war began, when Donahue's show was cancelled and replaced with a program titled "Countdown: Iraq." Although the network cited poor ratings as the reason for dumping Donahue, the *New York Times* reported that Donahue "was actually attracting more viewers than any other program on MSNBC, even the channel's signature prime-time program, *Hardball* with Chris Matthews."[2] A different story appears, however, in an internal NBC report leaked to *AllYourTV.com*, a web site that covers the television industry. The NBC report recommended axing Donahue because he presented a "difficult public face for NBC in a time of war . . . . He seems to delight in presenting guests who are anti-war, anti-Bush and skeptical of the administration's motives." It went on to outline a possible nightmare scenario where the show becomes "a home for the liberal anti-war agenda at the same time that our competitors are waving the flag at every opportunity."[3] At the same time that Donahue got the heave-ho, MSNBC added Michael Savage to its line-up, who routinely refers to non-white countries as "turd world nations" and charges that the U.S. "is being taken over by the freaks, the cripples, the perverts and the mental defectives." In one broadcast, Savage justified ethnic slurs as a national security tool: "We need racist stereotypes right now of our enemy in order to encourage our warriors to kill the enemy," he explained – a fairly straightforward summary of Sam Keen's thesis.[4]

---

1. Sam Keen, "To Create an Enemy" (poem), cited in "Healing the Enemy 2001" (sermon), preached at Grace North Church, Berkeley, CA, January 21, 2001 (http://www.apocryphile.net/homily/sermons/enemy01.html).

2. Bill Carter, "MSNBC Cancels Donahue," February 25, 2003 (http://www.nytimes.com/2003/02/25/business/media/25CND-PHIL.html).

3. Rick Ellis, "Commentary: The Surrender of MSNBC," AllYourTV.com, February 25, 2003 (http://www.allyourtv.com/0203season/news/02252003donahue.html).

4. "GE, Microsoft Bring Bigotry to Life," FAIR Action Alert, February 12, 2003 (http://www.fair.org/activism/msnbc-savage.html).

The patriotism police also patrolled American radio. Clear Channel Communications owns more than 1,200 radio stations (approximately half of the U.S. total), five times more than its closest competitors, CBS and ABC. Its executives have not hesitated to use their power to impose ideological direction. Days after the 9/11 attacks, a Clear-Channel executive circulated a memo with a list of songs that stations were asked to avoid playing in the wake of the tragedy, including "Peace Train" by Cat Stevens and "Imagine" by John Lennon.[1] In the weeks leading up to war with Iraq, Clear Channel stations offered financial sponsorship and on-air promotion for pro-war "Rallies for America."[2] A number of Clear Channel stations also pulled the Dixie Chicks from their playlists after the group's lead singer, Natalie Maines, told fans in London that they were ashamed to be from the same state as President Bush. Only a few days previously, Clear Channel Entertainment, the company's concert tour promotional arm, had been enthusiastically promoting its co-sponsorship of 26 upcoming concerts in the Chicks' upcoming "Top of the World Tour."[3] In Colorado Springs, two disk jockeys were suspended from Clear Channel affiliate KKCS for defying the ban. Station manager Jerry Grant, admitted that KKCS had received 200 calls from listeners, 75% of which wanted the ban lifted. Nevertheless, he said, he gave the DJs "an alternative: stop it now and they'll be on suspension, or they can continue playing them and when they come out of the studio they won't have a job."[4] Cumulus Media, another radio conglomerate that owns 262 stations, also banned the Dixie Chicks from all of its country stations.[5] Nationally syndicated radio talker Don Imus told his producer to screen out guests "who come on and whine about how the President failed to explore all diplomatic avenues. Just drop it, because I'm not interested in having that discussion."[6]

1. Stephen Marshall, "Prime Time Payola," *In These Times*, April 4, 2003 (http://inthese-times.com/comments.php?id=148_0_1_0_C).

2. John Schwartz and Geraldine Fabrikant, "War Puts Radio Giant on the Defensive," *New York Times*, March 31, 2003 (http://www.nytimes.com/2003/03/31/business/media/31RADI.html).

3. "Dixie Chicks' 'Top of the World Tour' a Great Success" (news release), Clear Channel Entertainment, Inc., March 7, 2003 (http://biz.yahoo.com/bw/030307/75279_1.html).

4. "DJs Suspended for Playing Dixie Chicks," *Washington Post*, May 6, 2003 (http://www.washingtonpost.com/wp-dyn/articles/A19571–2003May6.html).

5. "Treatment of Dixie Chicks by Some Radio Stations Raises Troubling Issues," *Citizen Times* (Asheville, NC), May 2, 2003 (http://cgi.citizen-times.com/cgi-bin/story/editorial/34115).

6. John Mainelli, "Tough Talkers," *New York Post*, March 21, 2003 (http://www.nypost.com/entertainment/71400.htm).

Greater diversity could be found in the print media, but not much. Journalism professor Todd Gitlin tabulated editorials that appeared in the *Washington Post* during a 12-week period shortly before the onset of war and found that "hawkish op-ed pieces numbered 39, dovish ones 12 – a ratio of more than 3-to-1."[1]

In addition to restricting the *number* of anti-war voices allowed to appear on television, the media engaged in selective presentation. The main voices that television viewers saw opposing the war came from a handful of TV celebrities such as Sean Penn, Martin Sheen, Janeane Garofalo and Susan Sarandon – actors who could be easily dismissed as brie-eating Hollywood elitists. Of course, the newspapers and TV networks could have easily interviewed academics and other more traditional anti-war sources, but they chose not to do so. In a speech in the fall of 2002, U.S. Senator Edward Kennedy "laid out what was arguably the most comprehensive case yet offered to the public questioning the Bush administration's policy and timing on Iraq," noted Michael Geler, the *Washington Post*'s ombudsman. "The next day, the *Post* devoted one sentence to the speech. Ironically, Kennedy made ample use in his remarks of the public testimony in Senate Armed Services Committee hearings a week earlier by retired four-star Army and Marine Corps generals who cautioned about attacking Iraq at this time – hearings that the *Post* also did not cover. Last Saturday, anti-war rallies involving some 200,000 people in London and thousands more in Rome took place and nothing ran in the *Sunday Post* about them . . . . Whatever one thinks about the wisdom of a new war, once it starts it is too late to air arguments that should have been aired before."[2]

Some peace groups attempted to purchase commercial time to broadcast ads for peace but were refused air time by all major networks and even MTV. (Some peace groups managed to partially circumvent the ban by buying local time for the ads in major cities.[3]) CBS network president Martin Franks explained the refusal by saying, "We think that informed discussion comes from our news programming." MTV spokesman Graham James said, "We don't accept advocacy advertising because it really opens us up to accepting every point of view on every subject."[4] Whereas pundits

1. Todd Gitlin, "The Pro-War Post," *American Prospect*, April 2003, p. 43.

2. Michael Getler, "Worth More Than a One-liner," *Washington Post*, October 6, 2002, p. B6.

3. Ira Teinowitz, "Battle Rages Over Anti-war TV Commercials," *Advertising Age*, February 24, 2003 (http://www.adage.com/news.cms?newsId=37202).

4. Nat Ives, "MTV Refuses Antiwar Commercial," *New York Times*, March 13, 2003, online.

from pro-war think tanks had ready access to talk shows where they sat in studios and expounded their views, it took mass protests of millions of people worldwide on February 15, 2003, before broadcasters gave more than cursory attention to the existence of a huge grassroots peace movement. Even then, coverage consisted of crowd shots and images of people waving banners, with little attempt to present the actual reasoning and arguments put forward by war opponents.

This does not mean that there was no diversity or no quality journalism in the United States. Actually, there was quite a bit of good investigative reporting, much of which we have drawn upon in writing this book. There were also a number of channels *outside* the mass media, such as web sites and email lists, through which alternative viewpoints were vigorously expressed. During the period following 9/11 and throughout the war in Iraq, however, the dominant tone and content of the American mass media was jingoistic and pro-war.

Gulf War II: The Sequel

Media coverage of the 2003 war in Iraq was a sequel, both in style and content, to the 1991 "CNN phenomenon" that occurred during the first U.S. war in the Persian Gulf. "For the first time in history, thanks to the shrewdness of Saddam Hussein, a television network became an active participant in the development of a major international crisis," observed former journalism executive Claude Moisy in a 1995 study titled *The Foreign News Flow in the Information Age.* CNN "became the channel of communication between the warring parties and the instant chronicler of the conflict. The impact on the international community was such that the expression 'global live coverage' was widely accepted as the description of what had happened and as the definitive hallmark of CNN."[1]

These trends continued and intensified with media coverage of the 2003 war in Iraq. "By a large margin, TV won in Iraq – even in areas that papers expected to win," reported John Lavine, director of the Readership Institute, a research organization funded by newspapers to help them increase the number of people who read them.[2] The Readership Institute conducted

---

1. Claude Moisy, "The Foreign News Flow in the Information Age," Discussion Paper D-23, Joan Shorenstein Center for Press, Politics and Public Policy, Harvard University, November 1996, p. 4 (http://www.ksg.harvard.edu/presspol/publications/pdfs/62062_D-23.pdf).

2. Mark Fitzgerald, "TV Trounced Newspapers During Iraq War," *Editor & Publisher*, April 30, 2003, online.

a study of media consumption patterns during the war and found that newspapers were being trounced by TV, which viewers regarded as more complete, accurate and engaging, offering the best experts and the greatest variety of viewpoints.[1]

Within the TV world, moreover, the cable networks dominated the traditional nightly news broadcasts on ABC, CBS and NBC. A survey conducted by the *Los Angeles Times* found that nearly 70 percent of Americans were getting most of their information about the war from the all-news cable channels such as FOX, CNN and MSNBC. Only 18 percent relied on the traditional nightly news.[2] Even MSNBC, whose market share was a distant third behind FOX and CNN, saw a 350 percent increase in viewership during the war.[3] But it was FOX, with its mix of belligerent hyper-patriotism, that won the ratings war.[4] And just as CNN's success in the first war shaped editorial policies throughout the broadcast world, the success of FOX triggered a ripple effect as other networks tailored their coverage to compete with what industry insiders called "the FOX effect."[5]

In many ways, however, the rise of round-the-clock cable TV news phenomenon reflected a *decline* in the amount and quality of foreign news available to American audiences. As Moisy pointed out, CNN by 1995 had a news gathering network worldwide of only 20 bureaus, with 35 correspondents outside the United States – "only half of what the BBC has had for a long time to cover world events on radio and television" and

> only a fraction of what the three largest international newswire services maintain on a permanent basis.... *The Associated Press*, a wire service in the United States ... can carry up to a hundred foreign stories a day. By comparison, CNN (including CNN International) never brings more than twenty foreign stories a day to its viewers, if for no other reason than the much higher cost of producing and transmitting video news.[6]

With the exception of wars and national disasters, notes *Washington Post* media critic Howard Kurtz, "many news executives, particularly in

1. *Ibid.*

2. Josh Getlin, "All-News Channels Find Big Audience," *Los Angeles Times*, April 5, 2003, online.

3. Eric Deggans, "Pride and Prejudice," *St. Petersburg Times*, April 25, 2003, online.

4. Allison Romano, "CNN Out-Foxed in War Coverage," *Broadcasting & Cable*, March 20, 2003 (http://www.broadcastingcable.com/index.asp?layout=story_stocks&articleId=CA286394).

5. Jim Rutenberg, "Cable's War Coverage Suggests a New 'FOX Effect' on Television," *New York Times*, April 16, 2003, online.

6. Moisy, *op. cit.*

television, concluded more than a decade ago that Americans had little interest in news beyond their borders." The time devoted to foreign coverage on ABC, CBS and NBC fell from 4,032 minutes in 1989 to 1,382 in 2,000, rebounding only slightly following the 9/11 attacks to 2,103 minutes in 2002. Once wars are over, countries fall quickly out of the spotlight. Afghanistan received 306 minutes of coverage while the war raged in November 2001, but within three months it fell to 28 minutes, and by March 2003 it was just one minute. Following the collapse of Saddam's regime, attention to Iraq went into rapid decline, as the cable and TV networks turned to covering the murder of pregnant California woman Laci Peterson and a miracle dog who survived being hit by a car.[1]

Round-the-clock live coverage also comes at the expense of detail, depth and research. It may be visually engaging and emotionally riveting, but viewers receive very little background analysis or historical context. While Operation Desert Storm was underway, a research team at the University of Massachusetts surveyed public opinion and correlated it with knowledge of basic facts about U.S. policy in the region. The results were startling: "The more TV people watched, the less they knew . . . . Despite months of coverage, most people do not know basic facts about the political situation in the Middle East, or about the recent history of U.S. policy towards Iraq." Moreover, "our study revealed a strong correlation between knowledge and opposition to the war. The more people know, in other words, the less likely they were to support the war policy." Not surprisingly, therefore, *"people who generally watch a lot of television were substantially more likely to 'strongly' support the use of force against Iraq."*[2]

The same can undoubtedly be said even more strongly about Gulf War II and the viewers in 2003 who tuned in to watch FOX anchor Neil Cavuto berating a professor who had written an anti-war letter as an "obnoxious, pontificating jerk," a "self-absorbed, condescending imbecile," and an "Ivy League intellectual Lilliputian."[3] Viewers may have *felt* that the coverage on TV was better than the coverage in newspapers, but there was actually an inverse relationship between the amount of emotional entertainment on display and the amount of actual information that viewers received. "FOX does

---

1. *Ibid.*

2. Justin Lewis, Sut Jhally and Michael Morgan, "The Gulf War: A Study of the Media, Public Opinion and Public Knowledge" (Center for the Study of Communication, University of Massachusetts, March, 1991). [Emphasis ours.—Ed.]

3. Neil Cavuto, "American First, Journalist Second," *FOX News*, March 28, 2003 (http://www.foxnews.com/story/0,2933,82504,00.html).

less news and more talking about the news than any other network," noted *Contra Costa Times* TV critic Chuck Barney after reviewing more than 200 hours of war coverage from different channels.[1] However, MSNBC was not far behind. In the excerpt below from an April 2 broadcast (edited here for brevity), note how little information is actually imparted as the program skips over the usual themes: Iraqi joy at being liberated, the evil nature of Saddam and his regime, the dangers of terrorism and weapons of mass destruction, the heroism of our troops, and the iron resolve of President Bush:

ANNOUNCER: And these are the very latest headlines of the top of the hour from MSNBC's continuing coverage of "Operation IRAQI FREEDOM" . . . .

CHRIS MATTHEWS (host): In southern Iraq, residents are still wary of the coalition forces, but they are starting to warm up. Here is ITV's Bill Neely, who is with the British troops in Umm Qasr.

NEELY: Another night, another raid, and another crack is made in the repressive and brutal state that is Saddam's Iraq. The Marines are targeting his henchmen in the south . . . . Saddam's secret police and paramilitaries are being rounded up. The old regime disappears, a new dawn, and some Iraqis are glad to see the last of them . . . .

MATTHEWS: Senator Saxby Chambliss of Georgia sits on the Armed Services Committee, and he is a member of the Senate Select Committee on Intelligence. Senator Chambliss, I'm going to ask you the bottom line: how's the war going?

CHAMBLISS: Chris, I think the war is going great. Our brave men and women are the best trained, best equipped, best prepared army in the world, and in only 13 days, we have moved further with greater speed than any army in the history of the world, and everybody knows what they've seen on TV with respect to the airpower that we're delivering to Baghdad and other surrounding communities. In Iraq, we're taking out the Republican Guard in a very surgical manner, and at the same time, not destroying civilian sites. We're not destroying a lot of the history of that country, and I think their folks are doing extremely well with a minimum of casualties . . . .

MATTHEWS: Was that the kind of war we should have expected though? A desperate regime, we are facing a desperate regime.

CHAMBLISS: That's right. When you've got a guy like Saddam, who is a murderer, a torturer and a rapist, you need to expect all of the worst from him, and now I think we do that, and our guys are prepared for whatever may be forthcoming . . . .

MATTHEWS: Have you got any information about whether they intend to use chemical [weapons]?

CHAMBLISS: I don't know. We know he has them. But whether or not he will use them now . . . we just don't know Chris, but it could come in any point in time.

---

1. Chuck Barney, "FOX Offering More News Talk Than News," *Knight Ridder*, April 11, 2003, online.

MATTHEWS: Is it fair to assume that the Iraqi government has direct ties to the terrorist camp that's in northern Iraq?

STEVE EMERSON, MSNBC TERRORISM ANALYST: They have found some precursors in some type of chem-bio development there. They're not a hundred percent sure; they're shipping it back as we speak for a chemical laboratory analysis. But it looks like – The Commander on site, for example, said, there was a precursor to ricin, as it was found in London . . . .

MATTHEWS: Let me ask about the dangers of ricin. How does it affect people? Just give me a basic fear that we should have of that.

EMERSON: It can totally immobilize you, kill you within 36 hours, if not treated within the first few minutes or first hour or so.

MATTHEWS: Once again, great having your expertise. Thanks for joining us. Let's go right now to the White House and NBC's Campbell Brown. How is President Bush handling his role as wartime commander in chief?

BROWN: *USA Today* . . . described the President as carrying a burden, as being very tense, and White House spokesman Ari Fleischer was quick to come out this morning and say he believed the story was too negative, that the President is a lot more steeled, a lot more confident than it made him out to be . . . .

MATTHEWS: Campbell, but the President in the middle of a war, with Americans getting killed, if he were bopping around the White House singing and whistling dippity doo da, wouldn't people think he was off his nut? Wouldn't you expect him to look a little turned off by what's going on?[1]

As in Gulf War I, the coverage of Gulf War II featured engaging visuals, some of which were familiar such as the green nightscope shots of Baghdad. Others were new, such as the live videophone images from embedded reporters of troops advancing through the desert. "The characters are the same: the President is a Bush and the other guy is Hussein. But the technology – the military's and the news media's – has exploded," said MSNBC chief Erik Sorenson. He compared it to "the difference between Atari and PlayStation." TV coverage, he said, "will be a much more three-dimensional visual experience, and in some cases you may see war live. This may be one time where the sequel is more compelling than the original."[2]

In Doha, Qatar, the Pentagon built a $1.5 million press center, where Brigadier General Vincent Brooks delivered briefings surrounded by soft-blue plasma screens. Networks quickly scrambled to give names to their war coverage, with corresponding graphic logos that swooshed and gleamed in 3D colors accompanied by mood-inducing soundtracks. CBS chose "America at War." CNN went with "Strike on Iraq." CNBC was "The Price of War," while

---

1. MSNBC, *Hardball* with Chris Matthews, April 2, 2003, transcript #040201cb.461.

2. Peter Johnson, "Media's War Footing Looks Solid," *USA Today*, February 17, 2003, p. 1D.

NBC and MSNBC both went with "Target: Iraq" – a choice that changed quickly as MSNBC joined FOX in using the Pentagon's own code name for the war – "Operation IRAQI FREEDOM." The logos featured fluttering American flags or motifs involving red, white and blue. On FOX, martial drumbeats accompanied regularly scheduled updates. Promo ads for MSNBC featured a photo montage of soldiers accompanied by a piano rendition of "The Star Spangled Banner." All of the networks peppered their broadcasts with statements such as, "CNN's live coverage of Operation IRAQI FREEDOM will continue, right after this short break." Every time this phrase came out of a reporter's mouth or appeared in the corner of the screen, the stations implicitly endorsed White House claims about the motives for war.

The networks also went to pains to identify with and praise the troops. FOX routinely referred to U.S. troops as "we" and "us" and "our folks." MSNBC featured a recurring segment called "America's Bravest," featuring photographs of soldiers in the field. Regular features on FOX included "The Ultimate Sacrifice," featuring mug shots of fallen U.S. soldiers, and "The Heart of War," offering personal profiles of military personnel.

Much of the coverage looked like a primetime patriotism extravaganza, with inspiring theme music and emotional collages of war photos used liberally at transitions between live reporting and advertising breaks. Bombing raids appeared on the screen as big red fireballs, interspersed with "gun-cam" shots, animated maps, charts and whizzy graphics showcasing military maneuvers and weapons technology. Inside the studios, networks provided large, game-board floor maps where ex-generals walked around with pointers, moving around little blue and red jet fighters and tanks.

"Have we made war glamorous?" asked MSNBC anchor Lester Holt during a March 26 exchange with former Navy Seal and professional wrestler turned politician Jesse Ventura, whom it had hired as an expert commentator.

"It reminds me a lot of the Super Bowl," Ventura replied.[1]

Overcoming the "Vietnam Syndrome"

During World Wars I and II, government censorship of military correspondents was routine, heavy, and rarely questioned even by the journalists themselves, who engaged in self-censorship and avoided graphic depictions of the gore and emotional trauma of war.[2] This was mostly true

---

1. "Operation IRAQI FREEDOM," transcript #032606cb.455, MSNBC, March 26, 2003.
2. "Press, freedom of the," *The Columbia Encyclopedia*, 6 ed. New York: Columbia

also of the Korean war, although censorship was less frequent and journalists began to report on negative aspects of war that previously went unmentioned, such as casualty rates for specific units and morale problems among American soldiers.[1] Vietnam was the first "television war" and also the first war in which serious differences emerged between the military and the reporters who covered it. After the war ended, in fact, many people concluded that television coverage undermined public support for the war by bringing disturbing scenes of death and violence into American living rooms.

This belief is largely a myth, according to University of California-San Diego professor Daniel Hallin, who has extensively studied the content of Vietnam war reporting. "Blood and gore were rarely shown," he states. "The violence in news reports often involved little more than puffs of smoke in the distance, as aircraft bombed the unseen enemy. Only during the 1968 Tet and 1972 spring offensives, when the war came into urban areas, did its suffering and destruction appear with any regularity on TV . . . . For the first few years of the living room war most of the coverage was upbeat . . . . In the early years, when morale was strong, television reflected the upbeat tone of the troops. But as withdrawals continued and morale declined, the tone of field reporting changed. This shift was paralleled by developments on the 'home front.' Here, divisions over the war received increasing air time, and the anti-war movement, which had been vilified as Communist-inspired in the early years, was more often accepted as a legitimate political movement."[2]

Regardless of whether television coverage *created* anti-war sentiment or merely *reflected* it, as Hallin suggests, the Vietnam war marked a watershed in the relationship between the military and the media. In subsequent wars, military planners placed considerable emphasis on controlling the information that reached the American public. Journalists were excluded from the wars in Granada and Panama until the fighting was already concluded. This in turn led to complaints from journalists, and in the 1990 war in Iraq, code-named Operation Desert Storm, the Pentagon adopted a "pool system" through which a hand-picked group of reporters were allowed to

University Press, 2003 (http://www.bartleby.com/65/pr/press-fr.html).

1. "How the War Changed the Way Military Conflicts Are Reported," *University Times* (University of Pittsburgh), vol. 32, no. 21, June 22, 2000 (http://www.pitt.edu/utimes/ issues/32/000622/15.html).

2. Daniel Hallin, "Vietnam on Television," The Encyclopedia of Television, Museum of Broadcast Communications (http://www.museum.tv/archives/etv/V/htmlV/vietnam-onte/vietnamonte.htm).

travel with soldiers under tightly controlled conditions. Between August 1990 and January 1991 only the "combat pools" – about 23 groups of reporters – were allowed access to military units in the field. The Pentagon's Joint Information Bureau, which was responsible for pool assignments, denied reporters access to some areas of the war zone on military orders. "For historic purposes, for truth-telling purposes, there were no independent eyes and ears" to document all the events of the war, recalled Frank Aukofer, former bureau chief of the *Milwaukee Journal Sentinel*.[1] As a result, the public saw a largely sanitized version of the war, dominated by Pentagon-supplied video footage of "smart bombs" blowing up buildings and other inanimate targets with pinpoint accuracy. Journalists who refused to participate in the pool system, such as photographer Peter Turnley, captured images of "incredible carnage" but were dismayed that their coverage of the graphic side of war went largely unpublished.[2]

By the time of the 2001 war in Afghanistan, however, reporters had come to identify with the soldiers they were covering. FOX war correspondent Geraldo Rivera went so far as to announce on air that he was carrying a gun (a violation of the rules of war for journalists under the Geneva Conventions) and told the *Philadelphia Inquirer* that he hoped to kill Osama bin Laden personally, to "kick his head in, then bring it home and bronze it." Just as reality TV crossed the boundary between journalism and entertainment, FOX and Geraldo crossed the boundary between reporters and combatants. Rather than exclude reporters from the battlefield, the Pentagon realized that it had little to lose and everything to gain by inviting them in.

Victoria (Torie) Clarke, formerly the Pentagon's assistant secretary of defense for public affairs, is credited with developing the Pentagon's strategy of "embedding" reporters with troops.[3] Clarke came to the military after running the Washington, D.C., office of the Hill & Knowlton public relations firm, which had run the PR campaign for the government-in-exile of Kuwait during the buildup to Operation Desert Storm a decade earlier. In a 13-page document outlining the ground rules for embedded journalists, the Pentagon stated that "media coverage of any future opera-

---

1. Namrata Savoor, "Persian Gulf War Press Pool Worked Well in Some Ways," *Newseum.org*, July 16, 2001 (http://www.newseum.org/warstories/exhibitinfo/newsstory.asp?DocumentID=14402).

2. Peter Turnley, "The Unseen Gulf War," World Association for Christian Communication (http://www.wacc.org.uk/publications/action/250/unseen_war.html).

3. Peter Johnson, "Who Won, and Who Lost, in the Media Battle," *USA Today*, April 13, 2003, online.

tion will, to a large extent, shape public perception" in the United States as well as other countries. The system of "embedding" allowed reporters to travel with military units – so long as they followed the rules. Those rules said reporters could not travel independently, interviews had to be on the record (which meant lower-level service members were less likely to speak candidly), and officers could censor and temporarily delay reports for "operational security."[1] Along with journalists, the Pentagon embedded its own public relations officers, who helped manage the reporters, steering them toward stories, facilitating interviews and photo opportunities.[2]

Overt censorship played a relatively minor role in shaping the content of reports from the field. Far more important was the way embedding encouraged reporters to identify with the soldiers they were covering. Part of the "point of view" to any journalistic account depends on the actual physical location from which reporters witness events. Since much of modern warfare involves the use of air power or long-range artillery, the journalists embedded with troops witnessed weapons being fired but rarely saw what happened at the receiving end. At the same time that an unprecedented number of reporters were traveling with American troops, there was almost no journalistic presence in Iraqi cities. Prior to the launch of war, Defense Department officials warned reporters to clear out of Baghdad, saying the war would be far more intense than the 1991 war. "If your template is Desert Storm, you've got to imagine something much, much different," said Gen. Richard Myers, chairman of the Joint Chiefs of Staff.[3] Although some print journalists remained in Baghdad, almost all of the television networks took the Pentagon's advice and pulled out in the days immediately preceding the start of fighting.[4] Of the major networks, only CNN still had correspondents in the city on the day the war began.[5] In the absence of their own news teams, the other networks were forced to

1. Robert Jensen, "The Military's Media," May 20, 2003 (http://www.progressive.org/may03/jen0503.html).

2. Douglas Quenqua, "Pentagon PA Staff Helping Out Embedded Reporters," *PR Week*, March 31, 2003 (http://www.prweek.com/news/news_story.cfm?ID=175623&site=3).

3. Douglas Holt, "Media Face Difficult Call on Reporters in War Zone," *Chicago Tribune*, March 12, 2003, online.

4. "NBC, ABC Pull Reporters from Baghdad After Comments Indicating War," *Associated Press*, March 17, 2003 (http://www.bayarea.com/mld/mercurynews/entertainment/television/5414596.htm); see also Jim Rutenberg, "US News Organizations Tell Employees to Leave Baghdad," *New York Times*, March 19, 2003, online.

5. Allesandra Stanley, "After a Lengthy Buildup, an Anticlimactic Strike" *New York Times*, March 20, 2003, online.

rely on feeds from CNN and Aljazeera, the Arabic satellite network once derided by Bush administration officials as "All Osama All the Time."[1]

Embedding also encouraged emotional bonding between reporters and soldiers. CBS News reporter Jim Axelrod, traveling with the Third Infantry, told viewers that he had just come from a military intelligence briefing. "We've been given orders," he said before correcting himself to say, "soldiers have been given orders."[2]

NBC News correspondent David Bloom (who died tragically of a blood clot) said the soldiers "have done anything and everything that we could ask of them, and we in turn are trying to return the favor by doing anything and everything that they can ask of us."[3]

"They're my protectors," said ABC's John Donovan.[4]

Oliver North, the former Marine lieutenant colonel and Iran/Contra defendant turned talk show host, became an embedded reporter for FOX, further blurring the line between journalists and warfighters. "I say General Franks should be commended – that's a U.S. Marine saying that about an Army general," he said in one broadcast.[5]

"Sheer genius," commented U.S. public relations consultant Katie Delahaye Paine, saying that the embedded reporters

> have been spectacular, bringing war into our living rooms like never before . . . .
> The sagacity of the tactic is that it is based on the basic tenet of public relations:
> it's all about relationships. The better the relationship any of us has with a
> journalist, the better the chance of that journalist picking up and reporting
> our messages. So now we have journalists making dozens – if not hundreds
> – of new friends among the armed forces.[6]

You're on Combat Camera

In addition to embedded journalists, the Pentagon offered combatants-as-journalists, with its own film crew, called "Combat Camera." In fact,

---

1. Jane Perlez with Jim Rutenberg, "U.S. Courts Network It Once Described as 'All Osama,'" *New York Times*, March 20, 2003, online.

2. Robert Jensen, *The Progressive*, "The Military's Media," May 20, 2003, online.

3. *Ibid.*

4. Howard Kurtz, "For Media After Iraq, a Case of Shell Shock," *Washington Post*, April 28, 2003, p. A1.

5. David Folkenflik, "*FOX News* Defends Its 'Patriotic' Coverage," *Baltimore Sun*, April 2, 2003, online.

6. K.D. Paine, "Army Intelligence," *The Measurement Standard*, March 28, 2003, online.

one of the biggest media scoops of the war – the dramatic rescue of POW Jessica Lynch – was a Combat Camera exclusive. *Baltimore Sun* correspondent Ariel Sabar watched the Combat Camera team at work: "A dozen employees at computer stations sift through the 600 to 800 photographs and 25 to 50 video clips beamed in each day from the front lines. About 80% are made available to the news media and the public," he reported.

> The images glisten from big screens at the news briefings in the Pentagon and the U.S. Central Command in Qatar. A gallery on the Defense Department Web site gets 750,000 hits a day, triple the number before the war. And for the first time, Combat Camera is emailing a daily batch of photographs to major news organizations . . . . In the battlefield of public opinion, experts say, images are as potent as bullets . . . . Photos of sleek fighter jets, rescued POWs, and smiling Iraqis cheering the arrival of U.S. troops are easy to find among Combat Camera's public images. Photos of bombed-out Baghdad neighborhoods and so-called "collateral damage" are not.[1]

"We've got a lot of good humanitarian images, showing us helping the Iraqi people and the people in Baghdad celebrating," said Lt. Jane Laroque, the officer in charge of Combat Camera's soldiers in Iraq. "A lot of our imagery will have a big impact on world opinion."[2]

Outside the United States, however, the imagery that people were seeing was quite different. Instead of heroic soldiers giving candy to Iraqi children and heartwarming rescues of injured POWs, the television networks in Europe and the Arab world showed images of war that were violent, disturbing, and unlikely to have the impact that Laroque imagined.

---

1. Ariel Sabar, "Military Crews Capture Images from Front Line," *Baltimore Sun*, April 18, 2003, online.
2. *Ibid.*

THE EDITORS' GLOSS: On August 5, 2005, an opinion piece appeared in *USA Today*, written by Larry DiRita, the Assistant Secretary of Defense for Public Affairs, arguing that it would be a mistake to make Congress "the arbiter of standards for interrogating captured terrorists." He was referring to amendments that Senators John McCain (R-Ariz.), Lindsey Graham (R-S.C.), and John Warner (R-Va.) proposed be added to the 2006 Defense Authorization Act to establish policies that would right some of the wrongs identified in this anthology's previous section. The McCain amendment says that "no individual in the custody or under the physical control of the United States Government, regardless of nationality or physical location, shall be subject to cruel, inhuman, or degrading treatment or punishment." Sounds good.

Dick Cheney met with the three Senators before their legislation was introduced to explain that it would usurp the President's authority and interfere with his ability "to protect Americans effectively from terrorist attack." The White House also sent a message to Capitol Hill threatening a veto of the defense bill if the anti-torture provisions were included. Obviously it hasn't really learned its lesson vis-à-vis Gitmo and Abu Ghraib. Yet it remains inconceivable that the tyrants in the White House would balk at a law that merely dictated that someone under American control be legally protected from abuse and mistreatment. Thus far has this country fallen.

What's most objectionable about DiRita's article – beyond the repugnant position it defends – is that it comes from an employee of the Defense Department (DoD). The issue is one of national policy, and those employed by the outfit chartered with defending the country shouldn't be wasting taxpayer dollars participating in a publicity campaign run out of the White House targeting the American public and members of Congress. DiRita's job is to inform the American people about DoD operations (read the DoD "principles of information" for a little education), not to persuade Congress. This is the fundamental problem, also, with the executive-branch conduct detailed in Col. Gardiner's essay. Happily, the colonel's piece was well received, as we understand it, by a few DoD "public affairs" (PAO) personnel, such as the top uniformed PAO for the Joint Chiefs, and Ken Bacon, who had DiRita's job a couple of terms ago.

Truth from These Podia:
A Study of Strategic Influence, Perception
Management, Information Warfare, and
Psychological Operations in Gulf War II
• • • • • • • • • •

Col. Sam Gardiner, USAF (ret.)

M Y INTENT WAS not to do this myself. The work had to be a combination of the kind of research I was doing and investigative journalism. I could do the outside part. Someone had to talk to those inside. After my return from an information warfare conference in London in July 2003 I began looking for interest from one of the major newspapers. I found that interest in Mark Fineman at the *LA Times.*

Mark had covered the war and previously had been bureau chief for the paper in the Philippines, India, Cyprus, and Mexico City. Although he had covered some of the stories I examined in my research, he saw very early the point I was making about the implication of their being seen as a whole: the strategic picture. We continued to exchange emails, talk by phone, and we met four times after our initial session. He shared information he was uncovering. I shared my developing research.

Mark Fineman died of an apparent heart attack while on assignment in Baghdad on September 23, 2003.

Introduction

It was not bad intelligence. It was much more. It was an orchestrated effort. It began before the war, was a major effort during the war and continues as post-conflict distortions.

When I began this study I thought it was going to be an analysis of Pentagon spin called "Truth from this Podium." That was to be a play on promises we were given before the war. The more I did, the more it became clear that it was not just the Pentagon. It was the White House, and it was Number 10 Downing Street. It was more than spin.

I thought about calling it "Apparatus of Lies," connecting to a title the White House gave a paper on Iraq's decade of fabrication, mostly about weapons of mass destruction. Although lies were part of the effort, that title would have been off the mark because the story is more about aversion to truth rather than the open lie.

I also missed on the subject. I thought it was going to be about spinning the stories of the conflict. The real essence of what I found was a much broader problem. It is a problem about the future as much as the past. This problem became the story of the study.

This study demonstrates that the United States and Britain conducted a strategic influence campaign that:

- distorted perceptions of the situation both before and during the conflict;
- caused misdirection of portions of the military operation;
- was irresponsible in parts;
- might have been illegal in some ways;
- cost big bucks; and
- will be even more serious in the future.

This is serious. I did not come to these conclusions lightly. It is because my plea is for truth in war, I have tried not to fall into a trap of describing exaggerations with exaggeration. I expect some will believe I have been guilty of the same sins. As long as we can have some discussion about truth in war, I accept the criticism.

My analysis and comments show I do not accept that the first casualty of war is truth. I think we have to have a higher standard.

In the most basic sense, Washington and London did not trust their peoples to come to right decisions. Truth became a casualty. When truth is a casualty, democracy receives collateral damage.

We have to restore truth as currency of government in matters as serious as war. My story would be important if it were the last chapter of the book. It's not. There is more to come. As the United States struggles with a post-conflict Iraq, distortions continue. Of more concern, major players in the game are working on ways to do it "better" in future conflicts.

In other words, it appears as if the issues of this war will become even more important for future wars. We have reason to be concerned.

Another way to summarize my conclusions is as follows:

(1) The assumption of some in the government is that the people of the United States and the United Kingdom will come to a wrong conclusion if they are given the truth.

(2) We have taken "Information Warfare" too far.

(3) We allowed strategic psychological operations to become part of public affairs.

(4) We failed to make adequate distinction between strategic influence and intelligence.

(5) Message became more important than performance.

The concepts of warfare got mixed up in this war. What happened is that information warfare, strategic influence, and strategic psychological operations pushed their way into the important process of informing the people. The United States and Britain became too good at concepts they had developed for future warfare.

The best way to describe my methodology is to use the words that came from Admiral Poindexter's unfunded project, "Total Information Awareness," later known as "Terrorism Information Awareness." What I have done in this study is look for "inconsistencies in open source data with regard to known facts . . . and goals."

The Terrorism Information Awareness program believed that by discovering linkages, it was possible to "identify intent, methods of operations, and organizational dynamics."

Through this methodology, it was possible to do what the Pentagon wanted to do, "to reduce vulnerability to open source information operations."[1]

Some would say I don't know – or am sloppy about – the definition of information warfare. It's not that I don't appreciate the clarity that comes from precise meaning. It's because almost all of the pre-war definitions were violated in implementation. I was left with these questions: "What was true, and who was affected by the non-truth?"

They told us what they were going to do. The Department of Defense created a storm early in 2002 when it revealed that there were plans to create

1. Report to Congress Regarding the Terrorism Information Awareness Program, May 20, 2003.

an office to do strategic influence. That attempt halted with White House agreement. On November 18, 2002, the secretary of defense announced on an aircraft going to South America, that he was just kidding when he said he would not do strategic influence:

> And then there was the Office of Strategic Influence. You may recall that. And "oh my goodness gracious isn't that terrible, Henny Penny the sky is going to fall." I went down that next day and said fine, if you want to savage this thing, fine I'll give you the corpse. There's the name. You can have the name, but I'm gonna keep doing every single thing that needs to be done and I have.

The White House gave a similar warning. Andrew Card, the President's Chief of Staff, told us they would undertake a major campaign to sell the war. Alastair Campbell, Tony Blair's then Strategy and Communications Director, was orchestrating the same in Britain. "From a marketing point of view, you don't introduce new products in August," White House Chief of Staff Andrew H. Card Jr. told the *New York Times* in September 2002. Card was explaining what the *Times* characterized as a "meticulously planned strategy to persuade the public, the Congress, and the allies of the need to confront the threat from Saddam Hussein." And it would cost over $200 million, according to the London *Times* (September 17, 2002).

We had, therefore, in our research for this study, to discover *what* they did and *how* they did what they said they were going to do.

I'm not going to address *why* they did it. I would like to ask them, "Why do it? Didn't you know there would be consequences?" It was not necessary. They could have told the truth. You don't defend democracy by making light of its most basic elements. Why do it?

Overview

The results of our investigations brought to light just over four dozen "stories" which were manipulated, managed, manufactured, or engineered that distorted the picture of Gulf War II for the American and British people. The list is not definitive. These four dozen are simply those on which I ended up doing detailed research. For each one of them, I attempted to look at when and where the story originated, which officials made statements related to the story, and then look at how it came out. Obviously my four dozen are those where the outcome – i.e., the facts of the story – ended up being different from the story that was told by the spokesmen. In what follows I'm just going to provide a number of examples, which will prove sufficient to demonstrate the validity of my thesis.

The following list summarizes the results of my investigation:

- Terrorism and 9/11
- Lt. Cmdr. Speicher
- Drones
- Mohammad Atta meeting with Iraqis
- Ansar al-Islam
- Chemical and biological weapons
  - Quantities
  - Location
  - Delivery readiness
- Weapons labs
- WMD cluster bombs
- Scuds
- Cutting off ears
- Cyber war capability
- Nuclear materials from Niger
- Aluminium tubes
- Nuclear weapons development
- Dirty bombs
- Humanitarian operations
- Attacking the power grid
- Russian punishment
  - Signing long term oil contracts
  - Night-vision goggles
  - GPS Jamming equipment
  - Saddam in embassy
- German punishment
- Attack and Surrender of the 507th Maintenance Company
- Uprising in Basra
- Red Zone
- Liberations of Umm Qasr and Basra
- Iraqi white flag incidents
- U.S. and U.K. uniforms to commit atrocities
- Execution of prisoners
- Salman Pak training facility
- Private Lynch rescue
  - Language
  - Holding the story
- Children soldiers
- 1000 vehicle attack from Baghdad
- Civilian casualties
- Woman hanged for waving
- French punishment
  - High precision switches
  - Smallpox strains
  - Signing long term oil contracts
  - Spare parts for aircraft
  - Roland missiles
  - Passports for Iraqi leaders
- British Parliamentarian attack
- WMD location
  - Moved to Syria
  - Hidden
  - Just-in-time program
- The post-conflict enemy
- Status of infrastructure repairs

What becomes important is not each story taken individually. If that were the case, it would probably seem to be only more of the same. If you were to look at them one at a time, you could conclude, "Okay we sort of knew that was happening." It is the *pattern* that becomes important. It's the summary of everything.

Recognizing that I said at the outset that I wouldn't exaggerate, it would not be an exaggeration to say the people of the United States and U.K. can find out more about the contents of a can of soup they buy than the contents of the can of worms they bought with the 2003 war in the Gulf.

The Theory

I'm not writing about a conspiracy. I'm writing about a well run and networked organization. My basic argument is that very bright officials found out how to control the process of governance in ways never before possible. I have no way of knowing *intent*. Those who believe the administration influenced by a small group could point out that, for that group, manipulating the truth is an important and even necessary dimension of governance.

Standing back from the details of the stories, the strategy of strategic influence and marketing emerges. It is *portrayed as a struggle between good and evil*. This is *the major theme* of the war on terrorism as well as Gulf War II. Terrorism is evil. We are good. The axis is evil, and we are the good guys. Ironically, the mirror of this is in the Muslim world where the U.S. is called the "Great Satan." The *subtle* theme throughout Gulf War II is that Iraq was behind the attack on the World Trade center. This is what propaganda theorists would call the "big lie." The plan was to connect Iraq with the 9/11 attacks, and make Americans believe that Saddam Hussein was behind those attacks. The effort followed the basic framework of effective propaganda. (And the mirror of this is the rumor that Israel was behind the Twin Towers bombing to produce an anti-Arab climate.)

Beyond the themes we can see certain strategic techniques, required by the 24/7 news cycle:

- saturate the media time and space;
- stay on message and stay ahead of the news cycle;
- manage expectations;
- no matter how bad the story, it tends to level; accelerate the process as much as possible; and
- keep the message consistent daily: Qatar, Pentagon, White House, London.

These come from John Rendon, of the Rendon Group, one of the media organizations hired by the Department of Defense. The Group was deeply involved in selling the first Gulf War, as well as this one. It has received nearly $200 million from the CIA and the Pentagon to turn public opinion against Saddam Hussein.[1] John Rendon calls himself an information warrior and a perception manager. Others within the administration have pushed another strategic technique: the use of information to attack and punish critics.

It's possible to get a sense of how strategic influence and the organization for combat came together by looking at a pattern from before the Gulf War II campaign.

In November 2001, the White House Coalition Information Center (WHCIC) sought to highlight the plight of women in Afghanistan. WHCIC became the Office of Global Communications officially in January 2003. It was in full operation, however, by the time the White House began its marketing campaign in September 2002. What we saw in the Afghanistan effort were patterns that would continue through Gulf War II. It was designed to "build support." As the *Washington Post* of November 16, 2002, said, the "women's campaign was designed to build support in countries in which there is heavy skepticism of the anti-terrorism coalition." It was not a program with specific steps or funding to improve the conditions of women.

On November 17, 2001, Laura Bush said: "Only the terrorists and the Taliban threaten to pull out women's fingernails for wearing nail polish." And on November 20, 2001, Cherie Blair confirmed: "In Afghanistan if you wear nail polish, you could have your nails torn out."

Jim Wilkinson, who was working with the WHCIC at the time, called this effort "the best thing we've done."

When he said it was the best thing they had done, it was not about something they did. It was about a story they *created*. Story was all important.

The other important pattern in the Afghanistan family campaign is the close coordination between the White House and Downing Street. The coordination was so close that Laura Bush and Cherie Blair used almost the same phrase in speeches only separated by three days. The message was coordinated in the Afghanistan campaign. It would also be coordinated for Gulf War II.

Another pattern emerged that we would see in the run up to the war. One might say they followed the concept that if you don't know the truth, fill the vacuum with speculation that would support policy. That certainly was true during the period of the anthrax scare; U.S. and U.K. "intelligence sources" told the press that everything pointed to Iraq.

---

1. James Bamford, *A Pretext for War* (New York: Doubleday, 2004), p. 295.

For instance, David Rose, writing in *The Observer*, October 14, 2001, said that, according to U.S. and U.K. intelligence sources.

> Iraq has the technology and supplies of anthrax suitable for terrorist use. "They aren't making this stuff in caves in Afghanistan," the CIA source said. "This is prima facie evidence of the involvement of a state intelligence agency. Maybe Iran has the capability. But it doesn't look likely politically. That leaves Iraq."

The story lingered. It was not until the middle of December 2003 that the White House put out a paper (not an announcement) that said it looked as if the source of the anthrax was domestic.[1] We would have expected to see the same kind of thing in Gulf War II. *If a story supports policy, even if incorrect, let it stay around.*

Based upon what went before, we would have expected to see the creation of stories to sell the policy, and to see the same stories used on both sides of the Atlantic. *We saw both.* The following summarizes what we noted from each category:

Parallel Storyline	Not Parallel Storyline
• Terrorism	• Aluminium tubes
• "Armed conflict" and "regime"	• Shock and Awe
• Materials from Niger	• Terrorist threat
• 45 minute release time	• Private Lynch
• Surrender of the 51st Division	• Lt. Cmdr. Speicher
• Uprising in Basra	• Cyber war capability
• Weapons labs	• Dirty bombs
• British Parliamentarian in pay of Iraq	• Woman hanged for waving
• US/U.K. uniforms (picked up from Wilkinson report)	• "Paramilitaries" and not "terrorist death squads"
• Baghdad neighborhood bombings	
• Executing prisoners	
• French & German precision switches (US in *NYT*; U.K. leaked UN Report)	

As I've said, the number of engineered or false stories from U.S. and U.K. sources is long. Those which follow are some of them. It's important, however, to point out that the U.K. did not always go along. And, of course, everything was not sinister, but when you begin with the small things, you

---

1. From the White House on December 18, 2001: it was "increasingly looking like" the anthrax sent through the mail came from a U.S. source.

again see a pattern that becomes important in understanding the larger distortions of the truth.

Engineered or False Stories

1. Characterizing the action

It was agreed, first of all, by the U.S. and the U.K. that the activity would be called "armed conflict." State Department documents used the term, as in an advisory that went to American citizens in Austria warning them that "armed conflict with Iraq began on March 20, 2003." Across the Atlantic, Alastair Campbell had a list of guidance items for Blair's press people. The "armed conflict" guidance was part of that list.[1] "Regime" was also on the list. Call the Iraqi government the "regime" rather than the "enemy."

As for the code, although a departure from the historical use of code names, it was not new that you would give the operation a code name that would be part of the marketing.

2. An assessment of the operation code name

The code name for the operation was transformed into a part of the strategic influence. In the past, these were used for security: OVERLORD, during World War II. This continued into the 1990s, with DESERT STORM and DESERT FOX. In these cases they were made of two words so the first word could designate the commander running the operation: DESERT = Central Command.

In the present case, though a departure from the historical purpose of the code operation's name, it was not unusual that it would be part of the marketing. We used names like Operation PROVIDE COMFORT in the past.

This time it was Operation IRAQI FREEDOM. The repetition and the visual quality added by the television networks became an effective memory producing technique in Gulf War II.

3. U.S. objectives as strategic influence

There were some dimensions of the marketing that were a little strange. Eisenhower's military objective was to "enter the continent of Europe and destroy the German Army." The secretary of defense said that what follows

---

1. Peter Stothard, *Thirty days: Tony Blair and the Test of History* (New York: HarperCollins, 2003).

were the objectives given to Central Command, but they were obviously meant for the press. As far as I am aware, this is the first time a military commander was given objectives that were about *justifying* a war.

The objectives released were these:

- End the regime of Saddam Hussein . . . .
- Identify, isolate and eventually eliminate Iraq's weapons of mass destruction.
- Search for, capture, drive out terrorists who have found safety in Iraq.
- Collect such intelligence as we can find related to terrorist networks in Iraq and beyond.
- Collect such intelligence as we can find related to the global network of illicit weapons of mass destruction activity . . . .
- End sanctions and deliver immediately humanitarian relief, food and medicine . . . .
- Secure Iraq's oil fields and resources, which belong to the Iraqi people . . . .
- Help the Iraqi people create the conditions for a rapid transition to a representative self-government . . . .

4. Private Jessica Lynch

From the outset it was called an "ambush." That lingered even in articles that questioned the official version of the events: "What really happened in the ambush of the 507?" *Assessment*: it's not an ambush when you drive a convoy into enemy lines. Though "terrorists" would do something like an ambush.

Military officers who are very careful about how they talk about operations would normally not be sloppy about describing this kind of event. This un-military kind of talk is one of the reasons we began doing this research. They just didn't cherish the truth.

There is still a great deal we don't know about the Jessica Lynch story, but there are some insights we can get once we grasp the pattern of how engineered or manufactured stories were handled during the war. It has the characteristics of a strategic influence campaign.

The first and unexplained part of the story is that just after she was returned to U.S. custody, the *first call* was to Jim Wilkinson, CENTCOM

Director of Strategic Communications. *Newsweek*, April 14, 2003, reported: "In the Joint Operations Center, Air Force Capt. Joe Della Vedova followed the raid as it happened, and as soon as Lynch was in the air phoned Jim Wilkinson, the top civilian communications aide to CENTCOM Gen. Tommy Franks. 'She is safe and in our hands,' he reported. The whole operation, expected to take 45 minutes, was over in 25. Next Della Vedova called Gen. Vince Brooks."

This is very strange for a military operation. Military friends often respond, "Do you suppose they staged it?" I don't have any information about it being staged, but we do know from Wilkinson that the President and secretary of defense were briefed immediately.

The story of Lynch's rescue broke on April 2, 2003. Truth got off track on the morning of April 3 with a story in the *Washington Post* that completely exaggerated what had happened. I have been told by a source that the *Washington Post* got the story from people in the Pentagon who were quoting communications intercepts from Iraq. In retrospect, the Iraqi reports were probably about the action of someone else in the convoy.

The question of releasing classified information has to be mentioned at this point in the Lynch story. If my source is correct, the information given to the *Washington Post* would have been highly classified, limited only to those who had a need to know. From the beginning of the marketing campaign throughout the war, it seemed "okay" to release classified information if it supported the message.

The April 3, 2003, *Washington Post* noted that Lynch "sustained multiple gunshot wounds" and also was stabbed while she "fought fiercely and shot several enemy soldiers . . . firing her weapon until she ran out of ammunition." The paper cited an unnamed U.S. military official as saying "she was fighting to the death." *The New York Times* also reported that she had gunshot wounds.

On the afternoon of the third when Rumsfeld and Myers gave their press briefing, the story on the street was that she was America's new Rambo. We know, however, that they had been briefed. We know they would have been aware of her injuries. When asked, Rumsfeld pulled back. "We are certainly grateful for the brilliant and courageous rescue of Sergeant – correction – Pfc. [Private First Class] Jessica Lynch, who was being held by Iraqi forces in what they called a 'hospital.'" He left the *Washington Post* story as *possibly* being right. ("Gen. Myers and I get briefed on these types of things," the Secretary said, "and there's an orderly process for debriefing and discussing them. And I have no intention of discussing it piecemeal.")

Again, we see the pattern. When the story on the street supports the message, *it will be left there by a non-answer.* The message is more important than the truth.

My friends who are graduates of the Air Force Academy agree that General Myers would have been taken before an honor board if he had been a cadet during this press briefing and did not speak up when he knew an untruth was being let stand.

Even Central Command kept the story alive by *not* giving out details. The April 5, 2003, CENTCOM briefing said simply that special operations forces, "in coordination with conventional forces from the Marine Corps and the Air Force and the Army, were able to successfully rescue Private First Class Jennifer (sic) Lynch out of a hospital and irregular military headquarters facility that was being used by these death squads in Nasiriyah and successfully return her to U.S. hands . . . . " Brig. Gen. Brooks also reported: "There was not a firefight inside of the building, I will tell you, but there were fire fights outside of the building, getting in and getting out." And his comments were picked up the same day by the Armed Forces Information Service: "There were no firefights inside the hospital, but plenty of action outside, Brooks said."

Meanwhile, there were no reports on her condition. The April 6, 2003, *Washington Times* reported that "the hospital where Pfc. Lynch was held was reported to be a stronghold of the Saddam Fedayeen, a guerrilla force sworn to martyrdom for Iraqi dictator Saddam Hussein. The rescuers arrived by helicopter, secured the building by gunfire and forced their way inside, CNN reported."

The exaggerated story was allowed to stay, and even appeared in the April 14, 2003, *TIME Magazine* article about her which read in part: "According to the *Washington Post*, Lynch, an Army supply clerk with only minimal combat training, shot several advancing Iraqi soldiers, emptying her weapon of ammunition and possibly incurring a series of gunshot wounds."

5. Saddam's Fedayeen

The most serious transformation of language was the direction from Washington to call the Iraqi irregular troops "terrorist death squads." One source told me this came in a letter from Rumsfeld. I've read in another place it was from the White House. On the 23rd of March, the troops were being called "Irregulars." The 24th had them as "Fedayeen." After March 25, the presenters changed the name. They were quickly "terrorist people dressed in civilian clothes," and then they became (on the 26th) "terrorist death squads."

Naming the irregulars seems to have been part of the strategic influence campaign. Calling them terrorists connected them with one of the major themes of Gulf War II. The structure of the argument and repetition are an effective implementation of the theory of creating memory in a population. This was part of the "big lie" to tie Iraq to 9/11. And it was successful. A majority of citizens believe Iraq was connected to 9/11. As the polls have shown, it continues to be effective. But what would be wrong with the truth?

6. Developing the terrorist theme

March 22, 2003, Gen. Franks, CENTCOM Briefing: "I can't really provide you a lot of detail. I can tell you that from time to time, in Iraq, we will come across what we believe to be terrorist-associated activity or people, and when we do so, we will strike them, and then we will exploit the site subsequent to the strike. I can tell you that in fact we did strike last evening a terrorist complex . . . . "

March 24, 2003, Deputy Secretary of Defense Wolfowitz, BBC World Service: "We've just taken some very decisive action against that pocket of al-Qaeda terrorists in Kramal."

March 25, 2003, Brig. Gen. Brooks, CENTCOM briefing: "The practices that have been conducted by these paramilitaries and by these others who are out there, sometimes in uniform, sometimes not in uniform, are more akin to the behaviors of global terrorists than they are to a nation. And that certainly is in our mind at this time."

Assessment: It is obvious why in an *Associated Press* poll conducted shortly after Gulf War II was declared ended, 53% of the nation pinned the 9/11 attacks on Saddam.

The "terrorist" connection took many other forms – many forms, but never the truth.

7. Operation TELIC production event

"The first image of the war will define the conflict," said one USMC spokesman. Much of the effort was about image. It might be called the marketing event that *never* happened. It was to be a big show when Basra fell. Sources in the BBC tell me the reason the U.S. 15th M.E.U. was given the task of attacking Umm Qasr and Basra, over the objections of the U.K., was so that an American unit could lead the way into the city. Although the reason for the assignment might not be true, it is almost as important a point that they believed that of the Americans.

Additionally, the following was supposed to have been done, according to what military officials said: marines were to carry packets of food to pass out to children; medics were to provide care as the occupation forces rolled in; journalists were to be bussed to the city; and television crews were to be flown into the city.

But the Battle of Basra took over two weeks, and the media event did not take place.

As an aside, the U.S. and the U.K. had a difference over the code name to give the conflict. The British chose to call it Operation TELIC, more consistent with the traditional methodology for naming combat operations. It was about image – so much effort and money on image.

8. Ansar al-Islam

When the pattern is recognized some of the stories have new clarity.

Ansar al-Islam was supposed to be a group of al-Qaeda terrorists. They were allegedly a Kurdish splinter group which found bin Laden's efforts heroic, and were formed "shortly after 9/11." Because a *single* source reported Republican Guard officers in their area, the group was tied to Saddam Hussein. And they were also supposed to be producing ricin in a "poison factory." Secretary of State Powell showed a picture of it in his presentation to the UN Security Council. The title was "Terrorist Poison and Explosives Factory."

They did eventually find rat poison in one of the buildings. Was it bad intelligence, or did they blur the line between a single source of information and the story they wanted to tell?

9. Salman Pak

The White House told us there was a terrorist training facility for non-Iraqi Arabs. This facility became a major part of the strategic influence and marketing effort. According to the White House White Paper, "Decade of Deception," September 12, 2002, "Former Iraqi military officers have described a highly secret terrorist training facility in Iraq known as Salman Pak, where both Iraqis and non-Iraqi Arabs receive training on hijacking planes and trains, planting explosives in cities, sabotage, and assassinations."

Why didn't we find compelling evidence? Seymour M. Hersh wrote in the June 18, 2003, *New Yorker:* "Salman Pak was overrun by American troops on April 6. Apparently, neither the camp nor the former biological facility has yielded evidence to substantiate the claims made before the war."

10. Attacking the Iraqi power grid

It was announced several times during the war that the United States had not struck the electrical power grid. This was simply not true. An April 3, 2003, release, Number: 03-04-38, headlined: "BAGHDAD ELECTRICAL SYSTEM NOT TARGETED BY COALITION," read: "News reports indicate that electrical power is out in Baghdad. Coalition forces have not targeted Baghdad's electrical system."

"We did not have the power grid as a target," Tori Clarke said at a DoD news briefing, April 4, 2003. "That was not us."

The facts are that the U.S. targeted portions of the power grid in the north during a special operations attack on the dam at Hadithah on April 1 or 2, 2003. According to Human Rights Watch, the attack included a Tomahawk strike using carbon fibers, which would have required approval in Washington.

11. Dirty bombs

The dirty bomb question surfaced a number of times during the marketing of the war. The Iraqi National Congress arranged for an interview of someone who said Iraq was working on a radiation weapon. In June 2002, Khidhir Hamza, an individual often quoted by the White House and the President himself, implied that Iraq was going to train terrorists to use a radiation weapon. "This environment is ideal for countries like Iraq to train and support a terrorist operation using radiation weapons," Hamza said, according to the *Wall Street Journal* of June 12, 2002. In a very subtle technique, "officials" did background interviews in which they said that radiation weapons were one of the things that kept them awake at night. "A few officials speaking on background, have engaged in what-could-go-wrong conversations, saying they are kept awake at night by the prospect of a dirty bomb," wrote David Sanger in the *International Herald Tribune*, February 28, 2003.

If it were not part of the pattern, you would almost have to admire this background technique as a way to reinforce a story. Additionally, some of the most extreme support for the message often came from individuals and groups with close connections to the White House or the Pentagon. This is one example.

12. Lieutenant Commander Scott Speicher

The case of Lt. Cmdr. Speicher is particularly painful. He was a naval aviator shot down early in the first Gulf War. There was some question about his status right after that war, but the evidence suggests his case was used to generate support and to market this war. A reporter told me that then-Deputy Secretary of Defense Wolfowitz had a list of 10 reasons for going to war. The Speicher case was on that list.

The story came to the surface with a *single* defector's report. Then, in a pattern typical of created stories, the *Washington Times* (January 11, 2002) reported that U.S. "intelligence agencies" had information that he was being held captive. The story was allowed to develop because of answers to questions by Wolfowitz and Rumsfeld. Rumsfeld's answer was particularly disturbing. When he was told in a question on March 25, 2002, that Iraq had denied they were holding Speicher as a prisoner, he responded by saying, "I don't believe very much that the regime . . . puts out." That answer was too clever not to have been formulated to leave the impression that he was alive. Why didn't Rumsfeld consider what he was doing to Speicher's family?

The President also raised the case in his presentation to the UN. Then, early in the marketing campaign, the Navy changed his status from "missing in action" to "captured." *ABC News* has reported that Navy officials say they were *pressured* to make this change.

In January 2003, "intelligence officials" continued to leak information that Speicher was alive and being held captive. In April, it was reported that his initials had been found on the wall of a cell. This was a very strange leak. Military POW recovery personnel are very careful about releasing information that would cause false hope in families.

The facts are that no trace has been found of him. DNA of hair fibers in the cell where the initials were found did not match. As the *Washington Times* reported on July 16, 2003, "[the lack of] evidence . . . casts doubt on the credibility of the defector." An April 5, 2005, follow-up story confirmed this assessment: " . . . information from a former Iraqi Special Security Organization informant . . . later was found to have been fabricated." A special 15-member Pentagon team was even established to search for Speicher after the war was over, but it was disbanded after coming up empty-handed.

Again, what becomes important is the pattern. It does not seem as if we were getting truth from the podia.

13. Chemical cluster bombs: a quick response

Then there were the chemical cluster bombs. The story didn't linger. It was around only a couple days. It was part of the attack on the second report from Hans Blix. On March 10, 2003, there were releases and statements by administration officials that the UNMOVIC report did not cover the Iraqi chemical cluster bomb program. These statements ran as follows:

"UN weapons inspectors in Iraq recently discovered a new variety of rocket seemingly configured to strew bomblets filled with chemical or biological agents over large areas, U.S. officials say" (*New York Times News Service*, March 10, 2003).

"Inspectors discovered cluster bombs and sub-munitions that appeared designed to deliver chemical or biological agents. Contrary to initial Iraqi statements, a number of bombs and over 100 sub-munitions were found" (State Department, March 10, 2003).

"Another is a videotape showing Iraq testing a cluster bomb that could disperse chemical weapons over a wide area" (*CNN*, March 10, 2003).

"Administration spokesmen said that chief inspector Hans Blix did not give details . . . of the possible existence of a cluster bomb that could deliver deadly poisons" *(Boston Globe*, March 11, 2003).

"The U.S. is also aware of UNMOVIC's discovery of Iraqi production of munitions capable of dispensing both chemical and biological weapons . . . " (Ari Fleischer, March 11, 2003).

But there was, according to a 1991 Office of the Secretary of Defense report on Patriot missile use during Gulf War I, "no evidence to conclude that Iraq has a warhead with chemical sub-munitions. No information on testing has been obtained, and experimentation with bursts at relatively high release points has not been seen." This follows, because these kinds of warheads are technologically very difficult to achieve, and there are better ways of delivering chemical or biological weapons.

Clearly, the information operation or strategic influence effort included attacking and discrediting those who did not support the story. This is also a good example of the concept of responding within the news cycle, although it lacked consistency. It was a "quick turn" response to the Blix report that got carried widely by print and broadcast media. The story did not have legs because it was rather weak, but it still served its purpose at the time.

It was probably worth the minor negative impact of the June 2003 Blix statement that it was part of a campaign to discredit him.

Again, the cluster bomb story fits the pattern and methods.

14. Iraqis in U.S. uniforms

We were told Iraq had acquired U.S. and U.K. uniforms. There was *one* report from an embedded reporter that a unit "thought" they had seen American uniforms; their fear was partly driven because some of their laundry had been stolen while they were in Kuwait. Since there were uniforms missing, it was assumed that they had gotten to the Iraqis. There is a generally accepted concept in press management that if something bad is predicted in advance, when it does happen the situation won't appear as bad as if nothing had been said. In this case the principle dictated a prediction that Iraqi soldiers were going to attack us wearing U.S. uniforms. My assessment was confirmed when I was told by an individual close to the chairman of the JCS that this story was fabricated. They had some information that Iraq *might* have some uniforms, so they made up the story to be protected if Iraq were to have used the uniforms to attack coalition forces.

Anyway, the reports went like this:

March 7, 2003: Iraq is acquiring military uniforms "identical down to the last detail" to those worn by American and British forces and plans to use them to shift blame for atrocities, a senior U.S. official said Thursday (statement by Jim Wilkinson, Tampa Florida).

March 26, 2003: "Soldiers in the U.S. 3rd Infantry moving north toward Baghdad say they believe they have been attacked by Iraqis wearing American uniforms. And they say they're worried that some of the uniforms were stolen several weeks ago while the U.S. troops were in Kuwait" (David Bloom, *NBC*).

But we have no reports of Iraq trying to shift the blame for atrocities. The way it was put by Jim Wilkinson, a name that keeps appearing in these questionable stories, it seems to fit a pattern of pre-blaming Iraq.

Then the story got turned into Iraqis wearing uniforms to get others to surrender, but even Tori Clarke, the Defense Department spokeswoman, cautioned about its validity. Two days later, Rumsfeld announced it as if it were true. Here are their statements, and note well Clarke's "caution." It all has the feel of being a created story.

March 26, 2003, Clarke: "Well, I remember several weeks ago out here talking about how we knew they were acquiring uniforms that looked like U.S. and U.K. uniforms. And the reporting was that they planned to use them, give them to the thugs, as I call them, to go out, carry out reprisals against the Iraqi people, and try to blame it on coalition forces. So just recently we have seen reports again that they may be wearing or using what looked like U.S. uniforms to confuse people, to confuse our forces, to confuse the Iraqi people.

"Q: Have you seen specific reports about them wearing U.S. uniforms accepting the surrender of Iraqi troops, and then executing them?

"Clarke: I have seen – I have seen at least one report.

"Clarke: I want to caution that and caveat that and say I have seen one report like that."

March 28, 2003, Rumsfeld: "They put on American and British uniforms to try to fool regular Iraqi soldiers into surrendering to them, and then execute them as an example for others who might contemplate defection or capitulation."

15. The Scud "threat"

Before the war, we were told Iraq had some number of Scuds left over. This was important because it would have meant the capability to attack Israel. It was a story consistent on both sides of the Atlantic, repeated a half a dozen times between September 2002, and April 2003.

For the first three days of the war, spokesmen were using the term Scud-*type* missiles to describe the missile attacks. They were not Scuds, and we have found no Scuds, *but for three days,* they kept the story alive.

A CIA report of October 2002 made the point that there were accounting discrepancies which *could* mean some hidden missiles. By the time of Powell's speech to the UN the missiles became a fact for the U.S. and U.K. The "Scud" storyline was carried through the war, probably as part of the strategic influence campaign.

Once the story had been created, it was hard to let go. But there were no Scuds.

16. Remotely piloted vehicles

We were supposed to be threatened by "remotely piloted vehicles" that could deliver chemical or biological weapons. In the October 2002 CIA report, these were *airplanes:* Iraq "attempted to convert some of its J-29 jet trainer aircraft into an RPV . . . that can be fitted with spray," it read. The President, in Cincinnati, also in October 2002 referred to drones that could be used to reach the United States. By the time of Powell's presentation to the UN the following year, they had become much smaller.

Later on, a USAF team, the 75th Exploitation Group, conducted "an investigation of reported drones with sprayers." They concluded that the remotely piloted vehicles were for reconnaissance. Their mission was to take pictures. "They quickly found the 'drones,'" the *Los Angeles Times* reported on June 15, 2003. "Five burned and blackened nine-foot wings dumped near the front gate. 'It could have been a student project, or maybe a model,' the team's expert, U.S. Air Force Capt. Libbie Boehm, said with a shrug."

17. Punishing the French

The evidence points to the French being the focus of punishment in the strategic influence campaign. There are at least eight times when false stories or engineered stories were aimed at them, the majority appearing *after their lack of support* in the UN for U.S. and U.K. actions.

In September 2002 the *New York Times* was told that the French (and Germans) had sold high-precision switches to Iraq that could be used for nuclear weapons. Keeping the cross-Atlantic dimension of the strategic influence effort, the same story appeared in the U.K. press. The fact is that although Iraq had requested these switches, they were *never* supplied.

"American intelligence sources" also leaked to the *Washington Post* in November 2002 the *incorrect* story that the French had prohibited strains of smallpox virus.

And in March 2003 a "US intelligence source" told the *Washington Times* that two French companies had sold spare parts to Iraq. The companies have said they did *not*. Of course no proof has surfaced.

Later in 2003, someone created a story that French Roland missiles were being used to shoot down American aircraft, and these missiles were new. According to an April 9, 2003, briefing presided over by Brig. Gen. Brooks, there was "found an underground storage facility containing an abundance of food and also Roland-type air defense missiles." Also, when an A-10 was shot down near Baghdad airport, a "Pentagon spokesman" pointed out they thought it was hit with a Roland missile; this was not mentioned in the Brooks briefing. In the April 21, 2003, *Newsweek,* it was reported that Lt. Greg Holmes, a tactical intelligence officer with the Third Infantry Division, told the magazine that U.S. forces discovered 51 Roland-2 missiles, made by a partnership of French and German arms manufacturers. One of the missiles he examined was labeled 05-11 KND 2002, which he took to mean that the missile was manufactured last year.

It turns out the story was not very well put together. The production line for the Roland 2 shut down in 1993. It is hard to explain, but this Roland fabrication keeps surfacing. It came up again in early October 2003 when a Polish unit was reported to have found recently manufactured missiles. After it bounced around for a couple of days, a Polish spokesman announced that it was *not true.*

We were also told that the French were helping Iraqi officials escape to Syria. The May 6, 2003, *Washington Times* reported that "an unknown number of Iraqis who worked for Saddam Hussein's government were given passports by French officials in Syria, U.S. intelligence officials said."

This story had some legs, and the *Washington Times* kept getting fed information to keep it alive. The story appeared in other outlets as well, such as *FOX News, Ireland onLine,* the *Charleston Post & Courier,* and the *Australian Broadcasting Corporation.* The May 7 *Washington Times* reported that "US intelligence officials are intensifying the search in Europe for officials of the Saddam Hussein government who fled Iraq with French passports," according to "U.S. officials." When Rumsfeld was questioned, he followed the pattern. When something is on the street that is part of the strategic influence campaign, let it *linger.* "France has historically had a very close relationship with Iraq," he said. And when asked *specifically* about the reports, "I have nothing to add to them." Clearly, the implication of that kind of answer is that he wanted people to believe the stories. *He* had nothing to add.

It was publicly reported on May 15 and 16, 2003, that the French had accused the United States of a smear campaign. As the *Washington Times* later reported, on May 17, 2003: "France's ambassador to the United States accused the Bush administration of starting a disinformation campaign against France."

Even the White House got into this strategic influence effort. One has to believe the administration knew by mid-May that the stories were not true, but at the White House press briefing, it was not stopped. The brief exchange on this topic on May 15, 2003, runs as follows:

> Q: Going back to France, the French have denied selling arms to Iraq and issuing passports to Syria to fleeing Iraqi officials. Are those charges valid?
>
> Mr. McClellan: Well, I think that those are questions you can address to France.
>
> Q: On that point, Scott, do you have any information that the French did, in fact, issue passports to people so that . . .
>
> Mr. McClellan: I think – no, I think that's a question you need to address to France.
>
> Q: Well, no, it's information the U.S. claims to have.
>
> Mr. McClellan: I don't have anything for you.

The technique for this campaign made effective use of the concept of "echo." Less-than professional journalism repeated the reports on the story *as a story* in hundreds of newspapers and on television.

I have been told by press sources that most of the leaks during the "armed conflict" that appeared in the *Washington Times* came from the Office of Special Plans in the Pentagon. Using the kind of methods Admiral Poindexter was going to do on information operations, there would appear to be some validity in this.

The secretary of defense told us before the war he was going to "do" strategic influence. It appears as if the French were a target.

18. White flag incident(s)

My research shows that the white flag story was engineered. Even more, it appears as if it were fabricated to cover a very serious friendly fire event.

Details of two incidents involving white flags have surfaced. The first was reported on March 23, 2003. General Abizaid, the Deputy Commander of Central Command, said that right after some Iraqi soldiers surrendered artillery fire came in on a Marine unit. He called it a ruse. On the surface the explanation seems strange. The Iraqi Army had trouble coordinating artillery fire at all. It is a stretch of the imagination to believe they could put together a plan in which a part of their force would surrender and *then* they would start firing artillery.

After this incident, however, it seems to have become *a matter of policy* to talk about white flag killing. It began the next day, with comments made at a briefing by Tori Clarke. Rumsfeld really got into the story on March 25, and it continued on the 27th.

The President came in and picked it up on April 5. The story had so much (many!) legs that it was even given as the reason for the death of a Marine at his funeral at Arlington Cemetery.

A disheartening aspect of the white flag story is what might have been the real cause of the Marine casualties near Al Nasiriyah on March 23, 2003. Marines are saying that nine of those killed may have been killed by an A-10 that made repeated passes attacking their position.

We know from a lessons-learned report released early in October 2003 that the death of nine Marines is under investigation as a friendly fire accident. From individual reports, we know that at least one of the Marines killed on March 23, reported as having been caught in the ruse, was hit directly in the chest with a round from an A-10 gun. We know at least one of the wives of a Marine killed that day is asking for the truth of her husband's death. We certainly need more truth on the white flag story.

19. Execution of prisoners

The most significant seemingly fabricated story dealt with the execution of prisoners. Tony Blair was in the United States meeting with the President at Camp David. He came out of the meeting and announced, at a joint press conference with the President, that two British prisoners had been executed. That same day, March 27, 2003, General Pace said almost the same thing on CNN.

That day (March 27) we began seeing statements attributing the story to one report. By the next day, the U.K. press began attacking the story as not true. One of the soldier's sisters reported that his colonel had said he was not executed. She was quoted in the *Daily Mirror* as saying that "we can't understand why people are lying."

The U.K. finally pulled away from the story, though the U.S. side stayed with it until April 7.

When Rumsfeld was questioned on April 7, the story began to change. The pattern of the *non-answer* surfaced. The press briefing at which SECDEF was questioned about this ran as follows:

Q: Mr. Secretary, you stated flatly that American POWs have been executed. On what basis do you make that statement? And now that there are at least nine remains that have come back from the ambush in Nasiriyah, how many of those do you believe were American soldiers that were executed?

Rumsfeld: Let me just see precisely what I said. (Looks through briefing materials.) I think I said they have executed prisoners of war. Did I say American prisoners of war?

Q: That was my – that's been the understanding here.

Rumsfeld: I didn't – you just said I said American prisoners of war, and I'm not sure I said that. (To General Myers.) Do you know?

Myers: I don't know.

Q: Are you saying that there have not been American prisoners executed then?

Rumsfeld: I'm not saying either. There may very well have been, but I'm not announcing that, if that's what you're asking. Would you check and see if I said that right now? You've got a copy of it; I'd be curious. If I did, I'd want to make it right.

Q: Well –

Rumsfeld: Just a minute. If I did say precisely American prisoners of war, I'd want to correct it, because I don't have the names of anyone who has – any

American prisoners of war who we know of certain knowledge has been executed. We do know they executed a lot of prisoners of war over the years. And that's what I –

Q: Do you know if any of the nine sets of remains that have been returned, if the forensics, preliminary forensics have shown any of those to have been executed?

Rumsfeld: I have not heard the report on that. Have you?

Myers: I have not seen any of that.

Rumsfeld: (Later in the briefing) Let me correct this. Your question was inaccurate. I had said, "They have executed POWs," and I did not say from what country.

By the end of the questioning, he implied they were not Americans.

I've talked to people who have seen the pictures taken when the individuals from the 507th were found. They described head wounds and fresh blood that could have been consistent with execution. Again, the pattern was that the story was more important than the facts. What is wrong with the truth? Why didn't these guys level with us? That frustrated me at the time, and it continues to frustrate me.

20. Shula district bombing

On March 29, 2003, 50 civilians were killed in a neighborhood in Baghdad. On April 2, 2003, the British *Independent* newspaper reports that its reporter, Robert Fisk, found a 30-centimeter piece of shrapnel at the site of the Shula bombing showing the serial number of the bomb, identifying it as a HARM built by Raytheon. On April 3, the CENTCOM cover story came from Jim Wilkinson. He said American forces have received "reliable information" that the Iraqi regime may be planning to bomb some Shiite Muslim neighborhoods of Baghdad, and then blame the U.S.-led coalition for the destruction. The U.K. side continued the "not us" line: on April 3 the U.K. Defense Chief Geoff Hoon said there was no evidence the market bombings were caused by coalition missiles.

It was part of the pattern. It is another one of those stories that is particularly painful. One keeps wanting to say, "Why did you do this?"

21. Capture of the 507th

General Pace did not have a very good day on March 27, 2003, on the *Larry King Show* on CNN. He said troops from the 507th were shot when they attempted to surrender.

It doesn't seem to have been true, though, according to the official Army report. It read, that "with no means to continue to resist, SGT Riley made the decision to surrender the two soldiers (Hernandez, and Johnson) and himself. PFC Miller moved beyond the crash-site, engaged the enemy, and was captured after being surrounded . . . . Hudson, also wounded, was immediately surrounded after the shooting stopped, and was pulled from the vehicle by Iraqis and captured."

22. The red zone

There was something about the "Red Zone" that caught a lot of people's imaginations. The discussion began with a question to Rumsfeld on March 21, 2003, about the probability of WMD use by the Iraqis. He provided a fairly good answer; it would not have stimulated much of a story. It was probably close to the truth. Three days later someone got to CBS with more (from David Martin, *CBS News*: "Iraqis have drawn a red line on the map around Baghdad, and once American troops cross it, the Republican Guards are authorized to use chemical weapons."), although that same day Franks with a statement tended to put it back in the box ("I actually think we don't know. There is a school of thought that says as the compression becomes tighter and tighter and tighter, the pressure will be greater and greater to use these weapons. So we don't know.").

By March 25, Rumsfeld began to pick up the theme. He said: "There has been intelligence scraps – who knows how accurate they are – chatter in the system that suggest that the closer that coalition forces get to Baghdad and Tikrit, the greater the likelihood, and that some command-and-control arrangements have been put in place. But whether it will happen or not remains to be seen." One can be alerted to strategic influence matter when he talks about "scraps of intelligence." By April 2, the Red Zone had taken on a life. Brig. Gen. Brooks's statement makes this clear: "First, the red zone or the red lines that we describe is simply a term that characterizes that there may be a trigger line where the regime deems sufficient threat to use weapons of mass destruction, weapons that we know are available to them, weapons that we've seen the regime use on their own people in the past, weapons we believe are in the possession of some of their forces now." Another official at U.S. Central Command said, on the same day, that "the imaginary red line, the conceptual trip wire for the danger zone, runs east from Karbala, about 50 miles south of Baghdad on the Euphrates River, to Kut on the Tigris River southeast of Baghdad."

After April 2, there were, incredibly, more than 1500 articles using the "Red Zone." By the middle of April, thousands of stories appeared in the written press about the Red Zone, including this representative *USA Today* piece from April 16:

> [A] salt desert strip west of the town of Karbala, the gap is only a little more than a mile wide. It also lies inside what the Army commanders came to call the "red line" – turf so close to Baghdad that Iraqi troops might defend it with chemical weapons. U.S. commanders feared that the Iraqis would sucker advance units through the gap, only to "slime" them from behind with chemical weapons, cutting them off to be killed.

Even if one grants the administration some room for not knowing Iraq didn't have chemical weapons it was immediately prepared to use against us at the beginning of the war, by April 16 it did know. Joint Task Force 20, whose mission it was to go to the WMD sites first, would have been to the majority of them. The coalition air forces had even stopped flying sorties against WMD areas. The evidence would have been coming back to Washington. But, they kept the story alive.

My sense on this one was confirmed in September 2004 based upon a conversation I had with David Kay, who had been the WMD searcher for the CIA. Quite off-hand he mentioned the Red Zone. He confirmed that it was fabricated. He discovered that it was a concept that had come out of a wargame done by the Pentagon. In the game, the U.S. side simply played that Iraq had established a Red Zone. That then became part of the message.

Psychological Operations

One element of the darker side was psychological operations. *Strategic influence* is aimed at international audiences (and possibly domestic audiences, too). *Psychological Operations* (PSYOPS), on the other hand, are targeted at the bad guys. The problem is that during this war PSYOPS became a major part of the relationship between the governments of the U.S. and the U.K. and the free press.

At the lower end of the scale, when Rumsfeld and London officials kept saying the days of the "regime" were numbered, they were talking to people in Iraq who might have been thinking of fighting. Comments like "The days of Saddam Hussein are numbered" (March 19, 2003); "the regime is starting to lose control of their country" (March 21, 2003); and "the outcome is clear. The regime of Saddam Hussein is gone. It's over" (Rumsfeld, March 21, 2003) were most likely part of the Strategic PSYOPS, with the U.S. press used to communicate the message.

Furthermore, when the British commander, Air Marshall Brian Burridge, gave a presentation to the international press on March 24, 2003, and talked about an uprising, he was not giving an assessment as a professional about likely outcomes, he was broadcasting to see if he could *inspire* that to happen. It was a psychological operation.

> It's probably unnecessary at this stage in the campaign to focus on him as one man. The key aspect is the regime itself. Once the regime recognizes that its days are up, then they will crumble. And while they are crumbling, others who for some years maybe have had designs on overthrowing the regime, will probably develop greater levels of courage themselves. So we'll see a crumble and Saddam's place in that is largely becoming immaterial.

Thus we can see where psychological operations begin to color the free press. It would have been wrong to conclude from his remarks that he was predicting overthrow. *His target audience was inside Iraq.*

1. A psychological operation?

A major example of PSYOPS distorting the free press with false information was the case of the 51st Division. On the 21st and 22nd of March 2003 their surrender was a major story. *It was told as if it were a truth.* It was told on both sides of the Atlantic. It had been coordinated. *It was not true.*

"The commander of Iraq's regular 51st Division," Washington *Reuters* reported on March 21, 2003, "on Friday surrendered to American Marines advancing through the desert toward Baghdad in southern Iraq, U.S. defense officials said . . . . The defense officials, who asked not to be identified, did not provide details but told Reuters that both the commander and vice-commander of the division had surrendered . . . the unit had been peppered in recent weeks with tens of thousands of air-dropped leaflets calling on the Iraqi military to give up."

CBS News followed this up on March 22, 2003: "An entire division of the Iraqi army, numbering 8,000 soldiers, surrendered to coalition forces in southern Iraq Friday, Pentagon officials said. The move marked the largest single unit to surrender *en masse.*"

However, by the 23rd of March, because of interviews with the commander who was supposed to have surrendered, it became clear the 51st *had not surrendered.* For instance, *Agence France-Presse*, on March 23, reported: "An Iraqi commander near the southern city of Basra said Sunday that his division, which Washington earlier said had surrendered, would continue to resist U.S. and British forces. 'I am with my men in Basra, we continue to defend the people and riches of the town,' Col. Khaled al-Hashemi, commander of the 51st Mechanized Division, told the satellite television channel Aljazeera." And *UPI,* on March 25, quoted Col. Chris Vernon, a U.K. spokesman, as follows: "It's quite clear elements of the Iraq regular army – the 51st Division that was west of Basra – have pulled back into the town, of what scale and size, we're not quite clear."

If the first unit the coalition encountered had surrendered as a group immediately, it would certainly have been a powerful message to the rest of the Iraqi military to do the same. Certainly, it was not an intelligence failure. You would know if you have an entire division.

The U.S./U.K. announcement of the surrender of the 51st Division was a psychological operation.

2. A psychological operation?

A story that appeared in the *Times* of the U.K., reporting that Saddam Hussein had worked out a plan to take members of his family to Libya, involving an alleged $3.5 billion deposited in Libyan banks, was planted.

In this case the British seem to have been given the lead on another strategic psychological operation, with the target most likely the people of Iraq.

Remember, the secretary of defense told us he was going to do this kind of thing.

Black Propaganda

I should also mention the black propaganda. There are some very powerful historical examples from the cold war. A former CIA manager for clandestine operations, Milt Bearden, has suggested that some of that kind of thing probably took place in this war. After one sees the pattern of the stories in the press, it is possible to see that some black operations might have been generated by the U.S. and the U.K. Both countries have *organizations* whose missions are to generate these kinds of stories.

Milt Bearden raises a profound question. If we would manipulate truth, would we also manipulate evidence? Is that what the secretary of defense meant when he said he was going to be doing strategic influence?

Here are some possibilities of black propaganda.

1. A black program?

There are, first of all, the Niger nuclear materials documents that came to the CIA through the Italians and the British, mentioned in the President's

State of the Union Message, and reported in the September 2002 U.K. dossier on the threat from Iraq. The chronology went something like this:

- February 2002. Joseph Wilson sent to Africa to investigate the reports.
- September 24. CIA to Congressional committee.
- September 26. Powell in closed hearing.
- December 19. State position paper; first public.
- January 28, 2003. State of the Union Message.
- March 7. IAEA reveals forgeries.

The Niger documents were forged. We have to ask: who would have benefited? For what groups was the fact that Iraq might be close to having nuclear weapons important? There are three possibilities.

The forgery could have been by someone inside the U.S. government probably other than the CIA. It could have been done by parts of the Department of Defense. It could have been done by Israeli intelligence. Israeli intelligence was participating with the Department of Defense in the Iraq information-collection effort. Israel had a great deal to gain. There was a pattern of bad intelligence from the Iraqi National Congress. This could have been part of that pattern. If it were any of the three, the American people certainly have a "need to know."

There was an interesting timing of the Africa connection. On September 9, 2002, the International Institute for Strategic Studies (IISS) released a report about nuclear weapons that said Iraq was "only months away if it were able to get hold of weapons grade uranium . . . from a foreign source." The U.K. dossier came out shortly after that, quoted the IISS report and mentioned that Iraq had tried to get nuclear materials from Africa. Someone gave IISS bad information. Their argument was compounded in the dossier by more bad information.

2. A black program?

And what about the case of George Galloway, a British Member of Parliament?

The April 22, 2003, *Daily Telegraph* (U.K.) reported papers retrieved from Iraq's Foreign Ministry which alleged payoffs to George Galloway, a long-time critic of taking a hard line against Hussein. Three days later, the *Christian Science Monitor* reported that Saddam Hussein had paid George Galloway $10M over 11 years. Documents were supposedly obtained from a retired general. On May 11, the British *Daily Mail* reported that it had received documents from the same source that were in fact forgeries. And on June 20 the *Christian Science Monitor* reported that their analysis also revealed that their documents were forgeries.

The nail in the coffin came when it was reported by the U.K. *Guardian* on December 2, 2003, that a British high court judge awarded George Galloway damages of £150,000 in a judgment against the *Telegraph*.

Who had something to gain? Is this part of the pattern of punishment?

The same retired general told the *Christian Science Monitor* that he had documents proving 6 of the 9/11 hijackers learned to fly in Iraq.

Documents were forged to suggest direct links between George Galloway and the Iraqi regime. Was this part of the pattern of punishment? Was this a black operation?

3. A black program?

Another story with a feeling of blackness was when Aljazeera reported that Saddam Hussein was in the Russian Embassy in Baghdad. The White House, however, picked up on the story and reported as if it were truth. Lines were "hot" to Moscow over the issue. There are, however, two possibilities. Either it was just a rumor, or it was a planted rumor. This latter possibility seems more likely because of the way the White House picked up on it. There is no other case that I know of where the White House picked up on an Aljazeera rumor.

More Strategic Influence

Voice of America serving the U.S. press

"The Iraq Crisis Bulletin" was a strange web site. It provided a daily update and reports from around the world about the crisis in Iraq, which could be subscribed to by email. It was not indicated on the site at all as to who was the sponsor of the site, but the articles were by *Voice of America* correspondents. It was fairly good and was even recommended to reporters by the American Press Institute. The problem is that the *Voice of America* is *prohibited* from providing communications for the American press, but during Gulf War II, it was getting the message to them.

To follow up, I contacted the press office at *VOA* and asked if they were aware of the "Iraq Crisis Bulletin" and who maintained the site. I got no response. So my question remains: *who* was maintaining the site? *Who* was paying?

Attack those who disagree

The thrust of the attack on Hans Blix was to focus on what he did *not* do or say. The personal attacks were left to affiliate organizations. The Dixie Chicks were attacked for remarks against the war at a concert in the U.K. The affiliates did the attacks. John Rendon, the veteran information operations professional, said of the retired military television commentators that they were one of the failures, because they took discussion of context away from the administration. Attacks on them were left to Cheney and Rumsfeld. Pierre Schori, the Swedish ambassador to the UN, opposed the war, and the U.S. refused to allow him to be considered as the EU envoy to Kosovo. Ambassador Wilson found the Niger yellowcake story to be without foundation, and the administration exposed his wife's cover at the CIA. An *ABC News* reporter interviewed soldiers who complained about their mission in Iraq, saying "if Donald Rumsfeld was here, I'd ask him for his resignation." The White House "communications shop" placed a call, telling Matt Drudge that he should review an article about the same *ABC News* reporter in a gay magazine. The first headline for the resultant piece was "ABC News Reporter who filed troop complaints – openly gay Canadian."

An example of strategic influence through no coverage

The White House was successful in keeping the images and the issue of civilian casualties off U.S. television and out of the public eye. This was not true in the rest of the world. Furthermore, emerging studies suggest Iraqi civilian casualties will end up being much greater than military deaths. A BBC poll showed that the rest of the world does not believe we were careful to prevent civilian casualties, despite that being a major theme in almost every CENTCOM and OSD briefing. Nevertheless, the White House was successful in keeping images of the bodies of soldiers returning home off the television. Casualties were mentioned only in a passing way at the beginning of the briefings. And neither the President, secretary of defense, nor Chairman of the JCS attended any funerals.

Strategic influence scorecard

One of the Pentagon media consultants said there were five separate audiences in the *perception* war. After all these efforts, it's possible to conclude that the truth is the best story. Only two audiences were influenced positively by the strategic influence campaign, and that influence is now diminishing.

According to the U.K. PSYOPS specialists I heard at a conference in London the first week in July 2003 they are convinced that one of the reasons we are currently having problems in Iraq is because we oversold our story. We told them too many times and too strongly that we would make it better and fix things.

Organizing for Combat

One way to view how the U.S. Government was organized to do the strategic communications effort before, during, and after the war is to use the chart (below) that was used by the assistant deputy director for information operations at the Joint Staff in his presentation at the London conference on July 2, 2003.

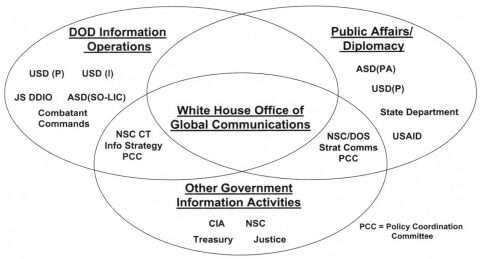

Players in USG Strategic Communication

Source: Capt. Gerald Mauer, Assistant Deputy Director for Information Operations, Joint Staff, 2 July 03

The center is the White House Office of Global Communications, the organization originally created by Karen Hughes as the Coalition Information Office. The White House is at the center of the strategic communications process.

It is important to note that there are two Policy Coordination Committees (PCC), one that deals with the information component of the war on terrorism, and one that deals with strategic communications in general.

In the Pentagon, in addition to the normal public affairs structure, the Office of Special Plans was deeply involved in this effort, supported (with information) by the Iraqi National Congress. This is illustrated below. There was the Rendon Group, headed by John Rendon, who gave media advice to OSD, the Joint Staff and the White House. Finally, there were connections to large PSYOPS activities. The names of individuals came from open reports. I was given the names of people in the Office of Special Plans by a press source.

Organizing for Combat

Special Plans Office
Abram Shulsky
Harold Rhode
Michael Rubin
Michael Pillsbury
Sven Kramer

Iraqi National Congress
(London)
Frances Brooke, Rendon Group

Advises OSD, Joint Staff and NSC

Rendon Group
(Connecticut Avenue & T Street)
(Catherine Place, London)
John W. Rendon
Sandra Libby (John's Wife)
David L. Perkins
Linda Flohr
Frances Brooke

Special Operations Command
• Directorate of Central Intelligence
and Information Operations
Brig. General James Parker
• 24 PSYOPS Group

Strategic PSYOPS Field Activity
(US Army INSCOM's Information Operations
Center at Fort Belvoir supported by DARPA
and John Poindexter)

The Rendon Group worked for the government of Kuwait during the Gulf I. John Rendon proudly tells that it was he who shipped small American flags to Kuwait for the citizens to wave as troops entered Kuwait City. He suggested the same technique for this war, but the Joint Staff IO (Information Operations) office turned down the idea.

The Rendon Group worked for both OSD and the Joint Staff during this war. John Rendon says he was part of the daily 9:30 phone calls with the key information players to set themes.

As illustrated on the chart on the following page, there was, inside the White House, an Iraq Group that determined policy direction, and then there was the Office of Global Communications itself.

Organizing for Combat

Coalition Information Center
(White House, London and Islamabad)

Executive Order in January 2003
Started Work ~ 6 months earlier

$200 Million: | Times of London

White House Iraq Group
Karl Rove
Karen Hughes
Mary Matalin
Jim Wilkinson
Nicholas Calio (Leg. Liaison)
Condi Rice
Stephen Hadley
Scooter Libby

Office of Global Communications
(White House, London)
CENTCOM Office in Qatar
Old Executive Office Building
Six Permanent People
•Tucker Eskew
•Dan Bartlett
Jeff Jones, Director of Strategic Communications
Peter Reid - Information Attaché, British Embassy
(Maybe 3 Brits)

White House Counterterrorism
Linda Flohr (moved from Rendon Group)

1) **Daily Messages**
2) **Communications Planning**
3) **Long Term Planning**

The London *Times* said the Office of Global Communications was a
$200 million program. That certainly raises the question of how much all
of this cost in total, including the $250,000 for the pressroom in Doha.

It's important to note that at times there were as many as three Britons
associated with the Office of Global Communications.

Organizing for Combat

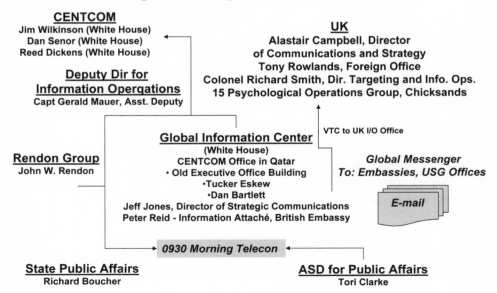

TRUTH FROM THESE PODIA

To ensure the military would be a willing part of the network, three people from the White House Office of Global Communications were sent to work with Central Command. This is shown on the preceding diagram. Jim Wilkinson became General Franks's Director of Strategic Communications.

What all of these illustrations collectively demonstrate is that *the war was handled like a political campaign. Everyone in the message business was from the political communications community. It was a political campaign.*

In London, there was even a parallel organization and a parallel coordination process. They kept the coordination with secure video teleconferences. This is illustrated in what follows.

UK Organizing for Combat

*0830 - UK Policy Meeting
0930 - UK Information Operations Cell
works the message for the day.
• For discussions with the US
• For their forces in the field
1300 - News Release Group Meeting
...ad hoc Targeting and Info. Ops.
discussions with Washington

Twice weekly - Iraq Media Group

Every Friday - VTC with Washington

White House Office of Global Communications

Direct Coordination

Coalition Information Center
**P. Hamill
**J. Pratt
**M. Khan
**Alison Blackshaw (Campbell's Personal Assistant)

*Source: Tony Rowlands, Foreign & Commonwealth Office, 2 July 03
** Drafted the February 3rd Dossier, *Telegraph*, 2/8/03

My concern about all of this became even greater when I attended the conference on Information Operations on July 3, 2003. This was John Rendon's list of things that need fixing:

- We were on the wrong side of expectations during the conflict.

- Embedded journalists were the equivalent of reality television, and they got air time.

- We allowed others to give the context too much.

[639]

- We were still behind the news cycle by four hours, particularly in other time zones.
- Lanes are not important as long as an agency with the capability contributes.

He said, additionally, that the embedded idea was great. It worked as they had found in the test. It was the war version of reality television, and, for the most part, they did not loose control of the story. He said one of the mistakes they made was that they lost control of the context. The retired people in the networks had too much control of context. *That had to be fixed for the next war.* He said he was made aware that lanes are not important. By lanes he meant not letting individual organizations take control of the story, and was hinting at a willingness to step across organizational boundaries in order to achieve his objective.

The Future

The information operations part of the future is frightening. Captain Gerald Mauer, Assistant Deputy Director for Information Operations at the Joint Staff, said, without a sense of the implications, that public diplomacy and public affairs are being integrated into information operations. He said he was looking ahead to the next war where the U.S. government will need a single fusion center that can integrate the story. He hopes to make more use of Hollywood and Madison Avenue in the future. The 15 Psychological Operations Group (U.K.) will grow, and strategic information operations will take on new importance.

He described a paper called the "Information Operations Roadmap" that was being coordinated in the Pentagon. He said when the paper was drafted by his office it said that information operations would be used against an "adversary." He went on to say that when the paper got to the office of the under secretary of defense for policy (Feith), it was changed to say that information operations will attempt to "disrupt, corrupt or usurp adversarial . . . decision-making." Adversarial . . . *decision-making* will be disrupted. In other words, we will *even go after friends* if they are against what we are doing or want to do, i.e., if their decisions are in any way "adversarial."

They seem to be documenting the practice that emerged during Gulf War II. If you don't agree with us, you could be the target of an information attack.

Leave Behind

If the democracies of the United States and the United Kingdom are really and truly based upon informed, open debate of the issues, we have a great deal of fixing to do.

A close friend always asks: what's your last chart? He means, what are your recommendations? What is your slide or chart that you're "leaving behind" for your audience, as a "take-home" message. He is right. It does not seem to be enough just to say things have gone bad.

Parliamentary Inquiry. In the U.K., it's not enough to look at the arguments about weapons of mass destruction before the war. There needs to be an inquiry into the broader question of how spin got to be *more important* than substance. What roles did information operations and strategic psychological operations play in the war? What controls need to be placed on information operations?

Information Operations. Someone inside the U.S. Government said to me that there were so many offices involved in information operations he couldn't even name them. We need a major investigation. We need restrictions on which parts of the government can 'do' information operations. We should not direct information operations against friends. We have to get this back under control.

Smith-Mundt Act. The law was written just after World War II. Its intent was that the American people would not become the target of our own propaganda. It no longer works. *We* became collateral damage, a target group of messages intended for other groups. The Internet and international media access have changed the conditions. We need to revise the laws.

Post Script

The reactions to my research have been very interesting.

When I show the material to individuals *inside* the government – mostly the career people who have been around more than one administration – they have an almost universal first reaction. They say something like, "Be careful with this; *they* will punish you." I don't hear that I have got it wrong. They don't correct my research. I keep hearing the notion, as I found in the research, that punishment of those who disagree is a dimension of the strategy.

Print media have been quite interested. I think reporters like the idea of someone confirming they had not been getting the true story. I have detected a major issue in these discussions in what reporters have not said to me.

I think the materials point to problems in the way newspapers did their job during the war. Why don't they react immediately by saying that they need to do some self-appraisal? I think one could take the stories I have highlighted and ask some direct questions. How was it that the *Washington Post* took classified information on the Jessica Lynch story and published it just the way the individual leaking it in the Pentagon wanted? Why did the *New York Times* let itself be used by "intelligence officials" on stories? Why did the *Washington Times* never seem to question a leak they were given? Why were newspapers in the U.K. better than those in the U.S. in raising questions before and during the war?

I have not heard any self-criticism from reporters to whom I have talked.

When I have talked to television producers and reporters my sense is they believe the whole story is just too complex to tell. That's sad but probably true.

Cynicism is the most disturbing reaction I have encountered. I got it from a limo driver who was taking me to the MSNBC studio for a debate on the no-WMD story. He said, "It's just what politicians do."

I gave a briefing on my research to one of the major Washington research organizations, a think tank. A major thrust of reactions was to keep asking: "What's new. This kind of thing always takes place." I think I heard laughter when I said there was no passion for truth in those who were taking us to war. Didn't *I* understand what goes on in government?

I pain for the limo driver because our leaders have pushed him to be so cynical. I pain even more for the senior researcher. He seems to have no sense of a higher vision. *I pain for our democratic process when I find individuals are not angered at being deceived.*

We either deal with terrorism and this extremism abroad, or we deal with it when it comes to us.

—Lt. Gen. John R. Vines, USA, June 22, 2005

. . . if we don't fight them here, we will have to fight them in Syria.

—Syrian fighter, to a reporter in Fallujah
in 2004 on why he was in Iraq fighting
American forces

THE OTHER SIDE OF THE STORY:
HONEST MEN CONSIDER THE
SITUATION OF IRAQ

THE EDITORS' GLOSS: As this volume goes to press, literally on the eve of the first deadline for Iraq's so-called "new" Constitution, Prof. Al-Qazzaz's comments look prescient beyond measure. Taken along with Mark Gery's essay on the first Iraqi "election," and the pieces by Col. de Grand Pré and Dr. Doebbler, which look tangentially at Ba'athism through the lenses of our continued occupation and our refusal to treat Saddam Hussein in accordance with the law – both international and American – al-Qazzaz's remarks about America's need to partition Iraq as a way of making sure it is not a rallying point for Pan-Arabism seems hard to argue with.

This is an aspect of things that few people grasp, and even fewer experts discuss. But it is there, behind the scenes, if those reading or listening have the eyes to see and the ears to hear. All the discussions that have taken place during the "dramatic" and "suspenseful" days leading up to the "new constitution" center around the possible division of Iraq into Kurd, Shiite, and Sunni statelets. Just recently (August 12, 2005) a radio interview with former CFR head Leslie Gelb and National Defense University scholar Judith Yaphe focused on the issue, arguing about whether it would be good for Iraqis to have their country split into three smaller, loosely united states. To her credit, Yaphe mentioned that only the extremists want that outcome, and when pressed to explain who those extremists are, she identified the Shiite cleric al-Hakim, head of the Supreme Council for Islamic Revolution in Iraq. Most Iraqis, she said, consider themselves to be Iraqis, not members of this or that sect, race, or religion. Nevertheless, self-interested U.S. designs for Iraq proceed, the desires of the Iraqi people notwithstanding . . .

As political developments in Iraq unfold, it will be important for us all to have a clear idea of what the truth really is, lurking behind popular media coverage and superficial "expert" analysis. We could do worse than to have as intellectual guides the clear perspectives of scholars such as Prof. Al-Qazzaz and others in this volume.

C H A P T E R
35

Behind the Smoke Screen: Why We Are in Iraq
. . . .
An Interview with Prof. Ayad S. Al-Qazzaz

PROFESSOR, THE HEART *of this interview will concern the current conflict with Iraq, and the reasons for the United States' attack upon that country. But before we turn to the conflict today in Iraq, it would be useful to know a little of your background. Could you describe your life in Iraq and your reasons for coming to the United States?*

AQ: I came to this country in January 1963 when I was 21 years old. I had just finished my Bachelor of Arts in Sociology at Baghdad University. I was very lucky to be accepted at the University of California, Berkeley, to pursue my graduate studies. In the late 1960s I decided to look for a job, and I accepted an offer from California State University, Sacramento. At which time I started several research projects and publications.

LID: Some of those publications involved Iraq, I assume?

AQ: Well, a number of them involved Iraq. The first article I published was in 1967 in the Berkeley *Journal of Sociology.* It was an article comparing Iraq, Syria and Egypt, and that article mainly explained why the military coup in Egypt stabilized the system in Egypt while the military forces in both Syria and Iraq led to instability.

LID: It seems to me that there is an attempt to link Iraq and al-Qaeda and then to compare Muslim countries in general with the historical period in which Muslim countries fought the West, consciously reviving the images and sentiments of the Crusades. This exploits widespread ignorance of the history of Iraq and of peaceful relations between Muslim countries and the West.

AQ: Iraq is an interesting country. On the one hand you can say it's a very modern country, dating it to 1921 when it was established *formally* under the British mandate.

LID: With the League of Nations.

AQ: Right. But on the other hand, the land of Iraq – and this is what people misunderstand – the land of Iraq is an ancient land. It's the cradle of civilization. The land of Babylon, the land of the Assyrian Empire, the land of the Akkadian and Sumerian Empire. The wheel was invented there, the first urban settlement was there, writing was invented there, the calendar was established, and in that region the Hanging Gardens were established, as well as the juridical Code of Hammurabi (1792–1750 B.C.) which is perhaps the "mother of all codes." Thus we are talking about a country with a very long, complex and rich history. If you look a little further into history, you find that Baghdad became the center of a huge Muslim empire, the Abassid Empire, in the eighth and the ninth century, under the Caliphates of Harun ar-Rashid (786–809). At that point the culture in Baghdad represented the highest of achievements, materially, intellectually, and so on. The Caliphate established the first university, called the "House of Wisdom," and in that university they did most of the translations of Greek documents. A lot of the Greek documents – Aristotle, for example – have been lost in the original, and all that we have is the Arabic translation for them.

But most of the time, between the 15th and 20th centuries, Iraq was controlled by the Ottoman Empire. Iraq at that time was divided into three provinces – Baghdad, Basra, and Mosul. Each one of them had its own governor, but Baghdad was the most powerful center. In 1914, the British invaded Iraq. They started by invading the south, and they completed the invasion of Baghdad in 1917. Interestingly, when the British invaded Baghdad, they issued a proclamation saying, Bush-like, "We came to liberate you." The British "liberation" turned out to be an occupation, a mandate, and the British practically did not leave until 1958.

LID: What about 1932?

AQ: Iraq became independent formally in 1932, but was tied by treaty to the British for 25 years. The treaty stipulated: firstly, that the British could maintain two military bases. Secondly, they could bring in troops at will during wartime. The British used this treaty on many occasions, naturally.

LID: Can we compare the British occupation and proclamation of liberation to the current public relations message that Iraq is now independent, with a Prime Minister and cabinet?

AQ: Yes. Iraq's government is a puppet government. It's amazing how history repeats itself. Remember the statements when we were invading Iraq: "We have no intention of occupying the country"? Then immediately after the fall of Baghdad on April 9, 2003, we went to the UN requesting that we be declared the official occupier. When the occupation, which has now lasted for two years, became very costly to us and very hard to justify and sell to the American people, we came up with the gimmick of establishing an interim government, claiming it represents the sovereign Iraqi people, and further claiming that we are in Iraq at the request of the Iraqi government.

LID: In spite of the occupation of Iraq by British forces, would you say, nevertheless, that there was a fairly cordial relationship between the broader Arab world and the West, which changed drastically with the creation of the Israel?

AQ: If you are talking about America, the reputation of the American – not only in Iraq, but throughout the Middle East – was very positive. Everyone remembers Wilson's principle – self-determination – and many Iraqis would have preferred America to be the mandate power rather than the British. But that goodwill started to evaporate in the Forties, and certainly with the establishment of the state of Israel. Unfortunately, the United States did not stop with the mere *establishment* of the state of Israel. American support for Israel, materially, commercially, economically and so forth, has increased over the years, thereby increasing the antagonism and the deep anti-American feeling found in the Middle East. It has poisoned the relationship tremendously.

LID: Would you say that it starts with the Palestinians being forcibly moved out of their country?

AQ: When the state of Israel was established, there were 600,000 Jews and 12,200,000 Palestinians. Israel then proceeded to kick out of their homes in one fashion or another some 800,000 of these Palestinians. Some of these refugees settled in Jordan; some of them settled in Syria; some of them elsewhere – but funny thing: despite the United Nations stressing that these Palestinians have the right to go home, Israel has refused to accept them. So they have never been back since then, and their numbers have grown to several million people.

LID: These were largely Muslims, but also some Eastern Rite Catholics and Nestorians?

AQ: They're basically Muslims and Christians. The Christian community in Palestine used to be a very big community. It represented 20 to 30 percent of the total population. But because of ongoing persecution, many of them were kicked out, and their cities in Palestine – like Ramallah and Bethlehem, completely Christian communities – have lost their Christian character. Ramallah was completely Christian; now it's completely Muslim because of outside immigration.

LID: It must be very difficult for Christian Palestinians to understand that there is a faction of supposed Christians in America who are actively supporting their oppressors.

AQ: That's correct. You see that bewilderment especially among the priests and the ministers of the Palestinian Christian community. They wonder why their co-religionists in the West are not active in spreading the word that Israeli policy is not a discrimination only against the Muslim but also against the Christian community; that not only the Muslim suffers, but also the Christian suffers. I remember talking to one member of the Christian community in Palestine – he said that if the situation continues, he can envision a time when there will be no Christian community there whatsoever. All that we will have is the church buildings staffed with a few people and nothing else, because the Christian community is finding it very difficult to live. Consequently many of them are emigrating.

LID: Let's talk about the intensifying of U.S. support for the Israeli state militarily and financially. We pour billions of dollars every year into that country, do we not?

AQ: We are giving Israel on average four billion dollars a year. That is the largest grant or loan to a foreign country in history. Technically, Israel is not eligible for foreign aid because it is a developed country. Foreign aid was established to help undeveloped countries, people who are in dire need. On average, every Israeli citizen receives about a thousand dollars of foreign aid.

LID: Let's look at U.S. foreign policy regarding the nuclear situation in the Middle East. We already know where the "weapons of mass destruction" are: Israel has weapons of mass destruction, has nuclear weapons.

AQ: Not only nuclear. They also possess chemical and biological weapons.

LID: We are putting pressure on Iran not to develop nuclear weapons, but no one is discussing Israel at all. The phrase "weapons of mass destruction" was only used in relation to Iraq in the recent past and now in the context of Iran, and never in respect of Israel with its obvious potential threat to peace in the Middle East.

AQ: You see, that's one of the tragedies, why people don't trust the U.S., and why they think that the U.S. is hypocritical because of their one-sided policy. For starters, if we, Americans, have weapons of mass destruction ourselves – if we have the nuclear bomb, if we have chemical and biological weapons – what right do we have to ask other countries not to have the same? Ethically speaking, if I have something, other people should have the right to the same thing. So, firstly, we cannot object on that basis. Secondly, when you talk about Iran – and I'm not defending the government of Iran – you must understand that if you are living in Iran – surrounded by countries like India, Pakistan and Russia which all have the nuclear bomb; when Iraq is occupied by a nuclear power, America; when Israel has a nuclear bomb – by what right can the U.S. tell other nations living in this situation that they, too, cannot have a nuclear bomb? If I were an Iranian I would pursue the bomb. In order to be trusted, the U.S. must pursue a coherent policy of seeking a nuclear-free zone throughout Middle East. Otherwise there is no way on earth they will be able to stop Iran pursuing the bomb unless, of course, they want to invade Iran.

LID: Why did we really invade Iraq given that the "weapons of mass destruction" was a pretext, and that there was no link between al-Qaeda and Saddam Hussein?

AQ: I can think of at least five or six different reasons.

LID: Okay, let's go into them all.

AQ: The first reason is oil. The second reason is to reduce Iraq's potential to be a regional power. The third reason is to solve the Arab-Israeli conflict on *Israeli* terms. The fourth reason is to fuel the American industrial-military complex. The fifth reason is to stop a trend which Iraq started: using the Euro instead of the Dollar to price oil. The sixth reason is to transfer military bases from Saudi Arabia to Iraq. We can talk about each one of them briefly if you want.

LID: Certainly.

AQ: Why is oil important? Oil is important because Iraq officially has the world's second largest proven reserves of oil. It has approximately 112 billion barrels or 13% of the world's proven reserve of oil. That's second only to Saudi Arabia, which has officially 260 billion. Now what does 112 billion mean? It means almost three or four times the proven reserves of oil in America. We have approximately 30 billion. But there's something else about the Iraqi oil. Because of the political instability in Iraq over the last forty years or so, oil exploration has been almost zero. Many oil experts who have some familiarity with Iraq think that Iraq is swimming with oil. There are some experts who say that Iraq's oil may even exceed Saudi Arabia's supply. The Iraqi oil is not only in the North. It is in the South, and they have it in the middle near Baghdad also. They have it everywhere.

There's another thing. The U.S. wants to *control* the Iraqi oil, not merely to have *access* to it. Whoever runs Iraq is still going to sell it on the market. So we will have access no matter who is in charge of Iraq. *But control is our objective, which is quite different from access.*

LID: *It's power and profit.*

AQ: It gives you all sorts of things. Iraqi oil is very cheap to produce. Until the latest war it cost about two dollars to produce a barrel of crude oil. In the U.S., it costs approximately 15 – 20 dollars. That gives you an idea why Standard Oil of California, along with other big fat oil corporations, wants to have its hands on Iraqi oil. The potential for profit is beyond belief.

Iraq also has gas. About 3 or 4 percent of the world's proven reserves of gas is in Iraq. So you put your hands not only on oil, but also on a lot of gas. What does this mean on the international oil market? It means you can almost control OPEC – the oil producing/exporting countries – because the country which really manipulates the market now is Saudi Arabia. They are the "swingers." They can destroy anyone; they can support anyone. They have the capacity to produce about ten million barrels a day. Iraq doesn't have it *right now,* because the oil industry was devastated during the sanctions period of the 1990s. But if they modernized the oil industry and if they updated the equipment, they could produce 6–7 million in three or four years time.

LID: *But we got the pipeline built following the invasion of Afghanistan.*

AQ: But that's not Iraq, that's Afghanistan. Iraq has several pipelines already, but they need to be updated. There's one through Turkey, one through Saudi Arabia, and there's one through Syria. But we stopped the

Syrian oil flow, because we wanted to punish Syria. If Iraq can do these things, it can affect the market. It can also be a "swinger" like the Saudis.

LID: If we have that capacity under our control, and we have the Afghanistan pipeline, what would be the significance of the two together?

AQ: Since Saudi Arabia is certainly still under our control, we would be able to control the oil market.

LID: That gives an immense amount of power to its holder.

AQ: Of course. Not only that. We can affect industrial Europe and we can affect industrial development in China, because we are going to be in charge of pricing the oil and also "suggesting" how much is going to be on the market. Thus controlling Iraqi oil gives us the ability to manipulate OPEC, and to become less and less dependent on Saudi Arabia. Once we become less beholden to the Saudis, we can talk openly about changing their government.

LID: At that point we would be in a wholly different relationship with them.

AQ: That was the aim, of course, but the trouble is that plans in Iraq did not develop the way they wanted.

LID: You mean Halliburton and the Dick Cheney connection?

AQ: Yes. We have the corporations. There is another reason why we want to control Iraq, which is very important in the world view of the neo-conservatives. They want to privatize that industry because the oil industry in Iraq is a state industry, as it is elsewhere throughout the Middle East. We wanted to start with Iraq and use it as a model to be followed by other Middle Eastern countries. As a matter of fact, one of the things which Bremer did with Coalition Provisional Authority Order Numbers 37, 39, and 40 was to try and privatize the whole Iraqi economy. The jewel of privatization was to be the oil industry, of course, but they haven't started the process yet because of the formidable Iraqi resistance.

LID: But of course it's about more than just the oil.

AQ: Of course. The second reason we invaded Iraq, which nobody really wants to talk about, is that we wanted to reduce Iraq's capacity to be a regional power. Iraq has the potential to be a regional power for three reasons. One: they have oil, which puts them ahead of the pack, and two: they have arable land, much more than other people. Iraq is not a desert – there is a big desert, but there are two rivers, and there is other arable land, and if that land is used efficiently and carefully, Iraq could be the breadbasket for the whole Middle East. The third reason: Iraq has the manpower, which is more or less well educated. Many people left Iraq in the 1990s because of the sanctions, but these are the three elements. Whosoever wields power in Iraq will feel the urge to exercise some regional influence. It didn't happen only under Saddam. It happened with Qassim, it happened with the monarchy. Regional power of this kind is not necessarily something to America's advantage. If there were to be any sort of unity between the Arab counties, that is not something which we could look upon indifferently – because *unity* means *power*. Part of the reason we opposed Saddam invading Kuwait was not because we loved the Kuwaitis, but because he would have had his hands on 25% of the world's proven reserves of oil. That would have made him a significant power. It's as simple as that. Iraq has that potential, and America is against any such form of unity *on principle.*

LID: Pan-Arabism?

AQ: Pan-Arabism, or any "ism:" Pan-Islamism, Pan-Arabism, Pan-whatever-it-is. *We are against them all.* We did not like Gamal Abdel-Nasser, Egypt's President, (1918–1970) because he was a Pan-Arabist. We oppose Arab nationalism because their unity means power. Imagine if all the Arab countries federated. Right now such a federation would include 300 million people. Area-wise it would be one and a half times the size of the U.S., and it would control 60% of the world's proven reserves of oil. They would be a power. You would have to listen to them. So it's not to our advantage. Go to the library and look at some of the books written by CIA people, about how much we want such unity out of our way, about how much we wanted to dismantle the unity between Egypt and Syria in 1958.

So we want to stop Iraq from realizing that potential. What are we doing about it? Many things. Firstly, we are encouraging sectarian tendencies, encouraging ethnic tendencies, in Iraq. I think we are, perhaps, going to divide Iraq. Possibly into a minimum of two states. There will be a Kurdish state in the North; in the South, God knows what it is going to be. But the Kurdish state is a matter of time. When is it going to be announced? I would say five to ten years from now. It all depends on Turkey. A time is coming when we will decide that Turkey is no longer a strategic ally for us. We will use the new Kurdish state as a place for ourselves, to build military bases and to influence neighboring countries.

LID: Because of its geographical position?

AQ: Well, it's going to be a very small state. It's going to be only inside Iraq, not in Turkey or Iran at that point. The new Kurdish state will not be stable in terms of borders – it will fight with the coming new government in Iraq over Kirkuk and other cities – so they will be in constant dispute. Then, because they will be a small state, they are going to ask a superpower to come and protect them, like Qatar is doing now.

Now if we split a Kurdish state off from Iraq, then Iraq becomes much smaller, because you remove about four or five million Kurds from a population of 24 million people. Iraq would be constantly "fighting the Kurdish state," and so we will severely hamper Iraq's potential to be a regional power. We want Iraq to become smaller and be busy fighting its neighbors. We are encouraging ethnic and sectarian tendencies. Suddenly now we are talking about Shiite and Sunni; we don't talk any longer about the *Arabs* of Iraq. We call them *Shiite* and *Sunni.* We are establishing a new construct, a new identity for the Iraqi people. And surprisingly we use it *only* in the context of the Arabs. Between 5 and 10 percent of the Kurds are Shiite, but we never call them Shiite. There are some Shiites among the Turkomen, perhaps up to 20 to 30 percent – yet we *never* call them Shiite or Sunni. We just call them Turkomen. We are playing games and employing gimmicks. We used the term "de-Ba'athification" for a while, and the purpose of that was to "de-Arabize" the country, to remove everything related to Arabism.

We are also, in one fashion or another, seeking to "normalize" Iraq's relationship with Israel. We are allowing the Israelis a free hand in Iraq. They are everywhere. The Mossad is everywhere, and there are many rumors that the Mossad was behind the killing of over 250 Iraqi professors and scientists. There are reports which indicate that the Mossad is very active in the Kurdish area of Iraq, along the border with Turkey, along the border with Iran, and they may in one fashion or another be stirring up some unrest among the Turkish Kurds, among the Iranian Kurds. It's already started happening among the Syrian Kurds.

LID: Sharon has successfully used September 11 to make a comparison: "We, the Israelis, also have to fight our 'war on terror' and so we will use this to solve our Palestinian problem once and for all."

AQ: That is correct. Another reason for the war in Iraq is to resolve the Arab-Israeli conflict on *Israeli* terms, because the Israelis regard Iraq as the only throne left. They have already taken Egypt and Jordan out of the equation; and Syria is not seen as that important since they are busy with Lebanon.

The Israelis will never forget that Iraq launched Scud missiles at them in the 1991 war. They have been acutely aware of Iraq's potential too.

Essentially, the Israelis thought that by taking Saddam out of the picture – taking Iraq out of the picture – the Palestinians would have no other support and would say, "Yes sir, we will sign whatever you want us to sign." The Israelis failed to predict correctly just as have the neoconservatives. The Palestinians did not give up despite all that is happening.

A fourth reason we went to war against Iraq – which apparently nobody talks about, save a few – is that we need a war every once in a while in order to fuel the industrial-military complex. Our last budget was 419 billion dollars, and it was passed with no discussion at all because "we are in a war situation." We need a war to test our weapons, but we also need a war to brag about our weapons so that we can sell them. We are the largest purveyor of military arms worldwide. I think it was two or three years ago, we sold in the neighborhood of 15 to 20 billion dollars worth of arms. This is partly because we brag about our weapons – "Hey, they are very effective. Look what they did in 1991. Look what they did last year." We need a war to find out how effective these weapons really are. War is good for business.

LID: A lot of "high tech" equipment was tested in this recent war.

AQ: Definitely. We tested some of it in 1990, and we tested more of it in 2003; and probably ten years from now we will come up with another war, so as to run more "tests" once again.

When you have a war, it's easy to pass laws, and it's easy to pass budgets. I remember the hassle which took place after the collapse of the Soviet Union, the controversy over continuing to justify a large military. But now nobody talks about it. We can keep raising the budget and nobody will talk about it. Democrat or Republican.

LID: Neither side.

AQ: No. This is a very important reason and few pay attention to it. Here's another reason for this war. At the end of the year 2000, Saddam started the trend of using the Euro to price oil in the international market. There was some discussion at that time that Venezuela and Iran might follow suit. If this had happened throughout OPEC it would have had a devastating impact on the dollar and on the U.S. economy.

[656]

LID: And the final reason for the war in your opinion?

AQ: Finally, we invaded Iraq in order to transfer the military bases from Saudi Arabia to Iraq. You see, having bases in Saudi Arabia is a problem. In a sense, that's what created bin Laden to some extent. He argued "Are you the protector of the Holy Places? You have the infidels here!" It must also be remembered that Saudi Arabia is much more restrictive and traditional. Iraq tended to be more open, more secular, etc., so the U.S. can "wheel and deal" within Iraq in a freer fashion. Both men and women can mingle and do all sorts of things. But what's happening now in Iraq is exactly the opposite. It's becoming more and more Islamisized. Another of their — the neoconservatives and Israelis — unforeseen, unintended consequences. *And where will the unforeseen and unintended end?*

THE EDITORS' GLOSS: Fr. Jean-Marie Benjamin has long been an activist on behalf of the beleaguered Iraqi people. His website (www.benjaminforiraq.org) chronicles some of his work. His work on behalf of Iraq also extended to interaction with a number of Iraqi government officials. Oddly enough, this gives pause to some, but is it any different than the activities of thousands of good-willed "public servants" in Britain and America who also "interact" – in exchange for a salary – with governments whose conduct is less than pristine?

Fr. Benjamin was praised by Angelo Cardinal Sodano, Secretary of State to the Vatican, for his work in assisting Tariq Aziz – a long-time friend – with his legal defense following the American invasion. Benjamin approached his bishops and superiors for permission (which they freely granted) to do so, and Sodano wrote him a warm letter thanking him for "building links with Iraqis and the wider Arab world." If only the goodwill extended by Benjamin and the Vatican towards the "wider Arab world" was mirrored by a like concern of British and American politicians for the fate of Arab Christians. Alas, the effects of their vile polices on members of our holy religion take a back seat to far less noble concerns, ideology, power, and money being foremost among them.

The *Washington Times*, surprisingly, chronicled the plight of Iraqi Christians in a March 29, 2005, article by Arnold Beichman. They have, he wrote,

> historically played an important role in the country. Tariq Aziz, 69, now in coalition custody, and once a familiar face on Western TV, is a Chaldean Catholic. During Saddam's dictatorship, he was Iraqi foreign minister and later deputy prime minister and at one time was even targeted in an assassination attempt by Iranian Islamic terrorists.

Quoting Nimrod Raphaeli, a senior analyst with the Middle East Media Research Institute, Beichman said that under Saddam "Iraqi Christians 'enjoyed considerable religious freedom,'" though Beichman believed that such freedom under Hussein was a "paradox." This fact alone sheds a disturbing light on the transformation of Iraqi society currently being wrought at the behest of Anglo-American politicians and occupying forces. In previous decades, Beichman noted, "successors to the dictator Abdul Karim Qassem, assassinated in 1963, employed Christian women . . . . They were practicing Chaldean Catholics under the guidance of a Belgian priest who conducted his office without let or hindrance." Perhaps if Fr. Benjamin had had the same freedom for his pre-war diplomatic mission, things today might be very different.

CHAPTER
36

A Priest Looks at the Former Regime

. . . .

An Interview with Fr. Jean-Marie Benjamin

FATHER BENJAMIN, TELL *us something, if you would, of how you first became interested in the subject of Iraq, and how your interest in it developed over the years.*

FB: I embarked upon a career as a composer and conductor in Paris in 1965. I am the author of about one hundred classical music and film soundtrack compositions, as well as having recorded some 30 albums. I wrote the official anthem of UNICEF which was played at a concert in Rome by the Orchestra and Choirs of the Italian state television channel, RAI. I accepted, thereafter, a post with the United Nations as the Special Events Officer for UNICEF, and was responsible for organizing television programs, and artistic events amongst others around the world. I terminated my artistic and United Nations work in 1988 to become a Catholic priest. I was ordained in Rome on October 26, 1991, at the age of 45. About two months before my ordination, Cardinal Agostino Casaroli, then the Secretary of State for the Vatican, invited me to assist him on his trips and missions abroad. Naturally, I thought that the experience would be both edifying and of great interest. So I accepted the offer and began to undertake a series of trips – which were about roughly fortnightly and spanned the globe – with the Cardinal up until January 1995. During one of the last of these trips – we went to Mexico and to New York – the Cardinal informed me of Pope John Paul II's intentions to go to the biblical sites of the Redemption on the occasion of the Jubilee in 2000A.D., a trip that would take him to the holy places ranging from the time of Abraham to the time of St. Paul. When I returned home, I contacted friends – two cameramen and a producer – and suggested to them the idea of going to Iraq to make a documentary film about Mesopotamia, the history of modern Iraq and the situation of the population in light of the economic embargo. It was thus that we produced the first documentary film, *Iraq: The Birth of Time*, and which led us to travel the country, from North to South, during a five-week period.

In the process I discovered a population of great gentility and refinement, a truly wonderful people. The welcome that we received everywhere was remarkable for us, Europeans, white from head to foot, and who "represented" in a certain way the West and the Embargo.

To travel across Iraq and to understand her people is to relive more than eight thousand years of history represented by more than ten thousand archaeological sites, and which are witnesses to our past, a fundamental patrimony for understanding the history of the human species. It is, too, to reflect upon the sixty centuries, which separates us from the Sumerian, Assyrian, and Babylonian civilizations. It is to relive the Bible and the accounts of Genesis, to walk in the footsteps of Abraham. It is to return to the first moments of Creation, to the first laboratory of the blossoming of future civilizations. It is to bring to mind that the great discoveries and the first inventions, which form the pedestal of our civilization – the culture of our planet, were born and grew up in Mesopotamia. It is in Iraq that the first civilization arose, the cradle of our culture and of our development.

We have heard American and European political leaders justify military intervention in Iraq by claiming that the military occupation of the country was intended to bring the values of "the civilized world" to Iraqis. Perhaps they don't know that Abraham was not born in Hollywood but in Iraq!

Before the last Anglo-American war of aggression in March and April 2003 and their unilateral occupation of the country, to travel in Iraq was also to enter into the mysterious world of Islam and to marvel in seeing side by side in any Baghdad street a church and a mosque. It meant being astonished to see students not wearing the burka, the chador, or the veil. Today bombs are exploding in churches, Shiite women are ordered to wear the veil, and every day there are bomb attacks against Christian-owned shops which sell wines and spirits. A strange way to "bring democracy" to a the country!

LID: As a Catholic priest how did you view things as the Anglo-American establishments began their political and media preparations for what became the Second Gulf War? Did you think that they had justice – of any kind or degree – on their side?

FB: To bomb, to invade and to occupy a country – a founding member of the United Nations, Iraq having joined on September 26, 1946 – on the basis of lies pushed day after day, for months on end, by the world's media about weapons of mass destruction which did not exist – *please!* Why wonder about an American administration which does not hesitate to create false documents conveyor belt-like in order to deceive UN inspectors, viz., the matter of uranium from Niger which Saddam Hussein was supposed to have bought and which was exposed as a crude hoax, or the false satellite photographs, or even the famous lorries in which the Baghdad government was supposedly manufacturing biological weapons, but which turned out to be for producing powered milk! Why wonder about an American administration which forced the UN Security Council to vote Resolution 1441 which sought to disarm Iraq of her few remaining conventional weapons on the basis of incredible lies in order to bomb and invade the country more effectively after it had been disarmed? The cowardice of a "superpower" which massacres through bombing a population already broken by 13 years of embargo, and invades a country whose army was totally defenseless because of the resolution of the U.N., is unique in the history of war. There is no reason to be surprised that the "Lords of War, Lies, and Torture" in Washington and London could only find the likes of Ahmad Chalabi and Iyad Allawi to put in power in Baghdad as their allies, these latter also being Masters of Lies who did not shrink from having their own people bombarded.

What is happening in reality in Iraq? There were no weapons of mass destruction. Saddam Hussein was arrested nearly two years ago, and yet every day F-15 fighters and Apache helicopters are bombing the indigenous population and piling up hundreds of victims in Fallujah, Samarra, Baquba, Najaf and other cities. Why? George W. Bush claims that it is a matter of a war against terrorism. If that is so, the men in Washington have not only deceived themselves, but they have placed Iraq in the hands of Islamic and terrorist organizations which, prior to the American invasion, had been rightly suppressed by the Rais of Baghdad, Saddam Hussein. The American Commission of Inquiry into the events of September 11, 2001, the Report of the American Senate, and the majority of the security services and diplomatic chancelleries around the world confirm: Iraq had no connection whatsoever with al-Qaeda nor had it any involvement in the attacks upon the USA on September 11. Osama bin Laden pointed the finger against Saddam Hussein and screamed: "Baghdad, this republic of scoundrels and infidels!" This took place at the time that Donald Rumsfeld visited Saddam in Baghdad to sell him arms and "pharmaceutical" products in 1983. Anyone can see and download the video of this historic meeting from the National Security Archive.[1] But, today, the country is seemingly in the hands of Islamic extremists. To this tragic situation one must add the organized criminal gangs, mafias of all kinds, and a resistance which is organized throughout the entire country, from Mosul to Basra, thanks to strategic alliances between Sunnis and Shiites, and between tribes and Kurds in the North.

Thus the administration in Washington justified the bombing of an innocent and civilized people and the occupation of a country by diffusing lies on a daily basis throughout the media so as to deceive public opinion. Today, during the present military occupation of Iraq – an occupation which remains illegal and contrary to international law – Washington and London continue to lie to the public about what is really happening in Iraq. But the most serious thing is that all of these lies and all of these deceptions are carried out in the name of peace, in the name of God, which is actually the greatest offence against God that one could commit since it is a matter of a sin against the Holy Spirit, the one unpardonable sin.

LID: We understand that you organized the visit of Tariq Aziz to meet the Holy Father in Rome just before the Anglo-American invasion. Can you tell us how the visit came about, how it was organized (especially given the blatantly anti-Catholic attitude of President Bush, and his attempts to eliminate anything that would have obstructed his war), and what you saw as the aim of the visit?

FB: On January 13, 2003, the crisis between America and Iraq was at its height. The situation was completely stalemated, and dialogue between Baghdad and Washington was non-existent. The U.N inspectors were working on the disarmament of Iraq, but each day brought new threats from George W. Bush. The War Party seemed to be gaining ground ineluctably. I decided, therefore, to try and create an opening by sending a fax to Mgr. Jean-Louis Tauran, Vatican secretary for relations between states, asking him to see if the Holy Father would agree to see in private audience Tariq Aziz, the Iraqi deputy prime minister.

Two days later I received the reply at my home in Assisi. The Vatican Secretariat of State informed me by fax that the request for an audience could be forwarded by the ambassador of the Republic of Iraq to the Holy See. Translated this meant the response was positive. I telephoned Tariq Aziz immediately.

---

1. See http://www.gwu.edu/~nsarchiv/NSAEBB/NSAEBB82/.

Benjamin: I have something important to convey to you.
Aziz: Are you coming to Baghdad?
Benjamin: I am taking the first plane to Amman.

The following Thursday I arrived in Baghdad in the evening. The next day I met the Deputy Prime Minister. I outlined my idea of an audience with the Pope. Rather surprised, Tariq Aziz asked me if I was sure that the Holy Father would be able to receive him. I told him that I had received a positive reply in writing. Tariq Aziz looked at me thoughtfully and in silence, his moustache not moving so much as a hair. He then thanked me for my help and told me that he would speak about it to Saddam. We then touched upon the practical details of a visit to Rome and I handed the Minister an official invitation from the *Beato Angelico Foundation,* of which I am the secretary-general, to come to Rome. I added: "After your audience with the Pope, I would like to suggest that you come to Assisi, as a Catholic, to pray for peace at the tomb of St. Francis and to announce a call for peace along with the Franciscan friars." Tariq Aziz replied: "Obviously I would be highly delighted to meet the Holy Father. I was received by him in the past on two occasions. As far as Assisi is concerned, if you think that it would be an important step in promoting peace, I agree. I invite you to co-ordinate the itinerary of the visit with our embassy in Rome."

Upon my return to the Italian capital, I got in touch with the Iraqi Ambassador to the Holy See, who had been put in the picture by Baghdad in the meantime. Events moved quickly. The Vatican stated that the audience would take place on February 14, 2003, at 11:00 a.m. Tariq Aziz would then meet Cardinal Angelo Sodano, secretary of state, and Mgr. Jean-Louis Tauran. The doors opened, not only at the Vatican, but also in Assisi where the three Franciscan communities agreed to my proposal to meet the Iraqi deputy prime minister. On February 13, Tariq Aziz arrived in Rome. We know the rest.

In my eyes – and not only mine – this visit was important. Obviously, it did not stop the bellicose intentions of the Washington administration, nor did it stop the American war machine in spite of repeated appeals from the Pope against this unjust war. But it did allow a new door for dialogue to be opened, to give greater force and momentum to the anti-war movements around the world, and to remind the world that in Iraq Christians and Muslims lived in perfect harmony. During this visit to Rome, Tariq Aziz was also able to meet Italian political leaders, journalists, and important figures from the church and the cultural world. All of them put questions to him, often difficult ones – but he was capable of answering them clearly and without evasion.

What also motivated me to undertake this difficult task of inviting Tariq Aziz to meet the Pope was that it was conducive to reminding the world that there lived in Iraq a Christian community which lives in perfect tranquility with the Muslims in spite of the embargo and the bombing, and that Iraq was one of the most conscientious countries in fighting Islamic extremism.

The Assisi visit was also important. For the first time the discussion passed from the political to the spiritual plane. Tariq Aziz was very moved. In the Golden Book of the Franciscan monastery he wrote: "Iraqis do not want war. They want peace. The world wants peace."

On Saturday, February 15, on my return from Assisi to Rome, I took the opportunity in a quiet moment of putting several questions to Tariq Aziz at the Iraqi embassy:

Benjamin: Are you expecting an American attack? Opposition at the United Nations and public opinion around the world is very strong.

Aziz: They will attack, with or without the United Nations.

Benjamin: Do you really think that they can do so without the agreement of the United Nations?

Aziz: Yes, they can. They are the most powerful. They have enforced the embargo for 13 years; they have bombed Iraq regularly; they have imposed "no fly zones" *without* United Nations agreement. They have enforced their will because they are the strongest. They want to invade Iraq for our oil and in order to control the region.

Benjamin: How are you going to defend yourselves?

Aziz: Their bombardments are going to destroy everything. But we will not fall once again into the trap of 1991. They are going to invade the country and they are going to discover a people which knows how to defend itself. With their military hardware and their technology, it won't be too difficult to occupy the country, *but* once they are inside a resistance will organize itself throughout Iraqi territory. There is also a risk that some extremist Muslim organizations will enter the country. The Americans are going to come up against tremendous problems.

Benjamin: Can I ask you if Iraq still possesses weapons of mass destruction?

Aziz: I repeated several times to the Pope that we no longer have weapons of mass destruction, either chemical or biological. They were all destroyed between 1991 and 1993. The chief of UNSCOM, Richard Butler, in December 1998, presented a false and twisted report to the Security Council of the United Nations, and thanks to the lies of Richard Butler, the Americans began to bomb our country once again, destroying our power stations, bridges, and water purification installations once again, when we had already had so much difficulty in rebuilding them after the Gulf War. In 1993 we had nothing left. Now they wish to disarm us – with the agreement of the United Nations – of the few arms left to us so as to attack and invade our country, probably without UN agreement.

In the light of events and what continues to be reported daily about the tragic situation in Iraq, along with the total failure of the American occupation and "democratization" of the country, the words of Tariq Aziz uttered a full month before the American-imposed war on Iraq ring out like a prophecy.

LID: In his discussions with the Holy Father, both on and off screen, can you tell us what Mr. Aziz proposed on behalf of his country's government as a solution to the crisis?

FB: Tariq Aziz repeated on several occasions to the Holy Father that Iraq no longer possessed weapons of mass destruction, and that the Baghdad government had accepted all the provisions of U.N Resolution 1441 without condition. Aziz told the Pope: "What more can we do?" He also gave a letter from Saddam Hussein to the Pope.

LID: We understand that you had visited Iraq on a number of occasions before the outbreak of this round of hostilities. Were you on good terms solely with Mr. Aziz, or were you acquainted with others in the Ba'athist government? How did you view the people that you knew: honest, open and cultured, or did you see them as substantially the bureaucrats of the ruthless regime that Mr. Bush has declared dominated the country before "Operation IRAQI FREEDOM"?

FB: During my many trips to Iraq between 1997 and 2003, I was in touch with Tariq Aziz, the health minister, Dr. Omeid Mubarak, and on only a couple of occasions with Mr. al-Sahaf, the minister of information. I did not meet Saddam Hussein at any time, nor did I seek to do so. But when I went to Iraq I was in touch above all with the population, as much with the Shiites of the south as with the Sunnis of the center and north. I also had the chance to meet some of the leaders of the Ba'ath Party on a couple of occasions.

From the Ba'ath Revolution of 1968, Iraq had a Constitution guaranteeing the same rights to all Iraqi citizens of the three monotheistic religions: Christians, Muslims, and Jews. Women had the same rights as the men, and took up positions of responsibility, even within the government. It was the foremost Arab country in terms of having the highest number of women in ministries, embassies and in positions of public office. The

Republic of Iraq was a secular republic – that is, a state without any one official religion – and the Ba'ath Party ensured that the secular nature of the state was completely respected. Islamic extremists were persecuted and driven from the country – a hard experience for the Shiites. School education was entirely free. For the poor villages of the south, electricity was also free. Social welfare was available to all classes in society. The Iraqi dinar was one of the strongest currencies in the world. Then, one Iraqi dinar was worth three American dollars. Today, one American dollar is worth 1,800 dinars.

The UNICEF report for 1989 confirms that the child mortality rate for the under fives was the lowest in the Arab world, and one of the lowest in the world. Today, child mortality is the highest in the Arab world and in the world at large.

Baghdad was regarded as one of the most important cultural centers of the Arab world. Universities in Iraq were attended by students from numerous Arab countries. The leading Iraqi scientists and doctors were the most advanced in their field in the world, whilst today they have practically all fled abroad. The man who was minister of health, whom I knew well, Omeid Mubarak, is a Kurd who has two doctorates in medicine from the United States. About thirty percent of the personnel in the Iraqi ministries were Kurds. Mr. Bush forgot to mention all these facts to the American people, or perhaps he never knew them.

LID: In your visits you undoubtedly met many ordinary Iraqis, Christian and Muslim. Did you ever hear them – or even sense in them – say that the country was a terrible oppression, or dominated by a small corrupt ruling class? In other words did you feel, as a Catholic priest and before God, that the place was a hellhole to live in?

FB: There was no more corruption in Iraq than there was in Italy, with its numerous scandals, like Parmalat, in recent years. There was never corruption in Iraq like the Enron affair in the U.S., or the ELF affair (oil-company money for the political parties) in Paris, or in Germany or Japan where bribes and financial rip-offs are at the head of the international corruption league. There was corruption just as in the rest of the world, and one thing is for sure: the administration in Washington was in no position to cast the first stone.

The kind of political oppression in Iraq under Saddam might be compared to that of certain Latin America countries during the last fifty years. Political opponents of Saddam Hussein were generally eliminated just as the CIA organized the elimination of certain political powers in Latin America or Asia, governments which were in opposition to Washington policy or which threatened the interests of the United States. In Iraq, however, political opposition to the status quo was not tolerated and was put down.

Of course this is not to put the actions of Saddam Hussein in his country on the same level as those of the CIA around the world. What it is important to remember is that the countries, governments, states, and individuals who opposed the policies of Washington have been eliminated: the states through aerial bombardment; the political leaders by the financing, organizing, and implementing of coups d'état and the overthrow of regimes; the individuals by paid assassins or members of the security services. It is for this reason that the United States is the last country in the world to lecture others about morals.

LID: Undoubtedly, you met many of the leading Christian dignitaries on your visits to Iraq. Did you feel that as a Christian minority they were being oppressed, or did they breath the air of freedom? We ask this question because Messrs. Bush and Blair made great play of their alleged "Christian faith," and because it appears that Christians are now suffering disproportionately under the occupation.

FB: Iraq was a model for peaceful co-existence between Christians and Muslims. For the last thirty years there was not a single example of conflict or rivalry between the two communities. There is nothing very Christian about either Tony Blair or George W. Bush, and I believe that for them to understand the true relationship between the Christians and Muslims of Iraq, they should spend several weeks holiday in Baghdad, Basra, or Mosul. In this way they would discover that the situation is no longer what it used to be. Today bombs are exploding in churches, and every week the children of Iraqi families are being abducted and held for extortionate ransoms. Since the occupation of Iraq, more than 80,000 Christians have fled the country. As one can see, this is the opposite of "democratization."

I think that it is useful to recall that it was in Iraq that the dialogue between the Muslim and Christian worlds *began.* A thousand years ago the dialogue between Christians and Muslims really began, and it is precisely in Baghdad that there took place the first attempt at *rapprochement,* of the study of Christian thought, of research on Western culture. It is precisely in Baghdad, during the ninth and tenth centuries, that a cooperation between Muslims and Christians grew up which took concrete form in the translation into Arabic of the science and philosophy of the Greeks. The close contact established between Muslim and Christian intellectuals resulted in the first theological efforts to pin down the points of agreement between the two religions. The work and the example of the intellectual community of Baghdad inspired Spanish and Sicilian thinkers to work for a new dialogue between the two communities at the height of the Middle Ages. The first translations of Arab philosophy into Latin were used in the work of St. Thomas Aquinas.

In 1076, the Sultan of Andalusia, al-Nasir, sent gifts and freed Christian slaves to Pope Gregory VII. The Pope replied to him by letter in terms which are surprising for the age:

> The Good Lord, Creator of all things, without Whom we would be unable to do anything or think anything, has inspired this gesture of your heart. He who enlightens all souls come into this world has enlightened your spirit. Because Almighty God, who seeks the salvation of all men and wishes to lose none, approves especially in us the fact that after loving oneself we should love our neighbor, and that we might do nothing to others that we would not wish done unto ourselves; and above all because we believe and confess equally one God who reveals Himself in different ways, and whom we praise and venerate daily as the Creator and Lord of this world. We pray, with our hearts and our lips, that after long life on earth, this same God will lead you to the bosom of happiness of the Most Holy Patriarch, Abraham.

This remarkable document, which predates the Second Vatican Council by nine centuries, contains all the elements of dialogue with Islam, proposes the unity of believers based upon the cult and prayer of one God, regarded as the basis of common belief in Abraham and in the hope of eternal happiness for Muslims and Christians. But the letter of the Pontiff goes beyond the belief in one God, and expresses concrete proposals: to seek to do good, to love one another reciprocally, to seek a peaceful world for the good of all.

Prior to the American invasion, Iraqi Christians could tell you that it was precisely on the basis of these proposals that they maintained and nourished a dialogue and a cooperation with their Muslim brothers. Iraq was one of the few Arab countries where this understanding and cooperation was carried out fully and openly. Today, everything has changed. It is, then, all the sadder to see this country, the first to have begun a religious dialogue between Christians and Muslims, attacked and persecuted so cruelly today by a "Christian" superpower. It is distressing to see thus compromised the work of centuries aimed at an authentic dialogue, and a reciprocal understanding and mutually beneficial cooperation for both religions.

LID: How were you received by the Muslim authorities in Iraq both before and after the invasion?

FB: In 1998, on a trip to the south of Iraq, I visited the Shiite Mosque of Najaf. Inside the Islamic sanctuary is the tomb of Ali, the son-in-law of Mohammed, and the founder of the Shiites. I asked the sanctuary's authorities if I might enter to see the tomb of Ali. After a few minutes of discussion between the Muslim authorities, I was granted permission. I think that I am the only Catholic priest who has ever entered this shrine, holy to Islam. I requested, too, that the cameraman who was accompanying me might enter likewise in order to film. They agreed and the splendid images that are to be found within the mosque are unique. I did not obtain this favor through menaces or arrogance, but through simplicity, through extending a friendly hand and speaking kindly. It is the anti-Arab politics of the United States this last thirty years which has created Islamic extremism, and a reaction from a good part of the Arab world against America. Only discussion, cultural and religious contact, and reciprocal respect and cooperation can destroy Islamic extremism and groups like al-Qaeda. The attack upon, and the invasion of, Iraq has only heightened the risks of terrorist action, exasperated the Arab peoples, and nourished the networks of Islamic organizations.

LID: Do you feel that Iraq under either of the puppet governments put in place by the Anglo-American forces possesses any legitimacy with the Iraqi population, be they Shiite, Sunni, or Christian?

FB: The Interim Prime Minister, Allawi, was not liked nor accepted by a large majority of the Iraqi people. The country no longer has a constitution. The main party in the country, the Ba'ath Party, has been forcibly dissolved and excluded from the life of the country. Many new parties were unable to present a candidate. Thanks to the chaos and anarchy which reigns throughout the country, the populations of several regions were not able to vote. In such a context, how can we imagine that these elections were democratic and representative of the wishes of Iraqis? It is not possible. These recent elections cannot be accepted nor seen as valid by the vast majority of the Iraqi people, and this has made the situation even more confused and dangerous.

LID: Do you believe that the country is better off or worse off since the overthrow of Saddam's government, as far as the population at large is concerned?

FB: When I used to go to Iraq, I could go out at 10 o'clock at night, call a cab by a simple gesture of the hand, travel to the other side of a town, and return to the hotel in the same way. I offer a free trip to Iraq to anyone who agrees to do the same thing today. I do not believe that I will have many takers! In the past, there were no bombs at the offices of the UN, or of humanitarian organizations, and no one was kidnapped. Now bombs are not merely aimed at the UN, at humanitarian groups, and at churches. People are kidnapped, bombs are exploding everywhere, and disorder and insecurity reigns throughout Iraq. And against this background, American planes continue to bomb villages and massacre hundreds of men, women, and children.

LID: Many have said that they expect that Saddam and the members of his government will be brought to trial soon, and that Saddam, at the very least, will be executed. How do you view this from a constitutional and legal point of view on the one hand, and from the moral and practical (in terms of how it will be received by Iraqis and the Arab world in general) point of view?

FB: I do not know how a country which does not possess a real constitution could possibly have an efficient legal system. I do not see what national legitimacy a court could have when it has been put in place by "a government" which is subservient to a force of military occupation. The secretary-general of the United Nations, Kofi Annan, has stated that the war against Iraq was illegal. Numerous countries have stated the same thing about the war against Iraq and her occupation. If the war against Iraq and the military occupation of the country is illegal, what legitimacy could a court possibly have to judge the President of a country – a member of the United Nations – who has been arrested illegally?

The Washington government does not want a trial of Saddam Hussein before an international court because, their war being illegal and in violation of international law, this would also necessitate bringing George W. Bush and his administration before the same court.

LID: What do you believe is the cause – or are the causes – for this Second Gulf War, and whose interests do you think they serve?

FB: I believe that this war has been, above all, a personal vendetta of the Bush family against Saddam Hussein. This whole gruesome affair has nothing whatever to do with weapons of mass destruction, or with "dictatorship," or with the "liberation of the Iraqi people." And it is no way a war against terrorism. Osama bin Laden is a Saudi, not an Iraqi, and there was no connection whatever between Iraq and al-Qaeda and its attack on America on September 11, 2001.

Also, there is a strategic factor: American military forces could no longer remain in Saudi Arabia; the American military presence in Iraq straddles the Arab countries of the Middle East; and with the same military presence in Afghanistan, it means that Iran finds itself with American forces on a couple of its borders. Nor is the question of oil an indifferent one. With oil at a record high in price, controlling Iraqi oil is most certainly good business.

LID: We understand that you were quite recently in Syria, and that you spoke to a large number of Muslims and their clerics? What did you say to them, and what do you hope came from such a meeting? Do you intend to continue such work?

FB: I travel regularly to Syria, but also to Lebanon and other Arab countries. I am often invited to conferences of religious exchange between Christians and Muslims. I have been invited to speak to Muslims at Friday prayer in Syria and other Arab countries in order to extend a fraternal hand to the Muslim world and to deepen and strengthen the contacts between Europe and the Arab world, and between Christians and Muslims.

LID: It seems increasingly possible that the Americans are going to try to force themselves upon the Syrian Ba'ath government. Do you think that the Syrians will fight if push comes to shove, especially in the light of the fact that American forces are not doing especially well fighting the Ba'athist insurgents in Iraq?

FB: Syria is not Iraq, and even less is it an Afghanistan under the Taliban. Another attack against an Arab country would be considered as an attack upon the entire Arab world. Such stupidity risks unleashing a terrible cataclysm throughout the Middle East and even beyond. On the other hand, Europe has important economic and cultural interests and exchanges with Syria and Lebanon, especially France. An attack on this Arab country could conceivably provoke a definitive split between America and Europe, which no one wishes.

LID: What in your opinion is needed to bring peace back to Iraq?

FB: The only way to bring peace back to Iraq is, firstly, to give it back to the Iraqi people. That means the withdrawal of all the occupation forces from the country and leaving the Iraqis to determine their future. Freeing the country of such occupation forces does not mean abandoning it; quite the contrary. Once the military forces have returned to their respective countries, an economic, industrial, social, and cultural cooperation could be developed between Europe and America, and Iraq, which could grow and flourish to the benefit of all. Throughout human history, a country occupied by the military forces of another country has only recovered its peace when the occupation forces left the country. Iraq will be no exception to this rule. One does not export "democracy" through bombing populations, through imprisoning and torturing those who oppose the occupation. Did not Jesus Christ Himself say: "Love your enemies, do good to those who persecute you"? Jesus Christ taught peace. George W. Bush taught war. It is for each of us to choose our camp.

THE EDITORS' GLOSS: Milton Viorst's recollection of the last months of 2002, and indeed the last months of Saddam Hussein's government, makes for sad reading. Tariq Aziz possessed, evidently, a clear sense of foreboding even though, in November of 2002, there was good reason to be optimistic. UN weapons inspectors had just returned to Iraq. France and others in the UN Security Council had succeeded in keeping the requirements of the "last-chance" UN resolution – 1441 – relatively moderate in form, over and against the "blustery and bellicose original draft," as Robert Dreyfuss put it in his December 30, 2002, piece for *American Prospect*. But Aziz seemed to know the future instinctively. He had seen it before in the frankly mendacious treatment he had had at American and British hands in the past.

In retrospect there's plenty of reason to understand why Aziz felt the way he did. Dreyfuss's chronicle of the background to Resolution 1441 should have been indication enough of what was to come for anyone paying attention. Kofi Annan warned of "hidden triggers" that the U.S. sought to implant in the resolution, providing an excuse for unilateral military action. "I think the discussions in the council made it clear we should be looking for something meaningful and not for excuses to do something," he said, knowingly, of American designs. In case that's not clear enough, Dreyfuss reports a comment that was overheard at a November 2002 meeting at the American Enterprise Institute, where, he says, the "mood wasn't good," thanks to the return of UN inspectors to Iraq, who might have defused war fever. "We can only hope and pray that this doesn't mean we are boxed in," Dreyfuss reported a high-level Department of Defense official, involved with planning Bush's war, as saying. With sentiments like that, one can only speculate as to who it was he was praying to.

Portrait of Noble Resignation:
Tariq Aziz and the Last Days of Saddam Hussein
• • • • • • • • •

Milton Viorst

TARIQ AZIZ SAW the dream of a lifetime vanishing before his eyes. "When we made this revolution we were young men in our thirties," he said during our meeting in Baghdad in September 2002, "and now we're in our sixties. We have made mistakes. Maybe we've been in power too long. But we've done good things for our country and we're proud of our work. Now we have to contemplate that an American attack will wipe it all out." Aziz's tone was free of defiance. It was, rather, a message suffused with despair.

Aziz was, like most Iraqis of his generation, imbued from childhood with a deep indignation of imperialism. A monarchy installed by Britain was still in power when, as a teenager, he enlisted in the revolution. Saddam Hussein, several years his junior, was shepherding goats among his clansmen in the village of Tikrit. By the time Iraq's king was overthrown in 1958, Aziz had sold his soul to Saddam, the up-and-coming leader of the Ba'ath Party, in the revolution's behalf. A few years later, Saddam came to power, and Aziz could exult in the fact that the goal of the revolution had been met: Iraq was sovereign, for the first time in centuries governing itself. Now, with American battalions poised on the horizon, Aziz foresees imperialism's return.

"I look at the situation philosophically," Aziz once said to me "The West is not prepared to accept a strong, modern, assertive developed country in the Arab world. I'm not a strong believer in conspiracies, but they do exist. And they exist more in our part of the world than elsewhere, because we have oil, a strategic position and Israel. This latest thing started with the collapse of the Soviet Union in Eastern Europe. Since then, America has become more and more arrogant. Our people are frustrated, our mood is fatalistic. It seems to be our tradition to suffer and to fail."

Tariq Aziz is known to the world as the voice – sometimes sooth-
ing, often irascible – of the government of Saddam Hussein. In the flow
charts of power, he was more than a spokesman. He was a member of
the Revolutionary Command Council, the state's highest authority. He
belongsed to the leadership of the Ba'ath Party, the ruling political body.
And he was the deputy prime minister, reporting only to Saddam, who
held the titles of Prime Minister and President. Yet, for all the power of his
offices, Aziz was regarded as an outsider in the ruling hierarchy. It was a
role that came to him naturally.

Born in a Christian village, Aziz was the son of a functionary in the
governorate of Mosul, a major city in northern Iraq. When he was ten, his
father, for unexplained reasons, left the bureaucracy and moved the family
to Baghdad, where he found work as a waiter in what has been described
as a seedy bar. The family's rootlessness, in a society that normally ties its
members for life to their place of birth, made Aziz a cultural misfit. This
role was reinforced by his Christian identity.

Aziz is a Chaldean Christian, one of 400,000 in a land of 20 million
Muslims. For Arab Christians to become Ba'athis was not unusual; many
were attracted to the party's secularism, which promised to erase religious
distinctions in the society. Michel Aflaq, the party founder, was himself
a Christian. Ethnically, Chaldeans are more closely related to the Biblical
Babylonians than to the Arabian tribesmen who settled Mesopotamia
in the seventh century; some Iraqis do not even regard them as Arabs.
Culturally, they tend to be richer, better educated and more widely traveled than other Iraqis. Many have emigrated to America, including at least
one in-law of Aziz. Iraqis say that Saddam sees Aziz's religion as an asset,
since a Chaldean could never be a rival for power in a Muslim land. Aziz
married a Chaldean and has three children, one of them named Saddam.
But it was politically useful for him to change his own Chaldean-sounding
name, Mikhail You Hanna, to the Arabic name by which he is currently
known.

Recruited by the Ba'ath Party while majoring in English at the Baghdad
College of Fine Arts, Aziz was from the start an intellectual in an organization dominated by roughnecks. Saddam himself rose through the ranks
on the strength of clan connections, an instinctive canniness, and a disposition to brutality. His circle was made up chiefly of friends and kin from
Tikrit, many of whom, like him, had not finished high school. Very early,
Saddam took a liking to Aziz and saw his intellect as potentially useful in
party struggles. But while Aziz climbed the civilian ladder to power after

the Ba'athis seized power, his party rivals established beachheads within the army and the secret police. Until even recently, he was unloved by the toughs who were closest to Saddam, but he benefited from the leader's protection and had access to his ear.

Aziz's first official post was editor of the party newspaper, *al-Thwart,* which he used to burnish Saddam's image. In 1974, he became information minister and, a few years later, foreign minister. In 1980, soon after Iran's Islamic revolution, he was the target of an assassination attempt by Shiite radicals linked to Teheran. Saddam, claiming the attempt was directed at him, replied by executing some 600 of the Shiite faithful and expelling 100,000 more. Saddam then used the episode to purge Shiites from the government, relying further on his Sunni base to tighten his tyranny. Aziz was among the few surviving outsiders. He often cites the assassination attempt as proof that Iraq cannot possibly sympathize with Islamic extremists, including Osama bin Laden. The episode, within the context of a struggle for preeminence between Iraq's secular and Iran's religious revolutions, was a factor in igniting the Iraq-Iran war.

As wartime head of foreign affairs, Aziz reached the pinnacle of his influence. Served by his mastery of English and finely honed negotiating skills, he lobbied for Iraq in the capitals of the world. He also shaped a foreign ministry that was acknowledged by the international community to be highly competent, with well-trained professionals rather than party hacks in charge of conducting Iraq's diplomatic business.

Aziz's efforts broke the ice with Egypt, from which Iraq had been estranged since Cairo's 1979 peace agreement with Israel. He supervised a deal that brought badly needed fighter planes and missiles from France, with which he has maintained a special relationship. He also presided in 1984 over the restoration of relations with the United States, which Iraq had severed during the Six-Day War of 1967. Received royally at the White House, Aziz predicted an extended "honeymoon" with America, and announced that Iraq's leaders, having matured, were ready to abandon diplomatic "rejectionism," even with regard to Israel. His rivals grumbled that he had become America's man, which seemed plausible enough from his statements that, when the war was over, Iraq would emulate the West in creating a free and democratic state.

Saddam's dictatorship did not become free and democratic, of course, and the "honeymoon" with Washington did not last much beyond the 1988 Iraq-Iran cease-fire. Washington collided with Baghdad over loan agreements, oil prices and arms purchases, and denounced Iraq for gassing Kurdish villagers, which Aziz vehemently denied. Saddam launched fiery rhetorical attacks on Israel and, over Western protests, Iraq executed Farzad Barzoft, an Anglo-Iranian journalist on charges of spying. Aziz's spin on the deterioration was that the U.S., profiting from the end of the cold war, decided to crush any ambitions Iraq might have to dominate the Persian Gulf, with its vast oil reservoirs. In 1990, Saddam raised the stakes by invading Kuwait. The first President Bush replied with a massive attack that decimated Iraq. A decade later, his son declared his intention to clean up the issues that the Gulf War had left unresolved.

In a government as tightly closed as Saddam's, it was not easy to determine where Aziz stood in deliberations on how to respond to Mr. Bush. Aziz, who answered a wide range of questions with candor, was notably evasive about relations among Iraqi leaders. Experts on the Iraqi system – diplomats, scholars, defected officials – mostly agree that after thirty years in power, the men around Saddam overcame their mutual antagonisms to work together smoothly. Part of the explanation is that each had his own domain, Aziz's being foreign relations. It is agreed that all were careful to suppress opinions, and even information, that Saddam did not want to hear. A Saudi intermediary at the negotiations to end the Iraq-Iran War relates that Aziz insisted that a Saudi prince dispatch to Saddam an unacceptable Iranian proposal, declining to deliver it himself. Certainly, no Iraqi doubts that, in the end, all decisions were made by Saddam, and by Saddam alone.

If there was any rearrangement of the power balance over the years, it was in favor of Qusay Hussein, Saddam's second son. Saddam is one of the aging Arab revolutionaries who, having overthrown kings, seek to pass power – under a system dubbed "dynastic republicanism" – to their sons. Assad in Syria succeeded in doing it; Mubarak in Egypt and Qathafi in Libya are working at it. Qusay was fingered as heir-apparent after a succession of well-publicized escapades left Uday, his elder brother, with a reputation for recklessness. Saddam relegated Uday to the direction of youth programs and an official newspaper, while Qusay was trained in the apparatus of the army, the party and the secret police, where real authority lies. Qusay held high posts in these organizations and, according to a British report, he might have been in charge of Iraq's chemical and biological weapons. Like his father, Qusay operated behind the scenes, rarely appearing in public. Iraqis see him as a shadowy figure who was ruthless, silent, cruelly ambitious and unlikely to change the way the regime conducted its business.

Qusay, for reasons that appear more related to family than policy, sought openly to undermine the influence of Tariq Aziz. A few years ago, he imprisoned Aziz's son, Ziad, on a charge of corruption, which Iraqis recognized – in a government riddled with corruption – as throwing down the gauntlet. Qusay, not Aziz, is said to have persuaded Saddam to undertake an offensive to circumvent the UN embargo in force since the end of the Gulf War and to reduce Iraq's diplomatic isolation. Begun in 1998, the initiative succeeded in improving Iraq's relations with its neighbors and with the Arab world, while swelling Saddam's support at home by raising popular standards of living. It also provided disturbing evidence to President Bush, who took office two years later, that Saddam's regime, unless disciplined, would in all likelihood grow stronger.

When Mr. Bush, in September 2002, appeared before the UN to put forth his series of demands on Iraq, however, it was Tariq Aziz, not the reclusive Qusay who was called upon to answer. In my meeting with him, Aziz declared that Iraq would not submit to any of Mr. Bush's demands, including the readmission of the UN weapons inspectors. "President Bush has made clear that even if the inspectors come back, there is no guarantee that they will prevent war," he said. "We know that Iraqis, not Americans, will be the major victims of a war, and maybe we can delay it. But if Bush wants it, war will come whatever we do." Saddam himself was quoted as telling an Arab foreign minister, "If I allow inspectors to return, I'm allowing the end of the regime." It was the same hard line he took with President Bush's father in refusing to evacuate Kuwait in 1990. Twice in an hour of talks with me, Aziz echoed this position with the grim explanation, "We're doomed if we do and doomed if we don't."

Aziz, like other Iraqi officials I met in Baghdad, made much of allegations that American spies had worked within the UN inspection teams. The allegations surfaced in 1998. UN records make a strong case that until then Iraq, in the hope of ending the embargo, had submitted, however reluctantly, to the inspectors, who made major progress in finding and destroying arms, especially chemical stocks. Based largely on leaks by the inspectors themselves, the charges of American infiltration changed the atmosphere, stiffening Iraqi resistance.

American authorities never denied the charges, arguing instead that spying was necessary to locate hidden weapons. Iraqi officials claimed that the espionage, far from targeting weapons, was directed at the whereabouts of Iraqi leaders. Late in 1998, Washington announced that it would bomb weapons sites throughout Iraq in response to Saddam's stonewalling. The

UN reacted to the warning by withdrawing its inspectors, and four days of bombing followed. Iraqis said the bombing was aimed not at weapons sites at all but at killing their leaders, particularly Saddam Hussein.

"By the time they left," Aziz said irritably, "what we had were not weapons inspectors but spies." The words brought me back to a remark he made to me some years before about the trial of the Anglo-Iranian journalist. "Barzoft was a spy," he said. "We punished him the way we punish others for this crime. We are very sensitive about security matters in our region. We react strongly, but that is how we are."

Saddam himself is famous for this sensitivity, especially as it regards his own safety. He was known to change bedrooms every night and desist from speaking on the phone. He almost never greeted his people in public. I have heard Iraqis mutter that, in his concern for his own skin, he abandoned the duties of leadership. Aziz himself told me the reason Saddam never went to the UN to speak out, as President Bush did, for his country's position was that he was sure the Americans would try to kill him. He acknowledged that the security issue complicated Iraq's options, making the first George Bush's insistence on withdrawal from Kuwait seem a cut-and-dried choice. Aziz left no doubt that, whatever Saddam's calculations for passing on the regime to his son, his belief that the weapons inspectors were a threat to his life stood as a barrier to ending the crisis.

After my talk with Aziz, I spent some time wandering through downtown Baghdad with an eye to comparing the public's mood with his obvious despair. The damage inflicted by the Gulf War had long since been repaired, and the larger-than-life tableaux of Saddam which leap out at every intersection had been refurbished, with the same face looking a little older. The tiny shops that dominate both the twentieth-century boulevards and the ancient souk which runs along the Tigris were vibrant with people. The city did not suggest a society living at the edge of impoverishment, much less of war. No gangs of workmen were digging bomb shelters or building walls of sandbags. The young men who stood smoking on street corners wore jeans, not uniforms. If Iraq was getting ready to resist foreign armies, it was mobilizing elsewhere, not in Baghdad.

Talkative as ever, the shopkeepers showed no animosity toward me, notwithstanding their daily dose of anti-American propaganda. All seemed to know of Mr. Bush's demands from listening to *Aljazeera*, VOA, the BBC, or Radio Monte Carlo. In 1991, after Iraq's defeat, the message I heard on the street – generally whispered, but sometimes delivered with bravado – was that it was time for Saddam Hussein to depart. But his support had obviously rebounded. The Iraqis I met on this visit directed their anger at the United States for a decade of bombing raids, as well as for the ongoing shortages that the embargo produced. If, in 1991, they understood that the world was reacting to the Iraqi occupation of Kuwait, a decade later they maintained they had no idea what sins Iraq had committed, or what America wanted. They seemed to speak as nationalists, not Saddam-lovers, in contending that the government, in defying Bush, was watching out for them.

Still, once past the anger, I heard an echo of Aziz's message of resignation. When I asked young men whether they would fight, their response was a shrug, or at best a dutiful yes. Merchants, after reminiscing about holidays in Italy when Iraq was rich, before the wars, said such days were unlikely ever to return. One evening I attended a gathering in the garden of a historic house along the river, where artists and intellectuals, conveying no obvious patriotism, much less personal loyalty to Saddam, nonetheless declared their gratitude to the government for distributing food rations at the beginning of every month, for keeping the schools running albeit with antiquated text books, and for maintaining medical services notwithstanding shortages of drugs and equipment. They talked of their pride in keeping their society intact. Yet they said they expected their lives to take a turn for the worse, without their being able to do anything to stop it.

One woman told me the public mood recalled to her the bleak days of the Gulf War when a reporter on an American ship would announce over the BBC that missiles had just been dispatched, inviting three or four minutes of sheer terror until they struck. "I feel President Bush has already launched the missiles," she said. "Whether they fall on me or on my neighbor is so random. But there is nothing we can do. We can only wait." Turning to metaphor she added, "When the Americans finish with us, we'll just get up, take our brooms, sweep away the rubble and start over again." A few Iraqis predicted wryly that after Saddam had been killed off, the Americans would present them with a fresh Saddam, scarcely different from the original.

Over the weekend that Tariq Aziz was telling journalists like me that Iraq would not readmit the weapons inspectors. Naji Sabri, Baghdad's foreign minister, was meeting in New York with the assembled foreign ministers of the Arab League. Sabri's older brother, once a high foreign ministry official, had been executed by Saddam in 1979 for involvement in a conspiracy; somehow Naji was pronounced clean by the security services and allowed to go on with his career. Through Sabri, the Arabs delivered to Saddam their belief that the impasse over the inspectors was providing President Bush with a pretext for starting a war that was likely to affect all of them. In the past, Saddam had not concealed his contempt for his fellow Arabs for submitting to Western power. Now the Arabs were telling him that, if he wanted their support, it was his turn to yield.

That Monday, Aziz had been scheduled to open an international conference of largely left-wing politicians and intellectuals who had converged on Baghdad to proclaim their solidarity with Iraq's defiance. But soon after the delegates read in the shabby English-language newspaper published daily by the information ministry that Saddam had been in non-stop session with the national leadership, an announcement was made that the conference was postponed. It was a tip-off that something big was afoot.

The next day, the world learned that Iraq, in a formal letter from Sabri to Kofi Annan, the UN secretary-general, had agreed to the weapons inspectors' unconditional return. Aziz had spent much of the weekend in long-distance consultation with Sabri and Annan, helping to draft the letter. It described the inspectors' return as "the indispensable first step toward an assurance that Iraq no longer possesses weapons of mass destruction." Mr. Bush reacted by dismissing the announcement's significance, but all Baghdad took the letter as a 180 degree turn, and seemed to breathe a sigh of relief.

When the international conference opened that afternoon, Aziz made a cryptic allusion to the New York meetings, the only reference to Iraq's change of position. The delegates responded with effusive speeches thanking Saddam for his wisdom. Later, I learned that Saddam had personally monitored every moment of the New York talks before yielding to the Arab insistence on his acceptance of the inspectors. His decision did not, of course, end the story. After September, with backing from France and the Arab states, Aziz's clients, Saddam waged a rear guard action in the Security Council over the terms of the return. In late November, the inspectors arrived in Baghdad, initiating what was expected to be months of work. Saddam had won a respite from the threat of war, though it was surely not enough to lift Tariq Aziz's foreboding about the fate of his life's mission. As we now know, his foreboding was proven sadly prophetic.

. . . we support the aspirations of the people to build a future based on democracy and to regain their sovereignty.
AND THAT REQUIRES . . . ANY FOREIGN OCCUPATION . . . TO END.

> —Scott McClellan, White House press
> secretary, March 4, 2005, evidently
> oblivious to the obvious parallel between
> the situation of Iraq and that of Lebanon, to
> which he was referring

We have had enough of his nonsense . . . . We don't accept that a non-Iraqi should try to enforce his control over Iraqis, regardless of their sect – whether Sunnis, Shiites, Arabs, or Kurds.

> —Sheik Ahmad Khanjar, leader of the Albu
> Ali clan in Ramadi, Iraq, August 2005,
> on the attempt by al-Zarqawi to provoke
> sectarian strife in Iraq

ENDURING INJUSTICE:
IRAQ AND THE
CURRENT POLITICAL LANDSCAPE

THE EDITORS' GLOSS: On July 28, 2005, Secretary Rumsfeld explained why he was so adamant that the new "Iraqi government" should get on with writing its constitution: "We have troops on the ground," he said. "People get killed." Yes, they do, Mr. Secretary: the price of imperial occupation and forcible "nation-building."

Col. de Grand Pré's essay answers the question that the secretary's remarks beg: troops on the ground get killed because they're not wanted in the country they're occupying. Who it is that doesn't want them is the subject of the Colonel's essay; why they are fighting follows as a plain enough conclusion. The press and the administration are taking great pains to portray our Iraqi opponents as "dead-enders" and "Islamist fanatics," in order to "prove" that those on the other side do not offer legitimate resistance but merely wreak terrorist havoc.

Neutral observers disagree. One unlikely voice in the debate is that of an Italian, Simona Torretta. She and her colleague from an aid group, "A Bridge to Baghdad," were seized by rebels on September 7, 2004, yet the experience didn't affect her point of view in the slightest. "I said it before the kidnapping and I repeat it today," she told *Corriere della Sera* in an interview published on October 1, 2004. "I am against the kidnapping of civilians," she said, but "you have to distinguish between terrorism and resistance. The guerrilla war is justified . . . . "

An Italian judge also made a name for herself by defending the right to resistance, even by means we might consider somewhat "over the top." According to *Reuters* (April 21, 2005), Clementina Forleo caught some flack earlier this year "by dropping charges against suspected Islamic militants accused of helping to recruit suicide bombers for Iraq – saying the alleged crimes amounted to foreign guerrilla activity . . . . " Her ruling pointed out, based on "conventional international doctrine," that "the differentiating factor [between guerrilla activity and terrorism] does not appear to be the instrument used, but the target in one's sights"; "terrorists" fail to distinguish between civilian and military targets. Foreign guerrilla activity, however, targets "a foreign occupying army or against a state structure held by the combatants as illegitimate." Reminiscent of the Bush-administration approach to such impertinence, her Reforms Minister called the ruling "stomach turning"; the Communications Minister said she was "extremely wrong"; and the Justice Minister opened an investigation looking for "negligence."

To Forleo's credit, she is suing them for defamation.

C H A P T E R
38

Nemesis and Name-Calling:
Who Are the Iraqi Rebels?
· · · · · · · · · ·
Col. Donn de Grand Pré, USA (ret.)

> "'Insurgency' is one of the most misleading words. Insurgency
> assumes that we had gone to Iraq, won the war and a group of
> disgruntled people began to operate against us. That would be an
> insurgency. But we are fighting the people we started the war against.
> We are fighting the Ba'athists plus nationalists. We took Baghdad
> easily. It wasn't because we won. We took Baghdad because they
> pulled back and let us take it, and decided to fight a war that had been
> pre-planned."
>
> —Seymour Hersh

THE IRAQI "RESISTANCE" is probably something of a mystery to most Americans, and this is largely thanks to the uninformative nature of our spineless media. Now some might think it "clever" to invade a country and then pretend that those who oppose the invasion by force of arms don't represent the people who have just been conquered, that they represent, rather, "a hatred of democracy," are "people who hate freedom," and practice "terrorism." It might also be "clever" to witness, on a daily basis, dozens of attacks on the occupying military forces and still insist that those attacks are the crazy "fringe" antics of misfits, jihadis, and "extremists" rather than the operations of a clandestine paramilitary force operating in defense of its country.

The problem with this vision of the situation in Iraq, however, is that it is not credible. Indeed, the facts of the case are all to the contrary, and only a willful denial of reality, or sheer delusion, permits it to be maintained. It stems from the ideological premise that the "American way" is so obviously superior that only misfits and "extremists" would presume to oppose it by force of arms. Complicit in furthering this viewpoint are the media and other "professional" commentators at think tanks and elsewhere. The terrorist targets of Bush's "Global War on Terror"(GWOT), such as al-Qaeda and Abu Musab al-Zarqawi – both of which are blown out of all proportion by the mainstream media – are also convenient allies, too, in the effort to portray the Iraqi resistance as something other than what it is.

The facts, as we will see, contradict this "official" vision of the resistance in Iraq. In spite of continual insistence that "we're not fighting the Iraqi people," the truth of the matter is that we *are* – along with their deposed, legally recognized government. Continued denial of the situation cannot and does not bode well for American prospects of "success" in Iraq – and there is no indication that things will change anytime soon.

Spinning Fact to Fit Ideology

The media problem

A classic illustration of the inadequacy of the media's approach to the Iraqi resistance was provided by a piece that ran in the *Christian Science Monitor* called "Coming to Terms with the Guerrillas in Their Midst." The author, Ruth Walker, provided – no doubt unwittingly – an important insight into the thinking of the Bush administration, and the way the American press, the Republic's Fourth Estate, reports that thinking in lockstep march.

Referring to a Donald Rumsfeld Pentagon press conference on June 30, 2003, she relates that the Defense Secretary bristled at the notion that the Iraq war was "a guerrilla war." He explained:

> I guess the reason I don't use the phrase "guerrilla war" is because there isn't one, and it would be a misunderstanding and a miscommunication to you and to the people of the country and the world.[1]

Even then, such an argument was less than credible, but it was part of the pattern of what passes for thinking in the Bush administration.

But back to Ruth Walker. She explains how the *CSM* staff – and by extension all mainstream hacks – anguished over the choice of words to describe the Iraqis fighting the American occupation. The word eventually settled upon was, of course, "insurgent," a term deemed "neutral" – as if the spilling of blood and brains could be written in neutral terms. It was chosen from a list of candidates. "Guerrilla" was unacceptable because it had taken on shades of Che Guevara; "rebel" was equally inappropriate

---

1. DoD News Briefing with Secretary Rumsfeld and Gen. Meyers, June 30, 2003 (http://www.defenselink.mil/transcripts/2003/tr20030630-secdef0321.html).

because it conjured up images of good ol' Johnny Reb; and "militant" didn't make the grade because it seemed too politically radical, although an isolated exception has been made for Abu Musab al-Zarqawi.

Yet the most peculiar conclusion was found in the penultimate paragraph where Walker wrote:

> "[R]esistance" is a term that popped up briefly in our newsroom a few months ago for consideration as a possible designation for the insurgents in Iraq. "Resistance," as the dictionary puts it, is "the organized underground movement in a country fighting against a foreign occupation, a dictatorship, etc."[1]

Any person who has followed the Iraq debacle will not fail to appreciate that "resistance" is *exactly* the word to use, and yet it was deemed "too positive" by our "objective" press. "We decided it wasn't the right word," Walker said. "[A]ssociations with the French Resistance during World War II make it too positive a term, we concluded."[2]

So the term chosen for the resistance was based not upon objective definition – indeed, what could be a *more* accurate way to refer to the Iraqi resistance than as an "organized underground movement . . . fighting against . . . foreign occupation" – but rather upon a sense of what might be "too positive" a portrayal of Iraqis fighting *American occupation*: a portrayal of them as fighting for a legitimate goal rather than for a retrograde, "un-American," "anti-freedom" agenda. The choice speaks volumes about the reluctance of the American press to speak the truth and challenge Bush-administration rhetoric.

Coincidentally, Norman Solomon made just that observation in a regular "Media Beat" column for Fairness and Accuracy in Reporting (FAIR). He wrote: "When misleading buzzwords become part of the media landscape, they slant news coverage and skew public perceptions."[3] He went on to ask: when is an Iraqi *not* an Iraqi? When he is actively *fighting* the American occupation. Solomon pointed out that all the main papers were constantly referring to things like "pitched battles between insurgents and American and Iraqi forces." In other words, those fighting alongside American troops merit the term "Iraqi forces," while those fighting the forces of Baghdad's puppet regime are variously "insurgents," "terrorists,"

---

1. Ruth Walker, "Coming to Terms with the Guerrillas in Their Midst," *Christian Science Monitor*, November 19, 2004, online.

2. Walker, *op. cit.*

3. Norman Solomon, "A Voluntary Tic in Media Coverage of Iraq," *FAIR*, November 18, 2004, online.

or "former regime elements." Solomon says that an accurate terminology is possible,

> but the Bush administration – striving to promote the attitude that only U.S.-allied Iraqis are actual Iraqis worthy of the name – is eager to blur exactly what good reporting should clarify. And America's major media outlets are helpfully providing a journalistic fog around a central fact: the U.S. government is at war with many people it claims to be liberating.[1]

Towing the party line

The penchant for repeating ideological dogma is not limited to the journalists who play along with the administration position, seeking to gain "access" to relevant officials and headline-grabbing stories. Numerous think-tank "thinkers" also pontificate on matters political to a tune piped by administration officials, along with a whole range of other hacks, politicians, experts, and sundry cheerleaders for the war. All are more or less complicit in portraying the Iraqi rebels as "terrorists" because these cheerleaders "believe" in the ideology they publicize. For them that ideology is a *blinding* vision, which prevents them from seeing the truth of a situation over their dogmatic interpretation of it.

The first and most notable fruit of this blindness is a profound hypocrisy. It is seen and heard most everywhere, a cheap attempt to portray Iraqis opposed to the occupation – whether fighting or not – as something other than legitimate adversaries or people opposed in principal (with every right to be so) to the prospect of forced "Americanization."

Rumsfeld demonstrated this hypocrisy from the outset, referring to our opponents in the initial invasion as "terrorist death squads."[2] Edward Luttwak, the "renowned strategist" at the Center for Strategic and International Studies (CSIS), demonstrated it in a pre-war op-ed pointing out that Saddam's forces consisted of "untrained civilians with small arms they scarcely know how to use," few who "could actually fight with enough skill to inflict casualties," and others who "will no doubt scatter as soon as they come under fire." Saddam's *Fedayeen*, according to Luttwak, were "poorly trained villagers."[3] Either Luttwak believed his own rhetoric then – which the facts of two years' worth of guerrilla war have clearly disproved

---

1. *Ibid.*
2. See Col. Sam Gardiner's essay detailing this and other "information operations" conducted before and during the war, on pp. 605–642 of the present volume.—Ed.
3. "Saddam Street Fighters Will Be No Match for Allies' Elite," *The Telegraph*, March 9, 2003, online.

– or his stance was simply a useful element of Bush's plan to lead America into war by convincing her people that it would indeed be a "cakewalk." Now that the "insurgency" is giving us a run for our money, we hear from the same range of hacks and "experts" that, rather than the work of the "Iraqi people," attacks on "coalition forces" are the work of "dead enders" and "former regime elements" like Ba'athists, members of the Special and Republican Guard, the Intelligence Services, and even the *Fedayeen*! Never mind that it's actually *the same people* being discussed; at once both incompetent (before the war) and dastardly (afterwards). How quickly the pre-war condescension shifts to shock, dismay, and feigned moral outrage that our "terrorist" and "extremist" opponents "won't fight fair"! The only thing worse than contradictions of this sort are those that appear in one single bit of "journalism" simultaneously, like the warning – coming over two years after Luttwak's – from chief neocon ideologue Max Boot, who cautioned[1] against building up the enemy "into 10-foot-tall supermen" and suggested that "we realize how weak they actually are," and then admitted that "the Iraqi uprising will [not] be quickly or easily defeated" and that "coalition military forces cannot hope to achieve a military victory in the near future"!

How to make sense of this nonsense? Two issues seem to be at play here. One is the assumption that anyone in Iraq possessing the temerity to oppose the "American experiment" in the Middle East is already a terrorist ideologically – this is why Boot says that headlines chronicling the ongoing conflict are really "about the rebels' *reign of terror*" (emphasis mine); why Bush says that "[o]ur mission in Iraq is . . . hunting down the terrorists;"[2] and the new "Prime Minister" of Iraq refuses even the *Christian Science Monitor* compromise, insisting on calling the Iraqi fighters "terrorists."[3]

To maintain this interpretation, the facts and statistics are selectively highlighted and interpreted to fit a blatantly ideological portrayal of what's actually going on in Iraq – namely, the opposition of a few deadbeats to "democracy," "progress," and "freedom." This is, of course, reminiscent of the way information was "cherry-picked" to get us into this catastrophic war in the first place. Bogeymen such as al-Zarqawi and isolated attacks on

---

1. "Why the Rebels Will Lose," *Los Angeles Times*, June 23, 2005, online.

2. President Addresses Nation, Discusses Iraq, War on Terror, Fort Bragg, N.C., June 28, 2005 (http://www.whitehouse.gov/news/releases/2005/06/20050628-7.html).

3. Robin Wright and Jim VandeHei, "Unlikely Allies Map Future," *Washington Post*, June 24, 2005, p. A25: the article reported explicitly that al-Jaafari "[rejected] the term 'insurgent.'"

civilians become the total embodiment of what we're fighting in Iraq, notwithstanding the evidence – which we'll look at later – that al-Zarqawi's role is seriously overplayed (and that's putting it mildly!), and that the bulk of the rebels have repeatedly condemned strikes against non-military or illegitimate targets.

The second issue at play is a healthy dose of good ol' American exceptionalism, which translates our successes into the triumph of justice and simple failures into our victimization. Luttwak's op-ed was entitled "Saddam Street Fighters Will Be No Match for Allies' Elite" from precisely this standpoint: where we're likely to win it's portrayed as a righteous vindication of our "elite" technological (and, implicitly, moral) superiority. Saddam's men "[lack] the skill to hold their ground," he said, a presumptuous comment if ever there was one, because no army decimated by a dozen years of crippling sanctions would square off face to face against the Pentagon's half-trillion-dollar war machine. Yet when Saddam's men do "hold their ground," even if it's accomplished by "poking out from behind trees," it's nothing other than a "reign of terror"!

This American exceptionalism is best illustrated by considering what we would do if the situation were reversed. Had the Soviets paratrooped into Georgia, you can bet that every man, woman, and child would have grabbed shotgun and pitchfork to drive out the Bolsheviks. We boast of having done the same thing to the British, who were appalled that we refused to obey the "laws of war" and confront squads of redcoated marksmen with neat and disciplined lines of "poorly trained villagers" (to use Luttwak's inspiring image). Hollywood at least got this right: the heroes of both Mel Gibson's *The Patriot* and the well-known *Red Dawn* didn't "fight fair"; they hid in the mountains, wore civilian clothes or casual militia garb, and their tactic of choice was the ambush. When *we* do it, though, it's just another proof of what Rumsfeld recently said about America: it's "the last best hope on earth."[1]

The Bush administration's obsession with this conception of America as not a simple member of the family of nations but as the divinely appointed savior of the world continues to have tragic consequences, not the least of which is the rising American military death toll overseas. Stubborn insistence upon seeing the resistance in Iraq as the fruit of "terror" and "ideological extremism" does nothing for our troops except give them a straw man to fight. It does, however, keep the neoconservative ideological thread from unraveling. Confronting our *real* enemy – the Iraqis who

---

1. Town Hall Meeting, June 29, 2005 (http://www.defenselink.mil/speeches/2005/sp20050629-secdef1684.html).

aren't "terrorists" but who simply oppose our occupation – would involve the unlikely admission that our adversaries might be simply legitimate opponents, who are fighting according to their wits and resources, in exercise of a right (theirs *no less* than ours) to live free of occupying forces, to control their own destiny, and to fight coercion, invasion, and foreign control. But this kind of realism is only heard on the ground. Spc. John Bandy, of Alpha Company, Task Force 2-2, 1st Infantry Division, Fallujah, said of his experience, "It's intense, that's all there is to say. The determination these guys have against our forces, these little bands of guys shooting at tanks, it's almost admirable."[1]

Meanwhile, those with their heads in the clouds remain tragically free of any such "reality check." The respect of the simple soldier for his legitimate adversary, ready to fight to the death against tremendous odds regardless of his political or religious beliefs, is not likely to infect Bush and Co. any time soon, or puncture their overwhelming pride. And so much the worse for our troops.

The "central front" in the "War on Terror": who are we fighting?

At the outset, it was said to be a question of a few "malcontents" or "criminals." Then it became small bands of "thugs and mugs," followed by "terrorists," "foreign fighters," and then, only towards the latter part of 2004, did it regularly become "FRE" – "former regime elements."

Nowadays, the media is fairly united in referring to "Saddam loyalists" *and* "foreign terrorists." The latter, though, have pride of place in administration rhetoric, given their connection to the all-encompassing "war on terror." How accurate is it, though, to make Iraqi fighters out to be footsoldiers in the allegedly global struggle of Islamic "misfits" against "the home of the brave"?

One book that bears critically on this discussion is *Imperial Hubris*,[2] written by Michael Scheuer, a CIA analyst with 25 years experience. It is well written and forthright, and it does not play according to the rules of political correctness. The book is essentially about Afghanistan, al-Qaeda,

---

1. Quoted by *Traveling Soldier* (www.traveling-soldier.org). In contrast, the Iraqi troops working with the puppet government in Baghdad seem humiliated by what they experience of the American attitude. A recent report on the training of the "Iraqi army" indicated that the Iraqi troops "complain bitterly that their American mentors don't respect them. In fact, the Americans don't: frustrated U.S. soldiers question the Iraqis courage, discipline and dedication and wonder whether they will ever be able to fight on their own . . . . " (Anthony Shadid and Steve Fainaru, "Building Iraq's Army: Mission Improbable," *Washington Post*, June 10, 2005, online).

2. Washington, D.C.: Brassey's, 2004.

and what Scheuer frequently calls "an intensifying Islamist insurgency." He examines the response of American foreign policy to that "insurgency," pointing out that it is essentially unthinking, incoherent, indiscriminate, and cowardly. One thing it is not, however, is based on clear objectives meshed to credible means.

Scheuer rightly insists that we should appreciate and respect the fact that our so-called enemies, the "Islamists," by and large, are not using "God" as a convenient "politico-marketing tool" to gain support. Rather, they are, generally speaking, people who have a sincere and in many cases deep belief in God. We may say that their conception of God is wrong, that their interpretation of His Will is wrong, or that they use means that contradict God's designs; but we cannot deny their very real convictions. An appreciation of this fact is of a piece with an honest and honorable assessment of our "enemy." Just because men are on "the other side" does not make them insincere or hypocritical. They too can cling to a creed with faithfulness and sincerity, even if that creed doesn't include an idolatry of freedom and democracy.

Scheuer also insists that America will obligate itself to fighting this Islamist insurgency across the globe *unless* the country is prepared to change the one critical part of its foreign policy that provokes that insurgency. Scheuer puts it in question form:

> Does unvarying military, economic, and political support for Israel serve substantive – vice emotional – U.S. interests, those that, by definition, affect America's security? Do we totally support Israel because it is essential to our security, or because of habit, the prowess of Israel's American lobbyists and spies, the half-true mantra that Israel is a democracy, the fear of having no control over a state we allowed to become armed with WMD, the bewildering pro-Israel alliance of liberal Democrats and Christian fundamentalists, and a misplaced sense of guilt over the Holocaust?[1]

His answer:

> Like America or any state, Israel has a right to exist if it can defend itself or live peacefully with its neighbors; that is not the question. The question is whether U.S. interests require Americans to be Israel's protectors and *endure the endless blood-and-treasure costs of that role*. Status quo U.S. policy toward Israel *will result in unending war with Islam* (emphasis mine).[2]

That question and answer demanded both clarity of thought and guts, because it pushed the envelope on the world's greatest taboo.

---

1. Scheuer, *op. cit.,* p. 257.
2. *Ibid.*

Notwithstanding this welcome "wake-up call," Scheuer's treatment of the problem has two major faults. Its first is overstating the strength and co-ordination of the "Islamist insurgency," and especially of al-Qaeda, both prime targets of the U.S.'s "global war on terror," or GWOT. By inflating (in my estimation) their scope, Scheuer's position unwittingly plays into the hands of those in whose interest it is to portray the struggle in Iraq as part of this "insurgency," and therefore one between American "freedom and enlightenment" and "terrorist dead-enders." But if the GWOT isn't what it's made out to be – as is my contention – we can be rightly suspect of any claim that Iraq is its "central front," or, as Bush put it more recently, simply its "latest battlefield."[1]

An opposite point of view from Scheuer's comes out in a May 2005 interview of Jude Wanniski with Professor Khalid Yahya Blankenship, a Muslim scholar at Temple University, Philadelphia, carried in Wanniski's "Memo on the Margin."[2] In the course of explaining that Muslims were not disproportionately active in warfare and terrorism around the world – contrary to popular opinion as fostered by the mass media – Blankenship said:

> An instructive book on this point is *My Jihad* by Aukai Collins, a white American Muslim soldier-of-fortune type who actually fought the Russians in Chechnya. Early in the book he avers that transnational Muslim fighters the world over insist that they do not amount to more than 10,000 persons, even though more than that went through the CIA-sponsored "American jihad" against the Soviets in Afghanistan, which is the original source of most of the inspiration and training of those people, as documented by John Cooley in *Unholy War.*

In other words, 10,000 people in a world Muslim population of 1.3 billion.

While it is certainly true that al-Qaeda had training camps in Afghanistan both during the anti-Soviet jihad of the 1980s and after, much of that training, equipment, logistics, and finance came from the CIA and the Pakistani ISI security service. Many now talk of "blowback" – the notion that the "spooks" set the scene, but did not foresee the consequences, namely, the al-Qaeda people turning on their American patrons. This may be partly true, but it is far from being the *whole* picture. More to the point is the general inflation of the "al-Qaeda menace" in the first

---

1. President Addresses Nation, Discusses Iraq, War on Terror, *loc. cit.*

2. "An Islamic Scholar Responds," *Wanniski.com*, May 10, 2005, online (http://www.wanniski.com/showarticle.asp?articleid=4352).

place, as compared to the testimony offered by people like Blankenship and Collins.

The term "al-Qaeda" is bandied around in a careless way by the mass media. Wherever there is an explosion or an assassination, and where there are Muslims on the ground, it is automatically taken for granted that "al-Qaeda is involved," or – on other occasions – something is "al-Qaeda linked," "al-Qaeda inspired," or "al-Qaeda style."[1] Following up these leads all too often reveals that the actions in question, if even caused by Muslim groups, are not carried out by people linked to al-Qaeda at all.

Jonathan Eyal, of the Royal United Services Institute – a British military think tank – commented in October 2004 that al-Qaeda was "being sustained by the way we rather cavalierly stick the name al-Qaeda on Iraq, Indonesia, the Philippines. There is a long tradition that if you divert all your resources to a threat, then you exaggerate it."[2] For his part, Bill Durodie, a leading security expert at King's College, London, says: "There is no real evidence that all these groups are connected."[3] In other words, this vast, global, coordinated Islamist conspiracy is largely illusory.[4] For the media, however, the equation is simple: Muslims + Violence = al-Qaeda.

The comments from these security experts are contained in a review, which ran in the British *Guardian*, of a three-part documentary by celebrated filmmaker Adam Curtis called "The Power of Nightmares," screened on BBC2 on October 20, 2004, and at the Cannes Film Festival on May 14 of this year. Robert Scheer, a contributing editor at the *Los Angeles Times*, thought enough of the program's content after seeing it that he wrote an opinion piece on it called "Is al-Qaeda Just a Bush Bogeyman?"[5]

---

1. The supposed links of terrorist events to al-Qaeda get very vague indeed, as illustrated by the current reporting on the Madrid train bombing. "A year after terrorists killed 191 people and wounded more than 1,500 at two Madrid train stations, both U.S. and Spanish officials say that there is no evidence that the al-Qaeda leadership authorized or even knew of the plan. Instead, say officials, their belief is that those responsible, while inspired by al-Qaeda, were local Muslims who took an opportunity to carry out an attack that would show their anger over Spanish involvement with the United States" (Robert Windrem, "No Evidence Al-Qaeda Knew of Madrid Plot," *NBC News*, March 11, 2005, online at *www.msnbc.msn.com*).

2. Andy Beckett, "The Making of the Terror Myth," *The Guardian*, October 15, 2004, online.

3. *Ibid.*

4. As a *Los Angeles Times* piece put it late last year, "Most of the descriptions of al-Qaeda [prove] more legend than fact" (Dirk Laabs, "A Dwarf Known as Al-Qaeda," *Los Angeles Times*, November 30, 2004, online).

5. *Los Angeles Times*, January 11, 2005, p. B13.

According to filmmaker Curtis, the explanation for the myth of terrorism can be traced to this: "In an age when all the grand ideas have lost credibility, fear of a phantom enemy is all the politicians have left to maintain their power."[1] His documentary argues – in a way consistent with the position taken by leading Islamic groups in Sudan and Lebanon on the question of al-Qaeda – that the alleged terrorist group

> is not an organized international network. It does not have members or a leader. It does not have "sleeper cells." It does not have an overall strategy. In fact, it barely exists at all, except as an idea about cleansing a corrupt world through religious violence.[2]

The review continues: "Curtis's evidence for these assertions is not easily dismissed." One important fact the documentary brings up, for example, is that al-Qaeda did not even have a name until early 2001 when the American government decided to prosecute Bin Laden *in abstentia* using anti-Mafia laws that required the existence of a named criminal organization. A second is the British Home Office's statistics that between September 11, 2001, and October 2004, 664 people were arrested on suspicion of terrorism, and only 17 of them were convicted, *none of whom were connected to Islamic terrorism.* Nor has anyone been convicted of membership in al-Qaeda.[3]

A similar air of unreality is found on other fronts of the GWOT. An article in the *New Yorker* by Jane Mayer[4] noted the failure of prosecutors to move forward in any serious way with prosecuting the alleged perpetrators of major terrorist acts. "The criminal prosecution of terrorist suspects," she noted, "has not been a priority for the Bush administration, which has focused, rather, on preventing additional attacks."[5] The trial of Zacarias Moussaoui – the only U.S. criminal trial of a suspect linked to the 9/11 attacks[6] – was stalled for several years because the Bush administra-

---

1. Beckett, *op. cit.*
2. *Ibid.*
3. *Ibid.*
4. "Outsourcing Torture," February 14, 2005, online.
5. *Ibid.*
6. The Moussaoui trial is indeed "an anomaly," as a *Christian Science Monitor* report put it. "For all the billions spent on investigations into the events of September 11, one might reasonably have expected more results," the report quoted Andrew Hess, Middle East expert at Tufts University's Fletcher School, as saying. "While Germany, and now Spain, have put accused terrorist logisticians and other figures in the dock for alleged crimes related to 9/11," it continued, "the nation where they occurred has only Moussaoui to show for its efforts" (Peter Grier and Faye Bowers, "Moussaoui: A Window On Terror Trials," *Christian Science Monitor,* April 22, 2005, online). [See also the comment of Lt. Cmdr. Charles Swift emphasizing this point, *supra*, p. 479, note 3.—Ed.]

tion refused to let Moussaoui call as witnesses alleged al-Qaeda members Ramzi bin al-Shibh and Khalid Sheikh Mohammed, who are being held by the American government. This, even though three years ago Moussaoui's indictment was "a chronicle of evil," according to then-U.S. Attorney General John Ashcroft. Government lawyers claimed that producing the witnesses would disrupt their interrogation process. But is it likely that interrogators would have been put at a disadvantage if these two were brought to a courtroom for a couple of weeks to testify in America's most important case, when they have been in prison for years already? As the recent Amnesty International report on the "war on terror" put it, "Is the government concerned that bringing such detainees into the light of day might also reveal to the public how they have been treated in custody?"[1]

Moussaoui pleaded guilty on April 22, 2005, to six counts of "conspiracy to engage in terrorism," though he maintains he intended to fly an airplane into the White House in what he said was "a different conspiracy than 9/11." During the course of his trial, he reportedly both requested and vowed to fight the death penalty,[2] and his testimony has been characterized by "unpredictable, often angry courtroom ramblings . . . ."[3] Counter-terrorism officials quoted by the *New York Times* said that, after having investigated for three years, they found no evidence of any kind of plot like the one to which Moussaoui referred. His guilty plea was made in the face of the U.S. government's not having waived pursuit of execution, raising additional questions (beyond those raised over the last several years) about his competence. As it stands now his sentencing trial won't take place until early 2006.[4] By pushing the conviction and execution of Moussaoui, the administration has highlighted its embarrassing record on actually doing anything to the people it believes are orchestrators of the events that launched the GWOT. Moussaoui's lawyers are expected to make just that point: "[He] now faces execution for his peripheral role in the conspiracy, while other captured operatives who were key planners of the attacks have yet to even be charged."[5] Even the *Reuters* story that reported his guilty

---

1. Amnesty International, USA, *Guantánamo and Beyond: The Continuing Pursuit of Unchecked Executive Power*, May 13, 2005, p. 83 (http://web.amnesty.org/library/pdf/AMR510632005ENGLISH/$File/AMR5106305.pdf).

2. Amnesty International, *op. cit.*

3. David Johnston and Neil A. Lewis, "Officials Say There Is No Evidence to Back Moussaoui's Story," *New York Times*, April 27, 2005, online.

4. Amnesty International, *ibid.*, p. 81.

5. Michael Isikoff and Mark Hosenball, "Got Him, Now What?" Newsweek, May 16, 2005, online.

plea noted that "[h]is intended role with al-Qaeda *has never been clearly explained*" (emphasis mine).[1]

The situation in Germany is much the same in the case of those allegedly involved in the 9/11 attacks. One of the defendants in Hamburg, Mounir El Motassadeq, who in 2004 became the first person to be convicted in the planning of the 9/11 attacks, had his conviction overturned by an appeals court because, as Mayer notes, "[they] found the evidence against him *too weak*" (emphasis mine).[2] The problem also relates to the U.S. government's refusal to produce bin al-Shibh and Mohammed as witnesses. All it has done is provide "edited summaries of testimony," something clearly unsatisfactory to Motassadeq's defense lawyer, Gerhard Strate, who told Mayer, "We are not satisfied with the summaries. If you want to find the truth, we need to know who has been interrogating them, and under what circumstances." He then added, "I don't know why they won't produce the witnesses. The first thing you think is that the U.S. government has something to hide."[3]

Though the U.S. has since then "finally" given Motassadeq's lawyers some of what they want, the same critique will no doubt apply. According to Sabine Westphalen, a German court spokeswoman, "A six-page summary of information [Mohammed and al-Shibh] had revealed under questioning"[4] will be presented in court, but it won't be any more reliable than previous summaries, absent an explanation of *how* it was obtained. One of the German court's concerns is that the witnesses may have been tortured, thus calling into question the reliability of their testimony.[5] Ultimately there's no reason to believe that any explanation will ever be provided, as "the Americans had turned down requests for other information . . . and made clear no more material would be forthcoming."[6]

All of this begs the essential question: why are people all over the world being bombarded by the myth of the terrorist threat if the Bush administration is failing to cooperate seriously with even the one or two trials

---

1. James Vicini, "Accused 9/11 Figure Moussaoui Pleads Guilty," *Reuters*, April 22, 2005, online.

2. Mayer, *op. cit.*

3. *Ibid.*

4. Mark Trevelyan, "U.S. Sends New al-Qaeda Evidence for German 9/11 Case," *Reuters*, May 13, 2005, online.

5. "U.S. Declassifying Documents for Motassadeq Trial," *Deutsche Presse-Agentur*, April 12, 2005, online.

6. Trevelyan, *op. cit.*

that will supposedly make "terrorists" pay for their crimes? Curtis replies: "Almost no one questions this myth about al-Qaeda because so many people have got an interest in keeping it alive."[1] Think about the fortunes to be made in security consultancy, security seminars, security gadgets, counter-terror weapons, anti-terrorist software, homeland security, security training agencies, and a host of related businesses, all dealing in colossal sums of money, with much of it coming out of the public purse. But Curtis goes further, citing

> the suspiciously circular relationship between the security services and much of the media since September 2001: the way in which official briefings about terrorism, often unverified or unverifiable by journalists, have become dramatic press stories which – in a jittery media-driven democracy – have prompted further briefings and further stories. Few of these ominous announcements are retracted if they turn out to be baseless. There is no fact-checking about al-Qaeda.[2]

The second main criticism of Scheuer's thesis is related to the first: his book seems to take at face value the official version of the event that launched the GWOT, the 9/11 terrorist attacks. It isn't necessary to enter into speculation or conspiracy theory to understand that there is a huge gap between the facts and the "official story." It is clearly problematic when people are said to make cellular phone calls on a plane from an attitude where it is technologically impossible to do so, or when steel girders are said to melt due to a fire that never reached the temperature required for them to do so. These and so many others are questions of fact, and not interpretation. It is all reminiscent of the Warren Commission, which concluded that there was no "conspiracy" in the murder of President Kennedy. Few believed that then, and even fewer believe it now.

So many inconsistencies relating to the "war on terror" and the event that kicked it off are available in the public domain, it is impossible to believe that an intelligent man like Scheuer would be unaware of them. Many were neatly summarized in a piece appearing in the British press some two years ago by British M.P. and former U.K. Environment Minister Michael Meacher, titled "This War on Terrorism Is Bogus" (*The Guardian*, September 6, 2003, online). Leaving them out of discussion in a book dealing with the GWOT seems hard to justify, but perhaps Scheuer's primary concern was to avoid the distraction of accusations of "conspiracy-mongering," and focus on the essential point: if 9/11 was the beginning of a

---

1. Beckett, *op. cit.*
2. *Ibid.*

global attack by Islamists against the U.S., it can't simply be attributed to an "intelligence failure." It is the fruit of what American policy has provoked. Much the way the Iraq debacle is neither the fault of "intelligence" agencies nor a question of participants in the "global Islamist insurgency" seeking an opportunity to fight American troops. It too is a disaster of a policy that we have chosen.

Internet warfare

Contributing to the "war on terror" mystique created by Bush and Co. is the frequent discovery by the press of Internet-based claims of responsibility for events in Iraq. Various and sundry cells of the global jihad, we are told, make routine postings indicating their role in this or that suicide attack or car bombing. More often than not these claims, as reported, are inconsistent and unverifiable. How, then, to take them seriously?

For instance: on January 19, 2005, the *CNN International* website carried the headline: "Wave of suicide blasts kills at least 25." The text declared:

> In 90 minutes, four suicide car bombings Wednesday killed at least 25 Iraqis in and around Baghdad, the U.S. military said.
>
> The terrorist network led by Abu Musab al-Zarqawi, who has ties to al-Qaeda, claimed responsibility for the bombings in postings on several Islamist Web sites.[1]

The next day that news had changed. According to Andrew Marshall, writing from Baghdad, for *Scotsman.com*, only three of the four car bombs were being "claimed" by al-Zarqawi.[2] Both *CNN* and the *Scotsman* insisted that al-Zarqawi and al-Qaeda were "linked" – yet the proof of that assertion to date has only been "postings" on "Islamic" or "insurgent" websites.

On January 14, 2005, Ellen Knickmeyer, writing for the *Associated Press*, reported that the assassination of the Shiite politician, Mahmoud Finjan, had been claimed by Ansar al-Islam "on a website used by insurgents." On January 16, 2005 a *Reuters* piece featured on *ABC News Online* stated that Ansar al-Islam had *denied* killing the politician![3] Then on January 20, Gareth Smyth's piece, "Ansar Wages War on 'Heretical' Iraq,"[4] posted on *FinancialTimes.com*, repeated that Ansar *had* claimed responsibility! Will the *real* Ansar al-Islam please stand up!

---

1. http://www.cnn.com/2005/WORLD/meast/01/19/iraq.main.
2. http://news.scotsman.com/international.cfm?id=69512005.
3. The *AP* and *Reuters* pieces are no longer accessible online.
4. http://news.ft.com/cms/s/dfd3d284-6a87-11d9-858c-00000e2511c8.html.

These reported Internet claims are by their very nature *unverifiable*.[1] Anyone can post anything on the Internet, claiming to represent anyone or anything. Rarely if ever is there follow-up by the media as to what is true or false about the claims they report. The reports themselves are conspicuous for their vagueness: what is "an insurgent website" or a "website *used* by Islamists"? Inconsistencies such as those in our examples are typical and unexamined. Thus, it wouldn't be an overstatement to say such claims are essentially useless in determining the facts of any particular case.

What they do manage to create, however, is a general impression of "mayhem" caused by conveniently elusive, unconventional, "terrorist" enemies. This is especially true because most individuals reading news reports will not follow each claim to the end to ferret out contradictions or even retractions. The general impression is useful enough for the Bush administration and its imperial press in reinforcing the sense that we are fighting not Iraqis who are simply resisting occupation, but rather "fanatics" who revel in beheadings on chat-rooms at "jihad-in-iraq.org." A deeper question still is whether or not some website or other that claims to be speaking in the name of Islamism or Ba'athism actually does so. "Black flag" or "false flag" operations – those carried out by one side in a conflict while pretending to be the other side – have been with us for decades. They have a well-documented history – just ask the CIA or the Mossad.[2] They are all the more effective in view of the increasingly prominent role of the Internet as a source of information.[3] It also goes direct to the "customer": while the old methods of claiming responsibility for terrorist acts involved phone

---

1. As the *New York Times* happily admitted when recently reporting an alleged al-Zarqawi Internet posting: "it is hard, of course, to be sure of the authenticity of Internet postings" (Robert F. Worth., "Jihadists Take Stand on Web, and Some Say It's Defensive," *New York Times*, March 13, 2005, online).

2. See, for example, ex-Mossad officer, Victor Ostrovsky's revealing book, *By Way of Deception* (St. Martin's Press, New York, 1990).

3. Recent polls indicate that 75 percent of young adults, when asked to choose between television and Internet as a source of information, opted for the latter compared to 15 percent for the former. See Neopets., Inc., "Youth Study 2004" (http://info.neopets.com/presskit/articles/research/ym2004.html#1). Neopets is a corporation formed around the Internet site Neopets.com, an online youth community boasting 25 million members. Numerous other studies confirm the gradual inroads that online news is making over traditional media. Other data show that a mere 22 percent of people in their 30s and younger seek news information from the nightly television news programs of the major networks. (Jacqueline Marcus, "TV News Viewership Declines, Internet Use Rises," CommonDreams.org, January 21, 2005). Finally, see information at the Center for the Digital Future, at the Annenberg School of the University of Southern California (http://www.digitalcenter.org), and various polls of the Pew Research Center for the People and the Press (http://people-press.org).

calls or letters to journalists and police, the Internet warfare of today is a handy form of direct selling.

Thus in this global war for "hearts and minds" we have to remember, especially as regards the Internet, that potential "black flags" are going up every day, not always the work of the parties whom they claim to represent, or even the work of those directly involved in the conflict. There are third parties out there with vested interests, so our question must always be: *who gains?*

Al-Zarqawi: "Terminator" or Wizard of Oz?

For the first couple of years after 9/11, the world was bombarded, day and night with one name: Osama Bin Laden. He was apparently running Islamic terror campaigns all over the world, in spite of the fact that he is known to have serious kidney problems and require dialysis twice a week (not easy, one suspects, in the Tora Bora mountains of Afghanistan). However, in the first part of 2004, Osama began to take something of a backseat in the media's "terrorist popularity stakes" to a new terror chief, Abu Musab al-Zarqawi. As the war in Iraq has widened and deepened, the column inches being devoted to al-Zarqawi have risen exponentially, while those of Bin Laden have declined dramatically. Scott Taylor, a former U.S. soldier and editor of *Esprit de Corps* magazine, emphasized al-Zarqawi's role as publicity front-runner for the terror war's "central front":

> The U.S.'s singular failure to apprehend the elusive al-Zarqawi has proven a major embarrassment for the U.S.-led forces, and in recent weeks he has become the symbolic figurehead for the Iraqi resistance – *at least in the American media reports*" (emphasis mine).[1]

What do we know about al-Zarqawi? He is Jordanian (though Judith S. Yaphe, a Senior Fellow for the Middle East at the Institute for National Strategic Studies in Washington, D.C., refers to him as *"allegedly* a Jordanian Islamic extremist"[2]). He is a Muslim terrorist with an evident penchant for chopping off the heads of infidels. He also appears to be an Arab "Scarlet Pimpernel" – "they seek him here, they seek him there" – who aspires to join the *Texas Chain Saw Massacre* crowd. As a journalist for New York's *Newsday*, Mohammad Bazzi, put it last year, "The Jordanian-born militant has achieved mythic status as a master of disguise and escape."[3] There's

---

1. "Fallujah – America's Hollow Victory," *Aljazeera*, November 23, 2004, online.
2. Judith S. Yaphe, "A Compendium of Iraqi Insurgent Groups and What It Is They Want," *Daily Star* (Lebanon), October 19, 2004, online.
3. "Where is al-Zarqawi?" *Newsday*, December 22, 2004, online.

no doubt that he's right, though emphasis needs to be put on the word "mythic" – the adjective derived from the word "myth" – as we will see shortly.

For his article, Bazzi spoke to Dana Ahmad Majid, the Head of Security of the Patriotic Union of Kurdistan, who said of al-Zarqawi:

> He can move around any number of Iraqi areas. He can change his appearance, he can change his papers. He could be moving around alone without any problem. Al-Zarqawi is a single man, and it is always extremely difficult to capture a single person.[1]

One can almost sense the breathless excitement of Majid in relating this stuff. Yet anyone who has traveled in that part of the world knows that story telling is a way of life, and stories will be told to anyone who *wants* or *needs* to hear them. If you are an Iraqi puppet-government official, you are likely to know that the Western media will want claims that things are going stupendously well and there is progress in all fields, along with lurid descriptions of just how bad the "bad guys" really are. While the claims of "progress" fall by the wayside almost immediately after they are spouted – the mortars and machinegun fire being all too "realistic" – the "lurid descriptions" live on, growing by day and night into monstrous fantasy beyond anything that Stephen Spielberg ever captured on screen. Since it is well known that the Kurdish clans around Barzani and Talabani have been playing fast and loose for decades with *all* the players in the region – America, Israel, Jordan, Iraq, and Iran – it wouldn't be a stretch to surmise that they have also developed their own cottage industry: spinning yarns.

During the second American assault on Fallujah, *Aljazeera.net* correspondent Roshan Muhammed Salih interviewed Abdel Bari Atwan, editor-in-chief of the London-based, Arab-language daily *Al-Quds al-Arabi*. Atwan is a "name" in the Arab journalistic world, the way Robert Fisk and Seymour Hersh are in the English-speaking world. His statements are not easily dismissed. Asked about al-Zarqawi, he replied: "There is no real proof that he is alive. If he is supposedly moving around freely in Iraq, why haven't Iraqis spoken about him? He cannot be that difficult to recognize with his wooden leg."[2] So our terrorist acrobat, doing his impressions of Harry Houdini on a never-ending tour of Iraq, has a *wooden leg*! Who

---

1. *Ibid.*
2. Roshan Muhammed Salih, "Al-Zarqawi: America's New Bogeyman," *Aljazeera.net*, July 1, 2004.

would have guessed, based solely on the "investigative journalism" of our intrepid media?

Doesn't Majid, the Kurdish "Patriot," know this? No doubt he does, but he is canvassed by hacks for outlandish al-Zarqawi headlines that will inspire "shock and awe" at home, and not for dull, factual accounts. And the Bush administration? They know it too. After all, who sent al-Zarqawi, bin Laden, and the rest of the so-called "Afghan Arabs" to Afghanistan in the 1980s? The *Guardian*'s Sunday *Observer* for February 2, 2003, details for the incredulous where poor old Abu picked up his wooden leg.[1] For those more inclined to believe an Arab or Islamic source, there is the informative comment of Sheikh Naem Kassem, the No. 2 in Hezbollah, offered during the course of his October 2004 interview in Beirut, Lebanon, with the Arab-French online news source, *Arab Monitor*. In reply to the question, "Is the al-Zarqawi phenomenon a consequence of Western political policy?" Mr. Kassem states: "He is a man who has escaped Western government control [as] happened in the past with other Mujahideen in Afghanistan. They were allied with the Americans, then they parted ways."[2]

Some deny that the ways have parted, believing rather that the phantoms of Bin Laden and al-Zarqawi actually serve U.S. policy by providing "justification" for intervention, or "revulsion" to grisly beheadings for those – now a decided majority in America – who are not sure that they want to "stay the course." Scheuer even says it's "fair to conclude that the United States of America remains Bin Laden's only indispensable ally."[3] Why? Because "Bin Laden" and "al-Zarqawi" do things and say things that allow the Bush Gang to point to "Islamic barbarism," thereby fireproofing their quest for "perpetual war for perpetual peace."

1. Ed Vulliamy, Martin Bright, Nick Pelham, "False Trails That Lead to the al-Qaeda 'Links,'" *The Observer*, February, 2003, online.

2. "Hezbollah Has Never Exceeded the Limits of the Occupation, and It Is an Acceptable Model for Europe," *Arabmonitor.com*, October 2004 (http://www.arabmonitor.info/approfondimenti/dettaglio.php?idnews=7241&lang=it). Accusations that American clandestine and paramilitary operations are the root of disturbances around the globe are not limited to the situation in Iraq. Of recent interest is a declaration by the government of Burma regarding three May 7, 2005, bombings there that "the terrorists . . . and the time bombs originated from training conducted with foreign experts at a place in a neighbouring country by a world famous organisation of a certain superpower nation." The *BBC News* remarked that "even though the [government information] minister refused to name the suspected country and organisation, correspondents believe he was referring to the United States and the CIA" ("'Superpower behind' Burma Blasts," *BBC News*, May 15, 2005, online).

3. Scheuer, *op. cit.*, p. xv.

John Pilger, a journalist who frequently comes up with both arguments and facts that no one else in the journalistic trade knows (or perhaps wants to know), took on the flurry of mainstream-media reports claiming that "the 'insurgents' are led by sinister foreigners of the kind that behead people," such as al-Zarqawi "said to be al-Qaeda's 'top operative' in Iraq."[1] It is what the Americans say routinely, he noted, and "it is also Blair's latest lie to Parliament." The irony is

> that the foreigners in Iraq are overwhelmingly American and, by all indications, loathed. These indications come from apparently credible polling organizations, one of which estimates that of 2,700 attacks every month by the resistance, six can be credited to the infamous al-Zarqawi.[2]

Besides, there are serious doubts about the relationship claimed between Osama and al-Zarqawi anyway. Judith Yaphe noted in her *Daily Star* report, "al-Zarqawi's current relationship with Osama Bin Laden is not known," and terrorism experts describe him "more as a rival than as a follower of the al-Qaeda leader."[3] So whether they are friends and colleagues or enemies and rivals depends, laughably, on which "terrorism expert" you consult.

Pilger further exposes the al-Zarqawi myth by referring to a letter written by the Fallujah Shura Council – which governed the city until the second American assault – to Kofi Annan at the UN on October 14, 2004. It said:

> In Fallujah [Americans] have created a new vague target: al-Zarqawi. Almost a year has elapsed since they created this new pretext, and whenever they destroy houses, mosques, restaurants, and kill women and children, they said: "We have launched a successful operation against al-Zarqawi." The people of Fallujah assure you that this person, if he exists, is not in Fallujah . . . and we have no links to any groups supporting inhuman behaviour. We appeal to you to urge the UN (to prevent) the new massacre which the Americans and the puppet government are planning to start soon in Fallujah, as well as in many parts of the country.[4]

While cynics and neocons will surely dismiss all this as lies, the open-minded will note from the foregoing that the Fallujans were not even sure that

---

1. John Pilger, "Iraq: The Unthinkable Becomes Normal," *New Statesman*, November 15, 2004, online.

2. *Ibid.*

3. Yaphe, *op. cit.*

4. Pilger, *op. cit.*

al-Zarqawi existed,[1] and if he had, they would have turned him over to the Americans. No doubt they would have done so mainly because they wouldn't have wanted their homes and businesses destroyed, but also because they disliked the al-Zarqawi "tactics," loathed in a country marinated in real religious toleration after decades of Ba'athist rule. But, as Pilger says, "not a word of this was reported in the mainstream media in Britain and America."

For those inclined to doubt the Fallujan's professed disapproval of "inhuman behavior," numerous reports exist to confirm it. One was filed by an *Associated Press* reporter, indicating that "[s]igns are growing of hostility between secular Iraqi insurgents and Muslim extremists fighting under the banner of al-Qaeda."[2] It continued to say, revealingly, that "Ramadi's insurgents argue that al-Qaeda fighters are giving the resistance a bad name and *demand they stop kidnappings and targeting civilians . . .* " (emphasis mine). In the mainly Sunni Azamiyah district of Baghdad, "another insurgency hotbed," the article also said, "residents have repeatedly brought down from walls and streetlight poles the black banners of al-Qaeda in Iraq." Another report from the *Washington Post* noted that over 1,000 Sunni clerics and political and tribal leaders, during a May 2005 meeting, issued a statement supporting the "legitimate right" of Iraqis to "[resist] the occupier" but *condemning* "all terrorist acts that target civilians, no matter the reason."[3]

With newspaper headlines regularly blaring that "X number of Iraqis died today," many people assume that civilians are routinely and indiscriminately targeted by any and all parties resisting occupation in Iraq. A careful read of most of these reports, however, indicates that "the civilians" involved are most often members of the Iraqi security forces – people regarded by the resistance as legitimate military targets because of their collaborating with the occupation. Such killings are a horrible fact of life, but they are typically found in all 20th-century warfare involving occupation forces and those collaborating with them, perhaps most memorably in Nazi-occupied Europe. Innocent people may be killed, but they are no more therefore *targets* than the innocent are the targets of U.S. air strikes on Iraqi cities. How else to explain the statements denouncing attacks on civilians from Iraqis who oth-

---

1. See also, on this point, the revealing piece by Middle East journalist Dahr Jamail, "Zarqawi: Everywhere and Nowhere," *Asia Times*, July 7, 2005, online.

2. Hamza Hendawi, "Insurgents Show Hostility to Extremists," *Associated Press*, April 10, 2005, online.

3. Ellen Knickmeyer and Naseer Nouri, "Sunnis Step Off Political Sidelines," *Washington Post*, May 22, 2005, p. A1. See also Nicholas Blanford, "Iraqi Resistance Tiring of Foreign Fighters," *The Daily Star*, July 16, 2004, online.

erwise maintain that resistance is legitimate? And how else to explain the reporting from Amariyah where it was detailed that resistance forces *overtly attempted to avoid targeting civilians?* "Where fighting took place," a report from the Baghdad Sunni neighborhood read, "it was intense." According to residents there, "insurgents shot in the air along residential streets, *warning people to stay inside*, then fought the [U.S.-backed] Iraqi forces."[1]

Some Iraqis who support the resistance have even suggested that the indiscriminate attacks on civilians are tolerated – if not orchestrated – by forces supporting the "new" Iraq, with hopes of delegitimizing the resistance. A report filed with the *New York Times* by Patrick Graham, a journalist who spent an extensive amount of time with Iraqi resistance fighters, pointed out that "[o]ne very religious Iraqi fighter I got to know . . . [l]ike many insurgents I met . . . believed car bombs to be the work of Americans trying to discredit a legitimate resistance."[2] A recent article appearing in the British *Guardian* confirmed this point of view. According to Sami Ramadani, senior lecturer at London Metropolitan University, "Zarqawi-style sectarian violence is . . . condemned by Iraqis across the political spectrum, *including supporters of the resistance*"(emphasis mine).[3] What's more, the al-Zarqawi approach is widely seen "as having had a blind eye turned to it by the occupation." In other words, according to Ramadani, many Iraqis think the "terror" is at least tolerated by the U.S. authorities as a part of a larger strategy to "dominate Iraqis by inflaming sectarian and ethnic divisions."[4] It cannot be denied that the havoc wreaked by the likes of al-Zarqawi does in fact aid those trying to both discredit the resistance and split the bulk of the Iraqi populace off from those supporting it. While such a contention may be "dismissed by outsiders," Ramadani says,

the record of John Negroponte, the [former] U.S. ambassador in Baghdad, of backing terror gangs in central America in the 80s has fuelled these fears,

1. Nancy Youssef, "As Sunnis Call Sweep Unfair, Iraq is Divided," *Philadelphia Inquirer*, June 4, 2005, online.

2. Patrick Graham, "The Message From the Sunni Heartland," *New York Times*, May 22, 2005, online.

3. Sami Ramadani, "The Vietnam Turnout was Good as Well," *The Guardian*, January 2, 2005, online. See also Ellen Knickmeyer and Jonathan Finer, "Iraqi Sunnis Battle to Defend Shiites," *Washington Post*, August 14, 2005, p. A01, on the unity of Iraqi Shiites and Sunnis in the face of foreign fighters' attempts "to spark open sectarian conflict."

4. *Ibid.* See Steve Negus and Dhiya Rasan, "Iraq Sunni Group Attacks 'State Terrorism,'" *Financial Times*, May 18, 2005, online, as one report among indicating how "Iraqi forces" and Shiite militia activities are increasingly taking on the character of targeted strikes, assassinations, and "Salvador"-option-style operations. [See also the article by Mark Gery on pp. 761–795 discussing the sectarian strife that has developed as a result of the political situation created by the U.S. occupation and its response to opposition to it.—Ed.]

as has Seymour Hersh's reports on the Pentagon's assassination squads and enthusiasm for the "Salvador option."[1]

As for the "foreign terrorist"/al-Qaeda/al-Zarqawi myth, its *coup de grace* came via telephone from an American Marine of the 1ˢᵗ Marine Expeditionary Force. Speaking to the Pentagon press corps from Fallujah on November 15, 2004, following the assault, the Force operations officer, Col. Michael Regner, said that of the "more than 1,000 insurgents" that had been detained by U.S. forces in the city, only 20 were foreigners.[2] The *AP* story that reported the colonel's remarks further detailed that officials of the then-Allawi-led puppet government in Iraq said that there were precisely 15 foreigners in detention in Fallujah – ten from Iran and one each from Saudi Arabia, Sudan, Egypt, Jordan, and the last possibly being from France. This is hardly "the flood" of foreign insurgents that Allawi claimed during his visit to the United States in September 2004 when he addressed Congress. Indeed, in one interview during the visit he estimated that foreign fighters constituted 30 percent of insurgent forces.[3]

According to an *L.A. Times* report from late 2004, U.S military and intelligence officials have said that Allawi's government tended to exaggerate the number of foreign fighters in the country to obscure the fact that large numbers of its countrymen have taken up arms against the American-backed puppet regime. This theme dovetails with statements made frequently by the Bush administration claiming the presence of foreign fighters "prove" that the war in Iraq is inextricably linked to the GWOT. No doubt the officials challenging this claim do not want to be named for fear of coming into the crosshairs of neocon zealots in Washington. But Army

---

1. *Ibid.* Peter Maass's "The Salvadorization of Iraq?" (with a "milder" title in *The New York Times Magazine*, May 01, 2005, online) lends credence to this view: James Steele, senior U.S. adviser to Gen. Adnan's commandos (*vide infra*, p. 733, n. 2), led special forces in El Salvador in the '80s and "trained front-line battalions that were accused of significant human rights abuses"; and Steve Casteel, senior U.S. adviser in the new Iraqi Interior Ministry – which has control of Adnan's commandos – is a former top official in the U.S. DEA "who spent much of his professional life immersed in the drug wars of Latin America." See also Michael Hirsh and John Barry, "'The Salvador Option,'" *Newsweek*, January 8, 2005, online, and Seymour M. Hersh, "The Coming Wars," *The New Yorker*, January 24 and 31, 2005, online. Even the mythic al-Zarqawi has been said to reject attacks on civilians, according to journalist Dahr Jamail. When on an al-Zarqawi fact-finding trip to Jordan, Jamail had his driver tell him, "Zarqawi doesn't instruct his followers in the killing of innocent people. If he did this, I would be the first to turn against him. He only targets the Americans and collaborators" (Jamail, *loc. cit.*).

2. *Associated Press*, "Few Foreigners Among Rebels Captured in Fallujah," *USA Today*, November 15, 2004, online.

3. See Mark Mazzetti, "Insurgents Are Mostly Iraqis, U.S. Military Says," *Los Angeles Times*, September 28, 2004, online.

Gen. John Abizaid, head of the U.S. Central Command, came to their aid indirectly when he said that military estimates of the number of foreign fighters in Iraq were below 1,000. He also said that

> [w]hile the foreign fighters in Iraq are a problem that have to be dealt with, I still think that the primary problem that we're dealing with is former regime elements of the ex-Ba'ath Party that are fighting against the government.[1]

A piece that appeared in the Australian *Age* implicitly confirmed the comment made by Abizaid while it simultaneously undercut the al-Zarqawi-insurgency line, saying that "American intelligence obtained through bribery may have seriously overstated the insurgency role of the most wanted fugitive in Iraq, Abu Musab al-Zarqawi."[2] Speaking to U.S. agents in both Fallujah and Baghdad, the reporter quoted one as saying,

> We were basically paying up to $10,000 a time to opportunists, criminals and chancers who passed off fiction and supposition about Zarqawi as cast-iron fact, making him out as the linchpin of just about every attack in Iraq . . . . Back home this stuff was gratefully received and formed the basis of policy decisions. We needed a villain, someone identifiable for the public to latch on to, and we got one.[3]

---

1. *Ibid.*

2. Adrian Blomfield, "Doubt Over Zarqawi's Role as Ringleader," *The Age* (Australia), October 2, 2004, online.

3. *Ibid.* Indications are that the American approach to al-Zarqawi still suffers from the same bad habits. After declaring in May 2005 that he went to Syria for "a summit with the heads of Iraqi insurgent groups to map out a new strategy of suicide bombings against U.S. and Iraqi forces," U.S. intelligence says instead as of June 2005 that it "now discounts reports" that al-Zarqawi ever crossed into Syria. Sounding eerily familiar to another intelligence scandal, U.S. officials now say that "U.S. intelligence was always skeptical of the military's assertions about Zarqawi, which they said were based largely on questionable information obtained during the interrogation of a detainee in Baghdad" (Robin Wright, "U.S. Doubts Zarqawi Went to Syria," *Washington Post*, June 4, 2005, p. A12).
   As the psychological impact of the al-Zarqawi phenomenon wears thin, it is perhaps likely that a new "Terror Chief of the Month" will be nominated to fill his shoes as Iraq-GWOT bogey man, much the way the emphasis shifted from Osama to al-Zarqawi in the last 18 months. One candidate might have appeared in an April 2005 piece for *NBC News* by Robert Windrem ("U.S., Iraqi Forces Hunt Alleged Insurgency Leader," *NBC News*, April 11, 2005, online at www.msnbc.msn.com), which noted that, "acting on fresh intelligence, Iraqi and U.S. special operations troops are hunting a senior leader of the Iraq insurgency, a man they believe is a senior aide to terrorist Abu Musab al-Zarqawi." The now-celebrated "U.S. official speaking on condition of anonymity" says in the report that "[Ahmed Ibrahim] al-Dabbash is well connected and a very, very bad dude," billing him a "Sunni fundamentalist," "mid-level financier of Islamic terrorism," and "commander in the Khalid Ibn Walid Brigade," said to be one of the most active terrorist cells in Iraq.
   Al-Dabbash got some publicity in Baghdad newspapers in April 2003 for setting up a group called the "Al-Dabbash Islamic Assembly" to protect the warehouses of the Ministry of Health in the al-Huriya district of the capital. Windrem notes that the assembly "prevented looters

Confirming General Abizaid's opinion, the agent additionally said that "[t]he overwhelming sense from the information we are now getting is that the number of foreign fighters does not exceed several hundred and is perhaps as low as 200." Retired Army Gen. Barry McCaffrey, returning from his third trip to Iraqi in June 2005, offered a similar estimate, noting in a telephone interview with the *Washington Times* that there were only "maybe 1,000 to 2,000 foreign fighters"[1] that needed to be dealt with by American forces. Anthony Cordesman, Pentagon consultant and Arleigh Burke Chair of Strategy at the CSIS, even criticized the President for mis-representing this aspect of the situation in Iraq in his Ft. Bragg speech:

> [The President] totally failed to mention the thousands of native Iraqis that make up the core of the insurgency, the fact we have only some 600 foreign detainees out of a total of 14,000, the fact most intelligence estimates put foreign fighters at around 5% of the total . . . .[2]

Why is it that credible military and intelligence reports from Iraq are being ignored in Washington? Probably because the idea that foreign fighters lead the fighting in Iraq is essential to the neocon plan to intervene in both Syria and Iran.[3] Since the neocons have *a priori* decided the "guilt" of

---

from robbing the warehouses and provided security for the workers," "[provided] security and electricity for the neighborhood," "fixed the main water pipes in al-Huriya, and distributed free food rations to 1,450 families," and "opened a health center." Al-Dabbash's mosque was attacked in December 2004 allegedly by members of prominent Shiite parties (probably SCIRI and al-Dawa); Windrem then points out that "U.S. military officials say it is not clear why or when al-Dabbash transformed into a terrorist." It would be more accurate to say that there is not a shred of evidence that al-Dabbash is "a terrorist" – in even the broad American sense of the term – or active in the Iraqi resistance. Included with Windrem's piece was a picture revealing that his becoming a first-class "terror master" may be quite a challenge. The picture shows 14 males with al-Dabbash: four or five are obviously teenagers, and one is a boy of about six, and al-Dabbash is one of only two carrying a weapon. Some militia!

1. Sharon Behn, "Retired General Estimates 20,000 Militants Are In Iraq," *Washington Times*, June 22, 2005, p. 14.

2. "The President's Speech on Iraq: Truth versus Spin," *CSIS*, June 29, 2005, online; CENTCOM's intelligence chief, Brig. Gen. John Custer, confirmed this figure explicitly ("Syria Increasing Efforts to Seal Border With Iraq," *Bloomberg.com*, July 6, 2005).

3. Patrick Seale explained for the London-based *Al-Hayat* how the results of the May/June 2005 operation in western Iraq, based on the idea that foreign fighters coming in from Syria make up a substantial part of the resistance, have failed to vindicate Bush-administration assertions. "A force of 1,000 U.S. Marines, supported by helicopters and jet fighters, swept this week through Iraq's North-West province of Anbar, on Syria's border, in a bid to destroy foreign jihadis and their safe havens . . . . The main target of the assault seems to be the town of Ubaydi and a string of villages on the north bank of the Euphrates, which are being given the Fallujah treatment – that is to say air strikes and tank fire against residential quarters, followed by house-to house searches to flush out the 'rebels' from the ruins . . . . The thinking behind the operation is that foreign fighters, together with their

Iran and Syria on anything and everything, it follows that any "intelligence," however vague or unconfirmed, will be seized upon. It is also difficult for the Bush administration to accept that Saddam's people are the very core of the resistance, for it strikes at the mythology of "Mission Accomplished," which says that the Ba'athist government suffered a clear defeat, the Iraqi people are "grateful" for their "liberation," and only misfits, "extremists," and "terrorists" resent the imposition of U.S.-style "democracy." Indeed, this was Bush's line when he spoke to the Army War College in Carlisle, Pa., on May 24, 2004:

> Zarqawi . . . and other terrorists know that Iraq is now the central front in the war on terror. And we must understand that, as well. The return of tyranny to Iraq would be an unprecedented terrorist victory, and a cause for killers to rejoice.[1]

It was still the line a year later when Bush addressed soldiers at Fort Bragg, N.C., on June 28, 2005: "Many terrorists who kill . . . on the streets of Baghdad are followers of the same murderous ideology that took the lives of our citizens in New York, in Washington, and Pennsylvania."[2]

The fact is, however, there is another force behind the opposition to our troops, as the President grudgingly (and somewhat inconsistently) conceded when he said the "terrorists" had made common cause with "Iraqi insurgents, and remnants of Saddam Hussein's regime who want to restore the old order" (i.e., the order before they were illegally deposed). As both the facts and numerous first-hand reports attest, Saddam's government never surrendered, it simply melted away – and adopted a new approach to a war that it could not win head-on. If the majority of Iraqis are actually fighting for the Ba'ath Party and its return, and if the insurgency is intensifying – and everyone says that it is – then it becomes obvious that the Hussein government was far more popular than Bush would have the world believe, and *certainly far more popular than the American occupation.*

---

weapons, explosives and funds, are continuing to infiltrate across the porous Syrian border; in other words, that Syria constitutes a 'rear base' for the insurrection . . . . The trouble with this theory is that there is little evidence to support it. Living in fear of an American attack, Syria has done its best to seal its border. Moreover the insurgency seems to be an overwhelmingly Iraqi enterprise . . . . Foreign-fighter involvement, numbered in the dozens rather than the thousands, would seem to be minimal . . . and the fighters at Ubaydi seem to have been professional, well-trained, and determined – clearly composed of former military personnel – before melting away into the desert in the face of superior American firepower" ("Can the United States Win in Iraq?" *Al-Hayat*, June 12, 2005, online).

1. "President Outlines Steps to Help Iraq Achieve Democracy and Freedom," Remarks by the President on Iraq and the War on Terror, May 24, 2004, online (http://www.whitehouse.gov/news/releases/2004/05/20040524-10.html).
2. President Addresses Nation, Discusses Iraq, War on Terror, *loc. cit.*

Neatly summarizing the foregoing, the former UN weapons inspector Scott Ritter wrote earlier this year:

> On the surface, the al-Zarqawi organization seems too good to be true. A single Jordanian male is suddenly running an organization that operates in sophisticated cells throughout Iraq. No one could logically accomplish this. But there is an organization that can – the Mukhabarat (Intelligence) of Saddam Hussein.[1]

Ritter is on target here, for the kind of resistance which bogs down the world's "superpower" in only 18 months is not one that was thrown together after the fall of Baghdad by unemployed soldiers, patriotic shop-keepers, and a gang of "thugs." It is the work of someone who foresaw what was coming and knew what would be needed to bring Ba'athism back to power. Only one person fits that bill: Saddam Hussein.

The Facts Speak for Themselves

The prescience of Saddam

Towards the end of 2004, the American government began to admit that much of what their troops were fighting was indeed a resistance support-ive of Saddam and/or the Ba'ath Party. U.S. spokesmen have also tended to frame the planning of such a resistance in the few months leading up to the war. Yet, as Ritter's observation intimated, it's hard to imagine that such a resistance movement could be put in the field to the degree and with the depth that we see in Iraq in such a short period. All logic says no.

Interestingly, Seymour Hersh knew *at the end of 2003* that the resis-tance was not, as one commentator put it early this year, "an incipient array of ill-organized holdovers from the ousted dictator's Ba'ath Party."[2] Hersh reveals this information in a few telling pages of his bestseller, *Chain of Command: The Road from 9/11 to Abu Ghraib*.[3] He relates that he met Ahmad Sadik, an Iraqi Air Force Brig. Gen. and a senior communications intelligence officer under Saddam, in Syria in December 2003.

Sadik revealed that Saddam had *not* organized the resistance in the months leading up to the war. He had drawn up the plans for resistance in

---

1. Scott Ritter, "The Risks of the al-Zarqawi Myth," *Aljazeera.net*, January 7, 2005.

2. Patrick McDonnell, "Iraqi Insurgency Proves Tough to Crack," *Los Angeles Times*, January 26, 2005, p. A8.

3. New York: HarperCollins Publishers, 2004.

2001! Astutely, he had understood that the officials brought into office by Bush were the same crew who had orchestrated the first Gulf War in 1991, and that they were intent on a sequel. Hersh continues:

> Huge amounts of small arms and other weapons were stockpiled around the country for use by the insurgents. In January 2003 . . . Saddam issued a four-page document ordering his secret police, the Mukhabarat, to respond to an attack by immediately breaking into key government offices and ministries, destroying documents, and setting buildings on fire. He also ordered the Mukhabarat to arrange for the penetration of the various Iraqi exile groups that would be brought into Iraq with U.S. help in the aftermath of the invasion.[1]

With American troops massed on the outskirts of Baghdad on April 7, 2003, and with the world now expecting ferocious door-to-door resistance, the final *coup de grace* to Saddam's regime appeared imminent. Hersh says further:

> Instead, the [Iraqi] troops, who included members of the Ba'ath Party hierarchy, the Special Republican Guard, the Special Security Organization, and the Mukhabarat were ordered to return to their homes and initiate the resistance from there.[2]

Hersh says he later received confirmation of this fact from a former high-level American intelligence official who said that Baghdad suddenly went quiet on the evening of April 7. Hersh writes: "Saddam loyalists had stopped chatting on satellite phones and other devices and simply melted away overnight."[3]

Sadik also revealed that in his 2001 directive, Saddam had ordered that the resistance be divided into three divisions made up of between two and four thousand people, working separately from one another, and organized into cells of only three or four members. The first division was headed by Izzat al-Douri and was composed of Ba'athists who were *not* publicly known as such. They were to remain in safe houses to be used later in operations. The second division was headed by Taha Yassin Ramadan, and was composed of Ba'ath Party members whose assignment was to back up the first division by providing operational instructions through a carefully constructed communications system, now commonly known in Iraq as "the thread."[4] Although Ramadan was captured in August 2003, it made

---

1. *Ibid.*, p. 258.

2. *Ibid.*

3. *Ibid.*, p. 259.

4. Hannah Allam, "Saddam's Ba'ath Party Is Back in Business," *Knight Ridder*, September 6, 2004, online.

no difference to the effectiveness of the division because it had been thoroughly broken down into cells. The third division's leader was not indicated, but its purpose was. It was the work of infiltration, and would involved the technocrats of the regime who had knowledge of the nation's infrastructure, such as power plants, water and sewage management, finance, and commerce. Finally, Sadik said that Saddam had given one final order: "They were never to come forward at the same time."[1]

This information was related to Hersh in December 2003, at a time when the U.S. government thought that it was only a question of mopping up remnants. Saddam's capture that month was also supposed to bring the resistance to an end, according to official wisdom. The facts tell another story.

What was being reported in the mainstream media a year later confirmed what Hersh knew the year before, and what Hersh's sources knew years before that. In fact the scenario described by Hersh's sources found confirmation in an article by Brian Bender published on Christmas 2004 in the *Boston Globe*:

> Iraqi insurgents and their informants have been infiltrating U.S. and coalition organizations, Iraqi security units, and political parties in growing numbers, posing a daunting challenge to efforts to defeat the guerrillas and create a stable Iraqi state, according to U.S. military officials, Iraq specialists, and a new study of Iraqi security forces.[2]

The study Bender referred to was by Anthony Cordesman of CSIS, who maintained that "penetration of Iraqi security and military forces may be the rule, not the exception." The reason for this penetration was lack of information as to who should and who shouldn't be allowed to become a member of the U.S.-backed Iraqi army. As noted by Army Colonel Paul Hughes, who served as a political adviser to U.S. occupation authorities, "[T]o vet properly [in Iraq], you have to have some sort of institution to keep track of Iraqis . . . . There is none of that over there."[3] And there was no information because, Hughes said, a memo that coalition forces found indicated that Saddam ordered the Mukhabarat to destroy all its files in the event of an American invasion. The *Boston Globe* journalist commented: "[T]he loss of that intelligence material was a major setback for the U.S.-led coalition as it began the process of weeding out individuals with ties to the former government or its security services."[4] American forces thus con-

---

1. Hersh, *Chain of Command*, p. 259.
2. Brian Bender, "Insurgents Infiltrating Coalition, U.S. Says," *Boston Globe*, December 25, 2004, online.
3. *Ibid.*
4. *Ibid.*

firmed what was said to Hersh earlier: Saddam's orders were followed in great detail. That they were is in part responsible for the intelligence troubles the U.S. has had, as well as the problems with infiltration of the new "Iraqi" security forces. We were forced to try weeding out "the bad guys" without knowing who they were. The situation has not shown any signs of improving, either. According to a *New York Times* piece that appeared five months after Bender's, American officials "acknowledge that they [still] have little understanding of who the leaders [of the insurgency] are . . . . "[1]

Also confirming the accuracy of Hersh's narrative is a comment of Dr. Rosemary Hollis of Chatham House, the renowned British think tank known formally as the Royal Institute of International Affairs.

> The idea that [the resistance] was organized before the war is beginning to reassert itself. There is a thesis that is gaining some currency with Arab nationalists that this definitely required a lot of preparation. There is also an increasingly long-term view, that they are playing a long game and, with a properly managed resistance, this is a conflict that can be won and that the Americans can be forced to go home.[2]

This comment dovetails with remarks made by Saddam Hussein himself to his lawyer, Khalil al-Dolaimi, during their December 2004 meeting, and published later that month by Mustapha Bakri, editor of the Egyptian *Al-Ousboua*. Appearing in a rough English translation on a Tunisian website, *Babnet Tunisie*, Saddam told al-Dolaimi:

> [Bush] will leave Iraq by the small door because the Iraqi resistance is well prepared. It was prepared well ahead of the war. I had joined the military and political commands, and we prepared this new page of the war against the Americans. What arrives today is not the fruit of chance.[3]

An interesting event of May 2005, reported by Tom Lasseter of *Knight Ridder*, confirmed that Saddam's remark was not merely the boasting of a fallen leader. Lasseter detailed that an enormous bunker used by Iraqi militants was discovered just 16 miles from Fallujah[4] – a stone's throw from the city whose violent siege and destruction was supposed to have been "a

---

1. Steven R Weisman and John F Burns, "Some Sunnis Hint at Peace Terms in Iraq, U.S. Says," *New York Times*, May 15, 2005, online.

2. Peter Beaumont, "Saddam Aide in Exile Heads List of Most Wanted Rebels," *The Observer*, October 17, 2004, online.

3. "Saddam in an Exclusive Interview: The Americans Will Leave Iraq by the Small Door," *Babnet Tunisia*, December 28, 2004, online (http://www.babnet.net/en_detail. asp?id=467).

4. Tom Lasseter, "Bunkers Reveal Well-Equipped, Sophisticated Insurgency," *Knight Ridder*, June 4, 2005.

turning point" in the struggle against the rebels in November 2004. Its discovery revealed "a sophisticated organization with a vast supply of weapons and enough confidence to operate near a major Marine base." Lasseter's report described "well-equipped, air-conditioned bunkers ... [that measured] 558 feet by 902 feet, the underground system of rooms featured four fully furnished living spaces, showers, and a kitchen with fresh food." The square footage of the complex was roughly equivalent to a quarter of the office space in the Empire State Building! According to Lasseter's article,

> [T]he weapons and high-tech equipment found inside the bunker was impressive: mortars, rockets, machine guns, night-vision goggles, compasses, ski masks and cell phones. Marines also found at least 59 surface-to-air missiles, some 29,000 AK-47 rounds, more than 350 pounds of plastic explosives and an unspecified amount of TNT in a five-mile area around the bunkers.

It is unlikely that this bunker is the only one of its kind, for there was no suggestion from military sources that it contained equipment that would have indicated it was the primary command and control facility. The odds have to be that there are more, especially in view of a comment made by a Marine Corps spokeswoman, who said that the bunker was "the largest underground system discovered in *at least the last year*" (emphasis mine).[1] Perhaps the comment Saddam made to al-Dolaimi – that "the Americans have seen nothing yet" – is worth considering seriously after all.

Looking at the resistance: the Ba'ath returns

On September 6, 2004, the *Knight Ridder* news service published a remarkable story called "Saddam's Ba'ath Party Is Back in Business." It begins:

> By day, Iraqis loyal to Saddam Hussein's much-feared Ba'ath Party recite their oath in clandestine meetings, solicit donations from former members and talk politics over sugary tea at a Baghdad café known simply as "The Party." By night, cells of these same men stage attacks on American and Iraqi forces, host soirées for Saddam's birthday and other former regime holidays, and debrief informants still dressed in suits and ties from their jobs in the new, U.S.-backed Iraqi government. Even with Saddam under lock and key, the Ba'ath Party is back in business.[2]

All this confirms what Sadik told Hersh, as does a piece from May 2005 by London-based Kurd Hiwa Osman. He wrote of the resistance that

> [t]hey have also infiltrated government institutions, facilitating assassination attempts in Baghdad and other cities of the Sunni triangle. Many government

---

1. *Ibid.*
2. Allam, *loc. cit.*

ministers and public officials have been stuck in their houses for weeks, even months. Some do not even visit their ministries.[1]

So while the rebels have both access to a whole slew of information about their enemies and evident ease of movement, the occupation forces have almost none. As put prosaically by Mark Mooney: "After two years, reliable intelligence about the enemy remains the Americans' glaring weakness."[2]

Hannah Allam's piece for *KR* continues:

> The Pan-Arab Socialist movement is going strong with sophisticated computer technology, high-level infiltration of the new government, and plenty of recruits in thousands of disenchanted, impoverished Sunni Muslims, according to interviews with current and former members, Iraqi government officials, and groups trying to root out former Ba'athists.[3]

Even the director general of the Supreme National Commission for De-Ba'athification (whose scope of authority barely extends beyond the Green Zone, despite its impressive name), Mithal al-Alusi, concurs that the Ba'ath is resurgent: "There are two governments in Iraq. The Ba'athists are like thieves, stealing the power of the new government. Their work is organized and strong."[4] Allam points out, too, that Ba'athists openly distribute price lists: burn a Humvee or detonate an IED and earn a couple of hundred dollars, kill an American soldier and earn $1000.

One interesting fact indicates that evidence for what Allam narrates is more than purely circumstantial. On April 7, 2004 – the 57th anniversary of the Ba'ath's foundation – a statement proclaimed via the Internet that the party intended to take back Iraq's Anbar province from the occupation forces: "The Ba'ath Party and resistance are to implement a series of military operations against U.S. Marines newly situated in western Iraq."[5] That same week the first clashes between Fallujah fighters and American troops erupted into a full-scale uprising, leading to the first U.S. assault on the city. Some postings on the Internet are to be believed, because they are born out by events.

Only a Sunni insurgency?

According to the media the resistance is almost exclusively confined to the Sunni heartlands – the famous "Sunni Triangle." Even if that's the case,

---

1. Hiwa Osman, "What Do the Insurgents Want?" *Washington Post*, May 8, 2005.
2. Mark Mooney, "Two Years and No End of Blood," *New York Daily News*, March 13, 2005.
3. Allam, *loc. cit.*
4. *Ibid.*
5. *Ibid.*

it is worth noting that 45 percent of the total population of Iraq is living in this "Triangle." If only 20 percent of all Iraqis are Sunnis – as is popularly accepted – and all of these Sunnis were in the Sunni triangle, there would still be fully another 25 percent of the total Iraqi population in this area. Meaning that if the Sunni Triangle is the "headquarters" of the resistance, the resistance is headquartered in an area where *more than half* of the people there are *not* Sunni. Food for thought, at least.

Intelligent journalists are now referring to the *"mainly* Sunni resistance" because it has become evident that it goes well beyond that particular branch of Islam.[1] An illustration of this is in the boycott of the January 2005 election, composed of widely varying ethnic and religious groups: according to a correspondent at *IslamOnline.net*, 47 different groups, Sunni, Shiite, Turkoman, and Christian, "declared their boycott" of the election.[2] Now it is likely that the ethnic or "sectarian" makeup of the boycott would correspond to the makeup of the resistance, which again suggests that support for the resistance goes well beyond Iraq's Sunnis. Indeed, statements of solidarity for the resistance – though mostly unreported – from numerous Islamic scholars in Saudi Arabia and around the globe also indicate a wide and substantial base of support throughout worldwide Islam.[3] Most telling, perhaps, is a June 2005 report by the *Boston Globe* that a "recent internal poll conducted for the U.S.-led coalition found that nearly 45 percent of the population supported the insurgent attacks, making accurate intelligence difficult to obtain."[4] Unless assertions that Sunnis make up only about 20 percent of the population of Iraq are substantially in error (and they might be), the broad base of support for the resistance is almost uncontestable.[5]

---

1. One example of the more intelligent recent media coverage is the interesting piece by Patrick Graham for the *New York Times*. The reporter claims to have spent some time with the "insurgents" and notes in his report inconvenient facts that dispel the myth that Shiites and Sunnis in Iraq are always and by definition diametrically opposed. He notes that Sunni Arab clans and subtribes sometimes have both Sunni and Shiite branches, that Baghdad is extremely mixed due to frequent intermarriage between Sunnis and Shiites, and that extreme fundamentalism, which views Shiites as "Muslim apostates" is "not as common among Sunnis I have met as having a grandmother who is Shiite" (Graham, *loc. cit.*).

2. Samir Haddad, "Capital Punishment for Anti-Occupation Iraqi Imams," *IslamOnline. net*, November 21, 2004, online.

3. "Scholars Defend Iraqi Resistance, Prohibit Collaboration," *IslamOnline.net*, November 6, 2004, online; Subhi Mejahid, "93 Muslim Figures Call for Democracy, Support Resistance," *IslamOnline,net*, August 23, 2004, online.

4. Bryan Bender, "Insurgency Seen Forcing Change in Iraq Strategy," *Boston Globe*, June 10, 2005, online.

5. Bender also reported that "[o]nly 15 percent of those polled said they strongly sup-

Other little-known facts support this notion. The Iraqi Ba'ath Party, in its earliest years, was led mainly by Shiites like Fu'ad al-Rikabi, who between 1951 and 1958 built it up into a force numbering around 12,000 supporters. The Turkomen have a vested interest in allying with the Arabs because of persistent Kurdish persecution. A Greek Orthodox Christian, Michel Aflaq, was the founder and spiritual leader of the party. He died in Baghdad shortly before the first Gulf War, insisting to the last that Saddam had upheld the "non-denominational" character of Ba'athism. And when Fallujah came under attack in November 2004, the resistance suddenly exploded in Mosul, which has the largest concentration of Christians outside Baghdad. It cannot credibly be maintained that simply because many American troops are nominally Christian, Iraqi Christians would hesitate to oppose them if otherwise inclined to do so.[1] Besides, under Saddam, Christians were protected, and were an influential body within the government, the bureaucracy, and the commercial world.

The pattern of attacks by the resistance also illustrates its broad support. A geographical study of those attacks, completed in September 2004 and discussed by the *New York Times*, revealed that

> [a]ttacks by insurgents have been directed against civilians and military targets in Iraq in a pattern that sprawls over nearly every major population center outside the Kurdish north, according to comprehensive data compiled by a private security company with access to military intelligence reports and its own network of Iraqi informants.[2]

According to the *NYT* piece, former Interim Prime Minister Allawi stood with President Bush in the White House in September 2004 declaring that, of Iraq's 18 provinces, "14 to 15 are completely safe," and that the others suffer merely from "pockets of terrorists." The study, produced by

ported the U.S.-led coalition," support that, one might surmise, comes chiefly from Kurds who have gained most from American intervention. It would also be reasonable to assume that the figures Bender reports understate the reality, since the poll was conducted for the U.S. authorities.

1. An example of the predicament faced by the Iraqi Christians in Mosul was provided by Sabah Guryal, a former executive of the Middle East Council of Churches in Mosul, who spoke to the *St. Petersburg Times* in May of this year. "Christians in Iraq paid twice after coalition forces entered. First, Iraqi Muslims accused the Christians of supporting the coalition because we are Christians like the American soldiers . . . . And we pay the second time because the American forces consider us all Arabs, not Christians" (Susan Taylor Martin, "Fleeing Iraqi Christians on Road to Damascus," *St. Petersburg Times*, May 23, 2005, online.)

2. James Glanz and Thom Shanker, "Iraq Study Sees Rebels' Attacks as Widespread," *New York Times*, September 29, 2004, online.

the Las Vegas-based Special Operations Consulting Security Management Group, Inc., revealed a different reality.

> The sweeping geographical reach of the attacks, from Nineveh and Salahuddin Provinces in the northwest to Babylon and Diyala in the centre, and Basra in the south, suggests a more widespread resistance than the isolated pockets described by Iraqi government officials.[1]

In the 30 days prior to the article's publication, the study shows that there were 283 attacks in Nineveh and 325 in Salahuddin, 332 in the western province of Anbar, 123 in Diyala, 76 in Babylon and 13 in Wasit. *There was not a single province without an attack in the 30-day period.* There are only two ways to explain this. Either the resistance is a kind of traveling circus, which is trying to give the impression of being omnipresent when it is not; or, more probably, it is the unfolding of the plan devised by Saddam for the spread of the resistance to all areas of Iraq as it grows in momentum and confidence. Those who maintain that, because the Shiite south is apparently all in favor of Ayatollah al-Sistani and pro-Iranian theocracy, the resistance has a purely Sunni composition are mistaken. Al-Sistani is an old and frail man who could pass from the scene at any moment. Once he does, the Shiites will split into various factions, and most will show themselves to be fundamentally Iraqi nationalists. The proof? On January 29, 2005, *Reuters* reported that Ayatollah Ahmed Hassani al-Baghdadi, one of the most eminent of Shiite clerics based in Najaf, opposed the puppet government and its then-upcoming elections, along with many others, such as al-Sadr, who for his part has even pointed recently to opposition to U.S. troops as a way to unite the country.[2] Al-Baghdadi said that such elections were "a conspiracy to divide and conquer Iraq," and he went on to say, "I am a son of Iraq, and I invite all Muslims and Christians to expel the Americans from Iraq."[3]

---

1. *Ibid.*

2. Carol J. Williams, "Radical Cleric Reaches Out," *Los Angeles Times*, May 23, 2005, p. 1.

3. Lin Noueihed, "Iraqi Shiite Cleric Urges Election Boycott," Reuters, January 29, 2005, online. Polling data from Zogby International from the same timeframe supports the view that majorities of both Shiites (69%) and Sunnis (82%) favor a withdrawal of American forces, and percentages slightly less than that indicated that the U.S. presence would "hurt" Iraq. See Zogby International Poll, "Survey Finds Deep Divisions in Iraq," Zogby International, January 28, 2005, online. The news release providing the results of the poll also noted that "[o]nly the Kurds seem to favor a continued U.S. presence, and are likely to outright reject violent resistance." [Dr. al-Obaidi expressed similar sentiments in personal correspondence to Jude Wanniski, as noted in the interview with Wanniski included in the companion to the present volume, *Neo-CONNED!*, pp. 3–79. The postscript to the

Some telling statistics

Dahr Jamail is a rare kind of journalist in Iraq these days, interested not in being "embedded," but taking his chances on the streets with his interpreter. Some of the most enlightening journalism on the invasion and occupation has come from him.

One of his Baghdad posts provided an interesting indicator of the resistance's strength. "The flight from Jordan feels all too normal," he wrote on November 5, 2004,

> until we arrive over Baghdad International Airport. The nose of the plane dips, the left wing drops, and the downward spiral begins – dropping us 4,000 feet per minute into the inferno that is occupied Iraq.
>
> Rather than an in-flight magazine, a lonely card is available to read in the seat pocket. It begins: "For those of you who have not traveled with us before, you need to be aware that, for your security and safety, not for your comfort, we do a spiral descent into Baghdad. This is carried out to avoid any risk from anti-aircraft missiles or small arms fire."[1]

This is the Baghdad where the American puppet government holds sway *in theory*; this is the Baghdad which is supposedly overseeing the creation of a free-market democracy in Iraq. This is the Baghdad where Bush says that progress is being made, citing the number of clinics open, the number of soccer balls distributed for free.

But it is also the Baghdad where Michael Ware, writing in *TIME Magazine*, says:

> The fact that insurgents . . . are patrolling one of Baghdad's major thoroughfares – within mortar range of the U.S. embassy – is an indication of just how much of the country is beyond the control of U.S. forces and the new Iraqi government.[2]

As is now well known, nothing has changed since Jamail chronicled his descent into the chaos of Baghdad, notwithstanding even the "success" of the January 2005 elections that claimed to give Iraq a sovereign government. "In many parts of the country, total insecurity remains the rule rather than the exception, to the great distress of the population," says Patrick Seale in the London-based *Al-Hayat*. "Shootings and car bombs take their dreadful

---

Wanniski interview also contains compelling testimony from Muhammad al-Baghdadi that there were numerous Shiites who were members of the Ba'ath Party.—Ed.]

1. Dahr Jamail, "Spiraling Into Occupied Iraq," *Dahr Jamail's Iraq Dispatches*, November 5, 2004, online (http://dahrjamailiraq.com/weblog/archives/dispatches/000105.php).

2. Michael Ware, "The Enemy With Many Faces," *TIME Magazine*, September 27, 2004, online.

toll. Some 350 people have been killed in the past two weeks. The numbers are uncertain because no one has the time to count them."[1]

A numbers game

Even though Lt. Gen. Thomas Metz remarked in January 2005 at a Baghdad press conference that "the thugs . . . are growing weaker," and that "[the enemy] is getting desperate,"[2] many of the major media outlets were then at least beginning to question just how true that was. Patrick McDonnell, for instance, admitted in a January 2005 piece for the *Los Angeles Times* that "the size of the insurgency has become a matter of debate as the war continues and casualties mount on both sides."[3]

When *Agence France Presse* published a story from Baghdad on January 3, 2005, with the headline "Iraq Battling More Than 200,000 Insurgents," it caused something of a minor sensation. The writer referred to an estimate given by Gen. Abdullah Shahwani, service director of the Iraqi Intelligence Service for the Allawi interim government. "I think the resistance is bigger than the U.S. military in Iraq," he said, "more than 200,000 people."[4] He went on to clarify his position by saying that he thought the hardcore fighters numbered around 40,000, and the rest of the total was made up of part-time fighters and volunteers, providing the rebels with everything they needed, from intelligence, to logistics, to shelter.

The *AFP* piece quoted the assessment of a RAND Corporation defense analyst, Bruce Hoffman, formerly an advisor to the U.S. military in Iraq, who said that Shahwani's estimate was not "completely out of the ballpark," given that his estimate referred "to active sympathizers and supporters and to part-time as well as full-time active insurgents."[5]

Anthony Cordesman, the CSIS expert, also said that Shahwani's figures are credible: "The Iraqi figures do . . . recognize the reality that the insurgency in Iraq has broad support in Sunni areas while the U.S. figures downplay this to the point of denial."[6]

1. Patrick Seale, "Can the United States Win in Iraq?" *Al-Hayat*, May 12, 2005.

2. Borzou Daragahi, "Destruction of U.S. Bradley Vehicle Raises Fears," *San Francisco Chronicle*, January 7, 2005, online.

3. Patrick J. McDonnell, "U.S. Apparently Underestimated Size of Insurgency, Top Commander Says," *Los Angeles Times*, January 27, 2005, online.

4. "Iraq Battling More Than 200,000 Insurgents," *Agence France-Presse*, January 3, 2005, online.

5. *Agence France-Presse*, "Iraq Battling More Than 200,000 Insurgents: Intelligence Chief," *TurkishPress.com*, January 3, 2005, online.

6. *Ibid.*

In early May 2004, the military was claiming that the rebels were around 5,000 in number, including both full and part-time fighters. By October 2004, the estimate was revised to 20,000 – an increase of 400 percent. And as of early 2005, the "top U.S. commander" in Iraq, Army Gen. George Casey, was claiming that "U.S. forces killed or captured about 15,000 suspected militants in Iraq last year."[1] Which means that the insurgency would have been virtually extinguished if the number of militants were indeed limited to 15 to 20 thousand.[2] While Gen. Casey admitted in a press conference in Baghdad that previous estimates of insurgent forces had been inaccurate, he nevertheless maintained that Shahwani's estimate was "inflated," saying, "It's not a number I would subscribe to."[3] Of course he declined to cite a number to which he *would* subscribe. McDonnell simply commented for the *Los Angeles Times* that "the reluctance reflects in part a lack of solid intelligence about the fighters." Casey did make one notable comment, though: "We cannot stay in front on this over the long haul and be successful. We're viewed by the people . . . as an occupation force."[4]

Independent confirmation of Shahwani's estimate comes from a U.S. special operations source who spoke anonymously to *Newsweek* in June 2005. If anything, Shahwani *underestimated* the breadth and depth of the resistance. The report including the U.S. official's comment ran as follows:

> New insurgents seem to spring up faster than the allied forces can cut them down. The Coalition has announced the killing of some 15,000 insurgents over the past year. Nevertheless, official briefers have recently estimated that between 12,000 and 20,000 insurgents remain active. According to a U.S. Special Ops source, who required anonymity because of the sensitivity of his work, the insurgents include an estimated 1,000 foreign jihadists, 500 homegrown Iraqi jihadists, between 15,000 and 30,000 former regime elements and as many as 400,000 auxiliaries and support personnel.[5]

---

1. McDonnell, *loc. cit.*

2. Adding to the somewhat ironic nature of the attempt to quantify the Iraqi resistance, retired Army Gen. McCaffrey said, after his return from Iraq in June 2005, that there are *still* "about 20,000 . . . adamant fighters" that need to be "dealt with" before the insurgency is finished off (Sharon Behn, "Retired General Estimates 20,000 Militants Are In Iraq," *Washington Times*, June 22, 2005, p. 14.). These batches of "20,000 fighters" continue to turn up, it seems, no matter how many the U.S. eliminates. As one career Marine officer told the *Christian Science Monitor* recently, "We've won every fight they've given us, but there always seem to be just as many people fighting us as when we got here" (Dan Murphy, "U.S. Strategy In Iraq: Is It Working?" *Christian Science Monitor*, June 21, 2005, p. 1).

3. *Ibid.*

4. *Ibid.*

5. Scott Johnson and Melinda Liu, "The Enemy Spies," *Newsweek*, June 27, 2005, online.

As for Shahwani himself, when asked by *AFP* if the insurgents were winning, he replied: "I would say they aren't losing."

A post-election wax or wane?

Concise figures for rebel attacks before the January election were provided by a *Knight Ridder* report. As of January 2005:

- U.S. military fatalities from hostile acts have risen from an average of about 17 per month just after Bush declared an end to major combat operations on May 1, 2003, to an average of 82 per month.
- The average number of U.S. soldiers wounded by hostile acts per month has spiraled from 142 to 808 during the same period . . . .
- Attacks on the U.S.-led coalition since November 2003, when statistics were first available, have risen from 735 a month to 2,400 in October 2004. Air Force Brigadier General Erv Lessel, the multinational forces' deputy operations director, told *Knight Ridder* that attacks were currently running at 75 a day, about 2,300 a month . . . .
- The average number of mass-casualty bombings has grown from zero in the first four months of the American occupation to an average of 13 per month.[1]

Since then, Bush administration officials have continued to say that they have got the insurgency by the throat, and its defeat is just a matter of time. The mood was best captured by Vice President Dick Cheney on May 30, 2005, when he declared on CNN's *Larry King Live* that "[t]he level of activity that we see today from a military standpoint, I think, will clearly decline. I think they are in the last throes, if you will, of the insurgency."[2] President Bush's approach is to admit an upsurge in violence since the "election" but to interpret it as "evidence that the insurgency is on its last legs."[3]

It wouldn't be a stretch to say that this is simply more wishful thinking, of the kind Iraq observer and University of Michigan professor Juan Cole has noted recently in President Bush. Bush has, Cole wrote for *Salon.com*, "repeatedly expressed wild optimism, utterly unfounded in reality, about the political process in Iraq and about the ability of the new Iraqi government and army to win the guerrilla war."[4]"

---

1. Tom Lasseter and Jon Landay, "Iraqi Insurgency Growing Larger, More Effective," *Knight Ridder*, January 16, 2005, online. Another interesting statistic was confirmed by American military spokesman: "since April, insurgents have fired [as of September 2004] nearly 3,000 mortar rounds" in the city alone; that is 125 rounds per week (Glanz and Shanker, *loc. cit.*).

2. "Iraq Insurgency in 'Last Throes,' Cheney Says," *CNN*, June 20, 2005, online.

3. Joe Galloway, "Administration Stubbornly Stays the Course in Iraq," *Salt Lake Tribune*, June 3, 2005, online.

4. Juan Cole, "The Revenge of Baghdad Bob," *Salon.com*, June 9, 2005.

What's more, the facts – and the statements of the professionals – contradict the administration line. Brig. Gen. Donald Alston, the chief U.S. military spokesman in Iraq, said almost two weeks after the vice president made his prediction,

> I think the more accurate way to approach this right now is to concede that ... this insurgency is not going to be settled, the terrorists and the terrorism in Iraq is not going to be settled, through military options or military operations.[1]

As for the statistics, there has been no substantial reduction in the number of attacks or other metrics since the January election, where the *Knight Ridder* report leaves off. Depending upon which source you go to, attack rates are somewhere between 60 and 70 per day.[2] In that vein, Defense Intelligence Agency Director Vice Admiral Lowell Jacoby told a Senate Armed Forces Committee in March of 2005 that

> [a]ttacks numbered approximately 25 per day one year ago .... Since the January 30 election, attacks have averaged around 60 per day .... It depends, therefore, on what time period you select. Compared to a year ago, the strike rate is double.[3]

The Admiral forgot to point out that most violent incidents in Iraq go *unreported.* In a couple of revealing paragraphs, Patrick Cockburn, writing for the British *Independent on Sunday,* noted that because of those omissions the attack rates cited by occupation authorities are open to serious question:

> We saw one suicide bomb explosion, clouds of smoke and dust erupting into the air, and heard another in the space of an hour. *Neither was mentioned in official reports.* Last year U.S. soldiers told the *IoS* that they do not tell their superiors about attacks on them *unless they suffer casualties.* This avoids bureaucratic hassle and "our generals want to hear about the number of attacks going down not up." This makes the official Pentagon claim that the number of insurgent attacks is down from 140 a day in January to 40 a day this month dubious (emphasis mine).[4]

1. Tom Lasseter, "Military Action Won't End Insurgency, Growing Number of U.S. Officers Believe," *Knight Ridder,* June 12, 2005, online.

2. Bryan Bender has written that "[d]espite U.S. estimates that it kills or captures between 1,000 and 3,000 insurgents a month, the number of daily attacks is going back up. Down to about 30 to 40 a day in February, attacks are now up to *at least* 70 per day, according to statistics of U.S. Central Command." See Bender, "Insurgency Seen Forcing Change in Iraq Strategy," *loc. cit.*

3. Paul Reynolds, "Iraq Two Years On: Endgame or Unending War?" *BBC News* (online), April 6, 2005.

4. Patrick Cockburn, "150 Hostages and 19 Deaths Leave U.S. Claims of Iraqi 'Peace' in

Cockburn continues by looking at the fact that in November 2004, roughly five American soldiers were dying per day, and by March 2005 it dropped to about one per day.[1] "This is the result of a switch in American strategy," he cautions, "rather than a sign of a collapse in the insurgency. U.S. military spokesmen make plain that America's military priority has changed from offensive operations to training Iraqi troops and police."[2] In other words, there are fewer regular patrols, fewer sorties beyond "fortified positions," so that it would be normal for the death rate to drop.[3] What

---

Tatters," *The Independent on Sunday*, April 17, 2005, online.

1. More recently *Boston Globe* reporter Bryan Bender tells us that "on average two U.S. soldiers continue to die each day [and] many more are wounded" ("Insurgency Seen Forcing Change in Iraq Strategy," June 10, 2005, online).

2. Cockburn, *loc. cit.*

3. Closely linked to the question of the number of attacks is the question of how many American troops are actually being killed and wounded. The Internet is awash with material claiming that the numbers of dead and wounded are *far higher* than the figures cited by the Pentagon. Much of the Internet is, of course, little more than a rumor mill. Controversial claims on sensitive subjects need to be approached with a healthy skepticism. That said, it is also obvious that there is a great deal of verifiably true material on the Internet which does *not* find its way onto the pages of the *Wall Street Journal* or into *FOX News*.

One Internet source that posts information beyond that available in mainstream news is *FreeArabVoice.org*. Of particular relevance is the Iraq Resistance Report, translated and compiled by an Arab named Muhammad abu Nasr. Recently, the State Department's official website took aim at Nasr and (along with a third) the site from which much of his report is developed, *IslamMemo*. The State Department's notice warned of "a trio of obscure websites and individuals has combined to spread deliberate disinformation, particularly about U.S. actions in Iraq," claiming furthermore that "the contents of his website make it clear that abu Nasr is a communist" who "champions Arab nationalist, anti-American, and anti-Israeli sentiments." His main source is also labeled "pro-al Qaeda," which would seem to be an overstatement indeed if Nasr's translation of the material he culls from *IslamMemo* is accurate. It appears to *report* the claims of al-Qaeda, much as *Aljazeera* and the *Washington Post* do. As for Nasr, no reasonable person could say, based upon *FreeArabVoice.org*, that his stance is pro-communist. In fact, the frequent media reports of complaints from Iraqi communists regarding elements of the Iraqi resistance make it unlikely that someone who sympathizes with the resistance – as Nasr obviously does – would be overly warm toward communism. As for his "anti-Israeli" position, one might ask why that is of concern to the U.S. government.

Why the rather absurd accusations? The issue seems to be Nasr's claims regarding U.S. dead and wounded, which the State Department says are far, far too high. Ultimately there is no way of knowing *who* is telling the truth. Nasr cannot prove what he says; neither can the State Department. What we can reflect upon is the motivations of those who make casualty claims. Supporters of the Iraqi resistance will want to believe that U.S. casualties are very high, but Nasr's figures at least must be limited by the reality on the ground, or he risks being seriously discredited. The Bush administration on its side clearly has a positive interest in denying Nasr's claims, for if they are even remotely accurate its legitimacy and survival would be jeopardized. It is impossible for an outside observer to take a position on who's telling the truth or what it is. It is simply worth noting that there is controversy on the issue, just as there is controversy over the secrecy pertaining to the return of U.S. wounded to Army hospitals and U.S. dead to Dover. There is little coverage of the dead and wounded coming out of Iraq. Is it really as result of the government's

gives Americans at home the impression that their troops control Iraq is the fact that sweeps like "Operation Lightning" – carried out in June 2005 by 1,000 Marines in Anbar Province – are given extensive media coverage, inevitably extolling "the huge success" that attended its conclusion. There is no hint of Cockburn's assertion in the mainstream media: "The U.S. army and Iraqi armed forces control *islands of territory* while much of Iraq is a dangerous no-man's land" (emphasis mine).[1]

While the general attacks have not diminished, and have in fact increased in sophistication, the incidence of "mass-casualty bombings" has soared exponentially. In mid-May 2005 a *New York Times* article noted that, according to a senior officer speaking in Baghdad, "the 21 car bombs [there] so far this month almost matched the total of 25 in all of last year."[2] Don't be shocked; it gets worse, because two weeks later the *Los Angeles Times* reported on the number of bombings that same month, but the number was much higher.

> Suicide bombings have become the Iraqi insurgency's weapon of choice, with a staggering 90 attacks accounting for most of last month's 750 deaths at the militants' hands, according to tallies by the U.S. military and news agencies.[3]

So in the space of just two weeks, 70 bombings took place. "Suicide attacks outpaced car bombings almost 2-to-1 in May," the *Los Angeles Times* piece further reported. In April "there were 69 suicide attacks – more than in the entire year preceding the June 28, 2004, hand-over of sovereignty."[4] It also noted that "the frequency of Iraq's suicide bombings is *unprecedented*, exceeding the practice through years of the Palestinian uprising against Israel" as well as "the Chechen rebellion in Russia" (emphasis mine). It also quotes Navy Cmdr. Fred Gaghan, the head of the Combined Explosive Exploitation Cell in Iraq, as saying: "At this time, there is nothing to indicate that the availability of volunteers is on the decline."[5]

As for who is carrying out these attacks, the answer again depends upon who you ask. Gen. Casey, commanding general of the multinational forces in Iraq, said that it might be Iraqis:

---

concern for "family and patient privacy," or is it something else altogether?

1. Cockburn, *loc. cit.*

2. John Burns and Eric Schmitt, "Generals Offer Sober Outlook on Iraqi War," *New York Times*, May 19, 2005, online.

3. Carol Williams, "Suicide Attacks Soaring in Iraq," *L. A. Times*, June 2, 2005, online.

4. *Ibid.*

5. As of August 4, 2005, David Cloud was reporting on the resistance's "increasingly deadly trend" ("Insurgents Using Bigger, More Lethal Bombs . . . ," *New York Times*, online).

> There is a kind of axiom out there that says that Iraqis aren't suicide bombers. I'm not sure that's the case. I believe there are Iraqi Islamic extremists . . . that are very capable of getting into cars and blowing themselves up.[1]

But Maj. Gen. John Defreitas, intelligence chief for the force commanded by Casey, said quite confidently that "[t]here is no evidence this is being done by Iraqis." In every case, he said, "the driver has been a foreigner."[2] What better illustration of the intelligence problem that the "allies" face in Iraq than the near diametric opposition between Casey's and Defreitas's assessment as to who is responsible for the spate of car bombings so much discussed in the recent news.

Ultimately it may well be impossible to get to the truth as far as these kinds of attacks are concerned, for – as illustrated in a July 2005 *AP* wire – the reporting is both politicized and attributed almost exclusively to U.S. and anti-insurgency, "Iraqi" sources, who clearly have a vested interest in how the conflict is portrayed. "The vast majority of suicide attackers in Iraq are thought to be . . . mostly Saudis and other Persian Gulf Arabs," the wire said,[3] quoting U.S. Air Force Brig. Gen. Don Alston who noted that "foreign fighters are the ones that most often are behind the wheel of suicide car bombs." Leaving aside the notable (but never discussed) difference between a "car bomb" and a "suicide attack," whatever those words are intended to mean,[4] maintaining this position is somewhat counterproductive for the Bush administration "message." While it highlights that "foreign fighters" play a sensational (if not substantial) role in the fighting in Iraq, it also concedes both that there are other "insurgents who are attacking U.S. troops because they are hostile to their presence"[5] and that "non-

---

1. *Ibid.*

2. *Ibid.*

3. Patrick Quinn and Katherine Shrader, "Iraq's Suicide Attacks Blamed on Foreigners," *Associated Press*, July 1, 2005, online.

4. Common sense alone dictates that a car bomb and a suicide attack are two different things, the former potentially but not at all necessarily implying the presence of a token "fanatic" willing to blow himself up to accomplish the mission. While suicide attacks themselves may involve Islamists seeking martyrdom, they do not imply a "freedom-hating" fanaticism that would link them irreversibly to the "war on terror." Neither car bombs nor suicide attacks necessarily imply "terrorism," since both may be used against solely military targets. Indeed, as an Italian judge, Clementina Forleo, recently (and inconveniently) pointed out, "militants who attack military or state targets, even with suicide bombers, cannot be considered terrorists in times of war or occupation." Even more inconveniently she noted that defining "every violent act" by irregular forces as "terrorist" risked "comprising people's right to self-determination and independence." See *Reuters*, "Terrorism Depends on Target: Judge," *The Australian*, April 22, 2005, online.

5. Dana Priest, "U.S. Talks With Iraqi Insurgents Confirmed," *Washington Post*, June 27,

Iraqis [are] behind most suicide missions."¹ If it is true, as "U.S. and Iraqi intelligence officials said," that there is "little evidence that Iraqis carried out the near-daily stream of suicide attacks over the past six months,"² it simply confirms that the mass of Iraqis supporting the resistance have no use for the famed "al-Zarqawi tactics."

Which raises the question: what about the "other" insurgents, simply "hostile to the presence of U.S. troops"? Kenneth Katzman, an analyst with the Congressional Research Service, thinks they make up the predominant part of the conflict.³ "I still think 80 percent of the insurgency, the day-to-day activity, is Iraqi: the roadside bombings, mortars, direct weapons fire, rifle fire, automatic weapons fire."⁴ It is this kind of activity since the January 2005 "election," beyond the sensational "Zarqawi-style" attacks, that has led observant commentators to speak more candidly and realistically about how well (or poorly) things are going in Iraq, illustrating by contrast the flights of fancy indulged in by Bush administration spokesmen when they speak of seeing a light at the end of the tunnel. Indeed, if the sampling of voices which follows is to be believed even reservedly, that light may very well be an oncoming train.

"In 2003, [the attacks] were random small-arms fire," writes Sharon Behn in the *Washington Times* for May 23, 2005.

> Then they escalated to roadside bombs – sometimes command-detonated or with tripwires. Then they escalated to car bombs that would run a ramp and pull into a convoy or traffic circle. And now they are very well organized, rehearsed, orchestrated, using a combination of rocket-propelled grenades, [roadside bombs] set in a daisy chain to get the wounded as they exit the vehicles, heavy machine guns, small arms and hand-thrown grenades.⁵

Writing for *Newsday* on May 12, 2005, Timothy Phelps said,

> With security experts reporting that no major road in the country was safe to travel, some Iraq specialists speculated that the Sunni insurgency was effectively encircling the capital and trying to cut it off from the north, south and west, where there are entrenched Sunni communities. East of Baghdad is a mostly unpopulated desert bordering on Iran.⁶

2005, p. A1.

1. Quinn and Shrader, *loc. cit.*

2. *Ibid.*

3. His is, of course, an unwelcome point of view for those interested in portraying the fighting as "an international struggle with militant Islam" (*ibid.*).

4. *Ibid.*

5. Sharon Behn, "Attacks Hit Vital Security in Iraq," *Washington Times*, May 23, 2005, online.

6. Timothy Phelps, "Experts: Iraq Verges on Civil War," *Newsday*, May 12, 2005.

Phelps quoted a number of experts who offered stark assessments. Professor Noah Feldman of New York University said of the insurgency that it has been "getting stronger every passing day. When the violence recedes," he continued, "it is a sign that they are regrouping . . . . I have not seen any coherent evidence that we are winning against the insurgency."[1]

Judith Kipper of the Council on Foreign Relations had the same view. "Everything we thought we knew about the insurgency obviously is flawed. It was quiet for a while, and here it is back full force all over the country, and that is very dark news."[2]

Tod Robberson's May 26, 2005, piece for the *Dallas Morning News* offered a similar perspective.

> Iraq's insurgents, described earlier this year by U.S. officials as a dwindling force, have resisted military efforts to halt their attacks and have an apparent new bombing strategy to inflict headline-grabbing casualties, according to diplomatic and academic experts . . . . The experts said the insurgents have shown patience as they regrouped, devised new strategies and repeatedly demonstrated an ability to thwart U.S.-led efforts to stabilize Iraq. The persistent campaign of attacks has demoralized the population while proving the insurgents can withstand repeated military offensives designed to defang them.[3]

These sentiments were echoed by John Yaukey of *Army Times* on June 6, 2005.

> The insurgent stronghold of Fallujah fell in November. The parliamentary elections of January 30 came and went. Iraq's new elected government took power in April. Each was touted as a major victory against Iraq's insurgents. And yet Iraqi forces, backed by U.S. troops, are now conducting the largest offensive in Iraq since Baghdad fell two years ago. The mission is to root out what has become an insurgency with proven staying power and evolving sophistication especially capable of exploiting political vulnerabilities.[4]

Patrick Seale, whose *Al-Hayat* piece from May 12, 2005, we noted earlier, spoke of the "conclusion reached by most military experts, whether American, European or Israeli":

> [T]here is no prospect of a quick U.S. military victory in Iraq. One informed British view is that it will take the Americans at least five years to train an

---

1. *Ibid.*

2. *Ibid.*

3. Tod Robberson, "Insurgents Regrouped and Refocused, Analysts Say," *Dallas Morning News*, May 26, 2005.

4. John Yaukey, "Iraq's Politically Savvy Insurgency Proves Its Staying Power," *ArmyTimes. com*, June 6, 2005.

Iraqi force strong enough to take on the insurgents. Another view, by a former Mossad chief, Efraim Halevy, is that the U.S. will have to maintain a strong military presence in Iraq and the region for at least a decade.[1]

A recent comment from Professor Juan Cole puts it this way: "[t]he guerrilla war in Iraq is far more active, professional and effective now than it has ever been. It routinely assassinates important government officials."[2] And Maj. Gen. Joseph Taluto, head of the U.S. 42nd Infantry Division, which covers "hot spots" like Baquba and Samarra, was quoted in a *Gulf News* piece for June 9, 2005, offering his thoughts on the size of the resistance.

> I stay away from numbers . . . . We can make estimates by doing some kind of guesswork . . . . Who knows how big these networks are, or how widespread? I know it's substantial enough to be a threat to the government and it will be for some time.[3]

In case the testimony of these voices is not sufficiently persuasive, one might consider a couple of recent, revealing incidents in order get a sense of the long arm of the Iraqi resistance.

In October 2004, the puppet Interior Ministry set up a new group called the Wolf Brigade, under the leadership of Abu Walid, a Shiite, whose real name is Maj. Gen. Mohammed Qureishi. It is variously described as a police commando unit, a counter-insurgency outfit, and a special-forces team, that is claimed to have 2,000 commandos (though many say its forces number in the hundreds). It has garnered substantial publicity in the Western media for its contribution to the GWOT; a Council on Foreign Relations expert called it "the most feared and effective commando unit in Iraq."[4] It is comprised of Shiites (though there are a number of Sunnis in its officer corps) who are considered "folk heroes to some Shiites, but an object of fear and mistrust for Sunnis."[5] Aside from being "at the centre

---

1. Patrick Seale, *loc. cit.*

2. Juan Cole, "The Revenge of Baghdad Bob," *Salon.com*, June 9, 2005.

3. Phil Sands, "Good and Honest Iraqis Fighting U.S. Forces," *Gulfnews.com*, June 9, 2005.

4. Waleed Ibrahim and Mussab Khairallah, "Elite Iraqi Police Leader Survives Suicide Attack," *Scotland on Sunday* (*Scotsman.com*), June 12, 2005.

5. Ibrahim and Khairallah, *ibid.* The reference to "some Shiites" is probably a reference to the Shiite Badr Brigade of SCIRI which was created, trained, and financed for years by the Iranian government. It is thus not unreasonable in the slightest to maintain that the Wolf Brigade is a sectarian outfit. Events in Basra relating to local security forces illustrate the problem posed by sectarian militias. As the U.K. *Guardian* reported, "[t]he chief of police in Basra admitted . . . that he had effectively lost control of three-quarters of his officers and that sectarian militias had infiltrated the force and were using their posts to assassi- nate opponents . . . . General Hassan al-Sade said half of his 13,750-strong force was secretly

of controversy about aggressive methods and accusations of a sectarian 'dirty war' on minority Sunnis,"[1] the brigade is unique because its commander has its own nightly reality-TV program, "Terrorism in the Grip of Justice," on *al-Iraqiya* TV, the State-run, U.S.-funded channel in Iraq. The program features confessions of alleged "terrorists," many of whom appear to be physically mistreated.[2] Whether they are guilty of anything is anyone's guess – but since the show is nightly one suspects that the "rules" are pretty flexible, if only to ensure a constant stream of "guests."

A recent attack on the Wolf Brigade by the resistance illustrates the latter's tenacity. It was targeted by a suicide bomber on June 12, 2005, in what press reports called "a failed bid to assassinate the leader of the anti-insurgent Wolf Brigade [that killed] three other policemen in the process."[3] The bomber was *a member of the unit itself,* and the Interior Ministry says that it is searching for two other former members in conjunction with the bombing. How many other members of the unit are linked to the resistance is an open question. The resistance missed its target – *this time.* But it will be back.[4]

I make that claim by extrapolation from a second incident. On June 9, 2005, Maj. Gen. Ahmad Jaff, the General Director of the puppet government's "Unit for Combating Terrorism" was killed by a suicide bomber – along with his accompanying officers – just after he had completed an

---

working for the political parties. 'I trust 25 percent of my force, no more. The militias are the real power in Basra and they are made up of criminals and bad people'" (Rory Carroll, "Basra Out of Control, Says Chief of Police," *The Guardian*, May 31, 2005, online). Carroll noted that in Basra "tranquility had been bought by ceding authority to conservative Islamic parties and turning a blind eye to their militias' corruption scams and hit squads." One can credibly conceive of the same pattern playing out at the national level in the case of the Wolf Brigade, especially in view of the fact that with the January 2005 "election" in Iraq, the U.S. practically ceded control of the country to the partisan Shiite groups SCIRI and al-Dawa, who dominate the coalition that received a majority of votes from the part of the population that did participate. [See the detailed discussion of this and other aspects of the January 2005 election in Iraq by Mark Gery on pp. 761–795 of the present volume.—Ed.]

1. Ibrahim and Khairallah, *ibid.*

2. Neil MacDonald, "Iraqi Reality-TV Hit Takes Fear Factor to Another Level," *Christian Science Monitor,* June 7, 2005, online. Peter Maass (*loc. cit.*, also at *www.petermaass.com*) reports that the program is also sponsored by Gen. Adnan Thabit, the Special Police Commandos Commander and former Ba'athist who spent 9 years in jail for participating in a 1996 attempted coup against Saddam, run by CIA-asset Iyad Allawi.

3. Ibrahim and Khairallah, *ibid.*

4. Provided, that is, that the brigade is still around and functioning. One example of why the proposition is doubtful is provided in a piece that appeared in the *Los Angeles Times,* indicating that recently "members of Iraq's elite police commando units, heralded by U.S. and Iraqi officials as a key to stemming the insurgency, staged a protest outside Baghdad's heavily fortified Green Zone, saying that they hadn't been paid for four months" (Borzou Daragahi, "Iraqis Look At Cuts in Payroll," June 6, 2005, online). So much for "winning hearts and minds."

inspection of a military post at ar-Ridwaniyah, southwest of Baghdad.[1] The bombing, which was not the first attempt on his life, received almost no publicity, no doubt – at least in part – because it does not reflect well upon the Iraqi "government" when leading figures in its counter-insurgency force can be so easily targeted. Indeed, when the anti-resistance forces lack "intelligence" on the rebels to this degree, what trust can be placed in anything they say?

Incidents of this kind provide credibility to the opinions of various experts who have been less than optimistic about the situation in Iraq. As Michael O'Hanlon of the Washington, D.C.-based Brookings Institution put it, "We are not winning, and the security trend lines could almost lead you to believe that we are losing."[2] Former NATO commander, Gen. Wesley Clark, was even more forceful, saying, "[T]here is no basis for the administration to crow that the guerrilla war is winding down."[3] Gen. John Abizaid's June 23, 2005, testimony before the Senate Armed Services Committee (SASC) – where he admitted that "the overall strength of the insurgency was 'about the same' as six months ago"[4] – was similarly, and thankfully, realistic. Toby Dodge, a senior fellow at the International Institute of Strategic Studies, maintains that there is no "viable exit strategy,"[5] and, bringing this whole discussion to a focused conclusion, Professor Feldman said simply that "[t]here is no evidence whatsoever that they cannot win."[6]

Truth or Consequences

Can the "superpower" lose this war?

One of the most germane questions, two years into the war in Iraq, is what remains of America's "superpower" status. No doubt the *pre-war* perception of American power is wholly different from the *post-war* perception of that power, and the difference is recognized the world over. While the Bush administration keeps on with its hectoring tone towards Syria,

---

1. "Resistance Attack Eliminates puppet General Director for fighting 'Terrorism,'" *FreeArabVoice.org*, June 9, 2005.

2. Lasseter and Landay, *loc. cit.*

3. Paul Reynolds, "Iraq Two Years On: Endgame or Unending War?" *BBC News* (online), April 6, 2005.

4. Liz Sidoti, "Commander: Iraq Insurgency Still Strong," *San Francisco Chronicle*, June 23, 2005, online.

5. Tod Robberson, "Insurgents Regrouped and Refocused, Analysts Say," *Dallas Morning News*, May 26, 2005.

6. Timothy Phelps, "Experts: Iraq Verges on Civil War," *Newsday*, May 12, 2005, online.

Iran, North Korea, and even Russia, can it really believe that its performance in Iraq has instilled *greater* fear into the armed forces of these more powerful countries?

We can admit that before the war there was a certain unknown quality about the military technology available to U.S. forces. Who could say for sure what the Pentagon's colossal budget had brought into being, out of view of even the most astute observer? The Bush regime could play upon the "be very afraid" theme so beloved of Hollywood screenwriters precisely because of that intangibility. The fear of something happening, however, is often more frightening than the actual event. The fear of "shock and awe" *no longer exists.* Iraqi rebels have shown its very real limits; and what Iraqis can do, others better armed and better trained can do too. There is now an undercurrent of quiet discussion that is nevertheless resonating all over the world, exploding the myth of American invincibility: "America can be defeated."[1]

It was therefore premature for Bush to declare before the invasion that "time is running out for Saddam." The entire Iraqi nation with its President had even at that point suffered over a decade of Anglo-American aggression, so the threat of "shock and awe" would not likely have seemed any more menacing than the dozen years of murderous sanctions and routine illegal bombing in the U.S.-U.K. "patrolled" no-fly zones. The probable Iraqi approach to Bush's threats reminds me of a scene I witnessed on TV of a foreign television crew filming a group of Iraqi military chiefs huddled over a table with a map of Baghdad as the March 2003 invasion approached the city. The nondescript room they were in had a heavy curtain over the window to avoid the attention of American planes bombing the city at night. When, with a deafening roar, the window blew in so that the curtain was blown up parallel to the ceiling, the television crew hit the floor, mouthing involuntary expletives. After they regained their composure, they looked around the room and found the Iraqi officers still huddled over the table discussing their moves as though nothing had happened. This scene, too, perhaps, they had seen before.

---

1. In spite of this growing consensus, Defense Secretary Rumsfeld maintains the contrary. Appearing before the House Armed Services Committee in March, 2005, he declared: "The world has seen, in the last three and a half years, the capability of the USA . . . . They have seen the United States and the coalition forces going into Iraq . . . . That has to have a deterrent effect on people . . . . If you put yourself in the shoes of a country that might decide they'd like to make mischief, they have a very recent, vivid example of the fact that the U.S. has the ability to deal with this" (Anne Scott Tyson, "U.S. Gaining World's Respect From Wars, Rumsfeld Asserts," *Washington Post*, March 11, 2005, online).

But what the world hasn't before seen is the U.S. Army with its 21st-century technology and multi-billion dollar equipment budget faced down by "poorly trained villagers." The world has seen it now, however, and insofar as the American place in the world is guaranteed by its military, we may speculate that its place is somewhat less certain than before.

The testimony of a wide range of intelligent commentators provides more than persuasive evidence for this interpretation. Late last year, Scott Ritter called the war one which "the United States cannot win, and which the interim government of Iyad Allawi cannot survive."[1] At much the same time, Professor Toby Dodge, an Iraq analyst at Queen Mary University, London told the BBC:

> [The Americans] have been saying that Fallujah is the source of and therefore the solution to their problems. The violence in Mosul has shown that to be a crassly stupid thing to say. Insurgency is a national phenomenon fuelled by alienation. I don't think this war is winnable because they have alienated the base of support across Iraqi society.[2]

The following month, Georgie Ann Geyer wrote in her column about "truth no one really wants to deal with," namely, that

> this war could very easily be lost by the United States. All the insurgents have to do is hang on another year. All we have to do is what the French and the British did in their colonies: let themselves be exhausted and finally destroyed by their hubris, their delusions, and their arrogant lack of understanding of the local people.[3]

Jim Lobe, Washington correspondent for *Inter Press Service*, wrote the next day that it must even now be "clear to friend and foe alike that . . . the American Colossus is not up to global domination."[4] For his part, Paul Craig Roberts, a former Republican assistant secretary of the treasury, seconded Lobe's understanding in a piece from the beginning of this year.

> The world is a vast place. The U.S. has demonstrated that it cannot impose its will on a tiny part known as Iraq. American realism may yet reassert itself, dispel the fog of delusion, cleanse the body politic of the Jacobin spirit, and

1. Scott Ritter, "Squeezing Jello in Iraq," *Aljazeera.net*, November 13, 2004, online.

2. Lin Noueihed, "U.S. Wins Fallujah but Struggles Elsewhere," *Reuters*, November 19, 2004, online.

3. Georgie Ann Geyer, "Maginot Minds in Washington Gloss Over the Truth in Iraq," *Universal Press Syndicate* (uexpress.com), December 28, 2004, online.

4. Jim Lobe (Inter Press Service), "Bye, Bye Unipolar World," *Antiwar.com*, December 29, 2004, online.

lead the world by good example. But this happy outcome will require regime change in the U.S.[1]

Sadly, the authority of these writers (with the numerous others who could be quoted) and the somber contents of their message don't seem to have sunk in with the career hacks or the legions of "Joe Sixpacks." Perhaps it will only be when they or their sons and daughters are drafted to "free the Iraqis" that they will get their heads out of the glue bag.

Effects of the resistance on the American military: Recruiting

Beyond the threat of the Iraqi resistance to the perception of so-called "American hegemony," other voices of warning have been raised about the effect of the Iraq misadventure upon other aspects of American national power, one aspect of which is the military which the Pentagon and Congress are struggling to maintain.

As of this writing, there are some 150,000 American troops in Iraq – that means that there are between 17 and 20 U.S. brigades in the country.[2] Of that number, some 40–50 percent are drawn from the National Guard and the Army Reserve. Many of those are at, or near the end of, their second consecutive year of active duty, and are soon due to return home and take up their civilian lives, *unless* the Pentagon comes up with something – more of the "back-door draft," or perhaps even outright conscription. Thus far, the U.S. has dealt with the pressure of keeping the Army together through a combination of financial incentives[3] and stop-loss initiatives,

---

1. Paul Craig Roberts, "How Americans Were Seduced by War," *LewRockwell.com*, January 18, 2005, online.

2. Regular American troop totals are not the sole guide to the number of military forces in Iraq, however. Much if not most of what goes by the name of "private contractors" are soldiers of fortune or paid mercenaries. There are an estimated 25,000 security "shooters" in Iraq, many of whom come from U.S. military and special-forces backgrounds. They are so numerous that the 60-plus private security companies (PSCs) in the country have their own lobbying association headed by Lawrence Peters. Recently they have been pressing for better armaments, with which to deal more effectively with the resistance. As a *Washington Post* article detailed recently, "PSCs, whose duties in Iraq increasingly mirror those of the U.S. military, are in some instances agitating for the right to arm themselves with heavy military-style weapons. Charged with the frontline responsibility of defending infrastructure projects, homes, personnel, and even U.S. military convoys, the companies operatives have become prime targets of terrorist attacks." The manager of one company asked for the PSCs to be equipped with "40mm grenade launchers, shoulder-fired anti-tank rockets, and M72 anti-armor Vietnam holdovers or AT4 bunker busters." The implications are far-reaching: there are tens of thousands more "troops" in the field in Iraq than indicated by the Army statistics – and it still isn't enough. See Sharon Behn, "Iraq Security Companies Lobby for Heavy Arms," *Washington Post*, June 6, 2005, online.

3. The scale of these incentives indicates just how serious the recruitment and re-enlist-

which force soldiers to stay in the army beyond their contractual obligations.[1] Thus, even now, the troops are being virtually press-ganged by the
government with the hope that these "grunts" in the field will save Bush's
bacon.

The incentives don't quite seem to be attractive enough, however. "The
Army is coming up short in its recruiting of National Guard forces," an
AP wire story indicated early this year, "and staffing the next rotation of
guardsmen and reservists to serve in Iraq will be difficult," according to
what top military officials told lawmakers.[2] The wire referred to an important meeting of a subcommittee of the House Armed Services Committee,
where officials from the Army National Guard and Reserve appeared to
explain the situation to politicians. Lt. General Roger Schultz, Chief of the
Army National Guard said that "recruiting is the area where we are falling
short," and added that the Army National Guard was currently 15,000 soldiers below its normal strength, with the recruiting total for January 2005
only 56 percent of the necessary target. Nor has the situation improved
over the last six months. A *Reuters* wire story described recent Pentagon
recruiting figures, showing that

> two-thirds through the fiscal 2005 recruiting year, which ends September 30,
> the regular Army was 17 percent behind its goal, the Army Reserve was 20
> percent behind and the Army National Guard was 24 percent behinds its end-
> of-May plans. The Army, which provides most of the U.S. ground troops in
> Iraq, had missed its fourth consecutive monthly recruiting goal in May.[3]

---

ment crisis is. According to a recent press account, "the Army has boosted some incentives, now offering up to $20,000 in signing bonuses and $70,000 toward college tuition"
(Nick Perry, "Big Drop in Seattle For Army Recruits," *Seattle Times*, June 6, 2005,
online). Army Secretary Francis Harvey has already spoken to lawmakers about increasing those incentives. If approved by Congress, the Army would "raise the maximum
cash bonus for new recruits to $40,000 and begin a pilot program to give up to $50,000
in home-mortgage assistance to people who volunteer for eight years active-duty service" (Will Dunham, "U.S. Army Slips Further Behind Recruiting Goals," *Reuters* (at
YahooNews), June 10, 2005, online). As for veteran special-forces non-commissioned
and warrant officers, "the Army offers a re-enlistment bonus of $197,000" (Joe Galloway,
"Administration Stubbornly Stays the Course in Iraq," *Salt Lake Tribune*, June 3, 2005,
online). It says something that *in spite of this huge sum* that "the backbone of the force,"
in the words of Galloway, "is leaving in droves" – attracted by the $20,000 *per month*
that they can obtain from "contractors" in Iraq.

1. See David Wood and Harry Esteve, "National Guard Stretched to the Limit," *The
Oregonian*, June 12, 2005, online: "Currently 27,495 Army National Guard soldiers are
being involuntarily kept on active duty, a status that can last months."

2. Liz Sidoti, "Top Military Officials say Forces Strained," *Associated Press*, February 2,
2005, online.

3. Dunham, *loc. cit.*

An Army Recruiting Command spokesman, Douglas Smith, commented: "We're having a really tough fight [to recruit] this year, and we're going to have an even tougher fight next year."

None of this bodes well for the Army Reserve's continued ability to meet the operational demands being placed on it. As a *Washington Post* correspondent noted gravely, "If the recruiting trends and the demand for forces persist, the Pentagon under current policies could eventually 'run out' of reserve forces for war-zone rotations."[1] Citing information supplied on February 2, 2005, to the House Armed Services Committee by Derek Stewart, director of defense capabilities and management for the Government Accountability Office, the correspondent noted that the Pentagon projects that some 100,000 reservists will have to be kept continuously mobilized over the next 3 to 5 years, something clearly problematic.

Regular Army statistics are not any better. A recent *UPI* wire story summarized them as follows:

> Defense Department figures at the end of April showed that 35,926 recruits had signed up this fiscal year, which began last October 1. This gives recruiters four months to sign up another 44,000 to meet their goal. Even worse is the number of reserves. Statistics show that 7,283 reserves have signed up. The goal is for 22,175 by the end of the year.[2]

Lt. General James Henly, the Army Reserve chief, sent a personal, detailed memo to Army Chief of Staff General Peter Schoomaker on December 20, 2004, confirming the concerns detailed above. The memo's stated purpose was "to inform [Schoomaker] of the Army Reserve's inability . . . to meet mission requirements," and he said in it that that the Reserve is "rapidly degenerating into a 'broken' force."[3] Add to this comments made by senior National Guard officers – like Lt. Gen. Steven Blum, the chief of the National Guard Bureau, who said recently, "My concern is that the National Guard will not be a ready force next time it's needed, whether here at home or abroad"; or head of the Maine National Guard, Brig. Gen Bill Libby, who said that "one can conclude that we're going to run out of soldiers" – and the picture is even more disturbing.[4] Pointing to the combined

---

1. Anne Scott Tyson, "Army Considers Extending Reserve," *Washington Post,* February 3, 2005, p. A22.

2. Philip Turner, "Army Faces Growing Recruiting Crisis," *UPI,* June 2, 2005, online.

3. Tom Bowman, *Baltimore Sun,* January 5, 2005, online.

4. David Wood and Harry Esteve, "National Guard Stretched to the Limit," *The Oregonian,* June 12, 2005, online. Elsewhere in this piece the authors say "the Army National Guard is hanging on by its fingertips. It provides half of the Army's combat power . . . but its battalions are struggling to scrape up enough soldiers and hand-me-down equipment to meet

psychological impact of Guantánamo Bay, Abu Ghraib, and U.S. casualties in Iraq, Philip Turner of *UPI* observed that "young men and women are not exactly banging down recruiting station doors to join the Army."[1] Retired Lt. Col. Charles Krohn, who worked at the Pentagon as a civilian public affairs official, spoke to veteran journalist Robert Novak, seconding Turner's assessment, and saying that recruiters are not to blame for current recruiting problems. But the war is. "Army recruiting is in a death spiral," he said, and it's "an unintended consequence of a prolonged war in Iraq, especially given the failure to find WMD."[2] Though Defense Secretary Rumsfeld has recently attempted to remind Americans that there were dark and pessimistic times even during World War II,[3] he forgets that far fewer Americans see Iraq as a war of necessity demanding sweeping national sacrifice. Charles Peña, director of defense policy studies at the Cato Institute, puts it more accurately: "This is *not* like World War II in that *the country is still split on this war* – there just aren't all those volunteers . . . and in Iraq, it's a situation that at best is treading water" (emphasis mine).[4]

Robert Novak cut to exactly this essential point in his piece for the *Chicago Sun-Times*." The Army's dilemma," he said,

is maintaining an all-volunteer service when volunteering means going in harm's way in Iraq. The dilemma extends to national policy. How can the United States maintain its global credibility against the Islamists, if military ranks cannot be filled by volunteers and there is no public will for a draft?[5]

---

overseas deployment orders . . . . " They cite internal National Guard documents indicating that "all 10 of its special forces units, all 147 military police units, 97 of 101 infantry units and 73 of 75 amour units cannot, because of past or current mobilizations, deploy again to a war zone without reinforcements." This translates into a need for "a staggering $20 billion worth of equipment to sustain its operations." The pool of soldiers available for assignment is also declining: "Fewer recruits are coming in, more soldiers are leaving the Army, and more troops are being drawn down. The pool is shrinking. Internal National Guard documents show that, in December 2004, 86,455 soldiers were available for duty. As of April 30, 2005, the number had shrunk to 74, 519. The current need for National Guard soldiers in Iraq alone is 32,000 . . . . On average each month, the Guard is enlisting three of the four recruits it needs." The number of soldiers coming into the Guard from the active force is also shrinking rapidly. In the first five months of this fiscal year, only 974 active duty soldiers switched to the Guard, while Col. Mike Jones, a National Guard manpower planner, said that "normally we're at 7,000" during the same period.

1. Turner, *loc. cit.*

2. Robert Novak, "Army's Recruitment Crisis Deepens," *Chicago Sun-Times*, May 26, 2005, online.

3. Testimony before the Senate Armed Services Committee, June 23, 2005 (http://www.defenselink.mil/speeches/2005/sp20050623-secdef1661.html).

4. Turner, *loc. cit.*

5. Novak, *loc. cit.* One sign of the panic setting in is the June 2005 coverage of the

If indeed they cannot, is outright conscription in the cards? Will the public accept it if it does come to that? How much will – and foolishness – does it take for the American public to "stay the course" under these kinds of conditions?

Effects on the American military 2: Equipment

The problem is not merely a question of men, it is also a question of equipment. Gen. Richard Cody, the Army's vice chief of staff, admitted earlier this year that his organization is "equipment-challenged right now."[1] He also highlighted the fact that the Army had drawn down "almost all" of its pre-positioned stocks of armored vehicles and other equipment to outfit seven Army National Guard brigades for deployment. His comments were seconded by Lt. Gen. Blum of the National Guard, who said that the Guard was "woefully under-equipped before the war started," and pointed out that the situation wasn't getting any better.[2] Reporters Wood and Esteve bring these assessments up to date in their June 2005 report.

> To fully equip units in Iraq, the Pentagon has stripped local Guard units of about 24,000 pieces of equipment, including helicopters, Humvees, radios, heavy trucks, night vision goggles, and weapons. That has left Guard units at home, already seriously short of gear, without equipment critical to state missions. The problem is especially acute in some Western states that cannot control forest fires without the National Guard.[3]

The "coalition of the willing" will not come to the rescue, either. After saying that one third of the British military was experiencing serious weaknesses, a report from the U.K.'s National Audit Office, covered by the British *Daily Telegraph*, further indicates that "there is a potential crisis facing the military with so many troops deployed in operations overseas."[4] With the resistance getting stronger by the day, and American and U.K. forces becoming more and more depleted, it may just be a question of who can hold on the longest.

Pentagon's move to set up a database of high-school students between the ages of 16 and 18 for more precisely targeted recruiting efforts. Privacy and government watchdog outfits have, not surprisingly, gone ballistic over the move. See "Pentagon Creating Student Database," Jonathan Krim, *Washington Post*, June 23, 2005, 2005, p. A1.

1. Tyson, *loc. cit.*
2. *Ibid.*
3. Wood and Esteve, *loc. cit.*
4. Thomas Harding, "Armed Forces Stretched Beyond Limit," *Daily Telegraph*, June 16, 2005, online at *news.telegraph.co.uk*.

Effects on the American military 3: Casualties

On January 6, 2005, an online news service compiled an article, based on Defense Department- and *CNN-* provided casualty information, that offered some sobering statistics. Even before the resurgence of the resistance after the claimed "lull" that followed the January 2005 "election," it reported that "the number of soldiers suffering combat injuries in Iraq had surpassed the 10,000 mark since the war began in March 2003."[1] The Department of Defense had at that time announced that 10,252 Americans had been wounded in the period, of which 5,396 were hurt seriously enough to be unable to return to the battlefield. The compilation continued by noting that "with a total casualty count of 11,601, and a permanently deployed force of 130,000, the chances of U.S. soldiers being killed or wounded in the conflict have been reduced to one in 11."[2] It went further, saying that with "the death toll [then] at 1,349, the chances of U.S. soldiers being killed in battle in Iraq stands at one in 96." A comforting thought for those sent to fight a war built on lies, especially considering that those statistics cover only 2003 and 2004.

"Iraq 2004 Looks Like Vietnam 1966" was the headline of another piece on U.S. casualties that appeared in December of last year on MSN's online magazine, *Slate.* The article offers an overview of research by Philip Carter and Owen West, respectively former Army and Marine Corps officers, and it is subtitled "Adjusting Body Counts for Medical and Military Changes." The authors' research compares Iraq casualties with those of Vietnam, taking into account factors such as improved body armor and more effective medical procedures. They conclude that

> [t]he casualty statistics make clear that our nation is involved in a war whose intensity on the ground matches that of previous American wars. Indeed the proportional burden on the infantryman is at its highest level since WWII.[3]

What they draw from this and other conclusions supported by their extensive research is that "today's fighting in Iraq may actually be more lethal than the street fighting in Vietnam," an assessment, they note, that "should not be taken lightly."[4]

1. "U.S. Troops Have One In 11 Chance Of Being Wounded Or Killed In Iraq," *BigNewsNetwork.com,* June, 23, 2005.
2. *Ibid.*
3. December 27, 2004, *Slate,* published at www.slate.msn.com.
4. *Ibid.* The magnitude of the problem is evident in the VA budget revision to provide medical care to the estimanted 80,000 more veterans than originally planned (Thomas B. Edsall, "VA Faces $2.6 Billion Shortfall in Medical Care," *Washington Post,* June 29, 2005, p. A19).

As in the case of recruiting and equipment problems, American forces are not alone in suffering severe casualties. As of early this year, the British Army had lost around 80 soldiers and suffered over 800 wounded.[1] When the number of British troops is scaled up proportionately to those of their American counterparts, their wounded rate is worse, even though they are not in the eye of the storm − at least for the moment. It is also worth noting that as of September 2004 some 700 British troops that served in Iraq were treated for mental health problems.[2] With less than 10,000 British troops in Iraq, this figure is close to 10 percent of the British force! As for American troops, "the Pentagon admits that as many as 100,000 new combat vets nationwide will suffer from mental issues,"[3] a figure not too far off from that mentioned by Dr. William Winkenwerder, Jr., assistant secretary of defense for health affairs, who said that "[t]he Department estimates between 8 and 15 percent of combat veterans suffer some *lasting* mental health trauma from their experience."[4] This is a tragedy both for the victims and for their families, hard enough to support in a just war. In an unjust war it is positively criminal that our young people are being sacrificed by a cabal of demonic warmongers.

The "Iraqi" army?

Pentagon chiefs and administration spokesmen regularly declare that America will be able to withdraw troops as soon as homegrown Iraqi forces are up and running. The goal in Iraq has long shifted away from "victory" to one of handing the problem over to native "Iraqi forces." This line comes from the top of the Bush administration[5] and is parroted down the chain of command.[6] Whether the competence of the new "Iraqi forces"

---

1. Michael Evans, "Toll of British Wounded in Iraq War Reaches 800," *The Times*, January 18, 2005, online.

2. Terri Judd, "Mental Health Problems For 700 Troops In Iraq," *The Independent*, February 5, 2005, online.

3. "Iraq War Vets Fight an Enemy at Home," Julian Guthrie, *San Francisco Chronicle*, January 17, 2005, online.

4. Leo Shane III, "DOD Adds Post-Combat Counseling Session to Diagnose Long-Term Trauma," *Stars and Stripes*, January 27, 2005, online.

5. See, e.g., Jim VandeHei and Peter Baker, "Bush's Optimism On Iraq Debated," *Washington Post*, June 5, 2005, p. 1: "[A] democratically elected Iraqi government protected by a better trained and equipped Iraqi military will hold off what remains of the insurgency and gradually allow U.S. forces to withdraw . . . . "

6. See, e.g., James Janega, "4,000 Marines, 30,000 Hostile Square Miles," *Chicago Tribune*, June 4, 2005, online: "'This is not something that we are going to solve. This is something where we can provide stability so that the government can form and resolve

are up to the task or not, there is an obvious political problem with this approach. Most recruits come from Kurdish or Shiite areas, and are themselves, according to most reports, predominantly Kurdish or Shiite. They and the militias they serve with tend also, in many cases, to identify historically and ideologically with Kurdish factions or radical Shiite sects such as SCIRI and al-Dawa.[1] Prior to the American invasion, these groups made it their mission to destabilize the legitimate government of Saddam Hussein, and they are seen by large numbers of Iraqis as having sectarian rather than generally nationalist, Iraqi motives. The fact that their activities were funded by the U.S., Iran, and others only adds to their suspicious character for many Iraqis. Their participation in an army supporting the American occupation can only be seen, by those who are anti-occupation, as just another chapter in the long saga of Kurdish and radical Shiite flirtation with foreign powers in order to further their own ends. Continued defense by the puppet Iraqi government of the use of Shiite and Kurdish militias (such as the Wolf and Badr Brigades) to "crack down" on insurgents can do nothing but fuel this antagonism, as we noted regarding the controversy surrounding the Wolf Brigade's treatment of Sunnis.[2] Even the recruits recognize this: one who until recently was part of a new unit called the Defense Force of Rutba, which was disbanded by the U.S. after recruits refused to attend training, admitted that many see him as an enemy for collaborating with his country's occupiers. Indeed this is why members of his unit feared to attend the required U.S.-military-conducted training. "The people here would believe that we were cooperating with U.S. forces," he said, "and that is a reason for anyone to be killed."[3]

---

it,' said Lt. Col. Lionel Urquhart, commanding officer of the 3rd Battalion, 25th Marines, whose troops occupy garrisons in Haditha and Hit."

1. See, e.g., Youssef, *loc. cit.*, and Sabrina Tavernise and John Burns, "As Iraqi Army Trains, Word In The Field Is It May Take Years," *New York Times*, June 13, 2005, p. 1. [Also see the essay by Mark Gery on pp. 761–795 of the present volume for a deeper discussion of the political landscape as regards the Kurdish and Shiite factions.—Ed.]

2. Also see Edmond Roy, "Iraq Insurgency Produces Better Trained Terrorists: CIA Report," *Australian Broadcasting Company* (www.abc.net.au), June 23, 2005, online. Roy interviewed Michael McKinley, senior lecturer in international relations and strategy at the Australian National University, who said that "the declared intentions and wishes of leading political figures in Iraq, that the best military would be the militia, that is, the Shiites in the south and the Kurds in the north. Now that doesn't bode well, especially when the principal enemy comes from the Sunni group. It's a recipe for dubious internal conflict bordering on civil war."

3. Fadil al-Badrani, "Unit Refuses To Train at U.S. Center," *Reuters*, June 5, 2005, online. See also Andrew Hammond, "Iraqi Army Fears Insurgents Outside Walls of Base," *Reuters*, August 8, 2005, online, quoting an Iraqi recruit: "We're all afraid. I can't go

Politics aside, the prospects of this ragbag Kurdish-Shiite puppet force taking over from the American forces is not promising. As of the beginning of 2005, U.S. officials were claiming that the Iraqi army numbered some 120,000 men. Journalists such as veteran Middle East writer Dilip Hiro immediately cast credible doubt on this number, pointing out that in actuality only 5,000 of them were both trained and reliable.[1] As for the "Iraqi Police Force," they were said to number some 135,000 on paper, but, again according to Hiro, over 45,000 of those on the payroll never report for duty, and of the remainder, only 50 percent are properly trained or armed. Many if not most never fight when rebels turn up – as Fallujah, Mosul, Ramadi, and other towns have long demonstrated.[2] A month after Hiro's piece, journalists writing for the British *Independent on Sunday* said that though the administration claimed that it was at the time "half-way to meeting the target of training almost 270,000 Iraqi forces, including around 52,000 troops and 135,000 Iraqi policemen," experts maintained that there were "as few as 5,000 troops who could be considered combat ready."[3] This number was seconded as recently as June 2005 in an editorial appearing in *Newsday*, which cited

members of Congress [returning] from a recent trip to Iraq [who] were told by U.S. commanders that only about 5,000 . . . Iraqi troops can be counted on to confront the insurgency with any degree of success. In too many skirmishes, Iraqi soldiers have fled at the first sign of resistance, some defecting as quickly as they signed up for the relatively generous pay offered them."[4]

Due to this embarrassing reality, the *Independent* journalists wrote, "the Pentagon has stopped giving figures for the number of combat-ready indigenous troops."[5] Instead, "only figures for troops 'on hand' are issued," which consist of the "overall total of Iraqis in uniform, [including] raw recruits and police who have gone on duty after as little as three weeks' training." This policy has continued up to now, with a *Bloomberg.com* report confirming that the "Pentagon has refused to release the percentage of Iraqi troops considered capable of conducting combat operations on their own or with

outside the base wearing these military clothes."

1. Dilip Hiro, "Cul-de-sacs All Around: Assessing the Iraqi Election," *Tomdispatch.com*, January 26, 2005, online.

2. *Ibid.*

3. Andrew Buncombe, Kim Sengupta, and Raymond Whitaker, "Pentagon Covers Up Failure to Train and Recruit Local Security Forces," *The Independent on Sunday*, February 13, 2005, online.

4. "Rummy in Wonderland," *Newsday*, June 19, 2005, online.

5. Buncombe *et al., loc. cit.*

minimal U.S. assistance."[1] Senator Carl Levin (D-Mich.) pressed Air Force Gen. Richard Myers for an answer as to "how many of the roughly 130,000 Iraqi forces were sufficiently trained and equipped" during a February 3, 2005, Senate Armed Services Committee hearing, but the general said he could not give an estimate.[2] Levin's own assessment was that "we have no way of measuring the capabilities" of our "allied" Iraqi forces. Senator Joe Biden (D-Del.) has also taken issue with the administration's characterization of the state of "Iraqi" forces; during Secretary of State Rice's confirmation hearing in January 2005, he said,

> Time and again this administration has tried to leave the American people with the impression that Iraq has well over 100,000 fully trained, fully competent military police and personnel, and that is simply not true. We're months, probably years, away from reaching our target.[3]

This was the assessment of a mid-June 2005 piece in the *New York Times*, which confirmed the statistics that the Pentagon has provided as well as the assessment of their reliability.

> [T]he American command says that there are now 107 battalions of Iraqi troops and paramilitary police units, totaling 169,000 men. The total is set to rise to 270,000 by next summer, when 10 fully equipped 14,000-man Iraqi army divisions are scheduled to be operational. But figures alone tell only part of the story, since *only three of the battalions now deployed are rated fully operational* by the Americans, and many others are far behind in terms of manpower, training and equipment" (emphasis mine).[4]

Reports from the visit of a congressional delegation to Iraq at the end of May 2005 reveal as well that the congressmen were told that "the United States is at least two years away from adequately training a viable Iraqi military."[5] Biden, who took part in the visit, reiterated the *NYT* statistic on ABC's *This Week*: of the "107 battalions . . . trained . . . and in uniform," he said, "only three – three – are fully operational, and three are close . . . . "[6] A recent newscast from Australia quoted Australian National University

1. Brendan Murray, "Bush, Iraq's Al-Jaafari to Meet Amid Concern Over War," *Bloomberg. com*, June 24, 2005.

2. Vicki Allen, "Wolfowitz Says No Iraq Nationalist Insurgency," *Reuters*, February 3, 2005, online.

3. Buncombe *et al., loc. cit.*

4. Tavernise and Burns, *loc. cit.*

5. VandeHei and Baker, *loc. cit.*

6. Borzou Daragahi, "Iraqis Look At Cuts In Payroll," *Los Angeles Times*, June 6, 2005, p. 1. See also Cordesman, *loc. cit.*

Lecturer in International Relations and Strategy Michael McKinley to the effect that

> there are too many reports coming out and openly expressed, it has to be said, by U.S. military enlisted men and by their officers, that the gearing up of a competent new Iraqi military is at least five to 10 years off. And that really is a figure that is just put forward because no one quite knows.[1]

The whole situation has about it the air of Hitler's bunker in the last months and weeks of World War II, when army units that only existed on paper were ordered into battle. David Isenberg of the British and American Security Council put his assessment quite bluntly: "[D]isaster is too polite a word."[2]

Regardless of how many there are, pro-"government" Iraqi forces are not much good to the U.S. if they're working for the insurgency, or dead. As for the former, a recent *Newsweek* paints a grim picture of what it calls the insurgents' most powerful weapon: "a vast network of infiltrators, spies, and recruiters." According to Baghdad intelligence officials who go unnamed to protect their clearances, Iraq's security services

> have hundreds of "ghost soldiers" – members who vanish, sometimes for months on end, but continue to draw their pay. The fear is that they are working for the insurgency while keeping up their ties in uniform. Early on, when training procedures were still being defined, U.S. forces tried to institute a program to screen Iraqi recruits . . . . [T]he process began with a preliminary interview with the enlistee. If he passed, vetting agents went on to do a background check on the individual as well as on key family members. But with pressure on to find an exit strategy for Iraq – and to build significant Iraqi forces fast – a lot of doubtful characters seem to have slipped through the cracks. Gaps in the process were quickly exploited in a strategic campaign of infiltration by the insurgency.[3]

This narrative is consistent with many of the reports that come from Iraq. The attempt on the life of the Wolf Brigade commander by one of its members, detailed above, is one such example. Another is the testimony of a U.S. Army captain who spent a year in Iraq as an intelligence officer and returned in February. "Infiltration of the police by insurgents poses a critical problem," he said, and "[s]ometimes the police even act in cahoots with the insurgents."[4] Any tally of effective Iraqi security forces should also

---

1. Roy, *loc. cit.*

2. Buncombe *et al.*, *loc. cit.*

3. Johnson and Liu, *loc. cit.* See also Patrick J. McDonnell, "Ranks Plagued by Infiltrators," *Los Angeles Times*, June 29, 2005, online, and CNN, "U.S. Study: Insurgents Infiltrate Iraqi Police," *CNN.com*, July 25, 2005.

4. Spencer Ante, "A Hole in Bush's Iraq Exit Strategy," *Business Week*, April 19, 2005, online.

exclude those such as "the 14,000 blue-uniformed Iraqi police in Nineveh Province, the capital of which is Mosul," where, according to comments made to the British *Independent on Sunday* by Khasro Goran, the deputy governor there, "the police had helped insurgents assassinate the previous governor." He further related that

> when guerrillas captured almost all of Mosul on November 11, 2004, the police collaborated, abandoning 30 police stations without a fight . . . . Some $40 million worth of arms and equipment was captured by the insurgents.[1]

The reporter who took Goran's testimony noted simply that "[i]t is a measure of how far the reality of the war in Iraq now differs from the rosy picture presented by the media that the fall of Mosul to the insurgents went almost unreported abroad."[2] As if the infiltration of security forces weren't enough, complaints have even surfaced that some Iraqi judges are meting out light sentences for those who "have hoarded or transported huge stashes of bombs, machine-guns, and rocket-propelled grenades" in order to show "a degree of sympathy with the insurgents."[3]

On February 3, 2005, Paul Wolfowitz confirmed before the Senate Armed Services Committee that 1,342 Iraqi police, soldiers and National Guards had been killed between June 2004 and January 2005.[4] The figure was out of date the moment it was uttered, as can be gauged from a June 2005 report from the *Boston Globe* which said, "So far this year, nearly 1,000 members of Iraq's police and security forces have been killed in attacks, almost as many as the total for the previous year and a half, according to Pentagon figures."[5] It is ultimately questionable how accurate these reports are, for reliable figures on the deaths of recruits and trainees are elusive, notwithstanding the statistics kept for every other part of the "Iraqi forces" training program. As the *New York Times* confirmed, "American officers, with statistics for virtually every other aspect of the program, say they have none on the numbers of Iraqis killed in attacks."[6]

1. Patrick Cockburn, "150 Hostages and 19 Deaths Leave U.S. Claims of Iraqi 'Peace' in Tatters," *The Independent on Sunday*, April 17, 2005, online.

2. *Ibid.*

3. Colin Freeman, "Saddam's Old Judges Provoke U.S. Fury with Their Lenient Sentences for Insurgents," *The Sunday Telegraph*, March 13, 2005, online.

4. *United Press International*, "1,342 Iraq Forces Killed Since June," *BigNewsNetwork.com*, February 4, 2005, online.

5. Bryan Bender, "Insurgency Seen Forcing Change In Iraq Strategy," *Boston Globe*, June 10, 2005.

6. Tavernise and Burns, *loc. cit.*

Two recent incidents relating to the formation of the new "Iraqi Army" are worth mentioning in some detail, for they demonstrate that recent U.S. officials' talk about "two years or so" until it is fully prepared for operations is "pie in the sky" at best – or downright lies at the worst.[1]

The first incident is described by a *Washington Post* piece in which the entire thrust of the article was ably captured by its headline, "Building Iraq's Army: Mission Improbable." The authors recap the U.S. government position, that "the reconstruction of Iraq's security forces is the prerequisite for an American withdrawal from Iraq." They then go on to say that in spite of how the administration "extols the continuing progress of the new Iraqi army, the project in Baiji . . . demonstrates the immense challenges of building an army from scratch in the middle of a bloody insurgency."[2]

Baiji is a desolate oil town located strategically in northern Iraq, where the Iraqi army's Charlie Company is being trained by American Army Sgt. Rick McGovern. He complains in the *Post* story that "[w]e can't tell these guys about a lot of stuff, because we're not really sure who's good and who isn't." The reporters explain what he means.

> An hour before dawn . . . the soldiers of . . . Charlie Company began their mission with a ballad to ousted President, Saddam Hussein. "We have lived in humiliation since you left," one sang in Arabic, out of earshot of his U.S. counterparts. "We had hoped to spend our life with you."[3]

These are supposed to be our "Iraqi allies," remember. Given their questionable loyalty, it is hardly surprising to hear not only that the entire Company disintegrated in December 2004 when its commander was killed by a car bomb, but also that

> members of the unit were threatening to quit en masse this week over complaints that ranged from dismal living conditions to insurgent threats. Across a vast cultural divide, language is just one impediment. Young Iraqi soldiers, ill equipped and drawn from a disenchanted Sunni minority, say they are not even sure what they are fighting for.[4]

But, of course, they *do* know – it is the relatively munificent $300–$400 per month that brings them, nothing else.

---

1. Beyond these two illustrative cases there are many others that could be cited. As noted above, a recent *Reuters* wire story noted how "an Iraqi national guard unit [in Rutba near the Jordanian border] had been disbanded after it refused to attend a military training academy overseen by U.S. advisers" (al-Badrani, *loc. cit.*).

2. Shadid and Fainaru, *loc. cit.*

3. *Ibid.*

4. *Ibid.*

When McGovern was asked when he thinks that the Iraqi soldiers such as those he trains will be ready to operate independently, he says with refreshing honesty: "There's part of me that says never. There's some cultural issues that I don't think they'll ever get through." McGovern provided an example of what he meant. When U.S. troops believed that the Rahma mosque in the town was being used by rebels, they sent in their Iraqi allies to search the place, something that they initially refused to do. When they were finally ordered to arrest everyone inside the mosque, the Iraqi platoon leader refused; the entire unit sat down next to the mosque in protest. Iraqi Cpl. Idris Dhanoun said simply that "you cannot enter the mosque with weapons. We have traditions, we have honor, and we're Muslims. You enter the mosque to pray, you don't enter the mosque with guns." If these are the kinds of "cultural issues" that Sgt. McGovern expects the Iraqi's to "get through" before being ready to operate successfully, one wonders indeed whether they'll ever measure up to the standards set by the Americans.

McGovern's pessimistic view of things was confirmed in a candid comment made to the *Post* reporters by his executive officer, 1st Lt. Kenrick Cato.

> I know the party line. You know, the DoD, the U.S. Army, five-star generals, four-star generals, President Bush, Donald Rumsfeld: the Iraqis will be ready in whatever time period . . . . But from the ground, I can say with certainty they won't be ready before I leave. And I know I'll be back in Iraq, probably in three or four years. And I don't think they'll be ready then.[1]

Part of the problem may lie in how our so-called Iraqi "allies" are being treated. "Due to a mix-up in paperwork, dozens of Iraqi soldiers went without pay for three months. Many lacked proper uniforms, body armor and weapons." Many "Iraqi forces" are currently

> housed at what they call simply "the base," a place as sparse as the name. Most of the Iraqis sleep in two tents and a shed with a concrete floor and corrugated tin roof that is bereft of walls. Some have cots; others sleep on cardboard or pieces of plywood stacked with tattered and torn blankets. The air conditioners are broken. There is no electricity. Drinking water comes from a sun-soaked camouflage tanker whose meager faucet also provides water for bathing.[2]

Baiji isn't an isolated example. Similar stories can be heard all over, one of which was covered by the *New York Times* at about the same time. This time it's about the "Iraqi Army" in Mahmudiya, a town south of Baghdad, which was charged with raiding a number of houses in a search operation

---

1. *Ibid.*
2. *Ibid.*

targeting actual or suspected resistance fighters. After one of the house raids ended, the *Times* chronicles, the Iraqi soldiers rushed

> to board pickup trucks they use as troop carriers [and] abandoned the blind-folded, handcuffed man they had come to arrest. "They left the detainee," an astonished American soldier said, spotting the man squatting in the dust along a residential street. "They just left him there. Sweet."[1]

Meanwhile, "American troops have been conducting night-time patrols to make sure the Iraqis stay awake" as a result of a recent incident where "Iraqi soldiers manning a checkpoint fell asleep [and] the checkpoint was ambushed by insurgents who tossed a grenade into the building, then stormed in and killed at least eight Iraqis . . . ."[2]

Sgt. Joshua Lower, a scout in the 3rd Brigade of the 1st Armored Division working with the Iraqis, is less than impressed. "I just wish they'd start to pull their own weight without us having to come out and baby-sit them all the time," he complained to the *NYT.* "Some Iraqi special forces really know what they are doing, but there are some units that scatter like cockroaches with the lights on when there's an attack."[3] The *NYT* reporters also discovered – like their colleagues from the *Post* – that the Sunni soldiers make "little secret of their support for Saddam Hussein and their contempt for the Americans."

Even the deployment of thousands of Iraqi troops in May 2005 across the Baghdad region by "Prime Minister" Ibrahim al-Jaafari, billed as the largest Iraqi-led military operation yet (aimed at the relentless rebel attacks on the capital), proved a very visible test of the validity of the American exit strategy. It had a less-than-impressive result, for it "underscored the raft of problems the American command has identified in the Iraqi force build-up."[4] Some of the problems noted were "hasty recruitment, insufficient training and a weak command structure, leading to breakdowns in discipline, especially under the stress of combat."

Summarizing this whole situation is a rather unexpected voice, though it is one that cannot be dismissed offhandedly. Speaking to a *Washington Times* reporter following his third trip to Iraq, retired Army Gen. Barry McCaffrey – of first Gulf War fame (or notoriety) – said that it will be at least another year before the violence subsides (many would critique that

---

1. Tavernise and Burns, *loc. cit.*
2. *Ibid.*
3. *Ibid.*
4. *Ibid.*

as optimistic). The problem with even that optimistic prediction is, according to Sharon Behn, who summarized McCaffrey's remarks for the *Times*, "[t]hat timetable may be cutting it fine for U.S. forces, which . . . [are] rapidly reaching the end of [their] rope."[1]

> "We are getting toward the end of our capacity," warned Gen. McCaffrey . . . . "
> The U.S. Army and Marine Corps are incapable of sustaining the effort. Our recruiting is coming apart. The National Guard is going to unravel."

Some economic effects of the resistance

For many people, the economic effects of this war are the least important of the war's evils. The life and safety of American troops ranks far higher than mere accountancy. Nonetheless, the war is having tremendous economic effects, and these should be thoroughly understood. At the end of the day – whether people focus on the problem or not – it is still the American taxpayer who is picking up the tab.

In the blizzard of lies that has characterized the Bush administration's war against Iraq, one of the snowflakes was a statement from former Deputy Defense Secretary, Paul Wolfowitz, who told the House Appropriations Committee on March 27, 2003, that Iraqi oil could generate $50–100 billion over two or three years: "We're dealing with a country that can really finance its own reconstruction, and relatively soon."[2] The reality?

UPI Senior News Analyst, Martin Sieff, summed up the financial catastrophe that the war represents in a compelling piece from the beginning of this year. "The liberation of Iraq," he wrote,

> was to have been the war that paid for itself in spades and gave U.S. corporations the inside track on the greatest energy bonanza of the twenty-first century. Instead, it has become a fiscal nightmare, a monetary Vietnam that already accounts for around 15 percent of the annual U.S. budget deficit, a figure likely only to grow remorselessly into the unforeseeable future.[3]

Details for Sieff's piece were provided by an analysis from Anthony Cordesman of CSIS. His comprehensive review of the war's costs completed in December 2004 offered some astounding figures.

The projected cost of the war to the end of 2004 was an incredible $128 billion, but this did not include the cost of replacing damaged or destroyed

1. Behn, "Retired General Estimates," *loc. cit.*
2. Matt Kelley, "Despite Pentagon's Low Figures, Outside Analysts Gauged Costs," *Portsmouth Herald*, November 1, 2003, online.
3. "How Bush Got Iraq War Costs Wrong," *Washington Times*, January 26, 2005, online.

equipment, the cost of upgrading equipment, or even the cost of major maintenance. Cordesman thus believed that another $5–10 billion more should be added to the $128 billion figure.

According to Cordesman, the projected cost of the war through the end of 2005 was going to be between $212 and 232 billion, again *not* including equipment replacement, necessary upgrading, and major maintenance. He concluded that the war was costing around $1–2 billion *a week*, and rising constantly. On April 21, 2005, the *Associated Press* announced Senate approval of an emergency supplemental funding bill of $81 billion, for the most part covering costs of the war in Iraq (though Afghanistan operations are merged into funding for personnel, operations, maintenance, etc.). This easily brings the total costs of war and reconstruction well past $300 billion, and it only covers expenditures foreseen as necessary through the end of the fiscal year on September 30, 2005.[1] The measure was approved through the House and Senate in early May and signed into law on May 11, 2005.[2] Moreover, the defense spending bill for 2005, totaling $409 billion for the fiscal year 2006, calls for "$45.3 billion in emergency funds to cover the ongoing cost of military operations in Iraq and Afghanistan from this coming October through March of next year."[3] This is yet another colossal sum of money to be spending on an unnecessary war at a time when too many Americans are suffering economic hardship, and when the nation's infrastructure is in an extremely poor condition.[4]

Another way of looking at this fiscal fiasco is to compare the war to that in Vietnam during the '60s and '70s. According to figures produced by the Congressional Research Service, the Vietnam War cost a total of

1. Liz Sidoti, "Senate OKs $81B for Iraq, Afghanistan," *Associated Press*, April 21, 2005, online. Cordesman (*loc. cit.*) predicted as of late June 2005 the need for another $200B to "stay the course" in Iraq.

2. See *Bill Summary & Status for the 109th Congress*, H.R.1268 (http://thomas.loc.gov/cgi-bin/bdquery/z?d109:HR01268:@@@L&summ2=m&).

3. William Watts, "White House Backs Defense Spending Bill," *www.marketwatch.com*, June 16, 2005.

4. Adding insult to injury is the fact that money earmarked for Iraq reconstruction is increasingly channeled towards security for reconstruction firms, due to the intractability of the resistance. An *Associated Press* report reveals that, according to Bill Taylor, director of the U.S.-led Iraq Reconstruction Management Office, "ceaseless attacks on contractors and facilities have also increased security demands, with up to 16 percent of all project costs now being spent on hiring armed guards, improving site protection, and providing equipment like hardened vehicles and telecommunications systems . . . . Since . . . 2003, the United States has earmarked $21 billion in resources for the country's reconstruction. So far $7.5 billion of this has been paid to contractors to perform works. Rebuilding, training and equipping Iraq's own security forces will eat up $5 billion alone" (Paul Garwood, "Insurgency Delays Reconstruction of Iraq," *Associated Press*, May 22, 2005, online).

$623 billion, using inflation-adjusted dollars. The current cost of Bush's war, following approval of the May 2005 supplemental, is about *half* of the Vietnam total.[1] What stands out, though, is that the Vietnam War went on for ten years, while Bush's war is only two years old and change.

Against Wolfowitz's estimate of $50–100 billion worth of oil revenue that would be available over two years to finance the war and reconstruction, what do we find? "Nineteen months after the invasion, Iraq has generated just $17 billion, according to [former] Oil Minister Thamer al-Ghadhban." The prediction at that point was that "Iraqi oil sales might not reach $25 billion by Wolfowitz's two-year mark."[2] The same report that provided the oil minister's remarks also indicated that because of rebel attacks, export revenue has been lost to the tune of $7–12 billion. Updating this figure is a comment from Ibrahim Bahr al-Uloum, Iraq's new Oil Minister, confirming that sabotage attacks against "Iraq's northern and central pipeline network [have led to] $1.25 billion of lost revenue in the *first five months* of this year" (emphasis mine).[3] "More than $1 billion in Iraqi oil revenues," the earlier report added, "also flowed to American and British companies, who landed expensive contracts from the now defunct U.S.-led occupation authority, often without competitive bidding."[4] And audits show that 60 percent of the large contracts financed by the oil funds went to Halliburton, Dick Cheney's old company.

As frustrating as the lack of oil revenue must be for those who banked on it as a way of funding the U.S. invasion and occupation, more frustrating still must be the fact that the Iraqi rebels know that by attacking the oil infrastructure they are hitting Uncle Sam in his wallet. The former Iraqi oil minister was quoted in a *Reuters* wire report as saying that "[w]e are up against people who plan every move and *know where to hit*" (emphasis mine).[5] Prefacing his remarks, the report candidly noted the motive for the attacks on Iraqi oil facilities by insurgents: "to deprive the U.S.-backed government of export revenue by choking off supply of fuels." Less than a month after the *Reuters* wire, James Glanz reported for the *New York Times* from Baghdad that

1. "Iraq, Afghan War Costs May Exceed $300B," *Associated Press*, February 16, 2005, online.

2. "Iraqi Pipelines Hit Again As Oil Losses Grow," *Daily Star* (Lebanon), October 25, 2004, online.

3. Khaled Yacoub Oweis, "Iraq Sees No Early Prospect of Oil Export Increase," *Reuters*, June 10, 2005, online.

4. *Daily Star, loc. cit.*

5. Khaled Yacoub Oweis, "Iraq Oil Industry Sabotage Worsening: Oil Minister," *Reuters*, January 26, 2005, online.

[i]nsurgent attacks to disrupt Baghdad's supplies of crude oil, gasoline, heating oil, water and electricity have reached a degree of coordination and sophistication not seen before, Iraqi and American officials say . . . . The new pattern, they say, shows that the insurgents have a deep understanding of the complex network of pipelines, power cables, and reservoirs feeding Baghdad.[1]

Al-Ghadhban told Glanz, furthermore, that "[t]here is an organization, sort of a command-room operation," and that "the scheme of the saboteurs is to isolate Baghdad from the sources of crude oil and oil products."[2] He also added: "they have succeeded to a great extent." The only reasonable conclusion, based upon the technical "savvy" of the attacks, then- Electricity Minister Aiham Alsammarae told Glanz, was that "the sabotage operation is being led by former members of the ministries themselves, possibly aided by sympathetic holdovers."[3] The reminiscence of this campaign to the third division of Saddam's resistance plan – the one involving the technocrats – is striking, and needs no additional comment. A June 2005 report detailed accusations that the tribes being paid to provide security for the northern oil pipeline running from the Kirkuk oil fields to the Turkish oil terminal of Ceyhan were actually themselves behind the attacks.[4] Meanwhile, the trend is towards an increase of these kinds of attacks: they numbered 77 in 2003, but were 246 in 2004.[5] Though reports indicate that they take place mainly in the Sunni areas in the north and center of the country, it is conceded – illustratively – that "facilities in the mostly Shiite south have not been fully secure either."[6]

What does the future hold?

Since we are not fighting the war to defend our homeland and we abuse so many of our professed principles, we face great difficulties in resolving the growing predicament in which we find ourselves. Our options are few, and admitting errors in judgment is not likely to occur. Moral forces are against us as we find ourselves imposing our will on a people 6,000 miles from our shores. How would the American people respond if a foreign country, with people of a

---

1. James Glanz, "Insurgents Wage Precise Attacks on Baghdad Fuel," *New York Times*, February 21, 2005, online.
2. *Ibid.*
3. *Ibid.*
4. Samah Samad, "Tribes Accused of Iraq Oil Protection Racket," *Environment News Service*, June 10, 2005, online. The story also notes that "[t]his big pipeline should be able to carry 800,000 barrels of oil per day, but because of the attacks it is currently averaging an eighth of that volume."
5. Khaled Yacoub Oweis, "Iraq Oil Industry Sabotage Worsening," *loc. cit.*
6. *Ibid.*

different color, religion, and language imposed itself on us to make us conform to their notions of justice and goodness? None of us would sit idly by. This is why those who see themselves as defenders of their homeland and their way of life have the upper hand regardless of the shock-and-awe military power available to us. At this point, our power works perversely. The stronger and more violent we are, the greater the resistance becomes.

So said Congressman Ron Paul (R-Tex.) before the House of Representatives on June 14, 2005.[1] It is only upon such an analysis that the United States can extricate itself from a disaster of its own making. Yet, sadly, it is probable that the Bush crowd will continue to listen to people expressing not facts, but fantasies. One good example is that uttered by David Phillips, a senior fellow with the Council on Foreign Relations, who said that "[t]he real struggle for power in Iraq is going to be over the constitution. It will define the country's future for decades to come."[2] That's nonsense.

The Iraqi resistance movement has shown itself to be a force that has exceeded every analyst's predictions. It has shown that how it sees the world, how it sees itself, and how it operates *do not mesh* with Western methods and conceptions. Put simply, the resistance has absolutely no interest in a new constitution for the good reason that if the resistance destroys the willpower of both the puppet Iraqi government and the U.S. government, the constitution will become what the American constitution has largely become in recent years – a scrap of paper of questionable utility. A constitution drawn up by whatever political constituency that does not have the agreement of the resistance leaders is a constitution destined for the waste basket. Talk of the constitution is an argument about where the deckchairs belong on the *Titanic*.

In the West, a respect for pluralism, democracy, the rule of law, and the other shibboleths of our vitiated political discourse still have some *limited* impact in our culture. In Iraq, *they have absolutely no resonance whatsoever.* To believe otherwise is not merely inane, it is to perpetuate the senseless sacrifice of our men and women on foreign fields to no good end and for no good purpose.

Can there be a "political solution" to the present conflict? Yes. But it consists only in acceptance by the U.S. of the need to get out of the country sooner rather than later. It might, of course, be objected that there are already tentative feelers between American officials and the resistance,

1. See http://www.house.gov/paul/congrec/congrec2005/cr061405.htm).
2. Yaukey, *loc. cit.*

issuing forth in a series of meetings, conferences, and behind-the-scenes rendezvous; that there is a desire on the part of much of the resistance movement to come "into the political process." It has appeared in articles with headlines like "Some Sunnis Hint At Peace Terms in Iraq, U.S. Says," published in May 2005 in the *New York Times*.[1] Such notions will appear, no doubt, with increasing frequency as the situation worsens.[2] Articles

---

1. Weisman and Burns, *loc. cit.*

2. Other examples of recent pieces in this vein are Ellen Knickmeyer and Naseer Nouri, "Sunnis Step Off Political Sidelines," *loc. cit.*; Adrian Blomfield, "Saddam May Escape Noose to Halt Insurgency," April 1, 2005, online; Priest, *loc. cit.*; and *Reuters*, "Troops Will Stay In Iraq, Bush Tells Americans," *Khaleej Times Online*, June 29, 2005. The focus of these and related articles tends to revolve around three themes: the insurgents themselves seeking "peace terms"; an alleged Sunni willingness to "participate" in the political process – with the implication that such a willingness signals a turning away from armed resistance; and an effort by the U.S. to "drive a wedge between the Iraqi and foreign insurgents" according to a "new" military plan allegedly approved back in August 2004 (Priest, *loc. cit.*). In all cases, the Sunni "representatives" allegedly participating in these initiatives cannot ever be proven to represent anyone other than themselves, and most if not all information about their activities is simply asserted by "U.S. officials."

In the piece by Weisman and Burns (*loc. cit.*), reference is made to the Sunni "National Dialogue Council" (NDC), said to be composed of 31 Sunni groups. The journalists themselves state plainly: "it is far from clear how much influence groups like the NDC have on insurgent leaders – and uncertain, too, whether even the council's leaders believe in the kind of majority rule democracy that the U.S. wants as its legacy in Iraq." Which means that the NDC could very arguably consist of a rag-bag of self-serving politicians who *claim* links in order to boost their "standing" in the quest for "position" (see also Tony Allen-Mills, "America Talks: But Are These the Real Rebel Leaders?, *London Sunday Times*, July 3, 2005, online, and Borzou Daragahi, "The Puzzle of Sunnis' Leadership Vacuum," *Los Angeles Times*, July 5, 2005, online, which illustrates the lack of credibility of the "self-proclaimed Sunni Arab leaders," and unwittingly reveals that the "leadership vacuum" is merely the unwillingness of insurgents to participate in the U.S.-dominated political process).

In many cases, if one reads past the headlines, one finds that the articles claiming the "Sunnis are seeking peace" state also that (see Knickmeyer and Nouri, *loc. cit.*) (1) senior Sunnis supporting the resistance do not take part in conferences held to facilitate "Sunni entrance into the political process," (2) the conferences themselves issue statements confirming the legitimacy of armed resistance, and (3) conference attendees shout down and prevent from speaking those Sunnis who (they say) have "sold out" and joined the U.S.-supported, Shiite-led Iraqi government. Much of this contradictory evidence is also apparent in the case of Ayham al-Samurai, a Sunni Muslim (from Chicago!) who served as electricity minister in the new "Iraqi government." Reports indicate that he has "supervised" meetings between insurgents and U.S. officials with the intention of silencing "skeptics who say there is no legitimate Iraqi resistance and that they cannot reveal their political face" (*Reuters*, "Troops Will Stay In Iraq," *loc. cit.*). At the same time he maintains "the right of the Iraqi people to resist the occupation by all possible means and to differentiate between terrorism and resistance" (*ibid.*). It is unlikely that U.S. negotiators involved in these alleged meetings share his assumptions; to the extent that they might, however, it would again reveal even their recognition that the conflict in Iraq is not simply an extension of the GWOT, as Bush makes it out to be. Regardless of what is true in all this, implying that it proves that there is a movement of Sunnis or resistance leaders away from armed conflict and towards a "political solution" is, quite frankly, a joke.

No less of one is the idea that, after Bush in June 2005 both renewed his commit-

claiming that insurgents are ready to "deal" invariably admit that it is the U.S government that is pushing for its Iraqi puppet to come to terms with the resistance. Evidence that the resistance is considering "negotiations" is sourced exclusively – and unsurprisingly – to "unnamed administration officials," "senior government sources," or, in one case, a "government-appointed overseer of Sunni religious sites." What these stories actually reveal is that *it is the Bush administration that needs a political resolution to the problem, not the resistance.* Even Central Command head Gen. Abizaid put it this way in June 2005, while speaking to *CNN*: it is "U.S. officials and Iraqi officials" who are "looking for the right people in the Sunni community to talk to."[1] Whether those "right people" will make themselves available, absent an immediate agreement to end the occupation, is another story.

As I hope the foregoing has demonstrated conclusively, there is no sense that the resistance is losing. There is, on the contrary, every indication that it is steadily gaining ground: partly through its own military efforts, partly through the ineptitude of the Bush government, and partly through the evident worthlessness of the puppet regime in Baghdad.[2] If the summer

---

ment to "completing the mission" (though it was already "accomplished") and refused to discuss a timetable for withdrawal from Iraq, the U.S. would be dealing honestly with insurgents who are reported to have "'[focused] their main demand' [in discussions with U.S. officials] on a guaranteed timetable of U.S. withdrawal" (Priest, *loc. cit.*).

It is, finally, interesting that some reports have "[o]ther parts of the U.S. government, including the State Department and CIA ... holding secret meetings with Iraqi insurgent factions" (Priest, *loc. cit.*), while others say that State Department officials at the U.S. embassy in Iraq "refuse to negotiate with insurgents or mediate between militants and the Iraqi government" (Mariam Fam, "U.S. Embassy in Iraq Refuses to Negotiate, *Associated Press*, July 1, 2005, online), even as the Iraqi "President" maintained that "[t]he Iraqi government has nothing to do with the negotiations with insurgents" ("Talabani Distances Himself from U.S. Talks with Insurgents," *Agence France-Presse*, June 28, 2005, online).

The upshot of this circus may very well be to create an acceptable political context for U.S. government's search for an escape from the Iraq mess, especially in light of Rumsfeld's admission that "victory" is not really our object in Iraq, as there is "no military solution to ending the insurgency" (Priest, *loc. cit.*). One wonders how the soldiers, sailors, airmen, and Marines in harm's way feel about how their leader has re-characterized their mission and that of their 1800 fallen comrades.

1. Priest, *loc. cit.*

2. An argument can be credibly made that even the current administration and associated neocon ideologues understand the inability of the current Iraqi "government" to deal with the situation in Iraq as it exists. Recently, the Iraqi "Justice Minister" Abdel Hussein Shandal accused the U.S. government of delaying Saddam Hussein's trial because, he said, perhaps referring to purported American support for Saddam during the Iran-Iraq war, "[i]t seems there are lots of secrets they want to hide" (*Associated Press*, "U.S. Attacked Over Saddam Access," *CNN.com*, June 22, 2005). The assertion is not vaguely credible, for the U.S. has been in the forefront of those pushing for a war-crimes trial for Saddam, and the kangaroo-court that is set up to try him is essentially

months of 2003 appeared as "dark days" to the Ba'ath Party, they must look less dark now that even experts are expressing concern that American forces are weakening, and more and more patriotic folks at home are demanding a withdrawal so as to preserve both their sons and daughters and America's security. Is it likely that they will give up at precisely the moment that victory is beginning to look more and more possible? Far more likely is the continuation of the U.S. attempt to hide its search for a way to give up on the Iraq experiment behind an attempt to encourage resistance leaders to "participate in the political process," especially now that Rumsfeld has made the scandalous admission that there will be "no military solution to ending the insurgency."[1] That the rebels are likely to see such an offer as simply an invitation to surrender their Iraqi identity and independence to a U.S.-backed government of unrepresentative Kurdish and Shiite factions illustrates both the slim prospect this approach has of success, and the U.S.'s ignorance of political reality on the ground.

We must, however, face that reality. What we are dealing with in Iraq *is* a domestic, nationalist resistance movement. It is the exact thing that Wolfowitz claimed in February 2005 did not exist, but which his unwitting parrot Max Boot effectively conceded in his June 2005 piece wherein he claimed the rebels would "lose."[2] This movement goes well beyond the false media designations of Shiite, Sunni, and Christian. Ba'athism in Iraq is the *national* vision; anything else is but a return to the sectarianism and division so beloved of Zionists and oil men. Ba'athism will return in Iraq, in some form or other, and its *return* will signal the American *departure*.

---

an American creation. Furthermore, the U.S. has been highlighting his role in allegedly exterminating Kurds in Halabja and elsewhere for years, without hesitation. If there *is* any conscious delay being injected into the process, it may in fact be because the Bush administration knows that the assassins and terrorists of al-Dawa and SCIRI, should they get an opportunity to put their hands on Saddam, will likely waste no time in executing him, not just in vengeance for his suppression of their subversive activities and his brutal (according to some) response to assassination attempts, but as a way to crush the Iraqi resistance through depriving it of its main icon. It is possible that the Bush administration sees Saddam as its ace in the hole. If there is one person who can bring the resistance to a halt, who can bring order back to Iraq, it is Saddam Hussein. The neocons may be crazy, but they are not unintelligent.

1. Priest, *loc. cit.*

2. Boot, *loc. cit.*: "The biggest weakness of the insurgency is that it is morphing from a war of national liberation into a revolutionary struggle against an elected government."

THE EDITORS' GLOSS: Defense Secretary Rumsfeld recently stated (London *Financial Times*, August 1, 2005), in response to the idea that the occupation of Iraq (among other things) gives rise to grievances that actually cause terrorism, that "coalition forces operate in Afghanistan and Iraq at the request of democratically elected governments."

But as Mark Gery details, the "democratically elected" government now in power in Iraq was put there by America and its allies, *not by Iraqis*: first by an invasion in contravention of the UN Charter and customary international law, and then via an "election" in which people were free to vote for *whomever we permitted to run for office*. Not coincidentally, these "allowable" candidates were mainly those who for years had conspired with the U.S., Iran, and Israel to overthrow Iraq's recignized government through bombings and assassinations, before we did it for them.

That "terrorists" are now in charge doesn't appear to matter to the American government. On *Meet the Press* (March 13, 2005) Tim Russert asked Condoleezza Rice if she was concerned about the terrorist past of the new "Prime Minister," Ibrahim al-Jaafari, and his Dawa Party. "He's an elected official," she replied, and "he has been very tough on the kind of terrorist activity that has been carried out by people like Zarqawi." Russert insisted: "So if he was a terrorist in his past, that's forgotten?" Condi's knowledge of recent Iraqi political history was on display here in all its grandeur: "Well, I don't know about the immediate past or about his past." She continued, "A lot of people in that period . . . who were fighters against Saddam Hussein were branded with various labels." Ah yes. Gratuitous labels. Like "terrorist."

The fruits of our electoral politics are becoming increasingly well known. Vivian Stomberg, executive director of the MADRE womens'rights group, felt compelled to admit that "the state of Iraqi women's human rights is worse today under U.S. occupation than it was under the notoriously repressive regime of Saddam Hussein" (*Detroit Free Press*, August 10, 2005). She defended her assertion admirably, proving what a disaster the recent American experiment in "nation-building" has become, and how much worse it might get with Iraq's new "constitution" looming ahead.

Before being "liberated" by U.S. forces, Iraqi women enjoyed rights to education, employment, freedom of movement, equal pay for equal work and universal day care, as well as the rights to inherit and own property, choose their own husbands, vote and hold public office. Ironically, these fundamental rights stand to be abolished in a "democratic" Iraq that has been ushered into being by our government.

C H A P T E R

39

The Politics of Electoral Illusion

• • • • • • • • •

Mark Gery

> "What do I do with democracy? Does it allow me to walk across the street without fear of being kidnapped, or being shot at, or being mugged or robbed? Would democracy feed my children? Would democracy allow me to quench my thirst? The U.S. has not done anything at all to improve the life of Iraqi people . . . . The shocking thing is that the conditions after 22 months of occupation are a lot worse in every single aspect of life than with Saddam Hussein after 12 years of sanctions."
>
> —Ghazwan Al-Mukhtar,
> retired engineer, Baghdad[1]

ON JANUARY 30, 2005, some millions of Iraqi citizens went to the polls and cast their votes for a Transitional National Assembly. The body's ostensible purpose would be to choose the country's new interim leaders and write a new constitution.

George Bush described the election as "a great and historical achievement." Was it? Timothy Bancroft-Hinchey, writing in *Pravda* on January 31, 2005, had one of the most insightful commentaries on the President's remark. If that were so, he wrote, "it says little for [Bush's] powers of judgment. In fact, this election confirms the worst-case scenario, a partition of Iraq, formerly held together by the Ba'ath government and now deeply cleft in three separate sections." Indeed, one might be tempted to ask whether President Bush's desire "to end tyranny in the world" is really sincere. We have heard about "Iraq and democracy and freedom," but we never hear about the repressive systems in the United Arab Emirates, Bahrain, Kuwait, Pakistan or of any other American *ally*. Could it be that the vision of former U.S. Secretary of State Henry Kissinger – that "Middle East oil is too

---

1. Interview with Amy Goodman, "The Election Was Shoved Down Our Throats," *Democracy Now!*, January 31, 2005.

important to be left in the hands of the Arabs" – has in fact been the *leit-motiv* of American foreign policy for decades, and that the hue and cry for selective "democracy" is simply the latest instrument for prizing control of Arab oil from Arab hands? A look at the difference between what has been claimed about the great success of the January 30, 2005, election and what has really been achieved by it gives us reason to suspect as much.

The Context of the Election

What Does International Law Say?

One of the most glaring features of Iraq's election was its obvious and blatant conflict with international law.

Following the 2003 invasion of the country by Anglo-American forces, Iraq was officially under foreign occupation. As such, it became subject to a whole group of edicts stemming from the 1907 Hague Convention, the Fourth Geneva Conventions (1949), and other documents of international law. As a signatory to the Hague and Geneva Conventions, the United States, the primary occupying power in Iraq, is legally bound to abide by their mandates in its administration of the country.

Since the chief purpose of this election was to *change* the Iraqi constitution (as U.S. representatives have repeatedly made clear), it was an *illegal enterprise* from the beginning. Article 43 of the annex to the fourth Hague Convention states that an occupying power can take no action that changes the laws of a country under its control: an occupier must "take all the measures in his power to restore, and ensure, as far as possible, public order and safety, while respecting, unless absolutely prevented, the laws in force in the country."[1] The Fourth Geneva Convention, hammered out after World War II, sharpened this point, saying, "The penal laws of the occupied territory shall remain in force, with the exception that they may be repealed or suspended by the Occupying Power in cases where they constitute a threat to its security or an obstacle to the application of the present Convention."[2] While Iraq's legitimate constitution, drawn up by the Ba'ath Party ("Ba'ath" being the Arabic word for "rebirth"), says much about realizing pan-Arab socialism for the Iraqi people, it contains noth-

---

1. Annex to Convention IV, *Regulations Concerning the Laws and Customs of War on Land,* The Hague, October 18, 1907.

2. Art. 64, Convention (IV) Relative to the Protection of Civilian Persons in Time of War, August 12, 1949.

ing that could possibly be construed as threatening U.S. security or contravening the letter or spirit of the Geneva accords.

Yet many of Iraq's laws have already been changed in accordance with American wishes.

On September 19, 2003, Paul Bremer, head of the Coalition Provisional Authority, issued Order 39, ordering, among other things, the privatization of many state-owned enterprises. Order 40 set in motion a process by which a number of Iraqi banks were to be available for purchase by foreign banking institutions. These and other proclamations stand in direct opposition to Iraq's constitution, which outlaws the privatization of key state assets to anyone but Arab citizens.[1]

Some may claim that elected Iraqis now call the shots in Iraq and that they, not American authority, will be responsible for implementing such sweeping changes in Iraqi law.

Such a view stands in stark contrast not only to international law, but to our own rules for warfare and occupation. According to American military law, as long as our forces occupy another country, we retain the status of a "belligerent occupant" and cannot employ any form of "puppet government" to sidestep the obligations placed upon us under international law. The U.S. Army's *Law of Land Warfare* makes this clear:

> The restrictions placed upon the authority of a belligerent government cannot be avoided by a system of using a puppet government, central or local, to carry out acts which would be unlawful if performed directly by the occupant. Acts induced or compelled by the occupant are nonetheless its acts.[2]

In other words, a "government" instituted or propped up by the American authority in Iraq cannot evade the limitations placed upon it by international law simply because it calls itself an "Iraqi government." The protests that came from UN officials in the days prior to the elections against the distribution by American military personnel of materials "urging Iraqis to vote in the country's elections" further illustrate the issue and highlight how even individuals who supported the election were concerned that it might be seen as a U.S.-orchestrated event.[3] In this light the boasting by

---

1. Antonia Juhasz, *The Economic Colonization of Iraq: Illegal and Immoral*, Testimony to the World Tribunal on Iraq, International Forum on Globalization, New York, May 8, 2004.

2. Field Manual 27–10, Chapter 6, Section II, para. 366, adopted by the Department of the Army, July 18, 1956.

3. Colum Lynch, "U.S. Troops' Role in Iraqi Elections Criticized: UN Official Assails Distribution of Material," *Washington Post*, January 27, 2005, p. A14.

Iraq's new "Transitional" President that the "provisional Ba'athist constitution of 1970" has been replaced with the "transitional Administrative Law, a progressive liberal interim constitution,"[1] is simply more evidence of the restructuring of Iraqi society being accomplished under the eyes (and arms) of American occupiers.

The central issue underscoring the election's illegality and illegitimacy in the light of international law is the well-known and openly admitted fact that the U.S. went to war against Iraq in order to change its government; this aim in and of itself is illegal under international law,[2] and it is the principal reason why the election of a new government is necessary in the first place: the U.S. abolished the previous one, and now finds it necessary to facilitate the installation of a successor. As prominent international lawyers such as Curtis Doebbler, Esq., Ph.D., have noted, "Until this question of the illegality of the use of force against Iraq has been decided, all actions that emanate from the illegal acts cannot be accepted."[3] This no doubt includes the recent Iraqi elections.

Eric Margolis, writing the day after the elections, put it neatly:

> No election held under a foreign military occupation resulting from an unjustified war is legal under international law. During the cold war, elections staged by the Soviets after invading Afghanistan, Hungary, and Czechoslovakia were rightly denounced by the U.S. as "frauds" and the leaders elected as "stooges."[4]

The American line is no different as regards Syria and Lebanon. On March 4, 2005, the White House spokesman, Scott McClellan, made the point very clear: " . . . in order to ensure that the Lebanese people have free and fair elections, Syria needs to get out." Substitute "Iraqi" for "Lebanese" and "U.S." for "Syria" and the conclusion is obvious: in order to ensure that the Iraqi people have free and fair elections, the U.S. needs to get out.

Until then one may rightly question the validity of any election in Iraq accomplished under both de facto and *de jure* American occupation.

History Repeated

Members of the Bush and Blair administrations have claimed that the Iraq vote was the country's first democratic election in 50 years. While

---

1. Jalal Talabani, "In Iraqis We Trust," *Wall Street Journal*, April 11, 2005, online.

2. See the extensive defense of this position by John Burroughs and Nicole Deller on pp. 361–371 of the present collection.—Ed.

3. See Dr. Doebbler's extensive look at the legal situation of deposed Iraqi President Saddam Hussein on pp. 797–817 of the present collection. —Ed.

4. "Iraq's Predetermined Elections," *Toronto Sun*, January 31, 2005.

it is true that an "election" occurred during the reign of King Feisal II (1953–1958), the King and his aides were bound to administer the vote within the framework laid out by a cadre of British "advisers" who had been stationed in the country for decades. According to historian Sandra Mackay, Feisal II was viewed as "a malleable monarch" by Britain "through which they could rule Iraq."[1] The 1955 "election" there, organized by the "American and British-appointed monarchy to select an advisory body[,] had no executive or legislative power. Its only function was to provide a façade of legitimacy to the puppet regime," as noted by a statement issued on February 2, 2005, by the International Action Center.[2] At any rate, a mere three years later the monarch was overthrown: "The *ancien régime* was swept away. The royal family was gunned down in the palace yard, and the Prime Minister, Nuri, literally was torn to bits by the mob."[3]

The present situation is not dissimilar. Some have referred to the January 30 election as a "demonstration," not unlike what the U.S. has orchestrated in the past in places like Honduras and Vietnam. Speaking of these historical examples, Frank Brodhead, co-author with Edward S. Herman of *Demonstration Elections: U.S.-Staged Elections in the Dominican Republic, Vietnam, and El Salvador,*[4] wrote:

> The purpose of these elections – organized, financed, and choreographed by the United States – was to persuade U.S. citizens and especially Congress that we were invading these countries and supporting a savage war against government opponents at the invitation of a legitimate, freely elected government. The main purpose of a demonstration election is to legitimize an invasion and occupation, not to choose a new government.[5]

It would be difficult to refute the suggestion that the Iraq election was not also a "demonstration election." As we noted above, the *raison d'être* of the American invasion was the disestablishment of Iraq's previous (i.e., pre-invasion) government. That vision necessarily shaped, and continues to shape, post-invasion policy. One instrument of that policy, though criti-

---

1. Sandra Mackay, *The Reckoning: Iraq and the Legacy of Saddam Hussein* (W.W. Norton & Co., New York, 2002, p. 112).

2. International Action Center, "The Election in Iraq: 'a tale, told by an idiot, full of sound and fury, signifying nothing,'" January 31, 2005, www.iacenter.org/iraqelection. htm). The International Action Center was founded by former U.S. Attorney General, Ramsay Clark.

3. Stephen Pelletière, *Iraq and the International Oil System* (Washington, D.C.: Maisonneuve Press, 2004), p.127.

4. Boston: South End Press, 1984.

5. Frank Brodhead, "Reframing the Iraq Election," *Znet* (www.zmag.org), January 21, 2005.

cized for its impetuousness, was the "Supreme National De-Ba'athification Commission," set up by the Iraqi Governing Council and headed by Ahmad Chalabi. Criticism notwithstanding, the policy remains effectively in force: as Douglas Feith, outgoing under secretary of defense for policy at the Pentagon, stated a year after the invasion, "the Saddam Hussein regime is gone and is not coming back."[1] The U.S. policy of "de-Ba'athification," he said, is a way "of communicating to the Iraqis that the Ba'ath regime is gone and is not coming back." Essentially this means that the political landscape in post-invasion Iraq is open to the participation of those who are content to take part in the U.S.-enforced expulsion – and continuing exclusion – of Iraq's pre-invasion government and broader political organization. Insofar as this *status quo* is maintained by the American occupation, it wouldn't be a stretch to see the election as merely a ratification of the occupation and the essential transformation of Iraq's government – the very activity forbidden by international law. Brodhead connects these dots in a way that's hard to argue with:

> As framed by the Bush administration, rather than being an election in support of a particular candidate or policy, the purpose of the January 30 election is to show Americans and the rest of the world that the Iraqi people support the theory and practice of democracy itself, and that they are willing to identify "democracy" with the *political process created by the United States.*[2] As this political process is, according to the Bush administration, the whole point of the occupation, the January 30 election is a drama to demonstrate Iraqi support for the occupation itself (emphasis mine).[3]

What Choices Did They Have?

The conduct of the election was largely determined by Iyad Allawi (Iraq's previous interim leader) who was obliged to follow clear parameters laid out by the United States. Before leaving his post in the summer of 2004, Paul Bremer established the High Commission for Elections, which in turn set the rules for the vote.

---

1. Keynote address at the American Enterprise Institute event, "Winning Iraq: A Briefing on the Anniversary of the End of Major Combat Operations," May 4, 2004.

2. The mechanism of voting and democracy are, of course two wholly different things, as the great English writer Hilaire Belloc pointed out in his book, *The Party System* (London: Stephen Swift, 1911, p. 15): "Votes and elections and representative assemblies are not democracy; they are at best machinery for carrying out democracy. Democracy is government by the general will."

3. Brodhead, *loc. cit.*

Most important is the fact that the American-appointed commission possessed the authority to disqualify any party or individual from the democratic process which did not meet with *Washington's* approval, and disqualifications could not be appealed. Based upon this set up, candidates for election were naturally those who were either long-time opponents of the Ba'athist government, or those who did not fundamentally object to participating in an American-sponsored process designed to crystallize the transformation of Iraq's political landscape.

Not surprisingly, the candidates who were allowed to run included such figures as ex-CIA asset, Iyad Allawi, and his Iraqi National Accord party, and convicted embezzler and former Pentagon poster boy, Ahmad Chalabi, and his Iraqi National Congress. Both groups were made up of Iraqi expatriates who had received American financial support for years. Prior to the election they drew upon their U.S. funding and training, as well as superior access to security and the media, to increase their position relative to indigenous Iraqi groups on the ballot. Other candidates included those affiliated with the United Iraqi Alliance (UIA), a broad coalition, backed by Grand Ayatollah Ali al-Sistani, of mostly Shiite Arab parties. The most prominent figure of the UIA is the leader of the al-Dawa party, Ibrahim al-Jaafari, described as "a 58-year-old doctor and a devout Shiite who fled into exile in 1980 on the day an arrest warrant was issued that would probably have sent him to the gallows."[1]

Beyond simply controlling the list of acceptable candidates, there was also the activity of two U.S.-funded organizations with long records of manipulating foreign elections – those in Venezuela and Ukraine being but some of the most recent examples[2] – on behalf of American inter-

---

1. John F. Burns, "A Crucial Window for Iraq: 15 Weeks to Pull Together," *New York Times*, April 29, 2005, online.

2. On Venezuela and Chavez, see Joshua Kurlantzick, "The Coop Connection," *Mother Jones*, November/December 2004 (www.motherjones.com/news/outfront/2004/11/11_401.html); Alan Bock, "Eye on the Empire," *Antiwar.com*, April 30, 2002; Benjamin Duncan, "Venezuela: What is the NED Up To?" *Aljazeera* (aljazeera.net), May 3, 2004; Irish Green Party statement, "Parties Must Break Links With U.S. Funders of Chavez Opponents," March 14, 2004 (www.greens-in.org/article/186); Andrew Buncombe, "U.S. Revealed To Be Secretly Funding Opponents of Chavez," *The Independent*, March 13, 2004. On the 2004 election in Ukraine, see Justin Raimondo, "The Yushchenko Mythos," *Antiwar.com*, November 29, 2004; Ian Traynor, "U.S. Campaign Behind the Turmoil in Kiev," *The Guardian*, November 26, 2004, online; Christine Stone, "Ukraine: The Diary of a Dissident Election Observer," *British Helsinki Human Rights Group Online* (www.bhhrg.org/LatestNews.asp?ArticleID=52); interview of Michael Ledeen by Chris Matthews, *Hardball*, February 8, 2005 (msnbc.msn.com/id/6941388/). In the interview Ledeen was perfectly open about how American funds, logistical support, and "training for demonstrators" were secretly used in the Ukraine election in favor of Yushchenko.

ests. These are the National Democratic Institute for International Affairs (NDI) and the International Republican Institute (IRI), "democracy-building" organizations established shortly after the creation of the well-known National Endowment for Democracy (NED).

The NED is, according to its own website,[1] a private, non-profit corporation funded by U.S. government appropriations. It acts as a grant-making foundation, distributing funds to private organizations for the purpose of "promoting democracy abroad." Two of the four "affiliated" institutions of the NED, through which most of the "democracy-promoting" grant money is funneled, are the above-mentioned NDI and IRI. The NED thus would serve as "the umbrella organization through which these . . . groups and an expanding number of other private sector groups . . . receive funding to carry out programs abroad."[2]

The White House originally intended to mobilize CIA assets to "aid U.S.-friendly candidates in the [Iraqi] elections."[3] When the secret "finding" exploring that possibility became known to U.S. members of Congress and others, "lawmakers from both parties raised questions about the idea . . . ."[4] *TIME Magazine* reported that, according to an official but anonymous U.S. source, "House minority leader Nancy Pelosi 'came unglued' when she learned about . . . a plan for 'the CIA to put an operation in place to affect the outcome of the elections.'"[5] A spokesman for former National Security Advisor Condoleezza Rice, Sean McCormack, told *TIME* that the plan was originally a vision to help "level the playing field" for candidates who would be trying to compete with those who the U.S. suspected of being helped by Iran. "In the final analysis," he declared (no doubt with an air of moral superiority reflecting the "nobility" of his government's decision in having renounced covert election-rigging), "we have adopted a policy that we will not try to influence the outcome of the upcoming Iraqi election by covertly helping individual candidates for office." But he only ruled out "covert" involvement. Another official U.S. source quoted in the same article revealed that "[o]ur embassy in Baghdad will run a number of overt programs to support the democratic electoral process.[6]

1. National Endowment for Democracy Website (www.ned.org/about/nedhistory.html).
2. *Ibid.*
3. Adam Entous, "Bush to Aid 'Moderate' Parties in Iraq Election," *Reuters,* October 8, 2004, online; also see Timothy J. Burger and Douglas Waller, "How Much U.S. Help?" *TIME Magazine,* October 04, 2004, online.
4. Burger and Waller, *loc. cit.*
5. *Ibid.*
6. Burger and Waller, *loc. cit.*

These overt operations included activities by the NDI and the IRI. In June, the IRI's "Baghdad team" hosted political party training conferences for the participants whom, it claimed, "represented the diverse spectrum of political parties."[1] This diverse spectrum, interestingly, included "the Patriotic Union of Kurdistan, the Supreme Council for Islamic Revolution in Iraq [SCIRI], [the] Da'wa Party, and dozens of small-to-medium sized organizations."[2] It is noteworthy that the major factions that received political and financial support from the U.S. are predominantly those that spent the better part of the last two decades trying to overthrow the Ba'athist government.

The activities of the NDI and IRI were not limited to hosting a few workshops. Beginning with "political party formation and civil society efforts in Iraq shortly after the spring 2003 invasion," the two groups would eventually receive – along with other organizations – "more than $80 million" from the U.S. Agency for International Development (USAID) "to provide technical and political assistance to the electoral process."[3]

Ken Wollack, President of the National Democratic Institute, made it plain that support would be available only to those who "are participating in the country's emerging political process."[4] As for those who feel obliged to continue an armed struggle against occupying forces, International Republican Institute President Lorne Craner said, "If you're a violent party outside the process, this is not the right place for you."[5] (Never mind that al-Jaafari's al-Dawa Party "was implicated by American intelligence in terrorist acts across the Middle East, including a 1983 bombing of the American Embassy in Kuwait."[6])

The heavy involvement of groups like NDI and IRI speaks volumes about the "objectivity" of the electoral and political process that the U.S. managed in Iraq. Experts see groups like the NDI and IRI as "extensions" of the U.S. State Department. Professor and author William I. Robinson of the Global and International Studies Program at the University of California, Santa Barbara said shortly before the election that NDI and IRI were prob-

---

1. "IRI in Iraq," International Republican Institute website (www.iri.org/countries.asp?id=7539148391).

2. *Ibid.*

3. Lisa Ashkenaz Croke and Brian Dominick, "Controversial U.S. Groups Operate Behind Scenes on Iraq Vote," *The New Standard*, December 13, 2004, online.

4. Entous, *loc. cit.*

5. *Ibid.*

6. Burns, *loc. cit.*

ably "trying to select individual leaders and organizations that are going to be very amenable to the U.S. transnational project for Iraq," a project that included "pacifying the country militarily and legitimating the occupation and the formal electoral system."[1]

Criticism of the NED and its sponsored organizations has come from the "right" no less than the "left." Barbara Conry wrote, for the conservative CATO Institute, that the NED's "mischief overseas" has amounted to U.S. taxpayers funding "special-interest groups to harass the duly elected governments of friendly countries, interfere in foreign elections, and foster the corruption of democratic movements."[2] Congressman Ron Paul (R-Tex.) noted in an October 11, 2003, article that the purposes for which NDI and IRI are used around the world "would be rightly illegal in the United States."[3]

A Glaring Omission

With the sponsorship of candidates and parties who opposed the "former regime" in Iraq and who support the continued American enforcement of its elimination, a large swath of the Iraqi people – those who do not sympathize with the America's plan for the "new Iraq" – found themselves disenfranchised during the election process. The Ba'ath Party – which had literally millions of members before the Anglo-American invasion – was totally excluded from the electoral process, in keeping with the "de-Ba'athification" process, on the grounds that it "preached hate" and was involved in "terrorist activities." (The fact that al-Jaafari's party is widely recognized as "terrorist" and has the dubious honor of having carried out the first modern suicide bombing is evidently not enough reason for it to have been forbidden to participate in this "peaceful" election. The U.S. Secretary of State dismissed those inconvenient truths as aspects of "the past."[4]) But if the current level of armed resistance is any indicator, the Ba'ath Party still enjoys a considerable measure of support in the country. In a truly fair election, should it not have also enjoyed a place on the ballot?

---

1. Croke and Dominick, *loc. cit.*

2. *Ibid.*

3. Congressman Ron Paul, "National Endowment for Democracy: Paying to Make Enemies of America," *Antiwar.com*, October 11, 2003.

4. See the discussion of al-Dawa's (and al-Jaafari's) history in the interview with Jude Wanniski, on pp. 3–79 of *Neo-CONNED!*, the companion to the present volume. See also the *Middle East Intelligence Bulletin*, Vol. 5, No. 6, June, 2003, and the interview of Secretary of State Concoleezza Rice by Tim Russert, *Meet the Press*, March 13, 2005.—Ed.

As Lew Rockwell pointed out, "when you think about democracy in Iraq, just remember that most real experts admit that Saddam Hussein would win if he ran."[1]

Keeping Ba'athists and other Iraqi "nationalists" out of the process turned the election into a more or less incestuous process of providing supporters of the U.S. role with an opportunity to vie for leadership of a country already politically and militarily dominated by it. That process by its nature put former dissidents at the forefront, and marginalized the former leadership of the country. As a *Los Angeles Times* piece put it quite directly, "Hussein's fall gave once-clandestine and now victorious Shiite and Kurdish movements an instant edge over the disparate Sunni Arabs."[2] An edge that they have not used subtly. For instance, Abdel Aziz al-Hakim, the leader of the SCIRI – a constituent part of the UIA – has insisted that "former regime" elements be denied any role in the new government, demanding that leaders not "hand over the country's assets to our enemies." He insisted the new government "de-Ba'athify Saddam's terrorists from all state institutions."[3]

In effect, what the U.S. has done by means of this election is hand a society over to those who opposed its former, legitimate authority. One can hardly claim that this is not what was in fact accomplished; right or wrong, under international law it is completely illegitimate. Even from a practical standpoint, the process seems hardly viable. A conservative estimate shows that at least a third if not half of the country was simply *left out* of the election by the terms under which it was conducted. "It isn't a real election," said retired Jordanian General Ali Shukri.

> Geographically one half of Iraq and demographically, one third of Iraq are not voting. There has to be a parliament that rules Iraq. How does that happen without the acquiescence of the Sunnis? Can you really write the constitution for all of Iraq in that circumstance? It's mission impossible.[4]

Indeed, as reported by Richard Boudreaux of the *Los Angeles Times,* "Most Sunni Arab groups shunned the election in hope of undermining the new government's legitimacy. An estimated 85% of eligible Sunni Arab

1. "Read the *Wall Street Journal* If You Can Stand It," *LewRockwell.com*, November 22, 2004.

2. Richard Boudreaux, "Iraq's Sunni Arabs Seek Their Voice," *Los Angeles Times*, March 28, 2005, online.

3. Burns, *loc. cit.*

4. Huda Ahmed and Soraya Sarhaddi Nelson, "Shiite Victory Threatens to Fracture The Arab Middle East," *Knight Ridder Newspapers*, January 27, 2005, online.

voters stayed home, out of principle or fear of insurgent attack."[1] Perhaps it would be more correct to invert Boudreaux's logic, and speculate that the Sunni Arabs, or Iraqi "nationalists" generally, shunned the election because they *already* doubted the legitimacy of the whole process. Either way, the election as it was conducted is hardly a recipe for rebuilding a cohesive and distinctly Iraqi society in the aftermath of the destruction of the government that held it together for so many years.

Occupation, Anyone?

The failure of the NED, NDI, and IRI to support any parties that offered serious political resistance to the occupation (such as al-Sadr's movement and Ba'ath Party members) is further proof of what many have suggested: that the election was conducted to legitimize occupation rather than provide a serious government. True or not, the legitimacy of any election which doesn't include a vote on the occupation is questionable at least. One would be hard pressed to find an issue more on the minds of the average Iraqi, and yet to leave it out of the picture simply brings us back to the stark fact that the U.S. never intended to "transfer" real power to Iraq by means of this election. Had it had such an intention it would have *facilitated* political opposition to the occupation by allowing known opponents of occupation to participate. Anyone claiming otherwise would run up against the fact that opponents of the occupation tend to concentrate around the groups that were sidelined by the electoral focus on those who for decades worked *against* the Ba'athist government. The election, from this perspective, was a self-serving enterprise omitting those who posed a credible threat to continued occupation.

The results of the election, in this regard, speak for themselves. Though the largest bloc in the new Iraqi "parliament" – the Shiite-dominated UIA – included in its platform a call for a timetable for withdrawal of occupation forces, President Bush's dismissal of the idea, just four days after the election, was loud and clear: "You don't set timetables."[2] The Alliance has since backed away from insisting on one,[3] Bush has tenaciously clung to his position rejecting it[4] (nevermind what the "freely elected" represen-

---

1. Boudreaux, *loc. cit.*

2. "President Discusses Strengthening Social Security in Montana," remarks at Montana Expo Park, Great Falls, Montana, February 3, 2005 (www.whitehouse.gov/news/releases/2005/02/20050203–13.html).

3. "Sadr Followers Plan Campaign To Oust U.S.," *Financial Times*, April 11, 2005, online.

4. Remarks by the President on the War on Terror, June 28, 2005 (http://www.whitehouse.

tatives of the Iraqi people might call for). Never mind that according to on-the-ground Baghdad journalist Dahr Jamail, those who voted "whether they be 35% or even 60% of registered voters, were not voting in support of an ongoing U.S. occupation of their country."[1] It was, rather, precisely the opposite. "Every Iraqi I have spoken with who voted," he wrote,

> explained that they believe the National Assembly which will be formed soon will signal an end to the occupation. And they expect the call for a withdrawing of foreign forces in their country to come sooner rather than later. This causes one to view the footage of cheering, jubilant Iraqis in a different light now, doesn't it?[2]

Nevertheless, both al-Hakim the SCIRI leader and al-Jaafari, the key al-Dawa figure, have since indicated that "Iraq will need American forces until its new army and paramilitary police can take over the war."[3] Many interpret that as meaning well into 2006, if not longer. Even before the election was conducted, the approved "Iraqi candidates acknowledge[d] that American and coalition support is vital to their new government, which will need to provide food, water, jobs and electricity for its constituents."[4]

What makes the omission of a vote on the occupation most glaring is the number of people in Iraq who actually oppose the continued presence of American forces. A poll conducted just before the election – which produced results that indicate what the vote would have been on the continued occupation, had one been offered – found that "[m]ajorities of both Sunni Arabs (82%) and Shiites (69%) . . . favor U.S. forces withdrawing either immediately or after an elected government is in place."[5] Of all of Iraq's ethnic and religious groups, it further indicated, "Only the Kurds seem to favor a continued U.S. presence, and are likely to outright reject violent resistance."[6] No wonder, then, that April 9, 2005 – over two months

---

gov/news/releases/2005/06/20050628-7.html): "Some contend that we should set a deadline for withdrawing U.S. forces . . . . that would be a serious mistake."

1. Dahr Jamail, "What They're Not Telling You About the 'Election,'" *Dahrjamail.com*, February 1, 2005.

2. *Ibid.*

3. Burns, *loc. cit.* Al-Jaafari was particularly "on message" (his and Bush's) during his June 2005 visit to the U.S., saying, according to the *Washington Post*, that "it would be a serious mistake to designate a specific date for the withdrawal of U.S. troops" (Robin Wright and Jim VandeHei, "Unlikely Allies Map Future," *Washington Post*, June 24, 2005, p. A25).

4. Ahmed and Nelson, *loc. cit.*

5. "Survey Finds Deep Divisions in Iraq," *Zogby International*, January 28, 2005 (www.zogby.com/news/ReadNews.dbm?ID=957).

6. *Ibid.* This poll also indicated that "half (49%) of Shiites and a majority (64%) of Sunni Arabs believe the U.S. will 'hurt' Iraq" over the next five years.

after the election – witnessed a massive turnout in protest at America's continued occupation of Iraq.

Bearing in mind both the statements of the Bush administration and the actual facts of what has occurred in the months since the election, it becomes harder not to see the election as a legitimization of the occupation rather than as a serious and independent vote on it. Frank Brodhead provided the most profound analysis of this point.

> President Bush and other administration officials have consistently stated that a U.S. exit from Iraq must await the establishment of political democracy and the creation of an Iraqi military force adequate to maintain order. Free markets and an open door to U.S. investments are core constituents of what "democracy" means for the Bush people, and their job will not be done until these goals are secured as well. Also, by definition, a democratic regime is run by "moderates," understood by the entire spectrum of the U.S. elite to mean political leaders who cooperate with U.S. interests. Moreover, a strong Iraqi security force, agreed by all to be a prerequisite for U.S. withdrawal, will be trained and equipped by the United States, historically a certain recipe for continued close links to the Pentagon and the CIA.
>
> Thus, when President Bush refuses to discuss a timetable for U.S. withdrawal, or links U.S. withdrawal to political and security benchmarks rather than to the calendar, or when U.S. general Tommy Franks states that U.S. troops will be in Iraq for at least 10 years, we should discard any assumptions that the United States will leave Iraq voluntarily unless and until its economic and military goals are secure. U.S. control of Iraq would be a stupendous achievement for the Bush administration and will not be lightly abandoned . . . .
>
> From this different perspective – that the United States occupation of Iraq is indefinite rather than limited – the Iraq election at the end of January assumes a different role and needs to be understood differently than the criticisms coming from mainstream or elite opinion.[1]

The Conduct of the Election

The Anomalies of Iraq's Allegedly "Landmark" Election

The Bush administration has talked long and loud about its intentions for the future in terms of foreign policy. The administration is committed to exporting what it calls the "global democratic revolution." In other words, it is seeking to establish democratic structures – the like of which are the norm in Western Europe and the United States, and which our citizens take for granted after long years of habit – in countries which have rarely if

---

1. Brodhead, *loc. cit.*

ever possessed such structures. Given the fledgling and tenuous nature of any attempt by the Bush administration to implement Western traditions in non-Western societies, a fine and particular attention to detail should be the order of day. Insofar as this election constituted an attempt to plant "popular" democratic traditions in foreign soil, it is not too much to expect that every part of the "first step" towards democracy should have been beyond reproach, in order to make that step a credible and effective one.

Such high standards were not met, however. Just how much of a departure from normal democratic procedures the Iraqi "election" was may be grasped from the following facts:

1. There were 7,785 candidates, and yet not even 50 of their names were known to the voting public.

2. There were no separate parties on the ballot, but only a number of lists made up of a number of parties whose participation in such lists was generally unknown.

3. There were no truly international observers.

4. There was no independent and impartial monitor to scrutinize the voting process, the integrity of the ballots, or the ballot count.

5. The only observers present were trained by groups like the National Democratic Institute, which had a direct and vested interest in ensuing a "positive result" for the authorities.

6. The UN election body was based not in the country but 200 miles away in a neighboring country.

7. There was a widespread curfew imposed on the eve of the election, and dozens of leading and influential figures, who denounced the "elections" under occupation conditions, were arrested for their opinions.1

Now some of these factors, such as the presence or absence of international observers, would not invalidate an election taking place in a Western

---

1. See Muhammad Abu Nasr, "Fraud Rife In Baghdad Elections," *Free Arab Voice*, January 31, 2005, online: "Just days before the ballots were cast, American and British occupation forces made a final show of force designed to quiet dissent. Fanning out across the country, they arrested at least twenty-eight Sunni religious leaders on charges of inciting the public to boycott the election, and encouraging armed jihad against occupation forces."

country, for the good reason that Western democratic structures have been in place for centuries. In the case of Iraq, however, we are talking of "fledgling democracies" and the mere planting of seeds, where every detail must be (and should have been) legitimate in order to give the process essential credibility, which would otherwise be lacking in a society not accustomed to foreign "democratic traditions."

The Fourth Estate

One way that the authorities might have provided some credibility for the process would have been to allow open and widespread media coverage of the event. Nevertheless, the decision was made to allow only large, approved networks to film in a very limited number of places. "The officially designated satellite companies were *al-Arabiyah* Satellite Network, the Iraqi *Qanat ash-Sharqiyah* – the Iraqi "government" TV station – and the American CNN," according to a *Free Arab Voice* report.[1] It continued by reporting that correspondents for the officially registered *Mafkarat al-Islam* challenged Iraqi and American officials to deny that coverage was limited to these "approved" networks, but no one did so.

Robert Fisk, writing before the vote, adds some detail to the picture:

> The big television networks have been given a list of five polling stations where they will be "allowed" to film. Close inspection of the list shows that four of the five are in Shiite Muslim areas – where the polling will probably be high – and one in an upmarket Sunni area, where it will be moderate . . . .
> . . . every working class Sunni polling station will be out of bounds to the press. I wonder if the television lads will tell us that today when they show voters "flocking" to the polls. In the Karada district, we found three truckloads of youths on Saturday, all brandishing Iraqi flags, all – like the unemployed who have been sticking posters to Baghdad's walls – paid by the government to "advertise" the election. And there was a cameraman from Iraqi State television, of course, which is controlled by Iyad Allawi's "interim" government.[2]

Coercion and the Count

One can be forgiven for suspecting that, had an election of this nature, with conditions of "objectivity" and procedural regularity as obviously deficient as in the Iraqi election, been held in a Western country, the reaction would have been cynical and unenthusiastic – and productive of a

---

1. *Ibid.*
2. Robert Fisk, "We'll Go On Cheering 'Democracy' – and the Iraqis Will Go On Dying," *The Independent*, January 30, 2005, online.

correspondingly low turnout – even in the face of massive media hype. Some would argue, however, that the allegedly "high" turnout in the Iraqi election proved such a suspicion to be unfounded. On the surface it's a fine point, but deeper analysis shows that things are not what they seem. The "high" turnout is clearly matter for debate, and whatever turnout there was may actually have been produced by coercion and intimidation.

The turnout has, of course, been hailed by journalists in the Anglo-American world. It has been claimed that the high turnout proves the yearning of Iraqis for "democracy," and is therefore justification alone for the illegal invasion of Iraq. Never mind that nobody in the White House or on Downing Street was talking about "democracy" in the long run-up to the attack on Iraq. It is a fact that has been quietly dropped.

Happily, a few in the press were watching with a skeptical eye. Greg Mitchell, editor of *Editor & Publisher,* a watchdog publication covering the print media, pointed out the way in which the main assertions regarding the election turnout were swallowed whole by the mainstream media, implicitly suggesting that the claimed figures didn't completely add up.

> In hailing, and at times gushing, over the turnout has the American media – as it did two years ago in the hyping of Saddam's WMDs – forgotten core journalistic principles in regard to fact-checking and weighing partisan assertions? It appears so."[1]

The reason for caution is that initially the media announced the statement from the Independent Electoral Commission of Iraq (IECI) that 72% of eligible voters turned out for the election. This figure was then rather quickly downgraded to 57%.[2] From then on the line was rigorously maintained that eight million Iraqis had voted and the turnout was in fact 57%. The question is, of course, 57% *of what?*

What is the population of Iraq? No one knows precisely. According to "some experts" it is 25 million or so; according to "other experts" it is 27.1 million. A discrepancy of some two million or more people – roughly 10% of the expert-estimated population – is hardly to be scoffed at.

Of this unclear population total, how many people were eligible to vote? According to the mainstream media, the number of eligible voters was 14

---

1. Greg Mitchell, "Officials Back Away from Early Estimates of Iraqi Voter Turnout," *Editor & Publisher,* February 2, 2005, online.

2. See Sami Ramadani, "The Vietnam Turnout Was Good as Well," *The Guardian,* February 1, 2005, online, and "Confusion Surrounds Iraq Poll Turnout," *Aljazeera,* January 30, 2005 (online).

million. Yet Howard Kurtz, writing in the *Washington Post,* pointed out that the number of adults in Iraq is closer to 18 million.[1] Nevertheless, in most of the media coverage of the event, no one seemed to know if the 14 million figure quoted was merely "registered" voters, adults over the age of 18, or what. Kurtz told Mitchell, who interviewed him for his *Editor & Publisher* piece, that even if his own estimate of 18 million adults was questionable (though it is based on work by Kenneth Pollack of the Brookings Institution), "the 14 million, the baseline, is a very fuzzy figure because there was no registration." Others raised the same question. Sami Ramdani noted in a piece the British *Guardian,* UN sources weren't able to explain how the number of people eligible to vote was arrived at or what it really signified:

> [W]hat percentage of the adult population is registered to vote? The Iraqi ambassador in London was unable to enlighten me. In fact, as UN sources confirm, there has been no registration or published list of electors – all we are told is that about 14 million people were entitled to vote.[2]

Now if the total population is *not* known, the number of eligible voters is *not* known, the basis for determining what makes a voter eligible is *not* known, and the number of registered voters is *not* known, discussing what *percentage* of the population turned out to vote is *meaningless:* it is like trying to do math without numbers! Kurtz actually notes in his piece for the *Post* that "election officials concede they did not have a reliable baseline on which to calculate turnout." If that is so, what faith can one put in any of the official declarations?

Nonetheless, the line from Baghdad and Washington has consistently been that 8 million people voted, and that this constituted a turnout of 57%.

Let's look at the 8 million figure, particularly as broken down by Mitchell's *Editor & Publisher* piece. The press initially quoted Farid Ayar, the spokesman for the IECI, as saying that "as many as 8 million" voted; this quickly became "about 8 million" in the media, and then, inevitably, simply "8 million." John Burns and Dexter Filkins, writing for the *New York Times* on the Friday after the election, reported that election officials had begun backtracking on the turnout "saying that the 8 million estimate had been reached hastily on the basis of telephone reports

1. "The Spinners, Casting Their Versions of the Vote in Iraq," *The Washington Post,* February 1, 2005, p. C1.

2. Ramdani, *loc. cit.*

from polling stations across the country."[1] What is remarkable about the "about 8 million" figure of Ayar, again following Mitchell's analysis, is that it corresponded perfectly with what he said *the day before* the election. Then, he suggested that between 7 and 8 million would turn out to vote, a prediction that might have given him some incentive to later find numbers that matched his forecast. Then again, if 8 million were expected to vote, Mitchell asks, why was the actual turnout greeted with such surprise?

As for the "57% turnout," Howard Kurtz points out in the *Post* that while the 14 million figure was the number of those said to be *registered* voters, in a normal election the turnout is calculated not on the number of registered voters but on the number of *eligible voters*. There is a huge difference, one which Greg Mitchell illustrated admirably:

> If say, for example, 50,000 residents of a city registered and 25,000 voted, that would seem like a very respectable 50% turnout, by one standard. But if the adult population of the city was 150,000, then the actual turnout of 16% would look quite different.

So if there were really 18 million eligible voters, and not just 14 million, the 8 million turnout counts for only 45% – less than half of the potential voters, quite different both politically and psychologically. And again this does not take into account the fact that the 8 million figure is doubtful at best – based upon a number of questions about the quality of the election in many technical and practical respects.

How many of those dealing with election figures outside of Iraq knew the difference between voter registration and voter eligibility? How many journalists drew their attention to the difference? Not without reason, then, did Robert Wiener, a Clinton White House veteran, declare: "It's an amazing media error, a huge blunder. I'm sure the Bush administration is thrilled by this spin."[2]

If the actual turnout was questionable, the way in which those who did vote were brought to the polls was no less so. The Iraqi Election Commission approved the use of the country's food-ration cards as the means by which all Iraqis would register and vote. Under pressure from the U.S. to speed the election process along, the Commission opted *not* to complete a comprehensive, nationwide census to determine voter eligibility – something

---

1. "Shiite Coalition Takes a Big Lead in the Iraq Vote," *New York Times*, February 4, 2005, p. A1.

2. Mitchell, *loc. cit.*

that should have been mandatory for an election of this size and importance, and indeed for any election that wished to be seen as legitimate.

Perhaps ironically, it was Saddam Hussein's Ba'ath Party which first created the food-rations system in 1991. In an effort to limit the devastating effects of UN sanctions, the Ba'ath Party issued a card to every Iraqi citizen, which entitled them to receive a free monthly ration of wheat, sugar, and other staples.

Throughout the nineties, as the situation became more dire, the food-ration cards constituted one of the few things Iraqis could rely on to make their daily lives tolerable. When the time came for Iraqis to vote in January 2005, one can only wonder what kind of internal discord many felt as they ventured forward with their precious food-ration card to choose leaders who would replace the very figures who produced the card.

Many Iraqis apparently voted only because they were convinced that their food rations might be cut if they failed to do so.

According *Al-Basa'ir*, a weekly publication of the Iraqi Muslim Scholars Council, people were expecting to have their 2004 ration cards renewed at the end of that year, as had occurred regularly for over a decade. But December came and went "without the Iraqis reading in the local papers or hearing in audio-visual media any mention of any invitation calling on them to replace these cards. This gave rise to many rumors as to why the issuance of these cards was delayed."[1]

Al-Basa'ir believed that the only plausible reason Iraqis found for the delay was that

> the government intends to withhold these cards from the families that will not participate in the elections. Many Iraqis affirm that the new ration card has been printed and that it will be distributed to the head of the family while he votes, and that those who do not go to the polling stations will not get their cards, and therefore will not receive the staples that are covered by the card, as a punishment.[2]

By late January, many Iraqis were convinced that their food supplies might be jeopardized if they did not show up for the vote. Amin Hajar, a small businessman from Baghdad, said, "I'll vote because I can't afford to have my food ration cut . . . if that happened, me and my family would starve to death."[3]

---

1. January 19, 2005, quoted by BBC Monitoring, January 24, 2005.
2. *Ibid.*
3. Dahr Jamail, "Some Just Voted for Food," *Inter Press Service*, January 31, 2005, online.

Saeed Jodhet, a 21-year-old Iraqi engineering student, had reason to believe he would lose out as well. "Two food dealers I know told me personally that our food rations would be withheld if we did not vote," he said.[1]

It matters little if such fears were without foundation. Large numbers of Iraqis believed them possible and took no chances on losing out. Given such a level of duress among the populace, one must question the validity of the choices made on election day.

Voting Day: What Else Was Fishy?

As if the questions about the actual turnout and the coercive methods by which it was achieved weren't enough to raise serious objections to the conduct of the election, other reports shortly after the elections revealed remarkably low turnouts in specific regions, as well as dubious voters and questionable voting practices in others. For instance:

- A mere 1,400 people voted in the predominantly Sunni city of Samarra, which boasts a population of over 200,000. This 1,400 *included* Iraqi soldiers and police, "most of whom were recruited from the [Shiite] south."[2]

- Four days after the election the *New York Times* was reporting that – with 60% of the count completed – turnout in Mosul, with its "diverse" population of Kurds, Shiites, Sunnis, and more, was slightly above 10%, or "somewhat more than 50,000 of Mosul's 500,000 estimated eligible voters."[3] The figure calls into question the refrain that maintains only Sunnis questioned, and therefore boycotted, the election.

- Of eligible Iraqis abroad, only 20% voted, according to the above-noted statement of the International Action Center. This gives the lie to the assertion that turnout was low in many areas simply because of security concerns.

- A correspondent for *Mafkarat al-Islam* reported that, according to the High Commission for Elections, the al-Karradah district of Baghdad was supposed to have 22,000 eligible voters. Of these only 700 voted. What makes this fact of particular interest is that

---

1. *Ibid.*

2. *Aljazeera*, "Confusion Surrounds Iraq Poll Turnout," *loc. cit.*

3. Christine Hauser, "In Diverse Mosul, Slightly More Than 10% Voted, but That's More Than Expected," *New York Times*, February 3, 2005, online.

the district is predominantly Christian, and not Sunni – which means that these too were *unenthusiastic* for the occupation and its political machinery.[1]

- Members of Ahmad Chalabi's party were seen escorting *non*-Iraqis to one polling station and issuing them false Iraqi citizenship certificates. In the span of just five minutes four people were observed participating in this counterfeit vote.[2]

- At another polling place every person who entered the site was asked to vote for a specific candidate. In some cases, according to one observer, election workers would actually mark the ballot form for the voter.[3]

- In another instance, armed men forced voters to cast their votes for a particular group, namely, the UIA.[4]

- In the north, Jalal Talabani's Kurdish PUK (Patriotic Union of Kurdistan) encouraged people to vote by distributing money and transistor radios to potential voters.[5]

- There was also a case in the north (quite possibly not unique) of a village that was supposed to have had 850 eligible voters, according to the authorities, but which managed to generate 4,500 votes. This fact was made known to the *Arab Monitor* news service by Hassan al-Zarqani, a representative of Moqtada al-Sadr.

Still other irregularities included insufficient ballots, votes cast without proper registration, polling stations not opening, pre-marked ballots, and multiple election cards.[6] Given the history of American government manipulation or staging of elections, going all the way back to Vietnam, it seems reasonable to assert that these elections, considered from an impartial and objective standpoint, cannot be considered credible.

---

1. Nasr, *loc. cit.*

2. *Ibid.*

3. *Ibid.*

4. James Glanz and Christine Hauser, "Election Complaints Fuel Protests in Iraq," *New York Times*, February 3, 2005, online; Tammuz Network for Election Monitoring, "Irregularities in Iraq's Election," January 30, 2005, quoted by *PoliticalAffairs.net*.

5. Nasr, *loc. cit.*

6. In this connection see: "Iraq Officials Admit Irregularities in Poll," *Aljazeera*, February 2, 2005, online; James Glanz and Christine Hauser, "Iraqis Report a Variety of Complaints About Irregularities on Election Day," *New York Times*, February 2, 2005, online; Tim Witcher, "Iraq Admits Vote Flaws as Rice Urges World to Unite on Future," *Agence France-Presse*, February 2, 2005, online.

The Results

According to the High Commission for Elections, 146 of the seats in the Transitional National Assembly went to members of the United Iraqi Alliance (UIA). The Kurdish alliance was second with 75 seats, and Iyad Allawi's "Iraqi List" – the presumed favorite of Washington – was third with only 40 seats. The remaining 20 seats went to nine smaller parties.

Interestingly, according to a report in the British *Independent*, Reuters reported a few hours before the election results were officially announced, on February 13, that "the United Iraqi Alliance said today it had been told by Iraq's Electoral Commission that it had won around 60 percent of the vote in the country's election."[1] The *Independent* report continued:

> This was later confirmed by the former U.S. chief UNSCOM weapons inspector in Iraq, Scott Ritter, who announced to a packed meeting in Washington State on 19 February that the United Iraqi Alliance actually gained 56 percent of the vote, and that "an official involved in the manipulation was the source."
>
> The significance of this voting maneuver is revealed in a *Washington Post* report (14 February): "A senior State Department official said yesterday that the 48 per cent vote won by the [Shiite] slate deprives it of an outright majority. 'If it had been higher, the slate would be seen with a lot more trepidation.'"

What makes the alleged 48% obtained by the al-Sistani-backed list of UIA Shiite parties even more suspicious is the fact that Shiites are supposed to comprise 60% of the population. Even more stunning is the fact that the leaders of the UIA – al-Jaafari and al-Hakim – did not complain about the inordinate delay in proclaiming the alleged results.

Given that the American-backed puppets did not perform well, it would have seemed reasonable to believe that the delay was a result of a downward "revision" of the results so that the al-Sistani list did not get an *outright* majority. Yet in this atmosphere of high tension, the al-Sistani list remained surprisingly – even unnaturally – quiet. One cannot help but wonder how much this has to do with the possible unreliability of what passes for standard demographic numbers in modern Iraq. A senior Sunni official, Fakhri al-Qaisi, a Baghdad dentist, longstanding member of conservative Islamic groups, and secretary-general of the National Dialogue Council, doesn't accept the standard "Iraq is 60% Shiite" line. As a recent *New York Times* piece put it, he contests

> even the demographics that suggest that any majority-rule government in Iraq will have to be led by Shiites. He argues that Shiites, generally considered

---

1. Michael Meacher, "America Is Usurping the Democratic Will in Iraq," *The Independent*, April 5, 2005, online.

to be about 60 percent of the population, are actually about half that, and Sunni Arabs closer to 40 percent than 20 percent, as most Iraqi studies have suggested.[1]

The Uncertain and Unstable Future

At the end of the day the process has crisis built into it, notwithstanding the questions regarding the election's legitimacy, integrity, and regularity. Why? Because the Bremer-imposed "Transitional Administrative Law" for formulating the new constitution declares that it can be accepted definitively *only if fewer than three* of Iraq's eighteen provinces reject it by a majority. Some have called this the "Kurdish veto," because they are the majority in three provinces. It could also be called the Sunni veto because they are the majority in at least three if not four provinces.[2] A relatively recent report has indicated that both Shiites and Sunnis are interested in having the law changed by the parliament, but the "TAL itself states that it can only be amended by a three-quarters vote in Parliament, which the Kurds, with more than a quarter of the seats, would be expected to block."[3]

One seems justified in asking whether this framework was a product of venality or stupidity on the part of Bremer and the Bush administration. In other words, were these "vetoes" built in deliberately by the U.S. in order to *guarantee* permanent constitutional crisis, for exploitation by American interests, or were they the product of the lack of foresight that this administration has demonstrated in so many other fields? In the abstract, a decent case could be made for both possibilities.

Meanwhile, a Successful Demonstration

The de facto American government in Iraq seems to have got what it wanted with the January 30 election. The election was billed as a "success" simply because a certain undetermined number of people participated. The whole thing was predictable, and it was in fact predicted with stunning precision by one of the world's most informed Middle East reporters, Robert Fisk:

> Yes, I know how it's all going to be played out. Iraqis bravely vote despite the bloodcurdling threats of the enemies of democracy. At last, the U.S. and

---

1. Steven R. Weisman and John F. Burns, "Some Sunnis Hint at Peace Terms in Iraq, U.S. Says," *New York Times*, May 15, 2005, online.
2. *Ibid.*
3. Meacher, *ibid.*

THE POLITICS OF ELECTORAL ILLUSION

British policies have reached fruition. A real and functioning democracy will be in place so the occupiers can leave soon. Or next year. Or in a decade or so. Merely to hold these elections – an act of folly in the eyes of so many Iraqis – will be a "success."[1]

The accuracy of Fisk's prediction was chronicled by, among others, Naomi Klein, writing for *The Nation* just 11 days after the election. "January 30, we are told, was not about what Iraqis were voting for," she noted.

> [I]t was about the fact of their voting and, more important, how their plucky courage made Americans feel about *their* war. Apparently, the election's true purpose was to prove to Americans that, as George Bush put it, "the Iraqi people value their own liberty." Stunningly, this appears to come as news. Chicago *Sun-Times* columnist Mark Brown said the vote was "the first clear sign that freedom really may mean something to the Iraqi people." On *The Daily Show*, CNN's Anderson Cooper described it as "the first time we've sort of had a gauge of whether or not they're willing to sort of step forward and do stuff."[2]

That the popular resistance movement and a tens of thousands-strong protest of American occupation don't qualify, for the American media, as the Iraqis "doing stuff" in defense of their own liberty and destiny is a testament to how well the election was packaged by those who orchestrated it. Clearly the idea that a free and independent people might reasonably reject a canned democratic process that is funded, organized, and enforced by American political and military might is not something that resonates with mainstream pundits. It is also a concept that is anathema to U.S. politicians, because the conceptual approach to the election has been designed to pit those who resist the occupation and the electoral process it created – the "terrorists," "dead-enders," and "former regime elements" – against those who submit to the U.S.-driven process and therefore prove that they "value their own freedom." Of all commentators, Frank Brodhead most convincingly sketched – 9 days in advance – how this dynamic works.

> [T]he dramatic tension of the January 30 election will focus on voter turnout. The U.S. mass media has already established this framing of the issue, and the election-day spectacle will pit the desire of the Iraqi people to vote *vs.* the violence of rebels opposed to democracy. Few of the long-term or background elements of a truly free election will receive any media play, and the idea that a free election is incompatible with U.S. military occupation will be completely off the agenda. That violence keeps many people from the polls, that many

---

1. Fisk, *loc. cit.*

2. "Getting the Purple Finger," *The Nation*, February 28, 2005 (posted online February 10, 2005, at www.thenation.com/doc.mhtml%3Fi=20050228&s=klein).

polling places will not be functioning, and that election officials, candidates, and even voters will be attacked by opponents of the U.S. occupation will be important preoccupations of the U.S. media on election day. (Anticipating these obvious problems, the United States has been taking steps to increase voter turnout – same-day registration, allowing voting at any polling place, allowing voting by Iraqis abroad, etc. – while at the same time trying to low-ball expectations of a strong voter turnout.) . . .

. . . the net effect of mass media coverage will be to frame the January 30 election to Bush's advantage, and to the advantage of continued U.S. military occupation. However flawed the election-day events, the media will accept the Bush administration's claim that its intention is to bring democracy to Iraqi, and that rebel violence shows that it is democracy itself that opponents of the U.S. occupation most fear.[1]

For the uncritical public eye, the election validated the political landscape engineered by the U.S. and demonstrated the continued need for American occupation to defend "freedom" and keep the democratic train on track. For the U.S., that train is a convenient vicious cycle; others would call it a train *wreck*. James Carroll noted in an article for the *Boston Globe* called "Train Wreck of an Election," how the intimate link between the electoral process, and the government it produced, on the one hand, and the occupation which maintains that government in power, on the other, results plainly in continued – perhaps indefinite? – occupation.

The chaos of a destroyed society leaves every new instrument of governance dependent on the American force, even as the American force shows itself incapable of defending against, much less defeating, the suicide legions. The irony is exquisite. The worse the violence gets, the longer the Americans will claim the right to stay.[2]

By that standard, assuming what Herman and Brodhead stated is true – that the purpose of a "demonstration election" is "to legitimize an invasion and occupation" – the January 30 Iraqi vote was a resounding success. Some even characterized the election as an outright "referendum in favor of peaceful politics,"[3] as if those who didn't vote were effectively voting *against* peace. It is perhaps not coincidental, however, that the journalist responsible for that description is an anti-Ba'athist, London-based Iraqi Kurd, for it is almost exclusively those like him who, having opposed the "old regime," now see something positive in the "demonstration" that cloaked its overthrow with legitimacy.

1. Brodhead, *loc. cit.*

2. James Carroll, *Boston Globe*, February 1, 2005, online.

3. See "What Do the Insurgents Want," by London-based Iraqi Kurd, Hiwa Osman, *Washington Post*, May 8, 2005, online.

The Facts on the Ground

The PR success that was the election doesn't for one minute alter the reality of the situation in Iraq. The country's real government, as Eric Margolis put it, "will continue to be the U.S. Embassy in Baghdad, the world's largest, and 150,000 occupation troops."[1] Recent calls from the new Iraqi "Transitional Government" for "more support and mediation" only serve to illustrate the dependence of the "liberated" Iraqi former-opposition groups upon Uncle Sam for help in policing the dysfunctional democracy that the "liberation" created.[2] American fears that heavy intervention in Iraq's post-election political arena would give the impression "that Iraqi government leaders were not acting independently" have since given way to a "new approach" that "[presses] hard for Iraq to move ahead."[3] As described by the *Los Angeles Times*, that new approach almost seemed dismissive of concerns that the Iraqis would seem insufficiently independent: while the Iraqis are "the ultimate determinants of their own destiny," a U.S. official was quoted as saying, "*we* have 140,000 troops here, and they are getting shot at" (emphasis mine). Ironically, the only time the new Iraqi "government" seems to flex its muscle vis-à-vis the U.S. is when the Americans suggest that a compromise on their anti-Ba'athist line – maintained by the dominant al-Dawa and SCIRI factions – might help reach out to the Ba'athist and Sunni leaders of the insurgency and encourage them to participate in the new Iraqi government. "This is not the business of the U.S.," a spokesman for al-Jaafari (now Prime Minister in the Transitional Government) said recently in response to such a suggestion. Many Iraqis also point to the intransigence of SCIRI leader al-Hakim (along with that of his Badr deputy, Hadi al-Amri[4]) as an obstacle to the Iraqi government's

---

1. Eric Margolis, "Iraq's Predetermined Elections," January 31, 2005.

2. See also Jim VandeHei and Peter Baker, "Bush's Optimism on Iraq Debated," *Washington Post*, June 5, 2005, online: "Iraqi Foreign Minister Hoshyar Zebari last week lobbied Cheney and others for a more assertive U.S. military approach in Iraq, as well as for more help meeting the fall deadline for writing and approving a constitution."

3. Paul Richter and Ashraf Khalil, "U.S. Moves to Reassert Itself in Iraq Affairs," *Los Angeles Times*, May 20, 2005, online.

4. *Agence France-Presse*, "Iraqi Shiite Party Poised for Power but Haunted by Its Past," April 12, 2005, online. SCIRI officials have also spearheaded the call to revamp the U.S.-backed "Iraqi" forces in order to ensure that their ranks are purged of individuals who served under Saddam Hussein or sympathizers with the insurgency. See Borzou Daragahi, "Iraqi Alliance Sets Sights on Revamping Police Force," *Globe and Mail*, March 26, 2005, p. A12.

GERY

ever extending a welcome to Sunni and Ba'athist elements.[1] The message would seem to be that the "new" Iraq is more than willing to follow America's lead, provided that lead does not dilute the newfound authority of those who, up until a couple of years ago, were defined by their opposition to the "former" Iraqi government. But transitional government has ultimately little to fear from American pressure as far as the "former regime" and the now disenfranchised Ba'athist organization are concerned. For the U.S. has made perfectly clear that there are certain "red lines" that its "partner" government in Iraq (as the *L.A. Times* tellingly put it) cannot cross. "The U.S. insists," the paper reported, "that the Iraqi government be democratic and that the country be pluralistic . . . ,"[2] according to an American official. "We constantly remind them that *we're working toward the same goal*" (emphasis mine), he also said.

As for those who maintain that the occupation will end when the Iraqi "security forces" can handle things on their own, it is hard not to question what resistance the Iraqi forces would have to oppose *after* the withdrawal of U.S. forces, since it is the latter's presence which is largely admitted as fueling the insurgency in the first place. This leads one to wonder whether the occupation will ever, in fact, end. Alternatively, the training and restructuring of the Iraqi "security array" by the American military training apparatus – which latest reports have as comprising 160,000 men (of, not insignificantly, mostly Shiite or Kurdish background[3]) funded by the U.S. at a cost of $5.7 billion,[4] and which includes "the national police force, . . . military units such as the Iraqi army, the Iraqi National Guard,

---

1. Weisman and Burns, *loc. cit.*

2. Richter and Khalil, *loc. cit.*

3. James Janega, "4,000 Marines, 30,000 Hostile Square Miles," *Chicago Tribune*, June 4, 2005, online. Other reports have indicated a predominantly Kurdish and Shiite makeup (both actual and desired by the current political leadership) of the new "Iraqi security forces." See, e.g., Edmond Roy, "Iraq Insurgency Produces Better Trained Terrorists: CIA Report," *Australian Broadcasting Company* (www.abc.net.au), June 23, 2005, online; Nancy Youssef, "As Sunnis Call Sweep Unfair, Iraq is Divided," *Philadelphia Inquirer*, June 4, 2005, online; Sabrina Tavernise and John Burns, "As Iraqi Army Trains, Word In The Field Is It May Take Years," *New York Times*, June 13, 2005, p. 1.

4. John F. Burns and Eric Schmitt, "Generals Offer Sober Outlook on Iraqi War," *New York Times*, May 19, 2005, online. See also Tavernise and Burns, *loc cit.*: " . . . with Iraq's unemployment rate at 30 percent or more, and as much as 60 percent among the poorest classes, a regular pay packet is a powerful incentive . . . . A common soldier's base pay can be up to $340 a month, rising to $950 for generals. Many doctors at Baghdad's best hospitals earn $500 a month or less, and many other Iraqis survive on $200 or less a month." Andrew Hammond ("Iraqi Army Fears Insurgents Outside Walls of Base," *Reuters*, August 8, 2005, online) quotes one recruit who makes it clear that we have simply "purchased" Iraqi participation in their new "army": "Most ordinary soldiers join just for the salary."

the Iraqi Prevention Force and Iraqi Special Operations Forces, and police-type units such as the Department of Border Enforcement and the Facilities Protection Service"[1] – may be simply another element of the American plan to reshape Iraq along U.S.-dictated lines: the element which in fact puts the mechanism to enforce that plan firmly in place.

Meanwhile, the January 30 election provided an entry point into the U.S.-created, post-"regime change" political landscape for the likes of al-Jaafari, Jalal Talabani, leader of the PUK (and now President), and the SCIRI leaders al-Hakim and al-Amri (respectively head of SCIRI and Badr), all of whom made names for themselves by fighting the legitimate government of Saddam Hussein over many years, with varying levels of support from Israel, Iran, and the U.S.[2]

By supporting those who opposed the now deposed Baghdad government and its network of popular Ba'athist, nationalist support, the U.S. has painted itself into an awful corner in Iraq, automatically cutting out of the political process any Iraqis who don't happen to support those formerly "opposition" parties. In fact they become borderline enemies of the (new) state and even possible targets for U.S. "counter-insurgency" forces. The fact remains, however, that the so-called "Iraqi forces" and "Iraqi government" sponsored and supported by the U.S. were imagined, not long ago, by a considerable number of Iraqis to be precisely the opposite: *anti-Iraqi*. Few touting the "new Iraq" remember the suspicion with which both SCIRI and al-Dawa are regarded by many Iraqis due to the role that both groups have played in Iraq's recent history as both destabilizing forces and agents of foreign powers. Illustrating the relationship between Iran, for instance, and the groups now controlling Iraq is a May 2005 visit there of Iranian foreign minister, Kamal Kharrazi, whose welcome by al-Jaafari and other "top" Iraqi Shiites was "suffused with references to the ties they formed during years of exile in Iran after fleeing the repression of Saddam Hussein."[3] Also illustrative was the early 2005 campaign of Hadi al-Amri, the head of the Badr wing of SCIRI (now a self-professed "political" organization, following the January 2005 election, though formerly, and some

---

1. Walter Pincus, "U.S. Says More Iraqi Police Are Needed as Attacks Continue," *Washington Post*, September 28, 2004, p. A23.

2. See the discussion by Jude Wanniski, on pp. 3–79 of the companion to the present volume, *Neo-CONNED!*, of the long-time support provided to the Kurdish Barzani and Talabani clans by third-party countries who were looking to encourage efforts to destabilize the Ba'athist government.—Ed.

3. John F. Burns, "Registering New Influence, Iran Sends a Top Aide to Iraq," *New York Times*, May 18, 2005, online.

say still, SCIRI's Iran-trained militia) for the post of interior minister of the Transitional Government. His bid for the position recalled memories – bad memories, for many – of the Badr Brigade's role in the Iran-Iraq war when it fought on the side of Iraq's enemy.[1] Though al-Amri didn't get the post, it sparked coverage in the press of Badr's alleged responsibility for torturing numerous Iraqi POWs during the Iran-Iraq war, with the intention of coercing them into joining Badr and fighting against Iraq.[2] Ironically, al-Amri maintains (according to *AFP*) that he was a "resistance" fighter and that, though he "could have stayed in Iraq, surrendered to the Ba'ath regime, and lived like an ordinary person" (one wonders how, given Hussein's alleged butchery), he remained "true to the resistance." Evidently, some resistance movements are acceptable to Iraq's new ruling coalition.

As if the U.S. embrace of pro-Iranian Shiite factions weren't enough to distance it from the rank and file of the Iraqi population, it has taken the same stance towards Kurdish separatists. U.S. Secretary of Defense Rumsfeld's visit to Iraqi Kurdistan on April 12, 2005, highlighted the attachment of the U.S. to Kurdish figures who led the effort to overthrow Baghdad's formerly recognized government. Rumsfeld, in his remarks, highlighted his opportunity

> to thank the Kurdish people and their leadership for the stalwart support over the many years now, and for their important role in liberating the Iraqi people from the repressive regime of Saddam Hussein.[3]

While Talabani, al-Jaafari, and his al-Dawa and SCIRI supporters now represent "acceptable" politics, still missing is what was marginalized by both the election and the process of "de-Ba'athification": the idea of a non-sectarian, nationalist Iraq held together by a vision other than ethnicity or religion.[4] The jockeying for power and position in the new "government" of Iraq might have been unseemly, but it was a wholly predictable outcome of the unleashing of destabilizing and sectarian forces in Iraq. What now seems to be the keynote of the new Iraqi politics is the pre-eminence of ethnic and religious concerns to the exclusion of an "Iraqi" vision.

---

1. Hannah Allam and Nancy A. Youssef, "Shiite, Sunni Leaders Trade Barbs," *Knight Ridder*, May. 19, 2005, online.

2. *Agence France-Presse, loc. cit.*

3. "Secretary Rumsfeld Press Availability with Mr. Barzani," April 12, 2005 (http://www.defense.gov/transcripts/2005/tr20050412-secdef2483.html).

4. Indeed, as pointed out by Boudreaux (*loc. cit.*), "no Sunni Arab leader known to have direct ties to the insurgents has taken part in the political talks or been mentioned for a possible role in the government."

Journalist Mark Danner called the election an "ethnic census,"[1] while Zogby pollsters characterized voting as "sectarian,"

> with Shiites voting for control of the government, and Kurds voting as an expression of their autonomy, the Sunni Arab failure to vote as a function not only of threats, but a clear expression of their growing sense of disenfranchisement."[2]

Concerns that currently predominate are similar, as indicated in the interesting *Knight-Ridder* report we have already cited.

> Shiite politicians will be under pressure from devout voters to enforce religious tenets and laws. Local officials who now control Iraq's heavily Shiite southern and central cities already have added traditional Islamic rules to secular laws governing public conduct there . . . .
> These moves have alienated Kurdish and Sunni voters and could fuel secession efforts that could split Iraq into three countries; a Kurdish state in the north, a Sunni one in the middle and a Shiite one to the south, said Jordanian political analyst Labib Kamhawi.
> Oil revenue is another point of contention.
> More than anything, Iraq's neighbors fear a civil war and a breakup of the country.[3]

These ethnic, religious, and territorial passions "can no longer be papered over," as John Burns warned in his April 29 piece for the *New York Times*. What lies ahead is "the hardest passage yet in the American enterprise in Iraq" (note he rightly calls the enterprise "American"), with issues hanging in the balance that are "basic to Iraq's future and its prospects of emerging as a stable democracy." At worst, what must be avoided is "civil war among Shiites, Sunnis, and Kurds."[4]

While much is made in the press of the potential for "civil war," it shouldn't be forgotten that one is *already* underway between Iraqis fighting for their right to self-determination and those collaborating with foreign occupation. This situation places the U.S. in the position, whether it likes it or not, of actively (and militarily) opposing the desires of many Iraqis, while working with those who have long sought (for whatever reason) to capture the reins of power in Baghdad. The internecine struggle between

---

1. "Iraq: The Real Election," *New York Review of Books*, April 28, 2005, online.

2. John Zogby and Dr. James Zogby, "The Real Meaning of the Iraq Elections: A Closer Look at the Details of the Abu Dhabi TV/Zogby International Poll in Iraq," *Zogby International*, January 31, 2005 (www.zogby.com/news/ReadNews.dbm?ID=958).

3. Ahmed and Nelson, *loc. cit.*

4. Burns, "Registering New Influence," *loc. cit.*

the Kurdish leaders Barzani and Talabani[1] is simply one illustration of the ongoing "power plays," as is the violence provoked by SCIRI reprisals against Sunni clerics, under the auspices of the Iraqi Interior Ministry, for their alleged support of the resistance movement,[2] all of which the U.S. is forced to take cognizance of as a result of its having sponsored the truly sectarian "opposition groups" as part of its effort to reshape Iraq. The obligation of U.S. Navy special operations forces to protect Transitional Prime Minister al-Jaafari from attack 24 hours a day[3] is perhaps an apt metaphor illustrating the larger task that the U.S. has signed itself up for.

No one who is "politically correct" will admit the sole solution to this predicament: the recognition by all concerned of the legitimacy of an Iraqi nationalism based on non-sectarian lines that claims for itself the freedom both to determine its own destiny and, if it chooses, to reject the occupying military force and its electoral public face. Though "sectarianism" is a problem, it is often overstated by the media, which insists on portraying the "insurgency" as a symptom of Sunni sour grapes rather than as what British journalist John Pilger terms a "war of national liberation." Such a war would necessitate a sense of *Iraqi* – rather than Sunni, Shiite, or Kurdish – identity, and such an identity cannot be reported upon if it is not conceived of as a legitimate option for the Iraqi people by American and puppet forces.

How else, then, to make sense of the early May 2005 refusal of Hashim al-Shibli to accept the post of Human Rights minister in the new "Transitional Government"? According to a *New York Times* report, al-Shibli felt that he was nominated for the post as part of "a quota system for Sunnis that would only make sectarian problems worse."[4] What's more, he only "heard about it watching TV," the report said.

---

1. According to a report posted on June 1, 2005, by Muhammad Abu Nasr, co-editor of *Free Arab Voice,* Kurdish sources told the London-based, Arab-language daily *Al-Quds al-Arabi* (edited by Abdel Bari Atwan) tensions between Barzani's KDP and the followers of Jalal Talibani in recent weeks flared over who should hold the post of "leader" of the Kurdistan separatist region [a post eventually granted to Barzani on June 12, 2005, in a what was widely seen as an exchange with Talabani for his having supported the latter's bid to become Transitional President of Iraq.—Ed.] As a result of these tensions, Kurdish sources blamed Talibani's forces for a May 31, 2005, attack on Barzani's motorcade. (See http://www.freearabvoice.org/Iraq/Report/report299.htm.)

2. Steve Negus and Dhiya Rasan, "Iraq Sunni Group Attacks 'State Terrorism,'" *Financial Times,* May 18, 2005, online.

3. Burns, "Registering New Influence," *loc. cit.*

4. Richard A. Oppel, Jr., "A New Political Setback for Iraq's Cabinet," *New York Times,* May 9, 2005, online.

"No one talked to me or asked me about it before. This morning they called me and tried to congratulate me on my 'new job,' but I said no. I refused this because this is sectarianism, *and I don't believe in sectarianism. I believe in democracy*" (emphasis mine).[1]

It is to the credit of the *Christian Science Monitor* that its May 10, 2005, editorial congratulated al-Shibli for his stance:

> Bravo for him. Perhaps Iraq's new leaders, like the U.S. occupation regime, cater too much to this notion that Iraqis identify themselves primarily by religion and ethnicity and not first as citizens of a nation called Iraq.[2]

The same plea for non-sectarian "democracy" was raised by a Sunni Arab member of the Iraqi National Front during the time the Transitional Government was being formed post-election. If the Sunnis were really just hoping to restore the "old regime" of allegedly exclusive Sunni dominance, what sense would it make for them to protest sectarianism? Yet according to Boudreaux of the *Los Angeles Times*, "Sunni Arabs worry that a more lasting – *and some say intentional* – legacy of U.S. intervention will be an increasingly violent sectarian and ethnic division of Iraq"(emphasis mine). Instead, Boudreaux writes, some Sunnis

> [advocate] a strategy to draw Shiites wary of their sect's pro-Iranian leaders into a pluralist movement.
> "Let us unite all Iraqi nationalists," said Hatim Jassim Mukhlis of the Iraqi National Front. "Otherwise, Iraq and its democracy will be lost."[3]

Looking Backwards and Forwards

It is ironic, to say the least, that the "regime" that the U.S. overthrew was acknowledged, even by its enemies, as having achieved the near impossible task of unifying the Kurds, Turkomen, Christians, Sunni Arabs, Shiite Arabs, and others that together constitute the Iraqi nation. A piece appearing just before the U.S. invasion in the Egyptian paper, *Al-Ahram*, commented that – speaking of a well-known Ba'athist writer – "Amal Khedairy summed up the feelings of most Iraqis when she said, 'This [Hussein] government has a hold on the country. The people who may come here to rule do not understand how to control Iraq.'"[4] It speaks volumes of the "former

---

1. *Ibid.*

2. The Monitor's View (editorial), "Iraq: More Than the Sum of Its Parts," *Christian Science Monitor*, May 10, 2005, online.

3. Boudreaux, *loc. cit.*

4. Michael Jansen, "Sleeping Splendour," *Al-Ahram Weekly Online*, Issue No. 625,

regime's" reputation in the Arab world that, in a *San Francisco Chronicle* piece criticizing Ms. Khedairy (on the occasion of her tour of the U.S. in the fall of 2003) for having been a columnist for the Ba'athist *Al-Thawra,* Medea Benjamin suggested to the American journalist that she should not "paint these women as Ba'athists, but instead . . . paint them as nationalists, *which they are*" (emphasis mine).[1]

At any rate, Khedairy's point is well made. Even mainstream sources reveal that the deposed Iraqi President's rule was not the monolithic tyranny of a Sunni bloc over its competitors; the Sunnis themselves "are splintered into dozens of groups and parties, some with just a few members,"[2] and even Hussein was able just barely to "[hold] their fractured community together."[3] Though he did do so, as he did in the case of the Islamic radicals who otherwise would have run rampant throughout Iraq. As Illana Mercer pointed out in a column last year,

> Whatever one might say about the al-Tawhid and Jihad (Abu Musab al-Zarqawi's outfit), the Islamic Army, the Khaled bin al-Waleed corps, the Green Brigade, the Islamic Response, Ansar al-Sunna and the Black Banners – they did not have the run of Iraq. Saddam Hussein did. Saddam was a brutal dictator, but he did provide Iraq with one of the foundations of civilization: order.[4]

If Saddam "just barely" managed to keep Sunnis together and the terrorists under his thumb, with his reputation as an iron-fisted dictator, what chance will the U.S. have of doing so when the Iraqi "nationalist" vision, which transcends ethnic and religious ties and which is the only practical common denominator around which to unite so many disparate clans, tribes, and loyalties, is officially and intentionally excluded by the new "government" and its U.S. backers?[5] Indeed, the vision for the "new Iraq" is a recipe for disaster, as the former Washington correspondent from *Al-Ahram Weekly,* Ayman El-Amir, pointed out recently.

February 13–19, 2003 (weekly.ahram.org.eg/2003/625/sc9.htm).

1. Debra J. Saunders, "Poster Women for Peace?" *San Francisco Chronicle,* November 16, 2003, online.

2. Boudreaux, *loc. cit.*

3. *Ibid.*

4. Ilana Mercer, "Liberation Has a Body Count," *Antiwar.com,* November 17, 2004.

5. As if American hypocrisy needed no further illustration, a recent *Daily Telegraph* piece indicated that Iyad Allawi was again becoming popular as a possible Iraqi leader, in spite of his "unyielding, belligerent . . . almost thuggish" manner, because many Iraqis recognize that "it is those slightly dictatorial tendencies that a successful leader in so diverse a country needs to have" (Adrian Blomfield, "Allawi's Star Rises Again as Iraq Counts the Cost of Insurgency Terror," *Daily Telegraph,* June 6, 2005, online).

On the home front Prime Minister al-Jaafari has stitched together not a government of national unity but a coalition of sectarian interests that attempts to balance the relative distribution of power in the country. It will result in a political formula more fragile than even the Lebanese model. Once ethno-religious sectarian interests are recognized and empowered, *no government or constitution will be able to guarantee the pursuit of unified national interests.* Such is the blood-stained lesson learned *at a staggering human cost* in both Lebanon and the former Yugoslavia (emphasis mine).

At any rate, it is difficult to conceive of a genuine and successful Iraqi nationalism that does not implicitly contain a healthy distrust of American motives, in view of the last 15 years of relations between the U.S. and Iraq. Though a generic and anodyne "democracy" may be foisted upon the Iraqi people by more electioneering and constitution-writing engineered by the occupying military and political forces in Iraq, one seems justified in hesitating to equate it with a real expression of the "popular will." Eric Margolis made this point as well as anyone: "We'll know for sure real freedom has dawned in Iraq when Baghdad orders U.S. troops out, raises oil prices, rebuilds its armed forces, and renews support for the Palestinian cause."[1]

---

1. Margolis, *loc. cit.* Evidence of Margolis's claim was proved in an interesting if round-about way by the Zogby survey (*loc. cit.*) of January 28, 2005, which reported, "While a majority of Iraqis believe relations can be improved between Iraq and neighbors Kuwait, Turkey, and Iran, all ethnic and religious groups overwhelmingly rejected improving relations with the State of Israel."

THE EDITORS' GLOSS: A perfect illustration of the "charges" now facing Saddam Hussein is the alleged "massacre" of villagers in the town of Dujail, 50 miles north of Baghdad. *AP* reported on June 13, 2005, that those killed numbered "at least 50 Iraqis . . . , in retaliation for a failed assassination attempt against [Hussein]." For its part, the London *Sunday Times* said (July 3, 2005) that "several hundred people were executed in cold blood in reprisal for a botched assassination attempt against Saddam," while John Burns of the *New York Times* maintains (June 6, 2005) that 143 people were executed, following sentencing by Awad al-Sadoun, chief judge of the Revolutionary Court. Burns later reported (July 3, 2005) that the attempt on Saddam's life had been carried out by the al-Dawa party, a "conservative Shiite religious party . . . with an armed wing that had opened up terrorist attacks against Mr. Hussein's government," and which had "strong support in Dujail," a town, he claimed, where many "despised [Saddam] for starting a war with Iran, Iraq's Shiite neighbor." The party regarded Saddam's visit to the town as "a chance to avenge the government's killing of hundreds of al-Dawa leaders and sympathizers." Burns records how one al-Dawa Shiite "confessed to his father before he died that he was one of those who had shot at the Iraqi ruler." Of 75,000 people in the town, 1,500 were arrested and somewhere between 50 to 143 were sentenced. Hussein reportedly told the people of Dujail, shortly after the incident, that "the people who had attempted to kill him were a small band of traitors, and that we don't want to confuse them with the good people of Dujail."

So some unclear number of people were convicted of attempted assassination of the Iraqi head of state, sentenced to death, and executed. Yet the Iraqi Special Tribunal – of which, Burns says, the "Regime Crimes Liaison Office, an American Embassy agency" is "the legal and financial mainstay" – is going to send Saddam to the gallows for this "massacre." But Burns admitted that Saddam's visit to Dujail amounted to "a venture into enemy terrority"; that he would be arraigned for dealing with sedition, attempted murder, and acts of terrorism there by unrepresentative, sectarian Shiites acting against their legitimate government is incredible indeed. It brings to mind what Ilana Mercer perceptively noted about another head of state in somewhat similar circumstances. "Over a million Americans died because Lincoln put down an insurrection in order to preserve the Union. If we hold Lincoln to the same standard the neocons hold Saddam to, then Lincoln must be universally acknowledged as one of history's greatest war criminals."

C H A P T E R
40

A Trial Indeed: The Treatment of Saddam Hussein vs. the Rule of Law
• • • • • • • • •

Curtis Doebbler, Esq., Ph.D.

> "I think it will be the modern-day equivalent of a lynching in the 'wild west.' I think that everybody more or less accepts the trial and the sentence is a foregone conclusion."
>
> > —Rime Allaf
> > Royal Institute of International Affairs, London

> "Saddam Hussein already has been convicted in the court of international public opinion for crimes against the Iraqi people."
>
> > —*The Associated Press*

> "It goes without saying Saddam's trial is going to be one of the most important trials of the last hundred years, *including Eichmann*."
>
> > —Paul D. Wolfowitz
> > former U.S. Deputy Secretary of Defense

THE LEGAL TEAM representing Mr. Saddam Hussein, the President of Iraq, consists of individuals chosen by his family and acting under the umbrella of ISNAD,[1] a body formed to coordinate the efforts aimed at ensuring respect for the rule of law in Iraq, and to draw attention to the illegitimacy and illegality of the Iraqi Special Tribunal (IST). The team consists of internationally distinguished lawyers, including former U.S. Attorney General, Mr. Ramsey Clarke, who joined the team in late December 2004, and former French Minister of Foreign Affairs Mr. Roland Dumas. The legal team has also been offered the support of numerous volunteer lawyers from the Arab world. It is headed by an Executive Committee whose administrative office is based in Amman, Jordan. The

---

1. ISNAD is the Defense and Support Committee of President Saddam Hussein, His Comrades and all POWs and Detainees in Iraq; the acronym is an Arabic word that means "support" for justice.

lawyers are currently all acting in volunteer capacities and on the basis of a power of representation provided by the family until they are allowed regular access to the President that allows him to make an informed choice as to the legal counsel he desires to represent him.

The first meeting between Mr. Hussein and a member of his legal team did not take place until more than a year after the start of his detention. Mr. Khalil al-Dolaimi, an Iraqi lawyer who is part of ISNAD, was allowed to meet with the President only under strict monitoring (both visual and audio) by U.S. military officials who were present at all times. Over four months after the original meeting, Mr. al-Dolaimi was finally able once again to meet with Mr. Hussein for several hours again under the inappropriate conditions of heavy surveillance.

This was only the President's second meeting with a member of the legal team after 16 months of illegal captivity. He has still not been allowed to see members of his family. He continues to be held by the United States government and its administrative arm in Iraq, the so-called Iraqi Transitional Government. Though the United States attempted to turn over "legal custody" of Mr. Hussein to the Iraqi "authorities" on July 1, 2004, under international law it is clear that both de facto and de jure custody is being maintained by the United States.

According to press reports, Mr. Hussein is being held at a location outside Baghdad, near Baghdad International Airport, within a vast American complex known as Camp Victory. Notwithstanding the two meetings he has been able to have with his lawyers, he is denied routine access to them and to the alleged evidence against him. Despite occasional statements that have been circulated in the press suggesting that he has been meeting routinely with his lawyers, no lawyers have met the President outside of the two permitted meetings, December 16, 2004, and April 27, 2005. Moreover, no lawyer chosen by the President has been able to meet him in confidence at any time since his arrest. At the same time the occupying forces continue to orchestrate a trial before the IST, a body that is neither competent, nor independent, nor impartial.

Despite these conditions, in which the rule of law is being significantly abused, efforts are continuing by the legal team and by ISNAD. Despite this context of the most dilapidated due process, some legal steps have been taken to try to encourage respect for the rule of law by the occupying powers in Iraq. Among these steps has been a petition for habeas corpus in the United States.

A Petition for a Writ of Habeas Corpus

On June 29, 2004, a petition for a writ of habeas corpus was filed with the United States Supreme Court by President Saddam Hussein (in legal terminology, the "Petitioner"), and served on U.S. President George Bush, U.S. Secretary of Defense Donald Rumsfeld, and L. Paul Bremer III, the former U.S. Administrator of the Coalition Provisional Authority in Iraq. All three officials (the "Respondents") have had the opportunity to order and ensure that Mr. Hussein is treated in accordance with law, but have failed to do so, and have contributed to his continued illegal detention. The filing also alleges that the United States is violating its own Constitution, its military law, and international law. It recognizes that the United States' aggression against the people of Iraq is illegal and that the occupation is illegal. It focuses, however, on the illegality of the treatment of the Iraqi President.

It is noteworthy that the filing and service on U.S. government officials of the petition took place before an attempt was made to transfer "legal" custody of Mr. Hussein to the Iraqi Interim Government on July 1, 2004, and before Mr. Hussein's appearance before an Iraqi judge. Ordinarily, when this kind of petition is filed, a prisoner may not be transferred until it is dealt with by the judicial authorities. The United States' actions subsequent to being served can thus be construed as an attempt to remove the jurisdiction of the Supreme Court and to suspend the writ of habeas corpus. So viewed, these actions alone by the United States government are a serious affront to the United States' highest judicial body and show a significant disrespect for the rule of law. Additionally, it is clear from known facts and from press reports as recent as April 27, 2005 (Jamal Halaby, "Lawyer Says Saddam Hussein in Good Health," *Associated Press*), that U.S. forces continue to maintain de facto custody of Mr. Hussein and determine who does and does not have the opportunity to meet with him. The U.S. government is therefore the effective authority over Mr. Hussein's continued detention, and thus the arguments that follow apply today no less than to the period prior to the attempted "transfer" of legal custody.

The petition is worth reading in full, but space limitations require that only its highlights are presented here. A review of the essential sections and their arguments will effectively illustrate the illegality of the treatment that was and still is being afforded Mr. Hussein, and will summarize the reasonableness of a request for a writ of habeas corpus in order to determine the legality of Mr. Hussein's continued detention.

The Court was requested to answer only two questions:

1. Is Petitioner's incommunicado detention, whereby he is prohibited access to family or to legal counsel, in accordance with law?
2. Is the turning over of the Petitioner to an authority that may reasonably be expected to violate his rights to a fair trial, due process of law, and his right to life in accordance with law?

The legal team believes that the answer to both questions is manifestly clear: *no*.

It may seem strange that the petition for habeas corpus was filed in an *American* court and not before some Iraqi institution. It should be remembered, though, that the petition was filed *before* the legal "transfer" of custody of Mr. Hussein to the Iraqi Interim Government, and thus there was no doubt that he was being held under U.S. authority both de jure and de facto. That the U.S. Supreme Court possessed jurisdiction over the matter was thus not in doubt. The relevant portions of the petition make this clear:

1. Petitioner brings this action under 28 U.S.C. §§2241(a) and 2242, and invokes this Court's jurisdiction under 28 U.S.C. §§1331, 1350, 1651, 2201, and 2202; 5 U.S.C. §702; as well as the Fifth and Fourteenth Amendments to the United States Constitution, the International Covenant on Civil and Political Rights (ICCPR), the American Declaration on the Rights and Duties of Man (ADRDM), the Third Geneva Convention Relative to the Treatment of Prisoners of War (GPW), and Customary International Law. For declaratory relief, Petitioners also rely on F. R. Civ. P. 57.

2. This Court is empowered under 28 U.S.C. §2241 to grant the Writ of Habeas Corpus under 28 U.S.C. §2242. This Court is further empowered to declare the rights and other legal relations of the parties herein by 28 U.S.C. §2201, and to effectuate and enforce declaratory relief by all necessary and proper means by 28 U.S.C. §2202, as this case involves an actual controversy within the Court's jurisdiction.

. . .

5. This case involves 28 U.S.C. §2241 that provides in relevant part:

(a) Writs of habeas corpus may be granted by the Supreme Court, any justice thereof, the district courts and any circuit judge within their respective jurisdictions . . . .

(c) The writ of habeas corpus shall not extend to a prisoner unless –

1. He is in custody under or by color of the authority of the United States . . . ; or

3. He is in custody in violation of the Constitution or laws or treaties of the United States . . . .

This case also involves the Due Process Clause of the Fifth and Fourteenth Amendment, U.S. Constitution, Amendments V and XIV; the Suspension

Clause, U.S. Constitution, Art. I, §9, clause 2; Army Regulation 190–8 (Enemy Prisoners of War, Retained Personnel, Civilian Internees, and Other Detainees), OPNAVINST 3461.6, AFJI 31-304, MCO 3461.1 (1 October 1997); the GPW, 6 U.S.T. 3316, 75 U.N.T.S. 135 (12 August 1949); International Covenant on Civil and Political Rights, 999 U.N.T.S. 171, U.N. G.A. Res. 2200A (XXI), 21 U.N. GAOR. Supp. No. 16, at 52, U.N. Doc. A/6316 (1966); the American Declaration of the Rights and Duties of Man, O.A.S. Res. XX, adopted by the Ninth International Conference of American States (1948), reprinted in Basic Documents Pertaining to Human Rights in the Inter-American System, OEA/Ser.L.V/II.82 doc.6 rhev.1 at 17 (1992).

The basic facts of Mr. Hussein's case are presented under eight points, numbered 6 to 13. These read as follows:

6. The detained Petitioner is the former President of Iraq. He was driven from power by an armed attack against his country by the United States which was ordered by the Respondents.

7. On 16 October 2002, a Joint Resolution of Congress authorized the Respondents "to use the Armed Forces of the United States as [the President] determines to be necessary and appropriate in order to . . . (1) defend the national security of the United States against the continuing threat posed by Iraq; and . . . (2) enforce all relevant United Nations Security Council resolutions regarding Iraq." Joint Resolution 114, To Authorize the Use of United States Armed Forces Against Iraq, Public Law 107–243, 116 Stat. 1498 (16 Oct. 2002).

8. The Resolution did not authorize the indefinite detention of persons seized on the field of battle. Although detention of individuals seized in the armed conflict is provided for under and according to Article 21 of the GPW.

9. Iraq, during the time that Petitioner was Head of State, was no direct threat to United States security. In fact at the time of the United States invasion in March 2003, Iraq was cooperating with the United Nations in relation to the inspection and destruction of specified aspects of its national defense system. It now appears, despite representations by the Respondents to the contrary, that Iraq and Petitioner had abided by the provisions of United Nations Security Council Resolutions calling for the destruction of weapons of mass destruction.

10. Furthermore, no American casualties were caused by the Iraqi government by acts of aggression directed against the United States under Saddam Hussein's presidency, prior to, or in the interim between the invasions of Iraq by successive American Presidents. Neither is there any significant evidence linking Iraq to al-Qaeda.

11. Nevertheless, on 19 March 2003, the United States, at the direction of Respondent Bush, began a massive military campaign against the Iraqi people and the Iraqi government headed by Petitioner.

12. In response Petitioner authorized the use of force against the United States military to repel invasions of his country and in furtherance of his

responsibilities as the Head of State of Iraq to protect the territorial integrity and political independence of Iraq from foreign invasion. These actions were taken in accordance with Article 51 of the Charter of the United Nations which provides for the right of self-defense.

13. The invasion that led to the arrest of Petitioner, on the other hand, was not in accordance with international law. It was a violation of the seminal Article 2, paragraph 4 of the Charter of the United Nations which prohibits the use of force against the territorial integrity and political independence of a country.

Summarizing the facts of the President's detention are an additional nine points.

17. Since his capture on or around 13 December 2003 Petitioner has been held incommunicado in Respondents' unlawful custody.

18. Petitioner's exact whereabouts are unknown because the United States government refuses to disclose this information.

19. Petitioner is being held incommunicado and is reportedly being interrogated repeatedly by agents of the United States Departments of Defense and Justice, though he has not been charged with an offense, nor has he been notified of any pending or contemplated charges. Petitioner has made no appearance before either a military or civilian tribunal of any kind, nor has he been provided counsel or the means to contact counsel. Petitioner is not known to have been informed of his rights under the United States Constitution, the regulations of the United States Military, the GPW, the ICCPR, or the ADRDM. Indeed, the Respondents have taken the position that the Petitioner should not be told of these rights. As a result, the detained Petitioner is completely unable either to protect, or to vindicate his rights under domestic and international law.

20. Petitioner has been allowed to write two or three very brief communications to his wife, one of which was dated 21 January 2004 and delivered by the International Committee of the Red Cross to Petitioner's family on or around 21 February 2004. This communication had nine out of fourteen lines censored out of it, making it hardly understandable.

21. Former Iraqi President Saddam Hussein was detained as a consequence of the illegal acts of aggression by the United States that were authorized and overseen by the Respondents.

22. The Respondents have also admitted that the Petitioner is a legitimate Prisoner of War to whom the provisions of the Geneva Convention on Prisoners of War apply fully.

23. Respondents have also threatened to turn over Petitioner to the Iraqi Interim Government on or about 30 June 2004.

24. At the same time Respondents have also threatened to turn Petitioner over to the Iraqi Interim Government despite the fact that this entity has indicated that it will not provide the minimum standards of due process that are guaranteed to Petitioner under United States and international law.

25. The detained Petitioner is not lawfully detained because his detention is in violation of international and United States law.

The petition then gets to the heart of the matter: requesting that the Supreme Court grant the writ of habeas corpus such that Mr. Hussein might challenge the legality of his continued detention. This request is made based upon three stipulations: (1) the President's due process rights under the Fifth and Fourteenth Amendments of the United States Constitution have been violated; (2) his due process rights under international human rights law have been violated; and (3) his due process rights under United States military law, Iraqi law, and international humanitarian law have been violated. These three stipulations are explained and argued in detail in the subsections to the petition devoted to each stipulation.

The essence of the first subsection is explained in four points dealing with the U.S. Constitution.

27. The Fifth and Fourteenth Amendments to the Constitution establish the most basic rights of individuals in the custody of the United States. These rights include, *inter alia,* the right to challenge one's detention and to be free of arbitrary detention, the right to legal counsel of one's choosing, and the right to know charges against oneself.

28. By the actions described above, Respondents, acting under color of law, have violated and continue to violate the right of the detained Petitioner to be free from arbitrary, prolonged, and indefinite detention, in violation of the Due Process Clause of the Fifth and Fourteenth Amendments to the United States Constitution . . . .

30. Although Petitioner was apprehended after Respondent George W. Bush announced the end of major hostilities on 1 May 2003, and therefore no longer constituted a threat to American security in Iraq, Petitioner has been and continues to be denied his basic Constitutional right to due process of law.

31. The detention of Petitioner violates the Fifth and Fourteenth Amendments of the United States Constitution.

The second subsection likewise details the violation of Mr. Hussein's rights under international human rights law. A few of the essential points are sufficient to give the thrust of the argument, though what follows are only eight of 21 points detailing the violation of Mr. Hussein's rights.

36. The widespread acceptance of the basic constituents of the right to fair trial by more than 150 states who have ratified [the International Covenant of Civil and Political Rights (ICCPR) and the American Declaration on the Rights and Duties of Man (ADRDM)] indicates that these rights have developed into Customary International Law.

37. All of these rights are violated by the regime under which Petitioner is being held and by the consistency and procedures of the court before which Petitioner is threatened with trial.

38. Petitioner's incommunicado detention denies him the right to challenge his arrest before any court . . . .

43. Despite being held incommunicado for more than six months Petitioner has not been informed of any charges against him.

44. Petitioner has . . . been denied the right to adequate facilities and time to prepare defense, including his right to consult a lawyer of his own choosing by his incommunicado detention.

45. Petitioner's right to a presumption of innocence has been violated by statements made by Respondent George W. Bush indicating that Petitioner is a very "bad person" who deserves to be executed.

46. The lengthy delays in charging Petitioner as well as the failure to allow him facilities to prepare his defense including access to lawyers violate his right to a trial without undue delay.

47. The fact that the prosecution is preparing a case against Petitioner, including questioning witnesses, while Petitioner lacks the basic necessities for preparing his defense also violates Petitioner's right to examine witnesses and to call witnesses under same conditions as the prosecution.

Finally, the petition points out the violation of the Petitioner's rights under the terms of United States Military Law, Iraqi law, and the GPW. Of the seven points comprising this subsection, three are sufficient to capture the nature of the rights violation.

55. United State Military Law, specifically Army Regulation 190–8 (Enemy Prisoners of War, Retained Personnel, Civilian Internees, and Other Detainees), OPNAVINST 3461.6, AFJI 31-304, MCO 3461.1 (1 October 1997) at Section 3-8, pp. 10 and 11, requires that captured enemy combatants be accorded the right to a fair trial, including being promptly charged and being given adequate facilities including counsel of their own choosing.

56. Article 15, especially paragraphs C through J, of the Law of Administration for the State of Iraq for the Interim Period (8 March 2004) provides for the protection of Petitioner's right to a fair trial before an impartial and independent court, the right to challenge his detention, with a public trial, and the full right of legal counsel of his choosing. No court, however, currently exists in Iraq that can ensure these guarantees.

57. Articles 84, 99, 100, and 105 of the GPW also require that a Prisoner of War be provided with the basic guarantees of due process including the right to be judged by an independent and impartial tribunal (Art. 84(2)); the right to adequate facilities and time to prepare defense (Art. 99); the right not to be punished for an act that was not a crime at the time of commission (Art. 99(1)); the right to counsel (Art. 99 and 105); and the right to be informed of criminal charges (Art. 100).

The second main contention of the petition is that any attempt to suspend the Petitioner's right to habeas corpus is a violation not only of the U.S. Constitution but also of international law. Two subsections detail the way in which each is violated by the Respondents' implicit attempt to deny Mr. Hussein the right to habeas corpus. In the first we have adduced a compelling discussion of the sacredness of the Great Writ in terms of the Constitution and the seriousness of its violation in this case.

61. To the extent that Respondents' actions prevent any challenge to the legality of the Petitioner's detention by way of habeas corpus, their action constitutes an unlawful suspension of the Writ, in violation of Article I of the United States Constitution.

62. The right to habeas corpus has been described by this Court as the most "precious safeguard of personal liberty" for which "there is no higher duty than to maintain it unimpaired." *Bowen v. Johnston*, 306 U.S. 19, 26 (1939). It is the most basic, and in this case, the ultimate, protection for the individual against arbitrary action by the government. Suspension of habeas corpus, even in extraordinary circumstances must not take place lightly.

63. Most recently this Court has held that detainees such as Petitioner have basic due-process rights, including habeas corpus. *Rasul v. Bush*, 542 U.S. __ (2004). Petitioner in this case is in a similar position to the detainees in Guantánamo in that action, as he is detained by the United States outside of the territory of the United States but under the exclusive jurisdiction and control of the United States.

64. In this case, Respondents have not suspended the Writ of Habeas Corpus by law, but instead are attempting to do so implicitly. Respondents deny Petitioner his right to habeas corpus by holding him incommunicado and refusing him access to his lawyer or the courts. Such an implied suspension of habeas corpus must be rejected, according to the longstanding jurisprudence of the Court. See, e.g., *Ex parte Yerger*, 8 Wall. 85, 105 (1869) and *Felker v. Turpin*, 518 U.S. 651, 660-62 (1996).

65. Moreover, even those rare precedents where the Court has allowed the suspension of habeas corpus in extraordinary circumstances, are distinguishable from the present case. See, for example, *Johnson v. Eisentrager*, 339 U.S. 763 (1950). In the present case Petitioner does not seek his release from custody or the exercise of any right that would jeopardize the national security of the United States. Instead, Petitioner merely seeks his basic rights of due process with this application for the Great Writ. As long ago as the nineteenth century, Chief Justice Taney held that the Great Writ applied even in wartime. *Ex parte Merryman*, 17 F. Cas.144 (1861). The human right to fair trial under International Law has evolved into a non-derogable human right in the time since both of the decisions just quoted were handed down. In view of this development the right to apply for habeas corpus has gained irrefutable weight to the argument that it is the right of every individual in a civilized country

showing even minimal respect for the rule of law to be able to challenge his or her detention.

The second habeas corpus subsection details the violation of international law implicit in the Respondents' conduct towards Mr. Hussein.

68. To the extent that Respondents prevent any challenge to the legality of the detention of Petitioner by way of denial of writ habeas corpus, their action constitutes an unlawful Suspension of the Writ of Habeas Corpus, in violation of International Human Rights and Customary International Law.

69. The Inter-American Court of Human Rights has repeatedly stated that the writ of habeas corpus cannot be suspended, as it is an essential guarantee of all other rights. Judicial Guarantees in States of Emergency (Arts. 27.2, 25 and 8, American Convention on Human Rights), Advisory Opinion OC-9/87 (October 6, 1987), Inter-American Court of Human Rights (Ser. A) No. 9 (1987) and Habeas Corpus in Emergency Situations (Arts. 27.2, 25.1 and 7.6, American Convention on Human Rights), Advisory Opinion OC-8/87 (January 30, 1987), Inter-American Court of Human Rights (Ser. A) No. 8 (1987).

70. The holdings of the Inter-American Court of Human Rights represent highly respected and authoritative interpretations of international law in the Americas. They indicate that the prohibition on suspending the habeas corpus has achieved the state of customary international law.

After a brief discussion of the violation of the Petitioner's rights to be treated humanely that is constituted by the Respondents' threat (since acted upon) to turn Mr. Hussein over to the Iraqi Interim Government, the petition concludes with a "prayer for relief." This "prayer" requests the U.S. Supreme Court to order that the Respondents: (1) refrain from turning the Petitioner over to any entity that will not safeguard his rights; (2) allow him to meet with legal counsel; and (3) cease all interrogations while the petition is pending. It further requests that the Court (1) cease all interrogations while the litigation is pending; and (2) declare that the detained Petitioner is being held in violation of (a) the Fifth and Fourteenth Amendments to the United States Constitution; (b) customary international law; (c) the ICCPR; (d) GPW; (e) the ADRDM; (f) the regulations of the U.S. military; and (g) international humanitarian law.[1]

On October 4, 2004, the U.S. Supreme Court rejected the Iraqi President's petition for a writ of habeas corpus with *in forma pauperis* status[2] without an affidavit. The writ had been filed in this way to highlight

1. Those who would like to see the entire content of the petition may access it on the Internet at www.uruknet.info/?p=7329.—Ed.

2. An *in forma pauperis* filing is one in which the individual making application warrants, usually via signed affidavit, that he does not possess sufficient monetary resources

the United States government's denial of the Iraqi President's right to his own monetary resources. The Court essentially stated that the legal team *must* have access to their client to obtain his signature on the affidavit attesting to his *in forma pauperis* status, *despite the fact that the United States government denied and continues to deny the legal team any serious access to its client.* The Court did not rule upon the motion to file *in forma pauperis,* nor upon the habeas corpus petition. The petition is thus still pending before the Court but must now be converted into a "paid" petition.

The Responsibility of Government Signatories to the Third International Geneva Convention

Another important initiative on behalf of Mr. Hussein was launched during the latter part of September and the beginning of October 2004. Representatives of the legal team met with the representatives of numerous UN missions in New York City, including the Iraqi mission. Only four – the United States, the United Kingdom, Italy, and the European Union (then chaired by the Netherlands) – refused meetings. These unaccommodating missions indicated that they did not believe international human rights law to be the concern of private individuals, but only of States. At other missions, ambassadors or legal advisors met with a representative of the legal team.

The meetings emphasized that the human rights of due process and fair trial encompassed both in international human rights law and international humanitarian law were not being respected. On October 4, 2004, the team sent a letter to the heads of thirty permanent missions to the United Nations emphasizing that the detention of individuals in Iraq was the result of an illegal invasion and occupation by the United States, and that the United States continues to be an illegal occupier as well as the detaining power over the deposed President of Iraq. The letter also points out the United States' and all other states' responsibilities for ensuring the protection of human rights.

The essentials are as follows:

> First and foremost, I respectfully draw your attention to the obligations your government has as a State Party to the GPW as well as under international human rights law, to take all necessary measures to ensure the rights of prisoners of war.

---

to pay for legal representation and other administrative fees.

Among these rights is the right of a prisoner of war to receive communications from one's family and lawyers, the right to effective legal representation by a lawyer, the right to know the charges against oneself, the right not to be charged for acts for which by law there was no criminal responsibility at the time they were committed, and, most importantly, the right to a trial before an independent and impartial court. Each of these rights has been, and continues to be, violated. Moreover, the violations are so serious that the damage has become irreparable and must have serious consequences for any future trial.

I also respectfully remind you that under both well-established customary international law and under Article 42 of the Regulations annexed to the Fourth Hague Convention on Land Warfare (1907) the United States remains the occupying power in Iraq. As is clear from Article 42, occupation is determined by a de facto evaluation of circumstances. Only an independent government that has been chosen by the people of Iraq – not merely by the occupying power – can bring the occupation to an end.

Moreover, the United States government undoubtedly remains the detaining power over the prisoners of war who we represent. The alleged transfer of authority over the prisoners of war that the occupying power attempted to effect on June 30, 2004, was no more than a further attempt to humiliate our clients in violation of the GPW.

As the United Nations secretary-general has recently indicated, and as an overwhelming number of the world's most senior international lawyers have repeatedly confirmed for months, the United States' use of force against the people of Iraq is unequivocally an act of aggression and a serious violation of international law. It is, therefore, an eminent matter of international peace and security that the rule of law be restored by your government taking all necessary measures in fulfillment of its treaty obligations to ensure that at the very least the rights of due process of persons suffering as a consequence of the United States' illegal action are guaranteed. Your failure to act sends an unmistakable message to the international community that the rule of international law is ineffective and that all legal means of redress have been exhausted. We implore you not to continue to send such a message.

It is hoped that these permanent missions to the United Nations will live up to their responsibilities to ensure respect for the rule of law and for the legal obligations they have agreed to uphold by ratifying the Geneva Conventions.

Other Legal Actions

On June 29, 2004, a case was filed with the Inter-American Commission on Human Rights, claiming that the United States was violating the right of Mr. Hussein to fair trial, under the American Declaration of the Rights and Duties of Man. (The ADRDM reflects customary international law.)

The case also claims that the United States' illegal aggression against Iraq violates the right of every Iraqi to life and to humane treatment. The Commission denied the precautionary measures requested to prevent the attempted turnover of Mr. Hussein to the Iraqi Interim Government. The Commission remains seized of the case, but has indicated that it will not take action on it for the time being.

Also on June 29, 2004, a case was filed with the European Court of Human Rights, claiming that the United Kingdom was violating the right of the President, under the European Convention on Human Rights, to be protected from the death penalty. The Fourth Chamber of the Court denied the legal team's request for interim measures on July 7, 2004. The Court did ask whether the legal team wished to keep the case on the list, and the team replied affirmatively, that it did wish the case to be considered. Subsequently, it was decided to bring all European states providing support for the American occupation of Iraq into the case. The case claims that these states, as co-occupiers, must take all necessary measures to ensure that the United States does not continue to violate the rights of Mr. Hussein and other Iraqis to life, humane treatment, and fair trial. On March 21, 2005, a communication was sent to the Court indicating that additional time would be needed to complete the submissions that joined the other European states to the case, and on May 23, 2005, the additional information was filed with the European Court of Human Rights.

Finally, on October 1, 2004, a petition was filed with the UN Working Group on Arbitrary Detention seeking that the detention and treatment of Mr. Hussein be declared a violation of international human rights law, which provides for the human rights of security of person and fair trial. On October 24, 2004, additional information was sent to the Working Group. On February 1, 2005, the Working Group indicated that it could not deal with the case because the case concerns a matter falling under the four Geneva Conventions relating to armed conflict and, as such, falls outside the group's jurisdiction. On February 5, 2005, the legal team, as "Applicant," responded, pointing out that although the United States declared the Iraqi President to be a prisoner of war, he is not being treated in accordance with the Geneva Conventions. On March 9, 2005, the Working Group indicated that the matter was being referred to the U.S. government for its comments. This is an indication that the Working Group believes there to be a *prima facie* violation alleged; it has now asked the U.S. government to respond. The U.S. has three months to respond after which the Working Group may make a determination.

The Iraqi Special Tribunal

Although the legal team continues attempts to establish regular access to the President of Iraq, as of June 2005 – almost 18 months after the detention began – only two meetings have taken place and both under strict monitoring (both visual and audio) whereby at least two U.S. military officials were present at all times. These meetings do not meet the minimum standards for access to legal counsel provided by international (e.g. Article 14 of the ICCPR) or Iraqi law. It is estimated that counsel needs at least several hours of *daily* contact with their client to be able to consult with him and to facilitate the preparation of his defense.

Legal counsel's inability to have routine and continual access to evidence or formal charges also contributes to the irreparable violation of the defendant's rights. Despite statements by United States and Iraqi government officials that huge amounts of evidence exist, after a year and a half still no access to any of this evidence has been granted to defense counsel.

The creation of the IST was announced on December 10, 2003, by the Interim Governing Council of Iraq – a body appointed by Coalition Provisional Authority Administrator Mr. L. Paul Bremer on July 13, 2003. According to the announcement, it is to consist of panels of five judges, along with up to 20 investigative judges and 20 prosecutors, to try Iraqi nationals and residents for alleged crimes against humanity, war crimes, and genocide committed between July 17, 1968, and May 1, 2003. The IST was reportedly provided by the U.S. government with a budget of $75 million, offices in the American command compound in Baghdad, and various levels of "support" from investigators and other officials.

In spite of his relative inexperience in war-crimes matters, Mr. Salem Chalabi, the nephew of Mr. Ahmad Chalabi, was named the head of the IST by Mr. Bremer and appointed to the position on May 8, 2004, by the Interim Governing Council. As should have been expected, Mr. Chalabi's appointment spurred immediate controversy.

According to a *New York Times Magazine* report,[1] Mr. Chalabi's involvement with Iraq and war crimes issues began in 1993 when, as a 30-year-old Northwestern law student, he was asked by an Iraqi dissident to draft an Iraqi National Congress (INC) report requesting that the UN Security Council investigate the Baghdad government on suspicion of war crimes. His anti-Ba'athist activities have also been documented, along with his links to the U.S. Defense, State, and Justice Departments.

---

1. Landesman, Peter, "Who v. Saddam?" *New York Times Magazine*, July 11, 2004, online.

Once appointed head of the IST, Mr. Chalabi began working with the State Department's Pierre-Richard Prosper, U.S. Ambassador-at-Large for War Crimes, to finalize the tribunal's statute. Mr. Prosper has been working for some time on behalf of the current U.S. administration to collect evidence against the Iraqi President with the clear intention, even before the U.S. invasion in March 2003, of prosecuting him for various crimes once he was forcibly removed from power.

In March 2004, Mr. Gregory W. Kehoe, a trial lawyer from Tampa, Fla., who had been a prosecutor for the International Criminal Tribunals at The Hague, was appointed as Regime Crimes Liaison to assist with the collection of evidence and development of the prosecution strategy.

In July 2004 a judge from Iraq's Central Criminal Court issued a warrant for the arrest of Mr. Salem Chalabi while he was outside Iraq for involvement in the murder of an Iraqi finance ministry official involved in an investigation of the Chalabi family's business dealings. Though the charges were reportedly dropped sometime around August 2004, then interim Prime Minister Mr. Iyad Allawi claimed, on 16 September 2004, to have demanded and "received the resignation" of Mr. Chalabi.

ISNAD maintains that the IST is not competent because it was illegally created, nor is it independent or impartial. It therefore constitutes a serious violation of international law.

1. The tribunal is the result of an illegal invasion of Iraq which unequivocally violated international law, namely Article 2(4) of the Charter of the United Nations. Attempts to justify this use of force as somehow justified by Iraq's reaction to UN Security Council (UNSC) resolutions are inconsistent with the statements of the majority of both the permanent members of the UNSC and the total membership of this body and are devoid of any legal basis.

2. The extraordinary nature of the IST is evidenced by the fact that it would have been illegal even under the Iraqi Administrative Law of March 8, 2004, except for the special dispensation which is given in that law. Despite the dispensation, however, the IST does not meet the minimum standards of international law required for a fair trial and is thus illegitimate.

3. The IST is also illegal because it is lacking in competency. It is not competent because it has been established outside the ordinary Iraqi judicial power by an occupying power, in violation of international law, as an attempt to usurp the sovereignty of the Iraqi people and to interfere with the existing judicial power in Iraq in a manner that renders it liable to violate international human rights and humanitarian law.

An occupying power is forbidden from destroying the judicial power of an occupied territory – especially as in this case, when courts and judges already existed in Iraq – and replacing it with a judicial power with allegiance to itself. Indeed, the IST was created by a decree of the occupying power from among judges that have been vetted for their political opinions and affiliations, and excluding those judges who disagree with the occupiers' political opinions. This action contravenes general international law that provides that an occupation is not sovereignty. It is also contrary to the responsibilities of the occupying powers to ensure the integrity of the judiciary in the country under occupation as established in Article 64 of the Fourth Geneva Convention. An occupying power is particularly prohibited from changing the institutions of government when those changes – in this case the establishment of a court that is not impartial nor independent, and does not guarantee the basic rights of the accused – contribute to a violation of international law.

It is worth noting that the "election" carried out in January 2005 does not change the legal situation in any fundamental sense. The election was carried out at the insistence of the occupation power, and in accordance with the methods and modalities prescribed by the occupation power – even to the point of deciding who could, and who could not, actually stand in the election. It is also important to recognize that the remit of the so-called Transitional National Assembly was determined by the occupation power, and thus it is difficult to assert that the occupation has ceased in any meaningful or legal sense.[1]

Another reason why the tribunal is not competent is that it will not be able to prosecute American officials who have committed crimes against peace, including American President George W. Bush, or American soldiers who have committed war crimes or crimes against humanity. To satisfy basic principles of justice, any courts concerned with trials in Iraq that have resulted from the United States' illegal use of force must be able and willing to do so. The international community has attempted to ensure this after learning the lesson from the tribunals established after World War II. Thus, in reaction to the criticism of the Tokyo and Nuremberg tribunals by Judge Bert V. Röllings – that they only dispensed victors' justice – the subsequent ad hoc tribunals that have been created by the UN Security Council can always prosecute all parties to an armed conflict. In the case of Iraq, how-

---

1. For a detailed look at the irregularities and insufficiency of the January 2005 Iraqi election, see the article by Mark Gery on pp. 761–795 of the present volume.—Ed.

ever, even allied soldiers who admit to committing grave breaches of international humanitarian law have been given inadequately light punishments by U.S. military tribunals, and they cannot be tried by the IST. Their commanders, right up to the commander-in-chief, have been given complete immunity. Only if the United States intends to provide every other governments' senior personnel the same immunity can such action be justified within the remit of the rule of law and especially under the principle of the equal protection of law. If the United States claims this immunity only for itself, grave damage is done to the rule of law.

To put the leaders of the Iraqi people on trial when the aggressors against the Iraqi people are not held responsible for their actions is the worst kind of vengeance, based on a violation of international law and mocking the rule of law in a manner that will damage it severely for decades to come. If that rule is to be preserved, the world needs to decide its priorities. Justice cannot be done by putting vengeance before the rule of law. The only way for the rule of law to be upheld is to decide upon the responsibility for *all* persons who have violated international law in relation to the situation in Iraq, starting with those who have perpetrated crimes that the Nuremberg Tribunal called "not only an international crime" but "the supreme international crime" that "contains within itself the accumulated evil of the whole." A legitimate tribunal should therefore have jurisdiction over the aggressors as well as their victims. As it stands, it is the *victims* of aggression in Iraq that are being brought to trial.

4. The IST is also illegal because it is not independent.

First, it has been established by the United States as the occupying power and not by a legitimate sovereign Iraqi government. The background to the formation of the tribunal is sufficient to illustrate its lack of independence.

In addition, there are already voiced suspicions that the occupying powers will use this tribunal for political ends. The *New York Times Magazine*, for example, reported that

> [w]ith the failure, to date, to find weapons of mass destruction, and the ties between Iraq's Ba'athists and al-Qaeda apparently not what the administration led Americans to believe they were, *the architects of the* invasion *are looking to the trials of Hussein and his lieutenants to vindicate the war and fulfill their vision of the taking of Baghdad as a transformative event in the region's history* (emphasis mine).[1]

---

1. Landesman, *loc. cit.*

Second, Mr. Salem Chalabi, architect of the IST and its charter, is a nephew of Mr. Ahmad Chalabi, the longtime U.S. government favorite who worked for years to encourage an American military overthrow of Mr. Hussein, and who was an associate of U.S. officials such as Mr. Pierre-Richard Prosper and others in the U.S. Defense, State, and Justice Departments who have been and are active in prosecuting alleged war crimes against Mr. Hussein on behalf of the U.S. government. Mr. Salem Chalabi was also involved in a Baghdad law firm called the Iraqi International Law Group, specializing in private-sector investment for Iraq. His partner in the venture was Mr. Marc Zell, former law partner of Mr. Douglas Feith, the outgoing U.S. under secretary of defense for policy. The insidious nature of the appearance of war profiteering in this triangular relationship creates an unfortunate environment for the IST.

Third, as a result of the refusal of the United Nations to aid in training Iraqi lawyers and judges, based upon concerns over U.S. violations of international law, the U.S. State and Justice Departments are now fulfilling this role with some less-than-adequate trainers and without the experience of the UN. Many of the lawyers involved are American lawyers. But when one looks at the state of American legal education in the realm of public international law, it is hard to imagine that there are many American lawyers qualified to provide the level of training needed by Iraqi judges and prosecutors. Indeed, one noted American legal scholar, Professor John Yoo at Berkley's School of Law in California, has written that the United States can unilaterally suspend the Geneva Conventions. Such a misunderstanding of the law does not bode well for the quality of his students and may unfortunately represent a serious problem in American international legal education. Perhaps it is because of their training that the judges of the IST have continued to deny the Iraqi President almost all of the due process rights to which he is entitled at this stage of the proceedings.

Fourth, since the judges have apparently been chosen from among those who have been vetted for their political allegiance to the occupying powers, they appear to serve at the convenience of the occupying power as a means of contributing to the occupation.[1] This assessment is supported by the failure of the IST to safeguard the rights of the President and other detainees. The failure is illustrated by the fact that the IST and those holding Mr. Hussein and others have denied them access to their lawyers, pre-

---

1. The ongoing attempt to purge "Ba'athists" from the IST is further evidence of its perception in the eyes of those running it as a means of eliminating any vestige of the "old regime." See Edward Wong, "Iraqi Leaders Vows to Block Purges," *New York Times*, July 29, 2005, online.

vented them from seeing the evidence against them, and withheld from them the means of preparing their defense. That these serious violations of due process over an extended period have been allowed by both the occupying powers and the judges of the IST raises a strong presumption of cooperation between the two entities.

Finally, it should be noted that the popular perception of the IST confirms its obvious lack of independence. Mr. Richard Dicker, the director of the international justice program at Human Rights Watch, was reported to have said that he "was enormously troubled that Mr. Salem Chalabi's appointment was announced by the I.N.C., a political entity with a political agenda."[1] Mr. Zuhair Almaliky, the chief investigative judge of Iraq's Central Criminal Court, was reported to have said, "This tribunal is not ours; it is somebody who came from abroad who created a court for themselves . . . . Chalabi selected the judges according to his political opinions."[2] Additionally, Professor M. Cherif Bassiouni, the former chairman of a United Nations commission to investigate war crimes in the former Yugoslavia, summarized the situation as regards the independence of the IST when he reportedly said,

> The trial could be an extraordinary opportunity to send a message to the tyrants of the Arab world . . . . But the deck is being stacked, and it's going to be obvious . . . . Where in the world can you say this is an independent judiciary, with U.S. proxies appointing and controlling judges, with U.S.-gift-wrapped cases? . . . In the Arab world there is already the perception this is a mockery.[3]

5. The IST is not impartial. The judges remain anonymous. The use of "faceless judges" has been held to be a prima facie violation of the right to fair trial[4] and of the requirement of impartiality. The court's impartiality is further impugned by the fact that its former administrator, Mr. Salem Chalabi, has been one of the main opponents of the government of Mr. Hussein and openly sought his removal by force as head of state of Iraq for more than a decade, in violation of both Iraqi law and international law.

6. The IST also violates international law because it denies its defendants' basic fair-trial and due-process rights. The defendants have not been able to meet their lawyers in any meaningful way or routinely. Evidence of the torture and mistreatment of defendants has not been investigated.

---

1. Landesman, *loc. cit.*
2. *Ibid.*
3. *Ibid.*
4. See, e.g., *Ricardo Ernesto Gómez Casafranca v. Peru*, Comm. No. 981/2001, UN Doc. No. CCPR/C/78/D/981/2001 (September 19, 2003) at para. 7.3.

The defendants have been denied facilities to prepare their defense; they have not been charged; they have been denied access to any of the alleged evidence against them. All of these failures constitute violations of the defendants' rights.

In conclusion, only a tribunal created by international mandate and with truly impartial judges sitting can try a head of state who has been captured pursuant to an illegal invasion of his country. Furthermore, a competent, independent, and impartial tribunal is one that applies a rule of law fairly to all persons who should fall under its jurisdiction. In the case of international aggression this must be the aggressor as well as victims of aggression. It is crucial that a determination about the legality of the use of force against Iraqis is a *conditio sine qua non* for the trial of any person accused of having committed crimes in Iraq.

That the United States' aggression against the Iraqi people is illegal is an opinion overwhelmingly, almost unanimously, shared among the world's legal scholars and world leaders. It is the first issue that should be litigated in any court of law in relation to the situation in Iraq. To act otherwise would not merely be to put the cart before the horse, but to shoot logic in the head in an attempt to cure a toothache.

Iraq had not attacked any other country. Iraq was, in fact, abiding by the law. According to UN Secretary-General Kofi Annan, UN weapons inspector Mr. Hans Blix, and the overwhelming majority of international jurists around the world, the United States and its allies are aggressors.

Already repeated attempts have been taken to use the courts of law to determine the illegality of the war. In Canada, American soldiers who have deserted from the U.S. military have claimed that their actions were justified because the war was illegal. Although blocking its immigration courts from addressing this question, the Canadian government admitted this question should be ruled upon by the International Court of Justice (ICJ).

Indeed, the General Assembly of the United Nations could consider the proposal of any member state to request an advisory opinion on the legality of the use of force in circumstances such as those surrounding the United States' attack on the Iraqi people. A majority of the General Assembly could then send the question to the ICJ.

If it is found that the situation in Iraq is the result of an illegal use of force then the aggressor must restore the situation to that which it was before the illegal act of aggression. Therefore, before any members of the Iraqi government headed by Iraqi President Saddam Hussein can stand trial, a determination should be made about the legality of the United States' use of force against the Iraqi people. Until this question of the illegality of the use of force against Iraq has been decided, all actions that emanate from the illegal acts cannot be accepted. The existence and popularity of the national liberation movement inside Iraq is testimony to this reality.

This brief resume of the situation concerning Iraqi President Saddam Hussein and his government colleagues demonstrates that they are being denied their most fundamental legal rights. There is no sophistry that can mask this fact. The fact that the American occupying power feels that it must go to such extraordinary lengths to deny the defendants their rights – rights that are based on the entire Western legal tradition that a man is held to be innocent until proven guilty – is most assuredly a measure of how indefensible their legal "case" really is. This is disrespectful of the entire corpus of international and United States law that has been carefully constructed over centuries to guarantee basic rights to individuals and to ensure that individuals are not subjected to arbitrary treatment by governments. The treatment of the Iraqi President is an unfortunate contradiction of the notion that the United States is guided and governed by the rule of law. If nations such as the United States do not abide by the laws they themselves decreed, how can they be surprised if a national liberation movement in Iraq resorts to the use of force to try to displace the foreign and oppressive occupation of its country?

To push forward with trials that have been widely referred to as "show trials" by prominent Iraqis themselves is a travesty of justice that will take generations to undo. Using a legal forum that fails to meet the most minimum basic requirements of justice is an insult to the rule of law and the legal profession. On the other hand, providing for a forum where all perpetrators of crimes in Iraq can be brought to justice, including those who have committed the most serious crimes against peace, would be a starting point for restoring justice in Iraq and restoring respect for the rule of law around the world.

The path of endless war will bankrupt our treasury, devour our soldiers, and degrade the moral and spiritual values of the nation. It is past time to change course.

—George McGovern, 1972 Democratic Presidential candidate and former U.S. Senator from South Dakota, and Congressman Jim McGovern (D-Mass.), June 2005

Appendices.
Perspectives on Gulf War I

THE EDITORS' GLOSS: This brief look at the legal issues surrounding the first Gulf War – adapted from the author's 1992 book, *War Crimes: A Report on United States War Crimes Against Iraq* – brings full circle the discussion of America's "thirteen-years' war" against Iraq. Immediately following Iraq's surprising "victory" in the Iran-Iraq war, America adopted a bellicose stance towards the Ba'athist government, the only satisfying explanation for which is the comment made by Edward Luttwak to Maurizio Blondet before Gulf War I:

After eight years of war against the Iranian regime of Khomeini, [Saddam] desperately needs to demobilize his Republican Guard, which incorporates so many of his technical elite, in order to rebuild the war-devastated country. These people are his technicians, his engineers. If they are put to work in the way Saddam wishes, they will rapidly make Iraq the most advanced power in the region, and we cannot allow this to happen.

Meanwhile, after having marginalized the UN in order to keep their invasion of Iraq on course, American neoconservatives are now rehabilitating UN regulations in order to prove they actually deposed a "bad guy." Saddam is condemned for having directed oil-purchase opportunities – permitted to him by the UN Security Council's "oil-for-food" scheme, set up to address the Anglo-American created humanitarian disaster in Iraq – to countries who "supported him." What nerve! He should, of course, have offered economic opportunities exclusively to those, like Britain and the U.S., who were bent on his destruction!

Now *we* would never offer economic incentives to other nations to encourage them to support our policies. This is why Ratner relates – based on an impeachment resolution filed by the late Congressman Henry Gonzales (D-Tx.) – that "President [Bush 41] paid off members of the UN Security Council in return for their votes in support of war against Iraq or to abstain from voting contrariwise." Egypt's debt was forgiven ($7 billion); a loan for China was agreed to ($140 million); Russia was promised aid (over $7 billion); Saudi Arabia was promised $12 billion in arms; and so the list goes on.

Readers will notice a reference in the text to the U.S.'s *continued* "embargo against food" and engagement "in battle after a cease-fire." Even from the perspective of 1992 it was apparent that this should have stopped once Gulf War I ended. It was probably hard to imagine then that it would continue through 2005, and constitute what is now even worse than thirteen years' worth of war.

Off to a Bad Start: International Law and War Crimes in the Case of Gulf War I

• • • • • • • • •

Michael Ratner, Esq.

I**N THE WORK** of the Commission of Inquiry for the International War Crimes Tribunal, we undertook an historic task. We inquired into and ultimately judged whether the United States, in the First Gulf War, violated laws that are fundamental to a civilized world; laws that are designed to protect people, human beings, from the barbarity of war. These laws prohibit war except in the narrowest of circumstances; they severely restrict who can be killed, the types of weapons that can be used and the appropriate targets. An indicia of a civilized country is adherence to these laws, not only by pious words but through actions. To act outside these laws, to disobey these laws, to flaunt these laws is to become *hostis humani generis,* an enemy of all mankind. In days past "enemies of all mankind" were slave traders and pirates. They could be brought to justice wherever found. Today such enemies include those countries and individuals who violate the fundamental laws that protect the peace and limit war. The testimony presented at the various Commissions of Inquiry here in New York and in other hearings throughout the world will determine whether the United States and its leaders are enemies of all mankind.

As people living in the United States we have an obligation not to close our eyes, cover our ears and remain silent. We must not and cannot be "good Germans." We must be, as Bertrand Russell said about the crimes committed by the U.S. in Vietnam, "Against the Crime of Silence." We must bear witness to the tens of thousands of deaths for whom our government and its leaders bear responsibility and ask the question – "Has the United States committed war crimes with regard to its initiation and conduct of the war against Iraq?" As investigators we believe that the United States and its leaders have committed international crimes. Although we cannot bring them to justice, we can reveal their criminal conduct to ourselves, to the people of the United States, and to the world with the hope that U.S. conduct will be repudiated, conduct, which by the way, still continues. The U.S. still occupies parts of Iraq, it continues an embargo against food, and it engages in battle after a cease-fire.[1]

Today I want to outline for you the legal framework in which we are operating and explain some of the broad principles of law applicable to judging the United States' conduct.

War crimes are violations by a country, its civilians, or its military personnel of the international laws of war. The laws of war are laws that must be obeyed by the United States, its officials and its military, and by the UN. The laws are contained in treaties that the U.S. has signed, for example the Geneva Convention of 1949 on Prisoners of War. They are reflected in what is called customary international law. This law has arisen over hundreds if not thousands of years. All countries must obey it.

War crimes are divided into two broad categories. The first are called crimes against peace. Crimes against peace include the planning, preparation, or initiation of a war of aggression. In other words one country cannot make aggressive war against another country. Nor can a country settle a dispute by war; it must always, and in good faith, negotiate a settlement. The second category are what we can call crimes against humanity; I am including here crimes against civilians and soldiers. These are violations of the rules as to the means and manner by which war is to be conducted once begun. These include the following prohibitions: killing of civilians, indiscriminate bombing, the use of certain types of weapons, killing of defenseless soldiers, ill treatment of POWs and attacks on non-military targets.

Any violation of these two sets of laws is a war crime; if the violations are done on purpose, recklessly or knowingly, they are considered very serious and called grave breaches; Germans and Japanese following World War II were hanged for such grave breaches.

First, I want to discuss crimes against peace and give you some sense of its application here. This prohibition is embodied in the Charter of the United Nations, the Nuremberg Charter, which is the law under which the Nazis were tried, and a treaty called the Kellogg-Briand pact. As the Nuremberg Charter defines:

---

1. See "The Thirteen Years' War" on pp. 3–11 of the present collection for a brief discussion of the sanctions, occupation, and bombing that began with the first Gulf War and continues through the second.

Crimes against peace:
Planning, preparation, initiation or waging of a war of aggression or a war in violation of international treaties, agreements or assurances;
Participation in a common plan or conspiracy for the accomplishment of any of the acts mentioned under (i).

The United Nations Charter is the highest expression of this prohibition on aggressive war and sets down very rigorous rules for avoiding the use of force – rules which were flagrantly violated by the United States and a Security Council it controlled. Article 2131 of the UN Charter requires that international disputes be settled by peaceful means so that international peace, security and justice are not endangered; Article 2141 requires that force shall not be used in any manner that is inconsistent with the purposes of the UN, and Article 33 requires that parties to a dispute shall first of all seek a solution by negotiation, inquiry, mediation, conciliation, arbitration judicial settlement, resort to regional agencies, or other peaceful means. Not until all such means are exhausted can force be used.

So, taken together we have two basic rules: a nation cannot plan and make war, and second, if there is a dispute, the nations must exhaust every means of settlement – every means. Even then, only the UN can authorize war. There is strong evidence, some of which is presented in the papers here, that the U.S. violated both of these basic laws. These facts are not hidden. Much of the evidence indicating that the U.S. set up the war with Iraq is contained in U.S. Congressman Gonzalez's impeachment resolution and brief in support presented to Congress and printed in full in the *Congressional Record* (H. Res. 86, February 21, 1991[1]). It is only the major commercial press that has ignored the facts. In part it includes the following revelations:

> As early as October 1989 the CIA representatives in Kuwait had agreed to take advantage of Iraq's deteriorating economic position to put pressure on Iraq to accede to Kuwait's demands with regard to the border dispute.
>
> [Kuwait was encouraged] to refuse to negotiate its differences with Iraq as required by the United Nations Charter, including Kuwait's failure to abide by OPEC quotas, its pumping of Iraqi oil from the Rumaila oil field and its refusal to negotiate these and other matters with Iraq.
>
> Months prior to the Iraqi invasion of Kuwait, the United States administration prepared a plan and practiced elaborate computer war games pitting United States forces against Iraqi armored divisions.

---

1. See Ramsey Clark, *et. al., War Crimes: A Report on United States War Crimes Against Iraq* (Washington, D.C.: The Commission of Inquiry for the International War Crimes Tribunal, 1992), pp. 146–157, for the text of the resolution.

In testimony before Congress prior to the invasion, Assistant Secretary Kelly misleadingly assured Congress that the United States had no commitment to come to Kuwait's assistance in the event of war.

April Glaspie's reassurance to Iraq that the dispute was an "Arab" matter and the U.S. would not interfere.

Even if we suspend judgment and believe that the U.S. neither planned nor prepared this war, it had no right to initiate war until all means of negotiation were at an end. The U.S., however, never wanted to negotiate. It wanted war. According to the *New York Times*, the U.S. wanted to "block the diplomatic track because it might defuse the crisis at the cost of a few token gains for Iraq."[1] Iraq at about this time made an offer to negotiate to settle the crisis. It offered to withdraw from Kuwait for some form of control over two uninhabited islands that would give it access to the Gulf and control over the Rumaila oilfield. The offer was, according to the some U.S. officials, "serious and negotiable." Offers continued until the eve of war and by that time Iraq was willing to withdraw totally from Kuwait. The U.S. instantly dismissed all offers to negotiate a settlement and refused to pursue them. "No negotiations" was the constant theme of U.S. President George Bush.[2] The U.S. and its allies wanted to see the crisis settled by force. It is the U.S. that chose war and not peace; it is the U.S. that committed a crime against peace.

I want to say a word about the UN Resolutions embargoing Iraq and supposedly authorizing the use of force. All of the UN Resolutions were suspect because of what Congressman Gonzalez called in his impeachment resolution the "bribing, intimidating and threatening of others, including members of the UN Security Council." Gonzalez cites the following outright bribes:

Immediately after the November 29 vote in the UN authorizing force, the administration unblocked a $140 million loan for the World Bank to China and agreed to meet with Chinese government officials.

The Soviet Union was promised $7 billion in aid from various countries and shipments of food from the United States.

Zaire was promised forgiveness of part of its debt as well as military assistance.

A $7 billion loan to Egypt was forgiven, a loan the President had no authority to forgive under U.S. law.

Syria was promised that there would be no interference in its Lebanon actions.

---

1. *New York Times*, August 22, 1990.
2. Michael Emty, "How the U.S. Avoided the Peace," *The Village Voice*, March 5, 1991.

Saudi Arabia was promised $12 billion in arms sales.

The U.S., which owes the most money to the UN, paid off $187 million of its debt immediately after the vote authorizing the use of force.

The administration attempted to coerce Yemen by threatening the cutoff of U.S. funds.[1]

But even were this not the case, can the UN apply measures of force such as the embargo, effectively a blockade and an act of war, and authorize all necessary means – which the U.S. saw as war – without negotiating first? It cannot do so according to the stipulations of its own Charter.

Nor was the UN permitted to embargo food and limit the importation of medicine. Neither the UN nor any country can take measures that intentionally or knowingly have the effect of starving and harming the civilian population. This is prohibited by every tenet of international law. It is well known that Iraq imports 60 to 70 percent of its food. As testimony presented elsewhere in books and in many reports from fact-finding missions to Iraq since the end of the war, many children died because of the lack of infant formula and adequate food and medicine.

And what of this infamous resolution that authorized all necessary means to remove Iraqi forces from Kuwait? Did this authorize war? Not by its own terms. The resolution was left specifically vague, stipulating only "all necessary means." Nowhere did it mention war and certainly many other means were readily available for achieving the goals of the UN resolutions. All other means were never exhausted. From the U.S. standpoint, massively violent war was the first and only option. All other means had to be precluded at any cost.

Finally, on the point of the U.S. commission of crimes against peace, even if we get over all of the other illegalities and assume that the UN had the authority to authorize war and did so in this case, what did it authorize? It authorized the use of force only to obtain the withdrawal from Kuwait. It certainly never authorized the incursion into, much less the occupation of, Iraq and the total subjection of that nation to the dictates of the UN acting out policies originating in the U.S. government. No one has authorized the U.S. to have even one soldier in Iraq. This is aggression in the classic sense. U.S. forces moved in from the north down to the 36th parallel and have set up camps for displaced Kurds. Nor did the resolution authorize any bombing of Iraq, certainly not the bombing of Baghdad or Basra or the near complete destruction of the economic infrastructure.

---

1. *Congressional Record*, January 16, 1991: H520.

The second broad category we are concerned with is what are referred to as crimes against humanity. By this I mean both crimes against civilians and combatants. There is a long history of outlawing certain kinds of conduct once war has begun. The principle is that the means and manner of waging war are not unlimited. In other words, while it is of primary importance to prevent war, once war has begun there are limits on the types of targets that can be attacked and the weapons that can be employed. Central to these laws of war is the desire to protect civilians, noncombatants, soldiers who are no longer fighting, and the resources and infrastructure necessary to their survival. Again, at Nuremberg, the Nazis were tried for crimes against humanity which included killings of the civilian population and the wanton destruction of cities, towns or villages and devastation not justified by military necessity.

These laws are embodied in various treaties, including most importantly the Hague Convention of 1907, the Geneva Conventions of 1949, and Protocol I Additional to the Geneva Conventions. They all reflect a similar set of rules, violations of which are war crimes. They are built around two principles. First, military operations are to be directed at military objectives – the civilian population and civilian objects are not to be targets. So, massive bombing, as was engaged in by the U.S., which kills civilians and destroyed the water supply, is illegal. In fact, when the dispute was barely a month old, in September, Air Force chief of staff General Michael J. Duggan was fired for leaking to the press suggestions that the U.S. was already planning bombing targets which would include Iraqi power systems, roads railroads, and petroleum plants.[1]

At the height of the war, this sort of bombing campaign was defended by Pentagon spokespersons in terms reminiscent of the Vietnam War. Many parts of Iraq became "free fire zones" in which everyone who remains in such a zone is declared unilaterally by the U.S. as a legitimate target for destruction. The entire city of Basra, Iraq's second largest, became such a free fire zone, as described by Brigadier General Richard I. Neal. The *Washington Post* story recounts:

In Riyadh, Marine Brig. Gen. Richard I. Neal gave a detailed explanation of why repeated allied pounding of the southern Iraqi city of Basra is causing "collateral damage." Basra, Neal said, "is a military town in the true sense, it is astride a major naval base and a port facility. The infrastructure, military infrastructure, is closely interwoven within the city of

1. Rick Atkinson, "U.S. to Rely on Air Strikes if War Erupts," *New York Times*, September 16, 1990: Al.

Basra itself." The destruction of targets in and around Basra is part of what Neal described as an "intensifying" air campaign against all "echelons of forces, from the front lines and all the way back . . . . There is no rest for the weary, for any of them . . . . There is no division, no brigade, there is no battalion that really is spared the attacks from our pilots."[1]

The second limit international law places on the conduct of war is the principle of proportionality – you can only use the amount of force against military targets necessary to achieve your objective. So, for example, destroying the retreating Iraqi army was disproportional for it was not necessary to achieve the Iraqi withdrawal from Kuwait. The whole conduct of the war, in fact, violates every conceivable notion of proportionality.

International law lays down rules for how the civilian population is to be protected. Obviously civilians cannot be intentionally attacked, but indiscriminate attacks are prohibited as well. Such attacks are defined as those that "employ a method of combat which cannot be directed at specific military objectives." While the mass media, especially TV news, gave the impression during the war that the U.S. was using only "smart" bombs that directly hit their military targets, in fact 93 percent of the bombs used were "dumb" bombs of which at least 60 to 70 percent missed their targets, killing lots of people. Such bombs cannot be directed exclusively at a military objective and in my view are illegal. Nor can bombs dropped from a B-52 flying at thirty to forty thousand feet hit their targets.

There is a special law protecting objects indispensable to the civilian population – the infrastructure of a country. This includes prohibitions on destroying food supplies, water and sewer systems, agriculture, power, medical services, transportation and similar essentials. These cannot be attacked even if there is some military goal, if the effect would be to leave civilians without the essentials for life. In fact, the U.S. government openly stated its goal of destroying the infrastructure of Iraq including water, food supplies, the sewer system, electricity and transportation. The story was not reported in U.S. newspapers until late June of 1991, but the facts were obvious to even a casual observer. According to the *Washington Post* story, U.S. officials admitted that

Some targets, especially late in the war, were bombed primarily to create postwar leverage over Iraq, not to influence the course of the conflict itself . . . . [T]he intent was to destroy or damage valuable facilities that Baghdad could not repair without foreign assistance.[2]

---

1. "Ground War Not Imminent, Bush Says: Allies to Rely on Air Power 'for a While,'" *Washington Post*, February 12, 1991, p. A14.

2. *Washington Post*, June 23, 1991, p. Al.

A report of the United Nations Mission to Iraq led by Under Secretary-General Martti Ahtisaari said that Iraq had been bombed into the pre-industrial age.[1] Thousands of additional people – all civilians and mostly children – are dying as a result.

Attacks are also to be limited to strictly military objectives. These are defined as those that make an effective contribution to military action and whose destruction offers a definite military advantage. Civilian objects are not to be attacked. In case of doubt, such as a school, it should be presumed that it is not used as a military object. What does this rule say about the bombing of the al-Ameriyah shelter? At least 300 children and parents were incinerated in a structure that the U.S. knew was built as a shelter for civilians. Its possible use as a military communications center was only a matter of speculation and weak supposition. Or, what are we to make of the destruction of the baby milk factory at the beginning of the bombing campaign? Again, an American general has admitted that this was a mistake – a mistake that has cost many, many babies their lives.

There are also a series of very specific laws:

The use of asphyxiating gases is prohibited. The U.S. violated this by its use of fuel-air explosive bombs on Iraqi frontline troops; these bombs are terror bombs which can burn the oxygen over a surface of one or two square kilometers, destroying human life by asphyxiation.

These fuel-air bombs and the U.S. use of napalm are also outlawed by the Hague and Geneva Conventions, which prohibit the use of weapons causing unnecessary harm to combatants. The level of U.S. evil is demonstrated by the sending to the Gulf of a stingray blinding laser system which is supposed to knock out optics on enemy weapons, but has the side effect of blinding soldiers as well who operate the weapons.

The bombing of peaceful nuclear power facilities is forbidden and particularly so because of the dangers of the spread of radioactivity. The UN International Atomic Energy Agency classified the reactors as peaceful, yet the U.S. bombed them, not caring about the spread of radioactivity. The bombing was intentional and planned in advance, clearly in violation of international law.

Both the Hague Convention of 1954 and Protocol I to the Geneva Conventions prohibit attacks against historic monuments, works of art, places of worship and sites which constitute the cultural and spiritual

---

1. Martti Ahtisaari, "Report to the Secretary-General on Humanitarian Needs in Kuwait and Iraq in the Immediate Post-Crisis Environment," United Nations Report No. S122366, March 20, 1991.

heritage of a people. Catholic churches, a 4th century monastery and a Sunni Moslem mosque represent just some of the massive violations that occurred. (See Fadwa El Guindi's essay on archaeological destruction, *Waging War on Civilization*.)

Protocol I of the Geneva Convention also requires protection of the natural environment against widespread and severe damage – the U.S. massive bombing, the blowing up of reactors, the hitting of oil storage facilities all violate this prohibition.

What I have tried to outline here, therefore, is the broad framework in which we can evaluate the criminal conduct of the United States.

THE EDITORS' GLOSS: This retrospect from the authors' book, *Toxic Sludge is Good For You*, should be mulled over in light of this anthology's section on the "Imperial Press." We often hear that things are getting worse in Iraq, but the message of this contribution, along with the one preceding it, is that things weren't great even 15 years ago.

The fact is that the first Gulf War, like the second, was sold to the American public with "creative lies." The notorious "incubator story" is no more honorable and no less outrageous than the British and American propaganda deployed in World War I, which claimed that German soldiers were gouging out the eyes of civilians, cutting off the hands of teenage boys, raping and mutilating women, giving children hand grenades to play with, bayoneting babies, and crucifying captured soldiers. Couple this with the pro-war propaganda, active censorship and the bullying of anti-war voices that seems sadly characteristic of wartime America throughout the last century of war – all sanctioned if not sponsored by the government and aided and abetted by the press – and you get a pretty grim picture of how a "democracy" manages its affairs in the mad rush to war.

The comment of a British general from World War I is axiomatic: "To make armies go on killing one another it is necessary to invent lies about the enemy." That his statement is now a truism is no reason for us not to be concerned about the truth it states. It will prove timely in the run-up to the next war no less than the present one. We would do well to prepare ourselves now for the propaganda blitz, that we may be the better prepared to resist it.

The Mother of All Clients:
The PR Campaign of Gulf War I
• • • • • • • • • •
John Stauber and Sheldon Rampton

O N AUGUST 2, 1990, Iraqi troops led by dictator Saddam Hussein invaded the oil-producing nation of Kuwait. Like Noriega in Panama, Hussein had been a U.S. ally for some years. Despite complaints from international human rights groups, the Reagan and Bush administrations had treated Hussein as a valuable ally in the U.S. confrontation with Iran. As late as July 25 – a week before the invasion of Kuwait – U.S. Ambassador April Glaspie commiserated with Hussein over a "cheap and unjust" profile by ABC's Diane Sawyer, and wished for an "appearance in the media, even for five minutes," by Hussein that "would help explain Iraq to the American people."[1]

Glaspie's ill-chosen comments may have helped convince the dictator that Washington would look the other way if he "annexed" a neighboring kingdom. The invasion of Kuwait, however, crossed a line that the Bush administration could not tolerate, for *oil* was at stake.

Viewed in strictly moral terms, Kuwait hardly looked like the sort of country that deserved defending, even from the likes of Hussein. The tiny but super-rich state had been an independent nation for just a quarter century when in 1986 the ruling al-Sabah family tightened its dictatorial grip over the "black gold" fiefdom by disbanding the token National Assembly and firmly establishing all power in the be-jeweled hands of the ruling Emir. Then, as now, Kuwait's ruling oligarchy brutally suppressed the country's small democracy movement, intimidated and censored journalists, and hired desperate foreigners to supply most of the nation's physical labor under conditions of indentured servitude and near-slavery. The

---

1. John R. MacArthur, *Second Front: Censorship and Propaganda in the Gulf War*, (Berkeley, CA: University of CA Press, 1992).

wealthy young men of Kuwait's ruling class were known as spoiled party boys in university cities and national capitals from Cairo to Washington.[1]

Unlike Grenada and Panama, Iraq had a substantial army that could not be subdued in a mere weekend of fighting. Unlike the Sandinistas in Nicaragua, Hussein was too far away from U.S. soil, too rich with oil money, and too experienced in ruling to be dislodged through the psychological-warfare techniques of low-intensity conflict. Waging a war to push Iraq's invading army from Kuwait would cost billions of dollars and require an unprecedented, massive U.S. military mobilization. The American public was notoriously reluctant to send its young into foreign battles on behalf of any cause. Selling war in the Middle East to the American people would not be easy. Bush would need to convince Americans that former ally Saddam Hussein now embodied evil, and that the oil fiefdom of Kuwait was a struggling young democracy. How could the Bush administration build U.S. support for "liberating" a country so fundamentally opposed to democratic values? How could the war appear noble and necessary rather than a crass grab to save cheap oil?

"If and when a shooting war starts, reporters will begin to wonder why American soldiers are dying for oil-rich sheiks," warned Hal Steward, a retired army PR official. "The U.S. military had better get cracking to come up with a public relations plan that will supply the answers the public can accept."[2]

Steward needn't have worried. A PR plan was already in place, paid for almost entirely by the "oil-rich sheiks" themselves.

Packaging the Emir

US Congressman Jimmy Hayes of Louisiana – a conservative Democrat who supported the Gulf War – later estimated that the government of Kuwait funded as many as 20 PR, law, and lobby firms in its campaign to mobilize U.S. opinion and force against Hussein.[3] Participating firms included the Rendon Group, which received a retainer of $100,000 per month for media work, and Neill & Co., which received $50,000 per month for lobbying Congress. Sam Zakhem, a former U.S. ambassador to the oil-

---

1. *Ibid.*
2. Hal D. Steward, "A Public Relations Plan for the U.S. Military in the Middle East," *Public Relations Quarterly*, Winter, 1990–91, p. 10.
3. "H&K leads PR charge in behalf of Kuwaiti cause," *O'Dwyer's PR Services Report*, Vol. 5, No. 1, January 1991, p.8.

rich gulf state of Bahrain, funneled $7.7 million in advertising and lobbying dollars through two front groups, the "Coalition for Americans at Risk" and the "Freedom Task Force." The Coalition, which began in the 1980s as a front for the contras in Nicaragua, prepared and placed TV and newspaper ads, and kept a stable of fifty speakers available for pro-war rallies and publicity events.[1]

Hill & Knowlton, then the world's largest PR firm, served as mastermind for the Kuwaiti campaign. Its activities alone would have constituted the largest foreign-funded campaign ever aimed at manipulating American public opinion. By law, the Foreign Agents Registration Act should have exposed this propaganda campaign to the American people, but the Justice Department chose not to enforce it. Nine days after Saddam's army marched into Kuwait, the Emir's government agreed to fund a contract under which Hill & Knowlton would represent "Citizens for a Free Kuwait," a classic PR front group designed to hide the real role of the Kuwaiti government and its collusion with the Bush administration. Over the next six months, the Kuwaiti government channeled $11.9 million dollars to Citizens for a Free Kuwait (CFK), whose only other funding totaled $17,861 from 78 individuals. Virtually all of CFK's budget – $10.8 million – went to Hill & Knowlton in the form of fees.[2]

The man running Hill & Knowlton's Washington office was Craig Fuller, one of Bush's closest friends and inside political advisors. The news media never bothered to examine Fuller's role until after the war had ended, but if America's editors had read the PR trade press, they might have noticed this announcement, published in O'Dwyer's PR Services before the fighting began: "Craig L. Fuller, chief of staff to Bush when he was vice president, has been on the Kuwaiti account at Hill & Knowlton since the first day. He and [Bob] Dilenschneider at one point made a trip to Saudi Arabia, observing the production of some 20 videotapes, among other chores. The Wirthlin Group, research arm of H&K, was the pollster for the Reagan administration . . . . Wirthlin has reported receiving $1.1 million in fees for research assignments for the Kuwaitis. Robert K. Gray, Chairman of H&K/USA based in Washington, D.C., had leading roles in both Reagan campaigns. He has been involved in foreign nation accounts for many years . . . . Lauri J. Fitz-Pegado, account supervisor on the Kuwait account,

---

1. "Citizens for Free Kuwait Files with FARA After a Nine-month Lag," O'Dwyer's FARA Report, Vol. 1, No. 9, Oct. 1991, p. 2. See also Arthur E. Rowse, "Flacking for the Emir," The Progressive, May, 1991, p. 22.

2. O'Dwyer's FARA Report, Vol. 1, No. 9, Oct. 1991, pp. 2.

is a former Foreign Service Officer at the U.S. Information Agency who joined Gray when he set up his firm in 1982."[1]

In addition to Republican notables like Gray and Fuller, Hill & Knowlton maintained a well-connected stable of in-house Democrats who helped develop the bipartisan support needed to support the war. Lauri Fitz-Pegado, who headed the Kuwait campaign, had previously worked with super-lobbyist Ron Brown representing Haiti's Duvalier dictatorship. Hill & Knowlton senior vice president Thomas Ross had been Pentagon spokesman during the Carter administration. To manage the news media, H&K relied on vice-chairman Frank Mankiewicz, whose background included service as press secretary and advisor to Robert F. Kennedy and George McGovern, followed by a stint as president of National Public Radio. Under his direction, Hill & Knowlton arranged hundreds of meetings, briefings, calls and mailings directed toward the editors of daily newspapers and other media outlets.

Jack O'Dwyer had reported on the PR business for more than twenty years, but he was awed by the rapid and expansive work of H&K on behalf of Citizens for a Free Kuwait: "Hill & Knowlton . . . has assumed a role in world affairs unprecedented for a PR firm. H&K has employed a stunning variety of opinion-forming devices and techniques to help keep U.S. opinion on the side of the Kuwaitis . . . . The techniques range from full-scale press conferences showing torture and other abuses by the Iraqis to the distribution of tens of thousands of 'Free Kuwait' T-shirts and bumper stickers at college campuses across the U.S."[2]

Documents filed with the U.S. Department of Justice showed that 119 H&K executives in 12 offices across the U.S. were overseeing the Kuwait account. "The firm's activities, as listed in its report to the Justice Department, included arranging media interviews for visiting Kuwaitis, setting up observances such as National Free Kuwait Day, National Prayer Day (for Kuwait), and National Student Information Day, organizing public rallies, releasing hostage letters to the media, distributing news releases and information kits, contacting politicians at all levels, and producing a nightly radio show in Arabic from Saudi Arabia," wrote Arthur Rowse in the *Progressive* after the war. Citizens for a Free Kuwait also capitalized on the publication of a quickie 154-page book about Iraqi atrocities titled *The Rape of Kuwait*, copies of which were stuffed into media kits and then featured on TV talk shows and the *Wall Street Journal*. The Kuwaiti embassy

1. *O'Dwyer's PR Services Report*, Vol. 5, No. 1, January 1991, pp. 8, 10.
2. *Ibid.*, p. 1.

also bought 200,000 copies of the book for distribution to American troops.[1]

Hill & Knowlton produced dozens of video news releases (VNRs) at a cost of well over half a million dollars, but it was money well spent, resulting in tens of millions of dollars worth of "free" air time. The VNRs were shown by eager TV news directors around the world who rarely (if ever) identified Kuwait's PR firm as the source of the footage and stories. TV stations and networks simply fed the carefully-crafted propaganda to unwitting viewers, who assumed they were watching "real" journalism. After the war Arthur Rowse asked Hill & Knowlton to show him some of the VNRs, but the PR company refused. Obviously the phony TV news reports had served their purpose, and it would do H&K no good to help a reporter reveal the extent of the deception. In *Unreliable Sources*, authors Martin Lee and Norman Solomon noted that "when a research team from the communications department of the University of Massachusetts surveyed public opinion and correlated it with knowledge of basic facts about U.S. policy in the region, they drew some sobering conclusions: the more television people watched, the fewer facts they knew; and the less people knew in terms of basic facts, the more likely they were to back the Bush administration."[2]

Throughout the campaign, the Wirthlin Group conducted daily opinion polls to help Hill & Knowlton take the emotional pulse of key constituencies so it could identify the themes and slogans that would be most effective in promoting support for U.S. military action. After the war ended, the Canadian Broadcasting Corporation produced an Emmy award-winning TV documentary on the PR campaign titled "To Sell a War." The show featured an interview with Wirthlin executive Dee Alsop in which Alsop bragged of his work and demonstrated how audience surveys were even used to adapt the clothing and hairstyle of the Kuwaiti ambassador physically so he would seem more likeable to TV audiences. Wirthlin's job, Alsop explained, was "to identify the messages that really resonate emotionally with the American people." The theme that struck the deepest emotional chord, they discovered, was "the fact that Saddam Hussein was a madman who had committed atrocities even against his own people,[3]

1. Rowse, *op. cit.*, pp. 21–22.

2. Martin A. Lee & Norman Solomon, *Unreliable Sources: A Guide to Detecting Bias in News Media* (New York: Lyle Stuart, 1991), p. xvii.

3. For somewhat of an alternative perspective on the accusations against Saddam in this regard, see both the article by Dr. Doebbler on pp. 797–817 of the present volume, and

and had tremendous power to do further damage, and he needed to be stopped."[1]

Suffer the Little Children

Every big media event needs what journalists and flacks alike refer to as "the hook." An ideal hook becomes the central element of a story that makes it newsworthy, evokes a strong emotional response, and sticks in the memory. In the case of the Gulf War, the "hook" was invented by Hill & Knowlton. In style, substance, and mode of delivery, it bore an uncanny resemblance to England's World War I hearings that accused German soldiers of killing babies.

On October 10, 1990, the Congressional Human Rights Caucus held a hearing on Capitol Hill which provided the first opportunity for formal presentations of Iraqi human rights violations. Outwardly, the hearing resembled an official congressional proceeding, but appearances were deceiving. In reality, the Human Rights Caucus, chaired by California Democrat Tom Lantos and Illinois Republican John Porter, was simply an association of politicians. Lantos and Porter were also co-chairs of the Congressional Human Rights Foundation, a legally separate entity that occupied free office space valued at $3,000 a year in Hill & Knowlton's Washington, D.C., office. Notwithstanding its congressional trappings, the Congressional Human Rights Caucus served as another Hill & Knowlton front group, which – like all front groups – used a noble-sounding name to disguise its true purpose.[2]

Only a few astute observers noticed the hypocrisy in Hill & Knowlton's use of the term "human rights." One of those observers was John MacArthur, author of *The Second Front*, which remains the best book written about the manipulation of the news media during the Gulf War. In the fall of 1990, MacArthur reported, Hill & Knowlton's Washington switchboard was simultaneously fielding calls for the Human Rights Foundation and for "government representatives of Indonesia, another H&K client. Like H&K client Turkey, Indonesia is a practitioner of naked aggression, having seized . . . the former Portuguese colony of East Timor in 1975. Since the

---

the interview with Jude Wanniski on pp. 3–79 of the companion to the present volume, *Neo-CONNED!*.—Ed.

1. Docherty, Neil, "To Sell a War," *The 5ᵗʰ Estate*, host: Lyndon MacIntyre, Toronto: CBC Television, 1991, pp. 3–4.

2. MacArthur, *op. cit.*, p. 60.

annexation of East Timor, the Indonesian government has killed, by conservative estimate, about 100,000 inhabitants of the region."[1]

MacArthur also noticed another telling detail about the October 1990 hearings: "The Human Rights Caucus is not a committee of Congress, and therefore it is unencumbered by the legal accouterments that would make a witness hesitate before he or she lied . . . . Lying under oath in front of a congressional committee is a crime; lying from under the cover of anonymity to a caucus is merely public relations."[2]

In fact, the most emotionally moving testimony on October 10 came from a 15-year-old Kuwaiti girl, known only by her first name of Nayirah. According to the Caucus, Nayirah's full name was being kept confidential to prevent Iraqi reprisals against her family in occupied Kuwait. Sobbing, she described what she had seen with her own eyes in a hospital in Kuwait City. Her written testimony was passed out in a media kit prepared by CFK. "I volunteered at the al-Addan hospital," Nayirah said. "While I was there, I saw the Iraqi soldiers come into the hospital with guns, and go into the room where . . . babies were in incubators. They took the babies out of the incubators, took the incubators, and left the babies on the cold floor to die."[3]

Three months passed between Nayirah's testimony and the start of the war. During those months, the story of babies torn from their incubators was repeated over and over again. President Bush told the story. It was recited as fact in Congressional testimony, on TV and radio talk shows, and at the UN Security Council. "Of all the accusations made against the dictator," MacArthur observed, "none had more impact on American public opinion than the one about Iraqi soldiers removing 312 babies from their incubators and leaving them to die on the cold hospital floors of Kuwait City."[4]

At the Human Rights Caucus, however, Hill & Knowlton and Congressman Lantos had failed to reveal that Nayirah was a member of the Kuwaiti Royal Family. Her father, in fact, was Saud Nasir al-Sabah, Kuwait's Ambassador to the U.S., who sat listening in the hearing room during her testimony. The Caucus also failed to reveal that H&K vice president Lauri Fitz-Pegado had coached Nayirah in what even the Kuwaitis' own investigators later confirmed was false testimony.

---

1. *Ibid.*
2. *Ibid.*, p.58.
3. *Ibid.*
4. *Ibid.*, p. 54.

If Nayirah's outrageous lie had been exposed at the time it was told, it might have at least caused some in Congress and the news media to reevaluate soberly the extent to which they were being skillfully manipulated to support military action. Public opinion was deeply divided on Bush's Gulf policy. As late as December 1990, a *New York Times/CBS News* poll indicated that 48 percent of the American people wanted Bush to wait before taking any action if Iraq failed to withdraw from Kuwait by Bush's January 15 deadline.[1] On January 12, the U.S. Senate voted by a narrow, five-vote margin to support the Bush administration in a declaration of war. Given the narrowness of the vote, the babies-thrown-from-incubators story may have turned the tide in Bush's favor.

Following the war, human rights investigators attempted to confirm Nayirah's story and could find no witnesses or other evidence to support it. Amnesty International, which had fallen for the story, was forced to issue an embarrassing retraction. Nayirah herself was unavailable for comment. "This is the first allegation I've had that she was the ambassador's daughter," said Human Rights Caucus co-chair John Porter. "Yes, I think people . . . were entitled to know the source of her testimony." When journalists for the Canadian Broadcasting Corporation asked Nasir al-Sabah for permission to question Nayirah about her story, the ambassador angrily refused.[2]

Front-Line Flacks

The military build-up in the Persian Gulf began by flying and shipping hundreds of thousands of U.S. troops, armaments, and supplies to staging areas in Saudi Arabia, yet another nation with no tolerance for a free press, democratic rights, and most western customs. In a secret strategy memo, the Pentagon outlined a tightly-woven plan to constrain and control journalists. A massive babysitting operation would ensure that no truly independent or uncensored reporting reached back to the U.S. public. "News media representatives will be escorted at all times," the memo stated. "Repeat, at all times."[3]

Assistant Secretary of Defense for Public Affairs Pete Williams served as the Pentagon's top flack for the Gulf War. Using the perennial PR strategy

---

1. *New York Times*/CBS News poll, as reported in *O'Dwyer's PR Services Report*, January 1991, p. 10.
2. "To Sell A War," *op. cit.*, pp. 4–5.
3. MacArthur, *op. cit.*, p. 7.

of "good cop/bad cop," the government of Saudi Arabia played the "heavy," denying visas and access to the U.S. press, while Williams, the reporters' friend, appeared to intercede repeatedly on their behalf. This strategy kept news organizations competing with each other for favors from Williams, and kept them from questioning the fundamental fact that journalistic independence was impossible under military escort and censorship.

The overwhelming technological superiority of U.S. forces won a decisive victory in the brief and brutal war known as Desert Storm. Afterwards, some in the media quietly admitted that they'd been manipulated to produce sanitized coverage which almost entirely ignored the war's human cost – today estimated at over 100,000 civilian deaths. The American public's single most lasting memory of the war will probably be the ridiculously successful video stunts supplied by the Pentagon showing robot "smart bombs" striking only their intended military targets, without much "collateral" (civilian) damage.

"Although influential media such as the *New York Times* and *Wall Street Journal* kept promoting the illusion of the 'clean war,' a different picture began to emerge after the U.S. stopped carpet-bombing Iraq," note Lee and Solomon. "The pattern underscored what Napoleon meant when he said that it wasn't necessary to suppress the news completely; it was sufficient to delay the news until it no longer mattered."[1]

---

1. Lee & Solomon, *op. cit.*, p. xix.

A veteran soldier protesting U.S. government Iraq policy with sign at the 2004 inauguration of George W. Bush.

About the Contributors

Joseph Cirincione is Senior Associate and Director for Non-proliferation at the Carnegie Endowment for International Peace in Washington, D.C. He holds an M.S. from the Georgetown School of Foreign Service, is the author of numerous articles and books including *Deadly Arsenals: The Threat from Nuclear, Biological, and Chemical Weapons* (Carnegie Endowment, 2005, second edition), and is co-author of *WMD in Iraq: Evidence and Implication* (Carnegie Endowment, 2004).

Scott Ritter is a former chief UN weapons inspector for the UN Special Commission (UNSCOM) in Iraq; he resigned in 1998, charging that the United States was purposefully obstructing completion of the UNSCOM mission there. He holds a B.A. in Soviet history from Franklin and Marshall College and is a former major, and intelligence officer, in the U.S. Marine Corps. Ritter is the author of *Endgame: Solving the Iraq Problem Once and For All* (Diane Publishing Co., 1999) and *Frontier Justice: Weapons of Mass Destruction and the Bushwhacking of America* (Context Books, 2003), and is co-author, with William Rivers Pitt, of *War on Iraq* (Context Books, 2002).

Alexander Cockburn was born in Scotland and grew up in Ireland. An Oxford graduate, he was an editor at the *Times Literary Supplement* and the *New Statesman* before becoming a permanent resident of the United States in 1973. Cockburn wrote about the media and politics for the *Village Voice*, and, through the 1980s, was a regular columnist for the *Wall Street Journal*. He co-edits the print and online magazine *CounterPunch*, and is the author of several books, including *Corruptions of Empire* (Verso Books, 1987) and, most recently, *Al Gore: A User's Manual* (Verso Books, 2000). His exclusive column appears fortnightly, among other places, on *Antiwar.com*.

Jeffrey St. Clair is an award-winning investigative journalist who co-edits *CounterPunch* with Alexander Cockburn. He is also a contributing editor to *In These Times*. A graduate in English and History of American University in Washington, D.C., he worked for many years as an environmental activist, organizer, and writer, and edited the influential *Forest Watch* from 1990 to 1994. He has written or edited several books both independently and with Alexander Cockburn, including *A Dime's Worth of Difference* (AK Press, 2004), *The Politics of Anti-Semitism* (AK Press, 2003), and *Been Brown So Long It Looked Like Green to Me: The Politics of Nature* (Common Courage Press, 2003). His most recent book, *Grand Theft Pentagon: How War Contractors Rip Off America and Threaten the World*, is forthcoming from Common Courage Press.

Robert Fisk, a world-renowned Middle East correspondent for London's *Independent*, received a Ph.D. in political science from Trinity College, Dublin, in 1985, and an honorary doctorate in literature and journalism from the University of Lancaster, England. He was *The Times*'s Belfast correspondent from 1971 to 1975, and Middle East correspondent from 1976 to 1987. Fisk has covered the conflict in the North of Ireland, the Israeli invasions of Lebanon, the Iranian Revolution, the Iran-Iraq war, the Soviet invasion of Afghanistan, the Gulf War, wars in Bosnia and Algeria, the NATO war with Yugoslavia, the Palestinian Intifadas, and the current war in Iraq. He was the winner of the Amnesty International U.K. Press Awards for his reports from Algeria (1998) and for his articles on the NATO bombing of Yugoslavia (2000). He was awarded the John Hopkins SIAS-CIBA prize for international journalism and has received the British International Journalist of the Year award seven times, most recently in 1996.

Maurizio Blondet holds a degree from the State University of Milan. After spending several years as a columnist, he became special correspondent on economics and finance for *Il Giornale,* a leading Italian newspaper, and is currently special correspondent on foreign affairs for the Italian Episcopal Conference's daily paper, *Avvenire.* After 9/11 he authored a trilogy on the attacks and related subjects entitled: *September 11ᵗʰ: A Coup d'Etat* (Effedieffe, Milan, 2002), *Who Really Governs America?* (Effedieffe, Milan, 2002), and *Osama Bin Mossad* (Effedieffe, Milan, 2003).

Noam Chomsky, Ph.D., received his doctorate in linguistics in 1955, and in 1961 was appointed Professor in the Department of Linguistics and Philosophy at MIT. He has written and lectured widely on linguistics, philosophy, intellectual history, contemporary issues, international affairs, and U.S. foreign policy. Chomsky has received literally dozens of honorary degrees and awards from many of the most prestigious institutions at home and around the world.

Claes G. Ryn, Ph.D., born and raised in Sweden, is currently Professor of Politics at the Catholic University of America, where he served for six years as Politics Department Chairman. He also taught at the University of Virginia and Georgetown University in the fields of ethics, politics, culture, and the history of Western political thought. Ryn is editor of the academic journal *Humanitas,* is a past president of the Philadelphia Society (2001–2002), and is chairman of the National Humanities Institute. He is widely published on both sides of the Atlantic with articles appearing in leading journals, magazines, and newspapers. His many books include *Will, Imagination and Reason* (Regnery, 1986); *Democracy and the Ethical Life* (Catholic University of America Press, 1990); *The New Jacobinism: Can Democracy Survive?* (National Humanities Institute, 1991); and *America the Virtuous* (Transaction Publishers, 2003).

Stephen J. Sneigoski, Ph.D., holds his doctorate in American history from the University of Maryland, with a specialty in American diplomatic history. He is the author of numerous articles dealing with World War II, the war on Iraq, and political philosophy that have appeared in such publications as *Telos, The World and I, Modern Age, Current Concerns, The Occidental Quarterly,* and *The Last Ditch.*

Justin Raimondo is the editorial director of *Antiwar.com.* He is also a contributing editor of *The American Conservative,* Senior Fellow at the Randolph Bourne Institute, and Adjunct Scholar with the Ludwig von Mises Institute. Raimondo writes frequently for *Chronicles: A Magazine of American Culture,* and is the author of, among other titles, *Reclaiming the American Right: The Lost Legacy of the Conservative Movement* (Center for Libertarian Studies, 1993) and *Terror Enigma: 9/11 and the Israeli Connection* (iUniverse, 2003).

David W. Lutz, Ph.D., graduated from the U.S. Military Academy in 1978 and served in the U.S. Army until 1983. In 1994 he received degrees in moral philosophy from the University of Notre Dame. He has held postdoctoral research positions at the University of St. Thomas in Minnesota and the Hanover Institute of Philosophical Research in Germany. Lutz currently teaches philosophy and management at the Catholic University of Eastern Africa in Nairobi, Kenya.

E. Michael Jones, Ph.D., has taught at both the high school and college levels in the U.S. and Europe. He received his doctorate in American literature from Temple University in 1979, and taught the subject as an Assistant

Professor at the University of Notre Dame through 1980. In 1981 he founded *Fidelity Magazine*, which was published by the Wanderer Forum Foundation until 1984 when he became publisher as well as editor. He currently edits *Culture Wars*, which succeeded *Fidelity* in 1999. He has written hundreds of articles and 12 books, the most recent of which is *The Slaughter of Cities: Urban Renewal as Ethnic Cleansing* (St. Augustine's Press, 2004).

Kirkpatrick Sale is a non-fiction writer, journalist, editor, and environmental activist, who focuses on political, economic, and ecological problems of contemporary society, proposing novel – and often controversial – solutions. Sale is the author of 12 books, including *Human Scale* (Perigee, 1982), *The Green Revolution* (Hill & Wang, 1993), and *Rebels Against the Future: The Luddites and Their War on the Industrial Revolution, Lessons for the Computer Age* (Addison Wesley Publishing Company, 1996). A contributing editor of *The Nation*, Sale writes for periodicals in the U.S. and the U.K., and is a board member of *The PEN American Center*, the *E.F. Schumacher Society*, and *The Learning Alliance of New York City*.

Naomi Klein, a Canadian, is an award-winning journalist and author of the international best seller *No Logo: Taking Aim at the Brand Bullies* (Picador USA, 2000). Her articles have appeared in publications such as *The Nation*, *The New Statesman*, the *New York Times*, and the *Village Voice*. Klein writes an internationally syndicated column for *The Globe and Mail* in Canada and *The Guardian* in Britain. She has traveled throughout North America, Asia, Latin America, and Europe, tracking the rise of anti-corporate activism.

William O'Rourke is Professor of English at the University of Notre Dame and Director of the Graduate Creative Writing Program there. He is the author of four novels and several non-fiction works, including *Signs of the Literary Times: Essays, Reviews, Profiles* 1970–1992 (State University of New York Press, 1993), *Campaign America '96: The View from the Couch* (reissued, University of Notre Dame Press, 2000), and *Campaign America 2000: The View From the Couch* (PreviewPort.com, 2001). O'Rourke has been writing a political column for the *Chicago Sun-Times* since 2001, and has been awarded two NEAs and a New York State Council on the Arts CAPS grant. He was the first James Thurber Writer-in-Residence at the Thurber House in Columbus, Ohio.

Lt. Col. Karen Kwiatkowski, USAF (ret.), has an M.A. in government from Harvard and an M.S. in science management from the University of Alaska. Before her recent retirement from the U.S. Air Force, her final assignment was as a political-military affairs officer in the Office of the Secretary of Defense, Under Secretariat for Policy, in the Sub-Saharan Africa and Near East and South Asia directorates. Lt. Col. Kwiatkowski also served on the staff of the Director of the National Security Agency.

Robert Hickson, USA (ret.), Ph.D., is a 1964 graduate of the U.S. Military Academy, retired U.S. Army Special Forces officer, and Vietnam War veteran. Following his retirement he served for many years in the intelligence and special-operations communities in varying capacities. His degree is in comparative literature and classics from the University of North Carolina, Chapel Hill, and he is a founding faculty member of Christendom College. Hickson has held professorships at the U.S. Air Force Academy, the Joint Special Operations University at U.S. Special Operations Command, the John. F. Kennedy Special Warfare Center and School, and the Joint Military Intelligence College.

Jack Dalton is a 60-year-old former Marine and disabled Vietnam veteran. He returned from Vietnam, he says, as "A real 'America, love it or leave it' type." But by the middle of 1967 he had changed drastically, after listening to what the American people were being told by their government about the war. Dalton wondered what war they were talking about, since "it sure wasn't the one I just came back from." Today he claims to hear the same kind of thing from those returning from Iraq. Only, in his opinion, "the level of government secrecy has increased," and "public discourse is once again being 'criminalized.'" Dalton is co-editor of *Project for the Old American Century,* a web-based, grass-roots organization that "strives to protect and strengthen democracy primarily by disseminating unreported and under-reported news stories from a perspective untainted by political or corporate sponsorship."

Chris Harrison is an ex-Army Reserve First Lieutenant of the Army Engineers. He did not serve in any conflict, and was honorably discharged September 1, 2004. **Tim Goodrich** joined the U.S. Air Force in April of 1999, and served for 4 years, being honorably discharged in April, 2003. His military specialty was as a maintainer of communications and navigation systems on the E-3 AWACS aircraft. He deployed to Saudi Arabia twice in support of Operation Southern Watch, and once to Oman in support of Operation Enduring Freedom (OEF). **Jimmy Massey** joined the Marines in January 1992, and served for 12 years with a specialty (MOS) in infantry. He was also an infantry instructor at the boot camp at Parris Island, S.C., and was a Marine recruiter in western North Carolina for three years. Upon the end of his recruiting duty tour, he left Twenty-nine

Palms, Calif., and was sent to Kuwait in January 2003, until the invasion in March. He was MedEvac-ed out of Iraq in May of 2003, and received an honorable medical discharge in December. **Dave Bischel** served as an active-duty MP in the Army in Germany from 1989 to 1993. He rejoined the military in March 2003 under the "try-one-year" option offered to honorably discharged veterans interested in being part of the National Guard. He was ordered to Iraq in May 2003, and came home in April 2004, when he was honorably discharged.

Petty Officer Pablo Paredes, USN, was raised in the Bronx, New York, and attended Catholic elementary and high schools where he developed an abiding respect for human life. He joined the U.S. Navy in 2000, and achieved the rank of Petty Officer Third Class, but his strong moral values put him at odds with the war in Iraq. On March 18, 2005, Petty Officer Paredes filed for conscientious objector status. He was convicted by a Special Court Martial on May 11, 2005, of missing his ship's movement and sentenced the following day to three months' hard labor.

Staff Sgt. Al Lorenz, USAR, first saw military service as a Marine Corps scout/sniper from 1976 to 1980. He transferred into the Army National Guard in the 80s, and to the Army Reserves in 1993. Refusing to serve under Bill Clinton, Staff Sgt. Lorenz resigned from the military honorably in 1994. Then on the first day of the Iraq invasion he volunteered to return from civilian life and requested combat duty with the specific aim of helping to take care of the young soldiers he had seen on TV. He deployed to Iraq from February to October 2004.

Col. W. Patrick Lang, USA (ret.), served in the Department of Defense as an Army officer in military intelligence and special forces, and as a member of the Defense Senior Executive Service. He is a highly educated Middle East specialist, and worked in that region for many years. He was the first Professor of Arabic at the United States Military Academy. In the Defense Intelligence Agency (DIA), he was the Defense Intelligence Officer for the Middle East, South Asia, and Terrorism, and later the first Director of the Defense HUMINT (Human Intelligence) Service. Col. Lang is currently President of Global Resources Group, and a regular analyst for many television and radio programs.

Ray McGovern is a graduate of Fordham University where he earned degrees in Russian studies and a commission in the Army as an intelligence officer. He spent 27 years as a CIA analyst, during which time he chaired various National Intelligence Estimates and, for a number of years, prepared the President's Daily Brief. McGovern is a founding member of Veteran Intelligence Professionals for Sanity, a group of 45 former intelligence-community members formed in January 2003, after it had become clear that intelligence analysis was being corrupted by political pressure to "justify" an unprovoked attack on Iraq. He now works at Tell the Word, the publishing arm of the ecumenical Church of the Savior in Washington, D.C.

Jeffrey Record, Ph.D., received his doctorate at the Johns Hopkins School of Advanced International Studies and was formerly a professor at Georgia Institute of Technology. During the Vietnam War he served as assistant province advisor in the Mekong Delta, and later as senior fellow at the Institute for Foreign Policy Analysis. Record also has extensive Capitol Hill experience having served as an advisor to Senators William Cohen and Gary Hart; as legislative assistant to Senators Sam Nunn, Bob Krueger, and Lloyd Bentsen; and later as a professional staff member for the Senate Armed Services Committee. He is the author of numerous books and monographs, including *Dark Victory: America's Second War Against Iraq* (Naval Institute Press, 2004).

Stephen Pelletière, Ph.D., holds a B.A. in English from the University of Vermont and a doctorate in Political Science from the University of California, Berkeley. He was the Central Intelligence Agency's senior political analyst on Iraq during the Iran-Iraq war, and was a professor at the Army War College from 1988 to 2000. He also served as the Middle East expert at the War College's Strategic Studies Institute during the same period. He has held positions in journalism and taught at the University of California, Berkeley, Ripon College, and Union College. Pelletière is the author of *The Kurds: An Unstable Element in the Gulf* (Westview Press, 1984); *The Iran-Iraq War: Chaos in a Vacuum* (Praeger Publishers, 1992); and *Iraq and the International Oil System: Why America Went to War in the Gulf* (Maisonneuve Press, 2004).

Gordon Prather, Ph.D., formerly worked as a nuclear weapons physicist at Lawrence Livermore National Laboratory in California and Sandia National Laboratory in New Mexico. He also served as a policy implementing official for national-security-related matters in the Federal Energy Agency, the Energy Research and Development Administration, the Department of Energy, the Office of the Secretary of Defense, and the Department of the Army. Prather was also legislative assistant for national security affairs to Senator Henry Bellmon (R-OK), a member of the Senate Energy Committee.

Roger Morris served on the senior staff of the National Security Council under Presidents Johnson and Nixon until he resigned in protest over the invasion of Cambodia. An award-winning investigative journalist and historian as well as a former diplomat, he is the author of several books including *Richard Milhous Nixon: The Rise of an American Politician* (Henry Holt & Co., 1989). Morris is currently completing a history dealing with U.S. policy and covert intervention in Southwest Asia for the publisher Alfred Knopf.

Mark and Louise Zwick, editors and publishers of the *Houston Catholic Worker,* take in immigrants and refugees at their Casa Juan Diego Houses of Hospitality in Houston. Casa Juan Diego provides a haven for thousands of immigrants and has made medical services, food, and clothing available to the poor of the community. The Zwicks' book on *The Catholic Worker Movement* will be published by Paulist Press later this year.

John Burroughs, J.D., Ph. D., holds his law degree from Boalt Hall School of Law and his Ph.D. in jurisprudence and social policy from the University of California, Berkeley. He is Executive Director of the Lawyers' Committee on Nuclear Policy, based in New York, and Adjunct Professor of International Law at Rutgers Law School. He is author of *The Legality of Threat or Use of Nuclear Weapons: A Guide to the Historic Opinion of the International Court of Justice* (Lit Verlag, 1998).

Nicole Deller, J.D., holds a law degree from New York University School of Law. She is program advisor for the World Federalist Movement in New York and chairs the Committee on International Security Affairs for the Association of the Bar of the City of New York. She is the principal editor of *Rule of Power or Rule of Law? An Assessment of U.S. Policies and Actions Regarding Security-Related Treaties* (Apex Press, 2003). Deller recently served as research associate and consultant for the Lawyers' Committee on Nuclear Policy.

Francis Boyle, J.D., Ph.D., holds his law degree and doctorate in political science from Harvard University. A scholar in the areas of international law and human rights, he is a professor at the College of Law, University of Illinois, and was a teaching fellow at Harvard and an associate at its Center for International Affairs. He formerly served as legal advisor to the Palestinian delegation to the Middle East peace negotiations, and has served on the board of directors of Amnesty International. Boyle is also attorney of record for the Chechen Republic of Ichkeria, conducting its legal affairs on a worldwide basis. His books include *Destroying World Order* (Charity Press, 2004); *Defending Civil Resistance Under International Law* (Juris Publications, Inc., 1987); and *Foundations of World Order: The Legalist Approach to International Relations (1898–1922)* (Duke University Press, 1999).

Immanuel Wallerstein, Ph.D., is Senior Research Scholar of Sociology at Yale University, former president of the International Sociological Association, and former chairman of the Gulbenkian Commission on the Restructuring of the Social Sciences. He writes in three domains of world-systems analysis: the historical development of the modern world-system, the contemporary crisis of the capitalist world-economy, and the structures of knowledge. His books include *The Modern World-System* (Academic Press, 1980), *Utopistics, or Historical Choices for the Twenty-first Century* (New Press, 1998), and *Unthinking Social Science: The Limits of Nineteenth-Century Paradigms* (Temple University Press, 2001). He holds his Ph.D. from Columbia University.

F. William Engdahl holds a degree in politics from Princeton, and has done graduate study in comparative economics at the University of Stockholm. A widely read freelance writer, he has appeared regularly in publications worldwide writing on energy, politics, and economics. Engdahl has attended numerous international conferences, from London to Jakarta to Moscow, speaking on geopolitical, economic, and energy issues. He currently lives in Germany and, in addition to writing and speaking, is active as a consulting economist.

Joseph Margulies, Esq., is a principal in the Minneapolis firm of Margulies & Richman and a faculty member at the University of Chicago Law School. He received his B.A., with honors, from Cornell University in 1982, and his J.D., *cum laude*, from Northwestern University School of Law in 1988. In 1989 he joined the staff of the Texas Capital Resource Center, where he represented men and women on Texas's death row, eventually becoming Senior Staff Attorney. In 1994 he moved to Minnesota, and he now specializes in civil rights and capital defense. He was lead counsel in *Rasul v. Bush,* which challenged the prisoner detentions at Guantánamo Bay, Cuba, before the Supreme Court. Margulies writes and lectures widely on capital defense and civil liberties in the wake of September 11.

Jeffrey Steinberg is a founding editor of the weekly *Executive Intelligence Review,* and has been senior editor since 1975. A graduate of Rutgers and

Montclair State University, Steinberg is author of *The Ugly Truth About the ADL* (Executive Intelligence Review, 1992) and *Dope, Inc.* (Executive Intelligence Review, 1992), as well as special reports on international terrorism, the drug trade, organized crime, and political corruption. He has lectured on national security affairs in Mexico, Peru, Guatemala, Italy, France, Germany, and Japan.

Jacob Weisberg is editor of *Slate*. He was previously *Slate*'s chief political correspondent and the originator of its "Strange Bedfellow" and "Ballot Box" columns. Before joining *Slate* in 1996, he wrote about politics for magazines including the *New Republic, Newsweek,* and *New York Magazine,* and has written as well for *Vanity Fair* and the *New York Times Magazine.* He is the co-author, with Robert E. Rubin, of *In an Uncertain World* (Random House, c2003). He is also the author of *In Defense of Government* (Scribner, 1996), the e-book *The Road to Chadville* (Slate, 2000), and the *Bushisms* series.

Col. Dan Smith, USA (ret.), graduated from West Point in 1966. He served as an intelligence advisor in Vietnam, and subsequently spent six years with the Defense Intelligence Agency. Among his many citations are a Bronze Star and Purple Heart. Colonel Smith is a graduate of the Army Command and General Staff College, the Armed Forces Staff College, and the Army War College. He retired from the Army in 1992, and in 2002 joined the Friends Committee on National Legislation as Senior Fellow on Military Affairs.

Rear Adm. John D. Hutson, USN (ret.), J.D., was commissioned in the U.S. Navy upon graduation from Michigan State University in 1969. He holds degrees from the University of Minnesota Law School and the Georgetown University Law Center, and was admitted to the State Bar of Michigan. Posts he held during his 31-year naval career include Director of Legislation for the Office of Legislative Affairs; Commanding Officer, Naval Legal Service Office, Europe and Southwest Asia; Commanding Officer, Naval Justice School; and Judge Advocate General of the Navy. Huston is currently President and Dean of Franklin Pierce Law Center.

Gabor Rona, J.D., Ll.M., was a legal advisor in the Legal Division of the International Committee of the Red Cross (ICRC) for 5 years. He frequently lectures at international conferences and has recently written articles appearing in the *Fletcher Forum on World Affairs,* the *Chicago Journal of International Law,* and the *Financial Times* on the role of the laws of armed conflict and on judicial guarantees in the U.S.'s so-called Global War on Terror. He is of Hungarian origin, having escaped with his family in the aftermath of the October 1956 Hungarian Revolution. He holds a B.A. from Brandeis University (1973), and law degrees from Vermont Law School (J.D., 1978) and Columbia University School of Law (Ll.M., 1996). Before moving to the ICRC in Geneva, he spent 15 years as a partner in a small civil and criminal litigation firm in Vermont and two years as a Senior Litigator in international human rights cases at the Center for Constitutional Rights in New York. He is currently International Legal Director at Human Rights First.

Tom Engelhardt is a graduate of Yale University and one of the country's most eminent book editors. Author of *The End of Victory Culture* (University of Mass., 1998) and *History Wars: The Enola Gay and Other Battles for the American Past* (Owl Books, 1996), he is widely published in such magazines as *Harper's*, *The Nation*, and the *Los Angeles Times Book Review*. He is also a former editor at Pantheon Books, and is currently a consulting editor at Holt/Metropolitan Books in New York City. He is a Koret Foundation Teaching Fellow working with the Editing Workshop of the University of California, Berkeley, Journalism School.

John Stauber is an investigative writer, public speaker, and democracy activist as well as the founder and Executive Director of the Center for Media and Democracy. He has worked with many citizen advocacy and public interest groups and, in 1993, launched *PR Watch*. Stauber lives and works in Madison, Wis., and has been featured, interviewed for, or quoted in practically all the major print and broadcast media. His recent books, in collaboration with Sheldon Rampton, include *Weapons of Mass Deception: The Uses of Propaganda in Bush's War on Iraq* (Jeremy P. Larcher/Penguin, 2003) and *Toxic Sludge Is Good for You: Lies, Damn Lies, and the Public Relations Industry* (Common Courage Press, 1995).

Sheldon Rampton is Research Director for the Center for Media and Democracy. A graduate of Princeton University, he has a diverse background as newspaper reporter, activist, and author. Since 1985 he has worked closely with the Wisconsin Coordinating Council on Nicaragua, and is co-author of *Friends In Deed: The Story of U.S.-Nicaragua Sister Cities* (Wisconsin Coordinating Council on Nicaragua, 1989).

Col. Samuel Gardiner, USAF (ret.), is a Vietnam combat veteran and former professor at the National, Air, and Naval War Colleges. He has been a consultant to the Department of Defense for over ten years, focusing on war games. Col. Gardiner was recently a visiting scholar at the Swedish Defence College, and has been a regular as a military analyst on the *NewsHour* with Jim Lehrer, BBC radio and television, CNN, and National Public Radio.

Ayad al-Qazzaz is Professor of Sociology and President of the Middle East Cultural Association at California State University, Sacramento. He holds degrees from the University of Baghdad and the University of California, Berkeley, and is currently president of the Arab American Chamber of Commerce of Sacramento. He is the author of several books and numerous articles published throughout the U.S. and the Arab world. Al-Qazzaz produces a half-hour TV show, "Focus on the Middle East," for the Access Channel in Sacramento.

Fr. Jean-Marie Benjamin is a former UNICEF special events officer and accomplished classical and modern composer. In 1988, in order to become a Catholic priest, he quit his UNICEF post and ended his artistic activities in favor of theological studies in Rome. He was ordained in 1991, at the age of 45, and is now a leading French cleric who is widely respected in the Arab world for his fight for justice for the Iraqi people, which he began in earnest in 1997. He has produced two revealing video documentaries exploring the depths of Anglo-American mendacity in their dealings with Iraq, and is currently involved in organizing the legal defense of Tariq Aziz, the deposed Deputy Prime Minister of Iraq.

Milton Viorst has, since the Six-Day War, written from the Middle East for the *Washington Post,* the *New York Times Magazine,* the *Atlantic,* and, as a staff correspondent, for the *New Yorker.* Among his six books on Middle East society and politics are *Sandcastles: The Arabs in Search of the Modern World* (Knopf, 1994); *In the Shadow of the Prophet: The Struggle for the Soul of Islam* (Westview Press, 2001); and *What Shall I Do With This People? Jews and the Fractious Politics of Judaism* (Free Press, 2002). His book on Arab nationalism will be published by Random House in 2005.

Col. Donn de Grand Pré, USA (ret.), served in Burma and China during World War II and was twice wounded commanding combat forces in Korea. Later, under then-Secretary of Defense Robert McNamara, he was chief arms negotiator for the Middle East as part of the International Security Affairs division in the Pentagon's Office of the Secretary of Defense, where he oversaw the sale of over a hundred billion dollars worth of military equipment. Since 1975, Colonel de Grand Pré has written a number of books, including his popular three-volume series, *Barbarians Inside the Gates* (GSC & Associates Publishing, 2000).

Mark Gery is an independent Iraq analyst and affiliate speaker for the Education for Peace in Iraq Center and for Foreign Policy in Focus. He is an expert on Saddam Hussein; the ideology, strategy, and history of the Ba'ath Party; and the geopolitical forces behind the war in Iraq. Gery is active in the anti-war movement in southern California and is currently writing a comprehensive text on the U.S.-Iraq conflict entitled *Desert Nightmare: The Truth About the Gulf War, the Middle East, and Saddam Hussein's Challenge to America.*

Curtis Doebbler, Esq., Ph.D., is an international human rights lawyer who holds law degrees from New York Law School and the Catholic University in Nijmegen, the Netherlands, and a doctorate in international law from the London School of Economics and Political Science. He is a member of the Bar of the District of Columbia, and his clients have included the Palestinian Authority, dozens of political activists in Sudan, the Democratic Republic of Congo, Peru, and Afghanistan, and numerous human rights defenders in countries around the world. His latest book is *International Human Rights Law: Cases and Materials* (CD Publishing, 2004). He has held professorships at the American University in Cairo, An-Najah National University in Palestine, the University of Pristina, Kosovo, and Tashkent State Institute of Law, Uzbekistan. He is currently serving on the legal defense team for deposed President Saddam Hussein of Iraq.

Michael Ratner, Esq., is president of the Center for Constitutional Rights and aggressively challenges the constitutional and international-law violations of the United States government after 9/11. He served as co-counsel in *Rasul v. Bush,* the historic Guantánamo detainees case that went before the U.S. Supreme Court. He is co-author of *Guantánamo: What the World Should Know* (Chelsea Green Publishing, 2004). Over the years, Ratner has litigated a dozen cases challenging a President's authority to go to war without congressional approval.

Acknowledgements

The editors wish to thank the following individuals for kind assistance rendered during the course of our work on *Neo-CONNED! Again*: Lindsey Carroll, Ted Schluenderfritz, David Brindle, Lynn Gonzalez, Anne Joyce, Robert Hickson, Tomas (for Dr. Doebbler), and Craig Heimbichner. This extremely important project was made easier, and its final result better, owing to their support.

We also gratefully acknowledge permission received from the following individuals or organizations for publication of material by the authors indicated in parenthesis: *The Independent* (Robert Fisk), *The New York Times* (Dr. Stephen Pelletière), The Royal Society (Dr. Noam Chomsky), Foreign Policy Research Institute (Dr. Claes Ryn), *Salon.com* (Roger Morris), *Middle East Policy* and Blackwell Publishing (Col. Patrick Lang, USA (ret.)), The Strategic Studies Institute of the U.S. Army War College (Dr. Jeffrey Record), *Human Rights Magazine* (Drs. John Burroughs and Nicole Deller), Dean Birkenkamp and Paradigm Publishers (Dr. Immanuel Wallerstein), *Current Concerns* (F. William Engdahl), *The Virginia Quarterly Review* (Joseph Margulies, Esq.), Washingtonpost Newsweek Interactive (Jacob Weisberg), and Peter Hastings, Common Courage Press, The Center for Media and Democracy, and *PR Watch* (John Stauber and Sheldon Rampton). We also thank Amnesty International, USA, for their permission to republish an excerpt from *Guantánamo and Beyond: The Continuing Pursuit of Unchecked Executive Power* (AI Index no. AMR 51/063/2005).

Finally, we would like to acknowledge Laryn Bakker and the webmasters and staff at www.informationclearinghouse.info, www.albasrah.net, www.einswine.com, and www.kein-plan.de for the images contained in this volume.

Further Resources

Given that the Iraq war remains tragically ongoing, readers of the *Neo-CONNED!* volumes may wish to continue their studies of the vitally important subjects relating to it. The editors herewith offer a few suggestions for further reading, included among which are also certain of our contributors' other related online and print publications. We do not necessarily endorse the opinions expressed in all the sources listed below. Readers should consult them with discernment.

Catholic reference works on matters of war and peace:

St. Robert Bellarmine, *De Laicis*, Kathleen E. Murphy, Ph.D., trans. (New York: Fordham University Press, 1928).

Catholic Encyclopedia (New York: Robert Appleton Company, 1907–1912; Online Edition Copyright 1999 by Kevin Knight), s.v. "War," at www.newadvent.org.

Rev. Cyprian Emanuel, O.F.M., Ph.D., and the Committee on Ethics, *The Morality of Conscientious Objection to War* (Washington, D.C.: CAIP, 1941); *The Ethics of War* (Washington, D.C.: CAIP, 1932).

John Eppstein, *The Catholic Tradition of the Law of Nations* (Washington, D.C.: CAIP, 1935).

Charles G. Fenwick, Ph.D., *A Primer of Peace* (Washington, D.C.: CAIP, 1937).

The International Union of Social Sciences, John Eppstein, trans. and ed., *Code of International Ethics* (Westminster, Md.: Newman Press, 1953).

Rev. Harry C. Koenig, S.T.D., ed., *Principles for Peace: Selections from Papal Documents, Leo XIII to Pius XII* (Washington, D.C.: National Catholic Welfare Conference, 1943).

James Brown Scott, *The Catholic Conception of International Law* (Washington, D.C.: Georgetown University Press, 1934); *The Spanish Origin of International Law* (Union, N.J.: Lawbook Exchange, 2000).

Franziskus Stratmann, O.P., *The Church and War* (New York: P. J. Kenedy and Sons, 1928); *War and Christianity Today* (Westminster, Md.: Newman Press, 1956).

Francisco Suárez, S.J., *De Caritate*, from *On the Three Theological Virtues: Faith, Hope, and Charity* (originally published, Coimbra: Nicolas Carvalho, 1621) in Gwladys L. Williams, et al., trans., *Selections from Three Works* (London: Humphrey Milford, 1944; reprinted, Buffalo: William S. Hein & Co., Inc., 1995), Disputation XIII (*De Bello*).

Francisco de Vitoria, O.P., *De Iure Belli*, in Ernest Nys, ed., and John Pawley Bate, trans., *De Indis et de Iure Belli Relectiones* (Washington, D.C.: Carnegie Institution, 1917; reprinted, Buffalo: William S. Hein & Co., Inc., 1995), parts V and VI of *Relectiones Theologicae XII* (published previously, Johan Georg Simon, J.U.D., ed., Cologne and Frankfort: August Boetius, 1696).

Recent and related books by the contributors:

Cockburn: *Imperial Crusades: Iraq, Afghanistan, and Yugoslavia* (with St. Clair)
Dime's Worth of Difference : Beyond the Lesser of Two Evils (with St. Clair)
The Politics of Anti-Semitism (with St. Clair)

Chomsky: *Hegemony or Survival: America's Quest for Global Dominance*

Ryn: *America the Virtuous: The Crisis of Democracy and the Quest for Empire*

Raimondo: *Terror Enigma: 9/11 and the Israeli Connection*

McGovern: "A Compromised C.I.A.: What Can Be Done?" in *Patriotism, Democracy, and Common Sense*

Pelletière: *America's Oil Wars*
Iraq and the International Oil System: Why America Went to War in the Gulf

The Zwicks: *The Catholic Worker Movement: Intellectual And Spiritual Origins*

Boyle: *Destroying World Order: U.S. Imperialism in the Middle East Before and After September 11th*

Wallerstein: *The Decline of American Power: The U.S. in a Chaotic World*
Alternatives: The United States Confronts the World

Engdahl: *A Century of War*

Engelhardt: *The End of Victory Culture: Cold War America and the Disillusioning of a Generation*

Stauber & Rampton: *Weapons of Mass Deception: The Uses of Propaganda in Bush's War on Iraq*

Viorst: *In the Shadow of the Prophet: The Struggle for the Soul of Islam*
What Shall I Do with This People?: Jews and the Fractious Politics of Judaism

De Grand Pré: *Barbarians Inside the Gates: The Black Book of Bolshevism (Book I); The Viper's Venom (Book II); The Rattler's Revenge (Book III)*

Ratner: "International Law and War Crimes," in *War Crimes: A Report on U.S. War Crimes Against Iraq*

Periodicals (subscription information available on the Internet):

Current Concerns

Culture Wars

Chronicles: A Magazine of American Culture

Houston Catholic Worker

The American Conservative

Occidental Quarterly: A Journal of Western Thought and Opinion

Middle East Policy

Websites:

Antiwar.com
LewRockwell.com
www.arabmonitor.org
www.freearabvoice.org
www.benjaminforiraq.org
www.albasrah.net
www.occupationwatch.org
www.mfso.org
www.vvaw.org
www.ivaw.org
www.bringthemhomenow.org
www.gsfp.org
www.counterpunch.org

www.sandersresearch.com
www.globalsecurity.org
www.oldamericancentury.org
www.iacenter.org
www.tompaine.com
www.tomdispatch.com
www.wanniski.com
www.sobran.com
www.ericmargolis.com
www.prwatch.org
www.robert-fisk.com
www.thornwalker.com/ditch